Internal Auditing Manual

SECOND EDITION

James D. Willson, CPA
Senior Vice-President—Finance (retired)
Northrop Corporation

Steven J. Root, CPA
Director—Corporate Audit
Northrop Corporation

WARREN, GORHAM & LAMONT
Boston • New York

Copyright © 1983, 1984, 1989 by
WARREN, GORHAM & LAMONT, INC.
210 SOUTH STREET
BOSTON, MASSACHUSETTS 02111

ALL RIGHTS RESERVED

No part of this book may be reproduced in any form, by photostat, microfilm, xerography, or any other means, or incorporated into any information retrieval system, electronic or mechanical, without the written permission of the copyright owner.

ISBN 0-7913-0079-X

Library of Congress Catalog Card No. 88-62094

This publication is designed to provide accurate and authoritative information in regard to the subject matter covered. In publishing this book, neither the authors nor the publisher is engaged in rendering legal, accounting, or other professional service. If legal advice or other expert assistance is required, the services of a competent professional should be sought.

PRINTED IN THE UNITED STATES OF AMERICA

Preface

IN THE PREFACE to the first edition of *Internal Auditing Manual*, we observed that internal auditing is largely a twentieth-century development, although it may be traced to the early civilizations of the world. The pace of change is such that internal auditing of the 1990s will differ markedly from that practiced earlier in the century. The difference will be so great that we must now declare that internal auditing, as we know it, is largely the result of developments occurring in the late 1970s and 1980s. These developments include:

- Growth in the professionalism of internal auditing as measured by the issuance of standards, a certified internal auditor program, a code of ethics, and increases in the membership of the IIA.
- Challenges to external, internal, and governmental auditors to deal with new demands for audit services. For external auditors, the challenge is to close what has been popularly referred to as the expectation gap—the gap between what the investing public expects from external auditors and what it is getting. For government auditors, the challenge is to develop a more integrated set of auditing standards to improve the effectiveness and efficiency of auditing in the government sector. For internal auditors, the challenge is to respond to the changing needs of management and a growing body of other interest groups in the work product of internal auditors.
- The increased perception of a decline in the ethical practices by which business is conducted. The instances of business fraud, such as financial reporting fraud, procurement fraud, inside trading, kickbacks, and bribery demand not only business solutions but also improved audit vigilance.
- Recommendations for company management teams, external auditors, internal auditors, the SEC, and the academic community by the Treadway Commission that point the direction to a business environment in which the public, shareholders, creditors, and others will be better protected from the effects of unscrupulous management.
- Technological advances in computers, telecommunications, and office and factory automation that have significantly changed the risks associated with computer-based business systems.
- Changes in the U.S. economy brought about by the growth in deficit government spending, the chronic unfavorable balance of payments, and periods of high interest rates.
- A new wave of mergers and acquisitions offering opportunities for internal auditors to assist in the execution of these transactions.
- Greater interest in the role of the audit committee in helping to ensure that the interests of shareholders are effectively protected, as evidenced by the efforts of the Treadway Commission.
- The increased importance of operational auditing as one way to enhance efficiency and effectiveness in business operations.

These changes have made the role of internal auditing more important than ever. The second edition of *Internal Auditing Manual* is written with the expanded role of internal auditing in mind. Among the areas afforded new or expanded coverage are:

- The identification and discussion of the three branches of auditing—external, internal, and governmental.
- The strategic approach to internal auditing in light of the Treadway Commission's report and other developments.
- The professional standards applicable to practice in each branch.
- The most common internal auditing areas, i.e., financial, operational, and specialized areas, such as information systems auditing. Separate parts of this book have been created for each of these.
- The subject of business ethics is presented in a new part that features expanded coverage of the principal forms of business fraud and suggestions for dealing with them from management and audit perspectives.

The operational auditing part of the book constitutes a complete guide to auditing areas of managerial responsibility generally recognized as critical to successful enterprise management.

It has been said that the more things change, the more they stay the same. Internal auditors must still plan, organize, and perform individual audit projects. Additionally, the internal auditing department must be properly managed. Technically skilled staff must be recruited, trained, and then motivated and supervised. Interfaces with interest groups must be established and maintained. *Internal Auditing Manual* provides guidance for accomplishing all of this.

The second edition of *Internal Auditing Manual* covers everything that internal auditing practitioners and their managers need to know to be effective in the 1990s. It is responsive to recent developments, such as the new standards issued by the Auditing Standards Board to close the expectation gap between what the public wants in an audit of financial statements versus what it has been getting. The work of the Treadway and Packard Commissions is also covered. The General Accounting Office's (GAO) role in setting new government auditing standards is discussed, as are the activities of the Defense Contract Audit Agency. Fraud indicators published by the Department of Defense Inspector General are also set forth.

Internal Auditing Manual, through the Warren, Gorham & Lamont policy of annual supplements, will continue to track the issues and developments of major importance to internal auditors. Important issues covered in this edition include congressional interest in legislative solutions to the problem of financial reporting fraud, actions by the SEC to require management reporting on internal control, court actions on the question of access by third parties to the work product of internal auditors, the effort by the GAO to rewrite standards for governmental audits, the war against waste, fraud, and abuse in government contracting, and the proper role of internal auditing regarding whistle-blowing.

This second edition benefits practitioners and others interested in the function of internal auditing in the following ways:

PREFACE

- Provides a perspective on how the practice of internal auditing fits into the family of auditing that includes external auditing and government auditing.
- Contains strategies for designing and performing programs of auditing coverage to meet the needs of management, audit committees, external auditors, and others.
- Discusses auditing standards applicable to all three branches of auditing.
- Reviews the technical aspect of auditing, such as how to perform statistical sampling, essential to effective auditing performance in the field.
- Offers detailed illustrations of audit programs, questionnaires, and reports for all of the most frequently performed financial and operational audits.
- Describes how to establish and maintain an effective program of information systems (also known as EDP) auditing.
- Includes definitions for all relevant auditing terminology.

In summary, this book is about successful internal auditing, which results from having a clear understanding of the role of internal auditing, committing to high professional standards of performance and ethics, mastering the requisite body of knowledge, managing internal auditing resources effectively, and performing internal audits that are designed to be responsive to the needs of interest groups. The second edition of *Internal Auditing Manual* is written to help internal audit practitioners achieve these objectives.

We gratefully acknowledge the contributions of the many persons who have provided advice and guidance in completing this work. In particular, we express our thanks to Joseph Comptois, recently retired from his many years of outstanding service to the GAO, for his work in authoring the new Chapter 5, "Governmental Auditing Standards." We also salute the helpful work of the editors, Brooks Donnelly and Anna Marie Muskelly. This book could not have been completed without the typing assistance of Jan Root and Nikki Magraudy, and the special administrative aid of Stephanie Sides. We also express our appreciation to the IIA and the AICPA for their permission to reprint relevant professional literature. In addition, we are grateful to the management and the internal auditors of Northrop Corporation, past and present, who contributed ideas on content. Finally, a special note of gratitude is given to Gene Simonoff, whose vision and confidence in this project through the years has been indispensable.

All opinions expressed in this second edition are those of the authors and not necessarily those of any corporation or institution with which we are or have been associated, directly or indirectly. The examples and illustrations, unless otherwise noted, represent original work of the authors. Any similarity between these materials and any actual circumstance is purely coincidental.

JAMES D. WILLSON
STEVEN J. ROOT

Los Angeles, California
August 1988

Summary of Contents

TABLE OF CONTENTS ix
LIST OF ACRONYMS xxxv

PART I—TECHNIQUES FOR EFFECTIVE OVERALL STRATEGY

1. The Audit Function — An Initial Perspective 1-1
2. Developing a Strategic Auditing Approach 2-1

PART II—AUDITING STANDARDS

3. Auditing Standards Development 3-1
4. Generally Accepted Auditing Standards 4-1
5. Governmental Auditing Standards 5-1
6. Standards for the Professional Practice of Internal Auditing 6-1

PART III—AUDIT MANAGEMENT

7. Organizing and Planning the Audit Function 7-1
8. Managing Audit Projects 8-1
9. Managing Human and Other Resources and Records 9-1
10. Communicating With the Audit Committee 10-1

PART IV—TECHNIQUES FOR THE PRACTITIONER

11. How to Perform Preliminary Work 11-1
12. How to Work Effectively in the Field 12-1
13. How to Communicate Results—The Audit Report 13-1

PART V—TECHNICAL ASPECTS OF AUDITING

14. Evidential Matter 14-1
15. Audit Sampling 15-1
16. Auditing Procedures 16-1

Part VI—FINANCIAL TYPE AUDITS

17. Internal Control—An Overall View 17-1
18. Auditing Internal Control 18-1
19. Billing, Accounts Receivable, and Collections 19-1
20. Accounts Payable and Payroll Processing and Accounting 20-1
21. Cost Accounting Systems 21-1

Part VII—ETHICAL BUSINESS CONDUCT

22. Business Fraud and Business Ethics—A General Review 22-1
23. Fraudulent Financial Reporting 23-1
24. Procurement Fraud: The Government and Private Sector 24-1
25. Computer Abuse and Fraud 25-1

Part VIII—SPECIALIZED AUDIT AREAS

26. Information Systems and Internal Control 26-1
27. How to Establish and Maintain an Information Systems (EDP) Audit Function 27-1
28. Information Systems (EDP) Audit Techniques 28-1
29. International Operations 29-1
30. Financial Analysis for Acquisitions, Mergers, and Divestments 30-1

Part IX—OPERATIONAL AUDITING

31. A Management Perspective 31-1
32. Financial Management 32-1
33. Credit and Collections Management 33-1
34. Inventory Management 34-1
35. Facilities Management 35-1
36. Program Management 36-1
37. Marketing Management 37-1
38. Information Systems Management 38-1
39. R&D Management; Engineering Management 39-1
40. Retirement Plan Management 40-1

INDEX I-1

Table of Contents

List of Acronyms xxxv

Part I — Techniques for Effective Overall Strategy

1 The Audit Function—An Initial Perspective

Auditing—An Overview 2
What is Internal Auditing? 2
   The IIA Definition 2
   Other Definitions 3
Purpose of Internal
   Auditing 5
Conflicts of Allegiance in Internal
   Auditing 6
Internal Auditing as a Profession 8
Auditing in General 10

Historical Overview 11
Early Auditors and Auditing 11
Forces Bringing Auditing to Its Current
   Position 12
Emergence of Audit Branches 12
Changing Focus of Auditing 13

Audit Branches 14
Identification 14
Common Characteristics 15
   Variety of Auditing Services 15
   Third-Party Assurance Regarding
      Conformity 16
   Common Techniques 17
   Gathering Evidence and Exercising
      Professional Judgment 17
Type of Assurance Differs Among
   Audit Branches 18
   Various Interest Groups 18

Different Technical Knowledge and
   Expertise 19

Government Audit Agencies 20
General Accounting Office 20
Defense Contract Audit Agency 23
Inspectors General 28
Internal Revenue Service 31
Significance of Government Auditing .. 32

Public Accounting 32
General 32
Role of the AICPA 34
Current Challenges 35
Congressional Interest 37
Self-Regulation 42
The Attest Function 45
Other Issues 46
Significance of Public Accounting 46

Internal Auditing 47
General 47
Services, Skills, and Experience 48
Certified Internal Auditor Program
   and the Code of Ethics 50
Role of Institute of Internal Auditors .. 51
The EDP Auditors Association 53
Significance of Internal Auditing 53

The Keys to Effective Practice 54

Suggested Reading 55

Fig. 1-1 Major GAO Functional Divisions 21
Fig. 1-2 DCAA Cross Service Arrangements 24
Fig. 1-3 Offices of Inspectors General 29
Fig. 1-4 Summary of Major Requirements for SECPS Membership 43

2 Developing a Strategic Auditing Approach

Reasons for a Strategic Auditing Approach 2
Effective Allocation of Limited Resources 2
Relevant and Reliable Results 3
Basis for Managing 3
Aid to Audit Staff 3

Relating Organization Needs and Auditing Objectives 4
Needs and Objectives Are Dynamic 4
The FCPA 4
Expanded Internal Control Perceptions 5
Renewed Emphasis on Operational Efficiency 7
Rapid Development and Application of Office Automation 9
Heightened Concern Regarding Government Spending Practices 9
Relevance of Financial Information 14
Business Ethics 17
Developing a Meaningful Statement of Objectives 21
   Supplementing the IIA Guidelines 21
   Three-Step Technique for Adding Specific Objectives 21

Overall Auditing Objectives 23
Correlating Needs With Auditing Areas 23
Financial Auditing 24
Operational Auditing 25
Information Systems Auditing 28
Ethical Business Practice Auditing 29

Financial Information Reporting Auditing Described 29
"Financial Information Reporting" Defined 29
Relevance of Financial Information 29
Contrasted Roles of External and Internal Auditors 31
The Interim Financial Report Audit 32

Ethical Business Practices Auditing Described 35
"Ethical Business Practices" Defined 35
The Ethical Practices Audit 36

Deciding How to Allocate Auditing Recources 43
Strategic Audit Planning 43
Surveying Universe of Auditable Areas 45
Identifying Risk Factors 48
   Impact on Decision Making 48
   Complexity of Systems 48
   Volume of Transactions 49
   Impact on Financial Statements (Materiality) 49
   Source or Use of Cash 49
   Regulatory Involvement 49
Prioritizing Risk Factors 50
Determining Audit Frequency 50
Guidelines for Allocation of Audit Resources 51
Maintaining Flexibility 54

A Word of Caution 54

Suggested Reading 55

Fig. 2-1   Milestones in Government Spending 10
Fig. 2-2   Federal Government Revenues, Outlays, and Deficits 11
Fig. 2-3   Size of Government and Economic Performance 12
Fig. 2-4   Statement of Responsibilities of Internal Auditing 22
Fig. 2-5   Audit Program for Limited Financial Review 33
Fig. 2-6   Audit Program for Review of Ethical Business Practices 37
Fig. 2-7   Audit Areas Selected From Transaction Cycle Functions and Policies—Financial Reporting Emphasis 47
Fig. 2-8   Weighted Ranking of Audit Areas 52
Fig. 2-9   Frequencies for Common Audits 54

Part II — Auditing Standards

3 Auditing Standards Development

Standards of Performance 1
Definition 2
Purpose 2

Importance of Audting as the Prerequisite 2

Table of Contents

Standard-Setting Process 3	**General Auditing Standards** 15
By Government 3	Independence 15
By Private Sector 4	SEC Definition 15
By Government and Private Sector 4	IIA Definition 17
Self-Regulation 5	Competence 17
	Due Diligence 19
Contributions of Professional	
Organizations to Standards Setting 8	**Final Comments on Professionalism,**
AICPA 9	**Standards, and Audit Techniques** 21
IIA 12	
GAO 13	**Suggested Reading** 22
IIA Standards Differentiated 13	
Internal Auditors' Reporting	
Relationships and Standards 14	

Fig. 3-1 Summary of Major Requirements for SEC Practice Section Membership 6
Fig. 3-2 Setting Auditing Standards: 1917–1987 10

4 Generally Accepted Auditing Standards

Definition 1	**Standards Applicable to Other Audit-**
Purpose 2	**Related Financial Statement Services** .. 14
	Unaudited Financial Statements 14
Elements of GAAS 3	Interim-Period Financial Statements ... 16
Identification of Elements 3	Prospective Financial Statements 17
The Code of Professional Ethics 3	**Attestation Standards** 18
The Role of the Auditing Standards	**Specialized Industry Auditing** 19
Board 4	
Approach in Standards Setting 4	**Standards for Other Services** 20
Impact of Congressional Inquiry 6	Tax Services 20
Impact of Other Inquiries 6	Management Advisory Services 20
Other Standards-Setting Activities of the	
ASB 7	**Recent Changes** 21
Other AICPA Standards-Setting	**Suggested Reading** 23
Groups 7	
The Ten GAAS 8	

FIG. 4-1 List of Authoritative Auditing Standards Pronouncements 10

5 Governmental Auditing Standards

Governmental Auditing Standards 1	A Summary of the 1981 Standards 8
Purpose of Governmental Auditing 2	Comparisons Between the 1972 and 1981
Historical Perspective 3	Standards 12
	Single Audit Act of 1984 14
Legislative Actions Expand Audit	**Nature of Major Revisions Proposed to**
Responsibilities 4	**1981 Standards** 17
Role of the GAO 5	**Suggested Reading** 18
A Brief Look at the 1972 Standards 7	

6 Standards for the Professional Practice of Internal Auditing

Definition and Background	1	**Internal Auditing Standards**	7
Purpose	2	The General and Specific Standards	7
		The SIASs	14
Applicability	3	The Codes of Ethics	17
The Role of the PSRC	4	Statement of Responsibilities	19
Organization and Methodology	5	**Suggested Reading**	22
The Treadway Commission	6		

Fig. 6-1 Internal Auditing Standards—Levels of Authority 5
Fig. 6-2 Developing and Approving Statements on Internal Auditing Standards 6
Fig. 6-3 The Institute of Internal Auditors, Inc. Code of Ethics 18
Fig. 6-4 The Certified Internal Auditor Code of Ethics 20
Fig. 6-5 Statement of Responsibilities of Internal Auditing 21

PART III — Audit Management

7 Organizing and Planning the Audit Function

Overview of Organizing and Planning the Audit Function	2	Existing Internal Control Environment	25
		Credibility of Management	25
Creating the Audit Charter	3	Significance of Corporate Accountability	25
Form and Content	3	Trends in Regulatory Activity	25
Importance of Management Support	5	Reporting Relationships Vary	25
Organization Structure	7		
Organizational Culture	8	**Obtaining Personnel, Facilities, and Other Resources**	27
Decentralization	10		
Business Combinations	12	**Long- and Short-Range Audit Planning**	27
Technology	13	Project Planning	28
The Changing Role of Internal Auditing	14	Resource Planning	28
Organizational Considerations	14	Organizational Planning	28
Skill Requirements	14	Scientific Planning Techniques	32
Administrative Requirements	16		
Geographical Considerations	16	**Creating the Right Image for the Audit Function**	33
Intradepartment Relationships	17	Selling the Benefits of the Department	33
Position Descriptions	19	Techniques	34
Reporting Relationships	22	Balancing Independence Against Acceptability	35
Independence vs. Conflict of Interest—A Constant Battle	23	**Quality Assurance**	36
Factors to Consider in Establishing the Audit Reporting Structure	24	Definition and Purpose	36
Capability of the Staff of the Audit Function	24	Background	37
What the Board of Directors or Senior Management Knows About Auditing	24	The Issues	38
		The Future	46
		Practical Guidelines	47
Accessibility of the Board of Directors or Senior Management	24	**Suggested Reading**	48

Table of Contents

Fig. 7-1	Audit Charter of a Manufacturing Company	4
Fig. 7-2	Excerpt From Corporate Bylaws Establishing Audit Committee	6
Fig. 7-3	Memo From Senior Management Soliciting Support for an Internal Audit Program	7
Fig. 7-4	The Public Company	15
Fig. 7-5	Chart of Audit Department in Centralized Organization	17
Fig. 7-6	Chart of Audit Department in Decentralized Organization	18
Fig. 7-7	Position Description—Director of Corporate Audit	19
Fig. 7-8	Position Description—Manager of Corporate Audit	21
Fig. 7-9	Position Description—Senior Corporate Auditor	22
Fig. 7-10	IIA Survey of Reporting Relationships of Chief Internal Auditors	26
Fig. 7-11	Annual Audit Plan	30
Fig. 7-12	Announcement of an Audit Seminar for All Interested Parties	36

8 Managing Audit Projects

Overview 2

Audit Manuals 2
Definition and Purpose 2
Contents 4

Questionnaires and Checklists 4
Purpose and Definitions 4
Questionnaires 5
   Typical Uses 5
   Method of Preparation 5
Checklists 7
   Typical Uses 7
   Method of Preparation 10

Personal Computers 12
Hardware 12
Software 13

Specific Project Controls 13
Background 13
Assignment Authorization 13
Detailed Project Budgets 14
Project Reporting 17
Developing Written Audit Programs ... 18
   Purpose 22

Techniques for Preparation 22
Time of Preparation 23
Project Review 23
   Definition 23
   Purpose 23
   Specific Objectives and Techniques to Improve the Review 23
Maintaining a Proper Attitude 24

Relationships With External Auditors ... 25
The Basis for the Relationship—A Historical Perspective 25
The Current Scene 26
   Direct Assistance by Internal Auditors 34
   Participative Auditing 34
   Direct Assistance by External Auditors 35
Specific Interactions Between External and Internal Auditors 35
Outlook for the Future 37

Data Security 39

Suggested Reading 40

Fig. 8-1	Contents for Corporate Audit Manual	3
Fig. 8-2	Excerpt of Questionnaire for Purchasing Transactions	8
Fig. 8-3	Closeout Checklist	10
Fig. 8-4	Audit Report Checklist	11
Fig. 8-5	Assignment Authorization Form	15
Fig. 8-6	Time Budget—Small Variance (Overrun)	16
Fig. 8-7	Time Budget—Favorable Variance	17
Fig. 8-8	Time Budget—Large Unfavorable Variance	18
Fig. 8-9	Project Revision Form	19
Fig. 8-10	Weekly Progress Report	20
Fig. 8-11	Weekly Work Planning Objectives	21
Fig. 8-12	Comparative Data on External Audit Fees	28
Fig. 8-13	The Extent to Which Internal Audit Hours Replace External Audit Hours	31

9 Managing Human and Other Resources and Records

Introduction 2

Personnel Management 2
Background 2
Recruiting 3
  Definition and Responsibility 3
  Dependence on Organizational
    Planning 3
  Other Factors 3
  Sources for Candidates 4
The Recruiting Process 8
  Searching Markets 8
  Screening Candidates 9
  Interviewing Candidates 9
  Testing and Evaluating 10
  Timing 11
  Offering and Acknowledging
    Acceptance 11
  Follow-Up 12
  Orienting New Employees 12
Performance Measurement 12
  Definition and Purpose 12
  Effect of Subjectivity 13
  Measurement Techniques 13
Professional Training 15
  Purpose and Techniques 15
  Other Considerations 16
Career Managing 17
  Purpose 17
  Techniques 18
  Other Considerations 18
Management of Other Resources 19
  Purpose 19
  Techniques 19
    Budgeting 19
    Organizational Performance
      Measurement 20
    Other New Techniques 22

Records Management 27
Purpose 27
Audit Report Follow-Up Records 28
  Purpose 28
  Techniques 28
  Related Files 28
Workpaper Records 29
  Purpose 29
  Techniques 29
Records Retention 33
  Purpose 33
  Opinion Regarding Retention 33
  Effect of IRS Efforts 33
  The DOD Access Offensive 34
  The DCAA Subpoena Power 56
  The Attorney-Client Privilege 59
  Implications for Internal Auditors ... 64

Suggested Reading 65

Fig. 9-1 IIA Survey of Internal Audit Recruiting Sources Among Industry
          Categories 6
Fig. 9-2 Professional Experience Reported by U.S. Internal Auditors 9
Fig. 9-3 Staff Evaluation Form 14
Fig. 9-4 Excerpt of a Performance Measurement Report 21
Fig. 9-5 Activity Report Segment 23
Fig. 9-6 Assignment Log 24
Fig. 9-7 Questionnaire for Evaluating Audit Services 26
Fig. 9-8 Retention Periods for Internal Audit Department Records 29
Fig. 9-9 Postaudit Report Follow-Up Form 30
Fig. 9-10 Report Log 31
Fig. 9-11 Categories for Filing Audit Reports 32
Fig. 9-12 Scope of the Government's Right to Contractors' Records 39
Fig. 9-13 NSIA Perspective on Attorney-Client Privilege 60

10 Communicating with the Audit Committee

**The Changing Activities of the Audit
Committee** 1

Functions of the Audit Committee 2
Recent Guidelines 2
  The IIA 2
  The Treadway Commission 3

Items Suggested for Attention 4
  Evaluation of the Internal Audit
    Staff and Organizational
    Structure 8
  Review of Audit Philosophy,
    Systems, and Procedures 9

Table of Contents   XV

Review and Monitoring of the
  System of Controls 9
Review of Proposed Audit
  Coverage 10
Review of Audit and Postaudit
  Activities 10
Independent Evaluation Might Be
  Helpful 11

Making the Audit Committee More
  Effective 12
Presentations to the Audit Committee ... 14
Types of Presentations 15
Suggested Coverage 15
Illustrative Segments of a Report to the
  Audit Committee 17

Suggested Reading 20

Fig. 10-1 Appendix I— GOOD PRACTICE GUIDELINES FOR THE AUDIT
           COMMITTEE 5
Fig. 10-2 Internal Audit Department Costs 18
Fig. 10-3 Percentage Increase in Sales, Income, and Internal Audit Costs 18
Fig. 10-4 Composition of Internal Audit Staff 19
Fig. 10-5 Planned Computer Systems Reviews 20

PART IV — Techniques for the Practitioner

11 How to Perform Preliminary Work

Background 1

Definition 2

Purpose 3

Elements of Preliminary Work 3
Overview 3
Routine vs. Nonroutine Efforts 4
Defining Objectives 6
  Recurring Audits 6
  Nonrecurring Audits 6

Reviewing Pertinent Department and
  Organizational Records 8
Researching Authoritative
  Literature 12
Interviewing Management 26
Preparing and Modifying Audit
  Tools 27
Coordinating Efforts 29
Developing the Audit Plan 31

Suggested Reading 32

Fig. 11-1 Categorizing Audit Project Preliminary Work 5
Fig. 11-2 Nonrecurring Audit Project Objectives 9
Fig. 11-3 Online Database Services 14
Fig. 11-4 Diagram of Computer Research Information Flow 25
Fig. 11-5 Examples of Survey Subjects 27
Fig. 11-6 Formal Communication of Year's Audits and Audit Arrangements 30
Fig. 11-7 Memo Communicating Specific Audit Arrangements 32

12 How to Work Effectively in the Field

Overview 1

Planning 3
Purpose 3
Techniques 3

Organizing 4
Definition and Purpose 4
Activities Involved 5
Techniques 5

Performing	7	Timing of Preparation	18
Activities Involved	7	Access Issues	18
Perspective	7		
Use of Portable Personal Computers	7	**Communicating Progress and Results**	24
		Perspective	24
Documenting: Preparing Workpapers	10	Communication Points	25
Purpose	10	Initial Conference	25
"Performing" and "Documenting"		Periodic Reporting	27
Distinguished	10	Exit Conference	28
Principle of Limited Record Keeping	11	Communication Modes	30
Common Workpaper Deficiencies	11	Criteria for Deciding What Is	
Techniques for Organization	12	Relevant	31
Criteria for Retention	17		
Suggestions in Creating Workpapers	17	**Suggested Reading**	34

Fig. 12-1	Communications Software Products	9
Fig. 12-2	Workpaper Contents Page	13
Fig. 12-3	Workpaper Summary Narrative	14
Fig. 12-4	Workpaper Summary of Findings	15
Fig. 12-5	Workpaper Evidencing Audit Testing	16
Fig. 12-6	Workpaper Evidencing Analytical Effort	19
Fig. 12-7	The Communication Triangle	26
Fig. 12-8	Project Status Report Form	29
Fig. 12-9	Techniques for an Effective Exit Conference	30
Fig. 12-10	Illustrative Actions for Specific Reporting Situations	33

13   How to Communicate Results—The Audit Report

The Audit Report as a Communication		Findings	21
Device	2	Recommendations	23
Requirements for Reports	2	**Conserving the Time of Higher**	
Basic Principles	2	**Management**	27
Accuracy	2		
Timeliness	3	**Oral Reports**	28
Adaptability to Proper Management		**Graphic and/or Pictured**	
Level	3	**Presentations**	28
Application of the "Exception			
Principle"	3	**Activity and Evaluation Reports**	32
Additional Guidelines	3		
		Preparing the Report	39
Classification of Reports	4	Writing the Report	39
		Physical Characteristics	39
Standards for Reporting	5	Editing	40
The IIA	5	Proofreading	40
The GAO	9		
		A Simple Program to Improve Audit	
Formal Written Reports on Activities		**Reports**	40
Examined	17		
Transmittal Sheet	18	**Replies to Audit Reports**	41
Summary or Highlights	18		
Statement of Purpose	18	**Suggested Reading**	43
Scope of Examination	19		
The Opinion	21		

Fig. 13-1	Transmittal Sheet	19
Fig. 13-2	Summary Section of Audit Report	20
Fig. 13-3	Complete Audit Report	24

Table of Contents   xvii

Fig. 13-4   Graphic Report on Capital Expenditure Performance 29
Fig. 13-5   Flow Chart Authorizing Travel 30
Fig. 13-6   Graph of Relative Operating Margin 31
Fig. 13-7   Written Annual Report to Audit Committee on Audit Activities 33
Fig. 13-8   Visual Aids Used in the Annual Report to the Audit Committee 35
Fig. 13-9   Audit Reply Evaluation Form 42

PART V — Technical Aspects of Auditing

14 Evidential Matter

Overview 1
The Importance of Evidential Matter 2
Definitions, Principles, and Concepts 3
"Audit Evidence" Defined 3
Selectivity 4
   Audit Risk 4
Reliability 7
Relevance 8

Differentiating Evidential Requirements
  of External and Internal Auditors 8

Basic Assumptions 10
Management Honesty 11
Management Competence 11
Authenticity of Documents 11
Senior Management Support 12
Arm's-Length Activities 12

Evidence Analyzed 13

Qualitative Characteristics 13
Quantitative Characteristics 13
Summary on Characteristics 14
Types of Evidence 14
  Primary Evidence 15
  External Evidence 15
  Recurring Internal Evidence 15
  Nonrecurring Internal Evidence 16
Evidence and the Internal Auditor 17
  Internal Control 17
  Internal Accounting Control
   Surveys 18
  Limited Financial Reviews 18
  Standards-of-Ethical-Business-
   Conduct Audits 18
  Operational Control Audits 18
  EDP Auditing 22
Other Considerations 22

Suggested Reading 22

Fig. 14-1   Examples of Primary Evidence 16
Fig. 14-2   Summary Narrative of Work Performed 19
Fig. 14-3   Comparative Analysis—An Example of Internal Evidence 21

15 Audit Sampling

Overview 2
Definitions 3
Background and Perspective 4
Concept of Limited Testing 4
Risk Considerations 5
Minimizing Risk—Cost vs. Benefit 6
Sampling Approaches 7
Nonstatistical Sampling 7
Definition 7

Performance Techniques 7
  Determining Sample Objective 8
  Determining Deviation
   Conditions 8
  Defining the Population
   Characteristics 9
  Determining Sample Size 9
  Selecting the Sample 10
  Performing the Test 11
  Evaluating Test Results 11
  Documentation Techniques 13
  Practical Suggestions 13

Statistical Sampling	15
Definition	15
The Evolution of Statistical Sampling	16
Advantages and Disadvantages	16
Concepts Involved in Statistical Sampling	17
Performance Techniques	19
Determining Sample Size	19
Selecting the Sample	20
Performing the Test	21
Evaluating the Results	21
Documentation Techniques	22
Statistical Sampling Methods	26
Attribute Sampling	26
Applicability	26
Methodology	28
Illustration	28
Variables Sampling	30
Applicability	31
Methodology	31
Other Sampling Techniques	35
Discovery Sampling	35
Combined Attribute Variables Sampling	35
Statistical Sampling Software	36
Conclusion	37
Suggested Reading	37

Fig. 15-1	Specimen Workpaper Evidencing Sample Size Determination	23
Fig. 15-2	Specimen Workpaper Evidencing Sample Tests Performed	24
Fig. 15-3	Specimen Workpaper Evidencing Analysis of Results	25
Fig. 15-4	Frequently Tested Attributes—Payroll and Procurement Functions	27
Fig. 15-5	Attribute Sampling Table	29
Fig. 15-6	Factors for Estimating Standard Deviation	33
Fig. 15-7	Variables Sampling Table	34

16   Auditing Procedures

Objective and Definition	2
Observation	2
Specific Forms of Observation Procedures	3
Techniques	3
Planning	3
Determining Sampling Method	4
Performing the Work	4
Documentation	5
Applicability to Specific Audit Approaches	5
Detailed Internal Control Audits	5
Internal Control Surveys	6
Limited Financial Reviews	6
Standards of Ethical Business Conduct	6
Operational and I/S Audits	6
Inquiry	7
Specific Forms of Inquiry	7
Interviewing	8
Researching	8
Analyzing	10
Special Types of Analytical Procedures	11
Techniques	19
Documentation	19
Applicability to Specific Audit Approaches	24
Inspection	24
Specific Forms of Inspection	25
Reading	25
Scanning	26
Reviewing	26
Vouching	26
Techniques	27
Planning and Preparation	27
Determining Sampling Method	27
Performing the Work	27
Documentation	29
Applicability to Specific Audit Approaches	29
Confirmation	29
Specific Forms of Confirmation Procedures	30
Confirming	30
Reperforming	31
Reconciling	31
Techniques	32
Documentation	32
Applicability to Specific Audit Approaches	35
Cost-Benefit Analysis	35
Definition and Background	35
Applicability	36
Techniques	36
Documentation	39
A Special Application	39
Suggested Reading	40

Table of Contents   xix

Fig. 16-1   Portion of an Audit Program for Observing Physical Inventory Counts 4
Fig. 16-2   How to Conduct an Interview 9
Fig. 16-3   Common Financial Ratios 12
Fig. 16-4   A Typical Trend Analysis 15
Fig. 16-5   An Example of a Linear Regression Analysis 17
Fig. 16-6   Forms of Regression Analysis 18
Fig. 16-7   Example of a Narrative of an Interview 20
Fig. 16-8   A Method of Evidencing Analytical Work 21
Fig. 16-9   Flow Chart With Objectives, Controls, and Evaluation Identified 22
Fig. 16-10   Example of a Workpaper Documenting Inspection 28
Fig. 16-11   Documentation of a Review of Reconciliations 33
Fig. 16-12   Documentation of Reperformance 34
Fig. 16-13   Table of Exposure Values 38

PART VI — Financial Type Audits

17 Internal Control—An Overall View

Introduction 2
Business Risks and Management Control 2
Internal Controls Defined 3
Foreign Corrupt Practices Act 7
General Provisions 8
Accounting Standards of the Act 8
Standards and Other Guidelines for Internal Controls 9
The AICPA 9
    The Form of the Accountant's Report 10
The IIA 14
    Summary 15
    SIAS No. 1—Control: Concepts and Responsibilities 15
The GAO 21
    Standards for Internal Controls in the Federal Government 21
    Proposed Revision to Audit Standards—Internal Controls Section 29
Report of the National Commission on Fraudulent Financial Reporting 30
The Institute of Internal Auditors Reports on Fraud 35
Variability of Control Systems 35
Elements of Internal Accounting Control Systems 37
Competent Personnel and Defined Responsibilities 37

Adequate Segregation of Duties 38
Existence of Adequate Documents and Records 38
Adequate Authorization Procedures ... 39
Levels of Business Activity 39
    Strategic Planning 40
    Tactical Planning 40
    Detailed Operational Control 40
Internal Accounting Control Objectives 41
EDP and Internal Accounting Controls 42
Cost-Effective Controls Needed 43
Responsibility of Senior Management and Directors 44
Role of the External Auditor 45
Internal Audit Department 46
Allocation of Responsibility for Adequate Internal Controls 47
Role of the Board of Directors 47
Role of Senior Corporate Management 48
Role of Financial Management 48
Role of Chief Internal Auditor 49
Role of Independent Accountant 49
Management Representations to the Public 50
Limitations on Internal Control 51
Suggested Reading 52

Fig. 17-1   Classification of Internal Controls 6
Fig. 17-2   Activities or Functions by Level of Business Activity 41
Fig. 17-3   Illustrative Declaration in Annual Report—Monsanto Company 51

18   Auditing Internal Control

Introduction 2	Need for a Combination of
Clarification of Terms 2	Techniques 28
Relevance of Internal Accounting Control 4	Detailed Auditing of Internal Control ... 28
Integration of the FCPA With Internal Accounting Control 4	Definition 28
	Objective 29
Aids for Auditing Internal Accounting Control 5	Unique Characteristics 31
	Focus Is on a Single Function, Cycle, or Activity 31
Approaches, Programs, Questionnaires, and Documentation 5	All Aspects of Control Are Included 31
Evaluations Used by Public Accountants 6	Questionnaires Are Used 32
Considering the Business 8	Tests Cover a Period of Time 32
Formulating Internal Accounting Control Objectives 8	Separate Audit Reports With Limited Distribution 32
Evaluating Whether Control Techniques Achieve the Objectives 9	Advantages and Disadvantages 36
	Internal Control Survey 37
Summary Checklist on Evaluating Internal Control 9	Definition 37
	Objective 37
The External Auditor's Responsibility For Internal Control 20	Unique Characteristics 39
	Focus Is on Accounting Entity 39
The Current Picture 20	Evaluation Limited to Accounting Controls 40
The Exposure Drafts 20	Limited Testing 41
The Concept of Control Structure 20	Absence of Questionnaires 41
Implications 22	Comprehensive Reports With Full Distribution 43
The Concept of Reportable Conditions 24	Audit Programs 43
The Effect on Internal Auditors 26	Advantages and Disadvantages 48
	Final Thoughts 48
Building on Techniques Developed by Public Accountants 26	Suggested Reading 49

Fig. 18-1   Approach to Internal Accounting Control Evaluation 7
Fig. 18-2   Operating Components of a Typical Commercial or Industrial Business 11
Fig. 18-3   Evaluation Process for Financial Management 12
Fig. 18-4   Evaluation Process for Financial Reporting 14
Fig. 18-5   Guide in Evaluating Cash Receipts 16
Fig. 18-6   Flow Chart Depicting the Cash Disbursements Cycle 18
Fig. 18-7   Sample Questionnaire on Internal Control for Sales, Billings, Receivables, and Collection Cycle 19
Fig. 18-8   Sample Detailed Internal Control Audit Report With No Findings 29
Fig. 18-9   Sample Detailed Internal Control Audit Report With Findings 30
Fig. 18-10 Internal Control Questionnaire for Cash Disbursements 33
Fig. 18-11 Audit Program for Cash Receipts 35
Fig. 18-12 Internal Control Survey Report 38
Fig. 18-13 Specimen Workpaper Documenting Internal Controls 42
Fig. 18-14 Illustration of Documenting Internal Control Evaluation 44
Fig. 18-15 Audit Program for Internal Accounting Control Survey 46

Table of Contents xxi

19 Billing, Accounts Receivable, and Collections

Overview	1	Reporting and Accountability	7
Definition and Background	2	Audit Techniques	8
The Business Environment	3	Preliminary	8
		Fieldwork	8
Risks	4	Illustrative Questionnaires	9
Internal Control Objectives	5	Sample Audit Program	18
Internal Control Techniques	6	Specimen Audit Report	22
Organization and Authorization	6		
Processing and Accounting	6	Suggested Reading	25
Safeguarding	7		

Fig. 19-1 Internal Control Questionnaire for Accounts Receivable Billing 10
Fig. 19-2 Internal Control Questionnaire for Cash Receipts 14
Fig. 19-3 Audit Program for Accounts Receivable Billing 18
Fig. 19-4 Report on Audit of Billing and Collecting Functions 22

20 Accounts Payable and Payroll Processing and Accounting

Accounts Payable Overview	2	A Specimen Report	13
Definition and Background	2	Payroll Overview	13
The Business Environment	3	Definition and Background	25
Management Objectives	3		
Current Financial Condition	4	The Business Environment	26
Type of Industry	4	Risks	27
Legal Considerations	4		
Risks	5	Internal Control Objectives	29
Internal Control Objectives	6	Internal Control Techniques	30
		Organization and Authorization	30
Internal Control Techniques	6	Processing and Accounting	31
Organization	7	Safeguarding	32
Authorization Controls	8	Reporting and Accountability	32
Processing and Accounting	8		
Accessibility and Safeguarding	9	Audit Techniques	33
Reporting and Accountability	9	Preliminary	33
		Fieldwork	34
Audit Techniques	10		
Preliminary	10	Illustrative Questionnaire	36
Fieldwork	11	A Sample Audit Program	36
Illustrative Questionnaire	13	Specimen Reports	45
A Sample Audit Program	13	Suggested Reading	51

Fig. 20-1 Internal Control Questionnaire for Accounts Payable 14
Fig. 20-2 Audit Program for Accounts Payable 17
Fig. 20-3 Audit Report—Accounts Payable Function 20
Fig. 20-4 Internal Control Questionnaire for Payroll 37
Fig. 20-5 Payroll Audit Program 42
Fig. 20-6 Audit Report—Corporate Payroll System Internal Controls 46
Fig. 20-7 Audit Report on Payroll-Related Transactions 49

21 Cost Accounting Systems

Overview	1	Processing and Accounting	10
Definition and Background	3	Accessibility and Safeguarding	13
Actual Job Cost System	4	Reporting and Accountability	13
Actual Process Cost System	4	Audit Techniques	14
Standard Cost System	5	Preliminary	14
The Business Environment	5	Fieldwork	15
Risks	7	Illustrative Questionnaire	16
Internal Control Objectives	8	Sample Audit Program	21
Internal Control Techniques	9	Specimen Report	21
Organization and Authorization	9	Suggested Reading	28

Fig. 21-1 Typical Cost Code Structure 11
Fig. 21-2 Illustrative Burden Pool Accounts 12
Fig. 21-3 Internal Control Questionnaire for Cost System (Cost Ledger) 17
Fig. 21-4 Cost System Review Audit Program 22
Fig. 21-5 Report on Audit of Manufacturing Job Cost Accounting System 25

PART VII — Ethical Business Conduct

22 Business Fraud and Business Ethics—A General Review

Introduction	2	Business Ethics and Internal Auditing	38
Fraud Defined	3	An Antifraud Checklist	40
Common Forms of Fraud	4	A Fraud Questionnaire	42
Circumstances That Encourage Fraud	5	Responsibility for Detecting Fraud	45
Indicia of Fraud	6	Independent Accountants	45
Standards for the Deterrence, Detection, Investigation, and Reporting of Fraud	11	Internal Auditors	47
		Government Auditors	49
		Management Accountants	51
General Preventive Measures	19	Special Fraud Investigations	54
Management Override	21	Definition	54
Consider Motivating Factors	24	Nature of the Work	55
Areas Vulnerable to Management Override	24	Standards and Procedures Employed	55
		Reporting	56
		Whistle-blowing	56
The Role of Business Ethics	25	SIAS No. 3	57
An Initial Perspective	25	Coordination With the Legal Department	58
Factors That Influence Business Ethics	27	Use of Informants	58
Misconduct—Why It Occurs	30		
The Risks	31	Summary	59
Techniques for Maintaining Effective Business Ethics	31	Suggested Reading	59

Fig. 22-1 Warning Signals of Possible Management Fraud 7
Fig. 22-2 The Red Flags of Possible Fraudulent Activity 9
Fig. 22-3 SIAS No. 3: Deterrence, Detection, Investigation, and Reporting of Fraud 13

Table of Contents   xxiii

Fig. 22-4   Corporate Policy Directive on Internal Controls—Responsibilities Section ...   22
Fig. 22-5   Business Ethics—A Hypothetical Situation   28
Fig. 22-6   Martin-Marrietta Corporation Code of Ethics and Standards of Conduct   33
Fig. 22-7   Defense Industry Initiatives Questionnaire and Illustrative Procedures   35
Fig. 22-8   Report of Peat Marwick Mitchell & Co.—Concluding Remarks   39

23 Fraudulent Financial Reporting

Introduction	1	The NCFFR	3
Conditions of Fraudulent Financial Reporting	2	Summary of NCFFR Recommendations	4
Participants in the Financial Reporting Process	3	Suggested Reading	10

24 Procurement Fraud: The Government and Private Sector

Introduction	1	Indicators of Fraud in DOD Procurement	5
Minimizing Fraud on Government Contracts	2	Labor Fraud Indicators	5
Some U.S. Government Publications	2	Material Fraud Indicators	5
		Defective Pricing Fraud	38
		Self-Policing by DOD Contractors	38

Fig. 24-1   Minimizing Vulnerability to Fraud   3
Fig. 24-2   Indicators of Fraud in Department of Defense Procurement   6

25 Computer Abuse and Fraud

Introduction	1	Detection	21
Definitions	2	Safeguarding Computer Data	22
Reasons for Growth in Computer Abuse and Fraud	2	An Operational Audit of Computer Security	22
Categories of Computer Abuse and Fraud	3	Developing Internal Control for a Minicomputer System	24
Computer Fraud—Causes and Techniques	4	Multilevel Controls	24
		Controlling Data Entry Errors	25
Computer-Related Crime	4	Preventing Unauthorized Access	25
The Role of the Computer in Crime	5	The Use of "Threat Teams" to Detect and Prevent Fraud	26
Where Does the Vulnerability Lie?	5	
Rapid Growth	5	Guidelines in Using the Threat Team Technique	26
Insufficient Auditing	5	
Inadequate Controls	6	The Advantages	27
Learning to Speak the Language	6	
A Question of Control and Responsibility	9	Legislative Relief	28
		State Legislation	28
		Federal Computer Crime Laws	29
Other Methods of Unauthorized Access ..	10	
Bulletin Board Systems	10	Computer Fraud Insurance Coverage ...	29
Reducing Computer Fraud	20	
Prevention	20	Suggested Reading	30

PART VIII — Specialized Audit Areas

26 Information Systems and Internal Control

An Overall Perspective	2
Definitions	2
Perspective	4
Functions That Benefit From I/S	7
Personal Computers	10
Explosion in Availability and Use	10
Risks and Concerns	12
Office Automation	13
Word Processing	13
Communication	14
Information Distribution	15
Communications Software	16
The Inherent Risks	17
Internal Control in an I/S Environment	23
Applicability of Internal Accounting Control Principles and Objectives	23
Variability of Control Techniques	24
Control Techniques Perspective	24
Internal Control Objectives in an I/S Environment	26
Detailed Objectives and Controls	31
I/S Organization Controls	31
Operations Controls	32
Resource Acquisition and Utilization Controls	33
Record-Keeping Controls	33
Accountability Controls	33
Security Controls	33
Systems Development Controls	34
Other Objectives and Techniques	35
Personal Computer Control Techniques	35
Implications for Auditors	41
Impact of Errors	41
Access Techniques	42
Specialized Knowledge	42
Audit Techniques	42
Independence	42
Changing Technology	43
Summary	43
Computer Crime—A Special Perspective	43
Glossary	44
Suggested Reading	53

Fig. 26-1	An MIS	3
Fig. 26-2	A Typical FIS for a Manufacturing Company	5
Fig. 26-3	Components of a Data Processing System	8
Fig. 26-4	An Example of an MIS Organization Structure	9
Fig. 26-5	Communications Software Packages	18
Fig. 26-6	Types of Security Exposure	21
Fig. 26-7	Preventive, Limiting, and Recovery Controls for Selected Exposures	22
Fig. 26-8	List of Controls by Area of Responsibility	27

27 How to Establish and Maintain an Information Systems (EDP) Audit Function

Role of Internal Auditing	2
Concern of Management	2
Response by Auditors	2
Objectives of I/S Auditing	4
I/S Audit Approach	4
Determining What to Audit	4
Relationship to Basic Internal Auditing Approach	5
Types of I/S Auditing	5
Detailed Functional Auditing	5
Installation Reviews	6
Applications Auditing	22
Developing Systems Auditing	22
Concurrent Auditing	23
Integrated Test Facilities	29
Embedded Audit Data Collection	29
Snapshot/Extended Record	30
Other Audit Forms	32
Prioritizing I/S Audit Projects	32
Suggestions for Allocating Audit Resources	33

Table of Contents

Managing the I/S Audit Function	35	Performance Measurement	46
Standards	35	Professional Training	47
Organizing and Planning I/S Audits	36		
Organizing	36	**Management of Personal Computers**	51
Planning	39	Automated Workpapers	53
Selling	40	Implementation Strategy	57
Project Management	42	**Performing I/S Audits**	58
Auditing Manuals	42	Applicability of Basic Audit	
Use of Questionnaires and Checklists	42	Approach	58
Specific Project Authorization and Monitoring	44	Preliminary Work	58
		Fieldwork	59
		Documentation	59
Quality Control	45	Evidential Matter	60
Management of Personnel	45		
Recruiting	45	**Suggested Reading**	62

Fig. 27-1	Top Management's Data Processing Concerns	3
Fig. 27-2	Questionnaire to Evaluate Controls in an EDP Installation	7
Fig. 27-3	Portion of a Developing System Control Questionnaire	24
Fig. 27-4	Flow Chart of the Snapshot Audit Technique	31
Fig. 27-5	Depiction of the Extended Record Technique	32
Fig. 27-6	Frequencies for I/S Audits	34
Fig. 27-7	Code of Professional Ethics	36
Fig. 27-8	General Standards for Information Systems Auditing	37
Fig. 27-9	Typical I/S Audit Function Organization Chart	39
Fig. 27-10	Excerpt of a Policy Statement Setting Forth I/S Audit Responsibility	40
Fig. 27-11	Audit Manual Contents Page—Excerpt Covering I/S Auditing	43
Fig. 27-12	Audit Software Packages and Vendors	55
Fig. 27-13	Spreadsheet Software	56
Fig. 27-14	Statistical Sampling Computer Report	61

28   Information Systems (EDP) Audit Techniques

Introduction	2	Integrated Test Facility	19
		Parallel Simulation	20
Overview	2	Parallel Simulation Using Generalized Audit Software	22
Definition and Purpose	4	Embedded Audit Routines	23
Sampling Applicability	4	Utility Programs	25
Nonstatistical Sampling	5	Other System Software	26
Statistical Sampling	7	Security Software	27
Traditional Auditing Techniques	7	**Improving Performance Efficiency and Effectiveness**	28
Observation	8	Generalized Audit Software	29
Inquiry	9	Utility Programs	35
Inspection	10	Other System Software	35
Confirmation	11	Embedded Routines	36
		Expert Systems	36
Computer-Assisted Audit Techniques	12		
Definition and Objectives	12	**Protecting Independence**	38
Applicability	13	The Audit Facility	38
		Utility Programs	40
Techniques for Auditing Controls	16	Program Verifications	40
Tracing	16	Operating System Reviews	41
Snapshot	17	Other Operating System Reviews	45
Test Data	18		

Audit Uses of Personal Computers 53
Criteria in Selecting
 MicroComputers 53
Audit Uses 55

Final Thoughts 58
Suggested Reading 59

Fig. 28-1	Use of I/S Audit Tools and Techniques	3
Fig. 28-2	Selected Activities for Which Nonstatistical Sampling Is Necessary	6
Fig. 28-3	Classification of Computer-Assisted Audit Techniques	13
Fig. 28-4	Narrative Workpaper Illustrating Difficulties in Applying Computer-Assisted Audit Techniques	15
Fig. 28-5	Flow Chart Depicting Parallel Simulation	21
Fig. 28-6	Depiction of Embedded Audit Routines	24
Fig. 28-7	A Tabulation of Generalized Audit Software Packages and Their Vendors	30
Fig. 28-8	Situations in Which Generalized Audit Software May Be of Use	32
Fig. 28-9	Comparison of Audit Techniques Common to I/S and Non-I/S Auditing Indicating the Potential for Independent Performance	39
Fig. 28-10	Suppliers of PC AT Compatibles	56
Fig. 28-11	Software Products for Downloading Data	57

29 International Operations

Introduction 2

Nature and Purpose of International Business 2

Characteristic Differences in International Operations 4

Advantages and Risks in Multinational Operations 5

Impact of International Operations on Management Functions 6
Impact on Financial Activities 6
 Organizational Matters 6
 Accounting Activities 9
 Financial Planning and Budgets 9
 Taxation 10
 Investment Decisions 11
 Obtaining Funds 11
 Controls 11
Impact on Marketing Activities 12
 Marketing Organization Structure .. 12
 Channels of Distribution 13
 Market 13
 The Product 13
 Marketing Tactics or Methods 13
Impact on Personnel Activities 14
Impact on Manufacturing, and Other Supporting Service, Activities 14

Managing the International Audit Function 15

Special U.S. Laws Relating to International Operations 15
Compliance With Legal Requirements of Host Countries ... 15
Special Need to Interpret Financial Policies and Procedures 16
Differences in Standards of Behavior 16

Performing International Audits 16
Preparation for a Foreign Location Audit 17
 Examples of Different Accounting Procedures 19
 Improving the Quality of the Overseas Audit 20

International Auditing Standards 21
Diversity in Auditing Standards and Procedures 21
Trends in International Auditing Standards 22
The Changing Multinational 23

Audit Questionnaires and Programs 24

Special Areas for Inquiry 24

Suggested Reading 29

Table of Contents xxvii

Fig. 29-1 Comparative Horizons or Viewpoints of Domestic (U.S.) vs. International Companies 7
Fig. 29-2 Chart of International Finance Functions—Centralized at Corporate Headquarters 9
Fig. 29-3 International Finance Organization Structure—Decentralized 10
Fig. 29-4 Audit Questionnaire—Foreign Agent Agreements 25

30 Financial Analysis for Acquisitions, Mergers, and Divestments

Introduction	2	Capitalized Earnings (P/E Multiples) ...	23
		Discounted Cash Flow	25
Acquisitions as Related to Corporate Objectives	3	Impact of Changes in Accounting Policies and Procedures	27
Acquisition Criteria	3	The Accounting Basis for Business Combinations	29
Reasons for Acquisitions or Mergers or Divestments	4	**Tax Considerations**	31
Selling a Business	5	Tax Methods of Consummating an Acquisition	31
A Trend Toward Concentration	6	An Asset Acquisition	32
Public Concern About Takeovers	7	A 338 Transaction	32
Diversification Can Be a Mistake	9	A Stock Acquisition	32
		Type A Reorganizations	32
Alternatives to Acquisitions	10	Type B Reorganizations	33
Leveraged Buyouts	10	Type C Reorganizations	34
		Impact of the Tax Reform Act of 1986	34
Greenmail	11		
Defenses Against Hostile Acquisitions ...	11	**Earnings Per Share**	35
		The Combination Package	37
Purpose of Financial Analysis	12		
Data Requirements	13	**The Audit Report**	39
Valuing an Acquisition	22	**Financial Analysis Necessary for Divestments**	45
Book Value	22		
Appraised Value	22	**Suggested Reading**	47
Market Value	23		

Fig. 30-1 Checklist for Acquisition Review 15
Fig. 30-2 Capitalized Earnings—Weighted and Unweighted 24
Fig. 30-3 Calculation of Purchase Price Based on Historical and Projected Earnings—as Adjusted 25
Fig. 30-4 Present Value of a Business Using the DCF Technique 26
Fig. 30-5 Summary of Comparative Factors for Merger Discussion 28
Fig. 30-6 Comparative Purchase Prices 28
Fig. 30-7 Rates of Return (DCF) 28
Fig. 30-8 Impact of Accounting Practices 30
Fig. 30-9 Increase in EPS With Acquisition 36
Fig. 30-10 Impact of Different Cash Securities Packages 38
Fig. 30-11 Impact of Various Growth Rates on EPS 39
Fig. 30-12 Illustrative Audit Report 42

PART IX — Operational Auditing

31 A Management Perspective

Internal Auditing—A Continually Changing Emphasis	1
A Workable Definition for Operational Auditing	3
Similarity of Activities in Both Financial and Operational Audits	4
Benefits of Operational Audits	6
Areas Suggested for Operational Audits	6
Securing an Engagement; Some Limitations	8
Knowledge Needed to Perform an Operational Audit	9
Good Management Practice	10
Standards for Operational Audits	11
Basic Steps in Operational Auditing	13
Preliminary Phase	14
Physical Tour of the Facility	14
Gathering of Written Data	15
Interviews With Management Personnel	15
Limited Financial Analysis	16
Preparation of Survey Memorandum	16
Progressively Difficult Levels of Operational Auditing	17
Operational Auditing	17
Management Auditing	17
Strategic Auditing	18
Reports on Operational Audits	18
Suggested Reading	19

Fig. 31-1 Nonfinancial Activities and Functions Audited by Internal Auditing, by Industry (282 Companies) 2
Fig. 31-2 Checklist for Expanded-Scope Audits 12

32 Financial Management

Introduction	1
Expanding Role of the Financial Executive	2
Environmental Changes	2
Technological Changes	3
Government Impact	3
Internal Business Changes	4
Nature of the Financial Function	5
Financial Management Objectives	6
Organizing and Managing the Financial Function	11
Basics for an Operating Audit	11
The Functional Outline	12
The Finance Organization Structure	12
Illustrative Audit Questionnaire for Financial Activities	15
Financial Management Audit Programs	27
Illustrative Audit Findings	45
Segment Operational Audits	55
Audit Program for Long-Term Liabilities	56

Fig. 32-1 Functional Outline—Senior Vice-President–Finance 13
Fig. 32-2 Financial Department Organization Chart 15
Fig. 32-3 Cash Management Control Questionnaire 16
Fig. 32-4 Quarterly Cash Forecasting Audit Program 28
Fig. 32-5 Audit Program—Financial Management 30
Fig. 32-6 Audit Report Recommending Improvements in Cash Management Procedures 47

33   Credit and Collections Management

Introduction	1	Elements of the Credit and Collections Operation	7
Nature and Role of Credit	2	Illustrative Audit Questionnaire—Credit and Collections Activity	8
Basic Objectives of Credit Management	2	Credit and Collections Operational Audit Program	14
Organizational Status	4		
The Three C's of Credit	6	Suggested Reading	20

Fig. 33-1   Functional Credit Organization in a Large Manufacturing Company 5
Fig. 33-2   Audit Questionnaire—Credit and Collections Activity 9
Fig. 33-3   Credit and Collections Operational Audit Program 14
Fig. 33-4   Some Selected Key Business Ratios Developed by Dun & Bradstreet, Inc. 19

34   Inventory Management

Introduction	2	Scope of Inventory Management	19
Pervading Impact of Inventory Management	2	Inventory Planning Applications	20
		Long-Range Plan	20
		Short-Term Plan	21
Key Components of an Effective Inventory Management System	4	Very Short-Term Plan	21
		Inventory Control Applications	21
Organization	5	Inventory Levels	22
Policies	5	The ABC Method of Inventory Management	23
Systems and Procedures	5	Material Requirements Planning	23
Functional Objectives and Procedures	6	Reorder Point Systems	24
Procurement and Inventory Management	6	The Order Quantity	25
		Importance of Adequate Data	27
Just-in-Time Inventories	7	Inventory Management Control Questionnaire	28
Procurement Objectives	8		
The Procurement Cycle	8	Inventory Management Audit Program	37
Role of the Internal Auditor	9	Inventory Management Audit Findings	41
Procurement Questionnaire and Audit Program	9	Financial Type Inventory Audits	54
Production Management Objectives	18	AICPA Study on Inventory Audits	57
Objectives of Warehousing and Distribution	19	Suggested Reading	59

Fig. 34-1   Illustration of an Integrated Planning and Control System 3
Fig. 34-2   Audit Questionnaire on Purchase of Materials, Supplies, and Services 10
Fig. 34-3   Audit Program for Procurement Review 15
Fig. 34-4   Illustration of EOQ Formula Application 26
Fig. 34-5   Inventory Management Control Questionnaire 28
Fig. 34-6   Audit Program—Inventory Management 38
Fig. 34-7   Audit Report on the Inventory Management System—Small Anodizing and Cutting Plant 41
Fig. 34-8   Audit Report on Inventory Management Showing Unacceptable Conditions —Telecommunications Manufacturer 43

xxx Table of Contents

35 Facilities Management

Objectives of Facilities Management 1
Facilities Organization Structure 2
Facilities Control Cycle 4
Long-Range Facilities Plan 5
Short-Term Facilities Plan 6
Project Evaluation Methods 6
Classifying and Ranking the Projects 7
Steps in the Capital Budgeting Procedure 9
Control and Monitoring of Capital Acquisitions 10
Custody and Administration of Facilities 11
Maintenance and Care 11
Optimum Utilization of Equipment 12
Records and Reports 12
Facilities Procurement Review 12
Facilities Management Questionnaire and Program 15
Facilities Management Audit Reports and Typical Findings 31
Internal Audit of Capital Investment Projects 34
Internal Audit of Ongoing Capital Projects 34
Post-Completion Audits of Capital Projects 37
Suggested Reading 38

Fig. 35-1 Functional Outline—Vice-President–Materiel, Facilities, and Services 3
Fig. 35-2 Priority Schedule for Capital Projects 8
Fig. 35-3 Audit Program for Facilities Procurement Review 13
Fig. 35-4 Facilities Management Audit Questionnaire 16
Fig. 35-5 Audit Program—Facilities Management 25
Fig. 35-6 Facilities Management Audit Report 32

36 Program Management

Introduction 1
Programs and Program Management 2
The Management Process and PERT 3
Determine and Define Objectives 4
Develop Plans 6
Determine Schedules 6
Progress Evaluation 7
Management Decisions and Actions 8
Recycle 8
PERT Networks 8
Indicated Final Cost 11
Program Management Control Questionnaire 11
Program Management Audit Program 19
Audit Findings 19
Program Management and Microcomputers 28
Suggested Reading 29

Fig. 36-1 The Management Process 5
Fig. 36-2 Work Breakdown Schedule Showing Work Breakdown Packages at Levels 1, 2, 3, 4 5
Fig. 36-3 Relationship of Work Breakdown Package to Functional Activities and Network of Steps 7
Fig. 36-4 PERT Network—Simplified 9
Fig. 36-5 PERT Network with Earliest and Latest Event Time 10
Fig. 36-6 Program Management Control Questionnaire 12
Fig. 36-7 Program Management Audit Program 20
Fig. 36-8 Program Management Audit Report 22

37 Marketing Management

Nature and Scope of the Marketing
  Function 1
Marketing Objectives 2
The Marketing Organization
  Structure 4
Marketing Policies and Procedures 5
Pricing Procedures and Controls 5
Effectiveness of the Sales Effort 5
Sales Planning 6
Performance Reports 6

Marketing Management
  Questionnaire 7
Marketing Management Audit
  Program 14
Role of the Internal Auditor 19
Using Computers in Marketing
  Management 20

Suggested Reading 20

Fig. 37-1   Relation of Marketing Objectives, Strategies, and Results 8
Fig. 37-2   Marketing Management Audit Questionnaire 7
Fig. 37-3   Operations Audit Program—Marketing Management 14

38 Information Systems Management

Overview 2
Information Systems and Its
  Management 2
Definitions 4
EDP Evolution: Impact on the
  Marketplace 4

Expanding Role of ISM 5
Technology Environment 7
User Environment 8
EDP Auditing Environment 9
A Perspective 9

Nature of the ISM Functions 9
Business Within a Business 10
Service Orientation 10
Dynamic Environment 11
Scarcity of Resources 12
Interface Challenges 12

ISM Objectives 13
Basic Mission 13
Supplemental Objectives 14

Risks and Concerns 15
Computer Fraud and Mischievous
  Acts 15
Violations of Laws and Regulations 16

Negligent or Ineffective I/S
  Management 17
Computer Dependence 17
Proliferation of Mini- and
  Microcomputers 18

Organizing and Managing the ISM
  Function 23
Planning 23
Auditing ISM Planning Functions 26
Organizing 28
Auditing the Organizing Process 28
Staffing 29
Auditing ISM Staffing 31
Controlling 31
Controlling Access—The Key 32
Auditing the Controlling Function 34

The Auditor's Role and Objectives 34

Audit Techniques 35
How to Maintain an I/S Audit
  Function 35
Techniques 35
I/S Auditing Tools 35

Suggested Reading 65

Fig. 38-1   Phases of I/S Organizational Growth 3
Fig. 38-2   Data Processing Evolution 6
Fig. 38-3   Survey Form for Microcomputer Usage 19
Fig. 38-4   Segment of a Strategic ISM Plan 25
Fig. 38-5   Excerpt From a Tactical ISM Plan 26
Fig. 38-6   Example of a Portion of a System Development Plan 27

Fig. 38-7	Example of a Simple Organization Structure	29
Fig. 38-8	A Typical Roster of Job Positions	30
Fig. 38-9	A List of Functional Areas for Operational Auditing	34
Fig. 38-10	ISM Questionnaire	38
Fig. 38-11	ISM Audit Program	55
Fig. 38-12	ISM Audit Report	64

39 R&D Management; Engineering Management

Introduction	2
R&D Activities Defined	2
Corporate Impact of Research and Development	3
Selected Subjects to Be Reviewed	4
Communication With Top Management	5
Amount Spent on Basic Research	5
Methods of Determining the Total R&D Budget	5
Establishment of the Operating Budget: Indirect Costs	8
Project Budgets	8
Quality of R&D Staff	9
Limited Use of Economic Measures	10
Organizing for Research and Development	13
Outside Resources	14
Increasing Research and Development Productivity	15
Financial Reports on Research and Development Activity	17
Performance Standards	17
Research and Development Management Audit Questionnaire and Program	20
An Operations Audit of the Engineering Function	34
Suggested Reading	41

Fig. 39-1	Interrelationship of Corporate Goals, Objectives, and the Research and Development Activity Plan	6
Fig. 39-2	Twenty-Five Factors Most Likely to Cause Serious Counterproductivity Within Research and Development Organizations	16
Fig. 39-3	Actual and Budgeted Research and Development Expense, by Department	18
Fig. 39-4	Research and Development Project Status Report	19
Fig. 39-5	Audit Questionnaire—Research and Development Management	20
Fig. 39-6	Audit Program—Research and Development Management	31
Fig. 39-7	Audit Questionnaire—Engineering Function	34

40 Retirement Plan Management

Introduction	2
Background	2
Definitions	3
The Employee Retirement Income Security Act and Other Laws	4
Overview	7
Purpose of Plans	9
Nature of Retirement Plan Administration	10
Establishing a Plan	11
Maintenance of Plans	12
Types of Plans	13
Defined Benefit Plans	14
Defined Contribution Plans	16
Retirement Plan Management Objectives	17
Basic Mission	17
Supplemental Objectives	18
Risks and Concerns	19
Retirement Plan Management Techniques	20

Table of Contents

Organization 20
Auditing Retirement Plan Management
  Organization 21
Staffing 22
Auditing Retirement Plan
  Administration Staffing 23
Planning 23
Auditing Retirement Plan Management
  Planning 25
Controlling 25
  Design Administration 26
  Participant Record Keeping 27
  Plan Management 30
Auditing of Retirement Plan
  Controls 31
Internal Accounting Control
  Surveys 31
Detailed Auditing of Internal
  Control 31
Information Systems Applications
  Auditing 31

**Operational Auditing of Retirement Plan
  Management** 32
Auditing Objective 32
Audit Tools and Techniques 33

Suggested Reading 59

Fig. 40-1 Retirement Plan Qualification Requirements Under the Internal Revenue Code 6
Fig. 40-2 Selected Reporting Requirements Under the Employee Retirement Income Security Act 8
Fig. 40-3 A Typical Organization Structure for Retirement Plan Administration 22
Fig. 40-4 Participant Record-Keeping System 28
Fig. 40-5 Flow Chart of Employee Benefits System 29
Fig. 40-6 Illustrative Retirement Plan Management Questionnaire 34
Fig. 40-7 Illustrative Operational Audit Program for Retirement Plan Management 51
Fig. 40-8 Illustrative Audit Report 58

Index I-1

List of Acronyms

A number of acronyms are found throughout this book. They are:

AAA	American Accounting Association
AICPA	American Institute of Certified Public Accountants
ASB	Auditing Standards Board
CIA	Certified Internal Auditor
CPA	Certified Public Accountant
DOD	Department of Defense
EDP	Electronic Data Processing
ERISA	Employee Retirement Income Security Act
FASB	Financial Accounting Standards Board
FBI	Federal Bureau of Investigation
FCPA	Foreign Corrupt Practices Act
FEI	Financial Executives Institute
FIFO	First-In, First-Out
FTC	Federal Trade Commission
GAAP	Generally Accepted Accounting Principles
GAAS	Generally Accepted Auditing Standards
GAO	General Accounting Office
GNP	Gross National Product
IIA	Institute of Internal Auditors, Inc.
IRC	Internal Revenue Code
IRS	Internal Revenue Service
LIFO	Last-In, First-Out
MBA	Master of Business Administration
NAA	National Association of Accountants
NCFFR	National Commission on Fraudulent Financial Reporting (Treadway Commission)
PC	Personal Computer
PPC	Professional Practices Committee
PSB	Professional Standards Bulletin
PSRC	Professional Standards and Responsibilities Committee

R&D   Research and Development
SAS   Statement on Auditing Standards
SEC   Securities and Exchange Commission
SIAS Statement on Internal Auditing Standards

PART I
Techniques for Effective Overall Strategy

PART 1

Techniques for Effective Overall Strategy

CHAPTER **1**

The Audit Function— An Initial Perspective

Auditing—An Overview 2	Different Technical Knowledge and
What is Internal Auditing? 2	Expertise 19
The IIA Definition 2	**Government Audit Agencies** 20
Other Definitions 3	General Accounting Office 20
Purpose of Internal	Defense Contract Audit Agency 23
Auditing 5	Inspectors General 28
Conflicts of Allegiance in Internal	Internal Revenue Service 31
Auditing 6	Significance of Government Auditing .. 32
Internal Auditing as a Profession 8	**Public Accounting** 32
Auditing in General 10	General 32
Historical Overview 11	Role of the AICPA 34
Early Auditors and Auditing 11	Current Challenges 35
Forces Bringing Auditing to Its Current	Congressional Interest ·.............. 37
Position 12	Self-Regulation 42
Emergence of Audit Branches 12	The Attest Function 45
Changing Focus of Auditing 13	Other Issues 46
	Significance of Public Accounting 46
Audit Branches 14	**Internal Auditing** 47
Identification 14	General 47
Common Characteristics 15	Services, Skills, and Experience 48
Variety of Auditing Services 15	Certified Internal Auditor Program
Third-Party Assurance Regarding	and the Code of Ethics 50
Conformity 16	Role of Institute of Internal Auditors .. 51
Common Techniques 17	The EDP Auditors Association 53
Gathering Evidence and Exercising	Significance of Internal Auditing 53
Professional Judgment 17	**The Keys to Effective Practice** 54
Type of Assurance Differs Among	
Audit Branches 18	**Suggested Reading** 55
Various Interest Groups 18	

Fig. 1-1   Major GAO Functional Divisions 21
Fig. 1-2   DCAA Cross-Service Arrangements 24
Fig. 1-3   Offices of Inspectors General 29
Fig. 1-4   Summary of Major Requirements for SECPS Membership 43

AUDITING—AN OVERVIEW

What Is Internal Auditing?

At the outset, it is important to establish what internal auditing is. This task is made difficult because internal auditing, often shortened in several organizations to the term auditing, is used by many to cover almost any undertaking that performs checks. Added to this is the fact that several organizations employ persons and give them the title of internal auditor but assign to them a variety of duties that do not entail auditing. Further, for those internal auditing functions that meet even the most stringent test of what internal auditing is, there is no uniform focus. Another complicating factor is that much internal auditing is performed by persons who do not intend to remain in the practice of internal auditing for the duration of their careers.

Evidence for the latter two points was developed in 1984 by a team of researchers under sponsorship by the IIA Research Foundation. The survey results, along with the conclusions of the research team, were published as *Internal Auditing: Directions and Opportunities* by the IIA in 1984.

According to Mssrs. Mautz, Tiessen, and Colson, members of the research team, internal auditing is a well-established and well-respected activity, but there is little indication that it is well defined or clearly directed in any overall professional sense.[1] Such an assertion sounds like an indictment of those who have worked to provide a professional basis for the practice of internal auditing. It is not. Rather, it serves to exemplify the point made at the outset that answering the question—"what is internal auditing?"—is difficult. This chapter, indeed this entire volume, is written to help provide the answer. In this chapter, we move toward that end by examining the various definitions of internal auditing, discussing the purpose of internal auditing, and providing an assessment of internal auditing as a profession. To understand what internal auditing is, it is helpful to consider it in the context of auditing in general. This chapter provides such an understanding by a brief historical overview of auditing and by describing the three principal auditing branches—public accounting, government auditing, and internal auditing. In so doing, this chapter presents a perspective on the balance of this edition and suggests keys to the effective practice of internal auditing.

The IIA Definition. Internal auditing is defined in professional internal auditing literature as follows:

> Internal auditing is an independent appraisal function established within an organization to examine and evaluate its activities as a service to the organization.[2]

---

[1] Robert K. Mautz, Ph.D., Peter Tiessen, Ph.D., and Robert H. Colson, Ph.D., *Internal Auditing: Directions and Opportunities,* (Altamonte Springs, Fla.: The Institute of Internal Auditors, 1984), pp. 6–7.

[2] The Institute of Internal Auditors, Inc., *Standards for the Professional Practice of Internal Auditing* (Altamonte Springs, Fla.: The Institute of Internal Auditors, 1981).

Most internal auditors probably accept this definition as covering the essential points. Terms such as "independent" and "evaluate" are present, and the notion that the function represents a service is also evident. More elaboration is necessary, however, to convey a better understanding of what internal auditing is.

Other Definitions. The challenge of devising an all-encompassing definition has stimulated writers on the subject.

Dr. Mautz and company suggest the following:

Internal auditing, which is ultimately responsible to the owners of the enterprise, is a service to senior management and other enterprise interest that includes (1) monitoring management controls; (2) anticipating, identifying, and assessing risks to enterprise assets and activities; (3) investigating actual and potential lapses of control and incidents of risk; and (4) making recommendations for improvement of control, the response to risk, and the attainment of enterprise objectives.[3]

This definition directly states that internal auditing is a service function. It also establishes the point that internal auditing is ultimately responsible to the owners of an enterprise.

There may be many arguments that can be advanced to support this view. However, at this point, not everyone agrees with that perception. For example, a case could be made that the internal auditing function owes allegiance to the corporate entity that employs it. This theory recognizes that a corporation has a legal existence with rights, duties, and obligations that must be accommodated. Part of that accommodation entails protecting its interests. It may be that the role of internal auditing eventually will be seen as existing primarily to help protect those interests.

Whether that theory is right is not really important. It merely serves to establish that it is not yet clear just what the ultimate responsibility of internal auditing is. Inserting a single view of responsibility of internal auditing into a definition of internal auditing, therefore, does not add insight—rather, it adds only a particular viewpoint.

Other terms are used in the definition, such as monitoring, anticipating, identifying, and investigating, which seem to reflect an attempt to tell how the function works. The more important question of why it exists—what purpose it serves—is not presented. In any event, the attempt falls short of the mark of presenting a balanced picture of the workings of internal auditing. Auditors do more in the way of inquiring, analyzing, corroborating, and confirming—terms that are not mentioned—than they do monitoring and anticipating—terms that are mentioned. The best that can be said of the alternative definition proposed by Dr. Mautz is that it has stimulated thought in the profession.

---

[3] Mautz, et al., *op. cit.*, p. 32.

Within the IIA, the PPC, predecessor to the Professional Issues Committee, considered altering the official definition contained in *Standards*. The PPC was the committee established by the IIA to consider matters affecting the professional practice of internal auditing and to form official IIA positions.

At its November 1984 meeting, the PPC resolved that the present definitions within the *Statement of Responsibilities, Standards*, and SIAS No. 1 are sufficient. Its reasons were:

- The Mautz definition does not differ in content but only in the specificity of the term.
- The definition in *Standards* is part of a total package made up of the introduction, specific standards, and any statements that are or will be developed.
- A total revamping of the definition along the lines suggested would be detrimental to the long-range success of this profession.

The Mautz definition has motivated others to offer definitions. For example, Larry Sawyer, in a letter to the *Internal Auditor*, suggested the following:

> Internal auditing is an independent appraisal of the diverse operations and controls within an organization to determine whether risks are identified and reduced, acceptable policies and procedures are followed, established standards are met, resources are used efficiently and economically, and the organization's objectives are achieved.[4]

Certainly, that definition covers the playing field of internal auditing better than the Mautz definition. In particular, it conveys the involvement of internal auditing with appraising efficiency, economy, and effectiveness. On the other hand, it seems to be extremely broad and somewhat vague. What sort of risks? Identified by whom? Acceptable to whom? Perhaps a complete, unassailable definition is unattainable.

In the first edition of this volume, a definition was not originally provided essentially for the above reason. However, in keeping with the times, it seemed appropriate to reverse course and advance a definition if for no other reason than to give some future critic an opportunity for dissent. Accordingly:

> *Internal auditing* is a service function. It is organized and operated primarily for the purpose of conducting audits, in accordance with professional standards, of systems of internal control, including operational controls and information systems processing applications and techniques. The evidential matter gathered from these audits forms the basis for furnishing opinions and other relevant information to affected members of management and the board of directors, or audit committees thereof, as is necessary in the opinion of the chief auditor and performing members of the audit team. Opinions and other information

---

[4] Larry B. Sawyer, "Letters to the Editor," *The Internal Auditor*, Aug. 1984, p. 6.

furnished may attest to the adequacy of internal control, the degree of compliance with established policies and procedures, and/or their effectiveness and efficiency in achieving organizational objectives. They may also recommend cost effective courses of action for management to consider in eliminating unnecessary risks identified by the audits.

Hopefully, no one will ever be required to memorize this definition. Its ponderous length serves as testimony to the fact that the practice of internal auditing is intricate and complex. It defies simple definition.

The definition, lengthy as it may be, builds on the definitions in professional literature and puts the essence of an internal audit into clearer focus. For one thing, it specifies that audits are conducted in accordance with professional standards. This means that internal audits performed in accordance with professional standards are of superior quality to those that are not. There are many "internal audits" that are performed by specialized functions, ad hoc groups, and others that are not conducted pursuant to these standards. Their efforts may produce useful results and are integral to the workings of particular functions—but they are not internal audits as the term is intended to be used here. Examples of such functions include quality assurance audits, subcontract audits, material audits, and self audits performed by management teams.

The definition also introduces the idea that the work product of internal auditing is opinions and other relevant information, which are based on evidence gathered during the performance of the audit. The other relevant information is comprised of findings and recommendations. The findings disclose the results of testing and may indicate areas where compliance with established procedures that are the focus of the testing differed from expected results and where existing procedures permit unnecessary exposures or risks of some sort. The recommendations are the internal auditor's reasoned ideas for improving compliance or reducing the identified risks and exposures to more tolerable ranges.

In essence, that is internal auditing. The definition also allows that the purpose of internal auditing is to conduct audits. However, value is derived from these audits. The primary beneficiaries are the managers of the enterprise. But there are others who also benefit from the work of internal auditors. Some may benefit at the expense of the enterprise—a perplexing dilemma that recently has begun to attract more attention. Such reality warrants further discussion. It is appropriate to do so in describing the purpose of internal auditing because the issue is most clearly visible in such a context.

Purpose of Internal Auditing

A good place to begin to understand the purpose of internal auditing is the *Standards for the Professional Practice of Internal Auditing*. It is stated in these standards that the objective of internal auditing is to assist members of the organization in the effective discharge of their responsibilities. To this end, internal auditing furnishes them with analyses, appraisals, recommendations, counsel, and information concerning the activities reviewed.[5]

It is noteworthy that the standards use the term "organization" in identifying who is being served by internal auditing. The organization could be a corporation, partnership, or proprietorship. It could also be a governmental entity of some type. But organizations are not persons. Which persons are being served in the final analysis is unclear in the minds of many.

It is unreasonable to expect the internal auditor to be a servant to the host of divergent interest groups that may exist at any particular point in time (see next section). The principal purpose of internal auditing, therefore, is or should be to conduct audits as a service to the enterprise. Enterprise interests are determined by the board of directors elected by the shareholders. Thus, to achieve the purpose of internal auditing, internal auditors must have access to the board of directors. Such access is achieved by periodic reporting to the audit committee of the board of directors.

With such reporting, the chief internal auditor is able to provide information to the board that it can use in discharging its responsibility for the interests of the company, its shareholders, and others. The increased focus on corporate accountability in recent years has introduced broader responsibilities and liabilities for directors. Thus, the directors of publicly held companies are suitably motivated to deal with issues of potential wrongdoing in an appropriate fashion, including external disclosure where appropriate. Under such circumstances, it is unnecessary to conscript internal auditing functions to a responsibility equal or superior to that of the board.

Conflicts of Allegiance in Internal Auditing

The problem here lies in the fact that there are many groups that may be interested in the work of the internal auditor, regardless of whether the internal auditor is employed by a governmental unit, a not-for-profit college or university, or a company whose stock is traded on the New York Stock Exchange (NYSE).

Private corporations, whether or not they are publicly owned or closely held, are often managed by persons who are not owners themselves or, at least, not majority owners. In the case of a publicly held corporation, it is much more likely that the managers are not the owners. Stated otherwise, most privately owned companies are small and are managed by the owner with the largest ownership interest. In most publicly owned companies, the chief executive is rarely the largest owner.

The interests of owners and managers should be the same. Most of the time they are. But there are times when they are not. When these interests

---

[5] *Standards for the Professional Practice of Internal Auditing, op. cit.*

diverge, to which group does the internal auditor owe allegiance? If the internal auditor in such a situation believes that his allegiance is only to the management that hired him, he probably is not an internal auditor as the term is intended by the professional standards. The standards use the term "organization" intentionally, to provide the internal auditor with the beginnings of a professional basis for departing from the interests of management, should there ever be a need to. Such occasions should be rare indeed. When they do occur, whose interests are to be served? The obvious answer is the owners. That is the view of Mautz, et al., as noted earlier. But what about the interests of others that may be relevant, depending on the specific situation? Other potential interest groups whose interests might differ from those of both the management and the owners of a publicly held corporation include:

- Taxing authorities
- Other regulatory authorities, such as the SEC or the Environmental Protection Agency
- Injured or potentially injurable parties, such as creditors, suppliers, customers, employees, or the general public
- Criminal investigatory authorities ranging from local police units to the U.S. Department of Justice
- One or more members of Congress harboring particular political viewpoints or sentiments
- Political office holders at the state and local level

The above list is extensive but it is by no means exhaustive. To which of these groups does the internal auditor owe allegiance? Is it reasonable to expect the internal auditor to recognize all the potential interest groups, discern their respective interests, and cater to them?

In earlier times, such questions as these were not foremost in the minds of internal auditing practitioners. The growth and expansion of internal auditing and its potential for future development and evolvement, however, make such questions relevant for current consideration.

Historically, internal audits have been considered confidential and proprietary information for use only within the organization. Times have changed. Now, such agencies as the IRS, the various Offices of Inspectors General (IGs), and the Defense Contract Audit Agency (DCAA) have gained access to the work products of internal auditors and so has at least one subcommittee of Congress.

One member of Congress, Rep. Ron Wyden (D. Or.), has expressed the view that internal auditors should be compelled to report their suspicions of management wrongdoing to appropriate authorities. In effect, he wants internal auditors to serve the interests of the public. There are many who support this view.

The actions of the IRS, IGs, and the DCAA have made internal auditing the focus of intense legal battles (a subject more fully discussed later in this chapter and in Chapter 9). The views of those represented by Rep. Wyden serve only to intensify the controversy.

For example, the work products of the internal auditing function of a NYSE company could be used by any of the interest groups cited to advance their interests. These interests may be at odds with those of the shareholders and/or the management of the company. Since these interests may be in conflict, there is no way to resolve the dilemma to everyone's satisfaction.

The focus of this discussion has been on the internal auditing functions that serve publicly held entities. However, as noted earlier, many internal auditing functions serve organizations that are not publicly held companies. For these, the question of who the internal auditor serves is much less critical, chiefly due to the absence of the public ownership. However, even for colleges, charitable organizations, governmental units, and closely held companies, there are a variety of interest groups. The internal auditors in these entities must serve the interests of the entity or, to use the term in the professional standards, the organization. In so doing, it will help the organization discharge its legal responsibilities. That, in turn, will help serve the interests of other groups over the long term.

Of course, in these situations, the internal auditing functions must have access to those responsible for the affairs of the organization involved. This may be a board of directors, trustees, or governors, or an executive head of some type. Whatever or whomever it is, it must have powers and duties equivalent to those of boards of directors of publicly held corporations.

The foregoing is possible only if internal auditing is permitted to practice in a professional manner. Internal auditing as a profession warrants further comment.

Internal Auditing as a Profession

The rise of internal auditing to the status of a profession is beginning to be recognized by a wide spectrum of the business community. Perhaps the most significant example of this growing recognition is contained in the report of the Treadway Commission. The report is discussed throughout this volume. It is noted here because the IIA was one of the sponsoring organizations, along with the AICPA and others. Such sponsorship is testimony to the emergence of internal auditing as a respected profession. It is also relevant because the Treadway Commission sees internal auditing as a potentially effective tool to help reduce the incidence of financial reporting fraud (see Chapter 23).

What basis does internal auditing have for claiming professional status? To answer that, it is necessary to consider what constitutes a profession. One authoritative source on the subject of auditing states that there is widespread agreement that a profession is characterized by:

THE AUDIT FUNCTION

- A body of specialized knowledge, usually acquired through formal education.
- Formal recognition of professional status by means of a license issued by a governmental body after admission standards have been met.
- A code of ethics to provide standards of conduct, and a means of enforcing compliance with the ethical code.
- Informal recognition and acceptance of professional status by the public and public interest in the work performed.
- Recognition by the professionals of a social obligation beyond the service performed for a particular client.[6]

The degree to which internal auditing qualifies on all counts is open to debate. Few would argue, however, that progress toward professionalism on most points is demonstrable. The IIA, an organization that is much discussed in this volume, has been the leading force in the movement toward professional status. The result is that:

- A body of knowledge exists and is being refined continuously.
- A program of certification exists.
- A code of ethics exists.
- As previously noted, recognition and acceptance of internal auditing as a profession is occurring.
- Many enlightened internal auditing practitioners believe that by performing a service to their organizations, society as a whole benefits.

Whether or not the practice of internal auditing passes all tests is not the argument here. The point is that the practice must strive in the direction of a recognized profession. Internal auditing will realize its fullest potential only when it is perceived by audit committees, senior managements, independent accountants, and others as a true profession or the equivalent of one. (More is said about the professional nature of internal auditing later in this chapter and in Chapter 6.)

There is one additional factor that evidences a profession. Each profession must employ some means to assure that its practitioners adhere to high standards of practice. The means must include a careful articulation of the standards, either on a cooperative voluntary basis or through some form of governmental expression. The means must also provide a way of enforcing compliance and, when necessary, disciplining members guilty of violations.

The practice of internal auditing as a profession under the leadership of the IIA has made strides in articulating standards and providing a basis for peer reviews (see Chapters 6 and 7). These strides, and even the practice of internal auditing, however, are best understood against the backdrop of auditing in general.

---

[6] Jerry D. Sullivan, Richard A. Gnospelius, Philip L. Defliese, and Henry R. Jaenicke, *Montgomery's Auditing,* 10th ed. (Copyright 1985, by Coopers & Lybrand, United States, published by John Wiley & Sons, Inc.), p. 61. Reprinted by permission of Coopers & Lybrand.

Auditing in General

Auditing is a familiar term. It is used, for example, by businessmen, government bureaucrats, educators, organized labor, politicians, lawyers, accountants, bankers, and investors. Even the general public has ideas of what comprises an audit. In this latter instance, it is likely that a survey would relate auditing to what an IRS examiner does. A banker, on the other hand, would probably define an audit as the function of a CPA. A government bureaucrat might describe an audit as something the government internal auditors do, or what the GAO does. A manager within a given company could be expcected to relate auditing to the role of the company auditors.

They are all correct. Auditing is a generic term used to identify all of these activities, and many more. In its broadset sense, it encompasses any action by an individual or group that checks the actions of some other individual or group for some particular purpose. Since it is such a broad term, many modifiers have sprung up over the years to distinguish one particular type of auditing from another. Here are some examples:

- Financial audit
- Managerial audit
- Operational audit
- Security audit
- Program audit
- EDP audit
- Systems audit
- Functional audit
- Self audit
- Cash audit
- Fraud audit

These terms have meanings that are not mutually exclusive. A managerial audit may be an operational audit. An EDP audit may be a systems audit. Aspects of a financial audit may be operational in nature and vice versa. Thus, efforts to help clarify the essence of auditing probably have done as much to confuse the picture. Perhaps it will always be so, owing to the diverse nature of human undertakings and the inescapable fact that humans are imperfect. Any decision, action, effort, or undertaking carries with it a risk, to varying degrees, that it will not achieve the result intended.

Checks and balances are the only means available to minimize the risk, to correct for the random unintended result, and to control the ever present possibility of human dishonesty. Hence, checks and balances are devised to foil all possible dishonest acts that can reasonably be anticipated. Auditing is but one of those checks and balances. Perhaps, a historical perspective might help to clarify this point.

HISTORICAL OVERVIEW

Early Auditors and Auditing

Accounting history records that the first audit function prior to 1500 A.D. involved services of validation for governmental and family units[7] in order to prevent defalcations from the treasuries of the ancient rulers. The technique commonly practiced was to employ two individuals to maintain independent records of the same transactions; in this way, the rulers had a reasonable level of assurance that any attempted defalcation would be promptly detected. This prospect of immediate discovery probably minimized thefts. From the foregoing, it can be seen that the indivisible relationship between internal control, auditing, and assurance was apparent at the outset. In this case, however, the rulers were primarily interested in preventing theft, fraud, and other malfeasance.

The primacy of fraud prevention as a business requirement and, therefore, as an audit objective, continued for several hundred years. It remains important to this day and, one suspects, it probably always will be. However, it is no longer considered to be the primary objective of auditing. Subsequent sections of this chapter will point out the forces that brought about this change.

It is interesting to note, in passing, that the earliest auditors were employed by property owners and rulers of society to provide full-time audit services to that particular owner or ruler. The concept of independent auditors or accountants did not evolve until the nineteenth century. Thus, it is accurate to say that the first auditors were, indeed, internal auditors.

The earliest audit techniques were quite simple by today's standards. In the days of the Roman Empire, the usual technique was to listen to the oral reports given by the quaestors, who were individuals entrusted with financial matters. The term "auditor" is thought to have derived from this "hearing" of accounts. This technique passed into extinction partially as a result of the development of a cheap process for producing paper. This enabled more events and transactions to be recorded for after-the-fact checking, but it did not alter the fact that in order to provide the desired assurance, considerable detail auditing was required.

It was not until the late nineteenth century that internal control techniques began to be practiced that considerably enhanced the accuracy and reliability of reported financial information. Auditors in that era encouraged the formation of these techniques, in part, because they believed the scope of their work could be restricted thereby.[8] Thus, the concept of limited test-

---

[7] Douglas R. Carmichael and John J. Willingham, *Perspectives in Auditing*, 3rd ed. (New York: McGraw-Hill Book Co., 1979), p. 2.

[8] Robert H. Montgomery, *Fifty Years of Accountancy* (New York: The Ronald Press Co., 1939), p. 21.

ing emerged, ultimately leading to the sophisticated sampling methods used by today's auditors.

Forces Bringing Auditing to Its Current Position

Auditing, despite its early origins, did not evolve into a significant factor in managerial control until the beginning of the twentieth century. The major forces that brought about this relatively recent and rapid transformation are as follows:

- The industrial revolution required a vast expansion in both capital and business operations. The significant growth in the United States and worldwide economics initiated a need for more advanced techniques in the organizing, planning, staffing, and directing of business activities.
- The growth period was accompanied by business practices that in some instances were abused, causing adverse economic consequences and, ultimately, the greatest depression in U.S. history. Examples included price-fixing, predatory trade practices, interlocking directorates, stock manipulating, and publishing misleading accounts of business performance.
- Regulatory actions by governmental units, such as the establishment of the Interstate Commerce Commission in 1887, the passage of the Sherman Antitrust Act in 1890, and the creation of the FTC in 1914, ushered in the era of increased administrative burden on both the government and the private business sector.
- Regulatory actions continued as more circumstances were identified as a result of the economic conditions of the 1930s, which include the various securities acts and the establishment of the SEC.
- The advent of EDP began to have major effects on business and auditors beginning after World War II. The impact of this technological development in shaping business and management techniques has continued to increase since that time.

Emergence of Audit Branches

The increasing activity of government in policing business conduct has had a profound impact on the role of auditing and accounting in the United States. For the developing public accounting profession, for example, the Securities Act of 1933 virtually assured that public accountants would play a vital role in the process of capital formation.

The enforcement of the numerous regulations caused the government to expand considerably. The increasing size and cost of government activities eventually raised questions about its efficiency and effectiveness. Thus, various audit groups were established within the administrative and legislative branches of the government to help identify and eliminate waste. The GAO and the DCAA are notable examples. Their roles are discussed later in this chapter.

In addition, the expanding size of private enterprise along with government regulatory impact combined to create a need for a function to perform audits of company operations on a full-time basis. As the service of public accountants became more costly and sometimes difficult to secure on a timely basis, the need for captive auditing was seen as a logical cost-effective answer. Thus, the era of modern internal auditing was born.

The explosive growth of EDP, now being widely referred to as I/S (information systems) has affected all three audit groups, requiring each to develop I/S audit expertise within a particular area of concentration.

Perhaps the most important point to be drawn from this brief historical account is that the practice of auditing has been constantly changing and evolving to keep pace with the shifting demands on business enterprise, caused by significant economic, social, and technological developments. Internal auditors, along with the managements they support, must continue to be as innovative and responsive as their predecessors have been. Only in that way will the organization's interest be effectively served.

Changing Focus of Auditing

The internal audit profession exists primarily to provide a broad variety of audit services to the management groups embodied in the organization it serves. What management[9] needs from an audit shifts in response to changing internal and external forces.

The initial internal audit efforts were directed at theft and fraud detection and, accordingly, served as a deterrent. This activity reflected the initial concern at the turn of the century of owners and managers who realized the potential for such acts. Improvements in control techniques over the years began to reduce the need for this service.

The concern in the post-World War II era expanded to operational efficiency. Internal auditors began to devote considerable attention to the effectiveness and efficiency with which component entities were performing. Auditors reported on such diverse subjects as production costs, production planning and control, purchasing, transportation expense, overtime analysis, and budgeting.

In the 1960s, concern developed about financial reporting. Many companies "went public" for the first time during this era. Internal auditors devoted increasing amounts of time to assisting external auditors in examining financial statements. Not only did this hold down the cost of external audits, but it also led to improved techniques in financial reporting.

In the 1970s, management's interest and concern regarding internal control led to still another shift in focus. This concern derived in part from the

---

[9] The term "management" as used in this discussion is intended to include the board of directors and audit committees. This is because, in many companies, the board includes strong representation by the senior management.

data processing revolution described earlier, but also from the growth of international business. Many companies found foreign business to be quite lucrative in the 1970s, but also they found that distance and separation led to an increased exposure to mismanagement and questionable activities.

The passage of the FCPA in 1977 was perhaps the most significant single event in terms of impact on internal auditing. It was the government's response to public concerns regarding corporate accountability that arose in the 1970s out of the post-Watergate disclosures of corporate wrongdoing. After 1977, internal audit services with respect to internal control evaluation and testing significantly increased in importance in the eyes of managements and their boards of directors.

The nature of internal auditing is such that it must constantly adjust its services to accommodate the observed needs to be of maximum value to the organization. The period of the 1980s continued this pattern.

Recent business failures in major banks and thrift institutions have produced renewed concern about how best to deal with the menace of financial reporting fraud. Other revelations, in aerospace and defense contracting, having to do with cost mischarging, defective pricing, substandard products, and procurement kickbacks, and in investment banking and stock trading, having to do with insider trading abuses, have resulted in wide public condemnation of American business ethics. Internal auditing is seen by many influential persons and groups as being one tool that can help deal with these matters. Indeed, internal auditors are responding to these new challenges in effective ways (see Chapters 2, 22–24).

While the spectrum of the internal auditor's services will continue to expand, the fundamental purpose or objective—to provide auditing services to the organization—remains as constant now as in the first days of auditing.

AUDIT BRANCHES

Identification

In practice, many management groups often cannot understand why they are audited by so many different auditors. How many different audit groups exist and why are there so many? What makes them different? This section answers these questions and provides some perspective that auditors may find useful in dealing with management concerns regarding redundancy. It also provides further insight into the nature and characteristics of each significant branch. Practitioners may find this section useful in understanding and explaining the distinctions between each type.

Three distinct branches of auditors have evolved as a result of the forces of changes described earlier: external or independent auditors, internal auditors, and government auditors. Various terms have evolved to identify each branch. For example, external auditors or outside auditors are also known as CPAs, independent auditors, or simply, public accountants. Internal auditors have been called operational auditors, management auditors, management services specialists, internal control analysts, and so on. The several divisions of the federal government auditors include:

- ☐ Legislative branch
  - General Accounting Office
- ☐ Executive branch
  - Inspectors General
  - Internal Revenue Service
  - Defense Contract Audit Agency

To these groups must be added the several audit organizations within each of the 50 states. In addition, the more populous counties and cities have provided resources for audit-type efforts by designated functions.

These various names and divisions imply that the practitioners of each serve different purposes and, in fact, the specific objectives of each branch and of each division within each branch are different. This is the predominant reason for the evolution of so many different types of auditors. However, there are also some similarities. In order to appreciate the differences between the branches, we must first identify the similarities.

Common Characteristics

The audit sectors may be likened to branches extending from a common base—much like the branches of a tree. In historical terms, the branching is a relatively recent event, occurring for the most part in the twentieth century. Yet, most practitioners within each branch or sector are not conscious of their shared heritage or commonality of purpose that exists today. All auditors

- Perform a variety of auditing services.
- Provide third-party assurance regarding conformity.
- Use common auditing techniques.
- Gather evidence and exercise professional judgment.

Each of these common areas is discussed in the following paragraphs.

Variety of Auditing Services. Each branch of auditing provides more than one type of auditing service. External auditors provide audits of financial statements, but they also may be retained for other attestation purposes or to render opinions regarding (1) interim period financial statements; (2) internal controls; (3) compliance with particular statutory, regulatory, or contractual requirements; (4) attributes of computer software; or (5) compliance with terms of financial instruments.

Government auditors may examine financial statements of government units or perform contract audits, program audits, and grant audits, as in the case of the GAO; tax audits, as in the case of the IRS; and contract audits, as in the case of the DCAA. In addition, regulatory audits by the major federal regulatory agencies are also part of the government auditing scene. These agencies include:

- Securities and Exchange Commission
- Federal Energy Regulatory Commission
- Federal Communication Commission
- Federal Maritime Commission
- Federal Trade Commission
- Interstate Commerce Commission

Internal auditors may perform such financial audits as examinations of financial statements, reviews of interim period financial information, and reviews of internal accounting control. They also perform operational audits, EDP or management information systems (MIS) audits, and audits of ethical business practices.

Third-Party Assurance Regarding Conformity. Anyone who performs audit services does so to provide a needed level of assurance that conditions actually encountered in the subject audit conform to some established concept, standard, or expectation. The need arises because of an interest in the subject by persons who are either not directly involved, or are not in a position to obtain such assurance directly. In other words, they are "third parties."

The parties in interest may be owners or creditors of a business, or corporate-based management of a decentralized company. They may be public office holders, such as members of Congress, or they may be the public itself. The established standard or expectation may be set forth in written form with great precision, such as that contained in laws, interpretive regulations, policies, and procedures. It may also be that the concepts are more generally stated, as in the case of GAAP. However, the endlessly growing body of authoritative literature that provides supporting detail with respect to accounting principles makes GAAP less of an example of generally stated concepts than it once was. Finally, it may be that the established concept or expectation has little or no formally developed and accepted guidelines, as is the case with the concepts involving internal control.

The assurance described above is always communicated in some effective fashion in order to be relevant to the user. Every audit must disclose the extent to which the conditions actually encountered deviate from the established concept or expectation. The method used to effect disclosure may vary, but the intent is constant. Thus, all audits involve some form of reporting relevant information to the parties in interest.

For example, public accountants report the extent to which financial statements present financial position and the results of operations of the entity under examination. The expectation by those who wish to use the financial statements is that they present fairly the purported information. By reporting that such information "fairly presents . . . in accordance with generally accepted accounting principles,"[10] public accountants have informed users of the extent to which the financial statements conform to their (the users') expectations.

If the public accountants found that the financial statements did not conform to GAAP, that finding and its impact would be stated in the report because it is relevant information to users.

Common Techniques. Not only do audits occur for basically the same reason, but also the fundamental procedures used in performing the audits are more or less the same. In fact, there has been no real change to the basic process since the origin of the function. The fundamental techniques are observation, inspection, inquiry, and confirmation. Even the advent of the computer has not changed the basics, although new detail techniques or procedures have been devised to observe, inspect, inquire, and confirm activities, and to control techniques involving computers.

Gathering Evidence and Exercising Professional Judgment. Why do auditors perform the audit techniques previously discussed? Quite simply, it is to obtain evidence regarding the degree to which the actual conditions encountered in the audit conform to expectations. With evidence, auditors gain a basis for expressing to interested parties their relevant findings and conclusions. Chapter 14 discusses the different types of evidential matter and the methods for organizing such evidence. At this point, it is only necessary to observe that gathering evidence is what occurs in every audit through observation, inspection, inquiry, and confirmation.

All audit projects require the frequent exercise of professional judgment in order to complete the project. Auditor's judgment occurs when determining the following:

- Audit objectives
- Standards by which encountered conditions are to be measured
- Nature and extent of audit procedure to be employed
- The relative importance of deviations
- Final opinions and conclusions
- Report content and distribution

In making the foregoing determinations, all auditors must seek assistance from authoritative sources. For example, the DCAA is guided with respect

---

[10] Statement on Auditing Standards No. 1 (Nov. 1972), Section 411.01 (AICPA, *Professional Standards,* Vol. 1). AU § 411.01.

to cost accounting principles in audits of contractor's disclosure statements by referring to the cost accounting standards promulgated by the Cost Accounting Standards Board (CASB). Likewise, internal auditors are guided by auditing standards promulgated by the IIA and by the many internally developed procedure manuals, to cite just two examples. Considerable authoritative literature regarding I/S has been published in recent years to assist I/S auditors. In making judgments, then, all auditors must continually develop their technical knowledge and information base in order that the determinations are made on the most practicable and credible base possible. Auditors of all types must be proficient in their field of practice and scrupulous in the diligent application of audit procedures in order to render assurance of the highest value. In a word, auditors must be professional.

Type of Assurance Differs Among Audit Branches

Various Interest Groups. Given the extensive similarities, it would seem that all audits are the same—that all auditors perform much the same function. This is a view frequently encountered by auditors in dealing with members of management of private industry, representatives of government agencies, and even the general public. Company managements are often baffled and frustrated by the seemingly endless audits to which their organizations are subjected. For example, banks may be subjected to audits by their own internal auditors, government-chartered audit functions, state-chartered audit agencies, and independent public accountants. Further, publicly held companies, including banks, are subject to SEC investigations. The smokestack segment of the economy, including steels, chemicals, oil and gas production, and paper mills, are prone to investigations by environmental agencies and Occupational Safety and Health Administration (OSHA) regulators. The aerospace industry is subjected to constant auditing by the DCAA in addition to other government auditing groups and independent public accountants.

Why all of these audits are necessary may be difficult to understand by those who are subjected to them. With some thought, however, it becomes apparent that each audit group conducts audits for objectives and purposes that differ from those of the other audit groups. As we have previously stated, the auditor's primary role is to provide assurance. What distinguishes or divides the various audit groups is the *nature* of that assurance.

In order to appreciate the distinctions, the question "assurance to whom with respect to what?" must be answered. Internal auditors provide boards of directors and company managements with assurance as to the sufficiency of the authorized control techniques to accomplish business goals and the degree of compliance therewith. The public accountants provide assurance to stockholders, creditors, and others regarding the fairness of the information contained in financial statements. Government auditors provide assurance to various units of the executive and legislative branches of government and to the general public. They assure that the relevant legislation, program, rule, or regulation is effectively administered as well as the degree to which compliance has occurred.

Different Technical Knowledge and Expertise. In order to provide the specific assurance needed, a specific body of technical knowledge must be involved and a specific set of procedures must be performed. These specific bodies of knowledge are different. For example, to perform an audit of an aerospace contractor's overhead for allowability, the DCAA representative must have sufficient knowledge of (1) applicable sections of the Federal Acquisition Regulations (FAR), (2) the DCAA Audit Manual, (3) cost accounting standards, and (4) the applicable procedures employed by the contractor. A DCAA auditor might examine some of the same supporting documentation that a staff member of a public accounting firm would examine. It is conceivable that the two could be performing their audits simultaneously—to the chagrin of management. The public accounting staff auditor, however, is thinking primarily about compliance with GAAP. He may have little or no knowledge of the FAR and probably would not detect violations of such regulations. The DCAA auditor, on the other hand, probably does not possess, and is not concerned with, an extensive knowledge of GAAP. He is impervious as to whether the overhead charged to a particular contract to date, when combined with costs yet to be incurred, will result in an unrecognized loss. On the other hand, the public accountant's audit program requires that this point be considered.

The development of the three main branches or sectors of auditing (internal, external, and governmental) was inevitable when one considers the evolution described in the foregoing. These branches may be further divided. The government auditing branch includes separate audit agencies at virtually every level—federal, state, and local. The division in expertise between internal and external auditors is not as clear-cut as for government auditors. The technical skills of internal auditors vary to some extent. For example, internal auditors skilled in EDP may be distinguished from financial and operational auditors. Also, internal auditors' skills are shaped according to the industry segments in which their companies are categorized. Finally, public accountants (external auditors) may be segmented according to the nature of their practice. Smaller accounting firms often tend to concentrate their practice in a particular industrial segment. While the major accounting firms practice public accounting in all business segments, individual partners within these firms tend to specialize.

In summary, the growth and expansion of the free enterprise system, paralleled by the expansion of the government bureaucracy, has created many and diverse interest groups. Each of these interest groups must be informed of the degree to which events and activities with which they are concerned conform to their standards or expectations. The audit function provides this information. To do so effectively, each group must be served by auditors with skill and training relevant to the subject.

GOVERNMENT AUDIT AGENCIES

This section of this chapter describes the important segments of the government sector, the public accounting sector, and internal auditing. This discussion provides additional insight into the specific similarities and differences among the significant branches of audit practitioners.

General Accounting Office

The GAO was established by congressional action in 1921. Its purpose then and now was to provide Congress with an ongoing source of objective assessments with respect to the efficacy of federally funded programs. The head of the GAO is the Comptroller General of the United States. He is appointed by the President, subject to the advice and consent of the Senate, for a nonrenewable 15-year term.

The GAO performs its services through various functional divisions, as outlined in Figure 1-1. Its activities are such that it is required to maintain significant administrative functions, including the Office of Congressional Relations, the Public Information Office, the Office of Human Concerns, the Office of Internal Review, and the Personnel Systems Project. In addition, the Office of the General Counsel provides advice to agencies and committees of both the legislative and executive branches and reviews all audit reports for legal sufficiency.

According to the 1986 Comptroller General's Annual Report, the GAO was initially little more than an offshoot of the Treasury Department's Division of Bookkeeping and Warrants. Its services, performed mostly by clerks, consisted of verifying financial transactions and determining the legality of individual vouchers. In the post-World War II era, the proliferation of fiscally undisciplined government corporations prompted legislation in 1945 directing that the corporation's financial operations be examined by the GAO. This legislation began the audits that grandfathered the evaluation work of the GAO today. Such work has grown and expanded over the years to include, in addition to traditional financial audits:

- Economy and efficiency audits
- Economic analyses
- Econometric modeling
- Actuarial Studies
- Program audits

One of the GAO's strengths is its ability to go where the programs, contractors, or recipients of federal funds are located. The GAO maintains 15 regional offices in the continental United States and 80 audit sites located

FIG. 1-1
Major GAO Functional Divisions

■ Logistics and Communications Division	■ Human Resources Division
	■ International Division
■ Procurement and Systems Acquisition Division	■ Accounting and Financial Management Division
■ Federal Personnel and Compensation Division	■ Energy and Minerals Division
	■ Program Analysis Division
■ General Government Division	■ Field Operations Division
■ Community and Economic Development Division	■ Claims Division

in federal agencies,[11] and performed assignments in 60 countries[12] in 1986.

The GAO has been a source of some controversy since is creation in 1921; during 1985 and 1986, the GAO became even more controversial because of the enactment of the Gramm-Rudman-Hollings deficit reduction legislation, which, among other things, gave the Comptroller General responsibility for reporting the results of an independent analysis to the President and Congress. The purpose was to determine where budget reductions were necessary to comply with the legislation. The determinations to be rendered by the Comptroller General were to be binding on the President. In January 1986, the GAO issued its first report under the Act. It called for spending reductions of $11.7 billion.[13]

Where to place the GAO became an issue of Constitutional proportion as a result of Gramm-Rudman-Hollings. The Comptroller General is appointed by the President and may be removed only by a joint resolution of Congress that is approved by the President. The GAO mainly performs services related to the legislative activities of Congress, although it also performs executive branch services. Many believe that the GAO is part of the legislative branch and, accordingly, cannot direct the President. Litigation to that effect was brought in federal district court by several members of Congress and federal employee unions. The Department of Justice joined in the argument and the federal district court accepted it. The case was appealed to the Supreme Court. In *Bowsher v. Synar*, the Supreme Court affirmed the lower court, ruling that the Comptroller General is subservient to Congress.[14] This decision has the effect of rendering the GAO role in Gramm-Rudman-Hollings inoperable. Still, the GAO continues to be a potent weapon in the fight to reduce deficit spending at the federal level.

---

[11] United States General Accounting Office, *Comptroller General's Annual Report 1986*, p. 3.

[12] *Ibid.*, p. 25.

[13] *Ibid.*, p. 6.

[14] *Ibid.*, p. 7.

With an annual budget approaching $300 million and a staff of some 5000 professional accountants, lawyers, engineers, and administrative staff, the GAO has come a long way.

GAO audits are conducted to (1) evaluate the efficiency, economy, legality, and effectiveness with which federal agencies carry out their financial management and program responsibilities; and (2) assist Congress and federal agency officials in carrying out their responsibilities by providing them with objective and timely information on the conduct of government operations together with conclusions and recommendations. In effect, the GAO performs for the government the roles of auditing that in the private sector are performed by professional internal and external auditors. The GAO also considers fraud to be an ever-present possibility and devises procedures to detect its occurrence.

The relevance of the GAO to government auditing extends beyond its auditing role. It is also actively involved in governmental auditing standards setting (see Chapter 5). The GAO's *Standards for Audit of Governmental Organizations, Programs, Activities, and Functions*, also known as the yellow book, originally issued in 1972, was nothing less than a major milestone in auditing achieved with an intergovernmental perspective.

The GAO responded to the Federal Managers' Financial Integrity Act of 1982 by issuing *Standards for Internal Controls in the Federal Government* in 1983. These standards (reprinted in Chapter 17) served to guide heads of executive agencies who, under the law, became required to submit annual reports to the President and Congress on the status of their systems internal control.

Though the interests of the GAO are in many ways similar to those of internal auditors within the agencies, the two are distinct. Within the federal government, internal auditing is considered an integral part of the management control of each agency. The GAO considers the effectiveness of governmental internal auditing in setting its scope.

The auditing work of the GAO, its activities in standards setting, the high caliber of its personnel, and its internal discipline for thoroughness and professionalism have made it a remarkably effective and well-respected organization. Its principal challenge seems to be to avoid being drawn into politically partisan issues and causes. Some critics contend the GAO often seems to reach conclusions in its audits that parallel the views of the particular members of Congress requesting the audits. In issues where different viewpoints exist between the legislative and executive branches, the GAO more often than not is drawn into the contest by Congress. Its views, expressed in its resultant audits, are frequently supportive of the legislative viewpoint and, thus, are frequently challenged by various executive agencies. This criticism is probably the result of Washington-style politics. Over the years, the high standards of auditing practiced by the GAO have earned for it a solid reputation for objectivity and professionalism.

Defense Contract Audit Agency

This agency was established by the DOD July 1, 1965, to perform all required auditing of DOD contracts. DOD Directive No. 5103.36, dated June 8, 1978, states the purpose in the following terms:

> 1. Perform all necessary contract audit for the Department of Defense and provide accounting and financial advisory services regarding contracts and subcontracts to all Department of Defense components responsible for procurement and contract administration. These services will be provided in connection with negotiation, administration, and settlement of contracts and subcontracts.
>
> 2. Provide contract audit service to other Government agencies as appropriate.[15]

The mission of the DCAA should not be confused with internal audit functions that each branch of the service maintains to perform needed audits within those branches other than contract auditing. The DCAA is also independent from the Defense Audit Services, an organization that performs noncontract audit services for the DOD. It is also separate from the DOD IG in an organizational sense. However, the IG does have oversight responsibility to the DCAA.

The head of the DCAA is a director who reports to the Assistant Secretary of Defense (Comptroller). He is appointed by the Secretary of Defense. The DCAA contract audit services are performed for a number of agencies, in addition to the DOD, through cross-service arrangements. (See Figure 1-2.)

The DCAA performs its services through an extensive network of field offices and regional offices throughout the United States and certain foreign offices. Its headquarters is located in Washington, D.C. The total staff strength approximates 4,000 personnel, and its budget exceeds $100 million.

The agency performs its audit services pursuant to audit standards contained in its audit manual. These were derived from audit standards published by the AICPA and those published by the GAO.[16]

The audit procedures to be used are also set forth in the manual in considerable detail. Sections of the manual specify procedures for the following areas, among others:

- Costs
- Evaluation of pricing proposals
- Terminated contracts

---

[15] *Contract Audit Manual* (Defense Contract Audit Agency, 1988), Vol. 1, p. 10.

[16] *Ibid.*, p. 201.

FIG. 1-2
DCAA Cross-Service Arrangements

■ ACTION (Peace Corps) ■ Agency for International Development Department of State ■ Community Services Administration ■ Department of Agriculture ■ Department of Commerce ■ Department of Education ■ Department of Energy ■ Department of Health and Human Services ■ Department of Housing and Urban Development ■ Department of the Interior ■ Department of Justice ■ Department of Labor ■ Department of State ■ Department of Transportation ■ Department of the Treasury ■ Environmental Protection Agency	■ Executive Office of the President, of Administration ■ Federal Emergency Management Agency ■ Federal Communications Commission ■ General Services Administration ■ International Communications Agency ■ National Academy of Sciences ■ National Aeronautics and Space Administration ■ National Science Foundation ■ Office of Technology Assessment ■ Selective Service System ■ U.S. Nuclear Regulatory Commission ■ U.S. Postal Service ■ U.S. Railway Association ■ U.S. Arms Control and Disarmament ■ U.S. Information Agency ■ Veterans Administration

- Grants and contracts with educational institutions
- Cost reimbursement

The importance of internal control is stressed in connection with each.

In addition to the identified sections, the manual contains an extensive appendix that provides guidance on a variety of advanced audit techniques, including statistical sampling, auditing automated data processing systems, and graphic and computational analysis techniques.

In practice, the DCAA performs a useful role for the DOD and other government agencies. Its audits assist in minimizing the cost to the government resulting from procurement activities of the various agencies. By concentrating its focus in the areas listed above, the DCAA is able to provide an independent assessment of the reasonableness of actual or estimated costs contained in contractors' claims and proposals. In addition, it provides an independent assessment regarding compliance with applicable provisions of the FAR and cost accounting standards. Numerous techniques used by the DCAA are specifically intended to alert the contracting officer to instances of excessive prices, profits, overcharges, and the like. As an example, the DCAA performs floor checks to determine if the contractor's employee's work corresponds to the cost objective, which is properly accumulating the related labor costs. Similarly, checks are made to determine that the costs of productive facilities are properly allocated between government and non-government (commercial) work.

DCAA auditors must be technically proficient in auditing and, in addition, must be knowledgeable of the government contracting process. They must have extensive knowledge of the FAR, cost accounting standards, and internal controls.

The professional approach of the DCAA to its tasks have earned it considerable respect among members of the government contracting community. Like all audit functions, it is not without its critics, who contend that it is too rigid in its interpretations of the FAR and the cost accounting standards promulgated by the CASB. As a result, it is argued that the DCAA often becomes unduly embroiled in time-consuming disagreements over insignificant matters. The vagueness of many of the CASB pronouncements has caused differing interpretations by contractors leading to varying practices. Consistency under present circumstances is proving to be difficult to achieve. The demise of the CASB and the force of experience to date may combine to cause future revisions in the cost accounting standards. This should permit the flexibility necessary to minimize the difficulties presented by the Cost Accounting Standards.

In recent years, the DCAA has pursued its role of performing contract audit services with increased intensity. Supporters of the DCAA claim that its effectiveness is rising. On the other hand, critics believe that its intensified efforts are adversely affecting the ability of defense contractors to fulfill contractual commitments.

This difference of opinion results from earlier criticism of the DCAA's performance as audit watchdog over the government's defense procurement system. Along with other alleged shortcomings in the system, the DCAA was seen by some as part of the reason for wasteful defense spending. Fuel for these claims was provided by numerous horror stories of exorbitant prices paid by the armed services for common everyday items. Examples include the $1,100 stool cap, the $400 hammer, and the $7,000 coffee pot. These stories, along with allegations of high level fraud in Navy submarine programs, widely publicized instances of defective parts, cost growth and overruns on certain other programs, and the sizeable increases in defense spending in general, have combined to compel the DCAA to adopt a more forceful audit strategy.

In 1985, news accounts of alleged improper billings of overhead and administrative expenses were widely publicized. Additionally, instances of labor cost mischarging, procurement kickbacks, and bid-rigging were publicized. In these latter cases, both the government and the prime contactors were victimized.

These events served to place further pressure on the DCAA, among others, for more rigorous auditing. It has responded by increasing its staff size and by making greater use of computer assisted audit techniques (see

Chapter 28). It is also extending its audits into new areas and concentrating its audit focus on topics where waste fraud and abuse are more likely to be found. Labor charging practices and overhead billing methods are two examples.

These actions have resulted in an increase in the number of audits performed by the DCAA. To illustrate, during the six-month reporting period ended September 30, 1986, the DCAA issued almost 40,000 reports, compared to 33,000 reports issued during the comparable period just two years earlier. This reflects an increase of more than 20 percent.[17] Auditing of forward pricing proposals seems to be the largest area of growth. This type of auditing increased from about 11,000 during the six months ended September 30, 1984 to more than 21,000 during the six months ended September 30, 1986—almost doubling the achievement in the earlier period.

The DCAA also is attempting to enlarge its scope of work to include operational audits and examinations of documents and records that in earlier years were considered to be outside its statutory and contractual boundaries.

To illustrate, in the six-month period ended September 30, 1986, the DCAA performed more than 250 operational audits. It claims that these audits resulted in cost-avoidance recommendations whose aggregate value exceeded $175 million.[18] Among the documents and records now being sought are company budgets and internal audit reports. The DCAA became particularly adamant about its demands for internal audit reports. Many believe that neither the statutes and regulations nor case law support the DCAA view that it is entitled to internal audit reports.[19]

Since 1965, when the DCAA was created, its rights of access to contractor records have been a source of controversy and contention between contractors and the DCAA. It is probable that the success of the DCAA has been hampered to some degree by resistance stemming from this controversy. Any audit group would be handicapped if its quest for information and evidential matter faced constant obstacles and resistance. Whether this resistance arose from historical experience suggesting that the DCAA misused and misunderstood the data or out of some more sinister concern is a matter of conjecture. Whatever the reason, there is little question that the DCAA has never enjoyed the right of access it believes necessary to better fulfill its watchdog role. Now that is changing. The rate of change dramatically increased as a result of two events in 1985. The first is the *Westinghouse* case and the second is federal legislation giving the DCAA subpoena

---

[17] The source for statistics in this section is from *Semiannual Reports to the Congress,* issued by the DOD IG. The six-month reporting periods run from April 1 to September 30 and from October 1 to March 31.

[18] Department of Defense Inspector General, *Semiannual Report to the Congress,* April 1, 1986 to September 30, 1986, p. 2-1.

[19] See, e.g., "The Scope of the Defense Contract Audit Agency's Access to Contractor Books and Records, A Growing Controversy," Author Unknown, *Memorandum,* Machinery & Allied Products Institute (Washington, D.C., Feb. 1985).

power.[20] Each event is discussed in detail in Chapter 9. To summarize here, in the instance of the *Westinghouse* case, Westinghouse refused attempts by the DCAA to gain access to internal audit reports. The DCAA, with no subpoena authority of its own at the time, enlisted the assistance of the DOD IG. The IG then subpoenaed the reports. Westinghouse refused to honor the subpoena. Thereafter, the Justice Department brought suit in federal court to force Westinghouse to honor the subpoena. The lower court decision was reaffirmed by an appeals court in favor of the government, resulting in the turnover of the reports to the IG originally sought by the DCAA.

The second event derived, in part from the first event. Congress, in enacting the 1985 Defense Authorization Act, bestowed subpoena power on the DCAA. Its early efforts to use the power, however, have been mixed. A U.S. District Court judge ruled in March 1987 that a defense contractor cannot be compelled by the DCAA to turn over internal audit reports for the period after January 1, 1986.[21] Interestingly, this same contractor, Newport News Shipbuilding, surrendered internal audit reports of earlier periods to the DOD IG pursuant to its subpoena. This court saw a difference between the respective powers of the two agencies when it comes to obtaining internal audit reports.

The extent to which the DCAA's new level of access and expanded audit scope will actually increase its effectiveness in terms of ridding fraud, waste, and abuse from defense procurement is unclear.

Proponents of more intensive DCAA auditing will no doubt be able to use new reports of abuses as evidence of the value of such efforts. Detractors will probably assert that the costs of these few abuses are overshadowed by the increased administrative efforts needed to cope with the greater auditing intensity.

One indicator of effectiveness is the amount of costs questioned. In the six-month period ended September 30, 1984, on a reports issued basis, the DCAA questioned about $14.8 billion in contract cost—mostly in forward price proposal audits (costs not yet incurred).[22] In the 1986 comparable period, it questioned over $16 billion in contrast cost—nearly a 10 percent increase.[23]

The implication of that increase is that audit effectiveness is increasing. The number of contract auditors, however, increased by nearly 20 percent during the same period. Thus, it could be inferred that audit effectiveness is dropping. Obviously, statistics do not tell the whole story.

---

[20] Pub. L. No. 99-145, Title IX, Part C ¶ 935, 995 Stat. 700, Nov. 8, 1985.

[21] "DCAA Cannot Subpoena Internal Audit Data, District Court Rules," *Federal Contracts Report* (Washington, D.C., Bureau of National Affairs, Inc., Mar. 30, 1987), p. 521.

[22] Department of Defense Inspector General, *Semiannual Report to the Congress*, April 1, 1984 to September 30, 1984, p. 2-5.

[23] Department of Defense Inspector General, *Semiannual Report to the Congress*, April 1, 1986 to September 30, 1986, p. 2-2.

It is still too early though to predict with any certainty what will emerge from this. However, another development that might be an indicator is noteworthy. The President's Blue Ribbon Commission on Defense Management (the Packard Commission) provided a report to the President in June, 1986. Among other things, the report's recommendations seek to achieve the following:

- Waste and delay in the development of new weapons can be minimized, and there can be greater assurance that military equipment performs as expected.
- The DOD and defense industry can have a more honest, productive partnership working in the national interest.

The recommendations seem to signal that the Commission expects the defense contracting community to take the lead in ridding itself of questionable procurement practices. The Commission noted the increasing public mistrust of private contractors, but it also noted that defense programs "too often suffered from lack of clear direction and cooperation among oversight agencies. Proliferation of uncoordinated contractor oversight—both administrative and congressional—has added unnecessary cost and inefficiency in the procurement process."

The Commission went on to say, "Government action should not impede efforts by contractors to improve their own performance. The Commission is concerned that, for example, overzealous use of investigative subpoenas by DOD agencies may result in less vigorous internal corporate auditing." This view is strikingly similar to that of the IIA, as reflected in its first amicus curae filed in connection with the *Westinghouse* case (see Chapter 9).

There is little question that both government and industry would be served by an arrangement in which government oversight was more directed toward and supportive of the internal oversight activities of the private sector, such as internal auditing. There is much room for development along these lines to occur.

Inspectors General

The Inspectors General Act of 1978 created 12 new audit entities, each headed by an IG. Subsequently, the number was enlarged to 19. Figure 1-3 lists the departments and agencies involved.

The purpose of the Act was to subject the administrative branch of government to the rigors of internal auditing. Specifically, the IGs are to:

- Provide leadership and coordination and recommend policies for activities designed (1) to promote economy, efficiency, and effectiveness in the administration of programs, and (2) to prevent and detect fraud and abuse in such programs and operations; and

THE AUDIT FUNCTION

FIG. 1-3
Offices of Inspectors General

Department
Agriculture
Commerce
Defense
Education
Energy
Health and Human Services
Housing and Urban Development
Interior
Justice
Labor
State
Transportation
Treasury
Agency for International Development
Environmental Protection Agency
General Services Administration
National Aeronautics and Space Administration
Small Business Administration
Veterans Administration

- Provide a means for keeping the head of the establishment and the Congress fully and currently informed about problems and deficiencies relating to the administration of such programs and operations and the necessity for and progress of corrective action.

The law requires that each IG appoint an Assistant IG for Auditing and an Assistant IG for Investigations. The law also requires that IGs submit semiannual reports to their respective department heads with copies transmitted to appropriate committees or subcommittees of Congress within 30 days of issuance. Copies of these reports are also available to the public at a reasonable cost 60 days after transmission to Congress. The various IGs have broad charters to appraise within their departments:

- Programs/operations
- Economy and efficiency
- Fraud, waste, and abuse
- Proposed legislation and regulations

The authority of the IGs is extensive and is greater than that of the

DCAA as noted earlier. In addition to having access to all records, reports, audits, and other material available to the applicable establishment, IGs, among other things, may:

- Conduct their own investigations.
- Request assistance of other federal, state, or local government agency or unit thereof.
- Subpoena from sources other than federal agencies all forms of information and documents necessary in the performance of their functions.

The power to subpoena is particularly strong and is causing some controversy, as noted previously in the discussion of the DCAA and later in Chapter 9.

However this controversy is resolved, the impact of the various IGs on ferreting out fraud, waste, and abuse has been impressive. The internal auditing activities of the DOD indicate that more than $2 billion in actual savings and cost avoidance is claimed in 1985 alone.[24] In 1986, savings mushroomed to more than $4 billion.

In addition, the IG's investigative efforts have led to nearly 1,000 convictions and over 550 debarments or suspensions in 1985.[25] For 1986, these numbers increased to 1,714 and 885 respectively.[26] It is worthwhile, in view of these numbers, to look at how IGs are organized.

Each IG is appointed by the President with the advice and consent of the Senate. Each reports to and is supervised by the department head he is authorized to audit. Each also has reporting responsibilities to overseeing congressional committees.

IGs are responsible for the auditing activities within their agencies. In many cases, internal auditing functions existed in the federal agencies as a result of the Budget and Accounting Act of 1950. The activities of these groups now are directed by the IGs.

Much of the activity of federal government internal auditing is aimed at grant funds. These are federal funds spent by state and local governments through specific grant programs. About $100 billion is spent each year in hundreds of programs. Often, the grant fund audits are required by the laws that establish the programs or are the result of directives from the Office of Management and Budget (OMB). All 50 state governments and over 80,000 local governments participate. The auditing challenge here is staggering.

To help deal with this challenge more effectively, Congress enacted the Single Audit Act of 1984 (discussed in detail in Chapter 5). While the mechanisms to implement the provisions of this Act are still being devised, the effect will be to alter the grant-by-grant style of auditing in favor of a single

---

[24] *Ibid.*, p. v.
[25] *Ibid.*, p. viii.
[26] *Ibid.*, p. i.

THE AUDIT FUNCTION

audit each year of each unit of government receiving in excess of $100,000 in federal assistance.

Under the 1984 Act, the OMB is responsible for developing implementation policy and for reporting annually to Congress on the status of implementation. The GAO and the state and local governments are to be consulted with by the OMB. Federal agencies' internal auditors are required to rely on and use the results of the single audit in planning and conducting additional work to avoid the duplication that previously existed and to enhance coverage. The single audit provides guideposts indicating where more in-depth auditing can be performed. It will be several years before the full benefits of the single audit concept will be realized.

On a combined basis, the IGs' staffs include nearly 7,500 auditors and investigators. Their annual budgets aggregate more than $400 million.

In recent years, the IGs, like the DCAA, have been criticized, despite their efforts and claims, of failing to significantly eliminate excessive waste and inefficiency, not to mention fraud, in their respective areas. One source of criticism was the President's Private Sector Survey on Cost Control (PPSSCC). Its review of IG activities found problems in the following areas:

- There should be better internal control auditing with a view toward preventing fraud, waste, and abuse.
- The current audit procedures of many IG staffs were not state of the art.
- The attraction of auditors with sufficient skills.
- Inconsistencies existed in administrative functions.

No doubt some of the findings of the PPSSCC are contentious. However, the unmistakable message is one with which all internal auditors can agree. That is: The government must eliminate mismanagement, fraud, waste, and abuse as part of the overall effort to cut government spending. The IGs must play an important part in this effort. Such a role parallels that of internal auditors in the private sector seeking to improve operational efficiency and effectiveness within their companies. To maximize IG effectiveness, the most up-to-date audit procedures must be employed by auditors with adequate skill and training, particularly in the EDP area.

This message is applicable to private sector internal auditors. The value of eliminating fraud, waste, and abuse is just as important for private enterprise as it is for government.

Internal Revenue Service

The IRS was established to oversee the orderly process by which income and estate tax returns are filed and amounts due are collected. A significant portion of the responsibilities and duties of the IRS pertain to its audit function for which it is primarily known. However, considerable resources are directed at the following additional functions:

- Executive direction
- Internal audit and security
- Management services
- Legal services
- Technical rulings and services
- Return processing
- Statistical reporting
- Taxpayer services
- Investigations and collections

The IRS is headed by a commissioner, who is appointed by and reports to the Secretary of the Treasury. Its audit function is performed through a series of local and district offices. Total manpower involved in the examination or audit function exceeds 30,000, not all of whom are auditors, however. It is by far the single largest audit force in the United States.

Significance of Government Auditing

This brief analysis of only the more substantial audit segments of the federal government illustrates three important points. First, the government audit sector representing, collectively, the largest and most diverse audit sector, repeatedly demonstrates the variety of circumstances in which auditing plays a constructive role. In many instances, the auditing is similar to internal auditing. Second, the audit agencies described offer outstanding testimony to what can be achieved by auditors in terms of organization, scope of work, and results. Finally, the fact that government auditors have borrowed liberally from standards and procedures originally introduced by the public accounting profession for their use suggests that such standards and procedures have very wide applicability.

PUBLIC ACCOUNTING

As indicated earlier in this chapter, the practice of public accounting in America began in the latter part of the nineteenth century. These additional comments amplify those in the earlier section.

General

Professional practice in the United States originated from branch operations of British accounting firms. The first national association of accountants in the United States, the American Association of Public Accountants, was established in 1887. This was a forerunner of what was to become in 1926, the AICPA. Today, there are some 250,000 individuals in the United States

THE AUDIT FUNCTION 1-33

who are members of the AICPA, about half of whom are public practitioners. The practice of public accounting ranges from that of sole practitioners and small partnerships to the practices of huge multinational accounting firms employing thousands of CPAs and earning gross fees in the $1 billion range.

The principal service offered by public accounting firms is the audit of financial statements. More is said about this service in a later section. Other financial audit-related services include compilation and review of financial statements, reviews of interim period financial statements, and prospective financial statements.

Public accountants offer other services similar to financial statement audit services. These are referred to as attestation engagements in which an entity may seek to have a CPA firm attest to a particular set of assertions by the entity other than in the context of financial statements. Examples include assertions regarding (1) compliance with particular statutory, regulatory, or contractual requirements; (2) attributes of computer software; and (3) compliance with terms of financial instruments.

CPA firms offer a variety of tax services, ranging from consultations to preparation of income and other tax return forms. They also offer management consulting services and actuarial services.

The extent of the services of public accounting firms and the significance of their principal service, the financial statement audit, make such firms invaluable and indispensable to the modern corporation, particularly publicly held corporations. Internal auditing, to a considerable degree, is shaped by the actions of these firms. It is essential that internal auditors possess a knowledge of the practice of public accounting. With that in mind, frequent references in this volume are made to public accounting and to the variety of other names used to identify public accountants, including independent accountants, independent auditors, and external auditors. Chapter 4 is devoted entirely to a discussion of GAAS developed by the AICPA. Understanding GAAS is necessary to an understanding of public accounting.

The practice of public accounting is regulated by the various states through boards of accountancy in much the same way that other public services are regulated. The principal form of regulation is the licensing authority. Each state has laws governing the licensing that each state board of accountancy is responsible for administering. In general, the states require that a license to practice accounting only be issued to individuals who:

- Possess a college degree.
- Have passed a uniform examination.
- Have satisfied experience requirements.

The uniform CPA examination is prepared by the AICPA as a service to the states. The exam is given twice a year, in May and November, under the supervision of the AICPA. The AICPA also offers a uniform grading service that all the states use.

The link between the state boards of accountancy and the AICPA is an important one. The states prescribe rules of conduct for the practice of public accounting that generally parallel the AICPA's Code of Ethics for its members. The effectiveness of the states' efforts in regulating public accountancy is enhanced by the National Association of State Boards of Accountancy. Each state Board of Accountancy is a member, as are the Boards of Accountancy of the District of Columbia, Guam, and Puerto Rico. Some states require, among other things, that audits be conducted in accordance with GAAS. GAAS (see Chapter 4) are promulgated by the AICPA. In view of this relationship, it is worthwhile to focus on the special role of the AICPA.

Role of the AICPA

The AICPA is the national professional organization for CPAs. Its mission, as set forth in its Mission Statement, is to assure that CPAs serve the public interest in performing quality professional services. The AICPA performs the following to achieve its mission:

- Promotes the uniform certification and licensing of CPAs
- Sets requirements for maintaining members' professional competence
- Assists members in the continuing development of professional expertise
- Provides standards of professional conduct and performance
- Monitors professional performance to enforce professional standards
- Promotes public confidence in the integrity, objectivity, competence, and professionalism of AICPA members and the services they perform
- Encourages highly qualified individuals to become CPAs and promotes the availability of appropriate educational programs
- Unites CPAs—whether in public practice, industry, education, or government—in their efforts to serve the public interest
- Serves as the national representative of CPAs to government, regulatory bodies, and other organizations
- Assists members in understanding and adjusting to changes in the economic, political, and technological environment

AICPA efforts in standards setting are more extensively detailed in Chapter 4. However, its involvement extends far beyond maintaining auditing standards. Until 1973, the AICPA, through designated committees and boards, issued authoritative pronouncements that constituted GAAP. In that year, the FASB, an independent standards-setting body, began operations. The FASB was charged with the responsibility of promulgating and maintaining the standards governing financial accounting and reporting. It was created in response to the recommendation of the Wheat Commission, a panel of seven distinguished individuals appointed by the AICPA. In effect, the panel concluded that the process of setting accounting principles could best be

THE AUDIT FUNCTION 1-35

improved by the AICPA by relinquishing it to the FASB.[27] Since 1973, the AICPA has exercised a strong voice in subsequent authoritative pronouncements by the FASB on accounting principles. The FASB is now the only body issuing pronouncements that have the authiority of GAAP.[28]

In addition to its historic role in standards setting, the AICPA provides these other useful services:

- Publication of the monthly magazine, *The Journal of Accountancy*
- Publication of a host of other technical material aimed at improving the body of knowledge existing in the financial community
- Maintenance of relations with other professional associations, such as Robert Morris Associates (bankers) and the American Bar Association (lawyers)
- Promotion of the well-being of members through self-study programs, meetings, conferences, and seminars to foster continuing education—both for those in public practice and in private industry
- Maintenance of a code of ethics for professional conduct
- Maintenance of an excellent library that is available to all members

These are but a few of the invaluable services furnished by the AICPA that benefit not only members but also state societies of CPAs, the public, and other audit branches.

The practice of public accounting is also affected by the various state CPA societies, the SEC, and last but not least, the courts.

Current Challenges

The professional practice of public accounting is undergoing considerable change in response to what it perceives as the current issues it faces.

In 1984, a report was submitted to the Board of Directors of the AICPA by the Future Issues Committee, which was established in 1982 for the purpose of articulating the issues. The report is aptly titled *Major Issues for the CPA Profession and the AICPA*. In 35 pages, it presents 14 issues that the committee believed to be an important starting point for the accounting profession to use to become more future-oriented. These issues are:

1. *Expansion of services and products.* How should the profession adapt its practices and standards so that firms can take maximum advantage of op-

---

[27] Marshall S. Armstrong, "The Financial Accounting Standards Board," in *Handbook of Accounting and Auditing,* John C. Burton, Russell E. Palmer, and Robert S. Kay, eds. (New York: Warren, Gorham & Lamont, 1981), Chapter 40.

[28] In 1984, the Financial Accounting Foundation (FAF) established the Government Accounting Standards Board (GASB) and the Government Accounting Standards Advisory Council (GASAC). The FAF assumed the same oversight responsibility for these groups as it does for the FASB and its advisory council—the Financial Accounting Standards Advisory Council. The 22-member GASAC provides advisory services to the GASB. The GASB issues pronouncements that have the authority of GAAP for financial statements of governments.

portunities to expand services and products in a manner appropriate to the professionalism and integrity of CPAs?

2. *Changes in the nature and extent of competition in the profession.* Can steps be taken to develop and implement strategies to maintain the viability and growth of practice units in an increasingly competitive environment, to adapt standards to make them more suitable to the new environment, and to alter the Institute's organizational structure and services to best meet the needs of its members in the changing environment?

3. *Widespread computerization and automation of business operations.* Can the profession adapt to take advantage of the widespread use of personal computers, and can the Institute provide leadership in those areas, while also developing technical performance standards and new services in those areas for the benefit of its members?

4. *Litigation and legal liability.* How can the accountants' exposure to liability arising from both audit and nonaudit work be limited in a manner consistent with the public interest?

5. *Increased specialization of accountants.* Should the profession establish a formal system for the recognition and accreditation of specialists beyond the CPA designation?

6. *Accounting standards overload.* Can the profession find the means, acceptable to all parties and consistent with the objectives of financial reporting, to alleviate accounting standards overload?

7. *The role of self-regulation.* What should be the appropriate role of the Institute in self-regulation?

8. *Upward mobility of women.* How can the profession strengthen the upward mobility of women in public accounting?

9. *Improving the quality of practice by CPAs.* How can general compliance with quality control standards be maintained in all areas of practice at a level sufficiently high to serve public needs adequately?

10. *Major reform of the federal income tax system.* What role should the Institute play in tax reform, and what strategies should the profession adopt to prepare for a major reform?

11. *Changes in the composition of institute membership and potential membership.* Can the Institute effectively serve the needs of its diverse membership and of non-CPA professionals, who are becoming an increasingly significant element in public accounting?

12. *Independence and objectivity.* Can independence and objectivity be maintained as the cornerstones of the practicing professional, or should broader concepts be emphasized?

13. *Diversity of CPA qualifications and performance requirements.* Can more effective initiatives be taken to achieve greater uniformity in the qualifications and performance requirements affecting CPAs?

14. *Mission, goals, and objectives of the Institute.* Do the stated mission, goals, and objectives of the Institute relate appropriately to all its mem-

THE AUDIT FUNCTION

bers—in public practice, industry, government, or education—considering, among other matters, if the traditional focus on public practitioners continues to be appropriate?[29]

The report of the Issues Committee goes on to recommend that the Institute:

- Undertake a comprehensive analysis of each issue presented.
- Establish a formal strategic planning process.
- Develop and implement a trend-monitoring system.
- Confirm the role of the Future Issues Committee as described in the report.
- Adopt an overall commitment to become future oriented.[30]

The work of the Issues Committee seems to have stimulated much attention and discussion among practitioners. It represents an important first step in taking the initiative to anticipate change and confront relevant issues in a timely fashion.

Of the issues identified in the preceding discussion, several either directly or indirectly deal with the AICPA. The Issues Committee omitted a direct discussion of one of these—Mission, Goals and Objectives of the Institute—since the AICPA established a separate Mission Committee to examine that issue.

The role of the AICPA has become an issue in the minds of the leaders of the profession for a variety of reasons. Perhaps chief among these is the fact that AICPA members in industry, government, and education now amount to almost half of total membership. That alone would be sufficient to cause a reevaluation of the role of the AICPA in serving this considerable sector. Other trends include:

- The emergence of women in large numbers in professional practice.
- The growth of computers.
- Increased specialization among members of the profession, which might indicate that perhaps other forms of recognition and accreditation might be appropriate.

Congressional Interest

The AICPA is not the only party interested in the issues confronting the practice of public accounting. At certain points in time, congressional committees have conducted hearings on the profession. In the mid-1970s, a Senate committee chaired by Senator Lee Metcalf and a House committee chaired by Congressman John Moss conducted separate hearings.

---

[29] Future Issues Committee, *Major Issues for the CPA Profession and the AICPA* (New York: AICPA, 1984) pp. 2–3. Reprinted by permission.

[30] *Ibid.*, p. 3.

No legislation came about as a result of these hearings, in part because the pressure exerted by these hearings and criticism from other sources (most notably the SEC) motivated the profession to adopt reforms. Many of these were recommended by the Commission on Auditors' Responsibilities, established by the AICPA to take a serious look at the profession. This commission was often referred to as the Cohen Commission, named after its Chairman, Manuel F. Cohen.

Out of that process came the Public Oversight Board (POB). The POB and the program for peer reviews perhaps were the most significant reforms. More is said about these reforms later in this chapter.

Once again, the profession has become the object of a congressional inquiry. In February 1985, the House Energy and Commerce Subcommittee on Oversight and Investigations initiated hearings focusing not only on public accounting but on the role of the SEC as well. These proceedings are the result of a growing perception among some members of Congress and others that accountants are not properly disciplined by the SEC for audit failures.

This concern has been fueled in recent years by instances of failures by banks and other businesses. It is alleged that audits in these instances did not provide sufficient warning of the imminent disasters to investors and other users of the audit reports.

Reports of the committee's proceedings suggest that opinions differ sharply on the quality of public accounting between practitioners and the SEC on the one hand and certain committee members on the other. In hearings held on February 20, March 6, April 2, and April 17, 1985, testimony by ranking members of the profession often clashed with members of the subcommittee. Those giving testimony included John R. Shad, Chairman of the SEC at the time; Philip B. Chenok, president of the AICPA; and Arthur M. Wood, then chairman of the AICPA's POB.[31]

In summary, the testimony noted that (1) the alleged audit failures comprised less than one percent of the 10,000 annual audits of publicly held companies; (2) the SEC is actively conducting enforcement actions against auditors; (3) the POB is effective in its efforts to provide oversight of the profession's self-regulating system; and (4) there is an important difference between business failures and audit failures.

Subsequent to the hearings, Representative Wyden (D. Or.) introduced legislation that, if enacted, would add significantly to the responsibilities of public accountants. As a result of further hearings held in 1986, the initial version of the bill was changed.

The revised version of the bill, H.R. 5439 (referred to by some as Wyden II), was thought to be more likely to gain passage. It contained far-reaching provisions and would have required the external auditor to bring possible fraudulent abuses to a corporation's audit committee. The audit committee would have time to conduct its own investigation and to direct management

---

[31] *Accounting News,* Summer 1985, p. 8.

THE AUDIT FUNCTION

to clean up any wrongdoing. Further disclosure by the external auditor may occur depending upon circumstances and the actions of the audit committee.

Corporate management would have been equally responsible with the external auditor for detecting fraud. The external auditor would have had to review any actions taken by management. Further, the bill would have required the external auditor to go to the authorities in instances where management failed to act adequately in investigating and correcting abuses reported by the auditor. The revised bill also contained a materiality standard. The standard was similar to that used by the GAO in investigating fraud. The materiality threshold envisioned would be less than that of financial statement materiality. It included both quantitative and qualitative factors.

Other provisions of the bill would have required affected companies to include in their annual reports an evaluation of systems of administrative and accounting controls. Further, it would have required external auditors to review such evaluations and report the results of such review.

The revised bill was not enacted. It died when the 99th Congress adjourned in 1986; so far it has not been reintroduced. Representative Wyden seems to be waiting to see what steps occur within the private sector to close the gap between public expectations of CPAs and what they can reasonably deliver. The statement by Wyden on introducing Wyden II gives a sobering view of the intensity of concern that gave rise to its development. A portion of his remarks follow:

> Mr. Speaker, in sixteen hearings conducted by the Subcommittee on Oversight and Investigations during 1985 and 1986, the subcommittee compiled an overwhelming record of devastating financial frauds. Again and again, the subcommittee found that independent auditors have failed to detect or to report fraudulent activities at a number of major corporations and financial institutions in this country.
>
> In one financial disaster after another, including E.F. Hutton, United American Bank, Penn Square Bank, E.S.M. Government Securities, Home State Savings Bank of Ohio, American Savings and Loan of Florida, Drysdale Government Securities, Saxon Industries and others, the disaster struck virtually on the heels of clean audit certificates issued by audit firms indicating that the companies were financially sound. The result? Hundreds of thousands of investors and creditors were out hundreds of millions of dollars.
>
> In spite of these and the many other major audit failures that have taken place in recent years, Mr. John Shad, Chairman of the Securities and Exchange Commission, said in his written statement to the subcommittee on June 23rd, 1986, "The evidence . . . suggests that the system is working well."
>
> Mr. Speaker, the many small depositors, investors, and others who are out in the cold because of these financial disasters do not share Mr. Shad's viewpoint. The fact is that SEC has failed to take the steps necessary to deal with financial fraud—even though both the Commission and the accounting profession have the authority to do so. Under current rules, when an auditor discovers a major

financial fraud, the auditor is required to do nothing but inform corporate management and consider resigning. While this rule may help protect accounting firms from lawsuits, it does very little to protect the consumer from fraud and illegal activity.[32]

Many in the profession are realizing the importance of the public's perceptions of CPAs. At the 13th annual AICPA National Conference on Current Developments in January 1986, SEC Commissioner Charles C. Cox said accountants "are beginning to realize that in 1986 it will be at least as important to look effective as to be effective." Further, he stated that the profession "realizes that public approval cannot be legislated or mandated by rule but must be sought and won." He went on to say that "[t]he profession's preoccupation with civil liability has contributed somewhat to its image problem. You will be more successful tackling the problems that have caused expanding liability than seeking to limit that liability directly." He added that "strict and clear audit standards should lead to reduced liability."

One response initiated in 1985 in all probability is directly attributable to this round of congressional inquiry. In the summer of 1985, the AICPA took the lead in the formation of a national commission to examine the specific issue of financial reporting fraud. Co-sponsors of the effort were the IIA, the FEI, and the NAA. The commission, renamed the NCFFR, was chaired by James C. Treadway, Jr., formerly an SEC commissioner. The five other members of the commission were drawn from the various interested sectors, such as banking, internal auditing, public accounting, industry, and Wall Street. The commission was supported by a 12-member advisory panel and was served by a professional staff.

The commission sought research assistance from sponsoring groups and from academic research bodies. Areas of concentration included:

- The independent auditing profession's response to fraudulent financial reporting.
- Effect of professionalism and codes of conduct on financial reporting.
- Role of the SEC in reducing the incidence of fraudulent financial reporting.
- Surprise write-offs.
- Expansion of nonaudit services and auditor independence.
- How to introduce the issue of fraudulent financial reporting to college business students.
- Opinion shopping and competition.
- Internal control.
- Role of the internal audit function.

The results of the research formed the basis for a broad-based report on the issues and suggestions for other private, public, and professional

---

[32] From remarks by Congressman Ron Wyden on the floor of the House of Representatives, Aug. 15, 1986.

groups to consider for implementation. Recommendations excerpted from the lengthy report are presented in Chapter 23.

The AICPA initiatives to respond to pressure for reform do not end with the Treadway Commission. Another important effort it undertook was to create in 1983 the Special Committee on Standards of Professional Conduct. The committee, also known as the Anderson Committee for its chairman, George Anderson (of Anderson, Anderson, Zurmuehlen & Co., Helena, Montana), was asked to:

- Evaluate the relevance of present ethical standards to professionalism, integrity, and commitment to both quality service and the public interest.
- Consider the role of the Institute in the process of establishing standards of professional conduct.
- Recommend a course of action.[33]

The report of the Special Committee was issued in 1986. Entitled *Restructuring Professional Standards to Achieve Professional Excellence in a Changing Environment*, its recommendations are comprehensive and bold. In summary, the recommendations call for the profession to:

- Restructure the Institute's Code of Professional Ethics to improve its relevance and effectiveness.
- Provide guidance to practitioners in making judgments regarding the scope and nature of services and in maintaining their adherence to professionalism.
- Establish a new program for the systematic monitoring of practice to improve the quality of service and to assure compliance with performance standards.
- Establish AICPA membership requirements for both continuing professional education and the basic education to enter the profession.[34]

Two of the recommendations of the Anderson Committee were controversial. The most significant of these was the recommendation for mandatory peer review. In October 1986, the AICPA Council, the Institute's governing body, voted to seek a full membership vote on a proposed bylaw amendment.

The amendment would require CPA firms that audit publicly held companies to belong to the AICPA's SEC Practices Section of the Division for CPA Firms. In so doing, all such firms would have to undergo a peer review once every three years. About 500 firms would have been affected.[35] As a bylaw amendment a two-thirds approval was required by those voting; the actual vote fell just short of that requirement.

The other recommendation would have allowed the membership to de-

---

[33] Special Committee on Standards of Professional Conduct for Certified Public Accountants, *Restructuring Professional Standards to Achieve Professional Excellence in a Changing Environment* (New York: AICPA, 1986), p. 5. Reprinted by permission.

[34] *Ibid.*, p. 1. Reprinted by permission.

[35] "Commission Issues Release on Proposed Mandatory Peer Reviews," *Security Regulation & Law Reports,* Apr. 10, 1987, p. 533.

cide whether to permit accepting nonaudit work on a contingent fee basis. The Council rejected the recommendation—by one vote.[36]

At the time of this writing, the AICPA board voted to ask the Council to authorize a ballot implementing the balance of the Anderson Committee recommendations. More discussion of the Anderson Committee Report appears in Chapter 7.

It is clear from the events surrounding the Anderson Committee activities that self-regulation of CPAs is a subject that is causing internal dissent within the AICPA. All CPAs probably would agree that services rendered to the public must be of the highest professional caliber. The extent to which some small firms feel compelled to demonstrate such high professional capability is at issue. This is particularly the case for those whose practice before the SEC is a minor portion of their overall practice. In effect, this group of CPAs appears to be reluctant to incur the costs necessary to demonstrate high professional capability. These costs would arise from joining or being required to join the SEC practices section (SECPS).

Self-Regulation

Practitioners of public accounting in the 1970s realized that actions were necessary to prevent the government from becoming directly involved in regulating their activities. Three of these subsequent actions that stand out and deserve discussion are:

1. The division in 1977 of the AICPA into two divisions—the SECPS and the private companies practice section (or PCPS).
2. The creation of the POB.
3. The establishment of a peer review program for SECPS member firms.

The first action saved a considerable segment of AICPA member firms from the costs of establishing and maintaining a peer review program. More importantly, however, it fostered the development of an organizational structure in which voluntary self-regulation could be exacted.

Self-regulation actions aimed at the SECPS were obviously more extensive and elaborate than those for the PCPS. Specific requirements for membership are given in the *Peer Review Manual* (AICPA, 1979). A summary of these requirements is presented in Figure 1-4.

The POB was created to serve as an overseer of the activities of the Executive Committee of SECPS and of the peer review program. It consists of five individual from outside the profession with established reputations for integrity and concern for public interest. The POB has access to all files, meetings, and other activities of the SECPS and the authority to hire staff.

---

[36] "AICPA Rejects Proposal to Mandate Peer Reviews as Membership Requirement," *Security Regulation & Law Reports*, Apr. 10, 1987, p. 510.

FIG. 1-4

Summary of Major Requirements for SECPS Membership

- The firm's quality controls over its accounting and auditing practice are to be subjected to peer review every three years, and at any other time as may be imposed as part of a disciplinary action.
- All partners and members of the professional staff resident in the USA must complete at least 120 hours of continuing professional education over three years, but not less than 20 hours in any given year.
- The audit partner in charge of an SEC engagement can serve in that capacity for a maximum of five consecutive years.
- A preissuance concurring review of an audit report for an SEC client must be made by a partner other than the audit partner in charge.
- The firm must provide specified information annually about its operations for inclusion in files open to the public.
- The firm must fulfill certain requirements set by the Executive Committee with regard to its independence.
- Total fees for management consulting services, and a description of their types, must be reported annually to the audit committee or board of an SEC client. Disagreements with management on material financial accounting and reporting matters and auditing procedures must likewise be reported.
- A firm must promptly report to the Special Investigations Committee any litigation against it or its personnel, or publicly announced investigations by regulatory agencies, where these matters allege deficiencies in auditing and reporting on SEC clients or former clients.

Source: John C. Burton, Russell E. Palmer, Robert S. Kay, *Handbook of Accounting and Auditing* (New York: Warren, Gorham & Lamont, Inc. 1981). Reprinted by permission.

The board exerts influence through its ability to express comments and criticisms publicly. Annually, the POB reports the results of its oversight efforts.

The current board believes that there has not been a serious breakdown in the quality standards of the accounting profession.[37]

Whether that view is sufficiently impressive to keep Congress from enacting legislation that would put the profession into a government regulated world is uncertain. As mentioned earlier, Representative Wyden, the author of the House bill that would have significantly altered these responsibilities of CPAs, criticized the POB during subcommittee hearings. In particular, he noted that the POB has never made a public pronouncement of any wrongdoing,[38] despite the fact that it is responsible for reporting findings of peer reviews. This system, in his view, could easily promote a conflict of interest among accountants.

---

[37] Author Unknown, "Public Oversight Board," *Journal of Accountancy,* May 1987, p. 43.

[38] "Dingell Hearings Continue to Probe Author's Role in Financial Reporting," *Accounting News,* Summer 1985, p. 8.

The number of firms joining SECPS represents a small percentage of all member firms of the AICPA. It is estimated that about 400 firms are current members of SECPS. These firms account for 85 percent of all SEC audit clients, however.[39]

Regardless of how the current congressional inquiry turns out, the AICPA can be proud of its role in recent years in responding to the challenges it faces. The peer review program its SECPS division has developed has done much to forward the cause of self-regulation. In the words of former AICPA Chairman Rholan E. Larson:

> Many firms that have undergone peer reviews will testify that it was a worthwhile process. Some have questioned the cost-benefit relationship of the process, but most believe in the value of peer review as firms use it as a foundation for quality control, practice growth and professional development. As a direct result of joining the division, many firms have developed well-thought-out systems of quality control that fit in with their emphasis on a strong and competent staff with effective partner leadership and supervision.[40]

In spite of the positive contributions that result from the peer review process, not all public accounting practitioners favor mandatory self-regulation. As noted earlier, the full membership rejected such a requirement in a 1987 ballot. The opposition seems to be represented primarily by small firms. One possible concern is that the increased cost of being a member of SECPS would place many firms at a competitive disadvantage in the non-SEC segment of the financial statement auditing market. These firms may fear that once they join they will be drawn into an ever-increasing cycle of regulatory activity—a cycle over which they would exercise little control—thereby increasing the competitive pressures they will face.

In this scenario, they would be dominated by the major firms in the SEC segment while being squeezed by non-SECPS practitioners in the non-SEC segment. Their options would indeed be bleak. The choice would be to reject joining SECPS with the probable result of losing their SEC practice, or join SECPS and risk losing not only their non-SEC practice but their identity as a separate practicing firm.

There may possibly be another alternative for these firms. It may be possible for them to create a separate self-regulating apparatus. Such an effort would not be easy, and there is no assurance that ultimately its cost would be less than that of SECPS. Finally, there is the question of whether such an apparatus would be acceptable to the SEC.

On that issue, the SEC seems to have spoken. In April 1987, the SEC proposed rules requiring CPAs who audit financial statements of publicly

---

[39] "AICPA Rejects Proposal to Mandate Peer Reviews as Membership Requirement," *op. cit.*, p. 510.

[40] Rholan E. Larson, "Self-Regulation: A Professional Step Forward," *Journal of Accountancy*, Sept. 1985, p. 60.

held companies to undergo a peer review every three years.[41] However, the proposed rules provide a choice for CPAs. They could have the review supervised by the SEC directly or by an acceptable peer review organization (PRO).

PROs would have to meet requirements set forth in the proposed rules. These rules provide that any PRO have a body of at least three independent individuals to represent the public interest in overseeing PRO activities. Such a body would be similar to the five-member POB that oversees the work of the SECPS. The rules also cover qualifications of peer reviewers, the study of the firm's quality controls, the documentation of the peer review, the peer review report, and the firm's response.

Such proposed rules make clear that any PRO will have to look very much like the one already established within the AICPA. The National Conference of CPA Practitioners is known to be developing such an organization for smaller firms.

Regardless of how successful this effort will be, it seems clear that the SEC and the AICPA are solidly supporting the concept of self-regulation.

One possible outcome of the current round of attention is some sort of public sanctioning mechanism for firms who fail to pass peer review or otherwise are involved in audit failures. How this might contribute toward improving quality is a hotly debated topic. Members are rightly fearful that public sanctions in the litigation-prone business environment in which CPAs operate will expose them to immeasurable new risks.

The Attest Function

It was noted earlier that the primary audit service performed by CPAs is the attest function. Historically, the attest function has most often been used to mean attesting to the fairness of financial statements prepared in accordance with GAAP.

Such a meaning for the term is still largely correct. However, CPAs are broadening their role and services to the public. With increasing frequency, they are being asked to provide assurance on something other than financial statements. In some cases, these engagements involve reporting on a more restricted basis. An example might be a report to management on its system of internal accounting control. Another might be an engagement to report on compliance with contractual or regulatory requirements. Not only the subject matter of these engagements varies, but also the opinion to be expressed may be other than positive. Forms of negative assurance may be appropriate, for instance.

The increasing scope of CPA attest services is such that it has kindled

---

[41] Securities and Exchange Commission, *Independent Accountants—Mandatory Peer Review* [Release Nos. 33-6695; 34-24289; 35-24360; IC-15655; IA-1064; File No. S7-13-86].

a rethinking of the basic GAAS. This subject is discussed in greater detail in Chapter 4.

Another action by the AICPA deserves mention here because it represents another in the series of efforts aimed at closing the "expectation gap" between what the public expects of CPAs and what they have been delivering.

In addition to the Treadway and the Anderson Commissions, the AICPA, through ASB, issued the most sweeping changes to general auditing standards since their original adoption in 1939. These new standards, 9 in all, deal with such matters as the scope of the study of internal control, the auditors standard report, communications with audit committees, illegal acts by clients, and the use of analytical procedures.

The proposals are intended to more clearly define the external auditor's responsibility for detecting and reporting fraud, to improve communications and understanding of the role of the auditor, and to improve the planning and performance of the independent audit of financial statements. More is said about these proposals in other sections of this volume, including Chapters 4 and 18.

Other Issues

There are still other issues facing the accounting profession. For example, the FTC is making inquiries concerning certain rules of professional conduct and antitrust concerns regarding rules of conduct for contingent fees, advertising, and direct solicitation of clients.

It is likely that the profession will continue to change in response to these and other pressures. These pressures are the unavoidable result of the increasingly complex environment in which the profession is expected to practice, fueled by growing and evolving demands by clients, the government, and the public.

Significance of Public Accounting

The assurance provided by CPAs is essential to orderly capital formation, a necessary part of the private enterprise system. This point warrants further comment here. Persons relying on such assurance for investment or other financial decisions related to the company may have a cause of action against the CPA should his assurance be improperly provided. CPAs, therefore, are exposed to considerable civil, and even criminal, liability in performing the attest function. This is unique among the audit branches. Actual cases are extremely rare, but when they do occur, they are often sensational and quite costly for the public accounting firm involved. This exposure is more than enough to have motivated the AICPA and its member firms to take the lead in establishing guidance to auditors. The efforts of the public accounting profession to develop the professional status of auditing has benefited all practitioners. Experience in a CPA firm is thought by many to be among the best career building blocks. Many executives in all areas of business, including chief executive officers, trace their starts to time spent in public accounting.

To summarize, the significance of external auditing, aside from its role in capital formation, is that it plays a lead role in standards setting, which affects all auditors. In addition, it serves as a training ground for careers in other financial areas, including internal auditing.

INTERNAL AUDITING

General

This branch is the least developed of the three. While some very large companies have developed sophisticated internal audit functions, taken as a whole, they are overshadowed by companies who have only recently created the function. To those must be added the companies that have perpetually allocated insufficient resources, thereby preventing the function from operating effectively.

There are no reliable estimates of the number of internal audit practitioners in the United States. In 1987, there were in excess of 30,000 members of the IIA worldwide. However, not all members are internal audit practitioners and, conversely, not all practitioners are members. It is unlikely, however, that the total exceeds 100,000 in the United States.

If we assume that the average size of an individual audit staff approximates 10, then simple division suggests that there may be as many as 7,500 separate internal audit organizations in the United States. In short, internal auditing has become a sizeable practice.

Internal audit departments are organized in a variety of ways. Some are functionally centralized, others are decentralized. Many are organized according to geographic divisions and still others are organized by industry segment. Chapter 6 discusses audit organizations and administration more extensively.

Normally, the department is headed by an individual occupying a relatively high and visible position in the management structure. According to a recent survey by the IIA, almost 20 percent of the surveyed departments reported that the chief internal auditor had attained the rank of vice-presient.[42] This is double the percent disclosed by a similar survey in 1979.

The internal auditing branch is affected by forces of change, although perhaps not to the degree that CPAs are being affected. (See Chapter 2 for a discussion of current forces of change.) The practice of internal auditing

---

[42] Kenneth R. White, Ph.D., and James A. Xander, Ph.D., *Survey of Internal Auditing: Trends and Practices* (Altamonte Springs, Fla.: The Institute of Internal Auditors, 1986), p. 27.

appears safe from the prying eyes of congressional subcommittees, for example.

Still, the practice is evolving, ever improving, and growing. One indicator that might be used as an overall barometer of the utility of internal auditing is to look at how it is affecting the character and extent of reviews by external auditors.

A 1984 study by Dr. Wanda Wallace of Southern Methodist University of the effect of internal audit activities on external audit fees provides much insight to the question. Dr. Wallace reported that, in 1968, a survey by the IIA showed that 12 percent of respondents indicated that internal and external auditors formally met. By 1981, that rate increased to 81 percent.[43]

According to the previously noted survey, the development of internal audit departments is resulting in greater use of internal audit reports by external auditors.[44] The survey disclosed, among other things, that in 1983, 67.9 percent of respondents indicated greater use of internal audit reports; in 1979, only 44 percent of respondents so indicated. If these responses are accurate, then it is appropriate to say that internal auditing is gaining in effectiveness.

Another indicator is the opportunity to meet with the audit committee. In 1975, 66 percent of survey respondents met regularly with audit committees. By 1979, that increased to 83.2 percent, and in 1983, it reached 89.7 percent.[45] Clearly, the trend is upward, suggesting that audit committees increasingly are accepting the notion that internal auditing contributes valuable information to aid in performing their oversight responsibility.

Consider reporting relationships. In 1979, 10 percent of respondents reported to the company president. In 1983, that percentage grew to 17 percent—a whopping 70 percent increase. By contrast, the number who report to the controller and chief financial officer seemed to decline slightly from the 1979 level.[46] This suggests that internal auditing is advancing organizationally. This can only result from improvements in the quality of the work performed by internal auditors.

Services, Skills, and Experience

Internal auditors perform a broad array of auditing and consulting services to their respective managements (including boards of directors). These ser-

---

[43] Wanda A. Wallace, Ph.D., CIA, CMA, CPA, *A Time Series Analyses of the Effect of Internal Audit Activities on External Audit Fees* (U.S.A.: The Institute of Internal Auditors, 1984), p. xiii.

[44] White and Xander, *op. cit.*, p. 13.

[45] *Ibid.*, p. 16.

[46] *Ibid.*, p. 17.

THE AUDIT FUNCTION

vices are the focus of this volume, so a lengthy discussion here is not intended.

Briefly, however, the auditing services performed by internal auditors are usually categorized as financial or operational. Both terms have wide meanings that are nearly as generic as internal auditing or auditing. Financial auditing consists of auditing of accounting records and controls, financial statements, and other financial information. Operational auditing, as defined in Chapter 31, is nonfinancial auditing for the purpose of appraising the managerial organization and efficiency of a company or a part of a company. Program auditing is a type of operational auditing (see Chapter 36).

In recent years, additional auditing services developed that do not easily fit into the categories of operational or financial auditing. One of these is EDP auditing, which has expanded to become more accurately identifiable as I/S auditing.

The concerns over corporte accountability and business ethics surfacing during the 1970s and 1980s spawned business conduct auditing. This type of auditing also does not fit well into the categories of operational and financial auditing. Finally, many internal auditing functions perform a type of auditing that checks controls and procedures for their sufficiency in reasonably assuring compliance with various applicable laws and regulatory requirements.

Internal auditing is under continuous change as a result of a combination of forces, as Chapter 2 makes clear. Within a given company, the function usually reports high in the organization structure and is directed by an individual who is skilled and proficient in auditing. The person may be an officer of the company. The position is known by various titles, such as general auditor, auditor general, director of internal auditing, vice-president–auditing, or simply, chief auditor. He is responsible for devising and implementing a program of auditing within the company that provides management, including the board of directors (usually through the audit committee), with opinions and other information to assist them in their stewardship of the organization. Internal auditing functions range in size from one or two individuals to large departments consisting of scores of auditors. The functions are managed using the same principles of management applicable to other functional disciplines. (Chapter 7–10 discuss the management of internal auditing functions in detail.)

It is imperative that internal auditing, like government auditing and public accounting, be performed in accordance with high professional standards. (Chapters 3–6 provide discussions of the development of standards as well as an elaboration of the standards applicable to all branches of auditing.)

An excellent discussion of the skill and experience of internal auditors is found in *The Practice of Modern Internal Auditing* by Lawrence B. Sawyer, CIA. (See "Selected References.") He describes the background and process by which the IIA adopted "The Common Body of Knowledge" in

1972. This statement, written by R.E. Gobeil,[47] describes the knowledge of internal auditors as existing on three levels intended to portray the knowledge of subject areas from a general to a more specific perspective. It resulted from a survey conducted by a subcommittee of the Institute's Education Committee, headed by Mr. Gobeil. The body of knowledge found to be common included accounting and finance, auditing, behavioral science, communications, computer systems and equipment, economics, legal aspects of business, quantitative methods, and systems and procedures.[48]

The most frequently encountered requirements in terms of skill include a formal business education from an accredited college or university, formal training and on-the-job experience as an auditor, and related business or accounting experience. The authors note a trend in recent years toward enhanced levels of skill and training possessed by internal auditors. Many now hold advanced degrees and professional credentials. A growing percentage of this group were formerly practicing CPAs. Also noteworthy has been the advent of the CIA Program and the Code of Ethics.

Certified Internal Auditor Program and the Code of Ethics

The CIA program was established in 1972 by the IIA. The program is intended to enhance the level of professionalism of the internal audit practitioners. Successful U.S. candidates must possess a college degree, a minimum of two years work experience, subscribe to the CIA Code of Ethics, submit a character reference from another CIA or from a supervisor, and pass a written examination. The examination is comprised of the following parts:

1. Principles of Auditing
2. Internal Audit Techniques
3. Principles of Management
4. Disciplines Related to Internal Auditing

Experience through 1980 reveals that about one candidate in five ultimately passes the exam.[49] There are about 14,000 CIAs worldwide.

The Code of Ethics for members of the IIA was developed in 1968. It was followed in 1972 with a Code of Ethics for CIAs. The Codes were

---

[47] R.E. Gobeil, "The Common Body of Knowledge for Internal Auditors," *The Internal Auditor*, Nov./Dec., 1972, p. 21. In addition to this work, an IIA Research Foundation study, entitled *A Common Body of Professional Knowledge for Internal Auditors: A Research Study*, was published in 1985. This study contains a framework for determining which staff members possess the knowledge and competence required for professional internal auditing.

[48] Lawrence B. Sawyer, *The Practice of Modern Internal Auditing*, 2nd ed. (Altamonte Springs, Fla.: The Institute of Internal Auditors, 1981), pp. 28–30.

[49] *Ibid.*, p. 35.

THE AUDIT FUNCTION 1-51

developed by the IIA and are a significant milestone in the effort to establish the practice of internal auditing as a professional practice.

The two Codes of Ethics are similar. The separate Code for CIAs is necessary because being a member of the IIA is not required in order to be a CIA—although most CIAs are members. The Code deals with such individual characteristics as honesty, objectivity, diligence, loyalty, and conflicts of interest. (The Codes of Ethics are reprinted in Chapter 6.)

Role of Institute of Internal Auditors

The IIA has already been mentioned several times and further comment regarding its activities is made throughout this book. The IIA has been a strong and vital force in lifting the practice of internal auditing to a professional status. Its role and services warrant special mention.

The IIA is an international association of professional practicing internal auditors. It is dedicated to the professional advancement of its members.

The services of the IIA are provided through an international network of local chapters and its international headquarters in Altamonte Springs, Florida. There are over 175 chapters in 46 states within the United States and 35 other countries. It offers a wide range of services to its members, including:

- Continuing educational programs through an extensive system of conferences and seminars.
- Current information through published research reports, the bi-monthly magazine, *The Internal Auditor,* and a monthly newsletter.
- Standards-setting activities.
- Maintaining a Code of Ethics.
- Marketing and promotional activities.
- Directing the CIA program.
- Providing quality assurance review services.

The IIA was founded in New York in 1941 by a small group of practicing internal auditors. In 1973, it moved its headquarters to Altamonte Springs, Florida, where it exists today. The IIA is governed by a board of directors comprised of 14 directors-at-large, 15 regional directors, and 31 district directors. These are drawn from the local chapters and elected by the members at the annual meeting. The board is headed by a chairman, three vice-chairmen—one of whom is designated as senior vice-chairman—a secretary, and a treasurer.

The board of directors is the policy-making group. It is supported by a host of special committees. Members of these committees are approved by the board to serve one to three-year terms on a voluntary basis. Examples of these committees include the Advanced Technology Committee, the College & University Relations Committee, and the Professional Conference

Committee. There are currently 20 such committees. The day-to-day operations of the IIA are managed by a full-time president and staff. The success of the IIA is attributable to the diligent efforts of this staff and the voluntary efforts of the members at the local chapter level and at the international committee and board levels. The IIA receives revenue from its dues structure, its publications, and its conferences and seminars. Much indirect support is provided by the network of private companies, colleges and universities, and governmental units that employ the members.

The voluntary nature of the IIA cannot be overstressed. There is no licensing requirement for internal auditors comparable to that described earlier in this chapter for CPAs. While some states have enacted laws mandating that internal auditing in governmental units conform with the IIA's standards, no statutory laws exist governing professional conduct of internal auditors in general. Moreover, there is no regulatory agency overseeing the IIA with power to affect the practice of internal auditing as the SEC does in the instance of CPAs. Finally, courts have yet to set any precedents in terms of civil and criminal liability as they have in the business of public accounting.

Therefore, the strength of the work of the IIA lies in the voluntary acceptance of its largely voluntary-produced services by its members.

The challenges this voluntary body must deal with are formidable. The practice of internal auditing is being promoted by many as being part of the solutions to such issues as corporate accountability, ethical business practices, and financial reporting fraud. At the same time, its readiness for this surge in responsibility is uncertain. The practice is still characterized by internal auditing practitioners who, for the most part, do not intend to remain in the practice. Rather, they seek experience in internal auditing as a building block toward a career in financial management. It is also characterized by risks for chief auditors who have the responsibility to report matters that may reflect poorly on members of management who outrank them. The effectiveness of internal auditing obviously suffers in such an environment.

Concern is also mounting that a properly functioning internal audit department may be a liability as much as it is an asset. Powerful government investigative bodies and others realize that a good internal auditing department will have files of reports and working papers that will serve as a road map to sensitive matters. It is in these areas that investigators look for evidence of wrongdoing to use against the company. The increasing frequency with which access to internal auditing records is occurring poses a threat to the effective practice of internal auditing. (See Chapter 9.)

Internal auditing is beginning to face the spectre of increased public attention and congressional scrutiny. As internal auditing responsibilities increase, so will the public interest in it. Regulatory and statutory action directly affecting internal auditing is not as impossible to imagine as it once was. Internal auditors accustomed to conducting their practice in a very closed environment must soon be prepared to face the world.

The IIA is aware of the challenges confronting the profession. It will require even greater efforts by the leaders of the profession—practitioners, educators, regulators, management, and external auditors—to maximize the opportunities presented by today's environment.

The EDP Auditors Association

The practice of internal auditing is also affected by other professional organizations. The AICPA affects many internal auditors who are both CPAs and members of the AICPA. The EDP Auditors Association (EDPAA) is also actively working to advance the professionalism and practice of EDP (I/S) auditors. This organization, founded in 1969 in Los Angeles, is now a worldwide association of information systems auditing professionals. It maintains a certification program bestowing the designation Certified Information Systems Auditor on those meeting the requirements. It also conducts research, develops and offers training courses, and publishes educational materials. In 1987, a milestone was achieved when the EDP Auditors Foundation (EDPAF) issued *General Standards for Information Systems Auditing* through the effects of its standards board. The EDPAF is the research and educational arm of the EDPAA. The EDPAF has also developed a Code of Ethics.

There are other organizations that have affected internal auditing but to a lesser extent. These include the NAA, the FEI, the American Management Association, the Association of Government Accountants, and the Bank Administration Institute.

Significance of Internal Auditing

From its independent vantage point, the internal audit function provides management, including the board of directors, with an ongoing stream of reliable information useful in appraising performance and measuring compliance with policies and procedures. This service, along with other reporting mechanisms, has fostered the growth and development of the modern-day corporation.

The expansion of corporate entities into multidivisional, multinational, multisegmented amalgamations could only occur through a combination of proper controls pinpointing responsibility and accountability. Auditors provide feedback to management, indicating the extent to which that combination is operating. The significance of internal auditing, then, is that it is a facilitating function; that is, it facilitates future growth and change to meet the objectives with which management is charged. This text discusses the important facets involved in effectively managing and performing the internal audit function.

THE KEYS TO EFFECTIVE PRACTICE

This volume is presented on the premise that, while internal auditing is practiced in a variety of situations, there are certain facets or keys that are applicable to all. These keys are essential to an effective internal auditing practice.

First, as established in this chapter, internal auditing is affected constantly by various forces. Change occurs in internal auditing as a result of economic, governmental, and technological developments. Internal auditors must recognize that change is inevitable and be responsive to it.

As Chapter 2 illustrates, it is necessary to allocate internal auditing resources in such a way as to maximize the utility of internal auditing services. This requires developing and implementing a strategic approach.

Part II of this volume is devoted to the subject of auditing standards. The importance of auditing standards to effective auditing is paramount. For that reason, four chapters are dedicated to presenting how standards are developed, and reviewing auditing standards applicable to each branch.

Effective internal auditing is the result of careful organizing, planning, directing, and controlling. In a word, internal auditing must be properly managed. Techniques to do this are the subject of Part III. Specific topics deal with organizing and planning the function, managing audit projects, managing people and other resources, and communicating with the audit committee.

Another key to effective practice is a knowledgeable cadre of performing internal auditors. Techniques for the performing auditor are presented in Part IV. The practical guidance provides answers to questions of how to perform preliminary work, how to work effectively in the field, and how to communicate results.

All auditors must be familiar with the tools of their trade—the technical aspects of auditing. Part V discusses these in three chapters. First, concepts of evidential matter are covered, followed by detailed explanations of audit sampling and auditing procedures.

Once the keys to effective internal auditing are presented, this volume moves its focus to the specific types of internal auditing and applies the keys. Part VI deals with financial auditing. It consists of illustrative descriptions of internal control and how to audit it. Detailed programs and questionnaires are included for the most common internal accounting control functions. Specimen reports are also set forth.

Part VII reviews the increasingly important subject of ethical business conduct. In addition to a thorough overview of the subject, separate chapters are devoted to discussions of the principal types of fraud. These include financial reporting fraud, procurement fraud, and computer fraud.

A book on internal auditing would be incomplete without an extensive coverage of specialized areas of internal auditing. The most important of these is information systems or EDP auditing. The growth of EDP in the last 30 years has been nothing short of spectacular. Never before in the history of mankind has there been any development with so pervasive an impact. Three chapters in Part VIII are given to a discussion of internal control concepts and how to audit in an information systems environment. Here too, detailed discussions of I/S audit techniques are included, as are examples of I/S audit tools. A glossary of terms is also provided to help with understanding the computer environment. Part VIII also covers two other specialized areas—international operations and financial analysis for business combinations.

Part IX is last but not least by any means. It presents 10 chapters that provide an in-depth look at operational auditing. This area of auditing is the most challenging and, often, the most rewarding. The challenge derives from the fact that improving operational efficiency and effectiveness—a principal objective—is very hard to do. Considerable innovativeness and resourcefulness are essential. Operational auditing also requires considerable experience and specialized knowledge. Operational auditing is susceptible to effective results, provided a systematic approach is followed and the proper tools are used. Chapters 31–40 present such an approach and reveal audit programs and questionnaires that may be used for many of the most critical management disciplines. These include finance, marketing, R&D facilities, and information systems.

One of the most challenging aspects of management is the management of inventory. The acquisition of materials, parts, and services, conversion of these into proprietory products and services, and the distribution of these to customers is what most businesses are formed to do. Chapter 34 presents a discussion of operational auditing in this area, embracing functions such as engineering, manufacturing, material, facilities, finance, security, and data processing.

This volume is intended to provide illustrative, practical guidance for use not only by internal auditors, but by governmental and external auditors as well. To meet the objectives of this work, this edition emphasizes definitions of terms. It also frequently explains the purposes or objectives of undertakings of all types in the belief that if the objective is clear, the techniques are easier to comprehend. Since this volume is predominantly practical, much guidance is offered in the form of techniques, illustrative programs, questionnaires, and specimen reports.

SUGGESTED READING

"AICPA Centennial Issue." *Journal of Accountancy,* May 1987.

Barrett, Michael J., DBA, CIA, Gerald W. Lee, CIA, CISA, CDP, S. Paul Roy, Ph.D., CA, and Leticia Verastegui. *A Common Body of Professional Knowledge for Internal Auditors: A Research Study,* Altamonte Springs, Fla.: The Institute of Internal Auditors, 1985.

Barrett, Michael J. "Internal Auditing and Corporate Financial Information Systems—Yesterday, Today and Tomorrow." *The Internal Auditor,* Vol. 37, No. 3, June 1980, pp. 26–32.

Brink, Victor Z. "Internal Auditing—A Historical Perspective and Future Direction." *The Internal Auditor,* Vol. 35, No. 6, Dec. 1978, pp. 23–35.

Briston, Richard J. "The Changing Role of the Internal Auditor." *The Internal Auditor,* Vol. 37, No. 1, Feb. 1980, pp. 23–28.

Burton, John C., Russell E. Palmer, and Robert S. Kay, eds. *Handbook of Accounting and Auditing,* Chapters 9, 39–43. New York. Warren, Gorham & Lamont, 1981.

Carmichael, Douglas R., and John J. Willingham. *Perspectives in Auditing,* 3rd ed. New York: McGraw-Hill, 1979.

The Commission on Auditors' Responsibilities: Report, Conclusions and Recommendations. New York: Commission on Auditors' Responsibilities, 1978.

Gobeil, R. E. "The Common Body of Knowledge for Internal Auditors." *The Internal Auditor,* Nov./Dec., 1972, pp. 20–28.

Mautz, Robert K., Ph.D., Peter Tiessen, Ph.D., and Robert H. Colson, Ph.D. *Internal Auditing: Directions and Opportunities.* Altamonte Springs, Fla.: The Institute of Internal Auditors, 1984.

Montgomery, Robert H. *Fifty Years of Accountancy.* The Ronald Press Co., 1939.

Sawyer, Lawrence B. *The Practice of Modern Internal Auditing,* 2nd ed., Part I. Altamonte Springs, Fla.: The Institute of Internal Auditors, 1981.

Scantlebury, D. L. "Federal Government Auditing." *Cashions Handbook for Auditors,* 2nd ed. McGraw-Hill, 1986.

Stettler, Howard F. "Have the Internal Auditors Arrived?" *The Internal Auditor,* Vol. 36, No. 3, June 1979, pp. 60–69.

White, Kenneth R., Ph.D., and James A. Xander, Ph.D. *Survey of Internal Auditing: Trends and Practices.* Altamonte Springs, Fla.: The Institute of Internal Auditors, 1986.

White, Richard, CIA, and William G. Bishop III. *The Role of the Internal Auditor in the Deterrence, Detection and Reporting of Fraudulent Financial Reporting.* Altamonte Springs, Fla.: The Institute of Internal Auditors, 1984.

CHAPTER 2

Developing a Strategic Auditing Approach

Reasons for a Strategic Auditing Approach 2	**Financial Information Reporting Auditing Described** 29
Effective Allocation of Limited Resources 2	"Financial Information Reporting" Defined 29
Relevant and Reliable Results 3	Relevance of Financial Information 29
Basis for Managing 3	Contrasted Roles of External and Internal Auditors 31
Aid to Audit Staff 3	The Interim Financial Report Audit 32
Relating Organization Needs and Auditing Objectives 4	**Ethical Business Practices Auditing Described** 35
Needs and Objectives Are Dynamic ... 4	"Ethical Business Practices" Defined .. 35
The FCPA 4	The Ethical Practices Audit 36
Expanded Internal Control Perceptions 5	**Deciding How to Allocate Auditing Resources** 43
Renewed Emphasis on Operational Efficiency 7	Strategic Audit Planning 43
Rapid Development and Application of Office Automation 9	Surveying Universe of Auditable Areas 45
Heightened Concern Regarding Government Spending Practices 9	Identifying Risk Factors 48
Relevance of Financial Information 14	Impact on Decision Making 48
Business Ethics 17	Complexity of Systems 48
Developing a Meaningful Statement of Objectives 21	Volume of Transactions 49
Supplementing the IIA Guidelines 21	Impact on Financial Statements (Materiality) 49
Three-Step Technique for Adding Specific Objectives 21	Source or Use of Cash 49
	Regulatory Involvement 49
Overall Auditing Objectives 23	Prioritizing Risk Factors 50
Correlating Needs With Auditing Areas 23	Determining Audit Frequency 50
Financial Auditing 24	Guidelines for Allocation of Audit Resources 51
Operational Auditing 25	Maintaining Flexibility 54
Information Systems Auditing 28	**A Word of Caution** 54
Ethical Business Practice Auditing 29	**Suggested Reading** 55

Fig. 2-1 Milestones in Government Spending 10
Fig. 2-2 Federal Government Revenues, Outlays, and Deficits 11
Fig. 2-3 Size of Government and Economic Performance 12

Fig. 2-4	Statement of Responsibilities of Internal Auditing	22
Fig. 2-5	Audit Program for Limited Financial Review	33
Fig. 2-6	Audit Program for Review of Ethical Business Practices	37
Fig. 2-7	Audit Areas Selected From Transaction Cycle Functions and Policies—Financial Reporting Emphasis	47
Fig. 2-8	Weighted Ranking of Audit Areas	52
Fig. 2-9	Frequencies for Common Audits	54

REASONS FOR A STRATEGIC AUDITING APPROACH

The subject of auditing strategy is a function of managing the internal auditing organization. As such, it could be covered in Part III. But it is also beneficial from the standpoint of perspective, and it contributes to the basis of overall understanding that is the objective of Part I.

This chapter explains why an overall strategic approach is important, identifies the forces that affect organizational needs, which are the determinants of the strategy, and provides details of how to develop a strategy. The discussions emphasize the point introduced in Chapter 1—that internal auditors must be responsive to those forces of change that affect organizational needs with respect to internal auditing. In that way, the internal auditing department stands the best chance of maximizing its worth to the organization.

There are four principal reasons why an overall strategy or plan is important. A plan:

1. Permits effective allocation of limited resources.
2. Assures that relevant and reliable information is provided.
3. Provides a basis for managing the function.
4. Helps the audit staff perform its role.

Effective Allocation of Limited Resources

One of the facts of life in the practice of auditing is that there is always more that can be audited than is permitted by time or resources. This status is common to all audit branches. In the government sector, for example, the IRS, despite its vast size, is able to audit only a fraction of the total income tax returns filed each year. Public accountants limit their examination to only those aspects of internal control that have a bearing on the financial statements they examine. Even then, the number of transactions and functions scrutinized is quite limited.

Similarly, internal auditing organizations—even the largest—will only be able to review a small fraction of the transactions, activities, and functions that occur in their respective companies. Decisions regarding the size of the organization, its structure, and its scope of services are largely a matter of judgment to be worked out by the chief auditor and the management to whom he reports. This judgment is made easier and more reliable if an overall plan exists.

Relevant and Reliable Results

The work of the internal auditor is most useful when the assurance and other information provided to third parties is relevant and reliable.

Relevant information, in this sense, is defined as that information in which management, including the board of directors, is interested. Generally, information is of interest to these groups if it assists them in effectively discharging their responsibilities. This requires that the information be timely and relevant in terms of subject matter. The obvious strategic significance of this point obliges the chief auditor to make every reasonable effort to position his organization so as to provide useful information of interest when it is needed.

Reliability, on the other hand, is intended here to mean that the information furnished is accurate, complete, and credible. The opinions and insights of the auditor add little to management's understanding if they deal in matters with which the auditor is not qualified to address. For example, the opinion of an auditor regarding the potential market for a new product or service would not be of much interest to most managements. This simply is not the auditor's field of expertise.

An overall strategy can go a long way toward assuring that the internal auditing function activities are properly directed to relevant areas and in such a manner as to provide reliable information.

Basis for Managing

Developing a strategic audit approach offers a great benefit to the internal auditing organization itself because it establishes the basis for effectively managing the department. In other words, decisions relating to such topics as organizational structure, personnel requirements, annual plans of audit coverage, reporting practices, and staff training are made on a more analytical and better-informed basis.

In addition, communications with senior managements and the board of directors is facilitated because the strategy, if it is properly formulated, will permit the chief auditor to easily compile and present to them the relevant information.

Aid to Audit Staff

Staff members, including directors, managers, seniors, and other performing auditors, are better able to perceive how specific audit projects relate to the basic audit plan. This perception results in their establishing specific audit assignment objectives that directly tie in to the overall plan, Also, staff members can explain to inquiring line managers how a given audit project fits into the "big picture."

RELATING ORGANIZATIONAL NEEDS AND AUDITING OBJECTIVES

Needs and Objectives Are Dynamic

The basic strategy, as introduced in Chapter 1, is simply to establish auditing objectives that directly relate to organizational (management and the board of directors) needs. As in making money in the stock market, the principle may be known, but the objective is difficult to achieve. That is because these needs are dynamic. Business enterprises operate in an environment of continually changing political, social, economic, and technological forces. Thus, the organization, under the direction of the board and management, is constantly changing and adapting to the influence of these forces. The chief internal auditor must see that the audit approach and objectives of the internal auditing function remain relevant in the face of these growing and changing needs.

Some factors that have influenced organizations and their internal auditing functions in recent years are as follows:

- The Foreign Corrupt Practices Act (FCPA)
- Renewed emphasis on operational efficiency
- Rapid development and application of office automation
- Heightened concern regarding government spending practices
- Relevance of financial information

The present effect of these forces, however, has changed from earlier times. The following discussions of each is intended to place them in their current perspective.

The FCPA

The FCPA was enacted in 1977 by the unanimous vote of both houses of Congress and signed into law by President Carter at the end of that year. It was widely hailed then as an essential action to halt the corrupt activities of U.S. companies in their dealings with foreign countries, a subject that had been making extensive headlines.

Little known at the time was the fact that the law contained provisions with respect to internal accounting control and record keeping. In effect, the Act made it illegal, with possible criminal sanctions, to knowingly or unknowingly fail to maintain adequate systems of internal accounting control. When the possible ramifications of the FCPA became apparent, virtually all publicly held companies, including even those without foreign operations, expended much effort to assess their systems. The perceptions of dire consequences were further fueled by proposals from the SEC, the agency given regulatory authority over the FCPA accounting section, to require public reporting by management of the adequacy of the company's internal accounting controls.

The concerns and activities of companies to voluntarily comply with the FCPA probably peaked by 1980. After that, events began to make it clear that the law would not nearly cause the consequences many had predicted. These events included a relaxation by the SEC of its proposal to require public disclosure of the adequacy of accounting controls. The SEC further calmed company managements by declaring its intent to cooperate with the Justice Department—the agency responsible for criminal enforcement—in providing guidance under the FCPA, in effect, toning down its zeal for enforcement.

While the SEC was redirecting its attention to other matters of concern, such as insider trading and financial disclosure fraud, others directed efforts focused on amending the FCPA to eliminate some of the troublesome vagueness it contains. These efforts were moderately successful. In 1988, the FCPA was amended by Public Law 100-418. The effect of the amendments was to eliminate the criminal sanctions for unknowing failure to comply with the accounting standards section of the Act.

Related to the post-1980 events noted above is the fact that the actual record of the SEC and the Justice Department in initiating civil and criminal court actions pursuant to the FCPA has been balanced. The 10-year time interval since the Act's passage seems sufficiently long to conclude reasonably that neither the SEC nor the Justice Department intends unreasonable enforcement of the FCPA.

Another contributing factor is that efforts by affected companies to assess and improve their internal controls had their desired effect. Internal auditors played an important part in helping managements eliminate practices incompatible with sound principles of internal control, thereby minimizing the potential for violations of the FCPA. Managements therefore have become less concerned with risks of failure to comply.

Expanded Internal Control Perceptions

Early authoritative writings distinguished internal controls in the broad sense from the internal controls involved in compiling accounting records from which financial statements are derived. These were defined in the literature as accounting controls. All other controls were administrative controls. This concept, devised by the accounting profession, served to focus the study primarily on internal accounting control as defined by GAAS. In that way, the audit was believed to be better suited and, at the same time, less costly.

Events occurring in the 1970s and 1980s are changing that concept. For some time now, many interested parties have held the view that the concept of distinguishing accounting control from administrative control was too restrictive and inappropriate. The SEC, for one, advised company managements and their accountants to employ as wide an interpretation of the former term as possible. Many public accounting firms developed approaches to the study of internal accounting control that included various controls that were administrative. For example, Chapter 18 describes one firm's approach that incorporates a consideration of the business as an element of the internal control evaluation. This includes such steps as (1) understanding the forces and factors to which a business must react, (2) identifying the key functions and personnel that are important, and (3) considering the administrative controls that have a bearing on the control environment.

The rash of business failures of the past few years brought new waves of criticism of the accounting profession. This is discussed in some depth in Chapter 1. The discussion includes the responses to date by the profession.

One of the most important responses is the series of new auditing standards by the ASB. Two of the standards deal with the subject of internal control. In effect, these standards discard the old concept of distinguishing internal accounting controls from internal administrative controls.

Replacing that concept is one that calls for the auditor to assess the control risk in terms of the overall control environment, accounting systems within that environment, and control procedures. Rather than communicate material weaknesses in internal accounting control as is now done, the new standards require communicating reportable conditions concerning the design of the control structure and the degree of compliance with it. That is a broader concept indeed.

As a result of these new standards, auditors will have to renew attention on auditing internal controls. Many internal auditing functions already embrace an expansive approach to assessing internal controls, as is recommended in the main volume. For these functions, the new proposals probably will not change their approach to any significant degree. Functions other than those, however, are certain to be more affected.

Overall, from a strategic standpoint, the subject of auditing internal control is apt to gain a fresh emphasis. In passing, it is relevant to note that the Treadway Commission recommended that management in the annual reports to shareholders acknowledge its responsibility for financial statements and internal control.[1] If this recommendation is adopted, boards of

---

[1] The National Commission on Fraudulent Financial Reporting, *Report of the National Commission on Fraudulent Financial Reporting* (Washington, D.C.: National Commission on Fraudulent Financial Reporting, 1987), p. 39.

directors, audit committees, and managements undoubtedly will devote greater attention to these matters. Internal auditors should prepare to be in a position to assist as may be necessary.

Renewed Emphasis on Operational Efficiency

During the years following the second oil crisis in 1976, the world economic picture became a recessionary scene characterized by high inflation rates, high unemployment, record numbers of business failures, and disenfranchised workers due to technological progress.

In the United States, this period was also marked by a weakening ability to compete effectively with Japan, Germany, Korea, Hong Kong, Switzerland, and other countries in industries once dominated by U.S. companies. The resultant loss of market share has been significant in such basic industries as steel, automobiles, electronic products, textiles, various manufactured items, and construction. The result has been a widening trade deficit that worries many economists, politicians, and businessmen.

This period also witnessed interest rates rising substantially. While easing the years after 1982, current rates remain above those of earlier times. Since interest rates in the United States are higher than those of most other industrial nations, U.S. companies' cost of obtaining capital is higher. These factors have combined to force company managements to place much greater efforts in devising ways to improve operational efficiencies. These efforts have included:

- Harnessing spiraling wage rates, which has been accomplished, for the most part, with the cautious cooperation of organized labor.
- Closing old, inefficient facilities and investing capital in new ones equipped with up-to-date resources.
- Employing greater and greater levels of automation in both the plant and the office.
- Acquiring or developing businesses in which the resource advantages and other factors offer a competitive edge (e.g., high technology).

In addition to these general efforts, individual companies are also actively studying and adjusting their managerial approaches, organization structures, and strategic plans to improve operational efficiency. As a result, changes in all these areas are occurring rapidly. Perhaps the most obvious example of adjusting strategic plans and corporate form is the massive restructuring of American Telephone and Telegraph into seven new, regulated local-service telephone companies and a new, unregulated long-distance communications company, A.T.&T. Clearly, in this instance, government antitrust and regulatory involvement also played a key role.

Many internal auditing departments are spending a proportionately greater amount of time assisting their managements in achieving improved operational efficiencies. Operational auditing, long a staple in the internal auditing business, is on the rise. Auditors are getting involved in measuring efficiencies and effectiveness in many functions that either barely existed a few years ago, were not as critical as they are now, or were somehow considered "off limits" to the internal auditors, including:

- Information systems management
- Telecommunications (network) management
- Inventory management
- Financial management
- Program management
- Research and development management

These and other specialized areas of operational auditing are covered in Chapters 31–40.

In working toward more efficient operations, many companies have found it necessary to effect new business combinations. Whether to gain entry to an emerging market, to acquire more economical access to desired resources, or to secure or enhance competitive position, companies have been acquiring and divesting business entities at record rates. These actions are markedly different from the acquisition fervor of the late 1960s and early 1970s, in that the primary objective in that era was diversification. Also important was the immediate earnings-per-share contribution that could be achieved under accounting rules prevalent at the time. Although recent leveraged buyout arrangements have led to some strange business combinations, the mergers and acquisitions have led to some strange business combinations, the mergers and acquisitions of this era are quite often strategically motivated, having operational advantages as a principal consideration.

To the foregoing must be added a new phenomenon: Business combinations and other long-term investment strategies do not always pay off immediately. Often, current earnings may be depressed as a result of these actions. This, in turn, can lower the price of a company's stock, and an opportunity for takeover attempts therefore exists. During the past few years, the financial press has been almost constantly dominated by such activity. In fact, the frequency of such actions and the variety of circumstances under which they occur have motivated many companies to institute measures aimed at preventing "raids."

Such actions have included reincorporation in states such as Delaware, where the legal environment is more permissive in terms of defense maneuvers. Other devices include staggered elections for board members, the abolition of cumulative voting rights, and the restriction of opportunity for shareholder initiatives.

Sometimes, these actions are not enough. Recently, a few companies have begun spinning off marginal performing units in an effort to unload the dead weight. Hence, dispositions are on the rise.

Auditors are finding that managements are looking to them to provide valuable assistance not only in effecting new business combinations but also in selling existing segments. Internal auditors are assisting management in this area by performing various review services. Chapter 30 is devoted to this subject.

Rapid Development and Application of Office Automation

The beginning of the 1980s has seen, quite literally, a minirevolution within a revolution. The larger revolution, of course, is the huge increase in data processing and information systems activity in general. This is noted in Chapter 26. The minirevolution is the swift advance of automation within the office in the principal form of small computers, both minicomputers and microcomputers, particularly the latter. In 1988 and 1989, it is probable that more than 10 million PCs will be sold.

In a large sense, the advent of mini- and microcomputers is but one example of the broader movement toward a more technologically oriented and operationally efficient economy. However, computers are a critical ingredient and deserve special mention here.

PCs and their eventual networking will soon result in complete office automation and a level of efficiency on a scale only dreamed of a few years ago. Any job or function, from the chief executive officer to the lowest clerk, will be made more efficient and effective.

Internal auditors are finding uses for PCs in auditing and in auditing administration. More is said on this point in Chapters 26–28. Internal auditors are also finding that management is becoming increasingly concerned about the control and security implications of the growing use of minicomputers and microcomputers. Finally, internal auditors are now beginning to spend time examining the ways by which mini- and microcomputer-related activities in their companies are being controlled and managed. These subjects are also covered in Chapters 26–28.

Heightened Concern Regarding Government Spending Practices

The fact that government spending is on a seemingly unstoppable pattern of constant, significant increase is widely acknowledged. Figure 2-1 illustrates this point rather dramatically.[2] It indicates that it took 186 years for federal, state, and local governments to spend $500 billion. It took less than 10 years to spend another $500 billion. Figure 2-2 isolates the increasing pattern of federal deficit spending during the past 20 years. It projects that

---

[2] From data released by the President's Private Sector Survey on Cost Control, Washington, D.C., 1983.

FIG. 2-1

Milestones in Government Spending

Billions of Current Dollars

Year	Federal	State and Local	Total	Milestones
1789	$ 0.002	$ 0.008	$ 0.010	First year of Federal Government.
1944	94.986	14.961	109.947	155 years later, World War II, spending first exceeds $100 billion.
1965	118.430	87.120	205.550	21 years later, spending exceeds $200 billion.
1975	324.245	235.855	**560.100**	10 years later, spending exceeds $500 billion.
1983E	805.200	492.200	**1,297.400**	8 more years, spending exceeds $1.2 trillion.
Extrapolated at 1965-1983E Rate				
1990	1,692.900	965.300	2,658.200	
2000	4,894.200	2,526.500	7,420.700	

It took 186 years to reach the first $500 billion milestone and only 8 years (1975–1983) to more than double that.

by the year 2000, if left unchecked, the spending pattern would produce an inconceivable annual deficit of over $2 trillion.

This clearly intolerable projection gives cause for concern. Not only do high deficits create extreme national financial problems, but also high government spending affects the capability of the nation and its system of private enterprise to compete successfully in the world marketplace. Figure 2-3 shows how government spending as a percentage of GNP compares among major free-world economies.[3] The low Japanese percentages in comparison with European countries and the United States translates into economic advantages for Japan. Some might argue that highly excessive government spending has little influence on private sector management, except perhaps in evaluating the impact of the resultant inflation and monetary risk. However, many believe deficit spending on such grand scales as are currently occurring and being projected will tend to keep interest rates high. This, in turn, will place even greater importance on improving operational efficien-

---

[3] *Ibid.*

A STRATEGIC APPROACH

FIG. 2-2

Federal Government Revenues, Outlays, and Deficits

($ billions)

	Revenues	Outlays	Deficit	Outlays as a Multiple of Revenues
1965	$ 116.8	$ 118.4	$ (1.6)	1.01X
1975	279.1	324.2	(45.1)	1.16
1983E	597.5	805.2	(207.7)	1.35
Average Annual Percentage Increase				
1965–1983E	9.5%	11.2%	31.0%	
1975–1983E	10.0	12.0	21.0	
Future growth rates the same as in:		*Results in 1990*		
1965–1983E	$1,127.8	$1,692.9	$ (565.1)	— 1.50X
1975–1983E	1,164.4	1,780.0	(615.6)	— 1.53
		Results in 2000		
1965–1983E	$2,795.0	$4,894.2	$(2,099.2)	— 1.75X
1975–1983E	3,020.0	5,528.5	(2,508.5)	— 1.83
		THE WIDENING GAP		

cies in order to remain competitive with foreign-based companies that have access to cheaper capital.

Concern over this dismal deficit picture has fostered combative efforts across a broad front, both in and out of government. Many proposals have emerged for dealing with the deficit. Effective resolution has been elusive, however, owing to the differing political perspectives that are unavoidably intertwined. Each year, the debates over the federal budget and where to cut it seem to become lengthier and more devisive, with the result that the government is often able to operate only on the basis of continuing budget resolutions.

In 1985, Congress enacted the Gramm-Rudman-Hollings bill. This bill, which was signed into law by President Reagan amid much controversy, holds some promise for forcing decisions on congressional budget action. That is because it provides for automatic across-the-board cuts if Congress fails to agree each year on deficit reduction measures that achieve the prescribed annual deficit reduction objectives of the Act.

The merits of this Act are apt to be argued for years. In the meantime,

FIG. 2-3

Size of Government and Economic Performance

	1973–1982			
	Government Spending as Percentage of GNP[a]	Average Investment as Percentage of GNP	Average Annual Percentage Increase	
			Industrial Output	Productivity
Japan	9.7%	32.1%	4.9%	5.5%
Germany	19.8	21.5	0.8	4.0
France	14.7	22.3	1.4	3.8
Italy	16.2	20.1	2.3	3.2
United Kingdom	20.9	18.2	(2.3)	2.4
United States	18.1	18.3	0.1	1.2

Japan Versus the United States

46 percent lower government expenditures
75 percent higher investment rate
49.0 times output growth
4.6 times productivity growth

[a] Federal, State and Local Current Spending Excluding Transfer Payments and Capital Spending.

it serves as a signal to all federal government organizations that achieving more and more economy and efficiency is the primary means by which the more oppressive effects of the Gramm-Rudman-Hollings bill may be avoided. Whether this signal is persuasive enough to cause the bureaucracies to act remains to be seen.

Another effort aimed at cutting federal spending was the President's Private Sector Survey on Cost Control (PPSSCC). J. Peter Grace and more than 150 private sector executives offered a Summary Report and 36 detail reports in 1984 to President Reagan. These reports provided numerous ideas for action that, if fully implemented, would generate savings in excess of $400 billion in three years.

Among the recommendations are the following:

- Scaling back military pensions
- Closing unnecessary military bases
- Closing domestic commissaries
- Increasing procurement competition
- Expanding use of multiple-year procurement

- Making fully private quasi-government agencies, such as the Farm Credit Bank System
- Slowing payments to defense contractors
- Using a fixed fee schedule for Medicare payments to health care providers
- Reducing the use of tax-free bond financing for hospitals
- Consolidating the Federal Highway Administration and the Urban Mass Transporation Administration

These and the other recommendations, as predicted, have generated more controversy than reform. Reactions seem to be based more on political perspective and special interest rather than reality. However, the PPSSCC has helped to shift the debate from the question of should government spending be cut to how it should be done.

One of the Grace Commission's principal targets for cost savings was defense spending. Subsequent to the completion of the work of the Grace Commission, numerous accounts of abusive and wasteful spending practices by the DOD and its three weapons acquisition branches came to light with alarming regularity. The public perception of the DOD's procurement process became one of incompetence, inefficiency, and ineffectiveness.

In July 1985, President Reagan formed yet another commission: the Presidents' Blue Ribbon Commission on Defense Management. It was headed by David Packard, co-founder of Hewlett-Packard, a widely respected maker of computers and other electronic items. This Commission was charged with conducting a study of current defense management and organization in its entirety, including the budget process, the procurement system, legislative oversight, and the formal and informal organizational and operational arrangements. The Commission's initial findings and recommendations were reported in an interim report issued in February 1986. A final report was rendered in June 1986. It expanded on the interim report conclusions. The recommendations of the Packard Commission were aimed at improving:

- The way in which the executive branch and Congress make critical defense determinations. Key components include a comprehensive statement of national security objectives, a five-year defense plan, and a two-year budget. Congress would be asked to approve the two-year budget.
- The military organization and command. The objective would be to strengthen the authority and control of the Chairman of the Joint Chiefs of Staff.
- The defense acquisition system. This would be accomplished by creating a new position: the Undersecretary of Defense (Acquisition). The Undersecretary would set overall policy for procurement and research and development, surpervise the performance of the entire acquisition system, and establish policy for administrative oversight and auditing of defense contractors. In effect, defense procurement would be centralized. Other key components

include multiyear procurement and prototyping. Full-scale engineering development would not be permitted until the prototypes had been evaluated.
- The accountability of both government and industry for the proper spending of public funds. Further comments on this segment are provided later in this Chapter.[4]

The report and the work of the Commission is noted here as one more significant event in the continuing battle to reduce government spending. One segment of the report is directly applicable to the interests of internal auditors and, in fact, internal auditing was mentioned specifically. This segment of the report, in which the Commission cautions against acts by DOD agencies that may result in less vigorous internal corporate auditing, is reprinted in Chapter 12.

Relevance of Financial Information

Information in relation to financial position, changes in financial position, and results of operations is perhaps the most sought-after data about a business entity. The importance of this information is so great that it exerts pressure on management to report favorable financial information, sometimes tempting overly optimistic management to employ accounting contrivances to mask the true nature of operating results.

At times, this over-optimism extends to the point where it becomes outright fraud. When this occurs, boards of directors, shareholders, creditors, and others are victimized. Whether known as financial disclosure fraud, management fraud, or some other name, it is almost always sensational news when it is revealed. The SEC, the body responsible for protecting the public from such acts, has always been concerned with this problem.

In a still relevant 1984 article in the *Journal of Accountancy*, John M. Fedders and L. Glenn Perry, the then Director of the SEC Division of Enforcement and the current Chief Accountant of the SEC Division of Enforcement, respectively, drew attention to the importance of fair and accurate financial information to the disclosure system. The title of the article, "Policing Financial Disclosure Fraud: The SEC's Top Priority," clearly indicates the SEC's awareness of financial disclosure fraud and the importance the SEC attaches to minimizing the occurrence of such fraud. In the article, the authors cite the following examples alleged in recent actions:[5]

- Creating and maintaining false records, including automated techniques to add false inventory, thus artificially inflating the carrying amount of inventory

---

[4] The President's Blue Ribbon Commission on Defense Management, *A Quest for Excellence*, Final Report to the President, June 1986, excerpted from the Final Summary Section, pp. xviii–xxx.

[5] John M. Fedders and L. Glenn Perry, "Policing Financial Disclosure Fraud: The SEC's Top Priority," *Journal of Accountancy*, July 1984, pp. 62–64.

- Making false statements to auditors
- Overstating earnings and otherwise misrepresenting financial condition through manipulation of loss reserves and adjustments to accrual and allowance accounts
- Falsifying corporate records by the recording as sales of unordered products
- Transferring nonexistent inventory from one division to another to avoid detection

These actions are typical of the proceedings undertaken by the SEC. They demonstrate the SEC's belief that financial disclosure fraud takes a variety of forms and is not restricted to any particular industry segment. The authors cite the following situations as being among the situations the SEC is sensitive to:[6]

    1. Liquidity problems, such as (a) decreased inflow of collections from sales to customers; (b) the lack of availability of credit from suppliers, banks, and others; and (c) the inability to meet maturing obligations when they fall due. Corporate disclosure must not minimize or fail fully to explain liquidity problems.

    2. Operating trends and factors affecting profits and losses, such as (a) curtailment of operations; (b) decline of orders; (c) increased competition; or (d) cost overruns on major contracts. Disclosure must include early notice of a significant reversal of previously reported sales trends. There must be an objective discussion of poor financial results.

Not only must material facts effecting a company's operations be reported, they must be reported promptly. Corporate releases that disclose favorable developments but do not describe material adverse developments do not serve investors' needs and may violate the antifraud provisions. In the case of an issuer making an offering or a continuous offering of its shares, the failure to disclose such material adverse developments also may violate the Securities Act of 1933, if there is not an appropriate updating of information.

Unless adequate and accurate information is publicly available, a company may not purchase its own securities or make acquisitions using its securities. Furthermore, insiders who trade in the securities of their companies under these circumstances violate the antifraud provisions of the Securities Exchange Act of 1934.

    3. Material increases in problem loans must be reported by financial institutions. Increased financial pressure on certain industries has caused a sharp increase in uncollectible and nonperforming loans. Disclosure must be made when there is a material increase in: (a) interest that has not been paid; (b) interest that is reduced or deferred; or (c) doubtful collections. When necessary, an increase in provisions for losses must be reported in a timely fashion.

    4. Corporations cannot avoid their disclosure obligations when they ap-

---

[6] *Ibid.*, p. 59.

proach business decline or failure. Economists report that the business failure rate is the highest since the trough of the Depression in 1932.

The principal method of projecting seeming economic well-being in the face of business decline and possible failure is through deceptive and fraudulent accounting practices. In order to hide fiscal difficulties and to deceive investors, declining and failing companies have: (a) prematurely recognized income; (b) improperly treated operating leases as sales; (c) inflated inventory by improper application of the LIFO inventory method; (d) included fictitious amounts in inventories; (e) failed to recognize losses through write-offs and allowances; (f) improperly capitalized or deferred costs and expenses; (g) included unusual gains in operating income; (h) overvalued marketable securities; (i) created "sham" year-end transactions to boost reported earnings; and (j) changed their accounting practices to increase earnings without disclosing the changes.

The professional response to the dilemma chronicled by Messrs. Fedders and Perry is also set forth in Chapter 1. In brief, the response includes:

- The creation of the Anderson committee. This committee has recommended (1) restructuring the AICPA Code of Professional Ethics, (2) a program to improve the quality of professional practice, and (3) new requirements to maintain professional competence.[7]
- Projects by the ASB of the AICPA. These resulted in nine proposed new standards that would improve communication in auditors' reports, provide improved guidance on auditors' judgments in control audit areas, and expand the auditors' concept of internal control. Chapter 5 contains further comments on this initiative.
- A study by the Accounting Standards Executive Committee of ways to modify GAAP. The objective is to aid users in assessing risks and uncertainties facing a reporting enterprise.
- The creation of a national commission to study the problem of financial reporting fraud and to recommend courses of action. The commission, known as the Treadway Commission, was cosponsored by the AICPA, the IIA, the FEI, and the NAA.

The last initiative mentioned above warrants further comment. The Treadway Commission, formerly known as the NCFFR, actively pursued its charter. It set up an advisory panel, created a staff, and researched issues. Its report was issued in the fall of 1987.

The report contains approximately 50 recommendations. These are directed variously to senior management, the accounting function and chief financial officer, the internal auditing function and the chief internal auditor, the board of directors and the audit committee, the independent public accountants, the SEC and other regulatory agencies, and, finally, the education system.

---

[7] The Special Committee on Standards of Professional Conduct for Certified Public Accountants, *Restructuring Professional Standards to Achieve Professional Excellence in a Changing Environment* (New York: AICPA, 1986), p. 1.

The objective of these recommendations is to improve the financial reporting process and the surveillance of that process. In so doing, the frequency of financial reporting fraud should be reduced.[8] Further comments regarding the work of this commission and its recommendations are provided in Chapter 23.

Internal auditors must follow developments in this area closely. That is because a change in the role of internal auditing regarding financial reporting fraud is likely to cause changes in the internal auditing strategies of many internal auditing functions.

Those internal auditing functions that employ strategic audit approaches similar to those suggested in this chapter are likely to be less affected than those that do not. It recommends a strategy for allocating audit resources that recognizes the importance and criticality of financial reporting. Accordingly, one of the major components of the strategy is a program of auditing interim-period financial reports and the key controls and documentation used to develop them. An audit program for this type of auditing is presented later.

The strategic audit approach also calls for extensive operational auditing. Operational audits are theoretically possible of even the most senior levels of management and the most strategic decisions, as presented in Chapter 31. It is worth restating here that in few companies is this type of operational auditing a reality. Indeed, it can only be present where there exists an enlightened management, a courageous board of directors, and, of course, a competent internal auditing function. The extent to which this can evolve will have a direct bearing on what will emerge as the role of internal auditing in financial reporting fraud prevention and how successful that role will be.

Another important way internal auditors can help their management (and board of directors) is to participate in the annual audit conducted by external auditors. While performing limited interim-period financial reviews and assisting external auditors in the year-end audit, internal auditors should remain alert to the attitude of the SEC role as financial fraud disclosure policeman.

Chapter 23 contains more detailed comments regarding management fraud, including a list of warning signals to watch for.

Business Ethics

Financial reporting fraud is not the only area of corporate accountability that is being questioned these days. A spate of stories has appeared in the last 18 to 24 months raising questions regarding the business ethics not so

---

[8] The National Commission on Fraudulent Financial Reporting, *Report of the National Commission on Fraudulent Financial Reporting* (Washington, D.C.: National Commission on Fraudulent Financial Reporting, 1987), p. 2.

much of company managements, but rather of company employees, suppliers, and vendors. Examples include:

- *Procurement kickbacks.* While most reports of kickbacks have been in the defense contracting sector, many believe the practice extends far beyond that business. Recent reports tend to give credibility to this view. For example, kickbacks were reported in the advertising and promotional activities of a major beer company. Kickbacks were also alleged in procurements at a university, a city government, and a municipal public transporation authority.

- *Product substitutions.* In these cases, some companies were reported as having delivered products that were inferior in terms of quality or that otherwise did not meet customer specifications. Examples have occurred in the semiconductor industry and in the defense contracting industry.

- *Labor mischarging.* Usually, this involves situations where government contracts improperly bear the costs of labor effort related to other government contracts or to commercial business. Embarrassing examples have been reported involving some of the most reputable companies in America.

- *Bank reporting failures.* Many accounts have been published that indicate that several of the largest and most respected financial institutions in the country have, for years, failed to comply with regulations that require reporting of large cash transactions. This failure enables the laundering by perpetrators of funds obtained through illicit activities, such as drug dealing.

- *Medical claims fraud.* Accounts of filing improper or invalid medical claims are not as sensational as other types of conduct mentioned in this section. Nevertheless, for those familiar with medical insurance administration, it is believed to be a serious and growing problem. Employees, doctors, and others have been increasingly victimizing company- and government-sponsored medical insurance plans.

- *Espionage.* Several instances have been reported in which company employees, government employees, and/or military personnel have been charged with having committed espionage activities.

Perhaps the most sensational example of breaching business ethics is the insider-trading scandal. Here, highly respected individuals within investment banking and brokerage firms with the most prestigious of reputations were found to be violating securities laws for personal gain. What is so astounding is that many of the individuals charged were already wealthy, by almost any standard. Add to this accounts of questionable conduct by lawyers[9] and accountants,[10] and a picture emerges of a business climate believed by many to be seriously flawed with ethical misconduct.

---

[9] See, e.g., William B. Glaberson, Pete Engardio, Stan Cook, and Scott Ticer, "A Question of Integrity at Blue-Chip Law Firms," *Business Week*, Apr. 7, 1986, pp. 76–80.

[10] See, e.g., Clement P. Work, "Accounting's Bottom Line: Big Troubles," *U.S. News & World Report*, Oct. 21, 1985, p. 58.

A STRATEGIC APPROACH

Many companies have responded by investing heavily in programs to promote improved ethical practices by their management and employees. Both inside and outside, government agencies have increased efforts to identify and eliminate improper and unethical conduct.

Defense contractors are among the first companies to act. In 1986, a group of 34 contractors voluntarily committed themselves to a series of initiatives. These initiatives were expressed in writing in the form of six principles:

1. Each company will have, and adhere to, a written code of business ethics and conduct.
2. The company's code establishes the high values expected of its employees and the standard by which they must judge their own conduct and that of their organization; each company will train its employees concerning their personal responsibilities under the code.
3. Each company will create a free and open atmosphere that allows employees to report violations of its code to the company without fear of retribution for such reporting.
4. Each company has the obligation to (1) self-govern by monitoring compliance with federal procurement laws and adopting procedures for voluntary disclosure of violations of federal procurement laws and (2) to take corrective actions.
5. Each company has a responsibility to each of the other companies in the industry to live by standards of conduct that preserve the integrity of the defense industry.
6. Each company must have public accountability for its commitment to these principles.[11]

The initiatives are discussed in Chapter 22. Principles 3, 4, and 6 are noteworthy here. In effect, the contractors agree to create an internal mechanism to enable employees to freely and anonymously report suspicions. Further, the mechanism must be sufficient to check each report. Those in which the evidence indicates that violations of federal procurement laws have occurred must be disclosed to appropriate government authorities. Such voluntary confessions are without precedent in the business world.

To accomplish this commitment, affected companies are investing heavily. Separate ethics committees are being formed. Each contractor is creating special ethics offices usually headed by an officer known variously as vice-president of business ethics, business practices, or some similar title. They are commonly referred to as ombudsmen. Internal hotlines or open lines are being set up to receive tips on unethical behavior. Techniques are being established to protect the caller's identity and to investigate the tips. In

---

[11] The President's Blue Ribbon Commission on Defense Management, *Conduct and Accountability*, A Report to the President, June 1986, p. 42.

addition, expensive orientation programs are being developed for new employees. Also, training programs are being used for all employees.

Principle 6 requires public accountability. According to the initiatives, each company for the next three years must engage an annual independent review of its ethical practices. The review may be performed by CPAs or by a similar independent organization. The resultant report along with the companies' responses to 18 prescribed questions must be furnished to an external independent body. The questions are intended to serve as a set of guidelines for a proper internal business practices function.

The external independent body reports the results for the volunteers as a whole. The report is released to the companies and the public simultaneously.

A working group of defense contractor representatives was formed to serve as an implementing force. Much detail needed to be worked out. With respect to the annual review, the group, along with a special task force of the AICPA's ASB, developed the procedures and the report language. It is also working to create the independent external body. These are set forth in Chapter 22.

Internal auditors within those companies (estimated to be 3,000 to 5,000) are involved in two ways. First, the companies may request the auditors to perform certain investigative duties as part of the mechanism to check out tips by informants. Second, they could monitor the mechanism as required by the initiatives to hold down the costs of such efforts.

Internal auditors can and should be active in this effort as a part of the strategic audit approach. A specimen audit program for this type of auditing is presented later in this chapter. Affected internal auditing functions may find it advisable to commence such a program.

The Defense Industry Initiatives are not the only action of note aimed at improving ethical practices. As indicated previously, procurement kickbacks occurred in the defense industry with a frequency unacceptable to Congress. Accordingly, it enacted the Anti-Kickback Enforcement Act of 1986.

This law toughens the civil and criminal penalties for any corporation, partnership trust, joint-stock company, or individual to provide, attempt to provide, or offer to provide any kickback. Also prohibited is any solicitation, acceptance, or attempted acceptance. The criminal penalties include provision for imprisonment for up to 10 years. Civil penalties are twice the amount of each kickback, up to $10,000 for each occurrence.

The new law also calls on contractors to have in place and follow reasonable procedures designed to prevent and detect violations of the Act. It also requires contractors and subcontractors to promptly report possible violations to the Inspector General (IG).[12]

Since the new law mandates a system of reasonable prevention and

---

[12] *Federal Register*, Vol. 52, No. 39, Friday, Feb. 27, 1987/Rules and Regulations, p. 6121.

A STRATEGIC APPROACH

detection, managements and internal auditors are advised to assess controls in this area. Chapter 24 contains a listing of fraud indicators in procurement as seen by the DOD IG. Internal auditors and managements should find this useful in performing such assessments.

The preceding discussion regarding current forces influencing internal auditing is important because it helps frame the background against which informed decisions regarding allocation of resources may be made. But before that can be done, it is necessary to establish an approach that enables the chief auditor to devise an effective program of coverage in the areas where organizational need exists. The embodiment of the approach is the statement of objectives.

Developing a Meaningful Statement of Objectives

Supplementing the IIA Guidelines. The enactment of the FCPA and the related events and issues discussed previously have caused many chief internal auditors to recognize the need to supplement the general objectives set forth in the IIA *Statement of Responsibilities* (see Figure 2-4) with objectives that are meaningful and practical within the context of their own organizations, the perceived needs of management, and the board of directors. Of course, many far-sighted chief internal auditors developed management-oriented specific objectives prior to the enactment of the FCPA. But the main point is that each chief auditor must be satisfied that the audit objectives being pursued in his company are appropriate. Many chief auditors have found that supplementing the IIA *Statement of Responsibilities* is an effective way to gain that satisfaction and, in fact, the development of specific objectives is not restricted to internal auditing. In the government sector, for example, the Defense Contract Audit Agency (DCAA) supplemented the broad objectives promulgated by the GAO with much more detailed subobjectives in order to assist the process by which prudent contracting (by the DOD and others) is accomplished.

Three-Step Technique for Adding Specific Objectives. Internal auditing department directors and managers who need to develop objectives to supplement those of the IIA and to meet the specific requirements of their management should:

- Identify organizational needs and concerns.
- Articulate clear, specific statements of objectives.
- Review the statements with management.

The first step can be accomplished by discussions with senior management, the audit committee, and/or the board of directors. External auditors may also be consulted. Such talks will probably be more productive if the audit manager or director has first obtained adequate information with re-

FIG. 2-4

Statement of Responsibilities of Internal Auditing

The purpose of this statement is to provide in summary form a general understanding of the role and responsibilities of internal auditing. For more specific guidance, readers should refer to the *Standards for the Professional Practice of Internal Auditing*.

Nature

Internal auditing is an independent appraisal activity established within an organization as a service to the organization. It is a control which functions by examining and evaluating the adequacy and effectiveness of other controls.

Objective and Scope

The objective of internal auditing is to assist members of the organization in the effective discharge of their responsibilities. To this end, internal auditing furnishes them with analysis, appraisals, recommendations, counsel, and information concerning the activities reviewed. The audit objective includes promoting effective control at reasonable cost.

The scope of internal auditing encompasses the examination and evaluation of the adequacy and effectiveness of the organization's system of internal control and the quality of performance in carrying out assigned responsibilities. The scope of internal auditing includes:

- Reviewing the reliability and integrity of financial and operating information and the means used to identify, measure, classify, and report such information.
- Reviewing the systems established to ensure compliance with those policies, plans, procedures, laws, and regulations which could have a significant impact on operations and reports, and determining whether the organization is in compliance.
- Reviewing the means of safeguarding assets and, as appropriate, verifying the existence of such assets.
- Appraising the economy and efficiency with which resources are employed.
- Reviewing operations or programs to ascertain whether results are consistent with established objectives and goals and whether the operations or programs are being carried out as planned.

Responsibility and Authority

Internal auditing functions under the policies established by management and the board. The purpose, authority and responsibility of the internal auditing department should be defined in a formal written document (charter), approved by management, and accepted by the board. The charter should make clear the purposes of the internal auditing department, specify the unrestricted scope of its work, and declare that auditors are to have no authority or responsibility for the activities they audit.

The responsibility of internal auditing is to serve the organization in a manner that is consistent with the *Standards for the Professional Practice of Internal Auditing* and with professional standards of conduct such as the *Code of Ethics* of The Institute of Internal Auditors, Inc. This responsibility includes coordinating internal audit activities with others so as to best achieve the audit objectives and the objectives of the organization.

Independence

Internal auditors should be independent of the activities they audit. Internal auditors are independent when they can carry out their work freely and objectively. Independence permits internal auditors to render the impartial and unbiased judgments essential to the proper conduct of audits. It is achieved through organizational status and objectivity.

> Organizational status should be sufficient to assure a broad range of audit coverage, and adequate consideration of and effective action on audit findings and recommendations.
>
> Objectivity requires that internal auditors have an independent mental attitude, and an honest belief in their work product. Drafting procedures, designing, installing, and operating systems, are not audit functions. Performing such activities is presumed to impair audit objectivity.
>
> The *Statement of Responsibilities of Internal Auditors* was originally issued by The Institute of Internal Auditors in 1947. The current *Statement*, revised in 1981, embodies the concepts previously established and includes such changes as are deemed advisable in light of the present status of the profession.
> Reprinted by permission of the Institute of Internal Auditors, Inc., 249 Maitland Ave., Altamonte Springs, Fla. 32701.

spect to the practices of others in the same or related industries. Such information could form the basis of discussion of a proposed set of objectives. The second step is largely a matter of reducing to writing the conclusions reached in the first step. Care should be taken to develop clear, specific statements. The last step is important to assure that both management and the audit department agree on the direction the department should take. A good practice is to embody the objectives in an audit charter. (See Chapter 7). From the detailed statement of objectives that is thus developed, the auditor is able to devise an overall strategy or approach to achieve each objective.

OVERALL AUDITING OBJECTIVES

Correlating Needs With Auditing Areas

The discussion of forces having an impact on the needs of the organization and, as a result, internal auditing, indicates the following correlations:

Forces Affecting	Type of Auditing
The FCPA	Financial
Expanded internal control perceptions	Financial
Renewal emphasis on operational efficiency	Operational
Rapid development and application of office automation	Information systems and EDP
Heightened concern regarding government spending practices	Operational
Relevance of financial information	Financial
Business ethics	Ethical business practices

From the correlation, it is evident that an auditing approach responsive to the given set of perceived needs entails the following auditing areas:

- Financial
- Ethical business practices
- Information systems (EDP)
- Operational

A statement of auditing objectives relating to these areas might be as follows:

Auditing Areas	Objectives
Financial	1. To determine the sufficiency of the system of internal control for assuring that internal control objectives pertaining to authorization, recording, and reporting of business activities and safeguarding of assets are attained.
	2. To determine the consistency of the reporting of interim period financial information with GAAP used in preparing annual audited financial statements.
Ethical business practices	1. To determine the extent of compliance with the company's standards and procedures for maintaining appropriate ethical practices in managing the affairs of the company.
Information systems	1. To determine the sufficiency of internal controls for reasonably assuring that EDP activities convert, process, store, and transmit data accurately and completely, in efficient fashion, with reasonable provision for security and backup of data and data processing assets and recovery in the event of loss of either.
Operational	1. To determine whether operational controls taken as a whole achieve a reasonable degree of efficiency and effectiveness, and the extent to which operational goals and objectives are accomplished.

Financial Auditing

Financial auditing necessary to achieve the stated objectives consists of auditing internal control and auditing financial information produced by those controls. An approach for auditing internal control is the subject of Part VI of this volume. How to audit financial information produced by those controls is discussed in the next section of this chapter.

A STRATEGIC APPROACH

Operational Auditing

Operational auditing necessary to achieve the stated objectives is discussed in Part IX of this volume. Operational auditing is the area of auditing that is the most variable. That is, the uniqueness of each business entity is such that truly effective operational auditing within each occurs only when the program of operational auditing is tailored to fit the unique circumstances. However, there are some operational or managerial responsibilities that are fairly common to a broad variety of businesses.

☐ *Financial management*. A critical element in the success of most business is an effective and efficient program of financial management. It may seem strange to list financial management as an area for operational auditing. The common perspective on operational auditing is that it is concerned with functional aspects of the organization more directly involved with buying raw materials, parts and services, converting them into proprietary parts and services, and delivering them to customers in accordance with agreed-on terms and conditions. Certainly, operational auditing must attend those direct aspects. Also important, however, is the contribution to the organization made by effective financing of inventory and receivables, and the arrangements for providing funds to finance long-term projects, such as capital assets, R&D, or other business ventures. The company that manages its sources and uses of funds in such a way that needed funds are always available, while the cost of providing those funds is kept low, will be doing much to maximize the competitive advantages of the entity. That is the responsibility of financial management. The potential for operational auditing of financial management is such that Chapters 32 and 33 are devoted to it. Related to financial management—in fact, many believe it is a part of financial management—is the special fiduciary responsibility exercised by many companies as a result of the many private welfare plans they offer as part of the compensation arrangements extended to their employees. The effective management of these plans has become a major responsibility. Chapter 40 offers a means for operational auditing of the most consequential of these plans—retirement plans.

☐ *Inventory management*. The effective and efficient acquisition of materials, parts, and services to convert them in accordance with engineered designs and specifications, whether owned or licensed, into proprietary products for sale in accordance with customer's orders is perhaps the most fundamental and important of all business endeavors. The effort requires the collective and coordinated actions of several functional elements that are usually separate organizational units within an enterprise. Thus, the effort covers the activities of engineering, purchasing of material, receiving and inspection, manufacturing, and quality assurance. Also contributing are such functions as data processing or information systems, and finance. Chapter 34 provides a basis for performing operational auditing aimed at measuring the effectiveness of the contributions made by these to the objective of effective and efficient inventory management.

☐ *Facilities management*. Like inventory management, many companies must manage their investments in facilities and capital assets by coordinating the efforts of several functional elements. These include the purchasing department, manufacturing, finance, and engineering. For these companies, the resultant investments in capital facilities is the largest item on the balance sheet. Decisions and commitments in this area affect companies for years. The competitive advantages and disadvantages produced by these decisions are a major factor in the overall success of the enterprise. Chapter 35 presents a program for operational auditing to evaluate the effectiveness and efficiency of the contributions by the involved functional organizations toward effective facilities management.

☐ *Program management.* For many businesses, delivery of products or services is accomplished through the efforts of differing functional disciplines that, organizationally, are made the responsibility of a specific authorized member of the management team. These efforts are known as programs, and the individual or group responsible is known as the program manager or program management. Programs occur in both industry and government. In the case of the federal government, for example, program grants to state and local government units exceed $100 billion annually. Programs may be short term in nature but often they are long term and involve a considerable allocation of internal resources in terms of management, facilities, and personnel. Efficient and effective program management is essential to achieve program goals and objectives. Chapter 36 describes a program for operational auditing within this important area.

☐ *Marketing management.* All enterprises, whether or not they are profit oriented, must provide things of value to those in need of them. A critical part of this is obtaining and retaining those who need the things the enterprise delivers, that is, customers. Finding and keeping customers is what marketing management is all about. Some argue that that is what businesses really are all about, for without customers, a business cannot exist. Chapter 37 discusses how operational auditing may be applied to measure the effectiveness and efficiency of a company's marketing management.

☐ *Information systems management.* In the past quarter century, technological developments in computers, telecommunications, and office automation have combined to produce information systems without which the modern business unit could not survive. These systems are developed and maintained at considerable cost and involve significant resources, including facilities, equipment, and personnel with unique technical knowledge and skill. The effective and efficient management of these dedicated resources is now an indispensable component for the success of the enterprise. In recent years, innovative information systems have enabled companies to gain competitive advantages over others in their respective industries. Examples are the flight reservation booking systems developed by certain airline companies—a decided advantage over those airlines who did not have such systems. Chapter 38 offers a means by which the efficiency and effectiveness of a company's information systems management may be measured through operational auditing.

☐ *Research and development.* Nothing stays the same. Change, and at an increasing rate, seems to be the only constant. All companies must strive to control the rate of change so as to preserve competitive advantage and continue to earn an acceptable rate of return for shareholders. To do this, companies must research scientific and technological developments. The objective is to find those that, on development, are most likely to yield improvements in proprietary products and services, and the methods necessary to produce them. That is what R&D are all about. A proper management of R&D activity today will assure that the company's future products and services will satisfy existing or future customers' needs. Since no one knows the future, decisions affecting the expenditure of resources for R&D carry a considerable degree of uncertainty. With that in mind, Chapter 39 details a program for the operational audit of R&D.

In providing the foregoing, this volume offers the internal auditing practitioner many practical techniques that may be used in conducting a broad-based program of operational auditing. This offering is not all-inclusive. Other topics for which operational auditing may be useful to certain enterprises include:

☐ *Human resource management.* Since companies are made up of people, their effective and efficient utilization in executing the will of management is vital.

☐ *Law management.* Companies operate in an era that is the most regulated that the world has ever seen. And it gets more so every day. The importance of knowing, understanding, and complying with all applicable laws and regulations involves yet another considerable investment in specialized talent, information systems, and, to some extent, facilities. The business of minimizing the exposure of the company to losses through litigation is big business.

☐ *Environmental management.* Problems of industrial pollution to the environment have become a major concern and a potentially huge area of business risk. The list of toxic substances grows almost daily. The regulatory apparatus aimed at assuring clean air and water also has proliferated, reflecting again the concern of society for a clean and healthy living environment.

Programs of operational auditing in these areas should be developed by the chief internal auditor, using the approaches described in Part IX. To these may be added other more functionally specific operational audits of such functions for a manufacturing entity as:

- Assembly inspection
- Budgets and analysis
- Cafeteria operations
- Capacity planning
- Cash management
- Configuration management
- Construction management
- Data administration
- Documentation support systems

- Employment verification
- Engineering
- Equipment and facility maintenance
- Forms administration
- General procurement
- Group insurance
- Inventory control
- Labor control

- Manufacturing
- Manufacturing engineering
- Master scheduling
- Material planning and scheduling
- Material procurement
- Night operations
- Numerical control systems
- Off-site activities
- Operations control
- Output control
- Overhead administration
- Payroll administration
- Personnel activities
- Plant protection
- Pricing
- Property control
- Quality assurance
- Receiving inspection
- Records management
- Risk management
- Safety
- Shipping inspection
- Special events
- Special projects
- Subassembly inspection
- Supplier control
- Systems management
- Telecommunications
- Tooling
- Traffic administration
- Training
- Transportation management

The list of functionally specific operational audits is limited only by the number of functions within a given entity. In some large companies, this numbers in the thousands. It is inconceivable that operational audits of each of these could be performed within any reasonable period. That is why the areas of operational auditing described in Part IX are so important. They are aimed at measuring the efficiency and effectiveness of the most consequential management responsibilities, those for which the detail functions are involved. Nevertheless, a proper program of operational auditing should include auditing at the detail functional level. How to decide which to audit is covered later in this chapter.

Information Systems Auditing

Information systems auditing to achieve the objectives described earlier entails a combination of specialized types of auditing that have come to be known as EDP auditing or information systems auditing. These specialized types are identified and discussed in Chapter 27. Techniques for performing them are the subject of Chapter 28.

Briefly, the types are identified as:

- Detailed functional auditing
- Installation reviews
- Applications auditing
- Developing systems auditing

Other related forms are also presented, including program verifications and post-implementation audits. Another important area, concurrent auditing, is also discussed, as well as how to prioritize the projects.

Ethical Business Practice Auditing

Ethical business practice auditing is discussed later in this Chapter and also in Chapter 22.

FINANCIAL INFORMATION REPORTING AUDITING DESCRIBED

"Financial Information Reporting" Defined

The term "financial information reporting" is intended to cover the variety of financial and other related information that is prepared by an organization, such as an accounting department, to inform interested members of management regarding events and activities within their areas of responsibility. These recipients might include corporate management, operational management, and other administrative management. The type of information varies from company to company. Examples include monthly and year-to-date financial statements, project status reports for major capital expenditures, overhead and burden studies, sales reports by facility or territory, and contract status reporting. For illustrative purposes, this section deals with the internal auditor's role in financial reporting.

Relevance of Financial Information

The importance of financial statements hardly needs further emphasis. As noted previously, information with respect to financial position, results of operations, and changes in financial position is perhaps the most sought-after data by many interested parties.

Publicly held companies spend millions of dollars each year to gather the basic data for disclosure in annual reports to shareholders. Millions more are spent supplementing that data with other information about the company—its products and services, its management, and its performance. The services of public relations firms are often obtained by the larger companies to help assure that the information is disclosed in a style that portrays the image that management wishes to convey to its shareholders and others.

The financial statements contained in annual reports and in filings with the SEC usually are audited by independent accountants. The disclosures contained in those statements have evolved over the past 75 years or so under the guidance of the accounting profession through AICPA designated committees or boards, the SEC and, for the past decade, by the FASB and others. One may rightfully ask, "Why, then, does the internal auditor concern himself with the financial statements?"

The answer is simple and twofold: Internal auditors usually are concerned with matters that are of concern to management. In effect, the financial statements are the report cards of management. Therefore, financial reporting is among management's chief concerns. Management may wish to delve into matters to a greater degree than is required for the annual audit.

Second, the consolidated financial statements seen by the public are but one category of financial statements. Most large industrial corporations are combinations of various entities that report interim financial data. In many cases, internally speaking, there are numerous reporting entities. For these companies, the financial reporting system is a critical mechanism. There must be sufficient internal controls to permit the preparation of financial statements in accordance with generally accepted accounting principles and in such form as required by management to effectively discharge its function.

Most managements have established elaborate systems for the internal reporting of financial information whether monthly, weekly, or even daily. These internal reporting systems usually gather and report considerable detail for each affected component. Naturally, the form and content varies from company to company and industry to industry.

This financial data must be accurate and complete. A reporting mechanism must be established and operated to reasonably assure that the information reported is just that—sufficiently accurate and complete so as to provide the executives with proper facts to make business decisions.

Sometimes, there is a temptation for overly optimistic management of profit centers to employ accounting contrivances to mask the true nature of operating results. Such misstatements could relate to unwarranted, overly optimistic assessments on such matters as the value of inventory, collectibility of accounts receivable, future performance on contracts, and outcome of litigation. Such contrivances also could include subtle changes in accounting methods (depreciation rates). More obvious techniques could include failure to record all costs in the proper period, or booking undelivered orders as sales of the current period.

Invariably, the intent in these cases is to disguise the true operating picture from senior management to afford the local management more time to solve their problems. At other times, however, simple intent to fraudulently divert company funds or resources is the reason.

As Chapter 1 explains in greater detail, and as Chapters 4 and 23 amplify, the incidence of financial reporting fraud in recent years has caused responsive actions that are continuing as this volume is being written. Chief among these is the effort by the Treadway Commission, mentioned briefly in the discussion of current forces. It was commissioned and sponsored by a joint effort of the AICPA, the FEI, the NAA, the IIA, and the AAA. Its 49 recommendations for improvements in financial reporting are directed at company managements, the internal auditing function, external auditors, the SEC, and the applicable educational curriculums of colleges and universities. It is clear that all of these groups must do more.

Internal auditors' involvement in financial information reporting, historically, was not extensive. Usually, internal auditing played a supporting role to external auditors. This consisted of providing staff assistance in connection with the latter's annual audit of the company's financial statements included in the report to shareholders. Some internal auditing departments did perform examinations of financial statements of divisions and subsidiaries. If this was done in connection with the annual audit, the units examined invariably were immaterial to the consolidated financial statements. It is the belief of the authors that the internal auditing function is much more useful in performing limited reviews of interim-period financial information. This role enables the internal auditing function to perform a valuable service that compliments the role performed by external auditors.

Contrasted Roles of External and Internal Auditors

External auditors are retained by companies to provide an independent opinion on the fairness of the financial statements contained in the annual report. Management looks to the external auditor to provide, in addition, guidance and counsel regarding its accounting principles. To a lesser extent, the views of the external auditor regarding internal accounting control are also sought.

Management should look to internal auditors to provide assurances and other information with respect to interim-period financial reporting, among other things, and the internal accounting controls used to generate such data. To some extent, each type focuses on different matters. However, the work of both the external and internal auditors must be coordinated to avoid redundancy and to maximize results. Chapter 9 provides techniques for effective audit coordination.

Because of the internal auditor presence throughout the year, his work can be of value to the external auditor by

- Informing appropriate representatives of the accounting firm regarding matters that could affect the scope of work. Examples include internal accounting control problems, deviations noted in applying accounting principles, changes in component entities, and changes in reporting procedures.
- Coordinating internal control auditing and other types of audit coverage related to the examination of financial statements to help minimize the scope of the external auditor's work.
- Accepting the guidance and counsel of the external auditors as to areas in which detail investigations seem warranted.
- Permitting the external auditors to have access to internal audit reports and workpaper files.

The external auditor, by virtue of his key role in influencing the selection of accounting principles and his independent relationship, can be helpful to internal auditors by

- Assisting in the resolution of interim-period financial reporting problems or inconsistencies.

- Coordinating internal control auditing.
- Allowing the internal auditor to have access to his workpapers to help minimize testing and other audit procedures that might otherwise be required.

The foregoing are not all-inclusive. The internal auditor-external auditor relationship has taken many forms in today's varied business environment. Internal auditors must realize that the relationship that evolves depends, among other things, on the degree of reliance that the external auditor believes can be placed on the work of the internal auditor. The GAAS by which the external auditor is guided require that this be considered.

The Interim Financial Report Audit

Internal auditors can help assure the accuracy and completeness of interim financial data if they conduct a reasonable program of limited review of the interim financial reports of various reporting segments or operating centers of the company. By applying objectivity and financial reporting knowledge to significant accounting matters that come to his attention during the review process, the auditor helps assure that financial data reporting during interim periods is reliable for use by senior management. An illustrative limited review program is shown in Figure 2-5. The reader should note that the program entails more work than would normally be performed by external auditors performing a limited financial review pursuant to SAS No. 36. In addition to comparative analyses and inquiries of management regarding financial reporting matters, evidence is examined indicating that the following specific control procedures are in effect:

- Reconciliations of cash accounts
- Balancing of general ledger control accounts with subsidiary records for accounts receivable, fixed assets, prepaids, and accounts payable
- Balancing of intercompany accounts
- Inquiries pertaining to risk management (insurance) program
- Analysis of payments for legal services

Other procedures could be added if warranted by circumstances.

The areas of accounting control examined in this approach are those that are critical to an adequate system. Any exceptions would signal potentially significant underlying problems. In most cases, the added procedures can be performed by experienced auditors in a minimum of time.

If there is other financial information of importance to management, appropriate audits of that data may be performed. Management of aerospace contractors, for example, are interested in the accuracy of estimates of final revenue cost and profit on major contracts. These estimates can be very detailed, and the accuracy of interim financial reporting is highly dependent

A STRATEGIC APPROACH

FIG. 2-5

Audit Program for Limited Financial Review

OBJECTIVE:
The objective of the limited review of interim financial information is to provide a basis for reporting to management those matters which should be brought to their attention. These matters are determined by applying auditor's objectivity and knowledge of financial reporting practices to significant accounting matters of which he becomes aware through inquiries and analytical procedures.

	Workpaper Reference	Done By

1. Accounting System:

☐ Obtain an understanding of the techniques used to record and report financial data for interim periods. Sources to be used for this may be prior reports and workpapers. Inquiries at the corporate office of finance and management personnel and in the field of profit center management may also be utilized. ....

- Note any inconsistencies between year-end procedures and interim procedures and any effect these differences may have on interim statements. Include such items as changes in management report format, chart of accounts, accounting or operating procedures.

- Particular attention should be paid to the consistency of handling deferrals, accruals and estimations between year-end and interim statements.

☐ Review management's assessment of internal accounting controls pursuant to the Foreign Corrupt Practices Act of 1977. ....

- Determine if there have been any significant changes in internal controls, or changes in policies and procedures which affect internal controls since the last year-end. If so, review the implications of the changes and perform tests to verify that key controls are in effect. ....

- Test key controls of the overall financial area by:
  a. Brief inspections of related accounting records and documentation, including general and subsidiary ledgers and account analyses for significant accounts. ....
  b. Observations of department activities or facilities. ....
  c. Oral confirmation by other personnel. ....
  d. A summary narrative of records or documents observed or narratives of inquiries usually will be sufficient documentation of the above procedures. ....

☐ Note any significant changes in controls or systems from the previous year-end which could affect the manner in which financial statements are prepared. ....

(continued)

FIG. 2-5 *(cont'd)*

	Workpaper Reference	Done By
☐ Note and thoroughly document any significant weaknesses resulting from steps in this section and by discussion with management, obtain concurrence with your evaluation or obtain explanations supporting contrary views and related documentation. Test as considered necessary.	....	....

2. Financial Statements:

	Workpaper Reference	Done By
☐ Obtain financial statements and management reports for the most recent interim period, the comparable period of the prior year and the most recent year-end. Compare the income statements and funds statements to the interim period; the balance sheet to the previous year-end balance sheet.	....	....
☐ For fluctuations disclosed by the comparisons in 1 above, obtain and evaluate explanations by such procedures as may be necessary in the circumstances. Verification work should be avoided. However, for unusually large or unique fluctuations, corroborating evidence should be examined.	....	....
☐ Review the narrative reports by management for significant financial items.	....	....
☐ Review the actual/plan comparisons and narrative variance analysis of the chief financial officer for the most recent interim period.	....	....
☐ Trace financial statement amounts to the general ledger. For large entities, this may be done on a test basis.	....	....

3. Specific Functional Areas:

	Workpaper Reference	Done By
☐ Determine that sales and cost of sales are recorded in accordance with generally accepted accounting principles and that practices are consistent between year-end and interim periods.	....	....
☐ Review changes in reserve accounts and inquire as to the adequacy of current provisions. Obtain a schedule of significant reserves displaying the beginning balance, ending balance and the major changes.	....	....
☐ Review for propriety the method of accounting for intercompany allocations.	....	....
☐ Obtain an analysis of any legal expenses paid by the profit center and review for indications of unusual items.	....	....
☐ Ascertain by inquiry and observation that all bank accounts are reconciled on a current basis.	....	....
☐ Inspect evidence to indicate that ■ Accounts receivable detail aging agrees with general ledger control accounts.	....	....

	Workpaper Reference	Done By

- Fixed asset detail records have been reconciled to general ledger control accounts.   ....
- Accounts payable trial balance agrees with general ledger control accounts.   ....
- Intercompany accounts are in agreement.   ....
☐ Ascertain that financial statement formats conform to established requirements.   ....
☐ Insurance:
  - Determine if there are procedures in existence for:
    a. Identifying insurable risks and/or assets.   ....
    b. Establishing insurable claims.   ....
    c. Identifying and submitting information regarding incidents which should result in the processing of claims by the insurance department.   ....
    d. Accounting for insurance transactions.   ....
  - Determine if balances in any prepaid or accrued insurance accounts are required to be analyzed and verified on a periodic basis.   ....

4. **Summary:**
   ☐ Summarize findings and recommendations for exit interview with cost center management.   ....
   ☐ Prior to leaving the field, prepare a draft report of findings and review with cost center management.   ....
   ☐ List recommendations for future audits.   ....

on such data. Internal auditors in aerospace companies frequently audit these estimates for reasonableness.

By undertaking a program of examining interim-period financial information, such as that suggested here, the internal auditing function would be responding to the call of the Treadway Commission, mentioned earlier, to become more involved in the financial reporting process. A reasonable frequency of involvement would be to conduct a limited review of financial reporting information once each year at each location within an entity for which financial reporting data is prepared. That includes the consolidated financial reporting data.

ETHICAL BUSINESS PRACTICES AUDITING DESCRIBED

"Ethical Business Practices" Defined

Ethical business practices is a term often used when referring to the conduct encouraged or condoned by business entities of their employees when dealing with each other and with customers, suppliers, and the general public. As previous comments in this chapter make clear, ethical business practices are a necessary and critical ingredient in the successful enterprise.

The Ethical Practices Audit

Many companies develop codes of ethics, policy statements covering a variety of topics, and internal mechanisms to monitor and enforce compliance. Examples of specific topics in which ethical practices procedural guidance may be found are as follows:

- Standards of procurement
- Conflicts of interest
- Gifts and gratuities
- Entertainment
- Political activities
- Fair trade practices
- Antiboycott activities
- Business travel and expense reporting
- Patents and licenses
- Use of the company name
- Public announcements and speaking engagements
- Antitrust activities
- Customer relations
- Minority businesses
- Supplier relations
- Government relations

The list is not complete, but it is sufficient to illustrate that ethical business practices extend to almost anything in which a business may be involved. Obviously, no program of auditing could be structured that would discover all instances of misconduct. But, through systematic inquiry and records inspection, a reasonably thorough auditing approach can be devised. The authors suggest a combination approach involving:

- A comprehensive review of compliance with standards of ethical practices. This entails a level of inquiry into all types of ethical practices to assess compliance and search for serious breaches.
- A series of separate audits involving in-depth, detailed auditing within a particular area.

An application of one or more of the specific detailed audits along with the comprehensive review should be performed at each operating element each year. An example of an audit program for performing a comprehensive review is provided in Figure 2-6.

(*text continues on page 2-43*)

A STRATEGIC APPROACH

FIG. 2-6

Audit Program for Review of Ethical Business Practices

OBJECTIVE:

To determine if profit center management is in compliance with corporate policies for ethical practices, including the use of company funds and resources; commitments, agreements, and communications with persons or organizations outside of the corporation and other sensitive matters.

SCOPE:

To establish the degree of audit work to be performed in each section of this program, consider other relevant audits performed by the internal audit department. Review the workpapers, reports, auditee's replies and auditor evaluations. For those areas with audit coverage sufficient to meet objectives of this program, so note in these workpapers. Obtain the approval of the audit manager.

Any matters disclosed by performing the procedures of this program which in the judgment of the auditor indicate questionable activity, must be immediately reported to the internal audit department management. Further instructions will depend upon the attendant circumstances. In conducting this program, any questions of law must be referred to the legal department.

	Workpaper Reference	Done By

1. Cash Disbursements:

☐ Review internal controls over payments:

- Obtain and read profit center written procedures and documentation of internal controls.   ....
- Update the previously completed internal control questionnaire or complete a questionnaire.   ....
- Inquire as to changes in procedures since the last internal control survey.   ....
- Evaluate the strengths and weaknesses of internal controls, test key controls as necessary and summarize.   ....

☐ Identify all bank accounts to provide a basis for reviewing receipts and disbursements in subsequent audit steps:

- Identify the purpose of each account and the nature and source of the receipt and disbursement.   ....
- Determine signatories and verify that they are properly authorized.   ....

☐ Review nonstandard journal entries; investigate any unusual transactions.   ....

☐ For specific accounts where unusual transactions may be found, review fluctuations from the prior year, and month to month relate these fluctuations to the business activity and investigate any unusual accounts. Include at least the following accounts: ....

(continued)

FIG. 2-6 *(cont'd)*

	Workpaper Reference	Done By
<ul><li>Miscellaneous</li><li>Professional service</li><li>Nonprofessional services purchased</li><li>Other direct charges</li><li>Charitable contributions</li><li>Dues and memberships</li><li>Research and development</li><li>Employee welfare</li><li>Entertainment, travel and business conference</li></ul>		
☐ Note any large petty cash funds and determine the business reason for their existence, use, location, and who controls. If the fund is unusual, review documentation of the fund's activity.	....	....

2. Consultants and Commission Agents:

	Workpaper Reference	Done By
☐ Obtain from the corporate secretary a list of all consultants and commission agents listing names, activity, territory, compensation and expiration date.	....	....
☐ Obtain from the profit center a similar list, as well as a list of payments made to the consultants and agents for the year.	....	....
■ Compare to the list obtained in 1 above and investigate any differences.	....	....
■ Agree payments made to the general ledger or expense ledger.	....	....
☐ Select a representative sample of consultants and perform the following:	....	....
■ Review the agreements for compliance with the recommended corporate format.	....	....
■ Trace payments made to supporting documents, noting proper approval for payment. For commission agents, verify sale and cash receipt.	....	....
■ Agree rates paid to agreements.	....	....
■ Ascertain that proper approval was obtained for agreements requiring such approval, paying particular attention to dollar amounts and sensitivity.	....	....
a. Ascertain that the consultant file has all the relevant documentation supporting the selection of the consultant as required by policy.	....	....
b. If the consultant is a former government or military employee, ascertain that there is proper compliance with applicable government regulations.	....	....
c. Ascertain that all required reports have been received and are maintained in the profit center.	....	....

A STRATEGIC APPROACH

	Workpaper Reference	Done By
d. Ascertain that the required conflict of interest paragraph is incorporated into the applicable agreement.	....	....
e. Ascertain that a written legal opinion together with supporting documents are on file.	....	....
f. Ascertain that the required corporate approval was obtained.	....	....
☐ From the commission agents selected above, choose a representative sample for further analysis for compliance with specific company procedures.	....	....
☐ For all consultants chosen above, ascertain by some examination of payroll records that they are not employees during the time of their agreement.	....	....
☐ Determine if there are any international joint ventures, partnerships, or other contracting arrangements.	....	....
■ Ascertain that such agreements executed by senior corporate executives follow the designated form as outlined by corporate policy	....	....
■ Review supporting documentation to determine that distributorships meet the criteria of corporate policy.	....	....
☐ Review list of agent and consultant payments and ascertain that those agreements in excess of $200,000 were properly approved by the board of directors.	....	....
☐ Review profit center disbursements (record period reviewed) and select large dollar payments not tested as consultants and agents and determine the nature and propriety of these payments. The purpose is to test that there are no payments to consultants and agents not so classified.	....	....

3. **Conflict of Interest:**

☐ Inquire of management regarding the existence of any conflict of interest; record their answers; and, where appropriate, ask for proof (forms used, procedures issued, etc.).	....	....
☐ Select key employees in the purchasing department and other departments having contact with vendors, and	....	....
■ By discussion, determine their awareness of the profit center's standards of procurement.	....	....
■ Ascertain that the individual has signed a representation to the company regarding absence of interest in vendors.	....	....
☐ Discuss with management and search executive, and/or buyer, correspondence files to determine if any understanding or agreements, expressed or implied,		

(continued)

FIG. 2-6 *(cont'd)*

	Workpaper Reference	Done By

☐ formal or informal, appear to have been made with suppliers or competitors in regard to fixing prices high enough to allow kickbacks or if any other arrangements or agreements have been made to permit/demand kickback payments to management or buyers based upon purchase agreements or awards of major subcontracts. ....

☐ Ascertain, through discussion and/or examination of files, the existence of lower management procurement decisions that were materially changed at higher levels. ....

- For large or unusual procurements, review documentations for rationale for the change. ....

- Discuss any that do not appear reasonable with appropriate levels of management. ....

☐ Select large dollar purchase orders and review the correspondence and bid files underlying the order for evidence of fair practices, such as competitive bids, analysis of price, quantity and quality considerations, unusual terms (larger dollars in the early state of the subcontract, or schedule of payments without consideration of performance or return of materials), etc. ....

☐ On a test basis, review cash received from vendors. Determine the nature of the receipt and evaluate the accounting entries. ....

4. **Expense Accounts:**

☐ From [*time period*], make a selection of expense reports to be examined. A stratified sample should be made to assure that key marketing, public relations and executive personnel are included. A judgment sample can then be made from the rest of the field. Record sample. ....

☐ Ascertain the following for each report selected:

- Expenses are charged at actual and are reasonable in amounts. ....

- Receipts are provided as documentation whenever possible and in all cases where expense item exceeds $25. Review documentation for authenticity. ....

    a. Original documents. ....

    b. Receipts are printed with the name of the restaurant. ....

    c. No evidence of alteration, duplication or repeat of serial numbers. ....

- Expense report is submitted on a timely basis. ....

	Workpaper Reference	Done By

- Expense reports properly approved by the employee's next higher level of authority. ....
- Expense report is reviewed by accounting for allowability as a deduction for tax purposes. ....

☐ For the reports selected, review them for the following items whenever applicable:

- Entertainment and business conference expenses

    a. Submitted on appropriate forms. ....

    b. Contain proper descriptions of the activity as required by the IRS. ....

    c. Agendas provided for all conferences, symposia, seminars or other meetings. ....

    d. No entertainment of government personnel. ....

    e. No payments to consultants or agents. ....

- Properly approved travel authorities are prepared for all business travel and adequate description of business purpose is provided. ....

- Expenses for travel of wives or other personal items are reported on a separate expense report, properly approved by the president or senior financial officer. Amounts should also be included in employee's W-2. ....

- Automobile expenses appear reasonable and limited to authorized items. ....

- Expenses for 1st-class air travel are properly approved by president or chief financial officer. ....

☐ Obtain a trial balance of employee advances. ....

- Investigate any large or old balances. (Note any officer's advances in particular.) ....

- Select several transactions and review documentation for proper approval. ....

☐ For the reports selected above, determine that advances are made in accordance with stated procedures. ....

☐ Review general ledger accounts (record time period) such as miscellaneous, business conference, entertainment, travel, etc., for entries from sources other than expense reports processed through normal accounting procedures. List any unusual items noted and investigate. ....

☐ Review cash receipt and disbursement records for any unusual or large amounts paid to, or received from, employees. ....

☐ Determine if loans have been made to officers and

(continued)

FIG. 2-6 *(cont'd)*

	Workpaper Reference	Done By
employees out of company funds other than for travel advances.	....	....
5. Other Areas. To determine the status of the following business practices, review of supporting files, executive or appropriate management correspondence files, and specific documentations (such as files on public announcements, contract acquisition schedules, correspondence, etc.), discussions with management or use other methods as may be appropriate in the circumstances. Document all work performed.	....	....
☐ Determine compliance with corporate policies of actions on committee memberships and government-industry memberships, public announcements correspondence with shareholders, publication of technical information, coordination and clearance of public speeches, distribution and control of brochures, and release of any other personal information regarding the corporation's activities to sources outside of the company.	....	....
☐ Determine that proper notification of reporting requirements has been made to former officers and employees of the U.S. Government and that copies of the applicable federal statutes and required reporting forms are available at company personnel offices. Obtain evidence that:	....	....
■ Records are maintained of all employees who are former government personnel.	....	....
■ Position descriptions and work to be performed have been prepared and reviewed by the company legal department representatives to assure that the scope of work excludes activity which would create a violation of applicable conflict of interest laws and regulations.	....	....
☐ Determine that the division general manager or subsidiary president has informed their employees in writing that corporate funds, facilities, and the corporate name shall not be used directly or indirectly for partisan political purposes on behalf of candidates for political office, political parties, or elected incumbent office holders at the federal, state, or local level.	....	....
☐ Determine if the cost center has any involvement in international joint ventures, partnerships, licensing agreements, distributorships, or other contracting arrangements with third parties involving foreign sales of the company's products and related services. Also determine if such agreements have been prepared, reviewed, approved, and signed in accordance with latest corporate requirements formats.	....	....

	Workpaper Reference	Done By
☐ Obtain and review schedule of all receivables due from officers and other employees to determine if any loans, advances, financial assistance or financial warranties have been provided in an aggregate amount of $5000 or more and having a duration of more than one year, excluding travel advances or revolving funds established for reimbursement of company expenses.	....	....
☐ Determine the following (1) whether the cost center has assigned legal counsel; (2) if so, are they reporting to the general counsel concerning any business or legal matters that arise within the organization that could involve either a significant legal exposure or business risk to the company; (3) company patent policies are adhered to; (4) does the general counsel report these significant matters directly to the offices of the chief executive officer and the chief operating officer, and monthly to the board of directors?	....	....
☐ Determine if procedures have been established to comply with the Export Administration Act of 1969 as amended and guidelines issued by the Treasury Department pursuant to Section 999 of the Internal Revenue Code. In reviewing documentation in other audit steps, such as purchase orders, contracts, shipping documents, correspondence, etc., be alert to any language which would compromise the company.	....	....
☐ By inquiry, determine whether there are any restrictive trade practices which are contrary to the antitrust laws.	....	....
6. Conclude:		
☐ Summarize the findings.	....	....
☐ Discuss the findings with appropriate management.	....	....
☐ Conclude as to the overall objectives of the audit.	....	....
☐ Prepare the report.	....	....

DECIDING HOW TO ALLOCATE AUDITING RESOURCES

Strategic Audit Planning

Let's review briefly what this chapter has developed to this point. First, it is important to develop a strategic approach. Second, various forces are at work that influence the establishing of auditing objectives. Third, auditing objectives relating to five areas of internal auditing are proposed that are responsive to current forces. These areas, which form the basis of the strategic approach, are financial auditing, operational auditing, information systems auditing, and ethical practices auditing. Other sections of this volume deal with specific aspects of each of these. However, specific comments and specimen programs were included in this chapter for interim-period financial reporting reviews and for ethical business practices audits. Suggestions for frequencies of coverage are now offered. The following summarizes these suggestions:

Area of Audit	Frequency
Financial:	
Interim-period financial reporting	Annually at each location where financial reporting occurs
Internal control reviews	Annually
Detailed functional audits	?
Operational:	
Multidisciplined management auditing (i.e, inventory management)	?
Detailed functional audits for efficiency and effectiveness	?
Information systems auditing:	
Installation reviews	Annually at each location where major processing installations exist
Developing systems auditing	?
Applications auditing	?
Detailed functional auditing	?
Ethical business practices auditing:	
Comprehensive reviews	Annually at each operating element
Detailed ethical practices auditing	?

It is evident from the foregoing that recommendations for broad-based auditing types, such as interim-period financial reporting or comprehensive reviews of ethical business practices, should be performed annually. But what about the rest? How does one decide from among the hundreds of potential detailed functional audits where to direct the specific auditing focus? That is where techniques of strategic planning come into play.

Strategic planning in the context of internal auditing may be defined as the process by which audit management decides how much auditing is required in particular circumstances or areas. Recognizing the five broad audit objectives described earlier in this chapter, the chief auditor and his assistants must decide what proportion of the total audit resource available should be allocated to each: internal accounting control, financial reporting, operational functions, standards of business conduct, and EDP.

The strategic planning process for auditing is largely a matter of professional judgment relying on the skill and experience of the audit management team. Knowledge of the company in general, and of management priorities in particular, will assist in making useful decisions. To systematically approach strategic planning, auditors should:

A STRATEGIC APPROACH

- Survey the universe of auditable areas
- Rank the audit areas into projects
- Prioritize the projects
- Assign audit frequencies

This process works particularly well in allocating resources for detailed internal control, operational, and EDP audits. Financial reporting and standards of business conduct are areas sufficiently important to warrant performing them at least once each year at each operating entity of the company. The rest of the audit coverage may be determined by applying the following process.

Surveying Universe of Auditable Areas

Auditable areas may be defined as those that are likely to provide useful, credible information to management and/or the board of directors as a result of an audit. The chief auditor and his assistants must identify all potential audit opportunities by surveying all relevant reservoirs of information from which prospective audit areas might be discerned. The following briefly describes some of the more fruitful sources:

- ☐ *Corporatewide policy statements.* These may define levels of authority for approving and executing internal transactions and activities of all types. They may also describe acceptable conduct, identify organizational goals, and prescribe permissible means of achieving them.
- ☐ *Corporatewide procedural manuals.* These usually spell out in considerable detail how a function is to be performed. They are written for all important functions such as procurement, labor relations, finance and accounting, quality control, production planning and scheduling, EDP, marketing, and manufacturing.
- ☐ *Organizational unit manuals.* These may contain useful information, such as interpretive procedural descriptions that indicate how the corporatewide policies are to be implemented within the division. If they exist, they usually are much more detailed than the corporatewide policies.
- ☐ *Flow charts and internal control documentation.* In many companies, management has directed the development of this type of documentation. Even if it does not follow standard formats, such as those variously recommended by the major public accounting firms, such documentation is an invaluable source of information.
- ☐ *Organization charts.* These depict, in chart fashion, the reporting relationships and identify the management structure of a company, subsidiary, division, department, or function. They are useful to auditors because they may identify the responsibility and authority of departments or functions.
- ☐ *Other documentation.* This would include, to the extent present, charts of accounts, published financial statements, internally reported financial data, data processing manuals, current lists of existing data processing applications, and even the functional telephone listing.

In addition to the above, the internal auditor may wish to make inquiries of the company's outside auditors regarding relevant areas of internal control as candidates for audit. Outside auditors welcome the opportunity to assist internal auditors in identifying such areas. In fact, many outside auditors permit internal auditors to inspect their applicable workpapers for this purpose.

During the process of identifying relevant areas, the auditor must realize that the accuracy and completeness of the search depends on the currency of the material searched. To eliminate the chance that the material is no longer relevant, the auditor should ascertain that mechanisms exist for keeping such material current. During the course of the search, evidence of updating should be noted.

Figure 2-7 is an example of a list of relevant audit areas that might be developed by this survey process. Note that the list is categorized to the extent practicable according to the way in which each component relates to operations. The term "operations" is used here in the same way it is used in financial reporting, where operations refer to virtually all management activities during a period. As a result, identification of all transactions and functions of consequence is reasonably assured. This is not intended to imply that other methods of categorizing are not equally effective.

Note also that all topics cannot be conveniently grouped in this fashion. That is because many relevant management activities do not result in a transaction accounted for by the financial reporting mechanism. In fact, financial reporting itself is an example of an extremely important function that cannot be grouped as though it is a type of transaction. Regardless of the approach used, there will always be some functions or activities that pose categorical problems.

Some transactions are included in more than one group in Figure 2-7. This redundancy derives from the use of a financial reporting orientation in the process (direct and indirect transactions for current operations and breakdown by prior and future periods). Again, this is no more or less of a problem than would be encountered by using any other grouping. The duplication does not mean that any redundant auditing will occur. It simply demonstrates that transaction cycles for *all* financial report groupings must be considered. The redundancy in the figure is simply to preserve the integrity of the separate categories.

There is one final point. The list of transaction cycles, functions, and so forth, in Figure 2-7 was developed for use by internal auditors in order to demonstrate the extent to which a thorough evaluation of internal control must be pursued. Accordingly, the list is much more extensive than the internal control areas of interest to public accountants. (See Chapter 18.)

The listing shown in Figure 2-7, when appropriately prioritized, permits developing a more detailed evaluation and testing than that produced by the more general approaches for which suggestions to coverage have already been offered. The listing is primarily useful for developing detailed financial

A STRATEGIC APPROACH

FIG. 2-7

Audit Areas Selected From Transaction Cycle Functions and Policies— Financial Reporting Emphasis

---

Direct Transactions and Functions Related to Current Operations

Payroll
Procurement — Subcontracts
Depreciation
Receivables billing & collection
Accounts payable
Cash control & management
Financial reporting
Cost accounting system
Inventory
Receiving
Warehousing
Shipping
Research & development
Capital asset transactions

Indirect Transactions and Functions Related to Current Operations

Procurement-related transactions
Payroll-related transactions
Production scheduling
Entertainment/Expense reports
Consultant/Commission agent activities
Joint ventures
Facilities management
Warranties
Budgeting
Advances to subcontractors
Business plans
Employee group benefit plans
Long-term investments
Stock transactions
Political activities
Corporate contributions
Long-term debt transactions
Retirement & savings plans
Income taxes
Litigation settlements
Insurance
Data processing
Security
Telecommunications
Marketing
Industrial relations
Record retention
Communications & graphics
Field offices
Community relations
Patent administration
Public affairs
Memberships

Transactions and Functions Related to Operations of Prior Periods

Contract terminations
Warranties
Financial reporting
Inventory
Litigation settlements
Cash control & management
Cost accounting system

Transactions and Functions Related to Operations of Future Periods

Research & development
Budgeting
Advances to subcontractors
Business plans
Bidding & estimating
Procurement — Subcontracts
Receivables billing & collection
Accounts payable
Accruals
Cash control & management
Financial reporting
Inventory
Production scheduling
Other indirect functions
Consultant/Commission agents
Joint ventures
Facilities management
Employee group benefit plans
Long-term investments
Stock transactions
Long-term debt
Capital asset
Other long-term assets
Income taxes
Litigation settlements
Insurance
Data processing
Marketing
Public affairs
Industrial relations
Regional offices
Community relations

audits of internal control. The same technique could be used to develop auditable areas for operational auditing, information systems auditing, and ethical practices auditing.

Identifying Risk Factors

All transaction cycles, functions, and policies are not of equal importance. Policies dealing with commitment authority and ethical conduct, major contracts, capital asset transactions, and long-term debt incurrence usually are of great importance. Others, such as the issuance of employee service commendations, control of office supplies, and memberships, dues, and subscriptions are less significant. To be sure, these areas must be sufficiently controlled. However, the chances of these areas posing significant problems to management are extremely remote.

Many of the topics could be intuitively ranked based on the knowledge, skill, and experience of the internal audit manager or director, and a reasonable ranking would probably result. On the other hand, there is also a chance that the intuitive process may err and that a potentially significant area might not receive audit scrutiny as soon as it might otherwise.

Other aspects of the audit approach, such as the internal control survey discussed in Chapter 18, would compensate somewhat for such an exposure. Thus, an intuitive ranking would probably suffice for small companies or organizations. However, the chief auditor may prefer a more systematic and documented method of ranking. This involves a process commonly referred to as risk analysis, a process described in the following paragraphs.

In practice, the relative importance or significance of a given transaction cycle, function, or policy is determined by considering the risk to the company. Several factors may be used to measure the risk.

Impact on Decision Making. Functions that provide useful and essential information to management as an aid in decision making tend to be of critical importance. Examples include aged accounts receivable listings for the credit and collection department, bank reconciliations for the cash manager or controller, comparisons of actual versus budgeted performance for department/functional managers, and financial statements for a variety of users.

Complexity of Systems. Simple systems usually do not pose challenges to management, whereas complex systems do. The greater the complexity of a system, the more important will be the controls necessary to reasonably assure that the system achieves its objectives. System complexity varies from industry segment to industry segment. A system for controlling cash receipts by an operator of a chain of retail stores or hotels is more elaborate than is the cash receipts system employed by a contractor. Payroll systems usually are complex. However, those for labor-intensive industries offer more opportunities for errors and omissions than do the systems for capital-intensive industries. Procedures to safeguard inventory are especially intricate for companies whose inventories are susceptible to pilferage, e.g., banks, jewelry companies, and stock brokerage firms. Conversely, heavy equipment manufacturers are less concerned with theft of inventory.

Volume of Transactions. As transaction volume increases, controls must be added to reasonably assure accurate and complete processing. A payroll system at a branch office may be maintained manually by a single clerk on a write-it-once pegboard system. A payroll for a large manufacturing plant may require extensive investment in personnel, equipment, and forms to be effective. Cash receipts and disbursements of a single location company usually can be handled relatively simply. The same transactions for a company with multiple locations calls for considerably more sophistication, including cash concentration accounts and electronic fund transfer capability.

Impact on Financial Statements (Materiality). Certain types of activities or transactions are more material than others because of their potential impact on financial statements. For contractors involved in long-term contracts, the estimates of final contract profit or loss are extremely important for income determination. Estimates of loan loss provisions for finance companies, or estimates of reserve requirements for insurance claims for casualty insurance companies, may be critical. On the other hand, errors in petty cash transactions and charitable contributions usually have little financial statement impact.

Source or Use of Cash. All company activities sooner or later involve either obtaining or spending cash. However, certain activities use or produce more of it than others. These activities receive considerable management attention and concern. Examples include capital projects such as facilities expansions, acquisitions of other business enterprises, major settlements of litigation, and major financing, such as issuing long-term debt and capital stock.

Regulatory Involvement. Almost any business undertaking involves considering applicable regulatory requirements. Some activities are affected by more regulations than others. For example, utilities, railroads, and banks are subject to considerable rules mandated by various federal and state regulatory agencies. Control systems in these industries must be responsive to regulatory requirements usually because the penalties for violations may be severe. Other industries are regulated, albeit, perhaps less extensively. Most are subject to federal regulations involving affirmative action, equal opportunity, and occupational safety and health, to name just three. Other significant business activities are regulated by the SEC, the FTC, the Federal Communications Commission, and the Food and Drug Administration, and all businesses are subject to actions of the IRS. Regulatory involvement is an important factor because it has a direct bearing on the type of information that must be collected and reported. Thus, it affects internal control.

Prioritizing Risk Factors

In order to use the above-mentioned factors for ranking purposes, the auditor may wish to first prioritize them. This requires identifying the comparative importance of the several factors—a difficult task and one in which there can be differences of opinion. The chief auditor should assign weights to the factors, based on his judgment of their importance. Such a weighting will make less likely the bunching of prospective audit projects in a vast middle area.

Once the weightings have been determined, it is only necessary to develop a matrix or schedule that ranks the prospective audit areas. Such a matrix is shown in Figure 2-8.

This technique of ranking is useful to help the auditor determine which subjects are more significant than others. It does not mean that all the important topics must be audited to the exclusion of the less important ones. However, in determining audit frequency, and to assure completeness of audit coverage, this or similar techniques are very useful.

Determining Audit Frequency

In order to assure that all areas are reviewed within a reasonable period, decisions must be made with respect to audit frequency. That is, the audit coverage within a given period—say a year—should be comprised of audit projects from all areas (i.e., internal control, financial reporting, operational policies and procedures, ethical business practices, and information systems. How much of each type to include depends on decisions as to how frequently specific audit projects within each area should be audited. For example, the payroll function is vital for most companies. Therefore, audits of the payroll system probably should occur at least once every two years and more often if control weaknesses exist. As stated earlier, interim-period financial reporting and comprehensive ethical business practices are subjects that should be reviewed each year at each significant location. On the other hand, audits of affirmative action plans may need to be performed only once every five to seven years under normal situations.

The criteria used to determine audit frequency is much the same as that used to rank the audit areas. That is because the higher the priority or ranking, the more frequent should be the audit coverage. An illustration of assigned audit frequencies to selected projects is shown in Figure 2-9.

Guidelines for Allocation of Audit Resources

A study of Figure 2-8 could lead to the conclusion that the plan of audit coverage for most internal auditing departments could be selected by simply choosing the topics with the highest ranking. If that were done, however, the audit areas of low rank would probably never receive audit scrutiny, due to the limited available audit resource. To compensate for the tendency to concentrate too many resources on high-ranking topics, some arbitrary guidelines may be useful.

In light of the emerging concern regarding business ethics and financial reporting frauds, it may be advisable for internal auditors to increase the amount of auditing in those areas. Since operational efficiency continues to interest management, internal auditing in this area should continue to receive a significant allocation of auditing resources.

Some internal auditing functions may use the foregoing to justify increasing the amount of available internal auditing resources. However, the increased auditing of financial reporting and ethical business practices may be achieved by other internal auditing functions by reducing the allocation of auditing resources of other areas. One possible candidate for such reduction is the auditing of internal accounting control (other than financial reporting). It is quite likely that a reduction is justifiable on the grounds that the extensive internal and external auditing of internal accounting control in recent years has resulted in the development of systems of internal accounting control that are sufficiently reliable, even for purposes of complying with the FCPA. Naturally, any proposed reduction in this area should be supported by management as well as the external auditors. The fact should be disclosed to the audit committee of the board of directors.

A strategic allocation of audit resources that considers the developments described in this chapter might be as follows:

Financial (including internal control and financial information reporting)	35%
Operational auditing	20
Information systems (EDP) auditing	20
Standards of ethical business practices	15
Special investigations and other (see Chapter 22)	10
	100%

There is no scientific basis for the suggested division of effort between the various types of internal auditing. The suggestions are based on considering the relative merits of each type of auditing and its significance to management and the board of directors. The chief auditor must exercise professional judgment to make similar decisions applicable to his particular situation. Such decisions serve to regulate decisions, within each auditing type, as to further opportioning the effort, as previously illustrated.

FIG. 2-8

Weighted Ranking of Audit Areas

Audit Area Weight	Level of Authority Involved 3	Complexity 2	Volume of Transactions 3	Materiality 3	Regulatory Involvement 2
Bidding & estimating	4	4	2	4	4
Financial reporting	4	4	1	4	4
Income taxes	3	4	2	4	4
Procurement	3	3	4	4	1
Cash	4	2	4	3	2
Payroll	1	3	4	4	3
Capital assets	4	4	1	4	2
Subcontracts	4	3	2	4	1
Inventory	3	3	4	2	2
Receivables	3	2	4	3	1
Telecommunications	2	4	4	2	2
Cost accounting	2	3	4	2	2
Accounts payable	2	2	4	3	1
Research & development	4	4	1	2	1
Patent administration	2	4	2	1	4
Shipping	3	2	2	3	1
Warehousing	1	2	4	2	1
Receiving	1	1	4	2	1
Depreciation	1	2	2	2	1
Public affairs	3	2	2	2	1

Some further guidelines must be established for determining a reasonable plan of coverage for any given year. These guidelines are as follows:

- Allocate a large proportion of time to projects with a ranking in the upper third of potential topics. Time allocated could be as much as 50 percent.
- Allocate a small proportion of time to projects with a ranking in the lowest third. Time allocated could be 20 percent or less.
- Allocate the balance of time to projects with a ranking in the mid-range.
- Consider past experience. If previous audit results indicate deficiencies and problems in a given area, allocate additional time to permit follow-up.

By following these guidelines, the chief auditor will find that, over time, all auditable areas will be covered pursuant to a rational, flexible strategy. How much time is required to cover the auditable areas varies, depending on the degree of control present, management attitude toward auditing, and similar factors.

There is one further consideration in determining audit frequency. Decisions regarding audit topics must be tempered by the credibility of the

A STRATEGIC APPROACH

Total			Legends
Raw Score	%	Rank	1. *Explanation of numerical factors:*
46	88	1	High-level extensive — 4
43	83	2	Above average — 3
43	83	3	Average (or equal hi/lo mix) — 2
41	79	4	Below average — 1
41	79	5	Insignificant — 0
39	75	6	2. "Weight" is judgmentally based on the circumstances of the company. This example assumes a large, complex manufacturing company, multiple profit centers, and numerous transactions.
39	75	7	
38	73	8	3. "Total" = Σ ["weight" × "numerical factors"]
37	71	9	
36	69	10	"%" = Total / Σ [weight × maximum numerical factor]
36	69	11	
34	65	12	
33	63	13	
31	60	14	
31	60	15	
30	58	16	
27	52	17	
25	48	18	
21	40	19	
27	52	20	

internal auditing function; that is, the topics to be included in the audit coverage must be reasonably susceptible to audit, given the general expertise of the audit department. Moreover, some areas that are susceptible to audit based on credibility may not warrant the internal auditor's independent assessment. This is the case in situations where management seeks such assessment from other sources. These other sources usually include other designated administrative functions, outside auditors, consultants, or other experts. In essence, the internal auditor must minimize auditing efforts in those areas in which the chance of value being added as a result of such effort is slight. While such areas vary from company to company, the following illustrative list is typical of many:

- Long-range planning
- Actuarial liabilities
- Financing alternatives
- Advertising
- Antitrust
- Labor relations
- Income tax reporting
- Occupational safety and health
- Equal employment practices
- Manufacturing quality control
- Litigation practices
- Community relations

FIG. 2-9
Frequencies for Common Audits

Function	Years	Function	Years
Procurement	1–2	Energy programs	3–4
Subcontract administration	1–2	Intercompany business management	3–4
Procurement-related transactions	1–4	Operations planning	2–3
Inventory management	1–2	Operations scheduling	2–3
Bidding and estimating	1–2	Risk management	2–3
Contracts	3–4	Risk reporting	1–2
Indirect cost control	3–4	Health-care plans	2–3
Budgeting	2–3	Company retirement/savings plan	2–3
Facilities management	2–3		
Cash forecasting	1–2	Flight operations	4–5
Field office review	4–5	Construction activities	3–4
Communication	4–5	Special reviews (as required)	
Transportation	3–4		

Needless to say, any exclusions from audit coverage should be clearly understood by management and the audit committee or the board of directors. Excluding topical areas from audit coverage is not intended to mean that the internal auditing function cannot perform useful assistance to affected management groups responsible for these functions. The auditor's objectivity and analytical ability can be a valuable aid in all of these areas to help develop special information of interest to each particular management group.

The strategic planning process is an indispensable aid in annual audit planning and in determining manpower requirements.

Maintaining Flexibility

It has already been established that circumstances change in ways that can significantly affect the practice of auditing. Therefore, the strategic plan and overall approach must be assessed anew annually. Perhaps the best time for this is immediately prior to planning the next year's audit coverage. Of course, major occurrences during the intervening period, such as a major business acquisition or divestiture, or a turnover in critical senior management, would require a more timely reassessment. In any event, flexibility in adapting to changed circumstances is essential if the audit function is to remain effective as a servant for management and the board of directors.

A WORD OF CAUTION

Throughout this chapter, emphasis has been placed on the desirability of an overall or strategic audit plan that effectively considered the areas or functions of greatest interest to the management or the board of directors. It is proper, and important to the well-being of the internal auditing organization, that these interests be serviced.

Professionalism also must enter into the planning. When the chief auditor believes certain activities seem improperly reported, or his innate audit sense says something seems wrong, or there are too many gaps in the evidential matter, for example, then he has a duty to explore these suspect areas—whether or not the management has requested it. (Of course, his supervisor and the appropriate members of management should be advised.) Some managements may not be alerted to matters that should properly be reviewed. It is up to the chief internal auditor to do the necessary explaining or "selling," and assure that the significant trouble spots that might embarrass the company or its executives, if not corrected, are examined. This type of situation does not arise very often, but it does occur and must be dealt with as diplomatically as possible. Services, yes; professionalism, yes also.

SUGGESTED READING

Barrett, Michael J., DBA, CIA. "Allocating Resources With Strength/Weakness Analysis." *The Internal Auditor*, Dec. 1984, pp. 43–48.

Cassell, Michael N., and Richard G. Schroeder. "An Effective Audit Program for FCPA." *The Internal Auditor*, June 1981, pp. 57–62.

DeMarco, Victor F. "How Internal Auditors Can Help CPAs Stamp Out Illegal Acts." *The Internal Auditor*, Feb. 1978, pp. 60–67.

Gillespie, G. Robert. "Questionable Payments." *The Internal Auditor*, Oct. 1979. pp. 61–65.

Gray, O. Ronald, Ph.D., CIA, CPA, CMA. "Audit Project Evaluation Methodology." *The Internal Auditor*, June 1983, pp. 31–34.

Kasparak, Wolfhart. "Developing an Audit Plan That Works." *The Internal Auditor*, Dec. 1981, pp. 62–67.

Macchiaverra, Paul. *Internal Auditing*, Chapter 1. New York: The Conference Board, 1978.

The National Commission on Fraudulent Financial Reporting. *Report of the National Commission on Fraudulent Financial Reporting*, Exposure Draft; Apr. 1987. Washington D.C.. National Commission on Fraudulent Financial Reporting, 1987.

The President's Blue Ribbon Commission on Defense Management. *A Quest for Excellence*, Final Report to the President, June 1986.

The President's Blue Ribbon Commission on Defense Management. *Conduct and Accountability*, A report to the President, June 1986.

Rittenberg, L. E. "Expanding Opportunities for Internal Audit Service." *The Internal Auditor*, Apr. 1980, pp. 73–80.

Southern California Gas Company Internal Controls Staff. "Application Risk Index." *The EDP Auditor*, Spring 1976, pp. 20–22.

The Special Committee on Standards of Professional Conduct for Certified Public

Accountants. *Restructuring Professional Standards to Achieve Professional Excellence in a Changing Environment.* New York: AICPA, 1986.

Storslee, Michael D., CPA, and Douglas W. Breckel. "The PDQ Prioritizer." *The Internal Auditor*, Apr. 1984, pp. 27–29.

White, Albert W. "Essentials of an Effective Internal Audit Department." *The Internal Auditor*, Apr. 1976, pp. 30–33.

Williams, Harold M. "The Emerging Responsibility of the Internal Auditor." *The Internal Auditor*, Oct. 1978, pp. 45–52.

Wilson, Paul W. "Planning and Operation of the Internal Audit Department." *Retail Control*, Jan. 1978, pp. 2–14.

PART II
Auditing Standards

CHAPTER **3**

Auditing Standards Development

Standards of Performance	1	GAO	13
Definition	2	IIA Standards Differentiated	13
Purpose	2	Internal Auditors' Reporting	
Importance of Auditing as the		Relationships and Standards	14
Prerequisite	2	**General Auditing Standards**	15
Standards-Setting Process	3	Independence	15
By Government	3	SEC Definition	15
By Private Sector	4	IIA Definition	17
By Government and Private Sector	4	Competence	17
Self-Regulation	5	Due Diligence	19
Contributions of Professional		**Final Comments on Professionalism,**	
Organizations to Standards Setting	8	**Standards, and Audit Techniques**	21
AICPA	9	**Suggested Reading**	22
IIA	12		

Fig. 3-1 Summary of Major Requirements for SEC Practice Section Membership 6
Fig. 3-2 Setting Auditing Standards: 1917–1987 10

STANDARDS OF PERFORMANCE

The intent of this chapter is to convey to the reader the critical role of auditing standards in managing an audit function. This chapter defines standards, provides a perspective on the standard-setting process, establishes the purpose of standards, compares and contrasts the published standards of the three branches of auditing (see Chapter 1), and comments on specific aspects of the general standards. Along with an overall audit strategy (Chapters 1 and 2), standards of performance form an indispensable basis on which other techniques are devised for effective audit management. These other techniques are discussed in Chapters 7–10.

Definition

Although auditing standards are enumerated and discussed extensively in professional accounting and auditing literature, the term "standards" is not actually defined. As used in such literature, it refers to a minimum set of conditions and practices required to be evident in the conduct of an audit to reasonably assure that the audit results will meet user expectations.

Purpose

Perhaps the best statement regarding the purpose of standards is found in the following excerpt from the Report of the Cohen Commission:

> Auditing standards have two important uses: communicating the requirements of auditing and evaluating the performance of auditors. [Ernest L. Hicks, "Standards for the Attest Function," *The Journal of Accountancy* (August 1974) pp. 39-40.] First, auditing standards provide guidance to auditors in their practice, to users who want to understand the work of auditors, and to educators who prepare people to become auditors. Second, auditing standards may be used by the profession's bodies charged with disciplining auditors, the courts, and the regulatory agencies to evaluate the performance of auditors.[1]

As the quotation implies, standards serve all parties that have an interest in the work of the auditor: the auditors themselves, the users (those for whom the audit is performed), and third parties, such as educators and government agencies. Standards serve these parties by articulating the expected level of effort required in the conduct of the auditor's services. In a sense, standards are objectives that must be met in the performance of service and, if properly set and meticulously followed, they produce the credibility necessary for effective service.

Importance of Auditing as the Prerequisite

It is interesting that the practice of auditing existed long before its significance evolved to the point where establishing formal standards became necessary. In 1949, more than 50 years after the AICPA (originally named American Institute of Accountants) was established, the organization formally issued the first standards, known today as GAAS. In 1972, the GAO issued formal standards for audit of government activities, and, in 1978, the IIA followed suit for its sphere of interest.

It should not be inferred that the professional branches of auditing op-

---

[1] The Commission on Auditors' Responsibilities, *The Commission on Auditors' Responsibilities: Report, Conclusions, and Recommendations* (New York: The Commission on Auditors' Responsibilities, 1978), p. 123.

erated without guidance, or performed poorly, prior to the adoption of formal standards. On the contrary, prior to the time of published standards, an informal body of general practices was in existence and was widely accepted. In addition, published literature specifying various audit procedures was present. The prestandard-setting period was characterized by the efforts of individuals of skill and foresight to whom current practitioners are indebted for their contributions to the overall practice of auditing.

In summary, although the importance of auditing services to society grew slowly and was interrupted by the Depression and World War II, with the increased recognition of the significance of the accounting and auditing functions, formal publicized standards eventually became necessary.

In the case of the government audit branch, the importance of that type of auditing became more critical as government spending increased. During the 1960s, both the number and dollar amounts of government programs substantially increased, generating, in turn, more demand for full accountability by those entrusted with the responsibility for administering the programs.[2]

In the case of the IIA, the pattern is similar. Internal auditors within companies established formal standards, often parallelling those of the AICPA, when the size and operation of each function required it. However, the need for a statement of standards that all members could embrace did not emerge until the growth of public concern regarding corporate accountability in the 1970s. This public concern led managements to place greater emphasis on the role to be played by internal auditors and increased the need for standards.

STANDARDS-SETTING PROCESS

By Government

Generally speaking, the way in which standards are set depends on the importance and the nature of the activity involved. If the activity is crucial to society as a whole, standards setting requires great care and will usually occur at the government level. For example, national defense is a matter of broad public concern that is critical to the well-being of those governed. Therefore, the government, through the various military branches, sets the standards, which are extensive and detailed, covering every aspect of military activity.

---

[2] Comptroller General of the United States, *Standards for Audits of Government Organizations, Programs, Activities and Functions* (Washington, D.C.: Government Printing Office, 1981), p. i.

By Private Sector

Similarly, comparatively less crucial activities are served by less rigorous processes. Accordingly, standards may be set entirely in the private sector, as in the case of the legal profession, or the responsibility may be shared. Who sets the standards in the private sector depends to a degree on the responsiveness of groups in the private sector. For example, standards pertaining to electrical and fire protection, hazardous chemicals, hazardous locations, air conditioning, heating, and refrigeration are set by the Underwriters Laboratories, a nongovernmental, independent testing laboratory. This organization was established nearly a century ago in direct response to the need for such standards. The work of this independent body is an excellent illustration of how effective standards-setting activity outside the government sector can be. Similarly, in recent years, standards setting for GAAP has been vested in a private sector body, FASB.

By Government and Private Sector

Standards setting in the field of public accounting is a complex process involving states, government agencies, state CPA societies, the AICPA, the SEC, and private firms. In the case of accounting, rules governing such matters as licensing or certification of accountants, continuing education, disciplinary proceedings, and forms of practice are set forth by state agencies. Boards of Accountancies of various states may also prescribe rules for specific aspects of accounting, such as (1) permission to use the practitioner's name, (2) incompatible occupations, (3) report context, (4) unaudited financial information, and (5) compilation and review of financial statements. While the states are empowered to prescribe rules of conduct, these legislative and administrative bodies are, in practice, considerably influenced by the viewpoint and action of the AICPA and the separate state societies of CPAs (i.e., the private sector).

Public accounting standards of practice are also promulgated by the AICPA, with careful monitoring by the SEC. At times, the SEC has taken more direct action, through Accounting Series Releases, to influence the AICPA to modify its body of GAAS. The large CPA firms supplement and interpret GAAS in order to achieve uniformity in practices among their numerous offices. Some of the areas in which interpretations have occurred include the following:

- Form and content of engagement letters
- Representation letters from outside legal counsel
- Confirmation practices
- Observation of physical inventories
- Study and evaluation of internal accounting control

- Use of statistical and judgment sampling
- Use of the firm name
- Form and content of representation letters
- Report qualifications
- Correspondence on technical matters
- Letters to underwriters

Over the years, the actions of the CPA firms, the AICPA, the SEC, and the states, through cooperative interaction, have developed the standards governing the practice of public accounting. Standards setting in government auditing is the responsibility of the GAO.

The practice of internal auditing is regulated by neither a governmental organization nor an independent organization. Hence, the development of standards for that branch of auditing is strictly a private sector voluntary effort.

Self-Regulation

Practitioners of public accounting in the 1970s realized that actions were necessary to prevent the government from becoming directly involved in regulating their activities. Three of these subsequent actions that stand out and deserve discussion are:

1. The division in 1977 of the AICPA into two divisions—the SEC practices section (SECPS) and the private companies practice section (or PCPS).
2. The creation of the Public Oversight Board (POB).
3. The establishment of a peer review program for SECPS member firms.

The first action saved a considerable segment of AICPA member firms from the costs of establishing and maintaining a peer review program. More importantly, however, it fostered the development of an organizational structure in which self-regulation could be exacted.

Self-regulation actions aimed at the SECPS were obviously more extensive and elaborate than those for the PCPS. Specific requirements for membership are given in the *Peer Review Manual* (AICPA, 1979). A summary of these requirements is presented in Figure 3-1.

The POB was created to serve as an overseer of the activities of the Executive Committee of SECPS and of the peer review program. It consists of five individuals from outside the profession with established reputations for integrity and concern for public interest. The POB has access to all files, meetings, and other activities of the SECPS and the authority to hire staff. Annually, the POB reports the results of its oversight efforts.

In 1984, the annual report of the POB came in two parts—one part was a report on the prior year's progress. The other was devoted to describing

FIG. 3-1

Summary of Major Requirements for SEC Practice Section Membership

- The firm's quality controls over its accounting and auditing practice are to be subjected to peer review every three years, and at any other time as may be imposed as part of a disciplinary action.
- All partners and members of the professional staff resident in the USA must complete at least 120 hours of continuing professional education over three years, but not less than 20 hours in any given year.
- The audit partner in charge of an SEC engagement can serve in that capacity for a maximum of five consecutive years.
- A preissuance concurring review of an audit report for an SEC client must be made by a partner other than the audit partner in charge.
- The firm must provide specified information annually about its operations for inclusion in files open to the public.
- The firm must fulfill certain requirements set by the Executive Committee with regard to its independence.
- Total fees for management consulting services, and a description of their types, must be reported annually to the audit committee or board of an SEC client. Disagreements with management on material financial accounting and reporting matters and auditing procedures must likewise be reported.
- A firm must promptly report to the Special Investigations Committee any litigation against it or its personnel, or publicly announced investigations by regulatory agencies, where these matters allege deficiencies in auditing and reporting on SEC clients or former clients.

Source: John C. Burton, Russell E. Palmer, Robert S. Kay, *Handbook of Accounting and Auditing* (Boston: Warren, Gorham & Lamont, Inc. 1981). Reprinted by permission.

the self-regulatory program of the AICPA.[3] The report was significantly longer than previous reports. Perhaps this reflects an awareness on the part of the profession of the importance of telling its self-regulatory story.

Whether that story is sufficiently impressive to keep Congress from enacting legislation that would put the profession into a government-regulated world is uncertain. Representative Ron Wyden, author of the House bill that would have significantly altered the responsibilities of CPAs, criticized the POB during subcommittee hearings. In particular, he noted that the POB has never made a public pronouncement of any wrongdoing,[4] despite the fact that it is responsible for reporting findings of peer reviews. This system, in his view, could easily promote a conflict of interest among accountants.

The number of firms joining SECPS represents a small percentage of

---

[3] Public Oversight Board, *Audit Quality: The Profession's Program* (New York: AICPA, 1984).

[4] "Dingell Hearings Continue to Probe Auditor's Role in Financial Reporting," *Accounting News,* Summer 1985, p. 8.

all member firms of the AICPA. It is estimated that about 400 firms are current members of SECPS. These firms account for 85 percent of all SEC audit clients, however.[5]

Regardless of how the current congressional inquiry turns out, the AICPA can be proud of its role, in recent years, in responding to the challenges it faces. The peer review program its SECPS division has developed has done much to forward the cause of self-regulation. In the words of former AICPA Chairman Rholan E. Larson:

> Many firms that have undergone peer reviews will testify that it was a worthwhile process. Some have questioned the cost-benefit relationship of the process, but most believe in the value of peer review as firms use it as a foundation for quality control, practice growth and professional development. As a direct result of joining the division, many firms have developed well-thought-out systems of quality control that fit in with their emphasis on a strong and competent staff with effective partner leadership and supervision.[6]

In spite of the positive contributions that result from the peer review process, not all public accounting practitioners favor mandatory self-regulation. As noted earlier, the full membership rejected such a requirement in a 1987 ballot. The opposition seems to be represented primarily by small firms. One possible concern is that the increased cost of being a member of SECPS would place many firms at a competitive disadvantage in the non-SEC segment of the financial statement auditing market. These firms may fear that once they join, they will be drawn into an ever-increasing cycle of regulatory activity—a cycle over which they would exercise little control—thereby increasing the competitive pressures they will face.

In this scenario, they would be dominated by the major firms in the SEC segment while being squeezed by non-SECPS practitioners in the non-SEC segment. Their options would indeed be bleak. The choice would be to reject joining SECPS with the probable result of losing their SEC practice, or join SECPS and risk losing not only their non-SEC practice but their identity as a separate practicing firm.

There may possibly be another alternative for these firms. It may be possible for them to create a separate self-regulating apparatus. Such an effort would not be easy, and there is no assurance that ultimately its cost would be less than that of SECPS. Finally, there is the question of whether such an apparatus would be acceptable to the SEC.

On that issue, the SEC seems to have spoken. In April 1987, the SEC proposed rules requiring CPAs who audit financial statements of publicly

---

[5] "AICPA Rejects Proposal to Mandate Peer Review as Membership Requirement," *Security Regulation & Law Reports,* Apr. 10, 1987, p. 510.

[6] Rholan E. Larson, "Self-Regulation: A Professional Step Forward," *Journal of Accountancy,* Sept. 1985, p. 60.

held companies to undergo a peer review every three years.[7] However, the proposed rules provide a choice for CPAs. They could have the review supervised by the SEC directly or by an acceptable peer review organization (PRO).

PROs would have to meet requirements set forth in the proposed rules. These rules provide that any PRO have a body of at least three independent individuals to represent the public interest in overseeing PRO activities. Such a body would be similar to the five-member POB that oversees the work of the SECPS. The rules also cover qualifications of peer reviewers, the study of the firm's quality controls, the documentation of the peer review, the peer review report, and the firm's response.

Such proposed rules make clear that any PRO will have to look very much like the one already established within the AICPA. The National Conference of CPA Practitioners is known to be developing such an organization for smaller firms.

Regardless of how successful this effort will be, it seems clear that the SEC and the AICPA are solidly supporting the concept of self-regulation.

One possible outcome of the current round of attention is some sort of public sanctioning mechanism for firms who fail to pass peer review or otherwise are involved in audit failures. How this might contribute toward improving quality is a hotly debated topic. Members are rightly fearful that public sanctions in the litigation-prone business environment in which CPAs operate will expose them to immeasurable new risks.

CONTRIBUTIONS OF PROFESSIONAL ORGANIZATIONS TO STANDARDS SETTING

If standards are to be effectively established outside the government, then those involved in the private sector must be organized for the purpose. Thus, standards setting is one of the principal services provided by private sector associations. The fact that numerous and varied standards have evolved through private sector effort supports the notion that the private sector is usually able to establish standards more effectively than are regulatory government agencies. This is particularly true for professional and industrial standards and, as a result, many technical associations and societies have the formulation and maintenance of standards as one of their primary functions. Examples include the American Society for Testing and Materials, the National Fire Protection Association, the American Association of Engineering Societies, and the American Society of Mechanical Engineering. The standards-setting activities of these and similar organizations occurs as

---

[7] Securities and Exchange Commission, Independent Accountants—Mandatory Peer Review [Release, Nos. 33-6695, 34-24289; 35-24360; IC-15655; IA-1064; File No. S7-13-86].

the result of voluntary efforts of individual members with appropriate qualifications. Similarly, professional organizations such as the American Medical Association and American Bar Association have established standards as have the AICPA and the IIA.

AICPA

In addition to establishing standards, these private sector organizations must continually interpret and update them in response to changing conditions. Among the professional accounting associations, the AICPA has by far been the most active in this regard. The history of the development of the practice of public accounting provides some insight as to the reasons for this activity. An interesting account of this history appeared in the AICPA Centennial Issue of the *Journal of Accountancy*. A portion of that article is reprinted in Figure 3-2.[8]

Another account of the history of auditing standards setting, written by John Carey, includes discussion of a 1929 court case that upset the widely held assumption that in cases of negligence, accountants could be held liable only to those with whom they had a contractual relationship. This now famous case—the *Ultramares* case—also established the principle that negligence might of itself be evidence from which an inference of fraud could be drawn, even though there was no evidence of intent to deceive anyone.[9] Shortly thereafter, in 1932, the U.S. insurance company that had agreed to provide indemnity insurance policies for accountants discontinued the coverage.[10] Eventually, another underwriter was found.

These events, which occurred during the height of the Depression, emphasized to public accountants that their role in auditing was unique and their liability exposure singular when compared to that of other audit practitioners, such as internal auditors or government auditors. The succession of landmark cases since *Ultramares* have broadened this exposure even further. It is little wonder, then, that public accountants have dominated the development of professional auditing standards.

In 1974, the AICPA began a loose-leaf service, *Professional Standards*, which has codified on an ongoing basis the pronouncements of the ASB. A list of the original pronouncements and their issue dates is set forth in Appendix B of Volume 1 of that service. It is evident from its record that the AICPA recognizes that maintenance of acceptable standards is an ongoing function vital to the practice of public accounting. Its activities in the area

---

[8] Sidney Davidson and George D. Anderson, "The Development of Accounting and Auditing Standards," *Journal of Accountancy*, May 1987, pp. 123–136. Reprinted by permission.

[9] John L. Carey, *The Rise of the Accounting Profession From Technical to Professional—1896–1936* (New York: AICPA, 1969), p. 257.

[10] *Ibid.*, p. 258.

FIG. 3-2

Setting Auditing Standards: 1917–1987

The process of setting auditing standards has been relatively smooth compared to that of prescribing accounting principles, although there has been an equal number of shifts in the rule-making body in each case. The first official pronouncement, "Uniform Accounts," published in 1917 in the Federal Reserve Bulletin and later retitled *Approved Methods for the Preparation of Balance Sheet Statements,* sought to deal with both accounting principles and auditing standards as described earlier. The booklet stressed detailed verification of individual items but contained no prescriptions on how such verifications were to be reported. No standard form of the auditor's certificate was prescribed or even suggested in the booklet.

Over the years there had been too many instances of auditor's certificates that contained the phrase "subject to the foregoing." The certificate might say, "We certify that, in our opinion, the financial statements of the XYZ Corporation are correctly set forth, subject to the foregoing, the financial position. . . ." The term "foregoing" might deal with such items as depreciation, bad debts or other valuations. John Carey quotes a jingle that some CPAs had jokingly circulated:

We have audited this balance sheet and say in our report
That the cash is overstated, the cashier being short;
That the customers' receivables are very much past due;
That if there are some good ones they are very, very few;
That the inventories are out of date and principally junk;
That the method of their pricing is very largely bunk;
That, according to our figures, the undertaking's wrecked,
But, subject to these comments, the balance sheet's correct.

A revision with greater emphasis on auditing standards entitled *Verification of Financial Statements* was published in 1929 by the Institute. In 1934 a second revision, *Audits of Corporate Accounts,* was released, followed two years later by a third revision entitled *Examination of Financial Statements by Independent Public Accountants.* This last revision included many recommended procedures that had been worked out in correspondence with the NYSE. The final version took an equivocal stance on two important auditing questions: observation of inventories and confirmation of receivables. The statement suggested that observation and confirmation would be desirable in many cases but not required.

The McKesson & Robbins case three years later showed that these two nonrequired audit procedures had contributed to a coverup of a gigantic fraud that had been going-on for years. At the end of 1937 the "certified" financial statements of McKesson & Robbins reported total assets of over $87 million, of which some $19 million—$10 million of inventory and $9 million of receivables—were later found to be fictitious. The case attracted widespread attention in the press and led to investigations by the SEC and the New York State attorney general.

The Institute promptly responded to the scandal, setting up the committee on auditing procedure (CAuP) in 1939. Recognizing the need for quick action by the profession, within months the CAuP had both prepared and published Statement on Auditing Procedure (SAP) no. 1. Calling for observation of inventories and the confirmation of receivables, SAP no. 1 suggested that the independent auditor either be selected by the board of directors or elected annually by the stockholders. The statement also recommended new wording of the standard form of the auditor's opinion and, even more important, emphasized the review of a company's system of internal control in order to determine how much reliance could be placed on company records.

The McKesson & Robbins case gave the profession much unfavorable publicity, but the response to it led to the creation of the highly constructive committee on auditing procedure. The fiasco also forced the profession to recognize that a dynamic program for developing auditing standards was sorely needed.

The SEC indicated its support of the CAuP when it issued ASR no. 21, requiring that "the accountant shall state whether the audit was made in accordance with generally accepted auditing standards applicable in the circumstances." In 1947 the committee issued its report, *Tentative Statement of Auditing Standards—Their Generally Accepted Significance and Scope*, listing nine auditing standards. Shortly thereafter a tenth standard was added to the report, which was approved by Institute members.

The committee continued to issue SAPs on various auditing topics and in 1963 issued SAP no. 33, a codification of the first 32 SAPs, entitled Auditing Standards and Procedures. It also issued 21 additional statements before it was replaced by the auditing standards executive committee (AudSEC) in 1972.

AudSEC was designated as the sole spokesman for the Institute on auditing topics. Rule 202 of the Code of Professional Ethics, entitled "Statements of Auditing Standards (SAS)," gave the pronouncements of AudSEC the same authority as the FASB statements—that is, a member must call attention in the attestation to a departure from the statements and must justify such a departure.

SAS no. 1 was a codification of all previous pronouncements on auditing standards, and between 1972 and 1974 three additional SASs were issued. Still, by 1974 some congressional critics, particularly Senator Lee Metcalf and Congressman John Moss, were beginning to raise the question of whether independent auditors were living up to the expectations of the investing public. Partly as a result of the questioning by congressional committees, in 1974 the Institute set up the Commission on Auditors' Responsibilities (the Cohen commission, so named after its chairman Manuel Cohen, a former SEC chairman).

The charge to the Cohen commission was to determine whether "a gap may exist between what the public expects and needs and what auditors can and should reasonably expect to accomplish. If such a gap does exist, it needs to be explored to determine how the disparity can be resolved." In its 1977 report the commission concluded that an expectations gap did exist, and it provided a list of recommended steps that would remedy the situation. The Institute adopted several recommendations, but two major ones weren't put into effect: to change the wording of the standard form of the auditor's report and to replace AudSEC with a smaller full-time board, much like the FASB.

Concerning the first of these recommendations, there was substantial agreement that the wording was far from perfect, but no consensus on improved wording could be developed. A compromise was reached on the second recommendation. In 1978 AudSEC was reduced in size, its name was changed to the auditing standards board (ASB) and it received additional research and administrative help. The ASB continued to use the SAS title for its pronouncements, and its numbering continues where AudSEC left off.

As a result of several publicized business failures, characterized by some as audit failures as well as an adverse report published by the Government Accounting Office, by 1985 congressional critics were again stirring. Committees chaired by Congressmen Jack Brooks and John Dingell are now studying the effectiveness of the audit process, focusing on the expectations gap. Partly as a result of the congressional inquiries and partly as an attempt to deal with the expectations gap, in 1985 the Institute—in cooperation with several other accounting and financial organizations—established the National Commission on Fraudulent Financial Reporting (the Treadway commission, named after its chairman, former SEC Commissioner James Treadway).

(continued)

FIG. 3-2 *(cont'd)*

> The Treadway commission plans to issue its report some time this year. It will undoubtedly contain recommendations for some changes in the standard-setting process and in the role of the independent public accountant. Meanwhile, the ASB continues to work actively to develop more effective standards.
>
> Almost two decades ago John Carey said: "In contrast with the turmoil in which statements on accounting principles were developed, the enunciation of authoritative guidelines for independent audits has been a steady, orderly process. One reason for this, no doubt, is that the extent and adequacy of their examinations are the responsibility of the accountants alone, whereas management, auditors, and regulatory bodies have shared responsibility for the representations made in financial statements."
>
> Congressional inquiries and two independent study commissions have reduced the full accuracy of Carey's statement. Yet, even today audit standard development can be described as a "steady, orderly process."
>
> The development of accounting and auditing standards has been an evolutionary process. On a few occasions the development of accounting standards has seemingly regressed, but it's important to note how much progress has been made in such a short time. The decades of developing accounting and auditing standards have helped to make Goethe's "one of the finest inventions of the human spirit" play an even more significant role in our economic society.

of standards setting influence not only its membership but also the form and content of standards set by the other branches of auditing.

IIA

The emphasis on standards-setting activity of the IIA differs from that of the AICPA. Not until 1978 did the IIA adopt a set of broad standards, which are presented in summary form in Chapter 6. It was not until 1983 that the IIA's PSRC offered the first SAS.

In part, this paucity in formal standards-setting activity is attributable to the fact that the IIA occupies a somewhat dissimilar position vis-à-vis its members than does the AICPA. The latter group requires conformity with GAAS and provides for enforcement under Rule 202 (Auditing Standards) of its Code of Professional Ethics. Further, the SEC uses GAAS as one means of regulating conduct of practicing CPAs. Finally, the various state laws governing the practice of public accounting invariably require audits of financial statements to be performed in accordance with GAAS. Failure to comply with these standards constitutes grounds for revocation of the license to practice accounting before the public.

There is no comparable enforcement apparatus in effect in the case of the IIA, nor does there seem to be any need for one. Failure to perform internal auditing in accordance with standards does not carry high public exposure. By contrast, failure by CPAs to perform the attest function in

AUDITING STANDARDS DEVELOPMENT 3-13

accordance with GAAS can have grave public consequences. Additionally, the absence of the constant pressure of regulatory and judicial forces evaluating internal auditor performance is another factor that contributes to the different approach to standards setting followed by the IIA. Thus, standards setting is much less critical a function to the IIA than it is to the AICPA. This is not to say that the IIA does not consider standards to be important; it does. However, it allocates more of its resources to such other beneficial membership activities as the CIA Program, a continuing development program, a program of seminars and self-study courses, and several research projects.

The IIA standards are beginning to receive broader recognition, a positive indicator that the profession itself is receiving broader recognition. In its discussion of the importance of internal auditing, the Treadway Commission encourages public companies to consider adopting the IIA standards.[11] It also provides the standards as an appendix to its basic report.[12]

GAO

The development of auditing standards for federal government auditing has evolved to become largely a service performed by the GAO. In 1972, the GAO issued "Standards Programs, Activities & Functions," better known as the yellow book. Since then, the GAO has issued various interpretive publications that demonstrate how the effectiveness and efficiency of government operations can be improved by auditing. To give the standards an authoritative boost, the Office of Management and Budget cited them in circulars as the basic audit criteria for federal executive departments and agencies to follow. Also, federal legislation requires that the standards be followed by the various federal inspectors general.[13]

IIA Standards Differentiated

A brief comparison of the IIA standards with those of the GAO and the AICPA serves to reinforce the point made in Chapter 1 that there are, indeed, three distinct branches of auditing. The IIA standards are similar to those of both the AICPA and GAO in that they cover independence, proficiency (or competence), and due professional care. In addition, they all require a study and evaluation of internal control and prescribe standards for the per-

---

[11] The National Commission on Fraudulent Financial Reporting, *Report of the National Commission on Fraudulent Financial Reporting* (Washington, D.C.: National Commission on Fraudulent Financial Reporting, 1987), p. 37.

[12] *Ibid.*, Appendix I, pp. 169–180.

[13] Comptroller General of the United States, *Standards for Audit of Governmental Organizations, Programs, Activities, and Functions*, 1981 revision, p. i.

formance of audit work. However, both the IIA and the GAO go beyond the AICPA in requiring an assessment of the quality of performance of assigned responsibilities.

The standards of the IIA differ from those of the AICPA and the GAO in that they are more generally stated, primarily in the area of reporting. This is attributable to the more varied types of auditing performed by internal auditors. Another uniqueness is that the IIA standards contain a section on managing the internal auditing department.

Internal Auditors' Reporting Relationships and Standards

A further comparison of the IIA standards with those of the other professional groups discloses an interesting difference regarding independence. Internal auditors, unlike their counterparts in public accounting and government auditing, are employed by the entities at which their audit efforts are directed. Thus, it is imperative that the internal audit department report to an officer sufficiently high in the hierarchy of the company and that it be reasonably independent in its conduct of audit programs.

In practice, actual organizational arrangements often fell short of this imperative. Until the late 1970s, the heads of internal audit departments most frequently reported to the controller or an assistant controller. Therefore, (1) they did not command sufficient attention; (2) they were not as independent of the accounting control system as desired; and (3) resources allocated to the audit department were sometimes insufficient to enable the function to fulfill its objectives.

In recent years, the independence of auditors has improved dramatically. Managements have elevated the reporting relationship of internal auditors, employed more professionally trained auditors, and taken greater interest in their activities and reports. By the same token, the quality of work performed by the internal auditor has improved immeasurably.

On the whole, these developments have been very favorable from the standpoint of the internal auditor. The elevated stature of internal auditors offers the exciting and rewarding potential for performing audits for a higher management level, although it also requires adhering to high standards. This fact has posed a challenge to many internal auditors. In response to past management comments regarding the quality of work, many internal audit departments found it necessary to establish their own standards. For the most part, these preceded the standards published by the IIA in 1978. Others have developed their own standards because they believe the various published standards must be supplemented.[14] Regardless of how they are developed, high standards are critical to the success of the function.

---

[14] Robert A. King, "A Practitioner Looks at Auditing Standards and Risk Analysis," *The Internal Auditor*, Oct. 1981, p. 60.

GENERAL AUDITING STANDARDS

The areas most commonly addressed by auditing standards may be divided into two categories:

1. General
   - Independence
   - Competence
   - Due diligence
2. Specific
   - Managing
   - Planning
   - Performing and testing
   - Reporting
   - Documenting

Discussions of the specific standards are provided in Chapters 7–10. Further remarks on the general standards are required here. As an overall comment, before beginning separate discussions, it must be made clear that the concepts of independence, competence, and due diligence are related. A lack of one—diligence, for example—presupposes a lack of competence. An auditor who is not independent is probably incapable of performing an audit with sufficient due diligence. The interrelationship must be kept in mind by the reader during the following separate discussions.

Independence

The concept of independence invariably discussed in reference works on auditing in terms of its value and importance to proper and effective auditing, but the concept is not often specifically defined. Perhaps that is because it is more informative to describe what independence is or is not than to define it.

In the AICPA *Professional Standards,* Vol. 1 (AU Section 220.02), independence is described as being without bias with respect to the client, since otherwise, the auditor would lack that impartiality necessary for the objectivity of his findings. The section goes on to state that independence does not imply the attitude of a prosecutor, but rather a judicial impartiality.

The dictionary definition offers some useful insight by defining the term "independent" as "not subject to control by others," or "not looking to others for one's opinion or for guidance in conduct."[15]

SEC Definition. Some have described independence by describing circumstances in which independence may be presumed to be compromised.

---

[15] Webster's New Collegiate Dictionary (U.S.A.: G. & C. Merriam, 1980), p. 577.

The best illustration of this is offered by the SEC which, according to Rappaport, deserves much of the credit for accelerating the development of the independence concept.[16] In Regulation S-X: Rules 2-01(b) and 2-01(c), the SEC provided the following regarding its view of the subject:

> (b) The Commission will not recognize any certified public accountant or public accountant as independent who is not in fact independent. For example, an accountant will be considered not independent with respect to any person or any of its parents, its subsidiaries, or other affiliates (1) in which, during the period of his professional engagement to examine the financial statements being reported on or at the date of his report, he or his firm or a member thereof had, or was committed to acquire, any direct financial interest or any material indirect financial interest; (2) with which during the period of his professional engagement to examine the financial statements being reported on, at the date of his report or during the period covered by the financial statements, he or his firm or a member thereof was connected as a promoter, underwriter, voting trustee, director, officer, or employee, except that a firm will not be deemed not independent in regard to a particular person if a former officer or employee of such person is employed by the firm and such individual has completely disassociated himself from the person and its affiliates and does not participate in auditing financial statements of the person or its affiliates covering any period of his employment by the person. For the purposes of Rule 2-01 the term "member" means all partners in the firm and all professional employees participating in the audit or located in an office of the firm participating in a significant portion of the audit.
>
> (c) In determining whether an accountant may in fact be not independent with respect to a particular person, the Commission will give appropriate consideration to all relevant circumstances, including evidence bearing on all relationships between the accountant and that person or any affiliate thereof, and will not confine itself to the relationships existing in connection with the filing of reports with the Commission.

Noteworthy in this SEC statement is the absence of the conditions in which the CPA is not, *in fact,* independent. Rather, in recognition of the concept that independence is a mental attitude or frame of mind, the SEC provides examples of conditions in which it will *consider* that the CPA is not independent. The significance of this distinction is that the SEC recognizes the value of the *perception* of the auditor's independence on the part of the public and others. The profession, through the AICPA, has also displayed a high awareness of the importance of the presumption of independence. The Institute's Code of Professional Ethics is, in part, a direct response to this awareness.

---

[16] Louis H. Rappaport, *SEC Accounting Practice and Procedure*, 2nd ed. (New York: The Ronald Press Co., 1966), p. 22–6.

IIA Definition. The IIA, too, has formally recognized the importance of independence in its Statement of Responsibilities, which reads in part:[17]

> Independence is essential to the effectiveness of internal auditing. This independence is obtained primarily through organizational status and objectivity:
>
> - The organizational status of the internal auditing function and the support accorded to it by management are major determinants of its range and value. The head of the internal auditing function, therefore, should be responsible to an officer whose authority is sufficient to assure both a broad range of audit coverage and the adequate consideration of and effective action on the audit findings and recommendations.
> - Objectivity is essential to the audit function. Therefore, internal auditors should not develop and install procedures, prepare records, or engage in any other activity which they would normally review and appraise and which could reasonably be construed to compromise the independence of the internal auditor. The internal auditor's objectivity need not be adversely affected, however, by determining and recommending standards of control to be applied in the development of the systems and procedures being reviewed.

In summary, independence is important to all auditors and those who benefit from their services because it reasonably assures that observations and opinions will be expressed free of prejudice or influence. In order to maintain an independent mental attitude, a healthy degree of skepticism must be exhibited by all auditors. The extent to which this healthy skepticism is practiced will normally be evident in the auditor's workpapers. (See Chapters 9 and 12.)

Competence

Competence is expressed in the professional standards of the three branches of auditing in terms of proficiency. It may be distinguished from independence in that competence has to do with a person's ability to do something properly, while independence may be thought of as the freedom to do it without bias. Auditing competence or proficiency may be defined as possessing sufficient technical knowledge and skill to be able to function effectively as an auditor.

Sufficient technical knowledge is obtained through formal education and subsequent professional training and experience. While levels of skill may have varied in earlier years, most internal audit departments now require that staff members possess a college or university degree, usually in a busi-

---

[17] From *The Statement of Responsibilities of Internal Auditors,* originally issued by The Institute of Internal Auditors in 1947. The continuing development of the profession has resulted in four revisions: 1957, 1971, 1976, and 1981.

ness-related field such as accounting or finance. The experience generally required for internal auditors is comprised of the following areas of expertise:

- Auditing standards and procedures
- Generally accepted principles of accounting
- Internal controls in general, and internal accounting control in particular
- Analytical skills
- Communications skills

In addition, internal auditors should have a general awareness of related business-oriented disciplines, such as financing, electronic data processing, business law, taxation, economics, security, and business management. In particular circumstances, the internal audit department may need to employ individuals who are experts in fields such as these.

In addition to the foregoing, internal auditors within each major industrial classification must possess or develop a knowledge of the distinguishing characteristics of those industries. This includes unique competitive aspects, key business factors, management styles, operational approaches, finance and accounting principles and methodologies, and regulatory requirements. Examples of industries requiring special awareness or knowledge are as follows:

- Banking
- Insurance
- Railroads
- Oil and gas
- Aerospace

- Retail merchandising
- Entertainment
- Automotive
- Health care
- Construction

Beyond that, each company has specific product lines, organizational structures and policies, procedures, and systems with which the internal auditor must be familiar. In summary, internal auditors share as a starting point a common body of knowledge. Within industrial segments and individual companies, that common body of knowledge is supplemented with further knowledge to enable auditors to be considered truly competent.

As the internal audit function evolves and changes in response to both professional and industrial developments, the requisite knowledge must change. All auditors should keep current with these changes through participation in continuing programs of professional education. The pace of change has been so rapid in recent years that keeping current with new developments or techniques requires considerable effort. A great many seminars, conferences, training programs, and self-study courses are available; however, care must be taken to avoid wasting time with courses presenting useless or invalid information. Chapter 9 discussed techniques applicable to staff training and development.

Due Diligence

If independence represents doing something in an unbiased, unrestricted fashion, and if competence represents the degree of knowledge and skill employed in a given audit, then due diligence is the extent to which such skills are applied in the specific circumstance. It may be thought of as self-discipline or attention to duty. Due diligence is also discussed or referred to in professional literature as due professional care. In AU Section 230.02 of the AICPA's *Professional Standards,* Vol. 1, it is stated that "due care imposes a responsibility upon each person within an independent auditor's organization to observe the standards of field work and reporting." The observation applies to internal auditors as well. However, as the following quotation from the *Standards for the Professional Practice of Internal Auditing* indicates, due professional care has its limits.

> Due care implies reasonable care and competence, not infallibility or extraordinary performance. Due care requires the auditor to conduct examinations and verifications to a reasonable extent, but does not require detailed audits of all transactions.[18]

These are general statements, to be sure, and applying them in particular circumstances can be extremely challenging. For this reason, skill, experience, and judgment are critical factors in any audit.

Over the years, the SEC and the courts have given additional shape and form to this general definition of due professional care (not to mention independence and competence), insofar as public accounting is concerned. This involvement has stemmed from a comparatively small number of business failures and frauds causing investor losses attributable in part to the external auditors' failure to detect or report the circumstances in a timely fashion. The applicability of many audit procedures widened as a result of these cases. Examples include the observation of inventories, confirmation of receivables, and the effects of EDP on the auditor's evaluation of internal control.

From a legal standpoint, the definition of due care is important. It is defined as "the performance of, and reporting on, professional engagements with at least the degree of care, competence, learning, and experience commonly possessed by members of the profession and required by professional standards."[19] The experience of public accountants and the legal definition is useful to internal auditors for information purposes, since future internal

---

[18] *Standards for the Professional Practice of Internal Auditing* (Altamonte Springs, Fla.: The Institute of Internal Auditors, 1978), p. 200-3.

[19] R. James Gormley, "Auditing and the Law," in *Handbook of Accounting and Auditing,* John C. Burton, Russell E. Palmer, Robert S. Kay, eds. (New York: Warren, Gorham & Lamont, 1980), p. 46-3.

auditors may be significantly involved in litigation involving the issue of due diligence. The internal auditor's rise in status and critical role in many companies in relation to internal control and standards of business conduct may bring increased legal exposure.

It is worthwhile, in view of the practical exposure, to briefly analyze the experience of public accountants with respect to audit failures to see what lessons are evident. The following is a partial list of the types of failures involving due diligence in various SEC proceedings:

- Failure to evaluate effectiveness of internal controls
- Failure to obtain sufficient evidence to confirm management's representations regarding material transactions
- Failure to employ adequate inventory observation procedures
- Failure to perform sufficient inquiry in taking on new engagements
- Performance of audits with a marked disregard for GAAP
- Failure to consider evidence readily at hand indicating the true nature of the transaction

It should be clear that, for the most part, these deficiencies involve aspects of auditing common to both internal and external auditors.

In searching for underlying causes, at least one factor seems to recur frequently. In each case, the need to complete the audit on a specific time schedule was perceived to be more important than the need to perform further work. This time pressure may have become great enough to have adversely affected auditors' judgments.

In its research, the Cohen Commission found that many practitioners "signed off" as having completed required audit steps without having actually performed them.[20] The Commission also found that new staff auditors are more prone to nonperformance than are more experienced auditors. In addition, the situations in which nonperformance might occur, according to the Commission, are as follows:

- Any area in which the individual concludes, without seeking concurrence or approval, that the audit procedure is unwarranted
- Where other sources of information have been reliable
- Where little workpaper documentation is required

The pressures leading to nonperformance invariably resulted from the belief that it was more important to get the job done and receive a good performance evaluation. Of course, intentional misrepresentation of performance is not necessarily involved in all cases of audit failures, but it is quite likely that time pressures account for much of it.

---

[20] The Commission on Auditors' Responsibilities, *op. cit.*, p. 179.

A study of 129 cases of audit failure by St. Pierre and Anderson suggests that some audit failures would have occurred even if there were no time pressures.[21] These include those involving errors in application of accounting principles. The authors asserted that time is not a factor in such situations, which is a debatable point. The proficiency of the auditor in dealing with conceptual matters was stated to be the critical factor in those cases. Whether proficiency, diligence, or both are involved is somewhat irrelevant. The point is that some evidence exists suggesting that professionalism may be sacrificed more often than is generally realized.

Internal auditors should learn from the experiences of their external counterparts. When diligence is exchanged for economy or other considerations, the risk of failure increases. The chief auditor must not sacrifice quality for quantity in conducting the practice of internal auditing. Accordingly, the importance of due diligence should be stressed in audit manuals, in staff training, and in project reviews. Sufficient time budgets for all aspects of audit projects should be developed to permit the entire planned program of required work to be performed, including adequate planning and preparation. Performing auditors must feel confident that they are suitably prepared to perform the work and that they understand and concur with all aspects of it. Compliance with these guidelines should be easier for internal auditors than for external auditors, since there are fewer reasons for time to become a limiting factor. That is because the type of absolute deadlines involved in external financial reporting are not usually encountered in internal audit projects.

FINAL COMMENTS ON PROFESSIONALISM, STANDARDS, AND AUDIT TECHNIQUES

This chapter presents a perspective of the broad standards by which each of the three audit branches—public accounting, government auditing, and internal auditing—perform their respective audit services. These standards serve both the branches and the users of the services of the branches. Standards, if followed, help to assure audits of high quality and enable the performance of the auditors to be evaluated.

As stated in this chapter, each body of standards contains similar pronouncements regarding competence, independence, and due diligence. It is these aspects of the standards that generate professionalism in any practice of auditing. In the case of internal and external auditors, the question may be asked, If the standards are similar and, if the two groups are equally professional, why do differences in practices exist between the two? It is

---

[21] Kent St. Pierre and James Anderson, "An Analysis of Audit Failures Based on Documental Legal Cases," *Journal of Accounting, Auditing and Finance,* Spring 1982, p. 241.

true that the public accounting profession has been more prolific in the production of authoritative pronouncements affecting that practice than its counterparts in internal auditing have been, for reasons previously explained. There are those who believe that internal auditors should strive to emulate the practices embodied in GAAS of the public accountants.[22] However, in contemplating standards for performance, one must consider the differences in management relationships and other inherent differences that distinguish the respective practices.

While independence is essential for effective internal auditing, the degree to which independence must be *demonstrated* is not as great as in the case of external auditors. This is because the primary user of the work product of the internal auditor is management, including the board of directors. This group is better informed and more knowledgeable with respect to the company than is the public, the primary users of the external auditor's work. Management also is close to, and aware of, the internal audit function and, as a result, can effectively appraise audit quality most of the time. The same cannot be said for the public vis-à-vis the external auditor. These differences translate into procedural and perhaps documentational differences. The distinction is difficult, if not impossible, to isolate in specific situations. Suffice it to say that substantive comparisons of workpapers between external and internal auditors would probably reveal less attention to documenting the supporting reasons for audit judgments in the case of the latter. Internal auditors realize the need for professionalism in the conduct of their work. However, they also realize that because their relationship with management and the board of directors differs from that of external auditors, questions regarding the nature and extent of work performed and the way in which it is documented take on less significance for their purposes. For this reason, internal auditors are often puzzled and, at times, frustrated by efforts on the part of external auditors to require internal audit approaches and workpapers to conform with external auditor formats and techniques.

Clearly, both external and internal auditors must employ high standards of professionalism, including independence, competence, and diligence. The extent to which this must be demonstrated is greater for external auditors. The extent to which high standards can be maintained through differing practices is a subject requiring further research before definitive conclusions can be made.

SUGGESTED READING

AICPA, *Professional Standards,* Vol. 1, *Historical Background* (AU Appendix A). AICPA, 1979.

---

[22] Paul W. Wilson, "Planning and Operation of the Internal Audit Department," *Retail Control,* 1978, p. 3.

Carey, John L. *The Rise of the Accounting Profession, From Technical to Professional—1896–1936*. New York: AICPA, 1969.

The Commission on Auditors' Responsibilities: Report, Conclusions and Recommendations. New York: The Commission on Auditors' Responsibilities, 1978.

Comptroller General of the United States. *Standards for Audit of Governmental Organizations, Programs, Activities and Functions*. Washington, D.C.: U.S. Government Printing Office, 1981.

———. *Standards for Audit of Governmental Organizations, Programs, Activities and Functions*, 1981 revision.

Robertson, Jack C. "Auditing Standards." *Handbook of Accounting and Auditing*, eds. J. Burton, R. Palmer, & R. Kay. New York: Warren, Gorham & Lamont, 1981.

Standards for the Professional Practice of Internal Auditing. Altamonte Springs, Fla.: The Institute of Internal Auditors, 1978.

Statement on Auditing Standards No. 1, *Codification of Auditing Standards and Procedures*. AICPA, *Professional Standards* AU §§ 150–561 (Nov. 1972).

CHAPTER 4

Generally Accepted Auditing Standards

Definition	1	The Ten GAAS	8
Purpose	2	Standards Applicable to Other Audit-Related Financial Statement Services	14
Elements of GAAS	3	Unaudited Financial Statements	14
Identification of Elements	3	Interim-Period Financial Statements	16
The Code of Professional Ethics	3	Prospective Financial Statements	17
The Role of the Auditing Standards Board	4	Attestation Standards	18
Approach in Standards Setting	4	Specialized Industry Auditing	19
Impact of Congressional Inquiry	6	Standards for Other Services	20
Impact of Other Inquiries	6	Tax Services	20
Other Standards-Setting Activities of the ASB	7	Management Advisory Services	20
Other AICPA Standards-Setting Groups	7	Recent Changes	21
		Suggested Reading	23

FIG. 4-1 List of Authoritative Auditing Standards Pronouncements ... 10

DEFINITION

The term "generally accepted auditing standards" (GAAS) is not defined in professional literature per se. It is however, the body of auditing standards accepted by members of the AICPA for use in performing independent examinations of financial statements for the purpose of expressing opinions regarding conformance by such financial statements with generally accepted accounting principles (GAAP). The term originated in a formal sense with the SEC. In 1941, the SEC issued Accounting Series Release (ASR) No. 21. That ASR supported the work of the AICPA's Committee on Auditing Procedure (CAuP), established in 1939. The CAuP published statements on

4-1

auditing procedures intended to improve the quality of auditing. The ASR, in effect, required that audits of financial statements filed with the SEC be performed in accordance with GAAS. At the time, it was unclear just what GAAS were. Auditing textbooks existed along with earlier official pronouncements (see Chapter 3). These were developed prior to the McKesson-Robbins scandal in 1937 which, among other things, highlighted the need for better and standardized auditing standards. No one could be certain to what degree procedures suggested by the textbooks and official statements were actually practiced.

The CAuP developed the "Tentative Statement of Auditing Standards—Their Generally Accepted Significance and Scope" to remedy the standards gap. The 10 GAAS were born from this effort. Their general acceptance derives from the affirmative action taken by the members of the AICPA in 1948.

Subsequent statements and interpretations by the committee and its AICPA-authorized successors have occurred over the years. These form the body of authoritative pronouncements that constitute the GAAS of today.

PURPOSE

Perhaps the best statement regarding the purpose of standards is found in the following excerpt from the Report of the Cohen Commission:

> Auditing standards have two important uses: communicating the requirements of auditing and evaluating the performance of auditors. [Ernest L. Hicks, "Standards for the Attest Function," *The Journal of Accountancy* (August 1974) pp. 39–40.] First, auditing standards provide guidance to auditors in their practice, to users who want to understand the work of auditors, and to educators who prepare people to become auditors. Second, auditing standards may be used by the profession's bodies charged with disciplining auditors, the courts, and the regulatory agencies to evaluate the performance of auditors.[1]

As the quotation implies, standards serve all parties that have an interest in the work of the auditor: the auditors themselves, the users (those for whom the audit is performed), and third parties, such as educators and government agencies. Standards serve these parties by articulating the expected level of effort required in the conduct of the auditor's services. In a sense, standards are objectives that must be met in the performance of service and, if properly set and meticulously followed, they produce the credibility necessary for effective service.

---

[1] *The Commission on Auditors' Responsibilities: Report, Conclusions and Recommendations* (New York: The Commission on Auditors' Responsibilities, 1978), p. 123.

ELEMENTS OF GAAS

Identification of Elements

Professional literature divides GAAS into categories of financial statement auditing and other services that are provided by CPAs. Thus, standards exist for:

- Audited financial statements
- Unaudited financial statements
- Reviews of interim financial statements
- Prospective financial statements
- Attestation engagements
- Specialized industry audit practices
- Tax services
- Management advisory services

Each of these categories is discussed briefly, as well as the effects of the courts on auditing standards.

The Code of Professional Ethics

The body of GAAS is binding. In other words, a CPA performing an audit of financial statements must perform the audit in accordance with GAAS. Why is this? For one thing, the AICPA Code of Professional Ethics compels it. The Code provides guidelines for members of the AICPA (only CPAs may become members of the AICPA) in conducting their professional practices. The Code and its interpretations were published by the AICPA over many years by actions of special committees, traceable as far back as 1906. A major restatement of the Code of Professional Ethics occurred in 1988. The Code prescribes guidance for general matters, such as independence, professional competence, due professional care, planning and supervision, and sufficient relevant data. More specific guidance is provided in the areas of confidentiality, contingent fees, advertising and other forms of solicitation, commissions, incompatible occupations, and forms of public practice (i.e., single practitioner, partnership, etc.) and name (i.e., the name of the practice). The Code also enumerates various acts deemed discreditable to the profession. Examples include committing a crime and the willful failure to file an income tax return.

With respect to GAAS, Rule 202 of the Code states in part:

> A member shall not permit his name to be associated with financial statements in such a manner as to imply that he is acting as an independent public accountant unless he has complied with the applicable generally accepted auditing standards promulgated by the Institute.

Thus, an act or failure to act that violates the GAAS also violates the Code of Professional Ethics. Such violation not only exposes the CPA to legal consequences but also to professional sanctions. These can run from the loss of membership in the AICPA to the loss of the right to practice public accounting. In the case of the latter, such loss would be by action of the State Board of Accountancy in the state in which the individual is licensed to practice. In addition, the SEC can censure the individual or firm, or both, from practicing before it. In summary, performing audits in accordance with GAAS is vital to the well being of the practitioner.

A word here about the recent activities of the Anderson Committee is important. The Committee, formally known as the Special Committee on Standards of Professional Conduct for Certified Public Accountants, was established in 1983. Its objective was to study the relevance and effectiveness of professional standards in the present environment.

The Committee, chaired by George D. Anderson, issued its final report in 1986, entitled *Restructuring Professional Standards to Achieve Professional Excellence in a Changing Environment*. The report recommended substantial reforms to the Code of Professional Ethics. The report forms one aspect of the AICPA's efforts to respond to concerns over the profession's ability to serve the public interest. Proposals to implement the recommendations were prepared for AICPA members' approval. The proposals were adopted and, in effect, restructure the Code of Professional Ethics into two sections, including new standards of professional conduct and revised rules of performance and behavior. The adopted proposals also provide new guidance in making judgments regarding professional services and adhering to professionalism. Also included are mandatory continuing professional education and post-baccalaureate education requirements. Finally, there is a new program for monitoring professional practice as a means of improving the quality of service and compliance with professional standards.

THE ROLE OF THE AUDITING STANDARDS BOARD

Before reviewing GAAS, it is worthwhile to consider the role of the ASB. The ASB was the successor in 1978 to the Auditing Standards Executive Committee (AUDSEC).

Approach in Standards Setting

The ASB is the official body responsible for promulgating auditing standards for the AICPA. It has 21 members, all of whom are members of the AICPA and serve voluntarily. The standards set up by the ASB are intended to:

- Define the nature and extent of the auditor's responsibilities.

- Provide guidance to the auditor in carrying out his duties, enabling him to express an opinion on the viability of the representations on which he is reporting.
- Make special provision, where appropriate, to meet the needs of small enterprises.
- Have regard to the costs that they impose on society in relation to the benefits reasonably expected to be derived from the audit function.

"The Auditing Standards Board will provide auditors with all possible guidance in the implementation of its pronouncements, by means of interpretations of its statements, by the issuance of guidelines, and by any other means available to it."[2]

SASs issued by the ASB follow a pattern in which the need for a pronouncement is first identified. Identification may result from litigation, comments by practitioners, suggestions by regulatory bodies, or other sources. Identification is followed by researching the matter. Research is conducted by the ASB staff and small task forces of practitioners and/or board members. Alternative approaches and a proposed pronouncement are then deliberated by the board. If at least 14 members approve, the proposed pronouncement is distributed to various interested parties, such as CPA firms, regulators, and academicians. This exposure period, which takes a minimum of 60 days, is followed by issuance, unless comments are raised as a result of the exposure period that require further deliberation or change. Finally, the draft is issued as one of a numbered series of SASs, with the approval of at least nine board members.

In response to a recommendation for broadened involvement in the standards-setting process, the AICPA established an advisory council to the ASB, whose conclusions are made public. Initial appointments to the 14-member council were made in 1979. The council includes financial analysts, lawyers, bankers, and government officials, among others. The functions of the advisory council are to:[3]

- Bring to the board's attention problems calling for new standards, for revision, or for interpretation of previous pronouncements.
- Review the board's agenda and offer guidance on the priorities implicit in the agenda.
- Review proposed pronouncements of the board in an advisory capacity.
- Recommend persons to serve on the board and on its task forces.
- Report at least annually on the work of the board and the extent to which it has fulfilled its charge.

---

[2] AICPA, *Professional Standards*, AU Appendix A (New York: AICPA, 1978), p. 2065.

[3] Douglas R. Carmichael, "Trends in Auditing Standards," *Journal of Accountancy*, Aug. 1982, p. 46.

Impact of Congressional Inquiry

Historically, the ASB standards-setting activities tended toward expanding the audit function rather than synthesizing good practice.[4] But events occurring subsequent to 1982 necessitated an abrupt departure from that trend. In essence, a series of unexpected bankruptcies in financial institutions and other businesses resulted in adverse publicity and criticism of the profession.

Congressional inquiry and the proposed legislative initiatives that would have significant effects on the accounting profession galvanized the ASB into action. The nine new standards that resulted in 1988 represented the most comprehensive set of changes ever issued by the ASB. Further comments on these are contained later in this chapter. With these changes, the ASB seems to be conceding the appropriateness of at least some of the criticism by many investors, federal regulators, financial analysts, and members of Congress who believed that outside auditors were not doing enough.

Impact of Other Inquiries

The ASB standards-setting process itself recently came under review. This was in connection with the study performed by the Treadway Commission. Among the 49 recommendations it proposed, to deal with the incidence of financial reporting fraud, the commission recommended that:

> The AICPA should reorganize the Auditing Standards Board to afford a full participatory role in the standard-setting process to knowledgeable persons who are affected by and interested in auditing standards but who either are not CPAs or are CPAs no longer in public practice.[5]

The Commission noted that the 10 proposed new standards issued by the ASB represented a tremendous effort. They demonstrate that the ASB must deal with policy issues that are of public interest. Expansion of the ASB to include meaningful participation by persons knowledgeable about auditing, but not in public accounting practice, is necessary. In so doing, these individuals would be assisting the ASB in fulfilling its public policy role. The Commission believes that its recommendation should be enacted under the continuing auspices of the AICPA.

This is not the first time that recommendations to change the ASB have

---

[4] *Ibid.*, p. 56

[5] The National Commission on Fraudulent Financial Reporting, *Report of the National Commission on Fraudulent Financial Reporting* (Washington, D.C.: National Commission on Fraudulent Financial Reporting, 1987), p. 60.

emerged. Previously, the Cohen Commission (see Chapter 1) recommended replacing the existing committee structure with a smaller, full-time, sufficiently compensated body. The profession did not adopt the recommendation.

More recently, the heads of seven major accounting firms presented recommendations to the AICPA that called for enhancing the capacity of the ASB. Clearly, auditing standards and the process by which they are established are becoming more important in terms of public interest. When unexpected business failures occur due to the fraudulent acts of management, the adequacy of auditing standards comes into question. The Treadway Commission seems to doubt that the ASB (as it is presently structured) is convincing in its efforts to protect the public interest. Put simply, the ASB may not go far enough fast enough. A standards-setting body with broader representation may be better positioned to differentiate the public interest from the self-interest of the profession.

Other Standards-Setting Activities of the ASB

In addition to issuing SASs, the ASB reviews Auditing Interpretations issued by the staff of the Auditing Standards Division. These interpretations are not considered to be as authoritative as the auditing standards issued by the ASB. However, members of the AICPA may have to justify any departure from an Auditing Interpretation if the quality of the member's work is in doubt.

The ASB also is involved in the issuance of Statements on Standards for Accountants' Services on Prospective Financial Information. Finally, along with the Accounting and Review Services Committee, the ASB jointly issues Statements for Attestation Engagements.

OTHER AICPA STANDARDS-SETTING GROUPS

The body of literature that comprises official guidance for AICPA members was primarily determined or shaped by the ASB and its predecessors, the Auditing Standards Executive Committee and the Committee on Auditing Procedures. This collection of promulgations, periodically codified, comprise the most authoritative guidance for AICPA members.

These pronouncements were not intended to provide the specialized guidance that might be required for special industry situations. Moreover, as the nature of audit services became more widespread, a need for guidance in specialized areas emerged. Thus, the body of GAAS includes pronouncements in various forms, by a variety of other AICPA groups. Generally speaking, these pronouncements are less authoritative than those of the

ASB. Nevertheless, members may be called on to justify any departures from these pronouncements. The following identifies the issuing bodies and the types of pronouncements they issue:

Issuer	Type of Issuance
Auditing Standards Division	Statements of Position Industry Audit Guides
Accounting and Review Services Committee	Statements on Standards for Accounting and Review Services (SSARS)
Accounting and Review Services Committee Staff	Accounting and Review Services Interpretations
Quality Control Standards Committee	Statements on Quality Control Standards (SQCS)
Executive Committee, Professional Ethics Division	Interpretations of Rules of Conduct
Professional Ethics Division	Ethics Rulings
Committee on Responsibilities in Tax Practice	Statements on Responsibilities in Tax Practice (SRTP)
Management Advisory Services Executive Committee	Statements on Standards for Management Advisory Services (SSMAS)

THE TEN GAAS

It is clear from the preceding paragraphs that the volume of statements on professional auditing standards for CPAs has steadily increased over the 30-plus years since the issuance of the AICPA general standards. However, GAAS have stood the test of time rather well and have remained essentially as originally adopted—a fact that is a tribute to the propriety of their original articulation. The AICPA defines them as follows:[6]

> *General Standards*
> 1. The examination is to be performed by a person or persons having adequate technical training and proficiency as an auditor.
> 2. In all matters relating to the assignment, an independence in mental attitude is to be maintained by the auditor or auditors.

---

[6] Statement on Auditing Standards No. 1, *Codification of Auditing Standards and Procedures* (Nov. 1972), § 150.02 (AICPA, *Professional Standards*, Vol. 1), AU § 150.02. Copyright © 1973 by the American Institute of Certified Public Accountants, Inc.

3. Due professional care is to be exercised in the performance of the examination and the preparation of the report.

Standards of Field Work
1. The work is to be adequately planned and assistants, if any, are to be properly supervised.
2. There is to be a proper study and evaluation of the existing internal control as a basis for reliance thereon and for the determination of the resultant extent of the tests to which auditing procedures are to be restricted.
3. Sufficient competent evidential matter is to be obtained through inspection, observation, inquiry, and confirmation to afford a reasonable basis for an opinion regarding the financial statements under examination.

Standards of Reporting
1. The report shall state whether the financial statements are presented in accordance with generally accepted accounting principles.
2. The report shall state whether such principles have been consistently observed in the current period in relation to the preceding period.
3. Informative disclosures in the financial statements are to be regarded as reasonably adequate unless otherwise stated in the report.
4. The report shall either contain an expression of opinion regarding the financial statements, taken as a whole, or an assertion to the effect that an opinion cannot be expressed. When an overall opinion cannot be expressed, the reasons therefor should be stated. In all cases where an auditor's name is associated with financial statements, the report should contain a clear-cut indication of the character of the auditor's examination, if any, and the degree of responsibility he is taking.

All of the subsequent SASs deal with aspects of these 10 GAAS. (There have been 60 to date, including codifications of earlier statements, the most recent being SAS No. 60, issued in 1988.) Figure 4-1 contains a chronological listing of the SASs issued through 1987 and the Statements on Auditing Procedure issued by the CAuP. The reader should keep in mind that SASs 1–23 were issued by the AUDSEC.[7]

All of the pronouncements identified in Figure 4-1 are brought together in volume 1 of a loose-leaf service published for the AICPA by Commerce Clearing House, Inc. A second volume contains SSARS, interpretations of SSARS, the Code of Professional Ethics, and the AICPA bylaws, among other items.[8]

---

[7] AICPA, *Professional Standards*, Vol. 1, AU Appendix B, pp. 2071–2076. Reprinted by permission from AICPA *Professional Standards*. Copyright © 1987 by American Institute of Certified Public Accountants, Inc.

[8] AICPA, *Professional Standards*, Vols. 1 and 2 (published by Commerce Clearing House, Inc., Chicago, Illinois, for the AICPA, © 1982).

FIG. 4-1

List of Authoritative Auditing Standards Pronouncements

Statements on Auditing Procedure

No.	Date Issued	Title
1	Oct. 1939	Extensions of Auditing Procedure
2	Dec. 1939	The Auditor's Opinion on the Basis of a Restricted Examination
3	Feb. 1940	Inventories and Receivables of Department Stores, Instalment Houses, Chain Stores, and Other Retailers
4	March 1941	Clients' Written Representations Regarding Inventories, Liabilities, and Other Matters
5	Feb. 1941	The Revised SEC Rule on "Accountants' Certificates"
6	March 1941	The Revised SEC Rule on "Accountants' Certificates" (continued)
7	March 1941	Contingent Liability Under Policies With Mutual Insurance Companies
8	Sept. 1941	Interim Financial Statements and the Auditor's Report Thereon
9	Dec. 1941	Accountants' Reports on Examinations of Securities and Similar Investments Under the Investment Company Act
10	June 1942	Auditing Under Wartime Conditions
11	Sept. 1942	The Auditor's Opinion on the Basis of a Restricted Examination (No. 2)
12	Oct. 1942	Amendment to Extensions of Auditing Procedure
13	Dec. 1942	The Auditor's Opinion on the Basis of a Restricted Examination (No. 3)—Face-Amount Certificate Companies
14	Dec. 1942	Confirmation of Public Utility Accounts Receivable
15	Dec. 1942	Disclosure of the Effect of Wartime Uncertainties on Financial Statements
16	Dec. 1942	Case Studies on Inventories
17	Dec. 1942	Physical Inventories in Wartime
18	Jan. 1943	Confirmation of Receivables From the Government
19	Nov. 1943	Confirmation of Receivables (Positive and Negative Methods)
20	Dec. 1943	Termination of Fixed Price Supply Contracts
21	July 1944	Wartime Government Regulations
22	May 1945	References to the Independent Accountant in Securities Registrations
23	Dec. 1949	Clarification of Accountant's Report When Opinion is Omitted (Revised)
24	Oct. 1948	Revision in Short-Form Accountant's Report or Certificate

GENERALLY ACCEPTED AUDITING STANDARDS 4-11

Statements on Auditing Procedure *(continued)*

No.	Date Issued	Title
25	Oct. 1954	Events Subsequent to the Date of Financial Statements
26	April 1956	Reporting on Use of "Other Procedures"
27	July 1957	Long-Form Reports
28	Oct. 1957	Special Reports
29	Oct. 1958	Scope of the Independent Auditor's Review of Internal Control
30	Sept. 1960	Responsibilities and Functions of the Independent Auditor in the Examination of Financial Statements
31	Oct. 1961	Consistency
32	Sept. 1962	Qualifications and Disclaimers
33	Dec. 1963	Auditing Standards and Procedures (a codification)
34	Sept. 1965	Long-Term Investments
35	Nov. 1965	Letters for Underwriters
36	Aug. 1966	Revision of "Extensions of Auditing Procedure" Relating to Inventories
37	Sept. 1966	Special Report: Public Warehouses—Controls and Auditing Procedures for Goods Held
38	Sept. 1967	Unaudited Financial Statements
39	Sept. 1967	Working Papers
40	Oct. 1968	Reports Following a Pooling of Interests
41	Oct. 1969	Subsequent Discovery of Facts Existing at the Date of the Auditor's Report
42	Jan. 1970	Reporting When a Certified Public Accountant Is Not Independent
43	Sept. 1970	Confirmation of Receivables and Observation of Inventories
44	April 1971	Reports Following a Pooling of Interests
45	July 1971	Using the Work and Reports of Other Auditors
46	July 1971	Piecemeal Opinions
47	Sept. 1971	Subsequent Events
48	Oct. 1971	Letters for Underwriters
49	Nov. 1971	Reports on Internal Control
50	Nov. 1971	Reporting on the Statement of Changes in Financial Position
51	July 1972	Long-Term Investments
52	Oct. 1972	Reports on Internal Control Based on Criteria Established by Governmental Agencies
53	Nov. 1972	Reporting on Consistency and Accounting Changes
54	Nov. 1972	The Auditor's Study and Evaluation of Internal Control

(continued)

FIG. 4-1 *(cont'd)*

Statements on Auditing Standards

No.	Date Issued	Title
1	Nov. 1972	Codification of Auditing Standards and Procedures
2	Oct. 1974	Reports on Audited Financial Statements
3	Dec. 1974	(Superseded by SAS 48.)
4	Dec. 1974	(Superseded by SAS 25.)
5	July 1975	The Meaning of "Present Fairly in Conformity With Generally Accepted Accounting Principles" in the Independent Auditor's Report
6	July 1975	(Superseded by SAS 45.)
7	Oct. 1975	Communications Between Predecessor and Successor Auditors
8	Dec. 1975	Other Information in Documents Containing Audited Financial Statements
9	Dec. 1975	The Effect of an Internal Audit Function on the Scope of the Independent Auditor's Examination
10	Dec. 1975	(Superseded by SAS 24.)
11	Dec. 1975	Using the Work of a Specialist
12	Jan. 1976	Inquiry of a Client's Lawyer Concerning Litigation, Claims, and Assessments
13	May 1976	(Superseded by SAS 24.)
14	Dec. 1976	Special Reports
15	Dec. 1976	Reports on Comparative Financial Statements
16	Jan. 1977	The Independent Auditor's Responsibility for the Detection of Errors or Irregularities
17	Jan. 1977	Illegal Acts by Clients
18	May 1977	(Withdrawn by Auditing Standards Board.)
19	June 1977	Client Representations
20	Aug. 1977	Required Communication of Material Weaknesses in Internal Accounting Control
21	Dec. 1977	Segment Information
22	Mar. 1978	Planning and Supervision
23	Oct. 1978	Analytical Review Procedures
24	Mar. 1979	(Superseded by SAS No. 36.)
25	Nov. 1979	The Relationship of Generally Accepted Auditing Standards to Quality Control Standards
26	Nov. 1979	Association With Financial Statements
27	Dec. 1979	Supplementary Information Required by the Financial Accounting Standards Board
28	June 1980	Supplementary Information on the Effects of Changing Prices
29	July 1980	Reporting on Information Accompanying the Basic Financial Statements in Auditor Submitted Documents

GENERALLY ACCEPTED AUDITING STANDARDS 4-13

Statements on Auditing Standards *(continued)*

No.	Date Issued	Title
30	July 1980	Reporting on Internal Accounting Control
31	Aug. 1980	Evidential Matter
32	Oct. 1980	Adequacy of Disclosure in Financial Statements
33	Oct. 1980	(Superseded by SAS 45.)
34	Mar. 1981	The Auditor's Considerations When a Question Arises About an Entity's Continued Existence
35	April 1981	Special Reports—Applying Agreed-upon Procedures to Specified Elements, Accounts, or Items of a Financial Statement
36	April 1981	Review of Interim Financial Information
37	April 1981	Filings Under Federal Securities Statutes
38	April 1981	(Superseded by SAS 49.)
39	June 1981	Audit Sampling
40	Feb. 1982	Supplementary Mineral Reserve Information
41	April 1982	Working Papers
42	Sept. 1982	Reporting on Condensed Financial Statements and Selected Financial Data
43	Aug. 1982	Omnibus Statement on Auditing Standards*
44	Dec. 1982	Special-Purpose Reports on Internal Accounting Control at Service Organizations
45	Aug. 1983	Omnibus Statement on Auditing Standards—1983**
46	Sept. 1983	Consideration of Omitted Procedures After the Report Date
47	Dec. 1983	Audit Risk and Materiality in Conducting an Audit
48	July 1984	The Effects of Computer Processing on the Examination of Financial Statements
49	Sept. 1984	Letters for Underwriters
50	July 1986	Reports on the Application of Accounting Principles
51	July 1986	Reporting on Financial Statements Prepared for Use in Other Countries

Statement on Standards for Accountants' Services on Prospective Financial Information

	Oct. 1985	Financial Forecasts and Projections

Statements on Standards for Attestation Engagements

	Mar. 1986	Attestation Standards

* Statement on Auditing Standards No. 43 has been integrated within sections 150.06, 320.50—.56, 320.59—.62, 331.14, 350.46, 411.05—.08, 420.15, 509.39, 901.01, 901.24 and 901.28.
** Statement on Auditing Standards No. 45 has created new sections 313, *Substantive Tests Prior to the Balance Sheet Date;* 334, *Related Parties;* and 557, *Supplementary Oil and Gas Reserve Information.*

STANDARDS APPLICABLE TO OTHER AUDIT-RELATED FINANCIAL STATEMENT SERVICES

AICPA members provide a range of financial statement audit-related services. Standards have evolved to deal with each type of service. Most standards setting has pertained to complete audits of financial statements. However, in certain types of SEC filings, the AICPA member may be associated with financial statements that have not been subjected to the application of any auditing procedures by him. Also, there may be occasions when the AICPA member may become associated with historical interim-period financial statements or with prospective financial statements.

Unaudited Financial Statements

Unaudited financial statements are generally understood to mean those for which auditing procedures were not applied or were not sufficient to permit expressing an opinion. SAS No. 26 provides reporting guidance for AICPA members whose names are associated with unaudited financial statements at public companies. SAS No. 26 requires the following disclaimer report when unaudited financial statements are involved:[9]

> The accompanying balance sheet of X company as of December 31, 19X1, and the related statements of income, retained earnings, and changes in financial position for the year then ended were not audited by us and, accordingly, we do not express an opinion on them.
>
> (signature and date)

The 10 GAAS apply to examinations of financial statements. Only certain of these standards are applicable, directly or indirectly, in situations where the auditor is associated with unaudited financial statements. Obviously, the general standards regarding proficiency, independence, and due professional care apply in an indirect sense. It is also obvious that an auditor would not be required to study the system of internal control nor would it be necessary to gather sufficient competent evidential matter to form an opinion. However, the work should be adequately planned and assistants should be properly supervised.

Only the fourth standard of reporting is directly applicable. That standard requires a clean opinion or an assertion that an opinion cannot be expressed. If, however, the auditor has reason to believe that the financial statements in some respect are not in accordance with GAAP or are inadequate with respect to informative disclosures, he must request that the

---

[9] AICPA, *Professional Standards*, Vol. 1, AU § 504.05 (New York: AICPA, 1987), p. 602.

financial statements be adjusted. If the client refuses, the auditor must not permit his name to be associated with the unaudited financial statements.

Unaudited financial statements also exist for nonpublic companies. The service an AICPA member may perform with respect to such companies may be in one of two forms—compilation or review.

Compilation refers to the service in which the report of the AICPA member indicates that an audit or a review was not performed and no opinion is rendered. A compilation occurs when the member prepares or assists in preparing financial statements without expressing any assurance as to their accuracy, completeness, or conformity with GAAP.

The other form of service (review) results in the provision in the report of a limited level of assurance that the financial statements are in accordance with GAAP.

The member must perform inquiry and analytical procedures so as to provide a reasonable basis for the limited assurance. The report identifies the financial statements reviewed, describes the review procedures applied, differentiates them from an audit performed in accordance with GAAS, and provides the limited assurance. The limited assurance in the standard form is expressed as follows:

> On the basis of our review, we are not aware of any material modifications that should be made to the accompanying financial statements in order for them to be in conformity with generally accepted accounting principles.

Prior to 1979, guidance pertaining to unaudited financial statements was lacking. Members were asked to permit their names to be associated with unaudited financial statements in a broad variety of circumstances with no indication of the degree of responsibility the member was taking. Concerns arose as to the implications, particularly legal, of such associations. In 1979, SSARS 1 was issued by the Accounting and Review Services Committee. It defined compilation and review services and provided standards for performing such services. At the same time, SSARS-2 was issued. It provided guidance for reporting on comparative financial statements. Three additional SSARS have been issued. These deal respectively with:

- Compilation Reports on Financial Statements in Certain Prescribed Forms (SSARS-3)
- Communication Between Predecessor and Successor Accountants (SSARS-4)
- Reporting on Compiled Financial Statements (SSARS-5)

AICPA members must comply with the SSARS when performing either compilation or review services. In effect, the SSARS require that the member must issue a report in all instances in which his name is associated with unaudited financial statements of a nonpublic entity. In addition to compliance with the SSARS, the member must comply with the general standards and with applicable portions of the Code of Professional Ethics. A member must be independent to perform review services but need not be for performing only compilation services. Even when performing compilation services, however, the member must have a general knowledge of applicable accounting principles and the business of the client. He must consider whether accounting services other than compilation are needed. He must also read the compiled financial statements for appropriateness, and check for obvious material compilation errors.

The AICPA member performing compilation services may not ignore significant questions that come to his attention, despite the fact that he is disclaiming an opinion. He must see that such questions are resolved to his satisfaction.

Interim-Period Financial Statements

Compilation and review services for nonpublic companies may be performed with respect either to annual financial statements or interim-period financial statements. With respect to publicly held companies, interim-period financial information is made public on a quarterly basis as required by the SEC. This information is not required to be audited. Further, in the annual report to shareholders, summarized quarterly financial information must be included in a footnote to the financial statements and labeled as unaudited. A review of interim-period financial information occurs when an AICPA member is asked by a public company to perform certain inquiries and analytical procedures with respect to such interim-period financial information. Such a service differs significantly from an audit. Guidance for such service is provided in SAS No. 36. In most instances, such service is a continuation or an extension of audit services performed for the prior period's annual financial statements. The results of performing the inquiries and analytical procedures required by SAS No. 36 is a report that contains a negative assurance that, based on the review, the member is not aware of any material modification that should be made to the interim-period financial information in order for it to conform with GAAP. Such an expression is similar to the limited assurance provided in performing review services for nonpublic entities.

The general standards pertaining to proficiency, independence, and due professional care apply to reviews of interim-period financial information. The standard of fieldwork pertaining to planning and supervision also applies. However, the standards of fieldwork pertaining to the study of internal control and gathering sufficient competent evidential matter do not apply.

The negative assurance reporting called for by SAS No. 36 obviates the four standards of reporting. However, if the AICPA member knows that the financial information is in some respect not in accordance with GAAP or is inconsistent with the annual financial statements, his report must so state.

Prospective Financial Statements

A prospective financial statement is either a financial forecast or a financial projection. A financial forecast is an entity's expected statements of financial position, results of operations, and changes in financial position anticipated during the forecast period. The forecast is based on the assumptions of conditions expected to exist and the course of action intended to be taken by the party involved. A financial projection reflects an entity's expected statements of financial position, results of operations, and changes in financial position based on the assumptions of conditions that would exist during the projected period if one or more hypothetical assumptions occurs and the course of action that would then be taken by the party involved. A prospective financial statement may be prepared as a single set of estimates or a range of estimates. Pro forma financial statements are not prospective financial statements but simply reflect the effects of a possible transaction or event on historical financial statements.

Prospective financial statements are often included in prospectuses and similar solicitations of financings and are used for other business purposes. Perhaps the most common usage in recent years is in connection with limited partnerships. Prior to 1980, little authoritative guidance existed to aid the CPA in associating himself with such financial statements. All that was available was SSMAS No. 3, "Guidelines for Systems for the Preparation of Financial Forecasts," and SOP 75-4 "Presentation and Disclosure of Financial Forecasts," both issued in 1975. These, along with a 1980 Guide for a Review of Financial Forecasts and a 1982 SOP on financial feasibility studies, were replaced in 1985. In October of that year, the ASB issued its first Statement on Standards for Accountants' Services on Prospective Financial Information. It was entitled "Financial Forecasts and Projections." In 1986, the Financial Forecasts and Projections Task Force issued an audit guide. It was entitled "Guide for Prospective Financial Statements."

Together, these pronouncements provide the standards to be employed by an AICPA member in performing services in connection with prospective financial statements. Services applied may be in the form of an examination, a compilation, or the performance of agreed-on procedures. In the performance of such services, the general standards of proficiency, independence, and due professional care apply. The work must be adequately planned and properly supervised. Sufficient evidence must be collected to determine the reasonableness of the assumptions used in the preparation of the prospective financial statements. A study of the system of internal control, however, is not required.

The reporting standards require that the following be included:

- Identification of the prospective financial statements presented
- Statement that the examination was made in accordance with AICPA standards with a description of the nature of the examination

- Accountant's opinion that the statements are presented in conformity with AICPA presentation guidelines and that the underlying assumptions provide a reasonable basis for the forecast or a reasonable basis for the projection given the hypothetical assumptions
- Caveat that the prospective results may not be achieved
- Statement that the accountant assumes no responsibility to update the report for subsequent events

ATTESTATION STANDARDS

There are a variety of circumstances in which an entity may seek to have a CPA firm attest to a particular set of assertions by the entity other than in the context of financial statements. Examples include assertions regarding (1) compliance with particular statutory, regulatory, or contractual requirements; (2) attributes of computer software; and (3) compliance with terms of financial instruments.

An attestation engagement, defined by the Standards for Attestation Engagements, was promulgated by the ASB in 1986. An attestation engagement is one in which a practitioner is engaged to issue or does issue a written communication that expresses a conclusion about the reliability of a written assertion that is the responsibility of another party.

Prior to these standards, guidance for such specialized forms of service did not exist. Conceptually, these standards are similar to the 10 GAAS in that they specify general standards, fieldwork standards, and reporting standards. In addition to the general standards of proficiency, independence, and due professional care, the attestation standards require knowledge of the assertion and the presence of reasonable criteria. Guidelines are suggested in the standards for the CPA to follow in determining the reasonableness of the criteria. Exceptions to this requirement for determining the reasonableness of criteria are also provided. It is not necessary to determine the reasonableness of criteria, for example, if the criteria is established by a body designated by the AICPA Council. Also, regulatory bodies that are composed of experts in their field that promulgate criteria pursuant to a due process are an acceptable source of reasonable criteria.

The fieldwork standards deal with (1) planning and supervision and (2) sufficient evidence. As such, they are similar to the fourth and sixth standards of fieldwork in GAAS. There is no assertion standard comparable to the fifth standard of fieldwork in GAAS, regarding the study and evaluation of internal control. Attestation engagements are not dependent on such a study to determine the extent to which auditing procedures are to be restricted. The standards provide that the extent of procedures to be employed in gathering sufficient evidence be based on an assessment of inherent risk control and detection risk. This is conceptually parallel to the 1988 standards for assessing control risk by the ASB.

The extent to which evidence is gathered is also affected by whether the attestation engagement is an examination or a review. The distinction here is similar to the difference between an audit engagement of financial statements and a review of financial statements.

The four reporting standards differ somewhat from the GAAS reporting standards. That is because the nature of the engagements differs. GAAS applies to examinations of financial statements and whether they are prepared in accordance with GAAP. Such criteria are not present in attestation engagements. Reporting standards for attestation engagements are directed at describing the character of the engagement, conclusions, significant reservations—such as scope deficiencies and presentation deficiencies—and, finally, restricted distribution. This standard applies when the distribution of the report is restricted. In such cases, the report must state that they are intended only for the use of those parties that participated in determining the agreed-on criteria or procedures.

SPECIALIZED INDUSTRY AUDITING

As mentioned earlier in this chapter, the body of GAAS provides broad guidance. The special auditing circumstances present in many segments of business require more specific guidance than is affirmed by GAAS. A number of industry audit guides applicable to both public and nonpublic entities have been prepared and issued over the years to provide their guidance. While not as authoritative as GAAS, members may be called on to justify deviations. The following identifies the industries for which guides are in existence to date:

- Property and liability insurance companies
- Hospitals
- Stock life insurance companies
- Colleges and universities
- Commercial banks
- Finance companies
- Investment companies
- Voluntary health and welfare organizations
- Service-center-produced records
- Government contractors
- Savings and loan associations
- Construction contractors
- Certain nonprofit organizations
- Airline companies
- Employee benefit plans
- Personal financial statements
- Casinos
- Securities brokers and dealers
- Credit unions
- Governmental units

In addition to the foregoing, specialized audit guidance in the form of audit guides has been developed for:

- Study and evaluation of internal control in EDP systems
- Computer-assisted audit techniques

- Audit sampling
- Guide for prospective financial statements

STANDARDS FOR OTHER SERVICES

Tax Services

SRTP are issued by the Committee on Responsibilities in Tax Practice and the Federal Taxation Executive Committee. These issuances are not enforceable under the Code of Professional Ethics. Since 1964, 10 statements have been issued, the first two of which have been withdrawn. Applicable topics include:

- SRTP-3 —Answers to Questions on Returns
- SRTP-4 —Recognition of Administrative Proceeding of a Prior Year
- SRTP-5 —Use of Estimates
- SRTP-6 —Knowledge of Error: Return Preparation
- SRTP-7 —Knowledge of Error: Administrative Proceedings
- SRTP-8 —Advice to Clients
- SRTP-9 —Certain Procedural Aspects of Preparing Returns
- SRTP-10—Positions Contrary to Treasury Department or IRS Interpretations of the Code

In addition to these statements, CPAs, like all tax return preparers, must comply with applicable provisions of the IRC. For those enrolled to practice before the IRS, its standards of conduct and rules of practice apply.

Management Advisory Services

SSMAS are issued by the Management Advisory Services Executive Committee of the AICPA. There have been three such pronouncements issued to date. Briefly, they are described as follows:

> SSMAS No. 1: *Definitions and Standards for MAS Practice*. This statement describes MAS as providing assistance to help a client achieve its objectives. It defines a MAS practitioner as a member of the AICPA who is in the practice of public accounting and who performs either a MAS Engagement or a MAS Consultation. A MAS Engagement is a service that is not incidental to another engagement and results in the application of an analytical approach or process that constitutes a study or project. A MAS Consultation is a service usually based on existing knowledge of the client, and the results of the consultation are communicated orally. This standard specifies the applicability of Rule 201 general standards to MAS Engagements. It also specifies the applicability of Rule 204 regarding other technical standards.

SSMAS No. 2: *MAS Engagements*. This standard relates three of the general standards of Rule 201 to MAS Engagements. The three are professional competence, planning and supervision, and sufficient relevant data. It also provides further guidance for applying other technical standards specified by Rule 204.

SSMAS No. 3: *MAS Consultations*. This statement provides guidance for consultation engagements with respect to due professional care, planning and supervision, and sufficient relevant data. In general, MAS Consultations are more informal than MAS Engagements.

In addition to these statements, the Management Advisory Services Executive Committee has issued a series of SSMAS. These represent the best thoughts of the profession as to the best practices. These were not promulgated under Rule 204, however. These statements were withdrawn in May 1982, on the issuance of SSMAS No. 1. However, some of the material in them may be incorporated in future MAS standards and practice aids. Practitioners may continue to consult these statements. Eight such statements were issued, dealing with topics ranging from personal characteristics to communication of results.

RECENT CHANGES

There have been no changes to the basic auditing standards since their original adoption. Since then, 60 SASs have been issued, including codifications of many earlier pronouncements.

In 1986, the Auditing Standards Division of the AICPA began to make available *Codification of Statements in Auditing Standards Nos. 1–49*. While not an SAS in itself, it should prove to be a handy reference source. It also includes auditing interpretations issued by the AICPA staff.

Earlier mention is made of the fact that in 1988, the ASB issued nine new SASs. Together, these represent the most sweeping set of changes to auditing standards since their original pronouncement.

The nine SASs deal with auditing standards. One additional exposure draft deals with the attestation standards, which were adopted by the ASB in 1986. The proposed change here provides guidance to independent auditors who are asked to examine and report on the "Management Discussion and Analysis" section of a client's annual report to shareholders. Such discussion is not now included in the scope of the audit of the financial statements.

The nine new SASs that deal with auditing standards are intended to:

- Improve the quality and timeliness of communications to interested parties.
- Improve the planning and performance of audits.

- Clarify the independent auditor's responsibility for detecting management fraud and other illegal acts.
- Provide early warning about the possibility of bankruptcy.

The nine SASs as reported by a recent issue of *Internal Auditing Alert* at the time they were proposed were:[10]

☐ *The Auditor's Standard Report.* This revision of the report would more clearly communicate the results of the auditor's work and the degree of responsibility assumed with respect to the financial statements.

☐ *The Auditor's Consideration of an Entity's Ability to Continue in Existence.* This proposal provides guidance for evaluating the continued existence of an entity in all audits, including the type of report to be rendered when the company is in financial difficulties.

☐ *The Auditor's Responsibility to Detect and Report Errors and Irregularities.* This proposal provides guidance for detecting errors and irregularities and material misstatements.

☐ *Illegal Acts by Clients.* This proposal clarifies the auditor's responsibility for detecting illegal acts and his communications to appropriate parties.

☐ *The Auditor's Responsibility for Assessing Control Risk.* This proposal would enhance audit effectiveness in planning an audit with regard to understanding the control environment, accounting systems, and control procedures.

☐ *The Communication of Control-Structure Related Matters Noted in an Audit.* This proposal is designed to improve the understandability of internal control reports and increases the flow of useful information by replacing the concept of material weaknesses in internal accounting control with a broader concept of reportable conditions concerning the design of the control structure and compliance with that structure.

☐ *Communication With Audit Committees or Others With Equivalent Authority and Responsibility.* This proposal would require the auditor to increase the flow of useful information regarding audit matters to audit committees or others with equivalent responsibility, such as owners of owner-management enterprises.

☐ *Analytical Procedures.* This proposal is designed to help auditors be more effective in detecting material misstatements by requiring the use of analytical procedures in the planning and final review stages of all audits.

☐ *Auditing Accounting Estimates.* This proposal provides guidance on evaluating the reasonableness of accounting estimates in historical financial statements.

Internal auditors are likely to be affected by these new standards. Those who work closely with external auditors will find it necessary to become familiar with the concepts and techniques involved.

---

[10] Editors, "AICPA Proposes New Auditing Standards," *Internal Auditing Alert*, April 1987, pp. 7–8. Reprinted by permission of Warren, Gorham & Lamont, Inc.

SUGGESTED READING

AICPA. *Code of Professional Ethics*. New York: AICPA, 1973.

AICPA. *Professional Standards*, Vols. 1 and 2. New York: AICPA, 1987.

Carey, John L. *The Rise of the Accounting Profession, From Technical to Professional—1876-1936*. New York: AICPA, 1969.

The Commission on Auditors' Responsibilities: Report, Conclusions and Recommendations. New York: The Commission on Auditors' Responsibilities, 1978.

Davidson, Sidney, and George D. Anderson. "The Development of Accounting and Auditing Standards." *Journal of Accountancy*, AICPA Centennial Issue 1987, May 1987, pp. 110-127.

Lowe, Herman J. "Ethics in Our 100-Year History." *Journal of Accountancy*, AICPA Centennial Issue 1987, May 1987, pp. 78-87.

Report of the National Commission on Fraudulent Financial Reporting, Oct. 1987. U.S.A.: National Commission on Fraudulent Financial Reporting, 1987.

Restructuring Professional Standards to Achieve Professional Excellence in a Changing Environment, Report of the Special Committee on Standards of Professional Conduct for Certified Public Accountants. New York: AICPA, 1986.

CHAPTER 5

Governmental Auditing Standards

by Joseph D. Comtois

Governmental Auditing Standards	1	A Summary of the 1981 Standards	8
Purpose of Governmental Auditing	2	Comparisons Between the 1972 and 1981 Standards	12
Historical Perspective	3	Single Audit Act of 1984	14
Legislative Actions Expand Audit Responsibilities	4	Nature of Major Revisions Proposed to 1981 Standards	17
Role of the GAO	5	Suggested Reading	18
A Brief Look at the 1972 Standards	7		

GOVERNMENTAL AUDITING STANDARDS

Generally accepted governmental auditing standards (GAGAS) are minimum guidelines set forth in a statement issued by the Comptroller General of the United States, entitled *Standards for Audit of Governmental Organizations, Programs, Activities and Functions*,[1] which is commonly referred to as the yellow book. In the context of GAGAS, the term "audit" expands on that work traditionally done by auditors and accountants in examining financial statements to describe work done by auditors in reviewing compliance with laws and regulations, economy and efficiency of operations, and effectiveness in achieving program results. The term "standard" in relation to

---

[1] Comptroller General of the United States, *Standards for Audit of Governmental Organizations, Programs, Activities and Functions*, 1981 Revision.

JOSEPH D. COMTOIS is Executive Director of the National Intergovernmental Audit Forum and Senior Group Director at the General Accounting Office.

GAGAS represents general measures of audit quality. They are not absolute measures to be rigidly applied, but are guiding principles requiring the application of considerable professional judgment in particular circumstances.

These measures relate to the scope and quality of the auditing effort and to the characteristics of professional and meaningful audit reports. GAGAS delineate the basic minimal standards for an audit organization or audit but not for procedures. For example, they do not provide guidelines for specific audit approaches and methodologies. Adherence to these standards, however, helps to assure users of audit reports that the auditor has adequately performed the audit and that the audit report can be relied on. The standards are also helpful in assessing the quality of an audit organization to produce useful reports, as noncompliance with the standards can cast doubt on the credibility and reliability of the audit, thereby reducing its usefulness.[2]

Governmental auditing standards present a codification of current practices and audit capabilities. But the concepts and areas of audit coverage that comprise such practices and capabilities are evolving as more responsibility is placed on governmental auditors by legislators and taxpayers. Initially issued in 1972, the standards underwent a major revision in 1981 and are currently undergoing another.

PURPOSE OF GOVERNMENTAL AUDITING

The concept of public accountability is central to the purpose of auditing in government. Government officials and employees should be required to render a full accounting of their activities to the public in accordance with generally accepted government accounting principles. Such an accounting would be particularly important in government because there is an absence of a market mechanism to guide the flow of services provided and, as a result, the profit measure cannot be employed as a primary indicator of performance. A wide range of measures relative to financial compliance with laws and regulations, efficiency, economy, and effectiveness are required to assess the stewardship provided by public officials. In general, there are three parties to an audit: the auditor, the auditee, and the party requesting a report on accountability, such as the legislature or head of a department.

Auditing is increasingly recognized by legislators and taxpayers as a critical part of our governmental system of checks and balances and is increasingly required by laws established at all levels of government. At the federal level, the GAO serves as the independent auditor for Congress over the executive branch. Within the executive branch, there are 19 Offices of Inspectors General (IGs) that also provide an audit function. IGs are required

---

[2] U.S. General Accounting Office, "CPA Audit Quality—Many Governmental Audits Do Not Comply With Professional Standards," 1001 AFMD 86-33, Mar. 1986, pp. 11, 12.

by law to report annually to Congress and the President.[3] All state governments have at least one independent audit organization.[4] With respect to local governments, the local representatives to the National Intergovernmental Audit Forum, in May 1987, published *Guidelines and Model Authorizing Legislation Regarding Audits of Local Governments*. This was issued to encourage more local governments to implement an independent audit function.[5] The pressure for auditing to be required by legislatures should further expand as a better understanding of this function improves and as resources (tax revenues) become scarcer.

GAGAS help ensure full accountability by establishing an expanded scope to provide for independent views, not only with respect to opinions on financial statements, but also as to whether resources have been applied in an efficient and effective manner. Legislators, taxpayers, and public officials desire, and need to know, not only whether government funds are properly safeguarded, reliably reported, and in compliance with all laws and regulations, but also whether government entities are achieving the purposes for which program funds were authorized and whether they are doing so economically, efficiently, and effectively.

HISTORICAL PERSPECTIVE

In the late 1960s and early 1970s, an exponential growth in federal financial assistance to state and local governments occurred. This growth created a strain on the administration, stemming from the introduction of hundreds of federal grants covering a wide array of programs. This strain engendered the need to establish a system to assure adequate accountability over the flow of the billions of dollars of federal financial assistance. Congressional officials and many federal program managers began to realize that the audit process could be an important tool for assuring greater accountability over complex funding and administration.

During this period, a proliferation of separate federal agency audit guides for auditing on a grant-by-grant basis evolved. Various audit philosophies were developed for legislation and regulations. The AICPA developed GAAS for auditing financial statements. Yet, there was a need for a more expanded set of standards that were unique to government operations.

In 1972, the Comptroller General of the United States issued *Standards for Audit of Governmental Organizations, Programs, Activities and Functions*. This was a major milestone in auditing achieved with an intergovernmental perspective. Since they were initially issued, these standards have

---

[3] Inspector General Act of 1978, Pub. L. No. 95-452.

[4] U.S. General Accounting Office, "Directory of State Audit Organizations," 1985.

[5] Local Government Representatives to the National Intergovernmental Audit Forum, "Guidelines and Model Authorizing Legislation Regarding Audit of Local Governments," May 1987.

been revised once and have been included in federal legislation or regulation and adopted by several states and local governments. The IIA has adopted similar standards (see Chapter 6). Several countries have translated them into their own language and the United Nations is in the process of adopting similar standards. The second major revision since 1972 is presently occurring, the nature of which is discussed at the end of this chapter.

LEGISLATIVE ACTIONS EXPAND AUDIT RESPONSIBILITIES

It is interesting to observe the trend of congressional legislation in relation to the expansion of responsibilities placed on governmental auditing in recent years. The standards were first incorporated in legislation in the Inspectors General Act of 1978. That act placed great emphasis on the need for preventing and detecting fraud, waste, and abuse.[6] The first major version of the yellow book in 1981 added a standard to make the auditors responsibility for detecting fraud and abuse in government programs and operations more specific.

In 1982, Congress enacted the Federal Managers' Financial Integrity Act. The goal of the legislation was to help reduce fraud, waste, and abuse, and improve the management of federal operations.[7] Paralleling the emphasis placed on internal controls by government auditors, the legislation made it necessary for government financial managers to identify and remedy longstanding internal control and system problems over accounting, administration, and programs that were frequently brought to their attention by auditors. A key requirement in the Act is that agency heads provide annual reports to the President and Congress on the status of internal controls and accounting systems. Thus, a legal requirement exists for internal control systems to provide means to prevent and detect problems early. This legislation also provides greater assurance to auditors that their reports and recommendations will receive priority attention and timely resolution.

Similar in nature to the issuance of government auditing standards, the Comptroller General of the United States, in 1983, issued *Standards for Internal Controls in the Federal Government* as guidance for heads of executive agencies in regards to their required annual reports to the President and Congress. The broad definition of internal controls developed for those standards goes beyond just accounting controls and includes those related to administration and program areas. For example, these standards refer to the internal auditing function as a most significant management control. This broader definition for internal controls is accompanied by an audit resolution

---

[6] Inspector General Act of 1978.

[7] Federal Managers' Financial Integrity Act of 1982, 31 USC §3512.

standard requiring the prompt resolution of findings and recommendations included in audit reports.[8]

In 1984, another significant milestone in the expansion of audit responsibility by the Congress occurred with the passage of the Single Audit Act of 1984.[9] This particular legislation is discussed more fully later in this chapter. However, the broad definition of internal control and the audit resolution standard emanating from the Federal Managers' Financial Integrity Act of 1982 was included in that legislation. The Single Audit Act places great emphasis on the need for improved assurances that accounting, administrative, and internal control systems over federal programs for financial assistance to state and local governments are managed in compliance with applicable laws and regulations.[10]

These legislative changes have also had either a direct or indirect impact on revisions to the AICPA's GAAS standards, which are incorporated in the yellow book. For example, as discussed in Chapter 4, the AICPA is in the process of expanding auditor responsibility in the areas of detecting and reporting errors and irregularities, and with respect to the concept of internal controls. The AICPA ASB is also developing a new standard for auditing for compliance with applicable laws and regulations such as the Davis-Bacon Act (this Act requires that workers employed by a federally financed construction project must be paid in accordance with minimum wage laws).[11] The public accounting response to the Anderson Committee Report, also discussed in Chapter 4, will provide the basis for increased leadership by the private sector in the future development and direction of audit responsibility. Public accounting professionals voted to adopt the recommendations of the Anderson Committee in early 1988.

ROLE OF THE GAO

The underlying survey and research work on which the 1972 yellow book was issued was conducted by an interagency working group made up of representatives of the GAO and federal executive departments and agencies that predominated in the federal grant programs. Assistance in their development was also obtained from audit representatives from state, county, and city governments visited during the survey and from leading professional organizations, including the AICPA, the IIA, the Federal Government Ac-

---

[8] Comptroller General of the United States, *Standards for Internal Controls in the Federal Government*, 1983.

[9] Single Audit Act of 1984, Pub. L. No. 98-502.

[10] Single Audit Act of 1984, Pub. L. No. 95-502, §§ 7501(9), 7502(d)(2)(B).

[11] Exposure draft issued by the AICPA on "Compliance Auditing: The Auditor's Responsibility for Testing Compliance With Laws, Regulations and Contractual Terms Governing Financial Assistance Certain Entities Receive From Government."

countants Association, the Municipal Finance Officers Association, and the AAA. Consultant assistance was obtained from such organizations as the Advisory Commission on Intergovernmental Relations, and from public interest groups, such as the Council of State Governments.

The 1972 standards were not mandated but were offered as guidance intended for application to audits of all government organizations, programs, activities, and functions, whether performed by auditors employed by federal, state, or local governments, independent public accountants, or others qualified to perform parts of the audit work contemplated under the standards. They were also intended to be applied to internal audits and audits of contractors, grantees, and other external organizations performed by or for a governmental entity. The standards of the AICPA that are applicable to audits performed to express opinions on the fairness with which financial statements present the financial positions and results of operations were incorporated into the yellow book.

A committee report of the AICPA that reviewed the standards in 1973 stated:

> "The members of this committee agree with the philosophy and objectives advocated by the GAO in its standards and believe that the GAO's broadened definition of auditing is a logical and worthwhile continuation of the evolution and growth of the auditing discipline." [12]

The first major revisions to the yellow book, made in 1981, resulted from the need to expand explanations of some standards, to separate the standards for financial compliance from those of economy and efficiency and program results, to incorporate standards for automatic data processing systems, and to add a standard to specify the auditors' responsibility for fraud.

In contrast to 1972, when the standards were not mandatory, the 1981 revision states that the standards must be followed by federal auditors for audits, when required by law or regulation, of federal organizations, programs, activities, functions, and funds received by contractors, nonprofit organizations, and other external organizations. The standards were merely recommended for audits of state and local governments performed by state and local government auditors or public accountants.

A very important comment contained in the 1981 standards is that the standards issued in 1972 withstood the test of time and proved to be sound and durable and have been generally accepted by all levels of government as well as by the accounting profession. As a result, the 1972 standards were, in fact, generally accepted by a broad base of government agencies and units for government auditing activities.

For example, the Office of Management and Budget (OMB) frequently

---

[12] *Standards for Audit of Governmental Organizations, Programs, Activities and Functions*, by the Comptroller General of the United States, 1981 Revision, p. 2.

cites the standards in OMB circulars as basic audit criteria for federal executive departments to follow. In addition, federal legislation incorporates the standards for Inspectors General to follow for audits of federal organizations, as well as for audits of federal funds received by state or local governments, contractors, nonprofit organizations, and other organizations. Many states also adopted the standards into their audit operations. Local government audit representatives to the National Intergovernmental Audit Forum have adopted the standards for incorporation in their publication, entitled *Guidelines and Model Authorizing Legislation Regarding Audit of Local Government*.[13]

Revisions included in the 1981 standards were also based on comments and suggestions that the GAO received after the standards were issued in 1972. These comments were considered in preparing a draft of the revised standards, which was then sent to audit officials at all levels of government, professional organizations, the public accounting profession, academia, and other interested groups and persons for review and comments. These comments were, in turn, reviewed and then incorporated, as appropriate, in the final revision of the standards.

The current revision to the standards is being developed with the assistance of an advisory council to the Comptroller General of the United States, comprised of individuals from a wide range of organizations from both the public and private sectors. The exposure draft revisions were again sent to a large cross section of audit officials for comments and, in addition, notice of the exposure draft was mentioned in the *Federal Register*, and public hearings were held.[14] Thus, a broad base of professionals have been afforded participation in this process.

A BRIEF LOOK AT THE 1972 STANDARDS

In comparison to similar standards issued by the AICPA, the 1972 version of the yellow book expanded the discussion of the general standards for qualifications, independence, and due professional care. This expansion encompassed the broader perspective of expanded scope auditing for government that goes beyond the development of independent opinions on financial statements. This broader perspective includes audit objectives regarding economy, efficiency, and effectiveness, in addition to audit objectives regarding financial statements. A new standard was developed within the general standards, called the scope of audit work standard. This standard was defined as follows:[15]

---

[13] Local Government Representative to the National Intergovernmental Audit Forum, *Guidelines and Model Authorizing Legislation Regarding Audit of Local Government*, May 1987, p. 1.

[14] *Federal Register*, Vol. 52, No. 67, pp. 11341, 11342, dated April 8, 1987; public hearings were scheduled for Washington, D.C., June 3, 1987; Phoenix, Arizona, June 9, 1987; Dallas, Texas, June 23, 1987; and New Orleans, July 2, 1987.

[15] 1972 *Standards*, p. 10.

The full scope of an audit of a governmental program, function, activity, or organization should encompass:

1. An examination of financial transactions, accounts, and reports, including an evaluation of compliance with applicable laws and regulations.
2. A review of efficiency and economy in the use of resources.
3. A review to determine whether desired results are effectively achieved.

In determining the scope for a particular audit, responsible officials should give consideration to the needs of the potential users of the results of the audit.

Separate examination and evaluation (i.e., fieldwork) standards and reporting standards relating to all three elements of the expanded scope were contained in the 1972 yellow book. The examination and evaluation standards related to planning, supervision, legal and regulatory requirements, internal control, and evidence. The reporting standards related to form and distribution, timeliness, content, and financial reports. Independent auditor opinions on financial statements were not specifically stated in the elements of expanded scope but were included as one of the financial reports.

A SUMMARY OF THE 1981 STANDARDS

The 1981 standards expanded explanation of some standards, separated the financial and compliance standards from other standards, incorporated standards for automatic data processing, and added a new standard with respect to fraud. These are discussed below:[16]

A. Scope of Audit Work

The expanded scope of auditing a government organization, a program, an activity, or a function should include:

1. *Financial and compliance*—determines (a) whether the financial statements of an audited entity present fairly the financial position and the results of financial operations in accordance with generally accepted accounting principles and (b) whether the entity has complied with laws and regulations that may have a material effect upon the financial statements.
2. *Economy and efficiency*—determines (a) whether the entity is managing and utilizing its resources (such as personnel, property, space) economically and efficiently, (b) the causes of inefficiencies or uneconomical practices, and (c) whether the entity has complied with laws and regulations concerning matters of economy and efficiency.
3. *Program results*—determines (a) whether the desired results or benefits established by the legislature or other authorizing body are being achieved and

---

[16] 1981 *Standards*, pp. 6–11.

(b) whether the agency has considered alternatives that might yield desired results at a lower cost.

In determining the scope for a particular audit, responsible audit and entity officials should consider the needs of the potential users of audit findings.

B. General Standards

1. *Qualifications:* The auditors assigned to perform the audit must collectively possess adequate professional proficiency for the tasks required.
2. *Independence:* In all matters relating to the audit work, the audit organization and the individual auditors, whether government or public, must be free from personal or external impairments to independence, must be organizationally independent, and shall maintain an independent attitude and appearance.
3. *Due professional care:* Due professional care is to be used in conducting the audit and in preparing related reports.
4. *Scope impairments:* When factors external to the audit organization and the auditor restrict the audit or interfere with the auditor's ability to form objective opinions and conclusions, the auditor should attempt to remove the limitation or, failing that, report the limitation.

C. Examination and Evaluation (Field Work) and Reporting Standards for Financial and Compliance Audits

1. AICPA Statements on Auditing Standards for field work and reporting are adopted and incorporated in this statement for government financial and compliance audits. Future statements should be adopted and incorporated, unless GAO excluded them by formal announcement.
2. Additional standards and requirements for government financial and compliance audits.
    a. *Standards on examination and evaluation:*
        (1) Planning shall include consideration of the requirements of all levels of government.
        (2) A review is to be made of compliance with applicable laws and regulations.
        (3) A written record of the auditors' work shall be retained in the form of working papers.
        (4) Auditors shall be alert to situations or transactions that could be indicative of fraud, abuse, and illegal expenditures and acts and if such evidence exists, extend audit steps and procedures to identify the effect on the entity's financial statements.
    b. *Standards on reporting:*
        (1) Written audit reports are to be submitted to the appropriate officials of the organization audited and to the appropriate officials of the organization audited and to the appropriate officials of the organizations requiring or arranging for the audits unless legal restrictions or ethical considerations prevent it. Copies of the reports should also be sent to other officials who may be responsible for taking action

and to others authorized to receive such reports. Unless restricted by law or regulations, copies should be made available for public inspection.
(2) A statement in the auditors' report that the examination was made in accordance with generally accepted government auditing standards for financial and compliance audits will be acceptable language to indicate that the audit was made in accordance with these standards. (See ch. V, par. 2b for AICPA-suggested language.)
(3) Either the auditors' report on the entity's financial statements or a separate report shall contain a statement of positive assurance on those items of compliance tested and negative assurance on those items not tested. It shall also include material instances of noncompliance and instances or indications of fraud, abuse, or illegal acts found during or in connection with the audit.
(4) The auditors shall report on their study and evaluation of internal accounting controls made as part of the financial and compliance audit. They shall identify as a minimum: (a) the entity's significant internal accounting controls, (b) the controls identified that were evaluated, and (c) the controls identified that were not evaluated (the auditor may satisfy this requirement by identifying any significant classes of transactions and related assets not included in the study and evaluation), and (d) the material weaknesses identified as a result of the evaluation.
(5) Either the auditor's report on the entity's financial statements or a separate report shall contain any other material deficiency findings identified during the audit not covered in (3) above.
(6) If certain information is prohibited from general disclosure, the report shall state the nature of the information omitted and the requirement that makes the omission necessary.

D. Examination and Evaluation Standards for Economy and Efficiency Audits and Program Results Audits

1. Work is to be adequately planned.
2. Assistants are to be properly supervised.
3. A review is to be made of compliance with applicable laws and regulations.
4. During the audit a study and evaluation shall be made of the internal control system (administrative controls) applicable to the organization, program, activity, or function under audit.
5. When audits involve computer-based systems, the auditors shall:
   a. Review general control in data processing systems to determine whether (1) the controls have been designed according to management direction and known legal requirements and (2) the controls are operating effectively to provide reliability of, and security over, the data being processed.
   b. Review application controls of installed data processing applications upon which the auditor is relying to assess their reliability in processing data in a timely, accurate, and complete manner.

6. Sufficient, competent, and relevant evidence is to be obtained to afford a reasonable basis for the auditors' judgments and conclusions regarding the organization, program, activity, or function under audit. A written record of the auditors' work shall be retained in the form of working papers.
7. The auditors shall:
   a. Be alert to situations or transactions that could be indicative of fraud, abuse, and illegal acts.
   b. If such evidence exists, extend audit steps and procedures to identify the effect on the entity's operations and programs.

E. Reporting Standards for Economy and Efficiency Audits and Program Results Audits

1. Written audit reports are to be prepared giving the results of each government audit.
2. Written audit reports are to be submitted to the appropriate officials of the organization audited and to the appropriate officials of the organizations requiring or arranging for the audits unless legal restrictions or ethical considerations prevent it. Copies of the reports should also be sent to other officials who may be responsible for taking action on audit findings and recommendations and to others authorized to receive such reports. Unless restricted by law or regulation, copies should be made available for public inspection.
3. Reports are to be issued on or before the dates specified by law, regulation, or other special arrangement. Reports are to be issued promptly so as to make the information available for timely use by management and by legislative officials.
4. The report shall include:
   a. A description of the scope and objectives of the audit.
   b. A statement that the audit (economy and efficiency or program results) was made in accordance with generally accepted government auditing standards.
   c. A description of material weaknesses found in the internal control system (administrative controls).
   d. A statement of positive assurance on those items of compliance tested and negative assurance on those items not tested. This should include significant instances of noncompliance and instances of or indications of fraud, abuse, or illegal acts found during or in connection with the audit. However, fraud, abuse, or illegal acts normally should be covered in a separate report, thus permitting the overall report to be released to the public.
   e. Recommendations for actions to improve problem areas noted in the audit and to improve operations. The underlying causes of problems reported should be included to assist in implementing corrective actions.
   f. Pertinent views of responsible officials of the organization, program, activity, or function audited concerning the auditors' findings, conclusions,

and recommendations. When possible their views should be obtained in writing.

    g. A description of noteworthy accomplishments, particularly when management improvements in one area may be applicable elsewhere.

    h. A listing of any issues and questions needing further study and consideration.

    i. A statement as to whether any pertinent information has been omitted because it is deemed privileged or confidential. The nature of such information should be described, and the law or other basis under which it is withheld should be stated. If a separate report was issued containing this information it should be indicated in the report.

5. The report shall:
    a. Present factual data accurately and fairly. Include only information, findings, and conclusions that are adequately supported by sufficient evidence in the auditors' working papers to demonstrate or prove the bases for the matters reported and their correctness and reasonableness.
    b. Present findings and conclusions in a convincing manner.
    c. Be objective.
    d. Be written in language as clear and simple as the subject matter permits.
    e. Be concise but, at the same time, clear enough to be understood by users.
    f. Present factual data completely to fully inform the users.
    g. Place primary emphasis on improvement rather than on criticism of the past; critical comments should be presented in a balanced perspective considering any unusual difficulties or circumstances faced by the operating officials concerned.

COMPARISONS BETWEEN THE 1972 AND 1981 STANDARDS

About nine years of experience with the 1972 version of the standards was obtained by federal, state, and local auditors and public accountants prior to the 1981 revision.

A significant input to the 1981 revision was made by the Intergovernmental Audit Forums, a network of about 1,000 members, many of whom are heads of audit organizations. These forums, comprised of a national and 10 regional forums, were supported by the Comptroller General of the United States since 1973. Most credit is due to a small number of state and local government auditors whose initiative was key to creating the forums. A major purpose of the forums is to improve the cooperation, coordination, and communication among all members of the governmental audit community. A major specific objective of the forums is to improve the development of national auditing standards. Thus, this input was broad-based in terms of federal, state, and local government audit officials, and was national in scope.

Significant input was also provided by the AICPA, whose major objective was to eliminate the confusion to public accountants and their clients concerning the broad definition of scope for the financial audit provided in the 1972 standards.[17] The 1972 standards related the financial audit to an unspecified scope dealing with financial transactions, accounts, reports, and evaluation of compliance with applicable laws and regulations. The public accounting profession desired a more specific relationship to the main objective of their work, namely, the rendering of opinions on financial statements. This change in the first element of expanded scope was not accompanied by a similar specificity for economy and efficiency or program results audits wherein objectives and scopes of audits had to be determined for each audit.

The 1981 standards included an additional area under the general standards category, which includes standards of qualifications, independence, and due care. The new area created was called scope impairments, and emphasized that the auditor should attempt to remove any restrictions or interference with the auditors ability to formulate objective opinions and conclusions.

Other changes were made to fieldwork and reporting standards that should be noted. While GAGAS required additional standards over GAAS, it did so mainly in the area of reporting. GAGAS called for a statement on internal control and a statement on compliance with laws and regulations (e.g., the Single Audit Act). The AICPA issued two statements on auditing standards to help close the gap between GAAS and GAGAS—SAS No. 22, "Planning and Supervision," and SAS No. 30, "Reporting on Internal Controls." It was also made clear by the AICPA, through its interpretation of its Code of Ethics, SEC 503-1, that it was an act discreditable to the public accounting profession if an auditor states he followed GAGAS when he did not do so.

As previously stated, 1981 standards emphasized a specific auditing objective and scope for the financial and compliance element. Reference was made to the rendering of opinions on financial statements in accordance with GAAP and to assessing compliance with laws and regulations that may have a material effect on financial statements. The four examination and evaluation standards that were added to GAAS for the financial and compliance audit included those related to planning considerations for all levels of government, the preparation of workpapers, the requirement that the auditor be alert to fraud, and a review of compliance with applicable laws and regulations to the extent they may have a material effect on the financial statements as a whole. No additional work was required for the review of internal controls over that called for in GAAS. As previously indicated, the

---

[17] Mortimer A. Dittenhofer, "The Revised Government Audit Standards," *GAO Review*, Spring 1982, p. 28.

reporting standards added by the yellow book required considerably more disclosure on the nature and extent of internal controls studied and evaluated, and a statement with respect to compliance with laws and regulations. It also required a disclosure of instances of fraudulent activities.

The examination and evaluation standards for economy and efficiency and program results, in comparison to 1972, added standards related to automatic data processing and fraud. Reporting standards included a specific statement with respect to the review of internal controls and compliance with laws and regulations.

The 1981 revisions state that it is not intended or feasible that every audit include all three elements and that the expanded scope audit should not be performed routinely, but rather selected to meet the needs of expected users. It was also noted that the 1978 Institute of Internal Audit Auditor Standards were compatible with the yellow book.

SINGLE AUDIT ACT OF 1984

Federal financial assistance to state and local governments of about $100 billion dollars flows every year to 50 states and to thousands of local governments. These funds provide for hundreds of different programs involving education, transportation, health, and a multitude of other areas. Attempts by Congress and the executive branch over the last several years to close significant gaps in audit coverage and to eliminate duplication of audit effort over these programs were not successful. The same governmental entity would undergo audits performed by different groups of federal, state, and local auditors and public accountants at the same time. A grant-by-grant approach to audits could not be curtailed, and a large number of federal grants were not subjected to any audit. The resulting audit products were fragmented, and were supported by different audit philosophies, audit guides, and legislative or regulatory requirements.

A report issued by the U.S. General Accounting Office in March 1984 discusses the reasons why legislation was needed to remove major obstacles to a more successful implementation of the single audit concept.[18] This legislation was needed to provide a clear definition of the purpose and scope of the single audit concept, to determine dollar thresholds to indicate which governments would be subject to the Single Audit Act, and to eliminate existing multiple federal audit requirements that were in conflict with the single audit concept. The responsibilities of many parties, including the GAO, OMB, federal agencies, state and local grantees, state and local auditors, and public accountants, had to be sorted out. Of course, the Act makes

---

[18] U.S. General Accounting Office, "Study of Progress Made in Implementing the Single Audit Concept," GAO/AFMD 84-21, Mar. 14, 1984.

it clear that the single audit would be performed in accordance with GAGAS. Passage of the Single Audit Act represents a major intergovernmental reform of the audit process. The purposes of the Single Audit Act are:[19]

1. To improve the financial management of state and local governments with respect to federal financial assistance programs,
2. To establish uniform requirements for audits of federal financial assistance provided to state and local governments,
3. To promote the efficient and effective use of audit resources, and
4. To ensure that federal departments and agencies, to the maximum extent practicable, rely upon and use work done pursuant to . . . this act.

An organizationwide, rather than a piecemeal, approach is a key aspect of the single audit concept. Thus, it is understandable that a major aspect of the Act is its emphasis on delineating the scope of the single audit. The single audit does not include such work as economy and efficiency or program results audits. It also excludes grant-by-grant auditing. However, it does include enough work to provide sufficient information on weaknesses in internal controls and in noncompliance with federal laws and regulations so that appropriate corrective action can be taken or additional work identified. The act provides three major components:

1. Financial statements of the government present fairly its financial position and the results of its financial operations in accordance with GAAP and whether the government has complied with laws and regulations that may have a material effect on the financial statements.
2. The government has internal control systems to provide reasonable assurance that it is managing federal financial assistance programs in compliance with applicable laws and regulations.
3. The government has complied with laws and regulations that may have a material effect on each major federal program.

Thus, the single audit builds on the traditional financial statement audit and requires an expansion of that audit to examine the internal control systems over federal financial assistance and compliance testing with respect to laws and regulations. The review of internal controls is not optional and must encompass not only accounting and administrative controls, but also controls applicable to the programs for which the assistance is intended. While the state or local entity is not mandated to follow GAAP, the auditors' report should indicate the extent to which financial statements do not do so.

Another significant aspect of the Single Audit Act is the change in the materiality levels related to federal financial assistance. Rather than a ma-

---

[19] Single Audit Act of 1984, Pub. L. No. 95-502, §§ 1(a), 1(b).

teriality level related to the entire financial statement, the Act requires compliance testing related to each major program. The aspects in such testing would include cost allocation charges, eligibility requirements, and other general and specific compliance requirements. The dollar thresholds for determining a major program are set forth in the Act.

An important feature of the Act is that federal agencies are required to rely on and use the results of the single audit in planning and conducting additional work to avoid the duplication that previously existed and to enhance coverage. The single audit provides guideposts to the conduct of additional work where more in-depth auditing on specific areas can be performed.

Adherence to these basic concepts should significantly improve the audit coverage of federal financial assistance throughout the nation. It will take several years before the single audit concept will reach its maximum effectiveness. However, it should, over time, provide an increased understanding and strengthening of internal control systems over federal grants at the entity level. When aggregated at the state level, single audits should identify patterns of noncompliance with laws and regulations that are statewide in scope. This aspect should provide an early warning on potential problems before they become major. The single audit provides an effective building block between the traditional financial statement audit and additional work that may be warranted. Such audits are usually costly to perform. Thus, a cost-effective audit policy on an intergovernmental basis has been established.

Several other aspects of the Single Audit Act include the requirements that:

- An audit is to be performed in accordance with the yellow book.
- An audit is to be performed annually.
- A unit of government must have a single audit if it receives over $100,000 in federal financial assistance. The definition of an entity or unit of government is left to the states and local governments.
- A unit of government has an option of not performing the single audit if it receives between $25,000 and $100,000 in assistance.
- Units of government receiving less than $25,000 are exempt.
- Major programs are defined according to dollar thresholds based on levels of expenditures.
- Nonmajor programs are to be tested for compliance with applicable laws and regulations only for the specific transaction being tested.
- Primary recipients of federal assistance must ensure safeguards over funds provided to subrecipients.
- A plan for corrective action must be submitted by the recipient to the relevant federal official to eliminate weaknesses or noncompliance found.
- Cognizant federal agencies, or those federal agencies designated by the OMB, are responsible to ensure timely reporting, proper corrective action, quality review over audits performed, and coordination of additional audits.

Several documents related to overall and procedural guidance are available to conduct the single audit, including:

- Several OMB circulars, including a compliance supplement.
- The OMB compliance supplement, which offers detailed guidance related to many particular grants on both general and specific areas of compliance, with applicable laws and regulations.
- Cognizant audit agency guidelines.
- Federal agency regulations.
- The yellow book.
- The AICPA industry audit guide for audits of state and local governmental units.

OMB is responsible for developing implementation policy and for reporting annually to Congress on the status of implementation. The GAO and state and local governments are to be consulted by OMB in the development of such policy guidance.

The most difficult part of the Act to be implemented will be the fieldwork and reporting standards related to audits of internal control systems and for testing for compliance with applicable laws and regulations because they involve not only accounting but administrative and program issues as well. As previously indicated, the AICPA is in the process of developing a broader concept statement for the audit of internal controls and a new standard for the audit of compliance with laws and regulations.

Considerable education and training is required to support the understanding of this concept by auditors and program managers at all levels of government. Cooperation at all levels of government and with public accountants will also be required for the single audit to work effectively. Additional major studies planned by the GAO, combined with reports by the OMB, and more experience by state and local government auditors and public accountants is needed before additional guidance can be developed.

The reader is referred to three published articles dealing more extensively with the single audit. The articles appear in the April 1985, April 1986, and July 1987 issues of the *Journal of Accountancy*.

NATURE OF MAJOR REVISIONS PROPOSED TO 1981 STANDARDS

The major proposed revisions now being considered for the yellow book include:

- Reference to the Single Audit Act of 1984
- Guidance on the procurement of audit services
- Clarification to the types of audit that might be performed

- Expansion of the requirements for continuing professional education and training
- Requirement of an internal quality control system and participation in an external quality control review program
- Further expansion on the concepts of audit risk and materiality
- Clarification to the auditor's responsibility for follow-up on findings and recommendations
- Clarification regarding the auditor's responsibility for detecting and reporting on fraud, abuse, and illegal acts
- Clarification to the auditor's responsibility on the study and evaluation of internal controls and reporting thereon
- Clarification to the auditor's responsibility for auditing computer-based systems
- Guidance for relying on the results of the work of other auditors

The last day for receiving comments to be considered in preparing the final revised standards was June 30, 1987. It is expected that the final revision will be issued sometime in 1988.[20]

It is clear that the auditor's responsibilities under GAGAS are being considerably expanded and refined. It is also clear that federal legislation and oversight activities are vitally concerned with the purpose and scope of governmental audits. The AICPA is also responding to the rapidly changing role of the public accountant involved in governmental audits.

SUGGESTED READING

Broadus, Jr., W.A., and Joseph D. Comtois. "The Single Audit Act: A Needed Reform." *Journal of Accountancy,* April 1985, pp. 62–71.

———. "Tools for the Single Audit." *Journal of Accountancy,* April 1986, pp. 73–81.

———. "The Single Audit: A Progress Report." *Journal of Accountancy,* July 1987, pp. 92–100.

---

[20] Draft of Proposed Revisions, Government Auditing Standards—Date for comments on the proposed revisions had to be sent to GAO by June 30, 1987.

CHAPTER **6**

Standards for the Professional Practice of Internal Auditing

Definition and Background 1
Purpose 2
Applicability 3
The Role of the PSRC 4
Organization and Methodology 5
The Treadway Commission 6

Internal Auditing Standards 7
The General and Specific Standards 7
The SIASs 14
The Codes of Ethics 17
Statement of Responsibilities 19

Suggested Reading 22

Fig. 6-1   Internal Auditing Standards—Levels of Authority 5
Fig. 6-2   Developing and Approving Statements on Internal Auditing Standards 6
Fig. 6-3   The Institute of Internal Auditors, Inc. Code of Ethics 18
Fig. 6-4   The Certified Internal Auditor Code of Ethics 20
Fig. 6-5   Statement of Responsibilities of Internal Auditing 21

DEFINITION AND BACKGROUND

"Standards for the Professional Practice of Internal Auditing" is the term the IIA devised to represent the internal auditing standards it approved in 1978. According to the foreword contained in the 1978 pronouncement, "The term standards means the criteria by which the operations of an internal auditing department are evaluated and measured."[1] These standards are more in the nature of goals. That is to say, they represent what the practice of internal auditing ought to be as determined by the IIA board of directors.

This body of standards differs from those of the AICPA and those of

---

[1] IIA, *Standards for the Professional Practice of Internal Auditing* (Altamonte Springs, Fla.: IIA 1978), p. iii.

6-1

the GAO. In those cases, the standards represent a minimum acceptable level of performance. In the instance of the AICPA, a member may be disciplined in the event he fails to abide by GAAS. In the instance of the GAO standards, federal legislation compels inspectors general and others who perform audits of federal organizations, programs, activities and functions to comply with them.

The distinction exists because the IIA, unlike the AICPA and the GAO, backed by state boards of accountancy and the federal government respectively, has no authority or clout to compel compliance. Instead, the board of directors developed the standards as a service to the profession. It actively promotes their adoption by internal audit departments of private companies and by other groups who perform auditing services.

Prior to the promulgation of these standards, there was no authoritative guidance for internal auditing practitioners. Practice could and did vary widely. On the one hand, there were many internal auditing departments that were observing high standards of performance and rendering high quality auditing services as a result. On the other hand, there were many who performed internal auditing with little apparent regard for the importance of high standards of performance and quality. Accordingly, in many organizations, internal auditing was a function held in low esteem. People with high skill and talent would tend to avoid it, or they would accept a stint in the department for only as long as it would take to find something better.

These circumstances operated to the detriment of the objectives of internal auditing for the organizations affected. They gave internal auditing a bad image. To some extent, that image remains perceptible even today, but it is much less so. And much of the credit for this changed circumstance traces to the issuance of these standards.

The balance of this chapter discusses these standards. It is imperative that internal auditing practitioners be knowledgeable of such standards. Beyond that, they must strive to comply with them.

PURPOSE

Internal auditing standards are intended to provide internal auditing practitioners with a set of goals to aim for. By specifying high ideals in all aspects of internal auditing involvement, the standards provide a useful gauge with which to measure performance of the internal auditing department.

A second purpose for the standards is to provide an authoritative communication device, informing practitioners of what they ought to be able to achieve. Not only are practitioners educated in the process, but also others who are involved in or affected by the internal auditing function, including members of management, boards of directors, external auditors, legislators, the courts, members of academe, and, to some extent, the public.

Perhaps the following, taken from the standards themselves, is the best statement of purpose for the standards:

"1. Impart an understanding of the role and responsibilities of internal auditing to all levels of management, boards directors, public bodies, external auditors, and related professional organizations.
2. Establish the basis for the guidance and measurement of internal audit performance.
3. Improve the practice of internal auditing."[2]

APPLICABILITY

The internal auditing standards promulgated by the IIA are intended to apply to departments, units, or activities established within an organization to examine and evaluate the organization's activities. For most companies, such departments, units, or activities are often referred to as the internal auditing department.

In many companies, there are functions or units that perform procedures and techniques similar to those of internal auditing but to whom these standards do not apply. One example is senior management. Its stewardship responsibility necessitates that it perform an ongoing evaluation of the appropriateness of its plans, strategies, products, commitments, and relationships. Other examples include such functions or departments as quality assurance, performance review boards, industrial engineering, product readiness groups, internal security forces, and self-audit groups.

Generally speaking, internal auditing standards are not intended to apply to such functions or departments because they are not organized to assist management and the board of directors. Usually, they are organized as an integral part of a line organization or function. As such, they have no contact with the board of directors and, in many cases, they even have little contact with members of senior management.

This is not to say that standards of performance are not important for these other functions. However, the IIA standards may not be wholly appropriate. For one thing, internal auditing must be organizationally independent of the entities, functions, and activities it audits, which is not possible for such functions as quality assurance. For another thing, the requisite body of knowledge differs for internal auditing departments vis-à-vis the other groups mentioned. It would be unwise for such groups to attempt to embrace the standards because it would tend to raise confusion as to whether the work product of the internal auditor is indeed independent from that of

---

[2] *Ibid.*, p. 2. Reprinted by permission of the Institute of Internal Auditors, Inc., 249 Maitland Ave., Altamonte Springs, Fla. 32701.

the other groups. These groups should develop standards more appropriate to their functional status.

The fact that internal auditing standards set forth by the IIA apply to certain internal groups and not others must be understood by all who may be involved with internal auditing. Another point that must be widely understood is that there is no law or regulation that requires private companies to have internal auditing departments, or that such departments follow the standards adopted by the IIA. To date, no court precedents have occurred in which one of the issues to be decided is whether compliance with IIA standards protects the practitioner in an instance where the work of the practitioner caused injury to another party.

Without such precedents and without the force of law or regulation, IIA standards apply only where those involved voluntarily adopt them. There is little question that the standards are widely employed by the voluntary actions of a growing body of practitioners. Some states, notably California and Florida, have mandated by legislative action compliance with the standards by state and local government auditors. Moreover, the SEC seems to have developed an interest in the function of internal auditing. Published statements by Robert Sack, Chief Accountant of the SEC, reflect this interest. According to reports, Mr. Sack indicated that "the turf of internal auditors may become the focus of more SEC activity in the future because of the SEC's continuing interest in the accounting provisions of the FCPA, and because CPA firms are focusing more on testing systems than testing account balances."[3] Whether the SEC will look to the standards of the IIA to evaluate the internal auditing departments of given registrants is not clear. But those who choose to ignore such standards may be called upon at some future date to justify such ignorance—with FCPA issues on the line.

THE ROLE OF THE PSRC

Standards setting by the IIA began with the adoption, by the IIA board of directors, of the *Standards for the Professional Practice of Internal Auditing*. These standards were developed for the board by the International Professional Standards and Responsibilities Committee. Later known as the PSRC, it is the senior technical committee designated by the IIA board of directors with authority to modify or amend the 25 specific standards and related guidelines.

The PSRC performs its role by issuing SIASs and PSBs. The IIA considers the SIASs to be as authoritative as the original general standards. It considers the PSBs to be semiauthoritative. That is because PSBs are ac-

---

[3] Michael J. Barrett, "Financial Reports and Quality Control," *Internal Auditing*, Summer 1985, p. 63.

FIG. 6-1

Internal Auditing Standards—Levels of Authority

Level of Authority	Type of Pronouncements	Process	Final Approval Authority
Authoritative			
Statement of Responsibilities	Statement	Research—exposure—PS&R approval	Board of Directors
IIA Code of Ethics	Code	Research—exposure—PS&R approval	Board of Directors
CIA Code of Ethics	Code	Research—exposure—PS&R approval	Board of Directors
Standards for the Professional Practice of Internal Auditing			
General standards	Standards	Research—exposure—PS&R approval	Board of Directors
Specific standards and guidelines	Statements (SIAS)	Research—exposure—PS&R approval	PS&R Committee
Semi-Authoritative			
Questions and answers	Bulletins (PSB)	Informal research—Standards Information Service subcommittee	PS&R Chairman—reviewed with Executive Committee designee

corded a reduced exposure process as compared to that for SIAS. The relationships are depicted in Figure 6-1.[4]

Organization and Methodology

The PSRC is an international committee of the IIA. Membership on the committee is appointed by the chairman of the IIA for a period of two years. At least two thirds of the committee must be CIAs. The membership historically has been approximately 15.

SIASs are released by the PSRC after a formal process that begins with project initiation and ends with a ballot draft voted on by each of the PSRC members. In between are steps entailing research, issuance of papers, initial drafts, exposure drafts, revised drafts, and finally, ballot drafts.

---

[4] IIA, *Standards for the Professional Practice of Internal Auditing* (Altamonte Springs, Fla.: IIA, 1985), p. iii. Reprinted by permission of the Institute of Internal Auditors, Inc.

FIG. 6-2

Developing and Approving Statements on Internal Auditing Standards

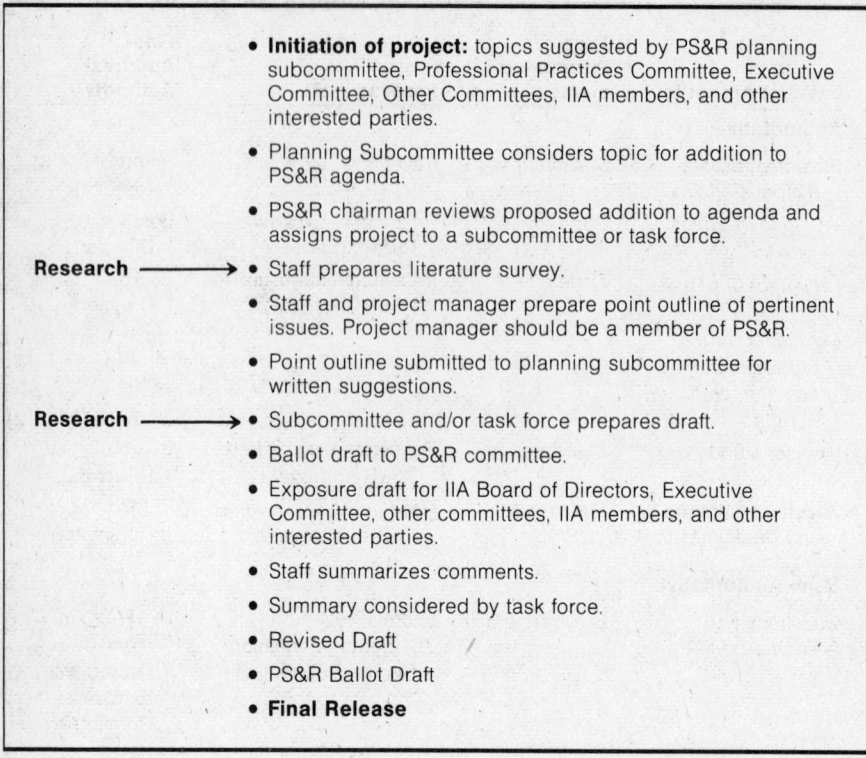

The PSRC is supported by IIA staff but much of the work is accomplished by voluntary efforts of task forces on a project basis headed by chairpersons or project leaders. The process is depicted in chart form in Figure 6-2.[5]

The Treadway Commission

The activities of the Treadway Commission are discussed in Chapters 1, 2, and 23. Its relevance in the context of internal auditing standards is such that it warrants emphasis here. The Commission voiced strong support for the contribution of internal auditing toward minimizing financial reporting fraud. With respect to standards, the Commission stated:[6]

---

[5] IIA, *The Role of the Internal Auditor in the Deterrence, Detection and Reporting of Fraudulent Financial Reporting* (Altamonte Springs, Fla.: IIA, 1987), p. 39. Reprinted by permission of the Institute of Internal Auditors, Inc.

[6] Treadway Commission, *Report of the National Commission on Fraudulent Financial Reporting*, October 1987 (U.S.A.: National Commission on Fraudulent Financial Reporting, 1987), p. 38.

The professionalism of internal auditors has been enhanced in recent years by the efforts of the Institute of Internal Auditors (IIA), the professional organization for internal auditors. Standards of the IIA offer excellent guidance for effective internal auditing and reflect some of the most advanced thinking on fraud prevention and detection. The Commission encourages public companies who have not done so to consider adopting the IIA standards.

The Commission included the standards as one of the appendices in its report.

INTERNAL AUDITING STANDARDS

Internal auditing standards include the general standards approved by the IIA board of directors in 1978 and the subsequent SIASs issued by the PSRC. The IIA also set forth a Code of Ethics for its members in 1968. Subsequently, in 1972, a Code of Ethics for CIAs was issued. Prior to developing internal auditing standards and the codes of ethics, the IIA published the Statement of Responsibilities of Internal Auditing. The statement was first prepared in 1947 and revised in 1957, 1971, 1976, and 1981. Technically, the statement of responsibilities is not a standard. However, it is identified by the IIA as authoritative because it provides, in summary form, an understanding of the role and responsibilities of internal auditing.

The General and Specific Standards

A summary of the standards published by the IIA is set forth in the following.[7]

> SUMMARY OF GENERAL AND SPECIFIC STANDARDS FOR THE PROFESSIONAL PRACTICE OF INTERNAL AUDITING
>
> 100 *Independence*. Internal auditors should be independent of the activities they audit.
>   110 *Organizational Status*. The organizational status of the internal auditing department should be sufficient to permit the accomplishment of its audit responsibilities.
>   120 *Objectivity*. Internal auditors should be objective in performing audits.
> 200 *Professional Proficiency*. Internal audits should be performed with proficiency and due professional care.

---

[7] From *Standards for the Professional Practice of Internal Auditing* by IIA International Professional Standards and Responsibilities Committee, pp. 3–4. Copyright, 1978 by the Institute of Internal Auditors, Inc., 249 Maitland Avenue, Altamonte Springs, Fla., 32701. Reprinted by permission of the Institute of Internal Auditors, Inc.

THE INTERNAL AUDITING DEPARTMENT

210 *Staffing.* The internal auditing department should provide assurance that the technical proficiency and educational background of internal auditors are appropriate for the audits to be performed.

220 *Knowledge, Skills, and Disciplines.* The internal auditing department should possess or should obtain the knowledge, skills, and disciplines needed to carry out its audit responsibilities.

230 *Supervision.* The internal auditing department should provide assurance that internal audits are properly supervised.

THE INTERNAL AUDITOR

240 *Compliance with Standards of Conduct.* Internal auditors should comply with professional standards of conduct.

250 *Knowledge, Skills, and Disciplines.* Internal auditors should possess the knowledge, skills, and disciplines essential to the performance of internal audits.

260 *Human Relations and Communications.* Internal auditors should be skilled in dealing with people and in communicating effectively.

270 *Continuing Education.* Internal auditors should maintain their technical competence through continuing education.

280 *Due Professional Care.* Internal auditors should exercise due professional care in performing internal audits.

300 *Scope of Work.* The scope of the internal audit should encompass the examination and evaluation of the adequacy and effectiveness of the organization's system of internal control and the quality of performance in carrying out assigned responsibilities.

310 *Reliability and Integrity of Information.* Internal auditors should review the reliability and integrity of financial and operating information and the means used to identify, measure, classify, and report such information.

320 *Compliance with Policies, Plans, Procedures, Laws, and Regulations.* Internal auditors should review the systems established to ensure compliance with those policies, plans, procedures, laws, and regulations which could have a significant impact on operations and reports and should determine whether the organization is in compliance.

330 *Safeguarding of Assets.* Internal auditors should review the means of safeguarding assets and, as appropriate, verify the existence of such assets.

340 *Economical and Efficient Use of Resources.* Internal auditors should appraise the economy and efficiency with which resources are employed.

350 *Accomplishment of Established Objectives and Goals for Operations or Programs.* Internal auditors should review operations or programs to ascertain whether results are consistent with established objectives and goals and whether the operations or programs are being carried out as planned.

400 *Performance of Audit Work.* Audit work should include planning the audit,

examining and evaluating information, communicating results, and following up.

- 410 *Planning the Audit.* Internal auditors should plan each audit.
- 420 *Examining and Evaluating Information.* Internal auditors should collect, analyze, interpret, and document information to support audit results.
- 430 *Communicating Results.* Internal auditors should report the results of their audit work.
- 440 *Following Up.* Internal auditors should follow up to ascertain that appropriate action is taken on reported audit findings.

500 *Management of the Internal Auditing Department.* The director of internal auditing should properly manage the internal auditing department.

- 510 *Purpose, Authority, and Responsibility.* The director of internal auditing should have a statement of purpose, authority, and responsibility for the internal auditing department.
- 520 *Planning.* The director of internal auditing should establish plans to carry out the responsibilities of the internal auditing department.
- 530 *Policies and Procedures.* The director of internal auditing should provide written policies and procedures to guide the audit staff.
- 540 *Personnel Management and Development.* The director of internal auditing should establish a program for selecting and developing the human resources of the internal auditing department.
- 550 *External Auditors.* The director of internal auditing should coordinate internal and external audit efforts.
- 560 *Quality Assurance.* The director of internal auditing should establish and maintain a quality assurance program to evaluate the operations of the internal auditing department.

An insightful discussion of the foregoing standards was provided as Appendix B to a report entitled, *The Role of the Internal Auditor in the Deterrence, Detection and Reporting of Fraudulent Financial Reporting,* prepared by the IIA for the Treadway Commission. The discussion is reprinted below.[8]

This section lists and summarizes the IIA's *Standards for the Professional Practice of Internal Auditing.*

Independence (100)

General Standard 100 states that internal auditors should be independent of the activities they audit. It includes guidance for enhancing independence and objectivity. *GS 100* specifies that:

---

[8] IIA, *The Role of the Internal Auditor in the Deterrence, Detection and Reporting of Fraudulent Financial Reporting,* Appendix B (Altamonte Springs, Fla.: IIA, 1987), pp. 41–44. Reprinted by permission of the Institute of Internal Auditors, Inc.

- Internal auditors should maintain a high-level reporting status. Although a specific level is not mentioned, the guidelines state that the internal audit director should report to an individual in the organization with sufficient authority to: (1) promote independence, (2) ensure broad audit coverage, and (3) provide adequate consideration of audit reports and appropriate action on audit recommendations.
- The audit director should have direct communication with the board of directors. The board should concur on the appointment or removal of the audit director. The internal auditing organization should adopt a charter or policy statement approved by management and the board, establishing an internal auditing position within the organization. This policy statement should define the scope of audit activities. It also should authorize access to records and to personal and physical properties under review.
- Senior management should approve audit work schedules, staffing plans, and the financial budget. The audit director should submit activity reports to management and the board and inform them of any limitations on scope.
- To ensure objectivity, internal auditors should:
  —Not subordinate their audit judgments.
  —Not make significant quality compromises.
  —Avoid conflicts of interests.
  —Rotate staff assignments.
  —Not assume operating responsibilities.
  —Not design systems.
  —Review audit work for objectivity.

Professional Proficiency (200)

GS 200 states that internal audits should be performed with "proficiency and due professional care." This section includes standards and guidelines for both the internal auditing department and the individual internal auditor. Guidelines for the internal auditing department encompass: staffing, knowledge, skills, disciplines, and supervision.

Relative to the individual internal auditor, this standard addresses: compliance with standards of conduct, knowledge, skills, discipline, human relations, communication, continuing education, and due professional care.

From the internal auditing department's viewpoint, individual audits should be assigned to persons who collectively possess the necessary knowledge and skills to properly conduct the audit.

Staffing (210)

Overall staffing is based on demand for audit services. Usually a manpower plan is established based on the supply and demand for audit skills. Internal auditing organizations compile a "skill inventory" by identifying staff members' skills and comparing them to skill requirements for future audit schedules. Additional training and staff are then acquired, if necessary.

The standards require that job descriptions should establish suitable educational experience criteria for filling internal audit positions.

Knowledge, Skills, and Disciplines—Audit Department (220)

This standard requires that audit department personnel possess the necessary collective skills to properly conduct an audit. Otherwise, outside consultants should be used. These standards help to justify the adoption of a formalized program of continuing education and training. A skill inventory is very helpful in identifying strengths and weaknesses in order to develop the staffing and training plans. For example, an audit department could be comprised of auditors with accounting degrees and CPA certificates.

This may be a problem if the staff does not have sufficient skills to perform EDP and operational audits. Conversely, EDP auditors may be very proficient in electronic data processing, but have little training in financial accounting and auditing.

Supervision (230)

This standard provides a quality assurance mechanism for the proper supervision of audits. As defined in *Specific Standard 230,* "supervision" includes: providing suitable instruction, approving audit programs, seeing that audit work is carried out, reviewing working papers and audit reports, and determining that audit objectives are being met.

Compliance With Standards of Conduct (240)

This standard requires compliance with professional standards of conduct and refers to The Institute's *Code of Ethics*. The *Code* includes provisions on:

- Objectivity, honesty, and diligence.
- Loyalty.
- Improvements in efficiency.
- Conflicts of interest.
- Sufficient evidence for rendering opinions.
- Using confident information for personal benefit.
- Not accepting gifts.

Knowledge, Skills, and Disciplines—Individual Auditor (250)

The standard on knowledge, skills, and disciplines for the individual auditor provides for various levels of proficiencies related to auditing standards, audit procedures and techniques, accounting principles and techniques, understanding of management principles, and appreciation of various other topics and disciplines such as accounting, economics, and EDP. This standard does not require each individual auditor to have all the knowledge, skills, and disciplines to conduct an audit. However, these characteristics should be possessed collectively by the audit team.

Human Relations and Communications (260)

The standard on human relations and communications requires internal auditors to maintain good relations with auditees and to possess clear and effective oral and written communications skills. This standard cannot be understated. The success of an audit depends on an individual's ability to deal with people throughout the audit. Research has shown that poor auditor/auditee relationships result from:

- Auditee's fear of performance evaluation and change.
- Auditor's behavior which is negative, superior, or unsympathetic.

Usually a participated auditing approach helps to improve auditor/auditee relations.

Continuing Education (270)

The standard on continuing education requires individual auditors to maintain their professional proficiency. The IIA has a voluntary continuing professional development program which requires 100 hours of participation every three years in educational programs, publications, oral presentations, and committee work.

Due Professional Care (280)

The standard on due professional care requires that auditors should consider:

- Extent of audit work needed to achieve objectives.
- Relative materiality.
- Adequacy and effectiveness of control.
- Cost benefit of auditing.

It also requires internal auditors to be alert to intentional wrongdoings, errors, inefficiencies, waste, ineffectiveness, and conflicts of interest. Internal auditors should be alert to those conditions and activities where irregularities are most likely to occur. In addition, they should identify inadequate controls and recommend improvements to promote compliance with acceptable procedures and practices.

Scope of Work (300)

This standard states that the scope of internal audit work should encompass: (1) the examination/evaluation of the adequacy and effectiveness of the organization's system of internal control, and (2) the quality of performance in carrying out assigned responsibilities. This standard encompasses a broad scope of work including the review of five internal control objectives. These objectives include:

- Reliability and integrity of information.
- Compliance with policy, plans, procedures, laws, and regulations.
- Safeguarding of assets.
- Economical and efficient use of resources.
- Accomplishments of established objectives and goals for operations and programs.

The review for adequacy determines whether the established systems of control provide reasonable assurance that the organization's objectives and goals will be

INTERNAL AUDITING STANDARDS

met efficiently and economically. The review for effectiveness ascertains whether the system is functioning as intended. The review for quality performance indicates whether the organization's objectives and goals have been achieved.

In discussing the scope of work, many auditors refer to conducting a comprehensive audit (or full-scope audit) which includes: (1) financial and compliance auditing, (2) operational and/or management auditing, and (3) EDP or information systems auditing.

Performance of Internal Audit Work (400)

This standard states that audit work should include: (1) planning the audit, (2) examining and evaluating information, and (3) communicating results and following up. *GS 400* requires that:

- Both the planning and audit processes are documented.
- An appropriate written audit report is issued, presenting the purpose, scope, and results of the audit (including audit opinions, where appropriate).
- Internal auditing follow up on audit reports to ascertain that either: (1) appropriate actions have been taken or (2) that management or the board has assumed the risk of not taking corrective action on reported findings.

Management of the Internal Auditing Department (500)

GS 500 states that the director of internal auditing should properly manage the internal auditing department. This standard includes specific standards and guidance on the audit charter, planning, policies and procedures, personal management and development, external auditors, and quality assurance. These items represent the elements that must be present to meet the general standard. The standard includes the typical management functions of planning, directing, and organizing the internal auditing function so that it will achieve its objectives.

Purpose, Authority, and Responsibility (510)

The standard on the audit charter is extremely important in relation to the independence of the internal auditing function and will have an impact on acceptance and support from auditing management. A strong written charter giving internal auditing proper authorization to perform its professional duties in accordance with the *Standards* will go a long way to aid the internal auditing department in achieving its objectives.

Planning (520)

The standard and related guidelines on audit planning define internal auditing with emphasis on developing goals, long- and short-range planning, audit work schedules, staffing plans and financial budgets, and activity reports for management and the board.

Policies and Procedures (530)

The guidance material on policies and procedures provides information for establishing both formal administrative and technical manuals.

Personnel Management and Development (540)

This standard provides information for establishing a program for selecting and developing the human resources of the internal auditing department. This standard is critical because people are the most important asset of any organization's internal audit function.

External Auditors (550)

This standard requires that internal auditing coordinate both external and internal audit efforts. This ensures adequate audit coverage and minimizes duplicated effort among independent public accountants, regulatory auditors, and internal auditors.

Quality Assurance (560)

The standard on quality assurance provides guidance in the areas of supervision, internal reviews, and external reviews.

The SIASs

The statements issued to date by the PSRC are:

- SIAS No. 1, "Control: Concepts and Responsibilities " (7/83)
- SIAS No. 2, "Communicating Results" (7/83)
- SIAS No. 3, "Deterrence, Detection, Investigation and Reporting of Fraud" (5/85)
- SIAS No. 4, "Quality Assurance" (11/86)

The aforementioned report, *The Role of the Internal Auditor in the Deterrence, Detection and Reporting of Fraudulent Financial Reporting*, provides the following discussion of these statements.[9]

1. Control: Concepts and Responsibilities

SIAS-1 provides guidance on the nature of control and the role of the participants in its establishment, maintenance, and evaluation. This statement is primarily definitional. It sets the stage for follow-up statements on how to assess control. Its major conclusions are:

- A "control" is any action taken to enhance the likelihood that established objectives and goals will be achieved.
- Control results from management's planning, organizing, and directing.
- The many variants of the term "control" (for example, administrative control, management control, internal control) can be incorporated within the generic term.
- The overall system of control is conceptual in nature. It is the integrated

---

[9] *Ibid.*, pp. 45–46. Reprinted by permission of the Institute of Internal Auditors, Inc.

collection of systems used by an organization to achieve its objectives and goals.
- Management plans, organizes, and directs in such a fashion as to provide reasonable assurance that established objectives and goals will be achieved.
- Internal auditing examines and evaluates the planning, organizing, and directing processes to determine whether reasonable assurance exists that objectives and goals will be achieved. All systems, processes, operations, functions, and activities within the organization are subject to internal auditing's evaluations. Such evaluations, in the aggregate, provide information to appraise the overall system of control.

This statement offers a broad definition of control and further reaffirms internal auditing's comprehensive full scope of work as stated in *GS 300*. Specifically, it adds a new dimension of describing internal auditing's examination and evaluation of the management functions of planning, organizing, and directing. It also provides for an overall evaluation of the system of control.

2. Communicating Results

SIAS-2 provides guidance on communicating results in the form of written and oral reports. This statement provides additional guidance on *Specific Standard 430* regarding such items as interim and summary reports, discussion of conclusions and recommendations, report content, attributes of a finding, and audit report approval and distribution. Although this statement does not add any new major material on audit reporting to internal audit literature, it does concisely summarize the recommended practices in internal audit literature and progressive companies.

3. Deterrence, Detection, Investigation, and Reporting of Fraud

SIAS-3 provides additional guidance on *SS 280* (Due Professional Care) and *GS 300* (Scope of Work). The major conclusions of this statement are:

A. *Deterrence of Fraud*

Deterrence of fraud is the responsibility of management. Internal auditors are responsible for examining and evaluating the adequacy and the effectiveness of actions taken by management to fulfill this obligation.

B. *Detection of Fraud*

Internal auditors should have sufficient knowledge of fraud to be able to identify indicators that fraud might have been committed. If significant control weaknesses are detected, additional tests conducted by internal auditors should include tests directed toward identification of other indicators of fraud.

Internal auditors are not expected to have knowledge equivalent to that of a person whose primary responsibility is to detect and investigate fraud. Also, audit procedures alone, even when carried out with due professional care, do not guarantee that fraud will be detected.

C. *Investigation of Fraud*

Fraud investigations may be conducted by or involve internal auditors, lawyers, investigators, security personnel, and other specialists from inside or outside the organization.

Internal auditing should assess the facts known relative to all fraud investigations in order to:

- Determine if controls need to be implemented or strengthened.
- Design audit tests to help disclose the existence of similar frauds in the future.
- Help meet the internal auditor's responsibility to maintain sufficient knowledge of fraud.

D. *Reporting of Fraud*

A written report should be issued at the conclusion of the investigation phase. It should include all findings, conclusions, recommendations, and corrective action taken.

4. Quality Assurance

SIAS-4 interprets *SS 560* on related guidelines on quality assurance. It provides detailed interpretation and guidance for implementing a quality assurance program in an internal auditing department. *SS 560* defines a program which includes: (1) adequate supervision, (2) internal review under the control of the director of internal auditing, and (3) external review by qualified persons, within or independent of the organization. The Institute provides a voluntary Quality Assurance Review Service for organizations interested in having an external review by peer internal auditors. The IIA also publishes a Quality Assurance Review Manual for Internal Auditing, which includes a checklist and forms for completing internal or external reviews of the internal audit function.

In March 1987, the PSRC issued for comment drafts of two new proposed SIAS. These are entitled, *Internal Auditors' Relationships With Independent Outside Auditors* and *Audit Working Papers*. The *Relationships* proposal provides guidance on such topics as:

- Coordination of audit work
- Meetings
- Access to programs and working papers
- Access to audit reports and management letters
- Common understanding

The *Relationships* draft supports the notion of maximum audit coordination and efficiency while emphasizing the professionalism of both internal and independent outside auditors.

The *Working Papers* draft provides guidance in preparing and using working papers. It covers such topics as:

- Contents
- Preparation techniques

- Review process
- Ownership custody and retention

The authoritative interpretations of the PSRC are not the sum total of IIA standards-setting activity in recent years. The information service subcommittee of the PSRC offers professional standards bulletins in each issue of *The Internal Auditor*. While the bulletins are not official pronouncements of IIA, they do provide information that practitioners may use in considering courses of action under specific circumstances. The bulletins are issued in a question-and-answer format and cover the entire spectrum of internal auditing practice. Topics covered in previous bulletins include:

- Being involved in systems development activity
- Maintaining objectivity in often-recurring audit projects
- Distinguishing between standards and guidelines
- Communicating with audit committees
- Reporting audit results in interim reports
- Signing reports

Other bulletins have dealt with questions involving managing the internal audit department, scope of work, independence, proficiency, and performance of audit work.

In addition to statements on internal auditing standards and professional standards bulletins, the IIA publishes Research Reports on timely topics of interest. This series of reports is intended to provide guidance and information on subjects of importance to the profession.

The PSRC is not the only IIA group that is involved in developing pronouncements, although it is the only group that interprets the standards. The PPC of the IIA is responsible for developing official positions for the Institute on a variety of subjects that affect the practice of internal auditing.

An example of the efforts of the PPC is the IIA position statement on audit committees. This statement, while not an internal auditing standard, sets forth the views of the IIA with respect to audit committees. The statement recognizes that a good working relationship between internal auditors and audit committees can aid the audit committee in discharging its responsibility to the board of directors, shareholders, and other outside parties. The statement encourages private sector companies and not-for-profit corporations and governmental units to establish audit committees or their equivalent. The full text of the position paper is presented in Chapter 10.

The Codes of Ethics

The Board of Directors of the IIA realized that high standards of moral conduct were essential to the proper practice of internal auditing. In 1968,

FIG. 6-3

The Institute of Internal Auditors, Inc. Code of Ethics

Introduction

Recognizing that ethics are an important consideration in the practice of internal auditing and that the moral principles followed by members of *The Institute of Internal Auditors, Inc.*, should be formalized, the Board of Directors at its regular meeting in New Orleans on December 13, 1968, received and adopted the following resolution:

WHEREAS the members of *The Institute of Internal Auditors, Inc.*, represent the profession of internal auditing; and

WHEREAS managements rely on the profession of internal auditing to assist in the fulfillment of their management stewardship; and

WHEREAS said members must maintain high standards of conduct, honor, and character in order to carry out proper and meaningful internal auditing practice;

THEREFORE BE IT RESOLVED that a Code of Ethics be now set forth, outlining the standards of professional behavior for the guidance of each member of *The Institute of Internal Auditors, Inc.*

In accordance with this resolution, the Board of Directors further approved of the principles set forth.

Interpretation of Principles

The provisions of this Code of Ethics cover basic principles in the various disciplines of internal auditing practice. Members shall realize that individual judgment is required in the application of these principles. They have a responsibility to conduct themselves so that their good faith and integrity should not be open to question. While having due regard for the limit of their technical skills, they will promote the highest possible internal auditing standards to the end of advancing the interest of their company or organization.

Articles

I. Members shall have an obligation to exercise honesty, objectivity, and diligence in the performance of their duties and responsibilities.

II. Members, in holding the trust of their employers, shall exhibit loyalty in all matters pertaining to the affairs of the employer or to whomever they may be rendering a service. However, members shall not knowingly be a party to any illegal or improper activity.

III. Members shall refrain from entering into any activity which may be in conflict with the interest of their employers or which would prejudice their ability to carry out objectively their duties and responsibilities.

IV. Members shall not accept a fee or a gift from an employee, a client, a customer, or a business associate of their employer without the knowledge and consent of their senior management.

V. Members shall be prudent in the use of information acquired in the course of their duties. They shall not use confidential information for any personal gain nor in a manner which would be detrimental to the welfare of their employer.

VI. Members, in expressing an opinion, shall use all reasonable care to obtain sufficient factual evidence to warrant such expression. In their reporting, members shall reveal such material facts known to them which, if not revealed,

INTERNAL AUDITING STANDARDS 6-19

> could either distort the report of the results of operations under review or conceal unlawful practice.
>
> **VII.** Members shall continually strive for improvement in the proficiency and effectiveness of their service.
>
> **VIII.** Members shall abide by the *Bylaws* and uphold the objectives of *The Institute of Internal Auditors, Inc.* In the practice of their profession, they shall be ever mindful of their obligation to maintain the high standard of competence, morality, and dignity which *The Institute of Internal Auditors, Inc.*, and its members have established.

it approved the issuance of the Code of Ethics. The Code of Ethics represents the basic principles in the several disciplines of internal auditing. The Code of Ethics for members of the IIA is reprinted in Figure 6-3.[10]

The IIA devised a certification program for internal auditors in 1971. It found it desirable to provide a separate Code of Ethics for CIAs because the IIA could not compel a CIA to be a member of the IIA and thus be subject to its Code of Ethics. The Code of Ethics for CIAs was developed to be certain that a code existed for CIAs. The principle difference between the two codes is that the Code of Ethics for CIAs omits the article that requires abiding by the *Bylaws* and upholding the objectives of the IIA. The Code of Ethics for CIAs is reprinted in Figure 6-4.[11]

Statement of Responsibilities

The Statement of Responsibilities of Internal Auditing sets forth the authoritative views of the IIA on the subject. Among other things, it asserts that internal auditing operates under the policies established by management and the board. The fact that the Statement cites a direct connection between the board and the function of internal auditing is an important evolutionary development. Earlier versions of this Statement did not articulate this relationship. The current version is reprinted in Figure 6-5.[12]

---

[10] IIA, *The Institute of Internal Auditors, Inc., Code of Ethics* (Altamonte Springs, Fla.: IIA, 1985). Reprinted by permission of the Institute of Internal Auditors, Inc.

[11] IIA, *The Certified Internal Auditor Code of Ethics*, (Altamonte Springs, Fla.: IIA, 1985). Reprinted by permission of the Institute of Internal Auditors, Inc.

[12] IIA, *Statement of Responsibilities of Internal Auditing,* (Altamonte Springs, Fla.: IIA, 1981). Reprinted by permission of the Institute of Internal Auditors, Inc.

FIG. 6-4

The Certified Internal Auditor Code of Ethics

Introduction

The Certified Internal Auditor has an obligation to the profession, management, and stockholders and to the general public to maintain high standards of professional conduct. In recognition of this obligation, The Institute of Internal Auditors, Inc., adopted this Code of Ethics for Certified Internal Auditors.

Adherence to this Code, which is based on the Code of Ethics for members of The Institute, is a prerequisite to maintaining the designation Certified Internal Auditor. A Certified Internal Auditor who is judged by the Board of Directors of The Institute to be in violation of the provisions of the Code shall forfeit the Certified Internal Auditor designation.

Interpretation of Principles

The provisions of this Code of Ethics cover basic principles in the various disciplines of internal auditing practice. Certified Internal Auditors shall realize that their individual judgment is required in the application of these principles. They have a responsibility to conduct themselves in a manner so that their good faith and integrity should not be open to question. Furthermore, they shall use the "Certified Internal Auditor" designation with discretion and in a dignified manner, fully aware of what the designation denotes and in a manner consistent with all statutory requirements. While having due regard for the limit of their technical skills, they will promote the highest possible internal auditing standards to the end of advancing the interest of their company or organization.

Articles

I. Certified Internal Auditors shall have an obligation to exercise honesty, objectivity, and diligence in the performance of their duties and responsibilities.

II. Certified Internal Auditors, in holding the trust of their employers, shall exhibit loyalty in all matters pertaining to the affairs of the employer or to whomever they may be rendering a service. However, members shall not knowingly be a party to any illegal or improper activity.

III. Certified Internal Auditors shall refrain from entering into any activity which may be in conflict with the interest of their employers or which would prejudice their ability to carry out objectively their duties and responsibilities.

IV. Certified Internal Auditors shall not accept a fee or a gift from an employee, a client, a customer, or a business associate of their employer without the knowledge and consent of their senior management.

V. Certified Internal Auditors shall be prudent in the use of information acquired in the course of their duties. They shall not use confidential information for any personal gain nor in a manner which would be detrimental to the welfare of their employer.

VI. Certified Internal Auditors, in expressing an opinion, shall use all reasonable care to obtain sufficient factual evidence to warrant such expression. In their reporting, members shall reveal such material facts known to them which, if not revealed, could either distort the report of the results of operations under review or conceal unlawful practice.

VII. Certified Internal Auditors shall continually strive for improvement in the proficiency and effectiveness of their service.

FIG. 6-5

Statement of Responsibilities of Internal Auditing

The purpose of this statement is to provide in summary form a general understanding of the role and responsibilities of internal auditing. For more specific guidance, readers should refer to the *Standards for the Professional Practice of Internal Auditing*.

Nature

Internal auditing is an independent appraisal activity established within an organization as a service to the organization. It is a control which functions by examining and evaluating the adequacy and effectiveness of other controls.

Objective and Scope

The objective of internal auditing is to assist members of the organization in the effective discharge of their responsibilities. To this end, internal auditing furnishes them with analysis, appraisals, recommendations, counsel, and information concerning the activities reviewed. The audit objective includes promoting effective control at reasonable cost.

The scope of internal auditing encompasses the examination and evaluation of the adequacy and effectiveness of the organization's system of internal control and the quality of performance in carrying out assigned responsibilities. The scope of internal auditing includes:

- Reviewing the reliability and integrity of financial and operating information and the means used to identify, measure, classify, and report such information.
- Reviewing the systems established to ensure compliance with those policies, plans, procedures, laws, and regulations which could have a significant impact on operations and reports, and determining whether the organization is in compliance.
- Reviewing the means of safeguarding assets and, as appropriate, verifying the existence of such assets.
- Appraising the economy and efficiency with which resources are employed.
- Reviewing operations or programs to ascertain whether results are consistent with established objectives and goals and whether the operations or programs are being carried out as planned.

Responsibility and Authority

Internal auditing functions under the policies established by management and the board. The purpose, authority and responsibility of the internal auditing department should be defined in a formal written document (charter), approved by management, and accepted by the board. The charter should make clear the purposes of the internal auditing department, specify the unrestricted scope of its work, and declare that auditors are to have no authority or responsibility for the activities they audit.

The responsibility of internal auditing is to serve the organization in a manner that is consistent with the *Standards for the Professional Practice of Internal Auditing* and with professional standards of conduct such as the *Code of Ethics* of The Institute of Internal Auditors, Inc. This responsibility includes coordinating internal audit activities with others so as to best achieve the audit objectives and the objectives of the organization.

(continued)

FIG. 6-5 *(cont'd)*

Independence

Internal auditors should be independent of the activities they audit. Internal auditors are independent when they can carry out their work freely and objectively. Independence permits internal auditors to render the impartial and unbiased judgments essential to the proper conduct of audits. It is achieved through organizational status and objectivity.

Organizational status should be sufficient to assure a broad range of audit coverage, and adequate consideration of and effective action on audit findings and recommendations.

Objectivity requires that internal auditors have an independent mental attitude, and an honest belief in their work product. Drafting procedures, designing, installing, and operating systems, are not audit functions. Performing such activities is presumed to impair audit objectivity.

The *Statement of Responsibilities of Internal Auditors* was originally issued by The Institute of Internal Auditors in 1947. The current *Statement*, revised in 1981, embodies the concepts previously established and includes such changes as are deemed advisable in light of the present status of the profession.

SUGGESTED READING

IIA. *The Institute of Internal Auditors Reports on Fraud,* Two reports by the Institute of Internal Auditors for the National Commission on Fraudulent Financial Reporting. Altamonte Springs, Fla.: The Institute of Internal Auditors, 1987.

Treadway Commission. *Report of the National Commission on Fraudulent Financial Reporting,* October 1987. U.S.A.: National Commission on Fraudulent Financial Reporting, 1987.

PART III
Audit Management

CHAPTER **7**

Organizing and Planning the Audit Function

Overview of Organizing and Planning the Audit Function 2	Existing Internal Control Environment 25
	Credibility of Management 25
Creating the Audit Charter 3	Significance of Corporate Accountability 25
Form and Content 3	Trends in Regulatory Activity 25
Importance of Management Support ... 5	Reporting Relationships Vary 25
Organization Structure 7	**Obtaining Personnel, Facilities, and**
Organizational Culture 8	**Other Resources** 27
Decentralization 10	
Business Combinations 12	**Long- and Short-Range Audit**
Technology 13	**Planning** 27
The Changing Role of Internal Auditing 14	Project Planning 28
Organizational Considerations 14	Resource Planning 28
Skill Requirements 14	Organizational Planning 28
Administrative Requirements 16	Scientific Planning Techniques 32
Geographical Considerations 16	**Creating the Right Image for the Audit**
Intradepartment Relationships 17	**Function** 33
	Selling the Benefits of the
Position Descriptions 19	Department 33
	Techniques 34
Reporting Relationships 22	Balancing Independence Against
Independence vs. Conflict of Interest— A Constant Battle 23	Acceptability 35
Factors to Consider in Establishing the Audit Reporting Structure 24	**Quality Assurance** 36
Capability of the Staff of the Audit Function 24	Definition and Purpose 36
What the Board of Directors or Senior Management Knows About Auditing 24	Background 37
	The Issues 38
	The Future 46
Accessibility of the Board of Directors or Senior Management ... 24	Practical Guidelines 47
	Suggested Reading 48

Fig. 7-1	Audit Charter of a Manufacturing Company	4
Fig. 7-2	Excerpt From Corporate Bylaws Establishing Audit Committee	6
Fig. 7-3	Memo From Senior Management Soliciting Support for an Internal Audit Program	7
Fig. 7-4	The Public Company	15

7-1

Fig. 7-5	Chart of Audit Department in Centralized Organization	17
Fig. 7-6	Chart of Audit Department in Decentralized Organization	18
Fig. 7-7	Position Description—Director of Corporate Audit	19
Fig. 7-8	Position Description—Manager of Corporate Audit	21
Fig. 7-9	Position Description—Senior Corporate Auditor	22
Fig. 7-10	IIA Survey of Reporting Relationships of Chief Internal Auditors	26
Fig. 7-11	Annual Audit Plan	30
Fig. 7-12	Announcement of an Audit Seminar for All Interested Parties	36

OVERVIEW OF ORGANIZING AND PLANNING THE AUDIT FUNCTION

The internal auditing department is often perceived by internal auditors to be unique and different from other departments within a company, and in many respects it is. For example, its services are not required to establish company policy, generate budgets, conduct business, manufacture or sell products, pay bills, or produce financial statements. Auditing is a staff service to the organization and an integral part of internal control. As discussed in Chapter 6, auditing services are most valuable when provided in an objective, unbiased manner, free from internal pressure. However, the audit function shares at least one common principle with other organizational units: It must be properly administered, or managed, if, like any other department, it is to meet its objectives. In fact, general standard 500 (see Chapter 6) requires it.

Auditing objectives are achieved effectively and efficiently through proper organizing, planning, staffing, and directing (i.e., by effective managing). The specific techniques that can be used for proper auditing function management are discussed in Chapters 7–9. The aspects of administering the function are arranged by functional areas to be managed. These include the following:

- Organizational management
- Project management
- Personnel management
- Records management
- Resource management

Organizing and planning the audit function are discussed in this chapter, since they are primary organizational management activities. Directing the activities of the department is discussed in Chapter 8 in terms of project management and in Chapter 9 as to resource and records management. Staffing is discussed in terms of personnel management in Chapter 9.

Large audit organizations, those employing scores of auditors with many and different skills in multiple locations, usually develop elaborate administrative procedures to be effective and efficient. On the other hand, small audit departments, such as those employing fewer than a half dozen auditors, do not need extensive formal procedures. The techniques described in this chapter recognize this variability in the management approach and are designed to be applicable to most audit organizations. It is up to each chief auditor to tailor them to fit individual circumstances.

The dictionary definition of the word "organize" is given as "to arrange or form into a coherent unity or functioning whole."[1] In the sense intended here, organizing refers to the actions needed to create the function. The formation of an internal auditing department involves the following activities:

- Creating and maintaining an audit charter
- Establishing a structure
- Defining job positions
- Arranging reporting relationships
- Obtaining personnel, facilities, and other resources
- Assuring quality

These activities are discussed in the next segment of this chapter.

CREATING THE AUDIT CHARTER

Audit charters may be defined as the formal document that describes objectives and responsibilities of the internal auditing function. It is the source of authority for the operations of the function.

Form and Content

All internal auditing organizations—large and small—require a clear statement of authority and responsibility. Also, the nature and scope of the activities of the department must be understood by the rest of the organization. These objectives are more easily attained when the nature and scope of activities are set forth formally, in writing, and when they are approved by the company's chief executive officer and/or board of directors. Therefore, it is desirable that the internal auditing organization secure a written audit charter, which should set forth the following:

- Company policy regarding the audit function
- Purpose or objective in establishing it

---

[1] *Webster's New Collegiate Dictionary*, (U.S.A.: G. & C. Merriam, 1980), p. 802.

FIG. 7-1

Audit Charter of a Manufacturing Company

I. **Policy.** It is the policy of the company to maintain a comprehensive program of internal auditing as an overall control measure and as a service to the organization. Its purpose is to aid corporate management and management at operational levels in achieving business goals without undue risk.

II. **Responsibilities:**

A. The Senior Vice-President–Finance is responsible for providing direction to the Corporate Director–Internal Audit in carrying out company policy in regard to the corporate audit function.

B. The Corporate Director–Internal Audit is responsible for the following:
  1. Designing and implementing procedural guidelines to assure that
     a. Internal controls of reporting entities achieve the objectives thereof and adequately safeguard the assets of the company.
     b. Financial statements of reporting entities are complete and accurate and comply with corporate policy, generally accepted accounting principles, requirements of government agencies such as the Securities and Exchange Commission and the Cost Accounting Standards Board, etc.
     c. Reporting entities are in compliance with operational policies and standards of ethical business practices that promote the well-being of the company.
     d. Controls over the development, maintenance, and operation of electronic data processing systems are sufficient to result in the processing of accurate and complete data.
  2. Coordinating coverage with independent outside auditors, division and subsidiary auditors, and others.
  3. Designing an annual plan for audit coverage that fulfills the responsibility of the department.
  4. Performing supervisory functions and staff training and development activities.
  5. Providing written reports of audit findings to such levels of management as may be necessary to effect remedial action.
  6. Performing and reporting on special reviews as may be required by the Audit Committee of the Board of Directors, the Senior Vice-President–Finance, or others.

C. The manager of each operating element is responsible for:
  1. Providing the Corporate Internal Audit Department sufficient access to records, documents, personnel, and facilities to enable the department to carry out its function.
  2. Providing timely written responses to the Corporate Internal Audit Department indicating actions taken or planned regarding the recommendations set forth in the audit report.

ORGANIZING & PLANNING THE AUDIT FUNCTION 7-5

- Responsibilities of affected management groups with respect to auditing, including (1) the chief internal auditor, (2) the office to whom he reports, and (3) other organizational management
- Organizational reporting relationships
- Any restrictions placed on the audit function or any of its members

The charter may exist in a variety of forms. In small companies with few formal written policies, the charter may take the form of a memorandum with general distribution. In larger companies, it may appear as a formal company policy statement or as part of an accounting or finance manual. The vehicle used to express the charter should be one that will most effectively communicate to all affected company segments the responsibilities of all involved parties as well as the degree of management support. An example of an audit charter is shown in Figure 7-1. In this case, the charter is in the form of a formal policy directive.

Importance of Management Support

The audit charter illustrated in Figure 7-1 should bear the signature of the chairman and chief executive officer. It is generally helpful if the charter is signed by the officer responsible for establishing policy. In most companies, this is the chief executive; in others, it may be the president and chief operating officer or the vice-president of administration. A formal board resolution should not normally be required, since these officers would be acting within their delegated authority. But a resolution does help to indicate to the organization the importance of internal auditing. Usually, the greater the interest of the board, the more potent are the audit recommendations. In recent years, many publicly owned companies have formally provided for ongoing contact between the board and the chief internal auditor. An example of a segment of a publicly owned corporation's bylaws establishing such a relationship is shown in Figure 7-2.

Satisfactory relationships must also exist among the senior management, other management levels, and the audit department if effective auditing is to be performed. It must be recognized that despite the need for an independent source of authority, the auditor's effectiveness is enhanced by the support of senior management. One way in which the support of senior management can be demonstrated is to prepare and distribute to all affected lower management levels a memo encouraging utilization of internal auditing. Such a device is shown in Figure 7-3.[2]

---

[2] Paul Macchiaverna, *Internal Auditing, A Research Report From the Conference Board.* Reprinted with permission.

FIG. 7-2
Excerpt From Corporate Bylaws Establishing Audit Committee

Section 3.14: AUDIT COMMITTEE. There shall be an Audit Committee of the Board of Directors which shall serve at the pleasure of the Board of Directors and be subject to its control. The committee shall have the following membership and powers:

1. The Committee shall have at least three (3) members. All members of the Committee shall be Independent Outside Directors.

2. The Committee shall recommend to the Board of Directors for its action the appointment or discharge of the Corporation's independent auditors, based upon the Committee's judgment of the independence of the auditors (taking into account the fees charged both for audit and nonaudit services) and the quality of its audit work. Approval by the shareholders of the Board of Directors' appointment of the Corporation's solicitation of proxies for the annual meeting of shareholders, if so determined by the Board of Directors. If the auditors must be replaced, the Committee shall recommend to the Board of Directors for its action the appointment of new auditors until the next annual meeting of shareholders.

3. The Committee shall review and approve the scope and plan of the audit.

4. The Committee shall meet with the independent auditors at appropriate times to review, among other things, the results of the audit, the Corporation's financial statements and any certification, report or opinion which the auditors propose to render in connection with such statements.

5. The Committee shall review and approve each professional service of a nonaudit nature to be provided by the auditors.

6. The Committee shall meet with the Corporation's chief internal auditor at least once a year to review his comments concerning the adequacy of the Corporation's system of internal accounting controls and such other matters as the Committee may deem appropriate.

7. The Committee shall have the power to direct the auditors and the internal audit staff to inquire into and report to it with respect to any of the Corporation's contracts, transactions or procedures, or the conduct of the Corporate Office, or any division, profit center, subsidiary or other unit, or any other matter having to do with the Corporation's business and affairs. If authorized by the Board of Directors, the Committee may initiate special investigations in these regards.

8. The Committee shall have such other duties as may be lawfully delegated to it from time to time by the Board of Directors.

When the purpose of the audit charter is kept in mind, the chief auditor should experience little difficulty in properly developing and maintaining it. Therefore, care should be taken to clearly state those objectives and responsibilities and mode of operation that are believed essential to a long-term, successful internal auditing department. A poorly constructed document would be counterproductive to the goals of the audit function.

FIG. 7-3

Memo From Senior Management Soliciting Support for an Internal Audit Program

---

TO: All Mead Personnel

This brochure has been designed to familiarize you with the responsibilities, objectives and approach of one of our important management control functions — the Mead Internal Audit Program. We depend upon the professional work of the internal audit staff to:

- Review and monitor administrative controls in the accounting, financial and operating functions of the company, and to make recommendations for improving the quality of our overall control system wherever possible.
- Direct the Internal Audit Program at Mead and coordinate the annual joint internal-external audit program.
- Keep management informed of field conditions through timely and appropriate reports.
- Follow up on audit recommendations.
- Hire and train professional personnel who have a broad business background and an aptitude for conducting internal audits, who later will be capable of assuming managerial responsibilities in other areas of the company.

It is my desire that all managers in the company look upon the Internal Audit Program as:

- An opportunity to improve the overall efficiency and effectiveness of their operation, by having an independent review and appraisal of the administrative controls in their major areas of responsibility.
- An opportunity to have qualified Mead personnel review their controls in the same manner that they would conduct the review if sufficient time were available. Our internal audit goal is to identify profit improvement opportunities, cost saving opportunities, and/or to identify potential problem areas in conjunction with our regular field audit work.
- An opportunity to benefit from and participate in a company-wide exchange of ideas concerning good methods and techniques observed by the audit staff at other locations.

Thank you for your continued cooperation with this important management control program.

Yours very truly,

J. W. McSWINEY
Chairman of the Board

ORGANIZATION STRUCTURE

Organization structure may be defined as the formal alignment of involved functions that is believed by management to be the most effective for accomplishing assigned tasks or objectives. Such a structure is usually expressed in charts and functional descriptions, which depict reporting relationships and lines of authority and responsibility in order to inform those involved with or affected by the organization. Internal auditing organization structures are affected by trends in basic managerial thought. These trends are discussed in the following paragraphs.

Organizational Culture

The existence of corporate culture is widely known and recognized. It is often used to help explain much of what goes on in organizations. Organizational culture is also a recurring theme in many of the best-selling management books that have burst upon the 1980s scene.

In *Organizational Culture and Leadership*, Edgar Schein defines organizational culture as "the deeper level of *basic assumptions* and *beliefs* that are shared by members of an organization, that operate unconsciously, and that define in a basic 'take it for granted' fashion an organization's view of itself and its environment."[3] Among other things, organizational culture is reflective of the dominant values of an organization. These might include such value categories as:

- Product quality
- Price leadership
- Employee consciousness
- Customer orientation
- Technological attitude
- Social awareness and involvement
- Work environment

It is not unusual for a large organization to have more than one culture. A company may have one culture for management, another for its factory workers, and still another for its dealers. Cultures may also vary by geography, nationality, and hierarchy.

Professional literature also recognizes the importance of corporate culture. The *Report of the National Commission on Fraudulent Financial Reporting* is a recent example. In discussing deterrents, the Commission noted that the attitude at the top is critical. In fact, according to the Commission, the tone set by senior management "is the most important factor contributing to the integrity of the financial reporting process."[4]

For internal auditing, organizational culture has many implications. The

---

[3] Edgar H. Schein, *Organizational Culture and Leadership* (San Francisco: Jossey-Bass, 1985), p. 6.

[4] The National Commission on Fraudulent Financial Reporting, *Report of the National Commission on Fraudulent Financial Reporting*, October 1987 (U.S.A.: National Commission on Fraudulent Financial Reporting, 1987), p. 28.

ORGANIZING & PLANNING THE AUDIT FUNCTION

kind of culture or cultures that exist in an organization will affect the development of:

- The audit charter.
- The acceptance of the audit function.
- The relationships that evolve between members of the audit group with others in the company.
- The development of the strategic approach to auditing in the organization.

Assessing or measuring the impact of organizational culture in any context is difficult. This is particularly true when it comes to considering the effect of organizational culture on how the internal auditing function is organized. The effect is not obvious, but it is a relevant factor. Perhaps the effect can best be portrayed by considering the likely organization that might be present in two culturally diverse hypothetical entities.

Assume that in Entity *A*, the management culture is such that innovation and new ideas are encouraged and are well-received. Management in Entity *A* is characterized by a willingness to adapt to changing forces (e.g., economic, technological, and regulatory). Failures are recognized and accepted as inevitable occasional occurrences. The entity has manifested a remarkable history of either dominating the markets it enters or becoming one of the major players in them. Intraorganizational coordination and cooperation are emphasized as being critical to the success of the entity. Managers have learned that promotion and development result from the sharing and pooling of efforts and ideas. It is rare when managerial positions are filled from sources outside the entity.

Entity *B* achieved its early success through the entrepreneurial efforts of its founder, an inventor who also was gifted in marketing. The founder is still a major force in the company, although his advanced years have forced him to turn over much of the operating authority to others. His personal viewpoints of diligence, thrift, and hard work have been indelibly imprinted on his organization.

Although Entity *B* is viewed as being innovative by outsiders, those within the company have learned to be careful about expressing thoughts or ideas that might differ from those of the founder and his handpicked group of powerful senior management aides. The history of the entity is repleat with examples of turnover resulting from such expressions. When the senior power group makes decisions, whether it be strategic planning, policy-making, goal-setting, or operating methodologies, they are not challenged. Managers in Entity *B* have learned that it does not pay to take risks, that is, to challenge the system. This is true even when they know a particular course of authorized action is likely to lead to failures. When failures occur in Entity *B*, someone usually gets blamed. As a result, managers spend a great deal of time and effort insulating and protecting themselves.

Under these circumstances, the internal auditing organization of Entity *A* is likely to be vastly different from that of Entity *B*. It is probable that it reports to a higher level in the organization. That is because, in Entity *B*, the founder has little regard for the contributions that can be made from any source outside his circle of loyal senior supporters.

It is also probable that the internal auditing organization of Entity *A* finds that obtaining resources and establishing appropriate relationships with key members of management are easier than in Entity *B*. Attracting and retaining competent, proficient staff members is likewise less difficult in Entity *A* in all likelihood.

It is obvious from the foregoing that the organizational culture of Entity *A* is more conducive to achieving internal auditing objectives than the culture of Entity *B*. The discussion here is not intended to imply that many internal auditing functions are actually being adversely affected by certain types of organizational cultures. More research and study is needed before that can be asserted with any certainty. At this point, it can only be claimed that organizational culture is an important factor, that organizational cultures differ among companies, and that these differences may affect internal auditing organizations in profound ways.

Decentralization

Domestic corporations of virtually every business segment are being challenged by foreign competitors. These challenges are forcing the affected managements to alter methodologies in an effort to defend and/or preserve market share. During the 1980s, many techniques have been advanced by business consultants and others to aid in this endeavor. For example, Theory Z—the art of Japanese management—coined by William Oichi in 1981, counseled American managements to make the management process more participative, that is to say, to involve those affected by decisions, workers and managers alike, in the decision-making process and provide appropriate job enrichment devices.

Other techniques advanced include Management by Walking Around, or MBWA, by Thomas J. Peters and Robert H. Waterman, in *In Search of Excellence*. The object here is to get out of the office and see what's happening rather than relying on reports from others. Other concepts include (1) "skunk works,"[5]—a means of accomplishing innovative objectives by authorizing a highly motivated and highly talented team to do it outside the normal channels for such efforts, (2) "star nurturing"[6]—the process of spot-

---

[5] The term is generally credited to Clarence L. "Kelly" Johnson, organizer of the Skunk Works Division of Lockheed Corporation, a unit that successfully designed and built the U-2 airplane and later the SR-70 for the U.S. government.

[6] This term appears, for example, in *The New Competitors*, by D. Quinn Mills (New York: John Wiley & Sons, 1985), Chapter 5.

ting and developing good managers, and (3) "intrapreneurship"—a term invented by Gifford Pinchot III in *Intrapreneuring* for anyone who takes hands-on responsibility for creating innovation of any kind within an organization.

If these terms and concepts have any common thread, it is probably that achieving them requires more in the way of decentralization. In other words, reliable decisions cannot be made often enough by individuals separated either physically or culturally or some other way from the focus of activities and people who are integral to carrying them out.

Some of the concepts may be faddish. Indeed, according to one recent article, Theory Z and MBWA are "out" while other concepts are "in."[7] Yet, many of the ideas have some value or merit and are changing the way companies think and act. Internal auditing functions are being affected as a result.

At present, there are no reliable indicators by which to measure the extent of the impact. Still, it is believed that when it comes to altering organization structures, more companies are deciding to decentralize internal auditing functions than the other way around. By decentralizing, companies can more closely match the internal auditing needs of diverse organizational unit managements with available internal auditing resources. This "localizing" of internal auditing offers advantages over centralized functions. First and foremost, internal auditing units reporting organizationally to local operating unit management are able to respond more easily to the needs of that management. Also, a dedicated internal auditing group is probably more knowledgeable about the local culture, systems, controls, and so forth. As a result, they may have a better feel for problem areas.

There are disadvantages that must be kept in mind, however. The most obvious one is the likelihood that internal auditing groups that report to local operating unit managements are less independent. Their "captivity" makes it seem as though they lose the valuable perspective possessed by those with no direct organizational ties to the unit. Another disadvantage is that it is more difficult to maintain uniform compliance with internal auditing standards. Finally, unhealthy turf battles can develop between local internal auditing groups and corporate-based groups.

These disadvantages can be compensated for by internal auditing management. Moreover, the presence of an active corporate-based auditing group tends to offset the perceived loss of independence of local auditing groups. The net result can be a combined auditing effort that, by design, is more likely to fulfill the needs of various levels of management. A decentralized internal auditing organization structured by distributing and sharing the challenges of organizing, planning, and directing internal auditing ac-

---

[7] Stuart Jackson, "Business Fads: What's In and Out," *Business Week*, Jan. 20, 1986, p. 58.

tivities is applying the essence of the management techniques advanced by the management gurus of the 1980s.

Business Combinations

Another factor that is affecting the way internal auditing functions are organized is the increase in large business combinations. The 1980s have been characterized so far by a number of sizeable business combinations. They have occurred in many sectors of U.S. business, ostensibly to improve competitive position.

When such combinations occur, a period of uncertainty arises as two formerly independent and self-sufficient organizations become one. Effecting a consolidation usually means some qualified and capable people will lose their jobs—thus, the uncertainty. All functional elements of a business are affected, including internal auditing.

At this point in time, there are no published research papers or other available public data on which the impact on internal auditing functions can be discerned. The chief auditor faced with the challenge of combining two formerly separate functions has little to go by in deciding how to proceed. Invariably, these organizations have different internal auditing strategies and probably have different approaches to such other relevant areas as:

- Staffing
- Planning
- Reporting
- Training
- Career development

Differing cultures of the companies may add to the challenge. In such situations, it is obviously preferable that the chief auditor of the acquiring company be involved, early on, in the considerations and decisions involved in the acquisition process. Unfortunately, this is not always done nor is it always possible to do so. Many acquisitions occur in ways that afford scant opportunity for effective, coordinated preparation efforts.

Under these circumstances, it is probably best to let the respective internal auditing organizations continue to function after the acquisition as though the companies were still separate. There are some good reasons for this. First, unless the acquisition is a rare exception, the organizational structure of the new entity cannot be anticipated with certainty. Any effort to change the internal auditing functions that preceded organizational changes in the new management structure is apt to be counterproductive. Second, it provides a period of time for the respective internal auditing functions to get to know one another. Third, it affords ample time for the chief auditor to consider organizational alternatives.

ORGANIZING & PLANNING THE AUDIT FUNCTION

Among the organizational issues that the chief auditor must work out are:

- The extent to which existing internal auditing personnel can continue to be effectively utilized.
- The extent to which existing locations and facilities can continue to be utilized.
- Whether or not the auditing management must be altered.
- The sufficiency and applicability of existing audit charters and strategic approaches.
- Whether or not changes must be made to the auditing manual.
- The effect, if any, on the relationship with outside auditors.
- The impact on the use of standard forms, programs, questionnaires, and generalized auditing software.

Needless to say, decisions regarding the foregoing require the best professional judgment possible. Those involved in the process might find it desirable to check the experiences of others who have been through this experience and can provide valuable advice as a result.

Technology

Not surprisingly, the force of technological change is affecting internal auditing organization structures. As is noted in Chapter 28, many internal auditing functions are adding information systems (I/S) auditing organization blocks. In fact, the growth and expansion of this segment of the overall internal auditing function has probably exceeded that of any other single segment. Many internal auditing organizations are acquiring personal computers, word processors, terminals, and various software packages (see Chapter 28).

To optimize the decisions regarding the acquisition and use of these devices, some internal auditing organizations are focusing such responsibility in a designated individual or group, depending on size and other considerations. Among other things, job responsibility might include:

- Developing in-house training programs for personal computer use by staff members.
- Designing and developing embedded auditing routines (see Chapter 28).
- Keeping current with respect to developments pertaining to FIS, telecommunications and office automation.
- Evaluating the merits of various competing auditing software products.
- Devising internal specialized software.

The Changing Role of Internal Auditing

In Chapter 1, the current forces affecting the practice of internal auditing are discussed. These forces have given rise to a dramatic increase in the importance and relevance of internal auditing in corporate affairs. In turn, organizational changes have occurred to accommodate the increase. More and more, chief auditors are gaining access to audit committees and senior management levels. The trend in reporting relationships for chief auditors is toward higher levels of management than was true in earlier times. Once again, the Treadway Commission points the way. The Commission's view of the internal auditing reporting relationship is depicted in a sort of organization chart. The chart is reprinted as Figure 7-4.[8] The figure shows internal auditing on an equal footing with the finance function and the law function. All are under the chief executive officer.

Few public companies are organized in this fashion today. The time may not be far off, however, when the more progressive managements begin to adopt this view.

Organizational Considerations

In addition to trends in managerial thought, there are other basic considerations that affect how internal auditing functions are organized. These are:

- Special skills required
- Administrative requirements
- Geographical considerations
- Intradepartment relationships

Skill Requirements

The organization of an internal auditing department is affected to some degree by the types of skills or specialties that are required to meet its objectives. The importance of internal control and financial reporting (see Chapters 17 and 18) requires most audit departments to develop a knowledge of accounting (e.g., internal accounting controls and GAAP) and finance. Many departments also employ electronic data processing specialists. Some use the services of lawyers, while others have engineers and other technical specialists. Also, particular industries may require the development of industry-specific skills. The number and types will depend upon the com-

---

[8] The National Commission on Fraudulent Financial Reporting, *Report of the National Commission on Fraudulent Financial Reporting,* October 1987 (U.S.A.: National Commission on Fraudulent Financial Reporting, 1987), p. 19. Reprinted by permission of the National Commission on Fraudulent Financial Reporting.

ORGANIZING & PLANNING THE AUDIT FUNCTION

FIG. 7-4
The Public Company

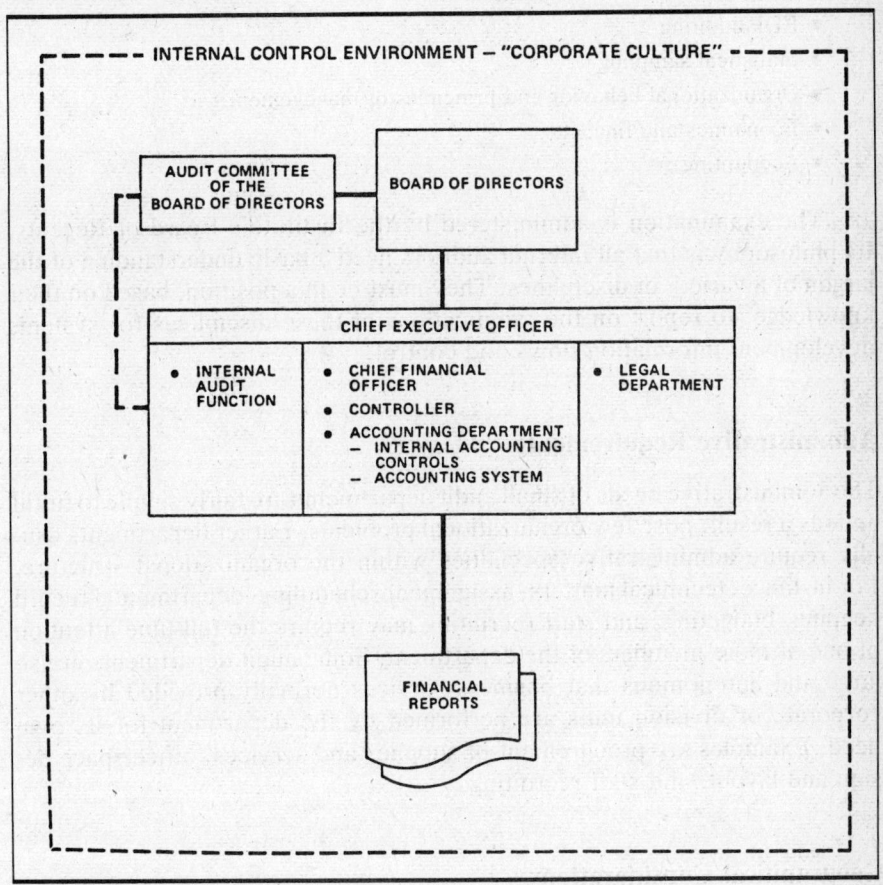

plexity of the industry, the inherent difficulty in making an examination, and the needs of the management group served by the department. According to a recent survey, other technical skills found in internal auditing from time to time include mathematics, statistics, marketing, economics, general management, production, personnel, and security.[9]

The IIA over the years has worked to help develop a body of knowledge and skills for internal auditors. Perhaps the best reflection of what these are is indicated in the IIA's CIA program. Beginning in 1974, the IIA began the program complete with requirement for written examination. Presently, the examination is given twice a year at locations around the world.

---

[9] Paul Macchiaverna, *op. cit.*, p. 79.

The CIA Examination reflects the current state of the art of internal auditing. Its four parts are designed to test the candidate's knowledge of:

- Internal auditing administration
- EDP auditing
- Statistical sampling
- Organizational behavior and principles of management
- Economics and finance
- Accounting

The examination is administered by the Institute's Board of Regents. Its philosophy is that all internal auditors need a basic understanding of the jargon of a variety of disciplines. They must be in a position, based on their knowledge, to report on the ramifications of these disciplines for systems development information flows and control.

Administrative Requirements

The administrative needs of small audit departments are fairly simple to fulfill and, as a result, pose few organizational problems. Larger departments usually require administrative specialties within the organizational structure. For instance, technical matters, assignment scheduling, departmental record keeping, budgeting, and staff recruiting may require the full-time attention of one or more members of the department. Some audit departments are so large and autonomous that business services normally provided by other corporate or division units are performed by the department for its own need. Examples are procurement of supplies and services, office space design and layout, and staff recruiting.

Geographical Considerations

Many companies have numerous divisions and subsidiaries located in geographically dispersed areas. In such cases, the chief auditor must consider whether it is more advantageous to operate from a single home office (which requires extensive travel) or from regional offices.

The most obvious consideration is the comparative cost effectiveness of the alternatives. Generally speaking, audit departments maintain branch or regional offices when the costs of travel to and from the areas exceed the cost of maintaining full-time local offices. However, factors other than simple cost comparisons may be important. For example, the sacrifice in quality control may be too great when a branch or regional office is maintained. Recruiting and turnover in the local area may prove troublesome and may require a disproportionate amount of attention from the central office. Geographic separation may unduly strain effective audit communication.

ORGANIZING & PLANNING THE AUDIT FUNCTION

FIG. 7-5

Chart of Audit Department in Centralized Organization

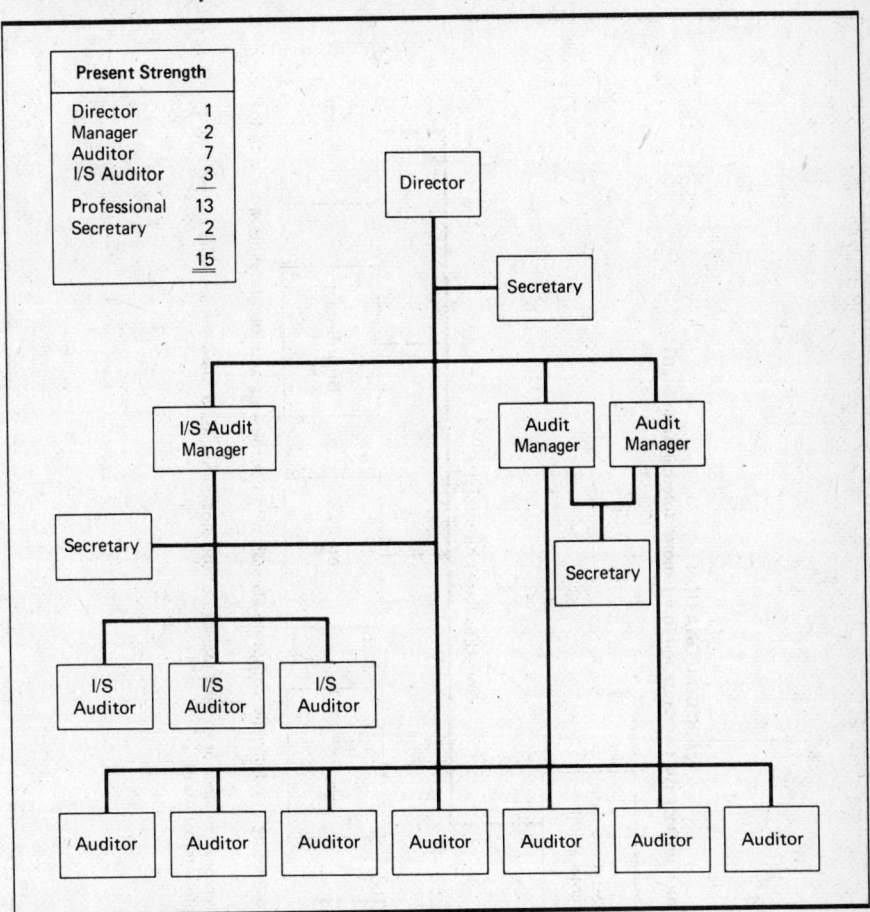

Intradepartment Relationships

The organization of small departments is often concerned primarily with assuring effective project management. The chief auditor in these departments doubles as a project manager and department head. In very small departments, the chief auditor may also perform many of the audits.

As audit organizations increase in size and complexity, the chief auditor usually retains authority for personnel administration, but delegates project management to others. In such departments, virtually everyone reports to the director from an administrative point of view. However, performing auditors may be assigned to one project manager for the duration of an audit

FIG. 7-6
Chart of Audit Department in Decentralized Organization

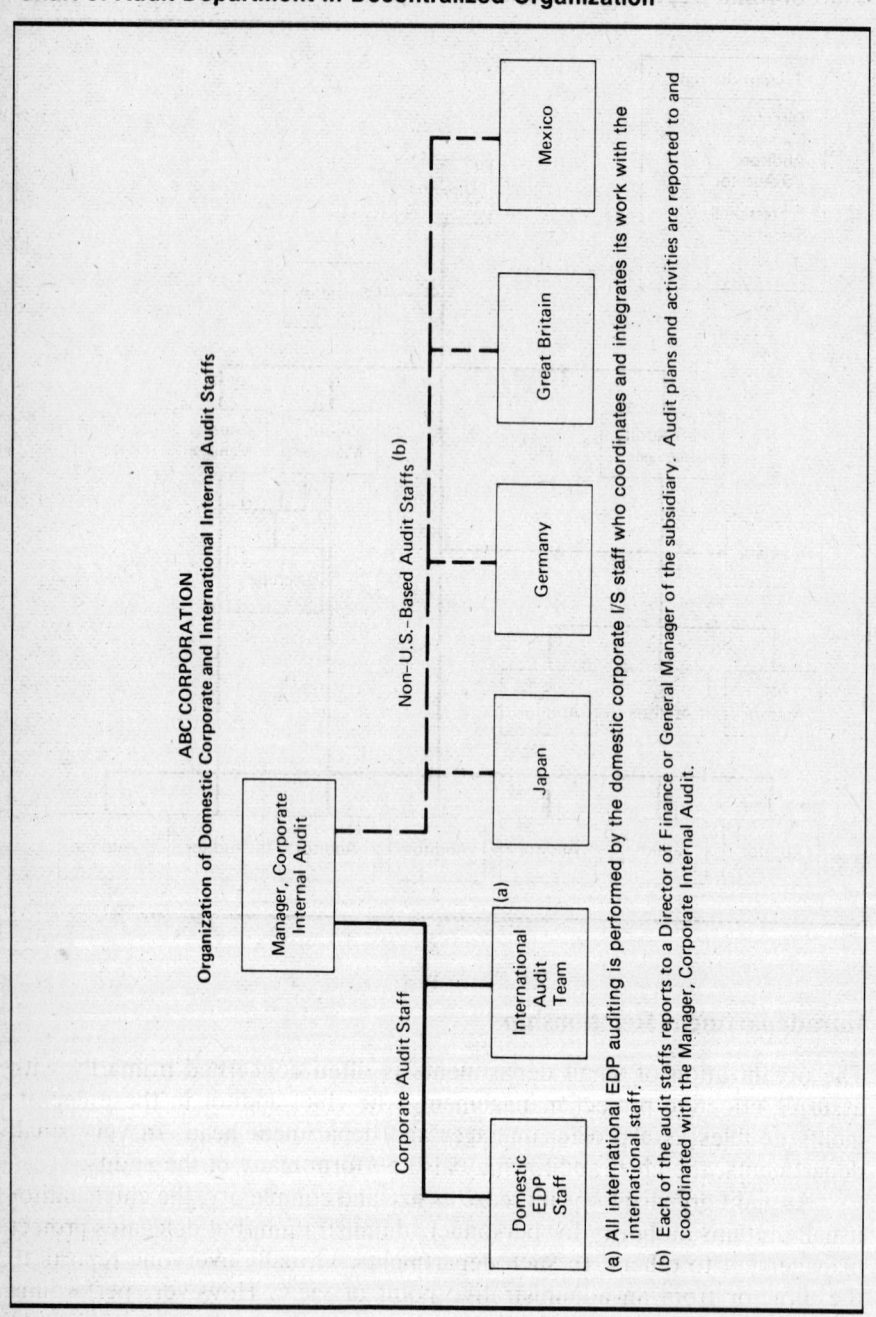

ORGANIZING & PLANNING THE AUDIT FUNCTION 7-19

project and then to another for the next project. This project reporting arrangement is similar to what exists in large public accounting firms. The organization of such a department is depicted in Figure 7-5. Note that the lines of authority are drawn in such a way that the reporting relationship of performing auditors permits reporting to any specific manager, depending on the project. In this type of organization, the auditors assigned to given projects (e.g., the manager, senior auditor, and staff members) combine to form a team, each fulfilling the role established by policy to result in a properly completed assignment.

Audit directors of other organizations might have to delegate to managers the authority for personnel management. This is usually required when multiple auditing offices are involved, or where employees with special skills (e.g., I/S technicians) are employed. An example of this type of organization is shown in Figure 7-6.

POSITION DESCRIPTIONS

Position descriptions are written statements of job responsibilities for the various job classifications within the department. They are a formal way to inform staff members of their duties. In this way, each person has a better understanding of his or her function, a result that fosters more effective performance. Position descriptions are of particular value in departments that experience heavy turnover because the descriptions facilitate the assimilation of new members. Beyond that, position descriptions are useful in recruiting and establishing a basis for evaluating staff members' performance. Position descriptions should be developed by the chief auditor or, if developed by others, should be reviewed and approved by him. Other suggestions are:

- Every position should be described.
- Specific responsibilities and duties should be enumerated.

FIG. 7-7

Position Description—Director of Corporate Audit

> SUMMARY:
> The Director–Corporate Audit is responsible for the development and implementation of an internal audit program designed to provide assurance to corporate management that, within economic limitations, (1) financial statements and reports comply with corporate policy; (2) internal accounting controls achieve the objectives thereof and are effective in promoting efficiency and protecting the assets
>
> *(continued)*

FIG. 7-7 *(cont'd)*

of the company; and (3) operational policies and standards of ethical business practice that promote the well-being of the company are enforced. In addition, the Director–Corporate Audit is responsible for reporting conditions which pose an inordinate risk of loss and for bringing to the surface any irregularities, fraud and other similar acts which are subject to detection through the application of normal audit procedures. In discharging the foregoing responsibilities, the Director–Corporate Audit reports to the Senior Vice-President–Finance.

SPECIFIC RESPONSIBILITIES:

1. Designs and implements procedural guidelines to assure that
    a. Internal accounting and financial controls of reporting entities achieve the objectives thereof and are adequate and efficient and can be relied upon to produce meaningful financial information of use to corporate management in discharging its responsibilities.
    b. Internal controls of reporting entities adequately safeguard the assets of the company.
    c. Financial statements of reporting entities comply with company policy, SEC requirements and generally accepted accounting principles, and are complete and accurate.
    d. Reporting entities are in compliance with operational policies that promote the well-being of the company, including policies regarding standards of business practice.
    e. Controls over the development, maintenance and operation of electronic data processing systems are sufficient to result in the processing of accurate and complete data.
2. Coordinates coverage with independent outside auditors, division internal auditors and others.
3. Designs an annual plan for audit coverage which fulfills the responsibility of the department.
4. Where appropriate, coordinates assignments with subsidiary and division management to facilitate efficient completion.
5. Establishes and maintains an internal auditing staff to perform in accordance with plans and guidelines.
6. Develops the professional capability of the staff by on-the-job training, staff meetings and seminars.
7. Directs and supervises the work of assistants to ensure that procedures are followed and that the work is performed in an efficient manner.
8. Assures that auditing objectives for specific projects and detail auditing programs proposed by assistants are reasonable.
9. Assures that workpapers prepared by assistants adequately document work performed and support conclusions contained in the reports.
10. Reviews report drafts prepared by assistants to maintain high quality and assure that matters requiring management action are brought to its attention in a timely fashion.
11. Follows up recommendations to determine that implementing action by affected management has occurred.
12. Directs the performance of such other special reviews as may be requested by the Audit Committee of the Board of Directors, the Senior Vice-President–Finance, or others.
13. Periodically and upon request, provides the Audit Committee of the Board of Directors with information, either orally in meetings or in written reports.

FIG. 7-8

Position Description—Manager of Corporate Audit

SUMMARY:

Responsible to the Director–Corporate Audit for assisting in the development and implementation of an internal auditing program designed to provide assurance to corporate management that, within economic limitations, (1) financial statements and reports comply with corporate policy; (2) internal accounting controls achieve the objectives thereof and are effective in promoting efficiency and protecting the assets of the company; and (3) operational policies and standards of ethical business practices that promote the well-being of the company are enforced.

SPECIFIC RESPONSIBILITIES:

1. Maintain high standards of quality on assigned audit projects by the following means:
    a. Review and approve audit programs and time budgets prepared by staff members.
    b. Monitor events and circumstances of assigned audit projects in progress and supervise the performance of staff members assigned.
    c. Review workpapers of completed projects assigned to be certain that adequate documentation has been gathered to evidence completion of the audit and that such workpapers form an adequate basis for reporting the results of that audit to management.
    d. Participate in exit conferences as required in the judgment of the manager and director.
    e. Review audit report drafts in connection with workpaper reviews to assure full and complete reporting of essential information in a professional manner.
2. Assist the director in accomplishing certain administrative functions as follows:
    a. Annual audit plans
    b. Coordination of plans with division internal auditors
    c. Recruiting efforts
    d. Staff performance evaluation
    e. Communication of plans with affected profit centers' managements
    f. Enforcing compliance with administrative practices, such as reports of weekly planning objectives and time reports.
3. Conduct audit examinations in accordance with department standards, effectively supervising the work of assistants, if any.
4. Assist the director in developing the technical skills and audit capabilities of the staff through informal on-the-job training techniques and through formalized instruction in topical areas during periodic staff meetings.
5. Keep current as to developments related to matters of interest to the department, such as pronouncements by the FASB, ASB, SEC, and others. Keep abreast of evolving audit techniques and practices.
6. Assist the director in contributing to the strength of the internal audit profession through attendance and participation in meetings of appropriate professional groups.

FIG. 7-9

Position Description—Senior Corporate Auditor

SUMMARY:

Senior corporate auditors are responsible for planning, performing, reporting and following up specific audit assignments under the guidance of an audit manager or the director. The responsibilities of the senior corporate auditor must be carried out in accordance with the Standards of Performance of the Corporate Audit Department. Such assignments are performed to provide assurance that, within economic limitations, (1) financial statements and reports comply with corporate policy; (2) internal accounting controls achieve the objectives thereof and are effective in promoting efficiency and protecting the assets of the company; and (3) operational policies and standards of ethical business practices that promote the well-being of the company are enforced.

SPECIFIC RESPONSIBILITIES:
1. Conduct feasibility studies and formulate plans for performing audit assignments.
2. Prepare or revise audit programs to accomplish audit objectives.
3. Prepare time budgets for completion of various audit steps.
4. Perform field work in accordance with approved audit program.
5. Review report draft and findings and recommendations with affected management.
6. Recommend areas for future audit efforts.
7. Evaluate responses to reports to determine reasonableness and suggest follow-up actions.
8. Keep current with developments in fields of expertise.
9. Participate in enhancing the status of the internal audit profession.

- As duties are changed, the descriptions should be updated.
- To assure understanding, descriptions should be discussed in recruiting, in staff meetings, and informally.

Examples of position descriptions for common job levels in internal auditing departments are shown in Figures 7-7, 7-8, and 7-9. These position descriptions illustrate the interrelationships and the sharing of responsibilities that must occur for effective audit results.

REPORTING RELATIONSHIPS

The preceding discussion with respect to organization structure makes it clear that a host of factors are involved in organizing an internal auditing function. In a sense, that discussion deals with factors that are more external to the particular internal auditing function and the organization it serves. In addition to these, there are factors that are more specific or focused to the organization and the internal auditing function.

ORGANIZING & PLANNING THE AUDIT FUNCTION

These are important because they directly affect the reporting relationship of the audit function and the extent to which it will be perceived as being independent. Independence must be attained if internal auditing standards are to be observed. Before discussing these factors, it is worth commenting further about the concept of independence and the struggle to maintain it.

Independence vs. Conflict of Interest—A Constant Battle

Chapter 6 presents the standard of independence that the internal auditor must maintain in the conduct of audit projects. Such a standard poses some unique reporting questions. The chief internal auditor must report organizationally to someone. Yet, that reporting relationship must not restrict the auditing function's access to any member of management or its full knowledge of company activities, when this access is relevant to the accomplishment of the auditing objectives.

This places the chief internal auditor in the awkward position of a dual reporting relationship and creates an ongoing potential for conflicts to arise between his need for maintaining independence and his reporting relationship. The audit director or manager is one of the few positions in the corporate hierarchy in which he has the opportunity to disclose information to more senior members of management, even to the board of directors when warranted, to remedy problems that lower levels of management either refuse to acknowledge or fail to prudently resolve—all within the context of the audit charter. One view holds that, depending on the circumstances, the internal auditor may need to report situations even to the SEC, the press, or law enforcement agencies.[10] The fact that such situations are rare, indeed, is of little comfort.

---

[10] John C. Corless, "Internal Auditors: The Conscience of Top Management," *The Internal Auditor*, Aug. 1978, p. 16.

In addition to Corless, Michael Meir and Larry Rittenberg, Ph.D., CIA, CPA, in May 1985, issued a paper on the subject of "The Internal Auditor's Responsibilities and Appropriate Actions for Dealing With Known Corporate Wrongdoing." They suggest that the CIA Code of Ethics provides a framework for guiding the internal auditor by encouraging the auditor *not* to be associated with illegal or improper activity. The authors suggest further that the auditor should consider that the need for more positive action may be necessary. The authors' advice is to seek assistance from legal counsel, but there is no direct recommendation that internal auditors report their information to outside agencies or authorities—by themselves. This seems consistent with recent testimony by the 1987–1988 IIA Chairman, Ronald Bell, before the House Oversight and Investigations Subcommittee chaired by John D. Dingell (D. Mich.) in July 1987. Rep. Wyden (D. Ore.) questioned what the internal auditor should do when auditors report the discovery of fraud but are ignored. Bell replied that the IIA has commissioned a study to look into "the role of internal auditors, their loyalty to their companies and their responsibility to report sensitive issues." Wyden pressed Bell by asking, "Shouldn't internal auditors be required to go to the public regulators?" Bell replied, "The internal auditor's reporting responsibility is to the organization. Our window to the outside world is through the audit committee and the board of directors."

To alleviate some of these complications or problems and to obviate the conflict-of-interest problem, several companies have arranged for the internal auditing function to report directly to the board, to the audit committee of the board, or to the chief executive officer. Many more have permitted the chief auditor unrestricted access to the audit committee or to the board, while retaining other administrative reporting relationships.

Factors to Consider in Establishing the Audit Reporting Structure

The proper location of the internal auditing organization in the corporate structure will evolve in each company, depending on the individual circumstances. Some of the factors that management must consider are discussed in the following sections. These factors are presented in what is believed to be a descending order of importance, although it is recognized that opinions as to the order of importance may vary.

Capability of the Staff of the Audit Function. Perhaps the most important factor is the capability of the chief auditor and his staff. If the board or senior management is skeptical about the capabilities of the staff of the audit, the function will probably be relegated to a lower and less influential reporting relationship.

What the Board of Directors or Senior Management Knows About Auditing. While some company executives have risen to head the business through the accounting or finance functions (some may have been auditors at one time), many others have followed different paths. Persons familiar with the technical aspects of accounting and finance have usually gained an understanding and appreciation of internal auditing. Such background enables more productive relationships to be built between the audit function and top management. All other factors being equal, the best management support and counsel will often come from an individual in senior management who has extensive knowledge and experience about auditing, although this can create the difficulty of undue interference. Thus, in an effort to maintain an independent function, the personalities and styles of the management should also be weighed.

Accessibility of the Board of Directors or Senior Management. In some circumstances, the chairman or the president is so actively involved in other significant company matters that he is unable to provide sufficient guidance and support to the audit function. In these situations, the function can drift and the relationships between it and other departments can become strained or ineffective. To avoid this in these cases, it is more prudent to have the function report directly to another senior officer.

ORGANIZING & PLANNING THE AUDIT FUNCTION

Existing Internal Control Environment. Companies with significant or chronic internal control problems or exposures to the risk of a lack of internal control have a greater need for a strong internal auditing function than companies in less demanding circumstances. The reporting relationship in such cases will probably be elevated to a higher level to assure adequate support and guidance of the function.

Credibility of Management. Companies whose managements have been marred by improper practices, unauthorized deviations from established policies, or illegal activities will also tend to raise to a higher level the reporting relationship of the audit function. In fact, the board of directors for these entities will usually insist on this.

Significance of Corporate Accountability. Companies that are frequently in the public eye, whether because of their products or services, the extent of public ownership, or for other reasons, are generally more sensitive to matters of corporate accountability than others. To be responsive to public interests, these companies may desire a high organizational status for the audit function. Other companies, whose business activities are less visible, may be less concerned with corporate accountability and may select that structure seen as most effective in carrying out the internal auditing mission. This structure may not have the same high status as in the case of the more publicly oriented companies.

Trends in Regulatory Activity. The actions of Congress, the SEC, the Justice Department, and others have had a profound effect on the way companies do business and on the role played by internal auditors. The FCPA, enacted in 1977, is an obvious example of how regulatory activity can affect reporting relationships. It was only after its enactment that many companies began critically focusing on the reporting relationships of their audit functions.

For the most part, the foregoing factors are not explicitly evident in published material regarding organization structure. The chief auditor's view of reporting relationships, if solicited by management or the audit committee, should be given only after carefully considering the advantages and disadvantages of the previous alternatives.

Reporting Relationships Vary

There is no single right answer for all companies as to the proper organizational placement of the audit function. Figure 7-10 indicates the spread of

FIG. 7-10

IIA Survey of Reporting Relationships of Chief Internal Auditors

4B. What is the title of the executive to whom the chief internal auditor reports functionally?

	U.S. — Canada				Other International				1979 Total
	Small	Medium	Large	Total	Small	Medium	Large	Total	
	%	%	%	%	%	%	%	%	
Vice-President–Finance	17.0%	14.3%	18.9%	16.8%	—	—	—	—	17%
Vice-President and/or Chief Financial Officer	6.6	15.5	14.1	12.8	0.0	16.7	0.0	9.5	13
Controller or assistant	9.4	8.1	8.1	8.4	0.0	0.0	20.0	4.8	8
President	14.2	12.4	3.8	9.3	0.0	8.3	0.0	4.8	9
Vice-President	2.8	4.3	6.5	4.9	—	—	—	—	5
Vice-President and/or Treasurer	9.4	2.5	1.6	3.8	—	—	—	—	4
Chairman of Board and Chief Executive Officer	7.5	6.8	8.6	7.7	0.0	8.3	20.0	9.5	8
Audit or Executive Committee	10.4	19.9	14.6	15.5	25.0	25.0	20.0	23.8	15
President and Chief Executive Officer	0.9	0.6	2.2	1.3	—	—	—	—	1
General Manager	2.8	1.2	0.0	1.1	25.0	33.3	0.0	23.8	2
Vice-President–Business Affairs	1.9	0.6	0.5	0.9	—	—	—	—	1
Inspector General	0.0	0.0	1.1	0.4	0.0	0.0	20.0	4.8	1
Deputy Minister	0.0	0.0	2.7	1.1	—	—	—	—	1
Director of Management Services	0.9	0.0	0.5	0.4	—	—	—	—	1
Financial audit committee chain	0.9	1.2	2.2	1.5	0.0	0.0	20.0	4.8	2
State Auditor	0.0	0.0	1.1	0.4	—	—	—	—	1
Company Secretary	1.9	0.0	0.0	0.4	—	—	—	—	1
No answer	9.4	8.7	9.2	9.1	25.0	8.3	0.0	9.5	10
Other	3.6%	3.0%	3.5%	3.2%	25.0%	0.0%	0.0%	4.8%	4%
Total mentions	106	161	185	452	4	12	5	21	497

* Not comparable

Comment: There is evidence to suggest that there are many dual-reporting relationships.

reporting relationships based on a 1979 survey by the IIA.[11] This data indicates that, overall, a strong preference exists for organizing the audit function under the company's chief financial or chief accounting officer.

Regardless of the organizational location in the company, the chief auditor must be reasonably assured of unimpeded access to appropriate levels of management, including the board of directors and, if necessary, the external auditors. Without such access, the potential for conflict of interest exists and the chief auditor may not be able to exercise sufficient independence.

OBTAINING PERSONNEL, FACILITIES, AND OTHER RESOURCES

Any discussion of organizing the audit function would be incomplete without mentioning the need to obtain the resources necessary to carry out its mission. In addition to personnel and facilities, this includes providing the essential auditing tools, such as auditing standards, questionnaires, audit programs, generalized audit software, and reference materials. These subjects are of sufficient importance to the successful management of an internal auditing function to warrant separate detailed discussions. (See Chapters 6, 8, 9, and 10.)

LONG- AND SHORT-RANGE AUDIT PLANNING

In a broad sense, planning means anticipating the course of future events and conditions and sequencing intended actions so as to achieve particular goals and objectives. Planning is such an integral part of daily activities of any organizational unit that it is easy to overlook the key role it plays. An audit department, like any other organizational unit, must devote considerable attention to planning if it is to be efficient and effective. Planning for audit activities occurs at several levels, as follows:

- Project planning
- Resource planning
- Organization planning

Project planning and resource planning are introduced generally in the fol-

---

[11] From *Survey of Internal Auditing 1979* (Altamonte Springs, Fla.: The Institute of Internal Auditors, 1980), p. 21. Reprinted by permission of the Institute of Internal Auditors, Inc., 249 Maitland Ave., Altamonte Springs, Fla. 32701.

lowing and are discussed in detail in Chapter 9. Organizational planning is discussed in some detail in the following.

Project Planning

Project planning may be defined as those activities involved in devising the plan of audit coverage for the entire entity for which the audit department is responsible for a given period. Project planning is done on both a near-term one-year and long-term (approximately three- to five-year) basis. Techniques for accomplishing this type of planning were set forth in Chapter 2. Basically, project planning requires systematically evaluating all relevant organizational units in terms of company policies, procedures, systems, and controls and then ranking areas in terms of importance. From this effort, frequencies of coverage of specific areas can be developed that result in satisfactory overall audit coverage over a specific period—say three to five years. This planning is critical because it will form the backdrop for the other types of planning. It must be accomplished, therefore, on an analytical and selective basis. An example of an annual audit plan is shown in Figure 7-11.

Project planning of a more detailed type occurs for every project assignment. In practice, assignment planning is usually the responsibility of project managers and performing auditors, and is discussed in detail in Chapter 11. Assignment planning includes planning work scope, developing the program of testing, and scheduling the interviews.

Resource Planning

Resource planning may be defined as the process of identifying the resources required to accomplish the objectives of the internal audit department. For this purpose, resources include manpower, facilities, equipment, supplies, and support services, such as data processing, reproduction, and graphics.

Resource planning can usually be done only when something is known about the extent of planned audit coverage. (See Chapter 2.) Resource planning entails the use of budgeting techniques and manpower planning. More is said about this subject in Chapter 10.

Organizational Planning

Earlier in this chapter, the subject of organizing is discussed in terms of the efforts required to establish a department. In order to sustain the department, however, organizational planning is required. Organizational planning may be defined as the process of estimating or anticipating the type of structure, reporting relationships, manpower, facilities, audit approaches, and so forth, that will be needed to direct an effective audit function over a long period.

ORGANIZING & PLANNING THE AUDIT FUNCTION 7-29

It is synonymous with strategic planning, a subject discussed in Chapter 2. However, in Chapter 2, the objective is to allocate auditing resources in the most effective manner. Organizational planning and strategic planning overlap, but, in terms of a time sequence, organizational planning comes first. Organizational planning should reflect the judgment of the director and should consider the needs of management, the audit committee, and the board of directors. Organizational planning is necessary to reasonably assure that the department will be responsive and effective as a management tool. Also, the type of planning is essential to help forge the strategic or overall approach discussed in Chapter 2.

Organizational planning is more general than the other planning discussed previously. It involves efforts to assure that the audit department keep pace with company growth, emerging problems, external developments, and so forth. As an example, the technological explosion in the field of data processing is revolutionizing business and office routines of all types. Most managements (and internal auditors) have not yet maximized the potential advantages that are currently available. Hence, the chief auditor must plan methodologies to facilitate more effective auditing of data processing, and a more effective utilization of the rapidly developing I/S technology.

Organizational planning requires that the chief auditor or his designee has sufficient information on which to shape the department into the desired position and maintain it. This may be done in the following ways:

☐ *Monitoring internal information.* Most managements generate considerable information that points out intended future directions of the company. This includes strategic or long-term plans and annual business plans. The audit department should be among the recipients of this data, which should be helpful in integrating the audit function with corporate growth plans. In addition, most company managements are furnished with a variety of financial data reflecting current performance against plans. The audit department should also be furnished this information regularly for identifying possible audit areas.

☐ *Keeping current with respect to external developments.* These include events that affect the general economy, the industrial or business segments in which the company operates, and the audit profession. Techniques for keeping current include the following:

- Subscribing to general business periodicals and relevant trade and professional publications
- Attending state-of-the-art conferences and seminars
- Participating in audit research projects sponsored by the audit profession, by academicians and others
- Experimenting with new techniques in on-the-job situations

☐ *Meeting with company management at all levels.* These may range from informal meetings with key department, division, and/or subsidiary managers to more formal, structured meetings with senior management, in-

FIG. 7-11
Annual Audit Plan

Corporate Audit — 19XX Audit Plan

Type of Audit	Manufacturing Group			Electronic and Systems Group			
	ABC	DEFG	HIJKL	MNO	PQR	STU	VWX
Financial:							
Cash control	X		X	X		X	
Accounts receivable							
Cost system							
Capital assets	X						
Depreciation							
Payroll	X		X			X	
Executive payroll							
Accounts payable	X						
Limited financial review	X	X	X	X	X	X	X
Internal control survey	X	(3)	X	X	X	X	X
Standards of Business Conduct:							
Comprehensive standards of business conduct	X	(3)		X		X	
Procural standards		X					
Trade practices		X					
Travel/Business conference/ Entertainment	X	X	X				
Consultant/Agent/Distributor	X						
Gratuity/Hospital	(2)						
I/S:							
Systems under development	XXXX	XX				X	
Installation Review			X	X		X	
Existing I/S application	XXXX					X	

(1) Various — per Attachment A [*omitted*]
(2) Project dependent upon feasibility determination
(3) Foreign program

ORGANIZING & PLANNING THE AUDIT FUNCTION

						Corporate				
YYZZ	AAA	BBB	CCC	DDD	EEE	FFFFF	GGG	HHHH	DP	CORP OFF
		X	X		X					X
X	X				X		X			
		X		X						
					X					
										X
					X			X	X	
X	X	X	X	X	X	X	X	X		X
X	X	X	X	X	X	X	X	X	X	X
							X	X		
X			X				X			X
X						X	X			X
X			X		X			X		X
	X	X	X				X	X		(1)
X		X	X	X						

cluding the president and the chief executive officer. The purpose of these meetings is to obtain information useful in organizational planning and to project the image of the audit department. More will be said on this latter point later in this chapter. Useful information could include intentions regarding expansion, new product lines, and developing systems.

Scientific Planning Techniques

As is noted in the preceding segment, an audit department must devote considerable attention to planning if it is to be efficient and effective. It is believed that many internal auditing practitioners employ the suggested techniques or variations of them.

Practitioners in need of more scientific techniques must look beyond these techniques. Such might be the case for extremely large internal auditing organizations and for lengthy and very complex internal auditing undertakings. In these instances, the commitment of resources may necessitate the enhanced reliability that is often claimed for more formalistic methods. Descriptions of these techniques were recently made available to practitioners by the IIA in *Planning for the Internal Audit Function*.[12] The following reprint from Chapter 6 of that publication identifies and briefly describes these techniques. They are classified into what the author sees as six main phases of planning.

1.0 Techniques for Enhancing Planning of the Role, Responsibility, and Approach of the Internal Audit Department
    1.1 Strategy-Set Transformation
    1.2 Delphi

2.0 Techniques for Enhancing Facilities and Procedures Management
    2.1 Analytical Hierarchy Process
    2.2 Rating Scales

3.0 Techniques for Enhancing Audit-Portfolio Management
    3.1 Variance Analysis Techniques

4.0 Techniques for Enhancing Personnel-Skills Management and Development
    4.1 Regression Analysis
    4.2 Management by Objectives

5.0 Techniques for Enhancing Planning and Budgeting
    5.1 Zero-Base Budgeting
    5.2 Simulation

6.0 Techniques for Enhancing Work Scheduling and Performance Monitoring
    6.1 Network-Scheduling Techniques
    6.2 Gantt Charts
    6.3 Mathematical Programming

---

[12] J. Efrim Boritz, Ph.D., *Planning for the Internal Audit Function* (Altamonte Springs, Fla.: The Institute of Internal Auditors Research Foundation, 1983), pp. 261–263. Reprinted by permission of the Institute of Internal Auditors Inc.

Strategy-set transformation was briefly discussed as a strategic planning tool in Chapter 2. This technique involves identifying and transforming key elements of organizational strategy sets into strategic departmental guidelines.

Delphi is a technique for eliciting an informal opinion and obtaining a consensus on a set of issues; for example, what should be the priorities of the internal audit department as viewed by external parties.

The analytical hierarchy process is a technique for hierarchically breaking down complex problems into sets of smaller, less formidable problems. It may be particularly useful for structuring audit-risk-exposure-concern evaluations.

Rating scales are used throughout auditing. Often, the theory of measurement and scaling is ignored; and the properties of measurement scales, both beneficial and restrictive, are not taken into consideration when constructing and using various types of scales. Misuse of rating scales can lead to unsupportable conclusions.

Variance analysis techniques have been proposed to aid in the discretionary allocation of audit attention to audit units. Two basic techniques introduced here will be control charts and Cusum charts.

Regression analysis is a useful statistical technique for estimating relationships. In particular, it may be used to arrive at reasonable estimates of audit-time requirements.

Management by objectives has been found to be useful for both directing attention toward desirable activities and as a basis for evaluating performance.

Zero-base budgeting is a tool for selecting subsets of desirable activities when resources are limited.

Network-scheduling techniques, including performance evaluation and review technique (PERT) and critical path method (CPM), are useful for planning as integrated set of activities so as to ensure that a work plan for a specified time period is achieved.

Gantt charts are useful graphic aids for organizing and monitoring ongoing work activities.

Mathematical programming permits the use of quantitative optimization techniques for best matching audit skills and hours available with specific audit requirements and other scheduling constraints.

These techniques are described more fully by Boritz in an overview or conceptual fashion. The discussions are sufficient to permit implementation. Detail applications are not provided. The intent is to expand the horizons of professionals seeking useful techniques to enhance planning capabilities.

CREATING THE RIGHT IMAGE FOR THE AUDIT FUNCTION

Selling the Benefits of the Department

It may seem surprising to find commentary on the subject of selling in a book about internal auditing. Obviously, the internal auditor does not sell in the same sense as the company's marketing staff. Nevertheless, all members of the internal auditing department must "sell" the services of the department. The most important salesman for this purpose is the chief internal auditor.

The importance of establishing and maintaining the proper image is better understood when viewed against the history of internal auditing. It has been said in a recent Conference Board survey that "[d]espite the general resurgence of top management interest in internal auditing, in a sizable minority of companies surveyed, inadequate management acceptance and support remain stumbling blocks to internal audit development."[13] While the resistance may have been justifiable based on past negative experiences with internal auditors, enhancements in professionalism over the years should now effectively minimize such experiences. What remains then is to convince doubters that internal auditing is beneficial and desirable, not only by audit projects, but by other activities as well. That is where selling comes in.

Techniques

Developing techniques for establishing and maintaining a proper image is an important responsibility of the Director of Internal Auditing. Staff members cannot be expected to project the proper image unless the chief auditor, by specific actions, sets the standard. Such obvious image-building qualities as attentiveness, responsiveness, dependability, and trustworthiness can be evidenced through the chief auditor's day-to-day activities. In essence, these and other related qualities not only contribute to a sound department, but also demonstrate the desired professional image; that is, they demonstrate independence, competence, and diligence.

There are several practical tips that should help the chief auditor establish an environment conducive to professionalism. In addition, there are some techniques that specifically relate to the conduct of audit projects that will also help. These are discussed in the following.

- ☐ *Involve management in shaping audit plans.* There is much to be gained from seeking management assistance in determining audit coverage. Not only is the actual audit plan enhanced, but the communication offers an opportunity to demonstrate the responsiveness of the audit function, which, in turn, nurtures the image the internal auditor seeks.

- ☐ *Discuss specific audit project objectives with management involved.* This technique demonstrates to affected management groups the auditor's competence in planning and organizing and, in addition, reveals the extent of the knowledge the auditor has obtained about the area under audit. Such discussion reflects the auditor's professionalism and builds a basis for mutual respect to develop.

---

[13] Macchiaverna, *op. cit.*, p. 11.

- *Inform management of audit progress timely.* Informing management of the audit progress is a way to maintain open communication between management and the auditor throughout the course of the audit. The nature of the discussions will be an indication of the auditor's judgmental ability (i.e., his ability to separate the important matters from the mundane ones).
- *Establish contact with management in nonaudit situations.* Contact with management may be established in nonaudit situations in a variety of ways. Telephone contact is useful, perhaps to elicit response to a relevant current event, to pay a compliment on operating performance, or to offer congratulations on reaching a special milestone. Sending informal memos for the same purpose is also useful. Getting together in after-hours informal discussions is also a good technique. The purpose of these get-togethers is to minimize apprehension or fear, and to let managers see that auditors are human beings who have a job to do.
- *Develop good listening habits.* Managers often believe that auditors ignore relevant, rational reasons offered as explanations for certain circumstances. Auditors can demonstrate that such explanations are worthwhile by altering the scope of work, the audit findings, or the indicated conclusion, or simply by changing wording in the audit report, as the case may be. Such actions suggest that the auditor is indeed responsive.
- *Avoid impasses to the extent practicable.* Contact with management should not end with unreconcilable points of view. Such conditions reflect poorly on both the auditor and auditee. Reasonable persons ought to be able to resolve major differences, or at least state them in specific, clear, and impersonal language.
- *Be open and communicative.* Auditors should be open and communicative, since unnecessary reticence on their part will appear to be unnatural to management and may raise questions of credibility.
- *Be responsive to requests for special assistance or consultation.* Responsiveness to requests for special assistance offers invaluable opportunities to demonstrate competence and willingness to serve management interests.
- *Accept criticism gracefully.* While some managers may offer unwarranted comments, they are far outnumbered by those who honestly seek improved relations with auditors. The chief auditor should periodically seek critical comments to reflect a responsive attitude and a desire to effect change where necessary.
- *Demonstrate technical competence.* Technical competence may be demonstrated in formal presentation to management groups in audit reports and other forms of communication, or by arranging for and conducting technical audit sessions for all interested parties. Figure 7-12 is an announcement of such a session.

Balancing Independence Against Acceptability

As important as is gaining acceptability, the chief auditor must not compromise independence as a result. The department must not develop a rep-

FIG. 7-12

Announcement of an Audit Seminar for All Interested Parties

> TO: Distribution
> FROM: K.H. Lewis
> SUBJECT: Cost/Benefit Analysis Seminar
>
> The Corporate Audit Department is planning a half-day seminar on Cost/Benefit Analysis to be presented to interested parties Monday, December 21, 19XX. This seminar will provide attendees an opportunity to enhance their knowledge of cost/benefit considerations through presentation of research conducted by Corporate Audit of available literature on the subject and through the exchange of viewpoints and procedures of other profit centers.
>
> The presentation will focus on techniques for identifying and measuring the costs and benefits associated with the planned implementation of alternative management decisions. These include such events as acquisition of assets (whether directly or through a make/buy process), installation of new EDP systems, and implementation of internal controls. Not only will there be discussions of cost/benefit applications as they apply to management decisions, but the seminar also can be a forum for discussions with Corporate Audit on improving considerations of cost/benefit applications as they apply to potential audit recommendations.
>
> Please inform me if you or anyone in your organization would be interested in attending. Extra copies are enclosed for distribution to others you feel may have an interest in attending. Further details regarding time and place will be communicated to respondents the first week of December. If there are any questions, feel free to call me at the Corporate Office on extension 401.

utation for vacillating. Informed management expects that the audit department will exhibit a healthy degree of skepticism and independence, and that it will challenge management when circumstances warrant.

QUALITY ASSURANCE

Definition and Purpose

The concept of quality assurance is widely recognized in government and private industry circles. It is a term whose definition is self-evident, perhaps explaining why most professional literature omits articulating it.

Quality assurance is used here to mean a series of control techniques to reasonably assure that the audit function is operating in accordance with the high standards established for it. Another way to state the same thing is to say that quality assurance is the process by which an interested party is assured that the work products are credible. The IIA suggests the following definition: "... the process of evaluating an internal audit organization's compliance with the *Standards for the Professional Practice of Internal Auditing* and other applicable company/departmental policies and procedures. This assessment encompasses the quality of independence, professional proficiency, scope of work, performance of audit work, and management of the internal audit department."[14] Thus, quality assurance is an important aspect of audit management.

Background

Quality assurance is necessary in all branches of auditing, but it has drawn the most publicity in public accounting, particularly in recent years. Audit failures during the 1980s have eroded the faith of investors and creditors in the ability of the accounting profession to perform the job that has historically been its unique function (the auditing of financial statements). It therefore seems as though quality assurance is more important to public accountants, to bolster the sagging confidence of users of financial statements.

While not nearly as widely publicized, the importance of quality assurance for internal auditing is equally high. Why is this so? For the answer one must look to the basics of auditing—any auditing.

As noted in Chapter 1, all auditors share some things in common regardless of whether they practice in the public sector, in government, or in private industry. One of these commonalities is that each auditor undertakes audit projects to gain information upon which to express opinions for reporting to others who intend to rely upon such opinions in deciding courses of action. These other parties in interest are not usually in a position to conduct examinations and, as a result, form their own opinions. In the instance of public accounting, the opinion has to do with the fairness with which financial statements present financial position and results of operations. The users of that opinion include investors and creditors, among others.

In the instance of internal auditing, opinions basically deal with the extent to which internal controls achieve the objectives. The users include management and the board of directors, among others.

In order for these opinions to be useful, they must carry a high potential for being relevant and reliable. Thus, it is necessary that such opinions are produced by a process designed to minimize the chance that the opinions are unreliable and/or irrelevant. For this reason, audits must be conducted in accordance with high professional standards of performance; these require proper planning and supervision of the work, professionally competent performers, and objective and independent mental attitude, due diligence, and so on (see Chapters 3 to 6 for a full discussion).

For users of the services of auditors, it may be necessary that, from time to time, they be informed in some way that the auditors in fact are

---

[14] Professional Standards and Responsibilities Committee 1983–1984, John K. Watsen, Chairman, *Quality Assurance Review Manual for Internal Auditing* (Altamonte Springs, Fla.: The Institute of Internal Auditors, 1984), p. IV.

performing their work in accordance with such standards. In essence, the auditors should be audited periodically.

The reports of such audits, often referred to as peer reviews, when furnished to the users of audit services, provide assurance to them that the opinions on which they rely meet the necessary quality conditions that can reasonably be expected. Thus, the objective of quality assurance is served.

The Issues

There are challenging issues involved in the delivery of quality assurance to those in need of it. These include (1) who should perform the work; (2) to whom should the results be made available; (3) what level of responsibility should be borne by those providing the assurance; and (4) who should audit the quality assurance reviewers?

Answering the first question is tricky. Auditing an auditor is not like other auditor-auditee situations. Auditees, in general, are not experts in auditing almost by definition. Forming an ad hoc group of auditee representatives to audit the auditors runs a high risk of their work being unreliable. Moreover, there is the question of objectivity that is ever-present. Auditors, on the other hand, are experts in auditing. They are required by standards to be technically proficient, not only in the practice of auditing but also in other subjects. Yet, it is somewhat difficult to assemble a team of auditors who are independent of the auditors being audited.

The manner in which this dilemma is being dealt with is somewhat different for public accountants and internal auditors. Public accountants who are members of the AICPA's SEC practices section (SECPS) are required to undergo a peer review every three years. Public accountants who are members of the AICPA's private companies practice section (PCPS) also must subject themselves to periodic quality assurance or peer reviews, but these are not subject to review by a peer review committee created for the purpose of oversight by the Public Oversight Board (POB). The function of the POB is discussed in Chapter 1. Members of SECPS may also be subjected to investigation by a nine-member special investigations committee, each of whom is a partner or retired partner of a different member firm. Investigations are triggered by filing with the committee reports of litigation against the firm alleging deficiencies. Peer reviews are usually performed by other CPA firms—a sort of you do me, then I'll do you approach.

Peer reviews, at the option of the reviewed firm, may also be performed by associations of CPA firms, provided the association meets the independence criteria established for such associations as set forth in the peer review manual. Also, such associations must submit for approval of the SECPS peer review committee its plan of administration and must be agreeable to administrative reviews by the committee.

Peer reviews may also be conducted pursuant to programs administered by state CPA societies. Such a society must satisfy the requirements for involvement specified by the peer review manual. Again, selecting this method of completing the peer review requirement is at the option of the firm to be reviewed.

The foregoing provisions for the AICPA's peer review program reflect an impressive response to criticisms of the quality of CPAs' work that arose in the 1970s. For a while, it seemed as though the program was effective. In the 1980s, however, a new wave of audit failures led to another round of congressional inquiry and public criticism of the quality assurance program. Many observers believe that the voluntary nature of the program and its seemingly steadfast avoidance of imposing sanctions against members who fail to remedy deficient conditions have compromised the effectiveness of the program.

Recently, a special AICPA committee, formed by Rholan E. Larson in 1983 to look at standards of professional conduct, recommended a different course. The committee, known as the Anderson Committee for its chairman, George Anderson, reported the results of its activities in 1986. The Anderson Committee concluded that the AICPA maintains an effective monitoring program of the firms in the AICPA's Division for CPA firms. However, many AICPA members in public practice are not subject to any form of quality review.[15] The Committee recommended that the Institute:

- ☐ Establish a quality review (QR) program and make participation in that program or in the peer review programs of the division a membership requirement for members in public practice.
- ☐ Adopt a requirement for AICPA members who practice in firms that audit one or more SEC registrants that would require those firms to be members of the SECPS.
- ☐ Establish more effective procedures for handling complaints and assuring compliance with performance standards by all members.[16]

These recommendations would have made peer reviews mandatory for firms that audit SEC registrants. A bylaw amendment to that effect was proposed. In October 1986, the AICPA Council decided to put the measure to a membership vote. It received a 61 percent favorable vote. Since the bylaws require a two-thirds majority vote, the measure did not pass.

The failed vote does not end the drive to forge a mandatory peer review program for firms auditing SEC registrants. In April 1987, the SEC proposed a rule that would achieve what the AICPA membership rejected.

The proposed rule would require CPA firms with SEC clients to have undergone a peer review within the three years preceding the date of the examination. A transition period of eighteen months is provided for firms

---

[15] Special Committee on Standards of Professional Conduct for Certified Public Accountants, *Restructuring Professional Standards to Achieve Professional Excellence in a Changing Environment* (New York: AICPA, 1986), p. 45.

[16] *Ibid.*, p. 45.

who have not had a peer review. The firms would have the option of having this review supervised by an acceptable peer review organization (PRO). The proposed rules provide requirements for what constitutes an acceptable PRO. No disciplinary authority is provided to PROs under the rules, but disciplinary action by PROs is not prohibited. In recent statements, it is clear that the AICPA will support these proposed rules.[17]

It is also clear that the leadership of the AICPA is intent on moving the program of quality assurance from a complaint-based system to a goal-oriented system featuring mandatory quality assurance monitoring. It also is clear that an assist from the SEC is needed.

For internal audit organizations, existing internal audit standards also call for quality assurance reviews. The approach entails internal reviews to be performed by internal auditors in the same manner as any other internal audit. Also, external reviews are encouraged. These are to be performed by qualified persons who are independent of the organization and who do not have a real or apparent conflict of interest. The suggested frequency of external reviews is three years.[18]

In 1986, the PSRC of the IIA issued for comment a proposed SIAS on quality assurance. In November 1986, that proposal was published as SIAS No. 4. It provides additional guidance for implementing an internal auditing quality assurance program. SIAS No. 4 is reprinted below.[19]

INTERPRETATIONS

Guideline 560.01

Guideline 560.01 states that the purpose of a quality assurance program is to provide reasonable assurance that audit work conforms with these *Standards*, the internal auditing department's charter, and other applicable standards. A quality assurance program should include the following elements:

Supervision
Internal reviews
External reviews

.1 The "reasonable assurance" mentioned in this guideline serves the needs of several constituencies in addition to that of the director of internal auditing. These may include senior management, the independent outside auditors, the audit committee, and regulatory agencies, each of whom may have reasons to rely upon the performance of the internal auditing function.

---

[17] See, for example, the remarks of J. Michael Cook, AICPA Chairman, appearing in *The CPA Letter,* April 13, 1987, which in part indicated that "the Institute will strongly support the thrust of . . . the SEC."

[18] *Standards for the Professional Practice of Internal Auditing,* (Altamonte Springs, Fla.: The Institute of Internal Auditors, 1978), p. 25.

[19] Professional Standards and Responsibilities Committee, *Statement on Internal Auditing Standards No. 4—November 1986 Quality Assurance* (Altamonte Springs, Fla.: The Institute of Internal Auditors, 1986). Reprinted by permission of the Institute of Internal Auditors, Inc.

ORGANIZING & PLANNING THE AUDIT FUNCTION

.2 Conformity with applicable standards is more than simply complying with established policies and procedures. It includes performance of the audit function at a high level of efficiency and effectiveness. Quality assurance is essential to achieving such performance, as well as to maintaining the internal auditing department's credibility with those it serves.

.3 As cited in Guideline 560.01, a key criterion against which an internal auditing department should be measured is its charter. Consideration of the department's charter should also include an assessment of the charter in terms of the elements specified in Standard 110, Organizational Status (110.01.4).

.4 The following are examples of "other applicable standards" and potential measurement criteria that should be considered in evaluating the performance of the internal auditing department:
- The Institute's *Code of Ethics*.
- The internal auditing department's objectives, policies, and procedures.
- The organization's policies and procedures that apply to the internal auditing function.
- Laws, regulations, and government or industry standards which specify auditing and reporting requirements.
- Systems for establishing the audit universe, assessing risk, and determining frequency and scope of audits.
- Audit planning documents, particularly those submitted to senior management and the audit committee.
- The plan of organization, statements of job requirements, position descriptions, and professional development plans of the internal auditing department.

Guideline 560.02

Guideline 560.02 states that supervision of work of the internal auditors should be carried out continually to assure conformance with internal auditing standards, departmental policies, and audit programs.

.1 Adequate supervision is the most fundamental element of a quality assurance program. As such, it provides a foundation upon which internal and external reviews can subsequently be built.

.2 The nature of and responsibility for supervision are set forth in the *Standards*, particularly 230, and related guidelines. As indicated in the guidelines under Standard 230, supervision includes among other things:
- Adequate planning and providing suitable instructions to subordinates.
- Determination that the approved audit program has been carried out and documented in the working papers and that the resulting report comments are appropriate.
- Adequate and properly documented supervision of all internal auditing activities, which is ultimately the responsibility of the director of internal auditing.

.3 In Guideline 560.02, the word "continually" indicates that supervision should be performed throughout the planning, examination, evaluation, report and follow-up process for all assignments. Supervision should also extend to training, employee performance evaluation, time and expense control, and similar administrative areas.

Guideline 560.03

Guideline 560.03 states that internal reviews should be performed periodically by members of the internal auditing staff to appraise the quality of the audit work performed. These reviews should be performed in the same manner as any other internal audit.

.1 Formal internal reviews are periodic self-assessments of the internal auditing department. These reviews generally are performed by a team or an individual selected by the director of internal auditing. Larger departments may have a person designated as "manager of quality assurance" or with a similar title and responsibilities.

.2 Internal quality assurance reviews primarily serve the needs of the director of internal auditing, but can also provide senior management and the audit committee with an assessment of the internal auditing function. These reviews should be structured so as to indicate the degree of compliance with the *Standards*, level of audit effectiveness, and extent of compliance with the organization and departmental policies and standards. The review should also provide recommendations for improvement.

.3 An internal review program, particularly in smaller internal auditing departments, will require adaptations that take into consideration the structure of the department and degree of involvement of the director in individual audits.

.4 When the foregoing formal internal reviews are not appropriate to the internal auditing department's needs, or to supplement such reviews, the following methods can provide elements of internal review coverage:

   a. Reviews by the director of internal auditing, audit managers, or supervisors, of a sample of audits (and areas of audit administration) where the work was performed under the direction of other managers or supervisors. As an ongoing process this can provide training, exchange of ideas, and greater uniformity, as well as provide assurance to the director of internal auditing.

   b. Feedback from auditees (in addition to that from personal contact) through the use of questionnaires or surveys, either routinely after each audit or periodically for selected audits. This process will elicit operating management's perception of the audit function and may also result in suggestions to make it more effective and responsive to management's needs.

.5 The director of internal auditing should initiate and monitor the internal review process. In selecting and instructing the team for an internal review, the director of internal auditing should ensure that the team is qualified and as independent as practicable.

.6 The director should receive a written report of the results of each internal review and ensure that appropriate action is taken. Although the purpose of internal reviews is to assess the effectiveness of the audit function for internal purposes, it may be appropriate for the director to share the results with persons outside the department, such as senior management, the audit committee, and the independent outside auditors. Internal reviews can also be useful as part of the self-assessment process in preparation for an external review.

.7 More detailed information about internal reviews is contained in other IIA pronouncements and publications including the *Quality Assurance Review Manual for Internal Auditing* which was published by The Institute of Internal Auditors in 1984.

Guideline 560.04

Guideline 560.04 states that external reviews of the internal auditing department should be performed to appraise the quality of the department's operations. These reviews should be performed by qualified persons who are independent of the organization and who do not have either a real or apparent conflict of interest. Such reviews should be conducted at least once every three years. On completion of the review, a formal, written report should be issued. The report should express an opinion as to the department's compliance with the *Standards for the Professional Practice of Internal Auditing* and, as appropriate, should include recommendations for improvement.

.1 External reviews can have considerable value to the director and other members of the internal auditing department. Another important purpose of external reviews is to provide independent assurance of quality to senior management, the audit committee, and others such as the independent outside auditors who rely on the work of the internal auditing department.

.2 The director of internal auditing should discuss with senior management and the audit committee the nature of an external review in the context of the overall quality assurance program and should involve them in the selection of an external reviewer.

.3 This guideline (560.04) states that external reviews should be performed by qualified individuals who are independent of the organization and who do not have either a real or an apparent conflict of interest. "Qualified individuals" are persons with the technical proficiency and educational background appropriate for the audit activities to be reviewed and could include internal auditors from outside the organization, outside consultants, or independent outside auditors. "Independent of the organization" means not a part of, or under the control of, the corporate entity or other organizations to which the internal auditing department belongs. In the selection of an external reviewer, consideration should be given to a possible real or apparent conflict of interest which the reviewer might have due to present or past relationships with the entity or its internal auditing department.

.4 Organizations of independent outside auditors in various countries have specified certain limited review procedures that they should consider in evaluating and using the work of the internal auditing function. These relate primarily to quality of work and degree of independence from auditees. These limited review procedures by independent outside auditors usually relate only to their audit of an organization's financial statements and generally would not constitute an "external review" for purposes of Guideline 560.04.

.5 Upon completion of an external review, the review team should issue a formal report containing an opinion as to the department's compliance with the *Standards*. The report should also address compliance with the department's charter and other applicable standards and include appropriate recommendations for improvement. The report should be addressed to the person or entity who requested the review. The director of internal auditing should prepare a written action plan in response to the significant comments and recommendations contained in the report of external review. Appropriate follow-up is also the director's responsibility.

.6 Guideline 560.04 states that external reviews should be conducted at least once every three years. However, there may be circumstances that justify a different interval. These circumstances include: (a) significant review and monitoring by the audit committee, (b) in-depth reviews by the independent outside auditors or others, and (c) the relative stability of the audit department's charter, organization, staff, and audit universe. The nature, scope, degree of independence, and overall results of the internal review program should also be considered in determining the external review interval.

.7 External review is an important element of the program for achieving quality assurance. However, if resources are limited, or for other reasons discussed above, the internal auditing department may be currently unable to obtain an external review. In these circumstances, more emphasis should be placed on supervision, periodic internal reviews, and other quality assurance methods that are available to the department. It is the responsibility of the director of internal audit to annually assess the conditions which restrict an external review. Another interim method is the use of qualified internal groups to conduct a review (e.g., former audit managers in the employ of the organization, other audit directors in a decentralized audit organization, or internal management advisory personnel). However, such a review should not be expected to achieve all of the objectives of an external review.

.8 More detailed information about external reviews is contained in other pronouncements and publications including the *Quality Assurance Review Manual for Internal Auditing* which was published by The Institute of Internal Auditors in 1984.

With respect to the second question—to whom should the results be made available—there is agreement that internal review reports should be addressed to the chief auditor and external review reports should be addressed to the audit committee. In fact, that is the way the specimen reports in the IIA Quality Assurance Review Manual are set up.

This is not to say that an internal review report could not be made available to persons other than the chief auditor. The same is true for the external review report. Other interested parties might include the external auditors, management, and various governmental agencies. It is not inconceivable that company shareholders, creditors, suppliers, and major customers may also be interested. Perhaps in the future even the general public will have to be informed in some appropriate fashion. Admittedly, that is a few years away—if it ever evolves at all.

Presently, for public accountants, reports of peer reviews of SECPS CPA firms, in addition to being given to the firm, are furnished to the peer review committee of the AICPA and are available to the POB. The SEC also has access to these reports. The reports are not required to be sent to clients of the CPA firm or the public. Also, the AICPA maintains files of these reports, member firm responses and peer review committee letters of acceptance, and other pertinent information.

The question of what degree of responsibility is to be taken by a quality assurance reviewer is potentially thorny in the instance of public accounting and unclear in the instance of internal auditing. Peer reviews in public accounting are conducted by peer review teams following a manual developed for the purpose.

Letters of arrangement are required and these contain, among other things, "hold harmless" clauses for the good faith acts of the team, the committee, and the AICPA. None of the documents that are available to the public (or the SEC for that matter) disclose the names of individuals, performing offices, or clients. It is not at all clear what would happen if the peer review process resulted in an unqualified opinion by the reviewing team of a CPA firm that was, in fact, failing to perform its work in accordance with GAAS in a situation in which the review process was deficient. If it could be proven that the review was not performed in good faith, some liability could result.

The POB reports and other events suggest that such a situation is not farfetched. It may be inferred from the POB that, while the majority of reviews are performed properly, a fraction are deficient. The POB staff has found it necessary to challenge several reviews that seemed not to have been properly performed.[20] Add to this the fact that, as far as is known, all of the CPA firms involved in the so called "audit failures" being investigated by the Dingell Subcommittee received unqualified peer review reports.[21] What are the chances of a peer reviewer being found by some future court to be liable for damages for failure to report substandard auditing? No one can say for sure.

With respect to internal auditing, the issue is much less clear and, perhaps, much less risky. That is because the responsibility of internal auditors has not yet been specifically reviewed in the courts. In other words, there have been no cases brought in which one of the issues to be decided was the role and responsibility of internal auditors and their liability, if any, should they fail to perform their determined responsibility in some relevant way. Hence, the peer reviewers of their performance are completely void of any reasonable guess as to what responsibility they are taking for their

---

[20] John C. Burton, Russell E. Palmer, and Robert S. Kay, *Handbook of Accounting and Auditing, 1983–1984 Update* (New York: Warren, Gorham & Lamont, 1983), p. 30-3.

[21] Editor, "Statements in Quotes," *Journal of Accountancy*, Aug. 1985, p. 142. The article quotes remarks by Arthur M. Wood, Chairman of the POB, to this effect.

work, although common sense suggests the number of times when the quality of the reviewer's work becomes an issue will be very few. In passing, it should be noted that the engagement letter section of the IIA's Quality Assurance Review Manual calls for protecting the review team and its members from any liability related to the review.

The fourth and last question to be discussed here asks who audits the peer reviewers. The answer is quite different for the two branches.

For public accountants in SECPS, peer reviews are themselves subject to review by the POB staff, as mentioned previously. Three types of monitoring programs are used by the POB staff to assess peer reviewers' adherence to the peer review standards:

1. Report review program, in which only reports are reviewed
2. Workpaper review program, in which workpapers of the reviewers are examined in addition to the report
3. Visitation-observation program, in which the scope of review includes visits to offices of the reviewed firm during the period of review

The results of these reviews are available to the POB. The SEC may also review the work of the staff, although, by special agreement, the names of the clients, the personnel, and the reviewed firm's offices are masked. The staff of the POB makes recommendations for improvements in the peer review standards that are often enacted by the POB.

This self-regulation program is aimed at improving quality, not disciplining members. This lack of sanction for substandard performance is being questioned by the same sources who are criticizing the voluntary nature of the program. Some see this as a factor in the perceived failure of public accounting to better protect the public from financial reporting fraud.

Perhaps in an effort to appease its critics, the profession may be moving toward some degree of sanctioning. The current peer review program empowers the executive committee of SECPS to impose sanctions ranging from requiring corrective measures to be taken by the reviewed firm to expulsion from membership. It was not until 1986 that the executive committee exercised its first use of these sanction powers. However, greater frequency of use in the future seems inevitable.

The quality assurance program of the IIA provides no comparable mechanism for monitoring the work of those who perform external reviews. The absence seems not to be posing any difficulties at present. That is because few internal auditing functions have undergone external reviews so far. In time, with greater frequency of occurrence and increased recognition of their value, the quality of these reviews is more apt to become a concern.

The Future

Quality assurance for public accounting has been in existence for several years. Yet, it is undergoing criticism and, as a result, is bound to change.

It must if CPAs are ever going to be able to close the gap that has developed between the public's expectation of quality performance and the level of performance that seems evident today. The reviews are going to become more systematic and probably less "friendly." Sanctions are going to become more frequent and more widely publicized. Whether this will serve to improve the quality of performance or further fuel the expectation gap is not clear. What does seem clear is the determination of the AICPA to demonstrate that it can clean its own house to avoid the imposition, through legislative means, of a mandatory house-cleaning apparatus under the control of the government.

The quality assurance program of the IIA, by comparison, is just getting started. Since the program is entirely voluntary, is not monitored, and lacks enforceability, it is not likely to gain widespread acceptance, endorsement, or use. For that to occur, a real need must emerge. This will occur only when the work of the internal auditor becomes more indispensible in the minds of company audit committees, directors, senior management, and, perhaps, the public. It is not inaccurate to state that, although internal auditing has made great strides, it is still underutilized and underappreciated. When these perceptions change, and the authors believe they will, the quality assurance mechanism of the IIA will also change.

Practical Guidelines

Chief auditors faced with maintaining quality assurance programs must decide whether and how to implement the recommendations of the IIA's Quality Assurance Review Manual. In other words, should the audit function undergo periodic internal and external reviews? The obvious answer is yes for internal reviews. Almost any size internal audit function can find the means to implement this type of program. The elements of the review include (1) the internal audit director's questionnaire, (2) the internal audit interview, (3) the administrative review, (4) the auditee interviews, and (5) the evaluation process. The procedures performed periodically should provide the chief internal auditor with much valuable information regarding the quality of his organization's work.

External reviews are also valuable, but they may not be for everyone. It may be that, in many cases, senior management and the audit committee are able to gain assurance regarding internal audit quality through other means. For example, impressions of quality may be obtained during presentations by the chief auditor, by reviewing written reports to the audit committee prepared by the chief auditor, and during question-and-answer sessions. Other, more direct means, such as inquiries of senior management and the external auditors, may also be employed.

If management and the audit committee are satisfied through informal means, little may be gained by conducting external reviews, particularly if the internal reviews do not reveal any quality problems. In other instances, senior management and the audit committee may see value in obtaining the assurance that comes from a formal external review. Or questions might arise regarding the quality of internal auditing—for whatever reason—that might necessitate an external review.

Whatever the reason, external reviews should only be undertaken, in the opinion of the authors, when all principal parties agree that such a review is desirable. The chief auditor, if given the opportunity, should encourage the audit committee and management to utilize the provisions of *Quality Assurance Review Manual for Internal Auditing*. However, he should also be prepared to cooperate with and accept external reviews that may be arranged and conducted in accordance with other review means.

SUGGESTED READING

Anderson, Urton. *Quality Assurance for Internal Auditing*. Altamonte Springs, Fla.: The Institute of Internal Auditors, 1983.

Boritz, J. Efrim. *Planning for the Internal Audit Function*. Altamonte Springs, Fla.: The Institute of Internal Auditors Research Foundation, 1983.

DeMeo, Joseph C. "The Need for an Internal Audit Quality Assurance Program." *Internal Auditing*, Winter 1986, Vol. 1, No. 3, pp. 14–22.

Glazer, Alan S., PhD, Henry R. Jaenicke, PhD, CPA. *A Framework for Evaluating an Internal Audit Function*. USA: The Foundation for Auditability Research and Education, 1980.

Pomeranz, Felix. "Internal Auditing—Organization and Planning," pp. 19-1–19-32, *Corporate Controller's Manual*, ed. Paul J. Wendell. Boston: Warren Gorham & Lamont, 1981.

Professional Standards and Responsibilities Committee, 1983–1984, John K. Watsen, Chairman. *Quality Assurance Review Manual for Internal Auditing*. Altamonte Springs, Fla.: The Institute of Internal Auditors, 1984.

The Special Committee on Standards of Professional Conduct for Certified Public Accountants, *Restructuring Professional Standards to Achieve Professional Excellence in a Changing Environment*, New York: AICPA, 1986.

CHAPTER **8**

Managing Audit Projects

Overview 2	Techniques for Preparation 22
	Time of Preparation 23
Audit Manuals 2	Project Review 23
Definition and Purpose 2	Definition 23
Contents 4	Purpose 23
	Specific Objectives and Techniques
Questionnaires and Checklists 4	to Improve the Review 23
Purpose and Definitions 4	Maintaining a Proper Attitude 24
Questionnaires 5	
Typical Uses 5	**Relationships With External Auditors** ... 25
Method of Preparation 5	The Basis for the Relationship—A
Checklists 7	Historical Perspective 25
Typical Uses 7	The Current Scene 26
Method of Preparation 10	Direct Assistance by Internal
	Auditors 34
Personal Computers 12	Participative Auditing 34
Hardware 12	Direct Assistance by External
Software 13	Auditors 35
	Specific Interactions Between External
Specific Project Controls 13	and Internal Auditors 35
Background 13	Outlook for the Future 37
Assignment Authorization 13	
Detailed Project Budgets 14	**Data Security** 39
Project Reporting 17	
Developing Written Audit Programs ... 18	**Suggested Reading** 40
Purpose 22	

Fig. 8-1	Contents for Corporate Audit Manual	3
Fig. 8-2	Excerpt of Questionnaire for Purchasing Transactions	8
Fig. 8-3	Closeout Checklist	10
Fig. 8-4	Audit Report Checklist	11
Fig. 8-5	Assignment Authorization Form	15
Fig. 8-6	Time Budget—Small Variance (Overrun)	16
Fig. 8-7	Time Budget—Favorable Variance	17
Fig. 8-8	Time Budget—Large Unfavorable Variance	18
Fig. 8-9	Project Revision Form	19
Fig. 8-10	Weekly Progress Report	20
Fig. 8-11	Weekly Work Planning Objectives	21
Fig. 8-12	Comparative Data on External Audit Fees	28
Fig. 8-13	The Extent to Which Internal Audit Hours Replace External Audit Hours ...	31

OVERVIEW

Project management involves the same managerial processes of planning, organizing, staffing, and directing that are identified at the beginning of Chapter 7. However, organizing and planning at the project level are essentially functions of the performing auditor or project leader and are covered in Chapters 11 and 12. Staffing is discussed in Chapter 9. Thus, the discussion of project management in this chapter is, for all practical purposes, a discussion of directing.

Directing may be defined as the effecting, implementing, or carrying out the activities of the organization[1] and is related to project management, since one of the principal activities of an internal auditing department is to conduct audit projects. These projects must be effectively managed or directed to reasonably assure that the standards of performance are met. (See Chapter 6.) This chapter provides a discussion of the more common techniques and devices used in managing or directing audit projects. These include:

- Audit manual
- Carefully designed questionnaires and checklists
- Personal computer (PC) software
- Project controls
- Written audit programs
- Quality-control reviews
- Data security

AUDIT MANUALS

Definition and Purpose

Effective project management begins with sufficient communication to the audit staff of the operating methodology to be used in managing and conducting audit projects. As audit departments grow in size, audit manuals become increasingly important as the means to inform the audit staff of the methods in use. In larger organizations, the organizational hierarchy puts distance between the management of the department and the performing auditors. Moreover, turnover is usually more constant in large audit departments than in their smaller counterparts.

An audit manual is a documented set of policies, procedures, and guidelines that establish the standards and methodology that constitute accepted internal auditing practice within the department. The principal value of the

---

[1] James D. Willson and John B. Campbell, *Controllership: The Work of the Managerial Accountant*, 3rd ed. (New York: John Wiley & Sons, 1981), p. 8.

FIG. 8-1
Contents for Corporate Audit Manual

Subject	Section	Date
Organization		
Objectives of corporate audit	100	12/11/xx
Allocation of company resources for audit purposes	110	12/11/xx
Organization chart	120	8/1/xy
Responsibilities of:		
Director	130	12/11/xx
Manager	131	12/11/xx
Supervising Senior Auditor	132	8/1/xy
Senior Auditor	133	8/1/xy
Staff Auditor	134	8/1/xx
Auditing standards	200	12/11/xx
First general standard — Technical training	210	12/11/xx
Second general standard — Independence	220	12/11/xx
Third general standard — Due professional care	230	12/11/xx
First standard of field work — Adequate planning and supervision	310	12/11/xx
Second standard of field work — Sufficient competent evidential matter	320	12/11/xx
First standard of reporting — Written report	410	12/11/xx
Second standard of reporting — Level to whom report is addressed and distribution	420	12/11/xx
Third standard of reporting — Identification of report contents	430	12/11/xx
Fourth standard of reporting — Conclusion on audit objectives	440	12/11/xx
Administration		
Administrative policy	500	12/11/xx
Audit plan	501	12/11/xx
Continuing education	502	12/11/xx
Professional memberships	503	12/11/xx
Record retention	504	1/1/xz
Auditor evaluations	505	1/27/xz
Audit Approach		
General	610	1/21/xy
Background and overview	620	1/21/xy
Business organization	630	1/21/xy
Business operations	640	1/21/xy
Nature of the business	650	1/21/xy
Principles for delegation of authority	660	1/21/xy
The control process	670	1/21/xy
Basic audit approach	680	1/21/xy
Bulletins	700	

audit manual is twofold. First, it serves as a ready reference for staff members to use in performing an audit—as an invisible, on-the-job, manager. Second, it helps the performing auditors and the audit management make decisions regarding a broad array of judgmental factors encountered in every audit. Some of these factors are (1) setting the work scope, (2) determining what needs to be tested and how much to test, (3) documenting the work, (4) deciding on exceptions and their impact, and (5) drawing conclusions regarding the testing.

Audit manuals also provide a beneficial by-product: they are tangible evidence of the professionalism with which the department seeks to discharge its responsibility. That is important because, among other things, the degree of professionalism is one of the factors considered by external auditors in evaluating the work of the internal auditors for possible use in performing the independent examination of the financial statements. Similarly, management may be more inclined to accept the work of an audit department whose methods have been codified in easily understood terms.

In preparing and maintaining the audit manual, the chief auditor must keep in mind that it is a quality-control device. The manual must be structured to reflect the level of quality expected. Therefore, care must be exercised in its design. To be effective, examples, discussions, and interpretations in the manual should be related to the company, its business, and its management philosophy and objectives.

Contents

A complete audit manual covers various topics. A typical table of contents is shown in Figure 8-1. Note that the manual covers organization (complete with objectives, charts, and position descriptions), auditing standards, administrative matters, and the audit approach. It is a good idea to arrange the manual so that bulletins or memoranda on emerging issues may be added at the end. (See Figure 8-1.) Placing the manual in ring binder makes it easy to add or replace material, so the manual can be updated as circumstances warrant. The issue date of each section evidences how current the manual is.

QUESTIONNAIRES AND CHECKLISTS

Purpose and Definitions

As stated earlier in this chapter, any auditor must make many professional judgments during the course of an audit. Decisions must be reached as to the scope of work, personnel to interview, questions to be asked, records and files to be tested, and so on. Experience shows that these decisions are more likely to produce useful and reliable results when they are based on a thoroughly structured examination of the relevant facts. Questionnaires and checklists are intended to provide the necessary structure. They are also quality-control devices that help to assure that projects are completed in accordance with the stated standards of quality. As defined in this discussion, a questionnaire is an organized list of specific questions and represents one of several ways to evidence the extent of inquiry or evaluation performed by the auditor in given circumstances. Flow charts, procedural narratives, and analytical spread sheets are examples of other forms of evaluation documentation. However, these are usually prepared during the course of the fieldwork, since the variety of actual circumstances precludes advance preparation. Questionnaires, on the other hand, are customarily prepared before entering the field (see Chapter 11) to serve as a sort of standard by which controls or other activities under investigation are to be measured. As such, a questionnaire, when completed, should constitute primary evidence that a reasonable assessment of control conditions occurred in the given circumstance.

Although the two devices are quite similar, checklists differ from questionnaires, as herein defined, in at least two respects. First, checklists are generally expressed in terms of statements rather than questions. Second, they are not expected to be a standard of measurement. Rather, they are intended in most instances and are defined in this context as reminder lists of important points to review or consider in completing the examination. Because of this, they ordinarily do not constitute primary evidence of the extent of any audit work performed. Questionnaires and checklists are discussed in more detail in the following paragraphs.

Questionnaires

Typical Uses. Preparation of questionnaires is a very important activity and should be accomplished by a staff member who has considerable auditing experience, usually the chief auditor or a project manager. Questionnaires are most frequently used in evaluating internal accounting controls. They are also used in evaluating economy and efficiency in operational auditing, and to a lesser degree, in situations in which the extent of inquiry must be documented, as in management interviews. Once developed, the questionnaires may be used repeatedly with little change, in most circumstances. Their longevity, coupled with their relative importance, requires the attention of high-level audit personnel.

Method of Preparation. The chief auditor will find the following steps useful in preparing questionnaires:

    1. *Establish objectives.* The preparer must have a clear idea of what the questionnaire is intended to accomplish. Otherwise, the questionnaire may include too many or too few control points, or may be illogically arranged.

For example, questionnaires designed to evaluate internal accounting control should include sufficient inquiry into controls over the following:

- Authorization of transactions
- Processing and recording of transactions
- Accountability aspects
- Safeguarding and security aspects

Note that these are the subject areas specified in the FCPA.

Questionnaires designed to evaluate operational controls—whether or not an EDP environment is involved—must clearly cover all relevant techniques useful in attaining effective and efficient operations.

2. *Perform research.* A great deal has been written on the subjects for which questionnaires are commonly drawn up. Examples of subjects are: all aspects of internal accounting control (such as cash receipts and disbursements), EDP, security, inventory control, procurement, and insurance management. Most college libraries have accumulated a sizeable sampling of this literature, as have the major public accounting firms. Many private companies have also established internal libraries where useful information may be found.

Published sources also provide questionnaires for some functions, which are usable in whole or in part. However, these questionnaires should not be adopted blindly. Although published questionnaires may be extensive, they are necessarily general, and must often be adapted to accomplish the specific objective intended. Each question should be reviewed by the auditor for its applicability in the specific situation in the company, and for its suitability for the purpose intended.

In addition to researching published sources, input should be obtained from company personnel who are knowledgeable in the particular subject area of the questionnaire. Also, inquiry might be made of other internal audit departments. Most chief auditors and their staffs are willing to share techniques and ideas, unless it compromises the company's competitive advantage or discloses confidential information.

3. *Prepare questionnaire.* After establishing the objective and obtaining sufficient background reference information, the chief auditor or project manager drafts the questionnaire. The following is a list of items to keep in mind:

- The questionnaire should be comprised of questions, not statements, and the questions should not be "leading" questions. However, explanatory comments should be provided, where appropriate.
- Questions should cover all relevant aspects of the subject, including EDP.
- Questions should follow a logical flow; that is, they should follow the sequence of whatever is happening (e.g., authorizing, executing, and recording).
- Questions should be phrased so that simple "yes" or "no" responses will answer them.
- Questions that require subjective judgment should be avoided (e.g., "Does the system provide sufficient or excessive user informa-

MANAGING AUDIT PROJECTS

tion?"). Although such questions may cover valid topical areas about which the auditor needs information, more detailed inquiry is required to develop a proper evaluative base.

- Questions should require that responses be referenced to procedure manuals, flow charts, or other evidence of the existence of the control.

4. *Review with management.* Management review and input can result in the disclosure of invalid, irrelevant, or inapplicable questions on questionnaires, as well as topics not covered. Enlisting management assistance is of value in obtaining proper answers. Enlisting management help also evidences the auditor's thoroughness.

5. *Keeping current.* Once developed, questionnaires must be kept current. They should be updated during each use. To do this, the auditor performs some or all of the techniques used in the original preparation, but only to the extent necessary to identify new or changed circumstances. Any departures from the questionnaire should be approved by the project manager of the chief auditor.

Questionnaires provide evidence of the extent of the auditor's evaluations. With careful preparation and execution, questionnaires attest to the professional care practiced by the auditor. A portion of a questionnaire on purchasing is shown in Figure 8-2 to illustrate the recommended techniques. Other more complete examples are provided in many chapters of this book. The reader may find it useful to check the index under the term "Questionnaires" for a complete listing.

Checklists

Typical Uses. Checklists are used to reasonably assure that an acceptable minimum number of points is covered by the auditor. In a sense, the audit program itself may be thought of as a checklist of audit procedures employed.

Checklists have been used advantageously by both external and internal auditors and others. For example, external auditors have used this type of aid in connection with the following:

- Tax planning
- Tax return preparation
- Tax accrual review
- Financial statement preparation
- SEC reporting

Contract administrators have found checklists invaluable in assuring that contracts contain all appropriate clauses and terms.

FIG. 8-2

Excerpt of Questionnaire for Purchasing Transactions

	Yes	No	Ref.
A. General:			
1. Are all purchases of materials and supplies required to be executed by a single purchasing group?	☐	☐	....
2. Is the purchasing function organizationally separate from receiving, accounting, and disbursing functions?	☐	☐	....
3. Are written procedures in existence and up-to-date for executing purchasing transactions?	☐	☐	....
4. Is an organization chart in existence depicting the reporting relationships?	☐	☐	....
5. Does the purchasing organization have adequate facilities and equipment to accomplish its function?	☐	☐	....
B. Authorization and Execution of Transactions:			
1. Are purchases of transactions initiated based upon approved requisitions from user groups or from some other original source, such as machine-generated reports or purchasing requirements?	☐	☐	....
2. Are requisitions or other source data for initiating purchase transactions retained in a manner which permits retrieval?	☐	☐	....
a. Is procurement action the result of considering:			
■ Quantities required as determined either by user or by some other appropriate means?	☐	☐	....
■ In-house fabrication?	☐	☐	....
■ Economic order quantities?	☐	☐	....
3. If purchasing transactions are accomplished by means of electronic data processing application,	☐	☐	....
a. Are the applicable procedures, forms, descriptions, and so forth set forth in a users' manual?	☐	☐	....
b. Is the organization responsible for processing source data the same organization responsible for all other data processing activity?	☐	☐	....
c. Were the systems or programs generated or acquired pursuant to the system development procedures, policies and standards applicable to system development?	☐	☐	....
d. Have there been or are there planned to be any changes of significance to the application?	☐	☐	....
e. Is the application a batch-oriented application with or without remote job entry features?	☐	☐	....

	Yes	No	Ref.
f. Do procedures require current and complete system and program documentation?	☐	☐	....

If the answers to the above questions are all "yes," then the auditor should proceed to obtain responses to the balance of the questions in this section. If the answer to any or all of these questions is "no," it may indicate that the application is too complex for this assignment. The auditor should not attempt further EDP evaluation and analysis without either assistance from a senior EDP auditor or approval of the manager or director.

	Yes	No	Ref.
1. Do procedures require that the user departments employ techniques to assure that data input and output are sufficiently controlled? *(Note:* In order to answer this question, it is necessary to complete forms for each relevant input form and output report.)	☐	☐	....
2. Do procedures require that techniques be employed to reasonably assure that programs, master files, other data sets, and related documentation are secure and may be reconstructed in the event of data loss or destruction?	☐	☐	....
3. Do procedures require that techniques be employed to reasonably assure that errors and omissions are detected and corrected within a reasonable time period?	☐	☐	....
4. Does the system documentation include steps to reasonably assure that the program executes all source data submitted?	☐	☐	....

In addition to audit programs, other checklists used by some internal auditors include:

- Project control
- Report writing
- Physical inventory observations
- Security checks

An example of a checklist used in project control is shown in Figure 8-3. The intent of this device is to provide a written record evidencing that important aspects of the project review have been performed. The project manager or the chief auditor can use the checklist to easily decide which aspects are satisfactorily completed and, more importantly, which are not.

Another example of a checklist, which relates to report writing, is shown in Figure 8-4. This checklist should be completed by the auditor after he prepares the initial draft of the audit report. It is an aid to self-editing and

FIG. 8-3
Closeout Checklist

Work Authorization No. .... Auditor ....
Description .... Reviewed by ....

Workpaper Contents   **Initial**

1. Assignment authorization — with objectives:
   a. A summary narrative describing work performed and audit opinions
      regarding each objective   ....
   b. Budget revisions   ....

2. A summary index to the workpapers:
   a. Numbered   ....
   b. Referenced   ....
   c. Audit programs approved and signed off   ....

3. Report findings referenced to the summary of findings   ....

4. Summary of findings:
   a. Discussed with person(s) to whom report will be sent   ....
   b. Referenced to the workpapers   ....

5. Organization charts for organization(s) involved — up to the chief
   executive officer.   ....

6. A copy or list of policies, procedures, and directives relating to the
   assignment.   ....

7. Copies of, or references to, prior audit reports for which follow-up has
   been performed.   ....

8. A list of recommended areas for future audit.   ....

9. A summary of potential areas for cost reduction.   ....

10. A summary of time spent with explanation for budget variances.   ....

11. Prior audit workpapers reviewed for retention disposition.   ....

---

its use by auditors during their report writing phase will minimize the manager's time in reviewing the draft.

Method of Preparation. Checklists are prepared in a manner similar to questionnaires. Effective preparation requires that the preparer (1) have objectives fixed in his mind, (2) perform sufficient research, (3) prepare the checklist, (4) review it with appropriate interested parties, and (5) keep it current.

FIG. 8-4
Audit Report Checklist

	Yes	No
1. Is the report addressed to the appropriate person?	☐	☐
2. Does the report identify the audit topic and organization involved?	☐	☐
3. Does the report state the purpose or objective of the audit?	☐	☐
4. Does the report state that the audit was conducted in accordance with the audit standards prescribed by the corporate audit manual?	☐	☐
5. Does the report concisely describe the scope of work performed, affording some specific insight into the extent of work performed?	☐	☐
6. Where applicable, does the report include a statement(s) describing any limitations on the scope imposed by project circumstances, management, time factors, etc.?	☐	☐
7. Does the report contain a brief summarization of the findings?	☐	☐
8. Is the summarization of findings phrased in a manner consistent with phrasing contained in the body of the report for each finding?	☐	☐
9. Does the report summarize the ramifications of the findings (i.e., summarize risks)?	☐	☐
10. Does the report contain an opinion appropriate in the circumstances?	☐	☐
11. Does the report request a written response to the recommendations within 30 days?	☐	☐
12. Does the report provide for distribution to all affected members of management of the profit center, group office, and corporate office?	☐	☐
13. Does the report contain a table of contents for ease of reference if there are four or more findings?	☐	☐
14. Is the sequence of findings in a descending order of significance?	☐	☐
15. Does each report finding headline clearly state the essence of the findings?	☐	☐
16. Does the narrative commentary for each finding fully develop the finding, including the ramifications or risks posed, if any?	☐	☐
17. Is the recommendation phrased in such a way that promotes understanding?	☐	☐
18. Is the recommendation phrased in such a way that would result in remedying the specific problem, if implemented?	☐	☐

(continued)

FIG. 8-4 *(cont'd)*

	Yes	No
19. Is the recommendation stated in the command tense?	☐	☐
20. Where necessary, are recommendations supplemented with examples of techniques which could be employed if more than one alternative exists?	☐	☐
21. Is it clear that the costs of implementing the recommendations do not outweigh the benefits?	☐	☐
22. Have you edited the report for punctuation, grammar, excess language, redundant thoughts, and typographical errors?	☐	☐

PERSONAL COMPUTERS

Hardware

The use of PCs in auditing is described in Chapters 27 and 28. The topic is only introduced here in the interest of identifying important devices and techniques used in managing audit projects. The application of PCs to audit management is a fast-growing area. It was only a few short years ago that PCs burst on the scene.

Few auditors at that time foresaw the opportunities that these devices presented. True, the earliest PCs were lacking in speed and memory capacity. But those machines were quickly replaced with faster and more powerful models. And the ownership costs continue to decline. It is safe to say that as recently as five years ago, few auditors made use of these devices. Today, however, it is the other way around. Most sizeable audit departments have at least one PC and may have several of the devices. Some are networked, that is, linked together via special software enabling expanded intercommunication capabilities and data storage opportunities.

PCs and laser printers have replaced word processors in several internal auditing departments. Another important hardware development is the portable lap top PC. These compact, lightweight and powerful units make the use of PCs in the field feasible.

From a project management standpoint, PCs offer a remarkable aid. Among other things, these devices facilitate communication between managers and auditors and between the department and auditee management. Questionnaires, checklists, and audit programs may be maintained using PCs. They can be used to monitor project status, to report relevant project information, to facilitate presentations, and to serve as central storage for important project information.

Software

The advances in PC hardware could not have been applied to auditing without corresponding PC software developments. The initial applicable software development was for word processing. Next came spreadsheet software and data base software. The communications software made the scene, followed by task-oriented software, such as for audit planning. It is no understatement to claim that with these software innovations, PCs are now indispensable tools for efficient and effective internal auditing. No internal auditor can afford to be in practice without access to them.

SPECIFIC PROJECT CONTROLS

Project controls may be defined as techniques to reasonably assure that each audit project will effectively and efficiently accomplish the intended results in accordance with established auditing standards.

Background

At any point, most audit functions have more than one project in process. The number of projects in process depends on the size of the function, and ranges from just a few in small organizations to several hundred in larger ones. To effectively control the increasing number of projects, the department's management must devise more sophisticated project control techniques. These are used to maintain effectiveness and efficiency (i.e., to minimize wasted time, unnecessary inquiry, and invalid or inaccurate conclusions).

Audit charters, standards of performance, audit manuals, and questionnaires are examples of such project control measures. All internal auditing projects are subject to these controls. The following project controls discussed herein supplement these measures and are intended to help achieve maximum efficiency and effectiveness:

- Assignment authorization
- Project budgets
- Project reporting
- Audit programs
- Project review

Assignment Authorization

Project control begins with assignment authorization. The intent is the same as for any productive activity, whether manufacturing, engineering, data processing, word processing, or reproduction. A means must be devised to assure that work is performed on only authorized activity.

Activities undertaken by small staffs, say up to six or seven auditors, may be easily and simply controlled at the personal direction of the chief auditor. In larger organizations, it is necessary to employ additional controls. These include numerical control over projects and use of authorization forms. An example of an assignment authorization form is shown in Figure 8-5.

The form provides for all essential information necessary to authorize an audit project. Of particular interest is the section on assignment objectives. These objectives should be clearly stated and understood by all persons involved. When objectives are established at the outset, there is much less chance of wasted effort during the project.

In addition, the form provides for summary budget information. As with any undertaking, there must be some common thinking as to how much time can economically be spent on the project. The form also allows for budget revisions, which are necessary in the event that circumstances change. Start and stop dates, also provided for in the form, assist in defining the project's time frame.

The form also provides for naming the participants and for approval of the project. The form should be prepared by the senior performing auditor in charge of the project. After approval, a work authorization number is assigned and the project is entered into the assignment log. These procedures establish the basis for project control.

Once a project is authorized, time is charged to it by the individuals assigned and working on the project. Thus, a continuing measurement of hours spent is initiated. The form provides for "closing," the end of authorization of time spent on the project. After closing, time may no longer be charged by staff for work on the project.

Detailed Project Budgets

Project budgets assist in planning and controlling each project. The level of detail in budgets may vary somewhat; however, the most common level of detail is man-hours by activity. Large projects may be budgeted in terms of man-days.

Budgets are intended to reflect the amount of time expected to be spent in carrying out the various segments of the audit. As such, the segment budgets need not be extensive or exhaustive in detail. There should be enough analysis so that the reviewer can appraise the allocation of effort over the different phases. Examples of time budgets are shown in Figures 8-6, 8-7, and 8-8. These budgets illustrate the level of detail in varying circumstances and present a slight overrun (Figure 8-6), a slight underrun (Figure 8-7), and a large overrun (Figure 8-8).

FIG. 8-5
Assignment Authorization Form

ASSIGNMENT AUTHORIZATION			
MANAGER	AUDITOR	DATE ASSIGNED	WA NO.
ENTITY	ASSIGNMENT TITLE		

ASSIGNMENT OBJECTIVES

COMMENTS ON SCOPE OF WORK (INCLUDING RECENT OR CONCURRENT AUDITS)

PROJECT BUDGET				ASSIGNMENT SCHEDULE	
ASSIGNED TO	START DATE	STOP DATE	BUDGET HOURS	START ON	
				WORK PAPERS TO REVIEWER	
				10 DAY DRAFT DATE	
*PROJECT LEADER IN ANNUAL PLAN ☐		TOTAL BUDGET BUDGET REVISION HOURS IN PLAN			

APPROVED BY	DATE
REMARKS	

PROJECT COMPLETION

REPORT MEMO NO	DATE	SIGNATURE

FIG. 8-6

Time Budget—Small Variance (Overrun)

Summary Record of Time Spent on a Standards of Business Conduct Audit		
	Hours	
	Budget	Actual
Review of applicable policies	8	8
Orientation	4	4
Follow-up on prior audit comments	4	4
Discussions with key employees	8	8
Review of small business activity and investigation of large, unusual amounts	4	16
Evaluation of small business reporting system	8	8
Limited review of purchase order documentation	8	8
Review of correspondence files	4	4
Review of conflict-of-interest forms	2	2
Review of open subcontracts files	2	2
Review of general procurement file (purchase orders)	4	4
Report preparation	8	16
TOTAL	64	84

Explanation: Encountered unexpected exceptions in compliance with company policy on relations with small business.

Prepared by: .... APPROVAL: ....

Budget: ....

Final: ....

In practice, the actual hours would be posted either during the course of the work or, for short projects, at completion. Any large variances would require explanation.

If, in performing the audit, it becomes apparent that the budget is insufficient, a revision may be in order. The budgeting control system should be flexible enough to permit changes when conditions warrant. It makes sense to adjust the budget when it no longer is a reasonable reflection of anticipated time requirements under the new conditions. Of course, budget adjustments should be subject to the same approvals as required for the original submission.

Changes to project budgets may be furnished, as shown in Figure 8-9. Figure 8-9 is similar in many respects to the assignment authorization form shown in Figure 8-5, and requires approval. Figure 8-9 also provides that the change be explained and its cost effect estimated. This is substantially similar to the original authorizations.

MANAGING AUDIT PROJECTS 8-17

FIG. 8-7
Time Budget—Favorable Variance

Summary Record of Time Spent on a Major Subcontracts Audit

	Hours	
	Budget	Actual
1. Planning the audit	18	12
2. Completing questionnaire	12	12
3. Audit program:		
a. General	6	4
b. Evaluation of internal control	20	12
c. Testing	80	64
Subtotal	136	104
4. Summary of findings, exit conferences, and report	20	16
Total	156	120

Explanation: Saved time by obtaining assistance of subcontract personnel in performing test designed to measure accuracy of subcontractor address file. Also, was able to have the manager of subcontracts complete the internal control questionnaire.

Prepared by .... APPROVAL: ....

                                                             Budget: ....

                                                             Actual: ....

Project Reporting

Effective project management requires that progress be monitored by the assigned manager or supervisor, and by the chief auditor. The extent of the monitoring depends on the size of the project and the size of the organization. There are informal techniques for project monitoring (such as by periodic telephone contact) and formal techniques as well. The latter involves some form of reporting by the performing auditors.

The two questions of interest to the manager are (1) Is the project on schedule? and (2) Are there any difficulties? Forms may be devised to help the manager obtain this information. Figures 8-10 and 8-11 are two examples of such forms. The weekly progress report (Figure 8-10) provides a record of time spent by project. It is submitted by each auditor, each week. In addition to reporting the time spent, the auditor must give estimates of the final hours and target dates for completion. Careful monitoring of this data will either assure the manager that progress is occurring as planned or that problems seem to be developing.

FIG. 8-8

Time Budget—Large Unfavorable Variance

Summary Record of Time Spent on a Contract Administration Audit

Audit Area	Hours Budget	Hours Actual
1. Orientation	8	12
2. Internal control review	16	12
3. Preparation — Audit program & internal control questionnaire	8	16
4. Testing	64	88
5. Clear findings and prepare report	16	16
6. Wrap-up	8	16
Total	120	160

Reason for overrun: Spent excessive time in reviewing contract files because the planned assistance to be obtained from contract personnel did not materialize due to a temporary undermanning caused by a leave of absence of two persons. Slight overrun in preparing questionnaire was due to resolving questions raised by manager review.

Prepared by .... APPROVAL: ....

Budget: ....

Final: ....

The weekly work planning objectives form (Figure 8-11) is also prepared by the performing auditor for each project. It enables both the auditor and the manager to monitor progress in accomplishing the objectives. It also provides insight into the auditor's ability to prioritize tasks in advance (i.e., to organize effectively).

At first glance, these reporting requirements may appear to be quite burdensome. However, well-organized auditors can prepare them with little difficulty. If assistance is needed, the manager or chief auditor should be consulted. Thus, the forms tend to force contact and focus attention where needed.

Developing Written Audit Programs

Audit programs may be defined as the auditor's written plan of inspection, observation, confirmation, and inquiry (see Chapter 16), which, upon performance, gathers the evidential matter (Chapter 14) required by auditing standards.

MANAGING AUDIT PROJECTS

FIG. 8-9

Project Revision Form

ASSIGNMENT REVISION			
MANAGER	ENTITY	WA NO.	DATE ASSIGNED
ASSIGNMENT TITLE			

BUDGET REVISION	
ACTUAL HOURS TO DATE	ORIGINAL BUDGET HOURS
ESTIMATE TO COMPLETE	INCREASE IN BUDGET
TOTAL HOURS	REVISED BUDGET HOURS

SCHEDULE REVISION	
ORIGINAL	REVISION
START ON	START ON
DRAFT REPORT DATE	DRAFT REPORT DATE
MANAGEMENT CONF	MANAGEMENT CONF
COMPLETION	COMPLETION

REASON FOR REVISION

SUBMIT REVISED ASSIGNMENT PLAN FOR BUDGET REVISION. DISCUSS CHANGES IN AUDIT SCOPE, PROBLEM AREAS, UNANTICIPATED EVENTS, PROFIT CENTER REQUESTS FOR REVISIONS, OR OTHER REASONS.

SUBMITTED BY	DATE	APPROVED BY	DATE
REMARKS			

FIG. 8-10
Weekly Progress Report

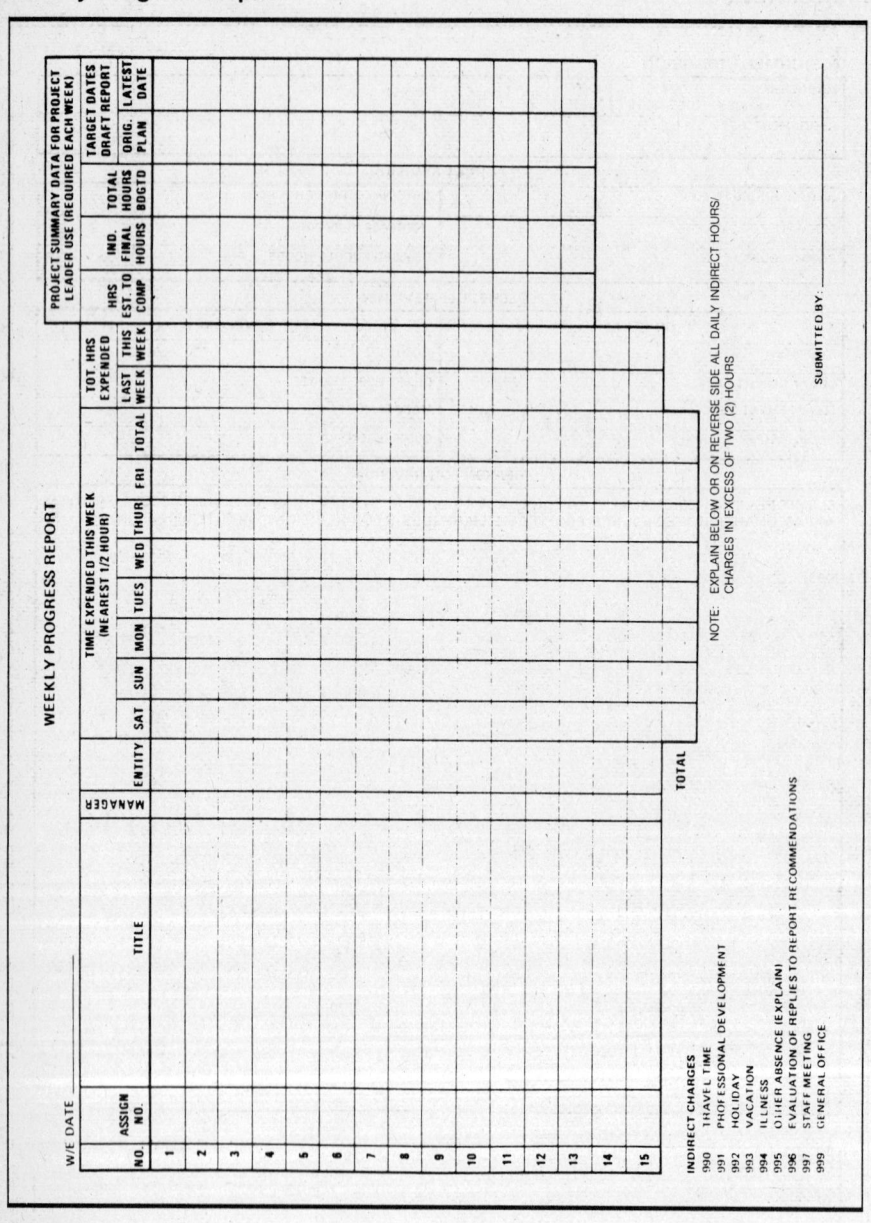

MANAGING AUDIT PROJECTS

FIG. 8-11
Weekly Work Planning Objectives

WEEKLY WORK PLANNING OBJECTIVES

WEEK BEGINNING (MONDAY): _____ 19___ NAME: _____

OBJECTIVE NO.	WA NO.	PRIMARY OBJECTIVES (SHORT DEFINITION)	PRIORITY RANKING	TARGET COMPLETION	
				DATE	EST. HRS
1					
2					
3					
4					
5					
6					

PRIOR WEEKS OBJECTIVES:

OBJECTIVE NO.	1	2	3	4	5	6
STATUS						

(CODE: C = Completed; W = In Work; P = Postponed; D = Dropped; N = Not Done)

Purpose. Written audit programs are another formal technique that help assure effective and efficient project control by spelling out the audit steps to be taken. They also indicate adherence to high professional standards. When signed off and dated by the auditor, the audit programs evidence completion of audit procedures and constitute primary documentation of the diligence exercised.

Techniques for Preparation. Audit programs should be prepared by the person most familiar with the intended scope of work. In most projects, that person is the project leader or the performing auditor. However, it is not uncommon to find that audit managers or the chief auditor participate as well because of their knowledge and experience. At a minimum, their involvement should include review and approval of audit programs—preferably before the work commences, but certainly before the project is completed.

Regardless of who prepares the program, it must be prepared in sufficient detail to clearly set forth the scope and degree of testing required to complete the audit objectives in each phase of the examination. Audit program steps must be expressed in the form of procedural statements, much like a set of instructions for assembling a child's toy. Anyone who has experienced this year-end holiday ritual can attest to the frustration caused by incomplete or illogical statements.

It is believed that a high correlation exists between unclear, poorly structured audit programs and poor results. The following thoughts should help to minimize the chances for unacceptable audit results:

- Be thoroughly familiar with and clearly state the audit objectives.
- Be familiar with all technical aspects involved and clearly stipulate what exposures and transactions must be examined.
- Determine that each audit step is feasible.
- Be certain that all necessary steps are included in the program—don't assume the auditor will know them.
- Arrange the steps in a logical sequential fashion and relate them to the specific audit objectives.
- Clearly state the kind of or extent of testing required.
- Where necessary, provide explanations for performing complex audit steps.
- Do not include questions in the audit program. (Questions belong in questionnaires.) However, it may be necessary to provide alternative procedures if certain conditions exist.
- Cross-reference program steps to procedure manuals or internal control documentation, where applicable.

In preparing the audit program, the auditor must consider (1) the reliability of the different types of evidential matter available (Chapter 14); (2)

MANAGING AUDIT PROJECTS 8-23

the materiality and relative risk associated with the particular project;[2] and (3) the possible applicability of sophisticated techniques, such as statistical sampling (Chapter 15) and computer-aided testing (Chapter 28).

Time of Preparation. To the extent practicable, audit programs should be prepared, or amended in the case of preexisting programs, prior to the actual commencement of fieldwork. This does not mean that the program cannot be prepared (or modified) in the field. In many circumstances, this may be the only effective procedure.

Ordinarily, audit programs should be approved in writing prior to the commencement of the fieldwork. Approval may be obtained orally if distance or other factors preclude obtaining written approval. The audit program should be filed as part of the audit workpapers. However, a copy should be forwarded to a centralized file of audit programs for reference and use by other auditors.

Project Review

Definition. The project review may be defined as the final check of the performing auditor's workpapers and report drafts prior to issuing the report—either in draft or final form. Project reviews are usually performed by the assigned project leader or manager with some participation by the chief auditor.

Purpose. The purpose of a project review is to reasonably assure that the auditing standards for quality performance are met for each project. In recognition of the importance of project reviews, experienced reviewers engage in project review activities throughout the course of the project. In that way, substantive, last-minute, follow-up exercises are minimized. A properly performed project review should, for example, detect and correct any invalid findings, unsupported conclusions, and insufficient testing in a timely fashion.

Specific Objectives and Techniques to Improve the Review. In order to properly perform project reviews, the supervisor or manager must thoroughly understand the specific objectives of the review and adopt an objective viewpoint. While this advice may seem obvious, in practice, the opposite—a lack of understanding and objectivity—is often the rule rather than the exception. The reviewer is, in effect, judging the performance and quality of the performing auditor's work. Few persons readily accept criti-

---

[2] Victor Z. Brink and Herbert Witt, *Modern Internal Auditing: Appraising Operations and Controls*, 4th ed. (New York: John Wiley & Sons, 1982), p. 273.

cism, a fact that makes the review process more difficult. Inexperienced auditors may mistake the review for unwarranted and unnecessary intervention and may feel threatened by the process. On the other hand, inexperienced reviewers may attempt to overcome their lack of experience by becoming unnecessarily assertive or demanding.

To minimize these problems and their effects and to secure an effective examination, the following specific objectives and the techniques to achieve them are given for an improved project review:

- ☐ To assure all audit steps required have been performed
  - Participate in design of audit program (nature and extent of testing).
  - Monitor progress.
  - Determine that audit program has been signed off during workpaper review.
- ☐ To assure evidence supports conclusions
  - Discuss and make inquiries as the job progresses.
  - Participate in the exit conference.
  - Review workpapers.
- ☐ To eliminate unresolved items
  - Discuss and make inquiries as the job progresses.
  - Participate in the exit conference.
  - Do research.
  - Review workpapers.
- ☐ To assure all relevant matters are reported
  - Discuss and make inquiries as the job progresses.
  - Review workpapers.
  - Review workpaper summarizations.
  - Review report drafts.

In addition, all of the above techniques are used to:

- Evaluate the performance of the auditor.
- Provide on-the-job training.
- Enforce department procedures.
- Contribute managerial skill and experience toward the completion of the project, thereby enhancing the project quality.

Maintaining a Proper Attitude

Reviewers should be skilled in conducting reviews and familiar with review objectives. The actual review must be performed without bias. Commentary and conduct that would embarrass, ridicule, or insult the performing auditor must be avoided. Instead, the reviewer must show courtesy and professional respect for the actions, thoughts, and contributions of the assigned auditor and, at the same time, must see that a proper examination occurs.

It must be remembered that the reviewer and the performing auditor are both members of a team in which each has a role to play. At times, the performing auditor has better knowledge than the reviewer about certain aspects of the project. The challenge for the reviewer in these circumstances is to channel the performing auditor's knowledge in a way that maximizes its worth to the project. The project supervisor or manager acts as an orchestra conductor—he does not know how to play all the instruments, but he does know how to blend and unite them to achieve the sound required by the musical score. With patience, practice, and self-discipline, a supervisor may similarly "orchestrate" a performing auditor's work.

RELATIONSHIPS WITH EXTERNAL AUDITORS

The Basis for the Relationship—A Historical Perspective

A discussion of techniques for managing audit projects would be incomplete without mentioning the special relationship between internal and external auditors and the needs of external auditors. The role of the external auditor is covered in Chapter 1, their responsibility with respect to internal control is set forth in Chapter 17, and their contribution to the development of auditing standards is outlined in Chapter 4. The relationship between internal and external auditors is best understood in light of the perspective provided in those chapters.

To summarize, the attest function performed by public accountants expanded rapidly after attestation became required for financial statements contained in filings and reports furnished to the SEC and others. The resulting increase in civil and criminal liability exposure to third-party users of such financial statements, coupled with the SEC's stringent enforcement of its rules of practice—particularly independence—led the public accounting profession to adopt rigorous standards of practice. These standards, together with the complex developments in accounting principles and reporting practices, had the effect of substantially increasing the effort required to perform an independent examination of financial statements. These increased efforts and increased pressures translated into higher costs for such examinations. Internal audit staffs were seen by many as one way to hold down audit costs. Other techniques included improving internal accounting controls and hiring more professionals in accounting departments in order to deal more effectively with the increased complexities in financial reporting. Internal and external auditors found it necessary to relate to one another in new ways to achieve their respective objectives.

The Current Scene

In 1975, the Auditing Standards Executive Committee of the AICPA issued SAS No. 9, "The Effect of an Internal Audit Function on the Scope of the Independent Auditor's Examination." This pronouncement reaffirms that the work of the internal auditor cannot be substituted for the work of the independent auditor. The clarity of that standard, however, expressed at the outset of the pronouncement in the first paragraph, is made unclear by the tenth paragraph, which provides:

> The independent auditor may make use of internal auditors to provide direct assistance in performing an examination in accordance with generally accepted auditing standards. Internal auditors may assist in performing substantive tests or tests of compliance. When the independent auditor makes such use of internal auditors, he should consider their competence and objectivity and supervise and test their work to the extent appropriate in the circumstances.[3]

The uncertainty over the meaning intended by the Auditing Standards Executive Committee in those two paragraphs produced two dissenting votes to SAS No. 9 from the 21 members. James I. Konkel dissented because he believed paragraph 10 could imply that the work of the internal auditor could be used virtually as a complete substitute for the work of the external auditor. He believed that when external auditors use the work of internal auditors, it is in reality a reduction of work scope in reliance on internal controls.[4]

Both Konkel and the other dissenter, Donald R. Ziegler, saw a need to provide guidance on the extent to which the independent auditor may make use of work performed by internal auditors in determining the scope of his own work. In addition, Ziegler felt that guidance was also needed as to when the work of internal auditors might cease to be a supplement to—and become a substitute for—the work of the independent auditor.[5]

In the absence of any clear-cut guidance, practitioners were free to form practically any relationship they wished. Many pursued a vigorous program of coordination aimed at reducing or slowing the growth of external fees; others did not.

The impact of SAS No. 9 on practice is interesting. The IIA Research Foundation recently published a study entitled, *A Time Series Analysis of the Effect of Internal Audit Activities on External Audit Fees*. The study was undertaken by Dr. Wanda A. Wallace of Southern Methodist University.

Dr. Wallace reported that:

> for the aggregate sample, a greater number of internal audit reports, a greater

---

[3] Statement on Auditing Standards No. 9 (Dec. 1975), "The Effect of an Internal Audit Function on the Scope of the Independent Auditor's Examination," ¶ 10 (AICPA, *Professional Standards,* Vol. 1), AU § 322.10.

[4] *Ibid.*, p. 5.

[5] *Ibid.*, p. 5.

number of CPAs as internal audit staff members, a higher level of internal audit expenditures, the use of formal audit manuals and programs, and the higher the percentage of assets being audited, the lower the external audit fees.[6]

In other words, high standards of internal audit performance translate into lower external audit fees. This is not surprising, given the advances in the professional practice of internal auditing occurring during the past 15 years. Among the most noteworthy are:

- Development of professional standards in 1978.
- CIA program.
- Adoption of a code of ethics.
- Increased body of professional literature.
- Emergence of professional development programs.

These events, along with the increased recognition by managements that professional internal auditing contributed significantly toward achieving corporate goals, enabled staffs to attract young professionals and retain them.

During the 1975–1981 test period of the IIA study, Wallace found that audit fees of the study group increased dramatically (see Figure 8-12).[7]

However, this raw data is inconclusive from the standpoint of whether the increase is real or merely reflects economic growth. Wallace found that comparisons of fee data standardized by the square root of assets and revenue revealed a more stable pattern. There were fluctuations across time and industrial segments that Wallace attributed to:

- Economic factors that differentially influence industry growth.
- Competition for audit services.
- Changes in regulation.[8]

Wallace saw an implication that the stabilization was explained to some degree by the presence of an internal audit function in all the sample companies.[9] This was attributed to increased reliance on internal auditors by external auditors, perhaps offsetting higher rates that would otherwise have occurred during the period. As mentioned earlier, the increases were deemed more pronounced for those situations where the internal auditors were perceived as more professional.

---

[6] Wanda A. Wallace, Ph.D., CIA, CMA, CPA, *A Time Series Analysis of the Effect of Internal Audit Activities on External Audit Fees* (Altamonte Springs, Fla.: The Institute of Internal Auditors, 1984), p. 198.

[7] *Ibid.*, p. 253. Reprinted by permission of The Institute of Internal Auditors, Inc., 249 Maitland Ave., Altamonte Springs, Fla. 32701.

[8] *Ibid.*, p. 74.

[9] *Ibid.*

FIG. 8-12

Comparative Data on External Audit Fees

External Audit Fee Information	1975	1976	1977	1978	1979	1980	1981
Audit services							
Budgeted fees	15	16	20	27	32	38	44
	121,800	133,475	164,500	199,509	204,069	233,929	267,098
	(165,908)	(165,003)	(201,263)	(210,950)	(228,948)	(264,559)	(308,429)
	50,000	51,500	85,250	131,510	118,500	150,500	150,400
	610,000	602,000	693,000	910,377	1.1M	1M	1.3M
Dollars (actual)	40	44	55	70	80	86	86
	247,845	262,076	353,621	403,904	432,669	444,901	482,947
	(347,041)	(372,644)	(583,734)	(656,564)	(715,115)	(767,369)	(812,333)
	78,500	90,150	100,100	131,510	135,000	135,109	149,933
	1.6M	1.8M	3.2M	3.6M	3.8M	4.13M	4.37M
Percentage of fees that are foreign vs. domestic	11	12	15	17	20	22	21
	39.3	35.4	38.4	35.4	34.3	34	36.2
	(17.4)	(16.7)	(18.9)	(19.6)	(20.9)	(22)	(21.2)
	41.3	40.5	47.8	37	38.5	36.5	39
	52	45	52	54	63	69	77
Hours (actual)	16	18	21	26	30	34	35
	8,107	7,640	7,594	8,865	7,771	7,514	6,827
	(12,596)	(11,564)	(11,277)	(11,104)	(9,756)	(9,426)	(8,737)
	2,200	2,693	3,647	4,018	3,802	3,806	3,000
	39,416	39,150	39,550	47,550	43,979	40,550	37,548
Expense reimbursements (actual)	10	10	12	15	18	21	19
	23,127	24,281	35,723	35,501	40,369	41,888	37,725
	(32,302)	(32,459)	(42,772)	(41,004)	(46,629)	(48,183)	(48,377)
	4,000	4,150	5,300	12,850	19,057	23,000	14,734
	96,300	87,000	102,825	101,606	142,760	163,061	152,975

MANAGING AUDIT PROJECTS

Accounting services other than the annual audit (please describe the nature of the services)							
Budgeted fees	4 24,275 (20,655) 11,300 40,200	5 27,960 (26,719) 17,000 65,200	6 34,883 (33,216) 81,000 81,000	9 30,811 (38,472) 18,000 122,000	13 28,425 (33,981) 19,225 113,000	17 32,024 (36,894) 22,000 135,000	14 26,600 (26,177) 14,613 92,000
Dollars (actual)	18 95,228 (146,694) 33,350 574,200	20 95,051 (148,899) 22,250 482,150	27 136,904 (236,467) 31,000 946,000	35 126,669 (274,088) 21,525 1.5M	43 157,782 (338,341) 26,000 1.9M	49 197,631 (530,487) 40,000 3.4M	47 201,566 (453,497) 50,000 2.6M
Percentage of fees that are foreign vs. domestic	5 27.8 (16) 24 42	4 26.8 (11.5) 27.5 28	7 38.3 (27.8) 30 86	8 52 (21.8) 56 57	8 50.5 (16) 55 42	8 46.5 (17.4) 46.5 53	8 42.8 (21.1) 32 61
Hours (actual)	4 983 (1352) 245 2800	4 983 (1352) 245 2800	4 1283 (1259) 650 2800	6 677 (1149) 215 2970	7 2224 (4222) 240 11,470	8 2330 (4199) 410 12,256	10 2042 (4309) 305 13,970
Expense reimbursements (actual)	—	—	—	1 500 (0) 500 0	2 11,383 (9,734) 11,383 13,766	1 5,000 (0) 5,000 0	2 2,955 (3,600) 2,955 5,091

Key: # of responses that were nonzero
Mean
(Standard deviation)
Median
Range

The results of this study, then, support the contention that reliance on the work of internal auditors by external auditors has been on the increase since the publication of SAS No. 9. It also demonstrates that reliance varies.

This may be attributable to external auditors' perceptions of the reliability of the internal audit functions, as the study seems to imply. It also could be that the variance in reliability is attributable to the vagueness of SAS No. 9 identified by Mr. Konkel and Mr. Ziegler.

The result of all these events and forces has been a notable improvement in the professional practice of internal auditing and a significant increase in the number of practicing internal auditors. Estimates of the population of practicing IAs in the United States alone are in the 25,000–50,000 range.

During the post-SAS No. 9 period of expansion and improved professionalism, relations between external auditors and internal auditors also improved. However, evidence is building that the rate of change in the relationship has not kept up with professional improvements.

In the previously mentioned Wallace study, the information presented indicates that the relationship is dominated by the belief that the more work internal auditors can perform under the direction of external auditors, the better. Figure 8-13, for example, is an analysis developed by one respondent in the study.[10] It analyzes the variety of services performed by internal auditors for external auditors. Three years of data are included.

The data suggest that the most effective result in terms of fee impact occurs when internal auditors work directly under the supervision of external auditors. The implication is that if internal audit organizations ran a sort of manpower pool for the external auditors, the impact on fees would be maximized.

Efforts to keep external audit fees within reason are desirable—even necessary—in today's competitive environment; however, such efforts have limits. Put another way, there comes a point when the incremental amount of internal cost required to perform a service for external auditors is greater than the increased audit fee that would otherwise occur. There are limits to the relationship as far as fee savings are concerned. This fact does not seem to be considered by either SAS No. 9 or the Wallace study.

Perhaps the most serious flaw, however, is that SAS No. 9 does not offer any means by which external auditors may determine the optimum arrangement. The absence of guidance has at times strained relationships. Those strains are produced by relationships characterized by an insufficient understanding of the internal audit function by external auditors. The external auditors' need to stay within budget frequently causes pressure to transfer more work to internal auditors. The very existence of budgets affords precious little time for the kind of external auditor planning and supervision that would achieve better relationships. Add to that the fact that

---

[10] *Ibid.*, p. 186. Reprinted by permission of The Institute of Internal Auditors, Inc., 249 Maitland Ave., Altamonte Springs, Fla. 32701.

MANAGING AUDIT PROJECTS

FIG. 8-13

The Extent to Which Internal Audit Hours Replace External Audit Hours

Types of Internal Audit Activity:

1 = Full scope operational and financial audit and detailed analytical review.
2 = Follow-up full scope operational and financial systems audit.
3 = Full scope operational audit on the manual portions of a revenue cycle.
4 = Limited scope operational and financial systems audit, including an in-depth data center review and a specific application review of the general ledger/financial reporting application.
5 = Limited scope operational and financial systems audit, including a data center review.
6 = Limited scope operational and financial systems audit.
7 = Follow-up data center review.
8 = Limited scope operational and financial audit.
9 = Follow-up limited scope operational and financial audit, including a data center review.
10 = Limited scope financial audit coordinated with external auditors.
11 = Limited scope financial audit directly under the supervision of the external auditors, performed specifically for the external auditors.
12 = Internal auditor assigned to the external auditor during the year-end engagement (number of internal auditors assigned).

Coding for Type of Internal Audit Activity	Total Internal Audit Man-hours	Replacement of External Audit Hours	Implied Substitution Ratio	Hourly Rate*	Extension**
1978 Audit					
1	425	60	7.08 : 1	$25	$ 1,500
10	920	450	2.04 : 1	25	11,250
3	375	125	3 : 1	22	2,750
11	575	450	1.28 : 1	25	11,250
12(1)	356	356	1 : 1	25	8,900
12(1)	104	60	1.73 : 1	25	1,500
12(1)	125	125	1 : 1	22	2,750
1979 Audit					
12(1 to 2)	95	95	1 : 1	$27	$ 2,565
12(1)	260	260	1 : 1	27	7,020
12(1)	72	72	1 : 1	30	2,160
12(1)	220	220	1 : 1	24	5,280
12(1)	170	170	1 : 1	27	4,590
12(1)	140	140	1 : 1	24	3,360
12(1)	80	80	1 : 1	30	2,400
12(1)	312	250	1.25 : 1	27	6,750
1	224	20	11.20 : 1	27	540

(continued)

FIG. 8-13 *(cont'd)*

Coding for Type of Internal Audit Activity	Total Internal Audit Man-hours	Replacement of External Audit Hours	Implied Substitution Ratio	Hourly Rate*	Extension**
5	1,000	500	2 : 1	27	13,500
9	832	250	3.33 : 1	27	6,750
6	584	450	1.30 : 1	27	12,150
2	440	200	2.20 : 1	25	5,000
2 (revenue cycle)	554	250	2.22 : 1	27	6,750
1980 Audit					
12(1)	45	45	1 : 1	$35	$ 1,575
12(1)	298	298	1 : 1	30	9,960
12(1)	331	331	1 : 1	30	10,935
12(1)	269	269	1 : 1	30	8,490
12(1)	174	174	1 : 1	30	5,430
12(1)	255	255	1 : 1	30	8,010
12(1)	277	200	1.39 : 1	30	6,000
7	1,040	650	1.60 : 1	30	19,500
8	632	350	1.81 : 1	30	10,500
8	512	350	1.46 : 1	30	10,500
6	528	350	1.51 : 1	30	10,500
4	400	120	3.33 : 1	30	3,600

* The cost of the staff level that would have otherwise performed the work.
** This is the estimated maximum amount of fee reduction.

the majority of staff members of external auditors (even managers and some partners) are in the learning, developmental phase of their careers. As a result, many internal auditors find external auditor actions at times shallow, naïve, or unsound.

A considerable number of internal auditors were originally trained in the service of CPA firms. They are experienced in external audit techniques and are knowledgeable concerning GAAP. The converse is not true, however. External auditors are much less familiar with internal auditing and its objectives; hence, their evaluations of internal audit functions are drawn largely from a single perspective, the external audit perspective.

In 1985, the IIA published the results of a study of the emerging practices being used by leading corporations to coordinate audit coverage of external and internal auditors. The study seems to be pointing in a somewhat different direction than the Wallace study. The research, conducted by Leonard Eugene Berry under authorization from the IIA Research Foundation, found acceptance of an earlier view that coordination between external and internal auditors has been around for some time. However, there is a gap between what should be optimal practice and what actually exists in practice.[11] Berry sought to find examples where practices seem to be working well. Fourteen large companies and six of their external auditing firms were selected by the researcher from recommendations made by advising members of IIA's International Research Committee.[12] The practices identified by this research have not gained wide acceptance, but suggest that, in the past five years, significant changes in coordination practices have occurred. Internal and external audit managers were working closely together to identify more cost-effective methods to reduce duplication and overlap.[13]

Berry noted as significant the trend toward what he described as coordinating total audit coverage in a "single audit" strategy. Under this approach, the single audit is comprised of the following five types of audit areas:

1. Overlapping audit areas apportioned to both external and internal auditors
2. Overlapping audit areas apportioned to internal auditors
3. Internal audits that don't overlap the external audit
4. Overlapping audit areas apportioned to external auditors
5. Areas of external audit that must be performed by the external auditor

Under the single audit approach, external auditors and internal auditors work together to plan, execute, and control all the audit work. The groups accept each other as equal partners. This concept seems preferable to that characterized by many external/internal auditor relationships, in which internal auditors simply work under the direction of external auditors. The extent to which the single audit concept catches on remains to be seen. It is difficult to see how single audits will apply to small or medium-size companies. Yet, the thought that the two professions relate to each other in an equal fashion is virtually unarguable and should become pervasive.

One last point should be mentioned. Berry also noted that several internal and external audit managers offered that, in their opinion, SAS No. 9 has not been revised to keep up with the new professionalism of internal auditors and the innovations in practices.[14] One can only hope that the IIA and the AICPA, together, can work to update it at some appropriate time in the near future.

---

[11] Michael J. Barrett and Victor Z. Brink, *Evaluating Internal/External Audit Services and Relationships* (Altamonte Springs, Fla.: The Institute of Internal Auditors, 1980), pp. 67–68.

[12] Leonard Eugene Berry, DBA, CIA, CPA, *Coordinating Total Audit Coverage: Trends and Practices* (Altamonte Springs, Fla.: The Institute of Internal Auditors Research Foundation, 1985), p. 4.

[13] *Ibid.*, p. 51.

[14] *Ibid.*, 51–52.

The following are areas of interest for both internal and external auditors:

- Study and evaluation of internal control
- Compliance with statutes
- Financial reporting
- Standards of business conduct
- EDP auditing

In each of these categories, there is a broad range of interaction within which specific relationships may fall. The variable factors that affect this determination include (1) the confidence the CPA has in the internal audit function, (2) the length of time the CPA has been retained (with increased contact, the two functions are more apt to develop a mutually agreeable relationship), (3) the attitude of management about the interrelationship, and (4) the nature of the business. The following three scenarios illustrate that range of interaction between internal and external auditors.

Direct Assistance by Internal Auditors. In this relationship, internal auditors perform audit work pursuant to the external auditor's audit programs, review, and direct supervision. Often, the external auditors furnish the type of workpapers and stipulate their formats and documentation techniques. Assistance is most frequently sought by external auditors in internal control compliance testing and in such substantive testing as verifying cash balances, accounts payable balances, and fixed asset transactions. External auditors find that such assistance helps to restrain increases in audit costs. Internal audit staffs that are composed primarily of experienced auditors often find some aspects of this assistance to be tedious and a waste of their skill and expertise. Care must be taken by the chief auditor in this relationship to avoid offending the internal auditor's professional sensibilities. Other chief auditors with less experienced staffs find that assisting the external auditors offers an excellent opportunity for their staffs to gain valuable audit experience and training.

Participative Auditing. Under this approach, the external and internal auditor together identify areas of mutual interest, establish objectives, and devise audit programs to accomplish them. The work may be performed by teams comprised of auditors from each staff, or segments of the job may be performed separately by the respective staffs. Supervision and review occur by each organization's management to the extent of its interest. These efforts put a premium on planning, coordination, and administration.

This type of auditing can occur in EDP auditing, reviews of international operations, limited scope financial reviews, and special investigations. External auditors find that this type of relationship can aid in holding down

MANAGING AUDIT PROJECTS 8-35

audit fees, provided that the savings are not offset by increased planning and coordination costs. Internal auditors find this approach preferable to the direct assistance relationship because they have greater voice in shaping the program and performing the audit.

Direct Assistance by External Auditors. Under this arrangement, the external auditor provides staff assistance, usually on a temporary basis, to the internal auditor, with the latter bearing overall responsibility. In these instances, the audit objectives, audit programs, and supervision are provided by the internal audit department. Examples of projects where this might occur include limited scope financial reviews, certain aspects of standards-of-business-conduct auditing (e.g., compliance tests of travel and business expense reporting), and compliance tests of internal controls. External auditors find that providing this assistance results in the absorption of costs of otherwise idle staff without compromising the auditor's independence, provided that the assistance is furnished by members of their staff not otherwise involved at any time with the independent audit of the financial statements. Chief internal auditors will find that such assistance can be useful in developing the supervisory skills of their staff and completing internal audits at distant locations (by obtaining staff from the office of the external auditor nearest to that location).

In any given circumstance, the relationship may involve a combination of the foregoing circumstances. However, the most common arrangement usually involves the external auditor obtaining some form of assistance from the internal auditors. A small but growing number of companies (customarily those with large corporate internal audit staffs) and their outside accountants are finding that the participatory relationship is mutually beneficial. It is believed that few companies, as yet, use external auditors to assist internal auditors.

In addition to direct or mutual assistance, some external auditors provide advice to internal auditors on how to establish programs of audit coverage, resolve issues pertaining to technical matters, and train staff members. In addition, many CPA firms make their workpapers available to internal auditors and permit internal auditors to use their time-sharing services, generalized audit software, questionnaires, and other audit tools.

Specific Interactions Between External and Internal Auditors

The board of directors, usually through its audit committee, provides oversight and has much to do with the selection of the external auditors (see Chapter 10). But, responsibility for establishing and maintaining effective working relations with external auditors is primarily that of the chief financial officer. The corporate controller and the chief internal auditor also have certain delegated duties regarding the annual audit.

In recent years, the internal audit function has played an increasingly important role in coordinating audit efforts with external auditors. The *Standards of the Professional Practice of Internal Auditing,* issued in 1978 by the IIA, make specific mention of coordination. In some companies, the cost of the independent financial audit is charged to internal audit department. In these instances, management holds the chief auditor accountable for the total auditing effort, both internal and external, and expects the chief auditor to maximize audit coverage and at the same time minimize total audit costs. Here, the coordination role the director of internal auditing plays is very important in maintaining overall relationships. In many other companies, the chief auditor is responsible for coordination, timing, and scheduling of audits with external auditors, but he is not accountable for the external auditor's fees.

Before devising techniques to effectively manage and coordinate the company's relationship with external auditors, the chief auditor must have a clear understanding of what management expects from him in this regard. This expectation, and the relationship with external auditors, should be explicitly defined in the audit charter. (See Chapter 7.)

The chief internal auditor's assigned responsibilities can often include the following functions:

- *Providing assistance.* As previously discussed, a common responsibility of the audit function is to provide assistance to external auditors. This assistance may range from performing compliance tests and substantive tests, to providing advice in formulating audit plans, to interpreting evidential matter.

- *Obtaining assistance.* The internal audit function may also obtain assistance, as discussed previously, from external auditors. Examples of such situations include compliance tests of expense reporting and limited financial reviews.

- *Coordination meetings.* Coordination meetings may be held by representatives of the two audit groups for a variety of reasons. These include meetings to (1) coordinate audit coverage, (2) monitor progress toward accomplishing audit objectives, (3) discuss problem areas, (4) exchange information, or (5) obtain advice. The frequency and timing of such meetings depends on the type of relationship that exists between the audit groups.

- *Formal communication.* Formal communication techniques include internal and external auditors forwarding copies to each other of annual audit plans and relevant audit reports. Direct communication may also occur to coordinate audit coverage, arrange services, or furnish information. Again, the extent of this type of communication depends on the nature of the relationship between internal and external auditors.

- *Accessing workpapers.* The work of internal and external auditors, in some respects, is so similar that they can both benefit from sharing their workpapers. Sharing workpapers may help avoid redundant effort.

- *Joint use of audit tools.* As noted earlier in this chapter, and in Chapters 17 and 18, external auditors have developed many useful audit tools, such as audit approaches, questionnaires, checklists, generalized audit software, time-sharing programs, and documentation formats. Most firms willingly permit their clients' internal auditors to use these tools at little or no cost. Conversely, some of the more progressive internal audit departments have developed specific tools that may be useful to the external auditor. These include special-purpose programs and questionnaires developed for audits of specific EDP applications (e.g., payroll or accounts payable) and operational audits.

☐ *Training.* Some of the very large independent accounting firms have developed numerous training courses to maintain and improve the audit proficiency of their staff. Often, these firms invite participation by their client's internal auditors. Such training courses may cover all aspects of auditing, including internal auditing. Some companies and their independent accountants have established programs where junior staff members of the CPA firm spend brief periods on the company's internal audit staff to gain valuable on-the-job training in aspects of auditing that are not available in the general practice of the CPA firm.

☐ *Technical assistance.* All of the major accounting firms provide their clients and other selected persons with a continuous stream of their own copyrighted data on such technically diverse subjects as income taxes, accounting and financial reporting, EDP, and other management-related subjects. In addition, many of the offices have libraries and offer research services. The internal audit department should take advantage of these publications and facilities to the extent possible and, in exchange, offer its reference material and files to the external auditor.

The chief auditor and the CPA firm should think of each other as a resource that, if effectively managed, can contribute mutually to their respective objectives.

Outlook for the Future

While some conditions, such as less than desirable coordination and communications, continue to act as impediments to improved relations, forces are at work that promise to change the situation for the better:

1. *Competition in public accounting.* CPA firms have changed markedly from the days when fees were thought not to be a basis for competing. It used to be considered unprofessional to solicit business or advertise directly. Today, accounting firms are pressing each other in a near no-holds-barred fee battle. The financial audit has come to be viewed as a commodity by many companies who compete for CPA firms much the way they do other types of procurement. This is forcing CPAs to look critically at how they perform the financial audit in a quest to gain a competitive advantage.

2. *The changing profession.* The pressure on CPA firms is compounded by the fact that the growth in its mainstay business—the financial audit—has disappeared. Many firms are seeking new ways to capitalize on their principal

product-attest services, by applying them to situations other than financial statements. As CPAs broaden the range of their services beyond traditional financial statement auditing, the more comparable they become to internal auditors.

3. *Evolution of internal auditing.* Since SAS No. 9 was adopted in 1975, internal auditing has evolved into a respected profession with a much clearer mission. The FCPA, among other things, gave internal auditors a significant opportunity to render assessments of internal controls as a vital service to management. Many members of management consider this service more important than the service internal auditors render to external auditors.

4. *EDP developments.* Not only do these developments challenge traditional approaches to financial audits, they offer the possibility to automate many manual audit techniques. It seems inevitable that external auditors will come to rely much more on internal auditors to effect embedded audit routines, extract data, and execute other automated audit routines.

5. *The Treadway Commission.* The Treadway Commission, in its 1987 report, recognizes that internal auditing is a service that is underutilized and underappreciated. It envisions a larger role for internal auditing in improving the defenses of public companies against the incidence of financial reporting fraud. If such a large role in fact emerges, the relationship between external and internal auditors must improve.

6. *GAAS changes.* The changes to GAAS enacted in 1988 (see Chapter 4) will necessitate better coordination. The changes will provide a basis in which the work of internal auditors will become even more relevant to external auditors.

7. *The IIA.* The efforts of the IIA over the years were an important factor in the rise of professionalism in the practice of internal auditing. These efforts will continue to advance the professional aspects of internal auditing in the future.

Both the AICPA and the IIA are aware of the difficulties and opportunities posed by the current scene. They are also conscious of the forces pushing for an improved relationship. In response, the ASB of the AICPA has joined with the Canadian Institute of Chartered Accountants to create a special task force to study the matter.

The joint task force is nearing completion of its work, and has sought input from the IIA. A task force of the Professional Issues Committee has been charged with providing that input. Expected to evolve from this effort is an Auditing Procedure/Audit Techniques Study. These are nonauthoritative but could provide much useful guidance to help point the way toward a more balanced and more effective relationship.

The increased professionalism of internal auditors, their expanded role in internal accounting control auditing, and the added complexities in conducting audit examinations, suggest that the need for a healthy professional relationship between external and internal auditors will continue and may perhaps become even more important.

MANAGING AUDIT PROJECTS 8-39

What seems likely in the foreseeable future is a continued sharing of interest between internal auditors and external auditors in (1) the adequacy of internal accounting control, (2) compliance with standards of business conduct, and (3) financial reporting. The rapid expansion of electronic data processing offers an obvious area for greater participation. Both groups need to increase their knowledge of EDP auditing. Due to the complexity in this area, the most successful results are likely to be through combined, coordinated efforts.

Beyond that, management will probably continue to look to internal auditors to make meaningful contributions in the area of operational auditing and for internal consulting. When one considers the entire spectrum of activities and operations of all types in which modern large businesses are involved, the possibilities for audit undertakings seem almost endless. Against this backdrop, internal and external auditors should easily be able to provide valuable services without infringing on their respective interests and responsibilities. Through mutual respect, cooperative spirit, and constant attention to improving the ways to work together, both audit groups should optimize their relationship and achieve their respective objectives.

DATA SECURITY

The Code of Ethics adopted by the IIA for its members (see Chapter 6) requires, among other things, that members shall be prudent in the use of information acquired in the course of their duties. The use of confidential information for any personal gain, or in a manner that would be detrimental to the employer, is explicitly prohibited. A properly functioning internal auditing department possesses information that highlights conditions and occurrences that are apt to be sensitive. Should this information be leaked to outsiders, the adverse consequences could be substantial.

The chances that this might occur were once thought to be remote. But with the increased litigious atmosphere that pervades the American business scene, the risk is greater. Moreover, in some industry segments, e.g., government contracting, federal legislation actually encourages whistle-blowing. The temptation for internal auditors to turn into whistle-blowers has resulted in at least one reported case in which an internal auditor leaked draft copies of investigative documents developed under the attorney client and attorney work product privileges to a newspaper and to Congress.[15]

It is imperative for internal audit managements to recognize that the information for which they are custodians is in demand. They must take steps to minimize the opportunities for the unauthorized diversion of con-

---

[15] Ralph Vartabedian, "Whistle-Blowing at Northrop Raises Questions on Auditor's Role," *Los Angeles Times,* Saturday, Oct. 31, 1987, Sec. IV, p. 1.

fidential information gathered during the course of conducting audits. There are several techniques that the chief auditor may wish to consider in dealing with this situation:

- Gather only information relevant to the audit objectives.
- Make sure that all affected members of management are orally informed of audit findings, conclusions, and recommendations.
- Take care in drafting reports so that the possibility for drawing misleading inferences is minimized.
- Exercise document accountability techniques to preclude easy unauthorized copying. Such techniques include (1) instructing recipients of drafts and final documents not to copy them, (2) marking each page of each document with the name or control number of each recipient, (3) requiring that all drafts be returned to the originator, (4) maintaining up-to-date logs of who is in possession of outstanding documents, (5) requiring that final reports be returned after their usefulness ceases, and (6) destroying all retrieved copies.
- Protect automated data bases of audit information by the use of passwords. Sensitive audit information should not be stored on PC hard disks.
- Devise and enforce strict accountability controls over floppy disks.
- Maintain termination procedures for internal auditors leaving the company to assure that all access devices (keys, passwords, and IDs) are retrieved as well as all outstanding floppies in the terminating employee's possession.

In addition to the above, the chief auditor may wish to consider the physical security within the department. It may be desirable for the department to be located in facilities that are physically separate or isolated from other organizations. Department files and records should be kept in limited access areas, such as locked cabinets, rooms, or vaults.

New auditors should be trained to be security conscious as part of the orientation program. Periodic reminders of the importance of data security for existing staff members is also a good idea.

SUGGESTED READING

Barrett, Michael J., DBA, and Victor Z. Brink, Ph.D. *Evaluating Internal/External Audit Services and Relationships.* U.S.A.: The Institute of Internal Auditors, 1980.

Berry, Leonard Eugene, DBA, CIA, CPA. *Coordinating Total Audit Coverage: Trends and Practices.* U.S.A.: The Institute of Internal Auditors, 1985.

De Marco, Victor F. "Will the CPA Wither Away?" *The Internal Auditor,* Oct. 1978, pp. 83–87.

Ferrier, R. J. "Developing a Working Relationship With Your External Auditor." *The Internal Auditor,* Dec. 1981, pp. 22–26.

Research Report 24, *Evaluating Internal Audit Services and Relationships.* Altamonte Springs, Fla.: The Institute of Internal Auditors, 1980.

Statement of Auditing Standards No. 9, "The Effect of an Internal Audit Function on the Scope of the Independent Auditor's Examination." AICPA, *Professional Standards,* Vol. 1, AU § 322 (Dec. 1975).

Wallace, Wanda A. *A Time Series Analysis of the Effect of Internal Audit Activities on External Audit Fees.* U.S.A.: The Institute of Internal Auditors, 1984.

Ward, D. Deweg, and Jack C. Robertson. "Reliance on Internal Auditors." *Journal of Accountancy,* Oct. 1980, p. 64.

"Who Needs External Audits?" *Forbes,* Dec. 1, 1977, p. 110.

CHAPTER **9**

Managing Human and Other Resources and Records

Introduction 2	Techniques 18
	Other Considerations 18
Personnel Management 2	**Management of Other Resources** 19
Background 2	Purpose 19
Recruiting 3	Techniques 19
Definition and Responsibility 3	Budgeting 19
Dependence on Organizational	Organizational Performance
Planning 3	Measurement 20
Other Factors 3	Other New Techniques 22
Sources for Candidates 4	
The Recruiting Process 8	**Records Management** 27
Searching Markets 8	Purpose 27
Screening Candidates 9	Audit Report Follow-Up Records 28
Interviewing Candidates 9	Purpose 28
Testing and Evaluating 10	Techniques 28
Timing 11	Related Files 28
Offering and Acknowledging	Workpaper Records 29
Acceptance 11	Purpose 29
Follow-Up 12	Techniques 29
Orienting New Employees 12	Records Retention 33
Performance Measurement 12	Purpose 33
Definition and Purpose 12	Opinion Regarding Retention 33
Effect of Subjectivity 13	Effect of IRS Efforts 33
Measurement Techniques 13	The DOD Access Offensive 34
Professional Training 15	The DCAA Subpoena Power 56
Purpose and Techniques 15	The Attorney-Client Privilege 59
Other Considerations 16	Implications for Internal Auditors 64
Career Managing 17	
Purpose 17	**Suggested Reading** 65

Fig. 9-1   IIA Survey of Internal Audit Recruiting Sources Among Industry
              Categories 6
Fig. 9-2   Professional Experience Reported by U.S. Internal Auditors 9
Fig. 9-3   Staff Evaluation Form 14
Fig. 9-4   Excerpt of a Performance Measurement Report 21

Fig. 9-5	Activity Report Segment	23
Fig. 9-6	Assignment Log	24
Fig. 9-7	Questionnaire for Evaluating Audit Services	26
Fig. 9-8	Retention Periods for Internal Audit Department Records	29
Fig. 9-9	Postaudit Report Follow-Up Form	30
Fig. 9-10	Report Log	31
Fig. 9-11	Categories for Filing Audit Reports	32
Fig. 9-12	Scope of the Government's Right to Contractors' Records	39
Fig. 9-13	NSIA Perspective on Attorney-Client Privilege	60

INTRODUCTION

Techniques for effective audit management are reviewed in Chapters 7 and 8 in the context of organizational management and project management. Attention is now focused on the single most important internal auditing resource—personnel, and how to manage it. Of course, to function effectively, internal auditing requires other resources in addition to competent professional staff. This chapter discusses human and other resources and records, and provides guidance for properly managing them.

PERSONNEL MANAGEMENT

Background

Since auditing is a service, it naturally follows that it is a labor-intensive activity. While utilization of other resources is involved, the success of the function is largely attributable to the capabilities of the people on staff and the skill exercised in managing them.

The importance of personnel management is not often recognized by practicing auditors. That is because the high standards of performance and professional ethics, to which all auditors subscribe, make the task less burdensome than it would otherwise be. Auditors are expected to be competent, self-motivated dedicated, and hard-working, and, for the most part, they are.

Nevertheless, staff members must be recruited, oriented, properly trained, effectively used, promoted when experience and performance warrant it, and eventually transferred to new positions to advance their professional careers.

The *Standards for the Professional Practice of Internal Auditing* enumerate the following activities, which are related to personnel management:[1]

---

[1] *Standards for the Professional Practice of Internal Auditing* (Altamonte Springs, Fla.: The Institute of Internal Auditors, 1978), pp. 500–502.

.1 Developing written job descriptions for each level of the audit staff.
.2 Selecting qualified and competent individuals.
.3 Training and providing continuing educational opportunities for each auditor.
.4 Appraising each internal auditor's performance, at least annually.
.5 Providing counsel to internal auditors on their performance and professional development.

Job descriptions are discussed in Chapter 7 in the context of organizing the department. The remaining activities are covered in this chapter as follows:

- Recruiting
- Performance measurement
- Professional training
- Career managing

Recruiting

Definition and Responsibility. Recruiting may be defined as the process by which qualified candidates are identified, screened, interviewed, evaluated, and hired. Since labor is a critical resource, it follows that recruiting is a crucial activity requiring that the recruiter be skilled and experienced.

Because of its importance, recruiting is usually done by the director of internal auditing, in all but the largest of departments. Even in instances when staffs are large, the chief auditor closely monitors the recruiting efforts of his designees—usually managers.

Dependence on Organizational Planning. Recruiting begins with knowing how many staff vacancies are to be filled, what skills are needed, and the qualifications of each—in other words, knowing the quantity and quality requisites of the organization. Identifying these requirements is largely a function of proper organizational planning and an established audit approach. The chief auditor, and those involved in recruiting activity, must have a good idea of what type of auditing is to be done, the extent or depth of the review, and the skills essential to accomplishing the task. Discussions of audit approaches and organizational planning have been presented in Chapters 2 and 7, respectively, which provide commentary on how to decide the extent of audit coverage. Chapter 3 describes auditor qualifications in the discussion of competence. The reader may wish to review sections of these chapters applicable to recruiting.

Other Factors. Proper functional outlines and sound organizational planning are basic to hiring the appropriate qualification and mix of staff. However, other factors are involved in shaping the nature and extent of recruiting.

These are the following:

- Expected turnover
- Competition in the marketplace
- Assistance by personnel departments and outside agencies

Expected turnover may be determined on the basis of historical experience, modified by the changes instituted to improve it. While all organizations experience some turnover, it can be minimized by fulfilling many of the professional and personal needs of the staff. This includes providing adequate compensation, suitable surroundings, adequate job opportunities, regular performance evaluations, proper training, and timely career consultation. These activities are discussed later in this chapter. However, other factors beyond the control of the chief auditor also affect turnover. Included are geographic area, type of industry, and company image.

Competition is also a largely uncontrollable factor, but it has an effect on the extent of recruiting that is necessary. For example, well-managed companies who lead in their industry may have a slight competitive advantage in attracting the best talent.

Finally, one other factor that merits mention is that large companies and the larger metropolitan areas are served by personnel departments and outside agencies. These groups can considerably ease the recruiting burden.

Sources for Candidates. Candidates may be recruited from a variety of sources, as is evident from Figure 9-1,[2] which depicts recruiting practices of internal audit departments in various industries. These sources can vary widely in terms of the qualities possessed by the candidates coming from each. As a result, not all audit organizations recruit from all markets. The sources listed in Figure 9-1 may be grouped into three categories for purposes of further discussion.

1. *Universities and colleges.* Universities and colleges are an obvious and excellent source for recruiting new personnel. Colleges and universities recognize the career potentials of internal auditing and are devoting an increasing proportion of their accounting and business administration curricula to better prepare graduates for careers in internal auditing. For the present and foreseeable future, however, the curricula is still heavily oriented toward preparing graduates for careers in public accounting and in private industry, to the exclusion of internal auditing. The major public accounting firms are formidable recruiting adversaries, and much of the most promising talent selects beginning careers in public practice. These facts must be recognized by those who choose to emphasize this source.

---

[2] From *Survey of Internal Auditing 1979* (Altamonte Springs, Fla.: The Institute of Internal Auditors, 1980), pp 134–135. Reprinted by permission of the Institute of Internal Auditors, Inc.

Another important factor involved in considering college graduates as a source is the need to supplement their formal education with the know-how that comes with experience. Good auditors are developed through a combination of proper training and experience, which is gained through carefully supervised and controlled on-the-job conditions. Some audit organizations are not able to offer this combination because the costs involved are simply too high.

For many companies, these limiting factors are more than offset by the fact that college graduates, particularly those with advanced degrees, learn more quickly, offer fresh insight, are more broadly trained in basic business, and are often more willing to get involved with unfamiliar subjects. To these pluses must be added the recent stirrings toward more emphasis on internal auditing in college courses.

The IIA is leading the way toward more college level training in internal auditing. In 1985, it inaugurated a program of support, including financial support. The program roots are traceable to the Louisiana State University Internal Auditing Program initiated in 1984. It was designated the LSU Internal Auditing Pilot School. The LSU program consists of four internal audit courses blended into the accounting curriculum.[3] It is expected that over 500 students will graduate from the program over the next 10 years.

That program led the IIA Research Foundation to approve a $15,000 grant to be awarded to a college or university in order to establish an internal auditing program similar to the LSU pilot program. Together, these developments suggest that college recruiting will be a more important source in future years.

2. *Internal sources.* A large number of companies prefer to fill open audit positions by transferring qualified personnel from within the company. The managements of these companies are of the opinion that knowledge of the company is a primary requisite to effective internal auditing. They further believe that a stint in the audit department is a useful building block leading to advanced positions in the management ranks. This approach is often more noticeable in very large and well-established companies. However, it is now practiced, although to a lesser extent, in a number of medium-sized companies.

3. *Other external sources.* Virtually all audit organizations fill many of their audit staff needs from the marketplace. Over the past 10 to 15 years, a growing percentage of candidates has been flowing to internal audit departments from public accounting firms, and the flow is not restricted simply to entry level and senior staff positions. The professional requirements of external and internal auditing are so similar that even managers and partners of public accounting firms have chosen to further their professional careers by joining internal audit departments in a management capacity. Thus, many audit functions are led and staffed by persons whose careers began in public accounting.

Of course, external sources other than public accounting firms can provide qualified candidates. Local chapters of the IIA usually assist prospective candidates and employers in identifying each other. Outside professional and executive consultant agencies, more commonly known as head hunters, offer a constant inventory of candidates. Use of these search firms involves a fee for services, which is paid

---

[3] Vincent C. Brenner and Glenn E. Sumners, "A New Development in Audit Education," *The Internal Auditor*, Feb. 1987, p. 45.

FIG. 9-1

IIA Survey of Internal Audit Recruiting Sources Among Industry Categories

6AI. From what sources do you recruit internal auditors for your department? (Check as many as apply.)

	Air/Auto	Bank	Chem	Cong	Educ	Elec	Food/Bev	Gen. Manu	Gov't St/Loc	Gov't Fed	1979 Total
Within the company	81.8%	81.4%	66.7%	62.9%	38.5%	69.6%	60.9%	56.3%	66.7%	76.9%	69.8%
Colleges (College recruiting)	54.5	52.5	41.7	60.0	15.4	43.5	39.1	34.4	50.0	46.2	42.7
Newspaper advertising	72.7	61.0	58.3	62.9	76.9	73.9	87.0	59.4	58.3	7.7	63.0
Other advertising	18.2	6.8	0.0	11.4	30.8	0.0	17.4	9.4	33.3	0.0	11.3
Employment agencies	54.5%	49.2%	75.0%	68.6%	30.8%	65.2%	69.6%	71.9%	8.3%	0.0%	58.1%
Sample size	11	59	12	35	13	23	23	32	24	13	497

6BI. Other (please specify)

	Air/Auto	Bank	Chem	Cong	Educ	Elec	Food/Bev	Gen. Manu	Gov't St/Loc	Gov't Fed	1979 Total
CPA firms	0.0%	20.0%	100.0%	20.0%	0.0%	66.6%	60.0%	66.6%	14.3%	0.0%	36.2%
Referrals	50.0	10.0	0.0	30.0	0.0	0.0	40.0	33.3	0.0	0.0	20.0
Company employment division	0.0	0.0	0.0	20.0	0.0	0.0	0.0	0.0	28.6	25.0	18.8
Institute of Internal Auditors	50.0	50.0	0.0	10.0	0.0	0.0	0.0	0.0	0.0	0.0	6.3
Executive search firms	0.0	0.0	0.0	10.0	0.0	0.0	0.0	0.0	0.0	0.0	2.5
State personnel department	0.0	0.0	0.0	0.0	0.0	0.0	0.0	0.0	28.6	0.0	2.5
Other government department	0.0	0.0	0.0	0.0	0.0	0.0	0.0	0.0	0.0	50.0	2.5
Intern programs	0.0	0.0	0.0	10.0	0.0	0.0	0.0	0.0	0.0	0.0	2.5
Civil Service Commission	0.0	0.0	0.0	0.0	0.0	0.0	0.0	0.0	0.0	25.0	1.3
Retired Military Officers Association	0.0	0.0	0.0	0.0	0.0	0.0	0.0	0.0	0.0	0.0	1.3
Farm Credit System	0.0	10.0	0.0	0.0	0.0	0.0	0.0	0.0	0.0	0.0	1.3
Technical schools	0.0	10.0	0.0	0.0	0.0	0.0	0.0	0.0	0.0	0.0	1.3
Seminars	0.0	0.0	0.0	0.0	0.0	33.3	0.0	0.0	0.0	0.0	1.3
Public service agency	0.0	0.0	0.0	0.0	0.0	0.0	0.0	0.0	14.3	0.0	1.3
Unsolicited applications	0.0%	0.0%	0.0%	0.0%	0.0%	0.0%	0.0%	0.0%	14.3%	0.0%	1.3%
Total mentions	2	10	1	10	0	3	5	6	7	4	80

6AI. From what sources do you recruit internal auditors for your department? (Check as many as apply.)

	Ins	Mach/Parts	Mining/Metals	Pap/Rub Text	Petro	Ret	Trans	Util	Health Care	Misc	1979 Total
Within the company	63.6%	76.9%	75.0%	78.9%	66.7%	68.0%	88.9%	84.6%	50.0%	70.5%	69.8%
Colleges (College recruiting)	40.9	23.1	41.7	36.8	16.7	48.0	44.4	56.4	25.0	36.1	42.7
Newspaper advertising	68.2	69.2	58.3	47.4	44.4	76.0	55.6	53.8	50.0	73.8	63.0
Other advertising	11.4	7.7	8.3	5.3	16.7	16.0	0.0	15.4	16.7	6.6	11.3
Employment agencies	72.7%	61.5%	50.0%	73.7%	61.1%	72.0%	44.4%	56.4%	33.3%	68.9%	58.1%
Sample size	44	13	12	19	18	25	9	39	12	61	497

6BI. Other (please specify)

	Ins	Mach/Parts	Mining/Metals	Pap/Rub Text	Petro	Ret	Trans	Util	Health Care	Misc	1979 Total
CPA firms	25.0%	0.0%	40.0%	0.0%	100.0%	66.6%	0.0%	33.3%	100.0%	71.5%	36.2%
Referrals	0.0	33.3	20.0	0.0	0.0	0.0	100.0	33.3	0.0	28.6	20.0
Company employment division	25.0	0.0	20.0	100.0	0.0	0.0	0.0	33.3	0.0	0.0	18.8
Institute of Internal Auditors	25.0	33.3	20.0	0.0	0.0	0.0	0.0	0.0	0.0	0.0	6.3
Executive search firms	0.0	33.3	0.0	0.0	0.0	0.0	0.0	0.0	0.0	0.0	2.5
State personnel department	0.0	0.0	0.0	0.0	0.0	0.0	0.0	0.0	0.0	0.0	2.5
Other government department	0.0	0.0	0.0	0.0	0.0	0.0	0.0	0.0	0.0	0.0	2.5
Intern programs	0.0	0.0	0.0	0.0	0.0	33.3	0.0	0.0	0.0	0.0	2.5
Civil Service Commission	0.0	0.0	0.0	0.0	0.0	0.0	0.0	0.0	0.0	0.0	1.3
Retired Military Officers Association	0.0	0.0	0.0	0.0	0.0	0.0	0.0	0.0	0.0	0.0	1.3
Farm Credit System	25.0	0.0	0.0	0.0	0.0	0.0	0.0	0.0	0.0	0.0	1.3
Technical schools	0.0	0.0	0.0	0.0	0.0	0.0	0.0	0.0	0.0	0.0	1.3
Seminars	0.0	0.0	0.0	0.0	0.0	0.0	0.0	0.0	0.0	0.0	1.3
Public service agency	0.0	0.0	0.0	0.0	0.0	0.0	0.0	0.0	0.0	0.0	1.3
Unsolicited applications	0.0%	0.0%	0.0%	0.0%	0.0%	0.0%	0.0%	0.0%	0.0%	0.0%	1.3%
Total Mentions	4	3	5	1	1	3	1	6	1	7	80

by the employer. Most companies are willing to pay these fees to secure qualified candidates on a timely basis.

Further insight as to sources for recruiting internal auditors derives from Figure 9-2. It is one of the results of a 1984 survey of over 6,500 IIA members. The survey was aimed at developing a profile of the internal auditing profession. The data reprinted in Figure 9-2 indicates that 92 percent of IIA members responding had at least one year of internal auditing.[4] This means that the most logical source for recruiting is from other companies. It also discloses that 34 percent have experience in public accounting. That means that public accounting firms continue to be a principal source of internal auditors. The figure indicates that corporate accounting offers another frequently used source, with data processing, production, tax/legal, quality control, and engineering used occasionally.

The Recruiting Process

The following steps are involved in recruiting:

1. Searching markets
2. Screening candidates
3. Interviewing candidates
4. Testing and evaluating
5. Offering the job and acknowledging acceptance
6. Following-up

Finally, timing is a relevant factor in all of the above.

Searching Markets. The nature and extent of the market search depends on the degree of involvement by recruiting firms. If such organizations are used, the employer's role is to manage its relationship with the companies so as to maximize the flow of candidates. If search firms are not used, the employer must conduct his own campaign. Techniques for the employer's own campaign are the following:

- Direct advertising
- Informal checks with associates—both inside and outside the company
- Inquiries of the IIA and other professional organizations (e.g., the AICPA)

Without outside assistance, searches can be time-consuming. It is not common for several months to lapse before positions are filled.

---

[4] Samuel L. Newman, Ph.D, CIA, *Salaries and Attitudes* (Altamonte Springs, Fla.: The Institute of Internal Auditors, 1984), p. 22. Reprinted by permission of the Institute of Internal Auditors, Inc.

FIG. 9-2
Professional Experience Reported by U.S. Internal Auditors

Field	Percentage With One Year or More Experience	Average Years of Experience
Internal auditing	92	7.1
External auditing	34	4.6
Corporate accounting	32	5.7
Data processing	12	5.9
Production	6	4.5
Tax/Legal	6	4.3
Quality control	2	3.3
Engineering	2	5.7
Other	19	5.4

Screening Candidates. Qualifications are usually evident from resumés and job applications. Both documents should be reviewed. There may be information on one that complements data on the other. Resumés, however, are the principal source of information about the candidate and should be used to screen qualifications against prescribed job requirements.

Interviewing Candidates. The interview is an important step in recruiting. It is the time when impressions will be made both by the candidate and by the recruiter. Despite its importance, the interview is often accomplished in a relatively short time span.

Experience has shown the following points are worth remembering when preparing for and conducting the interview.

- Pick a mutually convenient time. This may sometimes be after normal business hours.
- Know as much as possible about the candidate before the interview.
- Make the candidate feel at ease; avoid criticisms and lengthy discussions that are not relevant to the purpose.
- Lead the conversation, but let the candidate talk. Let him ask questions, and answer them as fully as possible.
- Ask questions that will permit the candidate to disclose his background, skill, and expertise.
- Be direct and positive, since otherwise, misunderstandings may result.
- Be honest, open, and communicative. Try to provide the candidate with the information he is seeking. Don't oversell the job or the environment.
- Respect the candidate's right to privacy. Avoid questions of a personal nature, as they could be construed as "prying."
- Offer advice if circumstances warrant.
- Cover the advantages of joining the company.

- Conclude the interview on a positive note. The candidate must not be dismissed without being told what will happen next—even if this means tactfully terminating further recruiting efforts.

A successful interview will usually enable the interviewer to evaluate the candidate according to the following:

- Appearance
- Poise
- Ability in oral expression
- Technical knowledge
- Judgment

The interviewer should keep in mind that first impressions can be misleading. Also, it is reasonable for most candidates to exhibit some nervousness and uncertainty. The conduct of the interviewer can do much to overcome this natural tendency. Because of these factors, and the brevity of the interview period, it is a good idea to have candidates interviewed by more than one person. A second or even a third interview is advisable for especially critical jobs. Invariably, the more contact there is between the interviewee and the potential employer, the greater the chance of a more accurate impression.

Testing and Evaluating. Many audit organizations supplement the interview with a short written test designed to provide further insight into the candidate's skill. These groups believe that the interview process is simply not a sufficient base on which to form an opinion about the candidate.

Others believe, in many cases, that testing is not only unnecessary, but may even be counterproductive. Unless the test is designed by experts, it may be an invalid measure of skill. Moreover, candidate uneasiness may materially affect test results. Finally, candidates for professional positions tend to resent being forced to demonstrate competence. Competence is usually evidenced by advanced degrees and CPA or CIA certificates. However, in the latter instance, the interviewer should understand that the vast majority of CIAs obtained their certification on the basis of experience, not by passing an examination.

The candidates should be evaluated against the prescribed job requirements. Most audit organizations are seeking extremely capable, highly qualified individuals. This is to be expected, since it is in the interest of the group and the company to do so, within economic limitations. Under these circumstances, the evaluator is entitled to expect candidates to demonstrate general qualities, such as:

- Clear thinking
- Prudent judgment

- Technical competence
- Professionalism

Beyond that, the evaluator should not expect specific detailed knowledge to surface. Also, he should consider whether the candidate will effectively represent the organization and whether he will "fit in." Many organizations use special forms for evidencing evaluations. However, unless the number of candidates to be evaluated is extensive, such a procedure is probably unnecessary. It is usually sufficient to record brief notes on the resumé or on the job application.

Timing. Timing is not so much a step in the process as it is a key point to keep in mind for proper management of the recruiting process. Timing is nearly as important in recruiting as the interview. Timing relates to the following:

- Length of the interview
- Length of the recruiting process
- Evaluation period
- Point at which the offer is made

If the timing of these activities or events is not reasonable, the candidate will be lost. Experience indicates that offers are usually accepted when they occur or as soon after the interview as practicable. Delays beyond two or three weeks (without frequent contact and follow-up) will usually lead the candidate to lose interest, particularly if other opportunities are in the picture.

Offering and Acknowledging Acceptance. In many companies, offering the job and acknowledging acceptance is handled by personnel departments. In others, the chief auditor or an audit manager may make the offer. If the audit department extends the proposal, it should be done only after checking references supplied by the candidate. Offers may be made in writing, in person, or over the phone. In the latter two cases, they should always be followed up in writing. All particulars should be clearly set forth in the document.

Acceptances are usually received orally. However, the department should require a follow-up acceptance in writing, by letter, or by telegram, if necessary. Such a requirement helps to terminate competition and more formally and clearly indicates a commitment.

The acceptance should be acknowledged by the chief auditor or his designee in the event the offer was extended by the personnel department. A warm and confident expression of pleasure at the candidate's decision serves to cement decisions.

Follow-Up. Usually several days or even a few weeks lapse before the new employee actually reports for work. Accordingly, it is courteous to contact the person once or twice before he reports for work to begin forming relations and to answer any remaining questions. It also helps resolve any transitional difficulties that may emerge.

Orienting New Employees. New employees must be allowed a few days in which to become oriented in their new positions. During this period, the new employee should be introduced to other members of the staff and management personnel, be exposed to company policies and procedures, audit manuals, and other reference material, be informed of administrative rules and procedures, and become familiar with the new surroundings. If practicable, it is helpful to let the new auditor review workpaper files and past records to get a sense for the department work style. This process rarely should take longer than a week.

Having become oriented, the new person can begin the planning process (see Chapter 11) for this first assignment. For the best results, the assigned supervisor or manager should work closely with the new employee during the planning efforts in this period. In that way, the new auditor will be more comfortable and will adjust more quickly. Care should be taken not to offend the new auditor's sense of professionalism or to give the appearance of lacking confidence in his ability.

Throughout the entire performance of the first assignment, the review and supervision should be a little more extensive than normal. The supervisor or manager must use his judgment as to the degree of involvement. As in planning the initial assignment, the sensitivities of the new auditor must be kept in mind.

This intensified control may be eased in subsequent assignments when it becomes clear that the new person is able to function effectively.

Performance Measurement

Definition and Purpose. Performance measurement, or simply measurement, has been described as measuring "the efficiency or effectiveness . . . in moving toward an objective. It involves the comparison with a standard of some sort. . . ."[5] Measurement of internal audit performance occurs primarily in order to determine compliance with performance standards established for the department. (See Chapter 6). However, other objectives or benefits are also involved, including the following:[6]

---

[5] James D. Willson and John B. Campbell, *Controllership: The Work of the Managerial Accountant*, 3rd ed. (New York: John Wiley & Sons, 1981), p. 9.

[6] Jerard A. Ward, "Quality Assurance Through Performance Appraisal or Vice Versa?" *The Internal Auditor*, Aug. 1982, p. 32.

- Basis for improving performance
- Improved communications
- Higher morale and lower turnover
- Less time and money spent on training

Performance measurement occurs on two levels: individual and organizational.

Effect of Subjectivity. Measuring and communicating something as subjective as individual performance is a difficult and necessarily delicate task. Audit performance is the result of personal service. The end product of the performance, usually a written report of some sort, is not readily susceptible to measurement in qualitative terms in the same sense as is a tangible or physical end product. A manufactured item, such as a car or an electric toaster, can be precisely measured against defined quality-control standards.

Tangible end products tend to perform satisfactorily as intended, if they meet the standard. But what are audits and audit reports supposed to do? The answer varies with each project. Sometimes audits provide assurance; sometimes they cause concern. Sometimes they motivate corrective action, and sometimes they don't.

Judging audit quality is not unlike judging works of art. In a sense, an audit is more an art than a science. Good auditing requires creativity and innovation on the part of the auditor—elements essential in any art form. Even in the best of circumstances, measuring audit performance can evoke resentment and hostility by the person being judged.

Measurement Techniques. The best approach in measuring performance is to adopt a systematic, rational methodology and apply it consistently. In other words, a standard measurement should be employed. The measurement effort should attempt to gauge separately each relevant component of performance. Figure 9-3 illustrates a form that can be used for this purpose. Of course, any other form that seeks to measure the components and includes the requisite information would also suffice.

Note the large space allocated for specific comments. The form recognizes the subjectivity involved and, by design, encourages supplementary comments. Yet, it also provides for rating specific qualities. Most of the evaluation categories shown in Figure 9-3 may be determined on the basis of evidence contained in the workpapers. It is essential that ratings be backed by adequate documentation. Such support is helpful in the discussion with the performing auditor. It enables the auditor to better understand what is expected of him and in what way performance was superior or deficient. Documentation to support superior performance is useful in securing merit increases and promotions for the auditor.

FIG. 9-3
Staff Evaluation Form

STAFF EVALUATION

AUDITOR	ASSIGNMENT NO (S)
ENTITY	ASSIGNMENT (S)

QUALITY OF WORK
- PLANNING
- ABILITY TO DEVISE PROPER PROGRAM OF TESTING
- DATA GATHERING (QUANTITATIVE)
- DOCUMENTATION (QUALITATIVE)
- ABILITY TO RECOGNIZE AUDIT POINTS & THEIR SIGNIFICANCE
- EVALUATION OF RESPONSE AND ADEQUATE FOLLOW-UP

COMMUNICATION
- ORAL – WITH AUDITEE
- WRITTEN – REPORT
- PROFESSIONALISM
- TECHNICAL KNOWLEDGE
- JUDGMENT
- DILIGENCE
- BUDGET PERFORMANCE

EXCELLENT – PERFORMANCE SIGNIFICANTLY EXCEEDED NORMAL EXPECTATIONS
GOOD – PERFORMANCE EXCEEDED NORMAL EXPECTATIONS
OK – MET EXPECTATIONS
FAIR – SLIGHTLY BELOW EXPECTATIONS
POOR – SUBSTANTIALLY BELOW EXPECTATIONS
N/A – NOT APPLICABLE

	START DATE	STOP DATE	HOURS
BUDGET			
ACTUAL			

COMMENTS (FOR ALL RATINGS OF EXCELLENT, FAIR OR POOR, CITE SPECIFIC CIRCUMSTANCES, OR REFERENCE TO SPECIFIC EXAMPLES IN THE WORK PAPERS TO SUBSTANTIATE THE RATING).

AUDITOR	DATE	REVIEWER	DATE

Professional Training

Another aspect of personnel management deals with professional training. Training helps assure that the entire staff attains and maintains proficiency as an auditor. The fast pace at which auditing and audit-related subjects are evolving is a widely recognized phenomenon. The following have occurred in just the past decade:

- The SEC has issued over 180 Accounting Series Releases (now embodied in its Codification of Financial Reporting Policies), causing a substantial overhaul of the form and content of financial information required to be filed.
- The FASB has issued over 60 Statements of Accounting Standards providing for significant additional accounting and disclosure requirements.
- The AICPA's ASB and its predecessor committee promulgated 60 statements on auditing procedure.
- The AICPA's Accounting Standards Division and various special committees have published Auditing and Accounting Guides for numerous industries, and Statements of Position on numerous other technical matters.
- The FCPA (1977), ERISA (1974), and several tax reform acts were passed. These are but a few of the federal laws that have had an impact on U.S. business, including the internal audit function.
- Numerous regulations by the Treasury Department and rulings by the IRS have been issued.
- An exponential increase in the application and use of technology of all types—most notably, EDP—gave birth to new products, new industries, and new markets.

Purpose and Techniques. Suffice it to say, the body of knowledge required for effective auditing is under constant and rapid change. To the extent practicable, the professional staff must continuously be kept current as to the more important relevant developments.

While each auditor is individually obligated by professional ethics to keep up-to-date, it is unreasonable to expect individual self-study efforts alone to maintain proficiency. Therefore, the chief auditor must establish and maintain an effective program to inform the staff. The techniques to do this include the five following items:

1. *Maintenance of an information distribution network.* The chief auditor must see that the staff is advised of important developments both inside and outside of the company. To do this, the chief auditor must establish a system for gathering the required data from appropriate sources. Relevant information can be gleaned from the following:
   - Daily, weekly, and monthly business publications
   - Professional literature
   - Government publications
   - Trade association publications

- CPA firm publications
- Research organization publications
- Text books

The sources of information are so varied that considerable effort and cost may be involved to keep current. It may be that only selected documents may be economically obtained.

2. *Periodic staff training meetings.* The chief auditor should hold periodic staff training meetings. Workpapers, testing, controls evaluation, I/S time management, cost-benefit analysis techniques, report writing, current developments, and miscellaneous administrative matters are examples of topics that lend themselves to effective in-house training.

3. *Outside training.* The chief auditor should make available supplemental training (at company expense) offered by the various professional associations and other external sources. There is a wide variety of topics covered in these one- to five-day seminars, conferences, and meetings. They are usually presented by individuals appropriately qualified in the subject.

4. *On-the-job training.* On-the-job training is perhaps the most effective technique. On-the-job training is the guidance and instruction given by department supervising auditors to the performing auditors during the job. Because of its informality, its value is easily overlooked. Audit management should emphasize the importance of on-the-job training to staff members who may prefer costlier and more structured training.

5. *Up-to-date audit library.* The audit function should provide an up-to-date audit library. Its contents will vary with the size of the organization and the proximity of other libraries within the company. At a minimum, a complete library of reference material on accounting, auditing, and data processing should be available.

Other Considerations. The training needs of each staff member differ. An effort must be made to identify the subjects that will provide the most benefit for each staff member. This is particularly important in choosing the right external training. Perceiving training needs may be done through careful observation, discussion with the staff member, and, if necessary, by testing.

Some subjects require timely reinforcement for everyone, even though all professional auditors are expected to be reasonably knowledgeable in them. These include such audit fundamentals as the following:

- Planning
- Interviewing
- Budgeting
- Documenting work performed
- Report writing
- Evaluating

These subjects are important from a training standpoint, not only because of their reinforcement value but also because their review keeps auditors current with the state of the art as it changes over time.

One particular source of training warrants special mention here. Over the years, the IIA has produced a number of seminars, conferences, and educational products to facilitate the job of keeping internal auditors properly trained. The IIA provides useful products because, for the most part, they are developed and presented by internal auditing professionals. As such, they tend to be practice-oriented as opposed to the theoretical. The following is a brief list of its products:

- ☐ Seminars
  - Tools and techniques for the beginning auditor
  - Skills for the new auditor-in-charge
  - Audit team-building through effective supervision
  - How to perform an operational audit
  - Current issues in internal audit management
  - Fraud detection and investigation for internal auditors
  - Effective auditing of construction activity
  - Concepts of oil and gas auditing
  - Information systems auditing—Concepts and application
  - Information systems auditing—Computer audit practices
  - Auditing computerized systems
  - Microcomputers and auditing
  - Productive uses of microcomputers in auditing
  - Auditing information processing facilities
- ☐ Conferences
  - Information systems audit and control conference
  - General audit management conference
  - Business issues and audit conference
  - Fraud: A conference on control, deterrence, and investigation
  - State-of-the-art conference
  - Contract auditing conference

Other educational products available from the IIA include video-assisted seminars and self-study courses. All of these products are described in detail in the Education Catalog prepared by the IIA annually. Copies are available by writing the IIA at P.O. Box 20099, Orlando, Florida, 32889-0003, or by calling (407) 830-7600.

Career Managing

Purpose. Hand in hand with the obligation to provide an effective program of training is the need to provide assistance in career development. While there are exceptions, the typical internal auditor in a given company is one whose career after college began in an area other than internal auditing. Also, most auditors do not expect to remain as internal auditors for the balance of their professional careers. They look forward to financial management or line management positions.

In the 1984 survey mentioned earlier in this chapter,[7] 74 percent of respondents indicated that they believe their job as an internal auditor provides an opportunity for promotion to fields outside internal auditing. Yet, as Figure 9-2 indicates, the average experience in internal auditing for the respondents is 7.1 years. The implication is that the vast majority of internal auditors expect to get into something else, but, in reality, most remain in internal auditing longer than they thought they would. In view of this, many companies have adopted career opportunities within the internal auditing organization and other opportunities outside it.

Career objectives must be balanced against the objectives of the department not only by each member, to be sure, but also by the chief auditor. The department requires knowledgeable, experienced, and dedicated staff in order to effectively perform its independent audit mission. If career objectives are overemphasized, the staff may become less independent, turnover may increase, and audit quality may deteriorate. On the other hand, if career objectives are not sufficiently recognized or considered, the staff will eventually cease to be motivated, turnover will increase, and audit quality will suffer.

Techniques. Proper career managing requires the chief auditor to:

- Stay abreast of career aspirations of the staff.
- Be informed of emerging opportunities within the company.
- Know the capabilities of each staff member.
- Develop the managerial potential of the staff through appropriate assignments and training.
- Expose the staff members to a variety of management personnel through meetings, conferences, and so on.
- Inform appropriate financial officers, management development officers, and others of the availability of internal audit staff for financial positions.
- Act as an advocate for staff members who are worthy of consideration for transferring to positions outside the department.
- Counsel staff members, as may be requested or required.

Other Considerations. Audit organizations may develop future managers for other departments or disciplines, but they cannot, and should not, be expected to be the sole source. The line organizations have an even greater responsibility for management development within their respective

---

[7] Newman, *op. cit.*, p. 53.

organizations. As a result, the career managing activities of the chief auditor must be realistic. Not all management positions—even in the financial area—will be filled with auditors.

Finally, the chief auditor should not attempt to force auditors to accept positions for which they are not qualified or in which they are not interested. If, in the judgment of the chief auditor, a particular member of the staff is not likely to advance his career in the company, the staff member should be so informed. This does not necessarily mean that the auditor must be terminated, unless there is cause for such action. However, the person should be encouraged to consider and explore other career-furthering options both within and without the company. In the authors' experience, the quality of work performed and the image of the department are enhanced when the staff members are comprised mainly of individuals whose careers are still developing (i.e., have not peaked).

MANAGEMENT OF OTHER RESOURCES

Purpose

In addition to manpower, the principal resource, there are supplemental or related other resources that require managing for effective and efficient utilization. These include cost-related resources, such as space, materials, and supplies; the services of other departments and outside groups; and expenses such as travel.

Techniques

The basic techniques used to control these resources are no different from those used by other organizations, some of which have already been discussed in detail in this and previous chapters. What remains to be covered in the context of resource management techniques are budgeting, performance measurement and reporting, and other techniques.

Budgeting. Budgeting is the long-established and widely practiced method of planning and controlling organizational expenditures. Budgeting includes the planning of staff and related costs, and the subsequent control of expenses to the end that they are maintained within planned limits. Budgeting in internal audit departments increases in importance with higher costs, and sound budgeting requires that the chief auditor, or his designee, perform the following:

1. Planning
    - Determine manpower requirements for the budget period, based on planned audit coverage.

- Estimate salary requirements and related fringe benefits.
- Analyze budget requirements for other key expense categories, such as:
  — Business conferences
  — Dues and memberships
  — Subscriptions
  — Professional services
  — Rent
  — Travel
  — Depreciation
  — Data processing
  — Miscellaneous
- Prepare the budget accordingly.

2. Control
   - Adopt those procedures that will keep expenses within the planned limits.
   - See that the expenses are kept within the limits planned.

Of course, the categories to be budgeted will vary from department to department, depending on company accounting and budgeting practices, relative costs, and responsibilities assigned. For example, some departments are not charged for space occupied; in some instances, the audit departments bear the fees of all audit services, including those of the external auditors. Other accountable categories could include report reproduction costs, telephone and telegraph charges, word processing expense, and outside non-accounting professional services (e.g., engineers).

Organizational Performance Measurement

As mentioned earlier in this chapter, performance measurement occurs on two levels: (1) individual and (2) organization. Individual performance measurement has been discussed. The objective of organizational performance measurement is to (1) monitor actual audit assignment progress against planned progress, (2) measure actual cost performance versus planned performance, and (3) monitor audit effectiveness. Put another way, the measurement of organizational performance should answer the question, Is the department doing its job? Measuring organizational performance requires not only planning and control, but also suitable records to facilitate measurement.

Measurement of cost performance against budget, and schedule performance against audit plans, is assisted by the proper systems of records and reports. Figure 9-4 compares actual and budgeted costs. Usually, this information is but a segment of a larger system. If such data are not available as part of the management information system, the audit department may need to develop and maintain it.

FIG. 9-4

Excerpt of a Performance Measurement Report

SUMMARY OF CORPORATE BUDGET & EXPENSES THROUGH JULY 31, 19XX
Responsibility: Director—Internal Audit

	Account	(1) Budget	(2) YTD Actual	(3) Indicated Final	(4) Budget Request
067	Services purchased — nonprofessional	$	$	$	$ .00
068	Meetings and other events	7,000.00	7,408.57	9,000.00	10,000.00
069	Subscriptions + books	1,500.00	1,190.42	1,600.00	1,600.00
071	Supplies	500.00	109.61	200.00	300.00
072	Franchise taxes			.00	.00
073	Taxes, licenses + permits		18.00	50.00	100.00
075	Freight, drayage + delivery				
077	Travel	108,200.00	53,500.96	93,830.00	117,000.00
078	Utilities			.00	.00
079	Residence expense			.00	.00
082	Overhead transfers from divs./subs.	3,000.00	3,302.11	4,500.00	4,000.00
083	Overhead allocation from NSP	3,000.00	1,101.63	2,500.00	3,000.00
086	Budget reduction			.00	.00
	Total	$1,318,300.00	$713,770.60	$1,288,405.00	$1,373,240.00

Figure 9-5 is an example of a report that measures actual assignment activity against the audit schedule. In order to prepare this data, it is necessary to keep a record of the assignments started and completed, as in Figure 9-6.

Information as to audit effectiveness is somewhat more difficult to come by. One measurement technique is to track the degree to which the department's recommendations have been implemented. A high ratio of acceptance ought to be above 90 percent. If the ratio is too low, it may suggest that the department is tending to be unrealistic in its proposed solutions, is not following up, or is not supported by senior management.

On the other hand, complete acceptance of all initial recommendations should not be expected. Although such a result is possible in an environment where the auditor and auditee work together diligently to implement all recommendations, it is not typical. If the ratio is too high, it may suggest that the department is getting too close to the auditees (i.e., is losing objectivity). Of course, these are only indicators that should signal the need for further investigation and, if necessary, remedial action.

Another technique used to measure audit efficiency is to periodically poll auditees for their opinions. This may be done informally during the many meetings between the internal audit department representatives and the auditees. Or, opinions may be sought in a more formal fashion, as illustrated in Figure 9-7. The questionnaire can be made more expensive if circumstances warrant, provided that it does not impose an undue burden on the auditee.

Some criticism should be expected. However, unusually harsh responses, or no responses, might suggest a need for more dialogue and inquiry to identify and resolve the causes.

Other New Techniques

Effective management of audit resources goes beyond techniques directly associated with quality and productivity. As has been shown, audit administration includes record-keeping duties, word processing, filing and retrieving data, and controlling and scheduling work.

In recent years, all of these activities have become candidates for EDP applications. For example, generalized programs exist that can assist in record-keeping requirements. Automated text processing has been a reality for several years. The trend of technical enhancements and declining cost for this equipment should make it within reach of most audit departments.

Now it is even possible to take advantage of available data processing capabilities in more innovative ways. For example, data bases may be established and maintained that contain the internal controls, systems, and procedures now present in more conventional forms. Another application could be audit reports, perhaps the creation of an automated audit report

FIG. 9-5
Activity Report Segment

TO: W.G. Henry
FROM: R.J. Stevens
SUBJECT: Third Quarter Activity

ASSIGNMENT ACTIVITY:

	Total	Plan	Prior Year
In process July 1, 19XX	42		31
Initiated	41	45–50	52
Completed	61	50–55	47
In process September 30, 19XX	24		36

COMMENTS REGARDING PERFORMANCE:

During the quarter, we emphasized completion of assignments in process. This was done to redress the imbalance in unfinished assignments noted at the end of the second quarter. As a result, our third quarter completions were the highest in history. The 61 completions reflect an almost 100% increase over the 33 completions achieved in the second quarter and even exceeded planned completions — a level which we thought would be difficult to attain.

The assignments in process at the end of September are more in line with expectations. The assignments initiated during the quarter were slightly less than plan due in part to the emphasis on completions and the loss of staff due to turnover.

On a year-to-date basis, our performance is keeping pace with our plan and is running slightly ahead of 19. . . . . A comparison of year-to-date information is as follows:

	Year-to-Date		
	19XX	19XX	19XX Plan
Projects begun	126	135	125
Projects completed	136	116	125

With respect to the age of the assignments in process at September 30, 19. . . ., all are current (less than 90 days old), except for the following:

Assignment Number	Date Started	Description
22-017	2/17/XX	Disaster planning — Corp.
22-070	6/24/XX	Cost reporting & control
22-071	6/24/XX	Data processing abends/reruns
22-072	6/24/XX	NASD computer installation
22-073	6/24/XX	Management control system — NASD
22-080	6/29/XX	NAS installation review

The Disaster Planning Project was initially intended only as a research project to determine the feasibility of performing a credible audit. It was subsequently

continued

FIG. 9-5 *(cont'd)*

> converted into an audit project without changing the assignment authorization. Its priority was not high, so we permitted the auditor to use it as a filler when gaps in scheduling occurred. The field work has been completed and a draft report has been provided to Industrial Relations for comment. It should be issued in the fourth quarter — probably in October.
>
> The other five assignments are just slightly in excess of 90 days old. The field work on all of them has been completed and reports will be issued in October and November. There are no unusual matters or events relating to these assignments which caused them to extend beyond 90 days. In each case, the auditor was asked to delay completion so that he/she might work on new projects with slightly higher priorities.

FIG. 9-6
Assignment Log

ASSIGNMENT CONTROL REGISTER

Assign. No.	Date Assigned	Assignment Title
22–121	9/17	Limited Financial Review
22–122	9/17	Limited Financial Review
22–123	9/17	Consultants/Lobbyist & Commissioned Agents
22–124	9/17	Executive Payroll
22–125	9/28	Employee Expense Report
22–126	9/29	Internal Accounting Controls
22–127	10/1	Computer Program Verification — Payroll
22–128	10/1	Sensitive Data on TSO
22–129	10/5	Limited Financial Review
22–130	10/8	Procurement Policies & Procedures
22–131	10/8	Accounts Payable
22–132	10/12	Security & Disaster/Recovery Follow-Up Review
22–133	10/12	Data Processing Installation Review
22–134	10/12	MMPC System Development Follow-Up Review
22–135	10/14	Data Base Management
22–136	10/14	Limited Financial Review
22–137	10/14	Inventory Management Audit
22–138	10/20	Internal Accounting Controls
22–139	10/22	Installation Review
22–140	10/22	Executive Expense Reports

reference file. This could be extremely useful not only in writing reports but also in researching subjects. (See Chapter 11.)

These and other automated techniques are within the grasp of some departments, but may be unattainable for others. Cost-benefit analysis will help determine the desirability of converting to automated methods. (See Chapter 16.) If the department can demonstrate that the benefits of automation greatly exceed the costs, the conversion should find little resistance from management.

The potential use of automated equipment is not the only means available to hold costs within reasonable limits. Actual costs should be reviewed in detail to see how further reductions could be made. Some examples of savings include these:

Mgr	Auditor(s)	Profit Center	Approval 10	Approval F	10-day Date	Report Date	Report Number
L	Westwood	050		x		9/30	219
L	Gathering	060			10/20		
L	Valdez	050			10/15	10/30	233
L	Jennings	050			10/19	10/30	232
L	Nellson	060		x		9/30	222
J	Gathering	080			11/20		
T	Gibson	040					
T	Gibson	040				11/17	242
J	Jennings	030			11/20		
J	Coxen	030					
T	Cuddles	040			10/13	10/27	228
T	Wilkins	040					
T	Wilkins	020					
I	Wilkins	020					
T	Inderson	050					
L	Valdez	090			10/20	10/30	234
L	Nellson	010			11/20		
J	Waller	030				11/25	245
T	Pierson	040					
L	Valdez	090					

FIG. 9-7
Questionnaire for Evaluating Audit Services

GENERAL:
1. Do you believe the frequency of audit coverage in your organization to be (select one):
   ☐ Sufficient?
   ☐ Excessive?
   ☐ Deficient?

2. Do assigned auditors perform their duties in a professional, business-like manner?
   ☐ Yes
   ☐ No

3. Do assigned auditors appear to be technically proficient?
   ☐ Yes
   ☐ No

4. Do assigned auditors appear to maintain an independent mental attitude in the conduct of their work?
   ☐ Yes
   ☐ No

FIELDWORK:
5. Is there sufficient communication prior to the start of the audit regarding audit subject, timing and general work scope?
   ☐ Yes
   ☐ No

6. Do auditors appear responsive to requests for changes in audit plans (i.e., timing change or subject change)?
   ☐ Yes
   ☐ No

7. Do auditors discuss findings and recommendations with all affected management prior to leaving the field?
   ☐ Yes
   ☐ No

REPORTS:
8. Do reports fairly portray findings and recommendations?
   ☐ Yes
   ☐ No

9. Are the auditor's conclusions reasonably derived from the facts and circumstances contained in the report?
   ☐ Yes
   ☐ No

10. Are affected members of management afforded sufficient opportunity to review draft reports?
    ☐ Yes
    ☐ No

11. Are recommendations for action sufficiently specific to be properly acted upon?
    ☐ Yes
    ☐ No

OTHER:

12. Do auditors provide useful commentary and other information to you which is not contained in the audit report?
    ☐ Yes
    ☐ No

13. Please provide us with any specific recommendation which you believe will enhance the quality of audit service to you and your organization. (Use back up sheet if necessary.)

    ....
    ....
    ....

- Plan and arrange air or other travel so as to take reasonable advantage of special discounts and excursion fares.
- Reduce out-of-town assignments to the minimum through proper planning and use of the latest techniques.
- Adopt reasonably prudent per diem policies. (Note: internal auditors should not be expected to endure inferior out-of-town conditions compared to those of other company travelers.)
- Minimize the amount of office space required. For example, it may not be necessary for each auditor to have a separate designated work area. Most auditors should be in the field the majority of the time. Hence, shared areas and equipment will reduce costs.
- Take advantage of centralized services and facilities such as reproduction, graphics, word processing, data processing, and meeting rooms.

RECORDS MANAGEMENT

Purpose

The audit function, like other organizational units, should maintain records that may have a bearing on its activities. These records are primarily for internal departmental use, but also may provide the information for activity reporting. Figure 9-8 is a list of some of the more commonly maintained internal audit records. A retention period for each record is also shown. The following discusses records management in terms of the more important records as well as record retention, with particular emphasis on workpapers.

Audit Report Follow-Up Records

Purpose. The most important products of the audit function are its reports on findings and recommendations. Small audit departments issue numerous such reports in any given year; large departments may issue hundreds. Each audit activity must devise ways to reasonably assure that the records maintained document the findings and any remedial actions that may result from reports. Such actions include the following:

- Follow-up efforts by the audit department to obtain management's response. Figure 9-9 contains a form to use for such follow-up.
- Management's response
- The audit department's evaluation of the response

Techniques. One way to effectively document corrective actions is to devise and maintain a report follow-up file. This file consists of a folder or pouch for each official (original) version of the report and related documents. The contents of each numerically arranged folder include, in addition to the report, management's response, the auditor's evaluation of this response, and any other pertinent correspondence. The file should document the resolution of all recommendations mentioned in the report.

The custodian of the file, usually an administrative employee of the department, should maintain a log of the official report files to help control its content and to facilitate locating specific reports. Such a log is illustrated in Figure 9-10. The log also serves as a cross-reference tool between reports and workpapers, which are usually filed in different sequences.

Related Files. The official report record file is not the only report file that might be maintained in an audit department. Reports contain information about subjects (such as accounts receivable, accounts payable, cash, and data processing) and about operational units of the company. Since auditors frequently must research both subjects and operational units in preparation for performing audits, cross-filing report files by subject and by operational units aids in research. Logs of these report files may also be maintained by the custodian to further aid the research effort. Examples of subjects into which reports might be categorized are shown in Figure 9-11.

As is the case for any valuable information, the custodian of report files must use appropriate means to make sure that the contents are not lost or misplaced.

FIG. 9-8

Retention Periods for Internal Audit Department Records

	Suggested Retention Period (years)		Suggested Retention Period (years)
Audit report files (including responses and evaluations)	3	Annual business plans of company	2
Audit report log	10	Annual budget data of company	3
Assignment log	10	Monthly budget reports	3
Work authorization file	10	Personnel folders	continuous
Audit report follow-up status log	3	Monthly financial operating reports	2
Reading (correspondence) file	3	Annual salary review data	3
Reading file log	5	Audit programs	continuous
Attendance log	3	Corporate audit manuals	continuous
Weekly time reports	2		
Weekly planning objectives	2	Corporate policy manuals	continuous
Reference library	as required	Corporate finance manual	continuous
Workpapers	3	Corporate office procedures	continuous
Management reports	2		
Consolidating financial statements	2		

Workpaper Records

Purpose. If reporting is the most important product of the auditing department, workpapers are the most important element in the production. Workpaper preparation is discussed in Chapter 14.

Not only are workpapers valuable as evidence, but also, like reports, they are an important source of relevant information. Workpapers are repeatedly referred to by the audit department and others. Accordingly, they must be retained in a manner that preserves their existence, restricts their availability, and facilitates their retrieval.

Techniques. A practical way of retaining workpapers is to file them by the work authorization numbers assigned during project initiation. Custody of the workpapers should be vested in a specifically designated person or persons. In larger audit organizations, this is usually an administrative employee or group.

FIG. 9-9
Postaudit Report Follow-Up Form

INTERNAL AUDIT REPORT FOLLOWUP			FOLLOWUP DATES	
(PREPARE ONE FOR EACH SOURCE OF REPLY)				
REPORT NO.		REPLY DUE FROM		ORGN NO.
REPORT DATE	ENTITY	FOR RECOMMENDATION NOS.		
REPORT TITLE				

PART I — FOLLOWUP REQUESTS

DATE	INDIVIDUAL CONTACTED	EXPLANATION RECEIVED	REVISED DUE DATE	DIR. APPVL.

PART II — REPLY RECEIVED RECORD

REPLY FOR RECOMMENDATION NOS.	DATE RECEIVED	EVALUATION FORM		DUE DATE FOR EVALUATION		DIR. APPVL.
		SENT TO	DATE	ORIGINAL	REVISIONS	

MANAGING HUMAN & OTHER RESOURCES　9-31

FIG. 9-10
Report Log

REPORT LOG

Report No.	Report Date	Report Title	Auditors	Assign. No.
221	9/30	Indicated Final Costs and Margin for Job 2394	Evans	22-105
222	9/30	Travel and Business Expense — Corporate	Smith	22-125
223	9/30	Travel and Business Expense — Northern Division	Jones	22-096
224	9/30	Review of Eastern Regional Office	White	22-101
225	9/30	Programming Standards	Johnson	22-042
226	10/21	Production Systems Documentation	Stone	22-085
227	10/22	Management Information Systems — Western Division	Wilson	22-080
228	10/27	Accounts Payable — Manufacturing Division	Becker	22-131
229	10/27	Accounts Payable — Services Division	Thompson	22-089
230	10/28	Business Systems — Corporate	Thompson	22-072
231	10/28	Management Control Systems Development	Franklin	22-073
232	10/30	Corporate Executive Payroll	Smith	22-124
233	10/30	Compliance With Policies Relative to Consultants and Lobbyists at the Corporate Office	White	22-123
234	10/30	Limited Financial Review — Manufacturing Division	Evans	22-136
235	10/30	Limited Financial Review — Services Division	Wall	22-117
236	10/30	Control of DP Reruns	Johnson	22-071
237	10/30	Business Data Processing — Northern Division	Stone	22-090
238	10/30	Standards of Business Conduct — Southern Division	Baker	22-116
239	11/5	Corporate–Wide Disaster Planning	Wall	22-017
240	11/5	Cash Control & Management — Manufacturing Division	Wilson	22-118

FIG. 9-11

Categories for Filing Audit Reports

AUDIT REPORT SUBJECTS

- Accounts payable
- Accounts receivable
- Bidding & estimating
- Business plans
- Capital assets
- Cash management
- Cash receipts & disbursements
- Consultants & agents
- Contracts & pricing
- Contributions, aid to higher education
- Cost systems
- Data processing functions
- Depreciation procedures
- Developing systems
- Disaster planning
- Executive expense reports
- Eastern regional office
- Factory overhead
- Facilities management
- Financial reporting & control
- Indicated final cost projections
- Indirect cost transactions
- Indirect payroll transactions
- Installation review
- Insurance
- Internal accounting controls
- Inventory management
- Limited financial reviews
- Material accounting
- Medical services
- NDP functions
- Overhead
- Payroll
- Procurement
- Records retention
- Retirement & savings plan
- Risk reporting
- Security
- Special reviews

Access to workpapers must be restricted to the audit staff and others authorized by the chief auditor or his designee. Typically, other interested parties include members of the audit committee, the company's outside auditors, other internal auditors within the company, in-house legal counsel, and, at times, senior members of financial management or operating management.

The internal audit function should resist efforts to access the department's workpapers by those who are unable to give a convincing reason to review them. The internal audit department has a broad spectrum of interests that essentially matches that of management. As a result, the workpapers contain confidential information. Moreover, there are also administrative reasons for carefully controlled access, such as minimizing the chances of losing or misplacing critical workpapers.

To reasonably assure restricted access, workpapers must be kept in a secure area. Storage facilities should be selected with due consideration to such risks as fire and theft. Lockable file cabinets are the most commonly used, although, in large organizations, vaults may be used. Workpapers on sensitive subjects may be secured in a separate area, such as in the office of the chief auditor or, in rare cases, in the office of the company's legal counsel.

The chief auditor or his designee should designate for the custodian those individuals who are authorized. The custodian should establish means to allow prompt access by authorized personnel. If the physical location of the department sufficiently isolates the audit function from other company activities, the honor system is probably adequate for this purpose. A more controlled approach involves the use of "out cards" inserted into the files. The cards identify the workpapers taken out of the files and bear the name of the person who has them. Very large audit organizations often have elaborate control schemes established, similar to those found in record centers or in libraries.

Records Retention

Purpose. A critical aspect of records management is deciding on their retention period. Records of any type should be preserved and retained only so long as they are useful in the operation of the business, or as long as they comply with all applicable laws and regulations or company policies.

Generally speaking, internal audit records should not be essential to the operation of the business. Any situation in which an audit department's record-keeping activities are found to be essential raises serious questions about the sufficiency of internal controls in that business or the adequacy of the function involved.

Opinion Regarding Retention. How long, then, should internal audit records be retained? The simple answer is that records should be retained only so long as they are useful. Deciding when records are no longer useful is largely a matter of judgment. Many internal audit practitioners are of the opinion that the key records, such as reports and workpapers, should be retained for long periods—up to 10 years or more. They believe that these records contain information that may be useful to future practitioners or to management.

Experience indicates that it is extremely rare when such records are of any practical value after a two- to three-year period. Moreover, many lawyers believe that internal audit reports and workpapers may contain information that, on subpoena, could aid causes of action by others against the company. They believe that the potential for adverse consequences outweighs the potential for beneficial advantage.

Effect of IRS Efforts. In recent years, governmental agencies, such as the IRS and the Defense Contract Audit Agency (DCAA) have become increasingly interested in the records of internal and external auditors.

According to Schnee and Taylor:[8]

---

[8] Edward J. Schnee and Martin E. Taylor, "IRS Access to Accountants' Work Papers—The Rules May Be Changing," *Journal of Accounting, Auditing and Finance*, Fall 1981, pp. 26–27.

The rulings in a number of recent court cases appear to be redefining the ground rules for the IRS's access to accountant's work papers. Cases that appear to have an important bearing on this are, inter alia, *United States v. First Chicago* (1978), *United States v. Noall* (1978), *United States v. Arthur Andersen & Co.* (1979), *United States v. Riley* (1979), and *United States v. Arthur Young & Co.* (1980).

In two of the cited cases (*First Chicago* and *Noall*), the issue was access to internal audit reports and workpapers. In these cases, the courts seem to indicate that the records are relevant if they throw light on the correctness of the tax return.[9]

While the vast majority of internal audit records would throw little light on tax return data, it is unwise to assume that they would be entirely void of information useful to the IRS. While the issue has more serious consequences for external auditors, it can have negative results for internal auditors as well. Internal auditors have become increasingly involved in auditing compliance with policies on business conduct, activities of commission agents and consultants used by the company, and other sensitive matters. Under the circumstances, internal audit inquiries into these areas could become more difficult because of management concerns over who might gain access to audit workpapers.

Since recent court decisions, the IRS has amended its manual of instructions to field agents. Examiners must obtain approval from the district chief before requesting access to tax accrual workpapers. However, the question of who has access to internal audit workpapers is still unresolved.

The DOD Access Offensive

In recent times, the DOD has increased demands for various records of contractors, including internal auditing reports and workpapers. These demands are but one aspect of a large campaign on the part of the DOD to eliminate waste, fraud, and abuse in the procurement of weapons systems, supplies, and services.

The demands originated in 1984 with the Inspector General (IG) of the DOD. Later, they extended to the DCAA, also an audit arm of the DOD (see Chapter 1). A discussion of the relevant events and their impact follows.

The authority of the IGs is extensive and is greater than that of the DCAA. In addition to having access to all records, reports, audits, and other material available to the applicable establishment, IGs, among other things, may:

- Conduct their own investigations.
- Request assistance of other federal, state, or local government agency or unit thereof.

---

[9] *Ibid.*, p. 22.

- Subpoena from sources other than federal agencies all forms of information and documents necessary in the performance of their functions.

The power to subpoena is particularly strong and is causing some controversy. One example is the action by Westinghouse Electric Corp. Here, the IG of the DOD subpoenaed internal audit reports and working papers of Westinghouse's internal audit function. This action was taken after Westinghouse refused to allow the DCAA access to them. Westinghouse further refused to honor the subpoena of the IG. Thereafter, the Justice Department brought suit in federal court against Westinghouse and asked the court to order Westinghouse to honor the subpoena.

Westinghouse, in its brief, asserted that the government improperly pressured it to release the documents. The company further stated that the subpoenaed reports and working papers represent its "innermost workings" and contended that the subpoena is so sweeping that it would require providing every planning and decision document.

The government maintained that the documents were relevant to determine the effectiveness of Westinghouse's methods for policing against fraud and abuse.

In mid-August 1985, the federal judge hearing the case in Pennsylvania ruled in favor of the government. Judge Louis Rosenberg's decision established that the IG of the DOD was entitled to see internal audits and other sensitive documents. He ordered Westinghouse to release the records. The order was stayed, however, pending the outcome of a Westinghouse appeal. On April 14, 1986, the Court of Appeals for the Third Circuit affirmed Judge Rosenberg's decision.

Providing unrestricted access to internal audit records could have a profound impact on the relationship between management and the internal audit function. It also could have a significant impact on the utility of internal auditing. In fact, the issue is so important that the IIA filed its first friend-of-the-court briefing in this case. In the brief, the IIA opposed the government's court action primarily because it believed that permitting the DCAA unrestricted access to internal audit reports and related records is not in the interest of the United States, contractor companies, or internal audit functions. The following excerpt of that brief establishes the IIA's point of view:

> To a large degree, management support for the internal audit process is based on the premise that internal auditing exists to serve management and that internal audit reports and working papers will remain confidential. If that premise were to become invalid, management would have to act to reduce the risks of having internal auditing work reviewed by outsiders and potentially used against the interests of the company. Confidentiality would clearly be lost if the DCAA were to be given unrestricted access, via the power of the IG's subpoena, to virtually any and all internal audit reports and related records.
>
> If the confidential element of internal auditing were removed, management might take actions which would reduce the effectiveness of internal auditing. Such actions might include discouraging the auditor's frankness or placing limits on

the scope of the auditor's work. It is conceivable that some management would opt for disbanding the internal audit function entirely. Clearly, actions in this range would decrease the effectiveness of internal auditing as a deterrent to waste, fraud and abuse.

If the effectiveness of internal auditing as a deterrent were reduced or eliminated, waste, fraud and abuse would increase (unless some other effective deterrent were substituted). This is hardly in anyone's interest.

It would seem, therefore, that the long-term interests of the government, as well as those of the contracting companies and internal auditing functions, are to be better served by avoiding actions that might damage or destroy an effective force working, among other things, to deter waste, fraud and abuse.

There is another extremely important dimension to this line of thought. Permitting unrestricted access by the DCAA to internal audit reports and related records introduces the possibility that these very private and sometimes sensitive files may, at times, mislead the DCAA. To understand how that might happen, it is necessary to explain the concept of "audit risk" and to understand the unique relationship that exists between the internal auditing function and the management it serves.

Audit risk is present in every audit undertaking. There are two aspects to audit risk. One aspect is that the work may fail to lead to the discovery of errors, omissions or other deviations even though such items are present. The other aspect is that the auditor may mistakenly claim that such items exist when, in reality, they do not.

Normally, by being competent and through exercising due professional care, internal auditors significantly reduce the incidence of audit failures. Due professional care entails the careful and complete gathering of documentary evidence to support reported findings, recommendations and conclusions. This is required by professional standards and is an approach common to all types of auditing.

Since the internal auditor is often encouraged by management to be "aggressive," audit reports and supporting audit working papers may contain, in addition to incontrovertible evidence, written narratives, recorded impressions, observations, and accounts of pertinent statements made to the auditor in interviews and meetings regarding assertions and representations by management.

Much of this commentary may be highly subjective and unsubstantiated. Few internal auditors prepare these records from the standpoint that the records may be studied by third parties and possibly used for purposes contrary to the interests of the company. Rather, internal auditors dutifully prepare their working papers in accordance with professional standards with the expectation that such papers will remain confidential.

Because auditors scrupulously adhere to high standards and perform assigned duties competently, the exposure to audit failure is most often kept to a tolerable minimum. The exposure cannot be completely eliminated, however, and its occurrence could easily mislead third parties who were not meant to have access to the internal audit work.

The effects of audit risk are controlled internally in two ways. First, the work of internal auditors is kept confidential. The second way is through the unique continuing relationship between the internal auditor and management. Audit findings, conclusions, and informal observations are commonly discussed with management and management already has the advantage of direct knowledge of both

> the operations under review and the internal auditors. Management, accordingly, is in a good position to assess the relative merits of the informal audit observations.
>
> The DCAA is not in any position similar to that of management and therefore could easily be misled by commentary in the audit reports and working papers.
>
> A related difficulty is that internal audit reports and related working papers often contain statements of a general nature or statements that require some familiarity with the specific subject matter in order to be understood in the proper context. Internal audit reports normally are written with the knowledge that the readership will be limited and that the readers—the affected management—are cognizant of the underlying circumstances. Such level of awareness cannot be expected of the DCAA to the same degree. As a result, audit information is susceptible to misinterpretation. With regard to access to internal audit working papers by a third party such as DCAA, the chances of drawing misleading inferences from audit working papers is even greater because such working papers contain a good deal of commentary of a subjective nature.
>
> The possible ramifications arising from misinterpretations of sensitive or controversial information taken from internal audit reports or their supporting records would clearly not be in the interests of the government or contractors.

In reaching a judgment in the *Westinghouse* case, Judge Rosenberg considered not only the position of the IIA, but also that of the U.S. Chamber of Commerce, which had also filed a brief in support of Westinghouse. The judge also considered the arguments of Westinghouse, which were numerous. Pertinent excerpts of his judgment follow.

> The government paid the respondent $554,000 in 1983 for its share of respondent's internal audit activities, as a proportion of the total auditing cost. This cost was paid by the government, although the DOD has not examined the actual reports and does not know what they actually purchased by that money—a *quid pro nihil*. Thus, as the IG stated, "... I had suspicion that there's something there that they don't want us to have" and "I want to see what the Government is getting for its money." (Document 18, page 144 and Sherick Affidavit, page 5).
>
> While it may be that the IG should not have used the DCAA because the DCAA had reasons of its own for getting information about the internal audit reports, it was nevertheless a discretionary right which Congress had given him, lacking his own personnel with which to act. He acted, he said, with the DCAA auditors because they were familiar with the subject matter, they were close to the source of the records, and they had long experience in reporting back to him on problems that they have found. Under such circumstances, it is not for this court to forbid the IG from using DCAA employees and to direct him to use some other agency employees or hire special employees for that purpose.
>
> Because the respondent has been brought into this action for enforcement of a civil writ, it must be understood that that does not presume any culpability on the part of the respondent. The respondent properly resorts to due process in this judicial proceeding to test its theories as to the correctness or the incorrectness of the IG's authority to issue the subpoena. Neither do I infer, in any way, any wrongdoing on the part of the respondent, because it is presently before

me or the public officials who are before me, when I state that the public has an irrefutable and absolute right to demand: that its money payments be returned to it in full money value of whatever kind for which it bargains; that its own officials and employees and those with whom it deals be honest and honorable; and, that its legislators provide determined and independent processes and functionaries to eliminate or at least to substantially lessen the infiltration of fraud and waste in its publicly budgeted spending.

Thus, when the Congress endows administrative agents and agencies with means and methods for improving the public welfare and provides resort for enforcement by court procedure, it becomes incumbent upon the judiciary to enforce the specific process in aid of the public's right to a remedy in accordance with law as it pertains to the facts.

To do otherwise would reinstate the public dilemma as it was as of the time when the Senators, concerned as they were, complained at the Hearing, Part 2, before the Committee on Governmental Affairs, on March 25, 1982, that if an IG for the DOD were created without strength and independence, it would be only for a "cosmetic" purpose. The Senators made it perfectly plain at the hearing and in the amending Act of 1982 that they intended and wanted an independent IG who would have power and purpose to prevent and detect fraud, abuse and waste in the government programs.

In view of the attitude of the Senators as translated into clear, determined words by Congress in the 1982 Amendment, and lacking any illegality or impropriety on the part of the IG in issuing the subpoena, and being abundantly obvious from the evidence as a whole of the circumstances which required the issuance of a subpoena within the discretion of the IG, it is not for this court to substitute its judgment for that of the IG.

With the assurance of the IG that the matter will be treated with professional confidence, and that only such matters will be reported as the law requires, I find that it is as much as the respondent may hope for.

We must remember that it is the auditing of the internal operations for which government money was spent and with which government resources, equipment and personnel have and are likely being used. Accordingly, the objections of the respondent will be denied, and the Petition for Enforcement of Administrative Subpoena by the Government will be enforced.

Recently, an excellent article providing insight and perspective into the access issue appeared in the *Federal Contracts Report*. The article, by Clarence T. Kipps, Jr., Jay L. Carlson, and Alan C. Brown, calls for defense contractors to examine the extent to which they will produce sensitive internal documents, their options if they refuse to do so, and the steps that can be taken prospectively to prevent disclosure of the documents. A major portion of this article is reprinted in Figure 9-12.[10] The article was written

(continued on page 9-55)

---

[10] Clarence T. Kipps, Jr., Jay L. Carlson, and Alan C. Brown, "Confronting the DoD 'Access to Records' Offensive," *Federal Contracts Report* (U.S.A.: The Bureau of National Affairs, 1985), pp. 1025–1035. Reprinted by permission of the Bureau of National Affairs, Inc., Washington, D.C.

FIG. 9-12

Scope of the Government's Right to Contractor's Records

Congress frequently uses expansive language in providing investigative authority to administrative agencies. Nonetheless, in scrutinizing an agency's demand for corporate records, the courts require, at a minimum, a showing that the inquiry is within the agency's authority, that the information sought is relevant to some legitimate investigative purpose and that the demand is no broader than necessary to achieve that purpose.[1]

Each request by an agency for corporate records must be considered in light of the particular function assigned to that agency by Congress. For example, in *U.S. v. Richards*,[2] the Fourth Circuit limited requests made by the Internal Revenue Service in an investigation of illegal foreign payments. Had a tax deduction been claimed for the payments, the information would have been relevant to a legitimate tax investigation. To the extent the information sought was unrelated to the company's tax liability, however, the summons would "obviously exceed the scope of authority granted the Service."

Similarly, in *CAB v. Frontier Airlines, Inc.*[3] the court rejected an agency's demand for *all* board of directors' minutes for a one-year period. Although the parties agreed that the specific minutes relating to matters which were relevant to a legitimate CAB inquiry should be produced, the court refused to allow plenary inspection by the government.[4]

What is "reasonably relevant" depends on the purpose and nature of the investigation undertaken by the agency.[5] Consequently, courts also have required that an agency subpoena or order disclose the purpose of the underlying investigation so that the relevance of the requested documents can be determined.[6]

Contractors are not powerless to prevent unwarranted intrusions into their affairs. Established legal principles delineate the scope of administrative investigative powers, and the courts will intercede when agencies exceed their authority or fail to establish that document requests are reasonably relevant to a lawful investigative purpose. Any request by the General Accounting Office, the Defense Contract Audit Agency, or the DOD Inspector General must be authorized by a specific statute or contract clause, and these provisions define and limit the purposes for which records may be sought. Requests for "all" board minutes, internal audit reports, or other noncost records simply do not meet those requirements.

In scrutinizing requests for records, it is also critical to recognize that audits which appear routine can quickly become criminal investigations, often without the contractor's knowledge. Material supplied to GAO, DCAA, or the IG in response to

---

[1] See, e.g., See v. City of Seattle, 387 U.S. 541, 544 (1967); U.S. v. Powell, 379 U.S. 48, 57-58 (1964); U.S. v. Morton Salt Co., 338 U.S. 632, 642-43 (1950); Oklahoma Press Publishing Co. v. Walling, 327 U.S. 186, 209 (1946).

[2] 631 F.2d 341 (CA4 1980).

[3] 686 F.2d 854, 859-60 (CA10 1982) (en banc).

[4] See also Burlington Northern, Inc. v. ICC, 462 F.2d 280, 287 (DC DC) cert. denied, 490 U.S. 891 (1972).

[5] Montship Lines, Ltd. v. Federal Maritime Board, 295 F.2d 147, 154 (CADC 1961).

[6] CAB v. United Airlines, Inc., 542 F.2d 394 (CA7 1976); Sunshine Gas Co. v. DOE, 524 F.Supp. 834 (DC NTex. 1981).

(continued)

FIG. 9-12 *(cont'd)*

a request or subpoena for documents may then be used by the Department of Justice in a criminal prosecution.[7]

DCAA's Audit Rights

DCAA does not possess subpoena power.[8] Its authority to audit contractors' records is derived solely from the statutes and regulations authorizing the examination of records by the Secretary of Defense or the contracting officer. The principal provision is paragraph (a) of the standard audit clause, FAR § 52.215-2, which entitles the contracting officer to "examine and audit," "books, records, documents, and other evidence and accounting procedures and practices, *sufficient to reflect properly all costs* claimed to have been incurred or anticipated to be incurred in performing this contract." (Emphasis added).[9] On its face, the sole authorized purpose for an audit under this paragraph is *a review of costs*.

Paragraph (b) of the clause is even more narrowly drawn and implements the access to records provision of the Truth in Negotiations Act (10 U.S.C. § 2306(f)). If cost or pricing data are required to be submitted, the statute authorizes the government to examine the contractor's books and records "for the purpose of evaluating the accuracy, completeness, and currency of cost or pricing data required to be submitted. . ."[10]

Similarly, if the contract requires the preparation of cost, funding, or performance reports, paragraph (c) of the audit clause entitles DOD to audit materials "for the purpose of evaluating" the reported data and the contractor's procedures for generating the reports.

Lastly, the standard Cost Accounting Standards clause, FAR § 52.230-3(c), authorizes DOD and GAO to examine the contractor's records "relating to compliance" with Cost Accounting Standards.

Evaluating Requests By DCAA. The two questions to ask when evaluating any DCAA request for records are (i) whether the audit is for a legitimate purpose authorized by one of the audit provisions of the contract, and (ii) if so, whether the materials requested are relevant to that purpose.

---

[7] See, e.g., Pickel v. U.S., 746 F.2d 176, 183–85 (CA3 1984); U.S. v. Merit Petroleum, Inc., 731 F.2d 901, 905 (TECA 1984); SEC v. Dresser Industries, 628 F.2d 1368 (DC DC), cert. denied, 449 U.S. 993 (1980); U.S. v. Art Metal-U.S.A., Inc., 484 F. Supp. 884, 886–87 (DC NJ 1980).

[8] Provisions that would give DCAA authority to subpoena records are included in the Senate version of the fiscal 1986 defense authorization and in HR 2397, approved by the House Armed Services Committee (43 FCR 968).

[9] This paragraph of the clause also implements 10 U.S.C. § 2313(a), which entitles the military departments and NASA to "inspect the plant and audit the books and records" of contractors performing cost type contracts and their subcontractors.

[10] Cost or pricing data are submitted on SF 1411. The instructions to this form entitle the contracting officer to examine *before award* the "supporting data" to "permit adequate evaluation of the proposed price." See Table 15-2, following FAR § 15.804-6. In addition, a clause equivalent to § 52.215-2(b) is applicable to formally advertised contracts. FAR § 52.214-26.

An increasingly common request which fails to meet these tests is DCAA's effort to obtain internal audit reports.[11] DCAA contends that access to audit reports and work papers is necessary to verify the accuracy of the costs of maintaining the internal audit function which are allocated to DOD contracts. The fallacy of this argument stems from a failure to recognize the obvious difference between auditing the *cost* of that function and reviewing the quality of the auditors' work product. DCAA's responsibility under the audit clause to examine records "sufficient to reflect properly all [such] costs" charged to DOD could be satisfied by examining the records reflecting the salary, travel, and office expenses incurred by the internal audit staff. DCAA's demand for audit reports and work papers is simply unrelated to the legitimacy of the costs incurred in preparing the reports and cannot be justified on that basis.

A second rationale offered by DCAA for seeking internal audit reports is its self-proclaimed "operational audit" mission. DCAAM ¶ 5-102(b). By DCAA's definition, an "operational audit" is not directed at costs, but at management efficiency. Since no audit clause authorizes this exercise, DCAA's attempts to rely on generally accepted auditing standards and, in particular, upon the AICPA's Professional Standards, Statements on Field Work. DCAA claims that the applicability of the AICPA standards has been recognized in four cases: *Grumman Aircraft Co.*[12], *Hayes International Corp.*[13], *American Business Systems*[14] and, *SCM v. United States.*[15]

However, none of these decisions eliminates the need for DCAA to establish a legitimate purpose for its audit under one of the audit provisions of the contract. Each merely supports DCAA's undisputed right to audit the costs charged to DOD contracts. Nor did these decisions hold that the audit clause constitutes a wholesale incorporation of the standards of the AICPA. The only case addressing those standards, *SCM*, concerned whether the audit function encompassed the right to remove information otherwise in the auditor's possession—not what information he was entitled to see.

Furthermore, the AICPA standards were established for use in conducting financial audits of companies subject to federal securities laws and are ill-suited to the narrow audits of contract costs which DCAA is entitled to conduct. In sharp contrast to the role of DCAA, financial auditors for public reporting purposes must examine management judgments, such as sufficiency of reserves, legal and tax positions, and projections of future performance. The function of DCAA, on the other hand, is to review the accuracy of the costs charged to the government—it has no role in reviewing the judgment or efficacy of management. Although DCAA is authorized to audit contractors' "accounting procedures and practices" to the extent necessary to assure that costs are properly charged, basic accounting

---

[11] Although this article focuses only upon access to documentary evidence, another area of recent controversy has been DCAA's attempts to conduct floor checks and employee interviews. See DCAA Contract Audit Manual ¶ 6-408.3. The Audit Clause entitles DCAA to review existing records and to examine the contractor's plant; it does not suggest any right to interrogate individual employees. The distinction between records and oral testimony is substantial, as recognized in U.S. v. Iannone, 610 F.2d 943 (CADC 1979) In *Iannone*, the court held that the broader subpoena power of the Department of Energy IG is limited to documentary evidence and does not include the power to compel testimony. As recognized in *Iannone*, had Congress intended to authorize the agency to compel testimony, it would have specified that power in the statute.

[12] ASBCA No. 10309, 66-2 BCA ¶ 5846.

[13] ASBCA No. 18447, 75-1 BCA ¶ 11,076.

[14] GSBCA No. 5140, 5141, 80-2 BCA ¶ 14,461.

[15] 645 F.2d 893 (Ct.Cl. 1981).

(continued)

FIG. 9-12 *(cont'd)*

records, not special internal audit reports, provide what is "sufficient to reflect properly all costs claimed to have been incurred or anticipated to be incurred in performing [a] contract." DCAA, in fact, routinely audits contractors' timekeeping, travel expense, and materials inventory systems in order to evaluate whether they result in proper recordation of costs. The audit clause does not, however, authorize far-ranging access to the company's internal analysis of its accounting procedures.

In short, DCAA's demands for internal audits fail to meet two critical access to records tests. First, review of "management efficiency" is not a legitimate purpose for a DCAA audit pursuant to the audit clauses and statutes. DCAA's function is only to audit contract costs and the procedures by which such costs are charged to government contracts. Second, internal audit reports are not material to any legitimate purpoce of DCAA, since they are irrelevant to a determination of contract costs.

Challenging DCAA demands for records. Refusal to comply with an administrative subpoena usually will be met with an enforcement action by the government in U.S. district court. Since DCAA has no subpoena authority, however, it has begun instead to suspend contract payments in order to obtain compliance with its document demands. If a DCAA auditor is not satisfied that sufficient documentation has been produced, he may issue a Form 1 "Notice of Contract Costs Suspended and/or Disapproved" and suspend payment of costs to a contractor under cost reimbursement or time-and-materials contracts. (FAR § 42.803(b)(2)). The Form 1 may be issued by an auditor without obtaining the approval of the contracting officer.[16]

This policy places the contractor on the horns of a dilemma—it can capitulate and surrender sensitive internal reports or else refuse to do so and face the suspension or disapproval of costs. While the contractor may file a claim pursuant to the Contract Disputes Act (FAR § 42.803(b)(3)(ii)), it must then await a contracting officer's decision and endure the delay inherent in resolving a dispute before the board or the Claims Court.[17] The inability to obtain injunctive or declaratory relief in these forums means that the contractor will likely be deprived of the payments in dispute throughout the period of litigation.[18]

Alternatively, there are substantial grounds for challenging the withholding of payment through suit in district court. This would provide a more expeditious resolution of the controversy as well as permit immediate injunctive relief. Under the doctrine of *Warner v. Cox*,[19] and its progeny, however, contractors face several obstacles.

---

[16] The use of the Form 1 as a basis for refusing to pay the costs to which the requested documents relate arguably is justified by DCAA's supposed inability, in the absence of the records, to verify the costs for which payment is sought. The Form 1, however, has also been used retroactively to disapprove costs previously paid, and the amounts have been set off against current invoices. The use of a Form 1 as justification to recover funds by way of setoff plainly contravenes § 6 of the Contract Disputes Act, 41 U.S.C. § 605(a), which requires that "all claims by the government against a contractor relating to a contract shall be the subject of a decision by the contracting officer." Such setoffs also contravene the Debt Collection Act of 1982. See DMJM/Norman Engineering Co., ASBCA No. 28154, 41 FCR 631, 658.

[17] The average time on docket for all ASBCA appeals disposed of during 1984 was 450 days. See ASBCA Statistics on Proceedings of the Board during Fiscal 1984. 42 FCR 846, 849.

[18] The Claims Court's authority to grant equitable relief is limited to preaward contract cases. See U.S. v. King, 395 U.S. 1 (1949); B.K. Instrument, Inc. v. U.S., 715 F.2d 713, 727 (CA2 1983).

[19] 487 F.2d 1301 (CA5 1974).

In *Warner,* the Fifth Circuit characterized a suit to enjoin the government's refusal to execute a deferred repayment agreement for overpayments claimed by the government as an order compelling the government to pay money, for which mandatory and exclusive jurisdiction resided in the former Court of Claims under the Tucker Act.[20] The court held (i) that review under the Administrative Procedure Act was unavailable when an "adequate remedy" existed under the Tucker Act and (ii) that the APA was not a waiver of sovereign immunity in a suit seeking money damages against the government.[21]

Nonetheless, the 1976 amendments to the APA and the federal question statute have diluted the impact of *Warner,* and recent cases have recognized that actions implicating contracts can be brought in federal district court. For example, the court in *B.K. Instrument, Inc. v. U. S.*[22] found, through cancellation of the prior award, jurisdiction over an action brought by a disappointed bidder and recognized "that it would be improper to classify all claims raising contracts issues as contract actions."

Similarly, in *Megapulse, Inc. v. Lewis,*[23] in which plaintiff sought to prevent the release of proprietary data under an upcoming procurement, the court rejected the contention that "*any* case requiring *some* reference to or incorporation of a contract is necessarily *on the contract* and therefore directly within the Tucker Act." Where there are possible bases for jurisdiction independent of the Tucker Act, a close and deliberate examination is required, the court said, to determine whether "the claim so clearly presents a disguised contract action that jurisdiction over the matter is properly limited to the Court of Claims."[24]

The Ninth Circuit recently employed a similar analysis in holding that reliance on statutory rights can keep a claim from being founded solely upon a contract, thereby avoiding the Tucker Act's implied restrictions on relief.[25] Under these decisions, therefore, a suit to vindicate statutory rights and obtain nonmonetary relief may be brought in a district court despite its relation to a contract controversy.[26]

A challenge in district court should be directed primarily at DCAA's unauthorized demand for records, rather than the withholding of contract payments. It should focus on the company's property rights in the records in dispute and on DCAA's lack of authority to force production thereof. It might also be based on 5 U.S.C. § 555, which states that an agency may not require reports, make inspections, or otherwise make or enforce any investigative act or demand "except as authorized by law." This provision prohibits agencies from making investigative demands or inspections unless their legal authority stems from some independent source.[27] It

---

[20] 28 U.S.C. §§ 1346(b), 1491(a).

[21] 487 F.2d at 1304.

[22] 715 F.2d 713, 728 (CA2 1983).

[23] 672 F.2d 959, 967-68 (CADC 1982).

[24] Id. at 968. *Megapulse* has been followed in several subsequent cases. See., e.g., Tennessee ex rel. Leech v. Dole, 749 F.2d 331, 335 (CA6 1984) ("The Court of Claims does not have exclusive jurisdiction over a suit merely because it raises contract related issues."); Minnesota ex rel. Noot v. Heckler, 718 F.2d 852 (CA8 1983).

[25] North Side Lumber Co. v. Block, 753 F.2d 1482 (CA9 1985); 43 FCR 559.

[26] Recently, in McDonnell Douglas v. United States, supra, the Federal Circuit also recognized that there are exceptions to the broad language "all claims . . . relating to a contract," as defined in the Contract Disputes Act, and held that a challenge to a GAO subpoena for records could be decided by a district court despite its foundation in a contract clause. 754 F.2d at 370.

[27] Pacific-Westbound Conference v. U.S., 332 F.2d 49, 53 n.10 (CA9 1964); University of Richmond v. Bell, 543, F. Supp. 321, 331–332 (DC EVa 1982).

(continued)

FIG. 9-12 (cont'd)

can be argued that DCAA, in demanding records which are beyond its authority, has violated this provision.[28]

In sum, the consequences of doing battle with DCAA can be significant. The potential for cost disallowances and suspensions, and the delay inherent in the disputes resolution process, create a substantial disincentive to an assertion of legitimate privacy interests. Although the availability of jurisdiction in the district courts is untested in this context, it may provide the most satisfactory solution to an otherwise difficult problem.[29]

Inspector General Authorities

In early 1984, DCAA requested access to Westinghouse Electric Corporation's internal audit reports. When Westinghouse refused to comply, the Defense IG, at the request of DCAA, issued a subpoena for the materials. The validity of that subpoena is now being litigated in the U.S. district court in Pittsburgh.[30]

The *Westinghouse* litigation and other recent developments present significant questions concerning the IG's subpoena authority. Principal among those questions are (i) whether the Westinghouse subpoena was issued for a legitimate, statutorily authorized purpose and (ii) what circumstances might justify issuance of an IG subpoena.

Statutory purpose. In *Westinghouse*, the IG subpoena demands, for approximately a two-year period, all "documentary evidence pertaining to internal audits . . . for which costs have been incurred by Westinghouse Electric Corporation and any of its segments and allocated to contracts awarded by the Department of Defense." Such evidence is sought, according to the boilerplate language on the printed IG subpoena form, because it is:

> necessary in the perforfance of the responsibility of the Inspector General under the Inspector General Act to conduct and supervise audits and investigations relating to, and to promote economy, efficiency, and effectiveness in the administration of, and to prevent and detect fraud and abuse in, the programs and operations of the Department of Defense.

In seeking judicial enforcement of the subpoena, the IG, in an affidavit submitted in the district court, acknowledges that DCAA requested him to compel production

---

[28] Failure to comply with the requirements of the Debt Collection Act of 1982 might provide a separate basis for challenging in district court the use of a Form 1 to withhold or set off payments. In Spectrum Leasing Corp. v. U.S., No. 83-3075 (DC DC 1984), the district court declined, however, to exercise jurisdiction over a Debt Collection Act challenge to GSA's withholding of liquidated damages. That decision is currently on appeal to the D.C. Circuit (No. 84-5371). The district court's rationale appears to be contrary to the Ninth Circuit's decision in *North Side Lumber*, as well as to several ASBCA cases holding the Act applicable to government contracts.

[29] It is significant that in upholding administrative subpoenas from Fourth Amendment challenge, the Supreme Court has relied on the party's ability to test the reasonableness of the subpoena in court *"prior to suffering penalties for refusing to comply."* See v. City of Seattle, supra, 387 U.S. at 544 (emphasis added). See also Donovan v. Lone Steer, Inc., 464 U.S. 408 (1984). By utilizing a Form 1 to withhold substantial payments until the records are provided, DCAA has created its own "punishment" for contractors who refuse to submit to its demands. By coercing compliance in this manner, DCAA denies contractors the judicial review to which they are entitled before penalties are imposed.

[30] U.S. v. Westinghouse Electric Corp., Misc. No. 11710 (DC WPa.) (43 FCR 497).

of Westinghouse's internal audit reports, but claims that he also "considered the matter to fall within the scope of [his] authority" to conduct and supervise audits and to investigate fraud, waste, and abuse.[31] He nonetheless "elected to request that DCAA pursue the matter in [his] behalf."[32] As a result, there was no substantive change in the staffing or conduct of the existing DCAA audit, except for the issuance of the subpoena.

The government's memorandum in support of its petition to enforce the subpoena relies principally on three provisions of the Inspector General Act that authorize the IG (i) "to make such investigations and reports relating to the administration of the programs and operations of the applicable establishment as are, in the judgment of the Inspector General, necessary or desirable" (§ 6(a)(2)), (ii) to "provide policy direction for audits and investigations relating to fraud, waste, and abuse and program effectiveness" (§ 8(c)(3)), and (iii) to "investigate fraud, waste, and abuse uncovered as a result of other contract and internal audits, as the Inspector General considers appropriate" (§ 8(c)(4)).

With respect to the Defense IG's authority under § 8(c)(4), there is no evidence in the affidavits submitted by the government in the *Westinghouse* litigation to show that the IG is investigating fraud, waste, or abuse "uncovered" as a result of a DCAA audit. That provision is thus inapposite. The other two provisions cited give the IG oversight responsibilities over DCAA and other DOD audit components. The question becomes, therefore—What actions may be taken by the IG in the name of oversight?

Neither the Inspector General Act, as amended, nor its legislative history suggests that Congress intended the Defense IG to take over DCAA's functions. Quite the contrary, DCAA's independence was to be maintained and the IG was "to *oversee* effectively and *review* the work of the Defense Contract Audit Agency." (emphasis added).[33]

In recently opposing a consolidation of DCAA and the IG's office, Defense Deputy Secretary Taft emphasized that "DCAA is an independent, but essential component of the procurement process. It should be kept separate from the Inspector General's organization to allow that group to conduct independently internal audit and program performance reviews of DCAA."[34]

Taft noted that the IG's "internal audit role" was designed to determine DCAA's "compliance with DOD policy" and to set "the standards by which contract audits are conducted."[35]

And, even the IG has recognized that: "Oversight reviews are not audits but rather an evaluation of the organization's quality control policies and procedures."[36]

The IG's attempt to use his oversight role to justify the subpoena is troublesome in at least three respects. First, the IG cannot, in the name of oversight, confer powers upon DCAA that Congress had refused to provide.[37]

---

[31] Affidavit of Joseph H. Sherick, ¶ 4.

[32] Id. at ¶ 0.

[33] Conf. Rep. No. 749, 97th Cong., 2d Sess. 176–77 (1982).

[34] [Management of the Department of Defense, Hearings Before the Committee on Government Affairs, United States Senate, 98th Cong., 2d Sess., Part 7, at 119 (DOD Management Hearings).]

[35] Id. at 120.

[36] Id. at 77–78.

[37] U.S. v. Iannone, 610 F.2d 943, 946 (CADC 1979). "[I]f Congress had intended to grant such power to [DCAA], it would have done so in specific language."

(continued)

FIG. 9-12 *(cont'd)*

Second, the Act and its legislative history plainly reject a use of subpoena power by the IG on DCAA's behalf. The Senate Committee Report specifically states: "The use of the subpoena power to obtain information for another agency component which does not have such power would clearly be improper."[38]
In addition, Section 6(a)(4), the Act provides that the IG subpoena power exists *only* to require the production of documents and information "necessary in the performance of the functions assigned by this act."

The IG cannot claim that DCAA's audit function was assigned to his office. Unlike other agencies covered by the IG Act, all DOD audit and investigative units were not consolidated into a single IG office. Rather, the routine contract audit function remains exclusively with DCAA, which continued as a separate, independent "agency component" with no subpoena power of its own. Thus, to the extent the subpoena is designed to carry out DCAA's audit function, it is not "necessary in the performance of the functions" assigned to the IG and is being improperly used on behalf of an "agency component" lacking subpoena power.

Third, if his function is to conduct internal audits and program performance reviews of DCAA, the IG's proper role is to evaluate the audits conducted by DCAA and to suggest changes where appropriate. Yet, insofar as DCAA's access to contractors' records is concerned, the IG has already prepared an extensive oversight report.[39] In addition, DCAA has already sought to obtain the Westinghouse internal audit reports. Under the circumstances, it is difficult to see what further oversight action by the IG is necessary, or why the Westinghouse subpoena is necessary to the IG's functions.

Circumstances that might justify a subpoena. In the area of detection and prevention of fraud, the functions generally assigned to Inspectors General are quite broad in scope. (See, e.g., § 4(a)(1), (a)(3)). These provisions are consistent with the original concept of combining all agency audit investigative functions into a single IG Office under the originally enacted statute. When applied to DOD, however, they must be read in the context of the unique separation of audit and investigative functions. As already noted, the Defense IG was given authority to conduct internal audits within DOD (§ 8(c)(2)) and to provide "policy direction" for audits relating to fraud, waste, and abuse (§ 8(c)(3)), but DCAA was retained as the separate entity responsible for routine audits of contractors. This dichotomy is reinforced by § 8(c)(4), which authorizes the Defense IG to "investigate fraud, waste, and abuse *uncovered as a result of other contract and internal audits.*" (Emphasis added).

The latter provision seems to recognize that detection of fraud in DOD contracts is, in the first instance, primarily the function of DCAA and other audit entities. In other words, it was not intended that the IG would usurp those responsibilities and conduct routine audits or fishing expeditions where no prior indication of improprieties exist.

Once a legitimate fraud investigation is commenced, however, the scope of the IG's power to subpoena documents in support of that investigation is quite broad. In *U. S. v. Art Metal-U.S.A., Inc.*,[40] that power was held to encompass such noncontract-related documents as tax returns, as well as documents in the possession of third parties. In support of a bona fide fraud investigation, the IG undoubtedly could subpoena nonprivileged internal company audit or investigative reports relating to the particular impropriety under investigation.

---

[38] S. Rep. No. 1071, 95th Cong., 2d Sess. 34 (1978).
[39] See DOD Management Hearings at 524, et. seq.
[40] Supra, 484 F.Supp. at 887.

In contrast, however, a request, as in the *Westinghouse* case, for all internal audit reports prepared over a period of two years, regardless of their relevance to the suspected improprieties or even to government contracts, would not be sufficiently related to an investigation or other proper purpose and would be unauthorized.[41] This conclusion is particularly apt where the IG has provided nothing more than a conclusory, boilerplate statement that the named documents are necessary to carry out his basic statutory functions.

Thus, unless the IG is able to identify a reasonably specific investigation that his office has actually and properly undertaken, and a reasonably specific set of documents it is seeking in connection with that investigation, there may be no lawful basis for use of the subpoena power.[42]

GAO Audit Powers

By statute, most negotiated contracts must contain an access to records clause entitling the Comptroller General or his representatives "to examine any books, documents, papers, or records of the contractor, or any of his subcontractors, that directly pertain to, and involve transactions relating to, the contract or subcontract."[43]

In *Bowsher v. Merck & Co.*,[44] the Supreme Court concluded that this clause, as applied to a fixed price contract for standard commercial items, entitled GAO to "inspect the contractor's records of direct costs, but not of indirect costs."[45] The Court analyzed the purpose and intended scope of GAO's audit power and determined that the "directly pertain" language used in the statute limits the type of records which GAO can review. The clause requires "some close connection between the type of records sought and the particular contract."[46]

---

[41] See CAB v. Frontier Airlines, Inc., supra, 686 F.2d at 859–60.

[42] See id. at 859 ("The CAB should not refuse to make its demands specific and should not refuse to disclose a purpose other than the statutory enforcement authority apparent on the face of the statute.").

[43] 10 U.S.C. § 2313(b); see also 41 U.S.C. § 254(c); FAR § 52.215-1. Since 1980, the Comptroller General has had authority to subpoena a contractor's records "to which the Comptroller General has access by law or by agreement." 31 U.S.C. § 716(c)(1). Subpoenas issued pursuant to this authority are enforceable through civil proceedings in the federal district courts, which are expressly authorized to punish, as a contempt of court, a failure to obey a court order. 31 U.S.C. § 716(c)(2). In McDonnell Douglas Corp. v. United States, 754 F.2d 365 (CAFC 1985), the Court of Appeals for the Federal Circuit confirmed that controversies regarding GAO subpoenas for records are not encompassed by the Contract Disputes Act and are beyond the jurisdiction of the boards of contract appeals.

[44] 460 U.S. 824 (1983).

[45] Id. at 826. The language in the opinion indicates that the Court defined "direct costs" more broadly and "indirect costs" more narrowly than is customary in government contract usage. The court used "indirect costs" to refer to costs, such as research and development, marketing and administration, which the contractor's accounting system did not "directly attribute" to any product or contract. Id. at 830 n.11. "Direct costs," on the other hand, were considered to be those expenses (including overhead) which were "attributable to a contract or product, either directly or by some method of allocation. Id. at 840.

[46] Id. at 831-32. The Court found that "Congress did not want unrestricted 'snooping' by the Comptroller General into the business records of a private contractor." The Court also stated, however, that in the context of a cost-based contract, "the contractor is in no position to complain of the intrusiveness of GAO inspection of direct costs records." Id. at 841 n. 17.

(continued)

FIG. 9-12 *(cont'd)*

> The Supreme Court in *Bowsher* recognized that it "must balance the public interest served by full GAO investigations against the private interest in freedom from officious government intermeddling..."[47] The decision effectively limits GAO's rights to cost records, and it is doubtful whether documents such as internal audit reports or board of directors' minutes could be demonstrated to be "directly pertinent" to any contracts so as to authorize a GAO inspection.[48]
>
> **SAFEGUARDING CONFIDENTIAL DATA**
>
> It is too late when the subpoena arrives to begin worrying about protecting confidential or sensitive documents. Preventive measures are the best insurance against the eventuality that such materials will have to be made available for scrutiny by government auditors and investigators or perhaps by a grand jury. Such measures are becoming all the more important as a result of DOD's plans to expand the terms of the audit clause, and of possible legislation providing subpoena authority to DCAA.
>
> **Creation and Retention of Documents**
>
> There are many documents over which a contractor has little discretion with respect to creation and retention. Various statutes, regulations, and contract clauses require contractors to maintain specified records for designated time periods. For example, the audit clause (FAR § 52.215-2(a)) requires contractors to maintain "books, records, documents, and other evidence and accounting procedures and practices, sufficient to reflect properly all costs claimed to have been incurred or anticipated to be incurred in performing this contract."
>
> In addition, individual contracts may require a contractor to generate various cost, funding, and performance reports during contract performance. Quality control requirements in contracts may also require contractors to maintain records of inspections for designated periods of time. Finally, FAR § 4.700 describes the general policies and procedures for retention of records by contractors.
>
> But in addition to these records, there typically are vast quantities of discretionary records generated within a contractor's organization. Uncontrolled creation and retention of data and documents by contractor personnel can produce a disjointed, incomplete, and confusing portrait of corporate actions and decisions—a portrait that can be very misleading and exceedingly harmful. Since record retention rules may require that a document be maintained once it is created, particular attention should be paid to limiting the generation of unnecessary or redundant records.
>
> **Informal Records**
>
> Many engineers and other technical personnel keep detailed journals, notebooks, or other logs of their activities. An engineer, for example, may keep notebooks recording his unofficial minutes of meetings and telephone conversations as well
>
> ---
>
> [47] Id. at 835.
> [48] The Eighth Circuit's recent decision in U.S. v. McDonnell Douglas Corp., 751 F.2d 220 (CA8 1984), while paying lip service to the Bowsher decision, adopted a much less restrictive view of GAO's authority. The error of the McDonnell Douglas decision becomes apparent by comparing the Supreme Court's denial of access to a large body of records of incurred costs with the Eighth Circuit's decision to permit access to the contractor's pre-contract estimates and projections of tooling hours. Despite the Eighth Circuit's opinion, the Supreme Court's decision in *Bowsher* remains the test by which GAO requests must be measured.

as his personal analysis of difficulties with contract performance. Contracts personnel may similarly maintain diaries of negotiations, telephone conferences, and discussions with government representatives.

The preparation and retention of these personal journals and memoranda create significant and uncontrollable risks during government investigations. They may reflect the writer's incomplete understanding of events and may also fail to distinguish between facts personally known to the writer and mere speculation or hearsay. The conclusions or opinions of the author may also be inconsistent with the official position of the company. Although the individual engineer may have considered his notebook to be personal and confidential, the government may nonetheless seek its production during audits, investigations, or litigation and will portray it as a reliable and "official" record of the contractor's actions and policies.

This risk demands a more structured approach to the creation of informal, unofficial, or "personal" records. Contractors should review the types of documents being maintained by their employees and decide whether the benefits outweigh the potential risks. Particular attention should be paid to documents that duplicate official records of the company. In many instances, a single, official record should be the only record, and informal parallel records should be prohibited. For example, a time card is the official—and should be the only—record of an employee's work effort. It is doubtful whether there is sufficient justification for an employee or department maintaining its own separate log of time charges.

Similarly, it may be desirable to assign one individual to take detailed minutes of a meeting that could be made part of the official contract file, rather than having each individual record his own observations or impressions. Preprinted phone memoranda forms could be used for recording contacts with government personnel. These could be maintained in the official files, rather than on a haphazard basis by individual employees.

With respect to informal records which the company may consider beneficial, guidance should be provided on the types of information to be included. Employees must be made aware that their notes and memoranda may someday be reviewed by the government or persons outside the company. Personnel might be instructed to limit journals to technical matters and to discuss only those facts of which they have personal knowledge, omitting speculation or hearsay. For example, where such events as test or inspection failures, specification deficiencies, or production problems are addressed in personal journals, the author should assure that the discussion is limited to matters of personal knowledge, that any conclusions are identified as preliminary, and that the final resolution of the matter, if known, is addressed. The problem, together with a copy of the personal memorandum, should be brought to the attention of responsible management.

Personnel could also be instructed to review their personal files periodically. Where retention of a memorandum, note, or other paper is desirable, or is required by a record retention rule, it could be made a part of the official files. If, on the other hand, there is no need to retain a document in the central contract files, it should not be retained at all. In this manner, the contractor would have better control over the full range of its records.

Self-Evaluative Records

Frequently, the most sensitive documents are those resulting from the contractor's review of its own activities. These reviews may be conducted for purposes of quality assurance, cost control, or auditing, and may be done on a routine basis or in response to specific problems.

During contract performance, for example, reports may be generated analyzing

(continued)

FIG. 9-12 *(cont'd)*

performance problems, reviewing production procedures, or making recommendations for the correction of problems. Some of the documents may be very preliminary, speculating on a number of possible sources of a production problem and on the possible resolution. If so, the preliminary nature of the findings should be clearly expressed, and speculation should not be stated as fact. Program management personnel may prepare weekly or monthly reports evaluating contract status, technical problems, and performance against budgets. Too often, the accuracy of these documents is clouded by the authors' efforts to pat themselves on the back. Again, it should be stressed that these documents may eventually be reviewed by the government, and accuracy and brevity should be the paramount considerations.

Of greater concern are the reports of those internal groups whose function is to detect fraud or other wrongdoing within the organization. These include the internal audit staffs common to most contractors. These groups typically operate as the company's "independent" inside auditors and report to a senior level of management. Frequently, these groups are joined by special ad hoc review teams whose charter is to conduct floor checks for compliance with timekeeping procedures or to spot check other areas of particular concern.

It must be recognized that these documents generally are not privileged and will be available to a grand jury or, in some circumstances, to the IG. The very subject matter of these reviews ensures that government investigators will seek their production.

Again, the purpose and need for these reports should be examined and their content controlled accordingly. If the goal of the internal audit or floor check reports is to detect whether problems exist and to recommend corrective or preventive measures, the findings can be expressed in generic or summary fashion. Details of specific incidents and identification of specific individuals or contracts may be unnecessary. There is usually little need for creating voluminous, detailed notes. Once a report is complete, moreover, there may be no need, under applicable record retention requirements, to retain the detailed notes and work papers underlying the report.

Most importantly, procedures should be established to ensure that at the *first indication* of fraud or other potential criminal conduct, the audit must stop and the matter must be brought to the attention of counsel. All too frequently, a company auditor will proceed to gather pertinent records, interview employees, and otherwise document potential improprieties before involving attorneys for the company. Unfortunately, the auditor's detailed report of the transgressions and his work papers generally are not privileged and may be available to the government investigators or to a grand jury. By the time it is certain that fraud has occurred, it may be too late. Accordingly, there should be a low threshold for stopping the review and referring the matter to company counsel.

Maintaining Confidentiality of Investigative Reports

Indications of improprieties may surface during a routine internal review, from complaints by employees or in government audit or investigative reports. The typical response is for the company to assign an internal group to conduct an investigation of the facts to determine the accuracy of the charges, delineate the scope of the problem, and recommend appropriate action.

The possibility that the allegations, if true, may result in criminal prosecution and debarment from government contracts mandates that these internal investigations be conducted in a highly confidential manner. Every step should be taken to maximize the ability to protect the investigators' notes, memoranda, and reports from involuntary disclosure to government auditors, the IG, and the grand jury. Three privileges which may be available under the circumstances are the attorney-client privilege, attorney work product privilege, and perhaps the privilege for self-evaluating materials.

Attorney-Client Privilege

Allegations of fraud or other wrongdoing will, in virtually every instance, necessitate obtaining legal advice. Management will undoubtedly seek advice as to, among other things, the statutory or regulatory provisions which may have been violated, the criminal, civil, and/or administrative penalties and sanctions which may be imposed, and the availability of defenses in preparing an effective response. The need for such advice provides the opportunity to protect the internal review of the allegations with the attorney-client privilege.

In general, the attorney-client privilege protects from disclosure (i) confidential communications, (ii) by a client to an attorney, (iii) made for the purpose of obtaining legal advice. The privilege is intended to encourage a full discussion of the facts by ensuring that the attorney will not later be compelled to disclose those facts absent client consent.[49]

When a communication is privileged, both the physical communication (e.g., the document) and the substance of the communication are privileged. However, the facts underlying the communication are not privileged, and their presence in a privileged communication does not protect them from disclosure. For example, while a disclosure by an employee to a company attorney that an invoice contained fictitious entries would be privileged, the invoice itself is an unprivileged business record and does not become privileged simply because it is given to the attorney.

The Supreme Court in *Upjohn* confirmed that privileged communications are not limited to those between attorneys and upper management. Thus, interviews between attorneys and lower level employees concerning matters relating to their employment with the company, conducted at the direction of the employees' superiors, for the purpose of supplying legal advice to the company, will also, with respect to the company, be protected by the attorney-client privilege.[50]

Two limitations to the privilege are of particular concern in the context of internal corporate investigations. First, to be privileged, the communications must be made for the purpose of obtaining *legal* advice. Second, the confidentiality of the investigation must be strictly maintained.

Merely assigning a lawyer or "deputizing" nonlawyers to conduct an investigation will not automatically envelop their work with the attorney-client privilege. If the lawyer is acting in a nonlegal capacity or if the advice sought is of a business or other nonlegal nature, the communications to the lawyer will not be privileged.[51] For example, in *In re Grand Jury Subpoena*,[52] the company, upon learning of

---

[49] See Upjohn Co. v. U.S., 449 U.S. 383, 389 (1981).

[50] There is serious doubt whether these conversations are privileged with respect to the employee. Consequently, the employee may be unable to object to the disclosure by the company of his statements to company counsel. See, e.g., In re Grand Jury Proceedings, 434 F. Supp. 648 (DC EMich. 1977), aff'd, 570 F.2d 562 (CA6 1978); Diversified Industries v. Meredith, 572 F.2d 596, 611 n.5 (CA8 1977) (en banc). This distinction raises ethical concerns regarding the manner in which the privilege is explained to employees during company investigations.

[51] See, e.g., U.S. v. Davis, 636 F.2d 1028, 1043-44 (CA 5), cert. denied, 454 U.S. 862 (1981).

[52] 599 F.2d 504 (CA2 1979).

(continued)

FIG. 9-12 *(cont'd)*

possible bribery of Mexican officials, assigned three senior company officials to conduct an internal investigation. They were to work under the direction of the company's general counsel, and all memoranda were to be addressed to the lawyer. After the results of this investigation were reviewed by the board of directors, the company retained a law firm to conduct a more extensive review with the assistance of the company's outside auditors.

The court, in considering claims of privilege regarding the memoranda of these two investigations, distinguished their essential purposes. Even though the first investigation was carried out under the auspices of a lawyer, its primary purpose was to report to the board of directors in the normal course of business—not to obtain legal advice. The results of this first "management" review prompted the company to seek legal advice, and the second investigation was conducted for the purpose of providing that advice. Consequently, the results of the second investigation were privileged, while the product of the first was not.[53]

This factor can be of greater import when the internal investigation is conducted by the company's in-house counsel instead of outside attorneys retained specifically for that purpose. While this fact alone does not affect the availability of the privilege, courts are prone to examine closely whether the attorney is also a part of the management team and is acting in a business rather than legal capacity.[54]

Strict confidentiality is also essential to protect the attorney-client privilege. Dissemination of the information should be on a strict need-to-know basis. For example, if investigative reports are distributed routinely through the normal management routing channels or if auditors assigned to assist the attorneys provide copies of their work to their superiors in the accounting department, a court may determine that the information was not treated as confidential by the company or that the privilege has been waived.[55] Discussion of the results of the investigation with outside accountants in connection with their financial audit of the company or for purposes of determining whether disclosures are required under the securities laws may also negate the attorney-client privilege.[56]

Work Product Privilege

Compared to the attorney-client privilege, the attorney work product privilege is broader in terms of the materials protected, yet less absolute in the protection provided. In general, the work product privilege protects from disclosure materials obtained or prepared by an attorney in preparation for litigation.[57]

The work product privilege is not limited to "communications." It can protect from disclosure work papers, analysis, and notes or memoranda of interviews with nonemployees that generally would not be protected by the attorney-client privilege.

In addition, it is much easier to bring within the umbrella of the work product privilege the reports of nonlawyer investigators, auditors, or technical specialists

---

[53] See also Diversified Industries v. Meredith, supra, 572 F.2d at 601; Resnick v. American Dental Assoc., 95 F.R.D. 372, 375 (DC NIII 1982).

[54] See, e.g., In re Sealed Case, 737 F.2d 94, 99 (CADC 1984); Computer Network Corp. v. Spohler, 95 F.R.D. 500, 502 (DC DC 1982); Valente v. Pepsico, Inc., 68 F.R.D. 361, 367 (DC Del 1975).

[55] Diversified Industries v. Meredith, supra, 572 F.2d at 609; SEC v. Gulf & Western Industries, 518 F. Supp. 675, 681 (DC DC 1981); In re Grand Jury Proceedings, 466 F. Supp. 863, 870 (DC Minn 1979).

[56] U.S. v. Bein, 728 F.2d 107, 112-13 (CA2 1984); In re John Doe Corp., 675 F.2d 482, 488 (CA2 1982).

[57] Hickman v. Taylor, 329 U.S. 495 (1947).

that have been prepared at the request of the attorney than it is to establish the attorney-client privilege for such documents. Unlike the attorney-client privilege, disclosure of the materials to a third party does not necessarily destroy the protection of the work product privilege.[58] But, like the attorney-client privilege, the work product privilege does not apply to planning documents, internal reports prepared routinely in the ordinary course of business, or to investigations conducted for business purposes by nonlawyer members of management.[59]

The essential element of the work product privilege is that the materials were collected or prepared in anticipation of litigation. It is not necessary that litigation have already commenced, but there must be a genuine threat or apprehension of litigation.[60] With respect to internal investigations of procurement fraud, the serious nature of the improprieties and the very real risk that the matter will result in criminal prosecution or a government suit to recover payment will in most cases create a sufficient risk of litigation to trigger application of the privilege.[61]

A principal shortcoming of the work product privilege is that it does not provide the absolute protection from disclosure that is afforded by the attorney-client privilege. The work product privilege can be overcome by a showing of substantial need for the materials and an inability to obtain the information by other means. Such a showing might consist, for example, of the fact that the author of the statement or questionnaire is deceased.[62] Most courts, however, hold that no showing of need is sufficient to warrant production of memoranda of oral statements of witnesses or other documents which might reveal the opinions or mental processes of the attorney.[63]

Self-Evaluative Privilege

A few courts, under the theory that companies should be encouraged to be self-critical and to improve or reform their business operations, have upheld a privilege for internal investigative reports.[64] Most of the cases in which the privilege has been successfully invoked have involved internal investigations of accidents, such as fires and airplane crashes, and the reports and proceedings of hospital medical review committees. Only a handful of cases (mostly private litigation) have upheld the privilege for evaluations of compliance with government regulation. Where documents have been sought by government agencies, the privilege has almost uniformly been rejected.[65]

The Supreme Court has never squarely addressed the self-evaluative privilege. But it has given strong indications that the privilege would not be available in the context of an Internal Revenue Service summons enforcement proceeding.[66] That decision may be explained in part, however, on the basis of the substantial deference normally afforded IRS summonses, and the IRS' own policies which would prevent requests for such materials from becoming routine or commonplace.

---

[58] In re Sealed Case, 676 F.2d 793, 809 (CADC 1982).
[59] See, e.g., In re Grand Jury Subpoena, 599 F.2d 504, 510 (CA2 1979).
[60] Binks Mfg. Co. v. National Presto Industries, 709 F.2d 1109, 1118–20 (CA7 1983).
[61] See, e.g., In re Grand Jury Investigation, 599 F.2d 1224, 1229 (CA3 1979).
[62] In re Grand Jury Investigation, supra, 599 F.2d at 1232.
[63] In re Sealed Case, supra, 676 F.2d at 811; In re Grand Jury Investigation, supra, 599 F.2d at 1231.
[64] See generally Murphy, The Self-Evaluative Privilege, 1982 The Journal of Corporation Law 489.
[65] See FTC v. TRW, Inc., 628 F.2d 207, 210 (DC DC 1980).
[66] See U.S. v. Arthur Young & Co., 104 S. Ct. 1495 (1984).

(continued)

FIG. 9-12 *(cont'd)*

Special Investigative Reports

The *Westinghouse* litigation and related actions by DCAA and the IG demonstrate that government investigators are seeking an ever-widening range of internal investigative reports. The internal audit reports sought in the *Westinghouse* litigation, however, are not the type of reports normally prepared in the context of an attorney-client relationship or in anticipation of litigation. The self-evaluative privilege may be the only privilege to be asserted. Whether it would apply to internal audit reports or whether the privilege itself will ultimately be recognized in the context of document demands by government investigators is far from clear. Thus, companies engaged in internal investigations may want to take steps to utilize the attorney-client and work product privileges to the fullest extent possible. The following actions are suggested:

(1) It must be recognized that the actions of DCAA and the IG are causing the routine audit function and the criminal investigative function to become increasingly intermixed. Any audit or investigation can, without the knowledge of the contractor, quickly develop into a criminal investigation, with the material supplied to DOD then provided to the Department of Justice. The threat of criminal prosecution and debarment demands that, at the *first sign* of improprieties, the matter be brought to the attention of company counsel and that all further investigation be conducted by an attorney or at his direction. This approach will maximize the extent to which the results of that review will be privileged and enable the company promptly to obtain the legal advice necessary to deal intelligently with the problem.

(2) The request to counsel for an investigation of suspected improprieties should be documented. Records (e.g., corporate minutes and resolutions, memoranda from corporate officials) should be prepared directing counsel to conduct any internal investigation, requesting legal analysis and recommendations regarding any possible problem and specifying the role and authority of counsel. The request should envision some form of legal analysis and should not be limited to mere factual development. To the extent litigation is anticipated, the basis for that expectation should be memorialized as soon as possible.

(3) Care should be taken to separate legal and nonlegal functions. For example, if a general counsel who is active is asked to undertake an internal investigation, company records should reflect that the investigation is being undertaken in a legal capacity. It may be desirable to appoint a subordinate attorney with no management responsibilities to head the investigative team and to provide the day-to-day direction.

(4) It is preferable for interviews of employees to be conducted by attorneys or by a team including at least one attorney. Memoranda from senior management should be provided to interviewees identifying the attorney and directing that the employee cooperate with the investigation as part of his employment duties. The interviewees should generally not be asked to sign a written statement nor should the interview be tape recorded or transcribed. Such documents might later be available to the government if the interviewee becomes a witness in a criminal trial. (Fed. R. Crim. P. 26.2). Instead, the interviewers should prepare summary memoranda of the interview.

(5) Once an investigation is undertaken, it should be carefully monitored. Counsel should supervise the type of documents created and the persons creating them. Notes of interviews should be marked confidential and retained by counsel. The notes should identify those persons present during the interviews. Employees should be instructed to treat the matter under investigation in confidence.

(6) The creation of sensitive documents should be supervised by counsel. Analyses

> and memoranda should be prepared only upon the direction of the attorney. The documents should be labeled "privileged, confidential, and for limited circulation only." Documents addressed to attorneys should use legal titles and identify the law department or law firm involved. Copies of sensitive documents (both received from and sent to the client) should be limited to those with a legitimate need for access, and care should be taken to avoid inadvertent waiver or release. Policies should be established for the filing, storage, and retention of confidential documents. Where feasible, such documents should be segregated from general files.
>
> (7) Meetings held in connection with an investigation should be limited to those with a need to know. When individual attendees have an interest only in certain aspects of a more general issue, they should not be present for discussion of matters in which they lack a direct interest. If third parties are deemed necessary, the discussion should be limited to information relevant to the purpose for which the third party is present.
>
> (8) If outside experts or consultants are to be used in the investigation, they should be retained by counsel. A written agreement should specify the relationship, ensuring that contacts, discussions, and all written materials will be communicated directly to counsel. The agreement should identify the need or purpose for using such experts or consultants.
>
> (9) Finally, procedures should be established for handling government requests for internal investigative documents. If such documents or oral or written summaries thereof are disclosed to the government, such disclosure may waive any claim of privilege for the entire investigative file.
>
> The access to records offensive is dramatically changing the relationship between DOD and defense contractors. Many of the potential offensive and defensive actions outlined above were unnecessary in a more cooperative environment, but are now essential to protect a contractor's interests.

in 1985, before the *Westinghouse* case was decided. That case is discussed in greater detail earlier in this chapter. In effect, the *Westinghouse* case made it apparent to Congress that the DCAA's lack of subpoena power needed a legislative remedy. In 1985, Congress bestowed subpoena power on the DCAA. The DCAA has resorted to using that power in only a few cases. More is said about this point later in this chapter.

Each company doing business with the government is being affected by the DOD access to records offensive. The issue of limits on DOD access is being pushed far beyond records directly pertaining to DOD contracts. As a result, it would be unwise to approach this matter as though only defense contracting segments of a company were affected. In the instance of Westinghouse, only 20 percent of its business is defense contracting; yet, the IG sought virtually all of its internal audit reports and workpapers.

The extent to which each company acts to protect itself will depend on its respective assessment of its individual situation. Mssrs. Kipps, Carlson, and Brown enumerate a number of considerations that must be taken into account, including the following:[11]

---

[11] *Ibid.*, p. 1024. Reprinted by permission of the Bureau of National Affairs, Inc., Washington, D.C.

- ☐ The courts generally will intercede when agencies exceed their investigative authority or fail to establish that their document requests are reasonably relevant to the lawful investigative purpose.
- ☐ The Supreme Court has recognized that an investigative agency's legitimate need for records must be balanced against a contractor's legitimate privacy interests.
- ☐ The standard audit clause limits the DCAA's review to those contractor records "sufficient to reflect properly all costs." It is doubtful whether that clause gives the DCAA authority to secure broad access to internal audit reports.
- ☐ There are substantial grounds for seeking immediate review in the district courts of the DCAA's suspension of contract payments to obtain compliance with its document requests.
- ☐ It is doubtful whether the DOD IG has subpoena authority to obtain plenary access to internal audit reports and similar internal records.
- ☐ Contractors should establish procedures to control the creation and retention of internal documents.
- ☐ Contractors should ensure that internal investigations are conducted in such a manner as to maximize the protections afforded by the attorney-client and work product privileges.

The DCAA Subpoena Power

The congressional action to provide the DCAA with subpoena power to access records is noted earlier in this chapter. The DCAA is now entitled to use that power for the purpose of evaluating the accuracy, completeness, and currency of a contractor's cost and pricing data.

The DCAA subpoena power, in effect, did not extend the DCAA right of access. It only served to strengthen the DCAA's hand in obtaining access to records to which it had a right via previous statutory authority and contract clauses. It has always been somewhat unclear just what the limits to this right of access are. This is evident from the article reprinted in Figure 9-12. In 1987, another court case brought this unclear picture into a better focus. The case involved the Department of Justice on behalf of the DCAA and Newport News Shipbuilding, a division of Tenneco. The reprinted article below provides background, details, and distinctions between this case and the *Westinghouse* case.[12]

DCAA CANNOT SUBPOENA INTERNAL AUDIT DATA, DISTRICT COURT RULES

The Defense Contract Audit Agency does not have authority to subpoena a contractor's internal audit reports, the U.S. District Court for the Eastern District of Virginia decides.

---

[12] Editors, "DCAA Cannot Subpoena Internal Audit Data, District Court Rules," *Federal Contracts Report*, March 30, 1987, pp. 521–522. Reprinted by permission of the Bureau of National Affairs, Inc., Washington, D.C.

Judge J. Calvitt Clarke distinguishes *Westinghouse*, in which the Third Circuit's held that the Defense Inspector General could subpoena internal audit data on behalf of DCAA. The Third Circuit did not decide whether DCAA could subpoena the audit reports, he points out. DCAA's subpoena power is not as broad as that granted the IG, he concludes. Congress, in giving DCAA subpoena authority, did not intend to expand its access to records authority (U.S. v. Newport News Shipbuilding & Drydock Co., DC EVa. No. Misc. 87-5-NN, 3/20/87; Newport News Shipbuilding & Drydock Co. v. Reed, DC EVa. No. 86-182-NN, 3/20/87).

Newport News Shipbuilding, a division of Tenneco, Inc., does virtually all its business with the Navy, and charges the cost of conducting internal audit reports against its government contracts.

The Defense IG and DCAA have maintained that they have a right to obtain these reports. The contractor filed suit last year, challenging an IG subpoena for its 1983–85 internal audit reports. The suit was settled after the Third Circuit ruled in U.S. v. Westinghouse Electric Co. (45 FCR 770, 793) that the IG could subpoena records on behalf of DCAA, provided the IG had exercised independent judgment in making the demand.

DCAA subsequently requested Newport News' internal audit reports prepared after Jan. 1, 1986. The contractor refused to furnish them, prompting DCAA to issue an administrative subpoena. Newport News filed suit to block enforcement of the subpoena. The Department of Justice subsequently went to court on behalf of DCAA, seeking to have the subpoena enforced (47 FCR 243).

Newport News argued that DCAA lacked the authority to subpoena its internal audit reports and that the subpoena was too broad.

Justice cited the FY 1985 Defense Authorization Act, 10 USC §2313, authorizing the DCAA director to require production of contractors' books and records, to the extent that access is provided to the Secretary of Defense under the statute.

DCAA said it had issued the subpoena to obtain documents needed by the agency in order to evaluate the reasonableness, allocability and allowability of Newport News' contract costs, and that it wanted to determine whether the contractor's certified cost and pricing data were accurate, complete and current as required by the Truth in Negotiations Act (47 FCR 243). The subpoena is within DCAA's statutory authority, and is both relevant and material to the agency's audit responsibilities, DOJ said.

"In short, DCAA is trying to determine Newport News' fitness as a defense contractor, and whether the government has received what it has paid for under its contracts," Judge Clarke observes.

DCAA's Subpoena Power

DCAA is entitled, under 10 USC §2306, to subpoena records for the purpose of evaluating the accuracy, completeness and currency of a contractor's cost and pricing data, the judge finds.

However, this provision does not, as the government has contended, authorize DCAA to subpoena all records that relate either directly or indirectly to a defense contract, Judge Clarke: "The court is convinced that §2306(f)(5) limits the DCAA's subpoena power to the extent that DCAA may not force Newport News to produce its internal audit reports and other related materials."

"Various congressional reports, hearings and commissions indicate that Congress intended to limit DCAA's subpoena power to those materials which are related to costs incurred in the negotiations, proposals and performance of particular contracts," the court stresses.

The Defense Authorization Act did not expand the scope of DCAA's access to records authority, the court adds. Rather, it merely provided DCAA with subpoena authority for enforcement of its existing rights to a contractor's books and records. Furthermore, the legislative history indicates that the congressional conferees wanted this enforcement mechanism to be used sparingly, the court notes.

Implementing Rules Support Restrictions

The implementing regulations also support the view that DCAA is not entitled to subpoena Newport News' internal audit reports, the court says.

The Federal Acquisition Regulation, 48 CFR §52-215, states that representatives of the contracting officer have the right to examine and audit books and records sufficient to reflect that all costs claimed were incurred in performing the contract. Under the FAR, these representatives have authority to examine those records pertaining to the negotiation, pricing and performance of the contract. "The right of examination shall extend to all documents necessary to permit adequate evaluation of the cost or pricing data submitted, along with the computations and projections used," the FAR states.

However, internal audit reports are used mainly for internal management control purposes, and are not pricing data subject to DCAA's subpoena, the court concludes. Although the government pays for internal audits, the payments represent general and administrative expenses charged to the government as overhead, Judge Clarke explains. "This overhead charge does not relate to any specific government contract."

Newport News has agreed to allow DCAA access to the salaries, hours worked, and other expenses incurred in preparing its internal audits, the court points out. "DCAA can fulfill its functions by reviewing the bid estimates, proposal packages and other contract records which Newport News has already made available."

Distinguishing Westinghouse

In *Westinghouse*, the Third Circuit ruled that DOD's Inspector General can subpoena books and records on behalf of DCAA, provided that he exercises independent judgment in making the demand. In affirming a trial judge's decision granting access to the audit reports (44 FCR 401, 424), the court stated that the subpoena was within the IG's authority as provided by the 1982 Inspector General Act. The audit reports also are relevant to determining whether the contractor is effectively combating waste, fraud and abuse records in government contracts, the Third Circuit added (45 FCR 770).

Judge Clarke points out that the Defense IG has broad investigatory powers. The *Westinghouse* case demonstrated that the IG can use DCAA personnel as its own when initiating, conducting and supervising audits and other investigations, he notes.

However, the *Westinghouse* court did not decide whether DCAA had authority to subpoena internal audit reports, the judge emphasizes. "*Westinghouse* in no way suggests that DCAA's subpoena power gives it authority to subpoena Newport News' internal audit reports."

"Instead, *Westinghouse* reveals that the Inspector General . . . would be the proper vehicle for gaining access to Newport News' internal audit reports," he concludes. "When DCAA's purpose under the statute and subpoena power are viewed along side the Inspector General's statutory purpose and subpoena power, the court must find that the DCAA is limited as to what materials it can and cannot subpoena." Whereas DCAA's access to contractors' records is limited to pricing and cost data, the Inspector General's subpoena power is not so limited, the court says in denying the government's petition for enforcement.

If this case is a reliable sign of court sentiment regarding DCAA access, it would appear that contractors may not have to divulge internal audit reports to the DCAA on a wholesale basis.

The Attorney-Client Privilege

In order to increase the protection of internal audit work products, many companies have expanded the use of the attorney-client privilege. As indicated in the article reprinted in Figure 9-12, this privilege offers protection from disclosure (1) of confidential communications (2) by a client to an attorney (3) made for the purpose of obtaining legal advice.

In June 1986, the DCAA General Counsel provided written guidance to its staff regarding denials of records based on the attorney-client privilege. In summary the guidance asserts that:

- The privilege does not extend to contractor documentation prepared in the ordinary course of business.
- The privilege applies in litigation settings only.
- The contractor's acceptance of a government contract waives the attorney-client privilege or the work product privilege.

The foregoing interpretations of applicable law and case history were forcefully rebutted by the National Security Industrial Association (NSIA). The NSIA, based in Washington, D.C., is a national organization of more than 400 industrial, research, legal, and educational organizations. It is a not-for-profit, nonpolitical, nonlobbying association. It functions to provide a close working relationship and effective two-way communication between government and the industry which supports it. A portion of a 1987 NSIA letter from its president, Wallace H. Robinson, Jr., to the DCAA is reprinted in Figure 9-13.

It is obvious that the NSIA believes strongly that the DCAA position on the issue of attorney-client privilege is faulty. It is likely that companies will continue to use the privilege wherever it best applies. The courts have yet another issue to settle regarding government access to internal records.

(continued on page 9-64)

FIG. 9-13

NSIA Perspective on Attorney-Client Privilege

A. The Attorney-Client Privilege Does Not Apply Only In Litigation Settings.

1. DCAA's Various Characterizations Of The Attorney-Client Privilege In Its Memorandum Are Inconsistent And Confusing.

DCAA's memorandum correctly states at one point that the attorney-client privilege attaches: (1) where legal advice *of any kind* is sought from a professional legal advisor in his capacity as such, and (2) where the communications relate to that purpose, and are made in confidence by the client. Under these circumstances, the communications are permanently protected from disclosure except when the privilege is waived by the client. The DCAA memorandum accurately states that this definition is "well settled in law." *See, e.g., United States v. Bein*, 728 F.2d 107, 112 (2d Cir.), *cert. denied*, 105 S. Ct. 135 (1984); *United States v. Kovel*, 296 F.2d 918, 921 (2d Cir. 1961); *B.D. Click Co.*, ASBCA Nos. 25609, 25972, 83-1 BCA ¶ 16,328 (1983).

However, this definition of the attorney-client privilege that DCAA agrees is "well settled in law" is completely contrary to the characterization of the privilege in paragraph (1) of the DCAA memorandum where DCAA states that the "privilege was judicially created primarily for the purpose of limiting disclosure of information in a *litigative setting*" (emphasis added). In fact, the privilege most certainly does *not* only pertain to litigation. As recognized in the first definition, the attorney-client privilege applies to any situation in which legal advice is sought from an attorney, and, contrary to the assertion, was created in large part to help clients resolve legal concerns while avoiding litigation.

2. The Courts Have Consistently Applied the Attorney-Client Privilege Well Outside Any Litigation Setting.

Courts have consistenlty upheld the use of the attorney-client privilege even where there is no foreseeable possibility of litigation. In *SCM Corp. v. Xerox Corp.*, 70 F.R.D. 508 (D. Conn. 1976), the court held specifically that the attorney-client privilege need not be limited to legal consultations in litigation situations:

> The privilege need not be limited to legal consultations between corporations *in litigation situations*, however. Corporations should be encouraged to seek legal advice in planning their affairs to avoid litigation as well as in pursuing it.

70 F.R.D. at 513 (emphasis added).

Similarly, the Eighth Circuit held that the attorney-client privilege attached to communications between attorneys and employees of a corporation when the attorneys were conducting an investigation to determine corporate wrongdoing. In *Diversified Industries, Inc. v. Meredith*, 572 F.2d 596, 610 (8th Cir. 1978), the court held that "the application of the attorney-client privilege to this matter and others like it will encourage corporations to seek out and correct wrongdoing in their own house." *Id.*

In *Fisher v. United States*, 425 U.S. 391 (1976), the Supreme Court held that "[c]onfidential disclosures by a client to an attorney made in order *to obtain any type of legal assistance* are privileged." *Id.* at 403 (emphasis added).

3. The Supreme Court Has Upheld A Broad Application Of the Attorney-Client Privilege In Order To Encourage Full and Effective Communication Between Attorney and Client.

The attorney-client privilege exists to encourage full and frank communication between attorneys and their clients, which will "promote broader public interest in the observance of law and administration of justice." *Upjohn Co. v. United States*, 449 U.S. 383, 389 (1981); *Tera Advanced Services Corp.*, GSBCA No. 6713-NRC, 84-1 BCA ¶ 16,936 at 84,249 (1983); *Radiant Burners, Inc. v. American Gas Association*, 320 F.2d 314, 322, (7th Cir.), *cert. denied*, 375 U.S. 929 (1963); *B.D. Click*, ASBCA No. 83-1 BCA at 81,173 (emphasis added).

Accordingly, there is no basis whatsoever to restrict the attorney-client privilege to litigation settings. Indeed, the Supreme Court has rejected any such restrictive applications of the privilege.

In *Upjohn*, the Supreme Court opted for an extremely broad reading of the atotrney-client privilege. The Court struck down the "control group" test[1] on the grounds that the test "frustrates the very purpose of the privilege by discouraging the communication of relevant information by employees of the client to attorneys seeking to render legal advice to the client corporation." 449 U.S. at 392. The Court held that use of the control-group test overlooks "the fact that the privilege exists to protect not only the giving of professional advice to those who can act on it but also the giving of information to the lawyer to enable him to give sound and informed advice." 449 U.S. at 390. The Court concluded that:

> [T]he narrow scope given the attorney-client privilege by the Court below not only makes it difficult for corporate attorneys to formulate sound advice when their client is faced with a specific legal problem but also threatens to limit the valuable efforts of corporate counsel to ensure their client's compliance with the law.

Id. at 392.

Since the late 1700's, the attorney-client privilege has served to alleviate a client's fear of disclosure in consulting his legal advisor in any area of the law. *Id.* In *Annesley v. Early of Anglesea*, 17 How. St. Tr. 1129, 1224 (Ex. 1743), B. Mounteney emphasized the necessity of "inviolable secrecy" by attorneys to enable clients to communicate fully and effectively with their attorneys:

> [a]n increase of legal business and the inabilities of parties to transact that business themselves, made it necessary for them to employ . . . other persons who might transact that business for them; *that this necessity introduced with it the necessity of what the law hath very justly established, an inviolable secrecy to be observed by attornies, in order to render it safe for clients to communicate to their attornies all proper instructions for the carrying on those causes which they found themselves under a necessity of instructing to their care.*

17 How. St. Tr. 1129, 1224; *see also* Wigmore at 546 (emphasis added).

---

[1] The control-group test was one of two tests previously utilized by the lower federal courts to determine who is the client for purposes of the attorney-client privilege when dealing with a corporation. The control group test restricted the application of the attorney-client privilege to counsel's communications with the "control group," or upper echelon of corporate management; lower-level employees were not considered representative of the corporate "client." *See, e.g., Philadelphia v. Westinghouse Electric Corp.*, 210 F. Supp. 483, 485 (E.D. Pa.), *petition for mandamus denied*, 312 F.2d 742 (3d Cir. 1962), *cert. denied*, 372 U.S. 943 (1963).

(continued)

FIG. 9-13 *(cont'd)*

Full and effective communication between attorneys and clients is essential not only in litigation, but also in the daily rendering of legal advice in non-litigation matters, including those relating to Government contracts.

4. DCAA's Guidance Confuses the Work Product Privilege With the Attorney-Client Privilege.

The attorney-client privilege preserves the confidentiality of attorney-client communications. In contrast, the work product privilege limits discovery of documents prepared by or for an attorney in anticipation of litigation. Unlike the attorney-client privilege the work product privilege applies *only* where there is some prospect of litigation. Indeed, the work product privilege was designed for the very purpose of giving limited protection to documents prepared in a litigation context.

The District of Columbia Circuit has recently highlighted the distinction between the two privileges:

> While the attorney-client privilege is intended to promote communication between attorney and client by protecting client confidences, the work product privilege is a broader protection designed to balance the needs of the adversary system to promote an attorney's preparation in representing a client against society's general interest in revealing all true and material facts relevant to the resolution of a dispute.

In re Subpoenas Duces Tecum, 738 F.2d 1367, 1371, (D.C. Cir. 1984). Similarly, the Boards of Contract Appeals have distinguished the two privileges in the same manner. *Amdahl Corp.*, GSBCA No. 7859-P, 85-2 BCA ¶ 18,054 at 90,617 (1985).

The prospect of litigation is an essential element of the work product privilege. However, whether or not a client may be faced with litigation has no bearing on whether or not the attorney-client privilege applies in a particular situation. DCAA's purported guidance to auditors confuses the two privileges.

B. Contractor Acceptance Of A Government Contract Does Not Waive The Attorney-Client Or Work Product Privilege.

DCAA's guidance asserts that "[b]y contractually consenting to permit examination of *all* necessary audit information in exchange for monetary consideration, a waiver of the privilege may have occurred" (emphasis supplied). Under this theory, once a contractor enters into a Government contract, he has forever lost the right to assert an attorney-client or work product privilege with respect to any document that DCAA might otherwise be entitled to examine under the "Audit-Negotiation" clause of FAR § 52.215-2.

DCAA's guidance is plainly wrong. Contractor assent to a Government contract containing the standard audit clause does not in and of itself waive the attorney-client privilege. A Government contract is a contract of adhesion.

James S. Lee & Co., ASBCA No. 18156, 79-2 BCA ¶ 14,036 (1979); *Building Maintenance Corp.*, ASBCA No. 14513, 70-2 BCA ¶ 8375 (1970) ("the very nature of a government contract makes it a contract of adhesion"). Contractors have no opportunity to negotiate the language of the Audit clause, and therefore give no voluntary consent to this particular contract provision. The clause does not speak to the matter of privilege directly and constitutes nothing more than a routine access to records provision.

It is well-settled that the Government's contractual or regulatory right to inspect records does not affect a client's right to assert the attorney-client privilege.

United States v. Louisville and Nashville Railroad, 236 U.S. 318, 336 (1915). *Louisville* involved an appeal by the Government from the District Court's denial of its motion for a writ of mandamus to compel the railroad's counsel to disclose certain confidential correspondence between the railroad and its attorneys. The demand for the writ was made pursuant to § 20 of the Act to Regulate Commerce, Ch. 3591, 34 Stat. 584, 594, 595 (1906) (codified as amended in scattered sections of 49 U.S.C. (1976)) which authorized agents of the Interstate Commerce Commission to examine the accounts, records, and memoranda of the railroads. 236 U.S. at 334. The railroad refused to disclose privileged communications between itself and its attorneys. The Court denied the writ, underscoring the importance of protecting the attorney-client privilege as a matter of strong public policy:

> *The desirability of protecting confidential communications between attorney and client as a matter of public policy is too well known and has been too often recognized by text-books and courts to need extended comment now. If such communications were required to be made the subject of examination and publication, such enactment would be a practical prohibition upon professional advice and assistance.*

Id. at 334 (emphasis added).

In *Louisville*, the railroad was forced to comply with the rules and regulations of the Interstate Commerce Commission as a condition of doing business as a railroad. Similarly, a contractor is required to accept the Audit clause in order to do business as a Government contractor. However, neither a railroad nor a Government contractor waives any right to invoke the attorney-client privilege merely as a condition of doing business. DCAA's guidance runs directly counter to seventy years of settled Supreme Court precedent.

C. Under The Work-Product Privilege, The Phrase "In Anticipation Of Litigation" Is To Be Broadly Construed.

The work product privilege is embodied in Federal Rule of Civil Procedure 26(b)(3), which provides:

> Trial Preparation: Materials subject to the provision of subdivision (b)(4) of this rule. A party may obtain discovery of *documents and tangible things otherwise discoverable under subdivision (b)(1) of this rule and prepared in anticipation of litigation or for trial by or for another party or by or for that other party's representative (including his attorney, consultant, surety, indemnitor, insurer, or agent), only upon a showing that the party seeking discovery has substantial need of the materials in the preparation of his case and that he is unable without undue hardship to obtain the substantial equivalent of the materials by other means.* (Emphasis added)

DCAA stated in its June 18 memorandum that "[t]he most important element of the [work product] rule is that the material be prepared *in anticipation of litigation*" (emphasis supplied). However, a business need not be engaged in actual litigation[2] before the work-product privilege can attach to attorney directed work. The Fifth Circuit has stated that litigation need not be imminent, so long as the primary motivating purpose behind the creation of the document was to aid in possible or prospective future litigation. *United States v. Davis*,

---

[2] Black's Law Dictionary defines litigation as "[a] lawsuit. Legal action including all proceedings therein. Contest in a court of law for the purpose of enforcing a right or seeking a remedy. A judicial contest, a judicial controversy, a suit at law."

(continued)

FIG. 9-13 *(cont'd)*

> 636 F.2d 1028, 1040 (5th Cir.), *cert. denied,* 102 S. Ct. 320 (1981). For the work product privilege to apply, it is necessary only to show that the information sought was prepared or obtained because of the *prospect* of litigation. *Amdahl Corp;* GSBCA No. 7859-P, 85-2 BCA ¶ 18,054 at 90,617 (1985).
>
> The Supreme Court has stated that there is a "strong public policy" which underlies the work product doctrine. *See Upjohn Co.,* 449 U.S. at 398; *United States v. Nobles,* 422 U.S. 225, 236-40 (1975). In *Upjohn* the Court held that "the work-product doctrine does apply in tax summons enforcement proceedings." 449 U.S. at 386. The Court's decision demonstrated that unless Congress specifically takes away the work product doctrine, it applies:
>
>> Nothing in the language of the IRS summons provisions or their legislative history suggests an intent on the part of Congress to preclude application of the work product doctrine.
>
> 449 U.S. at 398. Further, the Court emphasized that Rule 26 of the Federal Rules of Civil Procedure "accords special protection to work product revealing the attorney's mental processes". *Id* at 400.
>
> A court's inquiry when considering the assertion of the privilege will focus on the primary purpose behind the creation of the document. *United States v. Gulf Oil Corp.,* 760 F.2d 292, 296 (Temp. Emer. Ct. App. 1985). It had been held, for example, that investigation by a federal agency presents more than a "remote prospect" of litigation and provides grounds for anticipating litigation sufficient to invoke the work product rule. *In re LTV Securities Litigation,* 89 F.R.D. 595, 612 (N.D. Tex. 1981). Accordingly, the phrase "in anticipation of litigation" in the work product rule has been and will continue to be broadly construed.

Implications for Internal Auditors

In view of the serious implications posed by the DOD offensive, internal audit functions are advised to monitor developments carefully. In addition, they should:

- Work with their legal counsel and management to develop a posture and strategy that fits their circumstances.
- Educate their staff members as to the issues involved.
- Practice even greater care in conducting audits and documenting work performed to minimize the potential for drawing misleading inferences.
- Increase attention and efforts in reporting findings and recommendations to guard against making further unfounded statements or unwarranted opinions.
- Review record retention practices in light of any changed policies regarding the production of sensitive information.

Also, the previous discussion underscores that the question of record retention as it applies to internal audit reports and workpapers is an important one.

Some believe that audit workpapers and audit reports should be kept for at least two and five years respectively and then be transferred to inactive storage for the same period.[13] However, as shown in Figure 9-8, retention periods as brief as three years may be appropriate. There is no single right answer for all companies. The retention period in each instance should be determined by the unique circumstances involved. The determination should be made by the chief auditor with the concurrence of management and the company's legal counsel. Among the factors to consider are:

- The availability of other company records containing similar information.
- The existence of litigation involving issues that certain of the workpapers address.
- The status of open tax years (it may be desirable to retain audit workpapers and reports until the later of settlement data or the stated retention period).
- The relationship that exists between the company and investigative government agencies.

The determination should establish guidelines that maximize the utility of the workpapers to the audit department and the company, while minimizing the potential that such records may be used against the company.

SUGGESTED READING

Schnee, Edward J., and Martin E. Taylor. "IRS Access to Accountants' Work Papers—The Rules May Be Changing." *Journal of Accounting, Auditing and Finance*, Fall 1981.

Willson, James D., and John B. Campbell. *Controllership: The Work of the Managerial Accountant*, 3rd ed., Chapter 36. New York: John Wiley & Sons, 1981.

---

[13] Willson and Campbell, *op. cit.*, p. 822.

CHAPTER **10**

Communicating With the Audit Committee

The Changing Activities of the Audit Committee 1	Review of Audit and Postaudit Activities 10
Functions of the Audit Committee 2	Independent Evaluation Might Be Helpful 11
Recent Guidelines 2	Making the Audit Committee More
The IIA 2	Effective 12
The Treadway Commission 3	
Items Suggested for Attention 4	
Evaluation of the Internal Audit Staff and Organizational Structure 8	Presentations to the Audit Committee ... 14
	Types of Presentations 15
Review of Audit Philosophy, Systems, and Procedures 9	Suggested Coverage 15
	Illustrative Segments of a Report to the Audit Committee 17
Review and Monitoring of the System of Controls 9	
Review of Proposed Audit Coverage 10	Suggested Reading 20

Fig. 10-1   Appendix I—Good Practice Guidelines for the Audit Committee 5
Fig. 10-2   Internal Audit Department Costs 18
Fig. 10-3   Percentage Increase in Sales, Income, and Internal Audit Costs 18
Fig. 10-4   Composition of Internal Audit Staff 19
Fig. 10-5   Planned Computer Systems Reviews 20

THE CHANGING ACTIVITIES OF THE AUDIT COMMITTEE

In recent years, the role of corporate boards of directors in the United States has changed significantly. Changes have come about as a result of pressure from a number of forces—increased business complexity, social demands, requests from shareholders for greater accountability, and legal and statutory requirements—which has brought the improvement in corporate governance.

One of the changes that has emerged from these circumstances is the establishment of audit committees composed primarily of outside or independent members of the board of directors. These committees have been delegated many responsibilities, including the selection or recommendation of the independent accountants, the review of various facets of the annual examination of financial statements with these external auditors, and the interface with the general and financial management and the internal auditors. This chapter deals chiefly with the relationship between the audit committee and the internal auditors.

The professional internal auditor should be concerned with two aspects of the relationship with the audit committee:

1. Those areas or subjects concerning the internal audit function about which the audit committee should reasonably be expected to inquire.
2. The nature and type of reports or communications that the chief internal auditor might make to the audit committee.

FUNCTIONS OF THE AUDIT COMMITTEE

There has been considerable variance among U.S. companies as to the extent of interface between the audit committee and the internal auditing group. However, the members of the audit committee are becoming more conscious of their responsibilities and more familiar with the functions of the internal audit staff (and more aware of the importance of internal controls).

Recent Guidelines

Since the mid 1970s, there has been an increased focus on the functions of the audit committees, and various guidelines have been issued. Some evolved, while others were encouraged as a result of a series of events deemed as unacceptable business practices.

The IIA. Recognizing the importance of audit committees in corporate governance, the Professional Practices Committee of the IIA in 1985 issued a statement regarding the formation and composition of audit committees and their primary responsibilities. Further, it defined the relationship that should exist betwen audit committees and the internal auditing function. The text of the statement (which was also republished in September 1986 as an appendix to "The Institute of Internal Auditors Reports on Fraud" prepared for the NCFFR) follows.[1]

---

[1] Professional Practices Committee, "The Institute of Internal Auditors' Position on Audit Committees," *IIA Today,* Oct. 1985, p. 19. Reprinted by permission of The Institute of Internal Auditors, Inc.

COMMUNICATING WITH THE AUDIT COMMITTEE

Purpose

The Institute of Internal Auditors recognizes that audit committees and internal auditors have common goals. A good working relationship with internal auditors can assist the audit committee in fulfilling its responsibility to the board of directors, shareholders, and other outside parties. This statement summarizes The Institute's views concerning the appropriate relationship between audit committees and internal auditing. The Institute acknowledges that audit committee responsibilities encompass activities which are beyond the scope of this statement, and in no way intends this statement to be a comprehensive description of audit committee responsibilities.

Statement

The Institute of Internal Auditors recommends that every public company have an audit committee organized as a standing committee of the board of directors. The Institute also encourages the establishment of audit committees in other organizations, including not-for-profit and governmental bodies. The audit committee should consist solely of outside directors, independent of management. The primary responsibilities of the audit committee should involve assisting the board of directors in carrying out their responsibilities as they relate to the organization's accounting policies, internal control and financial reporting practices. The audit committee should establish and maintain lines of communication between the board and the company's independent auditors, internal auditors and financial management.

The audit committee should expect internal auditing to examine and evaluate the adequacy and effectiveness of the organization's system of internal control and the quality of performance in carrying out assigned responsibilities. Internal auditing may be used as a source of information to the audit committee on major frauds or irregularities as well as company compliance with laws and regulations.

To ensure that internal auditors carry out their responsibilities, the audit committee should approve and periodically review the internal audit charter, a management-approved document which states internal audit's purpose, authority and responsibility. The audit committee should review annually the internal audit department's objectives and goals, audit schedules, staffing plans, and financial budgets. The director of internal auditing should inform the audit committee of the results of audits, highlighting significant audit findings and recommendations. The audit committee should also determine whether internal audit activities are being carried out in accordance with the *Standards for the Professional Practice of Internal Auditing,* adopted by The Institute of Internal Auditors, Inc.

To help assure independence, the director of internal auditing should have direct communication with the audit committee. The director should attend audit committee meetings and meet privately with the audit committee at least annually. Independence is further enhanced when the audit committee concurs in the appointment or removal of the director of internal auditing.

The Treadway Commission. Since October 1985, the NCFFR (also known as the Treadway Commission) has studied the financial reporting system in the United States for causes of fraudulent financial reporting and steps to reduce its incidence. In its final report issued in October 1987, the Commission provided some guidelines that were quite specific as to audit committee duties and responsibilities, as a segment of the lengthy report. The full text of Appendix I, which contains such information, is provided in Figure 10-1.[2] It should be noted that in the General Guidelines, the report mentions three subjects calling for direct communication between the audit committee and the chief internal auditors: audit plans, EDP, and areas requiring special attention.

Items Suggested for Attention

Given the greater importance of the audit committee and the evolving attention being paid to corporate governance, a trend has developed for longer, more frequent, and more productive meetings between the two groups. Particularly in corporations governed by the Securities Act of 1933, there is a propensity for the charter of the audit committee to change from the general charge, "Review the internal audit function" to more specific duties. In any company, of course, the audit committee's responsibility should be to *monitor* the internal audit organization and activities, and not to engage in day-to-day direction of the function. Assuming the current tendency toward more involvement, the folllowing list indicates those duties which, based upon the authors' experience, should properly lie within the interest of the audit committee:

- Evaluate the internal audit staff as to professional background, experience, size, effectiveness (in communicating), and professional development activities.
- Review the departmental philosophy of audit and its systems and procedures.
- Review and monitor the corporate system of controls, with emphasis on internal accounting controls, as well as administrative and operational controls.
- Review the proposed program of audit coverage, planned budget, and schedule for the coming year; coordinate with the independent public accountants.
- Review the internal audit activities of the past year, comparing planned and actual audits and utilization of manpower (e.g., on regular financial, operational, and EDP audits).
- Request and review special audits or investigations as may be necessary.
- Provide free access to the chief internal auditor, as requested, to discuss sensitive audit findings or other matters of major importance.
- Support, as deemed necessary, the independence of the internal auditing activity.

Of course, there will be meetings with the independent accountants and

---

[2] *Report of the National Commission on Fraudulent Financial Reporting,* Oct. 1987, pp. 179–181. Reprinted with permission.

FIG. 10-1

Appendix I—Good Practice Guidelines for the Audit Committee

Introduction

Primary responsibility for the company's financial reporting lies with top management, overseen by the board of directors. To help boards of directors carry out this oversight responsibility, the Commission recommends that all public companies establish audit committees consisting of independent directors. Establishment of such committees, of course, does not relieve the other directors of their responsibility with respect to the financial reporting process. The Commission therefore reinforces its general recommendation with more specific recommendations for audit committee duties and responsibilities.

First, specific recommendations directed to audit committees highlight the need for the audit committee (1) to be informed and vigilant, (2) to have its duties and responsibilities set forth in a written charter, and (3) to be given resources and authority adequate to discharge its responsibilities. Among other things, the audit committee should review management's evaluation of factors related to the independence of the company's public accountant, help preserve that independence and review management's plans for engaging the company's independent public accountant to perform management advisory services during the coming year, considering the types of services that may be rendered and the amount budgeted for such services.

In addition, the Commission highlights other important audit committee functions throughout Chapter Two. The audit committee should review the company's process of assessing the risk of fraudulent financial reporting and the program that management establishes to monitor compliance with the code of corporate conduct. The audit committee should have open lines of communication with the chief accounting officer and the chief internal auditor. In fact, the chief internal auditor's direct and unrestricted access to the audit committee is vital to his objectivity. Management should advise the audit committee when it seeks a second opinion on a significant accounting issue. Audit committees should oversee the quarterly reporting process. Finally, the chairman of the audit committee should write a letter describing the committee's activities and responsibilities for inclusion in the annual report to stockholders.

The Commission developed this set of recommended audit committee duties and responsibilities from a review and consideration of the practices many well-managed companies follow today, of the extensive guidance the public accounting and legal professions have published on the subject, and of practices suggested by the results of the Commission's research projects, and by presentations made to the Commission.

The Commission believes that more detailed delineation and description of responsibilities is best left to the discretion of management and the board of directors to tailor to the needs and circumstances of each company. In the course of its research and deliberations, however, the Commission has identified additional, more specific practices and procedures that can help audit committees perform their oversight role effectively. The Commission is not prescribing these additional measures, and therefore has not included them as recommendations, but offers this guidance in the form of the following Good Practice Guidelines, which companies can consider within the exercise of their judgment. To companies that already have audit committees, the guidelines will serve as a standard for review and assessment. Other companies — those just establishing audit committees or those seeking to

(continued)

FIG. 10-1 *(cont'd)*

improve their committees' effectiveness — may find them to be helpful in suggesting practical ways for audit committees to discharge their responsibilities.

General Guidelines

- *Size and Term of Appointment.* An audit committee normally should consist of not fewer than three independent directors. The maximum size may vary, but the committee should be small enough so that each member is an active participant. The term of appointment is at the discretion of the board of directors, but it is desirable to have terms arranged to maintain continuity while bringing fresh perspectives to the work of the committee.
- *Meetings.* The committee should meet on a regular basis and special meetings should be called as circumstances require. The committee should meet privately with the internal auditor and the independent public accountant.
- *Reporting to the Board of Directors.* The committee should report its activities to the full board on a regular basis, such as after each meeting, so that the board is kept informed of its activities on a current basis.
- *Expand Knowledge of Company Operations.* A systematic and continuing learning process for audit committee members will increase their effectiveness. One way is to review various financial aspects of the company on a planned basis.
- *Company Counsel.* The committee should meet regularly with the company's general counsel, and outside counsel when appropriate, to discuss legal matters that may have a significant impact on the company's financial statements. In a number of companies the general counsel and/or outside counsel attend meetings.
- *Audit Plans.* The committee should review with the chief internal auditor and the independent public accountant their annual audit plans, including the degree of coordination of the respective plans. The committee should inquire as to the extent to which the planned audit scope can be relied upon to detect fraud or weaknesses in internal controls.
- *Electronic Data Processing.* The committee should discuss with the internal auditor and the independent public accountant what steps are planned for a review of the company's electronic data processing procedures and controls, and inquire as to the specific security programs to protect against computer fraud or misuse from both within and outside the company.
- *Other Auditors.* The committee should inquire as to the extent to which independent public accountants other than the principal auditor are to be used and understand the rationale for using them. The committee should request that their work be coordinated and that an appropriate review of their work be performed by the principal auditor.
- *Officer Expenses and Perquisites.* The committee should review in-house policies and procedures for regular review of officers' expenses and perquisites, including any use of corporate assets, inquire as to the results of the review, and, if appropriate, review a summarization of the expenses and perquisites of the period under review.
- *Areas Requiring Special Attention.* The committee should instruct the independent public accountant and the internal auditor that the committee expects to be advised if there are any areas that require its special attention.

Selection of an Independent Public Accountant

A primary responsibility of the audit committee should be the selection of an independent public accountant for the company. The actual selection generally is proposed by management, with the audit committee confirming management's selection, and is ratified by the stockholders. Suggested below are a number of considerations that may enter into the decision. There will be variations, of course, including those that depend upon whether the committee is considering management's proposal to retain the present independent public accountants or management's proposal to appoint a new public accounting firm.

Issues related to this audit:
- Opinions on the performance of the public accounting firm by appropriate management and the chief internal auditor
- The proposed audit fee and the independent public accountant's engagement letter; explanations for fee changes
- The expected level of participation by the partner and other management personnel in the audit examination, the mix of skills and experience of the staff, and staff rotation policy
- If a new public accounting firm is being considered, the steps planned to ensure a smooth and effective transition.

Issues related to the firm generally:
- The report of the public accounting firm's latest peer review conducted pursuant to a professional quality control program
- Any significant litigation problems or disciplinary actions by the SEC or others
- The public accounting firm's credentials, capabilities, and reputation and a list of clients in the same industry and geographical area.

Post-Audit Review

- The committee should obtain from management explanations for all significant variances in the financial statements between years. (This review may be performed at a meeting of the entire board.) The committee should consider whether the data are consistent with the Management's Discussion and Analysis (MD&A) section of the annual report.
- The committee should request an explanation from financial management and the independent public accountant of changes in accounting standards or rules promulgated by the Financial Accounting Standards Board, Securities and Exchange Commission or other regulatory bodies, that have an effect on the financial statements.
- The committee should inquire about the existence and substance of any significant accounting accruals, reserves, or estimates made by management that had a material impact on the financial statements.
- The committee should inquire of management and the independent public accountant if there were any significant financial reporting issues discussed during the accounting period and if so how they were resolved.
- The committee should meet privately with the independent public accountant, to request his opinion on various matters including the quality of financial and accounting personnel and the internal audit staff.
- The committee should ask the independent public accountant what his greatest concerns were and if he believes anything else should be discussed with the committee that has not been raised or covered elsewhere.

(continued)

FIG. 10-1 *(cont'd)*

> - The committee should review the letter of management representations given to the independent public accountant and inquire whether he encountered any difficulties in obtaining the letter or any specific representations therein.
> - The committee should discuss with management and the independent public accountant the substance of any significant issues raised by in-house and outside counsel concerning litigation, contingencies, claims or assessments. The committee should understand how such matters are reflected in the company's financial statements.
> - The committee should determine the open years on federal income tax returns and whether there are any significant items that have been or might be disputed by the IRS, and inquire as to the status of the related tax reserves.
> - The committee should review with management the MD&A section of the annual report and ask the extent to which the independent public accountant reviewed the MD&A section. The committee should inquire of the independent public accountant if the other sections of the annual report to stockholders are consistent with the information reflected in the financial statements.
> - The committee and the board of directors should consider whether the independent public accountant should meet with the full board to discuss any matters relative to the financial statements and to answer any questions that other directors may have.

the chief financial officer of the company, without the chief internal auditor being present. Among other things, these meetings may include discussions of the internal audit activities, so that the audit committee may form an independent appraisal. However, any conclusions should be deferred until the internal staff is provided ample opportunity to tell its story. Circumstances will occasionally arise wherein it is desirable for the chief internal auditor and selected staff members to meet with the audit committee without either members of management or the independent accountants being present.

The remainder of this chapter will deal in more depth with the areas involving the audit committee interface with the internal auditors.

Evaluation of the Internal Audit Staff and Organizational Structure. Obviously, the quality of internal audits will depend in large measure on the educational background, professional training and experience, organizational structure, and skills of the chief internal auditor and the staff members. Hence, the audit committee should be concerned in its overseer role with these matters. While the committee will naturally ask the external auditors and company management about the qualifications of the internal audit staff and structure, it is the primary responsibility of the chief internal auditor to assemble the proper talent, according to his assessment of the departmental needs. However, he must also make sure the audit committee knows and accepts the rationale. Improper selection may lead to substandard audits and mere checking of the financial records, in contrast to the thrust of modern internal auditing toward improved quality and more professionalism. Subjects to be considered by both the audit committee and the chief internal auditor include:

- A high level of professionalism, evidenced by the presence on the staff of a significant number of CPAs and CIAs, as well as personnel having advanced degrees, such as a MBA and, in some cases, a few graduate engineering degrees for project studies. Generalists with an operating background to assist in operational audits, and personnel skilled in EDP auditing, may also be on staff.
- An in-house training program or access to training programs by professional societies such as the IIA or those sponsored by the major independent accounting firms.
- Proper organizational structure to most effectively and economically audit operations in distant locations, including those outside of the United States, if applicable.
- An adequate performance and evaluation system of the staff members.

The qualifications should include, as to each auditor, (1) technical knowledge, (2) good professional communicating skills, both written and spoken, (3) acceptable work habits, and (4) good interpersonal skills. The matter of qualifications is also discussed in Chapters 6 and 9.

Review of Audit Philosophy, Systems, and Procedures. While the audit committee cannot be expected to be comprised of fully qualified auditors (although such a background on the part of some members would be helpful), the group should explore, within limits, such matters as:

- Do the internal audit activities extend beyond the traditional financial audits into, for example, operational audits or EDP auditing?
- Are modern auditing techniques (computer audit techniques and programs, statistical sampling, and so on) used?
- What is the basis of selecting areas to be audited? Are those activities likely to generate large exposures covered every year? Is every significant location (from the accounting and exposure viewpoint) visited at least once a year?
- How are audit programs developed?
- What use is made of manuals?

In summary, to the extent possible, the audit committee should ascertain that the department has the approach of a captive professional accounting firm, and not one whose principal function is that of routine checking of financial transactions.

Review and Monitoring of the System of Controls. The responsibility of the board of directors regarding controls, whether accounting, administrative, or operational, and the importance thereof, is discussed in Chapter 17.

Most directors are cognizant of their oversight responsibilities and are becoming increasingly aware of the role that the internal audit department can, and should, play with respect to controls. Frankly, it usually is the internal auditors who are more knowledgeable of, and in tune with, the internal control systems and their weaknesses—administrative controls, internal accounting controls, and operational controls—than management or, indeed, the public accountants. Accordingly, the audit committee should solicit the viewpoint of the internal auditors and the impact of suspected weakness on the internal audit programs.

Review of Proposed Audit Coverage. One of the most common functions of the audit committee in recent years has been to review the proposed areas of examination by the internal auditors for the coming audit period. With the committee's knowledge of past trouble spots, areas of improper activity, if any, locations with an inadequate profit or performance history, and its own ideas of management weaknesses, it should review the program of audit coverage and schedule at least once each year.

Topics to be covered should include:

- Total auditing budget, including comparison with the past year.
- Specific geographical areas and functions to be visited.
- Expected man-hours to be spent in specified areas, with comments on the special talents being utilized in the examination, if appropriate.
- Specific areas of weakness the audit committee wishes examined.
- Degree of coordination with the independent accountants, and amount of assistance to be given them.

Parenthetically, the point made in Chapter 6 regarding the tendency to use the skilled or professional internal audit staff to perform routine chores under the direction of the independent accountants deserves to be mentioned again. This practice is not to be encouraged; other clerical staff can render such assistance. With this approach, the internal auditors should tend not to dilute their professional efforts. Also to be mentioned is an apparent trend toward increased reliance by the independent accountants on the reviews by the internal auditors, when establishing the scope of examination.

Review of Audit and Postaudit Activities. Having made an overall review of the audit staff and related organizational matters, the systems and procedures, the internal controls, and the audit program and schedule, a major remaining oversight activity is a top scrutiny of the actual audits and results thereof. This may involve these aspects:

- ☐ Review of actual audits made as compared with program—man-hours expended vs. plan, and the planned examinations that were not accomplished, together with the reason therefor.

- ☐ A review of some of the major conditions found to exist.
- ☐ A spotcheck examination of some audit reports, particularly those areas that are of most concern to the audit committee.
- ☐ Obtaining a brief summary of the recommendations made, corrective or implementing action taken by management, and items where either no corrective action was taken or where there is disagreement as to the adequacy of the type and amount of follow-up activity necessary.

In these discussions, the chief internal auditor should brief the committee on the potentially significant problems, exposures, or deficiencies.

Independent Evaluation Might Be Helpful

The audit committee and, indeed, the entire board of directors and top management, want to be certain that the internal audit function is meeting the company's needs satisfactorily. This requirement to be informed extends not only to the organizational structure and qualifications of the staff, but also to the proficiency with which assignments are executed, as well as the scope of the work, extent of assignments, and the proficiency in communicating. The audit committee also should be assured that the management has assigned the proper responsibilities and resources to the function. Further, it should be satisfied that the function is achieving in a reasonable degree the goals set forth by the profession itself in the Standards for the Professional Practice of Internal Auditing adopted in 1978 by the IIA. (See Chapter 6 for example.) Of course, the chief internal auditor also would want to be satisfied on these matters.

Given the technical aspects of the internal audit function, it may be helpful and desirable to periodically have an evaluation of the function by a knowledgeable outside group. Who should do the evaluating, how it should be performed and how it should be reported should be decided by the audit committee and perhaps senior management—with input from the chief internal auditor or others.

Those to be considered for evaluators could include: peer groups of internal auditors employed outside the company or by affiliated entities; independent public accountants, either employed by the company, from another office of the same firm, or from another firm; or professional consultants. Some companies have formed internal teams comprised of management members for this purpose. There are advantages and disadvantages associated with each alternative because of the variables involved. These variables include cost trade-offs, degree of objectivity, knowledge of the company, and knowledge of auditing. Audit committees or their designees must consider these in light of their individual circumstances and must choose accordingly.

In any event, a competent evaluation team should provide valuable input to those concerned as to the internal audit function's compliance with the responsibilities established by management and with the *Standards*.

Making the Audit Committee More Effective

The purpose of the preceding sections was to alert the reader as to the type of queries an audit committee might direct to the chief internal auditor. It was provided so that he would be fully prepared to respond with complete and forthright answers. However, aside from this reactive posture and the formal presentations to the audit committee (discussed in the next section), there is one other type of assistance that the chief internal auditor, if circumstances make it prudent, may provide to the chairman of the audit committee. This relates to suggesting agenda items for audit committee meetings.

Very often, it will be helpful to the chairman of the audit committee if he is provided with a suggested agenda for the periodic meetings. Ordinarily, he may seek the suggestions from the chief financial officer, but he may also ask the chief internal auditor, the controller, or others. In any event, either directly or indirectly through others, the internal auditor should suggest any timely items about which the audit committee should be informed. With his broad knowledge of the financial and accounting activities of the company, he should be aware of the important or significant events that have transpired and, accordingly, he should communicate his ideas on possible topics for discussion. Very often, the chief financial officer will be knowledgeable about all subjects that ought to be reviewed, but not necessarily so. In any event, it is better to have some duplication rather than have a serious omission.

The agenda suggested by the internal auditor need not be restricted to those activities directly involving the internal audit function, but should extend to any that properly should be brought before the committee. For the planning meeting, or any follow-up meeting, the following provides a list that contains matters usually discussed if they are germane at the time:

1. General areas for Audit Committee discussion
   - ☐ Changes in accounting principles, practices, or applications that either have had a significant impact on financial statements for the current year or are expected to have in future years (e.g., FIFO to LIFO inventory valuation, depreciation rates, and tax accruals)
   - ☐ Reporting requirements, such as:
     - Annual report to shareholders
     - Reports to regulatory agencies (e.g., SEC and Department of Labor)
     - Management report (if included in annual report to shareholders)
   - ☐ Major adjustments to current financial statements that do *not* involve a change in accounting principles or practice
   - ☐ Major adjustments that were considered, or proposed to management, but were not made—and the reasons for the decision
   - ☐ Adequacy of disclosure in the financial statements of such sensitive matters as:
     - Transactions of an unusual nature with corporate officers

COMMUNICATING WITH THE AUDIT COMMITTEE

- Prohibited transactions (e.g., illegal payments)
- Possible litigation that may have a material effect on the financial position of the company
- Probable accounting treatment of forthcoming major transactions (e.g., acquisitions or divestments)
- Comparability, and degree of conservatism, of accounting practices compared with competitors or the industry in general
- Adherence to GAAP and their significance
- Impact on the company of new or recent FASB, SEC, IRS, or other regulatory body pronouncements

2. Plan and scope of audit activities
   - ☐ Areas in which the internal auditors or independent accountants found it necessary to expand the scope of the examination by reason of unsatisfactory results of the initial test of transactions
   - ☐ Degree to which organizational changes or changes in the level of activity have been reflected in modified audit plans
   - ☐ Extent to which the reviews of the financial information system has on the audit plan
   - ☐ Degree to which fraudulent activity has resulted in a change of audit plans
   - ☐ Extent to which changes in the internal control system have affected or have been affected by changes in the computer system
   - ☐ Degree to which the independent auditors have relied on the internal audit staff and coordinated the audit tests with the internal audit activity

3. Internal controls—accounting, operational, and administrative
   - ☐ General evaluation of each, to extent reviewed:
     - Administrative
     - Accounting
     - Operational
   - ☐ Balancing cost of controls and risks assumed by the company
   - ☐ Discussion of management override possibilities and instances revealed
   - ☐ Detailed review of areas and findings where unsatisfactory test results or inadequate accounting records required extended or alternative accounting—both by independent accountants and internal auditors
   - ☐ Recommended changes of significance in internal controls that either group of auditors believes will increase adherence to management policies as well as the safeguarding of assets
   - ☐ Acceptability or adequacy of conflict-of-interest policy and procedure of annual review with management individuals
   - ☐ Adequacy of internal controls over cash receipts and disbursements, including computer transfers and computer security
   - ☐ Adequacy of information security in computer applications
   - ☐ Observations about operational or administrative controls that were not within the scope of examination of the independent accountants or the internal auditors

- Observations on the management reporting system with particular reference to management reviews, management influencing, and management override
- Adequacy of bond coverage—fidelity bonds on employees, and computer security
- The auditors' (internal and external) appraisal of the efficiency and effectiveness of the accounting and/or financial functions and financial management
- Internal controls in the computer area—selection of personnel, organizational structure, control of inputs and outputs in sensitive or exposure areas
- Adequacy and timeliness of compliance with prior-year recommendations in the controls (or other) areas

4. Management relations
   - Degree to which information requested by the independent accountants or internal auditors was withheld or provided
   - Degree of access of either auditing group to the Audit Committee (and to top management)
   - Extent to which financial management advised either group on matters germane to its activities (e.g., year-end audit, fraud, other improper activities, and change in organization responsibility)

5. Other areas
   - Effectiveness and organization of the internal audit staff training
   - Degree of systems and/or tax effort, if any, suggested to be performed by the independent accountants

These are just some of the suggested topics that might be appropriate for review by the audit committee. The extent to which some or all of them are covered in any single meeting will depend on the circumstances and the professional judgment of the chief internal auditor.

PRESENTATIONS TO THE AUDIT COMMITTEE

The chief internal auditor, as well as his staff members, should welcome the opportunity to make presentations to the audit committee. In the correct environment, and with the right attitude, a presentation of this sort offers the following opportunities:

- The audit committee has the chance to obtain an insight into operations of a company that simply would not ordinarily be available from other company representatives or even the external auditors.
- The chief internal auditor is able to:
  - Enlighten and educate the audit committee members on the significant risks, control systems and procedures, and certain operational methods.

COMMUNICATING WITH THE AUDIT COMMITTEE 10-15

- "Sell" the need for the department's activities, display his capabilities and competence, and, in general, foster good will towards the function and its staff.
- Encourage support for well-thought-out proposed changes in policies and procedures, and for a carefully planned budget for departmental needs.

Well-prepared presentations encourage mutual respect and confidence between the audit committee and the audit function that should help establish credibility and solve problems.

Types of Presentations

Presentations to an audit committee may be informal or formal, written or oral. In the opinion of the authors, face-to-face meetings are the most desirable. To be sure, much will depend on the wishes of the audit committee itself. However, given the technical nature of the subject and perhaps the lack of specific knowledge on the part of many audit committee members, person-to-person meetings where participants are well-prepared are suggested as a better forum to give explanations and discuss plans and findings. The chief internal auditor is encouraged to promote this type of interchange.

Just what subject matter is covered depends on the purpose of the meeting. The general content is suggested, in part, by the preceding discussion of the responsibilities and interests of the audit committee.

It is suggested, generally, that visual aids be used liberally (see Chapter 13), that significant matters be covered, devoid of unimportant details, and that summarized data be presented. If the chief internal auditor concentrates on what he believes is important, and what the audit committee should know in fulfilling its responsibilities, then concise and rapidly moving oral commentary can be made. An agenda of topics to be covered should preferably be worked out ahead of time with the chairman or secretary of the committee. Some useful devices or techniques in making reports are also discussed in Chapter 13.

Suggested Coverage

Topics covered in the planning meeting for the coming year audits (based on the knowledge and experience of the audit committee with the internal audit function) might include data on:

1. Scope of planned audit coverage
   ☐ Master audit schedule:
     - Manpower
     - Month of accomplishment

- ☐ Planned regular audit coverage:
  - At the corporate level
  - By profit center
  - By functions
  - By type (e.g., financial, operational, and EDP)
- ☐ Headquarters coverage:
  - For other activities (e.g., pension funds, insurance affiliate, and credit union)
  - By general type (man-hours), including:
    —EDP audits
    —Operational audits
    —Management audits (in corporation with others)
    —Financial audits
  - Special audits
- ☐ Special security audits:
  - Computer fund transfers
  - Precious metal coverage
  - Temporary investments
- ☐ Other reviews:
  - Conflict-of-interest matters
  - Special subcontractor checks

2. Review of policies and procedures
   - ☐ Audit philosophy
   - ☐ Policy reviews
   - ☐ Procedure reviews
   - ☐ Typical audit procedure:
     - Internal controls
     - Operating review
     - Financial audits
     - Questionnaires
     - Monthly management (financial) report

3. Trends in audit practice
   - ☐ New developments
   - ☐ New techniques
   - ☐ Computer audit innovations or adoptions

Near the end of the year, a progress report might cover such subjects as:

1. Audits completed and in progress
   - ☐ Summary by location and function:
     - Generally satisfactory conditions and corrective actions
     - Significant negative findings or lack of implementation

COMMUNICATING WITH THE AUDIT COMMITTEE 10-17

☐ Review of selected audits:
- Those of special interest to audit committee
- Sensitive activities
- High or sustained exposure
- Unusually good circumstances or conditions observed

2. Freedom of activity report
   ☐ Access to records, including special contracts (need to know)
   ☐ Access to board, audit committee, and top management
   ☐ Independence in report preparation

The oral reports to the audit committee may be preceded by a highly summarized "annual report." Discretion in wording and content of any report made in writing, especially on sensitive subjects, is an important consideration. Examples of audit reports are illustrated and discussed in Chapter 13.

Illustrative Segments of a Report to the Audit Committee

The immediately preceding section contains suggestions of topics regarding the internal audit function or related matters that might be presented to the audit committee by the chief internal auditor. Chapter 13 discusses very briefly activity and evaluation reports to the audit committee, in which emphasis in the illustration is on internal controls. This section covers another subject that might be included in an activity report.

To a greater extent than before, in a more formal manner, U.S. corporations are planning activities several years in the future. Quite properly, the audit committee should be knowledgeable about the longer term plans for the internal audit activity and how the actual and planned increases in costs compare with other corporate measures of growth. Illustrated in Figures 10-2 through 10-5 are segments supporting the five-year plan, including:

- Graph of total internal audit department costs.
- Percentage increase in departmental costs versus operating profit and net sales.
- Proposed trend in audit staff composition.
- Planned computer system review.

Figure 10-2 indicates that total direct costs of the internal audit department for the past five years (1983-1987), and planned on proposed expenses for the next five years (1988-1992). Because it is a department of the financial division, a rather constant share of the total division costs are shown. As is explained in the meeting, despite significant expansion in foreign operations, the growth in audit function costs has not significantly increased in its share of the financial operations budget.

FIG. 10-2
Internal Audit Department Costs

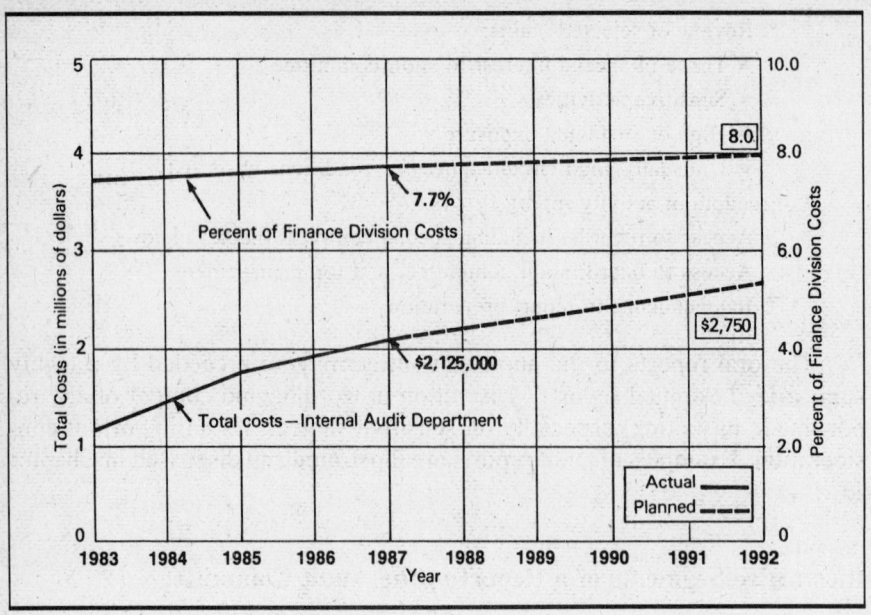

FIG. 10-3
Percentage Increase in Sales, Income, and Internal Audit Costs

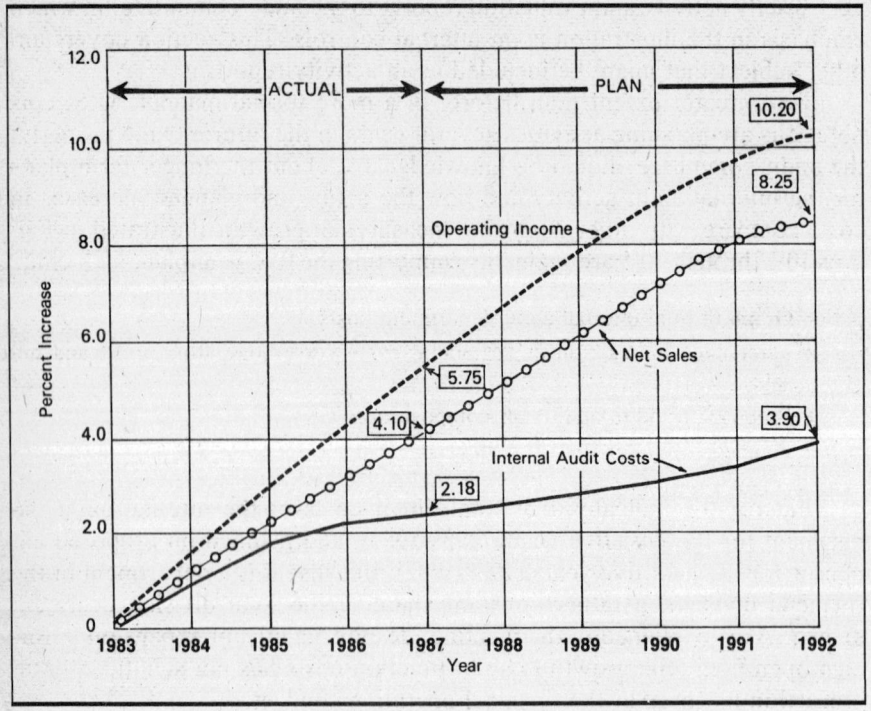

FIG. 10-4
Composition of Internal Audit Staff

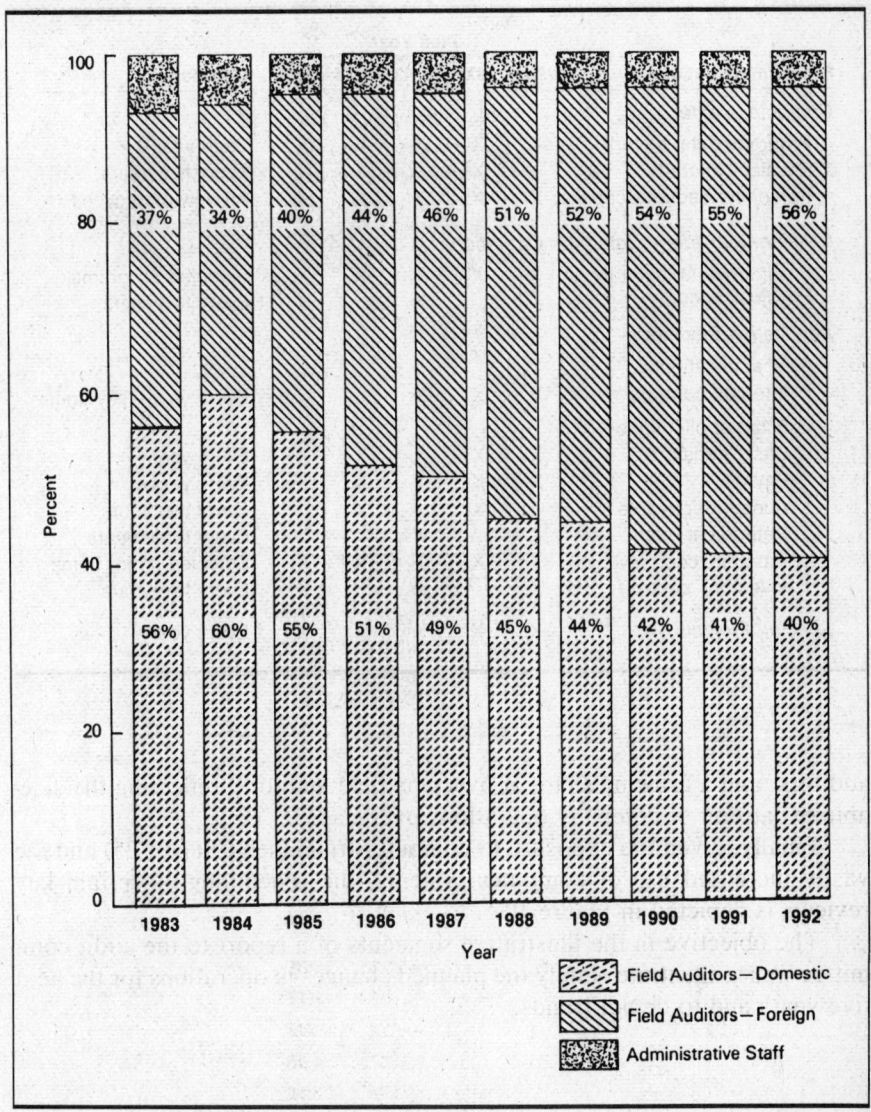

Figure 10-3 reflects the slower growth of internal audit department costs, as compared to net sales or operating income. This, of course, is generally expected.

By means of a percentage bar chart, the change in composition of the internal audit staff is portrayed in Figure 10-4: a decreasing share of administrative personnel, a relative decline in the number of domestic field

FIG. 10-5

Planned Computer Systems Reviews

| | Plan Year | | | | | |
Function/Operation	19X1	19X2	19X3	19X4	19X5	Commentary
Computer Center						
Program/data security	X	X	X	X	X	Each year
Physical security		X		X		Every two years
Personnel security checks	X	X	X	X	X	All new employees
Division/Subsidiary Computer Operations						
Program/data security	X	X	X	X	X	Selected programs
Physical security	X		X		X	Every two years
Application Reviews						
New applications						
Internal controls	X	X	X	X	X	Every year—key items
Existing applications						
Cash transfers	X	X	X	X	X	Every year
Payroll	X	X	X	X	X	Every year
Accounts payable		X		X		Every two years
Retirement plan			X			Every three years
Program cost reviews	X	X	X	X		Selected major items
Inventory control	X		X		X	Every two years
Special Projects	X	X	X	X	X	Every year

auditors, and a growing share of overseas field auditors, reflecting the sizeable expansion of company operations overseas.

Finally, given the exposure to computer fraud (see Chapter 25) and the vastly increased use of computer systems, the scheduling of certain key reviews is depicted in Figure 10-5.

The objective in the illustrative segments of a report to the audit committee was to illustrate simply the planned changes in operations for the next five years and to depict trends.

SUGGESTED READING

Audit Committee, The. The Board of Directors and The Independent Accountant. New York: Price Waterhouse & Co., 1973.

Audit Committees. Current Practices in Canada, the United Kingdom, and the United States. Accountants International Study Group, 1977.

Bacon, Jeremy. *Corporate Directorship Practices: The Audit Committee,* Report No. 76C. New York: The Conference Board, 1979.

Braiotta, Louis, J. *The Audit Directors Guide.* New York: John Wiley & Sons, 1981.

Connor, Joseph E., and Burnell H. DeVos, Jr., "The Monitoring Function—Audit Committees and Internal Auditing." *Guide to Accounting Controls, 1981 Supplement.* New York: Warren, Gorham & Lamont, 1981.

PART IV
Techniques for the Practitioner

PART IV

Techniques for the Practitioner

CHAPTER 11

How to Perform Preliminary Work

Background 1	Reviewing Pertinent Department and Organizational Records 8
Definition 2	Researching Authoritative Literature 12
Purpose 3	Interviewing Management 26
Elements of Preliminary Work 3	Preparing and Modifying Audit Tools 27
Overview 3	Coordinating Efforts 29
Routine vs. Nonroutine Efforts 4	Developing the Audit Plan 31
Defining Objectives 6	
Recurring Audits 6	Suggested Reading 32
Nonrecurring Audits 6	

Fig. 11-1 Categorizing Audit Project Preliminary Work	5
Fig. 11-2 Nonrecurring Audit Project Objectives	9
Fig. 11-3 Online Database Services	14
Fig. 11-4 Diagram of Computer Research Information Flow	25
Fig. 11-5 Examples of Survey Subjects	27
Fig. 11-6 Formal Communication of Year's Audits and Audit Arrangements	30
Fig. 11-7 Memo Communicating Specific Audit Arrangements	32

BACKGROUND

Up to this point, discussion has centered on developing a broad perspective on the audit function, and an understanding of the approaches and other techniques for effective internal audit management. With few exceptions, little has been said about how to perform an effective audit. The focus now shifts to a discussion of techniques for actual audit performance.

One might question why a book on managing the audit function would devote space to the subject of audit performance. The explanation is simple: Audit managers as well as practitioners must understand how audits are performed if each is to be effective. Also, for some audits, managers must perform some or all of the fieldwork themselves. This is true for external auditors and government auditors, as well as for internal auditors at private companies. As an example, this may occur in some special investigation requested by the board of directors or other high-ranking management members. The discretion, confidentiality, and professional competence required during such an investigation may mean that the chief auditor or an audit manager perform the audit. In some companies, internal auditing is performed by teams of managers of other disciplines who have been assembled on a temporary basis for the purpose of studying and reviewing specific aspects of the company's operations. Because these managers must not be familiar with techniques for effective auditing, the discussion in this chapter should also be helpful to them.

Audits of foreign operations of multinational firms are another example of situations in which audit managers or the director may be asked to perform the fieldwork. In these situations, the costs associated with performing fieldwork in distant locations may warrant that the work be performed by the most competent members of the staff to minimize the risk of an inferior product. Of course, audit managers in audit organizations that have foreign-based audit sections are not as susceptible to this situation as are audit organizations whose foreign audit requirements do not justify establishing such a section.

To facilitate the discussion of techniques, the audit is divided into the following topical areas that reflect the broad steps involved in virtually all audits:

- Preliminary work
- Fieldwork
- Communicating results

These areas are discussed in Chapters 11 (preliminary work), 12 (fieldwork), and 13 (communicating results). All relevant matters and practical techniques involved in performing audit projects are covered in these chapters. The more technical aspects of fieldwork are discussed in Chapters 14 (evidential matter), 15 (audit sampling), and 16 (audit procedures). The audit approach in Chapter 2 is emphasized throughout, particularly in Chapter 16. Chapters 14–16 also discuss the fieldwork requirements of limited financial reviews, detailed internal control audits, internal control surveys, and business conduct reviews. This chapter deals with the first phase of fieldwork: the preliminary phase.

DEFINITION

While preliminary work is involved in virtually every audit project, the term "preliminary work," like many other widely used audit terms, is not defined precisely by the professional literature. As the term implies, it covers the activities involved in getting ready to perform the actual audit work. These activities are preliminary because they are the first steps that must be taken, and because the nature of each audit makes the initial preparations subject to change as unexpected events and circumstances arise.

A workable definition for purposes of this chapter is as follows: Preliminary work comprises the efforts by assigned project members to devise a feasible audit plan that, upon performance, will reasonably assure the completion of the assignment in accordance with the standards of the department. (See Chapter 6.)

PURPOSE

Simply stated, the purpose of preliminary work is to prepare the auditor to perform the required fieldwork. However, that is not the only purpose. When properly completed, preliminary work establishes the feasibility of the assigned project. Preliminary work enables the performing auditor to determine that the objectives are attainable and that the planned procedures are workable.

Preliminary work also helps assure the audit department standards, which in turn help assure that the audit performed is of the highest quality. In essence, preliminary work entails planning, which is central to the success of any audit engagement.[1]

ELEMENTS OF PRELIMINARY WORK

Overview

The elements or components of preliminary work typically include the following:

- Defining objectives
- Reviewing pertinent department and organization files
- Researching authoritative literature
- Interviewing management
- Preparing or modifying audit tools
- Coordinating efforts
- Developing the audit plan

---

[1] J. W. Martin, "Documenting Key Audit Decisions," *The National Public Accountant*, Mar. 1981, p. 18.

These elements do not necessarily occur sequentially during the preliminary phase. For example, the objectives may not be defined finally until after affected management is consulted. Moreover, some activities, such as coordination, may occur throughout. It is important to realize the dynamic nature of the preliminary phase. Information gathered from any given source may change plans for other procedures, timing, scope, and so on.

Routine vs. Nonroutine Efforts

Audit projects may be divided into those that are routine and those that are not routine. Routine audits are those that recur according to some specified internal schedule (e.g., annually or biannually), and those that are nonroutine (i.e., those that do not recur, or, if they do recur, it is after so long an interval that the value of the prior work is practically nil for purposes of preliminary work). This distinction between routine and nonroutine projects is important because the preliminary work tends to be divided into either routine or nonroutine work, depending on the nature of the assignment.

Of course, some projects will fall between these two extremes. Figure 11-1 illustrates this point. It categorizes the required effort in terms of preliminary work into routine (R), somewhat routine (SR), or original (O) for the most common types of auditing discussed in this book. It can be seen that limited financial reviews, standards-of-business-conduct audits, and internal control surveys are classified as routine (R). That is because these assignments recur with great frequency. The auditor's familiarity with their objectives and requirements should be complete. Since these projects recur, the organizations and departments to be audited should also be familiar with what is intended in these audits.

On the other hand, preliminary work associated with nonrecurring audit efforts, such as special investigations, many operational audits, and certain aspects of EDP auditing, requires more originality because they recur with much less frequency.

Detailed internal control audits fall in between. Some of these recur with a high frequency, such as audits of payroll, procurement, and cash receipts and disbursements. Others occur less frequently. These include depreciation procedures, indirect cost transactions, and insurance.

Even though the preliminary work is more routine in many instances, it is no less important. In recurring preliminary work, the performing auditor must be alert for anything that will have an impact on the traditional plan. He must be prepared to alter the plan accordingly. Blindly accepting what has been done in the past can cause adverse consequences. Systems, products, people, and requirements all change over time and must be identified, reexamined, and evaluated against previous plans to assure the plans' continued utility.

HOW TO PERFORM PRELIMINARY WORK

FIG. 11-1

Categorizing Audit Project Preliminary Work

	Recurring					Nonrecurring		
	Limited Financial Review	Business Conduct	Internal Control Survey	Detailed Internal Control	EDP Installation	EDP Operations	Operational Auditing	Special
Planning	R	R	R	SR	SR	O	O	O
Defining objectives	R	R	R	R	R	O	O	O
Review prior workpapers	R	R	R	R	R	NA	NA	NA
Research literature	R	R	R	SR	SR	O	O	O
Interview management	R	R	R	SR	R	SR	O	O
Prepare/Modify audit program	R	R	R	SR	SR	O	O	O
Prepare/Modify questionnaires	R	R	R	SR	SR	O	O	O
Prepare time budget	O	O	O	O	O	O	O	O
Coordination	O	O	O	O	O	O	O	O
Modifying	O	O	O	O	O	O	O	O

R = Routine
SR = Somewhat routine
O = Original
NA = Not applicable

Defining Objectives

Recurring Audits. Auditors must define objectives as soon in the preliminary work as is practicable. Early definition of objectives minimizes confusion, avoids wasting time, and saves wear and tear on auditors and auditees alike.

Objectives for recurring assignments are relatively easy to deal with. Generally speaking, if the objectives were appropriate in the previous assignment, they will also be appropriate for the current assignment. Examples of objectives for recurring work are as follows:

- ☐ Limited financial review
  - To determine the consistency of application of accounting principles between interim and year-end financial statements.
  - To determine compliance with applicable company policies pertaining to financial reporting.
  - To provide other information of use to management.
- ☐ Internal control survey
  - To evaluate the adequacy[2] of internal accounting controls.
  - To determine the extent to which evidence indicates that accounting controls operated during the period under review.
- ☐ Detailed internal control audit
  - Same as for the internal control survey.
- ☐ Ethical business conduct audit
  - To measure compliance with applicable policies.
  - To provide information of use to management in evaluating compliance with company policy.

Nonrecurring Audits. The less frequently recurring or nonrecurring audit activities require more effort to define the objectives properly. Because of the variety of circumstances in which these activities may occur, it is not practicable to generalize or standardize the objectives much beyond the following:

- ☐ I/S application audits (see Chapter 27) tend to be concerned with evaluating whether or not the controls within the application:
  - Process the subject information completely and accurately.
  - Fulfill user needs.
  - Employ data processing resources effectively and efficiently.
  - Sufficiently safeguard data and related equipment.
- ☐ I/S installation audits (see Chapter 27) are more broadbased and cover

---

[2] Adequacy as used here is defined in accordance with AU § 320.28 of the *Professional Standards*, Vol. 1, published by the AICPA. See Chapter 3.

HOW TO PERFORM PRELIMINARY WORK

virtually all aspects of data processing within a given EDP facility. However, the objectives are similar to those stated for application audits.

☐ Operational audits (see Chapter 31) are performed to provide information with respect to efficiency and effectiveness. However, specific objectives can and do vary, depending on the operation selected for review.

☐ Special reviews are undertaken to provide information of use to management. The specific objectives in these reviews also vary.

To establish objectives in nonrecurring assignments, the performing auditor must work closely with the audit manager or director and management and conform to the following principles.

☐ *Objectives must fulfill management's needs.* This, of course, is the fundamental purpose of internal auditing. (See Chapter 2.) Internal auditors must remember that differing management levels have differing needs. Thus, assurances with respect to internal control in an overall scope may be very useful to audit committees and senior managements. However, line managements are interested in more specific assessments. Because of their closer association with company operations, their concerns and interests tend to be more focused. For example, line management may be interested in information that would help identify causes for a buildup in inventory, a deterioration in collections, or some other operating problem. At other times, they may be interested in having compliance with recently complemented procedures measured, or they may wish the effectiveness of other procedures to be evaluated. Sometimes, managements may be uncertain of what their needs are vis-à-vis internal auditing. Managements are usually most willing to receive the assistance of the audit department in defining these unstated needs. This assistance is particularly useful to those management members who may not be completely familiar with the capabilities of the audit function.

☐ *Objectives must be feasible.* Auditors cannot do the impossible. In being willing to serve management needs, care must be taken to avoid becoming overzealous. Management expectations may not be feasible for various reasons. The audit department may not possess the requisite knowledge, the timing may be inappropriate, or the objectives may simply be unattainable. For example, no auditor can "identify fraudulent activities, to the extent they exist," even though some managements may wish it.

☐ *Statement of objectives must state objectives.* It is easy to confuse objectives with procedures. Objectives should be thought of as the end product; procedures are the means to attain them. A statement such as "to examine canceled checks" sounds like an objective but is not. The following also sound like objectives, but *are not*:

- To review internal control
- To evaluate security measures
- To observe physical inventories
- To analyze accounts receivable

Each of the foregoing requires that procedures be performed to accomplish them. They are *not* objectives, however, because they are not end products; that is, they do not result in fulfilling a management need.[3] For example, reviews of internal control and security evaluations are done to provide information to management as to their sufficiency. Physical inventories are observed to establish their existence and accounts receivable may be analyzed for a variety of reasons. By relating objectives to management needs, questions are avoided as to why the auditor is undertaking a particular course of action.

Examples of objectives for nonrecurring audit projects are shown in Figure 11-2. In each example, the reader should be able to imagine a tentative series of steps that could be employed—some simple and some complex—to achieve the objectives. These should be steps that will differ markedly in each case. These tentative series of steps represent the initial definition of the scope of work. This is the acid test of defined objectives—whether they permit the formation of a tentative work scope. If they do, the objectives have been adequately defined; if they have not, more defining is in order.

Reviewing Pertinent Department and Organizational Records

The auditor's objective in reviewing pertinent files and records is to obtain background information relevant to the particular assignment. The extent of the review depends on the auditor's familiarity with the assignment before commencing the preliminary work. Normally, the auditor is more familiar with recurring work. Also, records are likely to have more information available for review pertaining to recurring work.

A thorough review of relevant documentation not only provides useful information, but also reduces the amount of time that otherwise would be required of the auditee. However, unless the auditor knows what he is looking for, the effort will be wasted. For this purpose, information is useful if it increases the auditor's knowledge in a twofold manner:

1. With respect to the auditee
   - Organization structure
   - Names and titles of personnel likely to be involved
   - Nature of the products or services provided
   - Procedures and methods of accounting
   - Trends in operating results
   - Business plans
   - Budgeting performance
   - Management concerns
   - Operational difficulties, if any

---

[3] Management need as used here includes the audit committee and the board of directors.

FIG. 11-2

Nonrecurring Audit Project Objectives

Nonrecurring Audit Type	Function or Operation	Specific Objectives
EDP OPERATIONS	■ Security	Evaluate whether security controls are sufficient to reasonably assure (1) protection of vital equipment and other resources against damage or destruction; (2) safeguarding of critical data against unauthorized access or misuse; and (3) maintenance of an effective disaster recovery capability in the event of an emergency, disaster, or other disruptive occurrence.
	■ Operating system	Evaluate whether controls over the operating system reasonably assure system integrity.
	■ Supplies	Determine that controls over data processing supplies reasonably assure availability for production use, proper recording and reporting of inventory transactions and status, and protection against loss or unauthorized use.
	■ Reruns	Evaluate whether controls over job and system failures (including reruns and abends) are sufficient to reasonably assure accuracy of information, quality of service, and reasonableness of cost (i.e., to minimize adverse effects upon data processing costs and services).
	■ Data base management	Determine the adequacy and effectiveness of existing data base management facilities administration and operations in providing and maintaining a reliable, effective, and secure data processing medium for the input, storage, and retrieval of information.
OPERATIONAL	■ Cash management	Determine that (1) investment activities meet management criteria; (2) interbank transfers occur pursuant to management guidelines; (3) investment transactions are properly recorded and reported; and (4) access to cash and investments is appropriately restricted.
	■ Facilities management	1. Evaluate the adequacy of corporate policy for major facility transactions including control over resource planning, monitoring of present use, preparation of

(continued)

FIG. 11-2 *(cont'd)*

Nonrecurring Audit Type	Function or Operation	Specific Objectives
OPERATIONAL (cont'd)		master plans, and monitoring of construction in progress.
		2. Determine that major investments in the facilities master plan are based upon an analysis of (1) the need to support production schedules; (2) return on investment; (3) adequate planning to anticipate future requirements; and (4) analysis of investment considerations including financing methods and tax effects.
		3. Determine that facilities transactions are properly approved, recorded and reported, and safeguarded.
	■ Travel cost	Survey the effectiveness and efficiency of present practices for providing travel services to company employees and to assess whether travel costs are the most reasonable to the company in the circumstances.
	■ Transportation	Evaluate the transportation energy conservation programs, and ascertain compliance with company objectives to support the national effort to reduce gasoline consumption.
	■ Engineering changes	1. Evaluate the control techniques to reasonably assure proper authorization and review of changes.
		2. Determine adequacy of procedures for timely and accurate recording and reporting and implementation of changes.
		3. Determine adequacy of techniques for identifying and disposing of surplus inventory created by such changes.
SPECIAL	■ Consigned inventory	Review inventory consigned to the ABC Company to determine whether (1) adequate safeguards exist to prevent loss from theft or misappropriation; (2) sales and remittances have been properly reported; and (3) balance of inventory on hand per physical count and inspection reconciles to records of consigned inventory.
	■ Supplier qualification	Provide information to purchasing and finance management regarding the financial capability of the ABC Company based upon an analytical review of

HOW TO PERFORM PRELIMINARY WORK 11-11

Nonrecurring Audit Type	Function or Operation	Specific Objectives
SPECIAL (cont'd)		financial statements and inquiries of ABC management.
	■ Claim support	Provide analytical assistance to the project team involved in documenting the claim for recovery on the ABC project.
	■ Management assistance	Assist management in investigating the cause of inventory shortage.
	■ Employee allegation	1. Determine if any sum is owed to John Doe.
		2. Gather evidence to confirm facts represented to Law Department by Mr. Doe.
		3. Determine level of service provided to Mr. Doe and the propriety of payments made to him.

2. With respect to the audit approach
   - Workable audit objectives
   - Audit procedures
   - Questionnaires and checklists
   - Analytical techniques
   - Nature and extent of testing
   - Requirements of auditee personnel
   - Tentative time requirements
   - Potential problem areas
   - Opportunities for using generalized audit software

The primary source for much of the useful information is the audit department's workpaper files (see Chapter 12). If the assignment is recurring or has been performed within the previous two or three years, the workpapers, if available, will be quite useful. If the specific project has not been recently performed, similar projects may have been performed at other locations, or other related projects may have been performed at that location. These workpapers may contain information of use to the current project, even though the current project may differ in several respects. If workpapers are not available, the auditor should not give up, for other files, if present, may provide useful information. These include the following:

- Report files, particularly if topical report files are maintained
- Monthly financial statement files
- Business plan files

- Procedural files (Note that not all audit departments maintain files of current company procedures. The cost is sometimes prohibitive. Usually, however, some corporate function is responsible for maintaining current procedural files that are easily accessible to the audit staff.)

Keeping these files and workpaper files intact in the face of their constant review is quite a task. The usefulness of the files is directly proportionate to their being available, intact, and current. Auditors making use of the files must properly care for them and must return them promptly when done.

Other sources from which relevant information can be gleaned include the following:

- Corporate policy statements
- Procedure manuals
- Organization charts
- Flow charts
- Interim financial reports
- Annual reports to shareholders
- Information reports filed with regulatory agencies
- Published news articles

Some of these files may be available in the audit department, but often, they must be obtained from other sources within the company. A knowledge of where to find relevant information is indispensable in performing preliminary work. If the performing auditor is unsure of where to look, he should seek assistance either from more experienced performing auditors, or from supervisory personnel.

Researching Authoritative Literature

The point was made in Chapter 7 and emphasized again in Chapter 9 that the pace of new developments that affect the body of knowledge requisite to proper auditing is both constant and rapid. Moreover, no auditor is completely familiar with all aspects of the body of knowledge. Therefore, it is usually helpful for the auditor to perform some research in connection with each project.

The recurring projects will not demand the same effort as the nonrecurring projects. However, there can be exceptions. For example, the Tax Reform Act of 1986 drastically changed income tax law with respect to depreciation, among other things. Auditors' review after 1986 of internal controls over depreciation accounting had to take into account the new requirements.

If the audit department maintains or has ready access to a business library (see Chapter 9), the research effort is greatly facilitated. However, in the absence of an internal library, information is otherwise available. Many offices of the large CPA firms maintain libraries. The firms are invariably willing to make these facilities available to internal auditors of their clients for reference purposes. Also, colleges and universities that offer a business curriculum have library facilities that might be accessed. Arrangements might even be made with nearby companies that maintain business libraries.

In recent years, electronic data processing developments have enabled automated information retrieval services to be offered by a small, but growing, number of vendors. These vendors have each assembled reference data onto magnetic tapes obtained from various government and other sources (known as data base producers). Some data bases are general as to subject matter, while others are more focused. The search and retrieval services are offered on a fee basis for customers to whom passwords have been issued. All the customer needs is a terminal, preferably one with a cathode-ray tube (CRT), or screen, a modem (to permit dial-up via the telephone), and perhaps a printer to enable on-site printing, as necessary, of information retrieved. In addition, the customer or user must become familiar with the simple query languages involved.

When suitably equipped, the audit department's research capability is increased dramatically by acquiring one or more of these computer research systems. Complete searches can be performed in less than 10 minutes with these powerful new systems.

Information data bases now contain a vast array of textual information. In addition, users are able to take advantages of related services, such as electronic mail, bulletin boards, and citizen band communications. Among the varieties of data available are the following:

- Wire service reports
- Stock quotations and related market data
- Financial newsletters
- Flight schedules
- Classified advertisements, such as those for jobs
- Consumer information
- Banking

Figure 11-3 provides a rather complete listing of such data bases. A more complete description of the services available is contained in the referenced article from which Figure 11-3 was excerpted.[4]

Costs for information data base services fluctuate with usage. Generally

(continued on page 11-24)

---

[4] Elizabeth M. Ferrarini, "Fingertip Power," *Micro Communications*, Feb. 1984, pp. 59–65. Reprinted by permission.

FIG. 11-3
Online Database Services

Company	Database	End Users	Subjects	Summary
Bibliographic Retrieval Services 1200 Route 7 Latham, N.Y. 12110 Tel: (518) 783-1161 (800) 833-4707	BRS	Business, academic	Life, physical, social and engineering sciences, as well as business, economics and general reference	Over 80 databases offered including Bibliographic and Source databases, *Harvard Business Review, Financial Times of London, Medicine, Books in Print, Chemical Abstracts,* and *Frost & Sullivan Market Research Report Abstracts.*
Bibliographic Retrieval Services same as above	BRS/After Dark	Computer hobbyists, business, researchers	Business, finance, education, energy, environment, news, patent information, medicine, psychology, science, technology, social sciences, humanities	Contains about 15–20 of the databases in the regular BRS service. This is a non-prime service only, accessible from 6 p.m. to midnight, and is designed for non-research and non-librarian personnel. Includes *Books in Print* and *Chemical Abstracts.*
Chase Econometrics/ Interactive Data Corporation 486 Totten Pond Road Waltham, Mass. 02154 Tel: (215) 667-6000	Insurance Forecast	Insurance companies	Insurance, insurance industry	Over 1,200 quarterly and annual time series of historical and forecast data on key variables affecting life, health and property-casualty insurance industries. Data obtained from American Council of Life Insurance and A. M. Best.

CompuServe Inc. Information Services Division 5000 Arlington Centre Blvd. Columbus, Ohio 43220 Tel: (614) 457-8600 (800) 848-8199	CompuServe	Computer hobbyists, business, financial institutions, government agencies	News, finance, educational information, stock market reports and commodities news, computer games, general reference materials	Articles from *Better Homes and Gardens* and *Popular Science*, text of the *World Book Encyclopedia*, *Archer Commodity Reports*. Reference and education-related information including weather service, airlines guide (OAG-EE), and movie reviews. New micro service for business users announced in mid-October 1983.
Data Resources Inc 24 Hartwell Ave. Lexington, Mass. 02173 Tel: (617) 863-5100		Business	Finance, economics	Bibliographic and Source databases, *Agriculture Data Base, Balance of Payments, Dodge Construction Potentials, Standard & Poor's Industry Financial Data Bank*.
Dialog Information Services Inc. 3460 Hillview Ave. Palo Alto, Cal. 94304 Tel: (800) 227-1927 (800) 962-5838	Dialog	Business, academic	Multidisciplinary, science, technology	Bibliographic and Source databases, *ABI/Inform, Federal Register Abstracts, Food Science and Technology, Adtrack, AGRICOLA, Book Review Index, Electronic Yellow Pages, Environmental Bibliography, Foundations*.

(continued)

FIG. 11-3 (cont'd)

Company	Database	End Users	Subjects	Summary
Dialog Information Services Inc. same as above Tel: (800) 227-5510 (415) 858-3796	Knowledge Index	Business, engineers, consumers, attorneys, physicians, students, teachers, hobbyists	Multidisciplinary	Contains about 12 of the databases in the regular Dialog service, including *Microcomputer Index*, *Standard & Poor's News*, *International Software Database*, *AGRICOLA*, *Books in Print*, *Magazine Index*, *Newsearch*, and *National Newspaper Index*.
Dow Jones & Company, Inc. Information Services Group P.O. Box 300 Princeton, N.J. 08540 Tel: (609) 452-2000	Dow Jones News/Retrieval Service	Business, some computer hobbyists	Finance, some general information, news, movie reviews	Abstracted articles from *The Wall Street Journal* and *Barron's*. Stock quotes within 15 minutes from the exchange. Other databases include *Media General Financial Services*, *Money Market Sales*, *Disclosure II*, movie reviews, sports, and weather, *Academic American Encyclopedia*.
Dun & Bradstreet, Inc. 99 Church St. New York, N.Y. 10007 Tel: (212) 285-7669	DunSPRINT	Financial and credit institutions, business	Finance, commercial credit	Information from over 4 million Dun & Bradstreet Business Information Reports on companies in U.S., including general descriptions and financial statement data. *Dun's Financial Profiles* and *Dun's Quest*.

HOW TO PERFORM PRELIMINARY WORK   11-17

General Electric Information Services 401 N. Washington St. Rockville, Md. 20850 Tel: (301) 340-4000	Over 47 databases available via Mark III Service	Business, financial institutions, communications	Economic, financial, demographic, science, engineering, petroleum	Databases offered include *Commodities Futures, International Economic Indicators Database, MIDS/Agriculture, MIDS/Banking and Finance, MIDS/Construction and Building Permits,* and *CITIBASE.*
I.P. Sharp Associates 2 First Canadian Place Exchange Tower, Box 418 Toronto, Ont., Canada M5X 1E3 Tel: (416) 364-5361	Over 100 numeric databases	Brokerage firms, publishing, insurance companies, airlines, governments, consultants, universities, trust companies	Financial information, aviation, energy, economic indicators, securities, insurance	Data provided for performing market share analysis, forecasting, analysis of trends, and route and schedule planning. Databases include *Actuarial Data Base, Australian Financial Data Base, Canadian Department of Insurance, CITIBASE,* and *DISCLOSURE*
National Library of Medicine MEDLARS Management Section 8600 Rockville Pike Bethesda, Md 20209 Tel: (301) 496-6193	MEDLINE (referred to as MEDLARS on BRS)	Medical profession, health care service personnel	Medicine, biomedicine, nursing, dentistry, research, clinical practice, administration, policy issues	Articles from 3,000 medical journals plus information on related audiovisuals. Service provides a chemical dictionary, *Hospital Literature Index, Index Medicus, Index to Dental Literature,* and *International Nursing Index.* Other databases include *Chemline, Toxline, Histline, Cancerdit,* and *Health Planning and Administration.*

(continued)

FIG. 11-3 (cont'd)

Company	Database	End Users	Subjects	Summary
Source Telecomputing Corp. 1616 Anderson Rd. McLean, Va. 22102 Tel: (703) 734-7500 (800) 336-3366	The Source	Computer hobbyists, business users	Financial monitoring and analysis, business and commodity news, consumer and leisure activities, employment and travel services, games	Full text databases for United Press International. Other databases include *Raylux Financial Advisory Service*, *Commodity News Services*, *Management Contents*, and *Wine Library*. Many other consumer programs offered.

INDUSTRY SPECIFIC DATABASES

Company	Database	End Users	Subjects	Summary
AgriData Resources 205 W. Highland Ave. Milwaukee, Wis. 53203 Tel: (414) 278-7676 (800) 558-9044	AgriStar	Agricultural industry	Agricultural engineering, meteorology, news, commodities	Eight files of agricultural business information. *AgriScan* is a database of over 12,000 entries covering business, financial, marketing, price, weather, livestock, and crop information. *Agridata News Service* database.
Bank Administration Institute 525 West 42nd St. New York, N.Y. 10010 Tel: (212) 943-6700 (800) 323-1321	InnerLine	Bankers, business and regulatory agencies	Banking, finance, commerce, industry	Articles covering daily financial news, opinion, and analysis reports from *American Banker* and *Bond Buyer*. Other special services include a news clipping service and access to the databases *Disclosure II* and *Citibase*.
The Bureau of National Affairs, Inc. 1231 25th St. N.W. Washington, D.C. 20037 Tel: (202) 452-4200	CHEMLAW	Chemical industry, research libraries, pharmacies	Chemical industry, U.S. federal government and law	Contains complete text of federal chemical regulations published in the *Code of Federal Regulations* and the *Federal Register*. Databases include PATLAW, LABORLAW,

HOW TO PERFORM PRELIMINARY WORK 11-19

Commodity News Services, Inc. 2100 S. 89th St. Leawood, Kan. 66206 Tel: (913) 642-7373	Commodity News Services	Brokerage firms, financial institutions, metals dealers, grain companies, farmers	Financial and commodity markets and the economic factors affecting those markets, including futures quotations, technical charts	Three commodity futures quotation systems (*Data Quote II, IV,* and *VII*), and 24 news wire services including *Financial Instruments News, Lumber Instant News, Global Weather Service,* and *UNICOM News.*
Conway Data, Inc. 1954 Airport Road, N.E. Atlanta, Ga. 30341-4996 Tel: (404) 458-6026	SiteNet	Corporate facility planners	Building site evaluations, inventories of buildings, analyses of incentive programs, numerical data on location factors	Area surveys provide details on markets, labor force, utilities, transportation, and other factors. Selected information from *Site Selection Handbook, Industrial Development, Site Report,* and *Corporate Facility Planning.*
Data Courier Inc. 620 South Fifth St. Louisville, Ky. 40202 Tel: (502) 582-4111 (800) 626-2823	ABI/INFORM	Business professionals, management, educational institutions, government agencies	Business management and administration	Summaries of articles from more than 500 international journals. Subjects include accounting, data processing, economics, finance, human resources, law and taxation, banking, and telecommunications.

Daily Tax Advance, Daily SEC Advance, and *Securities Law Advance.*

(continued)

FIG. 11-3 *(cont'd)*

Company	Database	End Users	Subjects	Summary
General Videotex Corporation 3 Blackstone St. Cambridge, Mass. 02139 Tel: (617) 491-3393	Delphi	Business and computer hobbyists	General	Complete text of *Kussmaul Encyclopedia* along with "gateways" to a research library of 200 searchable databases on legal resources, life sciences, and medicine.
GTE Telenet Medical Information Network 8229 Boone Blvd. Vienna, Va. 22180 Tel: (703) 442-1000	AMA/Net	Medical personnel, individual practitioners, hospitals, clinics, medical schools	Clinical, administrative, and medical practice information; biomedicine, health care, life sciences, pharmaceuticals and pharmaceutical industry	Articles and general information from *American Medical Association* publications and medical literature, including drug and disease information, medical procedure coding and nomenclature, and socio/economic bibliographic information.
Human Resources Selection Network, Inc. 20 Park Plaza Boston, Mass. 02116 Tel: (617) 338-6313	HRS:Net	Data processing consultants and engineers	Data processing personnel	Personnel database provides consultant's rate range, technical and applications skills, previous assignments, and resumé. Clients search database and contact consultants directly.
E.F. Hutton One Battery Park Plaza New York, N.Y. 10004 Tel: (212) 742-5000	Huttonline	E.F. Hutton clients	Account data and investment information	Daily account updates include securities transactions, portfolio positions, cash and margin balances, open orders, and available assets.
ITT Dialcom, Inc. 1109 Spring Street Silver Spring, Md. 20910 Tel: (301) 588-1572	Daily Tax Advance	Business	Taxes	Articles from *Daily Tax Report*, covering business accounting, tax news, pension legislation, and Internal Revenue and Treasury policy. Other

Management Contents 2265 Carlson Drive, Suite 5000 Northbrook, Ill. 60062 Tel: (800) 323-5354 (312) 564-1006	Management Contents	Business managers and administrators, consulting firms, educational institutions, government agencies	Accounting, finance, marketing, personnel, and production	Index and abstracts from over 560 journals, proceedings, transactions, books, and courses. *The Computer Database* covers articles from over 500 publications of consumer and technical information covering computer products, companies, and people.
Mead Data Central 9333 Springboro Pike P.O. Box 933 Dayton, Ohio 45401 Tel: (800) 227-4908 (513) 859-1611	NEXIS	Business and advertising executives, public relations officers, newspersons, lawyers	Business, industry, economic, and general news	Daily news summaries from *Financial Times, Morgan Guaranty Survey, National Journal,* wire services, magazines, government publications, and newsletters, includes *Advertising & Marketing Intelligence (AMI)* database.
Mead Data Central same as above	LEXIS	Law firms, judges, federal and state agencies, corporate law departments, law schools	Federal and state law, as well as tax, securities, labor, communications, bankruptcy, patent, trade, and copyright law	Full text of federal cases plus case law of all 50 states and District of Columbia. Citation searches possible in *Shepard's* and *AutoCite, Federal Register, Encyclopedia Britannica,* and selected publications.

(continued)

Note: databases offered include *UPI Datanews, ABI/INFORM,* and *UNISTOX*.

FIG. 11-3 *(cont'd)*

Company	Database	End Users	Subjects	Summary
NewsNet 945 Haverford Rd. Bryn Mawr, Pa. 19010 Tel: (800) 345-1301 (215) 527-8030	NewsNet	Business	Electronics and computers, finance and accounting, investment, publishing and broadcasting, and telecommunications	Text of 150 specialized newsletters in 40 different business categories. Includes *Bank Network News, Cable News, Advanced Office Concepts,* and *Executive Productivity*.
Official Airline Guides 2000 Clearwater Drive Oak Brook, Ill. 60521 Tel: (800) 323-3537	Official Airline Guides Electronic Edition (OAG-EE)	Business travelers	Flight schedules, fares, route information	Schedules of over 600 North American and 40 international airlines, for passenger and cargo flights. Available by itself or through CompuServe, Dialcom, I.P. Sharp, and Dunn & Bradstreet.
Photonet Computer Corporation 250 West 57th Street New York, N.Y. 10019 Tel: (212) 307-6999	Photonet	Photographers, advertising agencies, graphic designers, publishers, stock agencies	Photojournalism, stock photography research, sales and marketing	News on trends and technology, monthly features, interviews, product and service information, and opinion polls. Provides access to local resource databases for pre-production planning.
Policy Studies Corporation P.O. Box 2206 Springfield, Va. 22152 Tel: (703) 455-5108	Electronet	Graphic artists, publishers, computer and office products industries	Technologies and technical transfers within the computer, telecommunications, graphic arts, photographic product industry	Electronic publishing merging business graphics with text. Articles from trade publications —*Technology Watch, Tech Alert,* and *Tech Extra*—plus Technical Newswire of current events and technical dictionary.

HOW TO PERFORM PRELIMINARY WORK 11-23

Professional Data Corporation 55 Wheeler St. Cambridge, Mass. 02138 Tel: (617) 492-1690	Connexions	Business, personal	Confidential recruiting and job-listing service covering more than 100 companies in such high technology fields as engineering and data processing, as well as sales, marketing, and finance.
Quotron Systems, Inc. 5454 Beethoven Street Los Angeles, Cal. 90066 Tel: (800) 624-9522	Quotdial "After Market" Service	Private investors	Access to market data including stock, bond, option, stock index, financial futures indexes, and commodities prices, plus leading market indicators and the most actively traded issues.
Reuters Ltd. 2 Wall Street New York, N.Y. 10005 Tel: (212) 732-7800	The Reuter Monitor	Banks, financial institutions, brokerage houses, individual brokers	Provides 13 services containing subsets from approximately 60 files of information, including securities, tickers, and contributed information.
University of Nebraska Lincoln, Neb. 68583 Tel: (402) 472-1892	AGNET	Farmers, ranchers, agricultural managers, agricultural business, rural bankers	Variety of databases cover weekly updated reports on commodities and production estimates. Decision aids and market charting programs written by agriculture specialists relate to farm buying, and current tax laws.

Careers, employment opportunities

Financial information

General news, financial and money market news and prices, stock and commodities market quotes, sports, weather

Agricultural business information, taxes, management programs

speaking, the more that is available in the data base, the more it will cost to gain access. Fee structures may include a one-time sign up that ranges from $10 to $150, although some are much higher. Some companies charge a flat monthly fee ranging from $20 to $50. Others charge a per-use fee. These fees are determined by the amount of time the user is connected. Per-hour rates are $6 to $30, with some higher. Practically any combination of these rates may be encountered. One supplier offering bibliographic and source data bases, with additional data bases such as Agricultural Data Base, Dodge Construction Potentials, and Standard & Poor's Industry Financial Data Bank, charges as much as $32,000.[5]

Figure 11-4 is a diagram depicting how computer research occurs.[6]

For success in computerized research, the researcher must know which resources (data bases) are likely to contain relevant information as well as how to formulate searches effectively.[7] The vendors of these research facilities offer training programs designed to familiarize the researcher with the techniques and special queries involved. Generally, the investment in equipment is not great and the cost for using it is small. Usage costs include a charge for dial-up and connection with the computer and a charge for the amount of time connected. Rates vary, depending on the specific data base accessed. Off-line printing costs are charged separately. A typical search can be completed in five to ten minutes and could range in cost from $5.00 to $15.00 for the least expensive data bases. Of course, the professional data bases such as LEXIS and NAARS are more costly and make it unlikely that internal auditing departments could justify subscribing. However, access to these data bases may be possible for a fee through offices of the major public accounting firms or through the AICPA.

If there is insufficient published information available on a particular topic (e.g., commonly practiced techniques for controlling business travel), other techniques may be employed to find the information. In fact, it may be more advantageous to use these techniques even if published information on the topic exists. These techniques include the following:

- Discussions with management
- Discussions with other members of the audit staff
- Surveys

Discussions with management are covered later in this chapter. Discussions with other staff members are straightforward and require no further comment. Some discussion is warranted on the subject of surveys, however.

---

[5] *Ibid.*, p. 59.

[6] Diagram is from a presentation by Sherry du Roy, Ernst & Whinney, to the Corporate Audit Department, Northrop Corporation, June 26, 1982. Reprinted by permission of Ms. du Roy.

[7] Andrew P. Gale, "Computerized Research: An Advanced Tool," *Journal of Accountancy*, Jan. 1982, p. 74.

HOW TO PERFORM PRELIMINARY WORK

FIG. 11-4

Diagram of Computer Research Information Flow

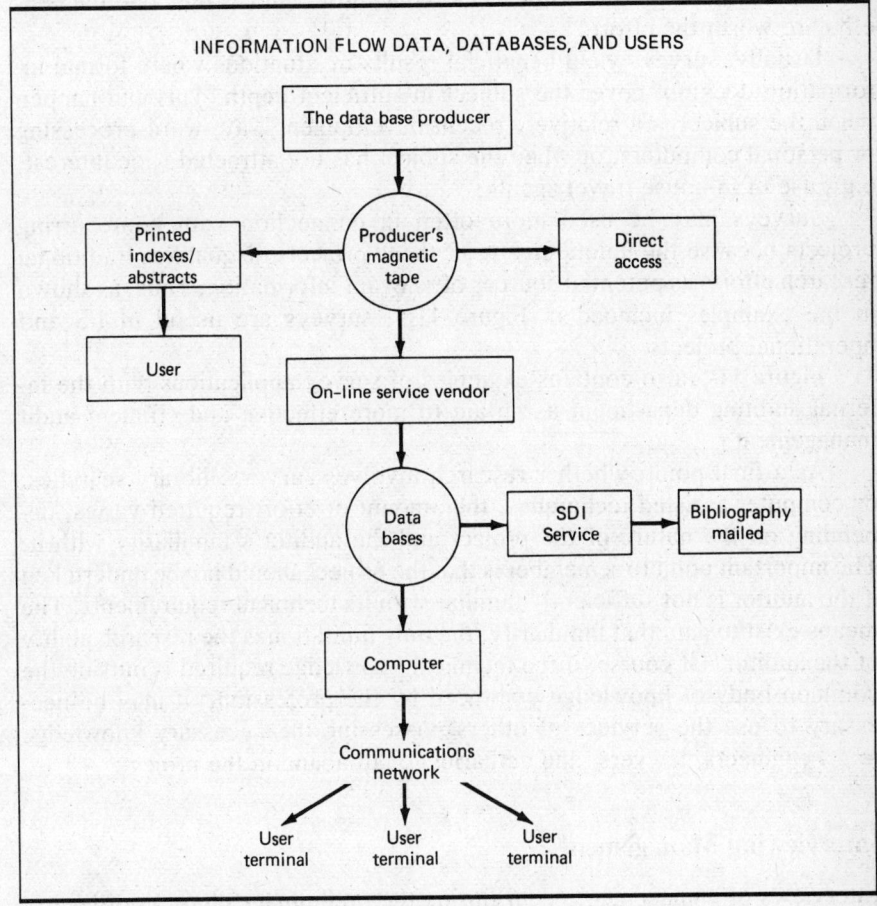

A survey is an effort to obtain comprehensive information about a specific subject from a representative sample of persons believed to be in possession of such information and who are believed to be willing to share it.

A survey is a most useful technique to obtain specific information about a subject from a variety of independent sources. As in the example of looking for techniques for controlling business travel, the survey may provide the only information, since no relevant published information exists. Surveys entail the careful preparation of a list of specific, easily understood, readily answerable questions. Considerable time is required to prepare for and conduct the survey, either by phone or by mail. The population surveyed inside and outside the company must be extensive enough to enable the construction of a sort of data base of information. The difficulties associated with each of these steps in the process make it one of the lesser practiced research techniques. However, despite the limitations, surveys should be used when other sources prove fruitless or when the auditor believes the potential benefits are worth the effort.

Usually, surveys yield beneficial results in situations where formal information does not cover the subject in sufficient depth. This can happen when the subject is a relatively recent development, say, word processing or personal computers, or when the subject has not attracted wide interest, e.g., use of in-house travel agents.

Surveys may be used more often in connection with nonrecurring projects because the unique nature of those projects disqualifies traditional research efforts as potential sources of relevant information. Thus, as shown in the examples included in Figure 11-5, surveys are useful in I/S and operational projects.

Figure 11-5 also contains examples of survey applications with the internal auditing department as an aid to more effective and efficient audit management.

As a final point, whether research involves surveys, library searches, or computer-assisted techniques, the amount of effort required varies, depending on the nature of the project and the auditor's familiarity with it. The important point to remember is that the project should not be undertaken if the auditor is not sufficiently familiar with its technical requirements. The means exist to gain that familiarity; the only limitation is the research ability of the auditor. Of course, if the technical knowledge required is outside the common body of knowledge embraced by the profession,[8] it may be necessary to use the services of others possessing the necessary knowledge (e.g., engineers, lawyers, and actuaries) or to abandon the project.

Interviewing Management

Interviews of management occur during the preliminary phase in order to:

- Gain additional information relevant to the project.
- Agree on audit objectives.
- Coordinate the timing of the audit.
- Obtain assistance needed, if any.

In order to accomplish the foregoing, the auditor and affected management may meet on more than one occasion and with more than one management representative. When possible, joint meetings with various management members may be desirable; however, many executives

---

[8] See R. E. Gobeil, "The Common Body of Knowledge for Internal Auditors," *The Internal Auditor,* Nov./Dec. 1972, pp. 20–28.

FIG. 11-5
Examples of Survey Subjects

PROJECT APPLICATIONS	
Survey subject:	*Used in the Audit of:*
■ Internal reporting practices	■ Any audit in which reporting practices are relevant, including financial reporting
■ Vital records protection practices	■ Data security, or any audit in which vital records are involved
■ Disaster recovery plans	■ Disaster planning
■ Experiences with quality-control circles	■ Manufacturing or production functions
■ Control practices regarding corporate contributions and memberships	■ Corporate memberships and contributions
■ Approaches to controlling construction costs	■ New facilities construction
■ Use of in-house travel agents	■ Travel practices
■ Back-up techniques in electronic data processing	■ EDP security
■ Approaches to word processing	■ Office administration techniques
■ Teleconferencing practices	■ Office administration techniques
AUDIT MANAGEMENT APPLICATIONS	
■ Organization structure	■ Relationship with other functions (e.g., in-house legal counsel)
■ Reporting relationships	■ Working paper retention policy
■ Size of department	■ Communication practices with audit committees
■ Audit approaches	■ Travel policies
■ Relationship with external auditors	■ Use of specialists

communicate more openly when other members of the management team are not present.

Interviews are more critical, of course, in nonrecurring audit projects. However, if the auditor prepares carefully and keeps in mind the objectives of the interview process, the necessary communication will occur without difficulty. A more detailed discussion of interview techniques is provided in Chapter 15.

Preparing and Modifying Audit Tools

Just as a fisherman checks his hooks, bait, and tackle before heading for the lake or stream, an auditor must check his tools to be sure they will function effectively. In the case of the auditor, the principal tools are the audit program and, if applicable, questionnaires and checklists. Of course, if these do not exist, he will have to build them.

For recurring projects, most of the tools should already be in existence. The auditor must not be unduly influenced by this existence. The sufficiency of audit programs, questionnaires, and any other tools, such as flow charts, organization charts, and checklists, should be carefully considered for each project. The changing conditions and differing circumstances in which recurring projects are performed warrant such consideration. In most instances, major revisions will not be necessary.

Techniques for preparing questionnaires and audit programs are discussed in Chapter 8. For purposes here, it is only necessary to reemphasize the importance of these tools. Audit programs are required for every project if professional results are desired. In many situations, the auditor will not be able to design the entire audit program before entering the field. The general thrust may be predetermined, but the specific tests and other procedures must await further discovery which can occur only in the field.

In some companies, audit programs are prepared by the audit manager or by a specially designated individual or group within the audit department. When the performing auditor does not personally prepare or ready the program for use, he should, nevertheless, review it to be sure it fits his objectives.[9]

Another audit tool that is becoming increasingly useful is generalized audit software, a device more fully explained in Chapter 27. Audit software includes general-purpose computer programs, which are available from private software suppliers and the major CPA firms, and that offer an opportunity to easily retrieve information from magnetic tapes, discs, or punched cards, using virtually any hardware and operating system. Several audit departments have designed their own internal, general-purpose programs. It is during the preliminary phase that their possible application must be considered, because successful utilization requires special planning and coordination, such as obtaining permission to access or copy data, obtaining the assistance of programmers, if necessary, and scheduling the "run."

One source of aid that is frequently overlooked is the assistance from the auditee or members of the auditee organization. Most auditees are interested in minimizing the amount of time the auditor must spend in their organizations. As a result, many are willing to assist the auditor in every possible way. Auditors need only realize that fact to make better use of the opportunity. Assistance may be obtained, for example, to do the following tasks that are involved in most adults:

- Locating items in files
- Sorting

---

[9] Charles J. Cater, Jr., "Performing the Internal Audit," *Corporate Controller's Manual*, Paul J. Wendell, ed. (New York: Warren, Gorham & Lamont, 1981), p. 20-7.

HOW TO PERFORM PRELIMINARY WORK

- Preparing schedules
- Completing questionnaires/checklists
- Typing

The foregoing items are rather obvious. However, other assistance may also be available. Some organizations are sufficiently large that one or more persons might be dispatched to assist the auditor in performing some of the testing. Independence need not be compromised, provided the auditor designs the test, sets the sample size, reviews the results, and derives his own conclusions.

Coordinating Efforts

In a sense, the efforts of performing auditors may be likened to those of a music arranger. Both the auditor and the music arranger must envision how a variety of resources may be combined to produce a pleasing effect. In addition to his own efforts, the auditor must coordinate the contribution of management, other auditors, auditees, the audit manager or director, and assigned specialists (e.g., I/S auditors). In some companies, there is more than one internal audit group, and external auditors are also present. Efforts by all these parties must be coordinated, overlap avoided, and performance measured against the audit program and audit objectives—as the arranger who must blend all musical efforts within the context of the written score.

A few broad suggestions can be stated to facilitate coordination. Beyond that, individual experience dictates what should be done. The realization that coordination is essential is the prime requirement. The following conditions are also helpful:

- Early and frequent auditee/management contact
- Flexibility in planning
- Resourcefulness
- Sensitivity

It is believed that the best results occur when auditing plans are disclosed well in advance. Not only does this enable advance preparation to begin, but it also provides an opportunity to disclose to affected management and others the overall approach and any limitations. This should be done in a formal fashion at least once each year. An example of an announcement of audits for a year is shown in Figure 11-6. An example of a memo communicating more specific audit arrangements is shown in Figure 11-7.

Some practitioners may be reluctant to follow this approach on the grounds that it sacrifices the element of surprise and results in conditions possibly being "doctored." The approach is defensible, however, inasmuch as the element of surprise has little value in most audit projects. As a matter of fact, in a high percentage of projects, the element of surprise can adversely

FIG. 11-6

Formal Communication of Year's Audits and Audit Arrangements

TO: Distribution
FROM: R.J. Stevens
SUBJECT: 19XX Audit Plan

The attached plan of audit coverage for the year 19XX has been developed in accordance with the requirements of PD No. 45 and certain other policy directives. The objectives of this plan are to provide assurance that

- Internal accounting and financial controls of reporting entities are effective and can be relied upon to produce meaningful financial information of use to corporate management in discharging its responsibilities.
- Internal controls of reporting entities adequately safeguard the assets of the company.
- Financial statements of reporting entities are complete and accurate and comply with generally accepted accounting principles.
- Reporting entities are in compliance with operational policies that promote the well-being of the company, including policies regarding standards of business practice.
- Controls over the development, maintenance, and operation of systems involving automated processing techniques are sufficient to result in the processing of accurate and complete data.

All planned audit assignments will require at least one to two weeks of actual field work by a member of the audit staff. The starting dates of the field work consider to the extent practicable other demands on organizational elements, such as monthly financial closing. The indicated starting dates are for assignments planned for the second quarter only. All other assignment starting dates will be communicated to you prior to the quarter in which they commence. In addition, our scope will consider the work scope of external auditors and, if applicable, that of division auditors.

Each audit assignment will be performed in accordance with internal audit standards that we have developed, and will include such tests as we deem necessary to accomplish the objectives of the audits, pursuant to written audit programs. Each audit will be adequately planned and will include discussions with organizational personnel prior to commencement of the work, where appropriate. Certain of our audits may be conducted on a surprise basis, however. These instances, which have not been included in the attached plan, will not entail prior communication.

Generally, the results of our audits will be reported in two ways. Detail reports of our findings and specific recommendations will be distributed to the organizational unit management so as to facilitate prompt remedial action. Summarized reports will be provided to interested corporate management on a periodic basis. These summarized reports will be by profit center and to the extent possible will cover more than one audit and will consider organizational unit responses. Summarized reports will not contain recommendations unless further action appears warranted in some specific circumstance.

Our findings and recommendations resulting from the audits will be discussed with appropriate management personnel prior to completion of our work. Draft versions of our detail reports will be provided to management prior to final issue to afford an opportunity to clarify our understanding of underlying factual circumstances.

Our audits are undertaken primarily for the purpose of determining compliance with

> existing procedures and policy statements and to evaluate their effectiveness. Such evaluations take into consideration the fact that the objective of internal accounting control is to provide reasonable, but not absolute, assurance as to the safeguarding of assets against loss from unauthorized use of dispositions, and the reliability of financial records for preparing financial statements and maintaining accountability for assets. This concept recognizes that the cost of a system should not exceed the benefits derived and recognizes that evaluation of these factors requires judgment by management.
>
> While our audits will be thorough for the purpose, inherent limitations in the audit process resulting from the concept of selective testing precludes us from discovering all matters that may be of concern. These limitations may also preclude the discovery of fraud, defalcation, or other similar irregularities, although such discovery is possible. However, we shall remain cognizant that such acts may have occurred or may occur as a result of weaknesses in control procedures.
>
> Unless you advise to the contrary, further communication regarding specific audit assignments will occur directly with the management of the organization element affected. Please see that a copy of this memo reaches all management members who are likely to be affected by the scope of this plan. Also, please ask that we be advised immediately of any proposed timing that will pose an undue hardship.

affect the conduct of the audit precisely because the important element of auditee coordination is forfeited. Constructive auditing requires preparation by both principal parties to the audit: the auditor and the auditee.

This is not to say that surprise audits are never worthwhile. In situations where fraud or other wrongdoing is suspected, the element of surprise is more than appropriate; it is essential.

Developing the Audit Plan

The final phase of preliminary work is developing the audit plan. This phase operates best when it is performed jointly with the assigned manager or director.

Depending upon the circumstances, the plan may be expressed formally in writing or it may be a simple oral agreement of the team members, including the assigned manager or the director. A completed plan will include (1) defined objectives; (2) a tentative audit program designed to accomplish the objectives, and that specifies the nature and extent of testing; (3) applicable questionnaires, checklists and other tools, and relevant reference material; (4) an awareness of potential risks and problem areas; (5) agreed start dates, targeted completion dates, and estimates of time requirements; (6) field locations to be visited; and (7) coordinated auditee assistance.

All phases of the planning should be checked by the manager or director, and particular emphasis should be placed on objectives, audit programs, questionnaires (if applicable), and any other special technique planned. Unique aspects should be fully explored and their impact on the scope of work resolved, to the extent practicable. Any other relevant matters should

FIG. 11-7

Memo Communicating Specific Audit Arrangements

TO: N. Smith

FROM: K.H. Lewis

SUBJECT: Corporate Audit Reviews at ABC Division

Enclosed are copies of the outlines of audit scopes and objectives and the Internal Control Questionnaires, if required, for the following audits to be commenced on April 12 and 13, 19XX at the ABC Division (ABC).

Audit	Auditor	Expected Arrival
Indirect procurement	Mike Rogers	Tuesday, April 13
Indirect costs	Ben Gomez	Monday, April 12
Accounts receivable	John Williams	Tuesday, April 13
Standards of business conduct	Adrian Marshall	Monday, April 12

The scope of all audits will be reviewed on a continuing basis by the auditors to assure that efforts are not duplicated. Mr. Rogers will discuss our overall approach with you upon his arrival on Tuesday, April 13.

As we discussed with you over the phone, it would be helpful if the Internal Control Questionnaires can be completed by the time we start our field work. In addition, we would appreciate your contacting those persons with whom the auditors will have primary contact to arrange for introductions and the availability of related policies and procedures, internal control documentation, organization charts, and other data and/or documents needed to expedite the reviews. In addition, it may be beneficial to have the auditors tour the facilities sometime on Tuesday, April 13.

I will be in Boston on Wednesday, April 21, and look forward to meeting you then. If you have any questions on the above matters, call me on extension 401 at the Corporate Office.

---

be discussed so that the performing auditors are in the most knowledgeable position possible before entering the field to start the audit.

Needless to say, the plan is not "set in concrete." Actual field conditions may even necessitate major changes, which should be cleared with the audit manager or director. But, for the great majority of projects, major changes will not occur, primarily due to the fact that the auditor has properly performed the preliminary phase of the audit.

SUGGESTED READING

Brenner, Vincent C., and Glenn E. Sumners. "A New Development in Internal Audit Education." *The Internal Auditor,* Feb. 1987, pp. 44–48.

Brownstone, David M., and Gorton Carruth. *Where to Find Business Information.* New York: John Wiley & Sons, 1979.

Gale, Andrew P. "Computerized Research: An Advanced Tool." *Journal of Accountancy,* Jan. 1982, pp. 73–84.

Garvin, Andrew P., and Hubert Bermont, *How to Win With Information or Lose Without It.* Washington, D.C.: Bermont Books, 1980.

Kagle, Arthur, R. "A College-level Course in Internal Auditing: Practitioner Perceptions," *The Internal Auditor,* Feb. 1987, pp. 41–43.

Newman, Samuel L. *Salaries and Attitudes: A Profile of the Internal Auditing Profession.* USA: The Institute of Internal Auditors, 1984.

Report of the National Commission on Fraudulent Financial Reporting, Chapter 5, Oct. 1987. U.S.A.: National Commission on Fraudulent Financial Reporting, 1987.

CHAPTER **12**

How to Work Effectively in the Field

Overview 1	Principle of Limited Record Keeping .. 11
	Common Workpaper Deficiencies 11
Planning 3	Techniques for Organization 12
Purpose 3	Criteria for Retention 17
Techniques 3	Suggestions in Creating Workpapers ... 17
	Timing of Preparation 18
Organizing 4	Access Issues 18
Definition and Purpose 4	
Activities Involved 5	**Communicating Progress and Results** ... 24
Techniques 5	Perspective 24
	Communication Points 25
Performing 7	Initial Conference 25
Activities Involved 7	Periodic Reporting 27
Perspective 7	Exit Conference 28
Use of Portable Personal Computers ... 7	Communication Modes 30
	Criteria for Deciding What Is
Documenting: Preparing Workpapers ... 10	Relevant 31
Purpose 10	
"Performing" and "Documenting"	**Suggested Reading** 34
Distinguished 10	

Fig. 12-1	Communications Software Products	9
Fig. 12-2	Workpaper Contents Page	13
Fig. 12-3	Workpaper Summary Narrative	14
Fig. 12-4	Workpaper Summary of Findings	15
Fig. 12-5	Workpaper Evidencing Audit Testing	16
Fig. 12-6	Workpaper Evidencing Analytical Effort	19
Fig. 12-7	The Communication Triangle	26
Fig. 12-8	Project Status Report Form	29
Fig. 12-9	Techniques for an Effective Exit Conference	30
Fig. 12-10	Illustrative Actions for Specific Reporting Situations	33

OVERVIEW

Fieldwork is the term usually intended to cover the auditor's activities in evidence- or fact-gathering that are performed at the auditee's place of business. The common perception is that fieldwork is the execution of the planned audit procedures (inspection, observation, inquiry, and confirmation). In actuality, these activities, which are discussed in detail in Chapters 14 through 16, are only a portion of total fieldwork. The other field activities are the planning, organizing, documenting, and reporting that must occur in order that the needed evidence is gathered smoothly and efficiently. It is these other aspects, which may be thought of in an overall sense as the conducting of the fieldwork, that are the subject of this chapter. In essence, these activities govern how effectively the fieldwork segment of an audit project is accomplished. The term "fieldwork" is a carryover from the early days of auditing, when most of the audit work was performed at the various locations of his clients and not in the accountant's office. A revealing and somewhat incredulous account of the conditions encountered by the early auditors in their field visits may be found in Montgomery's *Fifty Years of Accountancy:*[1]

> We had a great many out-of-town engagements. On our arrival we slept where we could and ate what they had. Even by old standards probably we were underprivileged but we were too busy to complain about it. One winter Adam Ross and I spent six weeks in a town in the mountains of North Carolina. And it was cold! We occupied a double bed and used one wash bowl. In the morning the water in the pitcher was frozen. It snowed right down the chimney into our room. In order to finish the job on time, we worked nights and Sundays and all night at the end. I distinctly remember making light of everything but the food. They cooked with rancid grease, so we had to live on boiled eggs. Our average was six or eight a day.

Thankfully, performing auditors today find field conditions vastly more hospitable than their forebears did. Also, the fieldwork component has declined somewhat as a percentage of total audit effort required to complete modern audits. The size and complexity of audits has grown as a direct result of the increasing size of business and the regulatory climate in which business is conducted. Thus, more time must be spent planning and preparing for audits, and finalizing them. Some planning and wrap-up activities are performed in the field, to be sure, but much more is done in the home office of the auditor.

In the future, the home office portion of the work is likely to expand even further. As computer technology evolves, more and more audit procedures, formerly possible only in the field, will be done at the auditor's desk—with a computer terminal, a set of programs, a small desk-top computer, and password access to relevant computerized data maintained by or for the auditee. It may eventually be that virtually the entire audit will be performed remotely (away from the auditee) with a minimum of auditee involvement. Of course, some contact with the auditee will always be required to maintain programs, investigate exceptions, and communicate re-

---

[1] Robert H. Montgomery, *Fifty Years of Accountancy* (New York: The Ronald Press Co., 1939), p. 21. Reprinted by permission of John Wiley & Sons, Inc.

HOW TO WORK EFFECTIVELY IN THE FIELD

sults. However, technological advances in communications may enable much of this to be done from the home office (e.g., through teleconferencing).

Hopefully, some aspects of fieldwork will always remain. There is something about the prospect of entering the field that kindles the auditor's spirit; it is akin to an adventure of sorts. This is particularly true if the fieldwork is conducted at some distant, unfamiliar location, which is often the case. The experiences in the field, meeting new people, observing the variety of human undertakings and business endeavors, and devising ways and means to achieve desired results sustain the adventure. They also mold character and form a solid foundation on which useful and productive managerial careers are built. This encountering, surviving, and solving the unknown is what fieldwork and auditing are all about.

Evidential matter (see Chapter 14) must be gathered in a controlled fashion. Thus, field activities include those related to project control and include planning, organizing, performing, documenting, and reporting. The following paragraphs cover each of these aspects in greater detail.

PLANNING

Purpose

In the field, planning activities become much more focused on specific audit procedures than is possible during preliminary work. (See Chapter 11.) That is because the actual field conditions are encountered. Those affect the planning and performance of audit steps. In contrast, such conditions could only be estimated in the preliminary phase. Field planning reasonably assures that the work can progress in a smooth, efficient fashion toward achievement of stated objectives. It involves sequencing events such as interviews, facility inspections, file searches, conferences, and other audit activities.

Techniques

For many audits, particularly those performed by a single auditor, field planning is an informal process. Like all persons whose daily activities are nonroutine, the auditor must think ahead, either at the end of the day, at the beginning of the next day, or when events require it. The stream of information coming to his attention and the dependency on the auditee for much of it require such flexibility to respond adequately to actual conditions.

For example, planned interviews may be canceled, interrupted, or made unproductive by other events. Sampling and other audit procedures may reveal facts and circumstances inconsistent with expectations. Finally, planned procedures may become unfeasible or inadvisable in the light of findings. Developments such as these must be assessed for their impact on the audit objectives and, if necessary, new courses of action devised. This thinking ahead is usually done spontaneously—almost subconsciously—by experienced auditors. However, their experience has taught them to distinguish between minor and major plan-altering events. In the latter circumstances, superiors assigned to the project should be consulted.

The most formal field-planning techniques might be preparing reminder lists, daily itineraries, and detailed time budgets. Reminder lists are short written statements or notes of important things to do either before the end of the day, the end of the week, or the end of the job. Such reminders help to organize the work and to minimize omissions of important actions.

Audit projects in which the auditee or others are integrally involved may require even more formal attention from a daily planning standpoint. For example, audits involving the application of computerized general audit software usually involve coordination and the assistance of programming personnel. Thus, coordination memos may be required to enable proper preparation to take place.

Detailed time budgets, another helpful planning technique, are estimates of time required to perform specific audit tasks. The estimates are expressed in man-hours (e.g., 2.5 hours) and may either be developed or modified in the field. Detailed budgets are essential to help control the time spent on each segment of the work, particularly that spent by assistants.

The following list offers additional suggestions on the subject of field planning:

- Make plans realistic; schedule only those items that can reasonably be accomplished within the envisioned time frame.
- Don't be too formal. Elaborate schedules or excessive detail gives the appearance of precision. This is wasted effort because even the best plans are subject to much uncertainty.
- Schedule and perform audit work so as to minimize disruption of the auditee's personnel and facilities.
- Early during the course of the field work, establish the date of the exit conference. Establishment of this date serves as a target and assures maximum attendance of all interested parties.
- Obtain approval from designated individuals (managers or project leaders) for significant changes in previously approved plans, whether such changes occur in the audit program, budget, or in some other aspect.

ORGANIZING

Definition and Purpose

Organizing is defined in Chapter 7 essentially as an administrative process of marshaling available resources in an orderly fashion. Organizing the field-

HOW TO WORK EFFECTIVELY IN THE FIELD 12-5

work is consistent with that definition and is closely related to planning. The purpose of organizing is to reasonably assure that the audit project objectives are achieved efficiently and effectively.

Activities Involved

Fieldwork organizing activities may be distinguished from preliminary organizing (see Chapter 11) in that organizing in the field is more task-oriented. Organizing in the field includes undertakings such as arranging workpaper filing formats and the following additional activities:

- Arranging for use of suitable space, such as desks, work stations, and conference rooms
- Obtaining administrative assistance (e.g., typing and filing)
- Prioritizing and scheduling work flow
- Coordinating efforts with outside auditors, auditee personnel, and others
- Summarizing work performed
- Filing and indexing of workpapers
- Referencing and cross-referencing workpapers

Techniques

The organizing tasks above involve varying efforts proportionate to the size and complexity of the work. Here are some practical suggestions to aid in organizing work in the field:

☐ *Develop a routine or pattern to follow in performing the fieldwork.* For example, allow time at the beginning or end of the day to plan that or the next day's activities. Allow time for administrative duties (e.g., filing, reporting to the supervisor or manager, giving guidance to subordinates, and preparing time reports), meeting with auditee personnel, testing, and other similar duties. Developing and adhering to work routines helps to assure that all matters are being timely attended.

☐ *Stay on track.* The field usually offers ample opportunity to become distracted. This is because the auditor's focus is often specific and, as a result, is concerned with only a portion of the business activities of the entity. However, there always exists a natural tendency to be absorbed by unrelated—albeit fascinating—events, transactions, or information. For instance, in reviewing contracts for the existence of any clauses that constitute an act in furtherance of illegal boycotts, it is difficult, if not impossible, to avoid becoming engrossed in the terms of the contract. Or, a review of lease files for proper approvals may evolve into a search for terms incompatible with the accorded method of accounting. While a certain amount of digression is to be expected, the auditor must exercise self-discipline in order to keep such occurrences to a minimum, and instead concentrate on the objectives.

☐ *Assign work to assistants that is commensurate with their skill and experience.* Generally speaking, work that involves considerable judgment should be done by more experienced auditors, or the in-charge auditor. Usually, compliance testing is suitable work for lesser skilled auditors, while seasoned auditors perform duties such as interviews and internal control evaluations.

☐ *Review the work of assistants promptly.* If a lengthy period of time passes, the subordinate may have more difficulty explaining matters and recalling circumstances. Moreover, the chance that latent findings may not be detected in a timely fashion is reduced when work is reviewed promptly.

☐ *Inform interested parties of test results in a timely fashion.* Providing the results of tests to those who have an interest minimizes pressures that otherwise build during the course of the field work. When interested parties are informed of test results, exit conferences are able to be conducted in a more enlightened atmosphere. Also, any reasonable conclusions drawn from the testing will be brought to light in a more timely way. Interested parties include audit supervision and interested auditee personnel.

☐ *Be punctual.* Normally, the hours of work observed by the auditee should also be observed by the auditor. However, extenuating circumstances, such as long commuting distances, must be taken into consideration. Arrive at scheduled conferences and meetings on time or, if necessary, a few minutes early. Punctuality not only enhances the auditor's professional image, but also facilitates more effective work routines.

☐ *Avoid monopolizing auditee facilities and/or personnel.* Unusually long (over one hour) meetings, discussions, and conversations could indicate inadequate preparation on the part of the auditor. This, however, is not always the case because substandard documentation and complex circumstances often require lengthy and repeated interrogations of knowledgeable personnel to obtain all relevant facts. Even in these circumstances, however, it may be preferable to divide the topic into more manageable elements. Long meetings usually entail unnecessary digressions and irrelevant commentary that can shroud meaningful dialogue. These should be avoided, if possible.

☐ *Do not become overworked.* Some auditors conduct fieldwork with the mistaken belief that long hours are required. Only under certain cirumstances should this be the case. "Work smart, not hard" should be the auditor's guiding thought. Long hours may be required when (1) a tight deadline is involved; (2) the work is being perfomed at a remote, inhospitable location, making prompt completion advisable; or (3) the work is unreasonably behind schedule. In all other situations, the work should be planned and organized to be completed in a normal working fashion (i.e., regular hours during which both auditor and auditee staff will be more efficient). Despite the auditor's willingness to work long hours, such a pace over an extended period will adversely affect job efficiency and, more importantly, might adversely affect the auditor's independent mental attitude.

PERFORMING

Activities Involved

"Performing" is a term applicable to the entire audit effort. However, as used here, it is intended to entail those activities related to gathering evidence. In essence, it involves the execution of audit procedures deemed necessary in the circumstances. Subsequent portions of this chapter and Chapters 14 through 16 discuss the nature of evidence and the techniques used to gather it. The intent here is simply to identify the subject as a key element involved in fieldwork and to discuss briefly how PCs are changing how audits are performed.

Perspective

It may provide some perspective to state that in most audit projects, the actual performance of audit procedures comprises less than 50 percent of the total time spent on the project. The common viewpoint is that this aspect comprises a much higher percentage of the total. However, in reality, the hours devoted to preliminary work, administrative work, and documenting and reporting activities is significant and, taken together, often exceed the time spent in gathering evidence.

Use of Portable Personal Computers

Although the age of automation and its effects on the work of the internal auditor are subjects that are discussed repeatedly throughout this volume, the pace of developments in this area warrants discussion here with respect to the conduct of fieldwork.

Many auditors perform fieldwork in much the same way they have for years. Any changes for this group are confined to improvements in office equipment, such as copying machines and calculators. However, an increasing number of internal auditors are making use of PCs for such tasks as word processing and spreadsheet analyses. Chapter 28 discusses these and other uses in greater detail. Until recently, computer-savvy internal auditors had to be content, for the most part, to make use of PCs while at their home office; opportunities for using them in the field were somewhat limited. PCs are not easily borrowed. While portable computers have been in existence for several years, most models were not compatible with home-based models. In addition, many were difficult to carry around despite their manufacturers' boasts to the contrary.

In the past three years, however, newer models have been available that promise much more effectiveness as tools for any auditor whose duties include performing fieldwork. These newer portables, often referred to as lap-top computers, retail in the two to four thousand dollar range, depending on features, and offer many advantages over older models. They are lighter and smaller, have larger storage and display areas, and are designed to be IBM PC-compatible.

Typically, lap-tops weigh between 8 and 13 pounds and can fit in a briefcase. They use three and one-half-inch disk drives, as opposed to the five and one-quarter-inch drives found on desktops; yet, these small disk drives can store more data. Standard internal memory of 256K is common.

The monitors or display screens provided for lap-tops are usually of the LED or LCD variety and can be difficult to look at for any length of time. Some models attempt to overcome this problem by enabling standard monitors to be attached. Thus, while these lap-tops are in the office, they can function like desktops. While enroute, their slim LCDs convert them to lap-tops. Yet, they offer a full 25 line display. Among the present manufacturers of lap-tops are IBM, Kaypro, Compaq Computer Corp., Hewlett Packard, Grid Systems, Inc., Data General, Epson, Toshiba, Apple, and NEC.

These machines are advancing auditors toward the day when conducting fieldwork without one will be all but unimaginable. Among the many tasks that can be facilitated by these devices are the following:

- ☐ Financial auditing
  - Preparation of trial balances
  - Consolidations
  - Aging schedules
  - Narratives of inquiries and observations
  - Statistical sampling selections
- ☐ Operational auditing
  - Trend analyses
  - Statistical sampling selections
  - Narratives
- ☐ EDP auditing
  - Terminal emulation
  - Data extraction
  - File scanning

Lap-top computers can also be useful in any type of auditing for such administrative tasks as keeping track of time spent, project reporting, and word processing.

Since most models offer modems as options, lap-tops can be made to communicate with other computers at the field work location, at the home office, or elsewhere. Thus, with appropriate software, downloading information from mainframes for analytical purposes or for other testing is practicable. Many software products are available that can be connected with each other. Others are available at greater cost that enable PCs and main-

HOW TO WORK EFFECTIVELY IN THE FIELD

FIG. 12-1
Communications Software Products

Product	Vendor	Operating System	Modes	Speed BPS	Protocols	Price	Comments
Apple Access II	Apple Computers, Inc. 20625 Mariani Ave. Cupertino, Cal. 95014 (406) 976-1610	Pro. DOS	PC to PC	—	Async	$75	Marks on Apple
Blast	Communications Research Co. 8939 Jefferson Hwy. Baton Rouge, La. 70809 (504) 923-9985	All	All	—	Full duplex sliding window	$250 $500+ $1300+	Micros Minis Mainframes
The Impersonator	Direct Aid, Inc. P.O. Box 4420 Boulder Colo. 80306 (303) 442-8680	MS/DOS PC/DOS	Main I/O, File transfer, etc.	300 1200	Xmodem	$245	Allows user to modify or create additional asynchronous emulations
Gammalink	Gammalink 2452 Embarkadero Road Palo Alto, Cal. 94303 (415) 856-7421	MS/DOS	PC to PC	9600	SDLC	$1995	Price includes hardware and software
Microgate APPC/BSC	Gateway Microsystems Inc. 9501 Capital of Texas Hwy, #105 Austin, Tex. 78759 (512) 345-7791	MS/DOS	PC to Mainframe	9600	Sync.	$695– $995	Allows users to generate custom communications
Smartcom II	Hayes Microcomputer Prods. P.O. Box 105203 Norcross, Ga. 30348 (404) 449-8791	MS/DOS 2.0 or 2.1	All	300 1200 2400	Xmodem	$149	Special version for Apple MacIntosh
Link I	Martin Marietta Data Systems IT Software P.O. Box 2392 Princeton, N.J. 08540 (609) 799-7500	MS/DOS PC/DOS	PC to PC PC to Mainframe	300– 9600	Async	$150	Emulates VT100 full-screen editor

Source: "Buyers Guide to Communications Software," *The Journal of Corporate Computing*, March/April, 1986, pp. 32–33.

frames to communicate. A tabulation of selected software products is presented in Figure 12-1.

DOCUMENTING: PREPARING WORKPAPERS

Purpose

Auditors, like practitioners of other disciplines, must document (i.e., make a record of) their activities. The most important objective in such documenting is to provide a record of information that supports the conclusions drawn by the auditor and presented in the report. In addition, the following purposes are also served:

- To facilitate quality-control reviews performed by audit management
- To provide information useful for future audit efforts
- To provide project control information, such as a comparison of actual versus budgeted hours by audit step

Clear, concise, and meaningful workpapers, which meet professional requirements and evidence the quality of the examination, make the reviewer's task easier. They also indicate the preparer's professional competence.[2] The professional requirements are simple. Professional standards require that the workpapers should record the information obtained and the analyses made and should support the bases for the findings and recommendations that are reported. Beyond these professional standards, workpaper principles and techniques have developed that warrant comment. Also, workpapers, when completed, constitute one of the most important auditor work products. In Chapter 9, a discussion of access issues is presented. There, the principal focus is on the audit report. The same access issues exist with respect to workpapers—a fact that requires further mention. But first, it is important to distinguish between performing audit work and documenting that work. For information purposes, some frequently encountered workpaper deficiencies are identified later in this section.

"Performing" and "Documenting" Distinguished

The documentation gathered constitutes the evidential matter referred to in auditing standards. (See Chapter 6.) The auditor should not confuse documenting activities with performing auditing procedures (inspection, observation, confirmation, and inquiry) mentioned previously and described in depth in Chapter 16.

Documenting is the actual organizing of evidence gathered and the writ-

---

[2] Paul M. Wilson, "Planning and Operation of the Internal Audit Department," *Retail Control*, Feb. 1978, p. 41.

ing down or recording of audit procedures performed. While it is possible to execute some audit procedures and make a record of the execution at the same time, it is more frequently the case that the documentation is constructed and put together after the fact. In other words, the process of documenting what was inspected, observed, confirmed, and so forth is usually a separate and distinct process from executing those tasks.

Principle of Limited Record Keeping

The process of documenting is commonly referred to as preparing workpapers. It is important to keep in mind that working papers do not contain all the evidence reviewed by the auditor. For example, in a test to determine compliance with approval requirements on purchase orders, the auditor may decide to examine numerous executed purchase order documents to note the presence of the appropriate approving signature. The auditor does not have to make copies of each of these documents for his workpaper files to evidence that, in fact, the signatures were present in the sample selected. The principle involved here is to limit the amount of evidence gathering or documenting to that which is sufficient to indicate that the actions taken by the auditor comply with his auditing standards. In this instance, a simple list of the purchase orders examined would suffice, along with a description of the tests performed on each and a conclusion. It is not necessary or economically feasible to reproduce everything encountered.

Common Workpaper Deficiencies

Constructing workpapers that sufficiently evidence work performed in an efficient and effective fashion requires judgment, skill, and experience. It is a task that many auditors find to be among the most difficult in performing an audit. Reviewers often note that workpapers are simply incomplete, unreadable, unintelligible, or unwisely constructed. Other more subtle deficiencies, such as the following, have also been noted:

- Narratives of discussions, meetings, and so forth, with no clear indication as to the relevance to the audit of the statements
- Comparative analyses that do not totally compare or totally analyze
- Written conclusions not supported by, or referenced to, evidence
- Copies of memos, invoices, purchase orders, and other forms of evidence with no reference or commentary as to why they are present
- Copies of computerized reports (in whole or in part) with no indication as to why they are present
- Copies of flow charts, procedural narratives, and policy statements, which do not clearly relate to the audit objective

The presence of any of these conditions adversely affects the utility of the workpapers for any of the purposes identified in the beginning of this section. Workpaper preparation must be given due professional care, for workpapers must stand the test of time. Long after the audit becomes a distant and foggy memory in the mind of the performing auditor, the workpapers must portray an accurate, recognizable picture of the relevant activities and events and must support the conclusions drawn without raising questions as to the adequacy of the work performed or the competency of the auditor, or both.

Techniques for Organization

Workpapers must be properly organized to fulfill their previously described objective and purposes. Organization such as the following will usually suffice:

- Table of contents
- Checklist evidencing completion of important quality-control tasks
- Final report copy
- Report drafts and related documentation
- Administrative section (project authorization, budget, actual time record)
- Audit program with all steps signed off as being complete
- Summary narratives of work performed
- Summary narratives of findings
- Organizational documentation (flow charts, policies, organization charts, as applicable)
- Questionnaires
- Tests

Specimen examples of certain of the foregoing have been provided in other portions of this book as follows:

- Checklists and questionnaires—Several chapters (see index)
- Final reports—Several chapters (see index)
- Administrative records—Chapter 8
- Audit program—Several chapters (see index)
- Flow charts—Chapters 18, 28

Illustrative examples of a table of contents, a summary narrative, a summary of findings, and a workpaper evidencing testing are provided in Figures 12-2–12-5.

(continued on page 12-17)

HOW TO WORK EFFECTIVELY IN THE FIELD

FIG. 12-2
Workpaper Contents Page

	WCR Division A/R Summary Index	Prepared By	Initials BB	Date 8/11/xx

A Administrative

    A-1   Close out checklist
    A-2   Assignment authorization
    A-3   Time budget
    A-4   Audit program
    A-5   Organizational Charts
    A-6   Personnel Contacted
    A-7   A/R Procedures
    A-8   Audit planning

B Report & Summaries

    B-1   Report
    B-2   Summary & Conclusions
    B-3   Discussion of Findings
    B-4   Exit Interview Notes

C Internal Control (see section index)

D Detail Testing (see section index)

FIG. 12-3
Workpaper Summary Narrative

KAR Division
A/R Summary & Conclusion

Prepared By: BD
Date: 8/11/XX

I have concluded my review of the accounts receivable functions at KAR. My review was done in accordance with the standard audit program for A/R, which included a detail test of A/R balances, detail test of shipping documents, review of sales journals & invoices, credit memo review, cut off tests of shipping & cost records, review of old A/R aged balances, and such other tests as considered necessary in the circumstances.

Three items were noted as audit findings from my review:

- credit memos had not been properly approved

- billing area had spent too much time chasing small dollar aged A/R balances

- no procedures existed for sale of scrap resulting in a bad debt due to a credit sale without approval.

Aside from the above matters, no additional items were considered significant for report inclusion. Based on my review, except for the above three items, KAR appears to have adequate internal controls surrounding billings, accruals, cash receipts and adjustments.

FIG. 12-4
Workpaper Summary of Findings

W/P Ref.	Audit Findings	Discussions w/ Management and Background Information	Report Recommendations	Prepared By	Initials	Date
		KIT - Corporate Fenton Cash System Summary of Findings			BB	8/11/xx
H-4 H-14	③ Procedures and controls over issuance of credit cards appear to be lacking or in disuse	Discussions were held with Mr. John Winters, VP of Finance and Accounting and Miss Shirley Ellsworth, Director of Corporate Accounting, concerning the controls over the company credit cards issued to employees. We pointed out that as the system currently exists, documentation authorizing issuance of a card cannot be easily located. Files of employees who were terminated are destroyed in a central file, and documentation concerning with the final disposition of the card cannot be located. Also, the listings in accounting of credit card holders was not current and included employees who had been terminated and did not include others who had recently received a card. They were receptive to our recommendations and recognize the need to have better controls over the system.	① Credit card authorizations should be maintained in the employee's credit card file, both in accounting and central files. ② When the employee is terminated or the card is returned to corporate, documentation should be placed in file as such. The file should be kept if employee is terminated and not destroyed as is current policy. ③ Listings of currently authorized credit card holders should be updated periodically and compared to the central files. This should be followed up during the next review.			
CD-1 CD-2	④ It was noted during our detail cash disbursement work that voucher packages were not being cancelled/stamped paid on a consistent basis.	This was brought to the attention the accounts payable clerk, Shirley Ellsworth, and John Winters. They agreed that all voucher packages should be stamped paid on all applicable source documents (check requests, invoices, monthly statements, purchase orders, etc.)	None			

FIG. 12-5
Workpaper Evidencing Audit Testing

JBR – Corporate
Cash Receipts Test

Prepared By: BB
Date: 8-17-8X

Date Rec'd	Amount		Date Trans. Out
2-5-81	20,000	✓	x
2-18-81	30,000	✓	x
3-19-81	85,000	✓	x
3-24-81	90,000	✓	x
4-2-81	80,000	✓	x
4-20-81	60,000	✓	x
5-6-81	30,000	✓	x
5-14-81	55,000	✓	x
5-29-81	95,000	✓	x
6-8-81	45,000	✓	x
6-11-81	125,000	✓	x
7-9-81	90,000	✓	x
7-23-81	20,000	✓	x
8-3-81	40,000	✓	x
8-5-81	35,000	✓	x

Purpose: The purpose of this test is to trace bank transfers recorded as cash receipts by JBR to the transfer out/disb. by the Corp. office.

Conclusion: Absence of exceptions tend to support assertion by management that corporate cash transfers are received intact and promptly deposited.

x — Traced amount to the Corporate disbursement account without exception.

✓ — Traced amount of cash receipt to applicable cash forecast statement and the applicable bank statement without exception.

Source: Cash Receipts Journal

Scope: Judgmentally selected 15 deposits at random during period 1-1-81 to 8-5-81. There were approximately 50 transfers executed during this period.

HOW TO WORK EFFECTIVELY IN THE FIELD 12-17

Criteria for Retention

A review of any given set of workpapers would indicate that only a portion of them is the auditor's original creation. Many are obtained, abstracted, or copied from existing sources. Examples of such workpapers include copies of policy statements, applicable sections of procedure manuals, flow charts, memorandums, contracts, and pertinent source documents such as purchase orders, invoices, and journal entries. Whether or not to retain copies of existing records depends essentially on the following considerations:

- Availability of the information in auditee files
- Period of time the information will be retained by the auditee (examples of records required to be retained for other purposes include journal vouchers, purchase orders, bank statements, invoices, check copies, trial balances, and financial statements)
- Whether the auditor believes the information will be retained
- Whether the auditor will make frequent use of the information contained in the record
- Whether the evidence might be relevant in some future legal cause of action

As a general rule, if the information is readily available and must be retained as part of the auditees' records, and if the auditor will not make frequent use of the information, the evidence (i.e., copies) should not be filed in the audit workpapers. In these cases, it is sufficient to identify the evidence examined by appropriate scheduling methods. Figure 12-5 illustrates this technique. On the other hand, if frequent use will be made, then copies should probably be retained. Workpapers that are copies of auditee memos, computer reports, and so forth should include comments by the auditor explaining their relevance to the audit. Also, if not clearly indicated, the auditor should state the source of the information and appropriately title it.

Suggestions in Creating Workpapers

With respect to creating evidence (as opposed to obtaining copies), the auditor should follow these guidelines:

1. Devise a heading or title for the workpapers that accurately identifies the content.
2. Initial and date all workpapers.
3. State purpose of objectives in each workpaper.
4. Identify or list the evidence in a clear and traceable fashion. In effect, an audit trail should be created that would enable the audit procedure to be duplicated by the reviewer.

5. State the appropriate conclusion.
6. Provide necessary references and cross-references to and from other relevant workpapers.

The foregoing guidelines are generally applicable to audits of information systems operations. However, workpapers for this type of auditing are different in some respects. These are covered in Chapter 27. Diligent application of workpaper techniques will result in documentation, which achieves workpaper objectives and minimizes the occurrence of deficiencies. Again, Figure 12-5, an example of audit testing, illustrates these principles. Another example of a workpaper prepared by a performing auditor is shown in Figure 12-6. In this example, analytical efforts are being documented as opposed to testing.

Timing of Preparation

Many auditors are able, first, to conduct their audit procedures, make appropriate notes, and then, near the conclusion of the audit, actually prepare the workpapers that form the evidence of record. These auditors may be able to properly and sufficiently recall and document work performed, and other relevant matters, long after the fact. However, there is a high risk that this approach may inaccurately portray portions of the work performed.

The most effective technique is to prepare the documentation during the performance of the audit procedure, if possible, or as soon after completion as practicable.

Access Issues

Efforts by various interested parties to obtain access to both audit reports and workpapers are noted in Chapter 9, which describes the efforts of the Defense Contract Audit Agency (DCAA) and others in this regard. Interest in the work products of internal auditors is not new and is not confined to agencies of the DOD. Others who may seek access from time to time include certain members of management, external auditors, congressional staff members, and other federal agencies. These include:

- Internal Revenue Service
- Federal Trade Commission
- Justice Department
- Securities and Exchange Commission
- General Accounting Office

It is clear from recent events that the level of interest is rising. Chapter 9 discussed the fact that the IRS was at that time thought to be the most

FIG. 12-6
Workpaper Evidencing Analytical Effort

```
┌─────────────────────────────────────────────────────────┬──────────┬──────┐
│              KAR Division                               │ Initials │ Date │
│  Material Handling - Estimate of Cost to Complete       ├──────────┼──────┤
│                                            Prepared By  │          │      │
└─────────────────────────────────────────────────────────┴──────────┴──────┘
```

	Material Base	Rate	Cost to Complete
To Complete FY'xx	2029 ✓	5.5% ①	1124
Future yrs CTC	9032 ✓	5.4% I-2.1	4884
Total			6008
			G

NOTE: Purpose of this workpaper is to calculate cost to complete and to determine reasonableness of rate used.
Above rates used appear reasonable and are consistent with prior periods.

① Per review of management's computation using actual amounts per the general ledger, the actual rate using year-to-date amounts is 5.3%. Rate of 5.5% used above appears reasonable, as difference between rates would only result in a difference of $4M. (5.5% - 5.3% = .2%; .2% × 2029 = $4M.)

✓ per material forecast @ w/p G
& calculation verified

aggressive agency in its attempts to access internal audit records. It may be that the DCAA has eclipsed the curiosity of the IRS.

Gaining access to internal audit reports and workpapers is a shortcut to discovering problem areas and sensitive matters, possibly accounting for an ardent interest in accessing work products. If valid, this thought is of concern to many internal auditors, corporate managements, and company lawyers. Some believe that comments and opinions contained in reports and workpapers will be used by groups seeking access to them in ways that could be adverse to corporate interests. Add to that the possibility that some of the information gained from these records can mislead those seeking access. The result could diminish the relationship between management and internal auditing that is so necessary to effective internal auditing. To date, however, little in the way of significant adverse consequences has emerged. In the meantime, internal auditors should realize that what they record in their reports and workpapers is not as confidential as they might mistakenly presume. Many interested parties have subpoena power and have used it. (See Chapter 9.) The following are suggestions that could limit or eliminate adverse consequences:

☐ *Observe high standards of professional practice*. Internal auditors who perform their assigned duties and responsibilities in accordance with the IIA's *Standards for the Professional Practice of Internal Auditing* or their equivalent will be best assured that the risks arising from third-party access will be minimal.

☐ *Perform an internal risk assessment*. The objective of this effort should be to identify inaccuracies, misstatements, unanswered questions, delinquent management responses, and similar items. By identifying these items, actions can be taken to correct the situation to minimize any chance of misleading third parties.

☐ *Educate management*. The objective is to make management aware that the traditional expectations of confidentiality are now history. Auditors and managements must work more closely to keep inaccuracies, disagreements, and the like to a minimum.

☐ *Work under the direction of lawyers where appropriate*. In-house lawyers, when performing legal services for their corporate client, possess what is known as attorney-client privilege (see Chapter 9). Under this privilege, the records and documents developed by the lawyer and those working under his direction are immune from search and subpoena. Many investigations, if properly structured, may be conducted under the lawyer's attorney-client privilege umbrella. It may be inappropriate, however, to attempt to force all internal auditing under this umbrella. According to one source, legal counsel, particularly outside counsel, may be less knowledgeable about corporate working and may not possess the ease of access and rapport with lower management that nonlegal managers may possess. Moreover, evaluation and correction are not counseling. Monitoring and implementing new ways of running a business are apt to be seen as management functions. This could put the attorney-client privilege relationship in jeopardy.[3]

☐ *Emphasize good workpaper techniques in staff training.* There are many techniques that can be covered in training sessions. Typical examples are:
- Draw conclusions where necessary and be sure all conclusions are adequately supported.
- Complete and sign off all steps in audit programs
- Fill out checklists and questionnaires in their entirety.
- Clear all open items, "to do" notes, and the like.
- Make sure all retained company documents relate to audit objectives.
- Eliminate, or better yet, do not generate extraneous notes and documents.
- Document management action in response to recommendations.
- Document all areas where apparent differences of opinion exist as to remedial action.
- Do not keep personal files at home or elsewhere to reinforce workpapers.

☐ *Review record-retention practices.* Internal auditing records should be retained only for as long as they are useful in the absence of any legal or contractual requirements. Chapter 9 offers further comments on the question of retention.

☐ *Follow the practice of reviewing draft reports with auditees.* Many errors and omissions will be identified by this technique. Also, comments that might be misleading to others may come to light for clarification and/or elimination.

In addition to the previous suggestions, it may be a good idea to establish a good working relationship with other interesting parties where possible. Some government agency auditors, such as the DCAA, have residencies in contractor facilities. A good working relationship in these situations will provide a basis for the kind of free-flowing communication that is essential to overcome bias, preconceptions, and similar notions that could be detrimental if they are present. Moreover, if third-party groups are able to see the professionalism with which internal auditing occurs, it may be a plus in their overall assessment of the quality of management.

One final thought on the subject of access must be stated here. Any auditor should have the right to access all records that in his judgment are relevant. For government auditors, this means that if they believe internal auditing records are relevant, they should be able to see them. However,

---

[3] Joseph E. Murphy, "The Self-Evaluative Privilege," *The Journal of Corporation Law,* Spring 1982, p. 497.

such a right carries a professional responsibility not to use it indiscriminately. Whether auditors are government-based, or internal, they must be professionally flexible on this point. It is often possible to gain alternate forms of evidential matter that provide insight into a desired subject. When those alternate forms avoid the possibility of adverse consequences, they should be employed.

In the case of internal auditing functions, it is possible to obtain evidence of the proficiency and effectiveness of the work of internal auditors by means other than reading reports and workpapers. Auditees could be interviewed, for example, or external auditors could be consulted. Also, the audit tools employed could be reviewed. Audit programs, checklists, questionnaires, and the like provide excellent indicators of professionalism and quality. Use of these techniques would reduce, if not eliminate, the need for examining reports or workpapers.

A willingness to seek alternatives will go far toward demonstrating professional concern for minimizing the damage that could otherwise occur. This point seems to have been recognized by the Packard Commission in its report. The section that deals with government industry accountability warns against government action that impedes efforts by contractors to improve their own performance. Specifically it expresses concern that "overzealous use of investigative subpoenas by DOD agencies may result in less vigorous internal corporate auditing."[4] The section is reprinted here to provide the reader with the full context in which the above quotation was made.

Government-Industry Accountability

In recent years there has been increasing public mistrust of the performance of private contractors in the country's defense programs. Numerous reports of questionable procurement practices have fostered a conviction, widely shared by members of the public and by many in government, that defense contractors place profits above legal and ethical responsibilities. Others argue that contractors have been unfairly discredited through ill-conceived official actions, exaggerated press, and mistaken public dialogue. The depth of public sentiment and prospect of continuing tensions and divisions between government and industry are cause for concern.

Our nation relies heavily upon the private sector in executing defense policy. Cooperation between government and industry is essential if private enterprise is to fulfill its role in the defense acquisition process. Contractor or government actions that undermine public confidence in the integrity of the contracting process jeopardize this needed partnership.

Aggressive and sustained enforcement of civil and criminal laws governing procurement punishes and deters misconduct by the few, vindicates the vast majority who deal with the government lawfully, and recoups losses to the Treasury.

---

[4] The Packard Commission, *A Quest For Excellence, Final Report to the President*, June 1986, p. xxvii–xxx.

As President Reagan emphasized in public remarks announcing the formation of this Commission, "Waste and fraud by corporate contractors are more than a ripoff of the taxpayer—they're a blow to the security of our nation. And this the American people cannot and should not tolerate." Specific measures can and should be taken to make civil and criminal enforcement still more effective.

Management and employees of companies that contract with the Defense Department assume unique and compelling obligations to the people of our Armed Forces, the American taxpayer, and our nation. They must apply (and be perceived as applying) the highest standards of business ethics and conduct. Significant improvements in contractor self-governance, addressing problems unique to defense contracting, are required. Contractors have a legal and moral obligation to disclose to government authorities misconduct discovered as a result of self-review.

Improvements also should be made in the Department's administration of current standards of conduct for military personnel and civilian employees. Additional enforcement and compliance, and complementary efforts to address the respective ethical concerns of government and industry, are required.

Despite an unquestioned need for broad administrative oversight of contractor performance, defense programs have too often suffered from lack of clear direction and cooperation among oversight agencies. Proliferation of uncoordinated contractor oversight—both administrative and congressional—has added unnecessary cost and inefficiency in the procurement process.

Government action should not impede efforts by contractors to improve their own performance. The Commission is concerned that, for example, overzealous use of investigative subpoenas by Defense Department agencies may result in less vigorous internal corporate auditing.

The Services and the Defense Logistics Agency are authorized to suspend or debar contractors, prohibiting the award of new government contracts for a particular period. Suspension and debarment are powerful administrative tools. Existing regulations provide insufficient guidance, however, as to when and how these sanctions should be used to protect legitimate government interests. If poorly administered, used for impermissible purposes, or applied too broadly, the sanctions can foreclose important sources of supply and inflict substantial harm on responsible contractors. A uniform policy and more precise administrative criteria are required to assure predictable and equitable application of these sanctions throughout the Department of Defense.

Recommendations

The Commission's recommendations address each of the above aspects of the Defense Department's relations with industry—law enforcement, corporate governance, official ethics, and contractor oversight.

We recommend continued, aggressive enforcement of federal civil and criminal laws governing defense acquisition. Specific measures can be taken to make enforcement still more effective, including the passage of Administration proposals to amend the civil False Claims Act and to establish administrative adjudication of small, civil false claims cases.

To assure that their houses are in order, defense contractors must promulgate and vigilantly enforce codes of ethics that address the unique problems and pro-

cedures incident to defense procurement. They must also develop and implement internal controls to monitor these codes of ethics and sensitive aspects of contract compliance.

The Department of Defense (DoD) should vigorously administer current ethics regulations for military and civilian personnel to assure that its employees comply with the same high standards expected of contractor personnel. This effort should include development of specific ethics guidance and specialized training programs concerning matters of particular concern to DoD acquisition personnel, including post-government relationships with defense contractors.

Oversight of defense contractors must be better coordinated among the various DoD agencies and Congress. Guidelines must be developed to remove undesirable duplication of official effort and, where appropriate, to encourage sharing of contractor data by audit agencies.

Government actions should foster contractor self-governance. DoD should not, for example, use investigative subpoenas to compel such disclosure of contractor internal auditing materials as would discourage aggressive self-review. The new Under Secretary of Defense (Acquisition) should establish appropriate overall audit policy for DoD agencies and generally supervise the DoD's oversight of contractor performance.

Suspension and debarment should be applied only to protect the public interest where a contractor is found to lack "present responsibility" to contract with the federal government. Suspension and debarment should not be imposed solely as a result of an indictment or conviction predicated upon former (not ongoing) conduct, nor should they be used punitively. The Federal Acquisition Regulation should be amended to provide more precise criteria for applying these sanctions and, in particular, determining present responsibility. Administration of suspension and debarment at DoD should be controlled by a uniform policy promulgated by the Secretary of Defense.

COMMUNICATING PROGRESS AND RESULTS

Perspective

Proper performance of many key steps produces successful audits. One of these is effective communication. The value of effective communication among performing auditors has long been recognized—and properly so. Victor Brink and James Cashin noted 30 years ago, in discussing the subject of audit conferences, that "no audit is better than its final presentation."[5] Although Brink and Cashin were referring to the final communication (i.e., the communication of audit results) (see Chapter 13), the comment extends to all forms of communication during an audit. The frequency and variety of communication requires skill. Richard Holman put it this way:

---

[5] Victor Z. Brink and James A. Cashin, *Internal Auditing* (New York: The Ronald Press Co., 1958), p. 87.

In order for internal audit to serve successfully its organization as a whole, internal auditors must recognize the need for good communication skills. These skills are necessary as auditors interact verbally with on-line and top management on a continuing basis and as they issue written reports of their findings and recommendations.[6]

As with other aspects of auditing, recognizing the importance of communication has not made the exercise any easier. On the contrary, it is one of the most difficult tasks of any audit, because of what may be called the fear factor, an understandably human condition. For his part, the auditor is worried, at the very least, that his findings and recommendations may be shown to be erroneous and, as a result, ridiculed by the auditee. Another auditor concern is that the auditee may allege auditor misconduct to higher management levels, thus threatening both job and career. The history of auditing is scarred with actual instances of this sort.

The auditee, on the other hand, is concerned that the findings and recommendations may reflect poorly on him in the eyes of his supervisors, thus adversely affecting his career. The history of auditing is not void of these instances, either. Thus, a kind of adversary relationship often emerges and inhibits what otherwise should be straightforward communication. Techniques to deal with this reality are discussed later. The intent at this point is to put the subject of communication into perspective as a prelude to examining the communication process.

Communication Points

The various official communication of findings to interested and affected management are often thought of as—and in fact are—the principal aspects of the auditor's communication process. Chapter 13 is devoted almost exclusively to the subject of this kind of communication. But communicating is an ongoing activity between the principal parties that can be depicted in a triangular fashion, as illustrated in Figure 12-7. There are two important communication points, or milestones, during the process in addition to the exit conference: the initial conference and continuous, periodic reporting.

Initial Conference. The initial conference is intended to get the project started on the proper footing toward the intended audit objectives. If the preliminary work has been done properly, the auditee will be keenly interested in the auditor's work. If this is the case, as it frequently is, the initial conference need only cover introductions, as necessary, and a brief review

---

[6] Richard Holman, "Communication: An Essential Element of Internal Auditing," *The Internal Auditor*, Dec. 1981, p. 39.

FIG. 12-7
The Communication Triangle

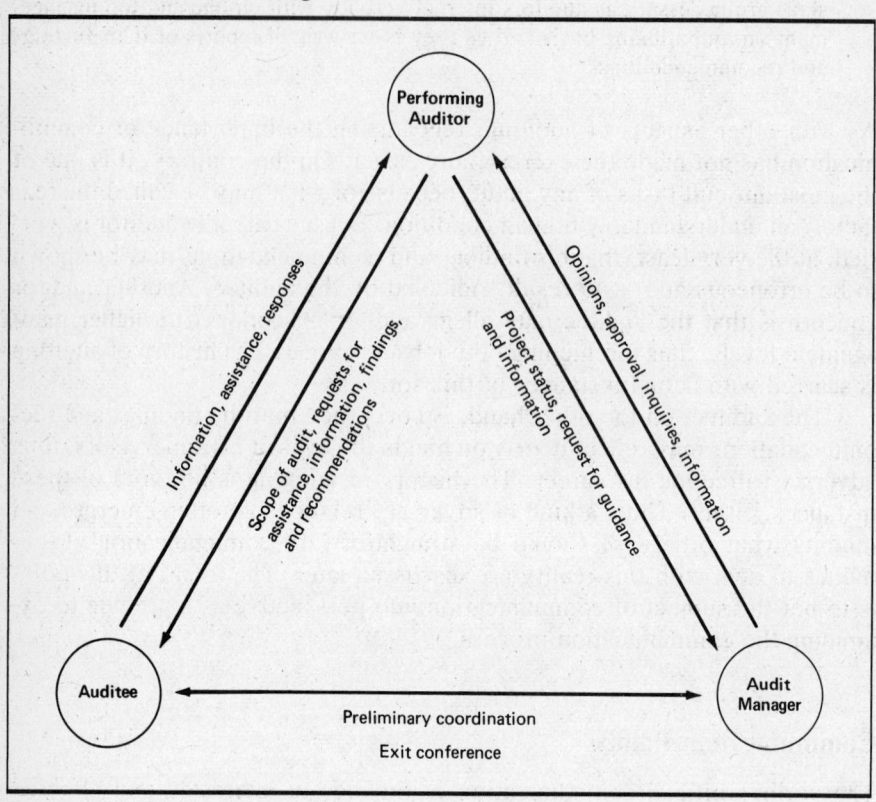

of previously agreed-on arrangements. Other topics for discussion might include:

- Last-minute developments affecting the plan
- General discussion of business conditions, operations, new products, and so on
- Preliminary concerns of the auditee, if any, or special requests by him
- Matters of particular interest or concern to the auditor

Because the initial conference is often the first face-to-face meeting, it is important that it be handled properly, since impressions drawn from it significantly affect the tone of the audit. The meeting should be conducted in a friendly, open atmosphere. The auditor should leave the auditee with the impression that he is knowledgeable about the auditee and his function, responsive, open-minded, and objective. Any behavior that appears to be patronizing or condescending on the one hand, or humbling or apologizing on the other, should be avoided. The auditor should be considerate, in deference to the disruption of normal activities caused by his presence. In summary, the initial conference should result in the development of mutual respect between the auditor and auditee. Techniques to assure a successful initial conference are similar to those involved in successful final or exit conferences.

Periodic Reporting. Periodic reporting occurs throughout the project. Items to be reported, the individuals to whom they are reported, and frequency of reporting, are all matters of judgment. Thus, the nature and extent of periodic reporting may vary with each assignment. The purpose of providing periodic information is to enable affected parties to evaluate progress and to assure that the completed project fulfills audit objectives. The interests of audit managers and auditee management are nearly identical. Both are interested in:

- Progress
- Problems
- Findings
- Recommendations
- Conclusions

In addition to the above, audit managers are concerned with any scope changes and budgeting information.

The auditor should be able to communicate the foregoing matters of interest at any time to those involved. In order to do this, the performing auditor must frequently ask himself:

- Where am I?
- What have I found?
- Do I need more information?
- Do I have a basis for reaching a conclusion?
- Have I informed everyone who should be informed?
- What is the solution?

The frequency with which these and similar questions are asked and answered varies with circumstances but should be sufficient in all cases to enable timely communication to interested parties. On short projects, it may be necessary to hold informal meetings or telephone conversations with interested parties every two or three days. On longer projects, weekly communication may suffice. An alternative is to provide feedback at the conclusion of each audit test or group of tests.

Any significant problems, findings, or scope changes should be discussed with the audit manager as soon as possible. The performing auditors must realize that the conduct of the audit is a team undertaking. The other members of the team (e.g., the chief auditor and the project manager) can perform their roles only if they are timely informed. Many audit departments have set up formal periodic reporting requirements to provide timely information. An example of a weekly reporting form is shown in Figure 12-8.

Communication may be made during meetings arranged for that purpose, over the telephone, or even by informal notes and memos. The technique employed depends on factors such as the availability of the interested party, the privacy needed, the complexity of the information to be communicated, and the distance involved.

Exit Conference. The exit conference is usually the last opportunity for oral communication between the performing auditors and the auditee before the auditors leave the field. The objective of this conference is to communicate results.

Some auditors approach exit conferences in the belief that all relevant information has been gathered and considered in forming their findings and recommendations. This group believes that resistance to their viewpoints is to be expected and must be overcome through assertive behavior.

This approach is invalid in most cases. The auditee is normally in an excellent position to judge the accuracy and appropriateness of the auditor's views. A reluctance on the auditee's part to accept findings and recommendations should be read by the auditor as a signal that something may be amiss in the audit work. The auditor should listen very carefully to the auditee in these situations. If the auditor becomes defensive or argumentative, the opportunity for real progress may be lost.

The better approach is to maintain an open mind—to consider views and recommendations as tentative and subject to change, based on the introduction of additional factual information. Of course, additional information usually comes in the form of management assertions. This may need to be corroborated by extending auditing procedures accordingly. If communications have been effective during the course of the fieldwork and if the proper exit conference approach is employed, the final meeting usually is mutually satisfactory.

The techniques essential to a good exit conference are not fundamentally different from the techniques necessary for any good conference: Adequate preparation is the key. The techniques for achieving the desired exit conference are set forth in Figure 12-9. In addition, the following suggestions may be useful:

- Assume that you are not going to be understood the first time; restate the point in different ways.
- Avoid generalities; be specific.
- Be tactful.
- Use visual aids, if appropriate and available.

HOW TO WORK EFFECTIVELY IN THE FIELD

FIG. 12-8
Project Status Report Form

PROJECT STATUS REPORT

WEEK ENDING _____ 19 ____   NAME _____

PROJECT NUMBER _____   TIME _____

PROJECT PROBLEMS
1. _____
2. _____
3. _____
4. _____
5. _____
6. _____

SCOPE CHANGES
1. _____
2. _____
3. _____
4. _____
5. _____
6. _____

BUDGET DATA

ACTUAL HRS TO DATE _____   FIELD WORK COMPL. DATE _____

ESTIMATE TO COMPLETE _____   REPORT DATE _____

TOTAL INDICATED FINAL _____

ORIGINAL BUDGET _____

OVER (UNDER) _____

NEXT WEEK'S OBJECTIVES

	TARGET COMPLETION	
	DATE	EST. HRS
1.		
2.		
3.		
4.		
5.		

FIG. 12-9

Techniques for an Effective Exit Conference

HOW TO HOLD AN EXIT CONFERENCE

1. Arrange a mutually convenient time, well in advance of field work completion.

2. Provide advance information to permit study and formulation of response.

3. Derive conclusions for each matter. The following categories indicate the variety of possible alternatives:
   - ☐ Eliminate the finding.
   - ☐ Perform further specific research or checking.
   - ☐ Alter the language used in particular sections.
   - ☐ OK as is.

4. Conduct the meeting as though it were for evidence-gathering purposes.

5. Avoid arguments, disagreements, or unpleasantness.

6. Listen and carefully observe reactions and responses.

7. Continually reassess findings and recommendations in light of discussion.

- Put yourself in the auditee's place; see the subject from his viewpoint.
- End the discussion on a positive note.

Despite applying all the techniques essential for a good conference, controversy may occur. It is inevitable that differences of opinion will arise over some issues, and these should be explored. However, the discussions must not become unproductive. The auditor should perceive when arguments become redundant; in this case, the issue may not be resolved at that time. He should find some common ground, be sure that he understands the view of the auditee, and acknowledge that it will be considered further.

Communication Modes

Initial conferences, progress reports, and exit conferences usually employ oral communication techniques. Although the information flows in two directions (auditor to auditee, and vice versa) most of the time, the primary flow is from the auditor to auditee. It is up to the auditor to pick the best method, or combination of methods, to communicate effectively.

Unaided presentations are perhaps the most common oral communication form used. This method is preferable when the interested parties are few and the matters to discuss are uncomplicated. If the subject matter is complex, or if the interested parties are many, communication aids may be useful. These can range from simple handout material, to carefully prepared slides, to videotape. Other aids include blackboards, flip charts, and overhead transparencies (view graphs).[7] For large presentations, the auditor may require the assistance of the audit manager and/or the director.

Criteria for Deciding What Is Relevant

There is no substitute for training and experience in deciding what information should be communicated to interested parties. Audit managers usually select the information they need to evaluate performance and job status. Since they are members of the audit team, their interests coincide with those of the performing auditors. Hence, the dialogues between manager and senior auditor are sufficiently free-flowing to effectively share the necessary information.

That is not necessarily the case with respect to the auditee. The fear factor described earlier presents obstacles to the unrestricted flow of information. To minimize any inhibitions, the auditor must have some idea as to what benefits or data the auditee wishes to obtain from the audit.

The auditor must exercise due care in deciding the form and content of the information to be communicated. He must give proper weight, among other things, to the consultative nature of his work. The objective in consulting is to furnish suggestions or observations that might remedy problems, improve accuracy, reduce costs, or produce some other similar benefit.

If the matter is significant enough, the auditor should conclude that it must be communicated formally in the written report. However, not all matters need be communicated in writing. Insignificant matters may be communicated orally during the exit conference or by telephone. But how can significant matters be discerned from insignificant ones? There is no right answer to that question. Management, accountants, auditors, lawyers, and others have wrestled with the concept of significance, or materiality, for decades. Recently, the AICPA adopted the following position regarding material internal control weaknesses:

> In this context, a material weakness is a condition in which the specific control procedures or the degree of compliance with them do not reduce to a relatively low level the risk that errors or irregularities in amounts that would be material in relation to the financial statements being audited may occur and not be de-

---

[7] A study by Edward J. Blocher, Ph.D., CPA, CMA, Robert P. Moffie, Ph.D., CPA, and Robert W. Smud, Ph.D., was reported in the February 1985 *Internal Auditor* under the title "How Best to Communicate Numerical Data" (pp. 38–42). The study concluded that task complexity was an important factor in considering the choice of presentation format for numerical data. Tabular presentations seemed more appropriate for complex numerical data, while color-graph formats were better when the data was relatively simple.

tected within a timely period by employees in the normal course of performing their assigned functions. These criteria may be broader than those that may be appropriate for evaluating weaknesses in accounting control for management or other purposes.[8]

If relevance is defined in terms of materiality, using the AICPA concept, then criteria may be devised that offer a useful way to help decide what to report and to whom. The criteria involve considering the following two questions:

1. Does the weakness pose more than a relatively low level of risk that a material error or irregularity might occur and not be detected within a reasonable period?
2. Does the estimated cost to remedy the circumstances (i.e., reduce the risk to a relatively low level) exceed the estimated cost impact of the error in the event of occurrence?

If the answer to question (1) is "yes," the auditor should formally report the matter in the manner required by auditing standards. If the answer to question (1) is "no," the action of the auditor is determined by considering the second question. A "yes" answer there means that no reporting responsibility exists. A "no" answer requires the matter to be reported to the level of management directly affected, possibly informally, depending upon the facts. If the answer is indeterminable, the auditor must use his best judgment. Probably, at a minimum, the matter should be informally reported Figure 12-10 portrays the alternatives in tabular form.

The process is simple enough once the relevant facts are known. The hard part is developing the factual information. The sources from which information is obtained are as follows:

Information need:	*Source:*
• Weakness	• Sampling results, internal control evaluation or management assertion

---

[8] Statement on Auditing Standards No. 30 (July 1980) *Reporting on Internal Control*, (AICPA, *Professional Standards,* Vol. 1) AU §§320.68, 642.62. As of November 1987, the ASB of the AICPA is proposing that in addition to reporting material weaknesses, the external auditor will be required to communicate "reportable conditions." Reportable conditions are defined as matters coming to the auditor's attention that in his judgment represent significant deficiencies in the design or functioning of the control structure that could adversely affect the organization's ability to record, process, summarize, and report financial data consistent with the assertions of management in the financial statements. This concept indicates that more matters will be communicated to audit committees than before. Some guidance as to judging what is a reportable condition is offered in the proposed standard. It suggests that, in making the judgment, the auditor should consider various factors, such as the entity's size, its complexity and diversity of activities, organization structure, and ownership characteristics. More is said on the subject of reportable conditions in Chapter 18.

FIG. 12-10
Illustrative Actions for Specific Reporting Situations

Situation	Action
■ Risk of material error is greater than "a relatively low level."	■ Matter must be reported formally to all levels of management.
■ Risk of material error is relatively low and cost to remedy exceeds estimated error impact.	■ No reporting responsibility.
■ Risk of material error is relatively low but cost to remedy is less than estimated error impact.	■ Matter must be reported to directly affected management in an appropriate fashion.
■ Risk of material error is relatively low and remedial costs and/or error impact is inestimable.	■ Matter may or may not warrant reporting to directly affected management, depending upon circumstances; informal reporting most frequently used.

Information need:	*Source:*
• Relative risk	• Analytical assessment, management assertion, or both
• Estimated cost to remedy weakness	• Obtained from management or proposal based upon data furnished by management
• Estimated impact of weakness	• Analytical assessment prepared either by auditor or management

Estimates produced in connection with the last three items may be simple or complex, depending on circumstances. Regardless of complexity, the methodology involved is similar to what is known as cost-benefit analysis. The subject is defined and discussed in detail in Chapter 16.

If the auditor decides to report matters informally pursuant to the criteria suggested here, a record of the subjects discussed and the recommendations made should be prepared and filed in the workpapers.[9] This record should include a description of the finding, the attendant risks, remedial cost/impact

---

[9] The criteria suggested here seem to be compatible with that included in the proposed standard for reportable conditions by the ASB of the AICPA, based on the fact that the criteria envisions reporting matters other than material weaknesses. The assessment of relative risk, estimated cost to remedy weaknesses, and the estimated impact of the weakness should develop the basis on which an informed judgment may be made. The auditor must also bear in mind the criteria indicated in SIAS No. 2, entitled "Communicating Results." In Guideline 430.04.6, the IIA sets forth its views on the attributes of findings (roughly akin to the reportable conditions described by the ASB). In brief, findings result from identifying differences between actual and expected conditions that produce risk to the auditee organization. SIAS No. 2 is reprinted in Chapter 13.

assessments and recommendations. In addition, the management response and intended action should also be stated. The record should not be considered complete unless it is reasonably certain that management action will be taken, or conversely, that action is unnecessary. In the latter instance, the reasons must be noted.

The informal nature of reporting insignificant matters should be performed with the intent of assisting local management, albeit from an objective, independent standpoint. Some form of periodic summarized reporting of informal recommendations may from time to time be made to senior management and/or the board of directors to inform these groups of this type of activity.

While the foregoing criteria and discussion for deciding what to report was adopted from AICPA criteria for reports dealing with internal accounting controls, these criteria may also be used for other reporting situations (e.g., operational auditing and EDP auditing). When followed in practice, internal auditors will find that the process is less complex than would appear to be the case for a majority of reporting situations.

SUGGESTED READING

Blocker, Edward J., Ph.D., CPA, CMA, Robert P. Moffie, Ph.D., CPA, and Robert W. Smud, Ph.D. "How to Communicate Numerical Data." *The Internal Auditor,* Feb. 1985, 38–42.

Fitzgerald, Gerald C. "Auto-written Audits." *The Internal Auditor,* June 1985, pp. 35–40.

Johnson, Gene H., CPA, CMA, and Frank Collins, Ph.D., CPA. "Getting the Right Information." *The Internal Auditor,* Aug. 1985, pp. 23–25.

Rittenberg, Larry E., and Donald L. Miner. "Performing Cost/Benefit Analyses of Internal Controls." *The Internal Auditor,* Feb. 1981, pp. 56–64.

CHAPTER **13**

How to Communicate Results—The Audit Report

The Audit Report as a Communication Device 2	The Opinion 21
	Findings 21
Requirements for Reports 2	Recommendations 23
Basic Principles 2	**Conserving the Time of Higher**
Accuracy 2	**Management** 27
Timeliness 3	
Adaptability to Proper Management Level 3	**Oral Reports** 28
Application of the "Exception Principle" 3	**Graphic and/or Pictured Presentations** 28
Additional Guidelines 3	**Activity and Evaluation Reports** 32
Classification of Reports 4	**Preparing the Report** 39
	Writing the Report 39
Standards for Reporting 5	Physical Characteristics 39
The IIA 5	Editing 40
The GAO 9	Proofreading 40
Formal Written Reports on Activities Examined 17	**A Simple Program to Improve Audit Reports** 40
Transmittal Sheet 18	
Summary or Highlights 18	**Replies to Audit Reports** 41
Statement of Purpose 18	
Scope of Examination 19	**Suggested Reading** 43

Fig. 13-1	Transmittal Sheet	19
Fig. 13-2	Summary Section of Audit Report	20
Fig. 13-3	Complete Audit Report	24
Fig. 13-4	Graphic Report on Capital Expenditure Performance	29
Fig. 13-5	Flow Chart Authorizing Travel	30
Fig. 13-6	Graph of Relative Operating Margin	31
Fig. 13-7	Written Annual Report to Audit Committee on Audit Activities	33
Fig. 13-8	Visual Aids Used in the Annual Report to the Audit Committee	35
Fig. 13-9	Audit Reply Evaluation Form	42

THE AUDIT REPORT AS A COMMUNICATION DEVICE

The tangible end product of an audit is usually a report, the purpose of which is to communicate the findings of the audit and, where applicable, to secure corrective action. Yet, if the report is never read, listened to, or acted upon, it will have failed to meet one of its principal objectives. For this reason, audit findings must be presented in such a way that they are easily understood, making it more likely that someone will implement the recommendations. Presumably, audit results are important to the level of management being addressed. The objective conclusions must alert management to conditions needing attention, or, at a minimum, ease its mind concerning activities that are functioning well.

Yet, excellent work is often lost because the addressee did not perceive the message—because it was not presented clearly, concisely, and in an inviting manner. The purpose of this chapter is to discuss the methods of motivating and informing management by means of the audit report.

REQUIREMENTS FOR REPORTS

Basic Principles

In all probability, many of the same principles applicable to effective financial reporting apply to good internal audit reports. While there may be differences in judgment as to what the basic principles are, there is probably general agreement on most of the desired attributes, whether basic or supplementary. The authors have selected the following four characteristics as being most fundamental:

Accuracy. The report must be accurate. Often there is nothing so disliked by management and so disheartening to the auditor than to find significant statements in the report that are successfully refuted by the auditee. Such events breed lack of confidence in the audit department. Consequently, it is important that reports be accurate and that statements be supported or supportable. Every categorical statement, every assertion, every figure must be factual and correct. It must be tested by the internal audit department, and should be documented by hard evidence. If statements are opinions, they should be expressed as such.

Generally, the internal audit department must earn the reputation that if it makes a statement, the odds are that the assertion is correct. It must be seen as reliable and trustworthy; it should have the distinction of not using secondhand evidence without identifying it as such, or not presenting inaccurate or incomplete data.

HOW TO COMMUNICATE RESULTS

Timeliness. The report must be timely. In general, late management reports that call for implementation are almost as bad as no report at all. Similarly, in the internal auditing field, a report should be timely to be most effective, since it ordinarily calls for action. If the audit is a relatively long one and tentative findings appear to indicate a critical condition, then it may be desirable to issue a progress or interim report. Any audit report should be carefully thought out and must be correct; hence, the accuracy factor must be weighed against the time factor, and appropriate qualifications must be included in the data, if necessary.

Adaptability to Proper Management Level. The report should be adapted to the management level receiving it. This principle has several facets:

- The higher the management level, the greater the degree of *summarization* that is desirable. Conversely, in the lower operating management range, more details are usually necessary and useful.
- The report should be expressed in *language* and *terms familiar* to the executive reading it. Thus, financial verbiage might be avoided, if possible, and operating expressions might be used, depending on the audience.
- The report *format* should be adapted to the executive. A sales executive, for example, might be more receptive to graphs or pictures, while a financial executive might prefer to read tabular or statistical information.

Common sense should be used in applying these suggestions. Since several echelons of managers may receive the reports, it is necessary to aim the presentation at the principal readers.

Application of the "Exception Principle." The exception principle should be applied. For most operations, the out-of-the-ordinary condition or operation should be emphasized. Where things are within an acceptable norm, little time should be wasted on long reports. In these circumstances, a one-sentence report might be applicable. An executive usually cannot and should not review or check every detail. Therefore, only those items needing attention should be emphasized, which is called the exception report.

Additional Guidelines

While the previously discussed report principles cover the more important aspects of audit reports, there are some other closely related characteristics that experience has shown are valid under most circumstances:

☐ *Reports should be concise and specific.* Executives do not like to read useless verbiage. Therefore, the language of the report should eliminate immaterial, irrelevant, or superfluous commentary. Only the explanations that are necessary to convey the message should be used. But conciseness does not imply a short report. If a lengthy explanation is required to develop an idea, it should be used. Also, although well-constructed long sentences may be used, short sentences may better convey the meaning. By the same token, vague generalizations should be avoided. Statements should be specific.

☐ *Reports should be simple and clear.* Reports should be so constructed that the reader may grasp the essential facts with a minimum of effort. Technical accounting terms should be avoided. Short, simple, common words should be used. For example, use "start" instead of "initiate," "stop" instead of "terminate," or "best" instead of "optimum."

☐ *Information should be presented in logical sequence.* As an example, discussion of a procedure or process should follow the steps of the physical activity. A labor report would comment on operations in their natural sequence.

☐ *The tone of the report should be constructive.* Nothing is gained by using a highly critical tone. While the unsatisfactory conditions can be described, emphasis should be placed on the needed improvements. The reader should not get the impression that he is being "talked down to." After all, auditors are not omniscient. The addressee should perceive the report as objective, thoughtful, and dispassionate.

☐ *Dull and trite expressions should be avoided.* The words, sentence structure, and organization of the report, should make it inviting. Clarity should be emphasized by using everyday language—the language of the reader—so that the idea is clearly conveyed.

☐ *The amount of care taken in preparing the report should be commensurate with its importance.* Reports going to top executives, from which important policy matters may be decided, should be prepared with great care and perhaps packaged in a better manner than others. Those dealing with lesser subjects do not need such close attention in preparation—although they should still be accurate.

☐ *Reports probably should be consistent in format.* The specific format to be used depends on many factors, including whether the report is oral or written, formal or informal, preliminary or final, financial or operational. It is also influenced by the characteristics of the recipient. But for all types of similar reports there is something to be said for consistency. With some experience, the reader knows what to expect. So consistency promotes a better understanding by the reader and facilitates the writing.

CLASSIFICATION OF REPORTS

The preceding comments on audit reports have been general in nature and are applicable to most types of reports. However, the following sections of this chapter discuss topics applicable to certain specific report formats.

Internal auditors have at their disposal some latitude in choosing a report form. For discussion purposes, they are categorized as follows:

HOW TO COMMUNICATE RESULTS

1. Audit reports on specific activities that were examined:
   - Written reports—formal or informal
   - Oral reports—formal or informal
2. Top management activity and evaluation reports concerning the internal audit department:
   - Written reports
   - Oral reports

Each of these report formats is discussed in detail in the following sections.

STANDARDS FOR REPORTING

The IIA

Before reviewing specific reporting formats, or discussing report preparation, the reader should be aware of an important standard for reporting. Given the growing importance of the internal audit function and the related need for effectively reporting on audit results, it is pleasing to see that the IIA has issued SIAS No. 2, "Communicating Results." The purpose of the statement is to provide guidance to internal auditors in communicating audit results in the form of oral and written reports. Basically, the statement discusses and interprets Guidelines 430 through 430.07. It reviews types, content, and attributes of internal audit reports. Included are discussions of findings, conclusions, recommendations, and report approval and distribution. It does not include guidelines on human relation aspects, communication skills, or the mechanics of report writing.

In view of the importance of the matter, the standard is quoted in full.[1]

> *Statement on Internal Auditing Standards No. 2*
>
> *Statements on Internal Auditing Standards* are issued by the Professional Standards and Responsibilities Committee, the senior technical committee designated by The Institute of Internal Auditors, Inc. to issue pronouncements on auditing matters. These statements are authoritative interpretations of the *Standards for the Professional Practice of Internal Auditing.*
>
> Organizations, internal auditing departments, directors of internal auditing, and internal auditors should strive to comply with the *Standards*. The implementation of the *Standards* and these related statements will be governed by the environment in which the internal auditing department carries out its assigned responsibilities. The adoption and implementation of the *Standards* and related statements will assist internal auditing professionals in accomplishing their responsibilities.

---

[1] From *The Internal Auditor,* Feb. 1984, pp. 10–12. Copyright © 1984 by The Institute of Internal Auditors, Inc., 249 Maitland Avenue, Altamonte Springs, Fla. 32701, U.S.A. Reprinted with permission.

FOREWORD

The Institute of Internal Auditors issued its *Standards for the Professional Practice of Internal Auditing* in 1978 "to serve the entire profession in all types of businesses, in various levels of government, and in all other organizations where internal auditors are found . . . to represent the practice of internal auditing as it should be. . . ." Experience and success have demonstrated the credibility of the basic principles promoted in the *Standards*.

The *Standards* establish a basis for the guidance and measurement of internal auditing performance. For Communicating Results, this basis is delineated in the *Standards* by seven guidelines related to the types, contents, and attributes of audit reports. This statement interprets Guidelines 430 through 430.07.

Summary

This statement provides guidance to internal auditors in communicating audit results in the form of oral and written reports.

It includes interpretation of Standard 430 (Communicating Results) related to types, contents, and attributes of audit reports; discussion of findings, conclusions, and recommendations with management; and audit-report approval and distribution.

430 STANDARD—COMMUNICATING RESULTS

Internal auditors should report the results of their audit work.
(The new interpretive guidelines are in bold print.)

   .01 A signed, written report should be used after the audit examination is completed. Interim reports may be written or oral and may be transmitted formally or informally.

      .1 Interim reports may be used to communicate information which requires immediate attention, to communicate a change in audit scope for the activity under review, or to keep management informed of audit progress when audits extend over a long period. The use of interim reports does not diminish or eliminate the need for a final report.

      .2 Summary reports highlighting audit results may be appropriate for levels of management above the head of the audited unit. They may be issued separately from or in conjunction with the final report.

   .02 The internal auditor should discuss conclusions and recommendations at appropriate levels of management before issuing final written reports.

      .1 Discussion of conclusions and recommendations is usually accomplished during the course of the audit and/or at postaudit meetings (exit interviews). Another technique is the review of draft audit reports by the head of each audited unit. These discussions and reviews help ensure that there have been no misunderstandings or misinterpretations of fact by providing the opportunity for the auditee to clarify specific items and to express views of the findings, conclusions, and recommendations.

      .2 Although the level of participants in the discussion and reviews may vary by organization and by the nature of the report, they will generally include those individuals who are knowledgeable of detailed operations and those who can authorize the implementation of corrective action.

HOW TO COMMUNICATE RESULTS

.03 Reports should be objective, clear, concise, constructive, and timely.

   .1 Objective reports are factual, unbiased, and free from distortion. Findings, conclusions, and recommendations should be included without prejudice.

   .2 Clear reports are easily understood and logical. Clarity can be improved avoiding unnecessary technical language and providing sufficient supportive information.

   .3 Concise reports are to the point and avoid unnecessary detail. They express thoughts completely in the fewest possible words.

   .4 Constructive reports are those which, as a result of their content and tone, help the auditee and the organization and lead to improvements where needed.

   .5 Timely reports are those which are issued without undue delay and enable prompt effective action.

.04 Reports should present the purpose, scope, and results of the audit; and, where appropriate, reports should contain an expression of the auditor's opinion.

   .1 Although audit report format and content may vary by organization or type of audit, they should contain, at a minimum, the purpose, scope, and results of the audit.

   .2 Audit reports may include background information and summaries. Background information may identify the organizational units and functions reviewed and provide relevant explanatory information. They may also include the status of findings, conclusions, and recommendations from prior reports. There may also be an indication of whether the report covers a scheduled audit or the response to a request. Summaries, if included, should be balanced representations of the audit report content.

   .3 Purpose statements should describe the audit objectives and may, where necessary, inform the reader why the audit was conducted and what it was expected to achieve.

   .4 Scope statements should identify the audited activities and include, where appropriate, supportive information such as time period audited. Related activities not audited should be identified if necessary to delineate the boundaries of the audit. The nature and extent of auditing performed also should be described.

   .5 Results may include findings, conclusions (opinions), and recommendations.

   .6 Findings are pertinent statements of fact. Those findings which are necessary to support or prevent misunderstanding of the internal auditor's conclusions and recommendations should be included in the final audit report. Less significant information or findings may be communicated orally or through informal correspondence.

      Audit findings emerge by a process of comparing "what should be" with "what is." Whether or not there is a difference, the internal auditor has a foundation on which to build the report. When conditions meet the criteria, acknowledgement in the audit report of satisfactory performance may be appropriate. Findings should be based on the following attributes:

Criteria: The standards, measures, or expectations used in making an evaluation and/or verification (what *should* exist).

Conditions: The factual evidence which the internal auditor found in the course of the examination (what *does* exist).

If there is a difference between the expected and actual conditions, then:

Cause: The reason for the difference between the expected and actual conditions (*why* the difference exists).

Effect: The risk or exposure the auditee organization and/or others encounter because the condition is not the same as the criteria (the *impact* of the difference).

The reported findings may also include recommendations, auditee accomplishments, and supportive information if not included elsewhere.

.7 Conclusions (opinions) are the internal auditor's evaluations of the effects of the findings on the activities reviewed. They usually put the findings in perspective based upon their overall implications. Audit conclusions, if included in the audit report, should be clearly identified as such. Conclusions may encompass the entire scope of an audit or specific aspects. They may cover but are not limited to whether operating or program objectives and goals conform with those of the organization, whether the organization's objectives and goals are being met, and whether the activity under review is functioning as intended.

.05 Reports may include recommendations for potential improvements and acknowledge satisfactory performance and corrective action.

.1 Recommendations are based on the internal auditor's findings and conclusions. They call for action to correct existing conditions or improve operations. Recommendations may suggest approaches to correcting or enhancing performance as a guide for management in achieving desired results. Recommendations may be general or specific. For example, under some circumstances, it may be desirable to recommend a general course of action and specific suggestions for implementation. In other circumstances, it may be appropriate only to suggest further investigation or study.

.2 Auditee accomplishments, in terms of improvements since the last audit or the establishment of a well-controlled operation, may be included in the audit report. This information may be necessary to fairly represent the existing conditions and to provide a proper perspective and appropriate balance to the audit report.

.06 The auditee's views about audit conclusions or recommendations may be included in the audit report.

.1 As part of the internal auditor's discussions with the auditee, the internal auditor should try to obtain agreement on the results of the audit and on a plan of action to improve operations, as needed. If the internal auditor and auditee disagree about the audit results, the audit report may state both positions and the reasons for the disagreement. The auditee's written comments may be included as an appendix to the audit report. Alternatively, the auditee's view may be presented in the body of the report or in a cover letter.

.07 The director of internal auditing or designee should review and approve the final audit report before issuance and should decide to whom the report will be distributed.

   .1 **The director of internal auditing or a designee should approve and may sign all final reports. If specific circumstances warrant, consideration should be given to having the auditor-in-charge, supervisor, or lead auditor sign the report as a representative of the director of internal auditing.**

   .2 Audit reports should be distributed to those members of the organization who are able to ensure that audit results are given due consideration. This means that the report should go to those who are in a position to take corrective action or ensure that corrective action is taken. The final audit report should be distributed to the head of each audited unit. Higher-level members in the organization may receive only a summary report. Reports may also be distributed to other interested or affected parties such as external auditors and audit committees.

   .3 Certain information may not be appropriate for disclosure to all report recipients because it is privileged, proprietary, or related to improper or illegal acts. Such information, however, may be disclosed in a separate report. If the conditions being reported involve senior management, report distribution should be to the audit committee of the board of directors or a similar high-level entity within the organization.

The GAO

Emphasis in this volume is on internal audit activities carried out to assist in the operation of the private enterprise system. Yet, there may exist occasions when the internal auditor may wish to follow reporting standards prepared by the U.S. government for the use of federal auditors. In early 1987, the GAO prepared a draft of proposed revisions to *Standards for Audit of Governmental Organizations, Programs, Activities and Functions*. This draft contains generally excellent directions on audit standards, including reporting standards, to be followed by federal auditors. Chapter VII of the *Standards* relates to the reporting standards and is reproduced below (proposed changes are in bold face type):

REPORTING STANDARDS FOR **PERFORMANCE** AUDITS

A. Form

   The first reporting standard for government **performance** audits is:

- Written audit reports are to be prepared giving the results of each government audit.[1]

---

[1] **Audit findings not included in the audit report should be reported in a letter to management.**

This standard is not intended to limit or prevent discussion of findings, judgments, conclusions, and recommendations with persons who have responsibilities involving the area being audited. On the contrary, such discussions should be encouraged. However, a written report should be prepared regardless of whether such discussions are held.

Written reports are necessary (1) to communicate the results of audits to officials at all levels of government, (2) to make the findings and recommendations less susceptible to misunderstanding, (3) to make the findings available for public inspection, and (4) to facilitate follow-up to determine whether **prompt and** appropriate corrective **actions** have been taken **by entity officials.**

When an audit is terminated prior to completion, the auditor should prepare a memorandum for the record briefly summarizing the results of the work performed, and explaining why the audit was terminated. The auditor should also notify the auditee and other appropriate officials, preferably in writing, that the audit has been terminated.

B. Distribution

The second reporting standard for government **performance** audits is:

- Written audit reports are to be submitted to the appropriate officials of the organization audited and to the appropriate officials of the organizations requiring or arranging for the audits unless legal restrictions or ethical considerations prevent it. Copies of the reports should also be sent to other officials who may be responsible for taking action on audit findings and recommendations and to others authorized to receive such reports. Unless restricted by law or regulation, copies should be made available for public inspection.

Audit reports should be distributed to as many interested officials as is practicable. In some cases, the subject of the audit may involve material that is classified for security purposes or is not releasable for other valid reasons. Generally, however, the report should be distributed to officials directly interested in the **results.** Such officials include those designated by law or regulation to receive such reports, those responsible for taking action on the findings and recommendations, legislators, and those of other levels of government that have provided funds to the audited entity. Also, unless restricted by law or regulation, copies should be available for distribution to or inspection by the public.

When **outside organizations** are engaged, the engaging organization must ensure that appropriate distribution is made to interested parties. If the **outside organizations** are to make the distribution, the engagement agreement should indicate what officials or organizations shall receive the report. Internal auditors should follow their entity's own arrangements. Usually, they report to their entity's top management and the entity is responsible for distribution of the report.

C. Timeliness

The third reporting standard for government **performance** audits is:

- Reports are to be issued promptly so as to make the information available for timely use by management and by legislative officials.

HOW TO COMMUNICATE RESULTS

To be of maximum use, the report must be timely. A carefully prepared report may be of little value to decisionmakers if it arrives too late. Therefore the auditors should plan and conduct the audit with this in mind. **In the planning phase of an audit, the auditor should plan for the timely issuance of the audit report.**

The auditors should consider interim reporting of significant matters to appropriate officials during the audit. Such communication is not a substitute for a final written report, but it does alert officials to matters needing immediate attention and permits them to take corrective action before the final report is completed.

D. Report Contents

The fourth reporting standard for government **performance** audits is:

- The report **should** include, **where appropriate:**
  1. A description of the objectives, scope, **methodology, results, and conclusions of the audit.**
  2. A statement that the audit was **or was not** made in accordance with generally accepted government auditing standards.
  3. **A statement identifying the significant internal controls that were studied and evaluated during the audit and a description of the significant weaknesses found in the internal controls.**
  4. **All** significant instances of noncompliance and all instances or **apparent** indications of fraud, abuse, or illegal acts found during or in connection with the audit. However, fraud, abuse, or illegal acts normally should be covered in a separate report, thus permitting **an audit** report to be released to the public.
  5. Recommendations for actions to improve problem areas noted in the audit and to improve operations.
  6. The underlying causes of problems reported should be included to assist in implementing corrective actions.
  7. Pertinent views of responsible officials of the organization, program, activity, or function audited concerning the auditors' findings, conclusions, and recommendations.
  8. A description of **significant** noteworthy accomplishments, particularly when management improvements in one area may be applicable elsewhere.
  9. A listing of any **significant** issues needing further study and consideration.
  10. A statement as to whether any pertinent information has been omitted because it is deemed privileged or confidential. The nature of such information should be described, and the law or other basis under which it is withheld should be stated.

Objectives, Scope and Methodology

The objectives, **scope and methodology** of the audit should be described in the audit report. **The statement of objectives should explain why the audit was made and state precisely what the report is to accomplish. This is essential to give the** reader the proper perspective—a background against which reported findings may be considered.

The statement of scope tells the reader what the auditors did and did not do. Explaining the depth and coverage of the audit work enables the reader to place the report's message in the proper perspective and understand any significant limitations. Every effort should be made to avoid any misunderstanding by the reader concerning the work that was or was not done to achieve the audit objectives, particularly when the work was limited by relying on internal controls or because of constraints on time or resources.

The statement on methodology should clearly explain to the reader how the auditors went about accomplishing the audit's objectives, and disclose any serious data limitations.

Results and Conclusions (Where Applicable)

Reports should contain sufficient information about findings and conclusions to promote adequate understanding of the matters reported and to provide convincing, but fair, presentations in proper perspective. Sufficient background information should also be included.

Readers should not be expected to possess all the facts that the auditor has, and therefore reports should not be written on the basis that the bare recital of facts makes the conclusions inescapable. Conclusions should be specified, rather than left to be inferred by readers.

Statement on Auditing Standards

A statement in the auditors' report that the audit was **or was not** made in accordance with generally accepted government auditing standards **is required.**

The above statement refers to all the applicable standards that the auditors should have followed during their audit. The statement need not be qualified to indicate that standards which were not applicable were not followed. However, the statement should be qualified in situations where the auditors did not follow a standard that should have been followed during their audit. In these situations the auditors should modify the statement, and disclose in appropriate sections of their report, that a required standard was not followed, the reasons therefore, and the effect not following the standard had or may have on the results of the audit.

Statement on Internal Control

The auditors' report should identify the significant internal controls that were studied and evaluated during the audit, and should describe the significant weaknesses found in the internal controls. Weaknesses should be reported if they are significant in relation to the audit objectives.

Compliance Statement

Compliance with laws and regulations, in many instances, assumes importance since recipients of the reports want to know whether funds were spent for authorized purposes.

HOW TO COMMUNICATE RESULTS

The auditors' report should include all significant instances of noncompliance **found during or in connection with the audit,** even those not resulting in a legal liability of the entity. **Minor instances of noncompliance should also be reported if illegal.** Other minor noncompliance need not be disclosed **in the audit report, but should be reported in a separate communication to the auditee.**

In reporting noncompliance, the auditors should place their findings in proper perspective. The extent of noncompliance should be related to the number of cases examined to give the reader a basis for judging the prevalence of noncompliance.

Fraud, Abuse, or Illegal Acts

If, during an audit or in connection with an audit of a government entity, external government auditors become aware of fraud, abuse, or illegal acts or **apparent** indications of such acts affecting the government entity, they should promptly notify the top official of that entity (unless the official is believed to be a party to such acts or otherwise implicated) and the appropriate law enforcement authorities. If the acts involve funds received from other government entities, the auditors should also promptly notify **the proper government** officials, **including the audit organization,** of those entities.

Internal government auditors auditing a government entity that is external to the government entity to which they are assigned should promptly notify officials and authorities in accordance with the preceding paragraph.

Outside organizations performing government audits will discharge their responsibility by promptly notifying the entity arranging for the audit. **However, if the acts involve funds received from other government entities, they should also promptly notify the proper government officials, including the audit organization, of those entities.**

Internal government auditors **auditing within the government entity to which they are assigned** should notify the top officials of the entity under audit.

It will be the responsibility of an entity, **both auditee and funding entity,** receiving the information **from the various organizations** to notify appropriate law enforcement authorities and other government entities whose funds may be involved.

In the case of an audit of government funds received by a nongovernment entity, the auditors should promptly notify the appropriate **governmental** entity **requiring or** arranging for the audit **and such other officials designated by law or regulation to receive the audit reports.**

All fraud, abuse, or illegal acts or **apparent** indications of such acts, whether significant or not, that auditors become aware of should be covered in a written report and submitted in accordance with the preceding paragraphs. Such information should normally be covered in a separate report, thus permitting **an audit** report to be released to the public. Auditors **generally** should not release reports containing information on such acts, or reports with references that such acts were omitted from reports, without consulting with legal counsel, since this could interfere with legal processes or subject the implicated individuals to undue publicity, **or might subject the auditor to potential legal action.**

Recommendations

The audit reports should contain recommendations whenever significant improvement in audited entities is possible. Also, recommendations should be made to effect compliance with laws or regulations when significant instances of noncompliance are noted. **If significant weaknesses are found in internal controls, the recommendations should contain constructive suggestions for improvement.** Reports which contain constructive recommendations can encourage improvements in the conduct of government programs and activities.

Management is primarily responsible for directing action and follow-up on recommendations. **In subsequent audits, the auditor's report should disclose the status of unresolved significant findings and recommendations from prior related audits that have an effect on the audit objective. To facilitate follow-up and reporting, government auditors should normally establish a system that enables them to track the status of their previous significant findings and recommendations.**

If the auditors cannot make appropriate recommendations because of limited audit scope or for other reasons, they should state in the report why they cannot and what additional work is needed to formulate recommendations.

Views of Responsible Officials

One of the most effective ways to ensure that a report is fair, complete, and objective is to obtain advance review and comments by officials of the audited entity. **The auditor should request that the responsible officials' views be submitted in writing.** This produces a report which shows not only what was found and what the auditors think about it but also what the responsible persons think about it and what they plan to do about it.

Advance comments should be objectively evaluated, and the report presentations and conclusions should recognize them. The comments and an analysis of them should be fairly presented in the report. A promise of corrective action should be noted but should not be accepted as justification for dropping a significant point or a related recommendation.

When the comments oppose the auditors' findings or conclusions and are not, in their opinion, valid, the auditors should state their reasons for rejecting them. Conversely, they should modify their position if they find the comments valid.

Recognition of Noteworthy Accomplishments

Significant management accomplishments identified during the audit, **which were within the scope of the audit necessary to accomplish the audit objectives,** should be included in the audit report, along with deficiencies. Such information is necessary to fairly present the situation the auditors find and to provide appropriate balance to the report. In addition, inclusion of such accomplishments may lead to improved performance by other government organizations that read the report.

Issues Needing Further Study

If during the audit, the auditor identifies significant issues that warrant further audit work, the auditor should:

(1) pursue the issues which are directly related to the audit objectives, or

(2) if not directly related, the auditor should consider changing the scope of the audit to pursue those issues identified[2] or refer the issues to the appropriate auditors within the audit organization responsible for planning future audit work, or

(3) if the auditor decides not to pursue or refer the issues, and in the auditor's opinion the issues could have a significant effect on the entity's programs, activities, and functions, the auditor should disclose these issues in the report and the reasons why they believe they need further study.

Privileged and Confidential Information

Certain information may be prohibited from general disclosure by federal, state, or local laws or regulations. Such information may be provided on a need-to-know basis only to persons authorized by law or regulation to **have** it.

If the auditors are prohibited by such requirements from including pertinent data in the report, they should state the nature of the information omitted and the requirement that makes the omission necessary. The auditors should obtain assurance that a valid requirement for the omission exists, **and where appropriate consult with legal counsel.**

Auditors should consult with legal counsel before releasing reports with references that fraud, abuse, or illegal acts or indications of such acts were omitted from reports.

E. Report Presentation

The fifth reporting standard for government performance audits is:

- All reports **should:**
    1. Present factual data accurately and fairly. Include only information, findings, and conclusions that are adequately supported by sufficient evidence in the auditors' working papers to demonstrate or prove the bases for the matters reported and their correctness and reasonableness. **Audit findings have often been regarded as containing the elements of condition, criteria, cause, and effect. However, the elements needed for a complete finding depends entirely on the objectives of the audit. Thus, a finding or set of findings is complete to the extent that the audit objectives are satisfied and the report clearly relates those objectives to the findings elements.**
    2. Present findings and conclusions in a convincing manner.
    3. Be objective.
    4. Be written in language as clear and simple as the subject matter permits.
    5. Be concise but, at the same time, clear enough to be understood by users.
    6. Present factual data completely to fully inform the users.
    7. Place primary emphasis on improvement rather than on criticism of the past (**use constructive tone**); critical comments should be presented in a

---

[2] See Footnote 3, Chapter V.

balanced perspective considering any unusual difficulties or circumstances faced by the operating officials concerned.

Accuracy and Adequacy of Support

The need for accuracy is based on the need to be fair and impartial in reporting and to assure readers that what is reported is reliable. One inaccuracy in a report can cast doubt on the validity of an entire report and can divert attention from the substance of the report..

Conclusions should be clearly identified and all facts, findings, and conclusions should be supported by sufficient objective evidence. Except as necessary to make convincing presentations, detailed supporting data need not be included. In most cases, a single example of a deficiency is not sufficient to support a broad conclusion or a related recommendation. All that it supports is that there was a deviation, an error, or a weakness.

Convincingness

Findings **should** be presented in a convincing manner and conclusions and recommendations **should** follow logically from the facts presented. The information in reports **should** be sufficient to persuade the readers of the importance of the findings, the reasonableness of the conclusions, and the desirability of their accepting the recommendations. Reports designed in this manner can do much to focus the attention of responsible officials on the matters in reports which warrant attention and to stimulate corrective actions.

Objectivity

Findings should be presented objectively and should include sufficient information on the subject to give readers a proper perspective. The audit report should be fair and not misleading and should place primary emphasis on matters needing attention. The auditor should guard against the tendency to exaggerate or overemphasize deficient performance noted.

The information needed to provide proper report balance and perspective should include:
1. Why the audit was made.
2. The size and nature of the activities or programs audited.
3. Correct and fair descriptions of findings. To avoid misinterpretations, the size of the sample of items tested and the methods of selecting the items should be **stated.**

Clarity and Simplicity

Reports should be written in language as clear and simple as practicable. Logical organization of material and accuracy and succinctness in stating facts, and in drawing conclusions are essential to clarity and understanding. Visual aids (such as pictures, charts, graphs, maps) should be used when appropriate to clarify and summarize complex material. Use of straightforward, nontechnical language is essential

to simplicity of presentation. If technical terms and unfamiliar abbreviations are used, they should be clearly defined.

Conciseness

The reports should be no longer than necessary. Too much detail detracts from a report, may even conceal the real message, and may confuse or discourage readers.

Although there is room for considerable judgment in determining the content of reports, those that are complete, but still concise, are likely to receive attention.

Completeness

Although reports should be concise, they should also be complete. Reports should contain sufficient information about findings, conclusions, and recommendations to promote adequate understanding of the matters reported and to provide convincing, but fair, presentations in proper perspective. Sufficient background information should also be included.

Readers should not be expected to possess all the facts that the auditor has, and therefore reports should not be written on the basis that the bare recital of facts makes the conclusions inescapable. Conclusions should be specified, rather than left to be inferred by readers.

Constructiveness of Tone

The tone of reports should encourage **the acceptance of the** recommendations. Titles, captions, and the text of reports should be stated constructively. Although findings should be presented in clear, forthright terms, the auditors should keep in mind that their objective is to obtain **acceptance of their recommendations** and that this can best be done by avoiding language that unnecessarily generates defensiveness and opposition. Although criticism of past performance is often necessary, the report should emphasize needed improvements rather than criticism.

FORMAL WRITTEN REPORTS ON ACTIVITIES EXAMINED

In the typical large industrial or commercial firm, the majority of the audit reports are formal written reports on the results of an examination. While the exact format of a formal written report may differ from company to company, the elements listed below are usually included:

- Transmittal sheet
- Summary or highlights
- Statement of purpose
- Scope of audit
- Opinion
- Findings
- Recommendations

Transmittal Sheet

The transmittal sheet, or cover, of the report should quickly do the following:

- Identify the document as an internal audit report.
- Name the function audited.
- Provide an audit number for ease of reference.
- Indicate the date of the report.
- Specify the distribution of the report.
- Indicate those who must take action, those who are to receive an informational copy only, and those who reviewed the report prior to release.
- Provide names of the auditors and approving supervisor.

While the exact format and content may vary, the transmittal sheet supplies critical information to the recipients. An example of such a sheet is shown in Figure 13-1.

Summary or Highlights

Most business executives are busy and do not wish to wade through masses of details to arrive at the significant conclusions and the action to be taken. Hence, a summary or highlights section is a useful device for encouraging reception of the report and action on its contents. The highlights spell out the major points and findings of an audit. The details are available later in the report for the executive who wishes to know more. Again, while the format may vary, these subjects are suggested for quick coverage:

- Scope of audit
- Significant findings
- Principal actions recommended
- Status of prior open items

An example of a summary section is illustrated in Figure 13-2. Care must be taken in preparing the summary section to avoid unwarranted conclusions by the readers.

Statement of Purpose

As a general rule, each audit report should contain a brief statement of purpose. It identifies the objectives of the audit so that the reader will know what items were and were not covered. As the findings are discussed and related to the purpose, the reader is assisted in understanding the report.

An example of a statement of purpose for an audit of accounts payable in a division would be:

FIG. 13-1
Transmittal Sheet

```
                    THE AIRCRAFT CORPORATION
                       INTERNAL AUDIT REPORT

                    Division:   Corporate Office
                    Function:   Supply Department

Audit No.  C 112-181                          Date:  Feb. 12, 19XX
```

Distribution	Action	Information	Reviewed Prior to Release
Chairman			
President		X	
Vice-President — Administration	X		
Director of Material	X		
Manager — Procurement	X		X
Manager — Supply Department	X		X
Vice-President & Controller		X	
Chief Accountant	X		X

Auditor: _____

Approved by: _____

Our examination was undertaken to obtain and confirm responses to the following control-related questions:

1. Did the division financial statement properly reflect the accounts payable balance as of September 30, 19XX?
2. Do receiving report documents support either the payment or the unpaid, but recorded, liability?
3. Are all cash discounts properly taken?
4. Are all purchase orders and vendor invoices properly matched? Are all numbers accounted for?
5. Is the aging of the accounts payable essentially correct?

Scope of Examination

A statement concerning the scope of examination is usually also included so that limitations may be identified. Unless this is done, either in combination with the statement of purpose, or as a separate statement, the reader might conclude that every aspect of the activity was reviewed. The phases of the activities that were audited should be mentioned. A discussion of the

FIG. 13-2
Summary Section of Audit Report

Corporate Headquarters
Insurance Department

SUMMARY:

The regular annual review of Insurance Department activities, covering the period 1/1/XX through 12/31/XX, was made.

PURPOSE:

The purpose of our review was to assess functional efficiency of the Insurance Department in terms of the use bidding procedures, reinsurance practices, coordination efforts, and rate of return on investments.

COVERAGE:

Included: 1. Corporate office
2. Insurance Subsidiary
3. Claims interface section — Electronics Group

SUMMARY OF FINDINGS:

1. Claims totaling $1,300,000 on damaged equipment in (country) have not been filed.
2. Insurance policy summary sheets are not completed for all coverage purchased after July 1, 19XX.
3. The detail prepaid insurance ledger is in excess of the control account by $560,000.

OVERALL OPINION:

With these administrative control exceptions, the department is functioning efficiently in that (1) insurance is being purchased economically through the bidding procedures recently put in place; (2) effective coordination with the Electronics division has been accomplished; and (3) the insurance subsidiary has secured advantageous reinsurance and a reasonable rate of income from its investments.

ACTION REQUIRED:

1. The new assistant manager should expedite claim filing.
2. The administrative assistant should complete the policy summaries.
3. The assistance of the Accounting Department should be sought in reconciling the subsidiary prepaid insurance ledger with the control account.

PRIOR AUDIT:

All matters have been successfully resolved

---

activity reviewed does not include a detailed statement of the audit steps taken.

An example of the scope of examination (for a pension fund activity) might be as follows:

> We confined our review to testing payments made to retirees and terminated employees for the six months ended June 30, 19XX as compared to provisions of the retirement plan. We verified investments by confirmation from the trustee of the trust assets, but we did not count the securities.

The Opinion

When an independent auditor performs an examination of the financial statements of a public corporation, most lenders, other major creditors, and shareholders expect a report that expresses an opinion on the statements. In fact, they hope for a "clean" opinion. And most sophisticated investors understand the limitations of the opinion; it is not a guarantee.[2]

By the same token, business managers expect an opinion from the internal auditors as to the activity reviewed. It is a concise, and usually brief, statement of the auditor's professional judgment—an assessment of the conditions he found. Obviously, the opinion should be supported by the facts, and should state precisely what the auditor intends to say. It should be responsive to the purposes of the audit.

Some sample opinions indicating (1) entirely satisfactory conditions; (2) generally satisfactory conditions with some minor exceptions; and (3) unsatisfactory conditions are presented below:

1. In our opinion, the system of internal control existent in the payroll department is sufficient to reasonably assure attaining the department objectives.
2. In our opinion, all company segments followed the commitment authority guidelines in all material respects except for three instances of precontractual expense incurrence totaling $2,870,000 in excess of authorized amounts occurring in the communications subsidiary.
3. In our opinion, the purchasing and inventory control functions are insufficient to reasonably assure attaining department objectives in that
   - ☐ Materials were not purchased in accordance with the current production schedule with a resulting excess inventory of $8,200,000 involving 320 items.
   - ☐ No attempt was made to use previously determined excess inventories, with a resulting estimated write-down of $1,400,000 now required.
   - ☐ Finished goods inventories of radio parts were not valued at the lower of cost or market. Consequently, the inventory adjustment will increase the annual loss by $1,982,000.

In some organizations overall opinions are not provided, but this practice appears to be declining.

Findings

The findings form the basis of the opinion and the recommendations. Obviously, the findings are crucial and must be accurate and factual. By implication, the findings are based on certain criteria, guidelines, or measures

---

[2] See John C. Burton, Russell E. Palmer, and Robert S. Kay, *Handbook of Accounting and Auditing*, Chapter 16 (Boston: Warren, Gorham & Lamont, 1981).

of propriety. In describing the conditions or result, the auditor must be sensitive to the particular attributes or uniqueness of the organization and its structure. There should be no limit on his right to challenge, to test, or to affirm the findings, even if a change in company policy may be necessary.

In setting forth the findings, the auditor must break down the problem into its several components. This strengthens the conclusion and forces a thinking through of the best procedure. It also provides a basis for giving the reader the elements that were weighed in reaching the judgment. Some of the parts or elements to be considered include these:

- ☐ *The objectives of the activity.* The purpose or objective of the activity must be known to judge whether or not it is being accomplished and is being done properly, effectively, and economically. Thus, the objective of the material department might be stated as follows: "The primary objective of the Material Department is to provide the production line with the raw materials and purchased parts at reasonable prices without causing excessive delays. The secondary objective is to maintain inventory levels as low as is possible while being consistent with the primary objective, so as to minimize investment." The auditor should consider whether the objective is proper, and properly stated.

- ☐ *The authority for the activity or procedure.* Under normal circumstances, someone authorized the function or activity under review. It may have been the board of directors, or chief executive officer, or some other member of management. Knowing specifically the authority and the bounds set for the activity permits the auditor to conclude that the activity has been operating within these limits, and in fact whether the proper source, from an internal control viewpoint, authorized the function. A written authority may be more easily checked or verified than an oral authorization.

- ☐ *A succinct and simple summary statement of the finding.* A one-sentence summary should simply and clearly state the finding. It should make the reader want to listen. For example: "The motor inventory was equivalent to four months production, and represented an excess investment of $29,300,000."

- ☐ *The criteria used should be cited if it is not inherently obvious.* Specification of the criteria assists the reader in judging the reasonableness of the conclusion. Criteria could include written procedures, established practices (which an auditor may find satisfactory), practices in other segments of the company, or industry practice.

- ☐ *The facts and results should be simply stated.* Whatever conditions were observed should be factually set forth. An example: "Excess materials were not returned to the stockroom, but were treated as scrap. Scrap ticket numbers, description, and date are summarized below showing a loss of $322,800 for the three-week period checked."

- ☐ *The cause should be identified if practicable.* When unsatisfactory conditions are uncovered, the natural question usually is: "How could that be?" or "Why did it happen?" The audit findings should include a statement of

HOW TO COMMUNICATE RESULTS 13-23

cause or possible causes, if identifiable, e.g., "The employees were not properly instructed on the correct procedure. The department supervisor did not monitor the process. The excessive work load occurring during the period under review as a result of the recent merger of the *ABC* Company may have been a contributing factor." The more important findings can be covered in a summary section, with substantial supporting details enumerated in an appendix, if it is desirable and the material is voluminous enough.

Recommendations

Having presented the findings, the next most important item of the audit report is the recommendations. The reader, having seen the conclusions, quite naturally needs suggestions on what should be done to correct the unsatisfactory conditions. Discussing a deficiency in activity without suggesting corrective measures is poor auditing, indeed.

The recommendations should be reviewed with the departmental manager and the staff as to such considerations as practicality. If the supervisor does not agree, his position should be clearly stated and the auditor's comment made thereon. These instances should be comparatively rare, since the intent of both auditor and auditee should be to resolve all disagreements over remedial actions prior to finalizing the report.

An example of a recommendations section of an audit report follows:

Based upon our review of the corporate office procedures for administrative office purchases, and discussions with the Contracting Officer (U.S. Air Force) we make three recommendations:

1. State the price on purchase orders for any items costing in excess of $500 for each item, or an aggregate value of $60,000. We estimate this will require pricing of about 250 items per month, on which figure the supervisor agrees. If this procedure is not adopted, there is some question about allowability of costs on government contracts.

2. Require that the receiving of materials and supplies be witnessed or supervised by a person other than the storekeeper.

   This segregation of duties, which can be handled on a part-time basis by the clerk in the administrative section, will improve the internal control on annual receipts of about $34 million.

   The supervisor believes this is an unnecessary check and control based on the assertion that pilferage and other unexplainable material losses average less than $25,000 per year. We believe, for the small cost involved, about $8,000 per year, the improvement in control is worth the effort.

3. In order to provide a more accurate accounts payable figure for the quarterly financial statements, price uninvoiced receiving reports on an estimated basis as of the end of each calendar quarter. The entry can be reversed for the succeeding period.

FIG. 13-3
Complete Audit Report

TO: R.S. Tatum

FROM: Corporate Audit

SUBJECT: Review of Capital Asset Transactions. Northern Assembly Division (NAD)

PURPOSE:

We have completed a review of capital asset transactions at NAD for the period January 1. 19X1 through March 31. 19X2. The purpose of our review was to determine that capital asset transactions are being executed in accordance with management's general or specific authorization. are recorded as necessary to permit preparation of financial statements in conformity with GAAP. that recorded accountability for assets is compared with existing assets at reasonable intervals with appropriate action being taken with respect to any differences. and that the related assets are appropriately safeguarded.

SCOPE OF AUDIT:

Our review was conducted in accordance with internally developed audit standards and included a review of related NAD policies and procedures. completing a capital asset internal control questionnaire. testing of controls identified. following up recommendations made in prior Corporate audit reports. and other procedures considered necessary in the circumstances.

FINDINGS — SUMMARY:

Our review disclosed the following matters which have been mentioned in previous audit reports and have not been resolved:

- Delays continue to exist in the transferring of completed equipment facilities requests (FRs) from the construction in progress (CIP) accounts to the completed fixed asset accounts. (External auditor's December 31, 19XX management letter and Corporate Audit Report No. XX-193. dated August 29. 19XX.)
- Several instances were noted where authorized FR amounts were exceeded and no supplemental FRs were prepared. (External auditor's December 31, 19XX management letter and NAD internal audit report #9010-XX-228, dated November 18. 19XX.) This matter will be discussed in more detail in a report on facilities management at NAD to be issued later this quarter.

In addition. the following matters which require management's attention were noted:

- More control and timely follow-up of move orders is needed.
- Two property accounting procedures are not in complete compliance with a requirement of CPD 36.
- Modification of the present computerized depreciation report should be investigated to accommodate the elimination of the manual calculation of depreciation expense.

The matters noted above (related to the nonissuance of required supplemental FRs and control over move orders) present weaknesses in controls which need to be resolved in order to assure that fixed asset amounts are properly authorized and accounted for. The other matters do not present weaknesses in controls, but relate to potential efficiencies and divisional procedure compliance with Corporate policies. Management has informed us that a physical inventory of fixed assets will commence in August 19X1 with a target completion date of December 31, 19X1. In addition they informed us of a planned automation of the property accounting system to be completed by late 19X1 or early 19X2. These planned actions, when implemented, will have the effect of greatly improving the existing control environment, and they have been taken into consideration in formulating our recommendations.

OPINION:

Subject to implementation of the recommendations related to the control weaknesses outlined above, it is our opinion that capital asset transactions are properly authorized, recorded, and reported to permit preparation of financial statements in conformity with generally accepted accounting principles, and that the related assets are appropriately safeguarded.

Our detailed findings and recommendations are presented in the balance of this report. A written reply to this report directed to Corporate Audit, 155/CC, is requested from the action party within thirty days.

DETAILED FINDINGS AND RECOMMENDATIONS

1. Delays continue to exist in the transferring of completed facilities requests (FRs) from the construction in progress (CIP) accounts to the completed fixed-asset accounts.

In our report No. XX-193, we noted delays in transferring completed FRs from construction in progress to the completed fixed asset accounts. NAD management's response to the report on this matter stated that a standard FR closure notice form was being developed to ensure prompt notification to property accounting of completed FRs. During our current review, we noted that delays continue to exist. Several instances were noted where FR closure notices were either not promptly received by property accounting or not closed out in a timely manner after being received. The manager of property accounting disclosed that in most instances he closes an item out based on costs accumulated to date. He may have a closure notice and no cost to date, as this information might not have been processed. This closure notice is then noted for future use. In instances where no closure notice is received, he uses his own judgment in closing these items out based upon review of charges on cost summaries. The entire cost accumulation and closing out of an FR is done on a manual basis. The manager of property accounting has informed us that due to the ever-increasing volume of FRs, it takes approximately 2–3 months to review and update all cost summaries and close items out. It is also time consuming to follow up with project engineers as to the status of projects and to determine why no closure notices have been received. Property management has informed us that automation of the property accounting system is currently in the developmental stages and should be completed by late 19X1 or early 19X2. This automation of the system should improve the timeliness of transfers from the CIP account to the completed asset account. It would also allow for more timely accumulation of cost summaries, thereby freeing up personnel for more reviews of cost summaries and follow-up of closure notice items. We believe that present efforts should be continued, particularly at year end, to assure timely transfers of FRs from the CIP to completed asset accounts.

Recommendation No. 1

Continue efforts to effect timely transfers of FRs from the CIP to completed fixed asset accounts, particularly at year end.

(continued)

FIG. 13-3 *(con'td)*

---

2. More control and timely follow-up of move orders is needed.

A control listing of all move orders is kept in property accounting. These move orders control the location of fixed assets and are used to adjust the master listing of fixed assets for any new location. Several instances were noted where prenumbered blank and unaccounted-for move orders were issued to various individuals. In addition, there is a considerable number of 'suspense' move order copies that are not being processed by property accounting because the original has not been received from the transferee. Property accounting management has informed us that they do not feel it necessary to implement more controls over move orders until completion of the physical inventory commencing in August, 19XX. While we concur with this opinion, we believe that more stringent controls should be implemented promptly upon completion of the physical inventory, as move orders are essential to the control of potential discrepancies between the records and physical location of the assets.

Recommendation No. 2

Upon completion of the physical inventory of fixed assets, establish more stringent controls over move orders by more accountability and timely follow-up of move orders.

3. Two property accounting procedures are not in complete compliance with a requirement of CPD 36.

CPD 36 states that Corporate approval of the disposition of an asset has to be obtained if the original cost is greater than $500,000 or its net book value is greater than $100,000. The division's SPP 3.0.0.1, in conjunction with its GPD 1-3.0.1, states that corporate approval is required if the original cost is greater than $25,000.

Recommendation No. 3

Revise division property accounting procedures and policies to assure that they are in agreement with the relevant Corporate policies.

4. Modification of the present computerized depreciation report should be investigated to accommodate the elimination of the manual calculation of depreciation expense.

Depreciation expense is calculated on a manual basis rather than by using an existing computerized depreciation expense report. This report is used for calculating "net book values" by asset and for reconciling asset costs per the property records to the general ledger. The report is not used for depreciation expense purposes because some items for the period 19X1 through 19X2 totaling $7,357,667 (net book value of approximately $2,452,000) are under "certificates of necessity" as required by the Air Force for cost reimbursement purposes. These items require a different depreciation calculation from NAD's stated policies as established and applied in the computerized depreciation report. The amounts subject to the "certificate of necessity" were arrived at from data on individual property cards that shows the portion subject to these certificates. The computerized report, however, shows the total as per individual property card and does not show the applicable amounts under their "certificates of necessity" separately to facilitate the separate depreciation-expense calculations required by the Air Force. The manager of property accounting informed us that he feels that too many items are involved to effect an update of the existing system.

While the volume of items may be substantial, we believe that modification of the computerized depreciation report should be investigated for possible use in

> calculating depreciation. This is based on the belief that the total value of items under "certificates of necessity" is too insignificant to forsake computerized calculations for all other capital assets, which total approximately $349 million as of March 31, 19X2. Computerizing the depreciation-expense calculation could improve the efficiency of property accounting as well as enhance existing controls by eliminating the risk of error inherent in a manual system.
>
> **Recommendation No. 4**
>
> Investigate the possibilities of modifying the computerized depreciation report in order to eliminate unnecessary manual calculations. As an alternative, due to the insignificant net book value of the "certificate of necessity" items and their effect on any cost reimbursement calculation, this situation could be discussed with the Air Force for possible acceptance of the more current depreciation methods.

An example of a complete audit report, encompassing some of the principles discussed herein, is presented in Figure 13-3.

CONSERVING THE TIME OF HIGHER MANAGEMENT

Management expects the internal auditor to gather the necessary facts, properly interpret them, and provide the analysis and recommendations so that the management processes or controls are improved for the company's benefit. Typically, the auditee explains the actions he has taken or will take, as well as their timing. When agreement between the internal auditor and operations manager cannot be reached, then higher management is called on to resolve the differences. However, the time of senior management that may be devoted to such audit-generated problems is limited by the demands of long-range planning, competitive forces, external influences, and the need to achieve the current business plan. Consequently, it is preferred that circumstances do not require the attention of higher management. To that end, these suggestions are made or reemphasized:

- To be of maximum assistance to line management, and to minimize interruption, the programs and procedures should be reviewed *before* they are installed. Or, performance should be checked *as it occurs*. There should be a sort of "on-line" review. Additionally, the internal auditor should be available for consultation by operating management or others *before* the proposed action takes place.
- Audit reports ought to be clear and concise to minimize the chances of misunderstandings. As previously stated, they should contain only relevant and significant points.
- Audit recommendations generally should focus on actions that can be taken by front-line executives. It is hoped that agreements on what can and should

be done will be worked out between auditor and auditee. Only rarely should the assistance of top management be needed.
- The auditor should be able to identify specifically the problem area so that the auditee will clearly understand the matter. References must be specific.

ORAL REPORTS

As previously stated, the majority of audit reports will be in written form. However, oral reports, especially when combined with visual aids, can be of immense value. Among their many advantages are these:

☐ They permit an easy interchange of information. The auditor can sense what is not clear and make clarifying statements immediately. Oral reports permit further explanations—questions and answers. They also serve to reveal attitudes on the part of those audited.

☐ They provide a device, especially for interim or informal reporting, to get information rather quickly into the hands of management—especially when management wants prompt action, without waiting for all the niceties of a written report.

☐ They present an opportunity for face-to-face meetings, which may be helpful for both parties. Often, they provide a means of establishing better rapport.

☐ Oral presentations may reveal inaccuracies in an auditor's thinking or approach, which can then be corrected.

Obviously, care should be taken, commensurate with the importance of the subject matter and audience, in preparing the report. Just as a salesperson prepares a talk to convince the prospect, so should the auditor organize the remarks to be delivered to management. They should be concise and to the point. Oral reports permit a certain amount of flexibility, depending on how the auditor perceives the report as being understood. Portions may be dropped or expanded as circumstances make advisable.

Visual aids usually permit the subject matter to be understood more quickly. These devices may include:

- Small, or large, flip charts
- Transparencies, such as vu-graphs, which may be quickly and inexpensively prepared, involving a projector for ease in viewing
- Regular photographic transparent slides

GRAPHIC AND/OR PICTURED PRESENTATIONS

Whether audit reports are oral or written, visual aids can be helpful in conveying a message. Photographs, for example, can quickly identify unsafe or

HOW TO COMMUNICATE RESULTS

FIG. 13-4
Graphic Report on Capital Expenditure Performance

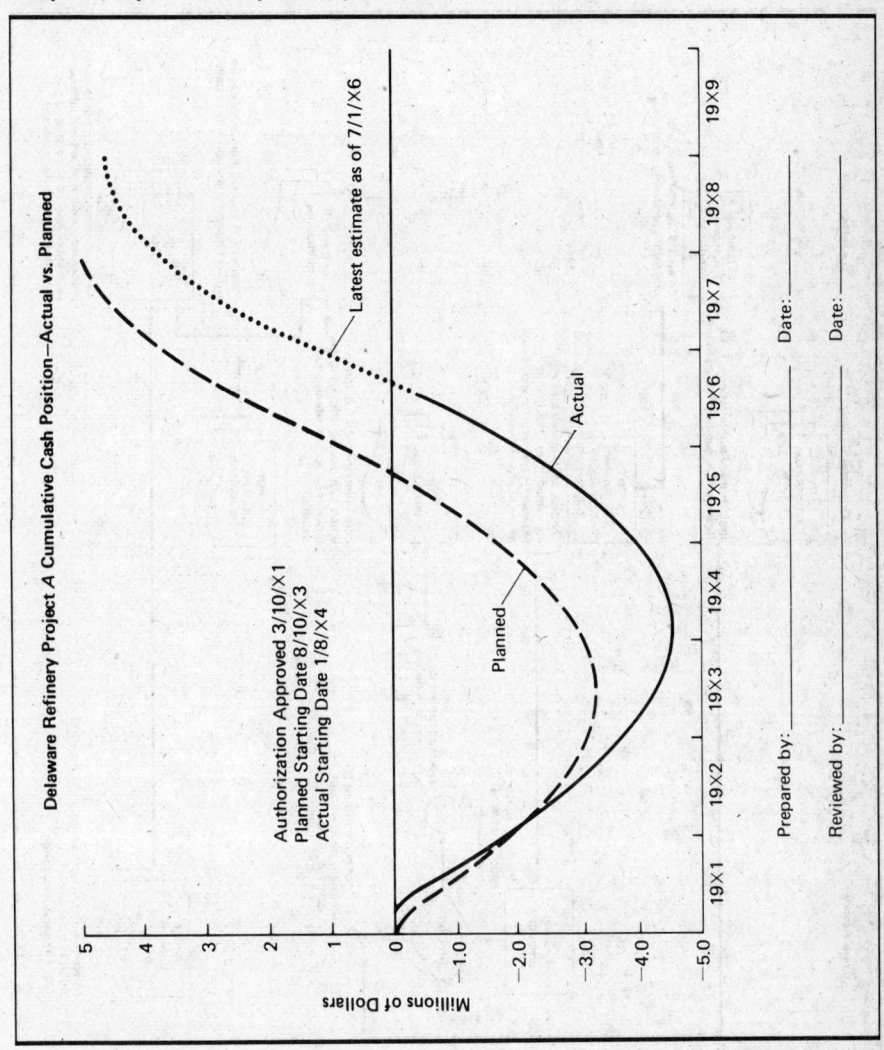

FIG. 13-5
Flow Chart Authorizing Travel

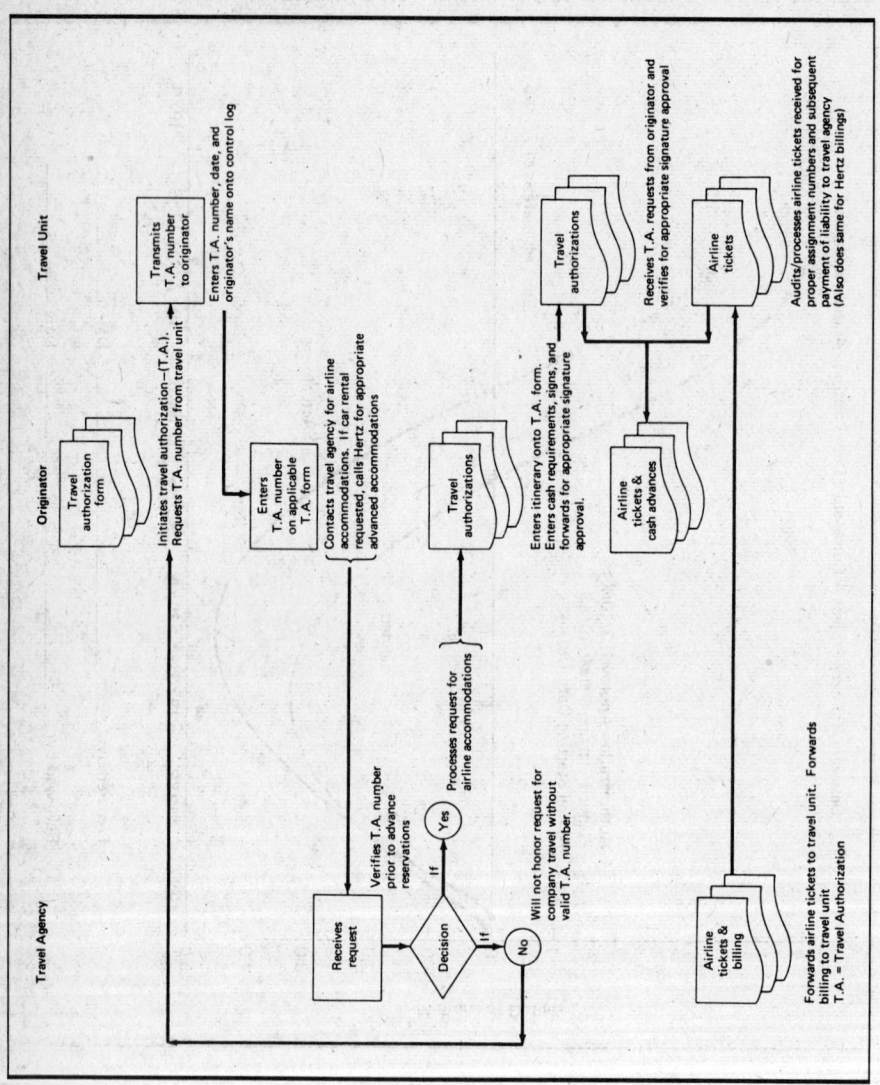

HOW TO COMMUNICATE RESULTS

FIG. 13-6
Graph of Relative Operating Margin

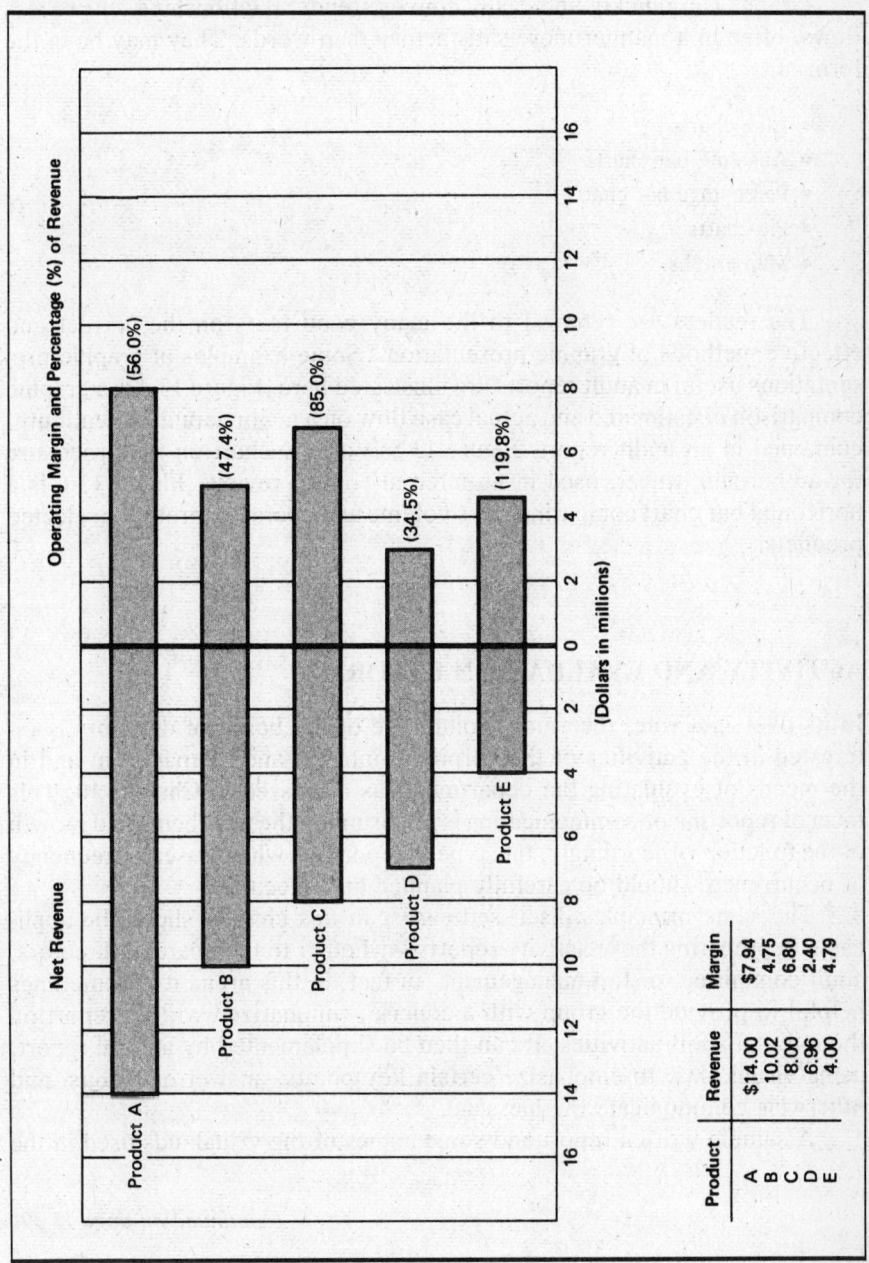

unsanitary conditions, wasteful practices, or an environment unsuited for storage of expensive inventory.

Graphs can quickly and easily convey trends, relationships, or process flows, often in a manner more satisfactory than words. They may be in the form of:

- Line charts
- Absolute bar charts
- Percentage bar charts
- Pie charts
- Map graphs

The readers are referred to the many good texts on the correct and effective methods of graphic presentation.[3] Some examples of graphic presentations useful in audit reports are illustrated here. Figure 13-4 is a graphic comparison of estimated and actual cash flow on a major capital expenditure, contained in an audit report. Figure 13-5 is a flow chart on the procedure for authorizing travel, used in an internal control review. Figure 13-6 is a horizontal bar chart comparing sales volume and operating profit for selected products.

ACTIVITY AND EVALUATION REPORTS

In its oversight role, the Audit Committee of the board of directors is interested in the activities of the corporate internal audit department and in the means of evaluating the department, as discussed in Chapter 10. This facet of reporting or communicating is important to the well-being and growth of the function. Accordingly, this type of reporting, while lesser in frequency of occurrence, should be carefully planned and executed.

The same principles discussed earlier in this chapter should be applicable in preparing these activity reports—whether to the board of directors, audit committee, or top management. In fact, in this arena it is sometimes helpful to provide the group with a concise, summarized written report on the internal audit activities. It can then be supplemented by an oral report, using visual aids, to emphasize certain key points, answer questions, and otherwise communicate the message.

A sample written report and some copies of the visual aids used in the

(continued on page 13-39)

---

[3] See, for example, Harry G. Costes, *Statistics for Business* (Columbus, Ohio: Charles E. Merrill Pub. Co., 1972); Arthur Lockwood, *Diagrams: A Visual Survey of Graphs, Maps, Charts and Diagrams for the Graphic Designer* (New York: Watson-Guptill, 1969).

FIG. 13-7

Written Annual Report to Audit Committee on Audit Activities

TO: Audit Committee
FROM: M. M. Smith
SUBJECT: Annual Report of the Director—Corporate Audit

We have completed our 19XX audit coverage in order to provide assurance that:
- Internal accounting and financial controls of reporting entities are effective and can be relied upon to produce meaningful financial information of use to Corporate management in discharging its responsibilities.
- Internal controls of reporting entities adequately safeguard the assets of the Company.
- Financial statements of reporting entities are complete and accurate and comply with GAAP.
- Reporting entities are in compliance with operational policies that promote the well-being of the Company, including policies regarding standards of business practice.
- Controls over the development, maintenance, and operation of systems involving automated processing techniques are sufficient to result in the processing of accurate and complete data.

During 19XX we provided such assurance to management by performing over 160 separate audit projects. These projects sampled compliance with all important Corporate policy statements and Executive Bulletins and financial and accounting policies set forth in the Corporate Finance Manual, and evaluated and tested internal controls over key functions and transaction flows. Audit projects were performed at every operating center location maintaining accounting records of any consequence. All audits were performed in accordance with our internally developed audit standards. The results of our audits were reported to the affected operation center and Corporate management. The reports contained over 400 specific findings and recommendations for remedial action by management. Of the 147 reports issued, 27 disclosed no findings while 50 disclosed only one or two findings.

In our opinion, none of the findings individually or in the aggregate are likely to cause errors or omissions which could materially misstate the consolidated financial position or results of operations of the Company. However, many of the findings are significant from the standpoint of the separate organizational units to which they relate. A summary of the most significant of these is provided in Attachment A along with an indication of management's planned remedial action.

On the basis of our evaluation of the responses to our reports that we have received, we believe that all of our recommendations have received reasonable consideration and action. There were 15 instances in which the affected management group concluded that the cost of the recommended action would exceed the benefits or for other reasons determined not to take action. While we do not necessarily agree with all of these determinations (we withdrew our recommendations in 5 instances), we are satisfied that significant exposure to the Company as a whole is not involved.

Our audit coverage pertaining to standards of business conduct disclosed no instances involving possible illegal or questionable activities. Our audit coverage of interim financial reporting disclosed no instances where adjustments were necessary to keep the reports from being misleading. We found no inconsistencies in the

(continued)

FIG. 13-7 *(con'td)*

application of accounting principles between the interim financial statements reviewed by us and the year-end financial statements.

Our audit coverage of the Company's various electronic data processing systems, operations and controls for 19XX disclosed over 100 findings for which recommendations for remedial action were made. Many of these findings and recommendations involve systems, operations, and controls at operational units not serviced by Central Data Processing. These stand-alone data processing facilities are considerably smaller than the CDP facility in New York, and consequently the impact of errors, omissions, and the like is considerably less. The findings disclosed in our reports pertaining to these units are typical of small to medium-size data-processing organizations. In our opinion, the EDP systems, operations, and controls of this group are excessively dependent upon the constant involvement of key managers. Also, the internal control techniques in effect are generally not sufficient to provide reasonable physical protection to EDP facilities and software. However, the risks involved, such as exposure to errors, omissions, and other irregularities, did not materialize in 19XX to any discernable extent. Responses from the various management groups affected indicate that our recommendations have been or will be enacted for the most part.

Our findings and recommendations pertaining to EDP systems, operations, and controls maintained by CDP most frequently reported the absence of sufficient controls over the process by which new systems are developed and existing systems are changed. This has caused the incurrence of excessive development costs and the development of systems which did not consistently satisfy all user requirements. Actions have been taken during 19X1 and more will be taken in 19X2 to minimize these conditions, which have persisted in recent years. The conditions were caused and persist in part by factors beyond the control of the data-processing community. These include the unforseeable rate at which data-processing technology is changing, which is enabling automated techniques to be applied to more and more functions. In addition, the advantages of on-line access and update capabilities are being recognized by the growing body of existing EDP users. This unforeseen increase in demand for high level EDP services and facilities has strained management and resources in attempting to satisfy that demand. As a result, resolving other recognized problems has required more time than it might otherwise. Unrelated organizational changes external to CDP have also indirectly slowed the process to some degree. However, it is unlikely that new systems, or changes to existing systems resulting from the systems development process, could cause significant adverse consequences in terms of existing internal accounting controls. This is because of compensating actions by knowledgeable personnel and other factors.

Other recommendations with respect to EDP dealt with security controls. In our opinion, reasonable progress has been made to improve physical security over data-processing facilities and software for which CDP is responsible. While there still exist neither a formal disaster recovery plan nor a suitable back-up facility, we believe management is working diligently to provide the additional security warranted. We do not believe that exposure to significant business interruption during the next few years is sufficiently likely to require more intensive efforts. We believe that exposure to unauthorized access and changes to data files, including programs, is of greater present concern. Affected management, while not believing the exposure to be inordinate, nevertheless plans to review its data security controls in 19X2 and implement any needed actions.

With respect specifically to internal accounting controls, we believe that during 19X1 such controls taken as a whole were sufficient to reasonably assure that transactions were authorized, recorded, and reported, and that assets were safeguarded consistent with requirements.

HOW TO COMMUNICATE RESULTS

FIG. 13-8

Visual Aids Used in the Annual Report to the Audit Committee

AUDIT COMMITTEE MEETING
December 18, 19XX

AGENDA:

- CONCLUSIONS
- CURRENT STATUS OF AUDIT WORK
- DETAIL EVALUATION
- SAMPLE FINDINGS
- RISKS

CONCLUSIONS:

- Management efforts to review and evaluate accounting controls have been sufficient, except for the XYZ Division.

- There are no control weaknesses whose potential for adverse consequences is likely to be material to the company taken as a whole, except for the XYZ Division.

- Sufficient controls will either be in place or in the process of being put in place on December 31, except at the XYZ Division.

(continued)

FIG. 13-8 (cont'd)

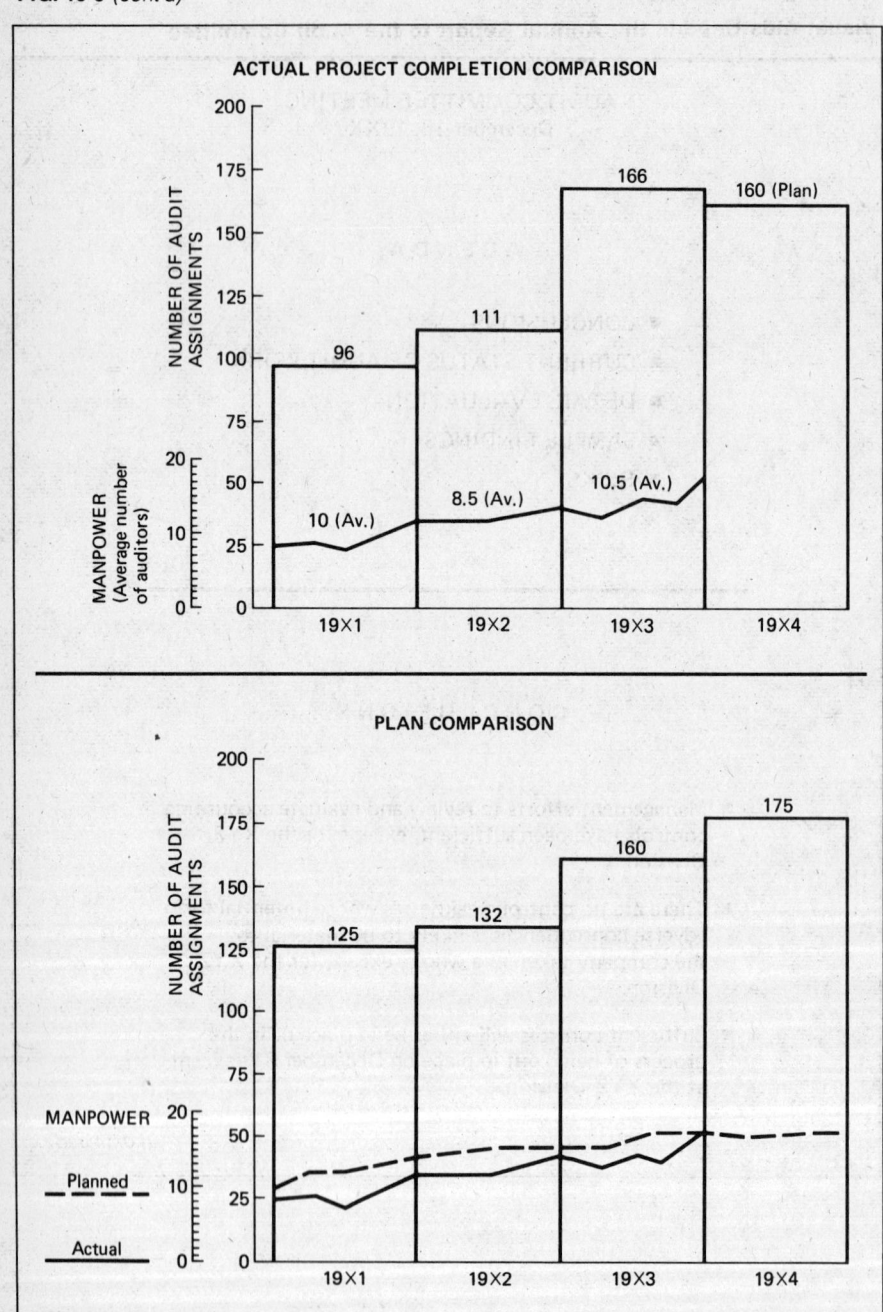

COMPLETED INTERNAL CONTROL SURVEYS

	Internal Control Survey Completed Through:				Detail Functional Audits
	Start	Field Work	Draft Report	Final	
Manufacturing Group:					
Main Manufacturing & Services Division	X	X			C
Foreign Division	X	X	X		–
Midwestern Division	X	X	X		C
Eastern Division	X	X	X	X	C
Technical Group:					
Avionics Division	X	X	X	X	C
Technical Systems Division	X	X	X	X	C
Computer Systems Division	X	X	X	X	C
Microwave Division	X	X	X		C
XYZ Division	X				SC
Construction Group:					
ABC Division	X	X	X	X	C
ABC–RMT Joint Venture	X	X	X	X	–
Architectural Services	X				C
Real Estate Group:					
Northern Division	X	X	X	X	C
Central Division	X	X			C
Southern Division	X	X	X	X	C
Corporate:					
Corporate Office	X	X			C
Research & Technology	X	X			C
Data Processing	X	X	X		SC

C – Complete   SC – Substantially Complete

EVALUATION OF DOCUMENTATION AND CONTROLS

	Evaluation Of:	
	Documentation	Controls
Manufacturing Group:		
Main Manufacturing & Services Division	Very Good	Sufficient
Foreign Division	Good*	Subject to
Midwestern Division	Very Good	Sufficient
Eastern Division	Very Good	Sufficient
Electronics & Communication Group:		
Avionics Division	Very Good	Sufficient
Technical Systems Division	Very Good	Sufficient
Computer Systems Division	Good	Sufficient
Microwave Division	Good*	Sufficient
XYZ Division	Poor	Questionable
Construction Group:		
ABC Division	Good	Sufficient, Subject to
ABC–RMT Joint Venture	Poor	Sufficient, Subject to
Architectural Services	Good*	Sufficient
Real Estate Group:		
Northern Division	Good	Sufficient
Central Division	Fair	Sufficient
Southern Division	Poor	Sufficient
Corporate:		
Corporate Office	Good	Sufficient
Research & Technology	Good	Sufficient
Data Processing	Good	Sufficient, but

*Assisted by Corporate Audit

(continued)

FIG. 13-8 *(cont'd)*

SAMPLE FINDINGS:

1. Lack of documentation of procedures followed by management in estimating future costs:
    - XYZ
    - Northern
    - Defense systems
    - Central
    - Eastern
    - ABC

2. Procedures for periodic physical verification of assets not set forth:
    - Northern
    - Main manufacturing
    - Southern

3. Concentration of incompatible functions:
    - XYZ
    - Avionics
    - Technical Systems
    - ABC

PRIMARY RISKS:

- Potential for improper management override

- Illegal acts

- Improper actions by employees

oral report are presented here. While the written report covered overall activities, the oral report shown here relates principally to internal controls—a subject of special interest at the time. The written annual report to the Audit Committee on internal audit activities is illustrated in Figure 13-7.[4] The selected simple visual aids used to accompany this report are shown in Figure 13-8.

PREPARING THE REPORT

Previous comments in this chapter have largely dealt with the report content, form, and method of expression. But a few words are in order on useful steps in the actual preparation.

Writing the Report

The basis for a good written (or orally presented) report is good thinking. Therefore, the ideas should be logically and carefully thought out and tested. One suggestion is to prepare an *outline* of the thoughts to be presented, making sure that they follow in natural sequence and that a logical relationship follows from cause to effect. This skeleton may then serve as the basis for writing the complete report (or planning the oral presentation).

Style is important, and wandering thoughts and needless words are to be avoided. In this context,

- Ideas should flow in logical succession.
- Words and sentence structure should be simple and clear.
- Repetitive words should be avoided; use synonyms to express the ideas.
- Short sentences and common words are desirable—with an occasional change in style for variety.
- Action words are preferable, as are positive statements.

In a nutshell, prepare the report from the viewpoint of the reader so that it will be understood.

Physical Characteristics

A report must be attractive and inviting to read. Among other things:

- The cover should be attractive.
- To avoid "heaviness," double spacing often should be used, with adequate margins, and plenty of "white space."

---

[4] For another extensive and excellent example of a report by the internal auditors to the audit committee, including the audit status of the year just completed and the five-year audit plan, see Joseph E. Connor and Burnell H. DeVos, Jr., eds., *Guide to Accounting Controls*, 1981 Supplement (Boston: Warren, Gorham & Lamont, 1981), pp. 91–119.

- Subject matter should be identified by headlines or paragraph structure.
- It should probably be signed by the auditor and the chief internal auditor or supervisor.

Editing

In most organizations, the report is drafted by the auditor and reviewed and/or edited by the supervisor or the chief internal auditor. This editing process is important because it is a means of securing a high degree of correctness and readability. In a sense, it is a quality-control device to add assurance to the conclusions and check the support for the facts.

Proofreading

After the report has been reviewed or edited, a final step should be careful proofreading to eliminate errors, such as misspelled words, incomplete sentences, and typographical errors. These types of errors in a final report reduce the auditor's credibility.

In summary, the same care and review used in preparing an audit report as typically issued by independent certified accountants should be taken by the internal audit department in preparing its reports.

A SIMPLE PROGRAM TO IMPROVE AUDIT REPORTS

Many internal audit departments spend one or two days each year at a seminar or conference as part of a professional development program. The objective might be to review the latest in audit standards, or the impact of a new FASB pronouncement, or new techniques in detecting fraud. Why not use the same forum for improving writing skills as applied to audit reports? It is entirely possible to do this in a cost-effective way. One company developed and implemented such a program, which encompassed two days at a cost of less than $1,000 for 35 people.[5]

An audit report may be described as the sales document of the internal auditing department. To be effective, to motivate the recipient to action, it must be inviting. This means that attention should be given to format, organization, content, and style—and these should be suited to those who will use the report. It must be appropriate to the particular organization.

Unless the chief internal auditor, or one of his staff, is an exceedingly capable writer, some limited outside help might be desirable. Thus, an internal auditor, who knows the organization and is experienced in internal

---

[5] For details of a program developed and used by the internal audit department of the Aluminum Company of America (Alcoa), see James C. Williams and Anita Brostaff, "A Cost-Effective Writing Program," *The Internal Auditor,* Dec. 1983, pp. 58–63.

auditing, might combine forces with a writing consultant, who might know little about auditing (yet is willing to listen) and is skilled in report formatting and writing. Additionally, an available videotaped program on writing skills may be a useful starting point. This combination for an in-house seminar is suggested because: (1) many people on their own simply will not read books about writing; (2) the use of extensive outside workshops can be expensive; (3) follow-up and personal guidance may be more easily handled on an in-house basis; and (4) the specific needs of the audit organization should be addressed (not only the general principles of good writing).

The in-house program consists of three phases:

1. *Planning and preparation.* This should involve not only the outside consultant and the "lead" internal auditing representative, but also the internal audit staff to the extent of identifying the expectations from the seminar and the objectives of the meeting, and of securing from them samples of their "best" writing, before and after the seminar. It includes preparing a detailed agenda to meet the specific needs of the internal audit department.
2. *The seminar.* This might be half a day or longer. At or before the seminar, the videotape might be viewed, and practice exercises could be undertaken. Depending on need, the following subjects could be discussed:
   - Executive summaries
   - Audit recommendations
   - Workpaper memoranda (keeping in mind possible court use)
3. *The evaluation.* This phase is suggested to see if the seminar met the group's needs, whether any of the provided checklists were used, whether the agenda should be changed or can be improved, and, most important, whether the session helped improve the quality of report writing.

REPLIES TO AUDIT REPORTS

An important managerial and audit department function is proper follow-up of audit reports to see that corrective action is taken, where indicated. There should also be systematic follow-up on internal audit reports. Corporate policy statements, or procedures or directives, should clearly stipulate the need for responding to an audit report. Whenever action is indicated in an audit review, instructions should provide guidelines on (1) who is to reply, (2) the form of the reply (in writing), (3) the procedure in replying (e.g., preparation, review, and signing), (4) who receives copies, and (5) the time limit for response.

By the same token, the audit department should maintain a follow-up system or file so that it knows when satisfactory replies have been received and the subject is a closed issue. A suggested form for this purpose is shown in Figure 13-9.

FIG. 13-9
Audit Reply Evaluation Form

CORPORATE AUDIT REPORT REPLY EVALUATION SUMMARY			
REPORT NO.	ASSIGNMENT NO.	ASSIGNMENT TITLE	
ASSIGNED TO	MANAGER		

RECOMMENDATION NUMBER	REPLY FROM	ORGN/PROFIT CENTER	DATE RECEIVED	DOES THE RESPONSE COMPLY WITH OR SATISFY THE RECOMMENDATION MADE (IF NO, ATTACH REPLY EVALUATION)		*REPLY EVALUATION CODE
				☐ YES	☐ NO	
				☐	☐	
				☐	☐	
				☐	☐	
				☐	☐	
				☐	☐	
				☐	☐	
				☐	☐	
				☐	☐	
				☐	☐	
				☐	☐	
				☐	☐	
				☐	☐	
				☐	☐	

*REPLY EVALUATION CODES
  A. MANAGEMENT CONCURS
  B. MANAGEMENT CONCURS, BUT ACTION NOT POSSIBLE
  C. MANAGEMENT DOES NOT CONCUR
  D. NO INDICATION OF CONCURRENCE OR NONCONCURRENCE
  E. ACTION TAKEN BUT FURTHER ACTION REQUIRED TO RESOLVE PROBLEM
  F. OTHER (SPECIFY)

COMMENTS

DISPOSITION:	POSTED TO FOLLOW-UP FILE		
FOLLOW-UP (AFTER)			
MEMO (IF APPLICABLE) TO:		DATE	NUMBER
PREPARED BY	DATE	DIRECTOR/MANAGER	DATE

When an auditor recommends corrective action, presumably most options have been considered and discussed with affected management. Occasions will arise, however, when the suggested course of action is not necessarily the best. As a practical matter, the audit department should be flexible in matters of implementing procedures. In many instances, the line people will be able to suggest effective alternative solutions. If these are likely to cure the deficiency, or at least the important aspects, then auditors should be willing to accept such an alternative solution. In the final analysis, of course, the internal auditor should have the right to declare a management-proposed remedy as inadequate. Procedures should exist to deal with such conditions—including the intervention of higher authority (on both sides) if necessary.

As a final word, most audit reports make reference to the disposition of prior recommendations. As a matter of internal procedure, it is suggested that a periodic written report be prepared for the cognizant executive responsible for the internal audit function to advise that executive of serious nonimplementation.

SUGGESTED READING

Braiotta, Louis, Jr. *The Audit Directors Guide,* New York: John Wiley & Sons, 1981.

Brink, Victor Z., and Herbert Witt. *Modern Internal Auditing,* 4th ed. New York: John Wiley & Sons, 1982.

Fielden, John S., and Ronald E. Dulek, "What Is Effective Business Writing?" *Business Horizons,* May/June 1987, pp. 62–66.

Sawyer, Lawrence B. *The Practice of Modern Internal Auditing,* 2nd ed. Altamonte Springs, Fla.: The Institute of Internal Auditors, 1981.

PART V
Technical Aspects of Auditing

CHAPTER **14**

Evidential Matter

Overview 1	Qualitative Characteristics 13
The Importance of Evidential Matter 2	Quantitative Characteristics 13
	Summary on Characteristics 14
Definitions, Principles, and Concepts 3	Types of Evidence 14
"Audit Evidence" Defined 3	Primary Evidence 15
Selectivity 4	External Evidence 15
Audit Risk 4	Recurring Internal Evidence 15
Reliability 7	Nonrecurring Internal Evidence 16
Relevance 8	Evidence and the Internal Auditor 17
	Internal Control 17
Differentiating Evidential Requirements	Internal Accounting Control
of External and Internal Auditors 8	Surveys 18
	Limited Financial Reviews 18
Basic Assumptions 10	Standards-of-Ethical-Business-
Management Honesty 11	Conduct Audits 18
Management Competence 11	Operational Control Audits 18
Authenticity of Documents 11	EDP Auditing 22
Senior Management Support 12	Other Considerations 22
Arm's-Length Activities 12	
	Suggested Reading 22
Evidence Analyzed 13	

Fig. 14-1 Examples of Primary Evidence 16
Fig. 14-2 Summary Narrative of Work Performed 19
Fig. 14-3 Comparative Analysis—An Example of Internal Evidence 21

OVERVIEW

Up to this point, methodologies for organizing and managing the audit function to serve management interests in an optimum fashion have been presented. In addition, techniques for managing and conducting specific audit projects have been covered. The principal aim has been to provide guidance to help chief auditors, audit managers, and performing auditors carry out their assigned responsibilities in an organized, cohesive manner—from strategic planning to conducting an exit conference. While the subjects discussed benefit all levels of internal auditors, they are, by themselves, not enough

14-1

to assure that high-quality auditing is achieved. Such a result is possible only if the chief auditor and his staff are familiar with the technical aspects of auditing and if they apply them effectively, in practice. These technical aspects are discussed in this chapter and in Chapters 15 and 16.

For purposes of this discussion, technical aspects include (1) evidential matter as it applies to auditing, (2) sampling, and (3) audit procedures. The topics are presented in this order because it is believed an understanding of the techniques used to gather evidence, including sampling and other audit procedures, is aided if the types of evidence to be gathered are understood first.

Those who are familiar with the technical aspects of auditing realize that, contrary to legal evidence, there are few detailed rules prescribing the forms of evidence that the auditor must obtain. For external auditors, auditing fieldwork standards simply require that it be sufficient and competent. (See Chapter 4.) For internal auditors, professional standards require that information be sufficient, competent, relevant, and useful. (See Chapter 6.) Over the years, some further guidance has evolved as to what constitutes sufficient and competent evidence, but professional judgment is still the primary determinant. This chapter provides definitions, discusses concepts and principles, specifies basic underlying assumptions, and analyzes types of evidence to provide a basis for understanding audit evidence so as to aid in judging its adequacy.

Since reference is frequently made to the auditor's need to gather evidence, it should be made clear at the outset that the auditor does not actually take possession of original documents, files, records, and the like, as might be imagined by those unfamiliar with the audit process. Rather, through observation, inspection, inquiry, and confirmation (see Chapter 16), he becomes exposed to the evidence in which he is interested. The process by which he records in his workpapers what he believes to be relevant is described in Chapter 12.

THE IMPORTANCE OF EVIDENTIAL MATTER

Evidential matter provides the documented basis for the internal auditor's conclusions and recommendations, as expressed in the report. Obviously, evidential matter is a critical indicator of the quality and usefulness of any audit project. Internal auditors are obligated by their professional standards to act objectively, exercise due professional care, and collect evidential matter to support audit results (Chapter 6). These standards put the internal auditor in a position not unlike that of a trial judge (as opposed to a policeman, the more common perception). Seen in this light, it is clear that the auditor, like a jurist, must objectively seek the information or evidence that in his professional judgment is both relevant to the audit purpose and reliable. To fulfill this requirement, the auditor must have an understanding of the various forms of evidential matter and their relative value. This enables him to prepare specific programs of procedures and tests designed to gather such evidence.

DEFINITIONS, PRINCIPLES, AND CONCEPTS

"Audit Evidence" Defined

The authoritative professional literature of the AICPA, GAO, and IIA does not define the term "evidence" per se. However, extensive guidance to help gather it is provided by these professional associations. In fact, the AICPA uses the term "evidential matter" as opposed to "evidence" in its GAAS, and the IIA uses the term "information" in its standards. If any difference between these terms is intended, it cannot be discerned explicitly from existing published material. Other reputable sources have offered definitions that provide some insight. Sawyer, for example, defines evidence as that which brings "to mind an honest belief about the truth or falsity of any proposition at issue."[1] However, to distinguish the term "audit evidence" from other evidential forms, a more precise definition is needed.

The AICPA describes evidential matter as consisting "of underlying accounting data (i.e., the underlying accounting or financial records) and corroborating information available to the auditor."[2] This narrows the focus to audit evidential matter gathered by external auditors examining financial statements. However, internal auditors are concerned with more facets of a company than financial reporting. A definition of evidence or evidential matter suitable for internal auditing might be as follows: documentation of any type, whether developed pursuant to established systems of control or pursuant to a subsequent special undertaking, and believed by the internal auditor to be (1) reliable corroborations of historical facts and circumstances and (2) relevant to the audit objectives.

Inherent in this definition are three principles that warrant further specific comment. These are as follows:

1. Selectivity (sufficiency)
2. Reliability
3. Relevance

The reader may recognize that two of these principles—reliability and relevance—are also involved in developing a strategic audit approach. (See

---

[1] Lawrence B. Sawyer, *The Practice of Modern Auditing* (Altamonte Springs, Fla.: The Institute of Internal Auditors, 1981), p. 200. This is an improvement on *Webster's New Collegiate Dictionary*, which defines evidence as "something that furnishes proof."

[2] Statement on Auditing Standards No. 31 (Aug. 1980), (AICPA, *Professional Standards*, Vol. 1), AU §326.13.

Chapter 2.) This results because the auditor must have relevant and reliable information in order to provide relevant and reliable service to management.

Selectivity

In this context, "selectivity" means choosing from available information that which is of interest to the auditor in sufficient quantity to permit forming an accurate conclusion, without looking at all of the available information. In other words, based on his professional judgment, the auditor selects only a portion of the available information to establish the basis for his conclusions. The principle may be stated as follows: The auditor may restrict his efforts to gather only that evidential matter sufficient to constitute an accurate representation of the conclusions that would be drawn from examining all available evidence.

The principle of selectivity, then, is synonymous with the concept of sufficiency as established in professional literature. Almost from the outset of auditing, it was clearly recognized that the auditor could not, indeed should not, examine all evidence contained in underlying records and data. It developed as an acceptable practice to examine only the evidence that in the judgment of the auditor was sufficient to afford a proper basis for a professional opinion or conclusion. The evidence examined, when aggregated, was intended to be persuasive as opposed to convincing.[3] Put another way, the cumulative evidential matter should be sufficient to be a credible basis for drawing conclusions or expressing opinions. It would not need to be sufficient to eliminate any possibility that the conclusions or opinions may be in error.

Audit Risk. The chance that the auditor's opinion or conclusion may be wrong introduces the concept of audit risk. The AICPA defines audit risk in SAS 47, "Audit Risk and Materiality in Conducting an Audit" (AU §312), as "the risk that the auditor may unknowingly fail to appropriately modify his opinion on financial statements that are materially misstated."

The concept, if not the definition, extends to government auditing and internal auditing as well. Much government auditing and most internal auditing is not concerned with reaching opinions on financial statements. Yet, the application of the concept for that purpose is worth understanding for government auditors and internal auditors so as to better grasp its application to their respective circumstances.

---

[3] For example, in *Montgomery's Auditing*, 10th ed., the authors comment that in an audit of financial statements an auditor usually relies on evidence that is persuasive rather than convincing. The auditor's decision as to how much persuasive evidence is enough is affected by the necessity of working within time constraints and by bearing in mind the cost of obtaining evidence and evaluating its usefulness. See Jerry D. Sullivan, Richard A. Gnospelius, Philip L. Defliese, and Henry R. Jaenicke, *Montgomery's Auditing*, 10th ed. (New York: John Wiley & Sons, Inc.), p. 176. Copyright © 1985 by Coopers & Lybrand, United States.

Audit risk, in an examination of financial statements, is the sum of component risks. These components are inherent risk, control risk, and detection risk. Inherent risk is defined in SAS 47 as the susceptibility of an account balance or class of transactions to error that could be material, when aggregated with error in other balances or classes, assuming there were no related internal accounting controls. Control risk, as defined by SAS 47, is the risk that error that could occur in an account balance or class of transactions and that could be material, when aggregated with error in other balances or classes, will not be prevented or detected on a timely basis by the system of internal accounting control. Detection risk, as defined by SAS 47, is the risk that an auditor's procedures will lead him to conclude that material error does not exist when, in fact, it does.

More recently, the ASB redefined these terms in its proposed SAS, entitled "Consideration of the Internal Control Structure in a Financial Statement Audit," revised draft of October 27, 1987, paragraph 24:

- ☐ *Inherent risk.* The susceptibility of an assertion to a material misstatement assuming there are no control structure elements.
- ☐ *Control risk.* The risk that a material misstatement that could occur in an assertion will not be prevented or detected on a timely basis by the entity's internal control structure.
- ☐ *Detection risk.* The risk that the auditor will not detect a material misstatement that exists in an assertion.

These refined definitions directly link audit risk to the underlying assertions that are embodied in financial statements. These assertions are set forth in SAS 31, "Evidential Matter," paragraphs 3–8. Briefly, the assertions have to do with (1) the existence of assets and liabilities at a given date and occurrence of transactions during a given period; (2) the completeness of transactions and accounts included in financial statements; (3) the rights and obligations at a given date; (4) the valuation and allocation of assets, liabilities, revenue, and expense components at appropriate amounts; and (5) the presentation and disclosure of financial statement components.

The process of risk assessment may be thought of as a series of defenses much like those of a football team defending against a forward pass. Inherent risk from the standpoint of the defense is the chance that the offense will complete a pass leading to a touchdown with no defense whatsoever. The chance of that occurring is very high. To reduce that risk, the defense employs various strategies aimed at providing coverage via man to man or zone assignments. Control risk in this example would be the chance that a pass may be completed that leads to a score, despite the fact that the defense is on the field.

Usually, defensive strategies provide for one person—the free safety—not to be assigned any specific areas or persons to defend. His role is to react to the play as it develops and to compensate for any missed assignments, misjudgments, and so forth that might otherwise permit a pass to be completed, leading to a touchdown. The free safety operates much as the auditor does. Both must assess what is happening on their respective fields and devise and execute a plan of action aimed at keeping the undesirable from occurring. For the auditor, it is audit procedures aimed at detecting a material error or omission regarding an assertion. For the free safety, it is the defensive maneuver he selects to prevent a touchdown. Detection risk for the free safety is the chance that he will fail to prevent the pass from being completed, leading to a touchdown.

The evidential matter that is sought by external auditors in an audit of financial statements is that which in their judgment is needed to corroborate the management assertions, given the level of audit risk that they perceive to be involved. A lower perceived risk means that less evidence needs to be obtained to persuade the auditor that the financial statements are free of material error. Conversely, if the auditor perceives a high risk, he will need much more corroborative evidence to persuade him that no material errors exist in the financial statements.

Audit risk for internal auditors must be understood in a different context. This is because internal auditors do not normally audit financial statements. Hence, the management assertions being corroborated by external auditors in an audit of financial statements is not necessarily relevant to the internal auditor.

To understand audit risk from the standpoint of the internal auditor requires expansion of the concept of management assertion. Such assertions exist for a variety of situations of which financial statements are only one. Such assertions may be expressed or implied. An example of the former would be a management assertion in an annual report that a given system of internal control is sufficient to achieve the objectives thereof. An example of the latter is the assertions that are inherent in financial statements.

Since there may be a variety of assertions, there may be a variety of internal audits. And, in point of fact, that is the case, as explained in Chapter 2. For the most part, internal audit reports of today do not take the form of attestations. There are those who believe they should, however, and are working within the profession to bring about the changes needed in the internal auditing standards to give recognition to this concept.

Whether or not internal auditing standards reflect the concept of attestation remains to be seen. For now, internal auditors must be content to manage audit risk without guidance from professional standards. If the internal auditor performs in the role of an attester to various management assertions,[4] then audit risk for the internal auditor is the sum of inherent risk, control risk, and detection risk.

Inherent risk for the internal auditor is the risk related to the funda-

---

[4] Management assertions are embodied in policies, procedures, flow charts, functional outlines, and manuals of various types.

mental characteristics of the internal audit assignment. For example, in operational auditing, a fundamental characteristic is to evaluate the effectiveness and efficiency by which an organization discharges its duties. Such evaluations are inherently risky because considerable expertise and judgment are involved. Finding a better way to accomplish something is not easy.

Control risk and detection risk for the internal auditor are not as present as inherent risk. This is because management assertions are not often expressed explicitly in an internal audit assignment. If they were, then control risk would be the risk that the process used to develop the assertions would fail to prevent a material misstatement in an assertion. Detection risk would be the risk that an internal auditor would fail to detect the misstatement that was not prevented by the techniques used to develop the assertions. For example, in an audit of internal controls, the procedures used by the organization to develop and maintain the documented procedures may be such that they do not accurately and completely reflect the procedures actually in effect. The internal auditor must take this into consideration in devising his program of tests. If there are significant errors in the procedures, the tests should detect them. But there is a chance that the internal auditor will not detect them because he cannot verify the existence of all procedures. Thus, we have come full cycle. The internal auditor must consider audit risk when selecting from available evidence only that evidence that appropriately minimizes the chance that his ultimate opinion or conclusion will be wrong. If he has reason to believe the risk is high, normally, he will need much evidence to persuade him that his assessment is reliable. Conversely, if he has reason to believe that the audit risk is low, he will need less evidence to persuade him that his assessment is reliable.

Reliability

Reliability of evidential matter is defined by the AICPA *Statement of Financial Accounting Concepts No. 2* as the quality of information that assures that information is reasonably free from error and bias and faithfully represents what it purports to represent.

While there are various types of evidential matter, as described later, all are not of equal reliability. To illustrate, in reviewing controls over accounts payable, an auditor might obtain evidence in the form of an assertion from management that all invoices are matched against receiving reports and that all differences are resolved before executing payment. Management assertions are evidential matter, whether expressed orally or as written procedural statements in manuals. However, such expressions are sometimes intended to convey what should be happening, rather than what actually happened. Actual conditions often deviate to some degree from asserted conditions. Accordingly, the reliability of this type of evidential matter for approximating the extent to which invoices and receivers are, in fact, matched prior to payment is less than for other types of available evidence. Such other evidence is usually present in paid invoice files in the form of executed receiving reports, completed purchase orders, and processed invoices, each of which contains evidence relevant to the matching question. This evidence is of high reliability in purporting to be, respectively, evidence of amounts billed, evidence of items received, and evidence of items ordered. By comparing or matching this evidence, the auditor can corroborate the assertion of management to the extent he deems necessary. The specific action performed by the auditor in matching these documents, when appropriately recorded in his workpapers (see Chapter 2) constitutes gathered evidence of suitable reliability.

Generally speaking, evidential matter is thought to be highly reliable if it is produced or developed externally. For example, an invoice from a customer is a more reliable indicator of what the supplier charged for a given transaction than is an internal report of amounts charged in which the transaction is listed. Also, the reliability of information is affected by the means used to generate it. To illustrate, a report developed pursuant to a system of adequate internal control is more reliable than a report produced by an inadequate system.

Relevance

Evidence is relevant if it is directly connected with and supportive of the auditor's objective. Stated otherwise, evidence is relevant to the extent that it has a bearing on considerations that the auditor must contemplate to form an opinion regarding a particular objective. The principle is stated as follows: The auditor must obtain sufficient evidential matter relevant to the objectives of the audit.

To illustrate the principle, assume the auditor is reviewing the internal controls of the purchasing function. An important consideration in such function is the various levels of purchasing authority established by management. Relevant information in this example would be evidence indicating the extent of compliance, in practice. This evidence might include a policy statement, a formal listing of commitment authority by management level, and signatures by those designated individuals on executory documents, such as purchase orders and contracts.

DIFFERENTIATING EVIDENTIAL REQUIREMENTS OF EXTERNAL AND INTERNAL AUDITORS

In Chapter 3, the substantial legal exposure of public accountants is described and the point is made that this exposure places burdens upon those practitioners, with respect to independence, which are not shared by their internal auditing counterparts. One principal reason for this difference, as stated in Chapter 3, has to do with relationships. The internal auditor and the primary interest group he serves—management—are closely related; both have extensive, intimate knowledge of the company. As a result, management is usually in a position to effectively appraise audit quality. In contrast, the primary interest group served by external auditors—stockholders, creditors, and the public—are not closely related to them and do not possess extensive knowledge of the company. As a result, generally speaking, this interest group is not able to appraise audit quality. There is insufficient basis to permit such an appraisal. This dissimilarity translates into differences in the nature and extent of evidential matter that needs to be gathered by each group. That is to say, the relational advantage enjoyed by internal auditors forms part of the basis for developing credible findings, recommendations, and opinions. Hence, the evidential gathering effort often need not be as extensive as that required for external auditors. Also, the attention paid to the manner in which internal auditors document the extent of their work performed may not be as great as that paid by external auditors, for the same reason. To be timely and useful, there may be occasions when information is furnished by internal auditors and accepted by management, based on only the most cursory of reviews. However, neither group would provide such information to the public. Sometimes, management may solicit the immediate views of the chief auditor based solely on his overall knowledge and experience with the company. Although such a procedure is valuable, interchanges of this type between external auditors and the public are almost inconceivable due to liability implications. Because management in most cases is positioned to judge audit risk and quality, it may alter its responsiveness as appropriate. In one situation, it may act immediately, while in others, it may wish to study the matter further or seek additional information from other sources, or it may reject the internal auditor's recommendations completely.

The foregoing comments should not be interpreted to mean that internal auditors are less professional or even less independent. It simply means that their relationship, background, and knowledge permit more flexibility and opportunity to provide a variety of information to management under differing degrees of uncertainty as to the accuracy of the information provided. It should be added that the judgment of the chief auditor or project manager is required in all cases to be certain that decisions regarding the extent of evidential matter gathered are based on considering management's perceived need to know and the risk of providing inaccurate information. The resulting evidential requirements could differ from those made by external auditors in accordance with GAAS.

It is interesting to note that recent events may be forcing internal auditors into positions more similar to external auditors. These events have to do with efforts by government investigative agencies, congressional committees, trial lawyers, and others to seek access to the work products of internal auditors. Chapters 8 and 9 discuss these efforts in some detail. As more and more internal audit reports become public information, the appropriateness of basing an internal auditing strategy on confidentiality and the close relationship of management and internal auditing must be questioned. It may become necessary to alter the audit approach and the audit reports so as to prevent the public from being unintentionally misled or misinformed simply because the work was performed and the report was prepared on the assumption that only management would see it. Whether that can be done and still provide useful information to management is unclear.

BASIC ASSUMPTIONS

In practice, there are at least five basic assumptions that are usually present in forming the plan of action to gather the necessary evidence. Unless information comes to the auditors' attention indicating the contrary, internal auditors may assume that:

1. Management is honest.
2. Management is competent.
3. Basic documents and records are authentic.
4. Senior management will support the audit.
5. Transactions and activities will occur in an arm's-length fashion (no collusion).

These assumptions afford the auditor an initial basis for deciding on the types of evidence that might be obtained in given situations, in turn permitting preliminary audit plans to be developed. (See Chapter 11.) In nonroutine audit projects, these assumptions are particularly useful because the auditor is unlikely to be familiar with the organizational unit or function that is the subject of the examination. In routine assignments, the auditor's previous experience affords a basis for modifying the assumptions, as deemed necessary.

Occasionally, even in routine assignments, the auditor may encounter circumstances when one or more of the basic assumptions is invalid. In these infrequent situations, the auditors' professionalism must be carefully exercised. For example, if management is dishonest or incompetent, or records and documents are not what they purport to be, the risk inherent in the audit process of drawing invalid conclusions is significantly increased. Procedures must then be devised to reasonably compensate for such conditions. The most common action is to increase the extent of tests performed to gather evidence. In some cases, the views and opinions of outside experts, such as engineers or lawyers, may be needed. In extreme cases, the auditor may be precluded from completing his work.

In addition to devising compensatory audit procedures, the auditor must inform senior management of the circumstances causing him to question the basic assumptions. Needless to say, the disclosure of this information must be discreet and should be kept confidential. If warranted, the chief auditor, or his designee, should offer recommendations for remedial action. Each of the five basic assumptions is discussed further in the following paragraphs.

Management Honesty

The entire sampling approach and the effectiveness of the concept of selectivity would be virtually invalidated if the auditor could not assume that management is honest. The Cohen Commission observed that public accountants should not make any assumption with respect to management honesty (or dishonesty), recommending instead that a "healthy attitude of skepticism" be maintained.[5] The closer working relationship between internal auditors and management, however, usually provides an adequate basis for assuming management's ongoing honesty. Nonetheless, while the internal audit scope may be structured with this assumption in mind, experienced internal auditors have learned that it is unwise to base audit findings and conclusions solely upon management assertions and representations. Many times managements make representations that they believe to be valid, only to be proved inaccurate by subsequent discovery of facts and circumstances of which they were unaware. In deciding upon audit scope, experienced auditors should consider not only the assumption of honesty, but also the principle of reliability, discussed earlier. Conditions that may alert the auditor to the potential for dishonest acts are set forth in Chapter 23.

Management Competence

Internal auditors initially assume that management is competent—meaning that it is able to discharge assigned duties and responsibilities in a capable manner. Of course, the existence of such factors as significant control weaknesses, poor operating performance, and high turnover in key positions within the management structure could raise questions regarding this assumption. If competence is in doubt, the auditor must extend the scope of the audit or make other arrangements.

Authenticity of Documents

Internal auditors examine many different forms of evidence, as set forth later in this chapter. Generally, the auditor is entitled to assume that the

---

[5] *The Commission on Auditors' Responsibilities: Report, Conclusions and Recommendations* (New York: The Commission on Auditors' Responsibilities, 1978), p. 10.

evidence is authentic; that is, that evidence is what it purports to be. Internal auditors cannot be expected to spot counterfeit invoices, purchase orders, stock certificates, and the like, although such detection is possible.

Senior Management Support

The auditor must be able to approach every assignment with the knowledge that senior management will support his right to conduct the audit as he deems necessary. This knowledge is gained through establishing and maintaining proper relationships and by maintaining a credible audit function. It is reinforced by designed-in accountability and performance reporting.

The chief auditor or his designee need not seek senior management support for every contemplated activity. However, it is a good idea to alert senior management or the audit committee, if appropriate, when there is reason to believe that certain investigations might evoke hostile reactions from any one of several management ranks. This is likely to occur, for example, when lower-level management competence or honesty is being questioned. When this happens, higher levels of management and the chief auditor must coordinate their respective actions to minimize the potential for adverse consequences.

Arm's-Length Activities

The term "arm's length" may be defined as a standard of conduct that will result in the execution of transactions and activities free of influencing bias, conflict of interest, or outside pressures. Thus, an arm's-length transaction involving two or more persons is one that would result if the parties, in representing their respective business interests, are motivated solely by such interests and are unrestricted in their freedom to pursue them.

In the real world, transactions and activities are rarely, if ever, conducted in such a clean environment. Everyone is biased to some degree in one way or another. However, excluding this element, the transactions that result are usually substantially identical with those that would result from circumstances free from any bias. Beyond this "normal influence," the impact, if any, that other, more severe, pressures have on executed transactions and activities cannot easily be discerned or measured. In the absence of evidence to the contrary, the internal auditor is entitled to assume that the transactions and activities he is examining are essentially arm's length.

In every organization, special intramanagement relationships evolve; some are positive, while others may potentially be destructive. Activities and transactions can be adversely affected by the latter. Decisions with respect to allocation of resources, organization structure, project assignments, promotions, and compensation levels are examples of situations where management bias can have a substantial effect. Internal auditors are in no position to establish the existence of these biases and their effect, usually because there are insufficient tangible clues evident. Experience, objectivity, and a proper level of inquiry will often be the means by which the auditor neutralizes the effect of such biases without actually identifying them. When there is clear evidence of undue influence, the appropriate executives, and perhaps lawyers, should be consulted.

EVIDENCE ANALYZED

The professional literature that has been developed on the subject of evidence has analyzed it in terms of qualitative and quantitative aspects.

Qualitative Characteristics

Qualitative characteristics have to do with how good the evidence is. Most writings on the subject use the term "competent" rather than "good" in discussing the quality of evidence. Thus, the auditor is interested in competent evidence. To be competent, evidence must be both relevant and reliable. These two concepts were previously discussed in this chapter.

Suffice it to reiterate here that not all evidence relates to the auditor's objectives. Through proper training and practice, the professional auditor has acquired the ability to distinguish relevance and to discern reliability in objectively judging the adequacy and appropriateness of evidential matter. That is what makes his service unique and valuable.

Quantitative Characteristics

Professional standards of public accountants require that competent evidence be obtained in sufficient quantity. Under the IIA standards, "internal auditors should collect, analyze, interpret and document information to support audit results."[6] Achievement of this is more easily said than done, in part because guidance as to what constitutes "sufficiency" in every audit situation is simply not available. Thus, the auditor must be prepared to decide whom he needs to talk to, what records and documents to examine, when to examine them, how much to examine, and what inferences can be drawn from such examinations. Practical experience, proper supervision, and effective quality control offer the best hope that the evidence gathered will be sufficient. Past experience also affords the auditor a reasonable starting point as to what evidence has been sufficient in past similar assignments.

---

[6] *Standards for the Professional Practice of Internal Auditing* (Altamonte Springs, Fla.: The Institute of Internal Auditors, 1978), p. 20.

Summary on Characteristics

There is a danger, however, in relying too greatly on past experience. The qualitative characteristics of evidence and the variety of underlying circumstances are such that some forms of evidence that are sufficient in one situation may not be sufficient in a subsequent audit. It is this fact, among others, that has proved so troublesome to public accounting firms in defending against allegations of negligence. (See Chapter 3.) The fact is no less true for internal auditors. Sufficiency, then, is largely determined by a rational, logical process on a case-by-case basis. For this reason, individuals who perform audits are expected to be properly skilled in their ability to exercise judgment.

In a general sense, it can be said that the auditor will have obtained sufficient evidence when he becomes reasonably certain, through the application of audit procedures to gather the corroborating evidential matter, that his understanding of relevant management assertions is proven correct.

Types of Evidence

Evidential matter for internal audit purposes may consist of virtually any type of documented information. As mentioned earlier, the AICPA *Professional Standards* identify evidential matter that supports financial statements as consisting of the underlying accounting data and all corroborating information available to the auditor.[7] The broader scope of auditing employed by internal auditors requires that underlying nonaccounting information be added to underlying accounting data.

Examples of accounting data include trial balances; the general ledger; books of original entry, such as a payroll or sales registers; source documents, such as invoices, payroll time cards, and vouchers; and various reports, such as an aged accounts receivable listing. Examples of nonaccounting data include budgets, policy statements, organization charts, status reports, cash forecasts, production schedules, productivity records, and authorization forms of various kinds.

Evidential matter has been described in many ways. Professional auditing literature describes evidential matter in terms such as "underlying" and "corroborative." Legal descriptions use terms such as "direct," "circumstantial," "primary," and "secondary." These and still other terms offer overlapping, yet authoritative, descriptions of evidence for particular purposes. From a practical standpoint, the auditor should be interested in obtaining the best, or primary, evidence, whether or not it originated outside or inside the company. Evidence originating outside the company is often called external evidence, while that originating inside the company is fre-

---

[7] Statement on Auditing Standards No. 31, *op. cit.*, AU § 326.13.

EVIDENTIAL MATTER 14-15

quently described as internal evidence. Internal evidence may be further subdivided between that which results from established recurring processes and systems and that which is developed from special nonrecurring efforts. These types may be referred to, respectively, as recurring internal evidence and nonrecurring internal evidence. The terms are discussed in greater detail in the following paragraphs.

Primary Evidence. Primary evidence is the best possible evidence relating to a particular situation. It is the most relevant and reliable evidence of a given transaction or activity and it has the highest possible value to the auditor. When primary evidence has been obtained, internal auditors may assume that it is what it purports to be without further verification. Figure 14-1 contains a listing of typical forms of primary evidence and the event to which each relates. Primary evidence may be either external or internal in origin, or a combination of both. Often, primary evidence is generated internally, as is clear from Figure 14-1. That is because internal source documents usually offer the best evidence of the existence of the activities from which they originated.

External Evidence. External evidence is that generated by an independent outside source, such as a customer, creditor, or party not in interest. External evidence is often primary evidence (e.g., customer orders, checks, and shipping advices) and, thus, is of the highest value. Other forms of external evidence may not be primary (e.g., some types of memoranda) but are still significant, since they are external. External evidence is highly valued because it is generated outside the company and is therefore considered to be very reliable. Other examples of this type of evidence include bank statements, vendor invoices, and some forms of correspondence.

Recurring Internal Evidence. Recurring internal evidence is that generated by the normal systems of internal control within the company. Examples of this type of evidence include most computer reports, financial statements, general ledgers, books of original entry, work sheets, schedules, and reconciliations. Internal evidence also includes some forms of primary evidence, such as purchase orders, receiving reports, and time cards. The reliability of internal evidence must usually be corroborated, often by employing sampling techniques, as discussed in Chapter 15. The extent of the corroboration is a matter to be decided by the auditor in the circumstances. As mentioned earlier in this chapter, evidence produced from established systems and routines, because it results from long-established control processes that are designed to assure accuracy and completeness, is more valuable than information developed only infrequently by special processes. Thus, cash receipts and disbursements journals, payroll records, and general ledgers are usually more reliable than specially developed data, such as an

FIG. 14-1
Examples of Primary Evidence

Form of Evidence:	Underlying Transaction or Activity:
■ Check	■ Receipt or disbursement of cash from a bank account
■ Invoice	■ Billing for purchase of material or services
■ Receiving report	■ Receipt of merchandise
■ Purchase order	■ Ordering merchandise or service
■ Time card	■ Performance of labor
■ Employment application	■ Employment
■ Personnel action notice	■ Various personnel transactions such as promotions, pay rate changes, terminations, etc.
■ Production order	■ Authority to produce something
■ Shipping advice	■ Delivery of merchandise
■ Sales invoice	■ Billing for material or services sold
■ Stock certificate	■ Purchase or sale of ownership interest
■ Bond	■ Borrowing or lending of capital
■ Minutes	■ Proceedings of a group such as a board or committee
■ Budget	■ Planning activities
■ Contract	■ Agreement of two or more parties for various purposes

analysis of credit memos issued during a given period or a schedule of inventory items showing no activity for a given period, e.g., a year.

Nonrecurring Internal Evidence. Nonrecurring internal evidence is that which is produced by the auditor or, at his request, by personnel of the unit under audit. Examples include account analyses, flow charts, narratives of interviews, and documentation of audit tests. Because it does not derive from established systems of internal control that have stood the test of time, this type of evidence is usually less reliable than other forms of evidence. Specially developed data are often properly and accurately prepared. On the other hand, they may also be prepared on a time-available basis by persons unfamiliar with the underlying records, and without proper review and supervision. Errors and omissions are more likely to occur in these situations and thus, on occasion, the information may be suspect.

Unfortunately, nonrecurring internally developed evidence is frequently necessary due to the unavailability of other documentation. For example, in a limited financial review, the auditor usually compares the most recent financial statement balances with balances from comparable prior periods.

EVIDENTIAL MATTER

Many operating units make such comparisons regularly, but do not normally make them in a documented fashion suitable for audit purposes. As a result, there is often no preexisting evidence indicating how balances of differing financial statements compare. Someone—either the auditor or an accountant in the audited organization—must prepare a schedule that makes such comparisons.

Even when other forms of evidence do exist, some form of scheduling or documenting is often necessary to effectively and efficiently create a workpaper trail (see Chapter 12) of the evidence examined. In the prior example, the schedule would be prepared from existing sources, such as the financial statements themselves, from trial balances, or from the general ledger, assuming these records exist. The schedule is a more effective way of evidencing the comparison because it is in a documentary form specifically for that purpose. As such, it is more valuable to the auditor than would be a simple management assertion that such comparisons were made but were not documented.

Auditors must exercise due care in preparing or obtaining such evidence in view of the higher probability of errors and omissions. It is usually necessary to corroborate this evidence in some fashion. Information contained in flow charts may be corroborated through compliance testing, for example.

Evidence and the Internal Auditor

In practice, competent evidence takes different forms, depending on the type of auditing activity, e.g., internal accounting control, operational control, information reporting, standards of ethical business conduct, or EDP. Some comments on the evidence usually sought in connection with each of the foregoing are presented in the following paragraphs.

Internal Control. Detailed reviews of internal control involve auditing segments of overall internal control systems (either functions, departments, or transaction cycles) for the purpose of evaluating the adequacy of control techniques asserted by management to be in effect and measuring compliance therewith. Since positive opinions are expected from the auditor, the evidence to be gathered is extremely important. Thus, in performing detailed reviews of internal control, the principal type of evidence to be gathered is primary evidence (i.e., direct evidence) that the controls were operative during the period under review. Primary evidence is the principal type because it is the best type of evidence (e.g., purchase orders, invoices, and checks) and, as indicated previously, it is routinely produced by the internal accounting control process. Other forms of internal evidence, such as flow charts and narrative descriptions, are also gathered in these audits. Little external evidence is sought. The extent of evidence collected may differ from that accumulated by external auditors on any single control point.

Internal Accounting Control Surveys. These surveys are in less depth than the detailed internal control reviews mentioned previously, and they focus on the overall system of internal accounting control for the purpose of evaluating the adequacy of control techniques asserted by management to be in effect and measuring compliance therewith. To the extent applicable, the scope of work performed in detailed reviews is considered in determining the extent of evidence required in surveys. Thus, even though positive opinions are expressed, the amount of evidence obtained can be reduced if several relevant detailed reviews occurred during the audit period covered by the survey. Stated otherwise, the extent to which controls are directly corroborated by detailed reviews and by examinations of internal evidence in connection with the survey may enable the auditor to draw inferences regarding management assertions about other controls that were not corroborated. The auditor must be certain that exceptions are resolved so that any inferred reliability is justifiable. If exceptions tend to indicate that such inferences cannot be made, the auditor must not make them. Primary and other internal evidence are most frequently gathered. Developed evidence, in the form of flow charts or control narratives, is also obtained or prepared. A portion of a summary narrative of work performed in an internal control survey is shown in Figure 14-2 to illustrate the type of work performed.

Limited Financial Reviews. Limited financial reviews seek to provide information to management as to the consistency of interim and year-end financial reporting. Since the financial statements are not being examined in accordance with GAAS, and since the reports issued by the auditor do not contain an overall opinion, the emphasis on corroborative evidence is less critical. The evidence required is usually internal evidence. An example is shown in Figure 14-3, which illustrates a special schedule analyzing financial statement data. This is an example of nonrecurring internally developed evidence.

Standards-of-Ethical-Business-Conduct Audits. Reviews of standards of business conduct involve gathering evidence of all types. That is because evidence that can indicate the existence of questionable activities can occur in any form.

Operational Control Audits. Operational auditing focuses more on internal evidence than on external evidence. Since primary evidence is infrequently involved in evidencing operational control techniques, it is less applicable, generally. As a result, operational audits may carry a somewhat greater risk of drawing invalid findings, recommendations, and conclusions. To compensate, auditors often work more closely with operational managements to obtain their concurrence with findings and, in particular, their recommendations for remedial actions. Operational findings are often pre-

EVIDENTIAL MATTER

FIG. 14-2
Summary Narrative of Work Performed

Summary Narrative — Work Performed

	Initials	Date
Prepared By	CH	2/2/xx

                                                                         Workpaper reference

1. Discussed with various JBR management personnel the status of management's evaluation of internal control.   C-14

2. Reviewed prior reports and workpapers of detailed internal control projects performed at JPR this year. These included:

    Procurement
    Cash disbursements / Accounts payable
    Payroll

In addition, a limited Financial review was performed which, among other things, indicated various tests of the financial reporting system. The scope of testing in this Review considered the tests and other audit procedures performed in the above projects. Follow-up inquiry and testing was performed to ascertain the extent of remedial actions to recommendations contained in the respective reports.

3. Various detailed tests were performed as follows:

<u>cash receipts</u>   E

Examined reconciliations of mailroom listings   E-3
Tested promptness of depositing   E-4
Tested postings of daily deposits   E-7
Discussed cash receipts procedures with Al Stevens, Supervisor, and compared responses to Standard Practices and Procedures # 9.2.4   E-10
Scanned files of deposit slips noting consistency of usage

<u>Cash Disbursements / Accounts Payable</u>   F

Brought Forward copies of tests performed in connection with recent audit project   F1-F14

(continued)

FIG. 14-2 *(cont'd)*

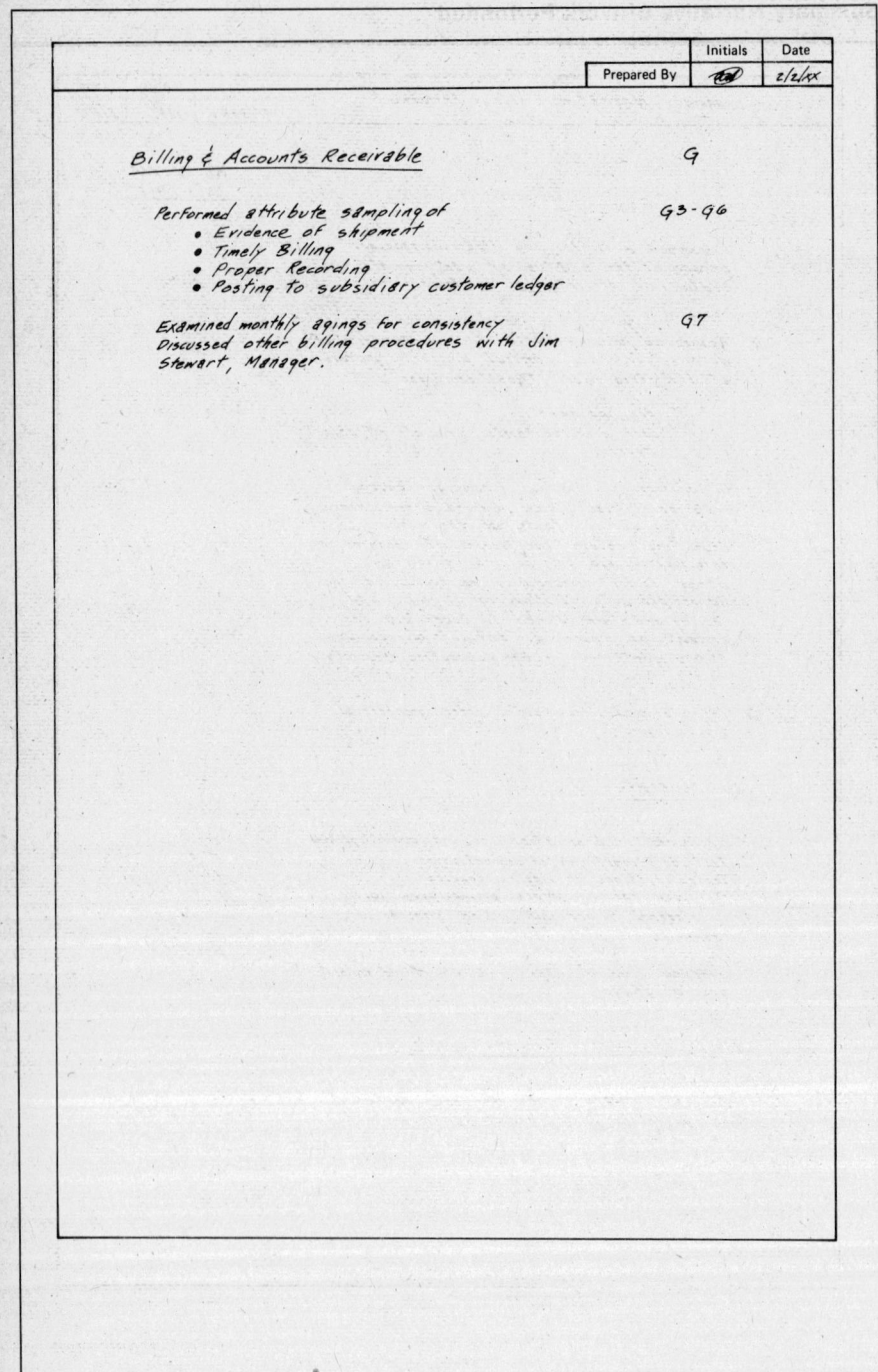

EVIDENTIAL MATTER

FIG. 14-3

Comparative Analysis—An Example of Internal Evidence

ABC Division
Comparative Analysis of Assets

Prepared By: JB Date: 10/14/XX

	August 19XX	December 19XX	Increase (Decrease)	%	EXPLANATION
CURRENT ASSETS					
Cash	⟨206⟩	⟨566⟩	360		Cash balance normally overdrawn due to outstanding checks (disbursement account only)
Temporary Investments	—	—	—		
Accounts Receivable	4901	7290	⟨2389⟩		Decrease due to collection of $1.2 million previously disputed receivable, and improved collection efforts, generally. Examined evidence of increased efforts in the form of enlarged staff, direct customer correspondence and improved cash flow in May–August period vs. year earlier.
Inventory – Raw Materials	9317	2583	6734		Substantial build-up in new product line in anticipation of customer demand and favorable raw material prices. Examined and compared acquisition quotes on five major commodity items with prior year, noting 20% reduction on the average. Also scanned approval by the group office for new product build up.
Inventory – Finished Product	16333	13187	3146		
Prepaid Expense	267	179	88		
	30612	22673	7939		
PROPERTY, PLANT & EQUIPMENT					
Accum. Depreciation	⟨3308⟩	⟨2985⟩	⟨323⟩		Normal provision for depreciation, compares favorably to prior years.
Land & Improvements	2895	2895	—		No current activity.
Buildings	2315	2830	⟨515⟩		For y/e reporting, construction in progress is reclassified here. Actual activity minimal.
Machinery & Equipment	4740	4592	148		Increase in accordance with planned and approved replacements.
Leasehold Improvements	482	401	81		Not significant.
Construction in Progress	5039	—	5039		Reflects progress to date on new plant. Examined contractors August progress billings. Toured jobsite – appears OK.
	12163	7733	4430		
OTHER ASSETS	5	5	—		Not significant.
	42780	30411	12369		Conclusion: Except for inconsistency in classification of construction in progress, nothing came to my attention indicating interim August Management Report was not consistent with year end report in terms of preparation.

Source: Management Report for August

Purpose: To ascertain consistency of report preparation between interim and year end by analyzing changes

sented orally; various alternatives are offered in a consultative fashion as possible solutions. For its part, management may seek information from other sources—within the company or outside it—to add credibility, as necessary. Further comments on operational auditing are provided in Chapters 29–37.

EDP Auditing. Since EDP auditing is, in reality, a highly technical form of operational auditing, EDP audits are similar to operational audits in terms of the types of evidence gathered. Internal and developed evidence are sought for the most part. This is discussed in greater detail in Chapter 27.

Other Considerations

Evidence gathering by internal auditors does not usually involve obtaining evidence directly from external sources, for reasons previously stated. Accordingly, internal auditors rarely correspond directly with banks, customers, outside legal counsel, and others who may have information relevant to external auditors about matters affecting the company. Invariably, the internal auditor can obtain sufficient, competent evidential matter from sources inside the company. The techniques for gathering this evidence are discussed in Chapters 15 and 16.

SUGGESTED READING

The Commission on Auditors' Responsibilities: Report, Conclusions and Recommendations. New York: Commission on Auditors' Responsibilities, 1978.

Sawyer, Lawrence B. *The Practice of Modern Internal Auditing.* Altamonte Springs, Fla.: The Institute of Internal Auditors, 1981.

Sullivan, Jerry D., Richard A. Gnospelius, Philip L. Defliese, and Henry R. Jaenicke *Montgomery's Auditing*, 10 ed., Chapter 5. New York: John Wiley & Sons, Inc. Copyright © 1985 by Coopers & Lybrand, United States.

CHAPTER **15**

Audit Sampling

Overview 2	Advantages and Disadvantages 16
Definitions 3	Concepts Involved in Statistical Sampling 17
Background and Perspective 4	Performance Techniques 19
Concept of Limited Testing 4	Determining Sample Size 19
Risk Considerations 5	Selecting the Sample 20
Minimizing Risk—Cost vs. Benefit 6	Performing the Test 21
Sampling Approaches 7	Evaluating the Results 21
	Documentation Techniques 22
Nonstatistical Sampling 7	
Definition 7	**Statistical Sampling Methods** 26
Performance Techniques 7	Attribute Sampling 26
Determining Sample Objective 8	Applicability 26
Determining Deviation Conditions 8	Methodology 28
Defining the Population Characteristics 9	Illustration 28
	Variables Sampling 30
Determining Sample Size 9	Applicability 31
Selecting the Sample 10	Methodology 31
Performing the Test 11	Other Sampling Techniques 35
Evaluating Test Results 11	Discovery Sampling 35
Documentation Techniques 13	Combined Attribute Variables Sampling 35
Practical Suggestions 13	
	Statistical Sampling Software 36
Statistical Sampling 15	
Definition 15	**Conclusion** 37
The Evolution of Statistical Sampling 16	**Suggested Reading** 37

Fig. 15-1	Specimen Workpaper Evidencing Sample Size Determination	23
Fig. 15-2	Specimen Workpaper Evidencing Sample Tests Performed	24
Fig. 15-3	Specimen Workpaper Evidencing Analysis of Results	25
Fig. 15-4	Frequently Tested Attributes—Payroll and Procurement Functions	27
Fig. 15-5	Attribute Sampling Table	29
Fig. 15-6	Factors for Estimating Standard Deviation	33
Fig. 15-7	Variables Sampling Table	34

OVERVIEW

Chapter 14 defines and analyzes the evidential matter that the auditor is interested in gathering in order to fulfill his objectives. The concept of selectivity—the notion that the extent of the auditor's efforts in evidence-gathering may be restricted or limited by him—is introduced there. Sampling occurs when the auditor is convinced the audit objectives pertaining to the entire population of a class of transactions or an account balance can be served by examining and gathering *less than all* of the available evidence.

This chapter discusses in detail the techniques applicable to the two forms of sampling—nonstatistical and statistical. The discussion distinguishes each form and describes the principal methods used in determining sample size, selecting samples, performing tests, evaluating results, and documenting work performed. The two major types of statistical sampling—attribute and variable—are also detailed.

Historically, many auditors have seen limited uses for statistical sampling and have preferred to rely on the auditors' judgment derived from knowledge of audit objectives and the characteristics of the subject matter.[1] This reliance on judgment and the special knowledge required to use statistical sampling has had the effect of slowing the expansion of its use.

The modern auditor is equipped with improved tools that ease much of the difficulty in applying statistical sampling. These include audit-related statistical tables (see Figures 15-5 and 15-6), reference material specifically addressing common situations in which statistical sampling is appropriate, and even EDP software that can perform much of the technical work. These developments and the growing concern by the courts, the SEC, and others as to the accuracy and precision of the work of the auditor have resulted in expanded uses of this form of sampling. This chapter also presents the evolution of statistical sampling to help in understanding it.

Some auditors will probably continue to debate the pros and cons of each sampling form—nonstatistical and statistical. However, the practical auditor should find that in the numerous and varied sampling circumstances encountered in field work, ample opportunity exists to make appropriate use of each. In other words, it may be better to think of nonstatistical sampling and statistical sampling not as alternatives, but rather as almost mutually exclusive tools to be used as dictated by conditions.

Regardless of which form is used, the objective in sampling is to infer

---

[1] Philip L. Defliese, Kenneth P. Johnson, and Roderick K. Macleod, *Montgomery's Auditing*, 9th ed. (New York: The Ronald Press Co., 1975), p. 146. It is interesting to note that in *Montgomery's Auditing*, 10th ed., the authors (Jerry D. Sullivan, Richard A. Gnospelius, Philip L. Defliese, and Henry R. Jaenicke) expand to all sampling the point made in the 9th edition as to the limited uses of statistical sampling to extend to all sampling. In effect, there are many types of tests performed by the auditor where less than 100 percent of a given population is examined that do not constitute sampling. Sampling is involved only when the objective is to project a conclusion about the sample to the entire population. The authors cite examples of this point on page 418, including some compliance testing.

conclusions about certain characteristics of a given population of like items, without examining the entire population. Sampling enables the auditor to derive reasonable conclusions and minimize the effort required to form the basis for those conclusions. Sampling is usually involved in inspection and confirmation, two of the principal techniques used in gathering evidential matter. These as well as the other techniques, observation, and inquiry, are discussed in Chapter 16.

DEFINITIONS

Audit sampling is defined in professional literature as the application of an audit procedure to less than 100 percent of the items within an account balance or class of transactions for the purpose of evaluating some characteristics of the balance or class.[2] (Note, however, that there may be other reasons to examine less than 100 percent of the population. This may occur, for example, when using an item or two to "walk through" the given system of controls.)

To better understand this definition, it may be helpful to define and distinguish the terms closely related to audit sampling. These terms are "audit procedures" and "testing." Audit procedures relate to all acts performed by the auditor in the conduct of his review. While they are described in more particular detail in Chapter 16, a summary preview at this point is needed. Audit procedures include such acts as reading, scanning, analyzing, evaluating, and even summarizing and reporting. These acts are designed to gather the necessary evidence. Some of these acts expose the auditor to large populations of rather homogenous items. Examples include canceled checks, invoices, purchase orders, and payroll time cards. Audit procedures may be performed using or scrutinizing information contained in these documents to determine compliance with some procedure, confirmation of some assertion, or corroboration of some relationship. It is in these instances that the auditor is apt to employ sampling techniques.

The term "testing" is often used interchangeably by auditors with the term "sampling." Indeed, testing does imply a limited, or less than total, application of some procedure. The expression "on a test basis" is frequently used by auditors in describing the extent to which a given audit procedure has been applied. For example, in a narrative of work performed, the auditor might state that he "examined approval signatures on employee time cards on a test basis" or, that he "traced postings to the general ledger on a test basis." In these situations, the concept of selective testing has been applied. However, such testing is not sampling according to GAAS

---

[2] Statement on Auditing Standards No. 39, *Audit Sampling* (June 1981) (AICPA, *Professional Standards*, Vol. 1). AU §350.01.

unless the auditor intends to project the results of the test to the entire population. This distinction is a technical one that is useful primarily to external auditors in deciding whether the disciplines required by SAS No. 39 apply to a given situation. The value to internal auditors, if distinguishing between sampling and testing, is much less. As a practical matter, most internal auditors as well as many external auditors continue to use the terms interchangeably. The interchangeability of testing and sampling as descriptive terms has not caused any discernible difficulties to auditors. The reader is cautioned not to impart different meanings to the terms as they are used throughout this chapter. Other terms are defined in this chapter when it is relevant to do so.

BACKGROUND AND PERSPECTIVE

Concept of Limited Testing

As noted in Chapter 1, the earliest audits checked everything because the systems of recording and summarizing transactions were fraught with errors and omissions. According to Montgomery:

> In the nineties we spent too much time on the routine checking of book entries. In some audits and not only the small ones, we verified every footing and every posting. Years later after we knew better, a British friend of mine said he still followed the same procedure and would not say he had made a complete audit unless he checked every item on the books.

Montgomery added:

> Frequently books have been out of balance for months or years, and the finding of errors was a terrific task. In the verification of postings one calls an amount from a ledger to another who compares it with an entry in a book of original entry. The function was referred to by those who did not like it as 'holler and tick.' One hollered the amount and the other ticked it off. The ticker often became sleepy and maybe an error was not discovered, which meant that the work had to be done over again.[3]

With improvements in control techniques, it soon became apparent that the reliability of the underlying records could be established by comprehensive tests. In the intervening years between then and now, testing has matured into a complex process.

---

[3] Robert H. Montgomery, *Fifty Years of Accountancy* (New York: Privately printed by the Ronald Press Co., 1939), p. 16. Copyright © 1939 by John Wiley & Sons, Inc. Reprinted with permission.

AUDIT SAMPLING

It should be noted that by employing the concept of testing, auditors are simply embracing the well-established management principle of considering the cost of an effort versus its benefit. The idea of testing is to maximize the assurance provided to third parties and minimize the effort required to do it.

Risk Considerations

Because a test may not be an accurate representation of the actual condition of the entire population from which the test was drawn, there is a risk that the auditor may draw the wrong conclusion from his testing. This risk is often referred to as sampling risk.

Authoritative literature defines sampling risk as the risk arising from the possibility that when an audit procedure is restricted to a sample, the auditor's conclusions may be different from the conclusions he would reach if the test were applied in the same way to all items in the account balance or class of transactions.[4]

Authoritative literature goes on to identify four varieties of sampling risk, two of which are associated with tests designed to validate balances of financial statement accounts, and two of which deal with tests designed to measure compliance with procedures. These are described as follows:[5]

1. *Risk associated with validation or substantive testing:*
   - The risk of *incorrect acceptance* is the risk that the sample supports the conclusion that the recorded account balance is not materially misstated when it is materially misstated.
   - The risk of *incorrect rejection* is the risk that the sample supports the conclusion that the recorded account balance is materially misstated when it is not materially misstated.

2. *Risk associated with compliance testing:*
   - The risk of *overreliance* on internal accounting control is the risk that the sample supports the auditor's planned degree of reliance on the control when the true compliance rate does not justify such reliance.
   - The risk of *underreliance* on internal accounting control is the risk that the sample does not support the auditor's planned degree of reliance on the control when the true compliance rate supports such reliance.

The inescapable presence of sampling risk makes it necessary to extend the previous statement on the testing objective, as follows: The complete objective is to provide the maximum level of assurance with the maximum practicable reliability with the least practicable level of effort. Once again,

---

[4] Statement on Auditing Standards No. 39, *op. cit.*, AU § 350.10.
[5] *Ibid.*, AU § 350.12.

judgment enters the picture. The extent of testing necessary to achieve any particular objective can be reliably determined only if the performing auditor is skilled and proficient in auditing. However, to reduce uncertainties over the adequacy of testing that are caused by the dependence upon the variable nature of the auditor's skill and proficiency, many techniques and guidelines have evolved. For example, audit testing today may be aided by the use of flow charts, questionnaires and checklists, generalized audit software, statistical sampling, and quality-control reviews.

Another risk factor involved in sampling, sometimes referred to as nonsampling risk, is that the auditor may make mistakes in performing the tests. These mistakes might take the form of failing to perform the proper test, failing to perform the test consistently or, as is more often the case, failing to note all exceptions. Even if all exceptions are noted, they may not all be properly resolved. Any of these possibilities may cause a similar result: an invalid conclusion. Due professional care and effective quality-control methods can reduce this risk to reasonable levels but cannot eliminate it completely.

Minimizing Risk—Cost vs. Benefit

The nature and extent of testing and other audit procedures necessary to minimize the ultimate risk of drawing the wrong conclusion, in turn, are dependent on the cost of performing the work and the value of the results to the overall audit objective. Obviously, the more critical the results are, the more extensive is the testing required. For example, evidence indicating approval of annual business plans is more critical in an audit of business planning than is evidence of analysis of future postage costs.

Also, the easier (i.e., less time-consuming and less costly) a test is to perform, the more likely it is that it is performed using larger samples. For example, bank reconciliations are usually performed monthly. If an auditor is reviewing cash controls for a given period—say, a year—it is almost as easy to see evidence that 12 reconciliations were prepared as it is to see just one. By looking at all 12, the auditor is in a much more confident position with respect to the preparation of bank reconciliations.

On the other hand, for company payrolls, time cards are usually present as primary evidence of the hours each employee works within a given payroll period. If the auditor is testing the control over approving time cards, he will be unable to examine all of them in most cases. Particularly is this the case for large payrolls covering thousands of employees. A weekly payroll covering 20,000 people would generate over one million time cards a year. It would also be impractical to examine a comparatively large portion of this population. How much testing is sufficient in this situation is covered in the next section.

Sampling Approaches

Two types of sampling approaches have gained acceptance in modern auditing—nonstatistical and statistical. Each is based on the premise that all evidence in support of a particular assertion need not be examined to confirm the assertion's validity. Both approaches have been described in detail by numerous authors in easy-to-follow texts. The following paragraphs provide general descriptions, illustrate each type and, perhaps more importantly, identify numerous applications. Thus, the manager and the performing auditor may make more informed decisions as to when each might best be applied.

NONSTATISTICAL SAMPLING

Definition

Nonstatistical sampling may be defined as the process of selecting a sample from a population of items which, in the judgment of the person making the selection, will result in a sampling whose characteristics are representative of those of the entire population. Nonstatistical sampling was formerly termed judgmental sampling, which is a term that may still be used by some auditors.

Whenever an auditor decides to examine less than 100 percent of the available data in order to project the results of the sample to the entire population, and statistical methods are not used, the sample is nonstatistical. The principal difference between the two is that, in statistical sampling, the degree of sampling risk is quantifiable, whereas in nonstatistical sampling, the risk is indeterminant. Another distinction is in the extent to which each can be used. Statistical sampling can be used only where the characteristics to be tested are believed to occur randomly throughout the entire population and where evidence of such occurrence exists. Also, the population must be large enough to permit the mathematical laws of statistics to operate. Nonstatistical sampling is comparatively easier to execute and may be used under almost any circumstance. For these reasons, nonstatistical sampling is more widely used, although statistical sampling is increasing in use.

Performance Techniques

The specific steps required to perform nonstatistical and statistical sampling are similar. It is thought to be easier to understand the process, however, if the steps are discussed separately. The steps are as follows:

1. Determine sampling objective.
2. Define the deviation conditions.

3. Define the population characteristics.
4. Determine the method of selecting the sample.
5. Determine the sample size.
6. Perform the test.
7. Evaluate the results.

In practice, the sequence of performing those steps is not necessarily the sequence shown above. For example, it is possible to determine the sample size before settling on the method of selecting the sample. But, generally, the sequence shown, if followed, will produce satisfactory results.

Determining Sample Objective. It is important that the auditor first determine the objective because that is where it becomes clear whether sampling is involved. Many tests of less than 100 percent of a population may be performed by the auditor for reasons other than projecting conclusions about the sample to the entire population. With respect to audits of financial statements, an auditor might, for example, perform substantive tests of large dollar value transactions within an account balance. The auditor may then decide to accept the risk of undetected error in the remaining unexamined transactions due to their immateriality. In other instances, tests of certain control conditions tend to offer cumulative evidence that the control condition operated during the period under review. Such instances are encountered by both internal and external auditors. Examples include checking certain types of error listings (such as a listing of improperly coded transactions during the period), examining reconciliations of detail records to control accounts, and ascertaining the existence of various types of reports (for instance, the existence of a monthly financial statement provides cumulative evidence that the transactions were recorded and that accounting records were closed, balanced, and reported).

If the auditor determines that the objective of the test is to develop a conclusion about the entire population, then sampling is involved.

Determining Deviation Conditions. The guidance here depends on the type of testing involved. In compliance testing, this step means figuring out for each control being tested just what evidence constitutes compliance and what constitutes noncompliance. This is relatively straightforward for most controls. The following list presents some of the more typical controls and the evidence of their operation:

Example	*Evidence*
• Control condition	• Written procedure
• Use of required form	• The form
• Properly executed form	• The completed form
• Approval	• Signature on form

AUDIT SAMPLING

Example	Evidence
• Evidence of checking for accuracy	• Tick mark, stamp, or initials
• Evidence of posting	• Tick mark, stamp, initials, or other notation on form
• Evidence of recording	• Entry in book of original entry
• Timeliness of processing	• Dates on form, date recorded
• Accuracy	• Error listings, correction entries, transaction traceability

Defining the Population Characteristics. The auditor must determine the period to be covered, the sampling unit, and have an idea of the size of the population. Usually, the identification of the period covered is established at the outset of the audit. For compliance auditing, the period is usually year to date, although any period could be selected.

Determining the sampling unit is, in most instances, simply a process of transaction identification. For example, compliance testing of purchasing transactions would require using the purchase order as the sampling unit. A test of cash disbursements usually would require using paid voucher packets as the sampling unit. A test of payroll would require using completed employee payroll transactions as the sampling unit, which, depending on the payroll, may be weekly, biweekly, semimonthly or monthly.

Determining Sample Size. Nonstatistical samples are determined by a largely intuitive process. Perhaps the most important determinant is the tolerable error rate. Tolerable error rate may be defined as the maximum rate of errors or exceptions that the auditor can encounter and still conclude that the control is operating as understood or, for example, if testing account balances, that the balance is materially correct. Sample size varies inversely with the tolerable error rate. That is, the larger the tolerable error rate, the smaller will be the sample.

The tolerable error rate must be determined in advance for each item or characteristic being tested. In recurring assignments, the auditor, or his predecessor, will have gained a feel for how credible the function is. In other words, he has some basis for anticipating what the error rate ought to be for that characteristic. For example, in performing a test of the accuracy of unit prices on sales invoices, the auditor may decide that an acceptable error rate is ±1% of extended value. In these circumstances, the auditor may be justified in selecting a smaller sample size than he might select in an initial review. On the other hand, in an initial review, the auditor must make some preliminary estimate of the rate of exceptions or deviations he is willing to live with and still confidently report that the control is functioning as expected. This estimate might be based on experiences elsewhere in similar circumstances, by discussion with management, or by consultation with the company's outside auditors.

In determining the tolerable error rate, the auditor should consider the relevance of the control to management, the risk posed by errors remaining undetected, and disciplinary controls involved. The latter are controls that reasonably assure the continuity of processing. Examples include supervisory reviews as might occur in a review of invoices prior to payment or a review of payroll listings prior to check preparation. Other examples are error detection and correction routines, such as validity checks on employee or vendor numbers, account numbers, and so forth. Still other examples would be balancing controls, such as reconciliations of bank accounts and general ledger control accounts with subsidiary records.

Another important determinant of sample size is the expected error (or deviation) rate. The expected error rate could be the same as the tolerable error rate but often is not. In most situations, it should be less than the tolerable error rate. It is the rate estimated by the auditor to approximate the true but unknown error frequency. The expected error rate affects sample size determination because the higher the expected rate is, the larger the sample must be.

In nonstatistical sampling, the sample size determination is a matter of judgment. The judgment also takes into consideration the reliability of the sample he selects as an indicator of the true but unknown condition of the entire population. In considering these three factors (tolerable error rate, expected deviation rate, and reliability), a sample size is determined.

Many auditors, when performing nonstatistical sampling, select sample sizes that fall within ranges. Under this approach, sample size will always exceed a certain minimum, say 25, and never exceed a certain maximum, say 200. Beyond 200, it may be that the auditor would be better off employing statistical sampling.

In determining sample size, it is interesting to note that the size of the population has little effect on sample size determination once the population is above 2,000 items.

In theory, the sample sizes will vary, depending on the results of considering the preceding factors. However, in practice, most auditors tend to select a single sample size for testing many related controls. The size of this sample should be not less than the largest deemed necessary by the auditor for any single control as determined by the process just described. For example, in testing controls for processing accounts payable, the auditor may select a sample size to test evidence of (1) ordering, (2) receipt, (3) matching, (4) audit, and (5) payment. If the most critical test (i.e., evidence of receipt) requires a sample size of 50 transactions, that sample size should probably be used for all related tests.

Selecting the Sample. Current professional literature requires that even in nonstatistical sampling, it is important that every item in the population has an equal chance of being selected.[6] In statistical sampling, this is usually

---
[6] *Ibid.*, AU § 350.24.

accomplished through some form of random sampling. Formal random sampling techniques may be used in nonstatistical sampling. These techniques, which include random sampling, stratified random sampling, and systematic sampling, are discussed later in the chapter. However, selection is usually accomplished in a less structured fashion. The auditor tries to be random, but stops short of using random number generators and the like because the resultant rigidity is not relevant to his purpose. Selections should be free of bias, however. Thus, the auditor should not concentrate his selection in a single month, if several months are under review. The sample should be drawn from the body of evidence for a given period so that it is representative. For instance, if a sample of 100 sales invoices is to be drawn from a year's sales transactions totaling 10,000, the sampling should be made from throughout the year, or 8–10 per month. If, however, the sales transactions are disproportionately high during the year-end holidays, then more of the sample should be taken from that period.

Performing the Test. Once the sample has been obtained, the actual testing can be performed. The types of compliance testing done by internal auditors usually involve some form of inspection or confirmation. Inspection and confirmation are discussed in Chapter 16. The objective in each case is to see if the documentation retained in the files includes evidence in each test case that the controls in which the auditor is interested were performed.

The actual performance of the test must be done with due care because much depends on it. Auditors often consider this aspect of auditing to be the most mundane of all audit tasks. It is true that the work can be boring because of its repetitive nature. Some less patient auditors may be tempted to falsify the testing, simply to avoid doing it. At times, budgetary pressures may influence the auditor to short-cut procedures or skip portions of the work. The diligence and professionalism of the auditor must be strong enough to resist these temptations. The following suggestions may also help:

- Spread the testing throughout the field work. If too much is saved or deferred to the end of the job, the pressures may become too great.
- Perform the testing at times when distractions can be minimized. For example, Monday mornings and Friday afternoons are often times when other thoughts may hold the auditor's attention. Also, tests should not be conducted when the auditor is tired. Therefore, late night tests should be avoided.
- Utilize the help of the organizational unit personnel to the extent possible to help with the test. Many are quite willing to help find and extract the needed evidence from the files. Some insist on doing it to keep the files in proper order.

Evaluating Test Results. The results of the test must be evaluated as to whether the evidence examined (i.e., the sample) is sufficient to draw reasonably accurate inferences therefrom. In other words, a total must be made of the number of instances in which the test was successful and the number of exceptions. In the case of the exceptions, each must be analyzed to determine the causes. If the rate of errors, for example, is within tolerable limits, the evaluation is quite simple. The auditor may conclude that he has examined sufficient convincing evidence that the control operated according to expectations during the period.

On the other hand, if the sample results disclosed a greater error rate than anticipated, the auditor must make further inquiry to understand the reasons, therefore, and to consider the implications of those reasons on the test results. There may be valid explainable circumstances as to why the sample was not representative. For example, the sample may be comprised disproportionately of transactions or activities occurring at a time when the individual or individuals normally responsible were absent. If the sample is deemed representative, then the auditor must attempt to isolate the reason or reasons for the excessive error rate in order to properly inform management.

In analyzing error rates, care must be taken to minimize the possibility of failing to detect temporary breakdowns in internal control. Evidence of such breakdowns may be manifested by the way in which the errors in the sample occur. A bunching of errors, for example, could mean that controls were ineffective for a brief period. If the auditor does not scrutinize the test data for clusters of errors, breakdowns could reoccur periodically at considerable cost to the company.[7]

Once the auditor is satisfied that the sample results are accurate, the results are projected to the entire population. If the sample error rate is 2 percent, the auditor projects that rate to the entire population. Should the auditor desire to know how many errors that would be, he need only multiply the number of transactions by the sample error rate. In a population of 10,000 items and with a sample error rate of 2 percent, the projected number of errors in the entire population is 200. If it is desirable to project the dollar value, the auditor may determine the average dollar error in the sample and extend that to the entire population. To illustrate, if the average error in the sample was $22, then the error in the population is $220,000. Another approach could be applied if the total population value is known. In the illustration, if the total value in the population is $38 million, the total value of the sample is $450,000, and if the total error amount in the sample is $2,640, then the error in the total population may be determined by the following:

$$\frac{\text{error in sample}}{\text{value of sample}} \times \frac{\text{error in population}}{\text{value of population}}$$

In this situation, it would be as follows:

---

[7] Roy Whittington and Steve J. Adams, "Temporary Breakdowns of Internal Control: Implications for External and Internal Auditors," *Journal of Accounting, Auditing and Finance*, Summer 1982, p. 312.

AUDIT SAMPLING 15-13

$$\frac{\$2,640}{\$450,000} \times \frac{X}{\$38,000,000} = \$223,000 \text{ (rounded)}$$

Documentation Techniques. Too frequently, auditors do not properly document in their workpapers the basis of selecting nonstatistical samples. Many times it is difficult, if not impossible, to understand the basis of selection solely by reviewing workpapers. This causes uneasiness on the part of the reviewer. The following items ought to be documented, at a minimum:

- Estimate of the population from which the transaction was drawn
- Factors that influenced the sample determination
- Identification of the sample in sufficient detail to permit the test to be duplicated
- Exceptions and their disposition
- Conclusions

Particular care must be taken in forming and documenting conclusions regarding nonstatistical samples. It is easy to infer more than is justified. Frequently, the following conclusions are encountered in auditors' workpapers:

- Existing evidence indicates that controls operated as understood during the period.
- No material errors or omissions occurred.
- [*Name of entity or function*] complied with applicable policies and procedures.

Note that these conclusions are worded too positively and place the auditor in the position of a guarantor. Each example implies that the auditor is positive that no deviations of any type have occurred. Such inferences are not possible in the context of sampling. Conclusions from nonstatistical sampling must be constructed to fit the circumstances. The foregoing examples need only slight modification to make them more accurate as follows:

- Existing evidence supports the understanding that controls over [*name of function*] operated during the period in all material respects.
- Evidence examined did not disclose material errors or omissions.
- Existing evidence indicates a high probability that [*name of entity or function*] complied with applicable policies and procedures in all material respects.

Practical Suggestions. Nonstatistical sampling is best used when the population from which the sample to be drawn is not large (say 0–1,000 items). Nonstatistical samples selected from this range would seldom exceed 50. If the population is between 1,000 and 10,000, a nonstatistical sample of 100 transactions usually will suffice. If the population is greater than 10,000, a sample size of at least 150 items is recommended. Sample sizes may vary considerably with circumstances. When circumstances permit, sample selection should be extensive to demonstrate prudence. Here are some examples of controls where tests may be devised in which the concept of selective testing does not normally lend itself to nonstatistical sampling. For these, the test should apply to most, if not all, applicable transactions.

- Bank reconciliations
- Authority to open bank accounts
- Authority to close bank accounts
- Authority to change accounting principles
- Authority to change authorized signatories of bank accounts
- Agings of accounts receivable
- Balancing of books of account
- Preparation of financial statements
- Preparation of budgets
- Preparation of minutes of meetings of the board of directors (or other groups)
- Reconciliations of control accounts with subsidiary ledgers (fixed assets, cost, accounts payable)
- Review and approval of officers' expense reports
- Approval for the use of foreign commission agents and consultants
- Retention and protection of vital records
- Settlements of major litigation

Every item in the population should have approximately the same chance of being selected for the audit sample—whether the sample is nonstatistical or statistical. Accordingly, in nonstatistical sampling, selection of the sample should occur throughout the period under review. Also, when possible, large samples of items should be tested. For example, consider the earlier example of a payroll audit in which the population of time cards exceeds one million for any given year. If the auditor wished to test for the existence of employee signatures on time cards, it may be almost as easy to riffle through a stack of 250 cards as it is to riffle through 50. Perhaps 10 stacks of 25 each could be randomly selected from the files in which the entire population resides. Also, the auditor may be able to estimate the population actually contained in the files to compare with the previous estimates made at the outset of the test. Such a procedure adds considerably to the evidence (and comfort) that the controls operated during the period as understood in all material respects. Other suggestions are:

- Decrease the sample size if supervisory controls exist, such as a requirement for supervisors' signatures on time cards, a requirement for time-keeping reviews of each time card, or an automated control that rejects time cards that do not bear employee signatures.

AUDIT SAMPLING 15-15

- Decrease the sample size if there is reason to believe that there are bound to be very few exceptions. In most payrolls, the presence of disciplinary controls makes the likelihood of exceptions to signature requirements remote.
- Increases in the sample size are not likely to produce added confidence despite the fact that the population is over one million. The size of the population has little to do with sample size determination.
- Use generalized or specialized audit software (see Chapter 28) where possible, in order to increase the scope and reliability of testing through the computer.
- Where possible, combine tests for maximum efficiency. In the previous example, in addition to time card approval, the auditor may also note (1) the signature of the employee, (2) consistent use of time cards, (3) completion of time card as per instructions, and (4) evidence of audit.
- Document the test results as near as practicable to the time of actual performance.
- Be sure to document all testing. Auditors invariably do more testing than they realize.

These are just a few thoughts. Keep in mind that nonstatistical sampling is a very flexible sampling approach and can be applied in virtually any situation. When properly applied and documented, it provides the essential evidence on which the auditor can draw rational inferences or conclusions regarding the population under audit. Also, it should be noted that the accuracy of nonstatistical sampling, like other aspects of auditing that require judgment, such as determining the extent of research required, deciding on audit procedures, evaluating results, drawing conclusions, and choosing the means to disclose findings, depends on the professional manner in which the work is performed. Adhering to the general standards of independence, competence, and due professional care, which are discussed in Chapter 6, is the best way to assure that proper judgments are made.

STATISTICAL SAMPLING

Definition

Statistical sampling, also known as scientific and mathematical sampling, may be defined as the process of selecting a sample from a population of items by applying prescribed mathematical techniques to produce a sample with a quantifiable precision and reliability regarding the extent to which the sample characteristics are representative of the characteristics of the entire population containing the sample.

The objective of statistical sampling is to obtain the quantity of evidence that, according to the mathematical laws of probability, is needed to satisfy the auditor's preferences for reliability and accuracy.

The Evolution of Statistical Sampling

Statistical sampling began to gain noticeable use among public accounting practitioners in the 1950s and 1960s. Its use increased considerably in the late 1960s and 1970s, perhaps as a response to frequent allegations of deficiencies in connection with audit scopes developed solely on the basis of judgment. To some practitioners, statistical sampling appeared to offer a more scientific—and, presumably, more defendable—testing method. Whether this view will convince the courts remains to be seen. In the meantime, its usefulness for audit purposes and its popularity continue to grow.

Advantages and Disadvantages

The proponents of statistical sampling believe it to be preferable to nonstatistical sampling, where applicable, because it offers the opportunity to quantify the risk of a sampling error.[8] Moreover, it is argued that the chance of performing too much or too little testing is eliminated by this approach.

While conceding that it is a less biased approach, other practitioners assert that it is useful in only a percentage of test situations.[9] Statistical sampling is also recognized as being more costly as a result of training costs and the additional work required in designing samples and performing selections.

In spite of early arguments asserting limitations on applicability, and in spite of the other arguments against statistical sampling, the approach is gaining in acceptance. This may be seen from briefly tracing its evolution in professional literature. In 1962, a special AICPA group, the Committee on Statistical Sampling, issued a special report in which it concluded: "A broader education in and knowledge of statistical sampling and further research as to its applicability on the part of the profession is desirable."[10]

In 1963, the AICPA Committee on Auditing Procedure issued *Auditing Standards and Procedures No. 33*, which suggested that the auditor might consider using statistical sampling techniques, which had been found to be advantageous in certain instances. Outright acceptance of the concept seemed imminent.

In 1964, the AICPA Committee on Statistical Sampling published another report, entitled "A Special Report by the Committee on Statistical Sampling of the American Institute of Certified Public Accountants," which appeared in *The Journal of Accountancy* in July of that year. In essence,

---

[8] Walter G. Kell and Richard E. Ziegler, *Modern Auditing* (New York: Warren, Gorham & Lamont, 1980), p. 152.

[9] Defliese et al., *op. cit.*, p. 147. In *Montgomery's Auditing*, 10th ed., the authors (Jerry D. Sullivan et al.) continue to reflect the view expressed in the 9th ed. that statistical sampling is a popular technique but that nonstatistical sampling is more widely used (see p. 446).

[10] Committee on Statistical Sampling, *Statistical Sampling and the Independent Auditor* (New York: AICPA, Feb. 1962), p. 2.

the report reiterated the position that the use of statistical sampling is compatible with, but not required by, GAAS. The report was included in SAS No. 1 as an appendix issued by the Committee on Auditing Procedures in 1973. This suggests that statistical sampling concepts were accepted, but the technique was not thought to be practiced to any significant extent. The Committee therefore included in SAS No. 1 another appendix, which provided application guidance, presumably to further actual practice of the technique.

In 1981, these appendices were superseded in Statement on Auditing Standards No. 39, entitled *Audit Sampling*. This pronouncement redefines some of the terminology and prescribes sampling techniques to be followed regardless of the sampling mode used. In essence, the two sampling types are given equal value. The pronouncement permits either the statistical or nonstatistical approach, as practiced by the techniques suggested, in order to gather sufficient evidential matter.

It appears from the foregoing that professional literature in recent years has moved toward favoring the unbiased objectives of the underlying disciplines involved in statistical sampling and perhaps the actual technique itself.

The reader must continue to bear in mind, however, that GAAS do not make sampling mandatory. The professional guidance for sampling only applied when the objective of the test is to project a conclusion or test result to the entire population or account balance.

Concepts Involved in Statistical Sampling

In order to use statistical sampling, it is necessary to be familiar with the underlying concepts involved. Statistical sampling is based on the principle that the accuracy of a sample as an indicator of the actual conditions of a given population is quantifiable by the use of mathematical formulas and tables. This quantification will provide the auditor with objective data that he can use in evaluating test results and in determining, if necessary, further courses of action. This means that an auditor employing statistical sampling may draw inferences with a precise reliability about a population he has not examined from the results of a sample of that population that he has examined. The auditor, in effect, is seeking the sample size necessary to examine in order to conclude with a prescribed confidence level that the actual deviation from perfection contained in the entire population falls within a tolerable error range. If, on selection and performance, the actual number of exceptions or deviations in the sample is greater than the tolerable range, then one of two alternatives must be adopted. Either the sample size or the tolerable range must be expanded.

Statistical sampling does not eliminate the need for exercising judgment. Like nonstatistical sampling, some advance determination must be made of the extent to which errors are tolerated and the degree of risk the auditor is willing to take that the sample does not truly represent the actual condition of the entire population. These factors are known to statisticians as precision and reliability.

"Precision" has been defined as the measure of the accuracy of a sample value as an estimator of the true population value.[11] For example, assume that in a sample of time cards in a test of supervisory approval, the auditor found a 3 percent error rate. That is, for 3 percent of the time cards examined, the supervisor's signature was not present. It may be that the 3 percent error rate was precisely the error rate of the entire population of time cards from which the sample is drawn. However, it is more likely that the actual error rate of the entire population is near to, but not exactly, 3 percent. The range, or interval, around 3 percent that contains the actual, but unknown, error rate is known as the precision interval. Precision intervals are set by the auditor prior to selecting the sample and performing the test. The interval selected should be large enough to accommodate the largest error range the auditor is willing to tolerate and still consider the results acceptable.

"Reliability" is the degree of confidence that the sample results are an accurate representation of the true condition of the entire population. Since the auditor is looking at only a portion of the population, he cannot be 100 percent confident that the sample accurately depicts the population. Statistical approaches involving mathematical formulas enable the auditor to determine sample size and sample results with a quantifiable level of confidence. In other words, he is able to quantify in terms of percentages the degree of confidence that his sample is an accurate representation of the population as a whole. The complement of reliability is risk. It follows that if the sampling reliability can be quantified, so can the sampling risk.

Professional literature of the AICPA used the terms precision and reliability until the ASB issued SAS No. 39 in 1981. SAS No. 39 uses the concept of risk instead of reliability or confidence level. That is because it is more in line with the underpinnings of GAAS. Thus, the terms "risk of underreliance on internal accounting control" and "risk of overreliance on internal accounting control" are used. These terms along with the terms "incorrect acceptance" and "incorrect rejection" are defined earlier in this chapter. The equivalent of precision in audit sampling is the tolerable error rate and sampling risk. Tolerable error rate is determined by the auditor to be the rate of errors the auditor is willing to encounter and still rely on the control to the extent planned. Internal auditors would modify this to be the rate the internal auditor is willing to encounter and still conclude that the control is operating effectively. Often, this rate is set at 5 or 10 percent. Sometimes, of course, it can be higher or lower.

Precision also comes into play in evaluating test results. In this context, the equivalent of precision is an allowance for the sampling risk concept previously mentioned. Internal auditors must be familiar with this interplay

---

[11] Kell and Ziegler, *op. cit.*, p. 154.

AUDIT SAMPLING

of terminology, since other literature on statistical sampling uses the traditional statistics terms.

The differing terminology that SAS No. 39 presents is intended to better relate the sampling work of the external auditor to GAAS employed in an examination of financial statements. In such an examination, the external auditor considers audit risk—the chance that the financial statements may contain a material error that has not been detected. In planning auditing procedures, the external auditor must assess control risk—the risk that a material error will not be detected and corrected by the control structure. Such consideration is principally analytical and evaluative but necessarily involves relying on those internal controls relevant to the process of recording transactions and preparing financial statements. To the extent such reliance is based on the results of sampling (both nonstatistical and statistical), the external auditor risks that he may erroneously conclude to rely on such controls when he should not and vice versa. This concept of over- and underreliance is relevant only in an examination of financial statements in accordance with GAAS. Chapter 4 discusses these standards, and Chapters 14 and 18 contain discussions of audit risk.

Internal auditors test compliance with internal controls to ascertain whether such controls operated effectively during the period of the test. The objective is to report the degree of compliance to interested management. For this, the concept of over- and underreliance is not involved. Nevertheless, the procedural aspects of sampling for this purpose are very similar to those used by external auditors. The guidance provided in the balance of this chapter is intended for internal auditors who are performing statistical sampling procedures primarily for the purpose of reporting the degree of compliance for a given period.

Performance Techniques

The steps involved in statistical sampling are similar to those used for nonstatistical sampling. Comments in the preceding discussion of nonstatistical sampling pertaining to determining sample objectives and deviation conditions and defining population characteristics also apply to statistical sampling. No further comments are offered for these. Additional commentary is warranted for determining sample size, reflecting the sample, performing the test, evaluating the results, and documenting the work.

Determining Sample Size. Sample size in statistical approaches is determined by mathematical formulas. Few auditors who perform testing under one of the various statistical techniques are aware of the mathematical equations and underlying theory, nor do they need to be. That is because tables have been constructed for virtually all types of situations the auditor may encounter. Examples of these tables are presented later in this chapter. The auditor simply must know how to use the tables.

In recent years, automated techniques have been developed so that the auditor doesn't even need the tables. All that is required is a terminal and access to one of the many software sampling programs that have evolved. Of course, this requires that the auditor know something about the available programs (i.e., how and when to use them). All of them come with descriptions and instructions so that the inexperienced practitioner may use them with little difficulty.

For example, Tymshare, Inc. maintains and makes available the following programs on a timeshare basis:[12]

    SAMGEN—for generation of random samples

   ATRES1—for determination of sample size and evaluation of sample results using attribute estimation

  VARES1—for determination of sample size and evaluation of sample results using variables estimation (i.e., mean-per-unit, difference and ratio estimation) with stratification

  VARES2—for determination of sample size and evaluation of sample results using variables estimation with stratification

Microcomputer programs that assist in sample size selection also are available. Naturally, use of these aids requires proper orientation and preparation. If the auditor is familiar with the programs, he will find that using them is quite simple. The procedures involve logging in and out via remote terminals, creating or inputting the required information, executing the program, and deleting the data when no longer needed.

Underlying each of the foregoing techniques are various mathematical equations, mathematical tables, and software programs. In order to determine which to use, the auditor must first define what is desired. Two objectives are most common for auditors. These include (1) drawing inferences regarding overall compliance with specific control requirements, and (2) estimating dollar values of a particular population. To achieve these objectives, auditors must employ, respectively, either attribute sampling or variable sampling. The differing methodology for each is described later in this chapter.

Selecting the Sample. In order for statistically valid conclusions to be drawn, it is essential that every item in the population under examination have an equal chance of being selected. To assure that this requirement is observed, various ways of making random selections have been developed:

☐ *Random sampling.* A technique where the sample is selected by using ran-

---

[12] Touche Ross & Co., *Instructions for Audit Sampling Timesharing Programs* (Touche Ross & Co., 1980), Preface.

AUDIT SAMPLING 15-21

dom numbers supplied by a random number table or a random number generator (a software program obtainable from time-sharing vendors).

- ☐ *Interval sampling.* Under this method, also known as systematic sampling, every nth item is selected. The interval is represented by n and is determined by dividing the total population by the sample size. A random number less than the value of n is used to find a starting point.

- ☐ *Stratified sampling.* A technique in which the interval of selection is varied according to predetermined criteria. The auditor may decide, for instance, that the sample should include all items over $10,000. The balance of the sample would be randomly selected from the rest of the population using one of the other methods.

More complex methods are available to accommodate other situations. These would rarely be encountered by the internal auditor and are beyond the scope of this book.

Whatever the technique used for sample selection, the principle of randomness must be observed. If the auditor has reason to believe that deviations (errors and omissions) do not occur randomly throughout the population, a statistical approach may be invalid. In a company where production volume fluctuates due to cyclical market conditions, errors in production scheduling or in completing and processing production orders may be more likely in peak periods. A random sample may not be desirable because each sample item may not have the same chance of detecting an error condition. Sometimes stratified sampling may compensate for such circumstances, but not always.

Performing the Test. Once the sample size is determined and the sample is obtained, the test is performed in much the same way as is the case for nonstatistical sampling. The same dedication to due diligence is necessary to reasonably assure an accurate and complete perormance of the test. To the extent practicable, the auditor should also perform the testing when distractions can be minimized and should utilize the help of organizational unit personnel. Also, like nonstatistical sampling, the testing should be scheduled to be performed throughout the fieldwork to avoid end-of-the-job rushes.

Evaluating the Results. The results of the test must be evaluated. This involves comparing the actual test results with the expected results. If the actual results fall within the precision range, the auditor may conclude, with the specified confidence level, that the actual error rate or dollar value is within acceptable, or tolerable, limits. The sample should be analyzed and checked for any errors or other circumstances that may affect its validity. If the sample results are found to be accurate and no other conditions affecting validity are identified, then other action is necessary. Either the sample size must be expanded, or the tolerable error rate or the confidence level must be adjusted.

If the sample size is expanded, the same random selection principle must be observed. The expanded sample may produce results that fall within the desired range. Of course, there is also the chance that the expanded results will also exceed the predetermined limits. If that happens, the auditor must analyze the sample errors and even the sampling method to identify any possible factors or conditions that may be distorting the results. If such factors cannot be isolated, the auditor must consider the implications of the sample results on the overall reliability of the system.

In practice, some auditors prefer to analyze the original sample without attempting to expand the sample in the belief that further testing is wasted effort. Regardless of the methodology, when the auditor is forced to conclude that the error rate is unacceptably high, he must attempt to identify the reasons therefor, because the matter must be reported to affected management and recommendations for remedial action must be made.

Documentation Techniques. Working papers evidencing statistical sampling techniques should include, at a minimum, comments on the following items:

- Controls or attributes being tested
- Sampling approach (attribute or variable)
- Population from which each sample is selected
- Selection method (random, stratified, etc.)
- Predetermined confidence level and precision interval
- Sample size
- Record of the tests performed
- Analysis of errors
- Conclusions

Figures 15-1, 15-2, 15-3, are specimen workpaper illustrations of the required documentation. For purposes of this illustration, tolerable error rate and expected deviation rate are the same—simply to be conservative. This results in a larger sample size, all other things being equal. Note that the conclusion expressed in Figure 15-3 projects, with a stated confidence level and precision, the auditor's opinion as to the number of exceptions contained in the entire population. Since the number of exceptions likely to be contained in the entire population is within tolerable limits, the auditor was satisfied. However, the results were still reported orally to management who, on learning of the results, took enforcement action. This situation points to one of the principal advantages of statistical sampling over nonstatistical sampling: The ability to provide highly reliable information about an entire population often motivates management to action. Had nonsta-

AUDIT SAMPLING

FIG. 15-1

Specimen Workpaper Evidencing Sample Size Determination

	KAR Division Procurement Testing	Initials	Date
		Prepared By TV	11/10/XX

Objective: Test compliance with competitive bid procedures.

Attributes tested: Evidence of competitive bid
Documentation of sole source justification
Cost Analysis
Approval

Source: Files of completed purchase transactions.

Size of population: Scan of purchase order logs indicates 4,000 purchases during the January – September period averaging 425/mo. No peaks or fluctuations noted.

Tolerable error rate: 10% on the basis that some buyers are extremely knowledgeable of sources of supply, and where the best deals can be made. As a result competitive bids may be waived on their judgment — without documenting the reasons.

Expected deviation rate: 10%

Confidence Level: 95%, to be conservative

Precision: ± 5%

Sample size required: 134

15-24 TECHNICAL ASPECTS OF AUDITING

FIG. 15-2

Specimen Workpaper Evidencing Sample Tests Performed

		Prepared By	Initials: TV	Date: 11/6/xx

KAR Division
Procurement Testing

No.	Date	Vendor	Purchase Order No.	Bid Sheet	Sole Source	Cost Analysis	Approval	Method of Selection:
1	1/21/xx	Jackson Instrument	92410	✓			✓	Random numbers table. Note: random numbers were selected from 4 digit tables, since the 9 is constant. Selected random numbers in sequence but discarded those below 92,388 and above 96,741. Ascending to the PO. i.e. PO #92,388 was the first written in January and #96,741 was the last written in September, which is our selected test period. Once the numbers were selected, they were arranged in ascending order to facilitate the test.
2	1/21/xx	Albertson Steel	92454	✓			✓	
3	1/10/xx	Franklin Supply	92471	✓			✓	
4	1/10/xx	Tate Inc.	92531	✓			✓	
5	1/12/xx	LYT Corp.	92565	✓			✓	
6	1/13/xx	Bryan Electric	92580	NA	✓	✓	✓	
7	1/12/xx	Nelson Equip. Co.	92612	✓			✓	
8	1/16/xx	NCT Corp.	92634	NA			✓	
9	1/21/xx	Albertson Steel	92688	✓			✓	
10	1/21/xx	Allied Mechanical	92701	✓			✓	Comment re: Attributes
11	1/22/xx	Bridges & Martin	92712	𝓃	𝓃	𝓃	𝓃	
...								
123	9/4/xx	Beamer's Mfg.	95916	✓			✓	This test considers that a purchase transaction evidenced by sole source justification and cost analysis of the sole source is equivalent to competitive bidding. Therefore, exceptions, for purpose of this test, are those for which there was no bid sheet present in the file and no evidence of sole source and cost justification analysis.
124	9/7/xx	Russell Supply	95978	NA			✓	
125	9/7/xx	Kelly Rigging Co.	95992	∅	∅	∅	✓	
126	9/7/xx	Thomas Int'l	96034	✓			✓	
127	9/8/xx	Evans Electric	96116	✓			✓	
128	9/9/xx	Toledo Plumbing	96201	✓			✓	
130	9/12/xx	Wendi Oil Int'l	96218	✓			✓	
131	9/13/xx	O.K. Repair	96307	✓			✓	
132	9/15/xx	Albertson Steel	96416	✓			✓	
133	9/18/xx	National Engineering Co.	96461	✓			✓	
134	9/21/xx	Atm Corp.	96518	✓			✓	
134	9/22/xx	Brown-Warner	96676	✓			✓	

Legend
✓ Attribute verified
NA Not applicable. Note: bid sheets are not present when decision is made to go sole source
∅ Exception. See w/p H-6 for resolution

FIG. 15-3
Specimen Workpaper Evidencing Analysis of Results

KAR Division
Procurement Testing

Prepared By: TC Date: 11/22/XX

Analysis of Results and Conclusions

Our tests resulted in identifying 7 transactions in which there was no evidence of any competitive bidding or compensating techniques such as price testing analysis or a record of negotiations. In three other instances, we noted sole source justification, documentation, and approval but no cost analysis was evident. We did not consider these to be exceptions to the primary attribute. Further tests of cost analysis at a later date appear to be warranted. Based upon our sample results and by reference to appropriate tables the redefined precision for the entire population at a 95% confidence level is 2.1%, to 10.1%. Accordingly the true # of errors is between 42 and 404 with a 95% confidence level. We believe this is a tolerable rate, given the fact that buyers' transactions were all approved and based upon the consideration that the absence of documentary evidence does not necessarily mean that competitive bidding did not occur or that the best price did not result.

Action

Reported the results to G. Torres, Purchasing Manager, who indicated some concern that the rate should be lower. He plans to hold a meeting with his buyers to emphasize competitive bidding and the proper documentation of it. No further action seems warranted at this time.

tistical sampling been used, the results could not have been similarly quantified and would not likely have been communicated to management in the same way. Although the auditor might have concluded that action was necessary, based on a nonstatistical sample and other factors, the chances of that happening are probably not high.

Note also that before he drew any conclusions, the auditor redefined the precision limits for the entire population based on the sample results. This is an important step in evaluating statistical sampling results that is often overlooked. Tables for this purpose have been published by the IIA, among others.

STATISTICAL SAMPLING METHODS

Two principal methods have gained wide acceptance among audit practitioners—attribute sampling and variables sampling. Each is described here in detail in terms of applicability and methodology. An illustration of attribute sampling—probably the most common statistical sampling method applied by internal auditors—is also presented. The reader is cautioned that this section is intended to be descriptive without being exhaustive. Individuals interested in developing sufficient skills to apply statistical sampling techniques must obtain training specifically designed for that purpose. Training is available from most accredited colleges and universities, from professional organizations such as the AICPA, and from some of the large public accounting firms.

Attribute Sampling

Attribute sampling, also known as frequency estimating sampling, is the technique to estimate the rate of occurrence of a given control or set of related controls (the attributes). For example, one attribute that might be tested might be approval of employee payroll time cards.

Applicability. This technique is more widely practiced by internal auditors than is variable sampling because it is, in essence, a device to measure compliance. The attributes or controls that must be tested are determined in much the same way as for nonstatistical sampling. The controls that must be tested are those that relate to the auditor's objectives. Examples of frequently tested attributes are shown in Figure 15-4 for payroll and procurement functions.

Note that the attributes shown do not comprise all of the attributes that might be employed to achieve the objectives stated. Other attributes involved do not necessarily leave audit trails, which are required to permit

AUDIT SAMPLING

FIG. 15-4

Frequently Tested Attributes—Payroll and Procurement Functions

Objectives	Attributes Tested
PAYROLL	
1. Changes to employee records (rate of pay, classification, etc.) should be authorized.	■ Use of proper form ■ Use of proper rate ■ Proper approval ■ Evidence of posting
2. Amounts due to employees should be accurately and completely calculated.	■ Use of proper form (e.g., time sheets) ■ Accurate completion of form ■ Signature of employee ■ Signature of supervisor ■ Evidence of timekeeper audit ■ Use of correct pay rates ■ Use of correct withholding rates ■ Evidence of error detection and correction
3. Payments to employees should be prepared accurately, authorized, and recorded.	■ Use of prenumbered checks ■ Posting of checks to payroll register ■ Use of designated check signatories ■ Evidence of error detection and correction
PROCUREMENT	
1. Only authorized items, quantities, terms, prices, and vendors are used.	■ Agreement with bill of materials ■ Agreement with authorized requisition ■ Agreement with authorized vendor files ■ Use of proper purchase order form ■ Agreement of price with catalog or other authorized source
2. Ordered items and services are timely received and reported.	■ Use or proper form (receiving report) ■ Evidence of proper inspection (i.e., checking of goods, reference to specifications, etc.) ■ Posting to receiving records ■ Evidence of handling of deviations
3. Amounts due to vendors are accurately and timely processed and recorded.	■ Evidence of matching of terms on invoice with receiving documents and purchase orders ■ Evidence of verification of invoice prices, extensions, and footings ■ Evidence of disposition of exceptions ■ Evidence of prompt recording

statistical sampling techniques. Examples of attributes not susceptible to statistical sampling include the following:

- Safeguards over blank check stock
- Operation of validity checks, limit tests, and run-to-run balancing controls
- Reconciliations
- Batch balancing
- Restrictions over access to confidential records (such as vendor files or employee earnings records)

Proper functioning of these and many other controls can only be done in a nonsampling manner through inquiry, observation, and confirmation procedures. These techniques are discussed in Chapter 16.

Methodology. Once the attributes to be tested are selected, the auditor must determine the sample size for each. The sample size is the same if all factors to be considered are equal, as they often are. However, it may be necessary to select different sample sizes because the factors are different. The factors to be considered are the reliability desired (confidence level), the precision interval desired, the expected deviation rate, and the expected tolerable error rate.

Invariably, auditors select 90 or 95 percent confidence levels to achieve a high degree of confidence. Also, the precision interval is usually between ± 1 percent and ± 5 percent. Unless the auditor has some basis for doing otherwise, it is often a good idea to set the expected deviation rate equal to the tolerable error rate. A lower rate would result in a smaller sample. Such a determination may be justified, however, based on past experience or as a result of discussions with knowledgeable management. Once all of the factors are determined, the sample size can be found by reference to a table, such as the one shown in Figure 15-5.[13]

Illustration. To illustrate, assume that an auditor is testing procurement procedures for the year. He is particularly interested in testing the use of competitive bidding procedures. Through preliminary work, he has learned that the purchasing department's policy is to follow competitive practices in all instances unless directed by a customer to purchase from a particular supplier. Occasionally, other factors, such as rush orders or lack of qualified bidders, may require sole source selection. In these instances, the reasons for the sole source selection are documented and approved. From discussions with management, it is determined that instances in which sole source

---

[13] Henry P. Hill, Joseph L. Roth, and Herbert Arkin, *Sampling in Auditing* (New York: Printed and published by Robert E. Krieger Publishing Co., 1979, from the original 1962 edition by arrangement with John Wiley & Sons, New York), Table 5. Copyright © 1979 by John Wiley & Sons, Inc. Reprinted with permission.

AUDIT SAMPLING

FIG. 15-5
Attribute Sampling Table

SAMPLE SIZES FOR SAMPLING ATTRIBUTES FOR RANDOM SAMPLES ONLY

Expected Rate of Occurrence not over 10% Confidence Level 95%

Number of Items in Field	Sample Size for Reliability of:				
	±1%	±2%	±3%	±4%	±5%
200				104	82
300				126	95
400			196	140	103
500			217	151	108
1,000		464	277	178	121
1,500		548	306	189	127
2,000		603	322	195	129
2,500		642	333	199	131
3,000		671	340	201	132
3,500	1739	693	346	203	133
4,000	1854	711	350	205	134
4,500	1955	725	354	206	134
5,000	2044	737	357	207	135
6,000	2193	755	361	208	135
7,000	2314	769	364	210	136
8,000	2413	780	366	210	136
9,000	2497	788	368	211	136
10,000	2568	795	370	211	136
15,000	2809	817	374	213	137
20,000	2947	828	377	214	137
25,000	3036	835	378	214	137
50,000	3233	849	381	215	138
100,000	3341	857	383	216	138

Expected Rate of Occurrence not over 10% Confidence Level 99%

Number of Items in Field	Sample Size for Reliability of:					
	±1%	±2%	±3%	±4%	±5%	±10%
200						46
300					133	50
400				193	150	52
500				214	162	53
1,000			399	272	193	56
1,500			460	299	206	57
2,000		855	498	315	213	58
2,500		935	525	325	218	59
3,000		997	544	332	221	59
3,500		1047	558	337	224	59
4,000		1087	569	341	225	59
4,500		1121	578	345	227	59
5,000		1150	586	347	228	59
6,000	2993	1196	598	351	230	59
7,000	3223	1231	606	354	231	59
8,000	3420	1258	613	357	232	59
9,000	3590	1281	618	358	233	59
10,000	3739	1299	622	360	233	59
15,000	4272	1358	635	364	235	59
20,000	4599	1389	642	366	236	60
25,000	4821	1409	646	368	237	60
50,000	5332	1450	655	371	238	60
100,000	5636	1471	659	372	238	60

procurement occurs without proper documentation would be fewer than 5 in 100. The purchase department writes about 100 purchase orders per week.

In assessing these circumstances, the auditor might conclude that competitive bidding is important to assure the lowest prices over the long run. Also, the arm's-length objectives of the transaction controls are reinforced through this technique. Hence, compliance is important. At the same time, he has been told that the purchasing department experiences extreme work load peaks from time to time caused by fluctuating production volumes, although no such peaks were experienced during the period of interest to the auditor. Moreover, the auditor has reasoned that the lack of competitive bidding from time to time does not necessarily mean that the resultant terms are not optimum. Experienced buyers, familiar with their suppliers, often know where to find the best price without resorting to competitive bid practices—a waste of time when the procurement backlog is high. Under the circumstances, he might conclude that a reasonable deviation rate might be 10 percent, double the rate management asserts is the actual rate. If the auditor desires a confidence level of 95 percent and a precision interval of ±5%, the required sample size can be found by use of a table similar to Figure 15-5.

To determine the sample, he first annualizes (remember, he is testing bidding activities for the full year) the number of transactions as 5,200 (100 purchase orders per week × 52). By reading down the first column to the line where the number of items in the field is 5,000 and then by reading across to the ±5% column, the tentative sample size in the table is 135. Since the actual population is 5,200, a slight interpolation is necessary. The next line indicates that even for a population of 6,000, the same sample size would be selected. Hence, the sample required to be tested to provide a 95 percent confidence level that the actual number of deviations is within the range of 494–546 is still 135. If the results of the test indicate fewer than 14 deviations (10.5% × 135), the inference is statistically valid. If the deviations are more than 14, further inquiry is in order and, possibly, additional testing. A reportable finding is evident to which a recommended solution would have to be developed.

Had we wished to use the expected error rate of 5 percent, suggested by management, our sample size would have been smaller. That is because the distribution of errors in the population under that assumption is much closer to the ideal standard of zero errors. The laws of statistics operate to produce a smaller sample in such circumstances because, when the distribution of the characteristics of the population is in a relatively narrow band, a smaller sample will generate the desired reliability. Thus, had we used 5 percent and a 95 percent confidence level, our sample would have been 111.

Variables Sampling

Variables sampling, also known as dollar estimation or mean estimation sampling, may be defined in simple terms as the technique used to estimate

AUDIT SAMPLING

the dollar value or some other unit of measure, such as weight, of a population from a sample portion of it. With variables sampling, it is also possible, when desired, to estimate the dollar value of errors contained in a given population. This variation is often referred to as differences estimation.

Applicability. Variables sampling may be of greater utility to external auditors in examining financial statements than it may be to internal auditors. The most frequent example cited is using the technique to develop an estimated value of inventory from a sample of items. This can be used as a reasonableness check against the recorded value of inventory.

For internal auditors, the method may be useful in estimating the dollar impact of errors. The following examples illustrate situations in which the dollar value of error conditions could be extremely informative:

- Lost revenue resulting from pricing errors
- Increased cost from failure to use materials on hand before changing requirements
- Dollar value of procurements made without competitive bidding
- Estimated dollar volume of procurements made from blanket purchase orders
- Estimated value of account distribution errors in recording expenses
- Estimated amount of lost discounts due to slow payment
- Estimated amount of unapproved or improperly documented expense report reimbursements
- The length of time required to accept delivered items
- The length of time required to pay vendors

As can be seen from the last two examples, variables sampling may be used to develop reliable estimates for values other than dollars.

Methodology. The following excerpt from *Sampling in Auditing* is a succinct description of variables sampling methodology.[14]

> Just as it is necessary in attributes sampling to estimate in advance the frequency of occurrence, so in variables sampling it is necessary to have some kind of estimate of the variability (standard deviation) of the values in the field to be sampled. One of the methods to obtain this variability estimate is to make a random sample of about 50 items from the field to be sampled. The preliminary sample values are then separated into groups of 6 or 7 values. These items must be grouped in the order or occurrence of their original random sequence. If the random numbers used have been arranged in sequence to facilitate locating the sample items, they must be returned to their original random sequence before grouping.
>
> The range (difference between highest and lowest value) is obtained for each group of 6 or 7 items and these ranges are averaged for all groups. The resulting

---

[14] *Ibid.*, pp. 32–34. Reprinted with permission of John Wiley & Sons, Inc.

average range may then be divided by the d_2 factor in Table 3 [Figure 15-6][15] to obtain the measure of variability (standard deviation). This value is then used in conjunction with Table 4 [Figure 15-7] in order to estimate the required sample size.

Table 4 [Figure 15-7][16] indicates, for a given field size and confidence level, the sample size estimated to be needed to achieve a given precision. To make the tables more flexible, the precision is expressed as a proportion of the estimated standard deviation.

To estimate the sample size required for a given sample reliability at a given confidence level in estimating an average value (or total value if multiplied by the number of items in the field), Tables 3 [Figure 15-6] and 4 [Figure 15-7] may be used. The following steps are required:

1. Decide on the sampling reliability or precision required per item, on the average ($\pm\$1.00$, $\pm\$10.00$, $\pm\$100.00$, etc.).
2. Select a confidence level (risk) which the auditor is willing to take (95%, 99%, or 99.9% if these tables are used).
3. Determine the field size (number of values or entries from which the sample is to be drawn).

Given the above, the estimated sample size can be determined as follows:

a. Obtain a preliminary random sample of about 50 items. The preliminary sample may be the first part of the ultimate sample to be used. Additional items may be sampled and added to the preliminary sample to secure the final sample, if later found necessary by these computations.

b. Group these items into groups of 6 or 7 items each, according to the order in which they occurred in the table of random numbers and secure the range of the values for each group (difference between largest and smallest).

c. Secure the averages of these ranges.

d. Using Table 3, obtain the appropriate d_2 factor. Divide the average range by this d_2 factor to obtain an estimate of the standard deviation.

e. Using Table 4 for the given field size and confidence level, the sample size can be estimated by determining the proportion of the standard deviation which will give the desired reliability. On the line with that proportion, the appropriate sample size is given.

For instance, let it be assumed that it is desired to check the total value of a group of inventory items numbering 5,000 to determine the reasonableness of the book value of these items which is stated as $4,256,821.68, by using a sample and estimating that total value.

An estimate with an accuracy of about $\pm 5\%$ of the true total value or about $\pm\$200,000$ is assumed to be sufficiently accurate for the purpose and a 95% confidence level is to be used. This means that the average value per item must be established to within $\pm\$40.00$ ($200,000 divided by 5,000).

A preliminary random sample of the balances of 48 accounts is secured.

---

[15] *Ibid.* Reprinted with permission of John Wiley & Sons, Inc.
[16] *Ibid.* Reprinted with permission of John Wiley & Sons, Inc.

AUDIT SAMPLING

FIG. 15-6

Factors for Estimating Standard Deviation

$$\text{Estimated Standard Deviation} = \frac{\text{Average Range}}{d_2 \text{ Factor}}$$

Group Size	d_2 Factor
5	2.326
6	2.534
7	2.704
8	2.847

Assume the following results when arranged in random groups of 6 each:

$1,233.42	$ 193.96	$ 790.91	$ 441.82
385.20	315.99	1,677.53	1,096.58
884.53	1,301.43	1,118.19	506.04
1,467.48	858.52	846.12	492.03
646.47	1,149.00	1,191.81	627.27
522.84	1,062.17	1,088.18	995.76
$ 264.00	$ 955.75	$1,108.58	$ 356.00
331.99	1,019.76	264.77	1,887.99
1,257.82	0	404.01	1,096.98
1,220.61	1,024.96	1,120.59	418.01
1,290.63	1,052.17	734.49	685.25
926.54	1,046.17	1,306.64	953.75

The ranges (differences between highest and smallest value) for these groups of 6 values are:

$1,082.28	$1,107.47	$ 886.62	$ 654.76
1,026.63	1,052.17	1,041.87	1,531.99

The average of these eight ranges is $1,047.97. Reference is now made to Table 3 where the factor for group size 6 is found to be 2.534. The average range ($1,047.97) is divided by this factor (2.534) to yield an estimate of the population standard deviation of $413.56.

The precision required here is ±$40.00. Dividing this desired precision (±$40.00) by the above estimate of the standard deviation, $413.56, the result obtained is .097.

Reference may now be had to Table 4, which is entered for field size 5,000. In the column "ratio of sampling error to standard deviation," the value .097 (in this case, use .10, the nearest value) is located. In the column headed 95% confidence level on that row, the required sample size is found to be 357.

It may then be estimated that, for this inventory, a random sample of 357 out of the 5,000 items will give an estimate of the true average value of the 357 items sampled to within $40.00 per item, and for the total value of all accounts, to within ±$200,000.00 (or $40.00 × 5,000) with 95% confidence level.

FIG. 15-7

Variables Sampling Table

Ratio of Sampling Error to Standard Deviation (Sampling Error/Standard Deviation)	Sample Size Required With Confidence Levels of:		
	95%	99%	99.9%
Field Size is 500			
.10	217	—	—
.15	127	186	246
.20	81	125	176
.25	55	88	129
.30	39	65	97
Field Size is 1000			
.10	278	399	—
.15	146	228	326
.20	88	143	314
.25	58	96	148
.30	41	69	108
Field Size is 2000			
.05	869	—	—
.10	322	499	705
.15	157	258	390
.20	92	154	240
.25	60	101	160
.30	42	72	114
Field Size is 3000			
.05	1016	1409	—
.10	341	544	799
.15	162	269	417
.20	93	158	250
.25	60	103	165
.30	42	72	116
Field Size is 4000			
.04	1500	—	—
.05	1110	1596	—
.10	351	570	856
.15	164	275	432
.20	94	160	255
.25	61	104	167
.30	42	73	117
Field Size is 5000			
.03	2303	—	—
.04	1622	2267	—
.05	1175	1734	2328
.10	357	586	894
.15	165	279	441
.20	94	161	258
.25	61	104	168
.30	42	73	118

SAMPLE SIZES FOR ESTIMATING AVERAGE VALUES FOR RANDOM SAMPLES ONLY

AUDIT SAMPLING   15-35

The preliminary sample of 48 is included as part of the sample taken, thus requiring 309 additional sample values.

The average value of the items in the sample is multiplied by the total number of accounts in the field (5,000) to secure the total value.

It should be evident from the foregoing that variables sampling, while useful, can require a fair amount of time and effort to complete. The auditor should be certain that its use will be of value in meeting the audit objectives before applying it.

Other Sampling Techniques

Other sampling techniques that, in reality, are variations of attribute and variables sampling are available for use by auditors, including discovery sampling, stop-and-go sampling, and combined attribute variables sampling. These will not be described in detail because their applicability to internal auditing objectives is considerably less than the techniques already described.

Discovery Sampling

This sampling technique is used when the auditor wishes to find at least one exception or deviation in a given population with a minimum of searching. Here too, the auditor must have in mind the confidence level (reliability) and the precision that he believes are warranted. Discovery sampling, also called exploratory sampling, is useful in the following situations:

- To check out an assertion by management that a given procedure is always performed, such as approval of personnel requisitions.
- As a tentative initial test to be expanded if an exception is actually encountered. This variation is often referred to as stop-and-go sampling.
- In other situations where the presence of at least one exception would be of interest or possibly suggesting misconduct or employee dishonesty. Examples include searches for unauthorized (1) pay rate changes, (2) payments to vendors and others, (3) changes to employee earnings records, and (4) changes to customer records.

Combined Attribute Variables Sampling

In the combined attribute variables sampling, the monetary unit becomes the sampling unit. This relatively new technique is also known as dollar unit sampling or monetary unit sampling. Since the sample is randomly selected from a population of dollars, large value transactions get more chances of being selected.[17] Auditors are often more interested in examining transactions with proportionately large dollar values. This is particularly true in the following situations:

- Examination of invoices for additions to property, plant, and equipment, or other major procurement items
- Selection of accounts receivable for confirmation purposes
- Performance of pricing tests of inventory

STATISTICAL SAMPLING SOFTWARE

Using sampling techniques to gather evidential matter attracts the attention of computer software developers and thus continues to be central to achieving internal auditing objectives. Simple, easy-to-use software packages could produce considerable benefits for their owners because such software would greatly facilitate applying statistical sampling concepts. Many generalized audit software packages (for a listing, see Chapter 28) have long offered statistical sampling options. In addition, microcomputer programs exist that perform statistical sampling routines.

Internal auditors, however, rarely use these tools. According to one source, the reason is that internal auditors often have problems in developing appropriate auditing objectives. Also, information systems auditors usually are not familiar with the technicalities of statistical sampling. Auditors do not always have the opportunity to interact with mainframes to develop their proficiency to the level necessary to be effective in using statistical sampling software. Finally, PC statistical sampling software is either too simplified or too complicated.[18]

One statistical sampling program is available that is easy to use and runs on an IBM PC.[19] The product is called AUDITSTAT, by DKC Inc.

AUDITSTAT is a menu-driven program requiring little training. The steps to operate the program include the same methodology as discussed earlier. Displays include:

- Total number of sample
- Population size and population value
- Total ledger value and total audit value
- Ratio of audit to ledger value
- Ratio of standard deviation

---

[17] Coopers & Lybrand, *Mathematical Techniques: A Guide for Auditors and Management* (New York: Coopers & Lybrand, 1981), p. 15.

[18] Editor, "Statistical Sampling Software—Part 1," *Internal Auditing Alert*, Nov. 1985, p. 3.

[19] *Ibid.*

- Correlation coefficient
- Precision percentage
- Degree of precision value
- Lower and upper dollar limits

The displays may be printed as well. Auditors may draw conclusions from the displays or printouts. Other available information includes average values, standard error, and coefficient of variations percentage. AUDIT-STAT is available through DKC Inc., 425 Farnsworth Dr., Broomall, Pa., 19008, (215) 356-8347. The cost is in the $1,000 range.

CONCLUSION

This chapter has discussed in detail the techniques applicable to the two forms of sampling—nonstatistical and statistical. They are used when it is desired to examine less than 100 percent of a given population of items when the auditor wishes to use the sample results to project to the entire population. Sampling is usually involved in inspection and confirmation, two of the principal techniques used by auditors in gathering evidential matter. Inspection and confirmation as well as the other principal techniques, observation and inquiry, are discussed in Chapter 16.

SUGGESTED READING

Arens, Alvin A., and James K. Loebbecke. *Applications of Statistical Sampling to Auditing*, Chapters 3–5, 9. Englewood Cliffs, N.J.: Prentice-Hall, 1981.

Kell, Walter G., and Richard E. Ziegler. *Modern Auditing*, Chapters 7 and 11. New York: Warren, Gorham & Lamont, 1980.

Rittenberg, Larry Eugene, and Bradley J. Schweiger. "Use of Statistical Sampling Tools—Parts I and II." *The Internal Auditor*, Aug. 1978, pp. 27–44.

Ritts, Blaine A., and Timothy L. Ross. "How Well Do Internal Auditors Know and Use Statistical Sampling?" *The Internal Auditor*, Feb. 1981, pp. 27–34.

Sampling for Modern Auditors, A Personal Study Course. Orlando, Florida: The Institute of Internal Auditors, 1975.

Statistical Sampling Subcommittee. "Audit Sampling," *Audit and Accounting Guide*. New York: AICPA, 1983.

Sullivan, Jerry D., Richard A. Gnospelius, Philip L. Defliese, and Henry R. Jaenicke. *Montgomery's Auditing*, 10th ed., Chapters 12 and 13. Copyright © 1985 by Coopers & Lybrand (United States), published by John Wiley & Sons, Inc.

CHAPTER **16**

Auditing Procedures

Objective and Definition 2	Specific Forms of Inspection 25
	Reading 25
Observation 2	Scanning 26
Specific Forms of Observation	Reviewing 26
Procedures 3	Vouching 26
Techniques 3	Techniques 27
Planning 3	Planning and Preparation 27
Determining Sampling Method 4	Determining Sampling Method 27
Performing the Work 4	Performing the Work 27
Documentation 5	Documentation 29
Applicability to Specific Audit	Applicability to Specific Audit
Approaches 5	Approaches 29
Detailed Internal Control Audits 5	
Internal Control Surveys 6	**Confirmation** 29
Limited Financial Reviews 6	Specific Forms of Confirmation
Standards of Ethical Business	Procedures 30
Conduct 6	Confirming 30
Operational and I/S Audits 6	Reperforming 31
	Reconciling 31
Inquiry 7	Techniques 32
Specific Forms of Inquiry 7	Documentation 32
Interviewing 8	Applicability to Specific Audit
Researching 8	Approaches 35
Analyzing 10	
Special Types of Analytical	**Cost-Benefit Analysis** 35
Procedures 11	Definition and Background 35
Techniques 19	Applicability 36
Documentation 19	Techniques 36
Applicability to Specific Audit	Documentation 39
Approaches 24	A Special Application 39
Inspection 24	**Suggested Reading** 40

Fig. 16-1	Portion of an Audit Program for Observing Physical Inventory Counts	4
Fig. 16-2	How to Conduct an Interview	9
Fig. 16-3	Common Financial Ratios	12
Fig. 16-4	A Typical Trend Analysis	15
Fig. 16-5	An Example of a Linear Regression Analysis	17
Fig. 16-6	Forms of Regression Analysis	18
Fig. 16-7	Example of a Narrative of an Interview	20
Fig. 16-8	A Method of Evidencing Analytical Work	21
Fig. 16-9	Flow Chart With Objectives, Controls, and Evaluation Identified	22
Fig. 16-10	Example of a Workpaper Documenting Inspection	28

Fig. 16-11 Documentation of a Review of Reconciliations 33
Fig. 16-12 Documentation of Reperformance 34
Fig. 16-13 Table of Exposure Values 38

OBJECTIVE AND DEFINITION

This chapter provides an understanding of the various procedures used to gather the evidential matter that is required by professional auditing standards. The applicability of these procedures to internal control audits, internal control surveys, limited financial reviews, standards of ethical business conduct, and operational and EDP or information systems (I/S) audits is also presented. Finally, cost-benefit analysis is discussed, not only as an aid in recommending courses of action to management, but also as a means to help decide the nature and extent of audit procedures to be employed.

Auditing procedures have been defined as the acts performed by the auditor to obtain corroborating information.[1] Numerous terms to describe auditing procedures have gained common usage. Among these are vouching, validating, reperforming, confirming, analyzing, and tracing. However, GAAS provides only four basic techniques:

1. Observation
2. Inquiry
3. Inspection
4. Confirmation

To be consistent with GAAS, the auditing procedures in this chapter are discussed in terms of these four basic techniques. The reader is advised that the many terms that have gained common usage among practitioners have considerable overlap in their definitions and applicability. Terms such as audit, review, and examine, for example, mean more or less the same thing. Similarly, analyze, inspect, observe, confirm, vouch, verify, validate, and substantiate have meanings that are somewhat similar. The overlapping and interrelated definitions of the terms used to describe audit procedures should be kept in mind throughout the chapter.

OBSERVATION

Observation may be defined as the body of techniques by which the auditor gathers evidence through what he sees or observes. Observation techniques are designed to obtain evidence in a real time, present-tense environment

---

[1] Walter G. Kell and Richard E. Ziegler, *Modern Auditing* (Boston: Warren, Gorham & Lamont, 1980), p. 81.

AUDITING PROCEDURES

to corroborate or substantiate management assertions or other data that the internal auditor intends to use or rely on. Although it is rarely mentioned, observations includes not only seeing what is happening but also hearing it.

Specific Forms of Observation Procedures

Observation procedures are often used by internal auditors when other types of procedures cannot be employed. This is usually because evidential matter corroborating the assertions does not exist. The only way to corroborate in these circumstances is to observe the actual occurrence. Controls that are verified in this manner include supervisory controls, segregation of duties, and controls that restrict access and otherwise offer safeguards.

Sometimes, observation provides the most effective and efficient means to obtain evidence. For example, there is usually abundant evidence to verify the physical existence of inventory. However, direct observation is usually thought to be the best of the available procedures. Audit programs of internal auditors whose companies have significant investments in inventory usually include procedures for observing physical counts similar to that illustrated in Figure 16-1.

Observation procedures are also used by internal auditors along with inquiry to gain an understanding about the entity or function under audit. The plant tour is an example of gaining an understanding by observation.

Another frequently employed procedure by internal auditors and government auditors is the floor check. These are performed when it is desired to test the reporting of labor hours on which labor cost distribution to final cost objectives is based. Floor checks involve checking current reported labor hours by visiting the areas where the reporting employees are working to see if the projects in which they appear to be involved correspond to the subsequent reports of their time spent.

Techniques

The techniques for effective observation of audit procedures are essentially the same, regardless of the specific type of observation being performed. The following paragraphs briefly discuss such techniques.

Planning. Most observations require careful preparation and coordination if their results are to be useful. This is true particularly when conducting physical inventory observations, floor checks, and plant tours. On the other hand, observations of security procedures and supervisory controls are usually performed in an impromptu and somewhat continuous fashion while fieldwork is being performed.

Matters to be considered in planning include (1) the length of time required to conduct the observation, (2) the number of persons required to be

FIG. 16-1

Portion of an Audit Program for Observing Physical Inventory Counts

	Performed by	Date
1. Obtain written instructions for count. Determine that a method exists for distinguishing items counted from those not counted (e.g., tagging or marking).	....	....
2. Tour facility to become familiar with count locations and to ascertain that arrangement of stock will facilitate accurate counting.	....	....
3. Observe count teams performing their assigned count routines for compliance with instructions.	....	....
4. Perform and record independent counts of randomly selected items for comparison with results of count teams and for later tracing.	....	....
5. Tour facility at completion noting that all items bear evidence of having been counted.	....	....

involved, (3) the timing of the work, and (4) the assignments and duties of those involved.

Determining Sampling Method. Observation techniques are not amenable to the concept of sampling, which is defined in SAS No. 39 (see Chapter 15). The auditor would find it difficult to determine a population size or identify a sampling unit or apply the randomness principle. On the other hand, the auditor cannot perform observation techniques on a 100 percent basis. For example, it is impracticable for the auditor to determine by observation that duties were, in fact, segregated in accordance with established procedures. To do so would require that the auditor be present on the scene constantly.

Performing the Work. Observation auditing procedures are relatively straightforward. They involve watching or witnessing the specific activities in which the auditor is interested. All that is required is to be alert and attentive. The auditor must be aware of what he expects to be seeing and must make quick decisions as to whether what is actually happening squares with his expectations (i.e., the required procedures).

Observation procedures work best when those being observed are not aware of what the auditor is looking for. However, sometimes it is necessary to disclose objectives in order to arrange the observance. For example, during floor checks it may be necessary for the auditor to reveal his identity

AUDITING PROCEDURES

to the supervisor or foreman and to make specific inquiry of employees being scrutinized. Thus alerted, unscrupulous employees and supervisors could conceivably alter their conduct during the course of the test, and thereby mislead the auditor. The auditor must realize the potential for real time tests to be unrepresentative of actual practices and must devise means to limit or minimize the adverse consequences that can occur. Repeated observations, unannounced observations, and the results of other tests, taken together, are often sufficient to reduce the risk to acceptable levels.

Documentation

Workpapers evidencing observation consist primarily of written narratives prepared by the performing auditor. These narratives explain what the objectives are, identify the specific procedures used, and state what was actually observed. Relevant discussions of follow-up investigations to resolve exceptions should also be included. If conclusions are evident, they should be carefully stated in view of all pertinent factual information presented.

Some observations are effectively evidenced and preserved in photographs. Photographs are especially useful in documenting damaged or unsalable merchandise, messy storage and arrangement of inventory items, lax physical safeguards, such as unattended guard stations, and unlocked gates to areas of restricted access.

Copies of documentation obtained from the entity's management or from other sources may also be retained. These include items such as diagrams of plant layouts (for use in plant tours and security checks), organization charts, and applicable written procedures.

Applicability to Specific Audit Approaches

Chapter 2 outlines an audit coverage that includes detailed internal control audits, internal control surveys, reviews of standards of ethical business conduct, operational auditing, and I/S auditing. The auditor's use of observation procedures in connection with each of these is briefly discussed in the following paragraphs.

Detailed Internal Control Audits. Detailed internal control audits involve extensive compliance testing by internal auditors. In connection with these compliance tests, observation procedures are used to generate evidence attesting to the existence of disciplinary controls for which there is no preexisting documentary evidence. Controls falling into this category include the following:

- Segregation of duties such as authorization, execution, processing, and recording of transactions.

- Segregation of other duties, including custody of assets and critical forms, such as negotiable instruments, from executory or accounting responsibilities.
- Supervisory controls that help to assure suitable ongoing performance of routine procedures. Examples include actions of supervisory and managerial personnel and built-in limit checks and edit routines for error detection and correction.

Documentation in working papers usually consists of brief statements on flow charts or narratives of work performed. An example of a narrative is shown later in this chapter in Figure 16-7.

Internal Control Surveys. Because internal control surveys are broader based than detailed internal control audits, the extent of testing is necessarily more limited. The same types of control techniques observed in detail in internal control reviews are also observed in surveys. If anything, these observation procedures are more important in surveys because of the minimal use of other forms of detailed testing.

Limited Financial Reviews. This type of auditing involves little or no observation procedures. The objective of the audit—to ascertain consistency in financial reporting between interim and year-end periods—can be achieved by applying other audit procedures, as shown later in this chapter.

Some internal auditors may modify this type of audit to include verification of physical assets, such as equipment and inventory. This might be done, for example, in companies having several branch office or multiple plant locations with centralized accounting and financial reporting. Observations would be an important audit procedure in those cases.

Standards of Ethical Business Conduct. Audits of this type typically do not require observations. Like limited financial reviews, the evidence needed is gathered through other auditing procedures.

Operational and I/S Audits. Operational and EDP audits usually include observations as an important part of the overall audit plan. That is because these audits involve compliance testing to a large extent, similar to internal control audits. The following is a list of operational and EDP activities that are susceptible to observation:

1. Operational
   - Cycle count activities performed by cycle count teams
   - Competitive bidding procedures performed by buyers (e.g., witnessing bid openings)
   - Field payroll distributions
   - Stores inventory stocking and issuing procedures

- Scrap sales procedures
- Dispositions of depreciated property
- Cash handling and sales recording procedures by retail sales clerks (applicable to department store chains, supermarket chains, hotels and casinos, and restaurants)

2. I/S
- Segregation of programming and operating personnel
- Rerun procedures
- Recovery or restart procedures after shutdown
- Hardware and software conversions
- Program testing by applications programmers
- Tests of safety equipment performed by EDP personnel (e.g., fire extinguishers and halon systems)

These are only a few suggestions. Observations can be made of many other operational routines and EDP as seen fit by the auditor in the circumstances.

INQUIRY

Though inquiry is identified in professional literature as one of the basic audit techniques, it is not specifically defined. This may be attributable to the fact that the term's meaning is self-evident. Inquiry involves those efforts to obtain information relevant to the auditor's purpose. Inquiry entails seeking answers and gaining insight into matters to enable the auditor to continue and, ultimately, to complete the audit project.

The sampling concepts outlined in Chapter 15 are generally not applicable to inquiry. The auditor's understanding that is gained through inquiry must be complete and total. The auditor must exercise professional judgment in deciding when sufficient knowledge has been gained. Generally speaking, the information obtained through inquiry must be corroborated through performing one or more of the other basic audit procedures (i.e., observation, confirmation, or inspection). Internal auditors also use inquiry techniques to corroborate information obtained from other sources. In practice, the various forms of inquiry, taken together, are used more extensively than all other audit procedures. It is critical, therefore, that performing auditors understand and master the subtle skills required.

Specific Forms of Inquiry

The principal method of obtaining information is the interview. Every audit project has at least one interview, but most require several to gain the necessary insight. There are other forms of inquiry that are also frequently used.

These include research, analysis, and review. The objectives and techniques of each are discussed in the following paragraphs.

Interviewing. Performed properly, interviews not only provide the auditor with needed information, but also establish the auditor as an attentive, competent professional in the minds of those being interviewed.

How to conduct successful interviews is a topic for which many seminars and conferences have been devised by various professional organizations and private enterprises. Internal auditors who feel the need to enhance their ability to conduct interviews should consider seeking the assistance offered by these courses. Others may find the techniques outlined in Figure 16-2 will provide all the assistance needed.

Interviews are normally performed near the beginning of the fieldwork. That is because it is the information thus obtained that must be audited. In order to audit the data, it is first necessary to know and understand it. In nonrecurring audits, such as some types of operational and I/S audits and special reviews, the interview is of even greater importance than it is in recurring audits. That is because in recurring projects, the auditor often has more information available to him from other sources (see Chapter 11).

Information obtained in an interview may be corroborated through inspection, confirmation and observation. It may also be corroborated through independent interviews with other knowledgeable personnel. When interviews are intended to corroborate previously obtained information, the auditor must be satisfied that all inconsistencies are resolved. Resolution may require other forms of corroboration.

Researching. Research is included here as a subtopic of inquiry. Others may prefer to think of research as a step in planning the work which, of course, it often is. It is discussed in this chapter as an auditing procedure because, like inquiry, the objective of research is to obtain information. Among the many topics for which research can provide benefits are:

1. Pervasive topics
    - Accounting principles and methods
    - Audit procedures
    - Internal controls
    - Rules and regulations
    - Company policies
    - General statistical data
2. Company-related topics
    - Policies and procedures
    - Accounting policies and methods
    - Internal control practices as evidenced by flow charts and other documentation

AUDITING PROCEDURES

FIG. 16-2

How to Conduct an Interview

---

1. Have clearly established objectives in mind before conducting the interview. In other words, know what it is that you need to find out.

2. Arrange for the interview to occur at a mutually convenient time, and tell the interviewee what you are interested in accomplishing. It will permit him to be better prepared.

3. Ask questions in a logical, rational pattern that will allow the information to be disclosed in a more easily understood fashion.

4. Give the interviewee feedback. Tell him what you think he told you. This will allow him to correct any misunderstandings.

5. Jot down key points for future reference and for use in preparing workpapers evidencing the interview.

6. Allow the interviewee to tell his story in his own way to the extent practicable. Some digression should be expected; however, the auditor must not allow valuable time to be wasted on irrelevant discussions. Keep the interview on track.

7. Listen carefully. Be alert for terms or phrases whose meaning is unclear. It is normal for people to talk in language that they know. If you are unfamiliar with the jargon, don't be afraid to admit it honestly and obtain clarification.

8. Be sure that you have achieved your objectives before ending the interview. If you have not achieved your objectives and if time will not permit continuing, state what is needed and arrange for a second session.

9. Document only the assertions and statements relevant to the objectives. Rambling narratives of every utterance raise questions about the auditor's ability to decide what is important.

- Information systems
- Prior-year audit workpapers
- Internal financial reports

In recurring projects, much of the research can be done as part of the preliminary work, as discussed in Chapter 11. However, the fact that the auditor is in the field does not preclude performing research if circumstances require it. In nonrecurring projects, the areas in which research is needed may not be apparent until the actual fieldwork commences.

Research should be considered whenever the auditor is in a situation of uncertainty. This may occur when deciding on which auditing procedures to apply, when evaluating the propriety of a particular method of accounting, when appraising the sufficiency of internal controls in particular circumstances, or when attempting to recommend remedial courses of action. A reasonable search of appropriate sources (see Chapter 11) usually provides information to help the auditor make up his mind with greater certainty.

Analyzing. Related to research are the techniques of analysis. Analysis, or analytical reviews as the term is used by public accountants, has a specific meaning.

In professional literature, analytical procedures are defined as tests of relationships among data that the auditor may reasonably expect to exist and continue in the absence of known conditions to the contrary.[2] Lack of these relationships provides evidential matter that may indicate the need for additional procedures, while strongly consistent relationships may indicate that the extent of other auditing procedures can be reduced.

Analytical reviews are categorized here as a form of inquiry because, in a sense, the auditor is inquiring into relationships. Analytical reviews are used as part of the substantive testing procedures used by public accountants in examinations of financial statements. Internal auditors who do not normally examine financial statements may nevertheless apply analytical procedures in many ways for a variety of other purposes, as follows:

- To isolate unusual relationships that might warrant further investigation
- To provide information that might lead to potential savings as, for example, in searching for excessive freight charges through comparative analysis
- To reveal errors in accounting as would be disclosed, for instance, by account analysis or by limited reviews of comparative financial statements
- To help appraise management effectiveness, as would result from analyzing records of production for comparable periods
- To obtain insight into fluctuations that may be of interest to the auditor and others, such as increases in the use of consultants or commission agents

Analysis, as the foregoing implies, involves an inquiry into a particular matter of interest by comparing relative data and understanding the causes for differences. The most common technique usually entails comparisons of the information of the current period with similar data from comparable prior periods of the same source, or with data from similar sources for the same period. Comparisons with prescribed standards or plans may also be performed. For example, the auditor may determine the average cost to prepare purchase orders for a given period with the planned or standard cost, or

---

[2] Statement on Auditing Standards No. 23, *Analytical Review Procedures* (Oct. 1978) (AICPA, *Professional Standards*, Vol. 1). AU § 318.03. At the time this chapter was written, the ASB had just voted to issue a proposed revision to SAS No. 23. The revision defines analytical procedures as consisting of evaluations of financial information made by a study of plausible relationships among both financial and nonfinancial data. The revision notes that analytical procedures range from simple comparisons to complex models. It continues the premise in the definition in the earlier SAS No. 23 that the plausible relationships among data may reasonably be expected to exist and continue to exist in the absence of known conditions to the contrary.

AUDITING PROCEDURES

with the comparable prior-period cost. Or, he may compare the cost of preparing purchase orders in one purchasing department with that of another department or with an industry standard.

Special Types of Analytical Procedures. Several types of analytical procedures are experiencing increased usage among auditors. Their growing appeal is attributable in no small part to the emergence of various computerized time-sharing programs now available. These programs automate the sometimes complex mathematical calculations otherwise required. These procedures include financial ratio analysis, trend analysis, regression analysis, and multiple regression analysis. They are used not only for the purpose of providing insight as mentioned earlier, but also for their predictive value (i.e., their ability to predict future results).

☐ *Financial ratio analysis.* This procedure expresses the relationship of two components of financial data by simply dividing one by the other. Versions of some of these ratios have gained widely recognized names, such as current ratio, quick ratio, and return on equity. Figure 16-3 contains a listing of these, states how they are calculated, and tells what they indicate.[3]

These ratios are most informative when they are compared with industry standards, prior years' ratios and planned ratios. Auditors may find value in financial ratio analysis anytime, but its value is particularly useful during the preliminary stages of an audit project (see Chapter 11) when the objective is to get as thorough an understanding of the organizational unit as possible. Needless to say, ratios and changes in comparative ratios are indicators, at best, and should be used only to supplement other audit procedures.

Trend analysis. Trend analysis, also called time-series analysis, is a technique that compares the results of some function, activity, or object for regular equal intervals of time. The comparison is usually expressed geographically, as illustrated in Figure 16-4, primarily to influence the focus of other audit procedures and to permit inferences to be drawn about likely future results. Almost any series of results can be compared in this fashion. Typical trend analysis involves the ratios described in the preceding discussion. Thus, a graphic presentation of current ratios, inventory turnover, or the ratio of net income to sales, for the past six months, past four quarters, or past five years could be developed. Of course, the components comprising the ratios could be similarly analyzed. Sales, cost of sales, net income, receivables, and long-term debt are often reviewed in a similar fashion. Operational data may be analyzed by trend also. Examples include trends in burden rates, production efficiency, capacity utilization, rework time, maintenance and repair costs, and sales returns.

(continued on page 16-15)

---

[3] Coopers & Lybrand, *Mathematical Techniques: A Guide for Auditors and Management* (U.S.A.: Coopers & Lybrand, 1981), pp. 23–24. Copyright © 1981 by Coopers & Lybrand, the international accounting firm, and reprinted with their permission.

FIG. 16-3
Common Financial Ratios

I. RATIOS INDICATING CURRENT POSITION

Description	Calculation	Indication
1. Current	$\dfrac{\text{Current assets}}{\text{Current liabilities}}$	Ability to meet current obligations from current assets as a going concern
2. Quick	$\dfrac{\text{"Liquid" assets + inventory}}{\text{Current liabilities}}$	Ability to meet sudden demands upon current assets
3. Receivables		
a. Receivables turnover	$\dfrac{\text{Net credit sales}}{\text{Net average receivables}}$	Efficiency of collection
b. Average collection period	$\dfrac{365 \text{ days}}{\text{Receivables turnover}}$	Average number of days to collect receivables
c. Days' receivables uncollected	$\dfrac{\text{Ending receivables} \times 365 \text{ days}}{\text{Net credit sales}}$	Number of days' sales uncollected
4. Inventory		
a. Merchandise turnover (retail)	$\dfrac{\text{Cost of goods sold}}{\text{Average merchandise inventory}}$	Effectiveness of inventory management
b. Finished goods turnover (manufacturing)	$\dfrac{\text{Cost of goods sold}}{\text{Average finished goods inventory}}$	

AUDITING PROCEDURES

c. Days' supply in ending inventory	$\dfrac{\text{Ending inventory} \times 365 \text{ days}}{\text{Cost of goods sold}}$	Number of days' supply in the ending inventory; may indicate over- or under-stocking
5. Working capital turnover	$\dfrac{\text{Net sales}}{\text{Average working capital}}$	Adequacy of and changes in working capital level

II. RATIOS INDICATING EQUITY POSITIONS

1. Owners' equity to total assets	$\dfrac{\text{Owners' equity (total net worth)}}{\text{Total assets (net of depreciation)}}$	Proportion of assets provided by owners; reflects financial strength and cushion for creditors
2. Creditors' equity to total assets	$\dfrac{\text{Total liabilities}}{\text{Total assets (net of depreciation)}}$	Proportion of assets provided by creditors and extent of "trading on the equity"
3. Long-term debt ratio	$\dfrac{\text{Long-term debt}}{\text{Long-term debt} + \text{owners' equity}}$	Percentage of total capitalization represented by long-term debt reflects degree of debt leverage being employed
4. Return on common stock equity	$\dfrac{\text{Net income} - \text{preferred dividends}}{\text{Common shareholders' equity}}$	Return on resources provided by common shareholders
5. Sales to owners' equity	$\dfrac{\text{Sales (net)}}{\text{Owners' equity}}$	Utilization of owner capital
6. Fixed assets to owners' equity	$\dfrac{\text{Fixed assets (net)}}{\text{Owners' equity}}$	Extent of capital invested in fixed assets

(continued)

FIG. 16-3 *(cont'd)*

Description	Calculation	Indication
7. Sales to fixed assets (plant turnover)	$\dfrac{\text{Sales (net)}}{\text{Fixed assets (net)}}$	Management's efficiency in using plant properties

III. RATIOS INDICATING INCOME POSITION AND OPERATING RESULTS

Description	Calculation	Indication
1. Net income to net sales	$\dfrac{\text{Net income}}{\text{Net sales}}$	Net productivity of each dollar of net sales
2. Income before taxes to total assets	$\dfrac{\text{Income before taxes}}{\text{Total assets}}$	Management's effectiveness in using available resources
3. Gross margin ratio	$\dfrac{\text{Gross profit (margin)}}{\text{Net sales}}$	Portion of net sales remaining after cost of sales expenses
4. Return on assets (based on Du Pont concept)	$\underbrace{\dfrac{\text{Operating income before interest and taxes}}{\text{Sales}}}_{\text{(Profitability)}} \times \underbrace{\dfrac{\text{Sales}}{\text{Total assets}}}_{\text{(Asset turnover)}}$	Overall measure of management's performance
5. Income before interest and taxes to interest expense	$\dfrac{\text{Income before interest and taxes}}{\text{Annual interest expense}}$	Ability to meet interest charges
6. Cash flow to current portion of debt	$\dfrac{\text{Net income + depreciation, depletion, and amortization}}{\text{Current portion of debt}}$	Ability to retire current portion of debt

AUDITING PROCEDURES

FIG. 16-4

A Typical Trend Analysis

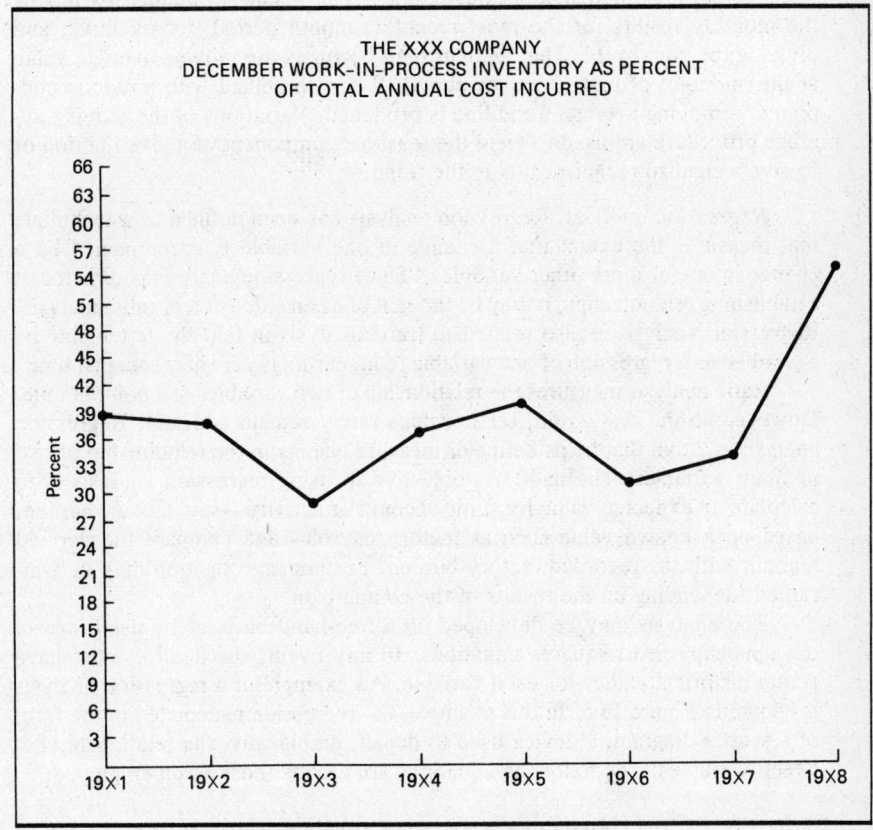

In performing trend analysis, the auditor must consider these segments:

- Long-term trends
- Cyclical changes
- Seasonal variations
- Random fluctuations

If the auditor is confident of the reliability of the trend, he may attempt, by extrapolation, to determine what the component may look like in future periods. At least two techniques are avoidable for this: the comparatively simple free-hand method and the more complicated least-squares method.

In the free-hand method, the auditor simply extends the line or curve in the manner that appears to him to be consistent with the past trend. In the least-squares method, mathematical formulas are used to derive the line or curve that minimizes the square of the differences between the actual values of data given and the values that would have been forecasted using the prediction equation.

Other predictive techniques include the moving-average method, which uses an averaging procedure (e.g., 12-month moving average) to minimize the effect of seasonal and random fluctuations. The result is obtained by adding the monthly results for the most recent 12-month period, for example, and dividing the sum by 12. That amount then becomes the moving-average value at the midpoint of that 12-month period. When combined with previous midpoints, a moving-average trend line is produced. Variations of the moving-average procedure are used to yield the seasonal component of a given period or to give weight to recent results in the trend.

Regression analysis. Regression analysis has been defined as a technique that measures the extent that a change in one variable is accompanied by a change in one or more other variables.[4] Since regression analysis is directed at establishing relationships, it may be thought of as an extension of ratio analysis. Regression analysis is also related to trend analysis in that the latter may be described as a regression of one variable (e.g., earnings per share) against time.

Ratio analysis measures the relationship of two variables at a point in time. However, in the real world, relationships rarely remain constant. Regression analysis is a tool that helps define or measure change in the relationship of two or more variables. The auditor's objective in using regression analysis is to calculate an expected value for some account or activity—say, factory burden, based on a known value such as factory payroll—and compare the derived amount with the recorded factory burden. Further investigation may be warranted, depending on the results of the comparison.

The analysis may be developed on a free-hand basis or by using one of the applicable least-squares equations. In any event, the auditor must have actual historical values for each variable. An example of a regression analysis is shown in Figure 16-5. In this example, the regression is depicted in the form of a scatter diagram, a device used to depict, graphically, the relationship between variables. The following equations are among those often employed:

$$\text{Straight line through the origin: } Y = BX$$
$$\text{General straight line: } Y = A + BX$$
$$\text{Quadratic function: } Y = A + BX + CX^2$$
$$\text{Power function: } Y = AX^x$$
$$\text{Exponential function: } Y = AB^x$$

where:

Y = Dependent variable
X = Independent variable
A = Y value at the point where the line or curve intersects the Y axis
B = Slope of the line or curve

---

[4] Lawrence B. Sawyer, *The Practice of Modern Auditing* (Altamonte Springs, Fla.: The Institute of Internal Auditors, 1981), p. 328.

FIG. 16-5

An Example of a Linear Regression Analysis

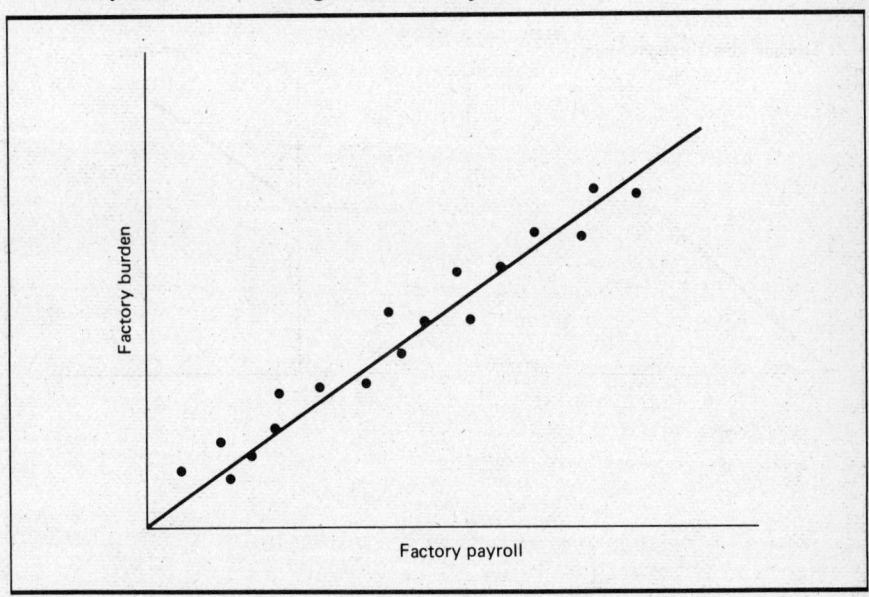

These various equations are illustrated graphically in Figure 16-6. Other equations are used for multiple regression analysis. However, those who are not adept at solving algebraic equations should seek assistance or use time-sharing or proprietary computer programs designed to make the calculations.

The number of situations in which regression analysis may be used are numerous. Here are a few examples:

1. Simple regression relationships
   - ☐ Dependent variable:
     - Sales commissions
     - Sales
     - Bad debts
     - Productivity
     - Worker's Compensation Insurance
     - Factory burden
     - Rework
     - Pilferage
     - Repairs and maintenance
     - Warranty cost
   - ☐ Independent variable:
     - Sales
     - Age of product
     - Credit sales
     - Investment in plant and equipment
     - Gross payroll
     - Size of plant
     - Production volume
     - Plant security cost
     - Age of facility
     - Quality control

FIG. 16-6
Forms of Regression Analysis

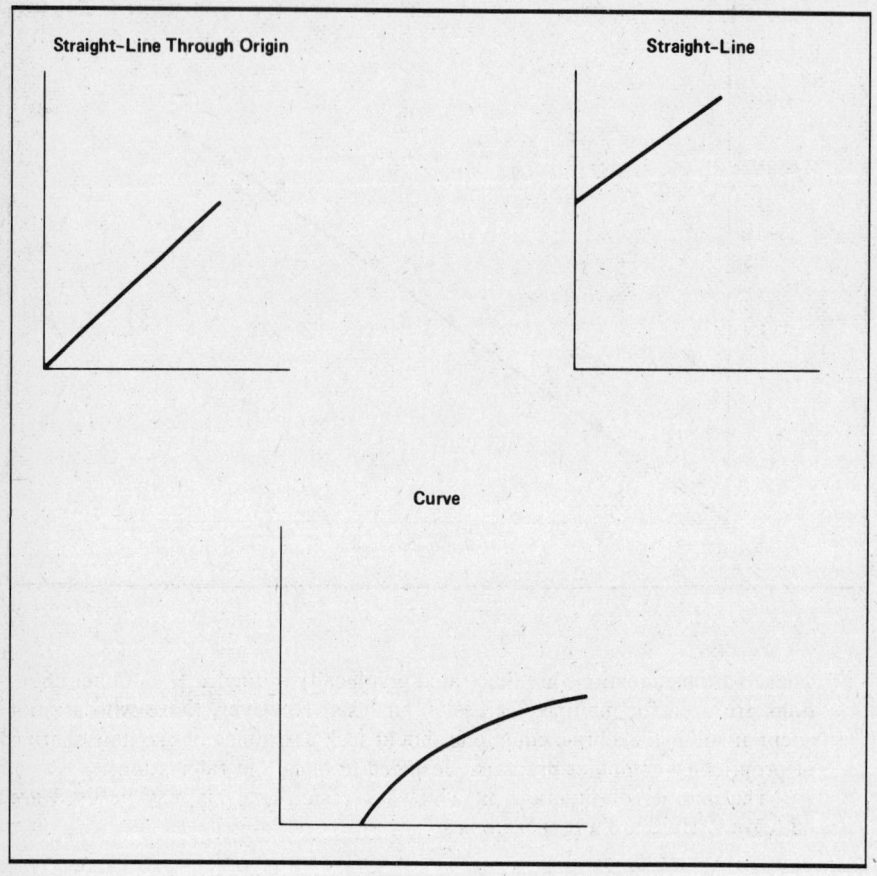

2. Multiple regression relationships
   - ☐ Dependent variable:
     - Investment in inventory
     - Transportation cost
     - Energy cost
     - Standard cost variance
   - ☐ Independent variable:
     - Production/sales
     - Number of vehicles; mean-distance traveled
     - Unit prices; consumption
     - Volume variance
     - Rate variance

Other techniques are available for determining the strength of variable relationships and for building models but are beyond the scope of this book.

The results of fitting different regression relationships to variable data must be assessed to determine which linear or curved relationship best ap-

AUDITING PROCEDURES 16-19

plies. The result that best fits the circumstances should appear to be reasonable in the context of the existing data. An improper fit increases the likelihood of drawing invalid conclusions. Properly applied, however, regression analysis can be a useful technique.

Techniques

The techniques for inquiry have been identified for the most part. However, there are a few general points to be made.

In view of the importance of internal controls, it is a good idea to formalize inquiry procedures by devising written questionnaires or checklists. (See Chapter 8.) These may serve as the basis for arranging and conducting interviews. Alternatively, they may be furnished to the appropriate auditee personnel for completion and subsequent review by the auditor.

While all forms of inquiry offer the best results when properly planned, the dynamics of the audit environment do not always afford such luxury. Much inquiry occurs in a spur-of-the-moment, reactive fashion. Good auditors learn to be quick on their feet and to be flexible and adaptive to fast-changing circumstances and perceptions.

To the foregoing must be added a word of caution. The ease and flexibility of inquiry can lead the auditor to rely on it excessively, without sufficient corroboration. Inquiry usually produces information that must be evaluated and, if necessary, corroborated either by further inquiry or by some other audit procedure.

The rapid movement in recent years toward on-line interactive information systems makes the analytical techniques described in this section virtually assured of an enlarged future role in the scope of internal auditing. Many internal auditors, even now, have available in their companies high-level query languages and programs aimed at aiding the analytical effort. These, coupled with large, detailed data bases, offer a vast opportunity for exploring relationships more fruitfully.

Documentation

Methods for documenting inquiry techniques include preparing narratives such as discussed in connection with techniques for interviewing earlier in this chapter. An example of such documentation is shown in Figure 16-7. A method for evidencing analytical work is shown in Figure 16-8, a simple columnar listing of the historical data obtained for the analysis illustrated in Figure 16-4. A unique method for documenting internal controls is flow charting. (See Chapter 17.) Many company managements have developed flow charts of internal controls as part of their responsibility for maintaining

(continued on page 16-24)

FIG. 16-7

Example of a Narrative of an Interview

WCR Division Interview with Chief Financial Officer	Prepared By	Initials WBT	Date 5/10/xx

Met with L.B. Smith, chief financial officer of WCR, to obtain an explanation of the causes for the substantial increase in inventory noted on W/P B-10. The following points are noteworthy:

- Ordering system in use up until January has not been based upon sound material requirements planning. Action has been taken in Jan-Mar time period to install a net requirements system whereby orders now consider on-hand and on-order items.

- Engineering change orders were often executed without considering the impact of the changes on existing quantities. For February, a new procedure now requires this impact to be shown in an attachment to the E.O. before it is approved.

- Several procurement decisions were made to buy excess quantities to take advantage of favorable prices.

- A portion of the increase is attributable to higher-than-expected demand for WCR's new Beta-B model, which required WCR to increase inventory levels.

To corroborate the above, test procedures were devised and performed as set forth in w/p C-1 through C-50. The results of this work are summarized in w/p A-15.

AUDITING PROCEDURES

FIG. 16-8
A Method of Evidencing Analytical Work

Exhibit

Worksheet to relate Cost incurred to inventory, analyze changes in operating margin, and compare year-end receivables to December sales for years shown.

The XXX Company

Prepared By: MV Date: 1-6-82

	19X1	19X2	19X3	19X4	19X5	19X6	19X7	19X8
I. Total Annual Cost Incurred	50376	56808	71172	58020	56064	78180	72696	50136
A. December Work-In-Process Inventory (WIP)	19616	21437	20854	21383	22666	24327	24930	27585
B. WIP as % of Annual Cost Incurred	38.9%	37.7%	29.3%	36.9%	40.4%	31.1%	34.3%	55.0%
	8-Year Average							
II. Total Annual Sales	55011	57552	45240	78096	52704	45696	67776	73404	19620
A. Total Annual Operating Margin	6227	5100	4884	7140	5064	5040	7920	11640	3024
B. Operating Margin as % of Sales	11.3196	8.8616	10.7958	9.1426	9.6084	11.0294	11.6856	15.8574	15.4128
C. Sales Increase (Decrease) From Average		2541	(9771)	23085	(2307)	(9315)	12765	18393	(3539)
D. Margin Change From 8-Year Average:									
* 1. Increase (Decrease) From Sales Volume		288	(1106)	2613	(261)	(1054)	1445	2082	(4006)
** 2. Increase (Decrease) From Rate Change		(1415)	(237)	(1700)	(902)	(133)	248	3331	803
Total		(1127)	(1343)	913	(1163)	(1187)	1693	5413	(3203)
III. Accounts Receivable At December	5070	6346	4611	4193	4718	4835	5361	6140	4326
A. Month of December Sales	4584	4796	3770	6508	4392	3808	5648	6117	1635
B. Accounts Receivable as % of Sales	110.6%	132.3%	122.3%	64.4%	108.1%	127.0%	94.9%	100.4%	264.6%

* Change in Sales Volume X 8-Year Average Margin Rate
** Change in Margin Rates X Total Annual Sales

FIG. 16-9
Flow Chart With Objectives, Controls, and Evaluation Identified

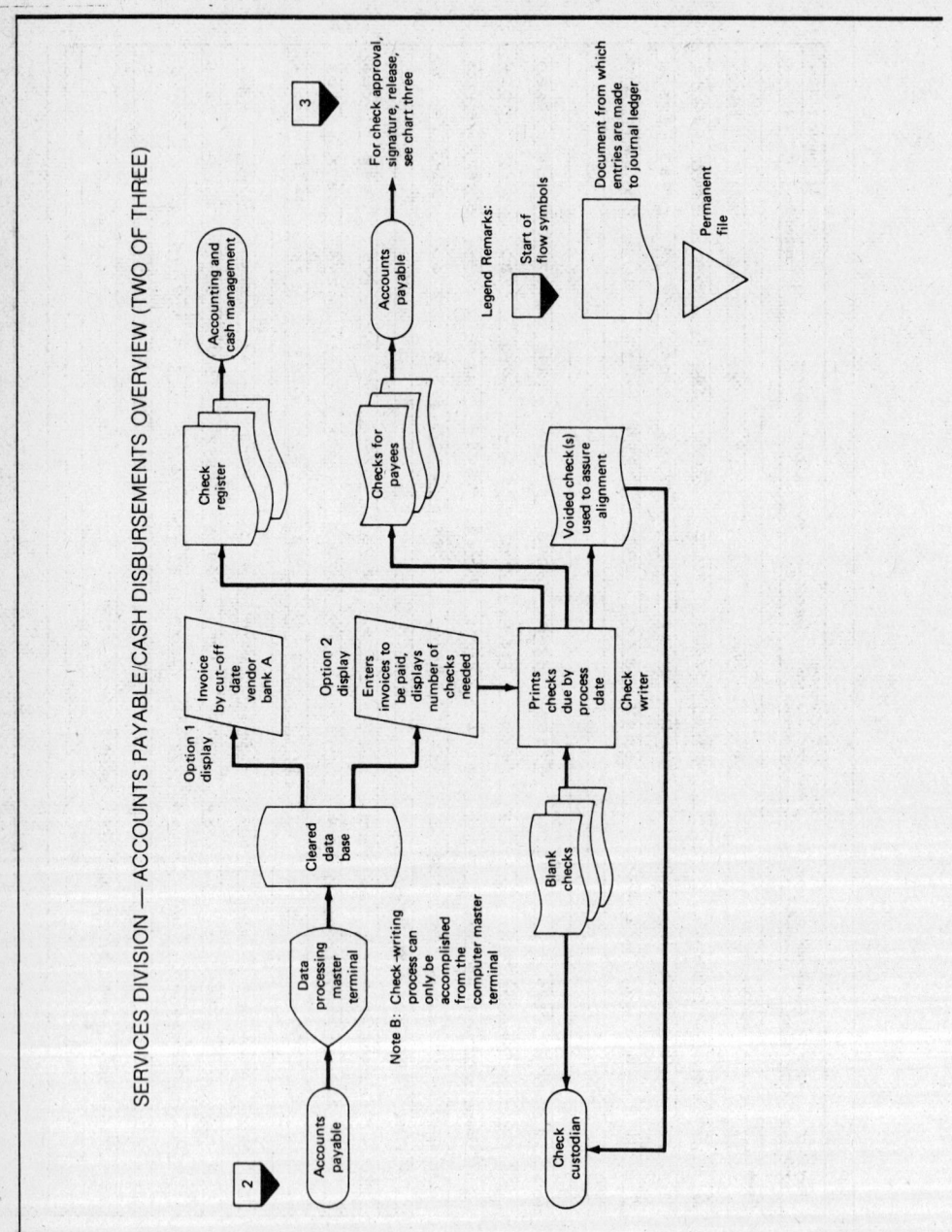

AUDITING PROCEDURES

CONTROL OBJECTIVES:

1. Recorded transactions are valid
2. Transactions are properly authorized
3. Existing transactions are recorded
4. Transactions are properly valued
5. Transactions are properly classified
6. Transactions are recorded at the proper time

CONTROL TECHNIQUES USED:

Objective 1 — New check stock is received, logged, and stored in secured area by finance personnel who are independent of accounts payable, cashier, and general accounting (latter reconciles bank accounts).

Objectives 1 and 2 — Cashier, who is independent of A/C payable, maintains signature plate, affixes signature after checks have been written by accounts payable, and mails checks.

Objectives 1, 2, 3, 4, 5, and 6 — A/C payable compares flimsy check copy with the payable documentation to determine accuracy of payment and approves release of checks to vendors by the cashier, after review and approval by accounting and cash management.

Objectives 1, 2, 3, and 5 — All checks written or voided are accounted for by finance personnel not associated with A/C payable or the cashier. Cashier maintains a log of checks signed and this is compared with log of checks issued, and inventory on hand at least monthly by general accounting personnel when reconciling the bank accounts, thus assuring that only authorized transactions have been recorded.

Objective 6 — Checks are written on computer indicated due dates.

EVALUATION OF CONTROL PROCEDURES:

	Risk		
	L	M	H
Objectives 1 and 2. Techniques used insure that there is adequate separation of duties in authorizing, approving, and processing the transactions.			X
Objective 3. Techniques in use assure that existing transactions are properly handled.			X
Objective 4. Procedures in use assure that a transaction processed and approved is properly valued.			X
Objective 5. Procedures in use provide reasonable assurance that transactions are properly classified.			X
Objective 6. Techniques used provide reasonable assurance that transactions are timely recorded.			X

adequate internal control. Copies of pertinent flow charts should be obtained for the auditor's permanent files. Some flow charts include documentation of control objectives and an evaluation as well. Figure 16-9 is an example of such documentation.

When flow charts do not exist, the auditor must consider preparing them. Preparation is time-consuming and will extend the time required to complete the audit project. If the project is an initial audit, likely to recur, flow charting may save time in the long run and would therefore be worth the effort. On the other hand, if the audit is nonrecurring, the effort required to flow chart controls may be a waste of time.

Applicability to Specific Audit Approaches

The use of inquiry techniques occurs in all types of audits. Interview and research techniques tend to be important in detailed internal control audits and in internal control surveys. That is because these audits are heavily dependent on gaining an understanding of the controls in which the auditor is interested. Interviews and research are also an integral part of operational and I/S auditing for much the same reason.

Analytical techniques are used extensively in limited financial reviews. Financial statement categories are compared with year-end audited amounts for balance sheet items and with comparable prior-period amounts for income statements. The fluctuations disclosed by these comparisons must make sense when account interrelationships are considered.

Analytical techniques are also employed in connection with operational audits. In addition to examples cited earlier in this chapter, such techniques, when combined with statistical sampling, may be used to:

- Determine the average length of time (in days) between receipt of cash and deposit.
- Estimate the average amount of disbursements by check and by cash.
- Determine the frequency with which petty cash accounts are replenished.
- Estimate the value of delinquent accounts receivable (if aging is not available).
- Estimate the dollar value of slow-moving, possibly obsolete, inventory.
- Ascertain the average age of accounts payable.

Analytical reviews can also be performed for management I/S functions. Analysis of abends, reruns, unauthorized attempts to access data, frequency of head crashes, and emergency program changes are but a few examples.

INSPECTION

Inspection is another basic auditing procedure identified by GAAS. Like inquiry, supporting authoritative literature does not provide a precise definition for the term. In most books, it is described in ways that relate it very closely to the term "observation."

It is true that both involve seeing what is actually occurring. For instance, one can observe a physical inventory count and one can inspect physical inventory. Perhaps the difference is that in observing, the auditor is merely seeing if what is occurring corresponds to what he expects to see. Inspection, while indeed similar, seems to imply more of a systematic search. It presupposes that specific information, objects, or activities that he wishes to see exist or might exist.

In audits of financial statements, CPAs use physical inspection procedures as part of their substantive testing to verify the existence of assets such as cash, marketable securities, and inventory. Internal auditors use inspection in connection with their examination of records and underlying data to corroborate the assertions and representations of management regarding internal control. Internal auditors also use forms of inspection for other purposes, such as to find evidence, if it exists, of errors, irregularities, and improper conduct.

Specific Forms of Inspection

Since inspection is only one of four auditing procedures required by GAAS, it follows that other procedures that have gained common recognition by auditors must fit into one (or more) of the basic four. It is believed that such procedures as reading, scanning, reviewing, and vouching are performed for purposes that are similar to those intended for inspection. Therefore, these procedures are discussed as forms of inspection.

Reading. Over the years, auditors have retained some of their early image as individuals who add columns and columns of numbers. In reality, as every practitioner knows, a significant amount of time is spent reading verbiage—not totaling numbers. In a typical audit project, an internal auditor may be required to read:

- Relevant external literature, such as applicable accounting principles, rules, regulations and interpretations, and case studies.
- Company policy statements and applicable procedural manuals.
- Previous internal audit reports.
- Prior-year workpapers.
- Contracts, management reports, miscellaneous memorandums, and other applicable internally generated documentation.

The truth of the matter is that on a comparative basis, less time is spent analyzing numbers than in reading verbiage. The extent of the material to be read in any particular circumstance must be judged by the auditor in light of those circumstances. The concept of sampling is not relevant here.

Much of the reading is done during the preliminary phase while researching and planning the scope of the work. Even so, it is not practicable for the auditor to read everything that may possibly contain relevant information; there are simply too many sources and too much volume of written data. However, through selective inspection, the auditor can usually focus his reading on that portion of the information most likely to be of value to him.

Scanning. This is a technique that is widely used to enable more information to be exposed to the auditor's eye than would be the case by systematic reading or analysis. Scanning requires that the auditor have in mind some idea of the characteristics of the item or items he is interested in finding. In most scanning efforts, the auditor is looking for out of the ordinary items or exceptions. In this situation, the auditor must have a clear idea of what ordinary is or what compliance is.

Scanning is highly dependent on the attentiveness of the auditor and on his ability to recognize what he is scanning for when it comes to his attention.

Reviewing. The term "reviewing" has been used in auditing literature and in practice in so many ways that it has come to be synonymous with virtually all audit procedures. If there is a unique auditing procedure applicable to the term, it would probably describe general audit efforts by performing auditors.

In most audit projects, if a facility or an activity or a record of some type is reviewed, it means that a more precise audit procedure was not performed unless otherwise specified. This might occur, for example, in reviewing expense reports for reasonableness, in reviewing account distributions for propriety, or in reviewing purchasing records for completeness. In the absence of more specific auditing procedures, reviews are performed primarily to establish the presence or absence of rather obvious, significant weaknesses, errors, and other deviations. Simple reviews have their merit when time is extremely limited. Conducting overseas audits may be one example where portions of the work can only be done on a review basis.

The nature and extent of review procedures are usually determined by the internal auditor's judgment. Sampling is rarely associated with this type of procedure.

Vouching. This procedure may be defined as the act of inspecting underlying documentary evidence in support of an account balance or of some other item of information of interest to the auditor. It is the best of the corroborative auditing procedures. Perhaps, for that reason, it is widely practiced among performing auditors.

The types of evidence that may be vouched have previously been described in Chapter 13, where it was noted that some forms of evidence are more valuable in terms of reliability than others. Proper vouching requires that the auditor realize the differing values of evidence and seek that which optimizes the reliability of the evidence while minimizing the effort to get it. Sampling concepts are particularly applicable to vouching.

Techniques

The various forms of inspection are best accomplished through adequate planning and preparation, selection of the proper sampling method, and diligent performance. These are similar to the steps involved in observation, described earlier. However, inspection involves a more systematic effort and, thus, requires more emphasis in planning and preparation. Also, many inspection auditing procedures are well suited to sampling techniques. Documentation techniques are discussed in the next section.

Planning and Preparation. In order to conduct a proper program of inspection, it is necessary to gain an understanding of the underlying system of procedures, controls, and records. This is usually done through inquiry procedures and is documented either by the organizational unit or by the auditor in flow charts and narratives. The auditor may wish to cement his understanding by selecting a single transaction and following it through the system. Misunderstandings of any consequence are likely to be surfaced by this technique—often referred to as transaction testing in auditing literature.

Determining Sampling Method. Some forms of inspection may be done on a 100 percent basis. This may be the case when the total number of items is small and they are relatively easy to inspect. For example, evidence of preparation of monthly financial statements would be easy to inspect for any given year. Also, when computer-assisted inspection occurs, it is often possible to verify the application of selected control points (limit tests and edit checks, for example) for an entire period quite easily.

For the majority of inspection efforts, less than 100 percent of the items will be inspected. Since the focus of inspection frequently is records and other evidential matter, sampling can be an effective way to perform the work. (See Chapter 15.) Often though, the preparation and effort required to perform statistical sampling will outweigh the advantage of precision. Nonstatistical sampling probably should be used in those cases.

Performing the Work. As with other auditing procedures, inspection must be done diligently and with professional care. This is particularly true when evaluating the results of the inspection. All items that may be possible exceptions should be considered in light of their impact on the auditor's understanding. Discussions with management or other knowledgeable per-

FIG. 16-10

Example of a Workpaper Documenting Inspection

WCR Division
Review of Travel Cost

	Initials	Date
Prepared By	BT	2/10/0x

Objective: To test controls over travel cost.
Inspected payments to the ABC Travel Agency covering the period from January to June 19xx. Noted evidence of the following:

- Detailed statement from ABC
- Supporting invoices
- No consistent indication of receipt of tickets
  See W/P L-14
- Accounts payable voucher
- Signature or initials of various reviewing persons
- Check copy prepared by data processing
- Check copy agreed to manually prepared accounts payable vouchers (input)
- Cancellation

Noted services of agency terminated in June. See inquiry on W/P L-15 for additional work performed

No other unusual items noted.

Source of test: Voucher Register & Vendor History File

Size of sample: Virtually all payments inspected, total population = ± 40

L-13

AUDITING PROCEDURES

sons may lead to further information, which may eliminate many of the items as actual exceptions.

Documentation

Methods of documenting inspection procedures in the auditor's workpapers are many and varied. Documentation may be in the form of copies of relevant auditee records or schedules to which the auditor adds tick marks and comments evidencing his inspection routines. In other cases, the auditor may prepare original schedules and worksheets in which the particular records are identified along with an identification of the control points corroborated. An example of this latter form of documentation is shown in Figure 16-10.

Applicability to Specific Audit Approaches

Inspection audit procedures are extensively applied to detailed internal control audits, operational audits, and I/S audits. To a lesser extent, the procedures are also applied to audits of standards of ethical business conduct and internal control surveys. As a result, these latter audit types are broader based and are more dependent on observation and inquiry procedures.

Inspection is perhaps least applicable to limited financial reviews, although even in these audits, important explanations of unusual fluctuations and nonrecurring items may require corroboration through inspection of underlying records.

CONFIRMATION

Confirmation audit procedures have different meanings to different auditors. To CPAs, it is most frequently associated with efforts to obtain written concurrence of balances receivable or payable of a client at a given date. The term is also used in a general sense by CPAs and internal auditors as a synonym for compliance testing. Thus, an auditor *confirms* his understanding of internal controls by performing selected compliance tests.

Some forms of compliance testing are more logically associated with inspection and observation, as was shown earlier in this chapter. Therefore, a narrower definition is necessary here. Confirmation procedures, as used in compliance testing, are those in which corroborative evidential matter is gathered from knowledgeable sources independent from those sources from which the evidence being corroborated was originally obtained. In simpler terms, confirmation procedures mean trying to get the same story from someone else. These procedures are generally an indirect way of corroborating an understanding. Inspection or observation procedures are more direct in that they are focused either upon the actual performance or the direct evidence produced by that performance. Confirmation procedures are indirect in that the confirming evidence is supplied by a person who may have been an independent party in the activity or transaction or may have seen direct evidence of it and is, therefore, in a position to make informed representations. The evidence may also be obtained from records or data that are independent of the evidence directly produced from the activity or transaction. Often, controls operate without producing any tangible evidence. However, in most situations, there is more than one person who is in a position to provide evidence in the form of representations as to the operation of such controls.

Confirmation procedures, then, are used when it is believed that the evidence obtained will be relevant and reliable, and when obtaining it will be more efficient than other types of audit procedures.

Specific Forms of Confirmation Procedures

The overlapping of meaning and use of the several terms used in describing audit procedures creates some confusion. The actual confirmation procedures themselves entail some form of inquiry, inspection, or observation. Because the procedures are aimed at obtaining indirect evidence, they are categorized here as confirmation-type procedures. Specific forms in this category are confirming, reperforming, and reconciling.

Confirming. This procedure means to obtain through inquiry representations or assertions from persons whose knowledge enables them to corroborate facts regarding matters of interest to the auditor. The representations or assertions may be obtained orally or in writing. Of course, oral representations would be reduced to writing by the auditor for retention in the working papers. The following four examples illustrate situations in which this procedure might be used:

1. The accuracy and completeness of data processed by the company computers might be confirmed with selected users.
2. Explanations obtained from controllers for unusual fluctuations in account balances might be confirmed by operations management or some other knowledgeable, independent source.
3. Representations regarding the absence of conflicts of interest furnished by employees may be confirmed by various line managers. (Procurement, marketing, and engineering are three examples.)
4. Assigned duties and responsibilities important to be segregated may be confirmed by various department managers (e.g., treasury, accounts payable, and purchasing).

The auditor must have reason to believe that the individuals corroborating his understanding are in a position either to know, or have reason to

AUDITING PROCEDURES 16-31

know, the accuracy of that understanding. Otherwise, the credibility of the corroborations will be in doubt, and the risk of drawing invalid conclusions is increased. When testing compliance, information to be confirmed and the number of confirmations are not susceptible to statistical sampling, normally. However, confirmation procedures used to validate account balances comprised of large populations of relatively small individual balances may be sampled statistically. Confirming customer accounts receivable for a utility or an oil and gas company are examples. The extent of the testing in most other situations is dependent on the auditor's judgment.

Reperforming. Often, there is no direct evidence that a particular control operated in the circumstances. For instance, audits of vendor invoices by accounts payable personnel (verification of price, quantity, extensions, and footings) cannot be documented. In these situations, auditors frequently duplicate the task, or reperform it sufficiently to be convinced, by the absence of excessive exceptions, that the control operated. The following controls may be tested in this fashion:

- Validity checks, such as for proper employee numbers in a payroll system or signatures on authorizing forms or negotiable instruments
- Numerical sequences (e.g., check numbers, purchase order numbers, and sales invoices)
- Balancing controls, such as in preparation of financial statements
- Mathematical accuracy of subsidiary ledgers and other accounting records requiring such accuracy

Obviously, the auditor is unable to reperform everything. Hence, the concept of sampling (see Chapter 15) applies here. Reperforming also includes such commonly performed procedures as tracing and recalculating.

Reconciling. The process of identifying elements that link two independent records of the same transactions or activities is known as reconciling. This technique takes advantage of the fact that information must be maintained in a variety of ways. Accounts payable must be kept by individual vendor and in total in the general ledger, for example. The result of reconciling one to the other, if successful, provides evidence that the controls that generated each operated satisfactorily.

In many cases, the system of internal control itself requires reconciliations to be made. The auditor's task is then one of simple scanning or reviewing the resultant reconciliations, assuming that a record is made of them. Reconciling is an important and valuable technique and, accordingly, is an integral part of internal controls and auditing. A few illustrative examples are noted below:

- Accounts receivable control total reconciled to detail customer account totals

- Accounts receivable debits to customer detail accounts reconciled with the total of credit sales for a given period
- Fixed asset control total reconciled to the subsidiary asset ledger totals for cost, accumulated depreciation, and net book value
- Cash receipt totals reconciled with credit postings to customer accounts for a given period

Reconciliations are typically performed infrequently (once per month is most common). As a result, it is often easy to inspect evidence of all of them. However, if time and circumstances preclude inspecting all, then a high percentage should be examined. Statistical sampling is inappropriate.

Techniques

The steps involved in obtaining evidence by confirmation depend on the form involved. The steps previously discussed for inspection, including adequate planning and preparation, selection of a sampling method, and performance of the work, are essentially applicable to *reperforming*. The techniques outlined earlier for inquiry apply to *confirming* as well.

Reconciling requires a thorough knowledge of the underlying records and the controls used to generate them if the auditor wishes to originate the reconciliation. Usually, differences between records result from timing differences. That is, an item recorded in the first record in one period may be recorded in the second record in another period. But differences may also occur for other reasons, including errors and omissions. Finding multiple errors can be extremely time-consuming, particularly if the number of transactions is large. This fact often precludes the auditor from initiating reconciliations.

Auditors are often content to permit some small differences to go unresolved or unlocated. When this is done, the auditor should be relatively confident that the difference is not likely to be the result of two or more large, but offsetting, differences. Assistance from knowledgeable personnel can expedite the reconciliation effort.

Documentation

The auditor's working papers evidencing oral or written confirmations include either the written confirmations themselves or narratives prepared by the auditor. The narratives need only document the relevant corroborating statements. A prudent practice is to permit the individual(s) making the representations to review the write-ups to assure their accuracy.

Some form of cross-referencing between the documentation evidencing the original understanding (such as flow charts or other narrative material) and the confirming documentation is helpful. The tick mark "C" meaning

AUDITING PROCEDURES

FIG. 16-11

Documentation of a Review of Reconciliations

WCR Division 7/8x vs 12/8x Test of Bank Reconciliations					Initials	Date
				Prepared By	BW	8/8/xx

A/C #	Type of account		7/82	12/81	Change	
101-01	Depository Transfer	∅	225.1 ✓	2.3	222.8	Normal Fluctuation
02	✓ ✓ Wash D.C.	Ⓐ	N/A	—	—	
04	Disbursement a/c	∅	(940.3)	✓(582.1)	(358.2)	✓✓
05	Freight a/c		9.2	✓ 29.0	(19.0)	✓✓
06	Depository Transfer - N.Y.C.		1.9	✓ 2.0	(0.1)	✓✓
21	Executive Payroll		(19.4)	✓ 0.1	(19.5)	✓✓
22	Bi Weekly Payroll	∅	258.0	✓ 0.7	(258.7)	✓✓
			(978.3)	(545.3)	(433.0)	
	Petty Cash		3.2	2.7	0.5	
	Per Financial Statement		(978.3)	545.3	(433.0)	

✓ Agreed amount per G/L to properly reviewed/approved bank reconciliation. Noted no unusual items. Reconciliations prepared in good form.

∅ Scanned file at bank reconciliations for the period 12/x1 - 7/x2. Noted that reconciliations were prepared for each month, reviewed, and approved without exception.

Ⓐ No transactions or balance. Agreed to bank statement

Conclusion: Evidence indicates bank accounts were regularly reconciled during period as required, with no unusual items evident.

Source of Test: Reconciliation files in Controller's office

FIG. 16-12
Documentation of Reperformance

JBR Division Test of Selected Accounts Payable Controls				Initials	Date
			Prepared By	VLM	12/11/xx
Date	Invoice Identification	Match to P.O.	Match to Receiver	Verify Math	Trace Posting
1/4/xx	ABC Supply #141619	✓	✓	✓	✓
1/7	American Steel Co. #818974	✓	✓	✓	✓
1/8	United Corporation #22468	✓	✓	✓	✓
1/9	Johnson International #3742	✓	✓	✓	✓
1/12	Technitron Inc. #187223	✓	✓	✓	✓
1/13	ATV Corp. #A21642	✓	✓	✓	✓
9/16	Franklin Steel #904062	✓	✓	✓	✓
9/26	Falmouth #3328624	✓	E9	✓	✓
9/27	Jenkins Maintenance Co. #1428	✓	✓	✓	✓
9/28	Metal Fabricators, Inc. #38387	✓	✓	✓	✓
9/28	Technitron, Inc. #264119	✓	✓	✓	✓

<u>Objective</u>
To document tests performed. See w/p B-1 for basis for selection

<u>Conclusion</u>
See w/p B-15

✓ Tested attribute O.K.
E Exceptions. See w/p B-14 for resolution

B-10

AUDITING PROCEDURES

confirmed, along with any explanatory remarks and references, is a widely used technique.

Work performed in connection with reviewing reconciliations may also be documented in the form of a narrative or as a schedule, as shown in Figure 16-11. In either case, the reconciliations reviewed should be identified. Some auditors even include copies of the reconciliations. If the reconciliation is originated by the auditor, the working papers should document the work performed, the objective, and any conclusions that are evident.

Reperformance is best documented by making schedules that identify the controls being duplicated and the transactions selected for reperformance. Figure 16-12 illustrates that technique.

Applicability to Specific Audit Approaches

Inasmuch as compliance testing is associated with all audit approaches, confirmation procedures are used in all, with the following exceptions.

Limited financial reviews are primarily analytical in nature. Therefore, confirmation is only necessary when, in the judgment of the auditor, it is necessary to corroborate explanations of large variances, nonrecurring items, or significant unusual fluctuations. On the other hand, internal control surveys, again because of their more general scope, require that compliance be measured to a large extent by discussions of control points with others, including management, outside auditors, and, if present, division or subsidiary internal auditors. These discussions are designed to corroborate the understanding of the existence of the controls obtained from other sources within the entity. Often, these discussions may save considerable time and effort so that the auditor can perform the entire survey.

The information gleaned from these discussions should be supplemented by reviews of working papers or other evidential matters to be certain that there is a reasonable basis for relying on them.

Under any audit approach, the factual accuracy of the auditor's findings should be confirmed with the affected members of the management responsible for the area under audit. Even though the findings may have been discussed and confirmed in the final exit conference, it is a good practice to reconfirm the findings in their final written form before issuing the report.

COST-BENEFIT ANALYSIS

Definition and Background

The term "cost benefit" has been defined as conveying "the abstract idea that one expects to receive value for value given. 'Cost-benefit analysis' is a general term which refers to any and all techniques used to examine alternatives and chooses the one that gives the greatest return for a given expenditure."[5]

The concept of cost versus benefit is based on the notion that the resources available for any given objective are limited. For example, internal auditing is a valuable function, a fact most managements recognize. Devoting resources to that function produces the beneficial effects desired by management. However, this process does not work indefinitely. At some point, the benefits from adding incremental auditors will be exceeded by the cost of such action. When that occurs, the prudent alternative would be to stop allocating resources to the internal auditing department.

Cost-benefit analytical techniques can range from intuitive informal judgments to rather detailed and complex mathematical processes.

The concept of maximizing benefits while minimizing cost has been in existence for a long time. Its importance to management and auditors grew as a result of the accounting standards section of the FCPA (see Chapters 17 and 18) and it is now thought to be one of the best techniques for deciding the extent to which internal accounting controls should be designed to keep within the perceived context of the law.

Applicability

As is evident in its definition, cost-benefit analysis is useful anytime the auditor or management is contemplating alternative courses of action. In addition to deciding whether to implement a control, the following are typical decision-making situations for which cost-benefit analysis is helpful:

- Development of I/S application
- Construction of a new facility
- Make or buy inventory decisions
- New business ventures

For auditors, cost-benefit considerations are useful in deciding on the nature and extent of audit procedures that should be performed in audit projects.

Techniques

As noted earlier, cost-benefit techniques range from intuitive informal judgment (perhaps the most common technique) to complex detailed analyses. Regardless of the degree of complexity, some common steps are involved.

---

[5] Joseph E. Connor and Burnell H. DeVos, Jr., eds., *Guide to Accounting Controls* (Boston: Warren, Gorham & Lamont, 1979), p. 1-38.

AUDITING PROCEDURES

These are as follows:

1. Identifying the cost and benefit factors
2. Assigning values
3. Drawing conclusions

In identifying costs and benefits, both quantitative and qualitative elements must be considered. A quantitative cost or benefit is one that can be measured or estimated in terms of dollars. Quantifiable costs of a prospective control might be added payroll and fringe benefits for any needed staff additions, additional communication expense, and incremental data processing costs.

Quantifiable benefits might include anticipated savings from improved efficiency (e.g., staff reduction) or the reduction in the risk of loss as a result of errors, omissions, or some other adversity that the prospective control is intended to remedy.

Qualitative elements are those that cannot be quantified, even in rough orders of magnitude. Examples are as follows:

Qualitative cost elements	*Qualitative benefit elements*
• Decreased employee morale	• Improved employee morale
• Adverse public reaction	• Enhanced public image
• Added pollution	• Cleaner environment
• Lower management confidence	• Improved reliability of data

Once the cost and benefit factors have been identified, dollar estimates can be ascribed to each. Costs, particularly out-of-pocket costs, are generally thought to be easier to dollarize than benefits. Internal auditors are encouraged to obtain the assistance of the organizational unit in question to derive the most reasonable estimates.

Benefits in the form of estimated savings are also comparatively easy to deal with, since they are often anticipated cost reductions. Benefits in the form of risk reduction are more difficult to estimate. The identification and analysis of risk, in itself, can range from the simple to the complex. An illustration of one useful technique is shown in Figure 16-13. Basically, two variables are involved: the frequency of occurrence and the impact of the loss. Developing precise estimates for these variables is impracticable. Therefore, Figure 16-13 presents a broad range of occurrences and impacts ranging from very small exposure to very great exposure. Very small exposure is evident if the rate of occurrence is once every 50 years and the dollar impact of such an occurrence is less than $60 per occurrence. However, if the rate of occurrence is 625 times per day and the estimated loss from each is $625, then the average annual exposure is more than $25 million. The purpose of the table is to present rough orders of magnitude, since precision beyond that would be of doubtful reliability. Thus, the table is

FIG. 16-13
Table of Exposure Values

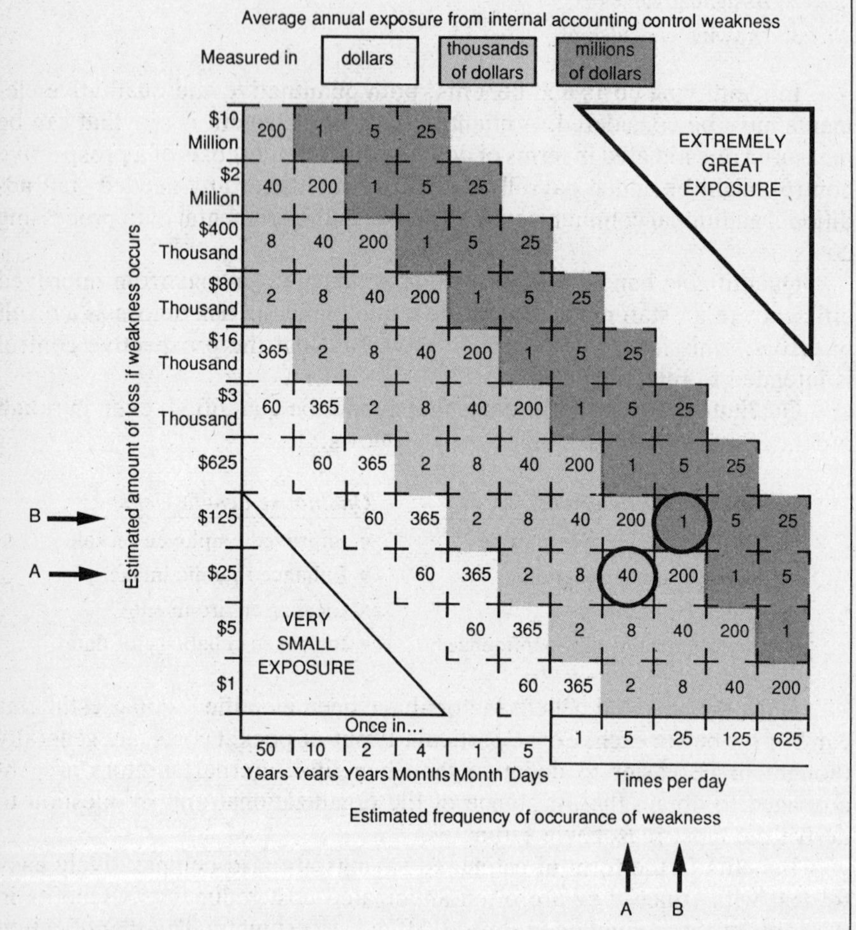

Note: The amounts, frequencies and exposures shown have been approximated at several points for purposes of using rounded figures. This does not adversely affect the usefulness of the table.

constructed in successive powers of 5. Powers of other numbers could be used to construct other tables. If the estimated frequency and estimated loss can be related to a table such as Figure 16-13, the average annual loss can be quickly derived.[6] In this figure, a loss of $25 occurring 5 times per day will accumulate to $40,000 in a year (see circled amount). Increasing each

---

[6] *Ibid.*, p. 1-50. Copyright © 1979 by Price Waterhouse & Co. Reprinted with permission.

AUDITING PROCEDURES

by a power of 5 would produce an annual loss of $1 million. If the auditor's estimates do not correlate with such a table, the auditor may calculate the annual exposure for his specific circumstance by multiplying the amount of each loss by the number of occurrences expected within a year.

When all quantifiable costs and benefits have been estimated and a net cost or a net benefit has been derived, the auditor must consider the qualitative or intangible factors. Some subjective consideration of their significance must be made and, in light of the quantifiable estimates, an informed decision can be made.

Cost-benefit analysis for most situations encountered by internal auditors need not be difficult or complex. As stated earlier, intuitive judgments are often sufficiently accurate and are frequently accepted by management. However, in instances where doubt exists, some estimation process should be employed to help select the appropriate course of action for management. It is alwo worth mentioning again that management is invariably in the best position to develop estimates for purposes of risk analysis. Its cooperation and assistance should be sought for that reason.

Documentation

When cost-benefit analysis techniques are employed, the working papers should evidence the fact. Simple narrative descriptions should suffice, supplemented, where necessary, by calculations of estimates used with appropriate references to sources where data were obtained.

A Special Application

Earlier, it was stated that cost-benefit analysis is useful to the auditor in deciding on the nature and extent of audit procedures to be applied in any given circumstance. In this context, the quantitative cost of a prospective audit procedure may be the estimated hours or days of incremental work required and any other incremental cost, such as travel cost, data processing charges, or other special outside assistance. The qualitative cost may be the impact of the particular procedure on the auditor's morale and the possible adverse impact that performance might have on the image of the function.

The principal benefit in performing incremental audit procedures is the increased level of assurance that the auditor will have on which to base his findings, recommendations, and opinions. Another benefit, equally difficult to quantify, is the possibility that by performing the additional procedure, the auditor may encounter an opportunity to offer cost-saving suggestions or ways to minimize unnecessary exposure to errors and omissions.

Although decisions regarding the application of auditing procedures are difficult, employing cost-benefit techniques can be a useful aid. However, it would be counterproductive to formally apply them in deciding on each and every auditing procedure, since there may be 50 or more involved in any given audit.

Instead, experienced and capable internal auditors have acquired the ability to follow the cost-benefit model in a more intuitive fashion. Their decisions in selecting from among the vast alternatives available and the specific auditing procedures to use in their audit projects are usually based on the following relationships:

- In performing testing procedures, the degree of assurance that can be obtained with respect to compliance varies inversely with the ease with which such compliance can be determined. Put another way, the more difficult it is to obtain evidence, the greater is the associated audit risk. These situations should be kept to a minimum and, if necessary, supplemented by other procedures.
- The need for testing a control varies directly with the importance of that control to the overall system. Stated otherwise, if the risk of loss due to noncompliance is great, the need for determining assurance is also great.

From the foregoing, it is evident that the ideal objective is to perform those auditing procedures that are easiest to test those controls and other areas of concern that are the most important. In practice, that ideal is not fully attained often, but if the auditor constantly strives for it, he will optimize his efforts.

SUGGESTED READING

AICPA. *An Auditor's Approach to Statistical Sampling.* Volumes 1–6 and supplements. New York: AICPA, 1974.

Albrecht, William Steve. "Analytical Reviews for Internal Auditors." *The Internal Auditor,* Aug. 1980, pp. 20–25.

———. "Ratio Analysis: An Audit Direction Finder—Part II." *Internal Auditing Alert,* Jan. 1982, pp. 5–7. Boston, Mass.: Warren, Gorham & Lamont, Inc.

Arens, Alvin A., and James K. Loebbecke. *Applications of Statistical Sampling to Auditing,* Chapter 10. Englewood Cliffs, N.J.: Prentice-Hall, 1981.

Bierman, Harold, Jr. *Financial Statement Analysis: Theory, Application and Interpretation.* Homewood, Ill.: Irwin, 1978.

Coopers & Lybrand. *Mathematical Techniques: A Guide for Auditors and Management,* Part II. U.S.A.: Coopers & Lybrand, 1981.

Curtis, Arthur B., John H. Cooper, and William James McCallion. *Mathematics of Accounting,* 4th ed., Chapter 15. Englewood Cliffs, N.J.: Prentice-Hall, 1961.

PART VI
Financial Type Audits

CHAPTER **17**

Internal Control—An Overall View

Introduction	2	Adequate Segregation of Duties	38
Business Risks and Management Control	2	Existence of Adequate Documents and Records	38
		Adequate Authorization Procedures	39
Internal Controls Defined	3	Levels of Business Activity	39
Foreign Corrupt Practices Act	7	Strategic Planning	40
General Provisions	8	Tactical Planning	40
Accounting Standards of the Act	8	Detailed Operational Control	40
Standards and Other Guidelines for Internal Controls	9	Internal Accounting Control Objectives	41
The AICPA	9	EDP and Internal Accounting Controls	42
The Form of the Accountant's Report	10	Cost-Effective Controls Needed	43
The IIA	14	Responsibility of Senior Management and Directors	44
Summary	15		
SIAS No. 1—Control: Concepts and Responsibilities	15	Role of the External Auditor	45
The GAO	21	Internal Audit Department	46
Standards for Internal Controls in the Federal Government	21	Allocation of Responsibility for Adequate Internal Controls	47
Proposed Revision to Audit Standards—Internal Controls Section	29	Role of the Board of Directors	47
		Role of Senior Corporate Management	48
Report of the National Commission on Fraudulent Financial Reporting	30	Role of Financial Management	48
The Institute of Internal Auditors Reports on Fraud	35	Role of Chief Internal Auditor	49
		Role of Independent Accountant	49
Variability of Control Systems	35	Management Representations to the Public	50
Elements of Internal Accounting Control Systems	37	Limitations on Internal Control	51
Competent Personnel and Defined Responsibilities	37	Suggested Reading	52

Fig. 17-1	Classification of Internal Controls	6
Fig. 17-2	Activities or Functions by Level of Business Activity	41
Fig. 17-3	Illustrative Declaration in Annual Report—Monsanto Company	51

17-1

INTRODUCTION

Those with experience in public accounting, in management positions within the finance function of private entities, or, indeed, in some aspects of government accounting or auditing, have long known that adequate internal controls are essential. In fact, many are familiar with the annual review of the internal control system made by the independent accountants in determining the extent of audit required to issue the usual Accountant's Opinion. But such reviews, however, often were considered routine.

As a result of the disclosure of improper actions by a few members of business management, among other things, the Foreign Corrupt Practices Act of 1977 was passed. Since then, other widely publicized bankruptcies and cases of embezzlement and fraud have caused an increased focus on internal controls. Within the past decade, several bodies either have issued standards or have made recommendations regarding internal controls.

It is the purpose of this chapter to provide a general review of internal controls by focussing on definitions, guidelines and standards, elements of the systems, objectives of such systems, and the responsibility of several business or management levels for an adequate system of internal controls.

BUSINESS RISKS AND MANAGEMENT CONTROL

This chapter deals with internal controls as an important device to assist management in achieving the business objectives of the company. In a narrow sense, the business objective under the private enterprise system has sometimes been described as that of earning the maximum profit over a designated period of time—or in more sophisticated terms, to optimize the return on assets employed, or on shareholders' equity, as the case may be. But in a broader sense, a business is an economic entity created principally to provide a needed or desired product or service. Only if it can furnish such an output on an economical basis will it survive and prosper.

In attempting to reach its goals, a business must take risks. In a sense, profits are the reward for successfully assuming and managing those risks. Risk results because activities may not turn out as planned; it may be due to external forces or internal forces. The manufacturing, marketing, or financial activities may encounter unexpected or unplanned obstacles. Some examples of external or internal forces that might have internal accounting control implications are these:

1. External
    - Inflation
    - General economic trends
    - Government regulation or intervention
    - Labor market upheaval
    - Raw material supply shortages

- Technology changes
- Availability of capital
- Market changes
- Armed conflict
- Natural disasters
- Foreign exchange problems

2. Internal
   - Change in company's organization or structure
   - Change in selected business policies
   - Employee turnover
   - Acquisition of new businesses
   - Cash depletion
   - Change in sales policies
   - New computer applications
   - Employee irregularities
   - Product failures

Sound business management involves assessing the risks, deciding which ones should be consciously assumed, and instituting appropriate measures to reduce the risks to the extent feasible. The system of policies and procedures designed to minimize the risks and report on the related business activities may collectively be called the internal control system. The objective of the system is to provide information to assist in reducing the unintentional and unnecessary exposure to business, financial, accounting, or other risks.

INTERNAL CONTROLS DEFINED

Business managements, including financial management as well as independent public accountants, have long been involved with internal control. Definitions have evolved, among other reasons, to clarify the scope of the independent accountants' review as it relates to an expression of opinion on the company's financial statements being audited. In the Statement on Auditing Procedure No. 29, issued in October 1958 by the Committee on Auditing Procedure of the AICPA (subsequently codified in SAS No. 1),[1] internal control was defined as follows:

> Internal control, in the broad sense includes . . . controls which may be characterized as either accounting or administrative as follows:
>
> a. Accounting controls comprise the plan of organization and all methods and

---

[1] Statement on Auditing Standards No. 1 (Nov. 1972) (AICPA, *Professional Standards*, Vol. 1). AU § 320.10. Copyright © 1972 by the American Institute of Certified Public Accountants.

procedures that are concerned mainly with, and relate directly to, the safeguarding of assets and the reliability of the financial records. They generally include such controls as the systems of authorization and approval, separation of duties concerned with record keeping and accounting reports from those concerned with operations or asset custody, physical controls over assets, and internal auditing.

b. Administrative controls comprise the plan of organization and all methods and procedures that are concerned mainly with operational efficiency and adherence to managerial policies and usually relate only indirectly to the financial records. They generally include such controls as statistical analyses, time and motion studies, performance reports, employee training programs, and quality controls.

However, in 1963, in clarifying the scope of study contemplated under GAAS by public accountants, the Committee stated in Chapter 5 of Statement on Auditing Procedures No. 33 (subsequently codified in SAS No. 1):[2]

The independent auditor is primarily concerned with the accounting controls. Accounting controls . . . generally bear directly and importantly on the reliability of financial records and require evaluation by the auditor. Administrative controls . . . ordinarily relate only indirectly to the financial records and thus would not require evaluation. If the independent auditor believes, however, that certain administrative controls may have an important bearing on the reliability of the financial records, he should consider the need for evaluating such controls. For example, statistical records maintained by production, sales, or other operating departments may require evaluation in a particular instance.

Hence, the practical effect of the statement is to include in the definition of accounting controls any administrative controls that have an important bearing on the reliability of the financial statements. Finally, in 1973, the Committee on Auditing Procedure revised, in SAS No. 1, the preceding definitions in Paragraphs 320.26 through 320.29 as follows:[3]

REVISED DEFINITIONS

.26 Based on the foregoing discussion, administrative control and accounting control are defined as indicated in the following two paragraphs.

.27 *Administrative control* includes, but is not limited to, the plan of organization and the procedures and records that are concerned with the decision processes leading to management's authorization of transactions. Such authorization is a management function directly associated with the responsibility

---

[2] *Ibid.,* AU § 320.11. Copyright © 1972 by the American Institute of Certified Public Accountants.

[3] *Ibid.,* AU §§ 320.26–320.29. Copyright © 1972 by the American Institute of Certified Public Accountants. This definition is intended only to provide a point of departure for distinguishing accounting control and consequently is not necessarily definitive for other purposes.

for achieving the objectives of the organization and is the starting point for establishing accounting control of transactions.

.28 *Accounting control* comprises the plan of organization and the procedures and records that are concerned with the safeguarding of assets and the reliability of financial records and consequently are designed to provide reasonable assurance that:

a. Transactions are executed in accordance with management's general or specific authorization.
b. Transactions are recorded as necessary (1) to permit preparation of financial statements in conformity with generally accepted accounting principles or any other criteria applicable to such statements and (2) to maintain accountability for assets.
c. Access to assets is permitted only in accordance with management's authorization.
d. The recorded accountability for assets is compared with the existing assets at reasonable intervals and appropriate action is taken with respect to any differences.

.29 The foregoing definitions are not necessarily mutually exclusive because some of the procedures and records comprehended in accounting control may also be involved in administrative control. For example, sales and cost records classified by products may be used for accounting control purposes and also in making management decisions concerning unit prices or other aspects of operations. Such multiple uses of procedures or records, however, are not critical for the purposes of this section because it is concerned primarily with clarifying the outer boundary of accounting control. Examples of records used solely for administrative control are those pertaining to customers contacted by salesmen and to defective work by production employees maintained only for evaluating personnel performance.

Some additional definitions appear among the section detailing standards and other guidelines for internal controls. Two of the components of the internal control system—*internal accounting* control and *administrative* control—have been defined first because it is in these areas that much of the work of the internal auditor will take place, and they are the types of controls emphasized in accounting literature. Yet, internal control may also be described as the exercise of a directing or restraining influence. In running a business, the principal direction and guidance on major policy matters comes from the chief executive officer and his top management. This control, the *primary operational* control of the business, lies in their hands, is *operational* in nature, and should be recognized as such. The administrative controls may be described as facilitating the operational controls by being concerned with operating efficiency and adherence to the stated policies. The internal accounting control is but another supportive facility concerning the safeguarding of the assets and the reliability of financial records. The relationship of these three controls, collectively described as internal control, is illustrated in Figure 17-1.

FIG. 17-1
Classification of Internal Controls

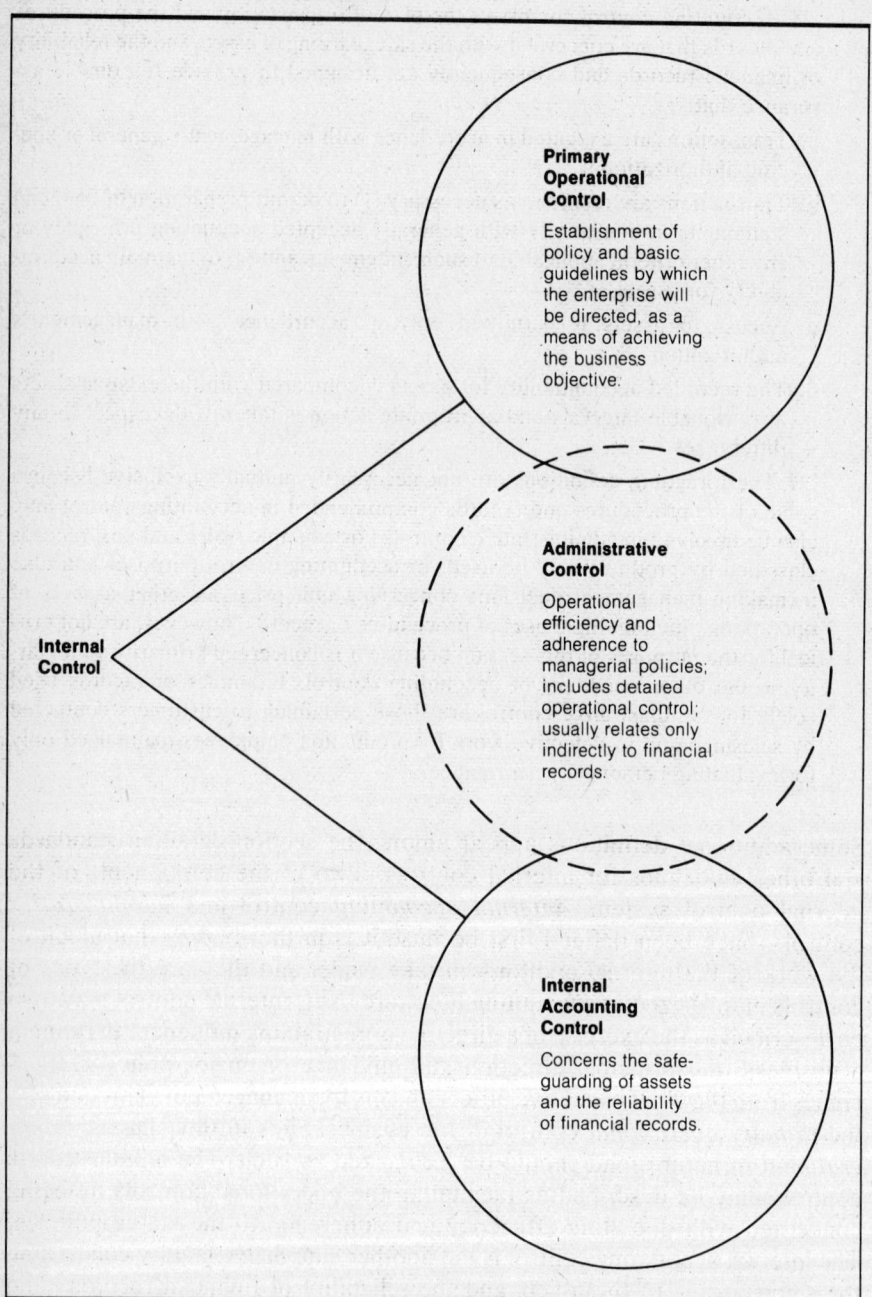

The importance of primary operating controls should be recognized. While the internal audit department is normally directly involved with both internal accounting controls and administrative controls for financial audit purposes, entry into the operational audit may focus on detailed operational controls. (See Chapters 31 through 40.)

From a practical standpoint, the classifications of internal control are largely irrelevant. What must be considered by management and internal auditors alike in a review of controls is the impact of the control system on the safeguarding of assets and the reliability of the financial statements.

Also, as a final comment, internal control consists essentially of the organization (including the people and the structures) and the procedures that cause or allow the company to operate—from broad overall policies and procedures, as established by the corporate charter and the board of directors, through the procedures for each department and each transaction or activity. Each business has an internal control system, however unsophisticated it may be, and whether or not it is evidenced in writing.

Each system is unique because of the nature of the business, the style of management, varying degrees of delegation of authority, differing extents to which responsibility is assumed, and differences in the experience and capability of the individuals making up the organization. Given these differences, even though superficially one business may appear nearly like another, the uniqueness most likely will often call for differences in the way internal control systems are evaluated.

FOREIGN CORRUPT PRACTICES ACT

Business management has long been responsible for reasonably assuring that an adequate system of controls was in place in the business organization, and was, in fact, operating. And, as later described, financial management had, and has, a particular role in establishing and maintaining adequate internal accounting controls. The role of independent accountants has been to review the system of internal controls primarily to determine the scope of examination considered necessary. Yet, the business executive had a continuing interest, day after day, in the effective operation of the controls. It was through his day-to-day observations that he knew if his policies and procedures were adhered to and carried out efficiently. As the size and complexity of the enterprise grew, and he was further removed from the scene of activity, these controls became more important. They were a necessary vehicle in achieving the business objective. Thus, business involvement with the control system in fact has existed for many years. However, in December 1977, Congress enacted the FCPA, which gave a new perspective to, and emphasis on, internal controls.

General Provisions

Briefly, the Act arose, among other reasons, from disclosures of unacceptable business practices and recommendations relating thereto from several sources:

1. The investigative results of the Office of the Watergate Special Prosecutor and the SEC, showing the use of corporate resources for domestic political contributions and for bribery of foreign officials.

    Some of the payments were illegal at the time, and others were at least questionable. Many were achieved through "off-the-books" funds or bank accounts and employment of methods that circumvented the internal accounting control systems.
2. The findings and recommendations of the SEC were disclosed in *Report on Questionable and Illegal Corporate Payments and Practices*, submitted to the Senate Banking, Housing and Urban Affairs Committee on May 12, 1976. In this document, the SEC recommended that Congress enact legislation to improve the accuracy of corporate books and records.
3. Hearings on illegal and questionable business payments conducted by the Senate Banking, Housing and Urban Affairs Committee. This committee proposed legislation that was, in part, incorporated in the FCPA.

Accounting Standards of the Act

Our concern in this text is principally with the accounting standards of the Act. In summary, if a company is subject to the Securities Exchange Act of 1934 (e.g., a company with publicly traded stock), the Accounting Standards Provision of the Act requires that the company keep in reasonable detail "books, records and accounts" that accurately and fairly reflect the company's transactions and dispositions of assets and maintain a system of internal accounting controls. Specifically, in the words of the law, every issuer covered by the law shall:

(A) make and keep books, records, and accounts, which, in reasonable detail, accurately and fairly reflect the transactions and dispositions of the assets of the issuer; and

(B) devise and maintain a system of internal accounting controls sufficient to provide reasonable assurances that—

(i) transactions are executed in accordance with management's general or specific authorization;

(ii) transactions are recorded as necessary (I) to permit preparation of financial statements in conformity with generally accepted accounting principles or any other criteria applicable to such statements, and (II) to maintain accountability for assets;

(iii) access to assets is permitted only in accordance with management's general or specific authorization; and

(iv) the recorded accountability for assets is compared with the existing assets

INTERNAL CONTROL

at reasonable intervals and appropriate action is taken with respect to any differences.

There are those who feel compliance with the Accounting Standards Provisions is difficult in that the law is unclear. Interpretations of the law are being provided with the passage of time, and some future statutory actions may help to further clarify matters. In considering compliance with the law, both congressional intent and the concept of reasonableness should be applied in determining action to be taken. It should be recognized that financial record keeping is not in fact separable from the internal accounting systems that generate the records. Therefore, in demonstrating compliance with the accounting standards of the Act, a company is well-advised to consider the entire internal control system and especially the internal accounting controls.

STANDARDS AND OTHER GUIDELINES FOR INTERNAL CONTROLS

As previously stated, writings on internal controls have been quite extensive in the past decade. Before analyzing some of the implications of the FCPA and other requirements inherent in a system of adequate internal controls, useful background can be found in the discussion of some of the publications.

Authoritative guidance regarding an evaluation of an entity's system of internal controls has emanated from these three organizations:

1. AICPA
2. IIA
3. GAO

In addition to the standards issued by these bodies, other reports have been made public, which probably will have a bearing on internal control evaluation. Two studies in this latter category include:

1. *Report of the National Commission on Fraudulent Financial Reporting* (Oct. 1987)
2. *The Institute of Internal Auditors Reports on Fraud* (Sept. 1986)

A limited discussion of some specific comments on internal control from each of these sources follows.

The AICPA

The responsibility of the independent accountant for detecting fraud (See Chapter 23), and hence, the guidelines relative to internal control, may be undergoing a bit of change. But the evolution of the standards and the present status of existing guidelines is important in any review of internal controls.

In November 1972, the Committee on Auditing Procedure of the AICPA adopted SAS No. 1, "Codification of Auditing Standards and Procedures." Section 320 of SAS No. 1 dealt extensively with the auditor's study and evaluation of internal control. In an earlier section of this chapter, the initial definition and revised definition of internal controls were quoted. Much of the published commentary on internal control standards and procedures has been strongly influenced by SAS No. 1 and related supplemental statements.

Three subsequently issued standards relating to internal control include: (a) SAS No. 3, "The Effects of EDP on the Auditor's Study and Evaluation of Internal Control" (Dec. 1974); (b) SAS No. 20, "Required Communication of Material Weaknesses in Internal Accounting Control" (Aug. 1977), which statement also amends sections of SAS No. 1; and (c) SAS No. 30, "Reporting on Internal Accounting Control." In fact, this latter source[4] specifically states that the guidance contained in Section 320 of SAS No. 1 and in SAS No. 3 also is generally applicable to engagements to report on internal accounting control.

The Form of the Accountant's Report. The reader is referred to SAS No. 30 for a complete and excellent discussion of procedures to be employed in studies of internal control and standards for reporting the findings. However, the general comments about the form of the accountant's report are informative in reference to standards to be observed by the independent accountant and may serve as a guide in some respects to the internal auditor:[5]

37. An independent accountant may express an opinion on a system of internal accounting control of any entity for which financial statements in conformity with generally accepted accounting principles, or any other criteria applicable to such statements, can be prepared.
38. The accountant's report expressing an opinion on an entity's system of internal accounting control should contain
    a. A description of the scope of the engagement.
    b. The date to which the opinion relates.
    c. A statement that the establishment and maintenance of the system is the responsibility of management.
    d. A brief explanation of the broad objectives and inherent limitations of internal accounting control.
    e. The accountant's opinion on whether the system taken as a whole was sufficient to meet the broad objectives of internal accounting control insofar as those objectives pertain to the prevention or de-

---

[4] Statement on Auditing Standards No. 30, "Reporting on Internal Accounting Control," July 1980, p. 1.

[5] *Ibid.*, pp. 13–14.

tection of errors or irregularities in amounts that would be material in relation to financial statements.

The report should be dated as of the date of completion of field work and may be addressed to the entity whose system is being studied or to its board of directors or stockholders.

STANDARD FORM OF REPORT

39. The following language should be used to express an unqualified opinion on an entity's system of internal accounting control:

We have made a study and evaluation of the system of internal accounting control of XYZ Company and subsidiaries in effect at (date). Our study and evaluation was conducted in accordance with standards established by the American Institute of Certified Public Accountants.

The management of XYZ Company is responsible for establishing and maintaining a system of internal accounting control. In fulfilling this responsibility, estimates and judgments by management are required to assess the expected benefits and related costs of control procedures. The objectives of a system are to provide management with reasonable, but not absolute, assurance that assets are safeguarded against loss from unauthorized use or disposition, and that transactions are executed in accordance with management's authorization and recorded properly to permit the preparation of financial statements in accordance with generally accepted accounting principles.

Because of inherent limitations in any system of internal accounting control, errors or irregularities may occur and not be detected. Also, projection of any evaluation of the system to future periods is subject to the risk that procedures may become inadequate because of changes in conditions, or that the degree of compliance with the procedures may deteriorate.

In our opinion, the system of internal accounting control of XYZ Company and subsidiaries in effect at (date), taken as a whole, was sufficient to meet the objectives stated above insofar as those objectives pertain to the prevention or detection of errors or irregularities in amounts that would be material in relation to the consolidated financial statements.

Copyright © 1980 by the American Institute of Certified Public Accountants, Inc.

As has been mentioned, the purpose, and usually the scope, of an independent accountant's engagement to express an opinion on a system of internal accounting control of a particular entity will differ from those related to the examination of the financial statements in accordance with generally accepted auditing standards. SAS No. 30 contains an illustrative auditor's report on accounting control when the auditor is requested to report on internal accounting control, even when the study and evaluation made as a part of the audit is not sufficient for expressing an opinion on the system taken as a whole. This standard is quoted as follows:[6]

---

[6] *Ibid.*, pp. 17–18.

49. The following is an illustration of an auditor's report on internal accounting control when the study and evaluation made as part of the audit is not sufficient for expressing an opinion on the system taken as a whole.

To the Board of Directors of XYZ Company:

We have examined the financial statements of XYZ Company for the year ended December 31, 19X1, and have issued our report thereon dated February 23, 19X2. As part of our examination, we made a study and evaluation of the Company's system of internal accounting control to the extent we considered necessary to evaluate the system as required by generally accepted auditing standards. The purpose of our study and evaluation was to determine the nature, timing, and extent of the auditing procedures necessary for expressing an opinion on the company's financial statement. Our study and evaluation was more limited than would be necessary to express an opinion on the system of internal accounting control taken as a whole.

The management of XYZ Company is responsible for establishing and maintaining a system of internal accounting control. In fulfilling this responsibility, estimates and judgments by management are required to assess the expected benefits and related costs of control procedures. The objectives of a system are to provide management with reasonable, but not absolute, assurance that assets are safeguarded against loss from unauthorized use or disposition, and that transactions are executed in accordance with management's authorization and recorded properly to permit the preparation of financial statements in accordance with generally accepted accounting principles.

Because of inherent limitations in any system of internal accounting control, errors or irregularities may nevertheless occur and not be detected. Also, projection of any evaluation of the system to future periods is subject to the risk that procedures may become inadequate because of changes in conditions or that the degree of compliance with the procedure may deteriorate.

Our study and evaluation made for the limited purpose described in the first paragraph would not necessarily disclose all material weaknesses in the system. Accordingly, we do not express an opinion on the system of internal accounting control of XYZ Company taken as a whole. However, our study and evaluation disclosed no condition that we believed to be a material weakness.

This report is intended solely for the use of management (or specified regulatory agency or other specified third party) and should not be used for any other purpose.

Copyright © 1980 by the American Institute of Certified Public Accountants, Inc.

The same source further provides this guidance when the study and evaluation discloses material weaknesses:[7]

50. If the study and evaluation discloses material weaknesses (as defined in SAS No. 20, as amended), the report should describe the weaknesses

---

[7] *Ibid.*, p. 18.

that have come to the auditor's attention and state that they were considered in determining the audit tests to be applied in the examination of financial statements. The last sentence of the fourth paragraph of the illustrative report should be modified as follows:

However, our study and evaluation disclosed the following conditions that we believe result in more than a relatively low risk that errors or irregularities in amounts that would be material in relation to the financial statements of XYZ Company may occur and not be detected within a timely period. (A description of the material weaknesses that have come to the auditor's attention would follow.)

These conditions were considered in determining the nature, timing, and extent of the audit tests to be applied in our examination of the 19X1 financial statements, and this report does not affect our report on these financial statements dated (date of report).

Copyright © 1980 by the American Institute of Certified Public Accountants, Inc.

A recent interpretation of paragraph 50 of SAS No. 30 makes these comments in response to the question, "May the auditor modify the wording of those illustrations (of reports) as he considers appropriate in the light of the circumstances of each engagement?"[8]

Interpretation—The auditor may modify the wording of the illustrative report on internal accounting control based solely on a study and evaluation made as part of an audit of financial statements provided it meets the requirements of paragraphs 48 and 50 of SAS No. 30, which are:

☐ The report indicates that it is intended solely for management, a specified regulatory agency, or other specified third party.[9]

☐ The report describes the limited purpose of the study and evaluation.

☐ The report disclaims an opinion on the system of internal accounting control taken as a whole.

☐ If the study and evaluation discloses material weaknesses, the report describes the weaknesses and indicates that they were considered in determining the audit tests to be applied in the examination of the financial statements.

The following is an example of a report on internal accounting control based solely on a study and evaluation made as a part of an audit that meets the minimum requirements of paragraph 48 of SAS No. 30:

To the Board of Directors of XYZ Company:

We have examined the financial statements of XYZ Company for the year ended December 31, 19X1, and have issued our report thereon dated

---

[8] Official Releases, Auditing Interpretations, *Journal of Accountancy*, Dec. 1983, p. 174.

[9] Footnote 7 of SAS No. 30 indicates that distribution of the report should be restricted to management or a specified regulatory agency or third party even though, by law or regulation, the report may be made a matter of public record.

February 23, 19X2. As part of our examination, we made a study and evaluation of the Company's system of internal accounting control to the extent we considered necessary solely to determine the nature, timing, and extent of our auditing procedures. Accordingly, we do not express an opinion on the system of internal accounting control taken as a whole. However, during our examination, we did not become aware of any conditions that we believe to be a material weakness.

This report is intended solely for the use of management (or specified regulatory agency or other specified third party).

If the auditor's study and evaluation or other aspects of his audit disclose material weaknesses, the last sentence of the first paragraph of the report example in the preceding paragraph should be modified as follows to comply with the requirement of paragraph 50 to SAS No. 30:

However, our examination disclosed the following conditions that we believe to be material weaknesses.[10] (A description of the material weaknesses that have come to the auditor's attention would follow.)[11] These conditions were considered in determining the nature, timing, and extent of the audit tests to be applied in our examination of the 19X1 financial statements, and this report does not affect our report on those financial statements dated February 23, 19X2.

In deciding on the wording of a report on internal accounting control based solely on a study and evaluation made as a part of an audit, the auditor should consider, among other factors, the intended distribution of the report, for example, whether distribution of the report will be limited solely to management or whether the report also will be distributed to a specified regulatory agency and will be made a matter of public record. In the latter case, the auditor may consider it desirable to include a description of the objectives and inherent limitations of internal accounting control and management's responsibility for maintaining the system as illustrated in paragraph 49 of SAS No. 30.

Copyright © 1983 by the American Institute of Certified Public Accountants, Inc.

The IIA

In the December 1983 issue of *The Internal Auditor*, the IIA announced the issuance of the first authoritative interpretation of *Standards for the Professional Practice of Internal Auditing*. It is entitled "Control: Concepts and

---

[10] Alternatively, this sentence may state, "However, our examination disclosed the following conditions that we believe result in more than a relatively low risk that errors or irregularities in amounts that would be material in relation to the financial statements of XYZ Company may occur and not be detected within a timely period."

[11] If management believes it is not practicable to correct the weaknesses, paragraph 9 of SAS No. 20 provides that the auditor may refer to the circumstances and summarize the weaknesses; a detailed communication of the circumstances and the related weaknesses is not required.

INTERNAL CONTROL

Responsibilities" (300.02 and 300.03), and provides three additional guidelines (300.06–300.08).

Summary. A summary of the statement provided by the IIA is as follows:[12]

> This statement provides guidance to internal auditors on the nature of control and the roles of the participants in its establishment, maintenance, and evaluation. Major conclusions include:
> - A control is any action taken by management to enhance the likelihood that established objectives and goals will be achieved.
> - Control results from management's planning, organizing, and directing.
> - The many variants of the term control (for example, administrative control, management control, internal control) can be incorporated with the generic term.
> - The overall system of control is conceptual in nature. It is the integrated collection of systems used by an organization to achieve its objectives and goals.
> - Management plans, organizes, and directs in such a fashion as to provide reasonable assurance that established objectives and goals will be achieved.
> - Internal auditing examines and evaluates the planning, organizing, and directing processes to determine whether reasonable assurance exists that objectives and goals will be achieved. All systems, processes, operations, functions, and activities within the organization are subject to internal auditing's evaluations. Such evaluations, in the aggregate, provide information to appraise the overall system of control.

SIAS No. 1—Control: Concepts and Responsibilities. The complete statement is reproduced below.[13] It should be observed that the new interpretive guidelines are in bold print.

> *Statements on Internal Auditing Standards* are issued by the Professional Standards and Responsibilities Committee, the senior technical committee designated by The Institute of Internal Auditors, Inc., to issue pronouncements on auditing matters. These statements are authoritative interpretations of the *Standards for the Professional Practice of Internal Auditing*.
> Organizations, internal auditing departments, directors of internal auditing, and internal auditors should strive to comply with the *Standards*. The implementation of the *Standards* and these related statements will be governed by the

---

[12] "The Institute Issues First Statement," *The Internal Auditor*, Dec. 1983, p. 8.

[13] *Ibid.*, pp. 11, 13–14. Note that as used in this statement, the term "management" includes anyone in an organization with responsibilities for setting and achieving objectives.

environment in which the internal auditing department carries out its assigned responsibilities. The adoption and implementation of the *Standards* and related statements will assist internal auditing professionals in accomplishing their responsibilities.

FOREWORD

The Institute of Internal Auditors issued its *Standards for the Professional Practice of Internal Auditing* in 1978 "to serve the entire profession in all types of businesses, in various levels of government, and in all other organizations where internal auditors are found . . . to represent the practice of internal auditing as it should be. . . ." Experience and success have demonstrated the credibility of the basic principles promoted in the *Standards*.

The *Standards* state that internal auditing is to assist members of the organization in the effective discharge of their responsibilities by providing them with information regarding control. However, differences of opinion have existed regarding the nature of control and the roles of the participants in its establishment, maintenance, and evaluation.

This statement provides guidance on these issues by focusing on Guidelines 300.02 and 300.03 and providing three additional guidelines.

BACKGROUND

Controls were defined early in the evolutionary process of organizational management as mechanisms or practices used to prevent or detect unauthorized activity. The purpose of controls was later expanded to include the concept of getting things done. Current usage leans toward any effort made to enhance the probability of accomplishing objectives.

Examples of "controls" abound. A partial list relating to protection of cash highlights the diversity of opinions: a safe, a locked safe, a requirement to lock cash in a safe, a procedure directing the storage of cash in a locked safe, restricted access to a safe and its contents, assignment of responsibility for protecting cash, authorizing cash disbursements, a record of cash disbursements and receipts, and unannounced cash counts. This diversity should not be construed as indicating a problem; in fact, the opposite may very well be true. All of these may be regarded as controls, depending on circumstances and the specific activity being reviewed.

As illustrated above, control is used as a noun, a verb, and an adjective; the term is used to describe a physical device, a method of performing an activity, a step in a process, a means to an end, and an end in itself.

Differences of opinion exist regarding the term "system of internal control." This term was used in a 1949 American Institute of Certified Public Accountants study titled *Internal Control—Elements of a Coordinated System and Its Importance to Management and the Independent Public Accountants*. From the external auditor's viewpoint, the importance of the system of internal control was "to establish a basis for reliance thereon in determining the nature, extent, and timing of audit tests to be applied in the examination of the financial statement." Since then, the term has been used by auditors to describe the set of controls within a specific system, operation, or department; it has also been used in the context of the organization's system of internal control.

It is clear that management and internal auditors are interested in both specific controls in specific systems and in overall control. It is generally agreed that their scope of interest (and responsibilities) extends beyond that of external auditors. To clearly delineate the difference between the broader control concerns of management and internal auditors and the narrower control concerns of external auditors, the broader concept of control will hereafter be referred to as the "overall system of control."

Differences of opinion exist regarding the specific nature of management's role in the establishment, maintenance, and evaluation of control. For example, it is commonly stated that management plans, organizes, directs, and controls. Thus, at least conceptually, controlling has been viewed as a separate activity. However, specific actions taken by management to enhance the likelihood that objectives and goals will be achieved, such as the setting of standards, the monitoring for compliance to those standards, and the related feedback to those in a position to take corrective action, are ongoing and fully integrated with planning, organizing, and directing activities. Therefore, controlling can be viewed as a part of planning, organizing, and directing rather than as a separate activity.

There is also diversity of opinion as to how much of the management process is subject to internal auditing's review. Since such diversity of opinion regarding the nature of control and roles played by the participants may cause or contribute to less than optimum performance by internal auditors, the following concepts were formulated to serve the profession. These concepts guide the interpretations contained in the remainder of this statement:

- Management plans, organizes, and directs in such a manner as to provide reasonable assurance that established objectives and goals will be achieved.
- Internal auditors examine and evaluate the planning, organizing, and directing processes to determine whether reasonable assurance exists that objectives and goals will be achieved. Thus, all systems, processes, operations, functions, and activities within the organization are subject to internal auditing's evaluations.
- External auditors evaluate "internal accounting control" within the parameters stated in their Generally Accepted Auditing Standards.
- Audit committees have guidance and oversight responsibilities related to internal and external auditings' performance.
- Boards of directors have guidance and oversight responsibilities related to subordinate management's performance.

300 STANDARD—SCOPE OF WORK

THE SCOPE OF THE INTERNAL AUDIT SHOULD ENCOMPASS THE EXAMINATION AND EVALUATION OF THE ADEQUACY AND EFFECTIVENESS OF THE ORGANIZATION'S SYSTEM OF INTERNAL CONTROL AND THE QUALITY OF PERFORMANCE IN CARRYING OUT ASSIGNED RESPONSIBILITIES.

(The new interpretive guidelines are in bold print.)

.01 The scope of internal auditing work, as specified in this standard, encompasses what audit work should be performed. It is recognized, however, that management and the board of directors provide general direction as to the scope of work and the activities to be audited.

.02 The purpose of the review for adequacy of the system of internal control is to ascertain whether the system established provides reasonable assurance that the organization's objectives and goals will be met efficiently and economically.

.1 Objectives are the broadest statements of what the organization chooses to accomplish. The establishment of objectives precedes the selection of goals and the design, implementation, and maintenance of systems whose purpose is to meet the organization's objectives and goals.

.2 Goals are specific objectives of specific systems, and may be otherwise referred to as operating or program objectives or goals, operating standards, performance levels, targets, or expected results. Goals should be identified for each system. They should be clearly defined, measurable, attainable, and consistent with established broader objectives, and they should explicitly recognize the risks associated with not achieving those objectives.

.3 A system (process, operation, function, or activity) is an arrangement, a set, or a collection of concepts, parts, activities, and/or people that are connected or interrelated to achieve objectives and goals. (This definition applies to both manual and automated systems.) A system may also be a collection of subsystems operating together for a common objective or goal.

.4 Adequate control is present if management has planned and organized (designed) in a manner which provides reasonable assurance that the organization's objectives and goals will be achieved efficiently and economically. The system design process begins with the establishment of objectives and goals. This is followed by connecting or interrelating concepts, parts, activities, and/or people in such a manner as to operate together to achieve the established objectives and goals. If system design is properly performed, planned activities should be executed as designed and expected results should be attained.

.5 Reasonable assurance is provided when cost-effective actions are taken to restrict deviations to a tolerable level. This implies, for example, that material errors and improper or illegal acts will be prevented or detected and corrected within a timely period by employees in the normal course of performing their assigned duties. The cost-benefit relationship is considered by management during the design of systems. The potential loss associated with any exposure or risk is weighed against the cost to control it.

.6 Efficient performance accomplishes objectives and goals in an accurate and timely fashion with minimal use of resources.

.7 Economical performance accomplishes objectives and goals at a cost commensurate with the risk. The term efficient incorporates this concept of economical performance.

.03 The purpose of the review for effectiveness of the system of internal control is to ascertain whether the system is functioning as intended.

.1 Effective control is present when management directs systems in such a manner as to provide reasonable assurance that the organization's objectives and goals will be achieved.

.2 Directing involves—in addition to accomplishing objectives and planned activities—authorizing and monitoring performance, periodically comparing actual with planned performance, and documenting these activities to provide additional assurance that systems operate as planned.

.2.1 Authorizing includes initiating or granting permission to perform activities or transactions. Authorization implies that the authorizing authority has verified and validated that the activity or transaction conforms with established policies and procedures.

.2.2 Monitoring encompasses supervising, observing, and testing activities and appropriately reporting to responsible individuals. Monitoring provides an ongoing verification of progress toward achievement of objectives and goals.

.2.3 Periodic comparison of actual to planned performance enhances the likelihood that activities occur as planned.

.2.4 Documenting provides evidence of the exercise of authority and responsibility; compliance with policies, procedures, and standards of performance; supervising, observing, and testing activities; and verification of planned performance.

.04 The purpose of the review for quality of performance is to ascertain whether the organization's objectives and goals have been achieved.

.05 The primary objectives of internal control are to ensure:

.1 The reliability and integrity of information

.2 Compliance with policies, plans, procedures, laws, and regulations

.3 The safeguarding of assets

.4 The economical and efficient use of resources

.5 The accomplishment of established objectives and goals for operations or programs

.06 A control is any action taken by management to enhance the likelihood that established objectives and goals will be achieved. Management plans, organizes, and directs the performance of sufficient actions to provide reasonable assurance that objectives and goals will be achieved. Thus, control is the result of proper planning, organizing, and directing by management.

.1 Controls may be preventive (to deter undesirable events from occurring), detective (to detect and correct undesirable events which have occurred), or directive (to cause or encourage a desirable event to occur).

.2 All variants of the term control (administrative control, internal accounting control, internal control, management control, operational control, output control, preventive control, etc.) can be incorporated within the generic term. These variants differ primarily in terms of the objectives to be achieved. Since these variants are useful in describing specific control applications, participants in the control process should be familiar with the terms as well as their applications. However, the methodology followed by internal auditing in evaluating such controls is consistent for all of the variants.

.3 The variant "internal control" came into general use to distinguish controls within an organization from those existing externally to the organization (such as laws). Since internal auditors operate within an organization and, among other responsibilities, evaluate management's response to external stimuli (such as laws), no such distinction between internal and external controls is necessary. Also, from the organization's viewpoint, internal controls are all activities which attempt to ensure the accomplishment of the organization's objectives and goals. For the purpose of this statement, internal control is considered synonymous with controls within the organization.

.4 The overall system of control is conceptual in nature. It is the integrated collection of controlled systems used by an organization to achieve its objectives and goals.

.07 Management plans, organizes, and directs in such a fashion as to provide reasonable assurance that established objectives and goals will be achieved.

.1 Planning and organizing involve the establishment of objectives and goals and the use of such tools as organization charts, flowcharts, procedures, records, and reports to establish the flow of data and the responsibilities of individuals for performing activities, establishing information traits, and setting standards of performance.

.2 Directing involves certain activities to provide additional assurance that systems operate as planned. These activities include authorizing and monitoring performance, periodically comparing actual with planned performance, and appropriately documenting these activities.

.3 Management ensures that its objectives and goals remain appropriate and that its systems remain current. Therefore, management periodically reviews its objectives and goals and modifies its systems to accommodate changes in internal and external conditions.

.4 Management establishes and maintains an environment that fosters control.

.08 Internal auditing examines and evaluates the planning, organizing, and directing processes to determine whether reasonable assurance exists that objectives and goals will be achieved. Such evaluations, in the aggregate, provide information to appraise the overall system of control.

.1 All systems, processes, operations, functions, and activities within the organization are subject to internal auditing's evaluations.

.2 Internal auditing's evaluations should encompass whether reasonable assurance exists that:

a. objectives and goals have been established;

b. authorizing, monitoring, and periodic comparison activities have been planned, performed, and documented as necessary to attain objectives and goals; and,

c. planned results have been achieved (objectives and goals have been accomplished).

.3 Internal auditing performs evaluations at specific points in time but should be alert to actual or potential changes in conditions which affect the ability to provide assurance from a forward-looking perspective. In

> those cases, internal auditing should address the risk that performance may deteriorate.
>
> From *The Internal Auditor*, Dec. 1983, pp. 8 and 11–14. Copyright © 1983 by The Institute of Internal Auditors, Inc., 294 Maitland Avenue, Altamonte Springs, Florida 32701 U.S.A. Reprinted with permission.

This statement is discussed further in Chapter 4. It is continued evidence of the attention being directed to controls, despite a lessening emphasis on the FCPA.

The GAO

Standards for Internal Controls in the Federal Government. It was in 1983 that the Comptroller General of the United States, Charles A. Bowsher, issued the internal control standards to be followed by executive agencies in the establishment and maintenance of systems of internal control as required by the Federal Managers' Financial Integrity Act of 1982. Because of their conciseness and clarity, the Foreword, the Introduction, and the Internal Control Standards, are reproduced in their entirety.[14]

> **FOREWORD**
>
> In 1950, the Accounting and Auditing Act was passed requiring, among other things, that agency heads establish and maintain effective systems of internal control. Since then, the General Accounting Office (GAO) has issued numerous publications to guide agencies in establishing and maintaining effective internal control systems. While the need for improved internal controls has continued, development of effective systems has been slow.
>
> In the past decade, numerous situations came to light that dramatically demonstrated the need for controls as the Government experienced a rash of illegal, unauthorized, and questionable acts which were characterized as fraud, waste, and abuse. It is generally recognized that good internal controls would have made the commission of such wrongful acts more difficult. Consequently, increased attention is being directed toward strengthening internal controls to help restore confidence in Government and to improve its operations.
>
> The Federal Managers' Financial Integrity Act of 1982 requires renewed focus on the need to strengthen internal controls. The act requires that agency internal control systems be periodically evaluated and that the heads of executive agencies report annually on their systems' status. These evaluations are to be made pursuant to the "Guidelines for the Evaluation and Improvement of and Reporting on Internal Control Systems in the Federal Government," issued by the Office of Management and Budget in December 1982, and the reports are to state whether systems meet the objectives of internal control and conform to standards established by GAO.

---

[14] Accounting Series, *Standards for Internal Controls in the Federal Government* (Washington, D.C.: U.S. General Accounting Office, 1983).

This document presents the internal control standards to be followed, and covers both the program management as well as the traditional financial management areas. From time to time, as may become necessary, GAO will issue interpretations and revisions to these standards.

We are grateful to the Government officials, professional organizations, public accounting officials, and other members of the academic and financial communities who provided us valuable assistance through their comments on our draft proposals.

INTRODUCTION

This document contains the Comptroller General's internal control standards to be followed by executive agencies in establishing and maintaining systems of internal control as required by the Federal Managers' Financial Integrity Act of 1982 (31 U.S.C. 3512(b)). Internal control systems are to reasonably ensure that the following objectives are achieved:

- ☐ Obligations and costs comply with applicable law.
- ☐ All assets are safeguarded against waste, loss, unauthorized use, and misappropriation.
- ☐ Revenues and expenditures applicable to agency operations are recorded and accounted for properly so that accounts and reliable financial and statistical reports may be prepared and accountability of the assets may be maintained.

The act directs the heads of executive agencies to:

- ☐ Make an annual evaluation of their internal controls using guidelines established by the Office of Management and Budget (OMB).
- ☐ Provide annual reports to the President and Congress that state whether agency systems of internal control comply with the objectives of internal controls set forth in the act and with the standards prescribed by the Comptroller General. Where systems do not comply, agency reports must identify the weaknesses involved and describe the plans for corrective action. The following concept of internal controls is useful in understanding and applying the internal control standards set forth and discussed on succeeding pages.

The plan of organization and methods and procedures adopted by management to ensure that resource use is consistent with laws, regulations, and policies; that resources are safeguarded against waste, loss, and misuse; and that reliable data are obtained, maintained, and fairly disclosed in reports.

The ultimate responsibility for good internal controls rests with management. Internal controls should not be looked upon as separate, specialized systems within an agency. Rather, they should be recognized as an integral part of each system that management uses to regulate and guide its operations. In this sense, internal controls are management controls. Good internal controls are essential to achieving the proper conduct of Government business with full accountability for the resources made available. They also facilitate the achievement of management objectives by serving as checks and balances against undesired actions.

In preventing negative consequences from occurring, internal controls help achieve the positive aims of program managers.

INTERNAL CONTROL STANDARDS

The internal control standards define the minimum level of quality acceptable for internal control systems in operation and constitute the criteria against which systems are to be evaluated. These internal control standards apply to all operations and administrative functions but are not intended to limit or interfere with duly granted authority related to development of legislation, rulemaking, or other discretionary policymaking in an agency.

General Standards

1. *Reasonable Assurance.* Internal control systems are to provide reasonable assurance that the objectives of the systems will be accomplished.
2. *Supportive Attitude.* Managers and employees are to maintain and demonstrate a positive and supportive attitude toward internal controls at all times.
3. *Competent Personnel.* Managers and employees are to have personal and professional integrity and are to maintain a level of competence that allows them to accomplish their assigned duties, as well as understand the importance of developing and implementing good internal controls.
4. *Control Objectives.* Internal control objectives are to be identified or developed for each agency activity and are to be logical, applicable, and reasonably complete.
5. *Control Techniques.* Internal control techniques are to be effective and efficient in accomplishing their internal control objectives.

Specific Standards

1. *Documentation.* Internal control systems and all transactions and other significant events are to be clearly documented, and the documentation is to be readily available for examination.
2. *Recording of Transactions and Events.* Transactions and other significant events are to be promptly recorded and properly classified.
3. *Execution of Transactions and Events.* Transactions and other significant events are to be authorized and executed only by persons acting within the scope of their authority.
4. *Separation of Duties.* Key duties and responsibilities in authorizing, processing, recording, and reviewing transactions should be separated among individuals.
5. *Supervision.* Qualified and continuous supervision is to be provided to ensure that internal control objectives are achieved.
6. *Access to and Accountability for Resources.* Access to resources and records is to be limited to authorized individuals, and accountability for the custody and use of resources is to be assigned and maintained. Periodic comparison shall be made of the resources with the recorded accountability

to determine whether the two agree. The frequency of the comparison shall be a function of the vulnerability of the asset.

Audit Resolution Standard

Prompt Resolution of Audit Findings. Managers are to (1) promptly evaluate findings and recommendations reported by auditors, (2) determine proper actions in response to audit findings and recommendations, and (3) complete, within established time frames, all actions that correct or otherwise resolve the matters brought to management's attention.

EXPLANATION OF GENERAL STANDARDS

General internal control standards apply to all aspects of internal controls.

Reasonable Assurance

Internal control systems are to provide reasonable assurance that the objectives of the systems will be accomplished.

The standard of reasonable assurance recognizes that the cost of internal control should not exceed the benefit derived. Reasonable assurance equates to a satisfactory level of confidence under given considerations of costs, benefits, and risks. The required determinations call for judgment to be exercised.

In exercising that judgment, agencies should:

☐ Identify (1) risks inherent in agency operations, (2) criteria for determining low, medium, and high risks, and (3) acceptable levels of risk under varying circumstances.
☐ Assess risks both quantitatively and qualitatively.

Cost refers to the financial measure of resources consumed in accomplishing a specified purpose. Cost can also represent a lost opportunity, such as a delay in operations, a decline in service levels or productivity, or low employee morale. A benefit is measured by the degree to which the risk of failing to achieve a stated objective is reduced. Examples include increasing the probability of detecting fraud, waste, abuse, or error; preventing an improper activity; or enhancing regulatory compliance.

Supportive Attitude

Managers and employees are to maintain and demonstrate a positive and supportive attitude toward internal controls at all times.

This standard requires agency managers and employees to be attentive to internal control matters and to take steps to promote the effectiveness of the controls. Attitude affects the quality of performance and, as a result, the quality of internal controls. A positive and supportive attitude is initiated and fostered by management and is ensured when internal controls are a consistently high management priority.

Attitude is not reflected in any one particular aspect of managers' actions but rather is fostered by managers' commitment to achieving strong controls through actions concerning agency organization, personnel practices, communication, protection and use of resources through systematic accountability, monitoring and systems of reporting, and general leadership. However, one important way for management to demonstrate its support for good internal controls is its

INTERNAL CONTROL   17-25

emphasis on the value of internal auditing and its responsiveness to information developed through internal audits.

The organization of an agency provides its management with the overall framework for planning, directing, and controlling its operations. Good internal control requires clear lines of authority and responsibility; appropriate reporting relationships; and appropriate separation of authority.

In the final analysis, general leadership is critical to maintaining a positive and supportive attitude toward internal controls. Adequate supervision, training, and motivation of employees in the area of internal controls is important.

Competent Personnel

Managers and employees are to have personal and professional integrity and are to maintain a level of competence that allows them to accomplish their assigned duties, as well as understand the importance of developing and implementing good internal controls.

This standard requires managers and their staffs to maintain and demonstrate (1) personal and professional integrity, (2) a level of skill necessary to help ensure effective performance, and (3) an understanding of internal controls sufficient to effectively discharge their responsibilities.

Many elements influence the integrity of managers and their staffs. For example, personnel should periodically be reminded of their obligations under an operative code of conduct.

In addition, hiring and staffing decisions should include pertinent verification of education and experience and, once on the job, the individual should be given the necessary formal and on-the-job training. Managers who possess a good understanding of internal controls are vital to effective control systems.

Counseling and performance appraisals are also important. Overall performance appraisals should be based on an assessment of many critical factors, one of which should be the implementation and maintenance of effective internal controls.

Control Objectives

Internal control objectives are to be identified or developed for each agency activity and are to be logical, applicable, and reasonably complete.

This standard requires that objectives be tailored to an agency's operations. All operations of an agency can generally be grouped into one or more categories called cycles. Cycles comprise all specific activities (such as identifying, classifying, recording, and reporting information) required to process a particular transaction or event. Cycles should be compatible with an agency's organization and division of responsibilities.

Cycles can be categorized in various ways. For example:

- ☐ Agency management
- ☐ Financial
- ☐ Program (operational)
- ☐ Administrative

Agency management cycles cover the overall policy and planning, organization, data processing, and audit functions. Financial cycles cover the traditional control areas concerned with the flow of funds (revenues and expenditures), related assets, and financial information. Program (operational) cycles are those agency activities that relate to the mission(s) of the agency and which are peculiar to a specific agency. Administrative cycles are those agency activities providing support to the agency's primary mission, such as library services, mail processing and delivery, and printing. The four types of cycles obviously interact, and controls over this interaction must be established. For example, a typical grant cycle would be concerned with eligibility and, if awarded, administration of the grant. At the time of award, the grant (program) and disbursement (financial) cycles would interface to control and record the payment authorization.

Complying with this standard calls for identifying the cycles of agency operations and analyzing each in detail to develop the cycle control objectives. These are the internal control goals or targets to be achieved in each cycle. The objectives should be tailored to fit the specific operations in each agency and be consistent with the overall objectives of internal controls as set forth in the Federal Managers' Financial Integrity Act.

In appendix B of its "Guidelines for the Evaluation and Improvement of and Reporting on Internal Control Systems in the Federal Government," OMB has provided a list of suggested agency cycles and cycle control objectives. Agencies should consider this and other sources when identifying their cycles and cycle control objectives.

Control Techniques

Internal control techniques are to be effective and efficient in accomplishing their internal control objectives.

Internal control techniques are the mechanisms by which control objectives are achieved. Techniques include, but are not limited to, such things as specific policies, procedures, plans of organization (including separation of duties), and physical arrangements (such as locks and fire alarms). This standard requires that internal control techniques continually provide a high degree of assurance that the internal control objectives are being achieved. To do so they must be effective and efficient.

To be effective, techniques should fulfill their intended purpose in actual application. They should provide the coverage they are supposed to and operate when intended. As for efficiency, techniques should be designed to derive maximum benefit with minimum effort. Techniques tested for effectiveness and efficiency should be those in actual operation and should be evaluated over a period of time.

EXPLANATION OF SPECIFIC STANDARDS

A number of techniques are essential to providing the greatest assurance that the internal control objectives will be achieved. These critical techniques are the specific standards discussed below.

Documentation

Internal control systems and all transactions and other significant events are to be clearly documented and the documentation is to be readily available for examination.

This standard requires written evidence of (1) an agency's internal control objectives and techniques and accountability systems and (2) all pertinent aspects of transactions and other significant events of an agency. Also, the documentation must be available as well as easily accessible for examination.

Documentation of internal control systems should include identification of the cycles and related objectives and techniques, and should appear in management directives, administrative policy, and accounting manuals. Documentation of transactions or other significant events should be complete and accurate and should facilitate tracing the transaction or event and related information from before it occurs, while it is in process, to after it is completed.

Complying with this standard requires that the documentation of internal control systems and transactions and other significant events be purposeful and useful to managers in controlling their operations, and to auditors or others involved in analyzing operations.

Recording of Transactions and Events

Transactions and other significant events are to be promptly recorded and properly classified.

Transactions must be promptly recorded if pertinent information is to maintain its relevance and value to management in controlling operations and making decisions. This standard applies to (1) the entire process or life cycle of a transaction or event and includes the initiation and authorization, (2) all aspects of the transaction while in process, and (3) its final classification in summary records. Proper classification of transactions and events is the organization and format of information on summary records from which reports and statements are prepared.

Execution of Transactions and Events

Transactions and other significant events are to be authorized and executed only by persons acting within the scope of their authority.

This standard deals with management's decisions to exchange, transfer, use, or commit resources for specified purposes under specific conditions. It is the principal means of assuring that only valid transactions and other events are entered into. Authorization should be clearly communicated to managers and employees and should include the specific conditions and terms under which authorizations are to be made. Conforming to the terms of an authorization means that employees are carrying out their assigned duties in accordance with directives and within the limitations established by management.

Separation of Duties

Key duties and responsibilities in authorizing, processing, recording, and reviewing transactions should be separated among individuals.

To reduce the risk of error, waste, or wrongful acts or to reduce the risk of their going undetected, no one individual should control all key aspects of a transaction or event. Rather, duties and responsibilities should be assigned systematically to a number of individuals to ensure that effective checks and balances exist. Key duties include authorizing, approving, and recording transactions; issuing and receiving assets; making payments and reviewing or auditing transactions. Collusion, however, can reduce or destroy the effectiveness of this internal control standard.

Supervision

Qualified and continuous supervision is to be provided to ensure that internal control objectives are achieved.

This standard requires supervisors to continuously review and approve the assigned work of their staffs. It also requires that they provide their staffs with the necessary guidance and training to help ensure that errors, waste, and wrongful acts are minimized and that specific management directives are achieved.

Assignment, review, and approval of a staff's work requires:

☐ Clearly communicating the duties, responsibilities, and accountabilities assigned each staff member.

☐ Systematically reviewing each member's work to the extent necessary.

☐ Approving work at critical points to ensure that work flows as intended.

Assignment, review, and approval of a staff's work should result in the proper processing of transactions and events including (1) following approved procedures and requirements, (2) detecting and eliminating errors, misunderstandings, and improper practices, and (3) discouraging wrongful acts from occurring or from recurring.

Access to and Accountability for Resources

Access to resources and records is to be limited to authorized individuals, and accountability for the custody and use of resources is to be assigned and maintained. Periodic comparison shall be made of the resources with the recorded accountability to determine whether the two agree. The frequency of the comparison shall be a function of the vulnerability of the asset.

The basic concept behind restricting access to resources is to help reduce the risk of unauthorized use or loss to the Government, and to help achieve the directives of management. However, restricting access to resources depends upon the vulnerability of the resource and the perceived risk of loss, both of which should be periodically assessed. For example, access to and accountability for highly vulnerable documents, such as check stocks can be achieved by:

☐ Keeping them locked in a safe.

☐ Assigning or having each document assigned a sequential number.

☐ Assigning custodial accountability to responsible individuals.

Other factors affecting access include the cost, portability, exchangeability, and the perceived risk of loss or improper use of the resource. In addition, assigning and maintaining accountability for resources involves directing and communicating responsibility to specific individuals within an agency for the custody and use of resources in achieving the specifically identified management directives.

EXPLANATION OF THE AUDIT RESOLUTION STANDARD

Prompt Resolution of Audit Findings

Managers are to (1) promptly evaluate findings and recommendations reported by auditors, (2) determine proper actions in response to audit findings and recommendations, and (3) complete, within established time frames, all actions that correct or otherwise resolve the matters brought to management's attention.

The audit resolution standard requires managers to take prompt, responsive action on all findings and recommendations made by auditors. Responsive action is that which corrects identified deficiencies. Where audit findings identify opportunities for improvement rather than cite deficiencies, responsive action is that which produces improvements.

The audit resolution process begins when the results of an audit are reported to management, and is completed only after action has been taken that (1) corrects identified deficiencies, (2) produces improvements, or (3) demonstrates the audit findings and recommendations are either invalid or do not warrant management action.

Auditors are responsible for following up on audit findings and recommendations to ascertain that resolution has been achieved. Auditors' findings and recommendations should be monitored through the resolution and followup processes. Top management should be kept informed through periodic reports so it can assure the quality and timeliness of individual resolution decisions.

Proposed Revision to Audit Standards—Internal Controls Section. In March 1987, the GAO drafted proposed revisions to the *Standards for Audit of Governmental Organizations, Programs, Activities and Functions*. As mentioned in Chapter 24, these standards, when finalized, are to be used for audits of federal establishments, organizations, programs, activities, and functions—and by state and local governments receiving federal assistance when conducting audits under the Single Audit Act of 1984—and are recommended for other audits of state and local government organizations, programs, activities, and functions performed by state or local government auditors or by public accountants. In any event, the *Standards* include these field work standards on performance audits as outlined in this draft of Chapter VI, Section D, of the government publication.

D. Internal Control

The fourth **field work** standard for government **performance** audits is:

- During the audit a study and evaluation **should** be made of the internal control systems of the organization, program, activity, or function under audit **that are applicable to the audit objectives.**

The lack of administrative continuity in government units because of continuing changes in elected legislative bodies and in administrative organizations increases the need for an effective internal control system.

Internal controls can be defined as the plan of organization and methods and procedures adopted by management to ensure that resource use is consistent with laws, regulations, and policies; that resources are safeguarded against waste, loss, and misuse; and that reliable data are obtained, maintained, and fairly disclosed in reports.

The focus of the review of internal control varies with the **objective of the** audit being **performed.**

Economy and efficiency—The auditors are to review those policies, procedures, practices, and controls applicable to the **programs, functions, and** activities, **under audit to the extent necessary, as determined by the audit objectives.**

Program—The auditors are to review those policies, procedures, practices, and controls which have a specific bearing on the attainment of the goals and objectives specified by the law or regulations for the organization, program, activity, or function under audit **to the extent necessary, as determined by the audit objectives.**

Internal Controls—Federal, state and local laws and regulations may require a study and evaluation of the adequacy of internal control systems, separate and apart from studies and evaluations made as a part of other audits.[2] **Auditors may be required or contracted to perform such studies and evaluations, and if so, the studies and evaluations should be made in accordance with the standards in this statement.**

Internal auditing is an important part of internal control, and the auditors should consider this in performing the audit. External auditors should consider the extent to which **the work** of the internal auditors can be relied upon to help provide reasonable assurance that internal control is functioning properly.[3]

In reviewing internal control in economy and efficiency audits it is common practice to identify problem areas first and then review controls that relate to the area in which the problem exists.

In view of the wide range in the size and nature of government organizations programs, activities, and functions and in view of their organizational structures and operating methods, no single pattern for internal audit **and review** activities can be specified. Many government entities have these activities identified by other names, such as inspection, appraisal, investigation, organization and methods, or management analysis. These activities assist management by reviewing selected functions. To prevent duplication of effort, all auditors should use, to the maximum extent practical, the work of internal audit **and review** personnel who are independent of the area under audit.[4]

[2] Examples include the Federal Managers' Financial Integrity Act of 1982, (Public Law 97-255) and the laws of several states.

[3] See Chapter V, section B.1.c. for guidance the auditor should follow for relying on the work of others.

[4] See footnote 3 above.

Report of the National Commission on Fraudulent Financial Reporting

In October 1987, the NCFFR issued its final report on fraudulent financial reporting. Chapter 23 of this volume contains a brief review of the purpose of the Commission and its complete recommendations. As would be expected, the Commission deals at some length with internal controls. It is suggested that the reader study the report itself. But, as a point of interest, Chapter Two discusses the importance the Commission places on maintaining internal controls "adequate to prevent and detect fraudulent financial reporting." However, the report broadens the traditional definition of internal accounting control to include the control environment. Appendix F

INTERNAL CONTROL 17-31

to the report provides some guidelines for assessing the risk of fraudulent financial reporting, and discusses internal control, including the control environment, as a factor to be considered in such risk.[15]

III. FACTORS TO BE CONSIDERED

A. The Internal Environment

The internal environment consists of the conditions, circumstances, and influences affecting the company's operations subject to management's influence. Internal environmental conditions include the company's (1) internal controls, (2) financial characteristics, (3) operations, (4) individual management characteristics, and (5) accounting policies and procedures.

1. Internal Controls

Chapter Two discusses the importance the Commission places on maintaining internal controls that provide reasonable assurance that fraudulent financial reporting will be prevented or subject to early detection. This chapter also notes that it refers to internal controls broader than the traditional definition of internal *accounting* control—it includes the control environment. Both internal accounting controls and the control environment are discussed here.

a. Internal Accounting Controls

A company's internal accounting controls consist of its accounting system and specific controls.

The accounting system comprises the methods and records established to identify, assemble, classify, analyze, record, and report an entity's transactions, and to maintain accountability for the related assets. An effective accounting system has both adequate physical documents and records, and adequate procedures to: (1) identify and record all valid transactions, (2) describe the transactions in sufficient detail to permit them to be properly classified, (3) measure the value of the transactions accurately, (4) ensure the transactions are recorded in the proper accounting period, and (5) present and disclose the transactions properly in the financial statements.

Specific controls are the individual policies and procedures pertaining to processing transactions that management establishes to provide assurance its objectives will be achieved. Effective specific controls help to ensure: (1) functions are adequately segregated, (2) all transactions are executed in accordance with management's general or specific authorization, (3) adequate physical control is maintained over assets and accounting records, and (4) regular, independent checks on performance, and comparison and reconciliation of assets to recorded accountability, are made.

Specific control procedures include clerical checks, document comparisons

---

[15] *Report of the National Commission on Fraudulent Financial Reporting,* Oct. 1987, pp. 156–159.

and cancellations, transaction approvals such as standard price lists or customer credit limits, computer comparison of run to run totals, reconciliations, reviews of data used to prepare management reports, independent asset counts, segregation of duties such as requiring that the bank reconciliation be performed by individuals with no cash receipts or disbursements responsibilities, and control over access to and use of computer programs and data files by procedures such as passwords and secured facilities.

The accounting system and specific controls a company establishes are influenced by its size, complexity, ownership characteristics, and business nature. A company designs its accounting system and specific controls to provide reliable financial statements. So internal accounting controls address many different types of situations. Some portions of the internal accounting controls, such as segregation of duties and clerical checks, are designed to prevent or detect inadvertent errors or corporate frauds such as embezzlements. Other portions of the internal accounting controls, such as review of management reports, are more closely associated with preventing and detecting fraudulent financial reporting.

Descriptions of methods of implementing effective accounting systems and specific controls abound within the accounting and auditing literature. Accordingly, this Appendix does not include extensive discussions of the merits of individual procedures. Because many portions of a company's internal accounting controls are important in preventing and detecting fraudulent financial reporting, however, they should be considered when assessing the risk of such fraud.

b. Control Environment

As Chapter Two makes clear, internal accounting controls are important, but a company also must look to its control environment to prevent and detect fraudulent financial reporting.

The company's control environment is the corporate atmosphere in which the accounting controls exist and the financial statements are prepared. A strong control environment reflects management's consciousness of and commitment to an effective system of internal control. While a strong control environment does not guarantee the absence of fraudulent financial reporting, it reduces the chance that management will override internal accounting controls. On the other hand, a weak control environment undermines the effectiveness of a company's internal accounting controls and may reflect a predisposition toward misrepresentations in the financial statements.

A company's control environment consists of its organizational philosophy and operating style, organizational structure, methods of communicating and enforcing the assignment of authority and responsibility, organizational control methods, and personnel management methods. (This description of the control environment is based in large part on the discussion in the Auditing Standards Board's proposed Statement on Auditing Standards on Control Risk.)

A company's organizational philosophy and operating style encompass a broad range of characteristics, such as (1) management's and the board of directors' attitudes and actions toward financial reporting, ethics, and business risks, (2) management's emphasis on meeting budget, profit, or other financial or operating goals, (3) management's preference for centralized or decentralized administration and operations and (4) the extent to which one or a few individuals dominate management. A company's philosophy and operating style are often the most important parts of the control environment.

An effective organizational structure gives the company an overall framework for planning, directing, and controlling its operations. It considers such matters as (1) the form, nature, and reporting relationships of an entity's organizational units and management positions, and (2) the assignment of authority and responsibility to these units and positions and the constraints established over their functioning. A key part of an effective organizational structure is a vigilant, informed, and effective audit committee.

Effective methods of communicating and enforcing the assignment of authority and responsibility clarify the understanding of, and improve compliance with, the organization's policies and objectives. These methods consider such matters as: (1) the delegation of authority and responsibility for matters such as organizational goals and objectives, operating functions, and regulatory requirements, (2) the policies regarding acceptable business practices and conflicts of interest, and (3) employee job descriptions delineating specific duties, responsibilities, and constraints. A key method of communicating employee responsibility is through a written code of corporate conduct.

Organizational control methods affect the company's ability to control and supervise its employees and operations effectively. Effective organizational control methods consider such matters as: (1) establishing adequate planning, accounting, and reporting systems, (2) requiring reports that communicate to appropriate individuals exceptions from planned performance, (3) establishing procedures to take appropriate corrective action when exceptions are identified, and (4) monitoring accounting and control systems so they can be modified when necessary. An effective internal audit function is often a particularly important organizational control method.

Personnel management methods influence the company's ability to employ sufficient competent personnel. Effective personnel management methods consider such matters as policies for hiring, training, evaluating, promoting, and compensating employees.

Because of the subjective nature of a company's control environment, assessing its individual components can be difficult. The overall strength of the control environment, however, can be assessed by an individual with sufficient wisdom, experience, and judgment to consider such matters as:

- The degree of emphasis placed on achieving earnings forecasts, meeting budgeted targets, and maintaining or manipulating the market value of the company's stock. Management may be unduly interested in the market price of the company's stock to assist the company with future financing, to prevent secured loans from being called, or to make stock options and other stock compensation more valuable.
- Turnover in key personnel, with special consideration given to unusual retirements or replacements of in-house counsel, internal auditors, or key individuals in the accounting department.

- Management's compensation plans. Plans featuring significant bonuses tied to reported earnings or other quantified targets warrant special attention, as do situations where a significant part of management's compensation results from stock options.
- The company's relationship with outside parties. This analysis considers, for example, how often the company changes independent public accountants, legal counsel, and bankers.
- The company's organizational structure. An unnecessarily complex organizational structure can be used to conceal fraudulent activities.
- Management's attitude toward financial reporting, particularly toward the selection and application of accounting policies.
- The company's delegation of authority and responsibility. This analysis considers whether operating unit management has adequate authority to manage the unit's operations, or whether one or a few individuals dominate the company's financial and operating decisions. Special consideration is given to whether management is so dominant that it impairs the ability of the board of directors and audit committee to exercise their oversight responsibility.
- The capabilities of the company's accounting department. This analysis considers the training and the experience of the key accounting personnel, and the adequacy of overall staffing levels for handling the department's day-to-day activities.
- The effectiveness of the company's internal audit department. This analysis considers such matters as whether the internal auditors have independent access to the audit committee and the CEO, whether the auditors have been adequately trained, and whether they have had sufficient experience. In large entities with decentralized operations, this analysis also can consider the focus and findings of recent internal audit examinations, and the operation's response to the audit findings.
- Management's concern for possible or existing weaknesses in the internal control system, and its responsiveness to known weaknesses in the system.
- The adequacy of the company's internal reporting system. This analysis considers such factors as the quality and the historical accuracy of the company's budgets, whether budgeted and actual amounts are regularly compared, and whether the responsible parties promptly pursue the resolution of any identified differences.
- The company's personnel policies and practices. This analysis considers, for example, whether background checks are made before hiring new employees, whether the company's promotion criteria are fair and adequate, and what the company's policies are for disciplining employees who violate company policies.
- The company's written code of corporate conduct, if one exists. This analysis also considers top management's attitudes toward the written (or unwritten) code of corporate conduct—the key factor determining compliance with the code.
- Management's attitudes toward compliance with laws and regulations affecting the company. This analysis might consider, for example, whether management strives to comply with the full spirit and the intent of regulations or attempts to meet only the minimum standards required.

- Whether the company maintains an established mechanism to report to upper management apparent violations of company policy. Methods frequently used to accomplish this objective include hotlines and ombudsmen. This analysis also considers how the company protects employees from reprisal.

The Institute of Internal Auditors Reports on Fraud

In September 1986, a paper, "Control and Internal Auditing," was prepared by Michael J. Barrett and Roger N. Carolus under the sponsorship of the IIA, and was presented to the NCFFR in association with another IIA-sponsored report. While the reader may wish to review the document and its concept of control, basically it argues that "control" is a "result." It states,[16] "As internal auditors view it, control (a result) is achieved by establishing and combining three control components with controlling activities."

The "essential control components" are stated to be:

1. The attitudes and behavior of the board and executive management;
2. A business plan, which is related to the planning and organizing activities of the board and executive management; and
3. A network of business fundamentals, which flows from the business plan "and establishes the elements and linkages needed to address business exposures in a prudent and cost-effective manner. This network of components and connections is used to direct individuals to perform their work to accomplish established objectives."[17] "The network of fundamentals involves all entities or parties to the organization—major customers, suppliers, and regulators, the board, executive and operating management, supervisors, and rank and file employees."[18]

A reading of the report may clarify the concept and the relationships among the elements.

VARIABILITY OF CONTROL SYSTEMS

Having provided a background on some current standards and other possible guidelines as to internal control systems, it may be helpful to review some of the basic factors and elements that shape the systems.

The manner in which a company is controlled will vary considerably, depending on a great many factors. Among these are:

- Overall size of company

---

[16] *The Institute of Internal Auditors Reports on Fraud*, Sept. 1986, p. 64.
[17] *Ibid.*, p. 68.
[18] *Ibid.*, p. 69.

- Geographic dispersion of operating units
- Degree of centralization or decentralization
- Style of management
- Type of industry
- Relative amount of foreign versus domestic operations
- Management philosophy

In a small company, the owners or management may observe and supervise the day-to-day activities. Usually, they will have a sense or feeling as to how the business is doing—whether shipments are made as scheduled and are properly billed; whether inventories are too high; whether or not quality is up to standard; whether receivables are being collected promptly; and whether the cash is effectively utilized. Under some circumstances, particularly in small companies, duties cannot be segregated as much as desired. Since personal observation by management usually will assure that control objectives are being achieved, extensive documentation of procedures may not be critical.

Yet, as a business grows, much of the personal involvement of owners or senior executives is lost. The senior management usually does not have the time or inclination to ascertain that controls are operating as expected. Its attention is often devoted to basic policy or strategy matters. Consequently, it must rely on the system of controls and the monitoring by others, including the internal auditors, to alert it as to basic failures or deficiencies in the control system.

Given these differences in circumstances, when judging the adequacy of internal control systems, in larger companies (subject to the Act) it probably is incumbent on the board of directors and top management to be more sensitive to the actions taken by each of them so that the appropriate control environment is created. The entire management and operating organization must sense the concern of top management with internal controls and adherence to policies and procedures. Hence, one public accounting firm is of the opinion that particular attention should be given to these factors in considering the control environment:[19]

- Code of business ethics
- Internal audit or monitoring function
- Formal, written control procedures surrounding transactions in areas of high business risk
- Written confirmation from executive and line management affirming compliance with policies and control procedures

---

[19] Joseph E. Connor and Burnell H. DeVos, eds., *Guide to Accounting Controls* (New York: Warren, Gorham & Lamont, 1979), p. 1-15.

ELEMENTS OF INTERNAL ACCOUNTING CONTROL SYSTEMS

The broad objectives of internal accounting control include:

- Safeguarding of assets against loss (or improper use).
- Production of reliable financial records for internal use and external reporting.

These general objectives may be developed into more specific control objectives for each type of asset, and for each transaction, function, or activity as later reviewed in this chapter. Generally, the systems and procedures of a company should provide, on a cost-effective basis, controls to achieve each of these objectives. The elements that make up the system are discussed below.

Competent Personnel and Defined Responsibilities

It is essential to have competent and trustworthy personnel who are given clearly defined lines of authority and responsibility. This is paramount in achieving the objectives of internal control. The people must understand their assigned functions and the prescribed procedures. An adequate number of competent people at each work level must exist. If employees are competent and trustworthy, then reliable financial statements can be produced, even if certain controls are absent. And, given a theoretically acceptable control system, incompetent and dishonest personnel can produce worthless financial statements. Of course, it is preferred to have competent people and an adequate control system.

A proper valuation and placement of personnel is critical. In fact, at each work level, management should be satisfied that the organization has:

- Screened the background of all prospective employees who may perform control functions.
- Determined the qualifications required for each position.
- Provided a clear statement of responsibilities and authority, and the reasons therefor.
- Hired, promoted, or assigned adequately qualified people to the tasks.
- Provided necessary supervision and training.
- Periodically appraised the quality of each individual's performance.

Of course, the proper environment in which the people are to work must be provided. For example, among other things, it means the necessity for following policy should be stressed. And management cannot say one thing in policy manuals and then "wink" at noncompliance, or instruct orally that matters be handled other than as stipulated by policy.

Adequate Segregation of Duties

To prevent either intentional or unintentional errors, duties should be segregated. Several types of segregation will be found helpful:

- ☐ *Separation within the financial function.* For example, separation of those functions relating to the general ledger should be made from those relating to the subsidiary ledger or records. Or, again, duties relating to the cash journals ought to be segregated from those involving the sales journals.
- ☐ *Segregation of the authorization of transactions from custody of the related assets.* For example, those who authorize the purchase of securities should not be custodians of the instruments. Or, those who authorize payment of an invoice should not sign the check.
- ☐ *Separation of operating duties from financial record-keeping.* For instance, those operating supervisors who maintain their own records and who prepare regular reports on their efficiency may be tempted to report biased performance. Where practical, separate financially originated reports should be generated.
- ☐ *Segregation of custody of the assets from maintenance of the related accounting records.* Separation of the accounting for the assets from actual custody of the assets should aid in preventing defalcation or theft. Thus, the segregation of the accounts receivable records maintenance from custody of cash or cash receipts is protective in reducing the conversion of cash to personal use (by kiting, lapping, or otherwise) and the adjustment of the specific customer account by means of a fictitious credit entry.

Existence of Adequate Documents and Records

Documents should be sufficiently specific and of a nature so as to provide reasonable assurance (through test-checking or other method) that the transaction is properly recorded and that the asset is adequately controlled. Thus, purchase orders, receiving reports, and related vendor invoices should exist. In addition, the records and documents should be:

- Sufficiently simple to reasonably assure that they are understood.
- Designed in such a manner that correct preparation tends to be assured. Thus, blank spaces should be provided for authorizations or approvals, and instructions should be provided on the form for proper routing and the disposition of each copy.
- Prenumbered consecutively, where practical, to facilitate accounting for all documents and later locating them when required.
- Designed for multiple use so as to minimize the need for different forms.
- Prepared within a reasonable time period after the transaction occurs, if it cannot be prepared before the event. Too much delay enhances the chance of error or omission.

Adequate Authorization Procedures

As stated earlier, each company has unique features. But each transaction must be properly authorized if control is to be adequate. Obviously, if any individual in an organization could acquire or dispose of assets at will, chaos would result.

These authorizations may be of a general or specific nature. Thus, the board of directors or top management may give general authorization to do certain things through the establishment of policies that the organization must follow. At lower levels within the company, certain supervisors must implement these policies by approving or disapproving certain transactions, depending on whether or not they are within the limits set by policy. Thus, a sales manager may issue fixed price lists for the sale of products within the criteria established by general policy.

In contrast to general authority, specific authority relates to individual transactions. For some types of transactions, for example, such as acquisition of a company or contracting for a multimillion dollar construction project, the board of directors may be unwilling to grant general authorization. Instead, it may insist on a case-by-case authorization. The type of authorization obviously will depend on many factors, for example, the management level of the person granted the authorization, the degree of confidence by the granting authority in the judgment and integrity of the grantee, the nature of the business, the geographical dispersion, and the degree of centralization, to name a few. Be that as it may, from a sound control standpoint, there must be an adequate system of authorization that is observed.

One should distinguish between authorization and approval. Approval merely constitutes assent—on the basis that the conditions required by the authorization have been met. Thus, approval of a sales order indicates that it seems to be in accordance with the terms and conditions required by the authorization. Review of the internal control system often will need to distinguish between authorization and approval and require an examination of the effectiveness of the approval process.

LEVELS OF BUSINESS ACTIVITY

In studying internal controls, it is helpful to recognize that planning and internal control are inextricably intermeshed or associated, and that the systems can be segregated into three activity levels:

1. Strategic planning
2. Tactical and short-term planning and control
3. Detailed operational control

These levels should be distinguished because each segment of an internal control system has certain objectives or goals. The purpose of the review is, among other things, to recognize these objectives, whether broad or functional; evaluate whether they are proper; and consider whether or not the control techniques employed are sufficient to achieve the objective sought.

Strategic Planning

Strategic planning may be defined as the process of determining the long-term major business objectives of a company and the policies and strategies that will govern the acquisition, use, and disposition of resources to achieve those objectives.

Tactical Planning

Tactical planning, or short-term planning, and its related control activities, relates to a period of perhaps one, two, or even five years in which detailed, coordinated, and comprehensive plans are made for the major functions of the business. The aim is to deploy or spend specific resources on a coordinated and controlled basis to reach short-term objectives that follow the policies or strategies laid down in the strategic planning.

Detailed Operational Control

Finally, detailed operational control in this context is related to the day-to-day routine transactions, functions, and activities and is intended to assure that such routines are conducted efficiently and effectively—as measured against standards, or the plan.

Detailed operational controls most frequently are reviewed as functions or activities, since this most often is the manner in which companies are organized; that is, companies are controlled by the segregation of functional authority and responsibility. A function or activity usually is represented by an individual or department of an organization that has specific and defined responsibilities for executing and processing transactions and for performing other activities related to operational objectives. Transactions as herein defined are the basic components of the business and include an exchange of assets or services with parties within the entity (i.e., conversion and transfer of inventory) or with parties outside of the business (i.e., sale and delivery of a product). Examples of functions or activities at each of the three activity levels are given in Figure 17-2. Sensitivity as to how actions in one level may have an impact on another level of control is desirable. Thus, fictitious sales must not be booked in order to meet the monthly profit plan.

It should be mentioned, finally, that detailed operational control as well as short-term tactical control must view both (1) the divisional or systems level controls in the profit centers or cost centers and (2) the corporate level

FIG. 17-2
Activities or Functions by Level of Business Activity

Strategic Planning
- Deciding business objectives or purposes
- Devising the strategy to achieve the objective
- Establishing and quantifying long-term goals
- Determining organization structure
- Establishing marketing plans
- Setting functional policies
- Deciding manufacturing policies

Short-Term Planning
- Formulating the annual profit plan
- Approving annual research budget
- Setting asset turnover goals for the year
- Planning staff levels
- Setting sales goals
- Determining working capital requirements
- Determining production levels

Detailed Operational Control
- Recording sales transaction
- Comparing departmental budget and actual expenditure
- Analyzing and checking inventory turnover of stock
- Hiring new personnel
- Comparing actual and planned sales goals for the month
- Controlling account receivable collections
- Scheduling the weekly production

---

controls that seek to assure that proper systems are operative at the various subsidiary areas.

INTERNAL ACCOUNTING CONTROL OBJECTIVES

Practically speaking, in a review of control objectives, while an overall view at all activity levels is necessary, most time is spent analyzing and evaluating rather detailed or lower-level transactions or functional controls. With respect to internal accounting controls, the detailed review is essential to see that the overall objectives of safeguarding the assets and assuring the reliability of the accounting records and information are achieved.

What, then, are the objectives of the accounting control system or the transaction cycle? What is the purpose of each control? While several classifications may be given, those specified or implied in the accounting standards provisions of the FCPA, enacted in 1977, are most valid and can be applied most readily to any type of transaction, activity, function, or account.

1. *Authorization*. Was the transaction authorized by management, either as a general authorization through the establishment of related policies or as a specific authorization? Thus, a construction contract may have been executed within the limits established by policy, or a specific authorization may have been necessary by reason of unusual risks.

2. *Recording*. Was the transaction properly recorded? All authorized transactions should be recorded in the correct amount, in the appropriate account (including amounts and quantities in related subsidiary records), and with a full and proper description. No fictitious transactions should be recorded.

3. *Safeguarding of assets*. Is responsibility for physical custody of the asset assigned to specific personnel who are independent of the related record-keeping functions? Direct physical access to assets should be limited to designated people, and indirect access to the assets (records or paperwork) should be limited to those properly authorized. Where applicable, as in handling cash or securities, are there appropriate physical facilities (e.g., vaults and locked storeroom)?

4. *Reconciliation*. Are records periodically compared with actual inventory or count? Thus, are bank reconciliations made with reasonable frequency? Are physical inventories compared with book quantities? Are detailed records reconciled to the control account?

5. *Valuation*. Are recorded amounts reviewed for impairment in value? Are provisions for loss or direct write-down, as may be appropriate, made so as to comply with generally accepted accounting practices?

These control objectives, together with an understanding of the basic functions or components of the business, provide the framework for evaluating the internal accounting controls. The *general* control objectives must be supported by *specific* control objectives of each major transaction cycle, function, or activity, and evaluated as discussed in the next four chapters.

EDP and Internal Accounting Controls

The types of records or information systems within a company do not affect the *objectives* of internal accounting control of each transaction system. But they do influence the *manner* in which the control objectives are achieved. With the growing use of computers or EDP, the reviewer of any system will

INTERNAL CONTROL

need to consider what controls and segregation of duties are necessary. For example, EDP can have an impact on the control system of a company in any number of ways[20]:

- In EDP systems, no documentary evidence is left of the performance of certain controls, or the evidence of performance is indirect.
- In EDP systems, information is often recorded only in machine readable form and cannot be read without the use of a computer and related computer programs.
- It may be more difficult to achieve an adequate segregation of duties in the EDP function.
- The decrease in human involvement in the processing of transactions in EDP systems may obscure errors that might otherwise have been observed in non-EDP systems.
- It is often difficult to make changes after an EDP system has been implemented. Thus, greater care is necessary in designing and changing EDP systems.
- With proper controls, EDP systems can provide greater reliability than non-EDP systems because EDP systems subject all data to the same procedures and controls. Non-EDP systems may be subject to human error on a random basis.

Although there are differences between EDP and other systems, these differences do not affect the objectives of internal accounting control for any transaction system. Rather, they impact on how the control objectives are achieved. In addition, the reviewer will need to consider procedural controls and segregation of duties within the EDP operations.

Cost-Effective Controls Needed

In instituting suitable accounting controls, the concept contemplates reasonable, but not absolute, assurance that the objectives to be attained by the system will in fact be achieved. As mentioned in the Statement on Auditing Standards,[21] "The concept of reasonable assurance recognizes that the cost of internal control should not exceed the benefits expected to be derived." In the normal institution of accounting control procedures, materiality is a factor most often considered by both management and the independent auditors.

However, with the imposition of the FCPA, materiality at present cannot be used by SEC-registered companies as a measure of the importance of the control. However, the cost-benefit relationship can be; and this is a prime determinant of whether a known weakness in internal accounting controls should be corrected, irrespective of any statutory requirement.

---

[20] *Ibid.*, p. 1-35. Copyright © 1979 by Price Waterhouse & Co. Reprinted with permission.
[21] Statement on Auditing Standards. No. 1, *op. cit.*, AU § 320.20.

The phrase "cost benefit" conveys the idea that costs should be measured against benefits, and business judgment would say that the costs expended should not exceed the benefits received. When a "weakness" is discovered in the internal accounting control system, the questions arise: What is the cost of correcting it? And is it worth the cost? For example, correcting a computer routine might be very costly. The weakness identified might be of two types: (1) instances where the transactions are not executed or recorded as they should be, resulting in errors and a potential asset loss; or (2) instances where the existing control system will not detect the error or irregularities on a *timely* basis after they have occurred. The amount of loss or exposure must be identified or measured to determine the importance of the weakness. This involves determining the probable magnitude of each "error" and the frequency of probable occurrence. Aside from removal of such quantifiable losses, the correction may produce other qualitative benefits, such as the confidence of the board of directors or management in the information presented.

Corrective action, of course, may take either of two avenues, or a combination of both:

1. Those actions taken that are not directly related to the accounting system; thus, continued inventory shortages might lead to purchase instead of manufacture
2. Changes to be made in the accounting control system, increasing the record keeping or changing points of control

Most cost-benefit determinations are just plain common sense. Others may be quite involved. The reader is referred to some of the literature on the subject.[22]

RESPONSIBILITY OF SENIOR MANAGEMENT AND DIRECTORS

The responsibility for assuring that an adequate system of internal controls is in place in a company and is operating effectively has been delegated to management. As to larger companies covered by the Securities Exchange Act of 1934, the impact of the FCPA perhaps serves to make this responsibility more real. In a general sense, management has the obligation to see that record keeping is adequate and sufficiently detailed to serve internal management purposes as well as for statement preparation for shareholders and other interested parties.

The board of directors is charged with the ultimate responsibility for all activities of the company, and acts as a general overseer of the various

---

[22] Connor and DeVos, *op. cit.,* pp. 1-45, 2-31, 3-30, 4-40, 5-38, 6-32, 7-34, 8-36, and 9-26.

INTERNAL CONTROL

management functions. Among other things, it must assure itself that management is carrying out its responsibilities. The board has a right to rely on management performing its proper function in the entire area of internal control. While more detailed statements of responsibility are included later in this chapter, the board of directors, perhaps through its audit committee, probably should review such matters as:

- The existence of a strong ethical climate—the tone at the top—to protect against fraud.
- The manner in which management has obtained reasonable assurances about the operation of the system of internal accounting control.
- From time to time, those actions the management believes necessary to correct weaknesses, if any, in the system.
- The rationale for not correcting specified weaknesses, if they exist.
- The conclusion of management as to the adequacy of internal controls, compliance with the FCPA, and the accuracy of the published financial statements, or any public report on internal controls.

ROLE OF THE EXTERNAL AUDITOR

Since the independent accountants review the system of internal accounting controls, often management is of the opinion that such a review is sufficient, and that it need not be further involved in an evaluation of internal accounting controls. As a general statement, the control evaluation performed by the external auditor in connection with the annual audit of the financial statements cannot be relied on to discharge management's responsibility as regards such controls. The purpose of such evaluation by the external auditors is to establish the amount of reliance thereon in determining the nature, extent, and timing of audit tests to be applied in the examination of the financial statements. Because there are inherent limitations in the internal control system, the independent auditor usually will employ additional auditing procedures to detect material errors or irregularities. Given the recommendations of the NCFFR (see Chapter 23) for the independent public accountant, some of the standards for detection of weaknesses in internal control may change.

As a summary, there are at least three ways in which the management viewpoint and involvement as to internal controls will differ from that of the independent public auditor:

1. *Scope and materiality.* The independent auditor basically is concerned only with significant weaknesses in those control systems on which he intends to rely in the examination. On the other hand, management has a responsibility for seeing that *each system* is in place and is operating properly. It is con-

cerned with each internal accounting control system dealing with financial activities and with many control systems not involving financial records.
2. *Reliance.* Management relies on many systems for decision making and to achieve the control objectives. It should not be limited to those that auditors have selected for testing in a given time period. Auditors usually do not test or rely on all systems.
3. *Alternative checks.* The external auditor must test for compliance those internal control systems on which he will rely. In contrast, management has alternative mechanisms to ascertain how a policy or procedure is adhered to. Among those may be internal audit programs, exception reporting, and selective personal involvement by management itself.

In general, then, it is incumbent on management to seek its own assurances as to the adequacy of the internal control system and not rely on the independent auditor.

INTERNAL AUDIT DEPARTMENT

In a text on internal auditing, special mention should be made of the role of the internal auditor.

Primary responsibility for compliance with the prescribed policies and procedures involving the control system, of course, must rest with the individuals who supervise the related daily activities. But business is dynamic and constantly changing. As activities become different in character, control procedures may need to change. As personnel changes occur, procedures are often dropped or not followed through lack of understanding. Yet, sound policies and procedures are of little value unless followed. Hence, there must be a rather continuous monitoring of the control system.

Management's responsibility for an effectively operating control system is a continuous one. Given changes in policies, procedures, environmental conditions, and personnel, the monitoring needs are ongoing.

The task of monitoring the control system, both administrative controls and internal accounting controls, often falls to the internal audit department. The ability to carry out this responsibility will, of course, depend on the independence of the department, the number and quality of internal auditors, the experience of the members and the leadership, and the quality of the management of the department. These topics are covered elsewhere, in Chapters 7 through 10. Suffice it to say that the increased professionalism and status of the internal audit practitioners permits greater management reliance on this function as an effective element in the control system. This improved status should be assisted by the recommendations of the NCFFR. (See Chapter 23.)

ALLOCATION OF RESPONSIBILITY FOR ADEQUATE INTERNAL CONTROLS

As stated repeatedly, the responsibility for reasonably assuring that an adequate system of controls is in place and is effective is that of management. Yet, the various members of management may not be sufficiently aware of their specific responsibilities. In any given company, the assignment of duties and responsibilities may vary. The following outline may be useful to those who must discuss placement of responsibility. It attempts to differentiate the various responsibilities.

Role of the Board of Directors

The board of directors is ultimately responsible for the governance of the corporation. It has responsibility for acting as a general overseer of all management activities. In reality, the board must ascertain that management is carrying out its responsibilities properly; but it has a right to rely on management in those areas where it believes the management is knowledgeable and competent. It must not get too involved in the details. In the area of controls, the board should

- Determine that the proper ethical environment and discipline exist within the company to make the controls effective.
- Be certain that the audit committee is informed, vigilant, and effective as overseers of the internal controls and the financial reporting process.
- Understand, in a general way, how the financial accounting system operates.
- Ascertain, again in a general way, how the internal control system (administrative controls and internal accounting controls) operates.
- Ascertain that the system is effective and sufficient to:
  —Safeguard the assets
  —Permit the issuance of accurate and complete financial reports for both internal and external purposes.
  In this connection, attention probably should be paid to the ability of management to "override the system" or circumvent the controls in important aspects.
  —Ascertain that a code of business ethics exists to govern conduct of employees.
  —Determine that an adequate monitoring system, usually performed by the internal auditing department, exists and that corrective action is instituted as necessary.
- Arrange for at least annual reviews to monitor compliance (with the general management, financial management, internal auditors, and independent accountants).

Role of Senior Corporate Management

Although the board of directors has ultimate responsibility for governing the corporation, it is the senior management that must assume primary responsibility for managing the company, and, in this context, for the operation of an effective control system. It is responsible to the board of directors for the safeguarding of assets and preparation of accurate financial reports in the context of the FCPA. It is this management group that is responsible for detailed implementation and enforcement of the systems.

Specifically, senior corporate management probably should perform the following in carrying out its duties:

- Identify the risks inherent in the business and the potential sources of significant errors and irregularities.
- Establish the proper environment for the control systems.
- Issue the code of ethics and the necessary policies and procedures for guiding the business, and be sure they are communicated to all levels of management.
- Direct the establishment of the necessary control systems, including:
  —Proper documentation
  —Periodic review
  —Overseeing of necessary changes
- Periodically review with the legal staff conformance to legal requirements.
- Assume responsibility for the issuance of financial reports and statements to the shareholders

Role of Financial Management

To be sure, the senior financial officer, as a member of top management, has the same responsibilities as senior management. But, in the real world, the financial management probably will be more heavily involved with the control systems than will other operating executives. Certainly, it will participate extensively in matters relating to internal accounting controls. This is a field in which the financial discipline can exhibit its professionalism and special knowledge in the controls field. But, in many instances, the financial officer will have a direct responsibility for reviewing and monitoring administrative controls as well as the accounting controls, and, to a degree, the operational controls.

As to internal accounting controls, the financial management, perhaps through the controller, normally should:

- Know the technical requirements of an adequate system of internal accounting control.
- Cause to be installed throughout the company, in divisions, departments, and subsidiaries, as well as at the corporate headquarters, effective internal control systems.

- Periodically review the system and monitor performance, perhaps through the use of the internal auditors. Make necessary changes, or correct deficiencies where feasible and practical.
- Enforce conformance to policies and procedures.
- Meet, as frequently as deemed necessary, with the independent accountants to gain their views as to the adequacy and effectiveness of the system.
- Work closely with the internal auditors in maintaining effective systems.
- Be responsible to the chief executive officer for the accuracy of the internal management reports of a financial nature, and for the reliability of the financial statements to the public and governmental agencies.

Role of Chief Internal Auditor

The role of the internal auditing department has been discussed earlier in this chapter. Suffice it to say, again, that the existence of a highly qualified internal auditing department is an important part of the internal control system. Among other things, this group is the eyes and ears of all management—particularly senior management and top financial management—in its role of monitoring the internal control system. To this independent group more than any others, the senior management and the board of directors will look for assistance in assuring that:

- An adequate system of internal controls exists.
- The system is effective for the purposes intended.
- Any deficiencies are brought to the attention of appropriate management.

Techniques for providing this assistance are discussed in Chapter 18.

Role of Independent Accountant

Up to this point, the discussion on responsibility for internal controls has rested on the role of various management levels or functions. An earlier discussion in this chapter centered on the differing viewpoint of management and the independent accountants in any review of the internal control system. Yet, this is not to say that there is no interface between the public accountants and company management. Although the independent auditors will review the control system to ascertain what reliance can be placed on it in rendering an opinion on the company financial statements, the outside auditor is in a unique position to counsel or provide assurance to the board of directors and other members of management, as to the adequacy of the internal accounting controls. The opinions expressed will presumably be objective and independent, and will be further grounded on the firm's experience with the control systems of other companies—some in the industry of the particular client and some outside of it.

As a summary, the independent auditor may perform these functions related to internal control:

1. *Review the system of internal control to:*
   - Determine the degree of reliance to be placed thereon in formulating the nature and extent of audit tests to be performed, regarding the opinion on the financial statements.
   - Communicate the significant findings to appropriate levels of management: the entire board of directors, the audit committee, senior management, and financial management at varying levels, as may be necessary or desirable.
2. *Provide technical assistance.* Independent auditors may provide instructional manuals and assistance on techniques for reviewing, documenting, testing, and evaluating internal controls.
3. *Training.* Independent auditors may conduct training programs for company financial personnel or internal auditors on techniques of review, evaluation, and cost-benefit trade-off calculations.

Thus, the independent accountants are in a position to assist company management and provide added assurance on the status of controls to the board of directors. And their responsibility, through the adoption of revised standards (see NCFFR recommendations) may increase.

MANAGEMENT REPRESENTATIONS TO THE PUBLIC

Given the importance of internal controls and management's responsibility for the financial statements and adequate controls, companies in recent years have increasingly included in the annual report to shareholders a statement concerning these subjects. As a matter of fact, the NCFFR recommends that such a statement be included in the annual report, and that it be signed by the chief executive officer and chief accounting officer. Illustrated in Figure 17-3 is the report by Monsanto Company contained in its annual report to shareholders for the year 1986.[23]

While the content may change somewhat, in the light of the NCFFR recommendations (see Chapter 23), several features contained in this statement, as well as that of numerous other companies, are of interest:

- Management acknowledges its responsibility for the financial statements (and not the independent accountants).
- Reference is made to the internal accounting controls that are designed to provide reasonable assurance of the reliability of the financial records and the proper safeguarding and use of its assets.

---

[23] Monsanto Company 1986 Annual Report. Reprinted with permission.

FIG. 17-3
Illustrative Declaration in Annual Report—Monsanto Company

> Monsanto Company management is responsible for the fair presentation and consistency of all financial data included in this Annual Report. Where necessary, the data reflect management estimates.
>
> Management also is responsible for maintaining a system of internal accounting controls to provide reasonable assurance that assets are safeguarded against material loss from unauthorized use or disposition and that authorized transactions are properly recorded to permit the preparation of accurate financial data. Cost-benefit judgments are an important consideration in this regard. The effectiveness of internal controls is maintained by: (1) personnel selection and training; (2) division of responsibilities; (3) establishment and communication of policies; and (4) ongoing internal review programs and audits.
>
> As ratified by shareowner vote at the 1986 Annual Meeting, Deloitte Haskins & Sells was appointed to examine, and express an opinion as to the fair presentation of, the consolidated financial statements. This opinion appears below.*
>
> Monsanto's Audit Committee, consisting of six nonemployee directors, meets with Controllership, Internal Audit and Deloitte Haskins & Sells personnel to review internal controls, financial reporting and accounting practices. Deloitte Haskins & Sells and internal auditors meet with the Committee, with and without management present, to discuss their examinations, the adequacy of internal controls and the quality of financial reporting.
>
> Richard J. Mahoney
> Chairman and
> Chief Executive Officer
>
> Francis A. Stroble
> Senior Vice-President and
> Chief Financial Officer
>
> February 27, 1987
>
> * Not included.

- A statement is made concerning the examination of the financial statements by the independent accountants.
- Finally, the nature of the audit committee, its functions, and free access to it by both the independent accountants and internal auditors is commented on.

LIMITATIONS ON INTERNAL CONTROL

A final word is in order with respect to internal controls. Prudent management will not rely solely on internal controls to the exclusion of other reviews—whether by management itself, or by the internal auditors, or by the independent accountants. To reiterate, there are three reasons why such periodic checks are desirable:

1. Any typical control system provides reasonable, but not absolute, assurance that the objectives of the system are met. Rare is the system that can "guar-

antee" that all errors or irregularities have been eliminated or corrected on a timely basis. The extensive detailed checking probably necessary to do this would be cost prohibitive. And, of course, human beings can be quite creative in circumventing the system if sufficient time, opportunity, and/or collusion, is present.
2. Given the human weaknesses in communication, mistakes in judgment, or other personal failures, and even acts by management itself, such conditions impose limitations on control procedures.
3. Because of continuous changes in personnel, procedures, and business operations, a given control system can become obsolete.

For these reasons, among others, a continuous vigilance and review are essential.

SUGGESTED READING

Broadus, W. A., Jr., and Joseph D. Comtois. "The Single Audit Act: A Needed Reform." *Journal of Accountancy,* Apr. 1985, pp. 62–70

Connor, Joseph E., and Burnell H. DeVos, Jr. *Guide to Accounting Controls.* New York: Warren, Gorham & Lamont, 1979, 1984.

Eichen, Susan P., and Mary Ann Domurachi. "Designing Internal Control Systems for Appropriate Management Control." *Corporate Accounting,* Fall 1986, pp. 20–28.

Jacobsen, Peter D., and Robert K. Elliott. "GAAS: Reconsidering the 'Ten Commandments.'" *Journal of Accountancy,* May 1984, pp. 77–88.

Johnson, Kenneth P., and Henry R. Jaenicke, *Evaluating Internal Control.* New York: John Wiley & Sons, 1980.

Kirby, Barbara J. "Establishing Control Through Computer Systems Development." *Corporate Accounting,* Summer 1983, pp. 39–43.

Loebbecke, James K., and George R. Zuber. "Evaluating Internal Control." *Journal of Accountancy,* Feb. 1980, pp. 39–46.

Statement on Auditing Standards No. 1, *Codification of Auditing Standards and Procedures.* New York: AICPA, 1973.

CHAPTER **18**

Auditing Internal Control

Introduction	2
Clarification of Terms	2
Relevance of Internal Accounting Control	4
Integration of the FCPA With Internal Accounting Control	4
Aids for Auditing Internal Accounting Control	5
Approaches, Programs, Questionnaires, and Documentation	5
Evaluations Used by Public Accountants	6
Considering the Business	8
Formulating Internal Accounting Control Objectives	8
Evaluating Whether Control Techniques Achieve the Objectives	9
Summary Checklist on Evaluating Internal Control	9
The External Auditor's Responsibility for Internal Control	20
The Current Picture	20
The Exposure Drafts	20
The Concept of Control Structure	20
Implications	22
The Concept of Reportable Conditions	24
The Effect on Internal Auditors	26
Building on Techniques Developed by Public Accountants	26
Need for a Combination of Techniques	28
Detailed Auditing of Internal Control ...	28
Definition	28
Objective	29
Unique Characteristics	31
Focus Is on a Single Function, Cycle, or Activity	31
All Aspects of Control Are Included	31
Questionnaires Are Used	32
Tests Cover a Period of Time	32
Separate Audit Reports With Limited Distribution	32
Advantages and Disadvantages	36
Internal Control Survey	37
Definition	37
Objective	37
Unique Characteristics	39
Focus Is on Accounting Entity	39
Evaluation Limited to Accounting Controls	40
Limited Testing	41
Absence of Questionnaires	41
Comprehensive Reports With Full Distribution	43
Audit Programs	43
Advantages and Disadvantages	48
Final Thoughts	48
Suggested Reading	49

Fig. 18-1	Approach to Internal Accounting Control Evaluation	7
Fig. 18-2	Operating Components of a Typical Commercial or Industrial Business	11
Fig. 18-3	Evaluation Process for Financial Management	12
Fig. 18-4	Evaluation Process for Financial Reporting	14
Fig. 18-5	Guide in Evaluating Cash Receipts	16
Fig. 18-6	Flow Chart Depicting the Cash Disbursements Cycle	18
Fig. 18-7	Sample Questionnaire on Internal Control for Sales, Billings, Receivables, and Collection Cycle	19
Fig. 18-8	Sample Detailed Internal Control Audit Report With No Findings	29

18-1

Fig. 18-9	Sample Detailed Internal Control Audit Report With Findings	30
Fig. 18-10	Internal Control Questionnaire for Cash Disbursements	33
Fig. 18-11	Audit Program for Cash Receipts	35
Fig. 18-12	Internal Control Survey Report	38
Fig. 18-13	Specimen Workpaper Documenting Internal Controls	42
Fig. 18-14	Illustration of Documenting Internal Control Evaluation	44
Fig. 18-15	Audit Program for Internal Accounting Control Survey	46

INTRODUCTION

The auditor's study and evaluation has long been a staple of auditing—whether it is external, internal, or governmental. It is a subject for which professional auditing standards of each branch of auditing provide guidance. The subject is also characterized by frequent refinements of underlying concepts, approaches, and techniques that continue right up to the present. This chapter offers discussions of internal control auditing from the standpoints of both external and internal auditors.

At the outset, it is important to note that the external auditor's study and evaluation of internal control required by the second standard of fieldwork (see Chapter 4) was revised in 1988. In fact, the question of whether the second standard itself should be revised or eliminated is under active consideration by the ASB. The effect, if any, of the revised guidance promulgated by the ASB on the internal auditor's objectives regarding internal control is being discussed by the IIA's PSRC. Thus, the subject of auditing internal controls promises to be one about which much will be said in the near future. Internal auditors must watch developments carefully and assess whether strategies continue to be appropriate.

Clarification of Terms

Chapter 17 provides definitions for internal control and associated terms. These definitions, taken from professional literature at different points in time, illustrate the evolutionary nature of the subject. They also punctuate the confluence of differing conceptual bases that has emerged for explaining internal control. The result is an often confusing mixture of terminology that means different things to different people. The following is a representative sampling of the terms that exist today regarding internal control:

- Control
- Internal control
- Internal accounting control
- Internal administrative control
- Management control

AUDITING INTERNAL CONTROL

- Operational control
- Preventative control
- Detective control
- Effective control

To this array of terms must be added a few new terms to keep pace with the ASB. In its draft proposal on *Consideration of the Internal Control Structure in a Financial Statement Audit*, these terms were born:

- Internal control structure
- Control environment
- Accounting system
- Control procedures

Simultaneously with the birth of these terms, the ASB drew the curtain on internal accounting control and internal administrative control. Yet, such terms remain in law if not professional literature. As Chapter 17 notes, the FCPA uses the term "internal accounting control" in the Accounting Standards Section. That section of the Act was borrowed from the AICPA AU Section 320 as it existed at the time. While the Act does not use the term "internal administrative control" explicitly, its existence is implied by use of the term "internal accounting control."

Why do these terms occur? In the author's view, they are the inevitable result of efforts to clarify or focus on the aspects of internal control in which there is particular interest by a particular body. In other words, the terms have relevance in the context of the objectives of the interest group. For external auditors examining financial statements, internal control needs to be assessed with an eye on what elements of internal control are relevant to the preparation of financial statements intended to portray financial position, changes in financial position, and operating results in accordance with GAAP. These internal control elements are also of interest to management and internal auditors. But, they are interested in other internal control elements. So it is not surprising that such terms as "management control" and "operating control" evolved.

Internal auditors and others interested in understanding internal control must first know that the terminology must be understood. To do so requires that the context in which the terminology is used be understood. In this chapter, the term "internal control" will be used in two different contexts. When discussing internal control from the external auditors' perspective, it is in the more limited context of internal controls applicable to the preparation of financial statements. In other instances, the term is used in the broader context inherent in the definition of the term control by the IIA. As Chapter 17 indicates, the IIA defines control as any action taken by management to enhance the likelihood that established objectives and goals will be achieved.

Relevance of Internal Accounting Control

While the term "internal control" is central to this chapter, the term "internal accounting control" continues to have special relevance. It derives from management's need to be informed in a timely fashion of those facts necessary to make business decisions and those relating to compliance with policies and procedures. Generally, the more distant is the management from the affected activities (both geographically and organizationally), the more critical is the need.

The type of information required varies with circumstances. Daily sales reports, weekly cash forecasts, daily labor distribution reports, cost versus budget analyses, and aged accounts receivable schedules are typical examples of differing needs. Whatever the content or format, the information must enable interested management to monitor the activities for which it is responsible.

The amount of information needed is often proportional to the size and complexity of the managing organization. In most companies, because there are so many varying activities and functions that must be managed, the volume is considerable.

In addition to satisfying internal management needs, information must be accumulated and reported to a host of external interest groups to comply with the numerous legal and regulatory requirements. Examples include annual reports to shareholders, SEC filings, FTC Reports, and income tax and other information returns filed with the IRS.

Obviously, information is useful to those who need it only if it is accurate, complete, and timely. Internal accounting control seeks to reasonably assure accuracy and completeness—within economic limitations. Because information is valuable, it is important that it be afforded sufficient protection. Thus, safeguarding information is also involved in internal accounting control.

Because maintaining adequate internal accounting control is mandated by the FCPA, it is of special significance to management and internal auditors. It is incumbent on all internal auditing functions of companies subject to the FCPA to develop and execute an ongoing program of internal accounting control evaluation and testing. The basis for such an approach follows.

Integration of the FCPA With Internal Accounting Control

To be meaningful in today's environment, any audit approach designed to provide information and assurance to management and the board of directors regarding internal accounting control must be integrated with the FCPA requirements. According to the Act, and as stated in Chapter 17, an adequate system of internal accounting control is one that is sufficient to provide reasonable assurance that:

AUDITING INTERNAL CONTROL 18-5

- Transactions are executed in accordance with management's general or specific authorizations.
- Transactions are recorded as necessary in order to:
  — Permit preparation of financial statements in conformity with GAAP or other applicable criteria.
  — Maintain accountability for its assets.
- Access to assets is permitted only in accordance with management authorization.
- The recorded accountability for assets is compared with existing assets at reasonable intervals, and appropriate action is taken with respect to any differences.

Integrating this concept of adequacy into an audit approach requires that any internal accounting control system be evaluated in terms of its:

- Authorization and execution objectives
- Transaction processing (recording objectives)
- Accessibility (safeguarding) objectives
- Accountability (reporting) and valuation objectives

Identifying sufficient internal accounting control techniques to achieve each of the foregoing objectives is a prerequisite in meeting the requirements of the Act.

Consequently, there is no reason why the foregoing could not be applied to the broader concept of internal control. That is because internal accounting control is a subset of internal control. If internal accounting control adequacy may be determined in terms of authorization, transaction processing, accessibility, and accountability, so may the adequacy of other internal control elements be determined. This important point permits an entire audit approach to be applied, as explained later in this chapter.

AIDS FOR AUDITING INTERNAL ACCOUNTING CONTROL

Approaches, Programs, Questionnaires, and Documentation

Effective auditing of internal accounting control requires that the auditor possess suitable audit tools. These include an organized approach to internal control auditing, an audit program for testing the existence of controls, and either a detailed internal control questionnaire or some other form of documentation to evidence the extent of evaluation. Other aids, usually available in the organizational unit, include organization charts, procedure manuals, flow charts, job descriptions, charts of accounts, and various record files and logs. These are self-explanatory and are mentioned only to remind the reader of their use for purposes of internal control auditing.

A considerable amount of information has been written in recent years to further aid the evaluation and testing of internal control. This information has been published by the AICPA, the IIA, government audit agencies (such as the Defense Contract Audit Agency), academicians, public accounting firms, and others. The chief internal auditor should draw from these sources, as well as internal sources and applicable industry sources, to develop the aids that in his opinion will enable professional internal accounting control reviews to occur.

While all audit aids are important, probably the most critical is the approach that is employed to conduct internal control auditing. Among the approaches available for use are the following:

- Using flow charts to identify controls, and evaluating in terms of prescribed, preferred practices to achieve specified control objectives for major transaction cycles (e.g., revenue cycle)
- Identifying and evaluating controls in terms of questionnaires designed according to specified classes of transactions (e.g., cash receipts and cash disbursements)
- Identifying and evaluating controls to achieve specified control objectives for operating components and related activities (e.g., administration, production, or service and finance)
- Identifying and evaluating controls necessary to prevent or detect errors that could occur for specific transaction types (e.g., similar to transaction cycles)

These approaches are similar in that specific controls are evaluated in terms of accomplishing identified control objectives. The principal difference between them involves the means employed in the evaluation and documentation process. Illustrative methodologies are described in the balance of this chapter.

Evaluations Used by Public Accountants

The concept of relating control techniques to specific control objectives within major divisions of internal accounting control was first developed by the large public accounting firms. A diagram of the approach of Price Waterhouse & Co. to the control evaluation is shown in Figure 18-1.[1]

This basic approach is applied to each major component or function of the business that is involved with accounting controls. (Some examples are provided later in this chapter.) Through a series of guides for each selected transaction system (e.g., revenues and receivables, purchases and payables, production costs and inventories, productive assets, employee compensation and benefits, financial management, and financial reporting, to name a

---

[1] Joseph E. Connor and Burnell H. DeVos, Jr., eds., *Guide to Accounting Controls* (New York: Warren, Gorham & Lamont, 1979), pp. 1-68–1-69. Copyright © 1979 by Price Waterhouse & Co. Adapted with permission.

AUDITING INTERNAL CONTROL

FIG. 18-1

Approach to Internal Accounting Control Evaluation

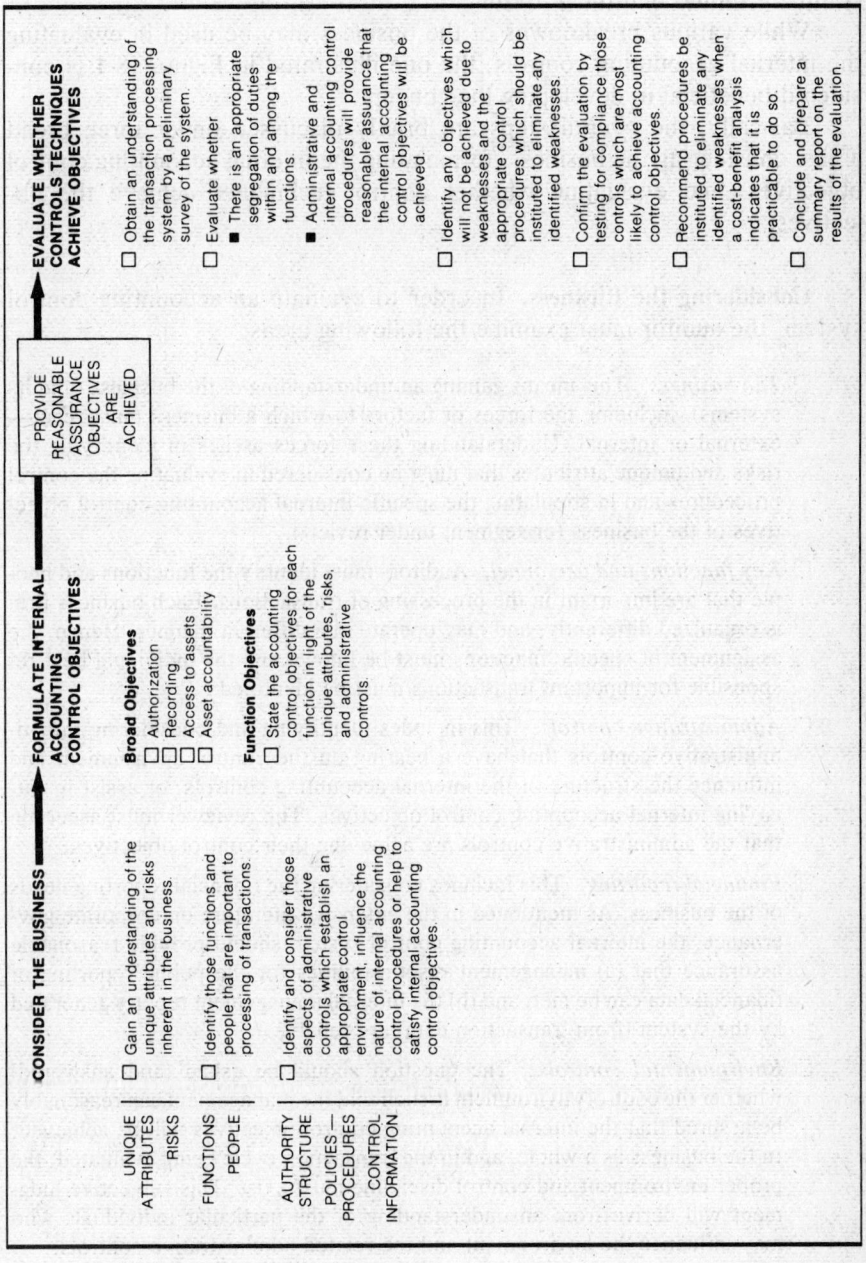

few), a road map is provided as a means of developing an evaluation program. The financial management and the internal auditors of almost any type of company should find them useful.

While various breakdowns of the business may be used in evaluating the internal accounting controls, the one illustrated in Figure 18-1 is considered beneficial in developing the concept.

Basically, the overall steps are briefly discussed under three broad areas: considering the business, formulating the internal accounting control objectives, and evaluating whether control techniques achieve the objectives.

Considering the Business. In order to evaluate an accounting control system, the auditor must examine the following areas:

- ☐ *The business.* This means gaining an understanding of the business (and its systems), including the forces or factors to which a business must react—external or internal. Understanding these forces assists in identifying the risks and unique attributes that must be considered in evaluating the control procedures and in stipulating the specific internal accounting control objectives of the business (or segment under review).

- ☐ *Key functions and personnel.* Auditors must identify the functions and people that are important in the processing of transactions. Each business firm is organized differently, and may operate in a different manner. Hence, the assignment of specific functions must be known and the individual held responsible for important transactions must be identified.

- ☐ *Administrative controls.* This includes identifying and considering the administrative controls that have a bearing on the control environment and influence the structure of the internal accounting controls, or assist in satisfying internal accounting control objectives. The reviewer must ascertain that the administrative controls are achieving their control objectives.

- ☐ *Financial reporting.* This includes considering the financial reporting needs of the business. As mentioned in the extensive literature on corporate governance, the internal accounting control system should provide reasonable assurance that (a) management responsibilities for the public reporting of financial data can be met, and (b) the internal management reports generated by the system (from transaction data) are reliable.

- ☐ *Environmental controls.* The question should be asked (and answered) whether the control environment is such that the management can reasonably be assured that the internal accounting control objectives will be achieved. In the business as a whole, and in the transaction cycle being evaluated, the proper environment and control discipline must exist. This subjective judgment will derive from an understanding of the particular individuals who may influence the environment and the related administrative controls.

Formulating Internal Accounting Control Objectives. Internal accounting control objectives must be formulated. In the Price Waterhouse & Co. guides, the typical functions in an organization have been grouped into transaction systems for which major internal control objectives are specified. These include:

- Financial reporting
- EDP
- Revenues and receivables
- Productive assets
- Purchases and payables
- Employee compensation and benefits
- Financial management
- Monitoring function

The listing is necessarily generalized in order to embrace the unique attributes and administrative controls of the diverse internal control environments present in business today. As a result, formulating control objectives is a phase of the review where creativity is important, and one that distinguishes the superior review from the mediocre one. Keen insight into the business often will detect methods by which the objective may not be achieved (and correction in procedures is needed).

Evaluating Whether Control Techniques Achieve the Objectives. The key ideas in evaluating whether techniques achieve the objectives are summarized in the following steps:

1. Secure an understanding of the transaction processing system through a preliminary survey of the system.
2. Evaluate whether or not:
    - There is an appropriate segregation of duties both within and among the functions.
    - The administrative and internal accounting control procedures will provide reasonable assurance that the objectives will be achieved.
3. Identify those objectives that will not be achieved due to weaknesses, and suggest the appropriate control procedures that should be instituted to correct the deficiency.
4. Confirm the validity, through tests, of those controls most likely to achieve the internal accounting control procedures.
5. Based on cost-benefit analyses, recommend those procedures that should be instituted to remedy the weakness and effectively reduce the risk.
6. Prepare the summary report on the evaluation. These aforementioned guides should be useful to internal auditors, or other monitors, in checking internal accounting control objectives, and in evaluating the internal control systems.

Summary Checklist on Evaluating Internal Control

The general background just presented is intended to introduce the reader to an approach generally regarded as useful in evaluating and testing internal accounting control systems. A restatement of the four basic steps, with some further elaboration is as follows:

1. Identify the principal activities in each operating component of the business (marketing, manufacturing, finance, and administration) and the related risks and exposures. Some of the risks related to financial accounting transactions include the following:
   - Embezzlement and fraud
   - Excessive costs
   - Insufficient revenues
   - Loss or destruction of assets
   - Statutory sanctions
   - Erroneous record keeping
   - Erroneous management decisions (based on inaccurate accounting data)
   - Competitive leaks of activities or information
2. Outline the control objectives related to each activity. This involves identifying what can go wrong and the controls needed to prevent the error or loss.
3. Identify and describe, by flow charts, or narratives, the various systems used to process transactions, safeguard assets, and prepare financial reports and statements. Included in this step is the identification of those attributes or ways that permit achieving the control objectives, and identified deficiencies.
4. Evaluate whether the system with the identified or recommended changes provides reasonable assurance that the control objective will be achieved.

The above procedure involves identification of the major functions, or components, and subfunctions of a business. A chart developed by one public accounting firm that illustrates components in a typical commercial or industrial company is shown in Figure 18-2.[2]

As mentioned earlier, there is extensive literature prepared by the several larger independent public accounting firms. Among other things, this literature provides reasonable detail on the evaluation process for each major function. Internal auditors may find the concepts and illustrations quite helpful. For example, a chart outlining the evaluation process for financial management is shown in Figure 18-3.[3] Another one dealing with financial reporting is presented in Figure 18-4.[4] Specific objectives, procedural controls, and risk considerations are outlined.

(continued on page 18-17)

---

[2] Ernst & Whinney, *Evaluating Internal Control, A Guide for Management and Directors* (Cleveland: Ernst & Whinney, 1982), p. 6. Copyright © 1982 by Ernst & Whinney. Reprinted courtesy of Ernst & Whinney.

[3] Connor and DeVos. *op. cit.*, pp. 9-4–9-5. Copyright © 1979 by Price Waterhouse & Co. Adapted with permission.

[4] *Ibid.* pp. 2-6–2-7. Copyright © 1979 by Price Waterhouse & Co. Adapted with permission.

AUDITING INTERNAL CONTROL

FIG. 18-2

Operating Components of a Typical Commercial or Industrial Business

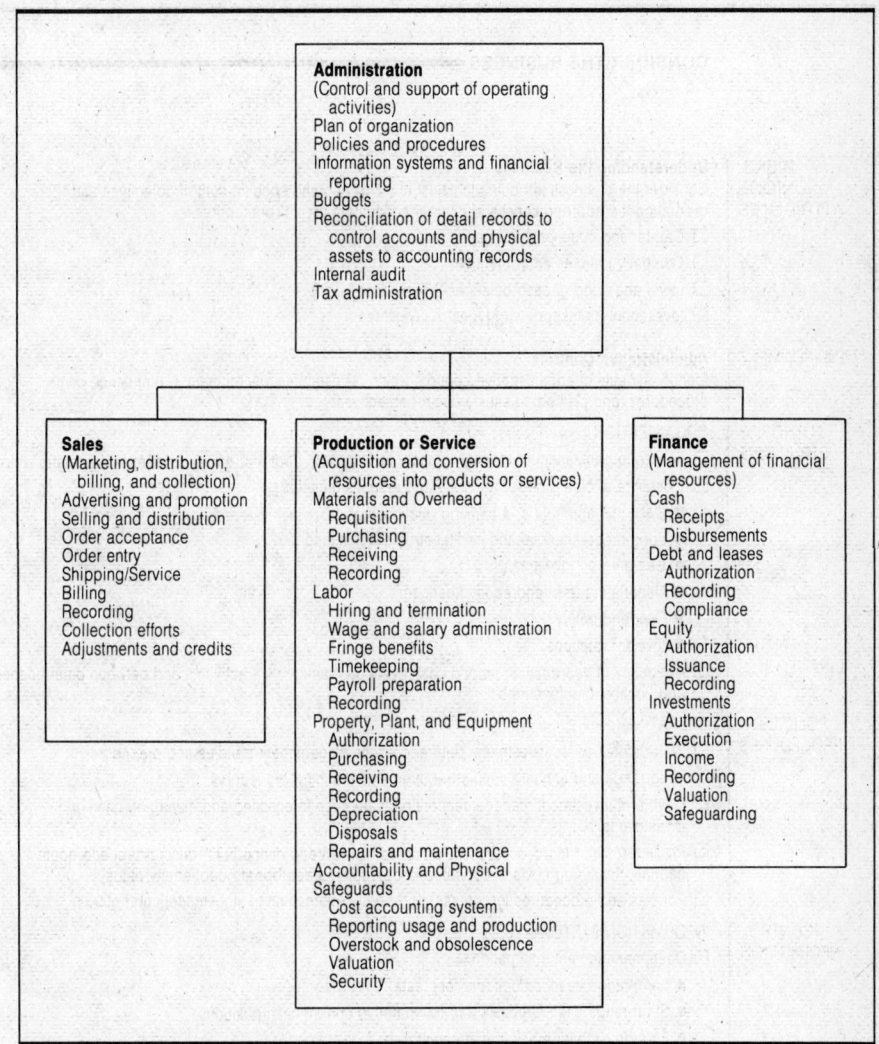

FIG. 18-3

Evaluation Process for Financial Management

CONSIDER THE BUSINESS

RISKS; UNIQUE ATTRIBUTES	**Understanding the Business** Consider the business attributes to assist in (1) developing specific control objectives and (2) evaluating the appropriateness of internal accounting control procedures. ☐ Capital and money market conditions ☐ Company policies and objectives ☐ Level and trend of cash balances ☐ Investment philosophy and types of investments
ENVIRONMENT	**Administrative Controls** Identify aspects of administrative controls which (1) establish environment; (2) influence control procedures; and (3) help to satisfy control objectives.

AUTHORITY STRUCTURE	ORGANIZATION
	☐ Form of organization for managing cash, investments, debt and equity, and reporting relationships.
	☐ Existence of clear lines of authority and responsibility for:
	  ■ Cash management and banking relationships
	  ■ Long-range financial and capital structure planning
	  ■ Deciding on investments
	  ■ Negotiating debt and equity financing
	  ■ Dividend policy
	  ■ Investor relations
	☐ Adequacy of coordination among cash resource management activities and between other financial and nonfinancial functions.

POLICIES — PROCEDURES	OPERATING ☐ Well-defined cash, investment, debt and equity management policies and procedures. ☐ Long-range and annual financial requirements planning procedures. ☐ Cash and investment management methods for cash forecasting and managing cash and investments. ☐ Procedures and techniques for determining sources and methods for raising debt and equity capital, measuring costs of capital, and determining appropriate debt/equity ratios. ☐ Policies and procedures for releasing corporate information to stockholders and others.

CONTROL INFORMATION	INFORMATION SYSTEM
	☐ Cash management information
	  ■ Long-range cash outlook and forecasts
	  ■ Short-range cash forecasts and comparative current cash positions
	  ■ Foreign exchange risk management data
	☐ Investment management information
	  ■ Investment portfolio analyses
	  ■ Comparison of investment yields with investment objectives
	  ■ Operating and financial data on investee companies
	☐ Debt management information
	  ■ Interest and principal payment schedules
	  ■ Comparisons of debt restrictions with current and projected status
	☐ Stockholder and equity capital information
	  ■ Stock trading information (including purchases and sales by insiders)
	  ■ Compliance information on equity restrictions
	  ■ Capital stock and dividend records

AUTITING INTERNAL CONTROL 18-13

➤ FORMULATE INTERNAL ACCOUNTING CONTROL OBJECTIVES → PROVIDE REASONABLE ASSURANCE OBJECTIVES ARE ACHIEVED → **EVALUATE WHETHER CONTROL TECHNIQUES ACHIEVE OBJECTIVES**

Broad Objectives

☐ Authorization
☐ Recording
☐ Access to assets
☐ Asset accountability

Financial Management Objectives

☐ *Approval*
All transactions are initiated by authorized individuals and are approved by appropriate levels of company management, the board of directors or shareholders.

☐ *Custody*
All negotiable instruments and permanent records are subject to effective custodial controls and physical safeguards.

☐ *Detail accounting*
All transactions are promptly and accurately recorded in adequate detail records, and appropriate reports are issued.

☐ *General ledger*
All transactions are properly accumulated, classified, and summarized in the accounts.

Internal Accounting Controls

Review internal accounting controls for:

SEGREGATION OF DUTIES

☐ Among major functions
☐ Between those and related functions.

PROCEDURAL CONTROLS

☐ *Initiation, evaluation and approval* — investment purchases and sales, bank borrowings, stock and debt issues and redemptions, dividends

☐ *Custody* — investment securities, unissued stock certificates, bank accounts, cash

☐ *Detail accounting* — cash, investment, debt and stockholder records; interest and dividend income, interest and dividend payments

☐ *General ledger* — procedures and bases for entries; reconciliation with bank statements and with detail investment and stockholder records

Risk Considerations

☐ Misappropriating cash receipts
☐ Diverting disbursement checks
☐ Falsifying bank reconciliation
☐ Using investment securities as collateral for personal loans
☐ Sale or purchase of securities at an improper price for personal gain
☐ Theft of investment securities
☐ Diversion of proceeds of borrowings
☐ Misappropriation of dividend or interest receipts or payments
☐ Sale or use as collateral of unissued or treasury stock for personal gain
☐ Failure to comply with debt or equity covenants

FIG. 18-4

Evaluation Process for Financial Reporting

CONSIDER THE BUSINESS ━━━━━━━━━━━━━━━━

RISKS; UNIQUE ATTRIBUTES	**Understanding the Business**
	Consider the business attributes to assist in (1) developing specific control objectives and (2) evaluating the appropriateness of internal accounting control procedures.
	
	☐ Financial reporting requirements
	  ■ Public reporting subject to rules and regulations by governmental and professional organizations
	  ■ Various internal reports
	
	☐ Financial reporting structure
	  ■ Multinational organization
	  ■ National organization
	  ■ Centralized accounting
	  ■ Decentralized accounting

ENVIRONMENT	**Administrative Controls** Identify aspects of administrative control which (1) establish control environments; (2) influence control procedures; and (3) help to satisfy control objectives.
AUTHORITY STRUCTURE	ORGANIZATION ☐ Financial reporting organization ☐ Financial reporting functions and activities
POLICIES — PROCEDURES	OPERATING ☐ Annual profit planning and budgeting ☐ Capital budgeting ☐ Cost accounting ☐ Comprehensive classification of accounts ☐ Responsibility accounting
CONTROL INFORMATION	INFORMATION SYSTEM ☐ Financial reports ☐ Highlights of activities ☐ Cash-flow information ☐ Status of capital expenditure programs ☐ Status of research programs ☐ Significant economic trends ☐ Financial forecasts

AUDITING INTERNAL CONTROL 18-15

▶ **FORMULATE INTERNAL** ▶ PROVIDE ▶ **EVALUATE WHETHER**
ACCOUNTING CONTROL REASONABLE **CONTROL TECHNIQUES**
OBJECTIVES ASSURANCE **ACHIEVE OBJECTIVES**
OBJECTIVES
ARE
ACHIEVED

Broad Objectives

☐ Authorizations
☐ Recording
☐ Access to assets
☐ Asset accountability

Financial Reporting Objectives

☐ *General ledger*
All transactions are properly accumulated, classified, and summarized in the accounts.

☐ *Closing*
All closing entries are initiated by authorized personnel and reviewed and approved in accordance with established policies and procedures.

☐ *Consolidation or combination*
All necessary data for consolidations and/or combinations is obtained and processed in accordance with established policies and procedures.

☐ *Preparation, review, and approval*
All internal and public financial reports are prepared on the basis of appropriate supporting data, provide the required information, and are reviewed and approved before issuance.

Internal Accounting Controls
Review internal accounting controls for:

SEGREGATION OF DUTIES

☐ Among major functions
☐ Between those and related functions

PROCEDURAL CONTROL

☐ General ledger — balanced, complete and supported by underlying records
☐ Consolidation or combination — data complete, appropriate elimination in consolidating the data, and accumulation of other information necessary
☐ Preparation, review and approval — complete, appropriate information, reviewed and approved for distribution

Risk Considerations

☐ Unauthorized entries
☐ Omitted entries
☐ Omitted data
☐ Errors in preparation
☐ Unauthorized use
☐ Unauthorized distribution

FIG. 18-5

Guide in Evaluating Cash Receipts

Finance

F-1 Cash Receipts are Recorded Correctly as to Account, Amount, and Period and are Deposited (Recording, Safeguarding)

System Attributes to Consider

Mail Receipts

Mail opened independent of cashier, accounts receivable bookkeeper, and other accounting employees who may initiate or post journal entries

Record of checks and cash received prepared by person opening the mail; list used as posting source and subsequently compared to daily deposit

Lock box used

Cash Sales

Independent check of prenumbered receipt and refund slips

Cash register tape totals compared with amount of cash in drawer

Clerks handling cash closely supervised

Cash refunds require approval

Receipts reconciled to stock sold

General

Employees handling receipts bonded

Cash receipts not handled or recorded by employees having access to accounts receivable records or general ledger

Cash receipts not handled by employees responsible for petty cash or other funds

General (continued)

Cash receipts remain with cashier until sent to bank

Each day's receipts deposited intact and without delay

Independent employees responsible for reconciling authenticated duplicate deposit slip, mail receipts listing, cash receipts book, bank statement

Cash funds (e.g., cash register, petty cash fund, non-company funds) each assigned to one individual, independent of other cash funds

Branch offices make deposits to home office account intact and without delay

Cash or checks not immediately deposited kept in fireproof vault or safe

Salesmen and/or drivers forbidden to accept or handle cash receipts

Miscellaneous receipts (scrap sales, rents, dividends) monitored to detect misappropriation

Bank accounts regularly reconciled independent of cash receipts, general ledger, or accounts receivable functions

Monthly statements sent to all (or delinquent) customers; complaints handled independent of cashier or accounts receivable bookkeeper

What Can Go Wrong

Errors

Cash or checks lost

Incorrect recording of cash receipts

Irregularities

Item sold for cash but no sale recorded or recorded at lesser amount; cash receipts misappropriated

Item sold for cash; cash refund documentation prepared and cash misappropriated

Checks received are deposited but not recorded; check written to employee for same amount, also not recorded

Collections on account misappropriated, concealed by debits to other than cash accounts (e.g., expense accounts), or by improper issuance of credit memo

Salesmen or drivers misappropriate cash received

Accounts Affected

Cash

Accounts and notes receivable

Sales

Other income

AUDITING INTERNAL CONTROL 18-17

F-2 Cash Receipts are Properly Applied to Customer Balances (Recording)

System Attributes to Consider

Employees responsible for posting receivable accounts have no access to cash receipts

Employees responsible for initiating or approving customer credits (including writeoffs) have no access to cash receipts or detail receivable records

Cash receipts applied to specific invoices rather than to current balance

Postings to receivable accounts independently reconciled to total of cash received

Monthly statements sent to all (or delinquent) customers; complaints handled independent of cashier or accounts receivable bookkeeper

Delinquent accounts followed up independent of cashier

What Can Go Wrong

Errors

Receivables properly stated in the aggregate, but individual customer accounts misstated

Irregularities

Collectible accounts written off or otherwise credited; customer remittances misappropriated

Lapping (cash receipts misappropriated; shortages covered by delaying postings)

Accounts Affected

Cash

Accounts receivable

Notes receivable

Another type of guide that may be used in evaluating control objectives, in this instance cash receipts, from the Ernst & Whinney publication, is shown in Figure 18-5.[5] An example of a transaction flow chart is illustrated in Figure 18-6.[6]

Some of the public accounting firms document the evaluation by using specific forms for each objective that client companies find useful in performing their own internal accounting control evaluations. As a point of departure for specific transactions, for example, typical objectives are specified, potential errors are listed, and provision is made for the working paper reference, which justifies the conclusion regarding the degree of control. An example is pictured in Figure 18-7[7] from the Touche Ross & Co. Accounting Control Evaluation (TRACE) approach.

---

[5] Ernst & Whinney, *op. cit.*, pp. 52–53. Copyright © 1982 by Ernst & Whinney. Reprinted courtesy of Ernst & Whinney.

[6] Connor and DeVos, *op. cit.*, p. 9-33. Copyright © 1979 by Price Waterhouse & Co. Adapted with permission.

[7] Touche Ross & Co., *Controlling Assets and Transactions* (New York: Touche Ross & Co., 1979), p. 36. Copyright © 1979 by Touche Ross & Co. Reprinted courtesy of Touche Ross & Co.

FIG. 18-6
Flow Chart Depicting the Cash Disbursements Cycle

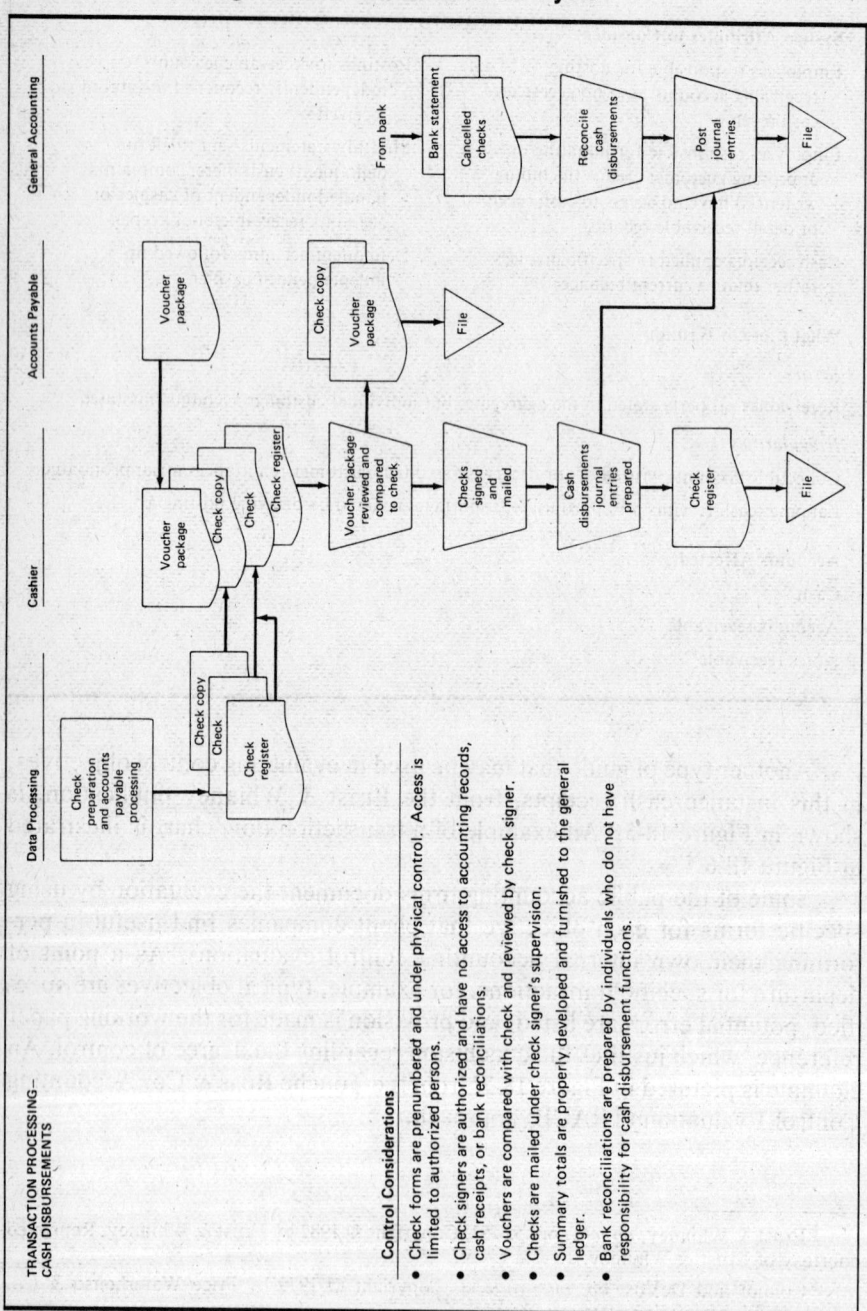

AUDITING INTERNAL CONTROL   18-19

FIG. 18-7

Sample Questionnaire on Internal Control for Sales, Billings, Receivables, and Collection Cycle

---

Touche Ross Accounting Control Evaluation

SALES, BILLINGS, RECEIVABLES AND COLLECTIONS CYCLE

Specific Objective

A. The authorization to ship goods or to provide services should result in the preparation, *to the appropriate degree of accuracy,** of accounting records including the:

— Pricing of goods and services

— Allocation to the correct customer's account, revenue accounts and time period.

Related potential error types

A1 Goods shipped but not invoiced
A2 Sales invoiced but not recorded
A3 Sales amount recorded incorrectly
A4 Sales not properly costed
A5 Sales misclassified
A6 Sales recorded in the wrong period
A7 Goods shipped to bad credit risk
A8 Others (detail below)

Degree of Control	Working Paper Reference

Specific objective achieved?

YES/NO	Working Paper Reference

---

* The qualifying phrase, "appropriate degree of accuracy" is used throughout this questionnaire to emphasize that precise accuracy for its own sake is not an objective. The need for accuracy should be assessed relative to the underlying objectives of internal accounting control and whether, in the last analysis, exactitude is necessary for that objective to be met. The underlying objective of all internal accounting controls is either: (a) the preparation of reliable financial information, or (b) the safeguarding of assets.

The illustrated approaches developed by public accountants in the preceding pages derive from GAAS and applicable professional literature. That professional literature is changing. It is necessary to incorporate a discussion of these changes at this point so that a complete and current understanding results. The discussion is presented from the standpoint of the external auditor's responsibility for internal control.

THE EXTERNAL AUDITOR'S RESPONSIBILITY FOR INTERNAL CONTROL

The Current Picture

Until 1988, the external auditor's responsibility for internal control was set forth in AU Section 320 of professional standards. It was entitled "The Auditor's Study and Evaluation of Internal Control." Briefly, this extensive section provides guidance to the external auditor for studying and evaluating internal control. The study was required by GAAS. In addition to examining financial statements, to which the auditing procedures are applied, the purpose was to afford a basis for determining to what extent the tests are to be restricted.

Section 320 defines internal control and two related terms, accounting control and administrative control. Chapter 17 provides a discussion of these definitions. The distinction between accounting control and administrative control is important primarily because the standards required a study of internal accounting control.

Over the years, practitioners recognized that it was not appropriate to be too restrictive in deciding the limits of this study. Recently, the ASB adopted two new standards regarding internal control. These new standards supersede AU Section 320.

The Exposure Drafts

In February 1987, the ASB of the AICPA exposed for comment 10 proposed new standards. Two of these deal specifically with internal control. They are:

- The auditor's responsibility for assessing control risk.
- The communication of control-structure related matters noted in an audit.

The Concept of Control Structure

The first of these standards is relevant to the subject of this chapter. It discards the definitions of accounting control and administrative control. It replaces them with the concept of control structure. Control structure consists of:

- The control environment
- The accounting system
- Control procedures

Control structure comprises all of the policies and procedures established to provide reasonable assurance that its objectives will be achieved. Generally, the policies and procedures that make up the control structure are those that relate to objectives pertaining to the company's ability to record, process, summarize, and report financial data consistent with management assertions in the financial statements.

Control environment consists of the overall attitude, awareness, and actions of the board of directors, management, owners, or others with similar authority. The specific matters of interest relate to:

- Management philosophy
- Operating style
- Organizational structure
- Audit Committee
- Methods of communicating authority and responsibility
- Management control methods
- Internal audit function
- Personnel management methods
- External influence

The accounting system is defined as consisting of the methods and records established to identify, assemble, classify, analyze, record, and report an entity's transactions and to maintain accountability for the related assets. An effective accounting system, according to the draft, will:

☐ Identify and record all valid transactions.
☐ Describe on a timely basis the type of transaction in sufficient detail to permit proper classification of the transaction for financial reporting.
☐ Measure the value of the transaction in a manner that permits recording its monetary value in the financial statements.
☐ Determine the period in which the transaction occurred to permit recording of the transaction in the proper accounting period.
☐ Present properly the transaction and related disclosures in the financial statements.[8]

Control procedures are defined as those policies and procedures in addition to the control environment and accounting system that management established to provide reasonable assurance that an entity's objectives will

---

[8] Auditing Standards Board, *Consideration of the Internal Control Structure, in a Financial Statement Audit*, Revised Draft, Oct. 27, 1987, para. 15. (New York: AICPA, 1987), p. 7.

be achieved. Among the objectives that are cited by the draft as being generally relevant for this purpose are:

- Proper authorization of transactions and activities, such as general or specific approval of transactions and approval for the reentry of transactions rejected by the computer.
- Segregation of duties so that procedures designed to detect misstatements are performed by persons other than those who are in a position to perpetrate them, such as separating the responsibilities for custody of assets from the responsibility for the related record-keeping, and separating computer programming from computer operations.
- Adequate documents and records, such as prenumbered documents.
- Adequate safeguards over access to and use of assets and records, such as secured facilities and authorization, for access to computer programs and data files.
- Independent checks on performance, such as clerical checks, reconciliations, comparison of assets with recorded accountability, computer-programmed edit controls, management review of reports that summarize the detail of account balances, such as an aged trial balance of accounts receivable, and user review of computer-generated reports.[9]

Implications

Clearly, the foregoing embodies the concepts of current authoritative literature. The objectives listed above are reconcilable to AU Section 320 and the FCPA. The initial draft was presented in such a way that such reconciliation was all but impossible. The draft was changed in response to comments that it seemed to convey a more radical departure from AU Section 320 than was intended. In the revised version, the concepts of authorization, recording, accessibility, and accountability that underlie AU Section 320 are identifiable. The proposed standard was issued in 1988 as SAS No. 55.

The guidance provided by SAS No. 55 is an improvement over AU Section 320 in that it makes it much clearer that the purpose of the external auditor's consideration of the internal control structure is risk-oriented. It makes explicit that the external auditor's consideration of the internal control structure is an integral part of his assessment of the risk that the assertions inherent in the financial statements he is auditing may be materially misstated. AU Section 320 did not make this relationship between the internal control structure and the audit of the financial statements as explicit.

Thus, the emphasis in the proposed standard is on risk assessment. If the external auditor determines that the control structure is sufficient and that the risk inherent in the management assertions embodied in a particular

---

[9] *Ibid.*, p. 10.

AUDITING INTERNAL CONTROL

account balance is low, the procedures that he employs to detect possible misstatements may be reduced. Such a judgment is made by considering the relationship of the elements of audit risk discussed in Chapter 14. These elements are inherent risk, control risk, and detection risk. The reader should refer to Chapter 14 for definitions and discussions of these terms.

What is important for internal auditors to understand is that, in this approach, the external auditor necessarily considers the activities of the internal auditing function as part of his assessment of the control environment. Therefore, in assessing a control environment in which internal auditing actively reviews internal control, the external auditor's decisions about the level of detection risk he will be willing to accept and the extent of audit procedures he will apply to attain that level are apt to be affected. Simply put, if all other things are equal, an external auditor will do less work in an environment in which an internal auditing function exists that effectively audits internal controls than in one in which the internal auditing function does not audit internal controls.

Presumably, the external auditor would spend little or no time in performing compliance testing in a situation like the one described in the preceding paragraph. Thus, the work of the internal auditor in assessing and testing internal control is likely to take on added significance. It is conceivable that internal auditors who adopt a management assertion based approach to auditing internal control will stand a better chance of influencing the judgments of external auditors. Such an approach is not expressly articulated in the present internal control pronouncements by the IIA. The position of the IIA is presented in its SIAS No. 1, "Control: Concepts and Responsibilities," reprinted in Chapter 17. That statement sees control as a result of activities involved in planning organizing and directing.

It is well developed in widely accepted principles of management that planning, organizing, directing, and controlling are inextricably linked. The IIA relates these activities to achieving established objectives. As such, the SIAS is conceptually relatable to the proposed ASB standards. But if it is possible to extend that concept, it may need to be articulated a little differently to make the relationship clearer.

A proposition can be advanced that internal auditing includes an ongoing responsibility to audit management assertions regarding its planning, organizing, and directing to reasonably assure attainment of objectives and goals. The assertions are not articulated explicitly, at present, in any management objective other than preparation of financial statements in accordance with GAAP. The expression of management assertions in this regard is provided by SAS 30, "Evidential Matter." If assertions can be articulated in this instance, they may be susceptible to articulation for other management objectives.

In practice, however, the feasibility of articulating specific objectives other than preparing financial statements in accordance with GAAP may be in considerable doubt. Moreover, it is unclear whether the assertions, once articulated, are susceptible to measurement against a reasonable criteria. For maximum effectiveness, such criteria should be developed by a recognized body.

Notwithstanding the practical difficulties, one area of management responsibility does appear susceptible to applying the theory. That area is internal control. Assertions by management regarding internal control are evident in the suggested management report on responsibility for financial reporting developed by the National Commission on Fraudulent Financial Reporting. Among other items, the suggested language states:

> Management of the corporation has established and maintains a system of internal control that provides reasonable assurance as to the integrity and reliability of the financial statements, the protection of assets from unauthorized use or disposition, and the prevention and detection of fraudulent financial reporting. The system of internal control provides for appropriate division of responsibility and is documented by written policies and procedures that are communicated to employees with significant roles in the financial reporting process and updated as necessary. Management continually monitors the system of internal control for compliance.[10]

Something akin to the foregoing provides articulated management assertions regarding internal control. What is not present, at this point in time, is a reasonable criteria against which such assertions could be measured. That may come in the future if the Treadway Commission has its way. Included in its *Report of the National Commission on Fraudulent Financial Reporting* is a recommendation that its sponsoring organizations should cooperate in developing additional, integrated guidance on internal control. Such guidance might provide the needed criteria. Internal auditors would then be able to use such criteria to measure management's internal control assertions. The results of this effort could be reported to the audit committee in an appropriate form. Such a report might be useful not only to the audit committee, but also to external auditors and other interested parties.

The Concept of Reportable Conditions

The second exposure draft (eventually issued as SAS No. 60 in 1988) is intended to make the independent outside auditor's reports on internal control (see Chapter 17) more responsive to the needs of boards of directors and others. For reporting purposes, it replaces the concept of material weakness in internal accounting control. In its place is a requirement for reporting conditions concerning the design of the control structure and compliance with that structure.

---

[10] National Commission on Fraudulent Financial Reporting, *Report of the National Commission on Fraudulent Financial Reporting*, Oct. 1987 (Copyright © 1987 by the National Commission on Fraudulent Financial Reporting), p. 184. Reprinted by permission of the National Commission on Fraudulent Financial Reporting.

The draft defines reportable conditions as matters coming to the auditor's attention that in his judgment represent significant deficiencies in the design or functioning of the control structure that could adversely affect the organization's ability to record, process, summarize, and report financial data consistent with the assertions of management in the financial statements. The reader may note the consistency of terminology and concept with the exposure draft on assessing control risk.

The draft also provides specimen forms that illustrate written reports that conform with its requirements under varying circumstances. The ASB encourages the use of written reports, although oral reports may also be used. In the event that oral reports are used, working papers must contain appropriate memorandum documentation. An appendix provides examples of possible reportable conditions.

These two new standards (SAS Nos. 55 and 60) promise to significantly alter the approach by which CPA firms perform and report the results of their required study of internal control. Another likely effect is to revive the annual financial audit. In recent years, it became a sort of yearly ritual. In the eyes of many, it was a virtual commodity—an indistinguishable product to be acquired by the cheapest means possible.

The effect on the quality of the audit process and on the audited financial statements is not reliably predictable at this time. It can be said that the new standards constitute a sensible new concept, and a much improved audit should be the benefit.

However, there are those who will be skeptical. There is a view that the current internal control concepts and definitions are effective. The new concept and definitions may serve only to increase the effort required to perform an audit in accordance with generally accepted standards. Accordingly, fees would go up.

Another concern is the possibility that outside auditors will be reporting more information to audit committees. There is no authoritative guidance to aid audit committees in dealing with conditions of risk reported by CPA firms. The obvious specter of increased liability for failing to act diligently may discourage qualified and capable persons from serving on such committees. Another concern is the time and effort required to act diligently. Since audit committees are comprised of outside directors, their resultant work load and their ability to discharge it could become a key part of the auditor's control risk assessment. The exposure drafts do not seem to envision that as a possibility. There is an unstated presumption that all audit committees will handle all reportable conditions timely and effectively, and there are those who do not accept this premise.

Another effect of these standards will be to make obsolete virtually all auditing textbooks and auditing curricula across the country. Academia will be forced to work very hard to catch up with these new concepts. In addition, practitioners will need training to bring them to a position of understanding. Those who do not update their practice will increase the possibility of their experiencing difficulty with the soon-to-be-required peer review.

The Effect on Internal Auditors

Internal auditors are bound to be affected by these new standards. Companies are likely to resist anything that would raise audit fees. Thus, there is every reason to expect internal auditors may become more important players in the game of annual financial statement auditing. In addition, it is not unrealistic to expect audit committees to involve internal auditors to monitor management actions to resolve reportable conditions.

The IIA will be pressured to consider the implications of the ASB's internal control concepts on its standards. It may be that revisions are unavoidable.

The effects of these standards on the practice of internal auditing applicable to internal controls auditing will become evident over time. Meanwhile, the techniques presently in use appear to be valid, given the fact that the concepts of authorization, recording, accessibility, and accountability of AU Section 320 are carried on in the proposed new standards. Therefore, techniques that build on these concepts continue to be appropriate. These techniques are discussed in the next section.

BUILDING ON TECHNIQUES DEVELOPED BY PUBLIC ACCOUNTANTS

Many company managements and their internal audit staffs have built on the conceptual approaches recommended by public accountants. Some have devised parallel methodologies. These efforts have involved applying the concepts to the specific circumstances and internal control environment within each company.

For instance, one internal audit department adopted a "top-down" approach, whereby it identified business cycles and the accounting systems within each cycle; then priorities were set for each accounting system in each division. The techniques employed were borrowed from a mix of Arthur Andersen & Co.'s business cycle concepts with Coopers & Lybrand's flow chart methodology.[11]

A midwestern bank modified its approach to auditing computerized systems and controls by coordinating the efforts of the internal audit staff with the efforts of the external audit staff. In devising the approach to auditing the installment loan function, specific cycles were identified within that func-

---

[11] Peter J. Choate, "Business Cycles: The Top-Down Approach to Accounting System Audits," *The Internal Auditor*, Apr. 1981, p. 30.

tion, which then were further divided into even more specific activities or functions.[12] In this instance, it appears the general approach of the outside auditors was modified to accommodate the unique requirements of an important bank function.

Although the approaches suggested by public accountants are useful, internal auditors are advised not to rely solely on them for evaluating and testing control systems. The principal reason for this view is that the approaches were designed primarily to evaluate internal accounting control in order to determine the nature and extent of audit procedures to apply in auditing financial statements. Evaluation of internal accounting control for purposes of ascertaining compliance with the accounting standards section of the FCPA involves more in-depth study. This point is inherent in the following statement contained in the Cohen Commission Report:

> The auditor's study and evaluation of the internal accounting control system should be expanded beyond what is now required by generally accepted auditing standards. The auditor should review and test the entire accounting control system. The objective of this study and evaluation would be to enable the auditor to reach a conclusion on whether controls over each significant part of the accounting system provide reasonable, though not absolute assurance that the system is free of material weaknesses.[13]

Another reason for caution in relying solely on this type of approach is the numerous subjective judgments regarding sufficiency that must be made by the performing auditor. The extent of difference in auditors' judgments has not been fully explored, but one research study, when testing auditors' sample size determinations, found substantial variability in the auditors' judgments about the materiality and relevance of various internal control strengths, and the degree of reliance they were willing to place on compliance-tested strengths.[14] The risk of making the wrong judgment would seem to be minimal in those broad areas of internal accounting control for which approaches are specifically designed (i.e., transaction cycles, including sales, procurement, payroll, treasury, and financial reporting). That is because considerable thought has been afforded those areas in terms of stating specific objectives and control techniques generally regarded to be indicative of sufficient control. Such is not the case for the more detailed functional aspects. For these, the absence of preidentified specific objectives and control techniques may very well suggest a greater risk of judgmental error (i.e., drawing the wrong conclusion).

---

[12] Howard D. Passage and Donald A. Fleming, "An Integrated Approach to Internal Control Reviews," *Management Accounting*, Feb. 1980, p. 31.

[13] *The Commission on Auditors' Responsibilities: Report, Conclusions and Recommendations* (New York: The Commission on Auditors' Responsibilities, 1978) p. 61.

[14] Theodore J. Mock and Jerry L. Turner, "Internal Accounting Control Evaluation and Auditor Judgment," *Auditing Research Monograph 3* (New York: AICPA, 1981), p. 122.

The following paragraphs discuss a combination of approaches that offer an expanded scope in light of the suggestion in that regard by the Cohen Commission, and that also minimizes the risk of judgmental error.

NEED FOR A COMBINATION OF TECHNIQUES

The nature and extent of internal accounting controls is such that a detailed study of every applicable function and activity would require more time and resources than the internal auditing department has available. On the other hand, a broad study may not entail sufficient depth to be a realistic evaluation tool. One solution to this circumstance is to employ a combination of practices, which permits both in-depth study to enhance the accuracy and reliability of the auditor's judgments, and broad coverage to permit study of all aspects of internal accounting control within a specified period, such as one year.

The combined approach requires that, for all given operational units of the company, a broad study or survey of the more important internal accounting control practices is performed at least once each year. To support the conclusions drawn by such a broad study and to help limit the extent of testing performed in connection with it, a series of one or more separate, detailed studies of specific aspects of the overall system is performed. Since the number of possible detailed reviews exceeds the available resources for studying them, those selected for study differ from year to year. The judgment of the audit department management is required to determine the scope, as described in Chapter 2.

DETAILED AUDITING OF INTERNAL CONTROL

Definition

Detailed auditing of internal control involves a process whereby each identifiable transaction cycle, function, and activity of consequence is evaluated and tested for compliance at least once within a two- to five-year period. Of course, if circumstances warrant, whether due to existing weaknesses or management preferences, more frequent coverage may be appropriate. In many large companies, several hundred separate audit undertakings are required to sufficiently apply this approach. In fact, there are so many auditable functions that no internal auditing staff of reasonable size could cover them all within one or two years. (See Figure 2-8 for a partial list of functional areas.) Each detailed audit involves planning, staffing, evaluating, testing, and reporting.

FIG. 18-8
Sample Detailed Internal Control Audit Report With No Findings

> TO: J.E. Welk
> FROM: Corporate Audit
> SUBJECT: Cash Control and Management, Western Division (WD)
>
> We have completed an evaluation of internal control techniques involved in cash receipts and disbursements at WD for the six months ended February 28, 19XX. Our review was performed in order to determine compliance with established corporate policies and to ascertain that existing internal controls are sufficient to reasonably assure cash transactions are properly authorized, recorded, reported, and safeguarded. Our work was performed in accordance with internally developed audit standards and included evaluation and tests of applicable controls; completion of internal control questionnaires for both cash receipts and disbursements; limited examination of documentation for selected receipts and disbursement transactions; and such other tests and review as we considered necessary in the circumstances. Our scope did not include cash disbursements related to payroll bank accounts.
>
> In our opinion, internal accounting controls over cash receipts and cash disbursements are sufficient to provide reasonable assurance that cash transactions are executed in accordance with appropriate authorization and are properly recorded; that access to assets is permitted pursuant to management's authorization; and accountability is appropriately maintained by various balancing and reporting techniques.

Objective

Detailed internal control auditing is performed in order to provide information to the management group immediately responsible for maintaining such controls. Such information takes the form of an opinion, expressed in a report, regarding the sufficiency of controls for reasonably assuring that the subject activity, function, or cycle is properly authorized, recorded, reported, and safeguarded. An example of such a report is shown in Figure 18-8. However, at times, the internal auditor will encounter situations in which the control environment is less than acceptable—either because of deficiencies in the controls, or because of a lack of compliance, or both. These findings, along with the auditor's recommendations for remedial action, must be included in the report.

The impact, if any, that these findings have on the overall opinion must also be stated. An unqualified opinion accompanied by a list of deficiency findings raises significant questions as to the reliability of the opinion. Conversely, a qualified opinion accompanied by findings appearing to be insignificant is equally questionable. Thus, judgment must be used in supporting the overall opinion with adequate detail of specific findings.

An example of a report containing a discussion of the impact on internal control of cited findings is shown in Figure 18-9. The discussion attempts to put the overall evaluation into perspective to enhance the reader's un-

FIG. 18-9

Sample Detailed Internal Control Audit Report With Findings

TO: K. Kasper

FROM: Corporate Audit

SUBJECT: Cash Control and Management, Western Division (WD)

We have completed an evaluation of internal control techniques involved in cash receipts and disbursements at WD for the nine months ended September 30, 19XX. Our review was performed in order to determine compliance with established corporate policies and to ascertain that existing internal controls are sufficient to reasonably assure cash transactions are properly authorized, recorded, and safeguarded. Our work was performed in accordance with a written audit program and included an evaluation and tests of applicable controls; an examination of reports and underlying documentation required by existing procedures; limited examination of documentation for selected receipts and disbursement transactions; and such other tests and reviews as we considered necessary in the circumstances. Our scope did not include tests of cash receipts and disbursements related to the payroll bank accounts and bank accounts in foreign countries.

Our review disclosed the following matters:

- Cash receipts recorded in general accounting records are not reconciled to the cashier's daily log.
- Checks received from customers are left unsecured in the mail room while awaiting pick up, and again in accounts receivable while being processed.

The above findings indicate a need for improvement in the areas noted. However, compensating factors, such as transaction controls over individual large dollar transactions, tend to minimize the exposure to errors and irregularities. The exposure could be further minimized to a more desirable level in our opinion without any significant incremental costs by implementing the recommendations of this report.

In our opinion, except for the matters noted above, the internal accounting controls over cash receipts and cash disbursements are sufficient to provide reasonable assurance that transactions are executed in accordance with appropriate authorization, transactions are recorded so as to permit preparation of financial statements in accordance with generally accepted accounting principles, access to assets is permitted pursuant to management's authorization, and that accountability is appropriately maintained by various balancing and reporting techniques.

The balance of this report contains a more detailed discussion of our findings and recommendations. A written reply to this report is requested from the action party directed to Corporate Audit within thirty days.

---

derstanding of the significance of the findings. The fact that the opinion is qualified does not mean that the company is in violation of the FCPA. The law recognizes that, at any one point in time, or even for a period of time, controls may be deficient. When this occurs, it is the degree of responsiveness to remedy weaknesses that determines compliance. If management reasonably acts to correct known weaknesses, the overall control system should not be violative of the FCPA. However, failure to act reasonably could constitute a violation, but this is a legal decision.

AUDITING INTERNAL CONTROL

Unique Characteristics

There are certain characteristics that distinguish detailed internal control audits from other types of audits. These are as follows:

- The focus is on a single function, cycle, or activity.
- All aspects of control are included in the scope.
- Questionnaires are used to document evaluation.
- Tests covering a period of time are performed.
- Separate audit findings are reported for each audit.

Each of these characteristics is discussed briefly in the following paragraphs.

Focus Is on a Single Function, Cycle, or Activity. Internal accounting control systems are a combination of transaction cycles, functions, and activities that are susceptible to specific identification. Each can be approached from an audit standpoint as a distinct component, despite the fact that in "the real world" the functions are interdependent. However, sufficient uniqueness exists to permit separate examination. Therefore, a detailed audit of internal control focuses on the components—one audit for each component. Examples include the following:

- Payroll
- Procurement
- Accounts payable
- Cash disbursements
- Employee group benefit plans
- Cost accounting
- Financial reporting
- Marketing
- Billing & collection
- Cash receipts
- Long-term debt transactions
- Capital stock transactions
- Capital asset transactions
- Data processing

All Aspects of Control Are Included. Detailed audits of internal control are not concerned with whether a particular control is defined as operational, organizational, administrative, managerial, accounting, or financial. Rather, the focus is on any type of control as it relates to the attainment of the objectives intended by prudent management. The objectives of internal accounting control contained in professional literature and adopted by the FCPA are believed to be applicable to virtually all functions. Hence, the approach herein suggested is based on considering whether internal controls are sufficient to reasonably assure that transactions and activities were authorized, properly recorded (or documented), properly reported, and effectively safeguarded. Each individual detailed audit, in effect, attempts to measure the degree of sufficiency of control techniques for that aspect of the overall system.

Questionnaires Are Used. Questionnaires document the degree or detail of examination by the auditor of the specific area under review. They must be designed in such a way as to evidence that the auditor reasonably considered control requirements necessary to achieve the objectives of authorization, recording, reporting, and safeguarding set forth earlier.

An example of a questionnaire for use in evaluating cash disbursement transactions is shown in Figure 18-10. Note that key EDP controls are included in the questionnaire along with non-EDP controls. Additional commentary on the design of internal control questionnaires is included in Chapter 11.

Tests Cover a Period of Time. Examinations of internal accounting control can provide the most useful information to management and others if they are designed to report on compliance over a designated period. Examinations designed to report on controls at a specific point in time (e.g., as suggested in Section 642.27 of SAS No. 30, issued by the AICPA ASB in July 1980) may be of interest but leave some doubt about the status of controls for the rest of the year. Managements would benefit to a greater extent if the report addressed the entire year. Accordingly, the auditor must design and extend his tests to cover a sufficiently large sample of the period for which he is measuring compliance.

An example of an audit program covering the audit of the cash receipts function is shown in Figure 18-11. Note in the example that the program calls for the auditor to perform his test procedures for the entire year (the period of review selected) where feasible. However, evidence that certain controls were performed throughout the year may be impossible to obtain. For example, in the cash receipts function, it is not possible to see evidence of the use of restrictive endorsements on checks. Hence, the auditor must examine what evidence there is (current day's deposits in this case) and evaluate the results in the context of the results of other test results. If other tests indicate compliance, the results of looking at the current day's deposits may be supportive. On the other hand, the other test results may contain errors and exceptions of such frequency and magnitude that the test of the current day's deposits may be meaningless.

Separate Audit Reports With Limited Distribution. Each detailed audit of internal control normally results in a separate report of findings. That is because each area usually involves separate segments of management who are responsible for a particular function. These management members have an interest in the audit findings and, accordingly, should be timely informed. It may not be necessary to inform all management members (e.g., senior management) at the same time and in the same degree of detail. However, all appropriate management must eventually be informed to the degree nec-

(continued on page 18-36)

FIG. 18-10

Internal Control Questionnaire for Cash Disbursements

1. **Authorization:**
   - ☐ Do procedures set forth the methods and appropriate approvals for establishing and closing bank accounts?
   - ☐ Are there procedures in effect covering the variety of ways disbursements may be accomplished (check, draft, letter of credit, etc.) and which clearly set forth authority for approval, execution and recording?
   - ☐ Do procedures designate the individuals empowered to designate bank signatories?
   - ☐ Do procedures require that requests to the corporate office for funds be reviewed and approved prior to execution?
   - ☐ If signatures on checks are accomplished by means of facsimile plates or similar devices, do procedures identify the individuals having custody and usage of the plates?
   - ☐ Do procedures identify the individual responsible for maintaining custody of blank check stock?

2. **Processing and Recording:**
   - ☐ Do procedures require that
     - All regular disbursements be made by checks prepared on the basis of adequate and approved documentation?
     - The check signer reviews evidence of adequate and approved documentation prior to signing?
     - All checks be prenumbered and that someone accounts for the sequence of numbers periodically?
     - Upon signing, are all checks recorded in a cash disbursement record in sufficient detail to permit accurate summarizing and posting?
     - If disbursements including check preparing and recording are accomplished by means of electronic data processing techniques, do procedures require:
       a. Control techniques such as item counts, hash totals or other means be used over each source document that is involved in the processing?
       b. A control log be maintained documenting key data such as transmitted number, date and control information?
       c. Rejected transactions and corrections be resubmitted in a manner similar to original transactions?
       d. In the event that terminals are used, sign-on/sign-off procedures and transaction entry procedures are included and that a log of terminal usage reflecting impartial data such as item counts and control totals be maintained?
       e. In the event that data conversion occurs within the profit center or accounting department, important data fields are verified and that converted data be transmitted directly to the processing center?
       f. The originating department be provided for reconciliation to control data evidence from the processing center that transactions were accepted (e.g., edit lists, proof listings, etc.)?

(continued)

FIG. 18-10 *(cont'd)*

     g. Reconciliations of output with control data?
     h. Maintenance of a current record of report distribution?
- The total of the record of cash disbursement be balanced periodically with the total of detail charges to vendor accounts?

3. Accessibility (Safeguarding):

☐ Do procedures require that
- All disbursements be by check or other negotiable instrument?
- Checks be used in sequence?
- Unused checks be stored in a restricted area in the custody of a specified individual?
- Checks be made of protective paper?
- Checks be prepared by persons independent of voucher approval functions?
- Checks be signed by persons independent of check preparation and voucher approval functions?
- Checks be made payable to specific payees?
- A check protector be used?
- Retaining voided/special or mutilated checks?
- Facsimile signature plates are kept in a restricted, secure place separate from blank check stock and are used only in the presence of the custodian, a specified custodian?
- Checks in excess of a stated amount be signed manually?
- Only completed checks be signed (never blank checks)?
- Supporting documents and vouchers be cancelled immediately after signing?
- Filing and accounting for the sequence of cancelled checks cleared by the bank?
- The segregation of the functions of disbursement from record keeping, cash receipts, computer processing (if applicable) and procurement?

4. Accountability (Reporting):

☐ Do procedures require that
- Each disbursement batch checks signed be totalled and compared to the cash disbursements journal prior to mailing?
- Periodically the total of the cash disbursements record be reconciled to bank records of checks cleared with appropriate investigation and resolution of differences? (Note that this procedure may be performed in connection with the reconciliation of the bank balance to the bank balance. However, a reconciliation of bank and bank balances can be accomplished without performing the subject procedure.)
- Periodic comparison of actual disbursements with forecasted disbursements with appropriate investigation of large or unusual differences?

AUDITING INTERNAL CONTROL

FIG. 18-11

Audit Program for Cash Receipts

1. **General:**
   - ☐ Obtain a copy of the current organization chart relative to the finance/treasury function for purposes of orientation and reference during the audit. This provides documentation of reporting relationships as well as the degree to which duties are segregated. Any differences noted during the audit should be discussed with management and resolved.
   - ☐ Obtain a copy of the written procedures and related documentation identifying and evaluating controls over cash receipts and disbursements.
   - ☐ By interviews with management, establish in what way, if any, procedures are not current or are not followed. Adjust documentation accordingly.
   - ☐ During the course of the audit, by observation, tours, etc., note any evidence of:
     - Resource problems
     - Personnel incompetence
     - Dishonest acts

2. **Authorization/Execution of Transactions:**
   - ☐ Select at random from the period under review at least 50 cash receipts transactions from cash receipts records, and check for evidence of the following:
     - Listing on duplicate deposit slip or remittance dvice
     - Authentication of duplicate deposit slip
     - Verification of amount by accounting or other personnel
     - Prompt deposit (Note: comparability of date deposited with date of remittance)
     - If processed via EDP:
       a. Inclusion in batch
       b. Recording of batch in control log
       c. Comparison of output with data in control log
   - ☐ Review journal entries which record cash disbursements for the year noting consistency and approval. Investigate unusual items.
   - ☐ Obtain the supporting data for the current day's deposit and test for:
     - Completeness of supporting detail
     - Agreement with listing prepared by person receiving cash (if any)
     - Unusual items such as stale deposits
     - Evidence of completed transaction (authenticated duplicate deposit slip)
     - Accuracy of deposit data by tracing to actual checks or cash received
     - Restrictive endorsement
   - ☐ Scan records of deposit activity such as cash receipt records, bank statements and bank reconciliations for any evidence which might indicate deviations from daily deposit activity requirements.
   - ☐ If terminals are used to record cash receipts, obtain log of terminal usage and review for consistent use and any unusual items.

(continued)

FIG. 18-11 *(cont'd)*

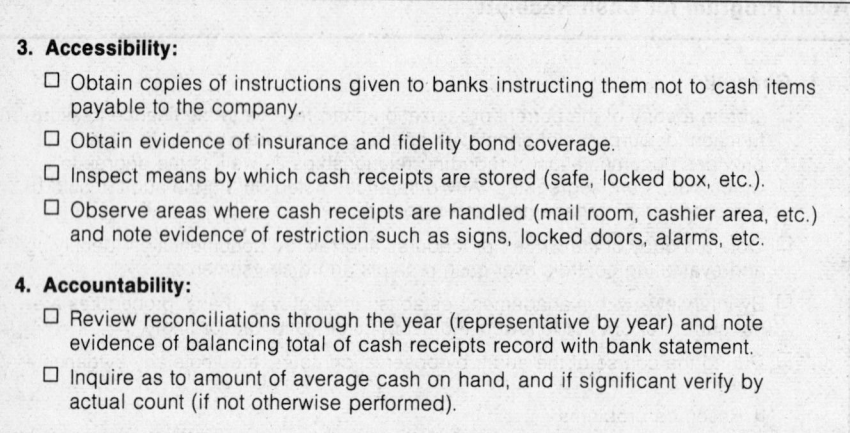

essary. Other reporting mechanisms may be used for that purpose, such as reports resulting from internal control surveys.

Advantages and Disadvantages

The level of detail suggested by detailed auditing offers both advantages and disadvantages. By way of advantage, it permits a depth of inquiry not offered by other methods. Because the approach systematically focuses on specific cycles, functions, and activities, it allows for easier coordination and poses fewer quality-control concerns. Moreover, the required scope of work can be performed by experienced auditors promptly. Complete audits can be performed typically in less than 30 days. Finally, the completed work may be used advantageously by outside auditors, thus restricting the extent of the work they must perform.

On the other hand, the number and variety of individual audits precludes performing them all in any given year. This problem becomes more significant for large, multidivisional, and multinational companies. Judgments must be made as to which functions should be audited each year. Despite the earlier suggestions as to how this can be done, a certain risk of omission is present; that is, by deciding to concentrate in one area, the auditor may not become aware of significant deficiencies elsewhere. In practice, the advantages tend to outweigh the disadvantages. However, the fact that certain relevant areas may escape scrutiny within any given year poses a risk that must be minimized if this approach is to be used confidently. The internal control survey is the device that effectively minimizes this risk.

INTERNAL CONTROL SURVEY

Definition

The internal control survey may be defined as an approach aimed at assessing the major components of an *overall* system of internal accounting control. Its use is particularly well-suited to companies with multiple business segments or operating units, both domestic and foreign. That is because each operating unit must have its own system of internal accounting control. The approach is based on the premise that virtually all business segment systems of internal accounting control may be appraised in terms of a few identifiable transaction cycles. Each transaction cycle is sufficiently controlled if techniques exist that attain prescribed control objectives. Among other things, evaluation includes assessing the degree of risk posed by failure of the techniques to achieve the objectives. Variations of this approach, used by many independent public accounting firms in connection with their required study and evaluation of internal accounting control, were illustrated earlier in this chapter.

Objective

The internal control survey is intended to complement the detailed audits of internal control in order to provide independent information to management regarding the extent to which internal accounting controls reasonably assure that

- Transactions are authorized in accordance with management's general or specific authorization.
- Transactions are recorded so as to permit preparation of financial statements in accordance with GAAP.
- The recorded accountability of assets is compared with the existing assets at reasonable intervals, and appropriate action is taken with respect to any differences.

The information is conveyed in the form of an opinion expressed in a report regarding the attainment of the foregoing objectives. An example is shown in Figure 18-12.

The auditor's opinion in normal circumstances is unqualified and is similar in many respects to that expressed in detailed audits of internal control. As a result, the same degree of care must be exercised in preparing it. Because the opinion covers the overall system, it must take into account any opinions expressed in connection with detailed internal control auditing and any other auditing projects that may have a bearing.

The approach is intended to provide evidence to the auditor that when combined with the detailed approach, affords the auditor a reasonable basis

FIG. 18-12
Internal Control Survey Report

TO: W.G. Evans
FROM: Corporate Audit
SUBJECT: Survey of Internal Accounting Controls — Corporate Office

We have performed a survey of the internal accounting controls in effect at the corporate office. Our review was performed in order to determine the extent to which such controls provide reasonable assurance that transactions are executed in accordance with management's specific authorization, and are recorded so as to permit preparation of financial statements in accordance with generally accepted accounting principles. Our review was also performed to ascertain that access to assets is appropriately restricted and that accountability is appropriately maintained over these functions.

Our methods and work performed are outlined on Attachment A. The scope of our work was reduced by considering work performed in previous projects completed by Corporate Audit during 19XX. These reports are listed on Attachment B.

The functions/activities reviewed included retirement and savings, tax administration, stock options and rights, risk management, procurement, accounts payable, general ledger, and financial reporting. Our review concerned itself with only those areas primarily impacted by internal accounting controls as opposed to administrative controls. As a result, we did not review such non-accounting functions as Industrial Relations.

In our opinion, the system of internal accounting controls reviewed by us is sufficient to provide reasonable assurance that transactions are properly authorized, executed and reported and that assets and records are appropriately safeguarded.

ATTACHMENT A

METHOD OF EVALUATING INTERNAL ACCOUNTING CONTROLS

In performing our review, attention was focused on:
- Evaluating the system of internal accounting controls and identifying any weaknesses which may cause errors that may have a material impact on the company's financial statements;
- Evaluating management's approach to and scope of assessment of their existing internal accounting controls; and
- Evaluating management's actions with respect to internal accounting control matters previously noted by the auditing department.

Our survey categorized the business activities into four broad transaction cycles. The following is a brief summary of the components of our work scope:
- Understanding the flow of transactions and accounting controls in place for each cycle;
- Ascertaining the adequacy of documentation of internal accounting control procedures and corresponding evaluations;
- Selecting several key functional systems and testing the internal control procedures;

AUDITING INTERNAL CONTROL 18-39

- Inspecting various internally created financial reports used by management for their review;
- Verifying corrective actions initiated in response to recent auditing department reports; and
- Such other tests considered necessary in the circumstances.

ATTACHMENT B

The extent and effort of our examination took into consideration the scope of work related to previous detailed internal control audits completed by the auditing department during 19XX. These efforts and results thereof were disclosed in the following reports:

Report No.	Date	Report Description
XX-125	March 21, 19XX	Consultants and Lobbyists
XX-131	March 30, 19XX	Contributions, Aid to Higher Education, and Corporate Memberships
XX-189	August 28, 19XX	Company-Funded Dental Plan
XX-193	August 31, 19XX	Facilities Management
XX-200	August 31, 19XX	Review of the Common Payroll Personnel System Internal Controls in Effect at the Corporate Office
XX-201	August 31, 19XX	Internal Controls Over Retirement System Corrections
XX-218	September 30, 19XX	Travel Practices
XX-219	September 30, 19XX	Limited Financial Review
XX-232	October 30, 19XX	Corporate Executive Payroll
XX-239	November 5, 19XX	Corporate-Wide Disaster Planning

for providing the independent information to management described in the preceding paragraph.

Unique Characteristics

The characteristics identifiable with this audit approach are as follows:

- Focus is on an accounting entity.
- Evaluation is limited to accounting controls.
- Testing is limited.
- Questionnaires are not used.
- Interests of external auditors are accommodated.

Focus Is on Accounting Entity. One of the primary objectives of the FCPA is to require internal accounting control systems that record transactions so as to permit the preparation of financial statements in accordance with GAAP. Therefore, the various financial reporting components that comprise the consolidated financial reporting entity must be examined separately. This applies to domestic reporting units and foreign reporting units as well. In the absence of clear-cut guidelines from the SEC, it is a good idea to cover virtually all reporting units each year. However, reporting units that are (1) clearly insignificant, (2) involved in business pursuits not likely to pose major risks of concern to corporate management, and (3) usually difficult to arrange for and conduct the survey may be excluded from this coverage. Some types of businesses involve many reporting units individually distinct, but more or less identical in organization, product, procedures, and so forth. Retail chains, for example, are comprised of numerous stores, which may be considered separate reporting units but that are also essentially clones of each other. For these businesses, reasonable coverage might be gained from a representative judgmental or statistical sampling.

Evaluation Limited to Accounting Controls. The focus of the survey covers all internal *accounting* controls within each entity. For convenience, the transaction analysis approach illustrated by the AICPA[15] and employed by many public accounting firms is extremely useful. To briefly recap, this approach divides the survey into transaction cycles or categories that are purported to be represented by financial statements and reports. Definitions and terminology vary somewhat among the firms. The following examples are typical:

- Procurement
- Payroll
- Conversion
- Revenue
- Treasury
- Financial reporting
- Organizational

For each category, internal control objectives are developed that support the broad objectives of internal accounting control. Sufficient control techniques for each objective are then identified, which reasonably assures attainment of the objectives in the auditor's judgment.

Only internal accounting controls falling into these or similar broad categories need be considered. Identifying these controls from all the other procedures and techniques that are present is the challenge inherent in this approach. The aids illustrated earlier in this chapter offer practical methods to meet this challenge by relating controls to identifiable control objectives that reasonably assure, in the opinion of the auditor, that such objectives are attained. The determination of the auditor in this regard is facilitated by considering the risks that are involved should the identifiable control objectives fail to be reasonably assured by the control techniques in effect. An

---

[15] Special Advisory Committee on Internal Accounting Controls, *Report of the Special Advisory Committee on Internal Accounting Controls* (New York: AICPA, 1979), p. 21.

example of how this process is documented for selected objectives pertaining to payroll is shown in Figure 18-13.

The SEC has declared that in enforcement actions it will not necessarily be restricted in its interpretations by definitions (such as that for internal accounting control) set forth in professional literature.[16] Considerable interest has developed as to the meaning actually intended by FCPA terminology. Until the courts or the SEC is able to provide more useful definitional guidance, a broad interpretation seems prudent to be sure all aspects of internal accounting control are covered.

Limited Testing. Because the focus of the survey is extensive, it cannot be validated by testing to the same degree as that for detailed internal control audits. To do so would require more time than the auditor has available. The purpose of survey testing is to gather sufficient audit evidence to determine whether key controls have operated during the period under review. If evidence tends to suggest that key controls have been operative, the auditor might reasonably conclude that other controls are also likely to be in effect. On the other hand, any errors or exceptions to management representations as to key controls actually practiced might require additional testing.

In determining the amount of testing, the auditor should utilize the work of other auditors, where relevant, to the extent practicable. Tests performed at the accounting unit in connection with relevant prior detailed auditing projects, as well as applicable work performed by other auditors, such as external auditors, should be considered. Needless to say, the auditor must also weigh the implications of any unremedied findings resulting from those reviews.

Tests actually performed must be similar in scope to those performed in connection with detailed audits of internal control. In other words, the tests must be designed to determine that the controls operated throughout the period under review. The difference between survey testing and detailed testing is this: In survey audits, the program of testing spans only the spectrum of internal accounting control but covers an entire entity. In detailed auditing, the testing is concentrated within the specific function or activity of an entity and may include all types of controls (i.e., organizational, managerial, operational, etc.).

Absence of Questionnaires. Internal accounting control surveys do not employ predetermined questions to evidence control evaluations. Instead, the evaluation is evidenced by documenting judgments as to specific control objectives on spreadsheets. The format of the working papers can be variable

---

[16] *Federal Register*, Vol. 44, No. 88, May 4, 1979, p. 25,704.

FIG. 18-13

Specimen Workpaper Documenting Internal Controls

Evaluation of Internal Controls

Functional Cycle: PAYROLL Division/Subsidiary: ____ CORPORATE OFFICE

Control Objective	Risk if Objective Not Achieved	Control Technique	Reference to Testing in W/P's	Evaluation of Control
Payroll processing procedure should be in accordance with management's criteria.	Circumvention of internal control techniques (unauthorized individuals or unauthorized changes to computer programs)	Policy/procedures manuals	B10	Manuals appear current and complete
		Computer security over programs and data	B15	D.P. Security is adequate
		Training of all employees	B1	Training is comprehensive and timely
		Periodic verification of approvals for all system and procedural changes	B17 and B22	All current systems and procedures are approved — appears adequate
	Loss of data	Periodic verification of actual payroll to expected results (budgets)	B30	Budget controls appear to be in effect
	Errors/omissions	Restricted access to payroll data (both computer and manual)	B18 and B24	Access appears adequately restricted
		Segregation of duties for manual procedures and also for computer processing	B25	Segregation of duties chart shows no weaknesses
Payroll should be accurately prepared and promptly and accurately recorded.	Unauthorized payments resulting in excessive costs, violation of laws, contracts, employee dissatisfaction, irregularities.	Documented procedures	B10	Manuals appear to be current and complete
		Verification methods of all data — check digits, reasonableness tests, exception tests (excess hours or pay, excessive deductions), key data checks (matching type of labor to pay rates, etc.), exception reports (one employee = one timecard or paycheck)	B50	All key data fields have check routines and tests of data indicate adequate procedures exist to test key data
	Accruals incorrect			
	Fines/penalties for law violations	Exception reports (hours paid but not charged, paychecks for individuals not on master list, etc.)	B55	Exception reports appear to be adequate and follow-up appears to be timely
	Inventory, property, and expense accounts may be misstated.	Reconciliation of hours and dollars paid to recorded payrolls and tax returns	B61	Reconciliations are performed for each payroll
		Budget, variance, and efficiency reporting	B30	Reports appear current and complete
		Review and approval of time changes and payroll		Review and approval is documented
		Payroll is approved and recorded in appropriate general ledger accounts	B60	Recorded amounts are approved

but should be designed to depict the following:

- Cycle under study
- Control objectives
- Control techniques employed
- Flow charts depicting the control flow
- Risks involved should the objective fail to be realized
- References to documentation within the organizational unit study identifying the control
- References to testing, where applicable

In many companies, such documentation is kept current by designated functions, such as a systems and procedures department, or by each involved unit itself. In other companies, management looks to the internal auditors to prepare the documentation evidencing controls. Flow charts and narratives are the primary means for accomplishing this. The time required for the auditor to prepare such documentation is extensive.

Such an undertaking is difficult in very large corporate entities. There is simply not enough time available to auditors to do a proper job. Moreover, there is a greater exposure to errors and omissions because auditors are less familiar than responsible management is with the various control systems. Despite these drawbacks, the auditor may find he must prepare this documentation. Figure 18-14 presents an illustrative format for preparing such documentation. This format is of value because it documents in one place the transaction or processing flow, the control objectives, the control techniques, and the auditor's evaluation.

Comprehensive Reports With Full Distribution. The results of the internal control survey should be reported to interested management. This may include various department level managers, organizational unit management, and corporate management and the cognizant accounting officer. In addition, the distribution may also include audit committees, external auditors, and others. Typically then, the distribution of survey audit reports is more extensive than that for detailed internal control audits.

Audit Programs. The broad-based nature of internal control surveys makes it impracticable to specify the full program of testing that is to be employed. Hence, the program is stated in general terms. An example of a survey audit program is shown in Figure 18-15.

It should be observed that the program is integrated with the FCPA requirements and that its general provisions can apply to almost any entity under review. It should be pointed out that the program requires that the control objectives as documented by management reconcile to the areas

(continued on page 18-47)

FIG. 18-14
Illustration of Documenting Internal Control Evaluation

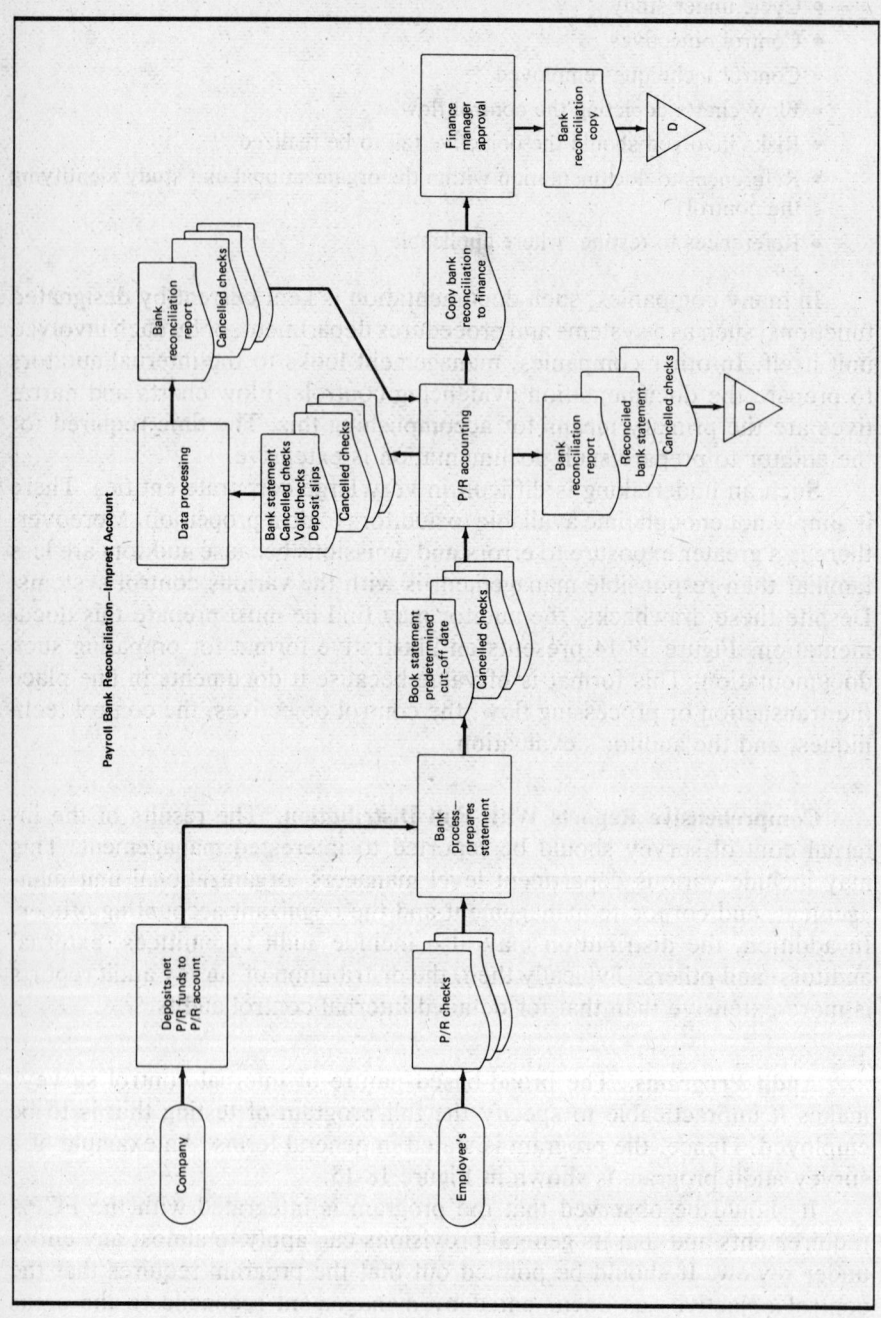

```
                                                              Risk
                                                           L  M  H
                                                              X
```

CONTROL OBJECTIVES:
1. To periodically assure that payroll transactions are properly processed and recorded.
2. To prevent and/or detect irregularities.

CONTROL TECHNIQUES:

Objectives 1 and 2
- ☐ Payroll account reconciled monthly
- ☐ Reconciliation performed by person independent of cash/payroll processing
- ☐ Reconciliation must be reviewed and approved
- ☐ All unreconciled differences are investigated
- ☐ Checks outstanding for more than 60 days are voided
- ☐ Automated reporting facilities reconciliation process (separate lists for cleared checks, outstanding checks and errors)
- ☐ Reconciliations are retained for three years

Objective 2
- ☐ Checks outstanding for more than 60 days are voided

EVALUATION OF CONTROL PROCEDURES:

Objectives 1 and 2. Procedures provide for adequate control over outstanding checks. Payroll accounts are reconciled on a monthly basis. The procedures and techniques used to provide reasonable assurance that the transactions are authorized, valid, and recorded. In addition, the separation of accounting duties in bank reconciliation is cue whenever possible. The forms and reports are deemed adequate for the purpose of entering the books at the proper time.

FIG. 18-15

Audit Program for Internal Accounting Control Survey

OBJECTIVE:

The evaluation of internal accounting controls is to determine if such system is sufficient to provide reasonable assurances that

1. Transactions are executed in accordance with management's general or specific authorization (Authorization);
2. Transactions are recorded as necessary to (a) permit preparation of financial statements in conformity with generally accepted accounting principles or any other criteria applicable to such statements; and (b) maintain accountability for assets (Recording and accountability);
3. Access to assets is permitted only in accordance with management's general or specific authorization (Accessibility); and
4. The recorded accountability for assets is compared with the existing assets at reasonable intervals, and appropriate action is taken with respect to any differences (Substantiation).

AUDIT PROCEDURES:

                                                                                                                  Done by

1. Obtain and review available publications dealing with the requirements of the Foreign Corrupt Practices Act (FCPA).   ....

2. Review the procedures used by the unit to gather and document the information needed to comply with the FCPA. Determine adequacy of the procedures and documentation.   ....

3. Obtain an understanding of the unit's business activity, flows of authority and responsibility, and flow of transactions through the accounting processes to the financial statements (flows of transactions by function within identification cycle of business activity).   ....

    ☐ Obtain management's evaluation of internal controls.   ....

    ☐ Obtain flow chart diagrams, procedures manuals, organization charts, memoranda, policies, and financial statements.   ....

4. Evaluate whether management's evaluation is complete as to the business environment controls and cycle of business controls.   ....

    ☐ Review the cycle control objectives applicable to the function within each business activity cycle as identified by profit center management, and document the internal control techniques used to achieve the objectives.   ....

    ☐ Determine that the control objectives are valid, all-inclusive, and that they encompass the four major areas required by the FCPA: ....
- Authorization
- Recording and accountability
- Accessibility
- Substantiation

	Done by
☐ Identify possible risk areas in each cycle, note offsetting controls, and determine the exposure to the company and probability of occurrence of all significant exposure areas.	....
☐ Evaluate the degree of achievement attained within each function in meeting objectives.	....
☐ In order to determine that all relevant functional areas have been documented and evaluated, obtain or prepare a schedule which cross-references functional areas documented to commonly recognized business cycles or functions as presented in authoritative literature.	....

5. Test compliance by verifying that internal control techniques are operating as discussed. ....
   (*Note:* The amount of review and compliance testing performed will in part be determined by the results of recent audits completed by the internal audit department, the outside audit company, and profit center internal audit groups. In each section of the file, a description of the work previously performed and its results will be included.)

   ☐ For all key controls, review documentation such as procedures which evidence that controls are in effect. ....

   ☐ Select limited representative transactions and "walk through" to validate the flow of transactions in instances where transaction flow is involved. ....

   ☐ Record all items tested in item above, and note exceptions and the effect such exceptions have on the evaluation of controls. ....

   ☐ To ascertain that controls were operational, review evidence that control was consistently followed during period under review. Workpapers should contain a clear description of the nature of the testing and the extent of coverage. This step can be accomplished by testing various transactions throughout the year or it can be accomplished by a cursory review of transaction documents for the year that would evidence the application of the control technique. ....

6. Summarize findings and recommendations for exit interview with the affected management. ....

7. Prior to leaving the field, prepare a draft of findings and review with profit center senior management. ....

8. List recommendations for future audits. ....

required by the accounting standards section of the FCPA. This procedure is necessary because the objectives may be documented in a variety of ways; that is, some managements may prefer to document objectives according to major transaction cycles, others may follow functional groupings, and still others may use departmental groupings. Some may use flow charts, others may use narratives, or both. Reconciling control objectives to the FCPA-required objectives of internal accounting control minimizes the potential for failing to consider important control aspects.

Advantages and Disadvantages

The principal advantage of the survey approach is that it enables the auditor to study all important internal accounting controls in the company. Any significant weaknesses—those that might cause a material misstatement in the consolidated financial statements—are likely to be identified by this process.

A corollary advantage is that the survey provides information to the auditor for use in planning future detailed audits. Its wide scope enables him to identify emerging problems, changing trends, and developing systems.

Another advantage is that, when properly documented, the survey can be of value to external auditors in conducting their study of internal control. In fact, some companies have found that through coordinating the internal control auditing efforts of internal and external auditors, a more extensive review results. The approach used in coordinating efforts is usually similar to the internal control survey approach just described. One such approach is followed at a midwestern bank.[17] Another has been employed by a major oil company.[18]

Finally, the survey is efficient. Surveys can be performed every year at every location where accounting records of consequence are kept while leaving considerable time for detailed audits, operational audits, and other work.

The principal disadvantage is the presence of a higher risk that the conclusions of the auditor, within a given area, might not be justified. That is because the lack of in-depth analysis and testing, combined with the absence of detailed internal control questionnaires, places a premium on the skill and judgment of the performing auditor. Also, considerable reliance must be placed on management representations. This advantage is partly overcome by the skill, experience, and judgment of qualified auditors.

The disadvantages of the survey approach are offset by the advantages of the detailed approach and vice versa. The combination of the two approaches provides the auditor with the basis needed for providing sound information to management regarding internal accounting control. It is a reasonable basis; however, it cannot absolutely assure that transactions have all been properly authorized, recorded, reported, and safeguarded.

FINAL THOUGHTS

It is clear that the importance of maintaining sound systems of internal control has gained widespread recognition and a foothold in U.S. law. Man-

---

[17] Passage and Fleming, *op. cit.*, p. 30.

[18] Albert S. Martin and Kenneth P. Johnson, "Assessing Internal Accounting Control: A Workable Approach," *Financial Executive*, May 1978, p. 24.

agements and other groups believe that internal auditors can provide a valuable contribution in this area.

In order to make the contribution, the chief auditor must have a well-conceived, systematic approach to afford a basis for presenting, in a professional fashion to management (including the board of directors and the audit committee), relevant and reliable opinions. Of course, other factors are also essential, such as competence, an independent mental attitude, and due diligence—in other words, professional standards. Also, the internal auditing department must obtain sufficient resources and effectively manage them. To be sure, these factors are necessary ingredients for all internal auditing projects; however, the increased status of the internal auditing function, resulting primarily from internal accounting control concerns, has served to highlight their importance.

SUGGESTED READING

Cassell, Michael N., and Richard G. Schroeder. "An Effective Audit Program for FCPA." *The Internal Auditor*, Feb. 1978, pp. 57–62.

Choate, Peter J. "Business Cycles: The Top-Down Approach to Accounting System Audits." *The Internal Auditor*, Apr. 1981, pp. 28–33.

Connor, Joseph E., and Burnell H. DeVos, Jr. *Guide to Accounting Controls*. New York: Warren, Gorham & Lamont, 1979.

Evaluating Internal Control, A Guide for Management and Directors. Cleveland: Ernst & Whinney, 1982.

Guide for Studying and Evaluating Internal Accounting Controls, A. New York: Arthur Andersen & Co., 1978.

Internal Accounting Control, An Overview of the DHS Study and Evaluation Techniques. New York: Deloitte Haskins & Sells, 1979.

Johnson, Kenneth P., and Henry R. Jaenicke. *Evaluating Internal Control*. New York: John Wiley & Sons, 1980.

Loebbecke, James K., and George R. Zuber. "Evaluating Internal Control." *Journal of Accountancy*, Feb. 1980, pp. 39–46.

Martin, Albert S., Jr., and Kenneth P. Johnson. "Assessing Internal Accounting Control: A Workable Approach." *Financial Executive*, May 1978, pp. 24–35.

Mautz, Robert K., et al. *Internal Control in U.S. Corporations: The State of the Art*. New York: Financial Executives Research Foundation, 1980.

Mock, Theodore J., and Jerry L. Turner. "Internal Accounting Control Evaluation and Auditor Judgment." *Auditing Research Monograph 3*. New York: AICPA, 1981.

The National Commission on Fraudulent Financial Reporting, *Report of the National Commission on Fraudulent Financial Reporting*, Oct. 1987. Copyright © 1987 by the National Commission on Fraudulent Financial Reporting.

New Management Imperative, The. New York: Touche Ross & Co., 1978.

Passage, Howard D., and Donald A. Fleming. "An Integrated Approach to Internal Controls." *Management Accounting*, Feb. 1980, pp. 29–35.

Sharpening Controls, Corporate Approaches to Complying With the Foreign Corrupt Practices Act. U.S.A.: Coopers & Lybrand, 1978.

Special Advisory Committee on Internal Accounting Control. *Report of the Special Advisory Committee on Internal Accounting Control.* New York: AICPA, 1979.

CHAPTER **19**

Billing, Accounts Receivable, and Collections

Overview	1	Reporting and Accountability	7
Definition and Background	2	**Audit Techniques**	8
The Business Environment	3	Preliminary	8
		Fieldwork	8
Risks	4	**Illustrative Questionnaires**	9
Internal Control Objectives	5	**Sample Audit Program**	18
Internal Control Techniques	6	**Specimen Audit Report**	22
Organization and Authorization	6		
Processing and Accounting	6	**Suggested Reading**	25
Safeguarding	7		

Fig. 19-1 Internal Control Questionnaire for Accounts Receivable Billing 10
Fig. 19-2 Internal Control Questionnaire for Cash Receipts 14
Fig. 19-3 Audit Program for Accounts Receivable Billing 18
Fig. 19-4 Report on Audit of Billing and Collecting Functions 22

OVERVIEW

In Chapters 17 and 18, the subject of internal control is introduced as an important device to assist management in achieving the business objectives of the company. In view of this importance, various approaches to auditing systems of internal control are described. One of the key aspects of internal control auditing, as described in Chapter 18, is to employ a combination of techniques that permits both *in depth* studies, to enhance the accuracy and reliability of the auditor's judgments, and *broad surveys*, to permit the study of all aspects of internal accounting control within a specified period.

Chapter 18 contains an example of an audit program and questionnaire suggesting how these tools may be applied in a detailed internal control review of cash receipts and cash disbursements. Sample reports are also presented. However, the importance of this type of internal control auditing warrants further explanation. Accordingly, this chapter and Chapters 20 and 21 provide guidance for conducting detailed internal control audits for the following functions:

- Billing and collecting accounts receivable
- Payroll accounting
- Accounts payable accounting
- Cost systems

Obviously, these four business functions do not comprise a complete menu for all internal control functions for any given business. However, it is believed that they represent functions applicable to a very broad segment of the business community and, at the same time, are considered to be vital applications for a large portion of that segment. Discussion of other applications may be provided in future supplements.

In this chapter, the functions of billing and collecting trade accounts receivable are presented from an auditing standpoint. It is acknowledged that there are other forms of receivables that occur in the normal course of business, including advances to suppliers, subcontractors, and employees for business purposes, receivables for tax refunds, amounts due from affiliated companies, claims receivable from insurance carriers and others, and balances owing from creditors. While it is important that these receivables be properly controlled, their infrequency of occurrence and small aggregate value compared to trade receivables result in less management concern for them generally. Accordingly, the focus of this chapter is restricted to trade accounts receivable.

From an operational standpoint, the billing and collecting of trade receivables is a small part of the large tasks of financial management and marketing management covered in Chapters 32 and 37, respectively.

DEFINITION AND BACKGROUND

The actions of billing and collecting accounts receivable must be defined separately, since they are distinct and separate functions. The process of billing involves those internal control techniques that result in informing customers and others of the sums legally owing to the billing entity for the performance of some contractual duty, or duties, expressed or implied, or by reason of the passage of time, or both. Usually, the billing occurs within a few days after an exchange of products or services between buyer and seller. On occasion, in instances where the rendering of the service or the delivery of the product occurs over an extended period, special billing arrangements may occur for periodic payments somewhat in advance of completion or delivery.

Collecting is the process of obtaining from customers payment for amounts billed within the time frame or credit period agreed to by the parties. Collecting activity continues until the funds are deposited in the company's designated bank account(s).

The significance of sufficient internal control over billing and collecting amounts due from customers cannot be overemphasized. Except for enterprises such as food retailers, and some restaurants and recreational enterprises, almost every product or service can be obtained on credit. Thus, virtually every business institution offers credit in some form as a sales inducement to customers. When one recalls that buying or selling on credit was practically nonexistent at the turn of the century, the growth of credit as a business tool is nothing short of spectacular. The cash and carry business of yesteryear has given way to businesses characterized by 30-, 60-, and 90-day terms, discounts for early payment, and use of accounts receivable as collateral for short-term loans.

THE BUSINESS ENVIRONMENT

The variety of circumstances in which billing and collecting functions occur are considerable. Therefore, the auditor must obtain an understanding of the particular circumstances of the entity as a starting point in devising his audit approach. Here are some of the factors to consider:

- ☐ *Management objectives.* Management objectives in using credit as a means to attain business goals vary, depending on such considerations as competitive conditions, industry practice, regulatory climate, business trends, and distribution methods.

- ☐ *Credit policy and practices.* The credit policy and practice of companies will differ, depending on many of the same factors that affect management objectives. That is because credit policy is set by management to coincide with its objectives. Credit policy is also affected by the nature of the business, the type of customer, and general economic conditions. For example, the credit policy of an automobile manufacturer, an oil company, a bank, an airline, and a leasing company are all different, primarily as a result of differences in the factors noted. Credit practice, in turn, is influenced by such factors as industry type, business cycles, and competitive status.

- ☐ *Customer base.* The customer base may be briefly defined as the population of customers that buy the company's products and services. The customer base significantly affects the internal control objectives and techniques that must be maintained. The customer base also affects the credit policy of the company. That is because some types of customers entail greater risks than others. Companies who do business extensively with the government, such as aerospace companies, are far less exposed to collection losses than are venture capital companies whose customers typically experience working capital problems and often experience business failure as a result. Generally speaking, offering credit to a few customers with known financial strengths is less risky than offering credit broadly to the public, as is done by utilities, for example.

- *Volume of transactions.* The volume of transaction activity also affects the nature and extent of controls. High-value product transactions occur much less frequently than do sales of materials and supplies consumed in short-term production cycles, but the individual transaction amounts are much greater. As a result, high-value products, such as heavy equipment and other durable goods, often require longer-term financing than is the case for materials, supplies, and services consumed in normal production cycles. The investment in accounts receivable by these companies is therefore much greater and requires more intensive checks of creditworthiness. On the other hand, small-value, high-volume products, such as energy consumption, require more intensive transaction processing controls.

- *Current working capital picture.* The current working capital picture of a company affects both the extent to which companies may be able to offer credit and the intensity of collection efforts. Companies experiencing working capital problems, whether due to general economic conditions, unsuccessful business ventures, or other reasons, will usually offer less generous credit terms and will use more extreme collection tactics than those companies free of working capital difficulties.

The value in considering the foregoing business environmental factors is that the internal control objectives and the underlying control techniques that are shaped by them can be better understood by the auditor.

RISKS

Another important set of considerations in understanding and evaluating internal controls related to billing and collecting accounts receivable consists of the risks inherent in the particular circumstances. These also vary among businesses; however, the following are often present:

- Billing
  - Failure to bill for services rendered or products delivered
  - Billing incorrect amounts
  - Billing the wrong customer
  - Failure to record amounts billed
  - Fraudulent conduct by one or more individuals involved in billing/collecting functions

- Collecting
  - Business losses arising from poor credit policy or practices
  - Failure to deposit remittances intact or promptly
  - Failure to record collections
  - Failure to post collections to proper customer accounts
  - Failure to effect collections in a timely fashion
  - Theft of remittances by employees or others

These and other risks must be minimized by the internal control objectives and techniques, which affected management must establish.

INTERNAL CONTROL OBJECTIVES

The internal control objectives with respect to billing and collecting accounts receivable vary with the business environment and the risks involved. Therefore, specific objectives applicable to all companies cannot be set forth in a general reference book. The chief auditor or his designee, with the help of management, must identify the objectives applicable to his organization. The following may be used as a guide:

- For accounts receivable billing
  - To bill only customers authorized to receive credit in accordance with established credit policies
  - To bill for all goods and services rendered to authorized customers in a timely fashion
  - To bill for goods and services in accordance with approved price structure.
  - To adjust billed terms and conditions only upon specific management authorization
  - To record all billings accurately and completely
  - To safeguard accounts receivable from loss due to fraud or other irregular acts by employees and others
  - To provide information with respect to amounts billed to authorized individuals to permit collection and to enable management to gauge the effectiveness of its credit policies
- For collecting accounts receivable
  - To pursue collection of accounts receivable in accordance with established policies
  - To promptly deposit all remittances
  - To record all collections accurately and completely
  - To safeguard collections from loss due to fraud or other irregular acts by employees and others
  - To properly record all cash receipts and discounts and credits to customer accounts

- To provide information with respect to amounts collected, to enable management to gauge the effectiveness of its collection efforts, and to provide a basis for establishing provisions for uncollectible amounts

INTERNAL CONTROL TECHNIQUES

The nature and extent of internal control techniques depend on the objectives of internal control noted in the preceding discussion. A significant number of companies have applied EDP techniques to billing and collecting. In some cases, the billing function is but one aspect of a larger, fully automated application in which invoices are prepared by the computer, involving large data bases for information such as price lists, customer files, and detailed accounting records. Depending on volume and other factors, billings may be made when items are shipped, on some periodic basis (e.g., daily, weekly, or semimonthly), or on a cyclical basis (a method whereby the total volume of customers to be billed is accomplished by billing approximately equal segments on specified days within the cycle).

Organization and Authorization

Typically, the responsibility for proper billing and collecting duties is that of the chief financial officer and is usually delegated to the controller or the treasurer. In large companies, the responsibility may be further delegated to the credit and collection manager. Most companies take care to reasonably assure that duties are assigned in such a way that specific billing and collecting routines are divided between two or more persons or subdepartments. Billing duties are often described in a procedural manual or in functional job descriptions and are made a matter of routine to the extent practicable.

Other internal control techniques include specifying the credit policy of the entity and identifying those individuals with credit granting authority. Credit policy is usually formulated at a high organizational level within the company—often receiving the attention of the finance committee of the board of directors and even that of the full board. Credit granting authority within the policy limits may be retained at a high level or delegated to midmanagement or lower, depending on the significance of each transaction and the total transaction volume.

Processing and Accounting

In many billing and collecting functions, the processing and accounting controls include:

- Use of prescribed documents and forms, such as shipping advices, delivery tickets, sales invoices, credit memos, and deposit slips, with preprinted instructions for completion. This helps to assure that the information for each type of transaction necessary to effect proper accounting is captured.

- A means to keep important data base and master file data intact and current. Such data might include customer files showing names, addresses, and payment history; product catalogs showing part numbers and descriptions; price lists; and contract terms and conditions, if applicable.
- An independent review or check of important information, such as customer data, product data, quantity, prices, and extensions on invoices for accuracy, completeness, and authenticity before processing and recording. This may be done manually or by automated means.
- A method whereby all items or services shipped or provided are invoiced or billed. The techniques for this vary considerably with the nature of the product or service. Generally, some form of prenumbered shipping advice is used with numbers being periodically accounted for. Some companies prepare the shipping advice and the invoice simultaneously; that is, one copy of the multiple copy invoice form is the shipping advice. Other controls to help assure complete invoicing occur prior to the actual billing process and have to do with the way in which customer orders are handled, the number of shipping points, and the controls in the shipping department. For services, the completeness of the billing depends on the system established to account for the services rendered. Usually, some sort of job order system is involved.
- The use of prescribed books of original entry, such as sales journals and cash books with column headings and layouts, which facilitate accurate and complete posting.

Safeguarding

Safeguarding controls include:

- Controls to minimize exposure to fraud and other irregularities, such as controls over the issuance of credit memoranda and write-offs of overdue balances, segregation of duties with respect to billing, collecting, depositing, and posting functions, use of restrictive endorsements on checks, use of lockboxes, and periodic reviews by internal auditors
- A means to protect forms, files, and records from damage due to natural disasters and from human acts, intentional or otherwise, and to enable recovery in the event of loss

Reporting and Accountability

Reporting and accountability controls include the following:

- A method to record billing and collection transactions (and related transactions, such as credit for returned merchandise) accurately and completely in the period in which they occurred.
- A reconciliation of the total debit entries to detail customer accounts with the total of credits to the credit sales accounts. This would bring to the surface errors in posting detail entries and could conceivably lead to the discovery of malfeasance.
- A reconciliation of total credit entries to detail customer accounts with the

total of debit entries to the cash account for collections. This serves the same purpose as the control technique described in the preceding paragraph.

AUDIT TECHNIQUES

The periodic auditing of control techniques over billing and collecting functions is an important audit activity in many companies. That is because cash received from billing and collecting activities is the primary source of working capital—the lifeblood of all business. Because of the vital nature of these functions, nearly all organizations have established adequate billing and collecting techniques to accelerate cash inflow. It is rare that auditors encounter situations in which this is not the case; however, when billing and collecting routines are inadequate, there is great cause for concern not only because of the questions regarding billing anad collection but also because of the questions regarding the capability of management.

In devising his approach to auditing the billing collection functions, the auditor must also keep in mind that these functions carry a slightly higher exposure to irregularities and malfeasance than do other accounting functions. Billing and collecting functions are also of interest to external auditors, so audit coverage should be coordinated to avoid duplication of effort.

Preliminary

The auditor must prepare for the audit by obtaining as much background data as possible. These would include a review of prior workpapers, if available, policy statements, procedure manuals, organization charts, and any regulatory requirements. Recent financial statements should be obtained and analyzed for trends in key ratios, such as current ratio, quick ratio, acid test ratio, and days sales outstanding (see Chapter 16).

Preliminary discussions and interviews should be conducted with various interested members of management and the audit management to learn of any particular management concerns. Also, the timing of the fieldwork can be coordinated by this process. The necessary audit tools intended to be employed should be gathered or devised, as the case may be. Flow charts, questionnaires, checklists, and audit programs must all be readied. Some aspects of billing, and possibly collecting, may be susceptible to testing via statistical sampling and generalized audit software. These should also be assembled to the extent practicable.

Fieldwork

Conducting the fieldwork involves performing various procedures, as called out in the audit program, associated with observation, inquiry, inspection,

BILLING, ACCOUNTS RECEIVABLE, & COLLECTIONS

and confirmation, to gather the evidential matter necessary to form an opinion regarding the adequacy of billing and collecting control techniques.

Observation techniques may occur generally throughout the fieldwork to provide an overall sense of the effectiveness and efficiency with which billing and collecting occur. Some specific observations with respect to physical arrangements, adequacy of work space, equipment, personnel, and other resources for carrying out billing and collecting duties in an effective fashion may be made. Also, important control considerations, such as the extent to which duties are segregated, may also be observed.

Inquiry procedures via questionnaires and interviews may be used to obtain an understanding of control techniques in effect and to evaluate their adequacy.

Inspection and confirmation techniques may be used to validate that the control procedures represented to be in effect are, in fact, operating as understood. In particular, the auditor should be interested in testing the control techniques covered earlier in this chapter. Attributes to be tested either judgmentally or statistically might include:

- Agreement of terms between sales invoices and shipping advices.
- Accuracy of pricing, extensions, and footings on invoices.
- Agreement of invoices with postings to books of account.
- Credit approval.
- Evidence of processing sales invoices.

Other tests may be devised for handling of credit memoranda and write-offs of bad debts.

As a general rule, internal auditors do not independently correspond directly with customers to confirm account balances, unless fraud is a significant concern to management. However, many internal auditors perform such procedures as a service to the company's external auditors. When this occurs, the internal auditors usually work under the direction of the external auditors and use their programs and confirmation forms. The workpapers evidencing this work are retained by the external auditors.

ILLUSTRATIVE QUESTIONNAIRES

The questionnaire in Figure 19-1 is intended to illustrate many of the questions that might be asked in connection with an evaluation of internal control over an accounts receivable billing function. A separate questionnaire covering cash receipts (i.e., collections) is also given in Figure 19-2.

(continued on page 19-18)

FIG. 19-1

Internal Control Questionnaire for Accounts Receivable Billing

A. Authorization:

Receivables are authorized by management through their sales, marketing, contract, and credit policies. Billing is determined by the accomplishment of certain contractual obligations, such as shipment of goods or performance of services. Each of these areas is subject to specific audits designed to evaluate and test the controls over accumulation and estimation of contract costs, and control over inventory. The authorization of billing is dependent on sufficient evidential matter generated by the above specific areas, and general controls. The cash receipt function is addressed in a separate questionnaire.

	Yes	No	Reference
1. Do procedures specify those individuals authorized to process accounts receivable billing transactions?	☐	☐	....
2. Do procedures specify all required documentation to initiate an invoice?	☐	☐	....
3. Are the following required in the accounts receivable department?			
a. Contract documents, if applicable	☐	☐	....
b. Agent contracts	☐	☐	....
c. Shipping documents	☐	☐	....
d. Financing and export	☐	☐	....
e. Appropriate accumulations of cost incurred	☐	☐	....
f. Selling schedules	☐	☐	....
g. Authorized price lists	☐	☐	....
4. Do procedures specify those individuals authorized to approve credit, both on contract sales and individual item sales?	☐	☐	....
5. Are all sales and credit policies defined?	☐	☐	....
6. Do procedures specify those individuals authorized to approve credit memoranda?	☐	☐	....
7. Do procedures specify the actions to be taken to verify a return of goods or credit against a billing and the documentation required?	☐	☐	....
8. Do procedures specify management's criteria for acceptance of sales orders and do procedures require comparison with the criteria?	☐	☐	....
9. Do procedures fix the responsibility for authorizing write-offs to billed and unbilled accounts receivable?	☐	☐	....

	Yes	No	Reference

B. Processing and Recording:

1. Are shipping and billing activities initiated from orders properly approved for credit or from properly approved contracts?   ☐ ☐ ....

2. Do procedures prevent goods from being shipped or withdrawn or services performed without authorization?   ☐ ☐ ....

3. Do the shipping procedures provide assurance that the goods shipped are shipped in the proper quantities of the right merchandise?   ☐ ☐ ....

4. Are all shipping orders accounted for to ensure that every shipment is billed?   ☐ ☐ ....

5. Are all invoices priced from authorized price lists, contracts, or schedules?   ☐ ☐ ....

6. Are billings reviewed as to prices, terms, freight or other charges, and clerical accuracy?   ☐ ☐ ....

7. Are all credit memoranda properly approved?   ☐ ☐ ....

8. Is every credit for returned merchandise supported by a receiving report, or appropriate technical appraisal field report, or similar evaluation?   ☐ ☐ ....

9. Are accounts charged off only after review and approval?   ☐ ☐ ....

10. Are collection efforts continued after receivable balances are written off?   ☐ ☐ ....

11. Do those who control collections have effective custody of incoming remittances from the time they are received until they are deposited in the bank?   ☐ ☐ ....

12. Do those who control collections forward cash receipts totals directly to general ledger accounting?   ☐ ☐ ....

13. Are all entries in the individual receivable records made only from copies of sales invoices, credit memoranda, remittance advices, and other properly authorized media?   ☐ ☐ ....

14. Are all sales invoices and credit memoranda accounted for to ensure that each is recorded in the customer, receivables controls, and sales accounts?   ☐ ☐ ....

15. Is every shipment-billing entry matched by entries for the relief of inventory and charges to cost of sales?   ☐ ☐ ....

(continued)

FIG. 19-1 *(cont'd)*

	Yes	No	Reference
16. Are all collections accounted for to ensure recording in the customer and receivable control accounts?	☐	☐	....
17. If data processing techniques are used to record accounts receivable:			
a. Do procedures require establishing batch controls for input documents (e.g., item counts and hash totals) prior to submission of data for processing?	☐	☐	....
b. Do procedures call for the use of transmittal numbers and control logs?	☐	☐	....
c. Do procedures require immediate transmittal directly to data processing of all batches?	☐	☐	....
d. Do procedures require prompt resolution and resubmission of errors, rejected data, and so forth?	☐	☐	....
e. If terminals are used, do procedures call for sign-on/sign-off procedures, maintenance of terminal logs of usage, and a means to control input such as built-in counters/accumulators, tapes, etc.?	☐	☐	....
f. If data conversion occurs with the accounts payable group or at the profit center, do procedures require data verification and prompt submission direct to the data processing center?	☐	☐	....
g. Do procedures require receipt of evidence that transactions were accepted for processing by EDP (edit listing, proofs, etc.)?	☐	☐	....
h. Do procedures require reconciling EDP listings to control data or some other technique to assure accurate and complete processing?	☐	☐	....
i. Are EDP reports reconciled to control data or are other techniques used to check the completeness and accuracy of processing?	☐	☐	....
j. Do procedures require resolving differences and exceptions disclosed by the two questions above in a timely fashion?	☐	☐	....
18. Do procedures require organized filing or other disposition of data-related processed accounts receivable transactions (invoice receiver, purchase order, EDP reports, etc.)?	☐	☐	....
19. Do procedures specify the period of time for retaining records related to completed accounts receivable transactions?	☐	☐	....

C. Accessibility:

1. Do procedures require that accounts receivable billing duties be performed by individuals independent of those responsible for:

BILLING, ACCOUNTS RECEIVABLE, & COLLECTIONS

	Yes	No	Reference
a. Initiating sales or contracts	☐	☐	....
b. Credit	☐	☐	....
c. Shipping	☐	☐	....
d. General ledger	☐	☐	....
e. Cash functions	☐	☐	....
f. EDP	☐	☐	....

2. Are shipping functions segregated from billing and initiation of sales?   ☐ ☐ ....

3. Are cash functions segregated from revenue and receivable functions?   ☐ ☐ ....

4. If data processing terminals are used, do procedures require the use of appropriate employee identification, such as passwords, keys, etc.?   ☐ ☐ ....

5. Is the data processing area adequately restricted to permit only authorized employees to enter?   ☐ ☐ ....

6. Are entries to control accounts other than by normal processing routines approved by a responsible individual?   ☐ ☐ ....

7. Are processed transactions reviewed periodically for compliance with prescribed individuals independent of accounts receivable functions (such as profit center internal audit)?   ☐ ☐ ....

D. Accountability:

1. Do procedures require periodic reconciliation or balancing of control accounts and individual customer account detail?   ☐ ☐ ....

2. Do procedures require prompt investigation and correction of differences disclosed?   ☐ ☐ ....

3. Are statements mailed periodically to customers and do procedures ensure that such statements are not altered or intercepted before mailing?   ☐ ☐ ....

4. Are accounts receivable accounts aged periodically and reviewed by appropriate levels of management?   ☐ ☐ ....

FIG. 19-2

Internal Control Questionnaire for Cash Receipts

A. Authorization of Transactions:

The receipt of cash is authorized in a general sense by management in connection with the determination of credit policy and related treasury matters such as short- and long-term borrowing, and so forth. In addition, management must specify the individuals authorized to receive cash, arrange for and execute deposits in appropriate bank accounts, effect the recording of cash receipts transactions and posting to accounts receivable accounts. Individual cash receipt transactions are not authorized by management in the same sense that it authorizes specific cash disbursements and other types of transactions. Cash receipts occur as the result of action by the Company's customers. Accordingly, controls over cash receipts transactions, insofar as management authorization is concerned, relate to general controls.

	Yes	No	Workpaper Reference
1. Do procedures authorize the variety of means by which cash is to be received (i.e., upon delivery, by mail, in currency, via banks, through letters of credit, etc.)?	☐	☐	....
2. Do procedures specify the methodology to be employed in receiving cash for each of the means identified in the previous question?	☐	☐	....
3. Do procedures authorize the organizational element(s) and/or individuals empowered to receive cash?	☐	☐	....
4. Do procedures set forth the means by which cash is to be deposited in banks?	☐	☐	....
5. Do procedures fix the responsibility for establishing depository bank accounts?	☐	☐	....
6. Do procedures set forth the means by which cash receipt transactions are recorded?	☐	☐	....
7. Do procedures require prior approval by responsible persons for deviations from established procedures?	☐	☐	....
8. Do procedures specify the means by which cash in depository or concentration accounts is transferred to disbursing accounts of the Company?	☐	☐	....
9. Do procedures covering cash transfers (previous question) require written management approval (or some similar alternate means) before execution?	☐	☐	....
10. Are there procedures in effect for handling the receipt of special items such as dividends, interest, proceeds from the sale of fixed assets, scrap, etc.?	☐	☐	....

BILLING, ACCOUNTS RECEIVABLE, & COLLECTIONS

	Yes	No	Workpaper Reference

B. Processing and Recording:

1. Do procedures require that a record be made of items of cash receipts by the individual who opens the mail? ☐ ☐ ....

2. Do procedures require that cash receipts be deposited promptly? ☐ ☐ ....
   (In most instances, daily deposits are sufficient; however, it may be that the volume of receipts does not warrant that degree of frequency. On the other hand, the volume and amounts may be such so as to warrant multiple deposits each day.)

3. Do procedures specify the method to be followed in effecting deposits? ☐ ☐ ....
   (Depending on the nature, volume, and amount of cash receipts, various means may be employed to affect the deposit. Among these are (1) direct receipt by the bank, (2) deposits by designated employees, (3) night deposits, and (4) armored car service, and so forth.)

4. Do procedures require that evidence in support of receipts, such as remittance advices, be retained? ☐ ☐ ....

5. Do procedures require that evidence of amounts deposited be obtained and retained (i.e., authenticated duplicate deposit slips, bank advices, etc.)? ☐ ☐ ....

6. Do procedures require that the evidence obtained in support of receipts be given promptly to accounting personnel for recording and filing? ☐ ☐ ....

7. Do procedures require that accounting personnel verify the accuracy and validity of deposits by reference to listings of mail receipts, remittance advices, or by other means prior to recording in cash journals or before input to data processing? ☐ ☐ ....

8. If receipts are recorded by means of electronic data processing, do procedures require that data input be controlled by item counts, hash totals, or by other means prior to submission? ☐ ☐ ....
   a. If input to data processing is achieved by means of terminals, are all input transactions required to be listed for review and approval prior to input, and is a separate record of input made by the terminal? ☐ ☐ ....
   b. If the Accounting Department or profit center is responsible for data conversion, do processing procedures require data verification and a means of cancelling source documents subsequent to conversion? ☐ ☐ ....

(continued)

FIG. 19-2 *(cont'd)*

	Yes	No	Workpaper Reference

c. Do procedures require that converted data be transferred immediately to processing center? ☐ ☐ ....

d. Do procedures require that accounting personnel receive evidence (i.e., edit listings, proofs, etc.) from the processing center that transactions were accepted and reconcile such evidence to control data? ☐ ☐ ....

e. Do procedures fix responsibility for error detection, correction, and resubmission in a timely fashion? ☐ ☐ ....

f. Do procedures require that output reports be reviewed and is control data required to be reconciled to manually prepared data? ☐ ☐ ....

9. If posting to cash journal is by means other than data processing, do procedures require that the source for posting be other than the items of cash receipts themselves? ☐ ☐ ....

10. Do procedures require the periodic balancing of the totals of the postings to the cash receipts journal (or comparable EDP report) with total posting credits to individual accounts receivable records? ☐ ☐ ....
    Note: This might be performed in connection with reconciling the bank account.

11. Do procedures cover the handling and recording of NSF checks? ☐ ☐ ....

12. Do procedures require that all cash items received, regardless of source, be promptly deposited and recorded? ☐ ☐ ....

C. Accessibility:

1. Is the authority to receive or transfer cash restricted to designated individuals? ☐ ☐ ....

2. Are persons who are authorized to receive cash independent of disbursement functions, persons who post accounting records, and persons involved in disbursement functions? ☐ ☐ ....

3. Do procedures require that cash items be stored in a secure area with restricted access until deposit (i.e., locked box, safe, locked cabinets, etc.)? ☐ ☐ ....

4. Are persons empowered to execute transfer of funds between bank accounts independent from related accounting functions? ☐ ☐ ....

5. Do procedures provide for appropriate protection for individuals effecting deposits by physically carrying cash items to the bank? ☐ ☐ ....

	Yes	No	Workpaper Reference

6. Does the method of deposit (direct receipt by bank, deposits by designated employees, night deposit, armored car service, etc.) appropriately safeguard cash items, given the nature of the cash items and the accounts involved? ☐ ☐ ....

7. Are persons who prepare and effect deposits required to be independent of receiving disbursement and accounting functions? ☐ ☐ ....

8. Is evidence of bank deposits (authenticated duplicate deposit slips, etc.) required to be received directly from the bank by individuals other than those making the deposit? ☐ ☐ ....

9. If recording of cash receipts is effected by means of data processing, are persons involved in receiving depositing and accounting for cash prohibited from entering the data processing area? ☐ ☐ ....

10. If terminals are used to record cash receipts, are there controls over sign-on/sign-off and transaction entry that restrict access ability (passwords, employee identifications, lock keys, etc.)? ☐ ☐ ....

11. If terminals are used, do procedures require periodic review of terminal logs or other control data by designated individuals independent of processing functions? ☐ ☐ ....

12. Do procedures require supervisory personnel or management to review and approve journal entries recording cash transactions and the balancing routine? ☐ ☐ ....

13. Do procedures prohibit cashing personal checks out of current receipts? ☐ ☐ ....

14. Have banks been instructed not to cash checks made out to the Company? ☐ ☐ ....

15. Are all negotiable items (checks, drafts, etc.) restrictively indorsed immediately upon receipt? ☐ ☐ ....

16. Are persons involved in depositing and recording cash receipts covered by insurance and fidelity bonds in appropriate amounts? ☐ ☐ ....

D. Accountability:

1. Do procedures require that records of cash receipt transactions be periodically reconciled to bank statements of cash receipts? ☐ ☐ ....

(continued)

FIG. 19-2 *(cont'd)*

	Yes	No	Workpaper Reference
Note: This procedure would normally be done in connection with reconciling bank and accounting department records. However, reconciliations of bank and accounting department records can occur without performing the procedure outlined above.			
2. Do procedures fix responsibility for investigation and correction of differences disclosed in the first question in this section?	☐	☐	....
3. Do procedures require periodic counts of cash items on hand?	☐	☐	....
4. Are periodic comparisons and evaluations made of cash actually received with projections of cash receipts for specified periods with investigation of large or unusual differences?	☐	☐	....

SAMPLE AUDIT PROGRAM

The audit program in Figure 19-3 is designed primarily for the audit of an accounts receivable billing function. An audit program for cash receipts is shown in Chapter 18. The program is integrated with the questionnaire illustrated in Figure 19-1 in this chapter, to the extent applicable.

FIG. 19-3

Audit Program for Accounts Receivable Billing

> The accounts receivable and revenue collection systems are reviewed and tested to make an evaluation of the following objectives:
> - All shipments are billed at authorized prices and terms. Billing adjustments for allowances, discounts, and returned merchandise have been authorized.
> - All collections are properly identified, control totals developed, and collections promptly deposited intact. *Note:* A separate audit program for cash receipts covers this aspect.
> - Billing, adjustments, and collections are properly recorded in individual customer accounts.
> - Revenues, collections, and receivables are properly accumulated, classified, and summarized in the accounts.

BILLING, ACCOUNTS RECEIVABLE, & COLLECTIONS

	Workpaper Reference	Done by

1. General:

☐ Obtain copy of organization chart and, by review of chart and discussion with management, determine the independence and reporting relationship of the accounts receivable function. ....

☐ Inquire into the existence of written procedures for accounts receivable. ....

☐ Review procedures, determine that procedures are current (noting last revision date), and document and evaluate the accounts receivable procedure. ....

☐ Prepare a schedule cross-referencing procedure to an internal control questionnaire. ....

☐ By interviews with management and personnel involved in the accounts receivable function, determine any deviations from written procedures or any other procedures that are not current. ....

☐ During the course of the audit, tour facilities and observe personnel at work for any indication of resource problems, personnel incompetence, or dishonest acts. ....

2. Authorization/Execution of Transactions:

☐ Select .... customer's accounts receivable balances and test for evidence of the following:
- Sales invoice agrees to account balances. ....
- Terms on .... individual sales invoices agree to contract terms. ....
- Prices, extensions, and footings are correct. ....
- Sales invoice agrees to shipping department records (shipping logs, bills of lading, customer acceptance or other authentic evidence of shipment). ....
- Sales invoice agrees to contractual billing schedule. ....
- Sales invoice agrees to cost incurred as evidenced in cost accounting records. ....
- Credit approval. ....
- Invoices are properly recorded to accounts receivable detail and control accounts, inventory or cost ledgers, and general ledgers. ....
- Any freight charges related to or included in the invoices selected have been approved by traffic department. ....

☐ Select .... shipments from shipping departments:
- Trace to invoice, noting timeliness of billing. ....

(continued)

FIG. 19-3 *(cont'd)*

	Workpaper Reference	Done by
■ Trace invoices to individual customer accounts.	....	....
■ Note any shortage reports and agree to customer invoices.	....	....
☐ Obtain sales journal for the most recent month end:		
■ Test foot (if manually prepared).	....	....
■ Trace totals to the general ledger.	....	....
☐ Review invoices for the month to determine numerical sequence.	....	....
☐ Consider confirming accounts receivable, particularly where controls are found to be weak, procedures are not being followed (substantiated by testing above) or old, outstanding, large, or numerous old accounts exist.	....	....
☐ Select sales credits and perform the following:		
■ Credit memos are promptly issued and properly authorized.	....	....
■ Credit memos agree in price and quantity to the original billing.	....	....
■ Entries are properly recorded to:		
a. Detail accounts receivable	....	....
b. Accounts receivable totals	....	....
c. Inventory	....	....
d. Sales	....	....
☐ Select a recent month end period and perform a test of sales cut-off.		
■ From shipping department records, trace shipments just prior to and subsequent to the approved cut-off date to sales invoices, noting recording of these invoices to the proper period.	....	....
■ From cost accounting records, trace costs incurred up to the approved cut-off date to recording as receivables in the proper time period. Determine that cost incurred subsequent to the cut-off is not recorded as sales until the next time period.	....	....
☐ Review old outstanding accounts receivable balances by selecting all old balances in excess of $.... and a random sample of		
■ Determine collection activity taken to date on each account.	....	....
■ Review the individual account with management and determine management's assessment of collectibility, including technical assessments, funding, disputes, claims, credit condition, contractual problems, etc.	....	....

	Workpaper Reference	Done by

- Review correspondence, contracts, and other substantive data that supports managements' assessments of collectibility.
- Determine provisions for specific accounts and evaluate the adequacy of such provisions.
- Review accounts written off in the past year. Determine that all were properly approved. Note the percentages of write-off to total receivable balance (or sales).
- Determine whether any provision unallocated to specific accounts is adequate to provide for the actual incidence of write-off in recent year.
- Determine which accounts have been placed for collection, and review the approval, accounting, and controls over recoveries.

☐ Inquire as to any organizational/system changes and check for evidence of proper approval.

☐ Check for evidence of approval for selected changes to vendor master files.

☐ Recording by automated system:
- Obtain control logs and review for evidence of reconciling batch controls to processed data.
- If terminals are used, inspect terminals, noting use of lock keys, passwords, sign-on/sign-off procedures, terminal logs, etc.
- Check for evidence of timely resubmission of errors and rejected transactions.
- Optional data processing testing. If the system review indicates substantial recent changes, significant control weakness are revealed by earlier inquiries, or significant processing or recording errors are noted in testing the detail transactions, consider requesting a system review by Corporate Audit data processing auditor.

3. Accessibility:

☐ Obtain audit reports issued by the profit center auditor and determine the nature of the finding, resolution of recommendation, and follow-up performed by the auditor and management. Determine what controls were changed to improve procedures or policies.

☐ Review entries to control accounts which arise from sources other than summaries of normal processing transactions:

(continued)

FIG. 19-3 *(cont'd)*

	Workpaper Reference	Done by
■ Determine the propriety of the entry.	....	....
■ Determine that all such entries are approved by a responsible level of management.	....	....
☐ By reference to organization charts and by observation, confirm the degree of segregation of duties.	....	....
☐ Inspect facilities for safeguarding negotiable instruments (if applicable) for compliance with established procedures.	....	....
4. Accountability:		
☐ Check for evidence of reconciliation of control accounts with detail subledgers and for investigation and correction of differences.	....	....
☐ Obtain accounts receivable trial balance for the most recent month end:		
■ Agree the total to the general ledger.	....	....
■ Test foot the trial balance.	....	....

SPECIMEN AUDIT REPORT

The report in Figure 19-4 is illustrative of typical findings that might be reported as a result of an audit of billing and collecting functions.

FIG. 19-4

Report on Audit of Billing and Collecting Functions

TO: A.R. Thompson

FROM: Corporate Audit

SUBJECT: Review of Accounts Receivable Billing and Collection — Sunset Equipment Company

We have reviewed the internal controls over the billing and collection functions pertaining to accounts receivable at Sunset Equipment Company (SEC). Our review was performed in order to determine that internal controls are sufficient to provide reasonable assurance that billings and collections are prepared in accordance with management's criteria; are recorded so as to permit preparation of financial statements in accordance with generally accepted accounting principles; and that balances and related data are properly reported and safeguarded. Our review was performed in accordance with internally developed audit standards and included tests and an evaluation of internal controls within the subject area, discussions with management, and such other audit procedures as we deemed necessary in the circumstances. Our review disclosed the following matters, which require management attention and action:

- Although sales orders are batched and control totals determined, there is no balancing of the sales order input to the sales invoice output generated by data processing. As a result, errors and omissions, which occur from time to time in data entry, are not detected until after the invoices are sent, if at all.
- Source documents (sales orders) are not individually cancelled at the time of data entry to preclude their resubmission.
- Credit memos for returned merchandise have not been consistently approved in accordance with the established approval authority matrix.
- Procedures for handling sales of scrap are not formalized in writing.
- System and user documentation is not sufficient for dependable and effective system maintenance and use.

While these findings may not, individually or in the aggregate, significantly impair the reliability and accuracy of billings and collections and the recording, reporting, and safeguarding thereof, they do present risks that can be more effectively controlled.

Our detailed findings and recommendations for corrective action are discussed in the balance of this report. A written reply to this report, including schedules for contemplated action, is requested within thirty days.

FINDINGS AND RECOMMENDATIONS

1. **Although sales orders are batched and control totals determined, there is no balancing of the sales order input to the output of sales invoices generated by data processing.**

    After orders are shipped, the audit copies of sales orders are sent to data processing to record the sales and generate invoices. Before submission to data processing, the accounts receivable clerk batches the sales orders and tabulates a batch balance of the total quantity of goods shipped. Following input, data processing generates an edit listing showing the total quantity processed.

    We noted that the accounts receivable clerk was not reviewing the edit listing for the purpose of ensuring that input and output quantities were in balance. Unless input and output quantities are balanced and differences investigated, erroneous processing could occur without detection. Since the structure of the control is already in place, the verification procedure can be instituted at minimal cost.

    ### RECOMMENDATION NO. 1

    Compare the input total of quantities shipped with the total processed per the computer generated edit listing and investigate any differences.

2. **Input documents are not individually cancelled at the time of data entry to preclude their resubmission.**

(continued)

FIG. 19-4 *(cont'd)*

Cancellation of individual input documents after the recording process is commonly practiced as a precaution against intentional or erroneous resubmission.

In the SEC accounts receivable systems, input documents (the sales orders) submitted to data entry in batches with a covering batch transmittal ticket. The transmittal form is eventually cancelled, but the input documents are not individually cancelled by stamping or punching.

RECOMMENDATION NO. 2

Cancel individual input documents at time of their entry into the Accounts Receivable System.

3. Credit memos have not been consistently approved in accordance with the established approval authority matrix.

All credit memos issued by the Billing area must be reviewed and approved according to the following matrix:

Item	Approval Required
External Credit Memos to be sent to the customer	Manager, General Accounting
Internal Credits adjusting accounts receivable records (up to $2,000)	Supervisor, Billing and Receivables
Internal Credits adjusting accounts receivable records (over $2,000)	Manager, General Accounting

Several instances were noted in our review of failure to obtain the necessary level of approval for internal credit memos. Although no evidence was found of an external credit memo (one that is actually sent to the customer) without the proper approval, both types of credit memos should be reviewed and approved by the proper level of management, as they both ultimately affect the amounts due from customer.

RECOMMENDATION NO. 3

Obtain the appropriate level of management approval for all credit memos issued by Billing.

4. No written procedures exist for handling sales of scrap material.

The informal and unwritten policy with regards to miscellaneous scrap sales is that the sale be collected on delivery. However, due to favorable past dealings with a particular scrap dealer, a sale of scrap generators was made on credit to the dealer. The receivable of $3,650 has subsequently become very doubtful of collection, with litigation now pending. Although the monetary exposure is relatively small, the lack of an adequate formal procedure that includes specified approval levels for credit sales of scrap material is the major internal control exposure. We also recognize, however, that implementation of controls for scrap sales should be based on cost-benefit analysis to assure that the costs of instituting controls do not exceed the benefits.

> **RECOMMENDATION NO. 4**
>
> Perform a cost-benefit analysis related to the implementation of procedures covering the controls over and approvals surrounding sales and disposals of scrap material and implement such controls to the extent the analysis indicates the need.
>
> **5. System and user documentation is not sufficient for dependable and effective system maintenance and use.**
>
> Complete and accurate documentation, consisting of a system description, system flow charts, edit routines, controls and audit trail descriptions, backup and recovery procedures, etc., is necessary for dependable and effective system maintenance. A User's Manual is also invaluable as a training aid and reference guide. Without such reference material, training of new personnel is dependent upon unassisted verbal instructions. Unavailability of knowledgeable, key personnel could result in unclear or overlooked instructions in the training process and a deterioration in the department's operating efficiency.
>
> Although the system flow charts were satisfactory, we were unable to locate additional necessary documentation items such as edit routines, control and balancing provisions, backup and recovery provisions, adequate system description, or a user's manual. As a result, the dependability and effectiveness of system maintenance is impaired.
>
> **RECOMMENDATION NO. 5**
>
> Prepare documentation for the billing system consisting of a system description, including edit routines, control and balancing provisions, backup and recovery provisions and user's manual.

SUGGESTED READING

Burton, John C., Russell E. Palmer, and Robert S. Kay, eds. *Handbook of Accounting and Auditing*, Chapter 18. New York: Warren, Gorham & Lamont, 1981.

Connor, Joseph E., and Burnell H. DeVos, Jr., eds. "Revenues and Receivables," in *Guide to Accounting Controls*. New York: Warren, Gorham & Lamont, 1979.

Kell, Walter G., and Richard E. Ziegler. *Modern Auditing*, Chapter 12. New York: Warren, Gorham & Lamont, 1980.

Willson, James D. *Budgeting and Profit Planning Manual*, Chapters 19–20. New York: Warren, Gorham & Lamont, 1987.

Willson, James D., and John B. Campbell. *Controllership: The Work of the Managerial Accountant*, Chapter 22. New York: John B. Wiley & Sons, 1981.

CHAPTER **20**

Accounts Payable and Payroll Processing and Accounting

Accounts Payable Overview 2	**A Specimen Report** 13
Definition and Background 2	**Payroll Overview** 13
The Business Environment 3	**Definition and Background** 25
Management Objectives 3	The Business Environment 26
Current Financial Condition 4	
Type of Industry 4	**Risks** 27
Legal Considerations 4	
Risks 5	**Internal Control Objectives** 29
Internal Control Objectives 6	**Internal Control Techniques** 30
	Organization and Authorization 30
Internal Control Techniques 6	Processing and Accounting 31
Organization 7	Safeguarding 32
Authorization Controls 8	Reporting and Accountability 32
Processing and Accounting 8	**Audit Techniques** 33
Accessibility and Safeguarding 9	Preliminary 33
Reporting and Accountability 9	Fieldwork 34
Audit Techniques 10	
Preliminary 10	**Illustrative Questionnaire** 36
Fieldwork 11	**A Sample Audit Program** 36
Illustrative Questionnaire 13	**Specimen Reports** 45
A Sample Audit Program 13	**Suggested Reading** 51

Fig. 20-1   Internal Control Questionnaire for Accounts Payable 14
Fig. 20-2   Audit Program for Accounts Payable 17
Fig. 20-3   Audit Report—Accounts Payable Function 20
Fig. 20-4   Internal Control Questionnaire for Payroll 37
Fig. 20-5   Payroll Audit Program 42
Fig. 20-6   Audit Report—Corporate Payroll System Internal Controls 46
Fig. 20-7   Audit Report on Payroll-Related Transactions 49

ACCOUNTS PAYABLE OVERVIEW

Accounts payable processing and accounting is yet another function basic to all business entities. It is associated with both the purchasing transaction cycle and the treasury or finance transaction cycle. From an operational standpoint, accounts payable is but one aspect of financial management (see Chapter 32). Accounts payable is a generic term covering not only amounts owing to trade creditors for purchases of materials, supplies, and services, but also amounts owing for rents, utilities, taxes, employee-incurred expenses, such as travel, and, in some companies, installment payments.

Accounts payable processing and accounting has always been an important part of any system of internal accounting control because of its significance to cash management and creditor relations. The timeliness with which companies pay their bills is one of the considerations used by creditors in deciding upon credit terms for their customers. In fact, tracking payment practices has become quite a business for some companies who report their results to interested parties for a fee.

The growth in the size of companies and the improvements in accounts payable processing over the years have transformed a once-simple task into one requiring a considerable investment in facilities, equipment, manpower, and systems to achieve internal control objectives. Since accounts payable processing and payment involves the use of cash, there is a higher continuing exposure to losses through fraudulent and other irregular acts on the part of employees and others. For these reasons, auditing the internal controls over accounts payable functions is a staple in most internal auditing organizations. This chapter defines the accounts payable function, describes the business environment, risks, and internal control objectives and techniques associated with it, discusses various audit techniques that may be used in auditing accounts payable functions, and offers an illustrative internal control questionnaire, audit program, and specimen audit report.

The discussions and illustrations in this chapter exclude the internal controls over actual cash disbursements—the actual preparation and recording of payment checks. For small organizations, the functions of accounts payable processing and recording and cash disbursements may be combined in a single audit undertaking. In these instances, the questionnaire shown in Figure 18-10 may be combined with that illustrated in this chapter.

DEFINITION AND BACKGROUND

Accounts payable processing and recording is a self-evident term intended here to mean the series of actions by which control is established and maintained over the readying of creditor invoices, bills and statements, and other forms of indebtedness for near-term payment.

Payment of creditors for services, products, and so on differs from payroll payments in that the latter claims on company cash are usually liquidated almost immediately as prescribed by law, bargaining agreements, and company policy. The former class of claims, because of the variety of circumstances in which they arise, first must be established as valid claims against the company, accumulated, and arranged so that payment is made in accordance with agreed terms. Trade accounts arising from the purchase of goods and services used in the business and certain other types of payments (telephone and other utility bills, rents, and employee reimbursements) are unsecured. That is, the company is not required to post any collateral to minimize the creditors' risk of loss in the event the company is unable to make payment. The company's previous record in making such payments and its business relationship with its trade creditors are prime determinants of the extent to which this class of creditors is willing to continue to offer similar terms. Companies experiencing work capital difficulties often become so strained for cash that specific arrangements must be made with its unsecured creditors. Sometimes, these arrangements must be worked out under the protection of federal bankruptcy laws. Under normal circumstances, internal auditors need know little more about the particulars of these laws other than to be aware of their existence and general purpose.

The specific nature of trade and other accounts payable vary from industry to industry and, to some extent, from company to company within specific industries. For example, accounts payable and the processes used to control them are thought to be somewhat different as between the automobile industry and the textile industry or the building materials industry.

THE BUSINESS ENVIRONMENT

Variations in the business environment account for much of the differences in the ways in which accounts payable are processed and recorded. It is believed, however, that the variances are not as great as is the case for the other areas of internal control discussed in other chapters (i.e., billing and collecting accounts receivable and cost systems). Virtually all companies must pay utility bills, rents, and taxes, and reimburse employees. The primary differences are caused by variations in the nature of the trade accounts.

Management Objectives

The objectives of management with respect to accounts payable vary from company to company. For example, many companies, including some large ones, attempt to optimize trade credit as a source of financing—even beyond stated terms—because it is interest-free. (There are, however, hidden costs, such as the adverse impact on vendor willingness to provide "extra" service in some instances and a higher price for the product or services in others.)

Other companies strive to stay within the stated payment terms. Some companies, by virtue of their commanding position in particular industries, use that position advantageously in negotiating trade credit. Others are less aggressive.

Current Financial Condition

The current financial condition of the company will often dictate the degree of flexibility open to management in using its leverage to secure advantageous trade credit terms. Poor financial condition produces serious doubts in the minds of creditors, making them less likely to extend their best terms. A sound financial picture provides management with the opportunity to establish the accounts payable policy best for their circumstance.

Type of Industry

The type of industry affects the control techniques that must be applied. Labor-intensive industries, certain governmental units, and financial institutions are examples of economic segments in which acquisition and conversion of raw materials, purchased parts, and supplies into some tangible finished product are not involved. Hence, trade payables are much less consequential. Even among manufacturing companies, where a high level trade payable activity occurs, variations exist due to differences in organization and in the nature of the basic goods and services being paid for. Some manufacturers, for instance, are more integrated than others, are thus able to fabricate larger proportions of their finished goods, and, as a result, require less trade with outside sources. Some others, in addition to purchasing basic raw materials (e.g., steel, aluminum, and petroleum), purchase many parts and subassemblies from major suppliers. Contractors use the work of subcontractors to perform certain segments of overall business projects. The purchases of still others, such as food processors, chemical producers, and beverage companies, are comprised to a large extent of bulk products. The processing of these and other types of trade payables requires specialized knowledge and skill within the payables department, and other unique methods to assure that management objectives are satisfied.

Legal Considerations

Legal considerations apply to accounts payable organizations in that due dates for payment of certain items, such as taxes, royalties, and dividends, are either fixed by law or otherwise regulated in some equivalent fashion. Moreover, some types of products or services are rendered pursuant to complex contractual arrangements. The accounts payable organizations of companies in these circumstances must employ more measures than would

ACCOUNTS PAYABLE PROCESSING

otherwise be necessary to assure that payment is made within the time specified and when all legal conditions have been met. Of course, the accounts payable department shares this responsibility in many companies with other disciplines, such as internal law departments.

RISKS

Another important set of considerations in understanding and evaluating accounts payable processing and accounting is the set of risks inherent in the particular circumstances. These also vary among businesses; however, the following are often present:

- Payment for goods and services not ordered
- Payment for goods and services not received or not meeting specifications
- Overpayments
- Duplicate payments
- Late payments
- Failure to record payments
- Fraud, theft and other irregular acts
- Unauthorized additions/deletions to vendor master files or other records
- Loss, theft, or destruction of vital accounts payable data
- Fraud, theft, and other irregular acts

Some of the ramifications of these risks include financial loss, misstated financial statements, decline in relations with vendors, and finished product quality. These risks and their ramifications are minimized by most companies through an effective application of resources, including systems personnel and equipment. Auditors often encounter isolated errors, such as instances of late payments and missed discounts, often occasioned by an increased volume in transactions requiring processing and payment. However, the risks previously identified, which are well-known to competent managements, make it highly unlikely that significant control weaknesses or major fraudulent activity will be encountered. The auditor performing an examination of accounts payable controls must keep this perspective in mind. At the same time, the auditor must remain alert to the possibility that significant problems might exist, particularly in entities experiencing unfavorable operating results or working capital difficulties and facing a bleak business outlook.

Many companies have applied EDP techniques to improve the effectiveness and efficiency of accounts payable processing and recording. These systems involve other specific risks, such as:

- Programming errors
- Processing delays due to machine downtime

- Insufficient controls to detect all errors resulting from data entry, conversion, storing, processing, and reporting
- Unauthorized changes to programs
- Unauthorized changes to computer master files
- Unauthorized access to sensitive vendor information
- Loss or destruction of data

It is not uncommon for auditors to detect control weaknesses where EDP systems are involved, inasmuch as controls within information system (I/S) departments, particularly small- to medium-sized installations, are often sacrificed to achieve "production efficiency."

INTERNAL CONTROL OBJECTIVES

The internal control objectives with respect to accounts payable processing and recording are thought to vary only slightly from company to company. The following objectives are invariably associated with this function:

- To process trade accounts and other amounts due in accordance with managements' authorization
- To process trade accounts and other amounts so as to effect payment in accordance with established terms, conditions, laws, and regulations
- To reasonably assure that only transactions resulting from properly ordered, received, and accepted goods and services are readied for payment
- To reasonably assure that vendors invoices, bills, statements, or other documents indicating amounts due are accurate and complete
- To reasonably assure that invoices, bills, and other related documentation are not lost or destroyed during processing
- To record accounts payable transactions in accordance with GAAP
- To restrict access to accounts payable records and files to authorized personnel
- To reasonably protect vital accounts payable records and files from loss or destruction
- In the event of business interruptions, to reasonably assure the return to normal processing with a minimum of adverse consequences
- To reasonably assure that accounts payable control accounts are reconciled to detail balances of periodic intervals, with appropriate follow-up differences
- To reasonably assure that actual processing activity and related costs are compared with budgeted activity with appropriate follow-up of differences

INTERNAL CONTROL TECHNIQUES

Internal control techniques over accounts payable processing and recording vary among companies, depending on the nature of the underlying transactions. From a control standpoint, regardless of the company, accounts payable processing is as integral a part of such transaction cycles as the purchasing or procurement cycle, the payroll cycle (taxes, withholdings, and insurance amounts calculated in the payroll cycle are routed for payment through the payables function in many companies), and the finance cycle. (Installment payments of long-term debt, leases, and other forms of indebtedness are also routed through the payables function in many companies.) As a result, accounts payable transactions are not authorized in a direct sense by management. Instead, these transactions are "authorized" by the operation of established control techniques within the related transaction cycles from which they originated. For instance, the recording of an accounts payable transaction for the purchase of materials derives from the fact that the accounts payable clerk has evidence, in the form of an approved, valid purchase order, a properly executed receiving report, and a correct vendor invoice, that the amounts being claimed must be paid. Accounts payable functions therefore must be organized and controlled in such a manner to reasonably assure that all such transactions, and other forms of indebtedness, are readied for timely payment and are recorded in the accounts promptly.

Organization

The accounts payable function is a finance function that involves both accounting and fiscal tasks. In small organizations, this poses few problems, since the finance organization is usually comprised of a single responsible manager or officer. In large organizations, where finance responsibility is divided between the controller's office and the treasurer's office, a more or less arbitrary arrangement evolves for managing the accounts payable function. In some companies, it is given to the controller; in others, it is given to the treasurer, and, in still others, the responsibility is divided in some fashion. Regardless of the arrangement, the auditor must be cognizant that the affected personnel are often sensitive about the arrangement and may be involved in ongoing disputes with other functional organizations involved in the payment process. It is not uncommon for auditors to be told by one organization that "we've always had trouble with the . . . . department. They never send us the information that we need in order to . . . ." The other organization may assert, "They don't know what they're doing over there. They ask for the same information three different ways and they always lose it." Occasionally these "family" squabbles can get out of hand to the point where it affects the timeliness and accuracy of the resultant payments. Performing auditors must be alert to this possibility and report any serious problems to affected management in an appropriate, discreet fashion.

Accounts payable organizations vary from company to company not only in terms of reporting relationships but also in terms of centralization. Some large companies follow the practice of centralizing the payment of all invoices and other amounts due in a single function for all operating units. Other large companies permit each operating element to organize and staff their own accounts payable function. Suitable, albeit different, control techniques can be devised regardless of the method used. The discussion of control techniques and the illustrative audit tools in this chapter are aimed at a decentralized arrangement.

Authorization Controls

As stated earlier, the authorization of accounts payable transactions derives from the operation of other functions. However, within the accounts payable department, authorization for access and changes to master file content and to basic procedures and systems should be spelled out. Also, if the computer is involved in the processing, then authority for accessing and updating computerized accounts payable files should be established. Virtually all companies use standard forms and records to "regularize" the processing activity. Reponsibility and authority for their use should be stated. Among the forms, records, and files associated with the payables function are:

1. Forms
   - Vendor invoices, statements, and bills
   - Freight bills
   - Requests for disbursements
   - Debit memos
   - Purchase orders
   - Receiving reports
   - Requests for information
2. Records
   - Accounts payable or voucher registers
   - Detail accounts payable ledger
3. Files
   - Unmatched files
   - Vendor master file
   - Paid files
   - To be paid files

Written procedures should exist covering the use of each of the foregoing. The procedures should also specify authority to effect changes in any of them. This is particularly important if EDP techniques are involved.

Processing and Accounting

Among the control techniques often used to reasonably assure accurate and complete processing of accounts payable transactions are the following:

ACCOUNTS PAYABLE PROCESSING

- Establishing or maintaining an invoice log to track the whereabouts of invoices received but not yet paid
- Establishing physical means to evidence processing activity (e.g., stamps, perforation devices, initialing to evidence matching, math verifying, and posting)
- Matching all relevant data, such as item number, part number, description, quantity unit price, and extended value for all appropriate documents
- Verifying mathematics
- Verifying approval signatures
- Use of accounting machines and computers
- Retention of all processed source data in a way to permit easy access and retrieval
- Use of charts of accounts and accounting manuals for determining account distribution
- Use of batch techniques to post books of original entry

Accessibility and Safeguarding

Among the control techniques applicable to accessibility and safeguarding are the following:

- Segregating duties associated with processing and recording of transactions from those associated with cash transactions
- Use of passwords and lock keys where applicable
- Use of lockable, fire-resistant file cabinets, where appropriate
- Physical segregation and protection of data processing function, where applicable
- Vital records protection procedures (e.g., duplicate records and off-site storage)
- Disaster recovery plan

Reporting and Accountability

Usually, reporting and accountability controls include periodic balancing between the general ledger control account and the subsidiary accounts payable ledger, which reflects individual vendor balances. Also, many accounts payable organizations maintain internal records of statistics, such as number of transactions received and processed in stated intervals, both in total and by clerk. Information with respect to the backlog of unpaid items may also be maintained. This information, when periodically reported to the treasurer, controller, or other responsible official, enables him to monitor the effectiveness and efficiency employed in processing accounts payable.

AUDIT TECHNIQUES

The significance of accounts payable processing and accounting is such that it is frequently included in the scope of internal auditing coverage. Performing auditors must bear in mind that accounts payable, like payroll, carries a higher exposure to irregularities and malfeasance than do other accounting functions. Accounts payable processing and accounting are also of interest to external auditors, so audit coverage should be coordinated to avoid duplicating efforts. For small organizational units, the auditor may be able to combine the review-related functions with the accounts payable review. These might include procurement, receiving, and cash disbursements.

Preliminary

As with other audit projects, the auditor charged with the responsibility for auditing accounts payable processing and accounting for purposes of testing compliance and evaluating the adequacy of controls must start by obtaining as much background information as possible. This would include prior workpapers, if available, policy statements, procedural manuals, organization charts, and pertinent financial data. Since accounts payable processing can vary, depending on the nature of the items being paid, the auditor must understand the particular circumstances of the organization to be reviewed.

If data are available, it is often informative to apply analytical techniques, such as trend or regression analysis, to such information as unpaid invoice backlog, transactions processed monthly, and average age of accounts payable transactions. It is also helpful to know the credit rating of the entity, if it is obtainable (from Dun & Bradstreet, for instance).

Preliminary discussions and interviews should be conducted with interested members of management and the audit management by the performing auditor(s) to learn of any particular concerns which they may have. Also, the timing of the fieldwork can be coordinated by this process.

Another aspect of preliminary work involves readying the audit tools intended to be used. These include audit programs, questionnnaires, and, to the extent applicable, I/S (EDP) audit techniques (see Chapter 28). Since processing and accounting for accounts payable transactions often involves EDP, such tools as generalized audit software and embedded audit routines are frequently useful. For example, generalized audit software may be used to:

- Extract information from computerized files, such as the vendor master file, and/or transaction files.
- Duplicate segments of programs, such as automated matching.
- Verify mathematical calculations.

Some accounts payable applications may involve on-line interactive techniques. For these, the auditor may not be able to use generalized software. Special extraction programs may have to be developed. Of course, the best alternative would be embedded audit routines. For example, a system control audit review file, SCARF (see Chapter 27), could be set up to accumulate all instances in which transactions were processed for vendors not appearing on the vendor master file, or were not matched to authorized purchase and receiving documents, or could statistically select random transactions for tracing and/or vouching routines. Needless to say, embedded audit routines are costly to establish and, as a result, are implemented during initial system design. Hence, the auditor must be farsighted enough to become involved during the design of the "host" application and establish the system auditability features he believes are warranted.

Fieldwork

Conducting the fieldwork involves performing various audit procedures as called out in the audit program associated with observation, inquiry, inspection, and, to a lesser extent, confirmation. The objective is to gather the evidential matter necessary to form an opinion regarding the adequacy of accounts payable processing and accounting controls.

Observation procedures may be used to observe the activities occurring in the accounts payable department and, if applicable, the I/S department. These general observations provide insight into the way in which duties and responsibilities are performed. If the department appears well-organized, disciplined, and prudent, the auditor may keep the scope of work at a minimum. However, if the department appears disorganized or ill-disciplined, the auditor may need to extend the scope of his work to be reasonably assured that the evidence he obtains is reliable. The extent to which duties are segregated may also be tested by observing the actual job routines of affected personnel.

Inasmuch as the accounts payable function is more susceptible to fraudulent acts than others, the auditor should be alert for any unusual behavior or activities occurring during the course of his work. While perfectly reasonable explanations may evolve, the auditor should question such unusual observances as:

- Clerks and supervisors with access to sensitive data frequently remaining on the job after hours.
- Extended absenteeism of key personnel during audit.
- Misplaced files and records.
- Numerous correcting entries.
- Chronic inability to reconcile accounts payable detail records with general ledger control accounts.
- Implausible explanations for out-of-balance conditions.
- Unprotected files, records, and sensitive forms.

The presence of one or more of these and similar findings that are incompatible with good control practices could be indications of much more serious difficulties. If the auditor has good reason to suspect fraud or embezzlement, he must discuss his findings and concerns with his audit management. Together, they should develop an appropriate course of action for the specific circumstances. It is quite unlikely that internal auditors, acting alone, can handle the matter suitably. Since management bears the responsibility for safeguarding the assets of the entity, the proper management members must be informed. Management may direct that the auditors work with the company's lawyers, special security investigators, or others to resolve the issue satisfactorily.

Inquiry procedures are used to gain an understanding of control techniques followed in processing and accounting for accounts payable transactions and reporting accounts payable information to interested parties. Inquiry procedures include interviewing key accounts payable personnel and management, obtaining responses to internal central questionnaires designed to evaluate the adequacy of controls, and researching applicable policies, manuals, and authoritative literature. Much of this may be done during the preliminary phase, but much may also be done during the fieldwork phase.

Inspection procedures may be used to selectively test, on either a nonstatistical or statistical sampling basis (see Chapter 15) the controls of importance in achieving internal control objectives. In an accounts payable system, these often include:

- Existence of approved purchase order (evidence of authorization)
- Existence of approved receiving report (evidence of receipt)
- Evidence of matching
- Evidence of audit
- Existence of coding for account distribution
- Evidence of recording
- Evidence of recording in proper period

In addition to the foregoing, the auditor may choose to inspect the controls used to physically protect unused checks, prepared checks awaiting signature, and other sensitive forms (e.g., debit memos). Some auditors may ask to review the contents of open files, such as unmatched purchase orders, receivers, and invoices for unusual items.

If the accounts payable processing steps occur without leaving an evidential trail, the auditor may have to reperform the critical steps (e.g., matching, verifying math, and determining the proper account distribution).

Confirmation procedures may be used by the auditor to check out explanations and assertions by accounts payable clerks and supervisors regarding deviations from established routines and to verify any special analysis or schedules prepared for the auditor by accounts payable personnel. Under certain circumstances, the auditor may wish to verify the accuracy

ACCOUNTS PAYABLE PROCESSING

of certain account balances by directly confirming the amounts with creditors. This might be done, for example, in situations where the nature of the relationship with the creditors involves frequent disputes over amounts owed. It may also be used when large balances outstanding are written off.

ILLUSTRATIVE QUESTIONNAIRE

The questionnaire in Figure 20-1 is intended to illustrate many of the questions that might be asked in connection with an evaluation of internal controls over accounts payable processing and accounting. The questionnaire is not designed to provide a basis for evaluating other related functions, such as procurement or cash disbursements.

A SAMPLE AUDIT PROGRAM

The audit program in Figure 20-2 is designed primarily for the audit of the accounts payable function and is integrated with the internal control questionnaire also presented in this chapter.

A SPECIMEN REPORT

The report in Figure 20-3 indicates findings typically encountered in an audit of the accounts payable function. It is rare that an auditor would encounter a payables department in which all of the sample findings are present. To the contrary, it is not unusual for the auditor to find no reportable matters in auditing accounts payable departments. The report is intended to be illustrative, not representative.

PAYROLL OVERVIEW

Payroll processing and accounting is basic to all business entities and represents but one aspect of the more general subject of employee compensation and related benefits and expenses. Among the functions involved are salary and wage administration, human resource development, health and welfare benefits administration, pension and profit-sharing plan administration, and labor relations.

The present-day importance and complexity of labor or manpower man-

(continued on page 20-24)

FIG. 20-1
Internal Control Questionnaire for Accounts Payable

A. Authorization:

Accounts payable transactions are not directly authorized by management. Rather, they are the result of authorized procurement and other business transactions. Accordingly, authorization controls are based upon authorized procurement and other business transactions. The control over such authorization is not within the scope of this audit questionnaire. A separate procurement questionnaire exists for that purpose.

	Yes	No	Workpaper Reference
1. Do procedures specify the individuals authorized to process accounts payable transactions?	☐	☐	....
2. Do procedures require that systems and system changes be reviewed and approved by appropriate management?	☐	☐	....
3. Do procedures require that standard forms and changes thereto be reviewed and approved by appropriate management?	☐	☐	....
4. Do procedures require the use of approved budgets?	☐	☐	....
5. Do procedures set forth the payment policy of the entity (e.g., a statement of interest to pay all accounts due vendors within prescribed credit period or to take advantage of all discounts)?	☐	☐	....
6. Do procedures require that deviations from established payment policy be approved in advance?	☐	☐	....
7. Do procedures require that accounts payable personnel be provided evidence of a properly effected procurement (this could be in the form of approved purchase orders (P.O.s), a computer report indicating receipt and matching of P.O.s, receivers and invoices, or some other documentation)?	☐	☐	....
8. Do procedures require that changes to vendor master files be authorized prior to making the change?	☐	☐	....
9. Do procedures require that accounts payable personnel be provided evidence of properly authorized debit transactions (e.g., returned merchandise)?	☐	☐	....
10. Do procedures require advance approval for subcontractor/vendor advance payments?	☐	☐	....

ACCOUNTS PAYABLE PROCESSING

	Yes	No	Workpaper Reference

B. Processing and Recording:

1. Do procedures require that all important data on invoices received, such as description, unit price or quantity, be matched to receiving reports and purchase orders? ☐ ☐ ....

2. Do procedures require verification of mathematical accuracy of vendor invoices or statements? ☐ ☐ ....

3. Do procedures call for other verification techniques for purchases of services and other items not involving receipt of physical merchandise? ☐ ☐ ....

4. Do procedures require that the accuracy and propriety of account distribution be initiated or confirmed? ☐ ☐ ....

5. Do procedures specify the method to be used in following up and resolving exceptions, such as unmatched invoices, receivers or errors? ☐ ☐ ....

6. Do procedures specify the method to be used for proper recording of vouchered accounts payable? ☐ ☐ ....

7. Do procedures require that all relevant data, such as date, vendor name, account distribution, and transaction amount be recorded? ☐ ☐ ....

8. If data processing techniques are used to record accounts payable:
   a. Do procedures require that batch controls for input documents (e.g., item counts and cash totals prior to submission of data for processing) be established? ☐ ☐ ....
   b. Do procedures call for the use of transmittal numbers and control logs? ☐ ☐ ....
   c. Do procedures require immediate transmittal of all batches directly to DP? ☐ ☐ ....
   d. Do procedures require prompt resolution and resubmission of errors and rejected data? ☐ ☐ ....
   e. If terminals are used, do procedures call for sign on/sign off procedures, maintenance of terminal logs of usage, and a means to control input such as built-in counters/accumulators and tapes? ☐ ☐ ....
   f. If data conversion occurs with the accounts payable group or at the profit center, do procedures require data verification and prompt submission directly to the DP center? ☐ ☐ ....

(continued)

FIG. 20-1 *(cont'd)*

	Yes	No	Workpaper Reference
g. Do procedures require receipt of evidences that transactions were accepted for processing by EDP (e.g., edit listing and proofs)?	☐	☐	....
h. Do procedures require reconciling EDP listings to control data or some other technique to assure accurate and complete processing?	☐	☐	....
i. Are EDP reports reconciled to control data or are other techniques used to check the completeness and accuracy of processing?	☐	☐	....
j. Do procedures require that the differences and exceptions disclosed above be resolved in a timely fashion?	☐	☐	....
9. Do procedures require the organized filing or other disposition of data-processed accounts payable transactions (e.g., invoice receiver, P.O., or EDP reports)?	☐	☐	....
10. Do procedures specify a method for recording unprocessed invoices received prior to the close of the period?	☐	☐	....
11. Do procedures specify the period of time for retaining records related to completed accounts payable transactions?	☐	☐	....
C. Accessibility and Safeguarding:			
1. Do procedures require that accounts payable duties be performed by individuals independent of those responsible for payment approval, purchasing cash disbursements, cash receipts, and DP functions?	☐	☐	....
2. Do procedures require the use of passwords, employee identification, lock keys, or other means for limiting access to terminals?	☐	☐	....
3. Do procedures call for appropriate safeguards for protecting negotiable instruments (such as safes and locked cabinets in limited access areas) in instances where accounts payable personnel have temporary custody of them?	☐	☐	....
4. Do procedures prohibit accounts payable personnel from entering the DP area?	☐	☐	....
5. Are entries to accounts payable control accounts other than by normal processing routines approved by a responsible individual?	☐	☐	....
6. Are processed transactions reviewed periodically for compliance with prescribed procedures and propriety by			

	Yes	No	Workpaper Reference
individuals independent of accounts payable functions (such as division internal audit)?	☐	☐	....
D. Accountability:			
1. Do procedures require periodic reconciliation or balancing of accounts payable control accounts with the total of detail vendor account balances?	☐	☐	....
2. Do procedures require prompt investigation and correction of differences disclosed by the above process?	☐	☐	....
3. Do procedures require periodic review and analysis of processed accounts payable transactions with planned transactions (actual vs. budget) by appropriate individuals?	☐	☐	....

FIG. 20-2
Audit Program for Accounts Payable

	Workpaper Reference	Done by
1. Preliminary:		
☐ Obtain a copy of the current organization chart of the finance/treasury function to refer to during the audit. This provides documentation of reporting relationships as well as the degree to which duties are segregated. Any errors or differences noted during the audit should be addressed to management and resolved.	....	....
☐ Obtain a copy of the written procedures and related documentation identifying and evaluating controls over accounts payable.	....	....
☐ By interview with management, establish in what way, if any, procedures are not current or are not being followed. Adjust documentation accordingly.	....	....
☐ During the course of the audit, by observation, tours, etc., note any evidence of:		
■ Resource problems	....	....
■ Personnel incompetence	....	....
■ Dishonest acts	....	....

(continued)

FIG. 20-2 *(cont'd)*

	Workpaper Reference	Done by
2. Authorization/Execution and Recording:		
☐ Randomly select accounts payable transactions from the payable register (either judgment or statistical sampling may be used) and review for the following:	. . . .	. . . .
■ Determine that documentation is available for:		
a. Authorization of purchase — purchase orders (and requisitions, if required by procedures)	. . . .	. . . .
b. Receipt of goods — receiving reports	. . . .	. . . .
c. Completion of services — formal reports and management approval	. . . .	. . . .
d. Authorization of miscellaneous purchase or service — request for disbursement (RFD)	. . . .	. . . .
e. Contract authorization — contracts on file in accounts payable department	. . . .	. . . .
■ Determine that there is evidence of:		
a. Approval for payment	. . . .	. . . .
b. Matching invoices with supporting documents for receipt of goods, quantities, prices, terms	. . . .	. . . .
c. Checking extensions and footings	. . . .	. . . .
d. Proper account distribution	. . . .	. . . .
e. Processing and recording	. . . .	. . . .
f. Cash discounts being taken, with timely processing and payment	. . . .	. . . .
g. Freight charges by traffic personnel	. . . .	. . . .
h. Accurate recording in the accounts payable register	. . . .	. . . .
■ Determine that the date, payee, and amount on the cancelled check agrees with the invoice and supporting documents, and that the disbursement appears proper.	. . . .	. . . .
a. Endorsement on the cancelled check agrees with the payee	. . . .	. . . .
b. Check was signed by an authorized check signer	. . . .	. . . .
c. All appropriate documents were marked to prevent their reuse	. . . .	. . . .
■ Determine that all accounts payable transactions tested are processed using standard procedures and forms, and that any deviations are properly approved.	. . . .	. . . .
■ Determine that vendors are properly listed in the master files.	. . . .	. . . .
■ Inquire into any unusual transactions, such as advance payments, and ascertain that they were properly approved and recorded so as to facilitate subsequent accountability.	. . . .	. . . .
☐ Select a statistical sample of receiving documents from the department.	. . . .	. . . .

ACCOUNTS PAYABLE PROCESSING

	Workpaper Reference	Done by
■ Determine that all items are properly matched with invoices, and investigate any receivers that cannot be so matched.	....	....
■ If available, obtain a list of unmatched receivers, and investigate any old, outstanding items.	....	....
☐ Select a random judgment sample of debit memos for testing, and:		
■ Determine that debit memos are properly supported by evidence of return of goods or that evidence for the reason for the debit is available, in the case of services.	....	....
■ Check for evidence of proper approval.	....	....
☐ For the most recent month-end, test cutoff procedures and:		
■ Review schedules of recurring items to determine that such items were properly accrued.	....	....
■ For invoices processed near the month-end, review receiving reports to determine that the cutoff was proper.	....	....
■ Determine the month-end balance of accounts payable and the accrued liability for the most recent month-end, quarter-end, and year-end, and obtain explanations for any significant variations.	....	....
☐ Inquire into any organizational/system changes and check for evidence of proper approval.	....	....
☐ Check for evidence of approval for selected changes to vendor master files.	....	....
☐ Review recording by automated system, and:		
■ Obtain control logs and review for evidence of reconciling batch controls to processed data.	....	....
■ If terminals are used, inspect them, noting use of lock keys, passwords, sign-on and sign-off procedures, terminal logs, etc.	....	....
■ Checks for evidence of timely resubmission of errors and reported transactions.	....	....
■ Consider requesting a system review by a corporate audit DP auditor, if the optional DP testing system indicates substantial recent changes, if significant control weakness are revealed by earlier inquiries, or if significant processing or recording errors are noted in testing the detail transactions.	....	....
3. Accessibility:		
☐ Review control account entries, noting any from sources other than routine processing of transactions.	....	....
■ For any significant entries note the propriety of the entry and check for evidence of approval.	....	....
■ Determine that entries are properly recorded.	....	....

(continued)

FIG. 20-2 *(cont'd)*

	Workpaper Reference	Done by
☐ Obtain audit reports issued by the profit center internal auditor and determine the nature and resolution of the findings and follow-up performed by the auditor and management. Determine what procedures or policies were changed to improve controls.	....	....
☐ By reference to organization charts and by observation, confirm the degree of segregation of duties.	....	....
☐ Inspect facilities for safeguarding negotiable instruments (if applicable) for compliance with established procedure.	....	....
4. Accountability:		
☐ Check for evidence of reconciliations of control accounts with detail subledgers and for investigation and correction of differences.	....	....
☐ For the most recent month-end obtain a trial balance of accounts payable:		
■ Agree the trial balance to the general ledger.	....	....
■ Review the trial balance for any large, old, or unusual entries and investigate them.	....	....
☐ Review budget reports for the most recent month-end and determine that management is aware of and has reviewed any significant fluctuations from budgeted amounts.	....	....

FIG. 20-3

Audit Report—Accounts Payable Function

TO: B.W. Smith
FROM: R.S. Reynolds
SUBJECT: Review of Accounts Payable Processing and Accounting — Warren Electronics, Inc.

We have reviewed the policies and procedures related to accounts payable and cash disbursements at Warren Electronics, Incorporated (WEI). Our review was performed in order to determine the adequacy of and compliance with established policies and procedures and to determine if existing internal controls are sufficient to provide reasonable assurance that cash disbursement/accounts payable transactions are executed with appropriate authorization, and are recorded so as to permit preparation of financial statements in accordance with generally accepted accounting principles (GAAP). Our review was also performed so as to ascertain that access to cash and related records and files is properly restricted and that accountability over these transactions and applicable functions is appropriately maintained. Our examination included a review of existing procedures, an evaluation of internal accounting controls, tests of selected transactions, discussions with

ACCOUNTS PAYABLE PROCESSING

management, and such other procedures as we considered necessary. Our examination, however, was limited in scope to accounts payable transactions at WEI's Denver office and did not include any transactions executed at field offices.

Our review disclosed the following matters that we believe should be brought to the attention of management:

- Evidence of proper authority for business travel is not always present.
- There is an excessively large number of credit cards outstanding.
- There are not adequate safeguards on blank check stock and blank traveler's checks.
- Not all invoices are sent directly to accounts payable and no invoice log is kept.
- Evidence of offsite services bureau utilization is inadequate and the purchase order authorizing use is an unlimited blanket purchase order.
- Voucher system is somewhat exposed to unauthorized payments.
- Not all practices are covered by procedures, and procedures issued are not all-inclusive.

These matters indicate weaknesses in controls, which (1) could permit the incurring expenditures on behalf of WEI without appropriate advance approval, (2) could increase the exposure to misappropriation of cash, and (3) tend to depend excessively individuals' knowing and remembering oral instructions in lieu of documented procedures.

In our opinion, the system of internal controls is not sufficient to provide reasonable assurance that Accounts Payable transactions are (1) executed in accordance with appropriate authorization and (2) recorded as necessary to permit preparation of financial statements in conformity with GAAP. Further, internal controls do not assure that accountability is appropriately maintained or that assets are appropriately safeguarded.

The balance of this report contains a more detailed discussion of our findings and contains recommendations which, if implemented, would result in sufficient controls to achieve the above objectives.

1. Evidence of proper authority for business travel is not always present.

We reviewed documentation supporting 12 separate trips by 12 different employees. Of the 12 files tested, only one contained a travel authorization form, and it was not approved by anyone. Further investigation revealed that travel authorization (Form 1092) is not received by Accounts Payable unless a travel advance is requested.

RECOMMENDATION NO. 1

Establish and implement a procedure whereby a travel authorization is required in advance of any business trip, regardless of whether an advance is required.

2. There is an excessively large number of credit cards outstanding.

Currently there are 87 Hertz credit cards, 99 air travel credit cards, 88 telephone credit cards, and 22 American Express credit cards issued to WEI employees. We believe the quantity of credit cards outstanding not only contributes to the

(continued)

FIG. 20-3 *(cont'd)*

amount of travel without documented advance authorization, but increases the exposure to unauthorized charges.

RECOMMENDATION NO. 2

Reduce the number of outstanding credit cards to a more manageable level or issue cards on an as-needed basis for approved trips only.

3. **There is a lack of adequate safeguards on blank check stock and blank traveler's checks.**

Blank check stock is located in a locked cabinet in the accounts payable storeroom. Additional blank check stock is kept (1) in a file cabinet in the office of the executive secretary to the Vice-President–Finance, (2) in a locked cabinet in the data processing (DP) storeroom, (3) outside the locked cabinet in the DP storeroom, (4) in an unlocked credenza in the payroll office, and (5) at night, in a locked credenza in the office of the Vice-President–Finance. At night the facsimile signature plates are stored in the same locked credenza in which some blank checks stored. During working hours traveler's checks amounting to $15,000 are stored in an unlocked file cabinet in the accounting department. During the audit, the manager of General Accounting obtained the key to the blank check storage file from the secretary to the Vice-President–Finance. We noted that neither is the custodian per WEI standards and procedures. We also noted that there is blank check stock for the First Bank of . . . . Account #04443-1 for a WEI subsidiary and we were unable to locate the check register or cancelled checks and were therefore unable to determine which was the last check written. Account #5529 was closed in August 1978, but the blank check stock has not been destroyed. With the exception of the Accounts Payable general account, logs are not maintained indicating quantity and check numbers received from printer.

RECOMMENDATION NO. 3

Implement the trade accounts payable standards and procedures titled "Check Control." Designate a secured area accessible only to the custodian of traveler's checks for the storage of traveler's checks. Prevent check signers from having access to blank checks. Do not store blank check stock with facsimile signature plates. Destroy all blank check stock for closed or unneeded accounts.

4. **Not all invoices are sent directly to Accounts Payable and no invoice log is kept.**

Vendor invoices for services are sent to the requestor of the services in many cases. This tends to delay payments. We noted that one department is directing vendors to send invoices directly to that department.

RECOMMENDATION NO. 4

Direct all employees who have vendor contact to request that vendors send all invoices directly to accounts payable. Revise subcontract instructions to state that all invoices should be

ACCOUNTS PAYABLE PROCESSING

submitted directly to the accounts payable department. Maintain an invoice log identifying all invoices leaving the Accounts Payable department for payment approval. This log should contain, at a minimum (1) date invoice received, (2) vendor, (3) invoice amount, (4) date sent out for approval, and (5) to whom sent.

5. Evidence of offsite service bureau utilization is inadequate and purchase order authorizing use is an unlimited purchase order.

Purchase order #123456 was issued 1/8/XX for machine usage at $45.00 per hour. This is a blanket purchase order with no dollar limitations. Invoices are approved for payment only by the manager of management information systems. The WEI signature authorization procedure indicates that a department manager has signature authority up to $500.00, and a director, up to $5,000.00. We noted that the total payments against the purchase order year-to-date is $25,282.00. There is no authorized approval for this level of expenditure to be found either on the purchase order or the invoice.

RECOMMENDATION NO. 5

Establish limits of expenditures authorized for each blanket purchase order and secure the authorizations as required by the guidelines in the statement of standards and procedures entitled "signature authorization." On purchase orders involving services, we recommend that the purchase orders establish who is authorized to approve payment on completion of services.

6. Voucher System is somewhat exposed to unauthorized payments.

Control over additions, deletions, or changes to the vendor master file is not sufficient. There is no evidence on vouchers to indicate who prepared them. Also, there are no procedures requiring appropriate authorization to submit vouchers for processing. We also noted that voucher processing appears inefficient: accounts payable matches the invoices with receivers, originates the vouchers, and then sends vouchers and supporting documentation to cost control; cost control performs the account distribution function on the vouchers, only to send 1) the originals and supporting documentation *back* to accounts payable and 2) copies of the vouchers to DP.

RECOMMENDATION NO. 6

Establish and implement a procedure whereby a document containing appropriate authorization to process accompanies all computer processing requests. Require that voucher entries be completed in person and require that person to sign or initial each voucher prepared.

7. Not all practices are covered by procedures, and procedures issued are not all-inclusive. There is no:

(continued)

FIG. 20-3 *(cont'd)*

- Procedure specifically requiring the traffic department to approve freight bills, currently purchase order terms "FOB DESTINATION" are not enforced on incoming shipments.
- Procedure requiring Accounts Payable to accrue unmatched invoices at each month-end.
- Procedure describing the return-to-vendor process or authorizations required to debit a vendor account.
- Procedure describing what course of action to take to resolve unmatched vendor invoice and/or unmatched receivers.
- Procedure requiring appropriate management's approval for system changes or current procedures for accounting for progress payments are not followed.
- Procedure requiring appropriate management's approval for system changes or for deviations from existing systems.
- Procedure documenting requirements for resubmission of items rejected by the computer.
- Procedures adequately documenting the desired segregation of duties between the individual having custody of check signature plates and the individuals having custody of blank check stock.
- Procedure covering the management policy on write-offs of uncollectible debit memos.
- Formalized procedure requiring that accounts payable be provided evidence that all transactions submitted for computer processing were accepted.
- Procedure that requires periodic comparison of actual cash disbursements with the planned disbursements.

RECOMMENDATION NO. 7

Formulate and implement procedures as required for the above items.

---

agement has evolved from the simple concept of a day's wages for a day's honest work as a result of developments over the last century or so that were brought about by the efforts of employee representatives, government regulation, and an enlightened management. While the fundamental objective remains more or less the same, that is, to compensate workers fairly for their services, the typical employee now receives a host of benefits over and above basic salaries or wages. These include:

- Overtime premium
- Shift differentials
- Incentive and deferred compensation arrangements
- Paid holidays
- Paid vacations
- Sick pay

- Wage continuation plans as a result of short- and long-term disability
- Health care coverage
- Retirement benefits
- Death benefits

While details with respect to the foregoing vary among companies, most employees are required by various laws, regulations, and other arrangements to contribute to the Old Age, Survivors' and Disability Insurance program (Social Security), to contribute to federal and state unemployment insurance funds and workmen's compensation funds, and to act as an agent for withholding taxes and other deductions for various federal, state, and local governments, and organizations such as unions, charities, and thrift institutions. Obviously, accomplishing the above requires a considerable investment in systems, management, and other resources. The heavy expenditures make the function a primary target for internal auditing. This chapter defines payroll accounting and describes the business environment, risks, and internal control objectives and techniques associated with payroll matters. It also discusses various audit techniques that may be used in auditing payroll controls, provides an illustrative internal control questionnaire and audit program, and presents a specimen audit report.

DEFINITION AND BACKGROUND

Payroll processing and accounting may be defined as the process of effecting payments to employees for their services and accumulating and reporting payroll-related information to interested third parties in compliance with various laws, regulations, and other arrangements. Payroll accounting, among other things, entails the maintenance of detailed records for each employee for such information as cumulative gross earnings, federal, state, and local income taxes withheld, state disability insurance withheld, Social Security taxes withheld, and other withholdings; and records, by employee, as may be required to effect payment of employer payroll taxes, insurance premiums based on payroll, such as workmen's compensation, liability insurance, and various welfare benefits.

Compensation for services rendered by employees takes several forms. A large number of companies offer a mixture or variety of remuneration. The most common form of compensation is payment on the basis of established hourly wage rates for each of numerous job classifications. Other methods include fixed salaries, which do not fluctuate with the number of hours actually worked, and piecemeal rates, which are based not on hours but on units of production completed. Additionally, some industries offer very unique methods of compensation. For example, airline flight attendants are paid a combination of a minimum periodic salary, to which an amount may be added for hours worked in flight status. Certain railroad employees are paid, in part, based on distances traveled. Many actors and actresses portraying small roles receive different compensation, depending on the number of lines spoken.

The variety of circumstances and the varying applicability of federal and state regulations makes it necessary for the performing auditor to become familiar with those circumstances, rules, and regulations that affect his company. In this way, his audit approach and his audit tools may be specifically tailored to the peculiarities of the organization. As a general rule, the following laws and regulations apply in many situations:

- Federal, state, and local income tax withholding laws
- Federal Insurance Contributions Act (Social Security)
- Federal Unemployment Tax Act and various related state unemployment laws
- State disability benefit laws
- Federal Wage-Hour Law (minimum wage law)
- Equal Pay Act (nondiscrimination)
- Walsh-Healey Public Contracts Act (minimum wages and other rules for employees working on government contracts)
- Davis-Bacon Act (minimum wages and other provisions affecting employees of contractors performing construction or maintenance work on public buildings or works for the United States)

These and other laws and regulations have evolved over the years for various reasons having to do with minimizing discriminatory employment practices, providing minimum wage levels, protecting certain classes of workers, such as minors, and providing an effective tax collecting mode.

THE BUSINESS ENVIRONMENT

From the foregoing, it is obvious that payroll accounting is affected by extensive and complex rules and regulations, and that considerable variance in compensation practices exists among business and governmental enterprises. The variances are such that it is probably safe to say that no two payroll systems are alike. The difference occurs not only because of varying rules and regulations but also because of dissimilarities in the business environments of the companies. Even within segments of the companies, varying practices may be attributable to the different business circumstances in which each must operate. For example, it is not uncommon to find different policies among individual business units of a company with respect to sick pay entitlements, health care plans, retirement plans, and so on. Even the method of payment (cash, check, or direct deposit) and the period covered by each payroll (weekly, biweekly, semimonthly, and so forth) may differ.

ACCOUNTS PAYABLE PROCESSING

The following are among the factors making up the business environment that affect payroll-related policies:

- *Management objectives.* Management objectives in using employee compensation as a means to attain business goals vary, depending on such considerations as competitive conditions, union pressures, regulatory climate, and general business trends.
- *Labor supply.* Labor supply, particularly that of skilled labor, affects the nature and extent of compensation packages offered by companies. In situations where shortages exist, management is often forced to add inducements to attract workers with the requisite skills in sufficient numbers.
- *Geographic location.* The geographic location in which the business operations must be conducted can also affect compensation arrangements. Certain parts of the United States, such as the "Sunbelt" and the Pacific Coast region, are thought by many to be preferable working and/or living areas. Some foreign locations are thought to offer comparatively less hospitable living environments than those offered by U.S. living. To entice people to work and live in those locations requires modifying basic compensation arrangements.
- *Current financial condition.* A company's current financial condition can affect the extent to which it can accommodate demands of unions for increased benefits. In the early 1980s, in fact, the adverse financial condition of many large U.S. companies required that their bargaining unions forego implementation of agreed-on increases to help stave off bankruptcy for the employers.

The value in considering these and other business environmental factors is that the internal control objectives and the underlying control techniques shaped by them can be better understood by the auditor. In turn, a proper understanding will help the auditor to formulate the tools and techniques necessary to effect an audit of payroll accounting of sufficient quality.

RISKS

Generally speaking, the business risks associated with the process of compensating employees are several and varied. However, from an historical perspective, losses resulting from payroll-related problems, or errors which were material to the financial statements of the company involved, are practically nonexistent. The comparatively low exposure to material errors and losses should not be construed to imply that management is not concerned with the risks associated with payroll accounting. To the contrary, most managements allocate considerable resources in the form of systems, manpower, and equipment to minimize the risks because of their potential for causing adverse publicity, poor employee morale, higher turnover, and, conceivably, loss of competitive advantage. Among the specific risks customarily associated with payroll processing are the following:

- Failure to pay all employees entitled to receive pay
- Errors in compiling gross earnings resulting in payroll amounts either greater or less than entitlements
- Effecting payments to individuals who are not employees
- Maintaining erroneous cumulative earnings and withholding information
- Loss or theft of sensitive payroll information, such as job classification and wage rates
- Loss or theft of blank payroll checks and signature plates
- Payments to fictitious persons
- Failure to properly report payroll information to various interested federal, state, and local governmental agencies and others
- Failure to accurately record payroll expenditures
- Failure to accurately record payroll-related accrued liabilities
- Failure to comply with laws and regulations affecting payroll administration

Auditors preparing to perform audits of payroll functions must keep a proper perspective on risk. While some violations of applicable payroll laws and regulations carry harsh penalties, the exposure to that potentiality is minimal for the vast majority of companies. That is because these companies have made available the necessary resources to achieve ongoing compliance. Some organizations, when faced with severe working capital requirements, have found irresistible the temptation to use withheld taxes illegally—as a source of funds for other purposes.

The more common compliance problems, which occur rarely in any given company, have to do with interpretations of regulations dealing with alleged discriminatory actions, wrongful terminations, and the like, some of which wind up being settled in court. These are not likely to be unearthed by auditors, although such a result is possible. It is more likely that auditors will detect intermittant instances of compliance violations, such as failure to obtain or retain employee deduction authorizations, failure by supervisors to approve time cards, or errors in coding labor distribution. Still, auditors must remain alert to the potential for more serious compliance problems and, in particular, to the various opportunities existing in many payroll systems for fraud, embezzlement, and the like to occur. In systems involving electronic data processing, this exposure can be even greater. While a complete description of dishonest acts involving payroll cannot be compiled, the following is indicative of the possibilities:

- Outright theft of cash payroll—often brought about by lax security measures
- Theft of blank checks—also facilitated by inadequate security measures
- Adding fictitious persons to the payroll

- Selling confidential payroll information to competitors
- Willful destruction of payroll records

Gauging the seriousness of the exposure in any particular circumstance requires judgment. Generally speaking, the easier it is to obtain payroll funds, the greater the exposure. Therefore, auditors should consider carefully the number of overt acts that a hypothetical perpetrator would have to execute to achieve his objective. For instance, if a person would find it necessary to (1) steal or fabricate a signature plate, (2) steal or counterfeit payroll checks, (3) obtain a phony I.D., and (4) forge signatures, all without detection, it is very unlikely that a payroll loss would occur. On the other hand, if the payroll is paid in cash once a month and if the cash is obtained several days before actual disbursement and kept in a location easily accessible to several persons, a hypothetical perpetrator would need only to gain access and remove the cash in a single overt action. A situation of this type would be exposed to a high risk of loss.

In the real world, most payrolls are reasonably controlled to minimize this type of risk; however, the fact that a payroll involves cash at some point makes any system ever vulnerable. Particular attention should be paid when old payroll systems are converted to new, EDP-oriented systems, to be sure that once-adequate control mechanisms are not rendered defenseless against the possibility of malfeasance by EDP personnel.

INTERNAL CONTROL OBJECTIVES

The internal control objectives with respect to payroll accounting vary with the business environment and the risks involved. Therefore, specific objectives applicable to all companies cannot be set forth in a general reference book. The chief auditor or his designee, with the help of management, must identify the objectives applicable to his organization. The following may be used as a guide to:

- Establish and maintain a routine for reasonably assuring that changes to payroll systems and payroll data occur pursuant to management authorization.
- Compensate only valid company employees who perform authorized work at authorized pay rates.
- Calculate amounts due to employees accurately, completely, and timely, in accordance with all applicable rules and regulations.
- Calculate payroll-related taxes and other related liabilities accurately, completely, and in accordance with all applicable rules and regulations.
- Effect adjustments to payroll calculations and records only in accordance with management's authorization.
- Process and record payroll and payroll-related transactions accurately, completely, and in accordance with (1) GAAP and (2) established cost system requirements.

- Restrict access to payroll data to personnel authorized by management.
- Segregate payroll duties so as to minimize exposure to fraud, theft, or other malfeasance.
- Protect payroll records, files, negotiable checks, and other forms from theft, loss, or destruction.
- Periodically report payroll information to interested management so as to permit effective administration of payroll and management of labor.
- Periodically report payroll and payroll information to interested third parties so as to comply with applicable rules, regulations, and contractual arrangements.

INTERNAL CONTROL TECHNIQUES

The nature and extent of internal control techniques over payroll depend on the objectives of internal control noted in the preceding discussion. Payroll accounting, invariably, is a finance function that reports to the controller. Some aspects of payroll accounting involve participation and coordination of other disciplines, such as the labor relations function, which is usually responsible for the administration of salary grades, pay rates, and other employee benefits. Retirement plan administration may be a shared responsibility between labor relations and the treasury or controller's functions.

Organization and Authorization

In order for the payroll department to achieve its objectives, it is dependent on other organizations to prepare and submit source information for each employee, each pay period, accurately and completely. There are a variety of techniques by which this may be accomplished. One of the most common practices involves the use of timecards, one for each employee for each pay period on which the employee's time is recorded each day, usually by some mechanical means, such as a time clock. In the best of these systems, both the employee and his immediate supervisor are required to sign the card as evidence of valid hours worked. Time keepers may be employed in some systems to verify the accuracy of the time recorded and balance it with labor distribution source data.

The success of the payroll department effort is also dependent on (1) the type of system established (manual or automated); (2) the clarity or simplicity of forms used; (3) the responsiveness of support organizations, such as labor relations, for maintaining current and complete job classifications and salary structures, for example; and, when applicable, (4) the EDP department for maintaining proper control of payroll programs, master file data, and transaction data, and to effect complete and accurate processing of payroll transactions. The effectiveness and efficiency of EDP for processing payroll transactions, and the availability of EDP services for this purpose, is such that the vast majority of payroll systems likely to be subject to the auditor's review will involve EDP techniques. Completely manual systems may be encountered in situations where access to such EDP services is impracticable. This may occur in some foreign locations and in remote field operations in the United States. Even these are fast disappearing with the trend toward distributed processing.

If an automated system exists, the duties of the payroll department probably involve review and checking of proof listings, maintenance of employee earnings data, processing of payroll adjustments, setting up new employees and handling terminations, and monitoring developments in the various federal and state agencies which establish the rules and regulations with which the company must comply. System changes necessitated by changes to rules and regulations are usually effected by the payroll department. In nonautomated systems, the payroll department performs many of the foregoing duties and, in addition, calculates each payroll, prepares checks, and distributes them to the various departments. From an accounting standpoint, in both EDP and non-EDP systems, payroll accounting entries to record the payroll are usually the responsibility of the payroll department. Accounting manuals, user manuals, and a chart of accounts are indispensable aids for this purpose. Most payroll departments are responsible for submitting payroll information to the various interested third parties, in addition to the duties previously described. Once source data are prepared and submitted (either by remote terminals or "over the counter" via mail or courier), they are generally checked for accuracy and completeness and controlled by means of some type of control total (document count, cash total) to prevent data loss and unauthorized transactions from occurring. This should occur in any payroll system. Large volumes of payroll transactions are often processed in batches, with counted totals established and logged for each batch.

Processing and Accounting

Accurate and complete processing of payroll transactions is best achieved by routinizing and sequencing, to the extent possible, the various actions that must occur for each transaction. Because each payroll involves numerous transactions—in some cases running into the millions, adequate provision should be made for checks and balances to minimize the errors that will occur. Some of these techniques involve:

- Verifying the validity of employee numbers.
- Checking the reasonableness of hours worked.
- Verifying the propriety of pay rates used.
- Checking extensions, footings, and cross footings.

- Reconciling payroll register net pay with the total of net pay per payroll checks.
- Reconciling gross pay totals with labor distribution reports.
- Reconciling transactions processed back to control totals recorded in control logs.
- Scanning payroll registers for unusual items.

Accuracy and completeness are also enhanced by using standard forms containing clearcut preparation instructions, having a user's manual available, and employing disciplinary controls to assure that established routines and procedures are followed. This includes not only the scanning and reconciling functions previously described, but also such techniques as balancing run-to-run totals in I/S systems, reviewing proof or edit listings, and balancing payroll registers, summary schedules, and journal entries. In addition, procedures for prompt correction and resubmission of detected errors are also important.

Safeguarding

Normally, payroll data is considered among the most sensitive of all company-owned data. Most companies take care to be sure that access to payroll data is kept to a bare minimum. If all payroll data are maintained by the payroll department, the task is comparatively simple. Payroll records in such cases are usually stored in a vault or a lockable, fire-resistant metal file of some kind. If the payroll data are stored on magnetic tape, or disk, they must be made secure against access by I/S programmers, operators, and managers. Where access is possible in an on-line system via remote terminals, the problem of accessibility is further compounded. Usually a data security software package, such as the IBM package known as Random Access Control Facility (RACF), must be installed to maintain effective security. Other techniques involve restricting programmers' access to payroll programs and data and operators' access to program documentation.

To assure continuous processing, controls such as physically protecting vital records and maintaining duplicates of master files stored in remote locations are often established. Formalized plans for recovery in the event of processing being interrupted are also a feature of many payroll systems, particularly automated systems.

Since extensive rules and regulations exist pertaining to retention of payroll records, methods must be established to assure that all necessary records are stored for the required length of time.

Reporting and Accountability

Controls must be implemented to enable management to monitor the effectiveness of payroll processing activities. In addition, controls must be es-

ACCOUNTS PAYABLE PROCESSING

tablished to assure that interested third parties are informed, as required of applicable rules and regulations. Some central techniques include employing persons having appropriate technical proficiency related to payroll accounting, establishing and maintaining routines, forms, manuals, and instructions as applicable. Keeping an up-to-date library of authoritative literature on the subject of payroll is also essential.

Other control techniques include supervisory review of payroll registers, reconciling payroll accounts, monthly closing routine review of labor reports by line management, and periodic audits by internal auditors.

AUDIT TECHNIQUES

The significance of payroll accounting in most companies is such that auditing payroll controls is high on the list of priorities for the auditors. In devising an approach to auditing payroll controls, the auditor must keep in mind that those functions, while often well-controlled, carry a much higher exposure to irregularities and malfeasance than do other accounting functions. Payroll functions are also a subject of interest to external auditors; consequently, audit coverage should be coordinated to avoid duplicating efforts.

Preliminary

As with other audit projects, the auditor charged with the responsibility for auditing payroll processing and accounting for purposes of testing compliance and evaluating the adequacy of controls must start by obtaining as much background information as possible. This would include prior workpapers, if available, policy statements, procedural manuals, organization charts, and pertinent financial data. Since payrolls involve extensive federal and state rules and regulations, the auditor must include in his preliminary work a study of those applicable to the specific payroll function to be audited. Most payroll and tax departments maintain libraries that contain the necessary reference material.

If historical financial and other data with respect to payroll exist, the auditor may wish to perform trend or regression analysis to highlight unusual relationships that might exist (see Chapter 16). Of particular interest for purposes of a review of controls might be trends in the frequency and dollar amount of payroll adjusting and correcting entries and unreconciled differences between otherwise reconcilable records, such as payroll cash accounts with bank statements and payroll registers with labor distribution reports.

Preliminary discussions and interviews should be conducted by the performing auditors with interested members of management and the audit management to learn of any particular concerns that they may have. Further, the timing of the fieldwork can be coordinated by this process.

Also, the audit tools intended to be used should be readied. These include audit programs, questionnaires and, to the extent applicable, I/S audit techniques, such as generalized audit software, test decks, and parallel simulation (see Chapter 28).

Payroll is one function for which these latter tools are of particular value, since most payroll systems today are automated. For example, generalized audit software may be used to:

- Extract data from master files for subsequent validation to source documents.
- Perform calculations such as gross and net pay for selected employees.
- Foot and cross-foot payroll records.

Some aspects of payroll testing are susceptible to statistical sampling. Necessary planning and preparation for such techniques should also be effected at this time.

Fieldwork

Conducting the fieldwork involves performing various procedures as called out in the audit program associated with observation, inquiry, inspection, and confirmation. The objective is to gather the evidential matter necessary to form an opinion regarding the adequacy of payroll processing and accounting controls.

Observation procedures may be used to good advantage in auditing payroll controls. During the course of the fieldwork, the auditor may observe the activities occurring in the payroll department and, if applicable, the I/S department, to provide insight into the way in which duties and functions are performed. The department may appear well organized, disciplined, and efficient, or it may appear to be the opposite. Such observations may affect the ultimate scope of work to be performed by the auditor and the extent to which he is willing to place reliance on the work of the department.

Observation procedures may also be used for specific purposes. For instance, the auditor may wish to observe the actual distribution of the payroll to the employees, particularly if the distribution is in cash. In large payrolls, this could only be done on a test basis, the extent of the observation being determined by the auditor's judgment. In addition to testing applicable controls to reasonably assure every employee receives his pay, the auditor is, in effect, testing for the possible existence of wrongdoing. If there are more payroll checks or pay envelopes than there are employees present to receive them, the auditor's suspicions could be alerted.

Other observation procedures include floor checks and check preparation routines. Floor checks are used to test compliance with controls for assuring that time worked is being accurately recorded and charged to proper account classifications. This procedure is usually performed on a nonstatistical sampling basis. Check preparation routines are observed to test compliance in this critical aspect of payrolling accounting. The extent of this type of testing is also determined by the auditor's judgment.

Inquiry procedures are used to gain an understanding of control techniques followed in processing and recording payroll transactions and in reporting payroll information to interested parties. Inquiry procedures include interviewing key payroll accounting personnel and management, obtaining responses to internal control questionnaires designed to evaluate the adequacy of controls, and researching applicable policies, manuals, functional descriptions, and authoritative literature. Much of this may be done during the preliminary phase, but much may also be done during the fieldwork phase.

Inquiry procedures may also be used when questions as to compliance with applicable rules and regulations arise. These questions can occur during compliance testing. For example, the auditor may discover practices that appear to him to be inconsistent with provisions of the minimum wage laws, discrimination laws, or wages and hours laws. Research helps to provide a better basis for drawing conclusions. Naturally, any serious questions should not be concluded without the benefit of legal opinions.

Inspection procedures are used extensively to test compliance with established control requirements. Among the controls often tested are the following:

- Compliance with hiring procedures, including use of employment requisitions, approvals, application forms, and approval for hiring
- Compliance with termination procedures, including proper approval and use of proper forms, and removal from current employee master files
- Compliance with procedures for preparation and submission of source data for processing payrolls
- Compliance with procedures for calculating gross and net pay and related payroll withholds and accrued liabilities

While both nonstatistical and statistical sampling techniques may be used for the foregoing, the volume of payroll transactions in many companies is such that many auditors are increasing their use of statistical sampling using the attribute method of sampling (see Chapter 15). In addition, this type of payroll testing may often benefit by the use of generalized audit software, as mentioned earlier, assuming payroll data are maintained on disks, magnetic tapes, or other machine media. Also, specialized routines, either automated or manual type, may be devised to test for the presence of evidence that may lead the auditor to suspect fraud. These tests are usually devised on the basis of the auditor's judgment and include:

- Verifying cumulative earnings for personnel assigned key payroll processing duties.
- Checking master files for the existence of names of terminated employees.

Other inspection procedures often include physical inspection of blank check stock and check signing devices to test compliance with access controls and to sample the numerical sequence of the checks. Also, it is not uncommon for auditors to inspect canceled checks for numerical sequence, agreement of payee and endorsement signature, and to note any unusual features, such as checks prepared in a manner inconsistent with established routines.

Confirmation procedures are used by some internal auditors to obtain independent external evidence as to balances in payroll bank accounts for use in testing the accuracy and propriety of bank reconciliations. Confirmation procedures are more frequently used to corroborate explanation by key personnel and others for deviations in established routines, and to substantiate the auditor's tentative conclusions as to findings of control weaknesses. Usually, confirmation procedures are employed on a nonstatistical sampling basis.

ILLUSTRATIVE QUESTIONNAIRE

The following questionnaire is intended to illustrate many of the questions that might be asked in connection with an evaluation of internal controls over payroll processing and accounting. The questionnaire, relating solely to payroll accounting, is not designed to cover other aspects related to employment practices. Coverage of related payroll transactions such as vacations, sick leave, holidays, incentive compensation, withholding, and payroll accruals is not included in this questionnaire because these require separate, specific control processes. However, general questions are included that require the auditor to explore the sufficiency of the controls in these areas, to the extent he deems necessary, to support an overall assessment of the adequacy of payroll accounting controls. Separate questionnaire could be developed to evaluate the adequacy of related payroll transaction controls if desired by the auditor.

The questionnaire is given in Figure 20-4.

A SAMPLE AUDIT PROGRAM

The audit program in Figure 20-5 is designed primarily for the audit of the payroll accounting function and is integrated with the questionnaire just illustrated.

(continued on page 20-45)

ACCOUNTS PAYABLE PROCESSING 20-37

FIG. 20-4

Internal Control Questionnaire for Payroll

	Yes	No	Workpaper Reference
A. Authorization:			
1. Do procedures require using prescribed forms for:			
a. Adding employees to the payroll	☐	☐	....
b. Deleting employees from the payroll	☐	☐	....
c. Changing employees pay rates	☐	☐	....
d. Changes in employee authorized deductions	☐	☐	....
e. Changes in important payroll information (e.g., classification, name, address, social security number)	☐	☐	....
2. Do procedures require that such forms include evidence of appropriate approval prior to processing?	☐	☐	....
3. Do procedures require that changes in established payroll rates and/or classifications be approved?	☐	☐	....
4. Do procedures fix the responsibility for the administration of payroll, personnel, and personnel related functions in appropriate individuals, groups, or departments including:			
a. Maintenance of records related to individual income tax and social security tax withholding	☐	☐	....
b. Maintenance of records related to EEO regulations	☐	☐	....
c. Maintenance of records related to employee welfare and benefit plans	☐	☐	....
d. Maintenance of records related to workmen's compensation, state disability, and other payroll based insurance coverage	☐	☐	....
e. Maintenance of records related to union agreements	☐	☐	....
5. Do procedures require that changes in incentive compensation and employee fringe benefit programs be approved by appropriate management or Board of Director levels?	☐	☐	....
6. Do procedures require that changes to systems and procedures including forms and documentation related to payroll and labor distribution processing be approved by appropriate management personnel?	☐	☐	....
7. Do procedures specify the method or methods for executing payroll disbursements?	☐	☐	....

(continued)

FIG. 20-4 *(cont'd)*

	Yes	No	Workpaper Reference
8. Are there procedures in writing for authorizing, establishing, maintaining, and closing payroll bank accounts?	☐	☐	....
9. Are payroll bank account signatories required to be approved?	☐	☐	....

B. Processing and Recording:

	Yes	No	Workpaper Reference
1. Do procedures require that additions, deletions, and changes to payroll master file information be evidenced by standard forms?	☐	☐	....
2. Do standard forms contain written instructions as to their use?	☐	☐	....
3. Do procedures provide for obtaining and retaining payroll information to facilitate preparation and submission of various employee information to interested agencies? This information includes, but is not limited to:			
a. Employee name, address, and social security number	☐	☐	....
b. Birth date	☐	☐	....
c. Date or dates of hire (if prior employee)	☐	☐	....
d. Prior termination date	☐	☐	....
e. Marital status	☐	☐	....
f. Participation in various employee benefit plans	☐	☐	....
g. Dependent information	☐	☐	....
h. Military status	☐	☐	....
i. Citizenship	☐	☐	....
j. Employment classification	☐	☐	....
k. History of employment, including prior job classifications and pay rates	☐	☐	....
l. Withholding information	☐	☐	....
m. Attendance record	☐	☐	....
4. Do procedures provide for maintaining up to date payroll related reference files and material such as a payroll tax administration library, federal wage-hour laws, wage control guidelines, state labor laws?	☐	☐	....
5. Do procedures specify the periods for which payroll transactions are to be summarized and processed?	☐	☐	....
6. Do procedures require that for all hourly paid employees, the amount of time for which compensation			

ACCOUNTS PAYABLE PROCESSING   20-39

	Yes	No	Workpaper Reference
has been earned be evidenced by a standard form such as a payroll time card?	☐	☐	....
7. Do procedures require that all source information (e.g., time cards) be checked for accuracy and approval?	☐	☐	....
8. Do procedures require that source information be aggregated in batches for further processing?	☐	☐	....
9. If processing involves automated techniques, do procedures require that:			
a. Up-to-date user's manual be maintained?	☐	☐	....
b. Alternate processing plans have been established in the event of interruption of normal routines?	☐	☐	....
c. Appropriate means to control batches are in effect (e.g., by hash totals, item counts, or transmittal numbers)?	☐	☐	....
d. Control data is recorded in a log for subsequent comparison to processed data?	☐	☐	....
e. Errors and rejected transactions be promptly investigated and resubmitted?	☐	☐	....
f. If processing includes use of terminals:			
■ Do procedures require use of sign-on/sign-off procedures, user identification, passwords, lock keys, etc.?	☐	☐	....
■ Do procedures require that a log of terminal usage be kept providing some indication of transactions processed thereby?	☐	☐	....
g. If source information is converted in whole or in part within the profit center:			
■ Do procedures require that all data to be processed be sent directly to the key processor group?	☐	☐	....
■ Do procedures require verification of converted data?	☐	☐	....
■ Are all source data cancelled?	☐	☐	....
■ Are all converted data transmitted directly to the processing center?	☐	☐	....
h. The payroll department receives evidence that payroll transactions were accepted for processing (e.g., edit list, proofs)?	☐	☐	....
i. Such evidence be reconciled to control data?	☐	☐	....
j. Prompt resolution of errors and rejected data?	☐	☐	....
k. Processed data (reports) are received back directly from the processing center?	☐	☐	....

(continued)

FIG. 20-4 *(cont'd)*

	Yes	No	Workpaper Reference
l. Processed data are required to be reconciled to control data or otherwise reviewed for completeness and accuracy?	☐	☐	....
m. Errors resulting from the preceding question are promptly investigated and corrected?	☐	☐	....
10. For manually processed payrolls:			
a. Are payroll calculations and extensions required to be checked?	☐	☐	....
b. Are rates of pay obtained from current approved pay rate files?	☐	☐	....
c. Is a method utilized which assures that the payroll register, employee earnings record, and pay checks data all agree?	☐	☐	....
d. Is a method used to assure that all and only current employees are included in the payroll? Note: Methods in effect would include use of payroll registers having preprinted employee names and numbers, retention of pay status changes, prior processing of pay status changes.	☐	☐	....
11. Are payroll register totals required to be balanced to tapes of payroll checks prior to check distribution?	☐	☐	....
12. Do procedures require that journal entries recording payroll data be supported by worksheets developing accrual information related to payroll, such as:			
a. Holiday accrual	☐	☐	....
b. Vacation accrual	☐	☐	....
c. Sick leave accrual	☐	☐	....
d. Group insurance accruals	☐	☐	....
e. Workman's compensation accrual	☐	☐	....
f. Other payroll related insurance accruals	☐	☐	....
13. Do procedures require that labor distribution per time cards or other source document be checked for accuracy and approval?	☐	☐	....
14. Do procedures require reconciling labor distribution reports with gross pay totals per payroll register?	☐	☐	....
C. Accessibility:			
1. Are persons who prepare payrolls independent of personnel files and are they denied access to personnel files?	☐	☐	....

ACCOUNTS PAYABLE PROCESSING

	Yes	No	Workpaper Reference
2. Is access to payroll change of status forms restricted to authorized personnel?	☐	☐	....
3. Are changes to payroll information required to be approved by persons independent of persons initiating the change of status form?	☐	☐	....
4. Are personnel records maintained by persons independent from approval functions and/or payroll preparation functions?	☐	☐	....
5. Are time cards or other evidence of time worked required to be approved by someone other than the employee?	☐	☐	....
6. Are time cards reviewed and checked by someone independent from the approval function?	☐	☐	....
7. Is access to payroll master file data restricted to authorized employees?	☐	☐	....
8. Are payroll forms and master file records retained in a physically secure area?	☐	☐	....
9. Is access to blank payroll check stock restricted to authorized employees?	☐	☐	....
10. Is blank check stock stored in a physically secure area?	☐	☐	....
11. Is blank check stock under numerical control?	☐	☐	....
12. If facsimile signatures are used, are the plates stored in a physically secure area in the custody of someone independent from custodial functions related to blank check stock?	☐	☐	....
13. Are custodians of signature plates precluded from obtaining blank check stock?	☐	☐	....
14. Are payroll bank accounts required to be reconciled by someone independent of other payroll functions?	☐	☐	....
15. If payroll disbursement is by cash, is evidence of employee receipt retained?	☐	☐	....
16. If payroll disbursement is by cash, are appropriate safeguards in effect to limit the exposure to theft?	☐	☐	....
17. If payroll disbursement is by cash, are persons involved in preparing cash envelopes disassociated from other payroll functions?	☐	☐	....

(continued)

FIG. 20-4 *(cont'd)*

	Yes	No	Workpaper Reference
18. Are personnel involved in preparation of payrolls covered by fidelity bonds?	☐	☐	....
19. Are duties related to payroll preparation, recording, and disbursement periodically rotated among personnel?	☐	☐	....
20. If payroll processing is accomplished by automated techniques:			
a. Is access to programs and master file data restricted to authorized personnel?	☐	☐	....
b. Are changes to programs required to be approved and reviewed prior to implementation?	☐	☐	....
D. Accountability:			
1. Are payroll registers required to be reviewed periodically by responsible officials not involved in preparation of the payroll?	☐	☐	....
2. Are there periodic reconciliations required to be made of gross and net pay amounts with amounts shown on payroll tax returns and the general ledger?	☐	☐	....
3. Are payroll cash accounts required to be reconciled periodically?	☐	☐	....
4. Are unused blank check stock required to be accounted for periodically?	☐	☐	....
5. Are reports of labor cost required to be compared with budgets and differences analyzed?	☐	☐	....

FIG. 20-5

Payroll Audit Program

	Workpaper Reference	Done by
1. General:		
☐ Obtain copy of organization chart and by review of chart and discussion with management, determine the independence and reporting relationship of the payroll functions.	....	....
☐ Inquire into the existence of written procedures for payroll.	....	....

ACCOUNTS PAYABLE PROCESSING

	Workpaper Reference	Done by
☐ Review procedures, determine that procedures are current noting last revision date, document, and evaluate the payroll procedures.	....	....
☐ Ascertain that clauses in procedures if any, are properly approved.	....	....
☐ Ascertain existence and use of standard forms used for processing of payroll.	....	....
☐ Prepare a schedule cross-referencing procedure to an internal control questionnaire.	....	....
☐ By interviews with management and personnel involved in the payroll function, determine any deviations from written procedures or any other procedures which are not current.	....	....
☐ Ascertain existence and currency of EDP user's manuals, procedures, contingency plans, etc.	....	....

2. Authorization/Execution:

☐ Select .... persons from the payroll register and test for evidence of the following:
- Properly approved employment agreement
- Hours worked agree to properly approved time cards
- Agree hours worked for one job code on time card to the labor distribution
- Wage or salary rates and employee classification agree to approved data in personnel folder
- Fringe benefits and/or incentive compensation amounts are properly approved
- Employee data agree to the personnel files and EDP master files
- Deductions from the payroll checks are supported by documents signed by the employee
- Agree gross pay to employee earnings record
- Agree net pay to cancelled check properly endorsed by employee

☐ Select .... terminations and verify the existence of the following:
- Termination notice in personnel file
- Termination interviews
- Ascertain that employee does not appear on following payroll registers
- Proper documentation supporting termination pay

☐ If payroll is manual, then for those selected items, test calculate the net pay.

☐ For selected payroll periods, perform the following:
- Review reconciliation of labor distribution to payroll register and investigate significant reconciling items

(continued)

FIG. 20-5 *(cont'd)*

	Workpaper Reference	Done by
■ Agree total net payroll amount to transfer of funds to payroll account and ascertain timeliness of such transfers	....	....
■ Agree amounts per the payroll register and labor distribution to the general ledger	....	....
☐ Select some payroll journal vouchers and verify the existence of the following:		
■ Agree amounts per the journal voucher to supporting documentation, such as payroll register, labor distribution, and accrual analysis	....	....
■ Note proper approval of journal voucher	....	....
☐ For EDP processed payroll perform the following additional tests for payroll registers tested at the third main item on page (beginning "For selected payroll periods").		
■ Ascertain use of batch control totals or other similar techniques by reconciling control totals to the EDP printout	....	....
■ Ascertain that differences, if any, arising from the previous question are resolved in a timely manner	....	....
■ Determine that batches were recorded in a log or similar control device prior to input into system	....	....
■ Obtain edit or error runs and ascertain that transactions that have been subsequently corrected in a timely manner can be done on a test basis	....	....
☐ For transactions transmitted by terminals observe the use of key identification numbers, passwords, and so forth. Also ascertain that terminal use is controlled by a log or similar device.	....	....
3. Accessibility:		
☐ By reference to organization charts and by observation, confirm the degree of segregation of duties.	....	....
☐ Inspect facilities and inquire of management as to procedures employed for safeguarding and restricting access to the following:		
■ Blank payroll checks	....	....
■ Payroll register	....	....
■ Personnel files	....	....
■ EDP master files	....	....
■ Passwords, codes, and so forth, for EDP terminals	....	....
■ EDP input documents	....	....
■ Payroll forms	....	....
■ Signature plates	....	....
■ EDP programs	....	....

	Workpaper Reference	Done by
☐ Inquire of management personnel the extent that employees are bonded and review appropriate documentation.	....	....
4. Accountability:		
☐ Determine that payroll register is reviewed and approved by appropriate levels of management.	....	....
☐ Review reconciliation of payroll register to payroll tax returns.	....	....
☐ For selected months, test payroll bank reconciliations as follows:		
▪ Agree amounts to payroll register and general ledger	....	....
▪ Review for arithmetical accuracy	....	....
▪ Determine nature of significant or unusual reconciling items	....	....
▪ Determine timeliness and approval of reconciliation	....	....
▪ Review signatures on checks and agree to signatories authorized by cash management at Corporate	....	....
☐ Compare labor distribution to prior year's amounts and to existing budgets. Investigate significant fluctuations.	....	....
☐ Review log of blank checks and compare it to checks on hand to ascertain that all checks used are accounted for.	....	....

SPECIMEN REPORTS

Two specimen reports are detailed in this section. Figure 20-6 is used to show how the scope of work of other efforts may be disclosed in the report and to display a method of reporting payroll auditing work scope in which the specific controls tested are identified. Since payroll is an area of high interest for management and others, such identification may be helpful to those groups in understanding the depth of the work performed. Figure 20-6 also illustrates that findings can affect the auditor's overall opinion on the sufficiency of controls.

Many auditors may find that the volume of payroll transactions and the complexities of payroll accounting is such that the study of payroll accounting controls may need to be divided into two or more audit efforts. Figure 20-7 indicates the type of report to provide data on a separate audit of payroll-related transactions. Payroll-related transactions for this purpose includes group insurance, incentive compensation, payroll accruals, and employee withholds.

(continued on page 20-51)

FIG. 20-6

Audit Report—Corporate Payroll System Internal Controls

> TO: R.R. Johnson
>
> FROM: Corporate Audit
>
> SUBJECT: Review of the Corporate Payroll System (COPS) Internal Controls in Effect at Northern Engineering Division (NED)
>
> We have reviewed the internal control techniques over COPS in effect at NED as part of an overall review of that system, including a review of the electronic data processing segment. The review was for the sixteen-month period ending April, 19XX. Our objective was to identify and to evaluate the key controls which reasonably assure that payroll and personnel transactions are properly authorized, recorded, reported, and accounted for, and that related assets are properly safeguarded. In order to meet this objective, we assessed the level of testing in other audits performed during our review period by Corporate Audit. Where prior audit work was performed, we relied on the results of that work and performed only additional work necessary to assure comprehensive coverage of those key control techniques over payroll transactions.
>
> Our work may be summarized as follows:
>
> - Evaluated all prior work performed by Corporate Audit, including related reports and action taken in response to these reports. See Appendix C for a listing of all reports considered. [*Appendix C omitted.*]
>
> - Determined key control techniques for payroll activities and assessed audit coverage.
>
> - Developed and completed an audit program and internal control questionnaire to test and evaluate key controls.
>
> - Discussed with management pertinent matters during the course of the review.
>
> - Performed such other work considered necessary in the circumstances.
>
> A broad summary of controls and procedures reviewed is provided in Appendix A.
>
> Our review excluded the processing of data in related systems, such as weekly labor accumulation or the Centralized Records Systems, which either provides data to, or is provided data by COPS. The review includes controls, such as run to run totals and performing reconciliations, over data transmission between COPS and other systems.
>
> During our review, we noted the following matters which we believe should be brought to management's attention:
>
> - The analysis of labor suspense and payroll clearing accounts has not been completed.
>
> - The labor distribution report is not reconciled to the payroll register.
>
> - Certain payroll input forms are not reviewed by anyone other than the preparer.
>
> As a result of the first two findings, the referenced accounts contain a small unresolved variance totaling $53,000. It is a reasonable likelihood that any significant erroneous or unauthorized transaction occurring as a result of any of the findings would be detected due to compensating controls such as discrepancy reports, review of departmental cost reports, or broader controls such as budgetary controls. However, the findings should be resolved to reduce the exposure, which

ACCOUNTS PAYABLE PROCESSING

does exist, of a smaller dollar unauthorized transaction or group of such transactions occurring, and remaining undetected.

In our opinion, subject to the resolution of the matters discussed above, the NED system of internal controls is sufficient to reasonably assure that personnel transactions and the vast majority of payroll transactions are properly authorized, recorded, and accounted for, and that related assets are properly safeguarded.

The balance of this report contains a more detailed discussion of our findings and recommendations. A written reply from the action party is requested within thirty days.

1. The analysis of labor suspense and payroll clearing accounts has not been completed.

We previously noted in our report, "Review of Cost System," Report No. XX-115, dated March 4, 19XX, that the labor suspense and payroll clearing accounts, were not analyzed on a monthly basis. As of June, 1981, we noted that the analysis of the payroll clearing account, was substantially completed except for an unresolved variance of $4,000 originating over two years ago. The analysis of the labor suspense account, (balance, $49,000), remains substantially incomplete. We were informed by accounting management that the analysis was complicated by the inclusion, within the account, of purchased or vendor (job shop) labor transactions. Those transactions belong in a separate account. Accounting management further stated that a combined effort with the Business Systems Department to resolve this system deficiency had been initiated, but that the effort had experienced some delays.

RECOMMENDATION NO. 1

Complete the analysis of the subject accounts, including appropriate corrective action regarding vendor labor transactions. Maintain such analysis on a current basis.

2. The labor distribution report is not reconciled to the payroll register.

Currently, labor distribution total dollars and hours are not reconciled to the payroll register. The two records do not directly agree due to such factors as adjustments, labor/payroll variances, corrections out of period, and so forth. We believe a reconciliation is an integral part of the control over labor and payroll transactions. Also, such a reconciliation might aid in the analysis of the payroll clearing account, which is discussed in the preceding comment.

RECOMMENDATION NO. 2

Reconcile labor distribution total hours and dollars to the Payroll Register.

3. Certain payroll input forms are not reviewed by anyone other than the preparer.

The following payroll input forms from which checks, or adjustments to payroll checks, can be generated are not reviewed and approved by someone other than the preparer:

(continued)

FIG. 20-6 *(cont'd)*

- Payroll/Labor adjustment transmittal
- Special payments, refunds, and termination advances

We believe that these documents are sufficiently important to warrant independent approval even though there are compensating controls in effect such as discrepancy reports, review of department cost reports, or broader controls such as budgetary controls which might detect significant erroneous or unauthorized inputs. While it is unlikely that any significant unauthorized transaction would occur, the possibility does exist of a smaller unauthorized transaction or group of such transactions occurring and remaining undetected.

RECOMMENDATION NO. 3

Require independent review and approval of the Forms indicated in the finding.

APPENDIX A: SUMMARY OF CONTROLS AND PROCEDURES REVIEWED

- ☐ Authorization of data input, such as master files changes, or other documentation.
- ☐ Key processing controls, such as data input/output verification techniques, and processing checks such as run-to-run totals.
- ☐ Security over data files, check signature plates, and payroll checks including related accountability.
- ☐ COPS programs/systems documentation including related program changes.
- ☐ Data transmission between COPS and the following systems:
    - Labor
    - Centralized Records Systems
    - Common Salary Review System
    - Corporate Savings Plan System
    - Group Insurance
- ☐ Payroll bank account reconciliations.
- ☐ Payroll tax returns.
- ☐ Segregation of duties.
- ☐ Reviewed following categories of employees selected from COPS computer files, using special automated programs developed by corporate audit, for week ending 3/27/XX:
    - Employees assigned to Personnel/Payroll functions
    - Employees with base rate greater than maximum rate range
    - Salaried employees with merit increases requiring vice president approval
    - Salaried employees with more than two increases in the year
    - Hourly employees with COLA and Automatic Progression Rates greater than maximum
    - Terminated employees with current pay

ACCOUNTS PAYABLE PROCESSING

FIG. 20-7

Audit Report on Payroll-Related Transactions

TO: F. Martini

FROM: S.J. Ford

SUBJECT: Review of Payroll Related Transactions — Wabash Energy, Inc., (WEI)

We have reviewed internal control techniques related to indirect payroll transactions such as group insurance, incentive compensation, payroll accruals, and employee withholding, and other items of a similar nature at WEI.

Our review was made to determine if existing internal controls are sufficient to provide reasonable assurance with respect to authorization, recording, and accountability of the mentioned payroll transactions and activity, and that accessibility to company assets insofar as it applies to indirect payroll and related transactions is appropriately restricted. Our examination was conducted in accordance with our internal audit standards and included obtaining an understanding of existing policies and procedures, detailed testing of selected payroll activities of recent periods, completing an internal control questionnaire, and other tests considered necessary in the circumstances.

Our testing encompassed the period August, 19XX, to April 19XX, and concentrated on those indirect payroll procedures which are outlined in the WEI policies and procedures manual which became effective August 1, 19XX. In addition, some testing of the general payroll system was made as it related to indirect payroll functions. Our review disclosed the following items which we feel warrant management's attention:

- Deficiencies appear to be contained in the existing EDP payroll processing program.
- Employee "status change forms" are not independently reviewed and approved prior to submission to data processing.
- The division of duties for payroll preparation does not reasonably assure detection of input clerical errors before issuing checks.
- The payroll department is not immediately notified of field employee terminations.

In our opinion, with the exception of the aforementioned matters, the internal control techniques pertaining to indirect payroll transactions are sufficient to reasonably assure that such transactions are executed in accordance with management's general or specific authorization, are recorded as necessary to permit preparation of financial statements in confirmity with generally accepted accounting principles, and that access to WEI's assets is appropriately restricted.

A written reply to this report is requested within thirty days.

1. Deficiencies appear to be contained in the existing EDP payroll processing program.

During our review, we noted differences between the totals for certain deductions per the payroll register and those totals provided in each payroll deduction summary report. These reconciling items are the result of what appear to be deficiencies in the existing data processing programs. Discussions with the Payroll Supervisor and data processing personnel revealed the following conditions existing in the EDP program that appear to be creating such differences:

(continued)

FIG. 20-7 *(cont'd)*

- Deductions in the salaried payroll are utilizing the same data fields as other types of deductions for the hourly payroll. This creates a comingling of deduction types in the payroll register when persons change from one payroll to the other.
- The deduction summary report appears to be prepared from a different data base than the payroll register. For example, terminations are deleted from the summary report in the period of termination even though a paycheck may have been issued for some reason, such as termination pay.

As a result of the foregoing, numerous reconciling items are identified and corrected each pay period in order that the payroll registers and deduction summary reports reflect proper amounts. Such time consuming activities can be avoided if corrections can be made to the existing EDP programs to assure the production of accurate EDP prepared reports. This would also allow more time for payroll personnel to concentrate on other matters such as rotating review functions as discussed in a latter point on the division of duties. Financial management has informed us that a new software package is being considered for purchase which should eliminate the existing problems. While this may be the case, we believe that during the time a new system is under investigation, program changes should be identified and implemented, if costs permit. We believe that elimination of the types of reconciling items noted should be expedited in order to avoid further inefficiencies from occurring within the payroll function.

RECOMMENDATION NO. 1

Expedite the means of eliminating reconciling items between the payroll register and deduction summary report.

2. Employee "status change forms" are not independently reviewed and approved prior to submission to data processing.

The Payroll Supervisor prepares the "status change form" which is a summarization of employee requests for voluntary payroll deduction. The "status change form" is then submitted directly to data processing without an independent review within the Payroll Department. In order to enhance the internal controls over the input to data processing, as well as minimize the possibility of clerical errors, we suggest a second person within the Payroll Department review the "status change forms."

RECOMMENDATION NO. 2

Require that "status change forms" be reviewed and approved by someone other than the preparer prior to submission to data processing.

3. The division of duties for payroll preparation does not reasonably assure detection of input clerical errors before issuing checks.

Clerical payroll activities have been divided into salary and hourly categories. Responsibility for all hourly payroll functions is assigned to one clerk and all salary payroll to another. Both clerks reconcile their own input documents to the initial reports and the final payroll register to the checks for those workers. Inasmuch as the clerks do not rotate functions, there are no controls in place to reasonably assure detection of input clerical error prior to issuing the final payroll.

> We realize there are inherent limitations in a small staff which prohibits the implementation of ideal segregated functions. However, we believe the reassignment of the payroll clerk functions would compensate for the lack of segregation of duties as well as enhance internal controls through increased clerical efficiency.
>
> **RECOMMENDATION NO. 3**
>
> Reassign payroll reviewing functions to persons other than those responsible for preparing the input document.
>
> **4. The Payroll Department is not immediately notified of field employee terminations.**
>
> For field personnel (all salaried) it is often the practice to issue pay checks prior to receipt of the employee's time sheet by the Payroll Department. In the event a salaried field employee terminates without immediate notification to the Payroll Department, the employee could leave WEI and still be liable for outstanding travel advances. If the Payroll Department were timely notified, outstanding advances, if any, can be netted against the last check issued to an employee.
>
> **RECOMMENDATION NO. 4**
>
> Implement policies and procedures whereby the Payroll Department is promptly notified of field employee terminations.

SUGGESTED READING

Connor, Joseph E., and Burnell H. DeVos, Jr., eds. "Employee Compensation and Benefits," in *Guide to Accounting Controls*. New York: Warren, Gorham & Lamont, Inc., 1979.

———. "Purchases and Payables," in *Guide to Accounting Controls*. New York: Warren, Gorham & Lamont, 1979.

Kell, Walter G. and Richard E. Ziegler. *Modern Auditing,* Chapter 10. New York: Warren, Gorham & Lamont, 1980.

Sullivan, Jerry D., Richard Gnospelius, Philip L. Defliese, and Henry R. Jaenicke. *Montgomery's Auditing,* 10th ed., Chapter 15. John Wiley & Sons, publishers. Copyright © 1985 by Coopers & Lybrand (United States).

CHAPTER **21**

Cost Accounting Systems

Overview	1	Processing and Accounting	10
		Accessibility and Safeguarding	13
Definition and Background	3	Reporting and Accountability	13
Actual Job Cost System	4		
Actual Process Cost System	4	**Audit Techniques**	14
Standard Cost System	5	Preliminary	14
		Fieldwork	15
The Business Environment	5		
		Illustrative Questionnaire	16
Risks	7		
		Sample Audit Program	21
Internal Control Objectives	8		
		Specimen Report	21
Internal Control Techniques	9		
Organization and Authorization	9	**Suggested Reading**	28

Fig. 21-1 Typical Cost Code Structure 11
Fig. 21-2 Illustrative Burden Pool Accounts 12
Fig. 21-3 Internal Control Questionnaire for Cost System (Cost Ledger) 17
Fig. 21-4 Cost System Review Audit Program 22
Fig. 21-5 Report on Audit of Manufacturing Job Cost Accounting System 25

OVERVIEW

Cost accounting is a function basic to any private business entity or governmental unit in which knowing the cost of an undertaking is relevant to achieving management objectives with respect to that undertaking. Cost accounting is an integral ingredient of the following:

- Companies engaged in extractive industries (mining, oil, and gas products)
- Producers of refined products (e.g., petroleum products)
- Manufacturers of durable goods (e.g., heavy machinery and trucks)

- Manufacturers of consumer goods (ranging from automobiles to furniture, etc.)
- Suppliers of commodities such as lumber, steel, and aluminum, and fabricated items such as steel and aluminum structural components
- Processors of chemicals, foods, and drugs
- Providers of services such as health care
- Aerospace and construction contractors

In addition to providing cost information for basic products or services, cost accounting techniques form an integral part of programs or project management (see Chapter 36) and overhead control. Accordingly, such project efforts as construction of a new factory or design of a new data processing system frequently are accompanied by cost accounting techniques. Also, cost systems are set up to accumulate and report departmental and/or functional costs for both planning and control. These vary from company to company but usually include such indirect functions as plant maintenance and related factory burden centers, engineering and R&D burden centers, and purchasing, receiving, and warehousing functions. Similarly, cost systems are often designed to account for general and administrative functions, such as public relations, finance and accounting, and labor relations. Naturally, the nature of the cost data accounted for in these examples varies considerably from inventory cost accounting systems.

The emergence of cost accounting as a function of significant value to management paralleled the emergence of the industrialized, corporate private enterprise system that now dominates worldwide economic activity. Timely, accurate, and complete cost data regarding such cost elements as labor, material, and overhead associated with such undertakings became a primary and indispensable tool for responsible management to use in controlling activities related to the undertaking—whether it is ongoing, such as the production of a beverage, or a nonrecurring project, such as the construction of a hydroelectric dam. Accurate and reliable cost data are essential in setting selling prices, valuing inventories and planning and controlling operations.

Cost accounting techniques, like many other control functions, have been enhanced by EDP, with the result that many systems today involve complex interractive data base systems, with significant investments in personnel, equipment, and other resources. These require a considerable, continuous managerial effort to keep the systems operating effectively. For these reasons, auditing the internal controls present in cost accounting systems is an important aspect for many internal auditing organizations. Most cost systems do not carry much exposure to loss through embezzlement, defalcations, and the like, although theft of sensitive cost data is a constant threat.

This chapter defines cost accounting, describes the business environment, risks, and internal control objectives surrounding it, discusses various audit techniques that may be used in auditing cost systems, offers an illustrative internal control questionnaire and an audit program, and presents a specimen audit report. Chapter 34 discusses the operational auditing of inventory management—the function in most companies with which cost accounting systems are most closely associated.

DEFINITION AND BACKGROUND

Cost accounting may be defined as the process of systematically classifying and accumulating the costs expended by an organization for labor, material, overhead, and other cost elements in connection with a particular identifiable work objective. The costs represent specific charges, such as for labor or materials, incurred directly for the objective. Also included are costs of a general or indirect nature which can be associated with the objective through one or more allocation processes.

Cost objectives may be defined as any end item or activity for which management desires cost information. Usually the system is an integral part of the manufacture of some product or delivery of some service. Depending on the type of company and other factors, costs may be accumulated for a given process or task, such as milling or annodizing; for a given department or function, such as fabrication, assembly, or inspection; for component parts, subassemblies, and final assemblies; or for specific jobs, projects, contracts, or customer orders. The variety of circumstances is such that it is unlikely that any auditor will see two systems that are completely alike, although some companies have multiple plants or operating locations producing the same items for which a single uniform cost system is used.

According to Connor and DeVos,[1] in addition to cost information, many cost control systems classify, accumulate, and report information with respect to:

- Economic order quantities
- Purchasing/manufacturing lead times
- Quantities received, issued, on hand, and on order
- Standard costs
- Inventory turnover and usage rates
- Slow moving inventory
- Stockouts
- Quantities of obsolete or unusable material
- Shop orders awaiting material
- Dollar inventory investment

---

[1] Joseph E. Connor and Burnell H. DeVos, Jr., eds., *Guide to Accounting Controls* (New York: Warren, Gorham & Lamont, 1979), p. 5-21.

Closely aligned with the operation of many cost systems is some type of performance measurement. Performance measurement involves identifying and analyzing deviations from expected results in order to enhance managerial effectiveness. Performance measurement mechanisms involve techniques such as budgeting and standard costing, and accounting for physical units produced, where applicable. Where physical units are not involved, performance measurement entails breaking down the scope of work into a hierarchical structure of interrelated but separately stated tasks for which budgets are developed. The cost accounting structure is then integrated to accumulate costs so as to enable progress to be tracked. Where products are involved, costs may be accumulated so as to report unit costs by part, production or customer order, or producing department. Many cost systems involve combinations of these basic modes.

While there are many variations, cost systems may be categorized into three basic types: (1) actual job cost system, (2) actual process cost system, and (3) standard cost system.

Actual Job Cost System

An actual job cost system is designed to accumulate actual costs of producing units on a job-lot basis. The lots are usually assigned a production or work order number and are evidenced by prenumbered order forms that specify what items are to be produced and how much. In addition, the forms often provide for specifying production instructions and provide space for approvals and sign-offs. Labor distribution records and material requisitions provide the source data for direct job charges.[2] Overhead is usually charged on the basis of its relationship to some direct cost item, such as labor hours, labor dollars, or total direct cost.

Actual Process Cost System

An actual process cost system is used in continuous process environments, such as the production of some chemicals, food and beverage products, and building materials. Costs are accumulated by cost element (i.e., direct labor, material, and overhead) for given periods (usually monthly) for each producing department. Source data for these charges include the labor distribution records and material usage records. In addition to cost data, a record of units in process at the beginning of the period, received into the department and completed by it, is maintained. By tracking both units and costs, unit cost data may be derived, which are then used to value units remaining in process at the end of the period and to determine production costs for the department.

---

[2] Paul J. Wendell, *Corporate Controller's Manual* (New York: Warren, Gorham & Lamont, 1981), p. 6-3.

COST ACCOUNTING SYSTEMS 21-5

Standard Cost System

A standard cost system is a more sophisticated form of costing in which the cost elements of production are accumulated based on unit standards for each task or operation. The standards are intended to approximate the actual costs of production. In the more advanced standard cost systems, actual costs are also accumulated to provide a basis for testing the accuracy of the standards.

Standard cost systems are usually found in mass production environments involving discrete, simultaneous production activities (i.e., departments or cost centers) of many parts, with staging of partially completed materials or parts between the related activities.[3] Standard cost systems may be found in either job cost or process cost environments.

There are various methods that may be employed to develop the standards and keep them current. Some companies employ industrial engineers for the purpose, while others base the standards on averages of historical cost experiences. Still others use a combination of these techniques. At some point in the cost system (e.g., at job closeout or at the time of physical inventory), the accumulated costs at standard are adjusted to reflect actual cost through a process known as variance accounting. Variances may be tracked for any relationship of interest to management. The most common variances are as follows:

- Labor rate
- Labor efficiency
- Material price
- Material usage
- Overhead rate
- Overhead capacity

Variances must be continuously analyzed to determine the causes and to provide a basis for adjusting standards, inventory values, and cost of sales.

THE BUSINESS ENVIRONMENT

Variations in the business environment account for most of the differences in the ways cost systems accumulate and report cost data. Hence, the auditor must understand the environment in which the company operates. The business environment factors that influence the cost system have already been hinted at and include:

☐ *The nature of the product or service.* The nature of the product or service affects the structure of the cost system. Factors involved include the life

---
[3] *Ibid.*, p. 6-7.

cycle of the product or service, the durability/perishability of the item, turnover rates, and price/elasticity.

- *Management objectives.* Management objectives are a prime determinant of cost systems because the systems will tend to track and report the information of interest to management.

- *The cost control potential.* The cost control potential is a concept that holds that the degree of control that may be exercised varies with the type and importance of the cost involved. Cost systems tend to be more elaborate for cost items that are more responsive to management control efforts. While all costs can be controlled, fixed costs, such as depreciation, some salary rates, and property taxes, are thought to be less controllable than those that vary more directly with the level of effort required. These include direct material and labor charges, equipment utilization costs, and payments to subcontractors. Generally speaking, management is more interested in obtaining information regarding variable costs because of their greater volatility and their greater susceptibility to managerial control efforts.

- *Market considerations.* Market considerations include the customer base (i.e., wholesale commercial or retail; domestic or foreign; private or government), the stability of demand, the degree of competition, the method of selling and delivering, and the nature of orders, including size, frequency, and other customer-originated requirements. These considerations play an important part in determining the ways in which cost information is gathered and reported.

- *Government rules and regulations.* Government rules and regulations affect cost systems in at least two different ways. First, as consumers of products and services, agencies and divisions of the federal government and those of state and local governmental units frequently issue complex rules and regulations affecting their procurement of goods or services. Many of these, such as the Federal Acquisition Regulations, specify detailed information requirements that, in turn, affect the way in which cost systems must be established. Second, some products or services exchanged between private entities and/or the public are regulated by governmental commissions and agencies. Examples include public utilities, railroads, broadcasters, financial institutions, and providers of health-care services. These regulations often specify requirements for accumulating and reporting cost data.

- *Manufacturing complexity.* Manufacturing complexity has a direct bearing on the type of cost system needed. If the manufacturing process is relatively simple—those involving few raw materials and only slight conversion—comparatively little detail cost information is required. Food and beverage processors and manufacturers of some consumable home products are examples. On the other hand, cost systems for manufacturers of complex items, such as automobiles, heavy equipment, and electronic products, and builders of complex items, such as buildings, airplanes, and ships, require more elaborate cost systems.

- *Capacity considerations.* Capacity considerations are important in industries where supply and demand changes occur more frequently and are more severe. Suppliers of basic commodities, such as steel, aluminum, petroleum, and chemical products, are often beset with cyclical swings in demand for their products. Cost accounting systems for these and other business entities similarly affected must be responsive to changes in capacity to properly account for the impact these changes have on the costs of the products involved.

The value in considering the business environment is to afford the auditor a proper understanding so that he can formulate the tools and techniques necessary to effect an audit of the cost accounting system that is of sufficient quality.

RISKS

Corollary to understanding the business environment is the need to understand the particular risks associated with a given function. The risks inherent in cost accounting systems differ somewhat from those described for receivables, payroll, and payables functions in other chapters, in that there is much less exposure to employee fraud, theft, and similar irregularities. There is, however, a greater exposure to management-induced fraud through overriding or manipulating cost systems to produce information intended to disguise poor performance. Auditors encountering systems that are easily susceptible to management influence must be alert to the presence of other circumstances that may suggest wrongful management acts. These circumstances are detailed in Chapter 23.

There are several risks associated with the effective management of inventory generally, including the risks of changing customer demands, general economic fluctuations, and producing or purchasing in excess of actual requirements. Other general risks involving inventory include the various exposures to damage or loss through natural or human acts. These general inventory management risks exist regardless of the cost accounting system in effect; however, they have an impact on the structure of cost systems.

Other risks or exposures more specifically associated with cost accounting systems include:

- Unauthorized changes to the cost system
- Insufficient resources allocated to permit the effective functioning of the system
- Incompetent personnel assigned to perform vital cost control functions
- Inadequate forms and manuals to minimize errors and omissions
- Absence of checks and balances to detect and correct costing errors
- Production activity which escapes recording in books of original entry
- Errors in assigning cost codes to cost input
- Inability to effect proper transaction cutoffs at period closings
- Inability to isolate and identify the causes for production inefficiencies

- Improper valuation of inventory balances
- Failure to account for infrequent inventory transactions, such as cost transfers, return of unacceptable merchandise, and write-offs of obsolete items
- Inconsistent application of accounting principles
- Failure to report cost information timely
- Failure to report sufficient cost information
- Inability to reconcile book balances with physical counts

These risks can cause profound difficulties for the business entity, such as the inability to successfully compete in the marketplace, erosion of customer base, failure to liquidate inventory balances, and even lawsuits. Business failure can often result unless remedial actions are taken. For other functions such as marketing, purchasing, shipping, and engineering, unreliable cost data can lead to improper decisions regarding the effectiveness of those functions. This, too, inevitably affects the competitive posture of the entity.

INTERNAL CONTROL OBJECTIVES

It is clear from the preceding discussions of business environment and risks that the principle objective of cost accounting systems is to provide timely, reliable, relevant cost information to interested management and other groups for planning and control purposes and to properly value inventories. Of course, there are a number of subobjectives that vary in importance among companies, depending on the particular risks and business environment involved. A summary of these objectives and subobjectives follows:

- To establish and maintain a cost system and effect changes thereto in accordance with management's authorization
- To record the actual or estimated cost of all transactions and activities, direct and indirect, involved in the construction, fabrication and/or production, and delivery of all products and services offered by the company
- To record the actual or estimated costs of all transactions and activities, direct and indirect, in accordance with GAAP, tax regulations, and other managerial or third-party requirements
- To report cost information to interested management accurately, completely, and timely, in formats that are relevant for its purposes
- To report cost information to customers, government agencies, and others as may be required by agreement, regulation, or other arrangement
- To segregate duties so as to minimize errors and irregularities
- To safeguard cost records and files from damage or loss due to natural or human acts
- To restore normal cost accounting routines in the event of business interruption

INTERNAL CONTROL TECHNIQUES

The importance of relevant and reliable cost information in most business entities is such that managements usually must allocate considerable resources to the function. However, the difficulties posed by the dynamic environmental and risk factors are such that few companies have continuously effective systems. Most companies are forced to supplement basic cost systems with other control techniques to enable them to maintain or increase competitive postures. These include special analyses, periodic performance reviews, frequent meetings of representatives of related disciplines, and occasional input from external sources, such as outside auditors and consultants.

The following discussion offers some of the more common control techniques found in cost accounting systems; however, the reader must bear in mind that the specific circumstances of each business unit determine the control techniques used.

Organization and Authorization

Typically, the cost accounting function is a primary duty and responsibility of the controller or chief accounting officer. In larger companies, the function is often redelegated to a section or department headed by a chief cost accountant or a manager, who reports to the controller. This individual is responsible for maintaining the cost system and the accuracy of the information produced by it. In many companies comprised of autonomous operating units, each one may have its own separate and distinct cost accounting function (as well as other accounting functions). Other companies, who produce a single product or a related family of products at multiple plant sites, may have only one basic cost accounting system.

Most cost accounting departments are comprised of accountants who possess review and analytical skills. Much of the data captured by the cost system for their scrutiny originate from transactions processed as part of other systems. For instance, labor transactions may originate with the payroll system; materials, services, and purchased parts may originate with the procurement system; and overhead pools are filled by transactions from both. Other costs may enter the cost system from general journal entries, e.g., equipment charges. The exact mix and methods vary, depending on whether the final cost objective is to determine the cost of a product, a customer order, a production order, a producing department, or a particular process.

Since cost systems process considerable volumes of transactions, the modern system often involves one or more electronic data processing applications. In such instances, cost accountants spend much time manually reviewing and analyzing computer-generated cost reports. If the system is sufficiently sophisticated, cost accountants may use automated techniques, via desk terminals and PCs, to perform such work.

Whether automated or manual, it is up to the cost department manager to be reasonably certain that the information feeding into its cost records is accurate and complete in all material respects. This often requires considerable inquiry of, and coordination with, other functional disciplines. Where standards costs are involved, the cost accounting function, in addition to its basic record-keeping responsibilities, is often responsible for keeping standards accurate and current. Additionally, some cost departments supply information on an "as requested" basis. This information may take the form of estimated costs of new products or services, or estimates of the cost impact of various marketing strategies or recommended price structures for enhancing profitability on current products.

Processing and Accounting

Achieving the objectives of internal control identified earlier for cost systems is possible only if the processing and accounting occurs in a standard routine fashion, with ample provision of checks and balances to catch all errors and omissions of any consequence. A primary ingredient in all cost systems is a transaction coding structure. The structure is usually comprised of numerical codes ranging in size from three or four digits in small systems to 12–14 digits in large systems. The code for any single transaction may be comprised of subcodes within the basic code to permit accumulating the cost transactions in various ways. In turn, this permits the summarization and reporting of costs for different purposes—i.e., by part, by department, by task, by production order, by cost element, and so on.

A typical simple cost code is shown in Figure 21-1. According to that structure, an item of material issued to the milling department in the Eastern Division may be coded "0255212004." The tasks in Figure 21-1 may be thought of as final cost objectives.

In addition to the cost code structure, most systems employ a variety of techniques to capture either the actual cost of each transaction or task, or an approximation of the actual cost. The specific details are frequently complex and may include some of the following:

1. Labor
   - Use of standard forms, such as timecards or time sheets
   - Use of standard rates by various categories, such as job classification, department, or product
   - Use of actual hours or fractions thereof by the same categories
   - Use of standard hours or fractions thereof for each task
   - A method to accumulate labor costs, such as the use of timecards filled out by workers and processed at regular intervals

FIG. 21-1
Typical Cost Code Structure

	XX	XXX	XXXX	XX	XXX
	Division	Department	Customer Order	Cost Element	Task

Division	Department	Element	Task
01 Northern	551 Cutting	11 Labor	001 Design
02 Eastern	552 Milling	12 Material	002 Tooling
03 Western	553 Boring	13 Purchased part	003 Scheduling
	554 Deburring	14 Subcontract	004 Fabrication
	555 Anodizing	15 Equipment	005 Inspection
	556 Paint	16 Scrap	006 Assembly
			007 Quality control
			008 Final test
			009 Rework
			010 Shipment

- A method to enable isolating variances between actual and standard labor changes

2. Material
   - Use of a standard bill of materials, including quantities for each material item
   - Use of standard unit costs
   - A system to record actual quantities issued at various production stages. For example, this may involve the use of issue slips generated by central stockroom personnel, coded at the time of issuance and processed at regular intervals
   - A method to enable isolating variances between actual and standard material charges

3. Equipment
   - Use of standard rates for each large piece of equipment used in the production process, based on costs of ownership, maintenance, and operation
   - A method to accumulate equipment charges, such as by use of timecards for each machine completed by operators and processed at regular intervals
   - A method to analyze variances between actual and standard equipment operating costs

For the most part, the preceding discussion covers techniques to accumulate direct costs. Another equally important aspect of cost systems is

FIG. 21-2

Illustrative Burden Pool Accounts

Expense Categories	Burden Pools			
	Manufacturing	Engineering	Use & Occupancy	Data Processing
Labor	X	X	X	X
Supervision	X	X	X	X
Fringe	X	X	X	X
Depreciation	X	X	X	X
Rent	X		X	X
Insurance			X	
Purchased services	X		X	
Supplies	X	X	X	X
Travel	X	X		X
Taxes			X	
Utilities			X	
Facilities allocation	X	X		X
Service center allocation	X	X		

the way in which indirect costs are accumulated. These may also be called burden costs or overhead. Indirect cost finding is important because the true cost of a product, operation, job, or department cannot be known without adding to its direct cost an amount intended to approximate its fair share of indirect costs. Usually, this is done by setting up one or more burden centers or pools comprised of identifiable expense categories associated with that center or pool. Figure 21-2 illustrates some of the types of pools and expense categories that may be encountered.

Cost departments charge these indirect costs to final cost objectives by various devices. One common technique is to devise rates for each burden center. These rates, expressed as percentages, derive by dividing the total burden pool expenses (actual or estimated for the period) by the total of the direct costs or the total of a direct cost element, such as labor. By applying these rates in the appropriate manner to the actual direct cost incurred, indirect costs become associated with final cost objectives. Included in the mechanics must be a means to adjust burden rates from time to time to keep them current and to eliminate over/underabsorption of burden by the direct cost objectives.

From the foregoing, it is obvious that cost systems can involve complicated structures, and require that discipline be exercised by the large

COST ACCOUNTING SYSTEMS

number of persons needed to "feed" the system. Even the best of systems is exposed to frequent errors and omissions that, taken individually, are usually insignificant. A number of techniques have evolved to help minimize these errors; however, no system will eliminate them completely. These include:

- A current and complete cost code structure
- A detailed explanation of the cost system—this may be included in the accounting manual or in a separate manual
- Use of prescribed forms, records, and ledgers, with instructions for each
- Organization charts and functional outlines
- Techniques to keep standards current, where applicable
- Use of timekeepers to "audit" the accuracy of labor time charges
- Use of automated devices to help assure accurate recording of time charges
- Computers to facilitate accurate and complete processing
- Use of standard procedures and entries to summarize and record cost transactions

Accessibility and Safeguarding

Since cost accounting does not involve access to cash or pilferable assets, the exposure to defalcations by personnel involved in cost accounting duties is nil. That is not to say, however, that cost accounting systems need not be safeguarded. Cost data are usually considered by managements to be among the most sensitive company data, and they must be protected from unauthorized access and use. If the cost system is completely manual, the records and files are usually kept within the cost accounting department and are locked away in fireproof metal files when unattended.

If the cost system is maintained on computer files, access is restricted by use of data security software and by other customary protective measures usually found in I/S installations (physical security techniques, segregation of duties, and provision for backup and recovery). Cost records and files are vital to most businesses and must be retained for sufficient periods to meet requirements of applicable rules and regulations of various agencies and commissions of governmental units and, if necessary, customer requirements.

Reporting and Accountability

The reporting of cost data is perhaps the most critical function of cost accounting systems. These systems are designed to provide abundant information to a host of interested parties, both internal and external. Reports may be prepared daily, weekly, monthly, quarterly, and annually. They may

or standard costs and may include explanations of variances. These reports enable the users to monitor and manage the activities occurring within their respective areas of responsibility.

The cost system is also used to enable comparisons to be made of recorded inventory values with amounts derived from priced physical counts of inventory items. These counts and comparisons may be done on a cyclical basis throughout the year, or once each year on a "wall-to-wall" basis. The differences disclosed by these comparisons tell much about the accuracy of the cost system and are thought to be among the most important of control techniques.

AUDIT TECHNIQUES

The significance of cost accounting systems is such that auditing cost accounting controls is usually assigned a top priority by many internal auditing functions. Cost systems are also a subject of interest to external auditors; consequently, audit coverage should be coordinated to avoid duplicating efforts.

Preliminary

As with other audit projects, the auditor assigned to audit a cost accounting system must start by obtaining as much background information as possible. This would include reviewing prior workpapers, if available, policy statements, procedural manuals, organization charts, flow charts, and pertinent financial data. Since the design of many cost systems is affected by applicable regulations and customer requirements, the auditor must include in his preliminary work a study of these. Such information is usually available in the cost accounting department.

If the historical financial data are available, they may be useful to analyze the trends of such indicators as inventory turnover rates, write-offs of obsolete inventory as a percentage of total inventory, and differences between book and physical inventory counts. This type of trend analysis may provide an initial indication of the effectiveness of the cost accounting system.

Preliminary interviews and discussions should be conducted with interested members of management and the audit management to learn of any concerns they may have. Further, the timing of the fieldwork can be coordinated by this process.

Another step usually performed during the preliminary stage is to ready the audit tools intended to be used. These include audit programs, questionnaires, and, to the extent applicable, computer-assisted audit techniques present cost data by division, department, inventory category, customer order, or cost element. The reports may contain comparisons with budgeted

COST ACCOUNTING SYSTEMS 21-15

(CAAT), such as generalized audit software, test decks, or integrated test facilities (see Chapter 28).

Cost accounting systems are particularly susceptible to the application of CAAT, since most cost systems are automated. Depending on the sophistication of the system, the following may be tested as indicated:

Control or Activity:	Method of Testing:
• Changes to system, such as standards and codes	• Test deck, or integrated test facility
• Accuracy of standards in master cost file	• Extracted via generalized or special audit software
• Processing of cost transactions (labor, material)	• Parallel simulation or generalized audit software
• Burden application	• Parallel simulation or generalized audit software
• Accuracy of cost system programs	• Program walk-throughs either manually or by using tracing or mapping utility programs

Of course, it is unlikely that all of the above techniques would be used in any single audit, but they may be performed over the course of several periodic audits.

Fieldwork

Conducting the fieldwork involves performing various procedures as called out in the audit program. The objective is to gather the evidential matter necessary to form an opinion regarding the adequacy of transaction processing and accounting controls. The procedures are discussed in the ensuing paragraphs in terms of observation, inquiry, inspection, and confirmation.

For most cost accounting system audits, observation procedures are limited to general observations regarding the segregation of duties and compliance with security measures (e.g., locking up books and records at night). In addition, the auditor may observe the manner in which assigned duties and functions appear to be carried out by cost accounting personnel. The appearance of diligent, competent performance may be a factor in evaluating the overall effectiveness of cost control techniques. On the other hand, the appearance of haphazard, disorganized work efforts may serve to arouse the auditor's concern regarding effectiveness. Observations made during plant tours may provide additional insight and understanding to that gained during preliminary work.

Inquiry procedures are used to gain an understanding of control techniques followed in processing and accounting for inventory and other transactions for which the cost system was devised. Inquiry procedures include interviews with key personnel and detailed reviews of applicable manuals and flow charts, if available. Inquiry also includes obtaining responses to internal control questionnaires designed to evaluate the adequacy of controls. Much of this work may be done during the preliminary phase, but much may also be done during the fieldwork phase.

Inquiry procedures may also be used to research and resolve questions that may arise during testing for compliance with policy, procedures, and external requirements. For example, the auditor may discover practices that may be inconsistent with tax regulations, GAAP, or contractual requirements. In addition to research, the auditor may seek the advice of external auditors and, if necessary, legal counsel where serious matters of law are involved.

Inspection procedures are used extensively to test compliance with established control requirements. Among the controls often tested are the following:

- Use of proper forms, such as production orders to authorize production, labor cards to record time charges, and material transaction slips to document material issues, transfers, and returns
- Compliance with established procedures for processing the foregoing forms
- Tests of transaction coding, summarizing, and posting to appropriate ledgers and subledgers
- Tests of the development and application of overhead rates
- Tests of other entries recording costs, such as waste, spoilage, scrap, and obsolete inventory, as applicable
- Tests of standard costs
- Tests of transaction cutoffs

Both nonstatistical and statistical sampling techniques may be used in connection with inspection routines as warranted by circumstances.

Confirmation procedures are used primarily to corroborate explanations by key personnel and others for deviations from established routines, and to substantiate the auditor's tentative conclusions as to findings of control weaknesses.

ILLUSTRATIVE QUESTIONNAIRE

The questionnaire in Figure 21-3 is intended to illustrate many of the questions that might be asked in evaluating cost accounting controls. The questionnaire, relating solely to cost accounting systems, does not cover the control aspects for the transactions or activities for which the cost systems

(continued on page 21-21)

COST ACCOUNTING SYSTEMS   21-17

FIG. 21-3

Internal Control Questionnaire for Cost System (Cost Ledger)

This questionnaire has been prepared for use with the Cost System Audit Program. Emphasis has been placed on determining that an adequate system of internal accounting control exists, and those controls are sufficient to provide reasonable assurances that cost accounting objectives are met.

	Yes	No	Workpaper Reference

A. Authorization:

1. Do procedures specifically authorize those who are responsible for approving:

    a. Changes to cost system procedures and manuals ☐ ☐ ....

    b. Changes to cost standards ☐ ☐ ....

    c. Entries to record standard journal entries ☐ ☐ ....

    d. Adjusting and correcting entries ☐ ☐ ....

    e. Entries to record reserves, and write-offs ☐ ☐ ....

    f. Revisions to forms and report formats ☐ ☐ ....

2. Are responsibilities and duties for cost accounting functions set forth in organization charts and functional job descriptions? ☐ ☐ ....

3. Are changes to organization charts and functional outlines required to be approved by designated individuals? ☐ ☐ ....

4. Are other administrative duties, such as hiring/firing/training of personnel and of department budgets, clearly set forth in functional outlines? ☐ ☐ ....

B. Processing and Recording:

1. Is the cost system described in manuals, flow charts or written procedural statements? ☐ ☐ ....

2. Is the process of recording costs integrated with other accounting applications such as purchasing and payroll? ☐ ☐ ....

3. Is the cost system designed to record all costs associated with final cost objectives of interest to management, completely and accurately? ☐ ☐ ....
Note: Final cost objectives usually include a specific identifiable work item or task (such as cutting, stripping, heat treating, annodizing, etc.) or it may be related to a function such as fabrication, inspection, assembly etc. Cost systems usually employ techniques such as the following to record costs accurately and completely.

(continued)

FIG. 21-3 *(cont'd)*

	Yes	No	Workpaper Reference
4. Labor:			
a. Use of a cost code structure sufficiently flexible to permit aggregating costs in several ways	☐	☐	....
b. Use of prescribed standards for work routines, or labor rates for each applicable job category, or both	☐	☐	....
c. Use of controls to account for physical movement of items of production	☐	☐	....
d. Use of production order system to serve as the cost-gathering medium	☐	☐	....
e. Use of labor cards or similar devices to serve as the source document for labor transactions	☐	☐	....
f. Use of timekeepers or other control techniques to check accuracy of time recording and coding	☐	☐	....
5. Material:			
a. Same techniques outlined above for items a–d dealing with labor	☐	☐	....
b. Use of a material issue methodology to approximate the actual adding or converting of material into salable proprietary products as it occurs	☐	☐	....
c. A means to assure that all material transactions are recorded. This might include such techniques as:			
■ Prenumbered forms for material issues, turn-ins, and transfers	☐	☐	....
■ Batch processing	☐	☐	....
■ Accounting for numerical sequence	☐	☐	....
6. Overhead:			
a. Use of overhead rates to charge indirect costs to final cost objectives	☐	☐	....
b. Use of overhead or burden costs and an accounting structure to gather overhead expenses	☐	☐	....
c. Use of clearing and/or account classifications and standard journal entries to apportion overhead to final cost objectives accurately and consistently	☐	☐	....
d. A means to minimize over/under absorption of overhead, including:			
■ Analysis of variances	☐	☐	....
■ Periodic overhead studies	☐	☐	....
■ Updating of overhead pools in light of changing conditions	☐	☐	....

7. Other Direct Cost:

Other direct cost may be charged to final cost objectives using techniques similar to those already outlined for

COST ACCOUNTING SYSTEMS 21-19

	Yes	No	Workpaper Reference

material and labor. Other direct cost may include charges for equipment operation and subcontracts.

    a. Does the processing and recording of costs incurred employ standard routines and techniques to assure consistent, accurate, and complete recording, including:

- Summarization forms designed to minimize errors and omissions ☐ ☐ ....
- Standardized journal entries ☐ ☐ ....
- Subsidiary cost ledgers ☐ ☐ ....
- Methods to assure proper cut-offs ☐ ☐ ....

    b. Does the processing and recording of cost incurred involve EDP? ☐ ☐ ....
(If the answer to this question is yes, see separate Section 10 of this questionnaire.)

8. Accessibility:

    a. Are cost accounting records maintained by personnel independent of other accounting functions such as payrolls, cash disbursements, and so on? ☐ ☐ ....

    b. Is access to cost records restricted to authorized personnel? ☐ ☐ ....

    c. Are cost accounting records and documents retained in a physically secure area? ☐ ☐ ....

    d. Are cost accounting records sufficiently protected from loss or damage due to natural or human acts? ☐ ☐ ....

    e. In the event of loss or destruction, do procedures plans provide for timely recovery? ☐ ☐ ....

9. Accountability:

    a. Is there a regular reporting and analysis of trends in amounts and types of charges? ☐ ☐ ....

    b. Are reconciliations performed between the general ledger and the cost system? ☐ ☐ ....

    c. Are reconciliations performed between the cost ledger and:

- Labor distribution ☐ ☐ ....
- Material charges ☐ ☐ ....
- Expense ledger ☐ ☐ ....

    d. Are reconciliations performed between manually prepared adjustments and computer-generated reports? ☐ ☐ ....

    e. Are procedures in existence that define responsibilities for the use of exception reports? ☐ ☐ ....

    f. Are the following exception reports used for controlling cost accounts on a consistent basis:

- Variance report — labor ☐ ☐ ....

(continued)

FIG. 21-3 *(cont'd)*

	Yes	No	Workpaper Reference

- Suspense report — production orders ☐ ☐ ....
- Overhead account analysis ☐ ☐ ....
- Credit balance report ☐ ☐ ....

g. Are standard costs or other methods used to control actual expenditures and usage of resources? ☐ ☐ ....

h. Are procedures in effect for regularly scheduled analysis of variances from budget and or standard amounts? ☐ ☐ ....

i. Are subsidiary accounts reconciled to the general ledger control accounts on a regularly scheduled basis? ☐ ☐ ....

j. Are reconciliations performed between:
- Labor and payroll ☐ ☐ ....
- Material transactions and inventory ☐ ☐ ....

k. Are comparisons made between applied and actual overhead charged? ☐ ☐ ....

10. Information Systems:

    a. Are instructions governing submitting, processing, correcting, resubmitting, and reporting contained in a written user's manual? ☐ ☐ ....

    b. Is system and programming logic documented in the form of flow charts, narratives, etc.? ☐ ☐ ....

    c. Are changes to the system governed by established program change control procedures that require user review and approval? ☐ ☐ ....

    d. Was the system developed pursuant to established system development standards? ☐ ☐ ....

    e. Does the system employ sophisticated complex processing methodologies (i.e., data bases, data base management systems, on-line interactive processing, remote job entry, etc.)? ☐ ☐ ....
    Note: If responses to the foregoing questions indicate a complex system likely to require the evaluation of a specialist, the balance of this questionnaire should not be completed. Instead, the assistance of an I/S audit senior should be obtained. If the responses indicate a batch-oriented system developed in accordance with applicable standards, well-documented and for which a user's manual exists, the balance of this questionnaire may be completed.

    f. If input is by means of remote job entry, are all transactions required to be listed or approved prior to submission and retained for future follow-up? ☐ ☐ ....

COST ACCOUNTING SYSTEMS 21-21

	Yes	No	Workpaper Reference
g. If input is by means of output (disk or tape) from another application (e.g., payroll), is there a method to assure all transactions are processed?	☐	☐	....
h. If the cost accounting department is responsible for data conversion, do procedures require data verification and a means of cancelling source documents to prevent re-entry?	☐	☐	....
i. Do procedures fix responsibility for and specify methods for timely error detection and correction?	☐	☐	....
j. Do programs for processing cost data contain edit routines, limit checks, run-to-run balancing routines, and other techniques to detect errors and omissions?	☐	☐	....
k. Do controls exist to assure that cost system reports and files are effectively safeguarded from unauthorized access and update?	☐	☐	....
l. Do back-up and recovery procedures exist to enable the I/S department to overcome data losses as a result of processing interruptions?	☐	☐	....
m. Are I/S files and records containing cost data afforded adequate protection from damage or loss due to natural or human acts?	☐	☐	....

are designed, such as procuring, receiving, warehousing, and manufacturing. These functions are covered in Chapter 34.

SAMPLE AUDIT PROGRAM

The audit program in Figure 21-4 is designed primarily for the audit of a job cost system of a manufacturing company. The program is integrated with the questionnaire, also illustrated in this chapter, to the extent applicable.

SPECIMEN REPORT

The report in Figure 21-5 is illustrative of typical findings that might be reported as a result of an audit of a manufacturing job cost accounting system.

(continued on page 21-28)

FIG. 21-4

Cost System Review Audit Program

	Workpaper Reference	Done by
1. General:		
☐ Obtain an understanding of the cost system and related procedures. Document with flow charts and/or narratives.	....	....
☐ Determine the existence of system documentation and evaluate adequacy of such documentation.	....	....
☐ Obtain organization charts for cost system related personnel	....	....
☐ Discuss with the management the nature of the operations of the profit center and note any unusual characteristics that may impact the evaluation of controls.	....	....
☐ Evaluate internal controls over cost system. Complete the attached internal control questionnaire in conjunction with the evaluation.	....	....
☐ Discuss with management and other appropriate persons the extent of any (1) reviews in this area by external auditors and (2) reviews of related areas by both external and internal auditors.	....	....
2. Authorization:		
☐ Review documentation indicating authority for:		
■ Changing cost system procedures	....	....
■ Changing cost standards	....	....
■ Preparing and approving entries	....	....
■ Preparing and approving adjusting and correcting entries	....	....
■ Preparing entries to record reserves and write-offs	....	....
■ Revising forms and report formats	....	....
☐ Review all changes in the above items for the year to date and note evidence of proper review approval.	....	....
☐ Read all applicable functional outlines and comment as to compliance with established requirements for managing the cost accounting function.	....	....
3. Processing and Recording:		
☐ Obtain and review for completeness documentation (procedural manual, flow charts, instructions) depicting the structure and transaction flow of the cost system.	....	....
☐ Perform the following with respect to the labor component:		
■ Select a random statistical sample of labor transactions processed by the system during the period and check evidence indicating compliance with the following attributes:	....	....

	Workpaper Reference	Done by
a. Use of time card as source document	....	....
b. Propriety of cost code	....	....
c. Evidence of timekeeper audit	....	....
d. Proper approval	....	....
e. Use of proper standard rate (if applicable)	....	....
f. Recording in proper period	....	....

☐ Perform the following with respect to the material component:
- Select a random statistical sampling of material transactions processed by the system during the period and check for evidence of: ....
  - a. Material transaction source document (issue/turn-in slip) ....
  - b. Proper approval ....
  - c. Proper cost coding ....
  - d. Proper standard, if applicable ....
  - e. Recording in proper period ....

☐ Perform the following with respect to overhead transactions:
- Trace overhead rates used in applying burden to evidence of approval. ....
- Review development of overhead rates for each overhead pool for compliance with established procedures. ....
- Test composition of overhead pools for compliance with established procedures. ....

☐ On a judgmental basis, review documentation evidencing periodic accumulation and summarization of cost data for: ....
- Use of consistent format ....
- Evidence of review ....
- Completeness and accuracy ....

Note: Documentation of this type usually takes the form of cost distribution spread sheets or work sheets and may be prepared separately for each type of cost component.

☐ On a judgmental basis, trace postings from general ledger control accounts to journal entries and to supporting distribution schedules, if applicable, or to other support. ....

☐ On a judgmental basis, trace postings from detail cost ledgers to source entries noting: ....
- Propriety of coding ....
- Compliance with summarization procedures ....
- Recording in proper period ....

(continued)

FIG. 21-4 *(cont'd)*

	Yes	No	Workpaper Reference

☐ Obtain a listing of cost transfers (between jobs) and on a judgmental basis, select a sample and perform the following detail tests:
- Review evidence of proper authorization. ....
- Test propriety of documentation. ....
- Trace posting to cost ledger. ....

4. Accessibility:

☐ Review functional outlines, job descriptions, and organization charts and observe cost accounting activities actually performed to ascertain compliance with established requirements for segregation of duties. ....

☐ Observe actual methods employed in the cost accounting section to protect cost records and data from unauthorized access. State physical protective measures observed. ....

☐ Inquire as to procedures and plans established to recover from loss or destruction of critical data. ....

☐ Inquire and, if available, examine evidence of any actual experiences with respect to loss or destruction. ....

5. Accountability:

☐ Obtain a listing of all required reports generated by the system and, on a judgmental basis, test for compliance by inspecting files of such reports to determine their existence and conformity with requirements for contents. Of particular interest are the following:
- Labor distribution reports ....
- Job cost summaries ....
- Production efficiency reports ....
- Completed jobs variance reports ....
- Aged open job reports ....

☐ Confirm on a judgmental basis with selected users of cost system reports that such reports are received timely, and that the data is accurate and complete to the best of their knowledge. ....

☐ On a judgmental basis, examine evidence of reconciliation of general ledger control entries with:
- Labor distribution report balances ....
- Material charges report balances ....
- Expense ledger balances (if applicable) ....

☐ On a judgmental basis, review evidence of analyses of variance reports and, where applicable, evidence of responsive actions to conditions detected (e.g., change in standards, change in production methods). ....

COST ACCOUNTING SYSTEMS 21-25

	Workpaper Reference	Done by
☐ On a judgmental basis, review comparisons between actual and applied overhead and inspect evidence of responsive actions such as overhead account analyses, overhead rate studies based on various assumptions, and changes to rates.	....	....
6. Electronic Data Processing:		
☐ Inspect system documentation and user manual for completeness, compliance with established requirements for such documentation, and currency.	....	....
☐ Review documentation for all significant changes to the cost system occurring during the year for evidence of:		
■ Proper authorization	....	....
■ Testing	....	....
■ User sign-off	....	....
☐ Consider using a generalized or specialized audit software package to simulate the processing of key program steps such as:	....	....
■ Application of overhead rates	....	....
■ Updating of standard costs of all parts and assemblies affected by changed standards	....	....
■ Cost report generation	....	....
☐ Consider developing or using a test deck to test the effectiveness of programmed edit checks, limit tests, and balancing routines.	....	....
☐ Inspect techniques actually employed to protect cost files and records.	....	....
☐ Examine evidence of backup and recovery compliance.	....	....

FIG. 21-5

Report on Audit of Manufacturing Job Cost Accounting System

TO: D.H. Fredericks
FROM: R.J. Sanchez
SUBJECT: Review of Cost System — Nevada Engine Division (NED)

We have performed a review of the control techniques used to classify and accumulate costs associated with final cost objectives at NED. The purpose of this review was to determine the sufficiency with which such controls reasonably assure that cost accumulation systems and data are properly authorized; costs are accurately accumulated and reported in accordance with applicable company policy and generally accepted principles of accounting; and that access to cost

(continued)

FIG. 21-5 *(cont'd)*

reports is appropriately restricted. The scope of our examination included (1) obtaining an understanding of the procedures in use for identifying and aggregating costs with final cost objectives; (2) completing an internal control questionnaire designed to evaluate cost systems; (3) detailed testing of cost accumulation techniques applicable to labor, material, and overhead; and (4) other tests considered necessary in the circumstances.

Our examination disclosed the following matters we believe should be brought to the attention of management:

- Analyses are not being done of the payroll clearing account and the fringe benefit allocation base.
- Material and overhead cost processes and procedures require additional documentation.
- Exceptions disclosed during floor checks raised questions as to the reliability of time reporting.
- Fabricated part material transfers are not processed on required forms and transactions are not batch balanced.

Subject to the correction of the foregoing matters, it is our opinion that internal controls are sufficient to provide reasonable assurance that cost transactions are executed in accordance with management's general or specific authorization, that they are accumulated and recorded accurately, and that access to cost records is appropriately restricted.

These matters are more fully described in the balance of this report. A written reply to this report from the action party is requested within thirty days.

1. Analyses are not being done of the payroll clearing account and the fringe benefit allocation base.

We noted that the payroll clearing accounts were not being analyzed on a monthly basis. Payroll costs are charged to the clearing accounts as incurred and are then distributed from the clearing accounts to the respective expense accounts via JV-30. Because of ongoing adjustment to the payroll accounts and because payroll costs are charged to the clearing accounts on an actual basis and distributed on an average cost (by account) basis, there is always a residual balance in the accounts. At the time of our review, the net balance of the two accounts was $86,441, which is immaterial to total annual payroll, as are normal adjustments and timing differences. However, to maintain proper control over the payroll system and to ensure accurate charging of costs, the clearing accounts should be analyzed monthly.

RECOMMENDATION NO. 1

Analyze payroll clearing accounts on a monthly basis as required by procedures.

2. Material and overhead cost processes and procedures require additional documentation.

The material accounting section must be updated to reflect the new costs system and expanded to include flow charts and/or narratives explaining the overall flow of material charges through the costs system. Also, a new section should be added to the Internal Control Manual that documents the burden accumulation and allocation process. Further, for both material and burden processing, key control points should be identified, such as reconciliations and approvals.

COST ACCOUNTING SYSTEMS

Documentation of the above procedures would ensure uniformity in costs system procedures and would enhance communication of the procedures to new employees and other interested parties.

RECOMMENDATION NO. 2

Update the Internal Control Manual to reflect the current flow of material charges through the cost system and document the accumulation, allocation, and flow of burden in the cost system.

3. Exceptions reported by the internal auditor raise questions as to the reliability of time reporting.

A review of the floor checks performed during the year revealed exceptions of time reporting on time cards. To determine the present status of time reporting, we performed a floor check and noted similar types of errors—namely, information missing or incomplete, or time cards not filled out on a daily basis. These matters, while not conforming to policy, do not represent areas where a misallocation of time results. Our review of the subsequent recording of the time cards reviewed during our floor check revealed that, except in one isolated instance, all were recorded to the appropriate cost objective. The exception we noted involved the recording of a direct supervisor's time to direct projects when in fact he was absent from work. The proper way to charge it is to personal business.

The low rate of errors in the sample test performed in our review does not necessarily mean that errors are not present. Accurate accumulation of time charges is a significant control objective. We believe that this audit and the floor checks raise questions as to the reliability of time reports. Management should take steps to reinforce its techniques for accumulating accurate time charges. These may include issuing instructions or reminders of proper approvals; periodic floor checks by managers and timekeepers; or enforcing discipline by returning any incomplete time cards to the originating department.

In addition, at the time this floor check was performed, none of the supervisors questioned had a copy of the timekeeping manual. This manual was last updated in July 19XX. Since that date new union contracts, changes in accounting procedures, and elimination of functions have occurred. For example, Appendix 4 mentions the timekeeping audit and follow-up function. A discussion with the Payroll Manager disclosed that the timekeeping audit and follow-up position was eliminated due to a budgetary reduction.

RECOMMENDATION NO. 3

Update the Timekeeping Manual and, to re-enforce existing procedures for the accurate recording of time, have managers review the instructions with employees, or employ other techniques as appropriate.

4. Fabricated part material transfers are not processed on required forms, and transactions are not batch balanced.

During our review, we noted material transfers of fabricated parts are not processed in accordance with Division Standard Procedure (DSP) No. 334, "Material Transfer." Since this procedure was issued, some forms and practices have changed. The following information is not provided for current fabricated part material transfers processed by inventory control:

(continued)

FIG. 21-5 *(cont'd)*

- Approval signature of manager of inventory control (or his designee)
- Signature of person preparing the material transfer
- Requirement authority
- Number of assembly, or part number, that requires the item
- Part description
- Date document is prepared

As a result, no evidence of the document's origination or approval is available when the material transfer is received in Contract Accounting.

Further, DSP No. 334 requires submitting a copy of the material transfer to Contract Accounting and retaining a copy for follow up. By not using the prescribed prenumbered form which has multiple parts, no record is presently kept in Inventory Control of the transfer sent to Contract Accounting. Using unnumbered forms does not enable batch balancing and control over such documents sent outside the Inventory Control and sent to Contract Accounting. There is no evidence of approval and no assurance that Accounting receives all such forms. Transactions usually number fewer than 100 per month. The amount can range from small dollar items to high-priced fabricated parts. Under the circumstances, it is unlikely that all fabricated part transfers are recorded.

(*Note:* There are many other types of material transfers that appear to be processed as specified in procedures and that are batch balanced and controlled.)

RECOMMENDATION NO. 4

Update DSP No. 334, Material Transfers, to incorporate recent forms and procedures and define approval levels. Establish fabricated material part transfer confirmation procedures in the revised DSP.

SUGGESTED READING

Connor, Joseph E., and Burnell H. DeVos, Jr., eds. "Production Costs and Inventories," in *Guide to Accounting Controls*. Boston: Warren, Gorham & Lamont, 1979.

Willson, James D., and John B. Campbell. *Controllership: The Work of the Managerial Accountant*, Chapters 17–18. New York: John Wiley & Sons, 1981.

Wendell, Paul J., ed. *Corporate Controller's Manual*, Chapter 6. Boston: Warren, Gorham & Lamont, 1981.

PART VII
Ethical Business Conduct

CHAPTER **22**

Business Fraud and Business Ethics—A General Review

Introduction 2	Business Ethics and Internal Auditing 38
Fraud Defined 3	An Antifraud Checklist 40
Common Forms of Fraud 4	A Fraud Questionnaire 42
Circumstances That Encourage Fraud .. 5	Responsibility for Detecting Fraud 45
Indicia of Fraud 6	Independent Accountants 45
Standards for the Deterrence, Detection, Investigation, and Reporting of Fraud 11	Internal Auditors 47
	Government Auditors 49
	Management Accountants 51
General Preventive Measures 19	Special Fraud Investigations 54
Management Override 21	Definition 54
Consider Motivating Factors 24	Nature of the Work 55
Areas Vulnerable to Management Override 24	Standards and Procedures Employed .. 55
	Reporting 56
	Whistle-blowing 56
	SIAS No. 3 57
The Role of Business Ethics 25	
An Initial Perspective 25	Coordination With the Legal Department 58
Factors That Influence Business Ethics 27	
	Use of Informants 58
Misconduct—Why It Occurs 30	
The Risks 31	Summary 59
Techniques for Maintaining Effective Business Ethics 31	Suggested Reading 59

Fig. 22-1	Warning Signals of Possible Management Fraud	7
Fig. 22-2	The Red Flags of Possible Fraudulent Activity	9
Fig. 22-3	SIAS No. 3: Deterrence, Detection, Investigation, and Reporting of Fraud	13
Fig. 22-4	Corporate Policy Directive on Internal Controls—Responsibilities Section ...	22
Fig. 22-5	Business Ethics—A Hypothetical Situation	28
Fig. 22-6	Martin-Marrietta Corporation Code of Ethics and Standards of Conduct	33
Fig. 22-7	Defense Industry Initiatives Questionnaire and Illustrative Procedures	35
Fig. 22-8	Report of Peat Marwick Mitchell & Co.—Concluding Remarks	39

INTRODUCTION

Unethical or illegal behavior by a limited number of people in business or government is nothing new. But in the past decade, the business community has become increasingly concerned about an apparent growth in business fraud. Headlines in business magazines and newspapers about white-collar crime seem to occur with greater frequency: "White Collar Crime: The Nation's Largest Growth Industry"; "Cooking the Books—A Popular Pastime"; "Computer Crime—The Spreading Danger to Business." Not only does there seem to be a greater incidence of fraud, but there may be a more significant amount of money involved.

One source reports that the price tag for reported white-collar crime was $50 billion in 1979, with an estimate that the amount by 1984 "will be $200 billion or more."[1]

The losses resulting from business crime have caused business management, government agencies, and professional accounting associations, such as the AICPA, the IIA, and the NAA, to rethink the role of auditors, management accountants, and of management itself, in dealing with the problem. Business ethics and the entire subject of corporate governance are receiving increased attention because, among other reasons, the presence of questionable ethics increases the possibility of fraud. For a long time, the principal business objective of the private enterprise system has been to maximize the return to shareholders through economically and efficiently satisfying the customers' needs or desires. This pursuit of profit for most businesses, however, generally has occurred within a framework of enlightened self-interest and social responsibility. The internal auditor should become more aware of the means of detecting and deterring business fraud, thereby assisting business in better meeting its social responsibility.

The purpose of this chapter is to provide a broad review of fraud and business ethics: types of fraud; conditions that encourage fraud; means of detecting and minimizing fraud; the role of business ethics and its relation to fraud; and the auditors' responsibility for detecting, deterring, and reporting fraud.

FRAUD DEFINED

"Fraud" has been used rather synonymously with such related terms as "swindle," "irregularities," "defalcation," and "embezzlement." Where extreme preciseness is needed, perhaps a legal source should be used. But

---

[1] Steven R. Schutt, "White Collar Crime: The Nation's Largest Growth Industry," *Financial Executive*, Feb. 1981, p. 17.

as an audit background, some general definitions are as follows: *Webster's Ninth New Collegiate Dictionary* defines fraud as "deceit, trickery, intentional perversion of truth in order to induce another to part with something of value or to surrender a legal right." This same source defines "defalcation" as "the act or an instance of embezzling," or "embezzle" as "to appropriate fraudulently to one's own use."

In reviewing accounting or auditing literature, the authors have found a clearly stated term as follows: "Fraud may be defined as an intentional deception, misappropriation of a company's assets or the manipulation of its financial data to the advantage of the perpetrator."[2] Another sort of definition is that of the IIA, contained in SIAS No. 3, "Standards for the Deterrence, Detection, Investigation, and Reporting of Fraud" (see Figure 22-3): "Fraud encompasses an array of irregularities and illegal acts characterized by intentional deception." Some other accounting or auditing publications sometimes distinguish types of fraud. Thus, "management fraud," as implicitly defined by the Auditing Standards Executive Committee of the AICPA, is described in this way:[3]

> The term *irregularities* refers to intentional distortions of financial statements, such as deliberate misrepresentations by management, sometimes referred to as management fraud, or misappropriations of assets, sometimes referred to as defalcations. Irregularities in financial statements may result from the misrepresentation or omission of the effects of events or transactions; manipulation, falsification, or alteration of records or documents; omission of significant information from records or documents; recording of transactions without substance; intentional misapplication of accounting principles; or misappropriation of assets for the benefit of management, employees, or third parties. Such acts may be accompanied by the use of false or misleading records or documents and may involve one or more individuals among management, employees, or third parties.

Another auditing source distinguishes between nonmanagement (or employee) fraud and management fraud in these words:[4]

> Nonmanagement fraud consists of dishonest actions that occur within a company despite management's efforts to prevent such actions.

---

[2] Marvin M. Levy, "Financial Fraud: Schemes and Indicia," *Journal of Accountancy*, Aug. 1985, p. 78.

[3] Statement on Auditing Standards No. 16, "The Independent Auditor's Responsibility for the Detection of Errors or Irregularities" (New York: American Institute of Certified Public Accountants, 1977), ¶ 3.

[4] Walter B. Meigs, E. John Larsen, and Robert F. Meigs, *Principles of Auditing*, 6th ed. (Homewood, Ill.: Richard D. Irwin, 1977), p. 8.

Management fraud occurs only when the top executives of a company deliberately deceive stockholders, creditors, and independent auditors. The purpose of management fraud is generally to issue misleading financial statements which exaggerate corporate earnings and financial strength. Such overstatements . . . may enable the management . . . to obtain increased salaries and bonuses. . . . The theft of assets may also be involved.

Finally, computer fraud is defined in this manner by Professor Brandt Allen:[5] "Computer fraud is—any defalcation or embezzlement accomplished by tampering with computer programs, data files, operations, equipment or media and resulting in losses sustained by the organization whose computer system was manipulated."

From these definitions, it is evident that fraud is not confined to those who have access to cash or cash equivalents. In some of the biggest embezzlements, the perpetrator had no access to cash (e.g., in computer frauds). In summary, fraud includes the intentional misrepresentation of facts undertaken to mislead auditors or users of financial statements, the misuse or misappropriation of assets, and other similar irregularities.

COMMON FORMS OF FRAUD

Fraud is a complex subject, and may involve different business groups or vehicles. Or, it may emphasize particular functions. For ease of discussion, and giving weight to the classifications in current literature, we will review these categories:

- Management fraud
- Employee fraud
- Computer fraud
- Financial reporting fraud
- Procurement fraud

In this general chapter, the first two types of fraud are reviewed in detail, but some of the conditions or causes will relate also to *all* types of fraud. The remaining three kinds of fraud and their special aspects are discussed in separate chapters.

CIRCUMSTANCES THAT ENCOURAGE FRAUD

Some awareness of the causes of fraud, or circumstances that may encourage it, may be of assistance to the internal auditor. There is no way to guarantee

---

[5] Brandt Allen, "The Biggest Computer Frauds: Lessons for CPS's," *Journal of Accountancy*, 143 No. 5, May 1977, p. 52.

BUSINESS ETHICS AND FRAUD

the absence of fraud, however defined, in most large U.S. companies, but the background on causes may provide new indicia that the auditor should watch for or at least be sensitive to.

From the experience of the authors, as well as from the perusal of current literature, there is some logic in concluding that fraud results from a combination of forces or pressures on the individual officer or employee concomitant with an environment that permits the act.

Some elaborations on circumstances that might contribute to irregularities include:

1. Weak internal control environment
   - Management does not emphasize the role of strong internal controls.
   - Management does not prosecute or punish identified embezzlers.
   - Management does not have a clear position about conflicts of interest.
   - Highly placed executives are less than prudent or restrained on expenditures for travel and entertainment, furnishings of offices, gifts to visitors and directors, etc.
   - Internal auditing does not have authority to investigate certain executive activities involving heavy "personal" expenditures.
   - Accounting policies and procedures are on the lax or loose side.
2. Financial pressures on individuals
   - Existence of heavy personal indebtedness, for whatever reason.
   - High inflation rates with absence of corresponding pay adjustments.
   - Family- or other-induced extravagant means of living.
   - Socially unacceptable behavioral excesses for business persons (e.g., gambling, drinking, extramarital affairs, and drugs).
3. Nonfinancial pressures (which induce management fraud)
   - A demanding board of directors or executive management that may have set unreasonable profit goals for divisions or subsidiaries.
   - Self-proclaimed goals set by the chief executive officer (CEO) that he feels must be met (e.g., earnings per share (EPS) and growth).
   - Rapidly declining sales or earnings, combined with heavy stock interests in a public corporation.
4. Other contributory conditions
   - Inadequate hiring practices—(e.g., lack of reference checks).
   - Undesirable personality traits that undermine personal integrity.
   - Possible connections with organized crime.

INDICIA OF FRAUD

An understanding of some of the circumstances that encourage fraud is helpful in being sensitive to fraud potential. But fraud is indeed difficult to detect, whether in connection with an examination under generally accepted accounting standards, or a special fraud investigation (discussed later). For example, the explanation of the nature of a particular transaction (e.g., need for a consultant) may be false, but nevertheless may sound quite reasonable. Hence, very often, an internal auditor must be suspicious about questionable circumstances of transactions, and must be alert for seemingly small telltale signs of fraud.

The absence of any indicia of fraud does not mean that no fraud exists; for most fraud goes undetected. On the other hand, the more that indicia of fraud do exist, the more alert the auditor should be, and perhaps the deeper the examination that must be made.

But what are some indicia of fraud? The AICPA has prepared a list of warning signals of possible *management* fraud, and these are presented in Figure 22-1.[6] Another excellent checklist of red flags of possible fraudulent activity by employees (management or otherwise) is provided in Figure 22-2.[7]

Aside from the indicators of fraud provided in the two figures, some new or related clues are:

- Failure or refusal to use serially numbered documents
- An excessive number of checking accounts without an apparent good business purpose—perhaps evidence of provision for a check-kiting scheme
- Excessive cash transactions
- Frequent and excessive use of exchange items, such as money orders and traveler's checks—often evidence of funding off-book operations or bank accounts
- Photocopies of invoices in file—perhaps evidence that the original was "doctored" and the copy does not show the change
- Excessive company checks bearing second endorsements—sometimes evidence of payroll fraud or purchase of stolen goods
- Assets sold for less than the real economic worth
- Excessive material charge-offs—evidence of theft or conversion
- High employee turnover rates in the accounting operation—where management might terminate employees before they become knowledgeable of the fraudulent system or where, having discovered fraud, the employee resigns

As a sort of summary, when considering the possibility of fraud, it is

---

[6] *The CPA Letter*, No. 5 (New York: American Institute of Certified Public Accountants, Mar. 12, 1979), p. 4. Copyright © 1979 by the American Institute of Certified Public Accountants, Inc. Reprinted with permission.

[7] Marshall B. Romney, W. Steve Albrecht, and David J. Cherrington, "Red-Flagging the White Collar Criminal," *Management Accounting*, Mar. 1980, p. 53. Copyright © 1980 by the National Association of Accountants. All rights reserved. Reprinted with permission.

BUSINESS ETHICS AND FRAUD

FIG. 22-1
Warning Signals of Possible Management Fraud

1. Highly domineering senior management and one or more of the following, or similar, conditions are present:
   - An ineffective board of directors and/or audit committee
   - Indications of management override of significant internal accounting controls
   - Compensation or significant stock options tied to reported performance or to a specific transaction over which senior management has actual or implied control
   - Indications of personal financial difficulties of senior management
   - Proxy contests involving control of the company or senior management's continuance, compensation, or status

2. Deterioration of quality of earnings evidenced by:
   - Decline in the volume or quality of sales (e.g., increased credit risk or sales at or below cost)
   - Significant changes in business practices
   - Excessive interest by senior management in the earnings per share effect of accounting alternatives

3. Business conditions that may create unusual pressures:
   - Inadequate working capital
   - LIttle flexibility in debt restrictions such as working capital ratios and limitations on additional borrowings
   - Rapid expansion of a product or business line markedly in excess of industry averages
   - A major investment of the company's resources in an industry noted for rapid change, such as a high technology industry

4. A complex corporate structure where the complexity does not appear to be warranted by the company's operations or size.

5. Widely dispersed business locations accompanied by highly decentralized management with inadequate responsibility reporting system.

6. Understaffing, which appears to require certain employees to work unusual hours, forgo vacations, and/or put in substantial overtime.

7. High turnover rate in key financial positions such as treasurer or controller.

8. Frequent change of auditors or legal counsel.

9. Known material weaknesses in internal control that could practically be corrected but remain uncorrected, such as:
   - Inadequately controlled access to computer equipment or electronic data entry devices
   - Incompatible duties that remain combined

10. Material transactions with related parties or transactions that may involve conflicts of interest.

(continued)

FIG. 22-1 *(cont'd)*

---

11. Premature announcements of operating results or future (positive) expectations.

12. Analytical review procedures disclosing significant fluctuations that cannot be reasonably explained, for example:
    - Material account balances
    - Financial or operational interrelationships
    - Physical inventory variances
    - Inventory turnover rates

13. Large or unusual transactions, particularly at year-end, with material effect on earnings.

14. Unusually large payments for services provided in the ordinary course of business by lawyers, consultants, agents, and others (including employees).

15. Difficulty in obtaining audit evidence with respect to:
    - Unusual or unexplained entries
    - Incomplete or missing documentation and/or authorization
    - Alterations in documentation or accounts

16. Unforeseen problems that are encountered in the performance of an examination of financial statements, for instance:
    - Client pressures to complete audit in an unusually short time or under difficult conditions
    - Sudden delays
    - Evasive or unreasonable responses of management to audit inquiries

---

helpful for the auditor to keep in mind some of the areas prone to fraudulent practices, and some of the means:

- Petty cash—use of false or inadequate documentation for disbursements
- Accounts payable—use of fictitious companies and dummy invoices; "adjustment" of invoices from existing suppliers
- Payroll—fictitious employees
- Kickbacks—for services or materials
- Cash transactions—such as alleged purchase of inventory items for cash rather than check
- Lopping—theft from one customer account receivable "covered up" by applying later receipts from another customer

FIG. 22-2
The Red Flags of Possible Fraudulent Activity

1. **Opportunity Red Flags:**
   - ☐ Employees against the company:
     - Familiarity with operations (including cover-up capabilities) and in a position of trust
     - Close association with suppliers and other key people
     - A firm that does not inform employees about rules or of the action taken to combat fraud
     - Rapid turnover (quit or fired) of key employees
     - No mandatory vacations, periodic rotations, or transfers of key employees
     - Inadequate personnel-screening policies when hiring new employees to fill positions of trust
     - An absence of explicit and uniform personnel policies
     - No maintenance of accurate personnel records of dishonest acts or disciplinary actions
     - Executive disclosures and examinations not required
     - A dishonest or overly dominant management
     - Operating on a crisis basis
     - No attention paid to details
     - Unrealistic productivity measurements
     - Poor compensation practices
     - A lack of internal security
     - Inadequate training programs
   - ☐ Individuals on behalf of the company:
     - Related-party transactions
     - A complex business structure
     - No effective internal auditing staff
     - A highly computerized firm
     - A firm in atypical or "hot" industries
     - A firm that uses several different auditing firms or changes auditors often
     - A firm that is reluctant to give auditors needed data
     - A firm that uses several different legal firms or changes legal counsels often
     - A firm that uses an unusually large number of different banks, none of which can see the entire picture
     - Continuous problems with various regulatory agencies
     - Large year-end, and/or unusual, transaction
     - An inadequate internal control system — or nonenforcement of the existing internal controls
     - Unduly liberal accounting practices
     - Poor accounting records and inadequate staffing in the accounting department
     - A firm that inadequately discloses questionable or unusual accounting practices

(continued)

FIG. 22-2 *(cont'd)*

2. **Personal Characteristic Red Flags:**
   ☐ Warning signals should go off when employees evidence characteristics such as:
   - Rationalization of contradictory behavior
   - Lack of a strong code of personal ethics
   - A "wheeler-dealer" personality
   - Lack of stability
   - A strong desire to beat the system
   - A criminal or questionable background
   - A poor credit rating and financial status

3. **Situational Pressure Red Flags:**
   ☐ Employees against the company:
   - High personal debts or financial losses
   - Inadequate income for lifestyle
   - Extensive stock market or other speculation
   - Excessive gambling
   - Undue family, company, or community expectations
   - Excessive use of alcohol or drugs
   - Perceived inequities in the organization
   - Resentment of superiors and frustration with job
   - Peer group pressures
   - Undue desire for self-enrichment and personal gain

   ☐ Management on behalf of the company:
   - Unfavorable economic conditions within the industry
   - Insufficient working capital, high debt
   - Dependence on one or two products, customers, or transactions
   - Severe obsolescence
   - Extremely rapid expansion through new business or product lines
   - Reduced ability to acquire credit or restrictive loan agreements
   - Profit squeeze — costs and expenses rising higher and faster than sales and revenues
   - Difficulty in collecting receivables
   - Progressive deterioration in quality of earnings
   - Significant tax adjustments
   - Urgent need for favorable earnings to support high price of stock or to meet earnings forecast
   - Need to gloss over a temporarily bad situation in order to maintain management position and prestige
   - Significant litigation — especially between stockholders and management
   - Unmarketable collateral
   - Significant reduction in sales backlogs (indicates future sales decline)
   - Possibility of license being revoked or imperiled especially if such is necessary for the continuation of business
   - Suspension or delisting from a stock exchange
   - Pressure to merge
   - Sizable inventory increase without comparable sales increases

STANDARDS FOR THE DETERRENCE, DETECTION, INVESTIGATION, AND REPORTING OF FRAUD

The preceding review of conditions conducive to fraud, and indicia of fraud, have been provided to assist in the deterrence or prevention of fraud. The objective is to eliminate or reduce fraud, and suggested measures are discussed later in this chapter.

But before more fully discussing preventive measures and the responsibilities of auditors and accountants regarding business fraud, a review of the position of the IIA may be valuable. It will probably add significance to the discussion of preventive measures and the detection and prevention of management fraud that follows.

With the wide publicity given to recent major fraud cases, and the seeming increase in acts of fraud, it is understandable that the IIA is seeking to provide guidance on the subject. In June 1985, the IIA issued SIAS No. 3, "Deterrence, Detection, Investigation, and Reporting of Fraud."

As most readers know, an SIAS interprets the Standards for the Professional Practice of Internal Auditing and thus establishes guidelines for the internal auditors. It does not provide specific audit procedures for conducting audits.

A summary of the major points of the Statement follows.[8]

> **Deterrence of Fraud.** The internal auditors take the same basic position as the independent auditors: Deterrence of fraud is the responsibility of the company's board of directors and its management. The internal auditors, however, acknowledge a responsibility for examining and evaluating the adequacy and effectiveness of actions taken by management to fulfill its obligation.
>
> In this regard, the auditor should:
>
> - Identify significant exposures;
> - Test mechanisms established to deter fraud and assess the adequacy and effectiveness of such mechanisms; and
> - Recommend the establishment of controls to help deter fraud.
>
> **Detection of Fraud.** The statement provides the following guidance for detecting fraud:
>
> ☐ Internal auditors should maintain sufficient knowledge of fraud patterns to enable them to be reasonably effective in identifying opportunities for potential perpetrators to commit fraud. They should be alert to such opportunities and evidence that indicates fraud might have been committed.
>
> ☐ If significant control weaknesses are detected, internal auditors should

---

[8] From *Internal Auditing Alert*, Nov. 1984, pp. 1–2.

expand their tests and look for other symptoms (transactions, situations, conditions, and danger signals) that could be key indicators of fraud. The presence of more than one indicator at any one time usually compounds their weight (i.e., the presence of any two together is usually more indicative of fraud than the weight of the two occurring separately).

☐ Internal auditors should pursue evidence that indicates fraud might have been committed by performing extended audit procedures to obtain additional evidence to decide whether (1) the initial evidence of suspected fraud was misleading; (2) to recommend an investigation; or (3) any further action appears necessary.

Undertaking detective audit procedures in the pursuit of conjecture serves neither the company's objectives nor the auditor's responsibilities. Plausible indicators of fraud, however, should always be pursued.

☐ Internal auditors cannot be expected to have knowledge equivalent to a person whose sole responsibility is detecting fraud and other irregularities. Even when audit procedures are carried out with due professional care, there can be no guarantee that the existence of fraud will be detected.

Investigation of Fraud. In deciding to investigate a possible fraud, the internal auditor should consider the following guidance:

☐ Once a determination is made that there is sufficient evidence of the commission of a fraud to recommend an investigation, the internal auditor should notify the appropriate authorities within the organization. The auditor should, however, first make a concerted effort to determine the probable level of complicity in the fraud within the organization. This can be critical to ensuring that the auditor's reporting of the situation is above the level of probable complicity.

☐ When a decision is made that internal auditing should investigate a possible fraud, the internal audit should carry out all the steps and procedures necessary to determine the specifics and to acquire sufficient competent evidential matter on the who, what, when, where, how, and why of the fraud.

☐ Internal auditing should take steps to ensure that the investigation is conducted by individuals having the appropriate type and level of technical expertise. This might require using the work of a specialist.

This section of the statement also includes a number of specific suggestions to aid the auditor in assigning personnel to a fraud investigation, gathering evidence, preparing working papers, and interrogating possible suspects.

Reporting of Fraud. While SIAS No. 2 "Communicating Results," is applicable to internal audit reports issued as a result of fraud investigations, this statement provides guidance that is particularly pertinent to reports on fraud.

☐ A formal report should be issued at the end of the investigation. The report should be distributed to the appropriate levels within the company to ensure

(continued on page 22-18)

FIG. 22-3

SIAS No. 3: Deterrence, Detection, Investigation, and Reporting of Fraud

Statements on Internal Auditing Standards are issued by the Professional Standards and Responsibilities Committee, the senior technical committee designated by The Institute of Internal Auditors to issue pronouncements on auditing matters. These statements are authoritative interpretations of the Standards for the Professional Practice of Internal Auditing.

Organizations, internal auditing departments, directors of internal auditing, and internal auditors should strive to comply with the Standards. The implementation of the Standards and these related statements will be governed by the environment in which the internal audit department carries out its assigned responsibilities. The adoption and implementation of the Standards and related statements will assist internal auditing professionals in accomplishing their responsibilities.

FOREWORD

The Institute of Internal Auditors issued the *Standards* in 1978 "to serve the entire profession in all types of business, in various levels of government, and in all other organizations where internal auditors are found . . . to represent the practice of internal auditing as it should be. . . ."

The *Standards* has been widely accepted and remains current despite continuous changes in business, society, and the profession of internal auditing. Promoted widely in management texts and used extensively in professional and technical symposia, such increasing acceptance and use demonstrate the credibility of the principles established by the *Standards*.

Fraud is a significant and sensitive management concern. This concern has grown in recent years owing to a substantial increase in the number and the size of the frauds disclosed. The tremendous expansion in the use of computers and the size of and publicity accorded computer-related frauds intensify this concern.

The internal auditor's responsibilities for deterring, detecting, investigating, and reporting of fraud have been a matter of much debate and controversy. Some of the controversy can be attributed to the differences in internal auditing's charter from country to country and from organization to organization. Another cause of the controversy may be unrealistic expectations of the internal auditor's ability to deter and detect fraud.

While several standards and guidelines directly or indirectly address the issue of internal auditors' responsibilities in cases of fraud, the following directly address these responsibilities:

SUMMARY

This statement interprets the *Standards* and establishes guidelines for internal auditors regarding their responsibility for deterring, detecting, investigating, and reporting of fraud. It does not provide guidance on specific audit procedures used in performing audits; rather, it establishes guidelines by which internal auditors conform their activities with the stated concepts of due professional care. Major conclusions of this statement are:

(continued)

FIG. 22-3 *(cont'd)*

Deterrence of Fraud

This is the responsibility of management. Internal auditors are responsible for examining and evaluating the adequacy and the effectiveness of actions taken by management to fulfill this obligation.

Detection of Fraud

Internal auditors should have sufficient knowledge of fraud to be able to identify indicators that fraud might have been committed.

If significant control weaknesses are detected, additional tests conducted by internal auditors should include tests directed toward identification of other indicators of fraud.

Internal auditors are not expected to have knowledge equivalent to that of a person whose primary responsibility is to detect and investigate fraud. Also, audit procedures alone, even when carried out with due professional care, do not guarantee that fraud will be detected.

Investigation of Fraud

Fraud investigations may be conducted by or involve participation of internal auditors, lawyers, investigators, security personnel, and other specialists from inside or outside the organization.

Internal auditing should assess the facts known relative to all fraud investigations in order to:

- Determine if controls need to be implemented or strengthened.
- Design audit tests to help disclose the existence of similar frauds in the future.
- Help meet the internal auditor's responsibility to maintain sufficient knowledge of fraud.

Reporting of Fraud

A written report should be issued at the conclusion of the investigation phase. It should include all findings, conclusions, recommendations and corrective action taken.

STANDARD 280	**DUE PROFESSIONAL CARE**
	Internal auditors should exercise due professional care in performing internal audits.
280.01	In exercising due professional care, internal auditors should be alert to the possibility of wrongdoing, errors and omissions, inefficiency, waste, ineffectiveness, and conflicts of interest. They should also be alert to those conditions and activities where irregularities are most likely to occur.
280.02	The possibility of material irregularities or noncompliance should be considered whenever the internal auditor undertakes an internal auditing assignment.
280.03	When an internal auditor suspects wrongdoing, the appropriate authorities within the organization should be informed. The internal auditor may recommend whatever investigation is considered necessary in the circumstances.

Thereafter, the auditor should follow up to see that the internal auditing department's responsibilities have been met.

STANDARD 300   **SCOPE OF WORK**

The scope of the internal audit should encompass the examination and the evaluation of the adequacy and the effectiveness of the organization's system of internal control and the quality of performance in carrying out assigned responsibilities.

330.01   Internal auditors should review the means used to safeguard assets from various types of losses such as those resulting from theft, fire, improper or illegal activities, and exposure to the elements.

CHARACTERISTICS OF FRAUD

1. Fraud encompasses an array of irregularities and illegal acts characterized by intentional deception. It can be perpetrated for the benefit of or to the detriment of the organization and by persons outside as well as inside the organization.

2. Fraud designed to benefit the organization generally produces such benefit by exploiting an unfair or dishonest advantage that also may deceive an outside party. Perpetrators of such frauds usually benefit indirectly, since personal benefit usually accrues when the organization is aided by the act. Some examples are:
   a. Sale or assignment of fictitious or misrepresented assets.
   b. Improper payments such as illegal political contributions, bribes, kickbacks, and payoffs to government officials, intermediaries of government officials, customers, or suppliers.
   c. Intentional, improper representation or valuation of transactions, assets, liabilities or income.
   d. Intentional, improper transfer pricing (e.g., valuation of goods exchanged between related entities). By purposely structuring pricing techniques improperly, management can improve the operating results of an organization involved in the transaction to the detriment of the other organization.
   e. Intentional, improper related party transactions in which one party receives some benefit not obtainable in an arm's-length transaction.
   f. Intentional failure to record or disclose significant information to improve the financial picture of the organization to outside parties.
   g. Prohibited business activities such as those which violate government standards, rules, regulations or contracts.
   h. Tax fraud.

3. Fraud perpetrated to the detriment of the organization generally is for the direct or indirect benefit of an employee, outside individual, or another firm. Some examples are:
   a. Acceptance of bribes or kickbacks.
   b. Diversion to an employee or outsider of a potentially profitable transaction that would normally generate profits for the organization.

(continued)

FIG. 22-3 *(cont'd)*

---

    c. Embezzlement, as typified by the misappropriation of money or property, and falsification of financial records to cover up the act, thus making detection difficult.

    d. Intentional concealment or misrepresentation of events or data.

    e. Claims submitted for services or goods not actually provided to the organization.

DETERRENCE OF FRAUD

4. Deterrence consists of those actions taken to discourage the perpetration of fraud and limit the exposure if fraud does occur. The principal mechanism for deterring fraud is control. Primary responsibility for establishing and maintaining control rests with management (See *SIAS No. 1,* Control: Concepts and Responsibilities).

Internal Auditing's Responsibilities

5. Internal auditing is responsible for assisting in the deterrence of fraud by examining and evaluating the adequacy and the effectiveness of control commensurate with the extent of the potential exposure risk in the various segments of the entity's operations. In carrying out this responsibility, internal auditing should, for example, determine whether:

    a. The organizational environment fosters control consciousness.

    b. Realistic organizational goals and objectives are set.

    c. Written corporate policies (e.g., code of conduct) exist that describe prohibited activities and the action required whenever violations are discovered.

    d. Appropriate authorization policies for transactions are established and maintained.

    e. Policies, practices, procedures, reports, and other mechanisms are developed to monitor activities and safeguard assets, particularly in high-risk areas.

    f. Communication channels provide management with adequate and reliable information.

    g. Recommendations need to be made for the establishment or enhancement of cost-effective controls to help deter fraud.

DETECTION OF FRAUD

6. Detection consists of identifying indicators of fraud sufficient to warrant recommending an investigation. These indicators may arise as a result of controls established by management, tests conducted by auditors, and other sources both within and outside the organization.

Internal Auditing's Responsibilities

7. In conducting audit assignments, the internal auditor's responsibilities for detecting fraud are to:

    a. Have sufficient knowledge of fraud to be able to identify indicators that fraud might have been committed. This knowledge includes the need to know the characteristics of fraud, the techniques used to commit fraud, and the types of frauds associated with the activities audited.

    b. Be alert to opportunities, such as control weaknesses, that could allow fraud. If significant control weaknesses are detected, additional tests conducted by internal auditors should include tests directed toward identification of other indicators of fraud. Some examples of indicators are unauthorized transactions, override of controls, unexplained pricing exceptions, and unusually large product losses. Internal auditors should recognize that the presence of more than one indicator at any one time increases the probability that fraud might have occurred.

    c. Evaluate the indicators that fraud might have been committed and decide whether any further action is necessary or whether an investigation should be recommended.

    d. Notify the appropriate authorities within the organization if a determination is made that there are sufficient indicators of the commission of a fraud to recommend an investigation.

8. Internal auditors are not expected to have knowledge equivalent to that of a person whose primary responsibility is detecting and investigating fraud. Also, audit procedures alone, even when carried out with due professional care, do not guarantee that fraud will be detected.

INVESTIGATION OF FRAUD

9. Investigation consists of performing extended procedures necessary to determine where fraud, as suggested by the indicators, has occurred. It includes gathering sufficient evidential matter about the specific details of a discovered fraud. Internal auditors, lawyers, investigators, security personnel, and other specialists from inside or outside the organization are the parties that usually conduct or participate in fraud investigations.

Internal Auditing's Responsibilities

10. When conducting fraud investigations, internal auditing should:

    a. Assess the probable level and the extent of complicity in the fraud within the organization. This can be critical to ensuring that the internal auditor avoids providing information to or obtaining misleading information from persons who may be involved.

    b. Determine the knowledge, skills, and disciplines needed to effectively carry out the investigation. Assess the qualifications and the skills of the internal auditors and of the specialists available to participate in the investigation to ensure that it is conducted by individuals having the appropriate type and level of technical expertise. This should include assurances on such matters as professional certifications, licenses, reputation, and that there is no relationship to those being investigated or to any of the employees or management of the organization.

    c. Design procedures to follow in attempting to identify the perpetrators, extent of the fraud, techniques used, and cause of the fraud.

    d. Coordinate activities with management personnel, legal counsel, and other specialists as appropriate throughout the course of the investigation.

    e. Be cognizant of the rights of alleged perpetrators and personnel within the scope of the investigation and the reputation of the organization itself.

11. Once a fraud investigation is concluded, internal audit should assess the facts known in order to:

    a. Determine if controls need to be implemented or strengthened to reduce future vulnerability.

(continued)

FIG. 22-3 *(cont'd)*

    b. Design audit tests to help disclose the existence of similar frauds in the future.
    c. Help meet the internal auditor's responsibility to maintain sufficient knowledge of fraud and thereby be able to identify future indicators of fraud.

REPORTING OF FRAUD

12. Reporting consists of the various oral or written, interim or final communications to management regarding the status and results of fraud investigations.

Internal Auditing's Responsibilities

13. A preliminary or final report may be desirable at the conclusion of the detection phase. The report should include the internal auditor's conclusion as to whether sufficient information exists to conduct an investigation. It should also summarize findings that serve as the basis for such decision.

14. *SIAS No. 2,* Communicating Results, which expands on Specific Standard 430 and provides interpretations, is applicable to internal audit reports issued as a result of fraud investigations. Additional interpretive guidelines on reporting of fraud are as follows:

    a. When the incidence of significant fraud has been established to a reasonable certainty, management or the board should be notified immediately.
    b. The results of a fraud investigation may indicate that fraud has had a previously undiscovered materially adverse effect on the financial position and results of operations of an organization for one or more years on which financial statements have already been issued. Internal audit should inform appropriate management and the audit committee of the board of directors of such a discovery.
    c. A written report should be issued at the conclusion of the investigation phase. It should include all findings, conclusions, recommendations, and corrective action taken.
    d. A draft of the proposed report on fraud should be submitted to legal counsel for review. In those cases in which the auditor wants to invoke client privilege, consideration should be given to addressing the report to legal counsel.

Note: As used in this statement, the term "management" includes anyone in an organization with responsibilities for setting and/or achieving objectives.

---

prompt and resolute action thereon; the internal auditor should ascertain if statutory or other official considerations dictate specific reporting compliance.

    ☐ The report should indicate all pertinent facts uncovered relative to the who, what, where, when, how, and why of the fraud. It should also include recommendations for control improvements to minimize the exposure to similar occurrences in the future.

The complete statement is reproduced in Figure 22-3.[9]

GENERAL PREVENTIVE MEASURES

To reiterate, the objective of this discussion of fraud detection is either the complete elimination of fraud—possibly a very difficult task—or at least a reduction of the occurrences.

Of course, primary responsibility for the prevention of fraud must rest with company management. It should take all necessary steps to set its house in order and install those safeguards that a prudent management should use—in a cost-effective way.

The internal auditor may assist in this implementation. Or, if the management asks for his suggestions as to what measures should be taken, he should, at a minimum, suggest these steps to deter fraudulent acts (whether management, other employee, or computer):

1. *Policies:*
    - ☐ See that a corporate policy statement exists on the subject of fraud or improper actions. This should set a high ethical tone, and provide the proper environment for dealing with fraud or improper acts. (See Chapter 17 on Internal Controls.) Some suggested topics to be included in the statement are:
        - Business philosophy
        - Impact of improper acts on business
        - Disposition of individuals involved in irregularities and fraud, etc.
        - Disclosure policies (e.g., SEC)
        - Completeness of financial records (no "off-the-books" funds)
        - Conformance to laws (U.S. and other, as may be applicable)
        - Precautions on management override of procedures
    - ☐ Take steps to be assured that the entire management is aware of corporate policies and procedures on the subject. Often the issuance of a policy statement, without follow-up, has little impact. Accordingly, some supplemental steps include these:
        - All levels of management must be made aware of the potential for fraud that exist in their areas of responsibility and the conditions conducive to it. The internal audit group or other financial and legal personnel can assist in this process through a limited number of meetings.

---

[9] Copyright © 1985 by the Institute of Internal Auditors, 249 Maitland Avenue, Altamonte Springs, Fla. 32701. All rights reserved. Printed in the United States of America. No part of this publication may be reproduced, stored in a retrieval system, or transmitted in any form by any means—electronic, mechanical, photocopying, recording, or otherwise—without prior written permission of the publisher. Reprinted with permission.

- Management must be motivated to monitor transactions or activities at the lower levels in their organization, and be on the alert for improper activities.
- Procedures must exist for dealing with conflicts of interest, discovery of irregularities, and what the management level is expected to do.

2. *Procedures.* While policies and management awareness are key elements in fraud deterrence and detection, they should be supported by proper written procedures. The extent and content of procedures may vary, but the following should be included:

- ☐ Provision for internal controls. This includes placing responsibility for proper internal controls and the principles (see Chapters 17 and 18) to be applied in each functional area.
- ☐ Provision for adequate computer systems review and operation. Given the susceptibility of computer systems to fraud, special care should be taken:
  - In systems design to provide for the necessary controls, perhaps with the assistance of both independent accountants and internal auditors.
  - In following the principle of separation of duties.
  - In the screening of computer and other personnel, when hired and trained.
  - In access to the computer and to computer data.
- ☐ Effective procedures on the discovery of fraud. These involve several facts:
  - Proper procedure for the *reporting* of fraud, when discovered, including audits, financial, and legal involvement.
  - Proper procedures for the *examination* of the circumstances (legal and internal audit, or others).
  - Proper procedures for disposition of the individual committing fraud. Only by prompt effective removal of a person found committing fraud can deterrence be effective. If it is known that a guilty party will not be punished (for whatever reason), then a major deterrent is removed.

3. *Organization.* A third factor in fraud deterrence and detection has to do with organizational considerations. Some suggested subjects are these:

- ☐ Existence of an independent audit committee of the board of directors.
- ☐ Existence of an internal audit department. Among other things, this function should check the internal controls and keep alert for fraud possibilities during audits.

  This group should assume responsibility for monitoring the internal audit activities, the system of internal controls and management controls, and accounting principles, to name a few functions.

- ☐ Access of the internal auditors to the audit committee, and to top management.

  To be most effective, an internal audit department must have a certain independence of action and access to top authority. It cannot be unduly restricted. Hence, even though the chief internal auditor may report, for example, to the senior vice-president–finance, he should have access to higher authority, when deemed necessary.

☐ Responsibility for the internal controls must be placed on the line executives. It may be a part of the functional outline or job description of each executive, and it may be a segment of appropriate policy directives. An example of the responsibility section for a corporate policy directive on internal controls is shown in Figure 22-4.

Management Override

As previously stated, the primary responsibility for preventing fraud rests with management. Yet, some of the most publicized instances of improper or illegal business practices are those carried on by a limited number of business managers themselves. Therefore, it may be worthwhile to briefly discuss some likely areas of management fraud.

The various controls—accounting, operational, and administrative—are designed so that all transactions are executed, recorded, and reported as authorized by management. The several methods reviewed in this chapter will ordinarily prevent or detect *unintentional* errors and deter fraud or defalcations by the continuous reviewing and strengthening of the control systems. Warning signals of possible management fraud are depicted in Figure 22-1. But irregularities committed by two or more persons, and especially individuals in different departments, are difficult to detect even by the best of auditors; this fact is again emphasized in this section. Perhaps the most difficult collusion and fraud to uncover is one in which management itself participates. Yet, such instances tend to be of significance to the investor. Management override occurs when executives with sufficient real or apparent authority cause subordinates to either improperly record or to conceal transactions or to process documents outside established procedures. These actions either can result in material misstatement of financial statements or can enable management to defraud the company. Management override occurs if requests for special processing of documents or other actions would be denied to other employees as a matter of routine. It is almost impossible to determine through standard auditing procedures transactions affected by management override. Auditors must, therefore, take a different approach in dealing with a potential problem of management override.

Evaluating the risk of management override. Auditors will have to evaluate the risk of management override, considering factors such as:

- Type of organization audited.
- General control environment and adherence to overall administrative controls.
- Susceptibility of the area under review.
- Circumstances that might motivate management to override controls.

FIG. 22-4

Corporate Policy Directive on Internal Controls—Responsibilities Section

---

RESPONSIBILITIES:

A. The Board of Directors is responsible for the determination, after appropriate review, that an adequate system of internal control exists, that the system is effective, and that a code of ethics applicable to the conduct of employees exists; it has the ultimate responsibility for monitoring compliance with the control system and taking appropriate actions concerning deviations from established policies, directives, and instructions.

B. The Chief Executive Officer, the Chief Operating Officer, and the senior vice-presidents are responsible to the Board of Directors for the creation and maintenance of a proper environment, including policies, directives, and other communications, and for the establishment, monitoring, and enforcement of the necessary internal controls. Their responsibilities include, but are not limited to, the following specific internal control functions:

 1. Providing direction to those who are responsible for business decisions

 2. Reviewing and approving risks inherent in existing or potential new business ventures

 3. Minimizing the potential for errors and irregularities in new and ongoing business transactions

 4. Providing direction to those who are responsible for the creation and maintenance of a documented internal control system

 5. Providing for the continuous review and evaluation of the system of internal control, including legal, accounting, or other technical review, by company personnel or independent consultants as appropriate

C. Division general managers and subsidiary presidents are responsible for the establishment, maintenance, and monitoring of the internal controls of their organizations and for annually providing the Chief Executive Officer with certification that the internal accounting controls and the internal administrative controls of the company element are adequate.

D. The chief financial officers of the company elements are responsible to their company element heads for the development, installation, documentation, evaluation, maintenance, and operation of an effective system of internal accounting control.

E. Vice-presidents and managers of nonfinancial functions within company elements are responsible for the development, installation, documentation, evaluation, maintenance, and operation of an effective system of administrative control for their functions.

F. The Vice-President and Controller is responsible for providing guidance to chief financial officers in developing, maintaining, and evaluating systems of internal accounting control.

G. In accordance with Policy Directive (PD) No. 45, the Director–Internal Audit is responsible for reviewing the internal control systems at various locations to determine that adequate systems exist in each operating center, that the systems are effective for the purposes intended, and that any deficiencies are brought to the attention of the appropriate management for corrective action. The Director–Internal Audit shall report his findings to the Senior Vice-President–Finance, the Executive Office, the Audit Committee, or the Board of Directors as appropriate.

> H. The Senior Vice-President–Finance shall coordinate the activities of Corporate Audit and the company's independent auditors in reviews of internal control for all company elements, exercise an overall review of the internal accounting control systems, and keep the Audit Committee and the Board of Directors advised, as necessary, of significant deviations as they may come to his attention.
>
> I. The Director–Government Financial Relations shall coordinate with the Director–Corporate Audit regarding the findings of government auditors related to the adequacy of internal control.
>
> J. Officers of the company, including officers of its divisions and subsidiaries, are responsible for insuring that they do not directly or indirectly make or cause to be made materially false or misleading oral or written statements to independent or internal auditors, or fail to state, or cause others to fail to state, any material fact which by its omission could mislead the independent or internal auditors.
>
> K. All levels of management are responsible for eliminating questionable methods of operation, financial or otherwise, possible conflicts of interest, and other actions that may circumvent internal control.
>
> L. Corporate Audit is responsible for the detection of unusual or questionable situations which may eventually be determined to be illegal or fraudulent acts or other similar irregularities in instances where the application of prudent audit procedures would likely result in their detection, and is responsible for alerting the Corporate Law Department that a particular action or event is questionable. The determination of appropriate action must be made by management after consultation with legal counsel and any other experts as deemed necessary. The Corporate Law Department may, at the request of management, undertake the responsibility to direct the investigation of any matter which reasonably could give rise to litigation involving the corporation. The responsibility of Corporate Audit with respect to detection of such situations does not relieve management of the responsibility for creating systems of internal control that, among other things, offer sufficient protection from fraud and similar irregularities. In addition, such systems must include techniques that are designed to detect such acts in a timely fashion. Corporate Audit is responsible for communicating to management any weaknesses which come to its attention which either could lead to questionable acts or delay or preclude their detection.

- Management judgments in determining amounts for accruals, reserves, and so forth.
- Prior audit experiences.

This evaluation is not intended to assess the probability that management is overriding the controls, but to determine whether the area being audited presents risks of override.

As an example, the auditor testing the reserve for obsolete and excess inventories will assess the risk of management override as being significant, even though he might be convinced that management of the particular organization would not engage in overriding internal controls. On the other hand, an auditor verifying payroll deductions might assess the risk of override as low, as insignificant gains could possibly accrue to management in this area.

Consider Motivating Factors

Except for outright fraud, which should not be considered the prime motivating factor for management override, a number of circumstances might lead management to engage in certain activities or action, which, within a normal environment, would not take place. Auditors should be aware of these circumstances:

- ☐ The audited facility operates in an industry that is experiencing a large number of business failures.
- ☐ The audited facility is under severe working capital pressure.
- ☐ The entity is sold, the price is based on the financial statements, and operating management will profit from this sale in some form.
- ☐ Management compensation is directly affected by the results of the operation, the compensation effected is substantial, and operating results tend to be erratic.
- ☐ Management is under pressure to meet budget, forecast, etc.

The internal auditor, more often than not, will be faced with the last two factors in his assessment of risks and circumstances for motivation. In almost all instances, operating managers' remuneration, or at least part of their compensation, is tied to the operating results of their operation, or is based on performance to budget. In the existing economic climate, almost all operations in any industry are faced with less than desirable or expected results. Countermeasures such as cost-containment programs might not be as effective as anticipated or might not have provided the effects on a timely basis. Often, management will engage in override actions, not because they are motivated by personal gain, but rather because they believe their superiors expect certain results, or because they are unable or unwilling to withstand corporate's legitimate pressure for improved results. "Improvement" of results through management override might not even be considered by local management as such. These actions are rationalized as "just following instructions from the top" (see Chapter 23 on Fraudulent Financial Reporting).

Areas Vulnerable to Management Override

If the auditor has evaluated the risk factors and determined that sufficient motivation for management override is prevailing, specific audit steps should be taken to scrutinize the following areas. These areas are the most common, but by no means the only ones in which management override could result in misstatement of financial activities:

- ☐ *Sales reporting.* Sales cutoffs, prebilling, reporting of advance sales, or shipments prior to required dates, causing customer dissatisfaction and possibly additional freight and handling costs.

- *Reserves.* Unjustified decreases, total elimination, or failure of setting up necessary reserves for inventory, allowances for bad debts, or litigation and tax reserves. Where inventory reserves or allowances for bad debts are established based on formulas, this override could also include alteration or exclusion of base data to which formulas are applied.
- *Accounts payable and accrued expenses.* Failure to record accounts payable vouchers within the proper time period (understatement of inventory levels or expenses) and establishing accruals of all types based on "what can the P&L take this month" rather than "what is the appropriate amount required."
- *Cost of sales.* Incorrect recording of cost of sales to provide higher margins, thus building up inventory differences that have to be faced up to in other reporting periods.
- *Manufacturing costs.* The capitalization of loss variances in inventory, causing inventory buildup during the year, but providing better than actual monthly results.
- *Deferring expenses.* Unjustified capitalization of current expenses, to be written off over a time period.
- *Change in accounting method for advertising expenses.* In organizations where advertising is a major expense, the change in accounting for these expenditures from the accrual method to actual invoicing can result in a major one-time cost reduction.

This list is by no means all encompassing but indicates to the auditors areas where management override can result in substantial distortion of financial reporting of results. External auditors will usually review these areas extensively at year-end, but are less concerned if corrections are made facing up to the facts at year-end. Internal auditors, however, are also concerned that financial reporting is correct throughout the year.

If these activities are brought to the attention of top management during the year, interim financial statements are more reliable and embarrassment is avoided at year-end. No organization is immune to management override of controls; it is the responsibility of internal audit to highlight such occurrences so that top management can take corrective action before variances become excessive. The potential effect on a company of management override has been highlighted in recent newspaper article disclosings made by Pepsico and other companies that discovered fictitious profits caused by division managers over several years.

THE ROLE OF BUSINESS ETHICS

An Initial Perspective

Business ethics is a term that has gained widespread attention in recent years. It is often used when referring to the conduct encouraged or condoned by business entities of their employees when dealing with each other and with customers, suppliers, and the general public. It is recognized as a critical ingredient in the successful management of an enterprise. Its importance stems not so much from the attention that results from doing things the right way. Good deeds and proper ethical conduct go largely unnoticed. That is because such is the expected norm—the societal standard. Rather, the importance stems from the attention that can result from doing things the wrong way. The adverse consequences that can befall a company, its management, those who engage in commerce with the company, and even the public provide a powerful motivator.

Such motivation accounts for the surging interest in business ethics. Many of America's top companies have been tarnished in recent years as a result of improper or unethical conduct by their managements or other employees. The range of incidents is broad indeed. Examples include:

- ☐ *Procurement kickbacks.* While most reports of kickbacks have been in the defense contracting sector, many believe the practice extends far beyond that business. Recent reports tend to give credibility to this view. For example, kickbacks were reported in the advertising and promotional activities of a major beer company. Kickbacks were also alleged in procurements at a university, a city government, and a municipal public transportation authority.

- ☐ *Product substitutions.* In these cases, some companies were reported as having delivered products that were inferior in terms of quality or otherwise did not meet customer specifications. Examples have occurred in the semiconductor industry and in the defense contracting industry.

- ☐ *Labor mischarging.* Usually, this involves situations where government contracts improperly bear the costs of labor effort related to other government contracts or to commercial business. Embarrassing examples have been reported involving some of the most reputable companies in America.

- ☐ *Bank reporting failures.* Many accounts have been published that indicate that several of the largest and most respected financial institutions in the country have, for years, failed to comply with regulations that require reporting of large cash transactions. This failure enables the laundering by perpetrators of funds obtained through illicit activities, such as drug dealing.

- ☐ *Medical claims fraud.* Accounts of filing improper or invalid medical claims are not as sensational as other types of conduct mentioned in this section. Nevertheless, for those familiar with medical insurance administration, it is believed to be a serious and growing problem. Employees, doctors, and others have been increasingly victimizing company- and government-sponsored medical insurance plans.

- ☐ *Espionage.* Several instances have been reported in which company employees, government employees, and military personnel have been charged with having committed espionage activities.

Perhaps the most sensational example of breaching business ethics is the insider-trading scandal. Here, highly respected individuals within in-

BUSINESS ETHICS AND FRAUD 22-27

vestment banking and brokerage firms with the most prestigious of reputations were found to be violating securities laws for personal gain. What is so astounding is that many of the individuals charged were already wealthy, by almost any standard. Add to this accounts of questionable conduct by lawyers[10] and accountants,[11] and a picture emerges of a business climate believed by many to be seriously flawed with ethical misconduct.

Many companies have responded by investing heavily in programs to promote improved ethical practices by their management and employees. Both inside and outside, government agencies have increased efforts to identify and eliminate improper and unethical conduct.

More is said about these efforts later in this chapter. The foregoing examples easily demonstrate that, to many, business ethics is in a sorry state. Yet, there is more. For some time now, the SEC has been concerned with the incidence of financial reporting fraud. In 1985, the subject attracted the interest of the House Subcommittee on Investigations and Oversight and its chairman, Rep. John Dingell (D-Michigan), and many committee members. One response was a bill proposed by Rep. Ron Wyden (D-Oregon). Its provisions would have added substantially to the disclosure requirements for managements and for independent auditors who examine financial statements. The bill did not become law. However, it is another indicator that there is a growing perception that the ethical practices of business must be dealt with. For the remainder of this section, the discussion examines the factors that influence business ethics, why misconduct occurs, the risks of not maintaining proper business ethics, techniques for maintaining an effective business ethics program, and some thoughts on what internal auditors can do to help.

Factors That Influence Business Ethics

Consider the following hypothetical situation set forth in Figure 22-5. The situation of Jack Smith is typical of many such situations being discussed in ethics courses in business schools. What Jack should do is determined by a variety of factors. Some are external, others are internal to the company. They are as follows:

- External factors
  - Society
  - Government
  - Economic

---

[10] See, e.g., William B. Glaberson, Pete Engardio, Stan Cook, and Scott Ticer, "A Question of Integrity of Blue-Chip Law Firms," *Business Week*, Apr. 7, 1986, pp. 76–80.

[11] See, e.g., Clement P. Work, "Accounting's Bottom Line: Big Troubles," *U.S. News & World Report*, Oct. 21, 1985, p. 58.

FIG. 22-5

Business Ethics—A Hypothetical Situation

> Most ethics training workshops ask participants to consider a hypothetical situation that poses several ethical dilemmas. Here, somewhat streamlined, are several case studies from recent seminars.
>
> **SECRET ENVELOPE**
>
> JACK SMITH, division vice president of a major defense contractor, opens a bulky envelope marked "Confidential and Personal." In it he finds a set of figures that appear to be cost data worked up by his company's major competitor for a Navy fighter-plane contract. An accompanying note from one of Jack's best marketing managers attests that the document is the real thing. Clearly, this could be a major advantage in preparing Jack's company's own bid.
>
> He calls in two trusted aides to discuss the pros and cons of using the figures. His marketing vice president sees no problem; everyone in the industry tries to get reliable intelligence on competitors' plans, and Jack himself had recently reminded his top managers how vital this was. But Jack's executive assistant warns of possible risks. The figures might have been bought or obtained with a promise of some quid pro quo; if so, it could blow up in the company's face if discovered.
>
> What should Jack do?
>
> Alan L. Otter, "Ethics on the Job: Companies Alert Employees to Potential Dilemmas," *Wall Street Journal*, July 14, 1986, Sec. 2, p. 19, cols. 3–6.

- ☐ Internal factors
  - Nature of the business
  - Management philosophy
  - Internal control
  - Audit committees

Each of these factors is discussed briefly in the following paragraphs.

Society. The role of society is extremely important in shaping business ethics. In the United States, the Judeo-Christian-inspired values of justice, equality, fairness, integrity, truthfulness, and respect for others provide the underpinnings for guiding ethical decision making. Americans expect business to be conducted in accordance with these values. Such expectations vary in societal segments in other parts of the world. Transnational companies doing business around the world are at times frustrated by clashing societal values. To illustrate, women have equal rights with men in the United States. This is not so in the Middle East and elsewhere.

Government. The actions by governmental bodies profoundly affect business practices. Government efforts to legislate and regulate business conduct are so voluminous as to defy categorizing and listing. Suffice it to say that virtually every form of commerce is regulated, some much more than others, and monitored. While the effects of these efforts may be debated, no one can deny that government agencies—federal, state, and local—are ever present.

Economic. Maintaining proper business ethics is in reality a battle to resist temptation. Resistance is relatively easy when the economic climate is healthy. Prosperity and security are welcome allies in the battle. When times get tough, those most imperiled are almost forced to act in ways they would not under better times. Thus, companies may close plants, terminate loyal employees, delay payments to suppliers, and restrict credit to long-term customers. While these actions are all legal, they strain the ethical value system. Such an environment could also lead to acts that are clearly improper and possibly fraudulent, such as defective pricing, labor mischanging, bribing customers and others, failing to make complete financial disclosures, and practicing trade in an unfair fashion.

Nature of the Business. To some extent, the nature of the business affects the ethics by which it is practiced. Defense contractors, for example, despite ethical adversities in recent years, are expected to hold to ethical values higher than other forms of business. That is because these companies assume unique and compelling obligations to the armed forces, the American taxpayer, and the nation.[12] The size of the company, the nature of its products, the types of customers served, the nature of the competition, its position in the industry, and the geographical areas in which it operates are all elements that, taken together, affect how the business of that company is conducted.

Management Philosophy. Management is responsible for the affairs of the company. Top management must set the tone or culture for the rest of the management team. Thus, if the CEO is obsessed with sales and earnings growth, expectations may be placed on managers to achieve targets that are unrealistic. Failure to achieve may not be tolerated. Such an environment creates the impetus for unnecessary risk-taking and, possibly, for management fraud. On the other hand, a philosophy of balanced commitments to customers, suppliers, communities, shareholders, and employees is more likely to translate into realistic expectations that are achievable through proper business conduct.

Internal Control. Internal control is discussed in detail in Chapter 17. Its presence here is in the sense that a system of adequate internal control provides an effective check against possible misconduct. It recognizes the fallibility of human behavior and designs means to help people from doing

---

[12] The Packard Commission, *Conduct and Accountability, a Report to the President*, June 1986, p. 3.

the wrong thing. A weak system of internal control fails to provide such protection. The risk of irregularities and dishonest acts increases proportionately.

Audit Committees. A large number of publicly held companies have formed audit committees, as noted in Chapter 10. Audit committees, by providing an oversight role on the actions of management, are an effective deterrent to improper ethical behavior. In many of the financial frauds reported by the SEC, audit committees were not present.

Misconduct—Why It Occurs

In a 1986 article in *Harvard Business Review*, Saul Gellerman suggested four rationalizations that managers have used through the ages. The Dean of the University of Dallas Graduate School of Management suggested that questionable conduct is justified by believing that:

- The conduct is not illegal or immoral.
- It is in the best interest of the individual and/or the company.
- It will never be found out.
- The company will condone it.[13]

In the hypothetical case cited in Fig. 22-5, it is easy to see how Jack's course of action could be rationalized by one or more of these excuses. If so, he would doubtless act to use the figures to gain an advantage, even though it would be thought by many to be unfair.

It is likely that in a great many cases, the morality or legality of a given course of action is difficult to discern. Thus, at times, people may be judged in hindsight to have been wrong, while they themselves believe they acted prudently. At other times, managers can legitimately misconstrue or misunderstand directives from above. Often, directives may seem conflicting. Managers may be confused but also may be afraid to seek clarification. Such an act may be viewed as indicative of incompetence—inability to accept responsibility.

Also, it is unfortunate, but nevertheless true, that managements historically have gotten away with much misconduct, even though they knew the act to be wrong. How much is conjecture? Whatever it has been, it has been sufficient to encourage the unscrupulous to perpetuate the problem. How to deter such thinking is what internal control systems are for. But every system to some extent depends on the honesty and integrity of the persons involved. Dishonest people, properly motivated and possessing the right skills, will always find a way.

---

[13] Saul W. Gellerman, "Why 'Good' Managers Make Bad Ethical Choices," *Harvard Business Review*, July/Aug., 1986, p. 85.

BUSINESS ETHICS AND FRAUD

It is no surprise to internal auditors that Gellerman suggests that surprise audits of control mechanisms are a good way to avoid management oversights.[14] More is said on this later.

The Risks

Before discussing techniques for maintaining sound business ethics, it is important to consider, more specifically, the attendent risks should such maintenance occur. Corporate misconduct, when detected, results in exposure to one or more of the following:

- ☐ *Sanctions.* Penalties, fines, damage awards, and other legal sanctions or restrictions imposed against the company. These, however, may be overshadowed by other exposures.
- ☐ *Absorption of management attention.* Inevitably, the most senior levels of management are often involved and for lengthy periods of time, which cuts into their capacity for managing the rest of the company.
- ☐ *Career impact.* Anyone who is accused of wrongdoing will most likely be tainted for the rest of his career. This is so even if he is later found to be innocent.
- ☐ *High legal costs.* The defense effort usually requires lengthy discovery proceedings and long court battles repleat with time-absorbing legal maneuvers. It all costs money. Law firms are expensive, and the more expert the firm is, the more it costs.
- ☐ *Damage to company image.* Companies work very hard to develop an acceptable, respected corporate image. Misconduct, even from the smallest component of a company, can tarnish the image of the entire entity.
- ☐ *Damage to employee morale.* The company's ability to attract and retain qualified, loyal employees can suffer greatly should misconduct occur.
- ☐ *Damage to the business.* Companies with soiled reputations may find customers and suppliers wary of doing business with them. The damage in the form of lost revenue or increased cost is inestimable.

Most companies realize these risks are such that it makes sense to take steps to minimize their chances of occurring. In recent times, the number of these steps has increased to help combat the public perception of business ethics as being in disarray.

Techniques for Maintaining Effective Business Ethics

How are company managements attempting to better their business practices? One group is making highly publicized efforts. Of the hundreds of

---

[14] *Ibid.*, p. 90.

companies that perform work for the DOD, 36 have jointly developed a voluntary program. Their actions are a response to a series of recommendations by the Packard Commission. Among other things, the Commission recommended that contractors "should adopt or revise, if they have adopted written standards of ethical business conduct to assure that they reasonably address, among other matters, the special requirements of defense contracting."[15] Appendix B in the *Report to the President* by the Commission provided details of findings from research sponsored by the Ethics Resource Center and others. It indicated that among 650 of the largest U.S. corporations, 73 percent had developed written standards of conduct or codes of ethics. The report further indicated that research of 279 major corporations by Bentley College in 1985 corroborated that finding. The report attributed this finding to the widespread development of codes in the 1970s in response to publicized misconduct in connection with the Watergate scandal, illegal political contributions, and overseas bribery payments.[16]

In general, the program that is recommended by the Commission, in addition to written codes, is being voluntarily implemented by the 36 contractors mentioned previously. This program includes the following:

- *Effective communication of ethics policies and procedures.* This includes dissemination of the code to all employees, informal discussions, new personnel orientation, group meetings and briefings, training and development programs, videotapes, and employee handbooks. The table of contents and first two pages of the Martin Marietta Corporation handbook are shown in Fig. 22-6.

- *Monitoring and enforcing ethics policies.* This includes such techniques as setting up ethics offices headed by an individual often reporting to the CEO or directly to the board of directors' ethics committee. This function is made responsible for developing and implementing standards of business conduct. According to the Packard Commission, 28 percent of defense contractors have set up ombudsmen. Generally, ombudsmen function at the corporate level, but some are resident in divisions as well. They are usually responsible for receiving and investigating allegations of violations. Additionally, they may be involved in monitoring compliance and assessing penalties.[17] Contract review boards have also been employed. Access by employees may involve walk-ins, interoffice mail, and use of hot lines. Hot lines are toll free telephone numbers leading directly to the ombudsman or ethics office.

One difficulty that remains to be resolved is the question of staffing. Most ethics offices, contract review boards, and ombudsmen have little or no staff to perform inquiries and follow-up work. Much of the time, members of the corporate counsel's staff of lawyers and internal auditors are used. In

---

[15] The Packard Commission, *Conduct and Accountability, a Report to the President*, June 1986, p. 10.

[16] *Ibid.*, p. 52.

[17] *Ibid.*, p. 57.

FIG. 22-6

Martin-Marietta Corporation Code of Ethics and Standards of Conduct

---

TABLE OF CONTENTS

	Page
Code of Ethics and Standards of Conduct	1
Commitments	2
Corporate Ethics Office	3
Bidding, Negotiation, and Performance of Government Contracts	3
Conflicts of Interest	4
Entertainment, Gifts, and Payments—Customer and Supplier Personnel	5
Complete and Accurate Books, Records, and Communications	8
Preservation of Assets and Cost Consciousness	9
Compliance with Securities Laws and Regulations	9
Compliance with Antitrust Laws	10
International Boycotts and Restrictive Trade Practices	10
Political Contributions	11
Compliance and Discipline	11

[page 1]

MARTIN MARIETTA CORPORATION CODE OF ETHICS AND STANDARDS OF CONDUCT

Martin Marietta Corporation will conduct its business in strict compliance with applicable laws, rules, and regulations, with honesty and integrity, and with a strong commitment to the highest standards of ethics. We have a duty to conduct our business affairs within both the letter and the spirit of the law.

This booklet provides a brief summary of the standards of ethics and conduct that are at the foundation of the Corporation's business operations.

Martin Marietta expects its employees, at all levels, to adhere to these standards.

[page 2]

COMMITMENTS

Martin Marietta is a community of well-trained and highly motivated men and women. We have significant commitments to our customers, our suppliers, the many communities of which we are a member, to society as a whole, to our shareholders, and to each other. These commitments, which are a prime element in any code of business ethics, are briefly summarized here:

☐ To our customers we are committed to continue to provide outstanding performance to produce quality products and services that meet or exceed requirements and specifications and to meet required schedules and budgets. We are also committed to the protection and handling of classified information in accordance with established rules and regulations.

(continued)

FIG. 22-6 (cont'd)

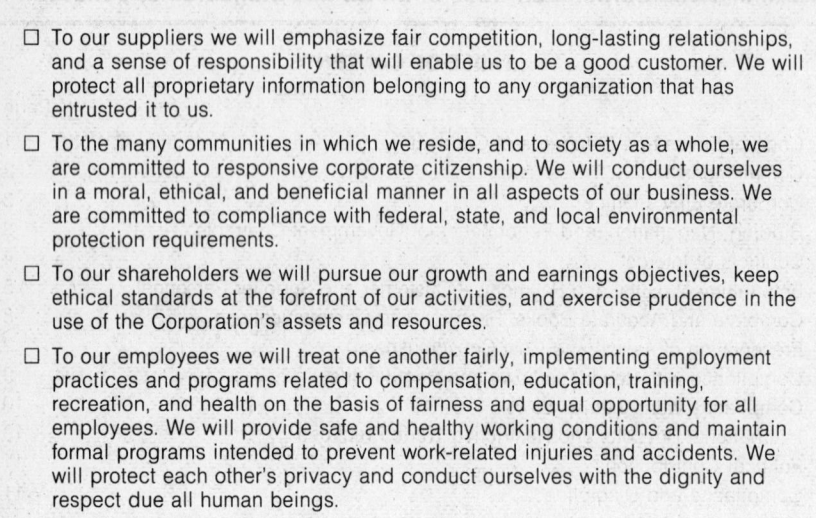

- ☐ To our suppliers we will emphasize fair competition, long-lasting relationships, and a sense of responsibility that will enable us to be a good customer. We will protect all proprietary information belonging to any organization that has entrusted it to us.
- ☐ To the many communities in which we reside, and to society as a whole, we are committed to responsive corporate citizenship. We will conduct ourselves in a moral, ethical, and beneficial manner in all aspects of our business. We are committed to compliance with federal, state, and local environmental protection requirements.
- ☐ To our shareholders we will pursue our growth and earnings objectives, keep ethical standards at the forefront of our activities, and exercise prudence in the use of the Corporation's assets and resources.
- ☐ To our employees we will treat one another fairly, implementing employment practices and programs related to compensation, education, training, recreation, and health on the basis of fairness and equal opportunity for all employees. We will provide safe and healthy working conditions and maintain formal programs intended to prevent work-related injuries and accidents. We will protect each other's privacy and conduct ourselves with the dignity and respect due all human beings.

most cases, the tips received turn out to be little more than employee grievances or misperceptions. The time required to check out these matters detracts from other work lawyers and internal auditors must do.

Another recommended technique is protection for whistle-blowers. Many believe that unless such protection is offered, managements will never be seen as seriously seeking a changed moral climate. One recent article suggests that "it is no secret, for example, that most senior executives are contemptuous of whistle-blowers, labeling them as 'snitches' and 'finks' and often demoting or firing them."[18] Uneven enforcement of codes is another pitfall. If executives are treated lightly, while lower-level employees are dealt with more harshly, the program is apt to fail. One answer may be to establish internal judicial boards empowered to judge violations, assure due process, and effect just punishment for wrongdoers.

While critics abound, companies such as the defense contractor group seem committed to enhance their business ethics. To emphasize that commitment, the contractors have agreed to a set of initiatives that includes publicizing annually the state of their ethics programs. The initiatives require that each contractor submit answers to a list of 18 questions to an external reviewer, such as a CPA firm, for review. The questions are reprinted in Fig. 22-7.[19]

---

[18] Thomas J. Murray, "Ethics Programs: Just A Pretty Face?" *Business Month*, Sept. 1987, p. 31.

[19] Official Releases, *Journal of Accountancy*, Aug., 1987, pp. 160–161.

FIG. 22-7

Defense Industry Initiatives Questionnaire and Illustrative Procedures

---

ILLUSTRATIVE PROCEDURES FOR REVIEW OF ANSWERS TO QUESTIONNAIRE

Defense Industry Questionnaire on Business Ethics and Conduct

Before performing procedures, the practitioner should read the *Defense Industry Initiatives on Business Ethics and Conduct.*

1. DOES THE COMPANY HAVE A WRITTEN CODE OF BUSINESS ETHICS AND CONDUCT?

Determine whether the Company has a written Code of Business Ethics and Conduct.

2. IS THE CODE DISTRIBUTED TO ALL EMPLOYEES PRINCIPALLY INVOLVED IN DEFENSE WORK?

Determine by inquiry of Company officials and/or by reading relevant documentation how the Company distributes the Code to all employees principally involved in defense work.

3. ARE NEW EMPLOYEES PROVIDED ANY ORIENTATION TO THE CODE?

Determine by inquiry of Company officials and/or by reading relevant documentation how the Company provides an orientation to the Code to new employees.

4. DOES THE CODE ASSIGN RESPONSIBILITY TO OPERATING MANAGEMENT AND OTHERS FOR COMPLIANCE WITH THE CODE?

Read the Code to determine whether it includes (a) the assignment of responsibility for compliance with the Code to operating management and others, and (b) a statement of the standards that govern the conduct of all employees in their relationships to the Company.

5. DOES THE COMPANY CONDUCT EMPLOYEE TRAINING PROGRAMS REGARDING THE CODE?

Determine by inquiry of Company officials and/or by reading relevant documentation how the Company conducts training programs regarding the Code.

6. DOES THE CODE ADDRESS STANDARDS THAT GOVERN THE CONDUCT OF EMPLOYEES IN THEIR DEALINGS WITH SUPPLIERS, CONSULTANTS AND CUSTOMERS?

Read the Code to determine whether it addresses standards that govern the conduct of employees in their dealings with suppliers, consultants, and customers.

7. IS THERE A CORPORATE REVIEW BOARD, OMBUDSMAN, CORPORATE COMPLIANCE OR ETHICS OFFICE OR SIMILAR MECHANISM FOR EMPLOYEES TO REPORT SUSPECTED VIOLATIONS TO SOMEONE OTHER THAN THEIR DIRECT SUPERVISOR, IF NECESSARY?

Determine by inquiry of Company officials and/or by reading relevant documentation whether a corporate review board, ombudsman, corporate compliance or ethics office, or similar mechanism exists for employees to report suspected violations.

(continued)

FIG. 22-7 *(cont'd)*

8. DOES THE MECHANISM EMPLOYED PROTECT THE CONFIDENTIALITY OF EMPLOYEE REPORTS?

a. Determine by inquiry of members of the corporate review board, ombudsman, corporate compliance or ethics office, or similar mechanism established by the Company whether they understand the need to protect the confidentiality of employee reports.

b. Determine by inquiry of Company officials and/or by reading relevant documentation how the procedures employed protect this confidentiality.

9. IS THERE AN APPROPRIATE MECHANISM TO FOLLOW-UP ON REPORTS OF SUSPECTED VIOLATIONS TO DETERMINE WHAT OCCURRED, WHO WAS RESPONSIBLE, AND RECOMMENDED CORRECTIVE AND OTHER ACTIONS?

Determine by inquiry of Company officials and/or by reading relevant documentation how the follow-up procedures established by the Company operate and whether an appropriate mechanism exists to follow-up on reports of suspected violations reported to a corporate review board, ombudsman, corporate compliance or ethics office, or similar mechanism to determine what occurred, who was responsible, and recommended corrective and other action.

10. IS THERE AN APPROPRIATE MECHANISM FOR LETTING EMPLOYEES KNOW THE RESULT OF ANY FOLLOW-UP INTO THEIR REPORTED CHARGES?

a. Determine by inquiry of Company officials and/or by reading relevant documentation whether an appropriate mechanism exists for letting employees know the result of any follow-up into their reported charges.

b. Determine by inquiry of members of the corporate review board, ombudsman, corporate compliance of ethics office, or similar mechanism whether the results of the Company's follow-up of reported charges have been communicated to employees.

11. IS THERE AN ONGOING PROGRAM OF COMMUNICATION TO EMPLOYEES, SPELLING OUT AND RE-EMPHASIZING THEIR OBLIGATIONS UNDER THE CODE OF CONDUCT?

and

12. WHAT ARE THE SPECIFICS OF SUCH A PROGRAM?
A. WRITTEN COMMUNICATION?
B. ONE-ON-ONE COMMUNICATION?
C. GROUP MEETINGS?
D. VISUAL AIDS?
E. OTHERS?

Determine by inquiry of Company officials and/or by reading relevant documentation the extent of the Company's ongoing program of communication to employees, spelling out and re-emphasizing their obligations under the Code. Note the specific means of communication and compare to the Company's response to Question 12 of the Questionnaire.

13. DOES THE COMPANY HAVE A PROCEDURE FOR VOLUNTARILY REPORTING VIOLATIONS OF FEDERAL PROCUREMENT LAWS TO APPROPRIATE GOVERNMENTAL AGENCIES?

Determine by inquiry of Company officials and/or by reading relevant documentation how the Company's procedures operate for determining whether violations of federal procurement laws are to be reported to appropriate governmental agencies.

> **14.** IS IMPLEMENTATION OF THE CODE'S PROVISIONS ONE OF THE STANDARDS BY WHICH ALL LEVELS OF SUPERVISION ARE EXPECTED TO BE MEASURED IN THEIR PERFORMANCE?
>
> Determine by inquiry of Company officials and/or by reading relevant documentation, such as position descriptions and personnel policies, whether performance evaluations are to consider supervisors' efforts in the implementation of the Code's provisions as a standard of measurement of their performance.
>
> **15.** IS THERE A PROGRAM TO MONITOR ON A CONTINUING BASIS ADHERENCE TO THE CODE OF CONDUCT AND COMPLIANCE WITH FEDERAL PROCUREMENT LAWS?
>
> Determine by inquiry of Company officials and/or by reading relevant documentation how the Company monitors, on a continuing basis, adherence to the Code and compliance with federal procurement laws.
>
> **16.** DOES THE COMPANY PARTICIPATE IN THE INDUSTRY'S "BEST PRACTICES FORUM"?
>
> Determine by inquiry of Company officials and/or by reading relevant documentation whether the Company participated in the "Best Practices Forum."
>
> **17.** ARE PERIODIC REPORTS ON ADHERENCE TO THE PRINCIPLES MADE TO THE COMPANY'S BOARD OF DIRECTORS OR TO ITS AUDIT OR OTHER APPROPRIATE COMMITTEE?
>
> Determine by inquiry of Company officials and/or by reading minutes of the Board of Directors or audit or other appropriate committee meetings or other relevant documentation whether Company officials have reported on adherence to the principles of business ethics and conduct.
>
> **18.** ARE THE COMPANY'S INDEPENDENT PUBLIC ACCOUNTANTS OR A SIMILAR INDEPENDENT ORGANIZATION REQUIRED TO COMMENT TO THE BOARD OF DIRECTORS OR A COMMITTEE THEREOF ON THE EFFICACY OF THE COMPANY'S INTERNAL PROCEDURES FOR IMPLEMENTING THE COMPANY'S CODE OF CONDUCT?
>
> Determine by inquiry of Company officials and/or by reading relevant documentation whether the Company's independent accountants or a similar independent organization are required to comment to the board of directors or a committee thereof on the efficacy of the Company's internal procedures for implementing the Company's Code.

The ASB of the AICPA cooperated with this initiative by issuing a set of procedures that may be employed by CPAs who are requested to perform such services. Reporting guidelines are also provided. They were published in the August 1987 edition of the *Journal of Accountancy* as an interpretation of the AICPA attestation standards.[20]

Whether the commitment by defense contractors is sufficient will become clear as time passes. What seems clear now is that without such com-

---

[20] Copies of the interpretation may be obtained from the AICPA, 1211 Avenue of the Americas, New York, N.Y. 10036. The first attestations were completed in October 1987. Figure 22-7 reprints illustrative procedures.

mitment, businesses may find greater government interference that may do more harm than good.

Business Ethics and Internal Auditing

The Packard Commission had much to say regarding the role of internal auditing in the context of business ethics. The basis for the commentary was formed from responses to a survey questionnaire received from a representative sampling of defense contractor internal audit functions. The survey was performed for the Commission by Peat Marwick Mitchell & Co., as the firm was then named. It inquired into the extent of internal auditing, profiles of the audit staff, independence and effectiveness of the internal audit function, and the level of performance in government-sensitive areas.

The survey provided much information of interest. Perhaps most noteworthy, however, is the overall observation that:

> Although the total internal audit effort shows signs of appreciable change from the traditional financial audit to one that encompasses those government-sensitive areas, there are indicators that more emphasis may be needed to attain an acceptable level of compliance with government requirements.[21]

One of the areas of particular interest to the government is the function of the ombudsman and the hot line. The survey disclosed that these functions are little recognized, as yet, by internal auditors as an important source of information regarding the functioning of the company's management system and controls. The report of Peat Marwick Mitchell & Co. went even further in its concluding remarks, reprinted below as Fig. 22-8:[22]

It is clear from the foregoing that internal auditors are perceived as an important element in a properly organized company effort to maintain ethical business practices that will satisfy public expectations. Such a perception goes beyond the traditional use of internal auditing. Traditionally, managements expected internal auditing, among other things, to be a deterrent against employee fraud of the type discussed earlier in this chapter.

The perception of internal auditing as an effective tool to validate compliance with business ethics policies brings the internal auditor face to face with assessing management compliance. Few internal audit functions at present have developed the capability to do this. Further, there is the obvious question of whether management will permit the internal audit function sufficient resources and access to personnel records that compliance validation calls for. For one thing, there is the disturbing problem of government access to the work product of internal auditors. Chapter 11 makes it clear that unimpeded access by the DOD Inspector General, the Defense Contract

---

[21] *Ibid.*, p. 78.
[22] *Ibid.*, pp. 81–82.

FIG. 22-8
Report of Peat Marwick Mitchell & Co.—Concluding Remarks

CONCLUDING REMARKS

The survey portrays an increasing awareness on the part of major defense contractors that compliance with statutory and regulatory requirements needs to be practiced to a much greater extent than was true in the past. Contract compliance is critical and vital for those engaged in government work; to perform the required surveillance over contractors' practices, the internal audit function is playing an ever-increasing role. In fact, internal audit is now regarded by most major government contractors as an essential monitoring device. Consequently, the scope of the internal audit function has been significantly broadened to embrace those areas that are sensitive to government contracting. The survey results also suggest the need for enhancement of the function to more speedily emphasize certain aspects of the current plans and programs.

As described earlier in this report, the internal audit function cannot achieve optimum contract compliance on its own. Its effectiveness is dependent on a sound, comprehensive system of policies, procedures, organization, and communication, all of which are consistent with government statutory and regulatory requirements.

A typical example and a vital factor in achieving contract compliance is a company statement of ethical practices that are expected of all employees. This company Code of Ethics should be issued as a formal document, clearly stating the company's policies and providing sanctions for violations. The implementation, in the form of procedures, should assign organizational responsibilities for conducting examinations, hearings, etc., for detecting violations, and the methods for imposing sanctions. These formal documents need to be disseminated to all personnel, including the newly employed. Moreover, there is a need for periodic acknowledgements by all personnel of their understanding of the Code of Ethics. The internal auditor would then periodically validate the above process, including the evidence that the practices are in place and in compliance with written policies and procedures.

Notwithstanding all efforts to use internal auditors more extensively and effectively, along with a continuing effort to keep the related policies, procedures, and organizational structure current, "full" or "perfect" compliance can never be achieved. Therefore, the measure of a contractor's compliance should consider appropriate criteria. In short, the following could be deemed acceptable criteria for contract compliance:

- The extent to which top management commitment to contract compliance is articulated and practiced.
- The efficacy of the organization's ongoing efforts as demonstrated by:
  —written policies that are current, complete, and clear;
  —procedures that are comprehensive and comprehensible at all need-to-know levels;
  —policies and procedures that are in compliance with government requirements;
  —an organization that produces an optimum degree of checks and balances;
  —a trained cadre of professionals to monitor all the above; and
  —an ombudsman and/or hotline procedure to augment the internal audit function.
- Prompt remedy of disclosed breaches.
- Prompt examination of all reported problem areas.

(continued)

FIG. 22-8 (cont'd)

> - Speedy, comprehensive, and vigorous pursuit, within the company, of suspected violations.
> - Sanctions against violators, appropriate to the irregularity.
> - Financial restitution and appropriate disclosures, made to the appropriate government officials.
>
> In such an environment, the company will have made an optimum effort to be in compliance with requirements.

Audit Agency, the GAO, congressional subcommittees, and trial lawyers will tend to influence management to restrict internal auditors' inquiries in sensitive areas. Unless reasonable restraints can be worked out, it is doubtful that many internal auditors will be permitted to perform in the fashion envisioned by the Packard Commission.

AN ANTIFRAUD CHECKLIST

Those who are engaged in internal auditing or other segments of the corporate financial function know from observation or experience that the detection of fraud is infrequent. In fact, a 1983 issue of *Corporate Controller's Report* indicates that most fraud probably is undetected, and that 95 percent of the disclosed occurrences are discovered only by accident.[23] Yet, the internal auditor, along with other members of management—especially the controller—has a responsibility for developing an effective plan to discourage the attempt at fraud and to increase the chances of detecting the action once it has occurred. This same publication includes a recommended list of actions from Coopers & Lybrand's *Executive Alert Newsletter*, which several segments of management should subscribe to in order to improve the antifraud environment. The action checklist is as follows.[24]

Senior Management and the Board of Directors

☐ Adopt conflict-of-interest and questionable-payments policies, communicate them to all employees, and establish a method of monitoring activities.

☐ Establish the responsibility and related policy for action if fraud is suspected. The security policy should include specific guidance to management on whom to inform and what action to take at the outset of any investigation. Management should also decide under what general circumstances it will prosecute those suspected of fraud.

---

[23] *Corporate Controller's Report*, Nov. 1983, p. 3.
[24] *Ibid.*, pp. 4–5.

☐ Seek reports on fraudulent activity and make sure affirmative measures have been taken to prevent recurrence.

☐ Make sure that the internal auditors have access to all activities.

☐ Distribute a written code of conduct and set an example for other employees by following not only the letter but also the spirit of company policy.

☐ Establish and maintain an adequate system of internal control that emphasizes appropriate separation of duties.

Personnel Management

☐ Screen job applicants, particularly for key positions that will have access to assets.

☐ Require periodic evaluations of employee performance.

☐ Set fair performance measurement standards.

☐ Promote mandatory vacations for sensitive positions.

☐ Promote regular rotation of sensitive duties through cross-training.

Security Management

☐ Establish working relationships with internal audit, insurance, and legal management.

☐ Develop a security policy and review it with senior management.

☐ Investigate all significant fraudulent activities and make special recommendations to strengthen control and reduce exposure to loss.

☐ Monitor physical security at outlying locations.

☐ Make sure that investigative skill is available within the organization.

☐ Establish working relationships with local law enforcement agencies.

☐ Make sure that security personnel are sensitive to all assets, not just inventory items. (Even the most sophisticated fraudulent scheme requires access to the targeted asset.)

☐ Consider establishing a hot line for employees to anonymously report suspected wrongdoing.

Legal Management

☐ Contribute to and guide the development of a security policy, a conflict-of-interest policy, and an ethics statement.

☐ Provide counsel at the outset of any investigation to ensure that all rights are properly considered.

☐ Monitor changes in the law and advise all affected members of management.

Insurance Management

☐ Periodically evaluate insurance coverage based on the assets' economic worth, which may differ from their recorded value.

☐ Maintain fidelity coverage for sensitive positions.

☐ Advise responsible employees of insurance carrier notification and documentation requirements if a fraud is suspected.

☐ Help investigate significant losses.

External Auditor

☐ Skeptically assess business and control risk at the audit planning stage to make sure audit procedures consider potential for fraud.

☐ Establish working relationships with the internal auditors and management to identify problem areas and to make certain that a well-coordinated and responsive overall audit plan is developed.

Internal Audit Management

☐ Foster an attitude of healthy skepticism in all audit personnel.

☐ Establish a means by which to be informed of all fraudulent activities.

☐ Make sure that the scope of normal internal audits includes sensitivity to fraud and follow-up of all danger signals.

☐ Identify the areas at risk in your particular industry, monitor the controls established, and provide appropriate audit coverage.

☐ Maintain scheduling flexibility and respond to management requests for special investigation when appropriate.

Implementation of the above courses of action may not eliminate the fraud threat but it should deter all but the most determined thieves.

As shown by the preceding checklist, all members of management should take necessary steps to discourage fraud. By the same token, the internal audit staff should reduce the opportunities for fraud by increasing the probability of detection. Perhaps every internal audit should include procedures that reveal areas where internal controls can be improved—those spots where fraud is more likely.

A FRAUD QUESTIONNAIRE

A helpful questionnaire to be used by internal auditors, which can supplement any questionnaire developed on the basis of the material in this chapter, covers the following selected areas.[25]

Questionable Behavior of Personnel

The potential for fraudulent acts can be reduced by "weeding out" those key executives and employees who display extremely questionable behavior. The fol-

---

[25] From "Evaluating the Potential for Fraud," *Internal Auditing Alert*, Feb. 1984, pp. 5–6.

lowing inquiries to an appropriate individual in the personnel department should aid the auditor in pinpointing such individuals for management's further consideration.

☐ Do personnel records indicate that there are executives who have frequently changed jobs and/or residences, which might be an indication of instability?

☐ Do any of the executives have poor credit ratings as indicated by referrals from credit agencies?

☐ Have any of the executive salaries been garnished in order to satisfy personal debts?

☐ Have there been complaints concerning excessive use of alcohol and/or drugs by executives?

☐ Have any executives indicated resentment toward superiors and/or job dissatisfaction?

Personnel Policies

In some cases, the impact of specific personnel policies on key executives and employees may create an opportunity for the perpetration of fraud. Therefore, consider the following inquiries:

☐ Have any of the key executives recently failed to take annual vacations of more than one or two days, or has the company failed to rotate or to transfer key personnel on a periodic basis?

☐ Does the company fail to use adequate personnel screening policies when hiring new employees to fill positions of trust (e.g., check on secondary references)?

☐ Does the company lack explicit and uniform personnel policies?

☐ Does the company have compensation policies and fringe benefits that are commensurate with other companies in the same industry?

☐ Does the company lack adequate training programs?

☐ Is the company experiencing a rapid turnover of key employees?

Operating Policies

In some cases, the way a company conducts business can pressure executives to commit fraud on behalf of the company. The following inquiries can reveal an atmosphere favoring fraud:

☐ Has the company recently experienced severe losses from any major investments or ventures?

☐ Is the company attempting to operate with insufficient working capital?

☐ Does the company depend heavily on only one or two products, customers, or transactions?

☐ Does the company have an excess of idle productive capacity?

☐ Does the company suffer from obsolescence (i.e., is a significant amount of the inventory or are the physical facilities obsolete)?

☐ Does the company have such unusually high debts that debt service poses a threat to the stability of the company?

☐ Has the company expanded rapidly through new business or product lines? If so, has the expansion been orderly or has it been done in an attempt to salvage profitability?

☐ Is the company caught in a profit squeeze (i.e., are costs and expenses rising higher and faster than sales and revenues)?

☐ Is the company experiencing undue difficulty in collecting receivables (i.e., is the receivable turnover slowing down)?

☐ Does the company face unusually heavy competition so that its existence appears to be threatened?

☐ Do existing loan agreements provide little available tolerance on debt restrictions?

☐ Has the company's quality of earnings been progressively deteriorating (e.g., adopting straight-line depreciation to replace accelerated depreciation without good reason, or reporting profits but experiencing cash shortages)?

☐ Has the company recently experienced significant adverse tax assessments?

☐ Is the company experiencing an urgent need to report favorable earnings (e.g., to support a high stock price or to meet forecasted earnings)?

☐ Does the company have a significant amount of unmarketable collateral?

☐ Is the company experiencing a significant reduction in sales backlog, indicating a future decline in sales?

☐ Is the company involved in long-term contracts that have a large potential for loss?

☐ Does the company have any revocable or possibly imperiled licenses that are necessary for the firm's existence or continued operations?

☐ Is the company highly computerized? If so, are there sufficient controls over hardware, software, computer personnel, etc?

Too many negative answers to these questions should require a reevaluation of internal accounting control.

Accounting Practices

A company's accounting practices can place it in a vulnerable fraud position. Consider the following inquiries:

☐ Does the company have a number of large year-end or unusual transactions?

☐ Does the company have an inadequate internal control system or does it fail to enforce the existing internal controls?

☐ Does the company have unduly liberal accounting practices?

☐ Does the company have poor accounting records?

☐ Does the accounting department of the company appear to be inadequately staffed?

☐ Does the company fail to disclose questionable or unusual accounting practices?

BUSINESS ETHICS AND FRAUD

Economic Conditions

Certain economic conditions can be a prelude to fraud. Consider the following inquiries:

☐ Are there currently or have there recently been unfavorable economic conditions within the company's industry; or is the company's performance running counter to industry trends?

☐ Has tight credit or high interest rates reduced the company's ability to acquire credit?

☐ Is the company in a high-risk industry (e.g., the coal or diamond industry, which have often experienced a large number of business failures or frauds)?

The internal auditor must be alert to the possibility of fraud, or conditions that may encourage fraud, as part of every examination of a company's records or operations.

RESPONSIBILITY FOR DETECTING FRAUD

After a general review of the conditions that encourage fraud, some fraud indicia, some general preventive measures, the role of business ethics, and some general antifraud checklists and questionaires, it may be well to conclude the general discussion of fraud by considering the role of auditors and management accountants in detecting fraud.

While management, including the board of directors and the audit committee, has a major responsibility in deterring fraud through providing the proper ethical environment and adequate controls, the following financially oriented groups have a special responsibility regarding the *detection* of fraud:

- Independent accountants
- Internal auditors
- Government auditors, where applicable
- Management accountants

Comments on the responsibilities of each of these groups are discussed briefly, albeit that some serious debate still continues, especially regarding the independent accountants or external auditors.

Independent Accountants

One of the popular misconceptions is that an audit by independent accountants will uncover any existent fraud. The fact is that several types of fraud, such as that involving collusion, forgery, or unrecorded transactions, probably would not be discovered by even the best of auditors. Be that as it may, given the high incidence of fraud and the numerous companies and individuals victimized, the financial press, courts, and regulatory agencies have been advocating that the public accountants be more effective in the detection of fraud.

With the attention being directed to the responsibility of the independent accountant in uncovering fraud, the Auditing Standards Executive Committee of the AICPA stated:[26]

> The independent auditor's objective in making an examination of financial statements in accordance with generally accepted auditing standards is to form an opinion on whether the financial statements present fairly financial position, results of operations, and changes in financial position in conformity with generally accepted accounting principles consistently applied. Consequently, under generally accepted auditing standards the independent auditor has the responsibility, within the inherent limitations of the auditing process (see paragraphs .11–.13), to plan his examination (see paragraphs .06–.10) to search for errors or irregularities that would have a material effect on the financial statements, and to exercise due skill and care in the conduct of that examination. The auditor's search for material errors or irregularities ordinarily is accomplished by the performance of those auditing procedures that in his judgment are appropriate in the circumstances to form an opinion on the financial statements; extended auditing procedures are required if the auditor's examination indicates that material errors or irregularities may exist (see paragraph .14). An independent auditor's standad report implicitly indicates his belief that the financial statements taken as a whole are not materially misstated as a result of errors or irregularities.

Note that this statement says, "an independent auditor's standard report implicitly indicates his belief that the financial statements taken as a whole are not materially misstated as a result of errors or irregularities." Thus, the report concluded that the independent auditor is not responsible for the detection of fraud if his examination was made in accordance with GAAS. The study includes as a criterion the concept of materiality. Along the same line, the Cohen commission concluded that an auditor has a duty to search for fraud and should be expected to detect those frauds that the exercise of professional skill and care would normally uncover. As the study states, "[a]n audit should be designed to provide reasonable assurance that the financial statements are not affected by material fraud and also to provide reasonable assurance on the accountability of management for material amounts of corporate assets."[27]

The independent public accountant has accepted the responsibility to design his audit to detect *material* errors in financial statements. However,

---

[26] Statement on Auditing Standards No. 16, *The Independent Auditor's Responsibility for the Detection of Errors or Irregularities* (New York: American Institute of Certified Public Accountants, 1977), ¶ 5.

[27] *The Commission on Auditors Responsibilities: Report, Conclusions and Recommendations* (New York: American Institute of Certified Public Accounts, 1978), p. 36 (also referred to as the Cohen Report).

BUSINESS ETHICS AND FRAUD

the degree of responsibility for designing the audit to detect fraudulent financial reporting has been the subject of continuing debate. While the matter of detecting fraudulent financial reporting is reviewed in Chapter 23, it should be stated here that the NCFFR has made this recommendation, among others:

> *Recommendation:* The Auditing Standards Board should revise standards to restate the independent public accountant's responsibility for detection of fraudulent financial reporting, requiring the independent public accountant to (1) take affirmative steps in each audit to assess the potential for such reporting and (2) design tests to provide reasonable assurance of detection. Revised standards should include guidance for assessing risks and pursuing detection when risks are identified.[28]

Internal Auditors

Just as attention has been recently focused on the role of the independent accountant in detecting and deterring fraud, so it was natural that the activities of internal auditors would come under scrutiny.

As a summary, suffice it to say that the IIA has promoted the detection and deterrence of fraud in recent years through the following efforts, among others:[29]

- Conducting an annual conference on fraud deterrence and investigation for the past several years
- Conducting professional seminars on fraud detection and investigation in various cities, on an ongoing basis
- Publishing a major study on fraud, "Deterring Fraud: The Internal Auditor's Perspective"
- Publishing Section 280, a segment of Standards for the Professional Practice of Internal Auditing, which deals, among other matters, with due care as related to intentional wrongdoing
- Publishing SIAS No. 3, "Deterrence, Detection, Investigation, and Reporting of Fraud," which establishes guidelines for internal auditors regarding their responsibilities in cases of fraud

Section 280 is quoted as follows, although a condensed Standard 280 is contained in SIAS No. 3:

> Internal Auditors should exercise due professional care in performing internal audits.

---

[28] *Report of the National Commission on Fraudulent Financial Reporting, Exposure Draft, Apr. 1987* (Washington, D.C.: National Commission on Fraudulent Financial Reporting, 1987), p. 46.

[29] Adopted in part from "The Role of the Internal Auditor in the Deterrence, Detection, and Reporting of Fraudulent Financial Reporting" (Altamonte Springs, Fla.: The Institute of Internal Auditors for the National Commission on Fraudulent Financial Reporting).

.01 Due professional care calls for the application of the care and skill expected of a reasonably prudent and competent internal auditor in the same or similar circumstances. Professional care should, therefore, be appropriate to the complexities of the audit being performed. In exercising due professional care, internal auditors should be alert to the possibility of intentional wrongdoing, errors and omissions, inefficiency, waste, ineffectiveness, and conflicts of interest. They should also be alert to those conditions and activities where irregularities are most likely to occur. In addition, they should identify inadequate controls and recommend improvements to promote compliance with acceptable procedures and practices.

.02 Due care implies reasonable care and competence, not infallibility or extraordinary performance. Due care requires the auditor to conduct examinations and verifications to a reasonable extent, but does not require detailed audits of all transactions. Accordingly, the internal auditor cannot give absolute assurance that noncompliance or irregularities do not exist. Nevertheless, the possibility of material irregularities or noncompliance should be considered whenever the internal auditor undertakes an internal auditing assignment.

.03 When an internal auditor suspects wrongdoing, the appropriate authorities within the organization should be informed. The internal auditor may recommend whatever investigation is considered necessary in the circumstances. Thereafter, the auditor should follow up to see that the internal auditing department's responsibilities have been met.

.04 Exercising due professional care means using reasonable audit skill and judgment in performing the audit. To this end, the internal auditor should consider:

- **.1** The extent of audit work needed to achieve audit objectives
- **.2** The relative materiality or significance of matters to which audit procedures are applied
- **.3** The adequacy and effectiveness of internal controls
- **.4** The cost of auditing in relation to potential benefits

.05 Due professional care includes evaluating established operating standards and determining whether those standards are acceptable and are being met. When such standards are vague, authoritative interpretations should be sought. If internal auditors are required to interpret or select operating standards, they should seek agreement with auditees as to the standards needed to measure operating performance.

Accordingly, internal auditors should exercise ordinary prudence when developing audit programs and when performing an examination. Among other things, the auditors should:

1. Upon discovering a significant internal control weakness, make tests to ascertain whether or not an irregularity occurred because of it.
2. In what appear to be unusual or special transactions or circumstances, adopt a skeptical attitude about the responses to questions. As the Cohen report states, "[t]he exercise of professional skill and care requires healthy skepticism." Search for evidence to support the statements made to the auditor (or perhaps contrary support).

BUSINESS ETHICS AND FRAUD

3. Generally, be alert in thinking about how fraud could occur in the particular environment: "Think like a thief."

For the purposes of this chapter, the most relevant and recent document is SIAS No. 3, "Deterrence, Detection, Investigation, and Reporting of Fraud," which is reproduced in full as Figure 22-3. The responsibilities of the internal auditor are detailed there and summarized in the "Standards" section. As a succinct condensation, however, the following conclusions are drawn:

- ☐ *Deterrence of fraud.* While this is the responsibility of management, internal auditors are responsible for examining and evaluating the adequacy and effectiveness of actions taken by management to fulfill its obligation.

- ☐ *Detection of fraud.* The internal auditors should have sufficient knowledge of fraud to be able to identify indicators that fraud might have been committed. If significant control weaknesses are detected, as in a normal audit, testing should be extended, and should include an effort to identify other fraud indicators.

- ☐ *Investigation of fraud.* Once the evidence is strong enough to indicate fraud, the appropriate executives should be notified. The facts should be assessed as to the need to (1) implement or strengthen controls and (2) design audit tests to help disclose other fraud.

- ☐ *Reporting of fraud.* A written report should be prepared that includes all findings, conclusions, recommendations, and corrective action taken.

Government Auditors

In early 1987, the Comptroller General of the United States issued a draft of proposed revisions to "Standards for Audit of Governmental Organizations, Programs, Activities and Functions." Among other things, the revisions to the standards clarify the auditor's responsibility for detecting and reporting on fraud, abuse, and illegal acts. The entire set of standards, not just those relative to fraud, are to be followed by federal auditors who conduct audits of federal organizations, programs, activities, functions, and funds received by contractors, nonprofit organizations, and other nonfederal organizations. Federal legislation further requires that the standards be followed by state and local governments receiving federal financial assistance when conducting audits under the Single Audit Act of 1984. Then, too, the audit standards set forth in the Statement are also recommended for other audits of state and local government organizations, programs, activities, and functions performed by state or local government auditors or by public accountants.[30]

---

[30] *Standards for Audit of Governmental Organizations, Programs, Activities, and Functions*, Draft of 1987 Revisions, pp. 1-1–1-2.

The draft of the seventh fieldwork standard for government performance audits, which is the one relating to fraud, abuse and illegal acts, is quoted below.[31]

> ### G. Fraud, Abuse, and Illegal Acts
>
> - Auditors **should** be alert to situations or transactions that could be indicative of fraud, abuse, and illegal acts, and if such evidence exists, extend audit steps and procedures to identify the effect on the entity's operations and programs.
>
> **In making audits in accordance with the standards in this statement the auditors choose and perform audit steps and procedures that, in their professional judgment, are appropriate in the circumstances to achieve the audit objectives. To achieve the audit objectives the auditors perform audit steps and procedures designed to obtain sufficient, competent, and relevant evidence that will provide a reasonable basis for their judgments and conclusions regarding the audit objectives.**
>
> **In planning and performing audits, the auditor should design steps and procedures to detect situations or transactions that could be indicative of fraud, abuse, or illegal acts that could significantly impact on the audit objectives.**
>
> When audit steps and procedures indicate that fraud, abuse, or illegal acts may have occurred, the auditor needs to consider the potential impact of these acts on the audit objectives. If these acts could have an impact on the audit objectives, the auditor should extend the audit steps and procedures, as necessary, to determine whether they exist and the extent to which these acts significantly impact on the audit objectives. If an audit contract does not permit the auditor to unilaterally extend steps and procedures, the auditor should obtain written approval to perform the necessary additional work. If such approval is not given to the auditor, a scope impairment generally exists which should be reported by the auditor. To protect the government's interest and to avoid unnecessary audit work it is important that auditors exercise due professional care and caution in extending audit steps and procedures so as not to interfere with potential future investigations and/or legal proceedings. Due care would include obtaining legal counsel and advice of the cognizant law enforcement organization, where appropriate, to make this judgment. If the auditor or audit team does not possess the necessary qualifications and skills needed to effectively extend audit steps and procedures, after obtaining legal counsel they should promptly consult with knowledgeable persons before extending audit steps and procedures.
>
> Circumstances may exist where laws, regulations, or policies require auditors to promptly report indications of fraud and illegal acts to legal or investigatory authorities before extending audit steps and procedures. The auditor may also be required to withdraw from, or defer further work on, the audit or a portion of the audit in order not to interfere with an investigation. This requirement would not be inconsistent with the standards. However, the auditor should consider whether this would restrict the completion of the remaining portion of the audit or interfere

---

[31] *Ibid.*, pp. 6-22–6-25.

with the auditor's ability to form objective opinions and conclusions. If it restricts or interferes, the auditor should discontinue further action until completion of the investigation or terminate the audit.

Most auditors are not trained to conduct criminal investigations. This is the responsibility of the investigator or law enforcement authorities. However, auditors are responsible for knowing the characteristics of, techniques used to commit, and the types of fraud, abuse, and illegal acts associated with the area being audited to be able to identify indications that these acts may have occurred.

An audit made in accordance with the standards in this statement will not guarantee the discovery of all fraud, abuse, or illegal acts that might have been committed. Nor does the subsequent discovery of fraud, abuse, or illegal acts committed during the audit period necessarily mean the auditors' performance was inadequate, **provided** the audit was made in accordance with these standards.

As evidenced by this Standard and other publications[32] (see Chapter 24), the GAO, the Inspector General of the DOD, and other agencies are vigorously pursuing the detection of fraud.

Management Accountants

In a volume directed largely to professional accountants and auditors, the authors probably would be remiss to discuss the responsibilities of management and of the various groups of *auditors* regarding fraud detection and deterrence without specifically addressing the ethics and desired conduct of the management accountants—those professionals who make the wheels turn, and who often are not members of top management.

Whether due to greater competition, the recent recession, the disastrous inflation, or other causes, there have been frequent accounts of management fraud recently. Even an issue of *The Wall Street Journal* had a featured article on the first page, entitled "Cooking the Books, SEC Charges Fudging of Corporate Figures Is a Growing Practice." Such expressions as "slush funds" or "cooking the books" give business in general, and accountants in particular, a bad name. Perhaps as a step to restoring trust in business and as a guide to management integrity, the NAA issued the following statement on ethical conduct for management accountants. Previously, management accountants were left to operate under their own instincts or conscience, as contrasted with CPAs who operated under a formal code of ethics. By articulating the responsibilities of management accountants, the new statement may assist internal auditors and help improve the control environment.

---

[32] *Standards for the Professional Practice of Internal Auditing,* Section 280, Due Professional Care (The Institute of Internal Auditors, 1979).

STATEMENT OF MANAGEMENT ACCOUNTING NO. 1C: STANDARDS OF ETHICAL CONDUCT FOR MANAGEMENT ACCOUNTANTS[33]

Preface

In accordance with the charge to the Management Accounting Practices (MAP) Committee to issue authoritative statements on accounting principles and practices, Statements on Management Accounting reflect official positions of the National Association of Accountants (NAA). The work of the MAP Committee is based on a framework for management accounting, whose principal categories are:

- Objectives
- Terminology
- Concepts
- Practices and Techniques
- Management of Accounting Activities

The NAA inaugurated its series of Statements on Management Accounting by publishing Statement No. 1A, *Definition of Management Accounting*. Statement No. 1B, *Objectives of Management Accounting*, embraces the definition and states in detail the NAA's view of the various roles and responsibilities assumed by the management accountant. Statement No. 1C, *Standards of Ethical Conduct for Management Accountants*, describes the ethical standards to which a management accountant is to subscribe in order to achieve the objectives of management accounting.

Competence

Management accountants have an obligation to the organizations they serve, their profession, the public, and themselves, to maintain the highest standards of ethical conduct. In recognition of this obligation, the National Association of Accountants has promulgated the following standards of ethical conduct for management accountants. Adherence to these standards is integral to achieving the *Objectives of Management Accounting*.[34]

Management accountants shall not commit acts contrary to these standards nor shall they condone the commission of such acts by others within their organizations. Management accountants have a responsibility to:

- Maintain an appropriate level of professional competence by ongoing development of their knowledge and skills.
- Perform their professional duties in accordance with relevant laws, regulations and technical standards.
- Prepare complete and clear reports and recommendations after appropriate analyses of relevant and reliable information.

---

[33] From *Management Accounting*, Sept. 1983, pp. 69–70.

[34] National Association of Accountants, *Statements on Management Accounting: Objectives of Management Accounting*, Statement No. 1B, New York, June 17, 1982.

Confidentiality

Management accountants have a responsibility to:

- Refrain from disclosing confidential information acquired in the course of their work except when authorized, unless legally obligated to do so.
- Inform subordinates as appropriate regarding the confidentiality of information acquired in the course of their work and monitor their activities to assure the maintenance of that confidentiality.
- Refrain from using or appearing to use confidential information acquired in the course of their work for unethical or illegal advantage either personally or through third parties.

Integrity

Management accountants have a responsibility to:

- Avoid actual or apparent conflicts of interest and advise all appropriate parties of any potential conflict.
- Refrain from engaging in any activity that would prejudice their ability to carry out their duties ethically.
- Refuse any gift, favor or hospitality that would influence or would appear to influence their actions.
- Refrain from either actively or passively subverting the attainment of the organization's legitimate and ethical objectives.
- Recognize and communicate professional limitations or other constraints that would preclude responsible judgment or successful performance of an activity.
- Communicate unfavorable as well as favorable information and professional judgments or opinions.
- Refrain from engaging in or supporting any activity that would discredit the profession.

Objectivity

Management accountants have a responsibility to:

- Communicate information fairly and objectively.
- Disclose fully all relevant information that could reasonably be expected to influence an intended user's understanding of the reports, comments, and recommendations presented.

Resolution of Ethical Conflict

In applying the standards of ethical conduct, management accountants may encounter problems in identifying unethical behavior or in resolving an ethical conflict. When faced with significant ethical issues management accountants should follow the established policies of the organization bearing on the resolution of such conflict. If these policies do not resolve the ethical conflict, management accountants should consider the following courses of action:

- Discuss such problems with the immediate superior except when it appears that the superior is involved, in which case the problem should be presented initially to the next higher managerial level. If satisfactory resolution cannot be achieved when the problem is initially presented, submit the issues to the next higher managerial level.

    If the immediate superior is the chief executive officer, or equivalent, the acceptable reviewing authority may be a group such as the audit committee, executive committee, board of directors, board of trustees, or owners. Contact with levels above the immediate superior should be initiated only with the superior's knowledge, assuming the superior is not involved.
- Clarify relevant concepts by confidential discussion with an objective advisor to obtain an understanding of possible courses of action.
- If the ethical conflict still exists after exhausting all levels of internal review, the management accountant may have no other recourse on significant matters than to resign from the organization and to submit an informative memorandum to an appropriate representative of the organization.

Except where legally prescribed, communication of such problems to authorities or individuals not employed or engaged by the organization is not considered appropriate.

Although corporate codes of ethics do exist, Statement on Management Accounting No. 1C may be helpful in creating a measure of consistency.

SPECIAL FRAUD INVESTIGATIONS

Definition

A special fraud investigation is defined here to mean an unplanned undertaking that is requested or directed as a result of a management concern stemming from a revelation suggesting the possibility of a dishonest act, irregularity, or illegality. Requests for such undertakings may come from any segment of management, although directed investigations usually come from senior management or the audit committee. The revelation may come in the form of a tip—perhaps via the company's hot line—or a letter. On the other hand, it may come through the routine oversight and review process performed by management. The revelation may be a direct allegation of kickbacks, for example, or of bid rigging. Or it may be more subtle, such as an uneasiness that senior management might feel about the disparity between reported business plans of a particular business segment and the expectations for that segment.

Special fraud investigations may be known by other terms, such as special investigations, special reviews, and inquiries. Many of these reviews may be performed in whole or in part by internal auditors.

Nature of the Work

By definition, special fraud investigations, usually, are not identifiable at the time the chief auditor prepares the annual plan of audit coverage. He may know on the basis of experience that such requests will be made. He can allocate time in a generic sense, but he cannot know in what form, where, or when such work might arise.

Another facet of special fraud investigations is that they often require fast action on short notice. Time is of the utmost importance. Thus, the chief auditor must develop a quick response capability. At the same time, however, he must be certain that the work performed is reliable and complete. Those involved in the investigative work are under much pressure to report progress, often to an impatient management. Care must be taken so that the auditor is not pressured into reporting what management wants to hear rather than what is.

Special fraud investigations more and more frequently are being directed by company legal counsel. In that way, the work product of internal auditors who may be involved will be protected from discovery by the attorney-client privilege or the attorney work product privilege (see Chapter 9). The chief auditor or project leader should make certain as early as possible whether the investigation is to be so protected.

Special fraud investigations may be short term in nature but a few may be quite time consuming and may disrupt considerably the planned audit work. The chief auditor or his designee must be certain that management and, if necessary, the audit committee are aware of the effects special fraud investigations may be having on other planned work. In extreme cases, it may be necessary for the chief auditor to seek additional manpower.

Standards and Procedures Employed

Special fraud investigations are performed in much the same way as any audit project. The work should be performed in accordance with the same high standards of auditing, such as those of the IIA (see Chapter 6). That means the work should be properly planned, performed by persons with appropriate skills, and the information gathered should be sufficient to support the findings and conclusions.

The specific audit procedures used are also similar to those used in routine audits. Inquiry and inspection of records are perhaps the most frequent procedures. Observation techniques are useful in some situations and, of course, confirmation techniques may be used to verify assertions and representations. Documentation of the procedures performed in the form of workpapers is done in much the same way as in regular audits.

Reporting

Special fraud investigations entail special reporting considerations. Obviously, any written reports are apt to have limited distribution. If the work is under attorney-client privilege, the report will probably be addressed or communicated to legal counsel. The form and structure of the written report will be determined by the nature of the work. Managements in these special situations are not likely to be interested in whether the auditor believes that fraud has occurred. They are more interested in finding out what the facts and circumstances are. The determination of fraud is a legal decision and one that internal auditors are not qualified to make. It is best to let the company legal counsel advise management on what the legal implications of the facts and circumstances are.

Whistle-blowing

In recent years, the question has arisen: To whom should the internal auditor report information that he believes suggests that fraud or other irregularities may have occurred? The authors choose to discuss the question in the context of special fraud investigations because it is in such contexts that internal auditors are more likely to ponder what their ethical responsibility for reporting is.

Whistle-blowing is a term that has come to mean informing persons outside the company—usually government regulators or authorities—about suspected wrongdoing. The problem has become more acute since the federal government created hot lines and actively promoted their use by anyone to report suspected fraud.

Ethically speaking, the authors believe internal auditors are under no general duty to inform outsiders of suspected wrongdoing. Internal auditors are under an ethical duty to report suspected wrongdoing to management. Management, in turn, is under an ethical obligation to investigate such suspicions—perhaps using the internal auditor, in part, as the investigating mechanism.

The authors believe the question of reporting suspected wrongdoing to outsiders must be decided by management. Such decisions must be made on the basis of all relevant facts and circumstances, including any legal requirements for such reporting.

If management fails to act prudently to discharge its ethical duty to investigate or if it investigates but fails to report when such reporting is required by law, the internal auditor is under an ethical duty to report such situations to the company's audit committee. The responsibility of audit committees is such that it is all but inconceivable that it would fail to make proper inquiry and disposition of the situation. In the very rare situation where internal auditors are not satisfied as to the course of action and resolution of the audit committee, the internal auditor should resign from the company and seek legal advice as to further actions he should take. In such situations, it is not unimaginable that the internal auditor may be advised to report his information to the proper authorities.

The question of reporting sensitive information is one in need of further research and guidance. The IIA, through its Research Foundation, is preparing a research paper on the subject. The issue is important because the role of internal auditors is such that they are more apt to become aware of wrongdoing than are other employees. The study is focusing on five questions:

1. Under what conditions do internal auditors report wrongdoing?
2. What pressures for and against reporting wrongdoing are experienced by internal auditors?
3. What consequences ensue for internal auditors who report wrongdoing?
4. How many negative consequences could be avoided or, at least, alleviated for internal auditors who report wrongdoing?
5. In what ways may discontinuation of the wrongdoing and an organizational change best be effected by internal auditors?[35]

The research should provide valuable information regarding current practice in this area.

SIAS No. 3

A short word is in order about special fraud investigations. SIAS No. 3, in the section relating to detection of fraud, indicates that, as to a *regular* audit assignment, internal auditing's responsibilities are to:

- Have sufficient knowledge of fraud to be able to identify indicators that fraud may have been committed.
- If warranted, conduct additional tests to detect further fraud indicators.
- Recommend whether a fraud investigation should be undertaken.

Paragraph 8 states, however, that internal auditors are not expected to have knowledge equivalent to that of a person whose primary responsibility is detecting and investigating fraud. It also states that audit procedures alone, even when carried out with due professional care, do not guarantee that fraud will be detected.

---

[35] From a draft report by Janet P. Near, PhD., and Marcia P. Miceli, D.B.A., *The Internal Auditor's Ultimate Responsibility: The Reporting of Sensitive Issues* for Institute of Internal Auditor's Research Foundation, dated Aug. 3, 1987.

SIAS No. 3, in the section relating to investigation of fraud, defines special investigation and outlines internal auditing's responsibilities. There is no need to restate here the pertinent comments from Figure 22-3, other than to note these two clauses:

- *From Section 9:* "Internal auditors, lawyers, investigators, security personnel, and other specialists from inside or outside the organization are the parties that usually conduct or participate in fraud investigations."
- *From Section 10d:* Internal auditing should "coordinate activities with management personnel, legal counsel, and other specialists as appropriate throughout the course of the investigation."

It seems that the IIA is alerting the internal auditors to the many potential traps as well as legal processes that must be observed. It seems to serve the interest of all concerned that the proper talent and procedures be selected to permit the reaching of correct conclusions and punishments in the deterrence of fraud.

COORDINATION WITH THE LEGAL DEPARTMENT

It is, of course, far better for an auditor to prevent fraud than it is to spend time and money searching out the facts and diverting company resources to recover the loss and punish the offender. However, trails of fraud must be pursued to a conclusion. Suffice it to say that there are legal hazards and pitfalls in the process. The auditor, not being a lawyer in most instances, should consult with and secure guidance from the company (or outside) legal department. Libel or slander, malicious prosecution, and false imprisonment are dangers to be avoided by both the auditor and the company.

An example of the need for close coordination of the internal audit department with the legal department is shown in Figure 22-4, an excerpt of instructions in a policy manual relating to the discovery of possibly questionable acts.

USE OF INFORMANTS?

For our purposes, an informant or concerned employee refers to those who report suspected fraud by going outside their normal reporting lines to such groups as security, top management, or internal auditors, whether done anonymously, by hot line or other means, or on an identified basis.

SIAS No. 3, discussed earlier in this chapter, relates to the deterrence, detection, investigation, and reporting of fraud. While the standard makes no reference to informants as such, in Section 6, relative to identifying indicators of fraud, it does refer to such acts that may arise—"as a result of controls established by management, tests conducted by auditors, and other sources both within and outside the organization." As in many criminal investigations, so also in internal auditing, it would be very difficult in some organizations to detect certain kinds of fraud without the information provided by concerned employees or other informants.

It seems that the internal auditor should discreetly use such third-party information either in searching for fraud or in assisting those who are trained in fraud detection. However, as one source states,[36] the auditor needs to be sensitive to the position and risks any employee, if his identity is known, is taking when he provides information.

SUMMARY

It is not possible to cover a subject as complex as fraud in a single chapter. We have attempted to discuss the circumstances that lead to fraud and the devices and conditions that should be used in deterrence and detection. The authors suggest the reader refer to the many books and articles in periodic literature on the matter—especially on the many ways in which fraud can be committed. (See Suggested Reading.)

It is to be stressed that the internal auditor now has a greater role to play in the prevention and detection of irregularities. While all management has certain responsibilities, as discussed, it may be that the chief internal auditor again may be the fountainhead for corrective action. Indeed, he should be much more familiar with the system and procedures of the company so that he can actively assist both management and the independent accountants in coping with the problem.

SUGGESTED READING

The Institute of Internal Auditors Reports on Fraud. Altamonte Springs, Fla.: The Institute of Internal Auditors, Sept. 1986.

Report of the National Commission on Fraudulent Financial Reporting, Exposure Draft. Washington, D.C.: National Commission on Fraudulent Financial Reporting, Apr. 1987.

Russell, Harold F. *Foozels and Frauds*. Altamonte Springs, Fla.: The Institute of Internal Auditors, 1977.

Levy, Marvin M. "Financial Fraud: Schemes and Indicia." *Journal of Accountancy*, Aug. 1985, pp. 78–87.

The Packard Commission. *Conduct and Accountability, a Report to the President*, June 1986.

---

[36] "The Auditor and the Informant," *The Internal Auditor*, Feb. 1987, p. 26.

CHAPTER **23**

Fraudulent Financial Reporting

Introduction	1	The NCFFR	3
Conditions of Fraudulent Financial Reporting	2	Summary of NCFFR Recommendations	4
Participants in the Financial Reporting Process	3	Suggested Reading	10

INTRODUCTION

In the mid-to-late 1980s, there have been a number of large and highly publicized bankruptcies caused by management fraud, and the occasional failure of public accounting firms to detect it. This has motivated many concerned groups to reexamine financial statement fraud and the steps that might be taken to prevent it. Such groups include the accounting profession, federal regulators, corporate management, and boards of directors.

Financial statement fraud has been defined by one authority as "deliberate fraud committed by management that potentially injures investors and creditors through materially misleading financial statements."[1] This definition identifies the class of perpetrator, the class of victim, and the means of perpetration; it excludes those instances where users of financial statements are injured by unintentional errors.

There has been a good deal of publicity about white collar crime that is not financial statement fraud (e.g., kickbacks, bribes, and embezzlements). However, this should not detract from efforts to detect and deter financial statement fraud. But, it does suggest that the number of such instances are relatively small compared to other fraudulent actions.

---

[1] Robert K. Elliott and Peter D. Jacobson, "Detecting and Deterring Financial Statement Fraud," *Corporate Accounting,* Fall 1986, p. 34.

The purpose of this chapter is to comment on the causes of financial statement fraud and to present recommendations by the prestigious Treadway Commission regarding the preparation of financial statements.

CONDITIONS OF FRAUDULENT FINANCIAL REPORTING

When the conditions that lead to fraud are better understood, then those responsible for detecting such events may know when and where to be more vigilant. Of course, this knowledge also provides guidance in determining what procedures should be examined and improved. To an extent, the same circumstances that encourage fraud generally (see Chapter 22) may be present in cases of financial statement fraud. The Treadway Commission (discussed later in this chapter under the NCFFR) indicates, however, that fraudulent financial reporting usually occurs when certain individual, institutional, or environmental forces and opportunities are present.

Some of the forces or pressures on an individual manager or on a company include:

- Desire to obtain a higher price from a debt or stock offering.
- Desire to postpone a financial difficulty (e.g., default on a restrictive bond covenant).
- Desire for personal financial gain (e.g., greater incentive pay, based on company or division earnings).
- Attempts to offset or cover up sudden decreases in market share or sales levels.
- Undue pressures to meet the annual profit plan.

Given these pressures, fraudulent financial reporting is much easier if, additionally, the environment or conditions seem to facilitate it. Circumstances that could encourage fraud include such matters as:

- Perception that top management is not too concerned about promoting an ethical environment and behavior.
- Weak or nonexistant internal accounting controls.
- Absence of a board of directors or an audit committee (composed of independent directors) that vigorously oversees the financial reporting process.
- An ineffective internal audit staff.
- Accounting estimates (revenues, costs, or expenses) that require substantial subjective judgment by company management (e.g., estimates of future costs, loan reserve requirements, or annual warranty expense provision).
- Complex or unusual transactions (e.g., the closing of a facility, or the sale of an operation).

The perpetrators of fraudulent financial reporting in a company could be any of several categories. In a majority of cases, however, it is top management itself. It might even include operating managers of a division, accountants, sales representatives, or other executives who have something to gain. In addition, very frequently, fraudulent financial reporting does not begin initially with the intent to deceive or distort statements. As operational difficulties become more intense, however, the final result can be pressure for more and more fraudulent reporting.

PARTICIPANTS IN THE FINANCIAL REPORTING PROCESS

Any review of fraudulent financial reporting should consider the role of each of the participants involved with the normal financial reporting process. Only when the functions of each segment are known can suggestions be made for possible improvements.

The principal participants are:

- The company and its management.
- The independent public accountant.
- Various regulatory and law enforcement agencies.

The primary responsibility for reliable financial reporting rests with the company and its top management. It must "set the tone" and establish the proper reporting environment. Included would be such practices as:

- Establishing a vigilant, informed, independent audit committee.
- Creating and maintaining an effective internal audit function.
- Providing a proper system of controls: accounting, operating, and administrative.

Also at interest are the independent public accountants. Although their role may be regarded as secondary, they do present an opinion on the content of the financial statements. Some of their responsibilities as regards detecting fraud are reviewed in Chapter 22. Of course, some of the public do not know just what the respective responsibilities of the independent accountant versus management are.

Finally, regulatory and law enforcement agencies, especially the SEC, provide some deterrence in reducing fraudulent financial reporting.

Then, too, although not directly involved, educators can provide some assistance in reducing fraudulent financial reporting by causing business and accounting students to be aware of the causes of such fraud and the controls needed to reduce it.

As will be deduced, improvements can be made in each functional area.

THE NCFFR

To delve into the subject of fraudulent financial statements, the NCFFR, a private sector initiative, was sponsored and funded by the prominent associations concerned with the subject: AICPA, AAA, FEI, IIA, and NAA. In October 1987, this Commission, also known as the Treadway Commission, issued its final report on how to reduce fraudulent financial reporting. Its recommendations are summarized below. By way of prefatory comment, the Commission focused on public companies, that is, companies owned by public investors. In this context, it had three principal subject areas to investigate:

1. The extent to which fraudulent financial reporting undermines the integrity of financial reporting, including the environment; forces contributing to the fraudulent acts; and, among other things, the extent to which it can be detected and prevented.
2. The role of the independent public accountant in detecting fraud.
3. Those attributes of the corporate structure that may contribute to acts of fraudulent financial reporting or to the failure to promptly detect such acts.

The scope of the study is indeed broad, extending from the complex multifaceted aspects of the corporate structure itself, to the independent public accountant, through the regulatory and legal environment, to even the education of the participants involved in the financial reporting process.

SUMMARY OF NCFFR RECOMMENDATIONS

The summary of recommendations should provide insight into the problem. In general it should be recognized, however, that (1) many of the more alert public companies are in fact doing largely (but not wholly) what is being recommended, and (2) in many of the recommendations, the Commission is extending somewhat the edges of the art or science in probing and detecting fraudulent actions.

A condensed summary of the recommendations follows.

1. Recommendations for the Public Company

☐ **The Tone at the Top**

Recommendation: For the top management of a public company to discharge its obligation to oversee the financial reporting process, it must identify, understand, and assess the factors that may cause the company's financial statements to be fraudulently misstated.

Recommendation: Public companies should maintain internal controls that are adequate to prevent and detect fraudulent financial reporting.

Recommendation: Public companies should develop and enforce written codes of corporate conduct. Codes of conduct should foster a strong ethical climate and open channels of communication to help protect against fraudulent financial reporting. As a part of its ongoing oversight of the effectiveness of internal controls, a company's audit committee should review annually the program that management establishes to monitor compliance with the code.

☐ **Accounting Function and Chief Accounting Officer**

Recommendation: Public companies should maintain accounting functions that are designed to meet their financial reporting obligations.

☐ **Internal Audit Function and Chief Internal Auditor**

Recommendation: Public companies should maintain an effective internal audit function staffed with an adequate number of qualified personnel appropriate to the size and the nature of the company.

Recommendation: Public companies should ensure that their internal audit functions are objective.

Recommendation: Internal auditors should consider the implications of their nonfinancial audit findings for the company's financial statements.

Recommendation: Management and the audit committee should ensure that the internal auditors' involvement in the audit of the entire financial reporting process is appropriate and properly coordinated with the independent public accountant.

☐ **Mandatory Independent Audit Committee**

Recommendation: The board of directors of all public companies should be required by SEC rule to establish audit committees comprised solely of independent directors.

Recommendation: Audit committees should be informed, vigilant, and effective overseers of the financial reporting process and the company's internal controls.

Recommendation: All public companies should develop a written charter setting forth the duties and responsibilities of the audit committee. The board of directors should approve the charter, review it periodically, and modify it as necessary.

Recommendation: Audit committees should have adequate resources and authority to discharge their responsibilities.

Recommendation: The audit committee should review management's evaluation of factors related to the independence of the company's public accountant. Both the audit committee and management should assist the public accountant in preserving his independence.

Recommendation: Before the beginning of each year, the audit committee should review management's plans for engaging the company's independent public accountant to perform management advisory services during the coming year, considering both the types of services that may be rendered and the projected fees.

☐ **Reporting on Responsibilities in the Annual Report to Stockholders**

Recommendation: All public companies should be required by SEC rule to include in their annual reports to stockholders management reports signed by the chief executive officer and chief accounting officer. The management report should acknowledge management's responsibilities for the financial statements and internal control, discuss how these responsibilities were fulfilled, and provide management's assessment of the effectiveness of the company's internal controls.

Recommendation: All public companies should be required by SEC rule to include in their annual reports to stockholders a letter signed by the chairman of the audit committee describing the committee's responsibilities and activities during the year.

☐ **Seeking a Second Opinion**

Recommendation: Management should advise the audit committee when it seeks a second opinion on a significant accounting issue.

Recommendation: When a public company changes independent public accountants, it should be required by SEC rule to disclose publicly the nature of any material accounting or auditing issue discussed with both its old and new auditor during the three-year period preceding the change.

☐ **Quarterly Reporting**

Recommendation: Audit committees should oversee the quarterly reporting process. This oversight should include approving financial results prior to public release.

☐ **Guidance on Internal Control**

Recommendation: The Commission's sponsoring organizations should cooperate in developing additional, integrated guidance on internal control.

2. Recommendations for the Independent Public Accountant

☐ **Recognizing Responsibility for Detecting Fraudulent Financial Reporting**

Recommendation: The Auditing Standards Board should revise standards to restate the independent public accountant's responsibility for detection of fraudulent financial reporting, requiring the independent public accountant to (1) take affirmative steps in each audit to assess the potential for such reporting and (2) design tests to provide reasonable assurance of detection. Revised standards should include guidance for assessing risks and pursuing detection when risks are identified.

☐ **Improving Detection Capabilities**

Recommendation: The Auditing Standards Board should establish standards to require independent public accountants to perform analytical review procedures in all audit engagements and should provide improved guidance on the appropriate use of these procedures.

Recommendation: The SEC should require independent public accountants to review quarterly financial data of public companies before release to the public.

☐ Improving Audit Quality

Recommendation: The AICPA's SEC Practices Section should strengthen its peer review program by increasing review of audit engagements involving public company clients new to a firm. For each office selected for peer review, the first audit of all such new clients should be reviewed.

Recommendation: The AICPA's SEC Practices Section requirement for a concurring, or second partner, review of the audit report should be revised as part of an ongoing process of review of this requirement. Standards for the concurring review should, among other things, (1) require concurring review partner involvement in the planning stage of the audit in addition to the final review stage, (2) specify qualifications of the concurring review partner to require prior experience with audits of SEC registrants and familiarity with the client's industry, and (3) require the concurring review partner to consider himself a peer of the engagement partner for purposes of the review.

Recommendation: Public accounting firms should recognize and control the organizational and individual pressures that potentially reduce audit quality.

☐ Communicating the Auditor's Role

Recommendation: The Auditing Standards Board should revise the auditor's standard report to state that the audit provides reasonable but not absolute assurance that the audited financial statements are free from material misstatements as a result of fraud or error.

Recommendation: The Auditing Standards Board should revise the auditor's standard report to describe the extent to which the independent public accountant has reviewed and evaluated the system of internal accounting control. The Auditing Standards Board also should provide explicit guidance to address the situation where, as a result of his knowledge of the company's internal accounting controls, the independent public accountant disagrees with management's assessment as stated in the proposed management's report.

☐ Reorganization of the Auditing Standards Board

Recommendation: The AICPA should reorganize the Auditing Standards Board to afford a full participatory role in the standard-setting process to knowledgeable persons who are affected by and interested in auditing standards but who either are not CPAs or are CPAs no longer in public practice.

3. Recommendations for the SEC and Others to Improve the Regulatory and Legal Environment

☐ Additional SEC Enforcement Remedies

Recommendation: The SEC should have the authority to impose civil money penalties in administrative proceedings [including Rule 2(e) proceedings] and to seek civil money penalties from a court directly in an injunctive proceeding.

Recommendation: The SEC should have the authority to issue a cease and desist order when it finds a securities law violation.

Recommendation: The SEC should seek explicit statutory authority to bar or suspend corporate officers and directors involved in fraudulent financial reporting from future service in that capacity in a public company.

☐ **Increased Criminal Prosecution**

Recommendation: Criminal prosecution of fraudulent financial reporting cases should become a higher priority. The SEC should conduct an affirmative program to promote increased criminal prosecution of fraudulent financial reporting cases by educating and assisting government officials with criminal prosecution powers.

☐ **Improved Regulation of the Public Accounting Profession**

Recommendation: The SEC should require all public accounting firms that audit public companies to be members of a professional organization that has peer review and independent oversight functions and is approved by the SEC, such as that specified by the SECPS of the AICPA's Division for CPA Firms.

Recommendation: The SEC should take enforcement action when a public accounting firm fails to remedy deficiencies cited in the public accounting profession's quality assurance program.

☐ **SEC Resources**

Recommendation: The SEC must be given adequate resources to perform existing and additional functions that help prevent, detect, and deter fraudulent financial reporting.

☐ **Financial Institution Regulatory Agencies**

Recommendation: The Office of the Comptroller of the Currency, the Federal Reserve Board, the Federal Deposit Insurance Corporation, and the Federal Home Loan Bank Board (including the Federal Savings and Loan Insurance Corporation) should adopt measures patterned on the Commission's recommendations directed to the SEC to carry out their own regulatory responsibility relating to financial reporting under the federal securities laws.

Recommendation: The financial institution regulatory agencies and the public accounting profession should provide for the regulatory examiner and the independent public accountant to have mutual access to information they develop about examined financial institutions.

☐ **Enhanced Enforcement by State Boards of Accountancy**

Recommendation: State boards of accountancy should implement positive enforcement programs that periodically would review the quality of services that the independent public accountants they license render.

☐ **Considering the Implications of Liability on Audit Quality**

Recommendation: Parties charged with responding to various tort reform initiatives should consider the implications that the perceived liability crisis holds for long-term audit quality and the independent public accountant's detection of fraudulent financial reporting.

☐ **Reconsidering Corporate Indemnification**

Recommendation: The SEC should reconsider its long-standing position, insofar as it applies to independent directors, that the corporate indemnification of officers and directors for liabilities that arise under the Securities Act of 1933 is against public policy and therefore unenforceable.

4. Recommendations for Education

☐ **Business and Accounting Curricula**

Recommendation: Throughout the business and accounting curricula, educators should foster knowledge and understanding of the factors that may cause fraudulent financial reporting and the strategies that can lead to a reduction in its incidence.

Recommendation: The business and accounting curricula should promote a better understanding of the function and the importance of internal controls, including the control environment, in preventing, detecting, and deterring fraudulent financial reporting.

Recommendation: Business and accounting students should be well-informed about the regulation and enforcement activities by which government and private bodies safeguard the financial reporting system and thereby protect the public interest.

Recommendation: The business and accounting curricula should help students develop stronger analytical, problem solving, and judgment skills to help prevent, detect, and deter fraudulent financial reporting when they become participants in the financial reporting process.

Recommendation: The business and accounting curricula should emphasize ethical values by integrating their development with the acquisition of knowledge and skills to help prevent, detect, and deter fraudulent financial reporting.

Recommendation: Business schools should encourage business and accounting faculty to develop their own personal competence as well as classroom materials for conveying information, skills, and ethical values that can help prevent, detect, and deter fraudulent financial reporting. Business school faculty reward systems should recognize and reward the contributions of faculty who develop such competence and materials.

☐ **Professional Certification Examinations**

Recommendation: Professional certification examinations should test students on the information, skills, and ethical values that further the understanding of fraudulent financial reporting and that promote its reduction.

☐ **Continuing Professional Education**

Recommendation: As part of their continuing professional education, independent public accountants, internal auditors, and corporate accountants should study the forces and opportunities that contribute to fraudulent financial reporting, the risk factors that may indicate its occurrence, and the relevant ethical and technical standards.

SUGGESTED READING

Elliott, Robert K., and Peter D. Jacobson. "Detecting and Deterring Financial Statement Fraud." *Corporate Accounting,* Fall 1986, pp. 34–39.

The Institute of Internal Auditors Reports on Fraud. Altamonte Springs, Fla.: The Institute of Internal Auditors, Sept. 1986.

Report of the National Commission on Fraudulent Financial Reporting. Washington, D.C.: National Commission on Fraudulent Financial Reporting, Oct. 1987.

Treadway, James C., Jack L. Krogstad, and Shirley A. Sunderland. "Financial Reporting and Public Confidence." *Corporate Accounting,* Fall 1986, pp. 4–8.

CHAPTER **24**

Procurement Fraud: The Government and Private Sector

Introduction	1	Indicators of Fraud in DOD Procurement	5
Minimizing Fraud on Government Contracts	2	Labor Fraud Indicators	5
		Material Fraud Indicators	5
		Defective Pricing Fraud	38
Some U.S. Government Publications	2	Self-Policing by DOD Contractors	38

Fig. 24-1 Minimizing Vulnerability to Fraud 3
Fig. 24-2 Indicators of Fraud in Department of Defense Procurement 6

INTRODUCTION

Headlines about fraud are not restricted to any one type. Embezzlements, swindles, management fraud, and procurement fraud all make the news. Given the heavy procurement budget by the U.S. government, it is understandable that much attention would be directed by the government to procurement fraud. With the tremendous buildup in the defense area, the Department of Justice and the DOD have been embarrassed on a number of occasions by disclosures about, among other things, illegal invoicing practices and overpriced spare parts. Of course, under some circumstances, the same improper activities can befall state and local governments as well as the private sector. Various agencies of the U.S. government, as a defense against fraud, have published some excellent material both on the indicies of fraud and on the auditing standards to be followed in detecting such activity.

It is the intention in this chapter to review procurement fraud in general and to provide some guidance on available literature that may be helpful to the auditor. Although much of the data is designed to assist the federal auditor, it may also be useful in the private sector.

MINIMIZING FRAUD ON GOVERNMENT CONTRACTS

With the heavy defense programs, a great many firms are engaged in business with the federal government. Given the possibility of damage to a company's reputation from some misunderstood, and often minor, transaction, even when there is no fraud, it is extremely important that nothing an enterprise does or says can be construed as fraud. Even though general policy statements and codes of ethics, in writing, prohibit fraud, it seems that some employees, for whatever reason, may attempt, or commit, fraudulent acts for which the company may be prosecuted. It is therefore imperative that an entity doing business with the U.S. government attempt to minimize its vulnerability. How? The independent public accounting firm of Touche Ross & Co. has published some suggestions on this subject. A portion of the article is presented in Figure 24-1.

SOME U.S. GOVERNMENT PUBLICATIONS

The U.S. government, and especially the DOD, has been increasingly concerned about those who would defraud the government. To assist DOD military and civilian personnel, especially those involved in the procurement process, in taking all reasonable steps to detect, deter, or eliminate fraud, a series of publications has been issued. Basically, the brochures deal with (1) the potential for fraud and (2) specific categories of fraudulent activities found in DOD programs. The Office of the Inspector General of the DOD has issued the following articles:

- "Indicators of Fraud in Department of Defense Procurement" (May 1984).
- "Handbook on Labor Fraud Indicators" (Aug. 1985).
- "Handbook on Scenarios of Potential Defective Pricing Fraud" (Dec. 1986).
- "Antitrust Enforcement in DOD Procurement" (Jan. 1987).

In March 1987, the Accounting and Financial Management Division of the GAO issued a draft of proposed revisions to the *Standards for Audit of Governmental Organizations, Programs, Activities and Functions*.

While brief comments on some of these documents are contained in this chapter, the readers are invited to secure the complete publication from the appropriate department or agency.

FIG. 24-1
Minimizing Vulnerability to Fraud

What Is Fraud?

While the law has not changed in years, the government's interpretation of what constitutes fraud is expanding rapidly. The law says fraud exists when claims are submitted to the government or statements are made to government officials that are:

- Written or oral;
- Shown to be false, concealing, or covering up a material fact; and
- Made knowingly and willfully.

Until recently, the law was not strictly enforced. But actions that were often previously accepted as a way of doing business are now prosecuted. Consider:

- If costs of $1.2 million are proposed to perform a government contract, when the proposer knows he can fulfill the requirements at a cost of $1 million, fraud may have occurred.
- If a contractor submits a progress payment for materials ordered but not yet received, fraud may exist.
- If an employee knowingly and willfully charges a different assignment than the account worked on, fraud **has** occurred.
- If a business misleads the government about residual inventory values under a flexibly priced contract, fraud **has** occurred.

What the Government Is Doing

Congress has mandated the establishment of an Inspector General's Office for the Department of Defense (DOD). This rapidly growing organization—it now has more than 800 people—has aggressively pursued fraud. Furthermore, DOD, with the Department of Justice, has set up a joint task force to make the investigation and prosecution of fraud easier.

The Defense Contract Audit Agency (DCAA) has also geared up to uncover fraudulent activities and, when it has done so, turn them over to the appropriate investigative organizations. Two areas that have received heavy DCAA emphasis are defective pricing and labor-charging practices.

Defective pricing. Two years ago, the DCAA tripled its efforts to ferret out defective pricing. The DCAA searches for contracts with high profits and targets them for audit because the agency believes that they have a high potential for defective pricing. Where it is uncovered, the auditors are instructed to further examine the findings for potential fraud.

It's important to realize that the primary distinction between defective pricing and fraud is intent. For instance, did the contractor's employees knowingly and willfully give proposal data to the government that was not current, accurate, or complete? Negligent misrepresentation may, at times, also constitute fraud.

Labor-charging practices. In the last few years, the DCAA has initiated "comprehensive labor audits." These are intended to analyze labor-charging patterns, and, often, in that process, they unearth fraud. The agency has established labor audit teams trained in such special audit techniques as risk assessment, intensified analysis of accounting data, and employee interview inquiries. And the agency has stepped up its review of labor-charging patterns at contractors' offsite locations where activity is distant from normal company scrutiny.

(continued)

FIG. 24-1 *(cont'd)*

Effect on Contractors

All companies are possible subjects for these reviews. And, the weaker the internal controls and management's oversight of the high-risk areas, the greater the probability that activities are being carried on that could trigger a fraud investigation.

Individual employees may, for example, engage in activities that could be defined as making false statements to the government. They may be motivated to do this for several reasons: to make their own performance look better or to accomplish misperceived company objectives.

Fraud investigations are extremely harmful to companies. They are also expensive. Costs include administrative support, outside counsel, consulting fees, and then, often, an ultimate monetary settlement with the government. The very investigation itself can also hurt a business's reputation. In addition, when the government is successful, it is sure to publicize its findings. Finally, there are severe penalties: the company can be suspended and barred from further government work and the guilty imprisoned.

Minimizing Exposure

A business can take certain steps [See "Minimizing Exposure to Fraud"] to reduce its vulnerability. Perhaps the most useful, immediate approach is a risk assessment to determine how much exposure the company may have. These reviews should look particularly hard at those critical areas where there is a greater possibility for employee acts that could expose the company to fraud. Primary risk areas are the labor-charging system, the estimating system, material control, and indirect cost allocations.

Minimizing Exposure to Fraud

Five pointers can help decrease your company's vulnerability to accusations of fraud:

- Conduct a risk assessment into areas where there is a high potential for fraud.
- Improve internal controls in those areas and monitor them on a continuing basis.
- Prepare written policies for all critical systems.
- Have an authority within your company to whom employees can go with suspicions of wrongdoing. The procedure should be written and communicated to employees.
- Review your cost-allocation practices with the eye of a government auditor, so that your judgment on allowability or cost allocation is less likely to be challenged and confused with fraud.

Government's Reach Is Longer

Companies today are focusing on fraud and its prevention as never before; however, the government is extending its investigations into areas it never before treated as fraud. This makes it imperative for companies doing business with the government to avoid even the merest appearance of fraud.

"How Can Contractors Minimize Vulnerability to Fraud?" *Washington Briefing*, Touche Ross & Co., Jan. 1985, pp. 4–5. Reprinted by permission.

INDICATORS OF FRAUD IN DOD PROCUREMENT

To be sure, while federal auditors are concerned with detecting and deterring fraud on government contracts, it should be recognized that the internal auditor employed by a defense contractor has similar interests—to prevent fraud not only in his company, but also on the part of subcontractors to his entity. When fraud indicia point to a particular type of illegal activity, guidance should be sought from any number of government sources, the company's legal department, or others (see Chapter 22). While an in-depth review is contained in some of the publications mentioned, an excellent review of the potential for fraud in the procurement process and the categories of fraud are contained in "Indicators of Fraud in Department of Defense Procurement," reproduced in Figure 24-2.[1]

Labor Fraud Indicators

In this mid- to late 1980s period, there are, from time to time, reports of a rash of white-collar crimes relating to defense contractors. The question remains: Has there been a general deterioration in business morality, an increased effort to prosecute such crime, or a combination of both? In any event, labor is a significant cost under government contracts, and often represents a difficult area to review. For this reason, among others, the useful *Handbook on Labor Fraud Indicators* was issued to stimulate the contract auditor's imagination regarding the detection of labor fraud indicators. As the preface states, in part:

> The handbook is a compilation of some of the more common labor fraud schemes. It highlights those fraud indicators which auditors need to be alert for and provides insight into the identification of labor fraud indicators. The scenarios help identify areas where the government's vulnerability to labor cost mischarging is particularly high. Testing for fraud indicators is a test for creativity. . . .

Material Fraud Indicators

In July 1986, the Office of the Inspector General issued the *Handbook on Fraud Indicators: Material* in an effort to stimulate the imagination of the contract auditors in a search for fraud. If material fraud is suspected, it can be a helpful source of information.

(continued on page 24-38)

---

[1] Office of the Inspector General, Department of Defense, May 1984.

FIG. 24-2

Indicators of Fraud in Department of Defense Procurement

PREFACE
FRAUD IN DOD PROCUREMENT

Deterrence remains the cornerstone of our defense policy. We continue to seek nuclear and conventional capability sufficient to convince any potential aggressor that the costs of aggression would exceed any potential gains that he might achieve.

Maintaining the necessary nuclear and conventional forces for deterrence is costly. It requires a tremendous commitment of our national resources. As a major custodian and dispenser of taxpayers' dollars, the Department of Defense (DOD) is a target of many who would seek to take advantage of any vulnerability.

The Secretary of Defense and the Inspector General, DOD, require the support and assistance of all DOD military and civilian personnel, particularly those in the procurement process, to take all reasonable steps to detect and eliminate fraud, waste and mismanagement and reduce DOD's vulnerability to zero. An initial step is learning to recognize indicators of the presence of fraud or of the potential for it. This publication is designed to assist DOD personnel to identify circumstances where fraud is likely to take place, or indicate fraud has already occurred. It describes actions that can be taken when fraud is found.

The first chapter discusses the potential for fraud in the procurement process through the contract award stage of a procurement. The next eight chapters discuss specific categories of fraudulent activities found in DOD programs. The final two chapters cover available actions that can be taken by DOD and other Government agencies to protect programs from future frauds, to recover resources lost through fraud, or to punish those who have perpetrated such frauds.

If Government interests are to be protected, fraud and illegal activity in Government procurement must be addressed by criminal, civil, administrative or contractual remedies, or a combination of these. Selecting remedies must be done not only by criminal investigators and prosecutors, but also contracting officers, technical representatives, managers, personnel officers, legal counsel, internal and contract auditors, and suspension and debarment authorities.

Remember that eliminating fraud, waste and abuse and reducing DOD's vulnerability to those who would compromise its programs requires cooperation from all employees within DOD. Achieving this goal depends on the alertness and sound judgement of DOD employees in using the tools and knowledge provided in publications like this one.

Joseph H. Sherick
Inspector General
Department of Defense

CHAPTER I: FRAUD IN GOVERNMENT CONTRACTS

A. Introduction.

The contract award process can and does take various courses to meet an end result, i.e., delivery of goods and services. This chapter discusses factors which may indicate the presence of or enhanced potential for fraud at various stages in the contract award process. The indicators included in this chapter are not intended, each taken by themselves, to establish the existence of fraud. Rather, the presence of any of these indicators, when taken in the context of the particular procurement action being conducted, should cause DOD employees to be alert to the possibility of impropriety and take appropriate actions to ensure the integrity of the process. Three later chapters will discuss in more detail the concepts of: (1) collusive bidding and price fixing; (2) defective pricing; and (3) bribery, gratuities and conflicts of interest. These activities are present in some of the indicators presented in this chapter and should be considered in light of the later explanations.

The motives and methods for fraud in the contract award process are varied. There are many instances where fraud is perpetrated to obtain a contract in order to create the opportunity to later engage in such activities as theft or embezzlement, product substitution, cost mischarging, fast pay or progress payment fraud. In some instances the fraud is perpetrated to obtain a contract at a higher price or with better terms than would have occurred in an award untainted by fraud. Still others commit fraud merely to get Government contracts because they need the business to keep their companies in operation when private sector activity is low.

Another factor to be considered is that frauds are sometimes committed by or with the help of DOD employees. The possibility should not be overlooked that a DOD employee has solicited or accepted bribes or gratuities or has a financial interest in a contractor. There have even been instances of DOD employees creating or participating in the ownership of outside businesses for the purpose of committing fraud through their ability to impact on or control the award process.

B. Fraud in the Identification of the Government's Need for Goods or Services.

Normally, procurement actions are initiated by formal or informal general requirements. These requirements consist of a brief description of the types and amounts of goods and services needed together with a justification for the need. Fraud may result here from decisions to buy goods and services in excess of those actually needed or possibly not needed at all. Needs determinations which are established for items that have scheduled disposal and reprocurement or have predetermined reorder levels may be particularly susceptible to manipulation. In addition, excessive purchases of items such as drugs or auto parts have been indications of other ensuing criminal acts such as theft or diversion of supplies.

Further potential for fraud is created where the needs assessment is not adequately or accurately developed. A Government agency which, with or without collusion, continually changes its mind about what it wants, will make it possible for a contractor to substantially increase the contract price.

Contractors may also charge the Government for "proprietary" data the Government already owns because it paid for the development on another contract, charge several agencies for doing the same job, or charge for "fixing" products or software which were deliberately made to meet defective or inadequate definitions of what was needed.

With respect to fraud in defining requirements and stock levels, the general fraud indicators include:

1. Requiring excessively high stock levels and inventory requirements to justify continuing purchasing activity from certain contractors.

2. Declaring items which are serviceable as excess or selling them as surplus while continuing to purchase similar items. (One documented scheme involved repurchasing the same items being sold as surplus on a recurring basis.)

3. Purchasing items, services, or research projects in response to aggressive marketing efforts (and possible favors, bribes or gratuities) by contractors rather than in response to valid requirements.

(continued)

FIG. 24-2 *(cont'd)*

4. Improperly defining needs in ways that can be met only by certain contractors.
5. Failing to develop "second-sources" for items, spare parts, and services being continually purchased from a single source.

C. Fraud in the Development of Statements of Work and Specifications.

Bid specifications and statements of work detailing the types and amounts of goods or services to be provided are prepared to assist in the selection process. They are intended to provide both potential bidders and the selecting officials with a firm basis for making and accepting bids. A well written contract will have specifications, standards and statements of work which make it clear what the Government is entitled to. Sloppy or carelessly written specifications make it easy for a contractor to claim that it is entitled to more money for what the Government later defines as what it really wants. Sometimes, there is deliberate collusion between Government personnel and the contractor to write vague specifications. At other times there is an agreement to amend the contract to increase the price immediately after the award. One contractor actually developed a "cost enhancement plan," identifying all of the changes he would make in order to double the cost of the contract, before it was even signed.

Fraud indicators include:

1. Defining statements of work and specifications to fit the products or capabilities of a single contractor.
2. Advance or selective release by Government employees of information concerning requirements and pending purchases only to preferred contractors.
3. Using statements of work, specifications, or sole source justifications developed by or in consultation with a preferred contractor (institutional conflict of interest).
4. Allowing architect-engineers, design engineers or other firms participating in the preparation of bid packages to obtain those same construction or production contracts or to be subcontractors to the winning contractors.
5. Release of information by firms participating in design and engineering to contractors competing for the prime contract.
6. Designing "pre-qualification" standards or specifications to exclude otherwise qualified contractors or their products.
7. Splitting up requirements so contractors each get a "fair share" and can rotate bids (See Chapter IV).
8. Splitting up requirements to get under small purchase requirements ($25,000) or to avoid prescribed levels of review or approval, e.g., to keep each within the contracting authority of a particular person or activity.
9. Bid specifications or the statement of work are not consistent with the items included in the general requirements.
10. Specifications are so vague that reasonable comparisons or estimates would be difficult.
11. Specifications are not consistent with past similar type procurements.

D. Fraud in Pre-Solicitation Phase.

Fraud indicators include:

1. Unnecessary sole source justifications.
2. Falsified statements to justify sole source or negotiated procurement.

PROCUREMENT FRAUD

3. Justifications for sole source or negotiated procurement signed by officials without authority or the deliberate by-passing of required levels of review.
4. Placing any restrictions in the solicitation documents which would tend to restrict competition.
5. Providing any advance information to contractors or their representatives on a preferential basis by technical or contracting personnel.

E. Fraud in Solicitation Phase.

Fraud indicators include:

1. Restricting procurement to exclude or hamper any qualified contractor.
2. Limiting time for submission of bids so only those with advance information have an adequate time to prepare bids or proposals.
3. Revealing any information about procurement to one contractor which is not revealed to all (from either technical or contracting personnel).
4. Conducting bidders conference in a way which invites bid rigging or price fixing or permits improper communications between contractors (See Chapter IV).
5. Failure to assure a sufficient number of potential competitors are aware of the solicitation. (Use of obscure publications, publishing in holiday season, providing a vague or inadequate synopsis to Commerce Business Daily, etc.)
6. Bid solicitation is vague as to the time, place, or other requirements for submitting acceptable bids.
7. Little or no control over the number and destination of bid packages sent to interested bidders.
8. Improper communication with contractors at trade or professional meetings or improper social contact with contractor representatives.
9. Government personnel or their families acquiring stock or a financial interest in a contractor or subcontractor.
10. Government personnel discussing possible employment with a contractor or subcontractor for themselves or a family member.
11. Special assistance to any contractor in preparing his bid or proposal.
12. "Referring" a contractor to a specific subcontractor, expert, or source of supply. (Express or implied that if you use the referred business, you will be more likely to get the contract.)
13. Failure to amend solicitation to include necessary changes or clarifications. (Telling one contractor of changes that can be made after award.)

F. Fraud in the Submission of Bids and Proposals.

Fraud indicators include:

1. Improper acceptance of a late bid.
2. Falsification of documents or receipts to get a late bid accepted.
3. Change in a bid after other bidders' prices are known. This is sometimes done by mistakes deliberately "planted" in a bid.
4. Withdrawal of the low bidder who may become a subcontractor to the higher bidder who gets the contract.

(continued)

FIG. 24-2 *(cont'd)*

5. Collusion or bid rigging between bidders.
6. Revealing one bidder's price to another.
7. False certifications by contractor.
   a. Small business certification.
   b. Minority business certification.
   c. Information provided to other agencies to support special status.
   d. Certification of independent price determination.
   e. Buy-American Act certification.
8. Falsification of information concerning contractor qualifications, financial capability, facilities, ownership of equipment and supplies, qualifications of personnel and successful performance of previous jobs, etc.

G. Fraud in the Evaluation of Bids and Proposals.

Fraud indicators include:

1. Deliberately discarding or "losing" the bid or proposal of an "outsider" who wants to participate. (May be part of a conspiracy between a Government official and a select contractor or group of contractors.)
2. Improperly disqualifying the bid or proposal of a contractor.
3. Accepting nonresponsive bids from preferred contractors.
4. Seemingly unnecessary contacts with contractor personnel by persons other than the contracting officer during the solicitation, evaluation, and negotiation processes.
5. Any unauthorized release of information to a contractor or other person.
6. Any exercise of favoritism toward a particular contractor during the evaluation process.
7. Using biased evaluation criteria or using biased individuals on the evaluation panel.

H. Fraud in the Award of the Contract.

Fraud indicators include:

1. Award of a contract to a contractor who is not the lowest responsible, responsive bidder.
2. Disqualification of any qualified bidder.
3. Allowing a low bidder to withdraw without justification.
4. Failure to forfeit bid bonds when a contractor withdraws improperly.
5. Material changes in the contract shortly after award.
6. Advance information concerning who is going to win a major competition can give advantages to persons trading in the stock of both the winning and losing companies.
7. Awards made to contractors with an apparent history of poor performance.
8. Awards made to the lowest of a very few bidders without readvertising considerations or without adequate publicity.
9. Awards made that include items other than those contained in bid specifications.

10. Awards made without adequate documentation of all preaward and postaward actions including all understandings or oral agreements.

I. Fraud in the Negotiation of a Contract.

There are a number of abuses which can occur in the negotiation of a contract. The first stems from the assumption of many personnel that once it has been determined that negotiated procurement procedures can be used (called procurement with discussions in the new FAR), that procurement on a sole source basis has also been justified. Whether a contracting officer is making the decision on a small dollar contract or a formal determination is being made by higher authority, competition is required unless specific justifications exist and are documented.

Fraud indicators include:

1. "Back-dated" or after-the-fact justifications may appear in the contract file or may be signed by persons without the authority to approve noncompetitive procurement.
2. Information given to one contractor which is not given to others which give it a competitive advantage.
3. Improper release of information (e.g., prices in proposals, technical proposals or characteristics of proposals, identity or rank of competing proposals, proprietary data or trade secrets, and Government price estimates) to unauthorized persons.
4. Weakening the Government's negotiating position through disclosures to the contractor selected for award.
5. Contractor misrepresentation as to costs during negotiations (See Chapter III).
6. Failure of Government personnel to obtain and rely upon a Certificate of Current Cost or Pricing Data.

CHAPTER II: CRIMES INVOLVED IN CONTRACT FRAUD

When the Government and its programs have been defrauded or corrupted, Federal investigators and prosecutors will usually find that one or more Federal statutes has been violated. It is their job to develop conclusive evidence that each of the elements of a specific crime exists. The most frequently violated statutes include:

A. 18 USC 1001—False Statements. Any one of three different types of acts can be covered under this statute if under the jurisdiction of any agency:

1. Falsifying, concealing or covering up a material fact by any trick, scheme or device;
2. Making false, fictitious, or fraudulent statements or representations; or
3. Making or using any false document or writing.

B. 18 USC 287—False Claims. This includes making any false, fictitious, or fraudulent claim against any agency of the United States. (In a related civil statute, 31 USC 3729, the United States can also recover double damages and $2,000 per false claim.)

C. 18 USC 1341—Mail Fraud and 18 USC 1343—Wire Fraud. These statutes make it illegal to engage in any scheme to defraud in which the mails or wire communications are utilized. (Even the **Government's** mailing of a payment check to a contractor can bring the scheme under this statute.)

(continued)

FIG. 24-2 *(cont'd)*

D. 18 USC 201–209—Bribery, Gratuities and Conflicts of Interest. These sections prohibit anyone from offering or giving a bribe to a Federal employee or agent and prohibit an employee from receiving either a bribe or gratuity. They also prohibit conflicts of interest during and after Federal employment. (New authority delegated by the President in November 1983, under 18 USC 218, permits agencies to rescind any contract tainted by bribery, graft, or conflict of interest after conviction.)

E. 18 USC 1905—Trade Secrets Act. This prohibits unauthorized release of any information a Federal employee receives confidentially in the course of employment. (Advance procurement information, prices, technical proposals, trade secrets or proprietary information, etc.)

F. 18 USC 641—Theft, Embezzlement or Destruction of Public Money, Property or Records. This prohibits the theft, embezzlement or destruction of any money, property or records of the United States or the receiving or concealing of such.

G. 41 USC 51, 54—Anti-Kickback Act. This prohibits the payment of any fee, compensation, gift or gratuity from a subcontractor to a prime contractor on any negotiated Government contract.

H. 15 USC 1—Sherman Antitrust Act. This prohibits any agreement to restrain trade in interstate commerce and includes price fixing, bid rigging or bid rotation schemes.

I. 18 USC 371—Conspiracy. This section prohibits any conspiracy to defraud the United States or to violate any Federal law or regulation (any offense against the United States). It prohibits either an unlawful objective or an unlawful means.

CHAPTER III: DEFECTIVE PRICING

A. Introduction: The Truth in Negotiations Act.

In the 1950's and early 1960's, the General Accounting Office (GAO) discovered numerous instances of overpricing by Government contractors on negotiated contracts. However, the Government had no legal redress of repricing contracts short of fraud or misrepresentation by the contractor. In 1959, the DOD adopted regulations requiring the contractor to provide cost and pricing data. However, subsequent GAO audits revealed noncompliance by the Military Services. In 1962, Congress enacted Public Law 87-653 (The Truth in Negotiations Act) designed to provide for examination by the Government of contractors' records. This enabled the Government to avoid excessive contract costs that result from contractors having in their possession accurate, complete, and current information when the Government does not possess the same data.

B. Cost or Pricing Data Provision: 10 USC 2306 (f).

The cost or pricing data provisions of the Truth in Negotiations Act are contained in 10 USC 2306 (f). It provides, in part, that a prime contractor or any subcontractor **shall** be required to submit cost or pricing data, and **shall** be required to certify that, to the best of his knowledge and belief, the cost or pricing data he submitted was accurate, complete, and current, under the following circumstances:

1. Prior to the award of any **negotiated** prime contract where the price is expected to exceed $500,000. Hence, the procedures are not applicable to advertised contracts or subcontracts under such contracts.

2. Prior to the pricing of any contract change or modification for which the price adjustment is expected to exceed $500,000 or such lesser amount as prescribed

PROCUREMENT FRAUD

by the head of the agency. Hence, the requirement applies to all prime contracts, negotiated or advertised.

3. Prior to the award of a subcontract at any tier, where the prime contractor and each higher tier subcontractor have been required to furnish such a certificate, if the price of such subcontract is expected to exceed $500,000.

4. Prior to the pricing of any contract change or modification to a subcontract covered by 3 above, for which the price adjustment is expected to exceed $500,000, or such lesser amounts as may be prescribed by the head of the agency.

The Act further requires that any prime contract or change or modification requiring a certificate of current cost or pricing data shall contain a price reduction clause, permitting the Government to adjust prices by the amount they were increased as a result of cost or pricing data that was inaccurate, incomplete, or not current.

Prime contracts, changes and modifications which fall within the mandatory requirements of the statute may avoid the above requirements of the statute if the price negotiated was:

1. based on adequate competition;

2. established catalog or market prices of commercial items sold in substantial quantities to the general public;

3. prices set by law or regulation; or,

4. in exceptional cases where the head of the agency waives the requirements.

Note, despite the presence of any or all of the above four exceptions, the Government can still insist upon submission of cost or pricing data if a certificate is required.

C. Regulatory Requirements: Federal Acquisition Regulations (FAR).

Section 15.801 of the FAR defines cost or pricing data and specifies the form and language for the certificate of current cost or pricing data. The clauses at FAR 52.214-27, 52.215-22, and 52.215-23, which are required contract clauses when the certificate is required, give the Government a contract right to a reduction in contract price to what it would have been if the contractor had submitted accurate, complete and current data.

Cost or pricing data is submitted to the Defense Department on the SF 1411, Contracting Pricing Proposal Cover Sheet. Along with that form the contractor (or offeror, if no contract award has yet been made) is required to provide a breakdown of his costs, disclose his basis for pricing these items of costs and submit supporting documentation such as vendor quotes or invoices. The contractor is required to submit the following certification as soon as practicable after agreement is reached on the contract or modification price:

> **CERTIFICATE OF CURRENT COST OR PRICING DATA**
>
> This is to certify that, to the best of my knowledge and belief, the cost or pricing data (as defined in Section 15.801 of the Federal Acquisition Regulation (FAR) and required under FAR subsection 15.804-2), submitted, either actually or by specific identification in writing to the contracting officer or to the contracting officer's representative in support of . . . . are accurate, complete, and current as of (day) (month) (year) . . . . This certification includes the cost or pricing data supporting any advance

(continued)

FIG. 24-2 *(cont'd)*

agreements and forward pricing rate agreements between the offerer and the Government which are part of the proposal.

Firm.........................
Name........................
Title.........................
Date of Execution........................

Note that, in accordance with FAR 15.801, the term cost or pricing data used in the certification specifically includes vendor quotations.

D. Defective Pricing Indicators.

In September 1983, the Director of DCAA issued a memorandum to DCAA auditors stating guidance in the area of defective pricing where certain conditions exist which might indicate fraud. Auditors were instructed that when **indications** of fraud are found, the case will be referred to the proper investigative agencies. They include:

1. Persistent defective pricing.
2. Repeated defective pricing involving similar patterns or conditions.
3. Failure to correct known system deficiencies.
4. Failure to update cost or pricing data with knowledge that past activity showed that prices have decreased.
5. Specific knowledge, that is not disclosed, regarding significant cost issues that will reduce proposal costs. This may be reflected in revisions in the price of a major subcontract, settlement of union negotiations that result in lower increases on labor rates, etc.
6. Denial by responsible contractor employees of the existence of historical records that are subsequently found.
7. Utilization of unqualified personnel to develop cost or pricing data used in estimating process.
8. Indications of falsification or alteration of supporting data.
9. Distortion of the overhead accounts or base information by the transfer of charges or accounts that have a material impact on Government contracts.
10. Failure to make complete disclosure of data known to responsible contractor personnel.
11. Protracted delay in release of data to the Government to preclude possible price reductions.
12. The employment of people known to have previously perpetuated fraud against the Government.

These indicators should be applied as well by contracting officers and others involved in the procurement process. Particular note should be made in defective pricing cases that the "intent" of the contractor will be critical to a determination of whether a criminal act occurred. The deliberate concealment or misrepresentation of a single significant cost element could constitute a prosecutable crime. The establishment of intent should be the function of trained criminal investigators; auditors and contracting officials should make no assumptions that defective pricing results from unintentional conduct.

CHAPTER IV: ANTITRUST VIOLATIONS: COLLUSIVE BIDDING AND PRICE FIXING

A. Introduction.

Collusive bidding, price fixing or bid rigging, are commonly used interchangeable terms which describe many forms of illegal anticompetitive activity. The common thread throughout all of these anticompetitive activities is that they involve any agreements or informal arrangements among independent competitors which limit competition. Schemes which allocate contracts and limit competition can take many forms and are only limited by the imagination of the parties. Common schemes, which will be discussed in more detail later, include bid suppression or limiting, complementary bidding, bid rotation and market division. Competitors can also violate the law by making any agreements among themselves as to the prices they will charge. This does not mean that all competitors have to agree to charge the same price for a violation to occur. Agreements among competitors which would violate the law include but are not limited to: (1) agreements to adhere to published price lists; (2) agreements to raise prices by a specified increment; (3) agreements to establish, adhere to, or eliminate discounts; (4) agreements not to advertise prices; and (5) agreements to maintain specified price differentials based on quantity, type or size of product.

B. Impact on the Procurement Process.

One of the cornerstones of the Federal procurement system is the requirement that Government contracts should be awarded, to the greatest extent possible, on the basis of free and open competition. The preference for competition in the procurement of goods or services on behalf of the United States was first set by statute in 1809. This preference still remains and has been specifically expressed in statutes concerning DOD purchases and contracts. Title 10 USC 2304(a) sets forth a specific requirement that, "Purchase of and contracts for property and services covered by this chapter shall be made by formal advertising, and shall be awarded on a competitive bid basis to the lowest responsible bidder, in all cases in which the use of such method is feasible and practicable under existing conditions and circumstances." In addition, subsection (g) of 10 USC 2304 requires that, except in certain limited circumstances, competition must also be obtained in negotiated procurements. These requirements are also contained in the basic DOD policy regarding competition as outlined in DAR 2-102 and now covered by FAR 14.103.

Further evidence of the importance of competition in the DOD procurement process is provided by the requirement for "Certification of Independent Price Determination," DAR 7-2003.1 and FAR 3.103-1. These regulations require contractors to certify that they have not engaged in certain specific activities which constitute what can generally be described as collusive bidding or price fixing.

It should be obvious that collusive bidding or price fixing among competitors completely undermines the Government's efforts to use competitive purchasing and contracting methods. The harm in this situation, however, is not limited to the mere circumvention of the important Government policies that encourage free and open competition. In fact, collusive bidding and price fixing result in increased costs, destroy public confidence in the country's economy and undermine our system of free enterprise. To illustrate the impact of these activities on DOD procurement, consider just a few of the recent cases:

1. In 1981, five corporations and their officers were convicted of collusive bidding involving 13 DOD contracts for asphalt paving work. The overcharges to the

(continued)

FIG. 24-2 *(cont'd)*

> Government as a result of the scheme were approximately $1,000,000 out of the total contract value of $16,500,000. The pattern of conduct ultimately involved almost 100 DOD contracts.
>
> 2. Sixteen corporations and their officers were convicted of collusive bidding on riverbank stabilization contracts. Evidence indicated that overcharges on the $56,000,000 worth of contracts ranged from 35 percent to 45 percent. ($19,600,000 to $25,200,000.)
>
> 3. Four corporations and their officers were convicted of collusive bidding on produce contracts valued at approximately $5,000,000. Based on evidence that overcharges for items sold ranged from 15 percent to 30 percent, DOD was overcharged between $750,000 and $1,500,000.
>
> It has been shown time and time again that collusive bidding and price fixing schemes cause DOD to pay much more for goods or services than it would have if true competition existed. Even though this is the case, the bids involved will often appear to be fair and reasonable. This should not mistakenly be accepted as proof that collusive bidding and price fixing are not occurring or that a violation of law does not exist because the harm in terms of monetary loss is not apparent. In fact, when such conduct is criminally prosecuted, the defendants are prohibited from introducing any evidence to justify their conduct or to demonstrate its reasonableness.
>
> **C. Indicators of Collusive Bidding and Price Fixing.**
>
> The following list of indicators is intended to facilitate recognition of those situations which may involve collusive bidding or price fixing. In and of themselves these indicators will not prove that illegal anticompetitive activity is occurring. They are, however, sufficient to warrant referral to appropriate authorities for investigation. Use of indicators such as these to identify possible anticompetitive activity is important because schemes to restrict competition are by their very nature secret and their exact nature is not readily visible.
>
> Practices or events that may evidence collusive bidding or price fixing are:
>
> 1. Bidders who are qualified and capable of performing but who fail to bid, with no apparent reason. A situation where fewer competitors than normal submit bids typifies this situation. (This could indicate a deliberate scheme to withhold bids.)
>
> 2. Certain contractors always bid against each other or conversely certain contractors do not bid against one another.
>
> 3. The successful bidder repeatedly subcontracts work to companies that submitted higher bids or to companies that picked up bid packages and could have bid as prime contractors but did not.
>
> 4. Different groups of contractors appear to specialize in Federal, state or local jobs exclusively. (This might indicate a market division by class of customer.)
>
> 5. There is an apparent pattern of low bids regularly reoccurring, such as corporation "x" always being the low bidder in a certain geographical area or in a fixed rotation with other bidders.
>
> 6. Failure of original bidders to rebid, or an identical ranking of the same bidders upon rebidding, when original bids were rejected as being too far over the Government estimate.
>
> 7. A certain company appears to be bidding substantially higher on some bids than on other bids with no logical cost differences to account for the increase,

PROCUREMENT FRAUD

i.e., a local company is bidding higher prices for an item to be delivered locally than for delivery to points farther away.

8. Bidders that ship their product a short distance bid more than those who must incur greater expense by shipping their product long distances.

9. Identical bid amounts on a contract line item by two or more contractors. Some instances of identical line item bids are explainable, as suppliers often quote the same prices to several bidders. But a large number of identical bids on any service-related item should be viewed critically.

10. Bidders frequently change prices at about the same time and to the same extent.

11. Joint venture bids where either contractor could have bid individually as a prime. (Both had technical capability and production capacity.)

12. Any incidents suggesting direct collusion among competitors, such as the appearance of identical calculation or spelling errors in two or more competitive bids or the submission by one firm of bids for other firms.

13. Competitors regularly socialize or appear to hold meetings, or otherwise get together in the vicinity of procurement offices shortly before bid filing deadlines.

14. Assertions by employees, former employees, or competitors that an agreement to fix bids and prices or otherwise restrain trade exists.

15. Bid prices appear to drop whenever a new or infrequent bidder submits a bid.

16. Competitors exchange any form of price information among themselves. This may result from the existence of an "industry price list" or "price agreement" to which contractors refer in formulating their bids or it may take other subtler forms such as discussions of the "right price."

17. Any reference by bidders to "association price shedules," "industry price schedules," "industry suggested prices," "industry-wide prices" or "market-wide prices."

18. A bidder's justification for a bid price or terms offered because they follow the industry or industry leader's pricing or terms, this may include a reference to following a named competitor's pricing or terms.

19. Any statement by a representative of a contractor that his company "does not sell in a particular area" or that "only a particular firm sells in that area."

20. Statements by a bidder that it is not their turn to receive a job or conversely that it is another bidder's turn.

D. Collusive Bidding and Price Fixing Examples.

The following sections describe common collusive bidding and price fixing schemes which DOD personnel may be able to recognize. These schemes relate to one another and overlap. Frequently an agreement by competitors to rig bids will involve more than one of these schemes.

1. **Bid Suppression or Limiting.** In this type of scheme one or more competitors agree with at least one other competitor to refrain from bidding or agree to withdraw a previously submitted bid so that a competitor's bid will be accepted. Other forms of this activity involve agreements by competitors to fabricate bid protests or to coerce suppliers and subcontractors not to deal with nonconspirators who submit bids.

(continued)

FIG. 24-2 *(cont'd)*

2. **Complementary Bidding.** "Complementary bidding" (also known as "protective" or "shadow" bidding) occurs when competitors submit token bids that are too high to be accepted (or if competitive in price, then on special terms that will not be acceptable). Such bids are not intended to secure the buyer's acceptance, but are merely designed to give the appearance of genuine bidding.

3. **Bid Rotation.** In "bid rotation," all vendors participating in the scheme submit bids, but by agreement take turns being the low bidder. In its most basic form bid rotation will consist of a cyclical pattern for submitting the low bid on certain contracts. This rotation may not be as obvious as might be expected if it is coupled with a scheme for awarding subcontracts to losing bidders, to take turns according to the size of the contract, or one of the other market division schemes explained below.

4. **Market Division.** Market division schemes are agreements to refrain from competing in a designated portion of a market. Division of a market for this purpose may be accomplished based on the customer or geographic area involved. The result of such a division is that competing firms will not bid or will submit only complementary bids when a solicitation for bids is made by a customer or in an area not assigned to them.

CHAPTER V: COST MISCHARGING

A. Introduction.

Cost mischarging is one of the abuses which is common because of the fact that most large Government research and development and production contracts are cost type contracts. Because the Government reimburses all costs which are allowable, allocable and reasonable, the contractor may increase profit by mischarging. If labor costs are mischarged, they may be multiplied by 100%–300% in indirect cost allowances. Sometimes a contractor is doing similar work for different agencies on fixed priced and cost type contracts. Any work which can be billed to the cost type contracts will be advantageous to the contractor. Sometimes these costs are shifted into indirect cost pools.

Frequently work that is being done by low level technicians is billed as being done by senior scientists or engineers at much higher rates. Some work may be billed to several contracts or indirect cost pools. The Government may be billed for the highest cost items by a contractor and these items may be diverted to its commercial work or the contractor may get "discounts" which are not passed on to the Government or which are applied to its commercial accounts.

The issue as to whether a mischarge was a "mistake" or a crime often depends on the issue of intent. Managers, auditors and contracting officers should not make assumptions about the good faith of a contractor. Investigators should examine the issue of intent. Prosecutors are likely to pursue cases where intent is established even though no substantial loss occurs particularly where the contractor has actively sought to conceal costs.

B. Allowable Costs.

Under cost type contracts, the Government reimburses the contractor's costs which are allowable, allocable to the contract and reasonable. These types of contracts include cost plus fixed fee, cost plus incentive fee, cost plus award fee, cost reimbursable and cost sharing contracts. In addition, contract changes and equitable adjustments to contracts are reimbursed on the basis of incurred costs even on fixed price contracts. Cost mischarging occurs whenever the contractor charges the Government for costs which are not allowable, not reasonable, or which cannot be directly or indirectly allocated to the contract.

The DAR 15-205 (FAR 31.205) identifies costs which are allowable and those which cannot be charged to Government contracts. Such costs may be direct costs, such as labor and materials used on one contract and no other, or indirect costs, which contribute to a number of different contracts. Indirect costs are placed in "cost pools" which are then allocated to contracts on some agreed basis (such as total cost or labor hours).

Unallowable costs include:

1. Advertising costs (except to obtain workers or scarce materials for a contract or to sell surplus or byproduct materials);
2. Bid and proposal costs in excess of a set limit;
3. Stock options and some forms of deferred compensation;
4. Contingencies;
5. Contributions and donations;
6. Entertainment costs;
7. Costs of idle facilities except in limited circumstances;
8. Interest;
9. Losses on other contracts;
10. Long-term leases of property or equipment and leases from related parties are limited to the costs of ownership;
11. Independent research and development costs beyond set limits; and
12. Legal costs related to a contractor's unsuccessful defense against charges of contract fraud.

C. Accounting Mischarges.

The fraud most frequently encountered by DCAA auditors is called an accounting mischarge. An accounting mischarge involves knowingly charging unallowable costs to the Government, concealing or misrepresenting them as allowable costs, or hiding them in accounts (such as office supplies) which are not audited closely. Another common variation involves charging types of costs which have their limits (such as bid and proposal costs or independent research and development costs) to other cost categories.

D. Material Cost Mischarges.

Material costs are sometimes mischarged. Numerous cases have been discovered where Government owned material was used on a similar commercial contract but the material accountability records showed that the material was used on a Government contract. Also there have been cases where Government owned materials were stolen and the thefts were concealed by showing the materials as being issued to and used on Government contracts. In other situations, materials have been ordered from Government supply depots, but upon receipt the materials were stolen and to conceal the theft entries were made to show that the order was cancelled.

Mischarges of materials are infrequent because the nature of the material items limit their use on other contracts. For example, a gyroscope for a C-130 cannot be used on a KC-135 aircraft. Accordingly, material mischarges are usually limited to raw materials such as aluminum sheets, steel, etc., which can be used on many different contract products.

(continued)

FIG. 24-2 *(cont'd)*

E. Labor Mischarges.

Labor costs are more susceptible to mischarging than material costs because the employees labor can readily be charged to any contract. The only way to assure that labor costs are charged to the correct contract is to actually observe the work of each employee to determine which contract he is working on and then determine from the accounting records that the employee's cost is charged to the proper contract.

Contractors have devised a number of ways to mischarge labor costs. The methods devised range from very crude to very sophisticated. Set forth below are some of the common methods of mischarging.

1. **Transfer of Labor Cost.** This mischarge is usually made after the contractor realizes that he has suffered a loss on a fixed priced contract. To eliminate the loss, a journal entry is made to remove the labor cost from the fixed priced contract cost and put it on the cost type contract. This type of mischarge is very easy to detect but is difficult to prove. The contractor will contend that the labor charges to the fixed price contract were in error and the journal entry, transferring the cost to the cost type contract, was made to correct that error. Frequently the dollar amount of the transfer is estimated.

2. **Time and Charges Do Not Agree With Contractor Billing to the Government.**
   a. This accounting mischarge method is probably the easiest to detect and prove. It is a simple matter of totaling the time and hours expended on the cost type contract and comparing them to the hours billed. For example, the time cards may show that 1,000 hours have been expended on the cost type contract when, in fact, the contractor has billed the Government for 2,000 hours of labor. The difference is obvious and the accounting records (time cards) will not support the billings.
   b. Contractor labor billings to the Government are normally supported by two accounting records. The source record is the individual employee time card. The other record is the labor distribution. The labor distribution is usually a computer printout that summarizes by contract the individual time card entries. Usually the contractor will use the labor distribution to support his Government billings. It is relatively easy to falsify a labor distribution but it is necessary to corrupt the entire work force to falsify the time cards. Hence, the individual time cards should be totaled and reconciled to the labor distribution at least on a test basis.

3. **Original Time Cards are Destroyed/Hidden and New Time Cards Are Prepared for the Auditor's Benefit.** This is a very successful method of concealing a labor mischarge. Mischarges of this nature are very difficult to detect. They are detected when:
   a. The hidden time cards are inadvertently given to the auditor.
   b. All of the old time cards are not destroyed and the auditor finds them.
   c. Employee signature on the time cards are carbon copies because the employee's original signature has been traced.
   d. Time card entries are compared to time records maintained by individual employees (copies of time cards, logs, etc.).

4. **Changes Are Made to Individual Time Cards.** A frequent labor fraud encountered by the DCAA auditor is where changes are made to the original contract charge numbers on employee time cards. Some of the changes are so well done that it is difficult to tell that a change has been made. In one

PROCUREMENT FRAUD

instance, the change was made so expertly that the auditor could not tell that a change had been made just from looking at the time sheet. The auditor detected the change by running his finger across the entry and noticed a difference in the "feel." Under magnification, the "white out" material used to cover the original entry could be seen. The auditors used a "light box" to determine what the original charge had been; i.e., by placing a light underneath the time sheet the auditor could read through the "white out" to determine the original charge. Just because changes are made on time cards, it does not necessarily mean that a fraud is being perpetrated. Many times innocent errors are made and corrected. In determining the possibility of fraudulent activity, one should:

a. Determine the magnitude of the changes. If only a few changes have been made then, in all probability, the changes were made to correct errors. However, if a significant percentage of the charges have been changed, the probability of fraudulent activity is increased.

b. A comparison of the original charge number to the revised charge number should be made. If the net effect of the changes is to increase the charges to cost reimbursable contracts, the likelihood of fraud is further increased.

c. Make a review of the sequence of events. For example, in one case the tail number of the aircraft that the employee worked on was posted to the time card in addition to the contract charge number. The following discrepancies were noted:

   (1) The original contract charge number corresponded to the contract for which work was to be accomplished on the specified aircraft, whereas, the changed contract charge number was for work on another contract for an entirely different type of aircraft, i.e., the original charge was to the C-130 aircraft and the tail number was a C-130 aircraft, but the new charge was made to the KC-135 aircraft.

   (2) Based upon the changed charge numbers, a ridiculous number of employees were working on the same aircraft during the same labor shift.

d. Identify the employee who made the changes, find out why the changes were made and what was the employee's source of information for the changed charge number.

5. Time Card Charges Are Made by Supervisors. One should be especially skeptical of timekeeping systems where time card charges are posted by supervisors. Management can exert pressure and influence on supervisors to accomplish certain goals. The pressure may influence the supervisor to falsify time charges in order to keep higher level management satisfied with his performance. An even more serious situation occurs when senior level management requires the supervisor to record time charges in a manner most profitable to the company. Management might even go so far as to provide supervisors with "budgets" of how to charge the time for each job. However, if individual employees post their time cards it would be difficult to corrupt the entire work force.

6. Impact of Labor Mischarges. When a labor cost is mischarged, so is the associated overhead and general and administrative (G&A) expenses. Overhead costs are allocated to labor costs based upon an overhead rate or percentage. Overhead costs usually exceed 100 percent of the labor cost. Therefore, any mischarging on labor rates also impacts upon overhead charges, which ultimately results in a greater than double loss to the Government. The same is true for G&A rates. In computing the dollar amount of the fraud, one must add

(continued)

FIG. 24-2 *(cont'd)*

the overhead and G&A cost because applied overhead and G&A will probably be more than the labor cost involved.

F. Cost Mischarging Examples.

1. An overhead audit conducted by DCAA disclosed substantial cost mischarging by a DOD acoustical research contractor. This mischarging principally involved shifting costs on both commercial and DOD contracts to the overhead category and then allocating the overhead to those contracts (principally DOD) which provided the best overhead rate. A thorough review of the audit work papers disclosed numerous examples of time sheets which had been altered by whiteouts. As a result of the audit and investigation, two senior company vice presidents were found guilty of violations of the Federal conspiracy statute and making false statements. Furthermore, the company was fined $706,000 and ordered to make restitution of approximately $2 million; the two senior vice presidents were fined $20,000 each and given six month sentences.

2. A major DOD contractor was found to have improperly shifted individual research and development costs (IR&D) on to cost type contracts. The corporation was convicted and fined $30,000. An accompanying civil and administrative settlement resulted in the company paying an additional $720,000 to DOD. The corporation also agreed to major revisions in corporate contracting practices and to increased DOD audit access to contractor records. Additionally, $300,000 in legal costs were disallowed.

CHAPTER VI: PRODUCT SUBSTITUTION

A. Introduction.

The term product substitution generally refers to attempts by contractors to deliver to the Government goods or services which do not conform to contract requirements, without informing the Government of the deficiency, while seeking reimbursement based upon alleged delivery of conforming products or services. It is the policy of DOD that goods and services acquired must conform to the quality and quantity required in the contract. Goods or services which do not conform in all respects to contractual requirements are to be rejected. It is **essential** that this policy be strictly adhered to, as failure to do so can result in providing substandard, untested and possibly defective material to our Armed Forces.

When a contract calls for delivery of an item produced by the original equipment manufacturer (OEM), then the contractor must furnish that item. This rule excludes even items that may be identical in all respects but are not produced by the OEM. If the contract requires the delivery of end products produced in the United States, then the contractor is obligated to supply items manufactured in the United States. This is required, even though comparable or identical items are available from foreign sources at lower costs to the contractor. Further, if the contract requires that certain tests be conducted to ensure that an item is suitable for its intended use and can be relied upon to perform as expected, those tests **must** be conducted. The contractor's ability to produce an item that will perform within acceptable limits regardless of whether actually tested is not relevant.

Contractors frequently argue that substituted goods or services delivered to the Government were "just as good" as what was contracted for even if specifications are not met, and that, therefore, no harm is done to the Government. There are several important fallacies to be noted when considering this argument. First and foremost, the substitute is usually not as good as what was contracted for. In cases of product substitution investigated to date, the substitute is usually one of

PROCUREMENT FRAUD

inferior quality or the workmanship is extremely poor because it was done by lesser qualified, and cheaper labor. Secondly, while the immediate harm that the substitute might cause or may have in fact caused is sometimes difficult to determine, its introduction into Defense supply channels undermines the reliability of the entire supply system. If, for example, a microchip were in use in larger components which failed, the cause of the failure might not be directly traceable to the inferior quality of the microchip. Third, even if the item is as good, there is harm to the integrity of the competitive procurement system which is based upon all competitors offering to furnish the item precisely described in the specifications.

B. Fraud Potential.

There are a wide variety of fraudulent schemes that may involve what is termed product substitution. Many of the recent product substitution fraud allegations involve consumable or off-the-shelf items. DOD employees should be aware of similar problems which have arisen in component parts and materials used in weapon systems, ships, aircraft and vehicles. Cases have included:

1. The nondelivery of supplies paid for pursuant to fast pay procedures;
2. The delivery of look-alike goods made from nonspecification materials;
3. Materials that have not been tested as required by the contract specifications; and
4. Providing foreign made products where domestic were required.

Product substitution cases sometimes involve Government employees. For example, gratuities and bribes have been paid to Government inspection personnel to accept items which do not conform to contract requirements.

The potential for a product substitution case is greatest where DOD relies upon contractor integrity to ensure that the Government gets what it has paid for. For example, fast pay procedures apply to small purchases. The Government pays contractors for goods based on certification of shipment. Quality assurance is frequently limited in scope, and is performed after payment has been made. Thus, small purchases such as these are particularly susceptible to unscrupulous contractors.

In large dollar value procurements, Government quality personnel often rely upon testing performed by the contractor. Falsification of the test documents may conceal the fact that a piece of equipment has not passed all the tests required by contract or has not been tested at all. False entries may also conceal the substitution of inferior or substandard materials in a product. When Government personnel actually witness or perform tests themselves, there is always the possibility that what they are seeng is a specifically prepared sample not representative of the contractor's actual production.

C. Product Substitution Examples.

1. A contractor allegodly employed two methods to bypass the Government inspection process to conceal intentional inclusion of substandard defective aircraft parts. The contractor would allow random unscheduled inspections of products prior to shipment and then substitute defective parts into the already inspected shipment. The second method was to ship the parts, including defectives, directly to distribution points before inspection took place.

2. A contractor was required to provide metal of specified type and grade for use in aircraft struts, ballast shields and bulkheads in ships. The contractor would

(continued)

FIG. 24-2 *(cont'd)*

purchase an inferior grade of required metal types or different types of metal entirely. False invoices and test results were created showing the required metals were being provided. The true specification stenciling was removed from the substituted metals and the required specifications stenciled on.

3. A contractor combined several schemes to conceal the production of substandard goods. Each of the schemes was aimed specifically at overcoming Government conducted quality assurance inspections (QAI). The contractor would: surreptitiously enter a locked area and substitute specially created samples for those the QAI personnel selected; move inspection tags to uninspected substandard goods after inspectors left; remove part of the good materials after inspection and add substandard or previously rejected materials; and disguise the true condition of substandard goods with chemicals the known inspection process would not disclose. Some of these tactics might have been neutralized by: unscheduled initial and repeat inspections; using inspection tags which would void automatically if moved; and requiring proof of or observing disposal of rejected goods.

4. A contractor was to provide instrument kits that were to be manufactured in the United States. Some of the materials were to be purchased from foreign sources, in compliance with the Buy American Act. The contractor showed the Quality Assurance Representative (QAR) raw forgings from which the instruments were to be made. The contractor then bought completed products from foreign sources. The markings of the country of origin were removed and the instruments marked showing United States manufacture. This scheme was not discovered by post production review by QAR personnel who randomly sampled the finished instruments. There were thousands of kits each containing 40 instruments, only some of which were altered. Users later found the original country of origin still on some items and obvious alterations on others. User complaints to quality assurance personnel led to specific inspections and discovery.

5. Two contractors, in separate cases, were required by their contracts to supply products that were domestically manufactured. In both instances, the contractors provided false documents establishing the purchase of raw materials in accordance with the contract requirements. Both contractors were in fact buying, in violation of Buy American provisions, finished products from foreign sources that manufactured them. One of the contractors also provided falsified test data to prove the product met specifications. The QAR in both cases suspected irregularities and made further inquiries which led to investigative referrals.

6. A contractor was required to provide parachute cord which would withstand certain strength tests. These tests were to be performed by a private laboratory. It was discovered that for six years the contractor had provided the Government with substandard cord and had covered up its conduct by giving the Government forged laboratory reports. Subsequent laboratory examination showed that the cord was over 25 years old and was completely inadequate. Immediate steps were required to remove all cord provided by this company from DOD inventories.

CHAPTER VII: PROGRESS PAYMENT FRAUD

A. Introduction.

Progress payments are payments made as work progresses under a contract based upon the costs incurred, the percentage of work accomplished, or the attainment

PROCUREMENT FRAUD

of a particular stage of completion. They do not include payments for partial deliveries accepted by the Government.

Fraud in progress payments occurs when a contractor submits a progress payment request based on falsified direct labor charges, on material costs for items not actually purchased, or on falsified certification of a stage of completion attained/work accomplished.

When a DOD contract contains one of the contract clauses in DAR 7-104.35 (FAR 52.232.16), a contractor may submit monthly progress payment requests and is entitled to receive a contractually specified percentage (95 percent if the contractor is a small business concern, 90 percent if the contractor is not small) of its "total costs." There are two definitions for "total costs," one for small businesses and the other for concerns which are not small. These costs include direct and indirect labor as well as material costs. For our limited purposes, the only significant difference between the two definitions concerns material costs—a concern that is not small must have actually paid for the materials for which the Government is being billed, while a small business need only have incurred an obligation to pay for the materials (although it must have acquired title to the materials).

Requests for progress payments are made on DD Form 1195. On this form the contractor identifies its contract costs and certifies that the statement of costs has been prepared from the contractor's books and records and is correct. In addition the contractor also makes a certification concerning encumbrances against the materials acquired for the contract.

The purpose of progress payments is to provide contractors with a continuing source of revenue throughout contract performance and to ensure that a contractor will have the necessary financial resources to meet its contractual obligations. Although some progress payment requests are audited before payment, for the most part DOD relies solely upon a contractor's integrity in making these payments. When a contractor requests payments for costs not actually incurred, the Government is harmed in many ways: (1) the contractor has the interest free use of money to which it is not entitled and which the Government itself may have had to borrow from the public; (2) the Government may lose its advances if the contractor goes out of business and there are no materials or completed products against which the Government may assert an interest; and (3) honest contractors lose their faith in the system and others, who are less scrupulous, are encouraged to take advantage of the system.

B. Progress Payment Fraud Indicators.

Firms with cash flow problems are the most likely to request funds in advance of being entitled to them. Progress payments which do not appear to coincide with the contractor's plan and capability to perform the contract are suspicious. This could indicate the contractor is claiming payment for work not yet done.

Another type of contractor fraud in this area is to submit a progress payment claim for materials which have not been purchased. The contractor may be issuing a check to the supplier, then holding it until the government progress payment arrives. One way to confirm this irregularity is to check the cancellation dates on the contractor's checks. If the bank received the check about the same time or later than the contractor received the progress payment, the check was probably held.

C. Progress Payment Fraud Examples.

1. A contractor, entered into an agreement with a Military Service to supply and install computer controlled material handling systems at various installations

(continued)

FIG. 24-2 (cont'd)

> located throughout the United States. The contractor then entered into an agreement with a subcontractor to locate and procure computers and computer equipment in order to satisfy the requirements of the contract. The contractor agreed with the subcontractor to provide false invoices for computers and computer equipment, which would be claimed and billed to DOD in progress payment requests. The contractor would receive payments from DOD and purported to pay the subcontractor based on false invoices. The subcontractor then returned the money to the contractor in the form of cashiers' checks.
>
> 2. A contractor conducted environmental impact studies for DOD as well as local governments and private concerns. The contractor directed employees to charge idle time and time from local government or private contracts against the DOD contracts thereby creating false documents to support requests for progress payments. In addition, the contractor directed employees to create overtime work and billed for noncompensated overtime worked by salaried employees so that funds allocated for labor costs could be "burned up." This overtime work did not relate to work on the DOD contracts and resulted in a $300,000 loss to DOD.
>
> 3. A contractor submitted false work reports which resulted in progress payments of $69,000 for work not actually performed on a $6.3 million contract to repair and renovate a sewage treatment plant. The fraud was discovered during performance of the contract due to a malfunction of the system. In correcting the malfunction it was discovered that sewer pipes had not been cleared or lined as required by specifications and reflected in the contractor's work reports.
>
> ### CHAPTER VIII: FAST PAY FRAUD
>
> **A. Introduction.**
>
> There are specific DOD regulations regarding fast pay. In general, the fast pay procedure is limited to contract orders that do not exceed $25,000. The fast payment procedure spelled out in DAR 3-606 (FAR 13.3) is designed to reduce delivery times and to improve DOD's relations with its suppliers by expediting contract payments. The procedure provides for payment based on the contractor's submission of an invoice. That invoice is a representation by the contractor that the supplies have been delivered to a post office, common carrier or point of first receipt.
>
> Fraud in fast pay occurs when a contractor submits an invoice requesting payment for supplies which have not been shipped or delivered to the Government. If the supplies are not in transit or actually delivered at the time the contractor submits his invoice, a criminal violation has occurred. It does not matter if the supplies are subsequently delivered to the Government.
>
> There are specific DOD regulations regarding fast pay. In general, the fast pay procedure is limited to contract orders that do not exceed $25,000. Fast pay orders are usually issued on the DD Form 1155. Regardless of the contract form used for the fast pay purchase, the contract will contain the following certification clause: "The Contractor agrees that the submission of an invoice to the Government for payment is a certification that the supplies for which the Government is being billed have been shipped or delivered in accordance with shipping instructions issued by the ordering officer, in the quantities shown on the invoice, and that such supplies are in the quantity and of the quality designated by the cited purchase order."
>
> The fast pay procedure benefits both the contracting community and DOD. However, contractor integrity and honesty is essential. Payments are made before

PROCUREMENT FRAUD

DOD is in a position to verify that it has received what it bargained for. In many cases, especially where overseas deliveries are involved, it may be weeks or even months before the DOD activity which actually issued the fast pay order is advised of either a nonconforming delivery or a nonreceipt. By that time an unscrupulous contractor may have had an opportunity to bilk the Government out of thousands of dollars and to drop out of sight. Because of the potential for large losses and the effect that such losses could have on continued use of the fast pay procedure, immediate detection of those who have abused the system is necessary.

B. Fast Pay Fraud Indicators.

How can DOD personnel dealing with fast pay identify possible fraud? The most obvious, and sometimes most difficult thing to do, is check for the correlation between the claim for payment and the delivery of goods. Since the claim for payment and receipt of goods occur at different locations this will require communication between paying and receiving points. An employee who becomes suspicious should check with the receiving point to verify that the goods have arrived. Some important things to check for include: not receiving the goods at all, receiving the goods later than would be expected if they were mailed when claimed, and receiving nonconforming goods. The latter sometimes occurs because the contractor has lost the incentive to perform fully to contract specifications after he has been paid.

DOD personnel should also be alert for indications that the invoice submitted by the contractor is forged or altered in some way to make it appear that the goods were sent. Information on the invoice may raise questions such as shipment on a weekend or holiday.

C. Fast Pay Fraud Example.

A contractor entered into an agreement with DOD for the supply of electrical cable protector and other electrical items under the fast payment procedure. The contractor submitted false invoices totaling $32,573.42 claiming goods had been mailed. The contractor was fully aware that this was not the case since its supplier had refused to honor any more purchase orders from the contractor for goods to be shipped to the Government.

CHAPTER IX: BRIBERY, GRATUITIES AND CONFLICTS OF INTEREST

A. Introduction.

This chapter is dedicated to the discussion of integrity awareness. It will inform managers and employees about their responsibilities to be alert for bribe offers, to avoid the acceptance of gratuities, and to recognize conflicts of interest. It calls attention to the relationship and impact of these issues on the procurement process. Further, the chapter discusses the existence and significance to the procurement process of bribery and kickbacks between non-Government entities, e.g., prime contractors and subcontractors.

B. Bribery.

In addition to being a crime, as discussed below, the use of bribery and gratuities in obtaining or doing business changes the nature of the Government's relationship with a contractor or potential contractor. It certainly bears upon the issue of contractor responsibility and possibly the retention of security clearances. How much reliability can be placed in later assertions made by someone who has attempted to bribe a Government employee or an employee of another firm? How can, in good conscience, such a person/company be certified as having the

(continued)

FIG. 24-2 *(cont'd)*

necessary business integrity to be a responsible bidder? It should be remembered that contractors using such methods to do business are usually doing so with the intent to further some form of procurement fraud they are committing or trying to commit. The Government should avoid business with contractors who must resort to kickbacks or bribery to obtain contracts. Where DOD must continue to do business with a contractor due to the circumstances of the procurement, e.g., unique product, stage of development or production of a major system, necessary actions such as increased inspection, review and audit activities should be considered to protect the Government's interests.

1. **Manager Responsibilities.** Managers have many responsibilities in the area of integrity awareness. They must set examples, not only of personal integrity and high ethical standards, but also of a willingness to participate in the referral and investigation process. Too often employees are discouraged from paying attention to or reporting possible bribe situations because it is thought that subsequent actions are time-consuming and disliked by managers because of the work involved. Instead of giving any impressions that they are unsympathetic to this process, managers should actively encourage their employees to be acutely aware of potential bribe overtures, encourage their employees to report bribe attempts immediately and indicate to their employees that they will have full support from management in any efforts to assist investigators in obtaining evidence of the offense.

   The tendency to treat less blatant attempts at bribery as ordinary occupational hazards or as routine innuendos which can easily be ignored or dismissed is another reason that many bribes are not reported. Another reason might include the sentiment that refusal of a bribe offer is deterrent enough. It is part of a manager's job to ensure that these conditions are not impediments to rapid, timely, and efficient reporting of attempted bribes.

2. **Employee Responsibilities.** There are some primary areas that should be focused on in discussing bribery awareness with employees. These areas of concern can be grouped into several questions.

   a. **What constitutes a bribe?** A bribe is an offer to employees of something of value to (a) do something they should not do or (b) fail to do something they should do, in their official duties. The something of value need not be money, it can be anything of value.

   b. **When is a bribe being offered?** People who offer bribes are generally astute and aware individuals. A blatant offer is a rarity. Generally, the party offering a bribe will make subtle overtures in a conventional fashion. They may begin by discussing the employee's life style, family, or salary. They are looking for a vulnerable area where they can exploit the employee. They may seek to establish that the employee has college age children and begin discussing the high cost of education. They may learn that the employee is a new homeowner and discuss high mortgage payments and the expenses of fixing up a new home. If unable to detect an area in which the employee is particularly vulnerable, they may move to more glamorous and alluring areas; cash, cars, and travel. In summary, if the employee feels that the individual is getting beyond mere civility and the professional purpose for the meeting, the employee should be alert to the possibility of a bribe attempt.

   The preliminary conversation may be an attempt to feel the employee out. The person attempting the bribe knows that bribe offers are illegal. They also know that a strong employee has an obligation to report the attempted bribe. Most importantly, the offeror of the bribe does not want to get caught. If the employee is not receptive to subtle overtures and alternative attempts fail, the person may not make any overt bribe offer. An employee has an obligation to determine the nature of the person's remarks. The very subtlety of these preliminary overtures makes the employee's job of detecting a bribe a delicate one.

c. What should be done if a bribe is offered? The first goal is to establish the nature of the person's remarks. Once the attempt to bribe has been determined, the employee should deftly negotiate out of the situation in order to report the attempt immediately to the appropriate investigative organization. An employee who firmly rejects the offer and then reports the attempt will only be faced with a later denial from the offeror. It is essential that an investigator be involved immediately. Employees may use any of several noncommittal excuses to extricate themselves from the meeting without closing out whatever business was the subject of the meeting. Further, the door should be left open for future contact with the offeror.

The response to the offer must be noncommittal. This allows the employee to break off the contact and return with an answer later so that the later meeting can be monitored by an investigator. It can be more difficult for the employee to be noncommittal if the offer is very blatant and direct.

A noncommittal answer like those suggested might be appropriate where a direct or blatant offer is involved:

—"I don't know, I've never done anything like this. I need to think about it."
—"I really need to look at some more information first, let me think about it."
—"I have to think about that carefully."
—"First I need to figure out what's involved here and then I'll get back to you."

After termination of the conversation, **immediately** contact the appropriate investigative organization and report the attempt.

d. Why not accept a bribe? The clear answer to this question is that the acceptance of a bribe is a criminal act which can result in prosecution, dismissal, fines and embarrassment to the family and friends of the employee. Is anyone's future and family worth the small amount they may receive, no matter how much the amount may seem at the time?

In addition, accepting a bribe leaves one always at the mercy of the person who paid it. There is no such thing as a one-time favor for one who accepts a bribe. Since the employee has committed a crime, the briber can ask anything later on under the threat of reporting the bribe, claiming it was solicited and threatening exposure.

e. Why not just refuse a bribe without reporting it? When an employee rejects a bribe, the offeror of the bribe may become concerned that the employee will report the attempt. They may decide that the best way to deal with the situation is to report that the employee tried to solicit a bribe and offer to cooperate in having the employee prosecuted or dismissed for it. If the employee has not reported the attempt, it would give credence to the offeror's allegation. Even though the employee has done nothing wrong, the allegation would have to be investigated and could cause undue problems and time to resolve.

Furthermore, since the attempt to bribe a Government official is in itself a crime, failure to report an attempted bribe, as well as other crimes, leaves the employee open to possible prosecution.

The failure to report a bribe attempt also leaves the offeror free to try again

(continued)

FIG. 24-2 *(cont'd)*

with another employee of the Government. The next employee may not be able to resist the offer. Further, there is no deterrent effect in refusal of the attempt. The offeror is free to try again without fear of the potential consequences. Investigation and prosecution of those who would try to corrupt our employees and our system of Government is the only way to deter others from believing that this is the way to do business with DOD.

3. **Bribes Are a Reality.** As a demonstration that the foregoing discussion relates to a very real problem, here are a few examples of recent DOD bribery cases.

   a. A Navy commander accepted several thousand dollars in money and goods to ensure the Government made purchases from a particular company.

   b. A DOD civilian employee accepted almost $90,000 over four years to make sure a specific company was awarded contracts.

   c. A corporate sales manager was sentenced to ten years in prison, fined $1,000 and ordered to make nearly $10,000 in restitution after conviction on multiple charges of bribing a DOD civilian employee relating to a scheme of false and inflated billings.

   d. A member of a corporate board of directors was sentenced to thirty days confinement and fined $1,000 after being convicted of conspiracy to bribe a civilian employee of DOD.

   e. A DOD civilian employee received a two year prison sentence for accepting over $17,000 for steering contracts to a favored corporation.

   f. A civilian quality assurance inspector was convicted of receiving over $2,000 from a contractor for accepting substandard goods.

   g. A GS-4 file clerk was convicted of receiving approximately $50,000 in bribes from various contractors to provide them inside information used to enhance their bid packages.

4. **Commercial Bribery and Kickbacks.** There are times when payments of bribes and kickbacks do not involve Government employees but still impact on the procurement process. Employees or officers of a prime contractor may solicit or be offered and accept payment of bribes or kickbacks in connection with the award or performance of subcontractors. Subcontractors may initiate such payments to prime contractor employees to obtain competitors' bid or technical data to gain an unfair competitive advantage. Such activities may impact on the procurement process in several ways. The price paid for the product or service may be higher because the subcontractor passes the cost of bribes and kickbacks through to the prime. In extreme instances, the kickbacks may be so significant that the subcontractor cannot perform the work in conformance with specifications or fails to perform at all due to underfunding. In these cases deliveries are delayed or prevented and the ultimate user deprived of the contracted for item.

   In addition to the contractual impact of commercial bribes and kickbacks, there is a statutory prohibition regarding such activities involving a negotiated Federal contract. The statute, known as the Anti-Kickback Act (41 USC 51-54), makes it a crime for a subcontractor to make a payment to a prime contractor in order to get the award of a subcontract.

   In a practical example of such a situation, the officers of a subcontractor agreed to pay substantial bribes to officers of a major DOD shipbuilder in order to get technical data enabling the subcontractor to get large subcontracts. Once the subcontracts were awarded, additional substantial kickbacks were paid to

PROCUREMENT FRAUD

officers of the prime to keep the subcontracts and influence the award of subsequent ones. The kickbacks were paid by creating phony companies. The subcontractor made payments to these phony companies for nonexistent services. The checks were negotiated through a series of nominees until the funds were ultimately deposited to Swiss bank accounts held by officers of the prime. The payments were so substantial they contributed greatly to the subcontractor going bankrupt before completing the required work. The officers of the subcontractor who paid the kickbacks formed a new company and had the subcontracts transferred to it. They continued to pay kickbacks to the same officers of the prime in order to affect this transfer. In addition to the bankruptcy of the original subcontractor, these schemes resulted in delays and incomplete work. Several individuals have pleaded guilty to criminal charges and the Government has filed a civil action to recoup monetary penalties and damages resulting from the scheme.

C. Gratuities

Gratuities are generally distinguished from attempted bribery in that there is usually no request for specific improper action in exchange for what is being given. Gratuities are generally given to assist in enhancing the "relationship" between the offeror and the Government employee. This "more favorable atmosphere" in which to do business may later move the employee to "lean" in the contractor's favor if needed. Some contractors have gone so far in providing gratuities as to actually budget substantial sums (in excess of $150,000 for a project in one case) to create a favorable atmosphere for their dealings with Government employees.

Dealings with those who seek to and who do business with the Government should be conducted in an objective manner, above reproach, and avoiding even the appearance of favoritism or other impropriety. Acceptance of gratuities of any kind should be avoided in order to maintain both the form and the substance of objectivity in official dealings. It should also be remembered that the offer or acceptance of a gratuity is a felony. Furthermore, the provision of a gratuity is a violation of a standard clause in DOD contracts (FAR 52.203-3).

D. Conflicts of Interest

DOD employees are generally prohibited by both criminal laws and standards of conduct requirements from taking official actions dealing with businesses in which they or their immediate families have a direct, financial interest. DOD employees should be alert to situations in which they suspect a possible conflict of interest and report these to appropriate authorities. The following recent cases are reflective of situations to which all DOD employees should be sensitive.

1. A buyer with the Defense Electronics Supply Center (DESC), along with his wife and sister-in-law, formed a company to represent various electronics companies in their efforts to obtain contracts with DESC. On numerous occasions, the buyer, who was responsible for bid solicitation and price determination for a selected series of electronic items, recommended awards of Government contracts to these same companies. The buyer also used an affiliate of the company he had formed to sell solenoids to DESC under approximately 50 contracts with the Government. As a DESC employee, he personally participated in the award of these contracts to his own company. No disclosure of his interest in this company was made to DESC. The buyer charged DESC over $70,000 as a result of these contracts. Based on a complaint from a co-worker at DESC, the buyer has recently been convicted under the Federal conflict of interest statute.

(continued)

FIG. 24-2 *(cont'd)*

2. A senior medical officer, who served as a consultant to the Surgeon General of a Military Department, recommended that DOD procure an item of medical equipment on a sole source basis from one company. At no time did the officer disclose that he was a director and major stockholder in the company. When the Surgeon General agreed to the recommendation, the officer sought to recapitalize the company in anticipation of receiving a large amount of new orders. When the officer learned that he was suspected of conflict of interest, he denied his ownership in the company, and had the company prepare false and backdated documents to show that he had no involvement with the company. In addition, the officer received payments from various drug companies for drug tests performed at a military hospital but failed to disclose to the hospital the receipt of this money, which is illegal under Federal law. The allegations in this case were made by two doctors at the hospital who became aware of the medical officer's conflicts of interest. The medical officer has been convicted of Federal violations of unlawfully supplementing his income, and charged with conflict of interest, tax fraud and obstruction of justice under the Uniform Code of Military Justice.

3. A military officer, working as the chief of a subcontracts branch in the resident office of a major DOD contractor, was assigned to assist in an inquiry into possible improper billing practices by the contractor. The officer, in anticipation of his pending retirement, solicited a job offer from the contractor. Negotiations took place between the officer and the contractor and a salary was agreed upon. The officer did not notify his superiors of his intention to retire nor did he disqualify himself from his duties relating to the inquiry of the contractor during his job negotiations. The officer took numerous actions during the inquiry which directly benefited the contractor. After submitting his notice of retirement, the officer commenced working for the company while on terminal leave from the military. In his new capacity, he headed up an internal audit group of the contractor and his main job was to identify improper billing practices including those which he had previously attempted to resolve as a military officer.

CHAPTER X: CIVIL, CONTRACTUAL AND ADMINISTRATIVE REMEDIES FOR FRAUD

A. Introduction.

Traditionally, Government contracting officials have relied upon the criminal justice system to police fraud by DOD contractors. This reliance has included forbearance from certain administrative and contractual actions until the criminal case is completed. However, this reliance is often misplaced for a number of reasons. First, a 1981 GAO report determined that two-thirds of all fraud cases which were referred to the Department of Justice (DOJ) for criminal actions were declined. The majority of cases were declined because the DOJ did not have adequate resources to prosecute the cases, and not because there was insufficient evidence to conclude that a fraud was committed upon the United States.

Second, criminal cases must be proven beyond a reasonable doubt. While there may be insufficient information to warrant a criminal conviction, contracting officials do not need that level of evidence in order to take administrative and contractual action.

Third, even if criminal action is taken, many serious cases are plea bargained down to minor offenses. This tends to confuse many people into incorrectly thinking that there was no proven serious offense. In one documented case, four nonappropriated fund officials pled guilty to accepting bribes from a contractor.

The contractor, however, pled guilty only to a misdemeanor—trespassing on a Federal reservation. Contracting officials believed the misdemeanor was an indication that the contractor's action was not serious. In fact, the actual evidence revealed the significant nature of this criminal conduct, despite the nature of his plea.

Finally, DOD contracting officials and not the DOJ are responsible for the integrity of the DOD contracting process. The FARs and DOD implementing regulations require DOD contracting officials to take positive action on any evidence of contractor impropriety and nonresponsibility. It is therefore necessary for managers and contracting officials to be aware of and utilize the civil, administrative, and contracting powers which are available to protect the Government, to prevent further loss to the Government and to recover Government funds lost through fraud.

B. Coordinated Approach to Remedies.

Because DOD officials are responsible for the integrity of DOD contracts, these officials must be prepared to take immediate action to protect the Government. This often includes positive action while a criminal investigation is under way, and before an indictment or a conviction has been obtained. Criminal cases often take years to complete and DOD can take many contractual and administrative actions on evidence less than that necessary for an indictment or conviction. Often, timely action by a contracting official, such as a preindictment suspension or a contract default termination, will aid the Government by precluding a contractor from continuing to benefit from fraudulent conduct while an investigation is under way.

Furthermore, by taking a coordinated approach to criminal, civil, contractual and administrative actions the Government is often able to induce guilty contractors into pleading guilty more quickly. Simultaneous consideration of all the remedies available to DOD and DOJ also enables the Government and the court to fashion a single comprehensive remedy package which will punish the contractor, protect the Government, and make the Government whole from any losses suffered.

While early action by contract officials is important, such actions must be coordinated with a variety of DOD and DOJ officials. For example, a recent case involved a Service member who was suspected of accepting bribes from a number of DOD contractors. While the criminal case was being investigated by the DOJ, the following related contract and administrative actions were also considered:

    a. Flagging of the Service member's record to preclude his retirement;

    b. Freezing of the Service member's retirement account to provide a fund against which the Government could recoup any monies lost;

    c. Termination of any contracts which the contractors had obtained through bribery; and

    d. Suspension of the contractors while the criminal case was under way.

In order to ensure that such coordination takes place, the Secretary of Defense directed on May 9, 1983 that each Military Department and Defense Agency appoint a centralized point of coordination for all criminal, civil, contractual and administrative actions in contract fraud and corruption cases. As a result of this memorandum, the following officials have been identified:

    Army—Contract Fraud Branch, Office of the Judge Advocate General

    Navy—Navy Materiel Command, Office of the Inspector General

    Air Force—Office of Review and Oversight, Air Force Inspector General

    DLA—Office of General Counsel

(continued)

FIG. 24-2 *(cont'd)*

C. Civil Actions

1. Civil False Claims Act. The Government has the right to take civil action against fraudulent contractors based upon a number of statutory grounds. These civil actions are filed by DOJ and may be filed in conjunction with, after, or instead of a criminal prosecution.

The submission of a false claim to the Government can make a contractor liable to the Government both criminally and civilly. The civil False Claims Act, 31 USC 3729-3731, establishes civil liability for false claims. The act provides for a civil penalty of $2,000 per false claim and double the damages suffered by the Government. For example, if a contractor falsely certifies small business status in order to get a small business set aside contract, every claim submitted on the contract is a civil false claim, even if the contractor performs satisfactorily. The Government may recover double the value of the contract, plus $2,000 for every invoice submitted.

2. Contract Disputes Act. Under the civil False Claims Act, the Government may only recover double damages when the Government has actually suffered damages, i.e., when a false claim is paid. If an audit or investigation determines that a claim is false and payment is not made, the Government is limited to the $2,000 penalty. However, under the Contract Disputes Act, 41 USC 604, a contractor is liable to the Government for the amount of any unsupported claim, if the claim is based on fraud or misrepresentation of fact. Under this statute the Government does not have to pay the claim in order to recover.

D. Contract Actions

Under contract law and principles, the Government has the right to insist upon certain standards of responsibility and business integrity from its contractors. Any indication that a contractor has violated these principles gives the Government the right to take a variety of actions. These actions may be taken in conjunction with, after, or instead of a criminal prosecution.

1. Termination for Default. The submission of a false claim or statement on a contract is clear evidence of a contractor's nonresponsibility and failure to perform on a contract. The contracting officer has the right and obligation to terminate the contract for default. Terminations for convenience are never appropriate when fraud is present on a contract.

Furthermore, certain improper actions also give rise to a statutory right to terminate for default. Under 10 USC 2207, the Government has the right to terminate any contract for default whenever a contractor offers a gratuity to a Government employee. (DAR 7-104.16 and Appendix D; FAR 52.203-3 and DFAR Appendix D.) This statute also gives the Government the right, in addition to all other default remedies, to penalize the contractor in the amount of three to ten times the value of the gratuity.

2. Denial of Claims. In addition to terminating a contract for default, DOD contracting officials also have an obligation not to pay claims which are tainted by fraud. Under the Contract Disputes Act, 41 USC 605, DOD is not authorized to "administer, settle, compromise, pay or otherwise adjust any claim involving fraud." Therefore, whenever fraud is detected on a claim, contracting officials should not take any further action on any portion of the claim without coordination with the DOJ.

3. **Findings of Nonresponsibility.** Under DAR 1-900 and FAR 9.1, contracts may only be awarded to responsible contractors. Contractors are required to affirmatively demonstrate their responsibility, including a satisfactory record of integrity and business ethics. Any evidence of fraud by a contractor is clearly a matter which should be considered by contracting officers in making responsibility determinations.

4. **Suspension and Debarment.** Under DAR 1-600 (FAR 9.4), contractors may be precluded from doing business with the Government for the commission of fraud or for various other actions indicating a lack of business integrity. Suspension is an interim measure designed to protect the Government while a criminal investigation or trial is under way and evidence of fraud is present. A contractor may be suspended for up to eighteen months while an investigation is under way, and once an indictment or civil suit is filed, the contractor remains suspended until the completion of all legal proceedings.

   Debarment is a final determination of a contractor's nonresponsibility. A contractor can be debarred, based upon a conviction of a crime, or upon sufficient evidence that a contractor has repeatedly failed to perform properly or has committed acts which indicate a lack of business integrity and honesty. Debarment can be in effect for up to three years.

   In order for the suspension and debarment procedures to be effective, it is essential for contracting officers to forward reports of improper contractor activity to the suspension/debarment authority at the earliest opportunity. Reporting procedures are set forth in DAR 1-608 (DOD FAR Supplement 9.472).

5. **Disallowance of Legal Costs.** Contractors who have engaged in fraud on cost type contracts are not entitled to recover legal and administrative costs relating to their defense against Government action. (DAR 15-250.52; FAR 31.205-5.) It is important for contracting officers to take prompt action to require contractors to identify such costs while an investigation is under way and to deny claims for such costs in all appropriate cases.

E. Personnel Actions.

The Government has a variety of remedies to take against Government employees who have colluded with contractors in fraudulent conduct or when a Government employee has engaged in improper actions such as receipt of bribes or gratuities or has been engaged in conflict of interest. These remedies include, but are not limited to:

1. Termination. The receipt of a bribe or gratuity, or actions indicating a personal conflict of interest, can justify the immediate termination of a Federal employee.

2. Revocation of a contracting officer's warrant. Contracting officers who engage in improper conduct can lose their right to contract on behalf of the Government.

3. Recoupment of funds lost. Whenever a contractor gives a bribe or gratuity to a Government employee, both the contractor and the employee are jointly liable to the Government for an amount equal to the value of the bribe or gratuity.

   Action should be taken to deduct the value of any such bribe or gratuity from the pension contributions of the employee, prior to the termination of the employee. Similar actions can be taken against military personnel and retirees.

(continued)

FIG. 24-2 *(cont'd)*

> **CHAPTER XI: CRACKING DOWN ON FRAUD IN DOD PROCUREMENT***
>
> A special investigation and prosecution unit to concentrate on fraud and corruption in procurement by the Department of Defense was formed and announced by Secretary of Defense Caspar W. Weinberger and Attorney General William French Smith.
>
> Since the Department of Defense spends millions of dollars every day for goods and services, both leaders are confident the unit will bolster the Administration's efforts to ferret out fraud, waste, and abuse.
>
> The interagency unit's primary objectives will be criminal investigation and prosecution. It will also assure early consideration of civil remedies, the primary means by which DOD can recover money lost as a result of fraud. DOD authorities are also expected to focus on the same cases for possible administrative sanctions, including suspension or debarment.
>
> The unit is staffed with attorneys, investigators and auditors from the Department of Defense and the Department of Justice.
>
> The need for the Department of Justice/Department of Defense Procurement Fraud Unit stemmed from a growing perception by officials in both departments for a way to manage more effectively the complex investigations and prosecutions resulting from DOD cases.
>
> First, while the four primary DOD investigative agencies—the Army Criminal Investigation Command, the Naval Investigative Service, the Air Force Office of Special Investigations, and the Defense Criminal Investigative Service—have all sought in recent years to emphasize the investigation of fraud cases, they have done so without the benefit of early consultation with Department of Justice prosecutors. Second, many fraud investigations languished for long periods of time without a judgment by the Department of Justice as to their potential for criminal prosecution. And third, civil and administrative remedies were often considered at a very late stage in the investigation, thus precluding effective mandatory recoveries or timely suspensions and debarments.
>
> These factors were compounded since the Department of Justice commitment in difficult fraud cases varied among the ninety-four United States Attorney's Offices throughout the country. The creation of a single Unit addresses these factors and embodies the type of commitment each department must provide for sustained success.
>
> Despite this concentration of resources in a single Procurement Fraud Unit, the need for the active and aggressive involvement of prosecutors in the United States Attorney's Offices continues. The number of cases actually prosecuted by the Unit will be small, limited to those which have the greatest potential significance or impact, but the majority of DOD fraud cases will remain the direct responsibility of the United States Attorney's Offices.
>
> The Procurement Fraud Unit will be able to serve as a central focal point, through which both departments can monitor and ensure timely consideration and disposition of cases referred directly to the United States Attorney's Offices. This monitoring ability should overcome one of the more substantial institutional obstacles confronted by DOD in the past—an inability to communicate its concerns to an organization dedicated exclusively to the overview of DOD fraud
>
> ---
>
> * This chapter is a reproduction of most of the text of an article by Mr. Joseph H. Sherick, the Inspector General, DOD. The article appeared in the January 1983 issue of *Defense '83*, a DOD publication.

cases. In addition, the Procurement Fraud Unit can assist the United States Attorney's Offices by supplying expert advice on certain types of complex DOD procurement cases and by generally monitoring their progress.

As with all organizational initiatives, the success of the Procurement Fraud Unit will depend on the commitment of the two departments and the talents of those individuals assigned to it. The Secretary of Defense has stated that his project is to receive the highest priority. Accordingly, the selection of DOD representatives has been a careful process. Special emphasis has been placed on obtaining investigators with solid backgrounds in fraud investigations and auditors with sensitivities to DOD programs and practices which are particularly vulnerable to fraud.

Investigators from the four DOD criminal investigative agencies and auditors from the Defense Contract Audit Agency and Defense Audit Service will be assigned to the Unit. Liaison has been established between the Unit and the Army Audit Agency, Naval Audit Service, and Air Force Audit Agency. The role of the Defense Contract Audit Agency will be particularly important in ensuring that potential fraud cases emanating from contract audits are given early attention by Department of Justice prosecutors.

The Army, Navy, and Air Force audit organizations will also play significant roles in specific investigations selected by the Unit for prosecution. Additionally, attorneys from the Army, Navy, and Air Force, with backgrounds in procurement and administrative remedies, have been assigned to the Unit. Their knowledge will complement the talents of the Department of Justice attorneys in developing complex cases and evaluating administrative remedies.

By making DOD investigators, auditors, and attorneys part of the immediate "prosecution team," it is expected that they will learn first hand what is required by the Department of Justice for a successful criminal or civil prosecution. They, in turn, will carry this information back to their respective organizations where it can be provided to the rest of the workforce.

While the ultimate impact of the new Procurement Fraud Unit will be measured primarily by the significant cases prosecuted, there should also be an immediate improvement in the effectiveness and timeliness of investigations, brought about by the Unit's emphasis and coordination ability.

While many investigations will not merit criminal prosecution, the sheer volume of investigations has often made screening for significant cases which warrant consideration for prosecution a difficult task. The Procurement Fraud Unit, through its representatives from the DOD investigative organizations, will perform this valuable early screening function and ensure that Department of Justice prosecutors are aware of serious allegations of fraud or corruption as soon as DOD investigations begin to establish evidence of such activities. This will help attorneys, investigators, and auditors work together to develop cases with the maximum potential for success. Alternatively, this process will identify cases which should be disposed of through civil or administrative actions without the need for protracted and resource-consuming criminal investigations.

By providing a multidiscipline approach to the investigation and proseccution of DOD fraud cases, the Unit also maximizes the potential sources from which good investigative leads might be developed. Just as importantly, the Unit will serve as a ready forum for the exchange of ideas and information between the participating agencies. Set in the midst of an organization which is directly involved in the prosecution of complex procurement fraud cases, it should provide an entirely new insight for DOD organizations into the effective development of cases of national significance. Investigators should particularly benefit by observing the means by

(continued)

FIG. 24-2 *(cont'd)*

> which the evidentiary requirements of prosecutors can be met to build the requisite elements of a fraud case. Of those elements, probably the most significant is that of "intent"; if investigators understand and anticipate the requirement to establish evidence of intentional fraud, the parts of an often-very-complicated criminal scheme can be pieced together quite effectively by an experienced prosecutor.
>
> Another significant by-product of the Procurement Fraud Unit will be the commitment of the Department of Justice to provide timely information derived from investigations to enable DOD to modify programs or procedures that are vulnerable to fraud and abuse. While such information should be naturally assimilated by the DOD participants in the Unit and related back to their respective organizations, the Department of Justice will also be encouraged to transmit formal reports of those findings which indicate program or procedural deficiences.
>
> The establishment of a Procurement Fraud Unit is a clear signal that efforts of the Government to curb fraud in DOD procurement activities have been intensified. Final success in our efforts will not hinge, however, on the creation of a single organization; it depends on the full participation of all our investigators and auditors and the complete support of all DOD employees and contractors. We must recognize that attainment of a national defense establishment second to none requires a system where the integrity of the participants is without question. And that every dollar provided by the taxpayers is spent prudently and wisely.

Defective Pricing Fraud

Another guidance document was issued by the Inspector General, Department of Defense in this mid- to late 1980s period. This one relates to defective pricing. As the preface states, it is not the responsibility of the contract auditor to prove fraud on the part of a contractor; that is the job of an investigator. But the finding and reporting of fraud indicators is the obligation of the auditor. Moreover, the auditor is encouraged to "think fraud." The short *Handbook on Scenarios of Potential Defective Pricing Fraud* is a useful reference.

Self-Policing by DOD Contractors

Quite naturally, the presence of federal auditors or the threat of a federal audit is a deterrent to fraud. Yet, given the magnitude of the task, it may be that enlightened self-interest on the part of defense contractors may encourage voluntary actions. A special study, "Conduct and Accountability, a Report to the President, by the President's Blue Ribbon Commission on Defense Management," (June 1986) prepared under the guidance of former Pentagon Chief David Packard, emphasizes such self-policing (see Chapter 22).

CHAPTER **25**

Computer Abuse and Fraud

Introduction 1	Reducing Computer Fraud 20
	Prevention 20
Definitions 2	Detection 21
Reasons for Growth in Computer Abuse and Fraud 2	Safeguarding Computer Data 22
	An Operational Audit of Computer Security 22
Categories of Computer Abuse and Fraud 3	Developing Internal Control for a Minicomputer System 24
Computer Fraud—Causes and Techniques 4	Multilevel Controls 24
	Controlling Data Entry Errors 25
Computer-Related Crime 4	Preventing Unauthorized Access 25
The Role of the Computer in Crime 5	
Where Does the Vulnerability Lie? 5	The Use of "Threat Teams" to Detect and Prevent Fraud 26
Rapid Growth 5	
Insufficient Auditing 5	Guidelines in Using the Threat Team Technique 26
Inadequate Controls 6	The Advantages 27
Learning to Speak the Language 6	
A Question of Control and Responsibility 9	Legislative Relief 28
	State Legislation 28
Other Methods of Unauthorized Access 10	Federal Computer Crime Laws 29
	Computer Fraud Insurance Coverage ... 29
Bulletin Board Systems 10	Suggested Reading 30

INTRODUCTION

Computer fraud is a large and growing business. Some of the more spectacular cases, such as those using electronic fund transfers (EFTs), involve computers and huge amounts of money, and often are hard to detect. One source quotes estimates of computer fraud losses to be between $3 billion and $5 billion annually in the U.S. alone.[1] Speed, ability to handle vast quantities of numbers, and flexibility have made the computer highly useful to businesses, as well as to the computer criminal. These same attributes make businesses vulnerable to heavy losses and serious disruption of operations.

This chapter deals with some of the causes and some of the steps that can be taken to deter, reduce, or prevent computer abuse and fraud.

DEFINITIONS

Some people use the terms "computer abuse" and "computer fraud" interchangeably. Although often, the same or common preventive measures are taken against both types of improper activities, it may be helpful to differentiate between the two categories.[2]

- ☐ *Computer abuse* may be defined as instances where actions are committed against computers and related software, making the computer the object of the crime.
- ☐ *Computer fraud* relates to actions where the computer is used as a tool or device to commit a crime.

Donn B. Parker, a computer criminologist of SRI International, defines computer crime as "any illegal act for which knowledge of computer technology is essential for successful perpetration." He defines computer abuse as "any intentional act involving a computer where one or more perpetrators made or could have made a gain and one or more victims suffered or could have suffered a loss."[3]

REASONS FOR GROWTH IN COMPUTER ABUSE AND FRAUD

There are any number of reasons why computer abuse and fraud have grown so much in the past several years, and why computer systems are so susceptible to criminal acts. Among these are the following:

1. More employees than ever have access to computers. This arises from more computer applications and the proliferation of the many random access computer terminals throughout a company.

---

[1] Stephen M. Paroby and William J. Barrett, "Reducing the Risk of Computer Fraud," *Corporate Accounting*, Fall 1987, p. 59.

[2] In part from Pamela R. Pfau, "Computer Abuse," *Corporate Accounting*, Fall 1985, pp. 46–47.

[3] *Ibid*, p. 47.

2. More and more people are being trained in the use of computers. In business schools or other universities, and even in high school and grade school, students are being taught how to use computers, and some students have become very sophisticated.
3. The potential growth of personal computers for use in the home—with ability to access other computer systems—is astronomical.
4. Computer security techniques have not kept up with technological advances in hardware and software. The emphasis on meeting the higher and higher work loads minimized the attention being devoted to security or antifraud matters.
5. As a rule, EDP personnel are not especially security-conscious and are not usually familiar with standard internal control procedures. Their specialty has been the rapid, economical, and unobstructed processing of data to the exclusion of security procedures.
6. In many instances, management has tended to let EDP personnel "do their thing" with little supervision or restriction.
7. With the absence of human intervention and normal audit trails, it has been easier to commit fraud without early detection. On occasion, complete files have been erased and it was not possible to trace transactions.

These are only some of the circumstances that have led to major computer frauds.

CATEGORIES OF COMPUTER ABUSE AND FRAUD

For those not specializing in computer fraud detection and the like, the following categories of computer abuse and fraud may be helpful explanations:

- ☐ *Use of a computer to embezzle funds or steal assets.* This may involve the use of EFTs, or employing a computer to fraudulently print coupons or tickets.
- ☐ *Use of a computer to commit fraud.* Examples could be the issuance of false checks by a computer, or the false alteration of payment files.
- ☐ *Unauthorized computer use.* Such actions could range from simple and limited personal use to massive operations, such as programming for business applications of another unrelated entity.
- ☐ *Unauthorized access to the computer.* This could involve relatively harmless "hacking" via phone lines to more extensive access, or a potentially harmful data loss.
- ☐ *The destruction, alteration, or interception of information or software.* This may not monetarily assist the transgressor, but it may cause operating and other difficulties for the firm whose records were accessed.
- ☐ *Theft of information, software, or hardware.* The theft of information or software may not be detected directly, although, in the hands of competitors,

it can cause significant loss. The theft of hardware may or may not involve large sums of money, but it is readily detectable.

COMPUTER FRAUD—CAUSES AND TECHNIQUES

Computer-Related Crime

As computer usage becomes more widespread, and as the systems become more complex, the potential for criminal activity is likely to grow. Moreover, the nature of computer crime is changing. White-collar workers were once the chief perpetrators. Now, however, law officials warn that organized crime is getting into the act. Therefore, it becomes doubly important that the internal auditor be aware of the various roles the computer can play in crime as well as some of the methods used. What better source for such information than the partner of a well-known accounting firm?

Some of the commentary in *Corporate Accounting* is essentially as follows:[4]

> In recent years, computer fraud has become quite profitable—for the computer criminal. Unfortunately, this sophisticated form of white-collar crime is costing America's businesses an estimated $75 billion a year. Moreover, as computer systems become more complex, the potential for crime is likely to increase.
>
> One indication that computer fraud is on the upswing is the formation of such groups as "data detectives"—a new breed of detective specializing in white-collar EDP crime. These agencies combine the clock-and-dagger aura of top-secret criminal investigators with the professional financial accounting and data processing expertise required to uncover white-collar crime in the EDP area.
>
> Public awareness of computer fraud is also on the upswing. Prior to 1970 there were very little data on the subject. Since that time, however, the Stamford Research Institute has been investigating computer abuse, and the AICPA recently sponsored two major studies of fraud in the banking and insurance industries. The studies indicated that a wide variety of methods are used by employees in both industries to commit computerized fraud.
>
> What steps can you take to prevent or detect computer crime in your organization? An increased awareness and understanding of EDP fraud techniques, and increased EDP audit involvement, will help you identify situations in your company that are susceptible to fraud, so you can take steps to prevent it.

---

[4] From David C. Goodyear, "Putting the Lid on Computer-Related Crime," *Corporate Accounting*, Summer 1983, pp. 82–86.

The Role of the Computer in Crime

Computer-related crime often falls into the same categories as traditional types of crime committed without a computer—i.e., fraud, larceny, embezzlement, theft, sabotage, espionage, vandalism, burglary, extortion, and conspiracy. However, relative to the occupations of the perpetrators, the environments in which computer-related crimes are committed and the forms of assets lost cause them to differ significantly from traditional crimes.

The nature of business, economic, and white-collar crimes is changing rapidly as computers provide the activities and environments in which these crimes occur. The computer can play four basic roles in crime:

1. *Object.* This normally includes the destruction of the computer, the data or programs contained in the computer, or even supportive facilities. While crimes of this type still occur, the number of such incidents is considerably smaller than it was 10 years ago because firms have taken steps to prevent such occurrences.
2. *Subject.* Here, the computer is the site or environment of the crime.
3. *Instrument.* In such situations, the method of crime is so complex that the computer is needed as a tool to pull it off.
4. *Symbol.* The computer is used to intimidate or deceive—e.g., false advertising of nonexistent services, such as in dating bureaus.

Where Does the Vulnerability Lie?

Rapid Growth. Large and small businesses alike are vulnerable to computer crimes. Firms that have experienced rapid growth, however, have proven especially vulnerable, because it takes time for conflicts, and their proper use, to catch up with the growth rate. In most businesses, those at the top are understandably removed from the computer and its operational systems, that there is no one in management close enough to them to deal with the issues that would prevent fraud.

Insufficient Auditing. Consider the following example: Company *A* buys Company *B* and, in the process, acquires its computer system, which happens to be vulnerable to computer crime. The Company *A* auditors, guided by Company *B*'s procedures manual, examine, test, evaluate, and make random checks on *B*'s system. However, they fail to ask if the procedures manual contains sufficient controls over the handling of data before they are entered into the computer system, or if it defines accurately the actual internal operations of the computer and its programs. If these areas are not probed, weaknesses in the system design, which could give rise to errors or irregularities, are not likely to be identified.

Some conscientious auditors will spot problems or inadequacies in manual procedures and suggest changes. Many, however, will audit "around" the computer, failing to spot system weakness that could later result in computer crime. They feel that their job is to audit the numbers—and not to test and critique the computer system.

Inadequate Controls. Say a corporation with annual sales of approximately $5 million buys a computer. The corporation is too small to hire a programmer so, instead, it purchases $3,000 of preprogrammed software to process paychecks, accounts payable, receivables, and so forth. Is there a vulnerability to computer crime here? Yes. Basically, the vulnerability lies in three areas: (1) computer access, (2) input controls, and (3) output controls.

Before the company's new computer was installed, a secretary typed 100 paychecks a week. When she was finished, the controller examined her work to make sure she hadn't typed an extra check for herself or made any errors. When the computer was brought in, management trusted it completely, thinking it was incapable of dishonesty or mistakes.

Management failed to consider that the secretary was completing the input being fed into the computer. Her function had remained the same in terms of control considerations, but because they had put a computer in the middle, management forgot about her. She still had the opportunity to enter an extra voucher for accounts payable—and the controller was no longer monitoring her work.

Learning to Speak the Language

Computer crime involves new methods of committing a crime, and so a new jargon has developed to identify various automated criminal methods. Become familiar with the major ones so that you can identify potential problems.

☐ *Data diddling* is by far the simplest, safest, and most common type of computer-related crime. It involves changing data before or during input to a computer. This can be accomplished by anyone associated with, or having access to, the process of creating, recording, transporting, examining, and checking data to enter the computer. For example, one might forge or counterfeit a document, exchange a valid computer tape, disk, or diskette with prepared replacements, and neutralize or avoid manual controls. In many systems, the visible audit trail tends to disappear, and such things as input documents are replaced with data entry through terminals, where it becomes more difficult to detect this type of fraud. If control totals are available to the perpetrator, the situation may be even more dangerous.

☐ *The Trojan Horse* method refers to the placement of extra statements in a computer program which causes the computer to perform unauthorized functions, while it continues to perform those primary functions which were intended without alteration.

This is one of the most common methods of computer fraud and sabotage—and one of the most difficult to detect. Why? Because instructions can be placed in the production computer program so that they are processed in the protected or restricted domain of the program and have access to all the data and files that are assigned for exclusive use of the program. The more clever individuals do not insert codes directly into the application program itself, which is where most auditors would look. Instead, they insert bogus statements in the operating system or utility programs, where they wait to interact with the application program while the application program is processing the data. Extra instructions are inserted for a few milliseconds of processing time. When the program is completed, there is no evidence these particular instructions were used. In addition, even if the crime is discovered, it may not be easy to identify the perpetrator. Note that this type of fraud requires a very high level of technical EDP knowledge. In most EDP installations, the person who can execute this type of fraud is unsupervised from a technical review standpoint.

If you suspect that a Trojan Horse exists in your company, there are ways to uncover it: (1) Periodically compare a control copy of an operational program with the program actually being run to determine whether or not they are the same. This comparison, however, would not uncover a Trojan Horse perpetrated through the operating system. To detect this would be a much more difficult task. However, it can be accomplished by following method (2). (2) Reprocess the individual application using a different operating system and processing at an off-site location. This would require reprocessing the application program and having the detailed results compared with the program previously run. Before using this means of identifying Trojan Horse fraud, other means, such as analytical review, might be easier to apply and might narrow the field of possible perpetrators.

☐ *A logic bomb* is a set of instructions inserted into a computer program and activated at appropriate or periodic times. For example, instructions may be inserted in a computer operating system, as in a Trojan Horse. The instructions test the date, by referencing the computer's day clock, to determine if a specific date has been reached. When the specified date arrives, the instructions are activated and cause one of several events to happen, such as the erasure of an entire personnel file or the crash of the operating system in an on-line environment. The result can be utter chaos.

☐ *Salami* techniques are an automated form of crime involving the theft of small amounts of assets from a large number of sources. For example, on a banking system, the demand deposit accounting system for checking accounts could be changed, using the Trojan Horse method, to randomly reduce a few hundred accounts by $0.10 or $0.15. The money is then transferred to a special account where it can be legitimately withdrawn through normal methods. Transactions of this magnitude are generally not reviewed by anyone, and, since all accounts would be in balance, there would be no indication that a problem existed.

☐ *Superzapping* derives its name from "Superzap," a computer utility program used in many IBM computer centers as a system tool. This particular type of utility is required because computers sometimes stop, malfunction or enter a state that cannot be overcome by normal recovery or restart procedures. Utility programs such as Superzap are extremely powerful—and, in the wrong hands, dangerous.

A classic example of "superzapping" resulted in a $128,000 loss for a New Jersey bank. The computer operations manager was using the Superzap program to correct errors by making changes to account balances. The regular error correction process was not working correctly because the demand deposit accounting system had become obsolete and error-ridden as a result of inattention in a computer changeover. The bank could not afford to wait until the new system was corrected and tested to update the accounts.

During the correction process, the operation manager discovered how easy it was to make changes without the usual control procedures or journal records. He took advantage of this by making changes and transferring money to the accounts of three friends. Finally, a customer noticed a shortage, and the fraud was discovered.

☐ *Scavenging* is a method of obtaining information that is left in or around the computer room after an application is processed.

Simple physical scavenging consists of the searching of trash barrels for copies of discarded computer listings or carbon paper. More technical and sophisticated methods of scavenging are achieved by searching through residual data left in a computer after an application is processed. For example, a computer operating system may not properly erase storage areas used for temporary storage of input or output data. Some operating systems do not erase magnetic tape storage media because that requires excess computer time. If one gains access to these files, it is possible to scavenge through the file for useful information.

This occurred in a Texas-based time-sharing service that had a number of oil companies as customers. The computer operator noted that each time one particular customer used computer services, he requested that a scratch tape be mounted on a tape drive. When the operator mounted the tape, he noticed that the tape light, indicating the tape was being read, always came on before the write tape light. This indicated that the user was reading data from a temporary storage tape before he had written anything on it. After awhile, the computer operator became curious and reported it to management. Simple investigation revealed that the customer was engaged in industrial espionage—obtaining the seismic data stored by various oil companies on temporary tapes and selling this highly proprietary and valuable information to competitors.

☐ *Data leakage* accounts for a wide range of computer-related crime involving the removal of data, or copies of data from a computer system or facility.

Here, the perpetrator is most vulnerable to exposure because he must retrieve the data from the computer in order to convert it to economic gain. In most computer installations, output is subject to examination by computer operators, and other data processing personnel and distribution is controlled.

Several techniques can be used by the perpetrator to leak data from the computer system. In some sophisticated situations, data are combined with otherwise innocuous data and removed from a computer facility. Usually the higher the level of security and risk within a particular installation, the more exotic the method used to extract data.

COMPUTER ABUSE & FRAUD

☐ *Piggybacking* and *impersonation* can be done physically or electronically. Physical piggybacking entails gaining access to sensitive areas. In a typical situation, an individual, usually with his hands full of computer-related objects, such as tape reels, stands by the locked door. When an authorized individual arrives and unlocks it, the piggybacker goes in with him. Turnstiles, mantraps (a double-door closet through which only one person can move with one key action), or a station guard will prevent this type of unauthorized access.

Electronic piggybacking takes place in on-line computer systems, where individuals are using terminals, and identification is verified automatically by the computer system. When a terminal is activated, the computer authorizes access, usually on the basis of a key, secret password, or the passing of required information, known as protocol. Compromise of the computer can take place when a remote computer terminal is connected to the same line through telephone switching equipment and used when a legitimate user is not using his terminal. The computer may not be able to differentiate or recognize the two terminals but senses only one terminal and one authorized user.

Piggybacking can generally be accomplished when the user signs off improperly, leaving the terminal in an active state or leaving the computer in a state where it assumes the user is still active.

An example of a clever impersonation occurred when a young man posed as a magazine writer and called on the telephone company, indicating that he was writing an article on the computer system in use by the utility. He was invited in and given a full and detailed briefing on all the computer facilities and application systems. As a result of this information, he was able to steal over $61 million worth of telephone equipment. One effective way to deal with this method of fraud is to have your computer break the line connection after a terminal is identified and call back the location where the authorized terminal resides. If it is an attempt at fraud, the perpetrator will not be successful because access to the computer is denied.

In another case, an individual stole magnetic stripe credit cards that required secret personal identification numbers. He would telephone the owners of the cards indicating that he was a bank official, had discovered the theft of the card and needed to know the secret personal identification number to protect the victim and issue a new card. Victims invariably gave out their secret numbers and the individual would proceed to withdraw the maximum amount from their accounts through automated teller machines.

A Question of Control and Responsibility

Most computer crime involves neither technical sophistication nor modification of any internal software programs. As can be seen from the examples, it is not the computer itself that is causing the problems; it is the lack of attention to what needs to be done in a rapidly changing EDP environment.

As to the question of why more sophisticated computer crime has not been uncovered, the reason may be fairly simple. There usually is no one person in the organization who is given the responsibility for overall security or the task of uncovering such crimes. Most frauds occur because of a lack of attention to fundamental control concepts, such as adequate segregation of duties. This is true even in a sophisticated EDP system. Although all the facts are not in yet, it appears that the recent $21 million theft at the Wells Fargo Bank occurred because one individual was intimately familiar with the bank's entire processing system and established controls. In addition, some of the bank's standard control procedures, such as mandatory vacation, were not being enforced.

When installing a new computer system, large or small, keep in mind that properly designed controls can provide assurance that data are complete, accurate, and protected. However, the auditor must determine that those controls established by management are functioning properly.

OTHER METHODS OF UNAUTHORIZED ACCESS

The preceding discussion of computer fraud effectively describes some of the techniques in use by employees or others closely associated with the company. Yet, comparative strangers have gained unauthorized access to large computers—commonly referred to as hacking—with the assistance of modems. Sometimes, such access is gained through networks, and sometimes not. The object usually is to gather information, not to secure funds or other property. Examples of computer hacking include the following:

- A company's customer file was reportedly pilfered electronically.
- A computerized motor vehicle file was entered and records of penalties given to bad drivers were erased.
- A group of teenagers accessed computer files of the DOD's Los Alamos nuclear test facility, a hospital, a bank, and an electronic mail service.
- Reports of FBI activity indicate that a teenager in San Diego County known as The Cracker supplied secret codes enabling others to break into the GTE Telenet network.

Computer hacking is said to have grown out of the phone phreaking of the 1960s.[5] Phone phreaking began with the advent of direct distance dialing, which permitted unauthorized use of long distance lines via "blue boxes." These were electronic devices developed by phreakers to effect unauthorized use. The first one discovered was blue, thus the name. The development of the personal computer and the introduction of time-sharing dramatically increased the potential for improper and illegal electronic activity.

BULLETIN BOARD SYSTEMS

The emergence of home computer "bulletin boards" in the early 1980s was an important factor in the spread of the related computer crime.

A bulletin board is a system that allows home computer users to com-

---

[5] John F. Maxfield, "Computer Bulletin Boards and the Hack Problem," Boardscan Report (Detroit: John F. Maxfield, 1984), p. 42.

municate and exchange information. Messages such as requests for help or equipment for sale could be exchanged on these systems. For various reasons established by the members or users of these systems, bulletin boards are private access.

A recent article appearing in *Boardscan Report* offers revealing insight into the dimensions of the problems posed by these bulletin board systems (BBSs). A segment of that article is reprinted below.[6]

> A BBS consists of a home computer such as a TRS-80, an Apple II, a Commodore C-64 or the like. Connected to the computer will be several floppy disc drives, a modem and, perhaps, a printer. A hard disc drive may be substituted for one or all of the floppy disc drives. Since information storage and retrieval is the main purpose of the system, the more disc drives and the larger the capacity of them, the more information (i.e. messages, programs, etc.) that can be stored for retrieval by on-line callers.
>
> A typical minimum system would consist of an Apple II+ with two disc drives and a modem. Cost of such a system would be about $2,000.00. At the other end of the spectrum would be a system with multiuser capabilities and multiple phone modems and lines. One such system in the Midwest has 8 phone lines and two 40-megabyte hard disc drives and runs on an Altos 68000 UNIX computer. Value of this home hobbyist system is about $25,000.00.
>
> It is very easy to become addicted to BBS's and the strange electronic underground that is associated with them. While a BBS is not inherently an evil thing, it does tend to contribute significantly to electronic crime. If a person becomes deeply involved in the BBS scene, one of their first problems is the size of the telephone bill. It is just too easy to obtain and use a billing code belonging to a customer of one of the alternate long-distance services such as SPRINT or MCI. Calls placed in this manner, where Equal-Access is not in effect, cannot be billed properly, nor can the originator be identified. If the long-distance service company tries to call the recipient of the fraudulent call, they will be answered by a modem and home computer. Even if the BBS operator is cooperative, learning the identity of the BBS caller is difficult since most fraudulent callers use a handle instead of their real name.
>
> Fraudulent calling is not limited to the users of the underground system, but is common to all BBS's. Large numbers of phreaked phone calls are placed to sexually oriented BBS's. BBS's by their very nature have to be classed as attractive nuisances if they are not policed or regulated. It would appear that laws regulating BBS's are needed. An analogy would be the laws governing the height and type of fencing to be used around a home swimming pool area. Unfortunately the large majority of BBS operators are juveniles which contributes significantly to the problem. Sadly, most parents haven't the slightest idea what their son or daughter is doing with the home computer!
>
> Any successful BBS almost always has a problem with a lack of sufficient disc storage space. Given the widespread use of credit cards and the availability of telephone order houses that carry computer equipment, it was inevitable that credit card fraud would enter the BBS scene. Credit card numbers are widely

---

[6] *Ibid*, pp. 3–9. Reprinted by permission.

traded and posted via the underground BBS's. Prime targets are the high credit limit cards that will allow the fraudulent purchase of a hard disc drive ($3,000–$5,000). There are many underground BBS's that openly brag about the new hard disc drive that was acquired for the system in this manner. It is hard to understand how a 14-year old boy could afford a $10,000 home computer system, yet BBS's with this such equipment owned by juveniles are quite commonplace.

Hardware alone does not constitute a BBS. There must be software also. Mention has already been made of the Ascii Express software for the pirate download systems. A normal BBS can use a wide variety of BBS software, either commercially produced or homemade. The various program types are not germane to this discussion, however, some of the more popular BBS programs are Networks and T-Net (and their pirated equivalents) for the Apple computer. All normal BBS software has most or all of these features: message base or bulletin section, text and data files, E-mail or private message section, program download/upload section, user listing.

The message base may consist of one or more sections dividing the messages into various categories. Typical categories are General, For Sale, Help, Meeting Announcements, etc. These sections are accessed from a menu of choices and the user may view the message titles, read any or all of the messages, post a new message, or delete a previously posted message. To limit objectionable messages, most systems will not allow posting until you have either been validated by the operator or have called the BBS several times.

In addition to the message base there are usually special files that may be viewed by the user but can only be placed there by the system operator. Examples of such files would be lists of other BBS systems, instructions for use of the system, news items, etc. Sometimes these files are combined with the program download section and may contain the documentation for the available programs.

The E-mail (electronic mail) section allows private communications between users. E-mail can only be read by the intended recipient or the system operator. On the underground boards the E-mail section is where much of the illegal information is exchanged, such as credit card numbers. E-mail will account for about half of the storage space on a typical system.

Most BBS's make a listing of the other users available to facilitate using the E-mail section. Obviously you cannot send mail to someone who does not use that particular BBS. Sometimes the user list will give the user's telephone number or address, but most often will merely list only the names or handles used by the various users.

Interestingly enough, BBS's are often the victims of the very hacker community they support. Crashing a regular BBS or even a rival gang's BBS is common. Due to the hacker problem and the anonymity of the user, most BBS's will assign a private password to each user and will only allow access to post messages if the new user gives his or her real name and telephone number to the system operator in a private message. Validation of the user typically takes 24 to 48 hours or more depending on the responsiveness of the system operator. Validation may also involve the raising of a user's security level so as to access parts of the BBS that otherwise would be off limits.

Why Does a Person Set Up A BBS?

Why would a private individual go to the expense of setting up a BBS? One major expense is the computer itself, which cannot be used for any other purpose while the BBS software is running. Some BBS operators have two or more computers so as to be able to perform other tasks without disturbing the operation of the BBS. Another expense is the telephone line, although this is minimal in comparison to the cost of the computer. Unless there is a computer club or some sort of commercial sponsor, all this cost has to be borne by the system operator. Some BBS's charge a nominal fee, say $5.00, in order to be validated, however these systems are not well patronized and are in the minority. There are a few underground BBS systems which charge a fee to access the program download section or the illegal information sections.

The operator of a popular BBS system is in a position to make lots of friends and acquaintances with mutual interests because he or she must communicate with the new users in order to screen them for subsequent validation. The operator of a dating service BBS obviously will have first pick of any newcomers.

A system operator can read any of the private mail messages on the system since he alone has full access to the contents of the disc drives. Even if the operator of a sexually oriented BBS did not directly participate in a communication with a user, he can certainly act as the electronic equivalent of a voyeur by reading the supposedly private correspondence between the users. If the system operator is discreet, the users will be completely unaware of any intrusion.

(This author ran an underground BBS for a while and found the E-mail to be an excellent source of intelligence.)

The operator of a pirate BBS will acquire a tremendous collection of free software from the users. Many of the early pirate boards would allow a user to download 4 or 5 programs only if they first uploaded one new program. This strategy ensured the system operator would always acquire the newest programs as they became available on the underground market. Software collections of over 1,000 programs are not uncommon. Most of the juveniles who set up BBS's do so for this reason alone. There are unscrupulous adults who obtain commercial and business software in this manner which they then resell to unsuspecting clients.

Most underground BBS's require a new user to prove that they too are a member of the underground by providing the BBS operator with some sort of illegal information, whether it be an MCI customer code, a credit card number, or something of similar nature, before granting full access to the BBS. The BBS operator is the one person most likely to benefit by permitting underground activity on the BBS.

Underground BBS's

How do you find an underground BBS? As a starting point, just attend a meeting of a local computer club and ask about BBS's. A few minutes' conversation will usually suffice to come up with the names and numbers of several pirate systems in the local area. All BBS's must advertise their presence in order to attract users and new information. Once you get validated on one system, you will usually be able to download a list of other systems from which you can get lists of more systems, ad infinitum. Most underground systems have obvious names such as Applecrackers, Twilight Phone, Forbidden Zone, Securityland, etc. There are a few which masquerade as normal legitimate systems or have nondescript names. If a BBS has menu selections which list special message bases such as Underground, Special Access, Phone Phreak, Hacking, Technical, Restricted, etc., you have probably found an underground system. Some BBS operators try to hide these illicit sections by making them invisible to a user who does not have the necessary security clearance. However, most users tend to be careless and if there is a hidden section, you will usually find reference to it in a message posted in another section. Another excellent way to tell if the BBS caters to the illegal, is to note whether or not the BBS operator has posted a disclaimer claiming freedom of speech absolving the operator from any liability due to message content. The tougher the wording of this disclaimer, the greater the illegality of the information stored in the BBS undoubtedly will be.

Here are a couple of disclaimers which I found to be rather comical:

The sysops take no responsibility for any messages, files, or other incriminating info on the boards, or in the General section, because those files were all uploaded by anonymous users.

DO YOU WORK FOR OR ARE YOU AFFILIATED WITH ANY GOVERNMENT, DETECTIVE, OR POLICE AGENCY, PUBLIC OR PRIVATE, OR WOULD YOU EVER REVEAL ANY INFORMATION GAINED FROM THIS BBS TO ANY OF THE ABOVE, OR DO YOU WORK FOR ANY TYPE OF LONG DISTANCE COMPANY, PUBLIC OR PRIVATE, AND/OR WOULD YOU RELEASE ANY INFORMATION GAINED FROM THIS BBS TO ANY SUCH LONG DISTANCE SERVICE OR ITS AFFILIATES?

PLEASE ANSWER YES OR NO > >

(if you answered YES, the computer would abruptly hang up.)

As mentioned previously, access to an underground BBS will usually involve giving the system operator proof that you too are a criminal. Also, the system operator will usually be more careful in screening and will almost always call you back at the phone number given to verify that you are really who you say you are. More than one telephone security person ran afoul of this when a secretary answered the phone! Some system operators will make use of the telephone company's CNA (Customer Name Address) bureau to verify whether you are using your home phone and to get your address. If you give the number of an unlisted residential phone, the CNA bureau will not give out any information other than to say that the number is unlisted. Another way to get validated with few problems is to have someone who is already established in the underground vouch for you. If you are the operator of an underground BBS, you will be validated instantly in exchange for similar privileges on your BBS.

Some of the nastier underground boards are limited to access by invitation only. If you are not a member of that particular hacker gang, you will not be allowed access. In most cases of this type, the BBS will not even permit a non-validated user to sign on. The only recourse here is to either become a member of the gang or to work through an informant who is a member. This is a tedious business at best and is the sort of thing better left up to experienced operatives. In the course of my work, I have gained access to private BBS's with as few as a dozen select hackers. Luckily, these private boards are in the minority and by their exclusiveness make themselves a highly visible target. Another factor which tends to work against this sort of BBS is that the amount of information, while it is usually of an extremely sensitive nature, is not widely disseminated, thus minimizing the potential for serious harm.

(In a few cases, this author found it harder to access a phreaker BBS than to access a high security government computer system!)

COMPUTER ABUSE & FRAUD   25-15

All sorts of illegal information can be found on these underground systems, such as:

- Lists of customer billing codes and common carrier access numbers.
- Plans and instructions for phone phreak blue, red, black, and silver boxes.
- Access numbers, passwords, and logon procedures for mainframe computer systems.
- Procedures for wiretapping and phone bugging.
- Instructions on how to pass oneself off as a computer or telephone repairman or other employee so as to gain information or access to be used for fraud.
- Plans and instructions in the art of lockpicking.
- Do-it-yourself instructions for the home manufacture of explosives, poisons, and incendiary devices.
- Lists of phone numbers of famous people, government installations, computer systems, and telephone operator call routing codes.
- Lists of credit card numbers (i.e. VISA and MASTERCARD) to be used to order merchandise over the phone for resale or trade.
- How to invade the privacy of anyone through access to their computerized credit and financial records.
- Ways to harrass and/or harm anyone you don't like either over the phone or by other means.
- Programs for downloading to convert your home computer into a blue box or to use for scanning for modem numbers or customer billing codes.

Don't worry about Orwell's Big Brother,
the problem today is with little brother.

Some of these BBS's have to be seen to be believed. As time passes and the BBS operators experience little or no control of their activities by law enforcement, they become more and more egregious. Some BBS's contain information of great use to both organized crime and enemy foreign powers.

Sources of Illicit Information

Many of the hacker gangs (who will be described later) set up group excursions to industrial parks or office complexes for the purpose of scavenging information and equipment from the trash dumpsters behind the buildings. Dumpster diving is a major source of passwords, system documentation, and other information. Credit card numbers are also obtained in this manner by salvaging and piecing together the carbons from the charge slips. Computer and electronic store garbage cans are a favorite hunting ground. Other major targets are telephone company switching centers and vehicle garages.

All too often, unscrupulous or careless employees of major corporations pass on details of computer operations to friendly hackers. In some cases the hacker, himself, has legal access to the computer center as, for example, an equipment repairman or delivery person. Hackers often pose as customers or employees and try to obtain information over the telephone about system access and passwords. Many times, this human engineering succeeds where other methods have failed.

As a last resort, physical theft is often attempted. A common ploy is the interception of mail containing customer account codes or passwords. Occasionally break-ins and theft of documentation, terminals or other equipment are a preliminary to a major hacker attack on a computer system.

Programmable smart modems which allow computer controlled phone number dialing and special software are used to find computer access numbers or customer billing codes. Numerous programs exist for almost any combination of home computer and modem that perform sequential or random dialing of trial numbers until a modem is located or a billing code is compromised. Some of these programs will test upwards of 1,000 numbers an hour. The recent movie Wargames showed in great detail the operation of one of these scanner programs.

Some hackers specialize in scanning and publish tremendous lists of codes and telephone numbers. Legislation is needed to control telephone scanning.

All of this information eventually winds up on an underground BBS. Once posted there, the information will be picked up and reposted everywhere. Some of the juveniles, in an effort to impress their peers, will gather up every little tidbit and repost it on all the boards that they call. Much of the information that is posted in this manner is old or useless because it has passed through so many hands. Any information of a sensitive nature or of extreme usefulness will not be publicly posted right away. Most of the hacker gangs will not post fresh information unless it is the gang's own BBS.

This author posted a test message one time on a California BBS. Only one hour and twenty minutes later, I discovered that the same message was now posted on a New York BBS. Within one week the message had been repeated on dozens of BBS's nationwide. It is useful to plant false or erroneous information in this manner so as to confuse the inexperienced hackers.

Your garbage is a hacker's gold.

Hacker Gangs

The early computer hackers tended to be of college age, as the exposure to computers occurred mainly at that educational level. With the advent of home computers and the teaching of computer basics in the lower grades, the average age of the beginning hacker has steadily dropped to a current level of only 14! The overwhelming majority of BBS owners and users are teenagers. Teens tend to form cliques and peer groups, so the formation of phone phreak and hacker gangs was inevitable. The parents of these bright teens usually do not, themselves, understand or comprehend the power of the computer. This means that the teens are not subject to the same parental restrictions that would govern their going out, the use of the family car, dates, etc. Many parents view the home computer as an excellent babysitting device. If their son or daughter spends the evening quietly in their room with the computer in lieu of a visit to the local pool hall or video parlor, the parents feel reassured that their offspring is not getting into trouble. In reality, these teens may be engaging in electronic gang activities that have serious implications. The losses to the software industry, alone, are staggering.

Unfortunately, many of the gang leaders are older more experienced teens, perhaps college students, who are interested in hacking, not for the intellectual challenge, but for the financial rewards. A few gang leaders are adults who are politically or financially activated. There are several adults who are major figures behind the cracking and distribution of pirated software for resale to the public. One adult gang leader openly solicited credit card numbers from the juvenile members in exchange for hard disc drives and other equipment that the adult would order fraudulently. Some of the teenage leaders bask in the tremendous notoriety and acclaim from their peers and strive to be the biggest phreaker or to have broken into the greatest number of computer systems.

The gangs may be local in nature, such as the infamous Milwaukee 414 gang, or they may be national in nature, such as the Inner Circle gang, or even international such as CHAOS, a Commodore C-64 cracking and pirating club, with headquarters in West Germany and the United States. In all cases, these gangs had a BBS that was their main base of operations and served as a (supposedly) secure communications center. The 414's had a private BBS that was so secret it didn't even have a name. The Inner Circle had the Securityland BBS and also illegitimately gotten accounts on BTE's TELEMAIL network, CHAOS operates on a variety of BBS's in both the U.S. and W. Germany. (I have had access to all of these BBS's and a large number of others.)

When modems are outlawed only outlaws will have modems.

Organized Crime and the BBS

Naturally the underground BBS would have its uses in organized crime in much the same manner as the teen hacker gangs would use one. This author has good reason to believe that organized crime is controlling a number of BBS systems in the Midwest, the New York City area and in Florida. One informant knows of a BBS that is located in an off-track betting parlor. The teens are easily recruited to act as information gatherers, who will work for little or nothing and in most cases don't even know they are being so used. This author and other adult hackers have been approached and offered large sums of money to tamper with banking and credit data computers. Organized crime is swiftly moving into this new and relatively untapped area of crime. There is a very real and present danger here if the BBS's are allowed to operate unchecked.

Private Underground BBS's

As law enforcement becomes more involved in prosecutions of hackers and phone phreaks, the illegal BBS operators become more paranoid. There is a slow trend toward all underground BBS's going to private invitation-only operations.

You will not learn of a private underground BBS from the normal sources mentioned earlier because the users are usually sworn to secrecy. Inevitably, there will be a leak, either an indiscreet message posted on an open system or from the apprehension of a suspected hacker who turns informant. Once entree has been established on a private board, it will usually be possible to find out about and gain access to the other private boards. The one downfall to the entire underground BBS network is that the systems must have users and the only way to get them is to pass the word around.

This author participated in several sting operations where informants posing as hackers joined (or were invited to join) several gangs. In another sting, a completely bogus gang was created which took over several smaller real gangs. The true identities of the gang members became known to the leaders of the bogus gang, of course. Mop up was then easy with the dissolution of the bogus gang.

The private BBS's use a variety of means to block access by unauthorized users. These methods are familiar to anyone who deals with mainframe system security and are borrowed from that technology. Special preliminary passwords changed at regular intervals, hidden sections within an otherwise normal appearing system, and even, in the case of one BBS, a primitive dialback system, are used. As time goes on, more sophistication will emerge; however, nothing beats an informant who is in possession of all the secret passwords and phone numbers. The teens are the mainstay of the underground but they are also its weakest link.

Controls

There are various legal remedies available, both civil and criminal. However, there is no uniform code of law from one State to the next. The Federal justice system lacks a central clearing house for computer and telecommunications crime control, and also cannot deal well with juveniles. Computer hacker attacks tend to be multi-jurisdictional nightmares that traditional law-enforcement does not handle very well. When the 414's were breaking into computers in New York, California, and New Mexico from their homes in Milwaukee, they were only caught through an intensive call tracing effort that took many hours and only after they had successfully penetrated some computer systems for months. As it turned out, the FBI in Detroit was in possession of the solution to the identity of the hackers, but neither Detroit nor Milwaukee were in communication with each other until the arrest of the hackers made nationwide newspaper headlines. Steps are being taken to prevent this unfortunate situation from recurring.

The BBS operator controls access to the system through the user validation process, is responsible for the format of the system, and decides what the various message base topics are to be . In the case of an underground board, the system operator is the person who made his BBS available for illegal information, not the users. If the system operator has to validate a user for special access to an underground section, it is clearly the operator who is a party to any wrongdoing, regardless of posted disclaimers.

The issue of freedom of speech is a sensitive one, however. Perhaps a licensing arrangement such as is used for ham radio operators and those who use Citizens Band radios is in order. Possession of an unlicensed BBS could be dealt with in a manner similar to that of possession of an unlicensed radio transmitter.

For a time, the State of Oklahoma had telephone tariff restrictions that charged an extra $50.00 for the connection of a modem to the telephone lines. This charge was subsequently dropped under protest by home computer owners. If this sort of charge were applied to lines used by a BBS, it would eliminate all but the few who were willing to pay extra for the privilege of owning a BBS. The telephone line connected to a successful BBS is always busy. Thus an extra tariff could be justified on the grounds that more than the normal amount of circuit time was being used up.

Finally, public awareness of the problem and the voluntary reporting of suspicious BBS's to the authorities and the closing down of teenage systems by concerned parents would go a long way toward controlling the problem. Several nasty BBS's were shut down last year when the leader of the 414's bragged about them on a network TV show. Only then did the father of one of the BBS operators find out what his son was really doing with the home computer.

Defeating a Mainframe Hacker Attack

Access attempts should be limited to only two or three tries per call. If someone is attempting to guess a password, this will slow them down considerably. A log must be kept of all attempts and an operator notified if the number of invalid logons exceeds a certain number in a given time period. Logs prove to be invaluable in tracking hacker activity since they may contain clues to the identity of the hacker or their location.

Backdoors into the system must be eliminated or fixed. Typically, juvenile hackers succeed only because common maintenance passwords or preset factory defaults are still present in the system.

If certain ID's are only used during certain hours, hacking can be curtailed by placing time restrictions on as many accounts as possible. Hackers typically are most active at night, on weekends or during school holidays. If the system is not normally accessed by the legitimate users during these times, it is best to block access entirely.

Naturally all standard precautions should be taken with passwords. However, sometimes management takes the view that the system should be easy to access. This is a serious mistake! A user friendly system is also hacker friendly. Do not prompt users at logon or give any clues as to the correct procedure until after the entire logon has been entered. HELP files should not be available unless a logon is successful. User friendliness is best left until after a logon has been validated.

Dialback systems will stop the average hacker cold. (The so-called Wizard of the Arpanet was completely frustrated in an attempt to crack a telephone company computer protected by a dialback system.) Dialback can be cracked, but the level of skill and equipment required is beyond that of the normal hacker. Dialback is extremely inconvenient to use, however.

The best way to catch a hacker is to set a trap. The 414's were caught only after their leader found a Star Trek game on a bank computer and played it for over 2 hours while the FBI traced the call. This author set a similar trap that resulted in the apprehension of a hacker in 1981. Suggestions for possible booby-traps are exotic games, a logon simulator that shunts the hacker off into a special compartment, a simulated operating system with dummy command menus and the like. Naturally, there should be suitable alarms given when the trap is sprung. It is high time that systems started fighting back!

The situation has increased the demand for insurance coverage to protect against losses as a result of thefts and damage due to hacking. Generally, these insurance policies cover the cost of reconstructing data losses due to damage or theft. However, if the data are only accessed but not destroyed, loss is not covered. For instance, if a customer file is accessed and copied, but not damaged in any way, the inevitable loss of future business would not be covered. From the insurer's standpoint, there is a natural reluctance to offer coverage in this new area where liabilities are difficult to fix and losses are hard to quantify. These problems will likely make it difficult for companies to obtain insurance coverage for all hacking risks.

The frequency of hacking incidents has motivated law enforcement agencies across the country, led by the FBI, to consider the threat a significant one. Many are employing computer fraud experts to help track down and prosecute perpetrators. Law enforcement activity against hacking is hampered somewhat by the fact that some states do not have laws making computer crime illegal and the existing laws differ widely in the acts they forbid. Comments on this subject are made later in this chapter.

REDUCING COMPUTER FRAUD

The preceding discussion of the types, causes, and techniques of computer fraud should provide useful background to the internal auditors. But more to the point, what can be done to reduce computer fraud?

The approach to the problem is twofold, and involves (1) means of deterring or preventing computer fraud and (2) methods of detecting the crime after its occurrence. Many of the same principles useful in deterring, detecting, investigating, and reporting fraud discussed in the preceding three chapters (as well as in Chapter 17 on internal control) should be helpful in preventing computer fraud. Some additional general suggestions are contained in the following overview on the prevention and detection of computer fraud.

Prevention

The magnitude of the problem is focusing attention on a solution. Among the developments that should assist in deterring fraud are these:

1. *Systems design.* Added core is needed in systems design. Briefly, independent accountants, internal auditors, and other computer specialists should be consulted in the design phase.

    Attention must be paid to inclusion of the necessary internal controls, not merely to processing the data. It is much cheaper to design the controls into the system than it is to add them later. Individuals well versed in what constitutes good controls and EDP should review the design and determine that the safeguards are present.

2. *Internal control.* Enforcement of the well-known internal control principles in the EDP organization should take place. Surprisingly, controls exercised in a treasury department dealing with securities, for example, have not been used in the computer department. Thus:

- Duties should be separated. Activities should be split so that no single person has exclusive responsibility for the complete processing of selected data. Thus, systems design and analysis, systems programming, systems operation, and data processing should be segregated. Once a program is completed, perhaps the programmer should be denied access to the computer and the files. Further, duties should be periodically rotated, as at vacation time.
- Personnel controls should be exercised in sensitive areas. Thus, new hires and transfers should be checked out for honesty and dependability. (See Chapter 17.)
- Bonding may be desirable. Management should stress the ethical and honesty standards required for the job. Also, it should be on the alert for signals of questionable activity. As employees are changed, codes and code words should be altered.
- Changes in programs or procedures should be properly reviewed before authorization.
- Access to the computer and the terminals should be properly controlled.

3. *Security devices.* Consideration should be given to using some of the new security devices that have been developed recently for use on the computer. Encryption hardware is now available, which will scramble messages so that only at the regular receiving station can the message be unscrambled (as in a bank wire room). Other software devices restrict access to the computer program or data. Based on codes or passwords, the software permits access to only certain individuals with a need to know. Where applicable, the computer audit and control procedures should be instituted to permit the computer to identify fraud automatically (e.g., no receiving report.) Finally, audit trails should perhaps be introduced.

Detection

Having taken steps to *prevent* computer-oriented irregularities, the last logical step relates to means to *detect* them. For example, the internal audit department should include EDP-trained personnel who would be active in the computer operations in these ways:

☐ Assuming a knowledge of internal controls, they should conduct periodic regular audits, being alert for suspicious transactions.

☐ They should use the new software programs, which permit an auditor to request reports from his own terminal—without the knowledge of the EDP staff. While audit software is usually employed extensively by the independent accountant, there is no reason why it should not also be a useful tool for the internal auditors.

☐ Given the rapid technological advances, it is incumbent on the staff members to keep up to date with current and future computer/software developments and to implement audit programs that take advantage of the developments.

SAFEGUARDING COMPUTER DATA

Because of the highly publicized nature of computer fraud, a number of articles have appeared, which are directed to the general business reader, as distinguished from auditors or accountants. One such writing suggests these commonsense rules for safeguarding computer data.[7]

1. Regularly change the password necessary to get into the computer files. This will limit a password's usefulness if it is obtained illicitly.
2. In addition to the password, require such personal information as an employee's name, birthday, or identification number. It is far more difficult for the thief to come up with two correct types of identification.
3. Limit the number of attempts that anyone can make in logging on to a system, in order to deter any guessing.
4. Keep a record of all user activity in a system and monitor this log to detect any unusual activity, such as repeated failures by someone to enter a correct password, unusual amounts of data retrieval, and attempts to enter confidential files.
5. Follow through at top-management level by allocating the money and staff necessary to carry out these steps continuously. Prosecute any security violators, whether employees or outsiders, even if it means unflattering publicity.

AN OPERATIONAL AUDIT OF COMPUTER SECURITY

Another article directed to auditors suggests steps for the internal auditor to take in an audit of computer security and in developing an internal control system for a minicomputer.[8] Evaluating the effectiveness of computer security and the cost-benefit relationships of the control system is a responsibility of the internal auditor. An operations audit in this vital area of communications and record keeping should be scheduled on a periodic basis. In most companies, new computer equipment and facilities are added from time to time and, often, the computer systems are revised to use the hardware more efficiently.

The following set of principles can be used as a basic operational auditing program to measure your company's current physical, operational, and procedural security system and plans. If the principles of sound security are not being followed, or if specific weaknesses or inefficiencies are disclosed, the auditor would develop further detailed audit steps to determine the causes of the problem and make suggestions to management for improvement.

---

[7] "Computer Security: What Can Be Done?" *Business Week*, Sept. 26, 1983, pp. 126–130.
[8] *Internal Auditing Alert*, Sept. 1982, pp. 6–8.

☐ *Identification of loss reduction.* Determine that a proposed safeguard adequately addresses a proven threat and lowers the risk.

☐ *Evaluation of performance degradation.* Determine the price paid for a safeguard in terms of its direct cost as well as the possibility that its use may lower the performance level of the EDP operation to be protected.

☐ *Minimum reliance on safeguard secrecy.* Do not base your security plan just on keeping the functions of a system secret. Often, criminals will know as much about the design and implementation of safeguards in a system as the designers of the system and safeguards themselves. For example, security is not in keeping secret how a lock works, but rather is in safeguarding the keys for the lock. Of course, do not unnecessarily disclose the workings of any system safeguard.

☐ *Least privilege.* This is the "need-to-know" principle. To follow it, restrict information about the system's safeguards to the smallest possible number of people. These people should know only enough to perform their jobs and to maintain the effective operation of the EDP system.

☐ *Separation of responsibility or dual control.* Sensitive functions within the EDP system should be broken down into the smallest effective work assignments. There should be little or no overlapping responsibilities for these assignments. An alternative is dual control over a sensitive function, where one person performs the function and another oversees the work performed. Accountability for all work done must be assured.

☐ *Completeness, consistency, and reliability.* A safeguard must perform all of its specified tasks and functions completely, consistently, and without conflict. It must perform reliably enough to warrant confidence in its continued use. Safeguards must be implemented in a "chain-of-protection" fashion because security is only as good as its weakest link.

☐ *Threat monitoring.* Each safeguard should be instrumented so that its performance and any threats against its performance (or the assets it is protecting) can be detected and reported. For example, if your company's terminal access is protected by requiring a user to enter by a password, the system should record and report all instances when incorrect passwords have been supplied.

☐ *Auditability.* A safeguard must permit an auditor to determine that it is functioning properly and is in compliance with its specifications. For example, your company's data processing personnel should be able to demonstrate that recovery from a disaster is possible by restating important computer applications from remotely stored copies of backup files and programs.

☐ *Personnel acceptance and tolerance.* Employees who are constrained in their work by a safeguard must be willing to accept constraint and tolerate its functions and purpose. For example, your company's programmers must abide by restrictions on access to the computer room.

☐ *Sustainability.* A safeguard must function effectively not only when it is first installed but on a continuing basis. For example, plastic covers to protect equipment during emergencies should not be moved or concealed.

☐ *Compartmentalization*. Safeguards must be compartmentalized so that the compromise of one does not lead to the compromise of another, much as the compartmentalization in the design of a ship's hull. It may be desirable, for example, to restrict physical access to functional areas within the EDP operation as well as the outside perimeter.

☐ *Isolation*. Security safeguards should be isolated so that personnel constrained by one safeguard are prevented from compromising or weakening another safeguard. Employees should not gain access to their own sensitive work area by passing through another sensitive area.

☐ *Legal and ethical constraints*. Safeguards must comply with legal and regulatory restrictions. They must not violate the ethical practices of employees or place them in position of trust beyond their resistance to temptation. The backgrounds of employees in positions of trust should be investigated only to the extent warranted by that degree of trust.

☐ *Mutual suspicion*. Employees in positions of trust and the security safeguards themselves must function as though they are in a hostile environment. Security becomes vulnerable when an employee is manipulated into cooperating in an unauthorized act. All personnel should be alert to this possibility and be able to resist such attack.

DEVELOPING INTERNAL CONTROL FOR A MINICOMPUTER SYSTEM

In a minicomputer environment, terminals are generally used for transaction, data entry, inquiry, and other interactive functions. Since these terminals are usually located in the user area, they may be readily accessible to company personnel. Unless proper controls exist, unauthorized access to data files and programs may result in errors due to improper use or manipulation of data files or computer programs.

Multilevel Controls

Control over access to a minicomputer usually starts with the person who has a key to unlock the system. Once the system is unlocked, the broadest level of control is the issuance of a pass code to log onto the system. Most minicomputers allow for levels of pass code access. There is usually one person who has access to the entire system, with the ability to make changes even to the operating system. Below that, there are levels of pass codes that give increasingly narrow levels of entry.

In an environment where there are multiple terminals, control can be established at the physical terminal level so that only certain terminals can be used for specific transactions. This could be accomplished through a combination of physical access controls and software. An example of this might be a terminal in the payroll section having the only access to the payroll master file.

Alternatively, the authority of persons to initiate transactions might be based on requiring the entry of user identification and passwords to execute specific transactions. Management should review and change these pass codes periodically to ensure that only the appropriate people have access to the system.

Controlling Data Entry Errors

Because transaction entry frequently represents the largest volume of activity, it usually accounts for the greatest number of potential errors. A well-controlled on-line entry procedure can provide a reliable means of controlling data entry errors. For example, in a loan application, the system might check to determine that a transaction contains a valid account number, that the interest rate quality does not exceed a specified rate, and that the loan amount is appropriate.

Some control techniques that could be applied to an on-line input system that would increase data integrity are:

- ☐ Use of forms that permit efficient recording of critical data before they are entered on the terminal.
- ☐ Validation of all input data at the time they are entered into the terminal, reporting errors to the operator to permit immediate correction and reentry.
- ☐ Use of formatted screens that guide the operator through the data to be entered and prevent the entry of data in invalid formats.
- ☐ Predefined interactive conversations that guide the operator through the data to be entered and ensure that all required data are entered. (This is sometimes referred to as a menu.)
- ☐ Redisplay of data entered (in either detailed or summary form) for visual verification by the operator before the data are accepted by the system.
- ☐ Batching of input to facilitate easier resolution of errors detected later in processing.

Preventing Unauthorized Access

Fraudulent entries and inquiries due to system accessibility may be avoided with the help of the following techniques:

- ☐ Identification of operators by the use of confidential passwords and denial of access to the system unless an authorized password is entered
- ☐ Restriction of system resources (e.g., programs for data entry or inquiry, data, and computer time) based on operator identity, password, terminal location, and time of day

- ☐ Regular cancellation of all passwords and assignment of new passwords only to those having current, authorized need
- ☐ Reporting and timely investigation of all attempts at unauthorized terminal use
- ☐ Logical disconnection of the terminal by the system following a set number of attempts to enter an invalid operator identity or password
- ☐ System analysis of all log-ons to prevent a single operator from gaining access to the system if that operator is already logged on at another terminal
- ☐ Logical disconnection of the terminal by the system following a reasonable time period of inactivity
- ☐ Automatic forced sign-off of all operators when a system failure is detected
- ☐ Transaction registers or posting reports of all sensitive or critical data, with procedures for management review of such reports and resolution of unusual or unapproved conditions.
- ☐ Field-level sensitivity masks that restrict the information displayed on a screen to only that permitted, as defined by operator access authorization tables
- ☐ Restrictions on the ability of data processing personnel to bypass or manipulate authorization requirements and stringent supervision of all such usage

With the continuing proliferation of minicomputer use in various areas of company operations, the internal auditor must develop a standard of internal controls that can be implemented at each location that a minicomputer is installed. Once the minicomputer is operating, the internal auditor should determine if there are any potential problems applicable to that location that require changes or additions to the standard control system.

THE USE OF "THREAT TEAMS" TO DETECT AND PREVENT FRAUD

A new technique, the threat team, is coming into use to cope with fraud, especially with computer-related fraud. A threat team is composed of experienced employees within the company who meet as a task force to identify holes in the security system that could create embezzlement opportunities and who discuss how to handle possible fraud scenarios. Use of such teams is based on the premise that the people in the best position to discover how to beat the system are those who work with it every day.

Guidelines in Using the Threat Team Technique

According to experts in the field, there are six important considerations when setting a team and using it effectively:

1. *Selection of a target system or function for study.* When the target is well-defined, the team will need less direction, and all group members are more likely to participate to the best of their ability.
2. *Choosing team members.* As a general rule, members should not be chosen from the following groups: (1) managers with overall, general responsibility for a function or operation under review but with little day-to-day contact with the details of transactions processing; (2) individuals who are new in their jobs or who have new supervisors; (3) security officers, internal auditors, and others who are responsible for the design and policing of internal controls; (4) observers and members of top management who might dampen the group's enthusiasm; and (5) those who have a stake in the outcome.
3. *Establishing ground rules.* A thorough briefing at the first meeting should supply sufficient background information and lay out basic procedures.
4. *Setting the meeting atmosphere.* Sessions should be conducted in a fairly open-ended manner. They should begin with a general question, such as: "If you were going to beat this company, how would you do it?" Having selected the right people, placed them at ease with the proper background briefing, stimulated their thinking with some examples, and established a supportive environment, the discussion should soon take off.
5. *Controlling the discussion.* The moderator should start the discussion rolling, control the pace, help to develop realistic hypothetical schemes, probe for variations, and review the material discussed at the end of the session.
6. *Analyzing results.* Often, it's possible to segregate actual problem areas from very remote, almost inconceivable, cases. Also, it's beneficial to prioritize or rank the possible schemes in order of importance, seriousness, and probability.

The Advantages

Among the many advantages of using threat teams are:

- ☐ The teams appear to uncover instances of poor internal control in systems design and operation, nonstandard or improper operating procedures, and vulnerable job positions.
- ☐ The technique makes team members more aware of the need for good control.
- ☐ The analysis can be completed quickly and at little cost.
- ☐ Companies get an indication of the vulnerability of their systems to embezzlement. Management is able to gauge the likelihood of various schemes, the possible losses, and the number of employees in a position to execute fraud schemes.

These advantages greatly outweigh any disadvantages. The only disadvantages known to the author are that (1) the team member is taken from his regular duties for a time and (2) in some instances, the member exerts less than desired effort "because it is not his regular job." It is up to the team captain to motivate the individual team members.

Note that while the internal auditor is not recommended as a member of the threat team, he can be an observer, and he should use its results as a guide to strengthen controls and focus his auditing efforts.

LEGISLATIVE RELIEF

While the internal auditor has a responsibility for identifying the indicators of computer fraud as well as other types of fraud (see Chapter 22), he is expected to work closely with the legal department of his company and other investigators whose special knowledge extends to fraud investigations. These sources, including outside counsel, normally would be more familiar with computer crime law, including federal and state law, relating to the particular site and type of suspected violation. The auditor, however, should have a general understanding of computer crime legislation.

State Legislation

As of early 1988, every state except Arkansas, Vermont, and West Virginia has enacted computer crime laws. Although these 47 states unanimously classify violations as criminal (misdemeanor or felony) their laws vary widely in (1) identifying specifically what acts they forbid and (2) the penalties meted out.

In a general sense, the acts not permitted relate to these categories as applied to the indicated phases:

Category	Phase
Access or use	Generally
	To obtain property
Alter, damage, or destroy	Hardware
	Software
	To obtain property
Alter, take or disclose	Computer items
	Data
	Access codes
	Services
Disrupt or deny	Services
	Critical services

The internal auditor may wish to review the laws of the particular states in which he is interested.

Federal Computer Crime Laws

In late 1984, the first federal computer crime law was passed. Basically it related to computers:

- Used in national defense, foreign relations, and atomic energy.
- Used in financial institutions.
- Operated for or on behalf of the U.S. government.

In late 1986, the second federal computer crime law, the Computer Fraud and Abuse Act of 1986, was passed. Among other things, the bill extends computer crime coverage to computers operating in interstate commerce, to certain medical computer systems, and to trafficking in computer access passwords that affect interstate commerce.

As such laws are subject to change, when appropriate, the auditor should consult the latest legal summaries and seek any necessary assistance.

COMPUTER FRAUD INSURANCE COVERAGE

Computer fraud insurance is one of the newest types of insurance coverage. As a vice-president of an insurance company says, "Computer-fraud coverage is the most sought after insurance in the crime area these days—the computer is the fad of the 1980's and computer insurance is the fad topic of the insurance world."[9]

Although computer fraud insurance does not prevent fraud, it does offer a company an element of protection and should be explored. The kinds of coverage available vary widely as insurance carriers develop their policies. Some cover only the cost of reproducing erased or damaged information. Others relate to the theft of trade secrets or customer lists. Initially, in 1981, computer crime policies related primarily to money and securities transferred by electronic means and were applicable only to financial institutions. The new policies relate to information rather than money.

There are problems to be overcome in relation to computer fraud coverage. One, of course, is that insurers prefer to restrict policies to quantifiable losses, such as those previously mentioned. Therefore, some more nebulous losses, such as confidence among customers or loss of confidentiality, may be noninsurable at present. If computer data is not damaged but is read—such as an unpublished stock appraisal report—then no insurance is applicable. Another problem is the cost of insurance premiums. Of course, if a company has a backup computer, alternate systems, records, or a good

---

[9] "Computer-Fraud Coverage Grows as Insurers Solve Policy Problems," *The Wall Street Journal*, §2, Oct. 18, 1983, p. 33.

system of internal control, premium cost should be lower. A discussion of computer search for fraud is presented in Chapter 28.

SUGGESTED READING

LeGrand, Charles H. "Discouraging Fraud Through System Design." *The Internal Auditor*, Apr., 1986, pp. 28–35.

Paroby, Stephen M., and William J. Barrett. "Reducing the Risk of Computer Fraud." *Corporate Accounting*, Fall 1987, pp. 59–62.

Pfau, Pamela R. "Computer Abuse." *Corporate Accounting*, Fall 1985, pp. 46–51.

Wolfe, Christopher, and Casper E. Wiggins. "Internal Control in the Microcomputer Environment." *The Internal Auditor*, Dec. 1986, pp. 54–60.

PART VIII
Specialized Audit Areas

CHAPTER **26**

Information Systems and Internal Control

An Overall Perspective 2	Operations Controls 32
Definitions 2	Resource Acquisition and Utilization
Perspective 4	Controls 33
Functions That Benefit From I/S 7	Record-Keeping Controls 33
	Accountability Controls 33
Personal Computers 10	Security Controls 33
Explosion in Availability and Use 10	Systems Development Controls 34
Risks and Concerns 12	Other Objectives and Techniques 35
	Personal Computer Control
Office Automation 13	Techniques 35
Word Processing 13	
Communication 14	**Implications for Auditors** 41
Information Distribution 15	Impact of Errors 41
Communications Software 16	Access Techniques 42
	Specialized Knowledge 42
The Inherent Risks 17	Audit Techniques 42
	Independence 42
Internal Control in an I/S	Changing Technology 43
Environment 23	
Applicability of Internal Accounting	**Summary** 43
Control Principles and Objectives 23	
Variability of Control Techniques 24	**Computer Crime—A Special**
Control Techniques Perspective 24	**Perspective** 43
Internal Control Objectives in an I/S	
Environment 26	**Glossary** 44
Detailed Objectives and Controls 31	**Suggested Reading** 53
I/S Organization Controls 31	

Fig. 26-1 An MIS	3
Fig. 26-2 A Typical FIS for a Manufacturing Company	5
Fig. 26-3 Components of a Data Processing System	8
Fig. 26-4 An Example of an MIS Organization Structure	9
Fig. 26-5 Communications Software Packages	18
Fig. 26-6 Types of Security Exposure	21
Fig. 26-7 Preventive, Limiting, and Recovery Controls for Selected Exposures	22
Fig. 26-8 List of Controls by Area of Responsibility	27

AN OVERALL PERSPECTIVE

Definitions

Information systems (I/S) is a term that has become common in the past 5 to 10 years. It has been defined as the procedures, techniques, and facilities employed in each function of an enterprise to gather, file, process, store, and analyze data for use in the operation and management of an enterprise.[1] I/S may be financial or nonfinancial, as Figure 26-1 illustrates. They also may be entirely automated, partially automated, or manual. However, the pace of technological development in the field of I/S spanning EDP hardware, software, telecommunications equipment, and office automation have made entirely manual systems all but extinct. This is true even for small businesses. The advent of mini- and microcomputers saw to that. In the first edition of this volume the *Internal Auditing Manual* used the term "electronic data processing" to describe one of the areas of internal auditing of major interest and concern. The developments since then make continued use of this term somewhat misleading because the area of interest is broader than is implied there. This is evident by comparing definitions.

EDP was defined in the first edition as follows:

> Electronic data processing is a commonly used term for the organized employment of specialized facilities, electronic equipment, programs, systems, procedures, and personnel for the purpose of creating, changing, executing, or storing data in an organized and controlled fashion, by automated methods for specific purposes and users.

The definitions are similar. But the definition for I/S suggests a multiplicity of systems for a variety of management disciplines, each having a set of applicable procedures, techniques, and facilities. EDP, on the other hand, suggests a more centralized perspective of a large data processing installation that performs data processing and related activities as a service to management. Migration to the term "information systems" is a reflection of the fact that the control and management of EDP functions is moving away from the centralized EDP center toward users. In effect, users are becoming more responsible for activities that formerly were the domain of the EDP organizations. Once again, technological developments in mini- and microcomputers, software, and telecommunications have led to this state of affairs.

Other terms have also emerged that convey the same message, more or less. These terms include "management information systems (MIS)," "financial information systems (FIS)," and "accounting information sys-

---

[1] Steven J. Root, "Perspectives on Financial Information Systems," Chapter 1, in *Financial Information Systems Manual*, James D. Willson and Jack F. Duston, eds. (Boston: Warren, Gorham & Lamont, Inc., 1986), p. 1-4.

**FIG. 26-1
An MIS**

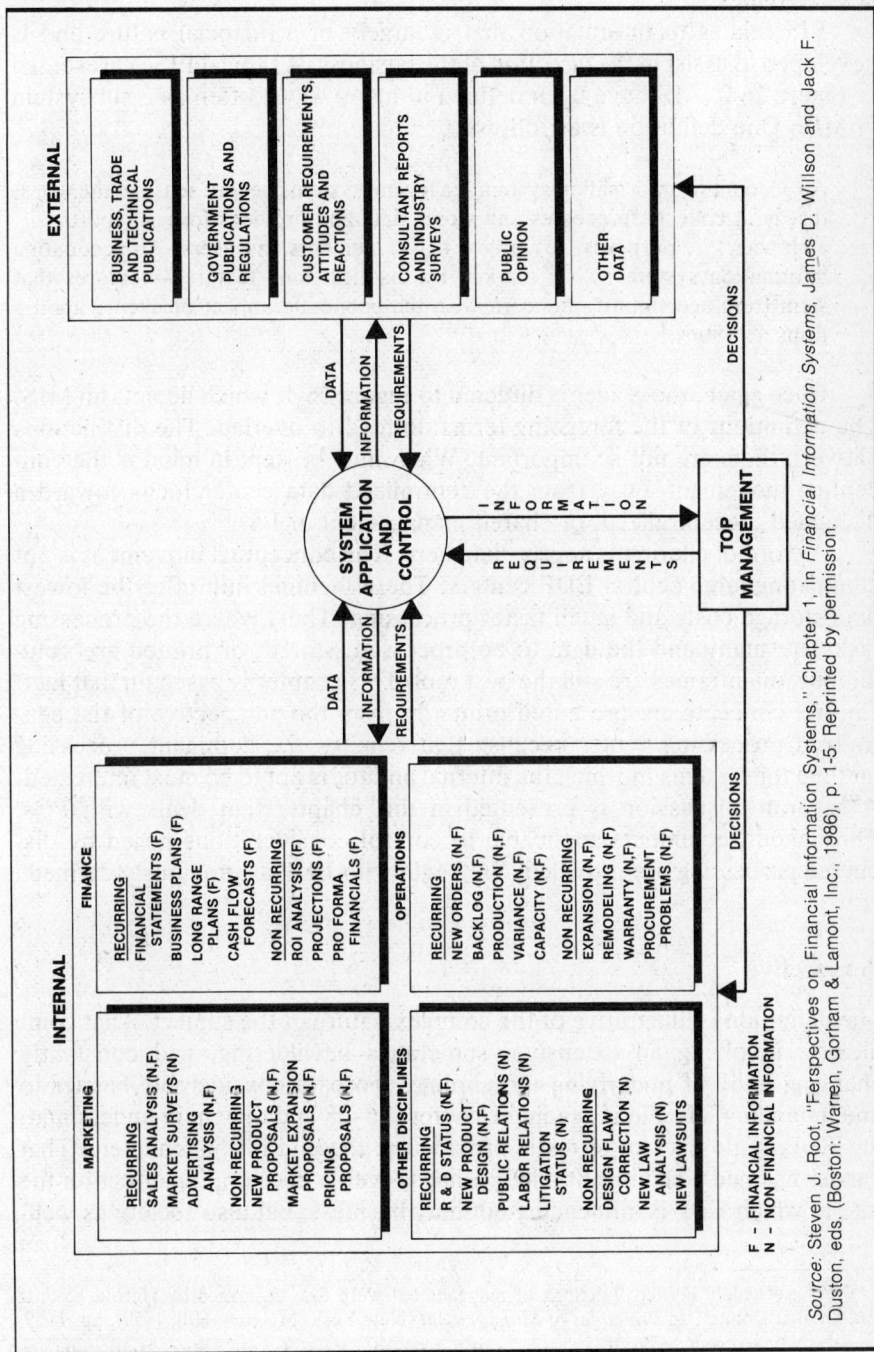

Source: Steven J. Root, "Perspectives on Financial Information Systems," Chapter 1, in *Financial Information Systems*, James D. Willson and Jack F. Duston, eds. (Boston: Warren, Gorham & Lamont, Inc., 1986), p. 1-5. Reprinted by permission.

tems (AIS)." MIS means the entire spectrum of information used by management in organizing, planning, directing, and controlling an entity's business activities.[2]

FIS relates to information that is largely of a financial nature and is developed to assist in the direction of the business. A typical FIS is presented in Figure 26-2. AIS have been defined in many ways, often as a subsystem of MIS. One definition is as follows:

> An accounting information system is a formal system in every sense of the word: that is, it collects, processes and stores data and provides formal reports . . . embraces . . . purposes, resources, tasks, elements and users. An accounting information system . . . is marked by distinguishing features—features that stem from accounting's concern with the economic impact of events upon a firms activities.[3]

Once again, the reader is directed to Figure 26-1, which depicts an MIS. The definitions of the foregoing terms do tend to overlap. The distinctions between them are not so important. What must be kept in mind is the conceptual movement away from the centralized data center focus toward a disbursed, decentralized, or shared management of I/S.

A word of caution is appropriate here. The conceptual movement is not eliminating large central EDP centers. These facilities still offer the lowest data storage costs and much faster processing. Thus, where the processing tasks are many and the data to be processed, stored, or printed are voluminous, mainframes are still the best tool. This chapter is based on that fact. Control concepts are presented primarily from the perspective of the centralized processing center because that remains the dominant processing method for systems in which the internal auditor is apt to be most interested. A separate discussion is presented in this chapter that deals with PCs. Throughout, comments applicable to control considerations posed by disbursed processing are provided. We begin with EDP as previously defined.

Perspective

The definition is illustrative of the complex nature of the subject. That complexity, involving an extensive, sometimes bewildering, and constantly changing body of underlying terminology, poses a considerable barrier to understanding. (To aid in reading Chapters 26–28 and to help in understanding EDP, a glossary of terms is provided at the end of this chapter.) That barrier has had a significant and, perhaps, even a decelerating effect on the rate at which EDP is influencing not only business, but also society as well.

---

[2] These widely quoted functions of management were first described by Harold Koontz and Cyril O'Donnell, in *Principles of Management* (New York: McGraw-Hill, 1959), pp. 1–59.

[3] Joseph W. Wilkinson, *Accounting and Information Systems* (New York: John Wiley & Sons, 1982), p. 9.

FIG. 26-2

A Typical FIS for a Manufacturing Company

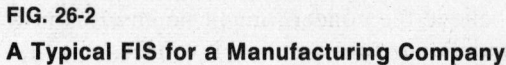

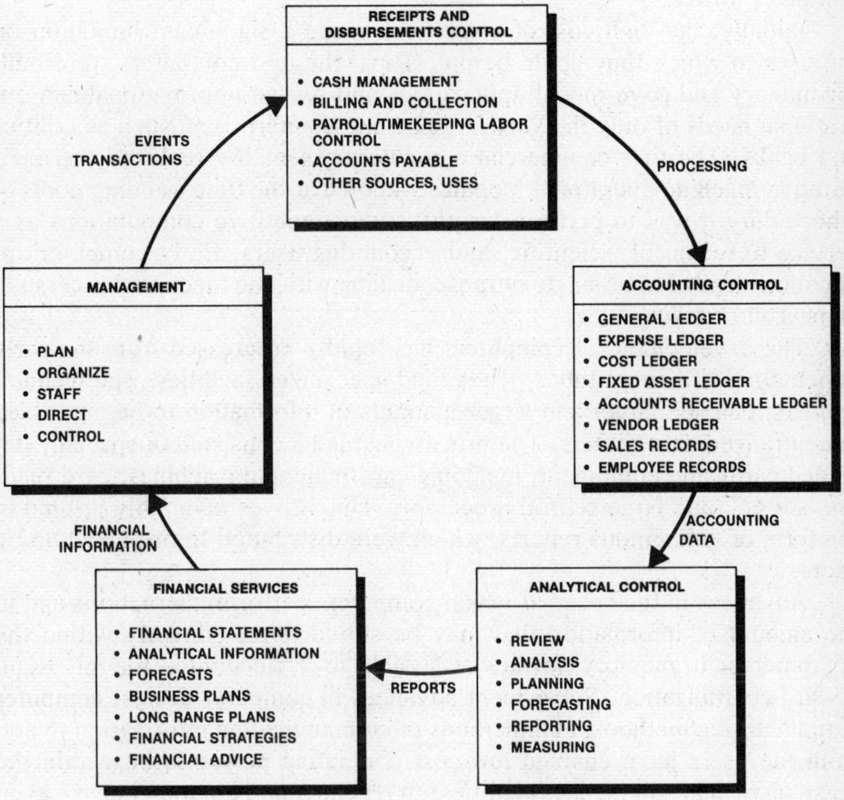

Source: Steven J. Root, "Perspectives on Financial Information Systems," Chapter 1, in *Financial Information Systems Manual*, James D. Willson and Jack F. Duston, eds. (Boston: Warren, Gorham & Lamont, Inc., 1986), p. 1-7. Reprinted by permission.

This is not to say that the rate of change has been anything less than spectacular. However, this change is occurring in the face of an ever-increasing concern on the part of management and auditors that the rapid pace may have some unanticipated adverse consequences of major proportions. In a 1980 survey of the state of the art of internal control in U.S. corporations, it was reported that the aspect of internal control that troubles executives most is the increasing dependence of companies on computers for operational effectiveness and for financial reporting.[4] While the authors found no comparable subsequent survey indicating the level of executive concern in

---

[4] Robert K. Mautz et al., *Internal Control in U.S. Corporations* (New York: Research Foundation of Financial Executives Institute, 1980), p. 8.

this area, there is no reason to believe the concern might be any less now than it was in 1980. In order to understand that concern, it is necessary first to trace the brief history of the computer and to describe the benefits of computer power.

Initially, the high cost of computers posed a significant limitation on the uses to which they could be put. Thus, the first computers were built for military and government applications and served informational and operational needs of only the very large business enterprises, such as utilities and banks. The first commercial computers essentially replaced the computation machine operators—popularly known at the time as comp pools—whose duty it was to perform lengthy and/or repetitive computations as a service to technical, scientific, and accounting users. Early computer applications tended to be single-purpose, dealing with one functional user, such as payroll or billing.[5]

The development of computers has rapidly progressed from the early behemoths of vacuum tubes, wires, and specialized facilities. The technology first enabled larger and larger amounts of information to be processed in centralized data centers. The processing media consisted of specially designed cards and equipment, including card-punching machines, card readers, sorters, and large central processors. Output was invariably printed in the form of voluminous reports, which were distributed to or picked up by users.

Advances in the speed at which computers perform instructions and in the amount of information that may be stored, either directly within the computer or in memory devices accessible to it, accounted for this trend toward centralization. Subsequent advances in computer design, computer manufacturing methods, and methods of communicating information to and from the users have enabled low-cost computing power to be within the grasp of virtually all business entities. In recent years, computers have even been designed for individual use.

The advances in computer design have been accompanied by improvements in the methods by which computers are instructed to perform their intended tasks (i.e., the systems and programming techniques).

Thus, the modern data processing organization is a complex mixture of terminals, modems, front-end processors, central computers, disk drives, tape drives, readers, printers, and telecommunications equipment.

The equipment is more than likely dispersed both organizationally and geographically throughout the company in an interconnected network using leased telephone lines, microwaves, and possibly even satellites as data links. Services offered may include local batch processing, remote batch processing, time-sharing, and interactive on-line facilities. Many data centers are operated around the clock and all must be supported by technical

---

[5] Auditing Advanced Systems Task Force, "Management, Control and Audit of Avanced EDP Systems," in *Computer Service Guidelines* (New York: American Institute of Certified Public Accountants, 1977), p. 5.

services, such as programming, I/S design, data administration, and security. An illustrative diagram of the components of a modern computer facility is shown in Figure 26-3.[6] An example of an organization structure of a major data processing organization is depicted in Figure 26-4.[7]

Functions That Benefit From I/S

Applications that benefit from I/S involving automated data processing techniques have increased remarkably from the simple military and government uses in the early years. Today, computers are being used to process accounting and financial information of all types. It is not unusual to find entities in which the entire financial records exist only in machine-readable form. Hence, financial statements, general ledgers, and original entry records (e.g., payroll registers, cash receipts, and disbursements journals) are all computerized. Most of these are processed in a batch mode, meaning that all homogenous transactions are grouped together in batches that are submitted to the EDP center, which then sets up and processes the data according to applicable instructions. A growing percentage of these applications is being converted to the faster, cheaper, and more useful, on-line processing mode. This method, made possible by the advances in memory storage, processing speed, and communication techniques, does not require accumulating transactions in batches. Rather, data is submitted to a data processing center located in the user organization through terminals to be processed instantly by the application programs, which are stored at the data center in a manner that enables processing to occur immediately without the manual setup procedure. Eventually, much information is likely to be processed in this fashion.

While the applicability of computers to financial information has been substantial, the ultimate worth of the computer to management goes far beyond finance functions. EDP technology has enabled undreamed-of progress to be made in basic and applied research of all types, product design and development, manufacturing, scheduling and production techniques, quality control, material control, marketing, industrial relations communication, and numerous other functions vital to business enterprise.

The technological advances in computer design combined with improvements in programming languages and techniques will considerably simplify the future development of new applications. Experiences in costly, lengthy, and frustrating system development efforts will be replaced by large data bases and facilities that will enable users virtually to develop their own applications. The power of the computer, in effect, will be an arm's reach

---

[6] Jerry Fitzgerald, *Internal Controls for Computerized Systems*, (San Leandro, Cal.: E. M. Underwood, 1978), p. 5. Reprinted courtesy of Jerry Fitzgerald, 506 Barkestine Lane, Redwood City, Cal. 94065

[7] William C. Mair et al., *Computer Control and Audit* (U.S.A.: Touche Ross & Co., 1976), p. 27. Copyright © 1976 by Touche Ross & Co. Reprinted with permission.

FIG. 26-3

Components of a Data Processing System

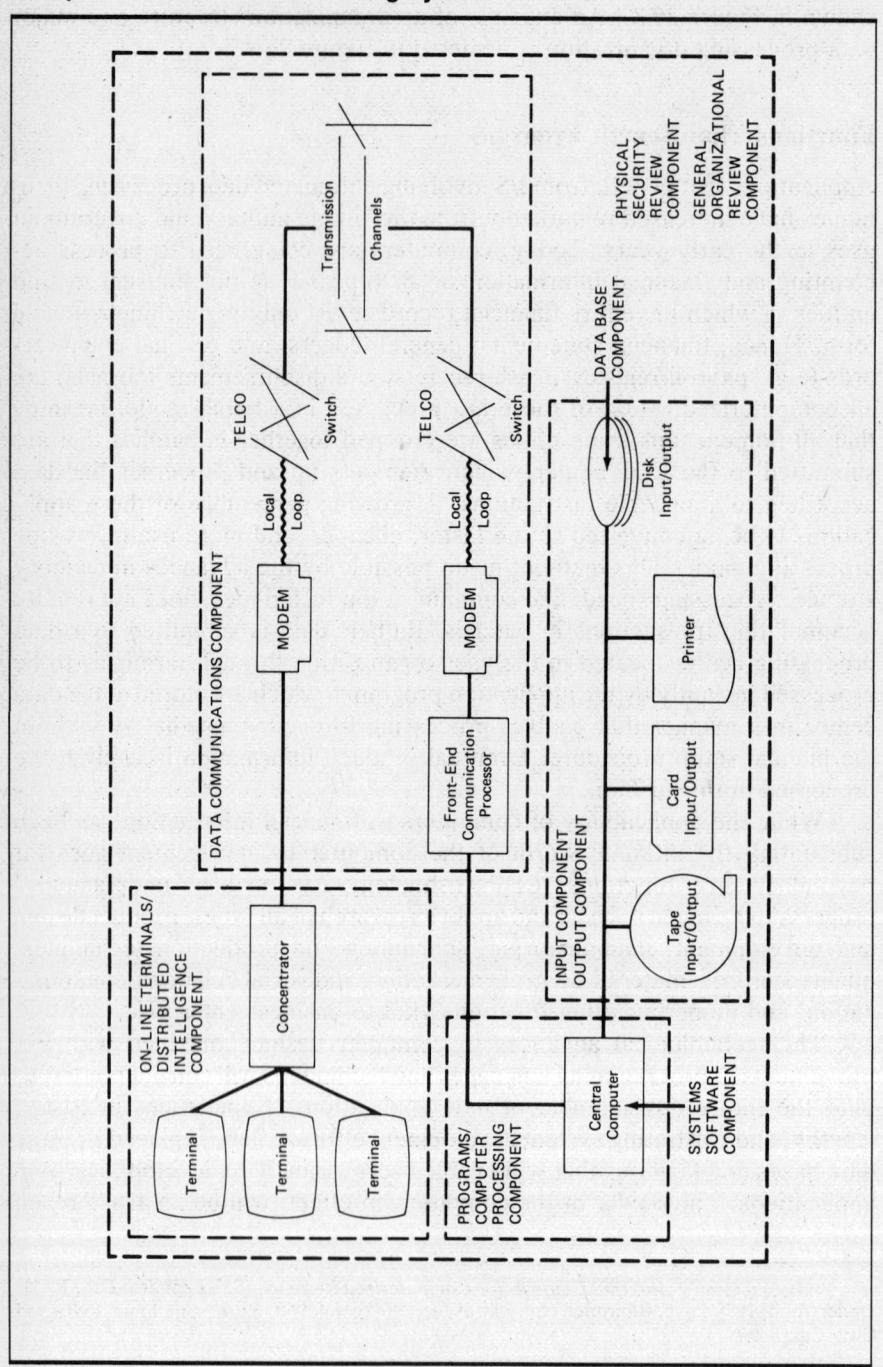

FIG. 26-4
An Example of an MIS Organization Structure

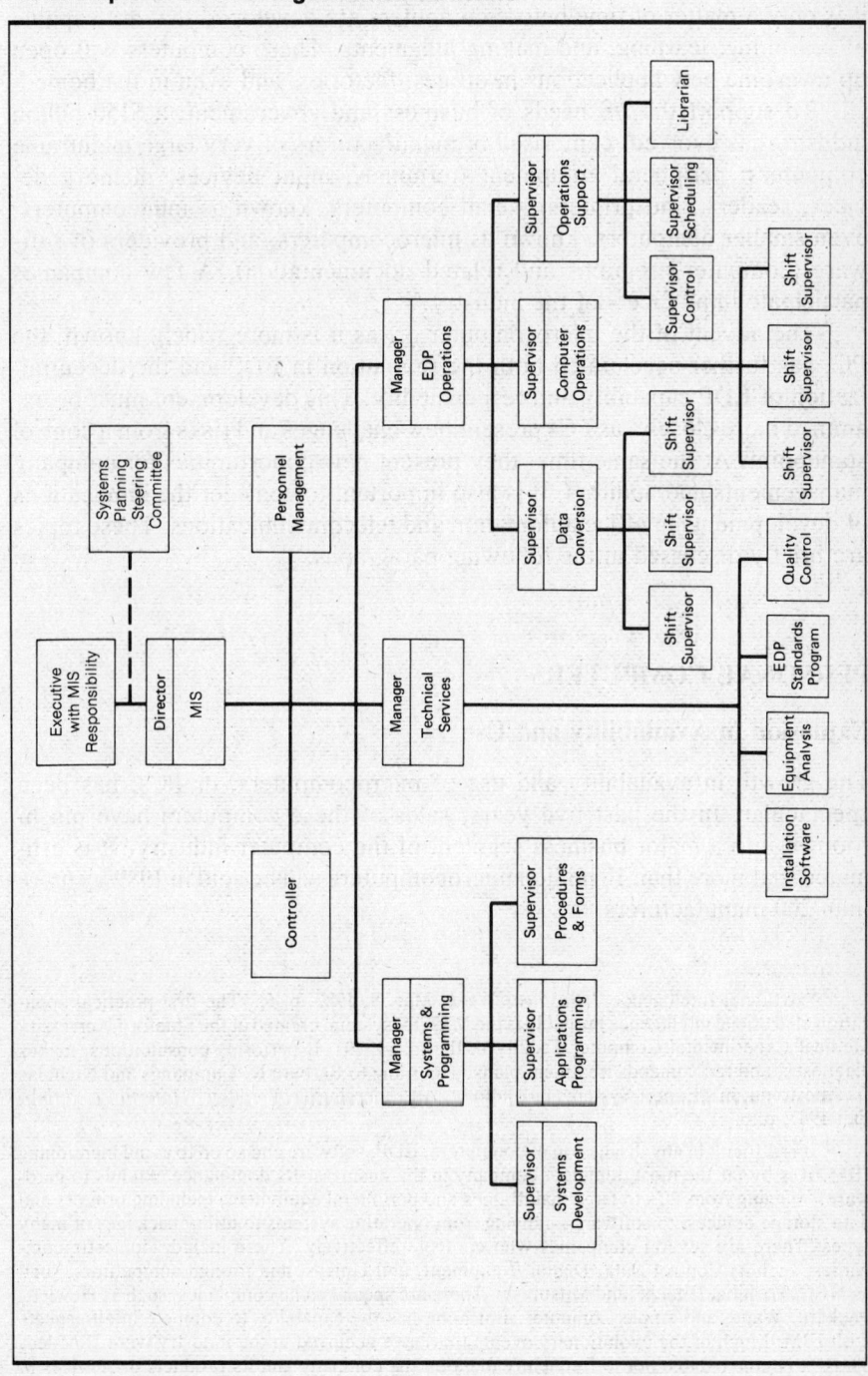

away from company executives, line management, and operational personnel to serve their individual informational needs. Experts are convinced that it is only a matter of time before computers are developed that are capable of reasoning, learning, and making judgments. These computers will open up awesome new applications in offices, factories, and even in the home.[8]

To support the I/S needs of business and government, a $150 billion industry has evolved, comprised of manufacturers of very large mainframe computers, peripheral equipment (terminals, input devices, memory devices, readers, and printers), small computers, known as minicomputers, even smaller computers, known as microcomputers, and providers of software (computer programs and related documentation). A few companies participate in all facets of the industry.[9]

The advent of the microcomputer or, as it is more widely known, the PC, has further accelerated both the revolution in EDP and the decentralization of EDP capability and responsibility. This development must be examined more closely, as PCs present new challenges and risks from a control standpoint. At the same time, they present new opportunities for company managements and auditors. It is also important to consider the implications of developments in office automation and telecommunications. These topics are briefly discussed in the following paragraphs.

PERSONAL COMPUTERS

Explosion in Availability and Use

The growth in availability and use of microcomputers, or PCs, has been spectacular. In the past five years, sales of these computers have mushroomed into a major business segment of the computer industry. It is estimated that more than 10 million microcomputers will be sold in 1989 by more than 200 manufacturers.

---

[8] "Artificial Intelligence," *Business Week*, Mar. 8, 1982, p. 66. The first practical application of artificial intelligence probably is the MYCIN system, created at the Stanford University Medical Experimental Computer Facility in the mid-1970s. It performs consultations, makes diagnoses, and recommends treatment plans, according to Barbara K. Cummings and Nicholas G. Apostolou, in "Expert Systems in Auditing: An Emerging Technology," *Internal Auditing*, Fall 1987, p. 6.

[9] It is difficult in any discussion of computers, EDP, software and so on to avoid mentioning IBM. It is by far the most dominant company in the business. Its dominance extends to hardware—ranging from PCs to large mainframes and peripheral equipment, including printers and data storage devices, to software—ranging from operating systems to utility packages of many types. There are several companies who compete effectively. These include domestic companies, such as Control Data, Digital Equipment, and Unisys, and foreign competitors, such as NEC, Toshiba, Hitachi, and Mitsubishi. There are special niche companies, such as Hewlett-Packard, Wang, and Apple Computer. But none has the capability to compete in all aspects with IBM. Much of the evolutionary events that have occurred in the industry were IBM-led. Thus, it is unavoidable not to frequently mention the company and its products or services in discussing information systems.

The success of these devices as a means to make desk jobs more efficient has itself spawned a new business. Many new companies and some established ones have found writing PC programs to be very profitable. It is estimated that more than 1,500 programs exist just for the IBM PC and its compatible rivals. Some believe there is an oversupply of software products that bewilders prospective users. In the rush to cash in on the software bonanza, products came to market that did not work properly. Users are becoming cautious and more skeptical when it comes to buying new products, even from well known suppliers. An industry shakeout is the inevitable result.

The impact of the first generation of PCs took the business scene by surprise. Initiated by the Apple Computer, the market for such devices was validated when IBM introduced its entry, the PC, in 1982. Based on the Intel 8088 microprocessor chip, the PC soon became the de facto industry standard spawning many PC compatibles.

Now, the second generation of PCs is upon us with the development of the IBM PC-AT and PC-XT. These microcomputers are based on a new chip, the Intel 80286, which offers more internal memory, faster processing speed, and a much larger storage capacity.

Like the PC, these new versions are attracting imitators. Several companies, including Compaq, Texas Instruments, and Kaypro, have joined the 286 club. These new processors are roughly priced in the $4,000 range. They promise to launch a new round of software that should continue the automation advances for the office. To offset the ability of companies building IBM "plug-compatible" PCs, IBM ushered in the third generation with its PS-2 line.

Not only are PCs commonplace in the office but, with the vast and growing array of PC software, they also do many things, even jobs once reserved for mainframes. In a recent survey of PC use by business, designed by Data Decisions and conducted by Beta Research Corporation, it was reported that substituting the PC for the mainframe will be the area in which growth in use will be the most dramatic.[10]

According to an analysis of PC buyers by Dataquest, 66 percent of computer buyers cited accounting as the principal purpose for their purchases.[11] The accounting software products that are available to these buyers are both numerous and varied. Not only are there scores of basic accounting packages, such as packages for processing payrolls and maintaining general ledgers, but there are also products for business management and financial applications. Examples of the former include products for project tracking, statistical analysis, and decision analysis. Examples of the latter include packages that provide investment record-keeping capabilities, portfolio evaluations, and investment analyses.

---

[10] Data Decisions, "Micros at Big Firms: A survey," *Datamation*, Nov. 1983, p. 172.

[11] Ken Greenberg, "Accounting, Business Management, and Financial Applications," *PC World*, Winter 1984/1985, p. 156.

Other functions for which PCs are used include new applications not suitable for mainframes, word processing, graphics, and functions formerly obtained via time-sharing. No longer is employment of PCs the exclusive province of technical specialists. Reports of uses by senior management, middle management, and clerical personnel are increasing. Increased use of PCs by internal auditors is described in Chapters 27 and 28.

Typical uses for PCs include:

- Preparing financial plans
- Preparing form letters and other correspondence
- Preparing reports
- Maintaining department logs
- Receiving or sending correspondence
- Performing research
- Accessing mainframes
- Preparing graphs and charts
- Maintaining department files
- Performing scheduling and analytical tasks

Of the several hundred packages that are available, the most popular are integrated software packages, which offer a combination of products in a single package. These products now number in excess of 50. Lotus 1-2-3, the first such package, integrated spreadsheets, graphics, and data base functions.

In addition to these functions, more recent software products integrate other functions, such as communications, with other PCs, word processing, calendars, and notepads. Still others integrate accounting functions, such as check writing and general ledgers.

Risks and Concerns

Microcomputer usage is becoming so widespread that it poses new risks and concerns for managements and auditors. Or, perhaps it is more aptly said that risks and concerns, once reserved for mainframes, are now attendant to microcomputers.

The growth of PCs means that data processing resources and controls are becoming widely dispersed in user companies. Many users formerly depended on centralized data processing departments to provide the needed EDP controls. With PCs, these users will need to develop and administer the necessary controls themselves. Some may not be technically ready to accept this responsibility, and the result will be a more dispersed potential for:

- Errors and omissions
- Illegal penetration of privacy and security controls

- Inconsistencies with respect to systems development and operating standards and procedures
- Inefficient use of resources
- Inadequate segregation of duties
- Inadequate backup records and files and documentation of systems and programs
- Data "pollution" and redundancy
- Equipment incompatibility

As the use of PCs inevitably evolves toward greater and greater interaction with and replacement of mainframes, the ramifications of these risks and concerns will multiply.

In addition to the preceding, the problem of software piracy is becoming more widespread. Software piracy involves unauthorized copying and disseminating of proprietary software. At one time, some users believed that software vendors were willing to tolerate a certain amount of piracy in order to gain market penetration.[12] Recent legal and other actions by software houses appear aimed at dispelling such myths and reducing the problem. One of those actions involves the formation of the Software Protection Fund (SPF). This association is comprised of software vendors' plans to actively combat piracy through a program of meetings with corporate users, a public-relations campaign, and an ongoing search to find and prosecute pirates.

OFFICE AUTOMATION

The revolution in PC usage is, in reality, part of a larger revolution in business offices. Automation of such tasks as word processing, voice, image and facsimile communication, and information distribution are among the fastest growing business segments. Each of these tasks is discussed separately in the following paragraphs.

Word Processing

Word processing is the process by which the thoughts of one person in an organization are prepared for communication to others in a documented form. Communication of this type, in the form of letters, memos, notes, reports, and so on, occurs daily on a substantial scale.

The developments in improving the efficiency with which information is documented have been a significant factor in the technological evolution of business and commerce. Inventions such as the printing press, typewriter, and copy machine are noteworthy examples.

---

[12] Marv Lincoln, "In Search of the 'Perfect' Software Protection Scheme," *dNews*, May 1984, p. 20.

Today, the computer, printer, and typewriter have been joined in the word processor and PC. These devices enable the user to prepare original drafts, add or delete data, and print final copy with a level of efficiency unattainable through conventional means.

Most word processing programs have similar features. These include automatic word-wrap, pagination, insertion and deletion of text, spell checks, and search-and-replace functions. There is a wide range of sophistication, however, within these features. Some word processing programs offer unique features, such as automatic indexing and table of contents preparing. More advanced features include automated recalling of frequently used text.

Word processing can be accomplished either with PCs or dedicated word processors. These latter devices were developed by manufacturers such as Wang and IBM. Their primary purpose is word processing, and they are used principally by secretaries and other clerical personnel. In many instances, companies have established centralized word processing groups. These groups provide word processing services, usually using dedicated word processors, to other using groups within the entity. Since these machines and supporting software exist only for word processing, they were at first superior in performance and ease of use to the PC word processing. More recent PC word processing programs are very close to dedicated word processors in terms of performance. As a result, it is likely that dedicated word processors will eventually be driven out of existence by PCs.

Communication

Deeply intertwined with the fast-paced advances in computers is the complex field of communication. Fifty years ago, it was simple to distinguish the various forms of electronic communication. These included the telephone, telegraph, phonograph, radio, television, and motion pictures.

Today, the application of computer and other technologies have all but eliminated the distinctions. Not only is it difficult to distinguish among communication media, it is difficult to distinguish between communications and computers. It is not by coincidence that the world's largest computer maker and the world's largest telecommunications company are becoming direct competitors. Nowhere is the competition expected to be more fierce than in the office. That is because there is an ever-increasing demand for immediate information in order to conduct business effectively.

In recent years, such inventions as communications satellites, microwave transmission, fiber optics, cable TV, digital and integrated switches, and many others have significantly changed what can be communicated, how much of it, and how fast. These and other developments have enabled the combining of two basic signals—voice and data. It is now possible to transmit and receive both voice and data using the same equipment, which eliminates the need for such items as modems, acoustic coupler, and line drivers. A number of manufacturers now offer computerized telephone switching systems to effect this technology, and many companies are installing them.

These developments enable word processors, data processors, copiers, and other devices to be electronically linked together in networks. Electronic mail—the electronic transmission of data normally carried through physical means—is a reality. *Infosystems* reported that an estimated 70 percent of Fortune 500 companies installed some form of electronic mail in the 1982 to 1984 period.[13] Communications management is likely to become an area requiring specialized management skill and expertise. Organization charts may have to make room for yet another critical discipline.

Information Distribution

This subject is really a subset of word processing and communication. The various telecommunication and computer developments have given birth to such terms as electronic mail, videotex, teleconferencing, and videoconferencing. These terms are discussed under the general topic of information distribution, since they each represent a different way of accomplishing that task.

"Electronic mail" is described in the preceding section. It represents the transmission of information to one or more destinations by electronic means that otherwise is transmitted physically. Electronic mail may be used for ordering goods and services, paying bills, moving funds, advertising, distributing reports, responding to inquiries, and so on.

"Videotex" is an automated way of obtaining information. The producer of the information usually develops and maintains a data base of information. Topics range from current affairs to law libraries and shipping movements. The producer markets this information by making it available in an on-line interactive fashion to users through a computer network.

"Teleconferencing" is simply a telephone conversation between two or more persons. While it has been available as a tool for a number years, teleconferencing use has been limited.

"Videoconferencing" is the answer to achieving two-way face-to-face communication between two groups geographically separated, without travel. In videoconferencing, image as well as voice is transmitted. At present, the economics of this mode suggest that only very large government and business entities can justify its use. However, the technology is constantly changing and improving the economics, and the time may not be far off when videoconferencing will be within reach of any organization.

Small- to medium-sized companies are not being passed by when it comes to information distribution by any means. This is particularly true for

---

[13] Lou Pilla, "Telecommunications Guide—New Directions," *Management World*, Mar. 1982, p. 12.

those companies in which communication is critical. For example, many phone systems commonly include such efficiency-inducing features as:

- *Call forwarding.* The automatic diversion of an incoming call to a number external to the office PBX (private telephone switchboard).
- *Call waiting.* A signal to a person engaged in a call that an incoming call is holding.
- *Speed calling.* Initiating calls for frequently dialed numbers using a two- or three-digit code.
- *Automatic route selection.* A facility that enables the system to select the most economical routing automatically.
- *Station hunting.* Automatically switches call to another number after a given number of rings.

Communications Software

Developments regarding communications hardware have been equaled, if not surpassed, by those affecting communications software. No matter how good the switches and other network hardware are, good communications software is indispensable.

Communications software works with modems (modulator/demodulator) to match the protocol of the sender with that of the receiver on the other end of the phone line. The most important of the protocols is transmission speed.[14] Originally, transmission speeds were the same as those for voice—300 bauds per second (BPS). Now, however, newer equipment permits much faster speeds. For PCs, speeds can range from 1200 BPS to as much as 9600 BPS.

Other important communications software features include file management, print buffers, and error checking. File management is the sending (uploading and receiving (downloading) of files (data). A print buffer enables the user to print information downloaded. Error checking is intended to detect errors caused in transmission. Auto-dialing is yet another feature. This permits keyboard dialing and avoids the use of a telephone.

Recent trends in communications software include micro-to-mainframe communications and North American Presentation Level Protocol Syntax (NAPLPS). NAPLPS permits the interactive communication of color graphics information.[15] Figure 26-5 presents a brief listing of communications software packages currently available.

While the advances have been impressive, they are still insufficient to permit communication networks involving incompatible equipment and software. Part of the difficulty is explained by the fact that there is no standard

---

[14] Eric Brown, "Communications," *PC World*, Winter, 1984/1985, p. 106.
[15] *Ibid.*, p. 108.

protocol agreed to and supported by public network vendors.[16] Also, some companies are settling for products that are less expensive and less functional, while others are investing in products that are more functional. Later, more capability is added in-house. For example, some products do not offer data extraction or file formatting. Of course, there are products available with these features, but at prices that many believe are too high.[17] Finally, there is the question of data security. Micro-to-mainframe communications raises the issue of data security. Specifically, it is necessary to decide the levels of security to afford downloaded data and to provide a mechanism for reasonably assuring appropriate levels are implemented.[18] Discussion of how to protect data in this emerging age of easy communication is provided in this chapter under "Personal Computer Control Techniques."

Despite the obstacles, there is general optimism that software links will evolve in the near future that will enable the easy movement of data from computer to computer regardless of make or model.

Obviously, the internal controls in a company whose I/S includes a combination of large data processing installations, other EDP capability disbursed throughout the company, data networks, and PCs differs markedly from companies without such systems. The concern of management about such systems is understandable. To put that concern in perspective, it is necessary to consider the inherent risks.

THE INHERENT RISKS

It is widely recognized that computers offer significant advantages in terms of speed, efficiency, and accuracy. However, these gains are not achieved risk-free. Computers and the data they store and process are exposed to many of the same risks that are present without them. Acts of God, such as fire and earthquakes, and human errors can cause damage and loss to a company, irrespective of the computer's presence.

Other types of risks arise solely because the computer is there. Examples of these include hardware failures, such as a computer outage, or software failures, such as program errors that alter or delete valid data.

Whether or not the risk is common to all business assets or unique to the computer is not an important distinction. The important point is that because computers enable the concentration of data of all types, any damage is likely to cause more profound adverse consequences, regardless of the cause. Therefore, any risk analysis must be inclusive of all types of risks.

---

[16] Joanne Kelleher, "Communication Software Tangles," *Business Computer Systems*, Mar. 1986, p. 53.

[17] *Ibid.*, p. 53.

[18] *Ibid.*, p. 56.

FIG. 26-5

Communications Software Packages

Product	Supplier	Protocol	Modes	Price	Requirements	Comments
LogOn	Ferox Microsystems Inc. 1701 N. Ft. Meyer Drive #611 Arlington, Va. 22209 (703) 841-0800	Async	PC-PC	$150	128K 1 disk drive serial port	Operates with UCSD Pascal only
Micro Link II	Digital Marketing Corp. 2363 Boulevard Circle Walnut Creek, Cal. 94595 (415) 947-1000	Xmodem	PC-PC time sharing	$99	32K 1 disk drive serial port	Communicates with information services, timesharing computers
PC-Talk III	Freeware The Headlands Press, Inc. P.O. Box 862 Tiburon, Cal. 94920	XON/XOFF Xmodem handshaking	ASCII-blmy file Xfer	$35*	64K 1 disk drive modem	Autodial and redial capabilities
Micro Gate 6530	Gateway Microsystems Inc. 9501 Capital of Texas Hwy #105 Austin, Tex. 78759 (512) 345-7791	Async	PC-PC PC-host	$2,500	128K 1 disk drive serial port	A Tandem Computer 6520/30 terminal emulator links PCs to any Tandem system
dBase/Answer	Ashton-Tate 10150 W. Jefferson Blvd. Culver City, Cal. 90230 (213) 376-6978	Async	PC-mainframe	$45,000	256K 2 disk drives modem serial port	Access, select, upload download IBM mainframe data base info in formats compatible with Ashton-Tate software
Compac	Frontier Technologies Corp. P.O. Box 11238 Milwaukee, Wis. 53211 (414) 964-8689	Async Bisync HDLC SDLC	PC-host	$40 $195	128K 1 disk drive Ad Com 2 board	Price depends on transmission speed (300–9600 BPS)
Asynchronous Communications Support 2.00	IBM Systems Products Division P.O. Box 1328 Boca Raton, Fla. 33432 (800) 447-4700	Async	PC-mainframe	$60	64K (128K for DOS 2.00 and later versions) 1 disk drive modem	Menu offers selections for Dow Jones News/Retrieval service, The Source and TSO

* Requested contribution

The Apple-IBM Connection	Alpha Software Corp. 30 B Street Burlington, Mass. 01803 (800) 451-1018	Async	PC-PC	$250	96K 1 disk drive modem serial port	Permits moving binary files and data between Apple II and/or IIe and IBM, Eagle, or Columbia PCs
The Impersonator	Direct Aid, Inc. P.O. Box 4420 Boulder, Colo. 80306 (303) 442-8080	Xmodem XON/XOFF 3 others	PC-mainframe	$195	192K 1 disk drive modem	A terminal emulation program with preconfigured emulations for several specific terminals; Permits access primarily
Crosstalk XVI	Microstuf, Inc. 1000 Holcomb Woods Pkwy #440 Roswell, Ga. 30676 (404) 778-3998	Async Xmodem	PC-mainframe	$195	96K 1 disk drive serial port	A terminal emulation program for many specific terminals
Auto-Mail	Jones Engineering Assoc. Inc. P.O. Box 26134 Charlotte, N.C. 28221 (704) 455-9616	Async	PC-PC	$100	64K 1 disk drive serial port Hayes smart modem	An electronic mail program

Source: Brown, "Communications," *PC World*, Winter 1984/1985, pp. 105–129.

Also, each risk must be assessed in terms of the consequences that are likely to result from its occurrence. The consequences might range from loss of a single record or file to the inability to continue processing. An excellent method for identifying and evaluating risk is illustrated in Figure 26-6.

Among other things, Figure 26-6 indicates that the areas of greatest exposure for the risks illustrated are programmer and operator errors that can cause damage to records and files but that pose no serious threat to facilities, equipment, and personnel. Of course, not all risks are illustrated, and risks that might occur frequently—more than once a week or several times daily—were excluded because they pose little overall exposure. Examples of this type of exposure include errors in data submission and errors in data conversion (keypunch mistakes).

It is impossible to provide absolute assurance that occurrences such as those depicted in Figure 26-6 will not occur. However, by identifying risks in terms of their potential for happening and their likely effects, controls may be instituted to minimize the chances of experiencing them. In addition, controls may be instituted to minimize the effects when they do happen and to facilitate returning to normal operations. Figure 26-7 illustrates preventive controls, limiting controls (i.e., those that limit the effect of the exposure), and recovery controls for selected exposures. The controls cited are not all-inclusive. Indeed, many risks require several techniques to reasonably minimize management's concern.

It can be seen from these examples that some of the controls cover more than a single exposure. It should also be evident that it is the risk attendant in the computer environment that is the primary factor in shaping I/S environment controls.

From an internal control standpoint, the primary concern is how to limit access to data files and records only to those who are authorized. Put another way, management cannot reasonably assure that, in an environment where access to information is widespread, sufficient protection against loss, destruction, and theft are effectively minimized.

The many evolving automated and electronic means of transmitting and receiving data offer increased security exposure. Messages transmitted over wire are susceptible to wiretap, the principal exposure. While wiretapping has been a means of eavesdropping for a long time, its use may increase, because data and other signals can now be intercepted in addition to voice messages. For nonwire transmission methods (e.g., microwave transmission), other electronic means exist to intercept data.

A related concern is controlling the updating of the information to reasonably assure its accuracy and completeness and to guard against unauthorized changes. Obviously, these concerns exist in any system, whether automated or not; however, in an automated system, the techniques employed to minimize them necessarily differ, as we shall see.

From an operational standpoint, perhaps the greatest concern is how best to apply the changing technology to individual circumstances. The costs

INFORMATION SYSTEMS AUDITING

FIG. 26-6
Types of Security Exposure

Risks	Loss of Funds*	Records Loss Minor	Records Loss Major	File Loss Minor	File Loss Major	F — Damaged E — Intact P — Intact	F — Intact E — Damaged P — Lost	F — Intact E — Damaged P — Intact	F — Damaged E — Damaged P — Damaged
External:									
Earthquake	0	1–2	0–1	1–2	0–1	0–1	0–1	0–1	0
Fire	0	0–1	0	0–1	0–1	0–1	0–1	0–1	0
Flood from storms	0	0	0	0	0	0	0	0	0
Act of war	0	1–2	0–1	0–1	0	0–1	1–2	1–2	0
Lightning	0	1–2	0–1	0–1	0	0–1	0–1	0–1	0
Explosion	0	0–1	0–1	0–1	0	0–1	0–1	0–1	0
Water supply loss	0	0	0	0	0	0	0	0	0
Nuclear accident	0	2–3	1–2	1–2	1–2	0	0	1–2	0
Power supply interruption	0	0–1	0–1	0–1	0–1	0–1	0	0	0–1
Airliner crash	0	0	0	0	0	0	0	0	0
Internal:									
Head crash	0	1–2	1–2	1–2	1–2	NA	NA	NA	NA
Program error	3–4	2–3	1–2	2–3	1–2	NA	NA	NA	NA
Operator error	3–4	2–3	1–2	2–3	1–2	NA	NA	NA	NA
Data control error	2–3	2–3	1–2	2–3	1–2	NA	NA	NA	NA
Magnetism	0	2–3	1–2	2–3	1–2	NA	NA	NA	NA
Criminal Acts:									
Vandalism	0	1–2	0–1	1–2	0–1	0–1	0–1	0–1	0
Espionage	1–2	1–2	1–2	1–2	1–2	0–1	0–1	0–1	0
Fraud	1–2	1–2	1–2	1–2	0	0	0	0	0
Theft	1–2	1–2	1–2	1–2	0–1	0–1	0–1	0–1	0
Terrorist activity	0–1	1–2	1–2	1–2	1–2	1–2	1–2	1–2	1–2
Sabotage	0–1	1–2	1–2	1–2	1–2	1–2	1–2	1–2	1–2

*Also other items of value such as negotiable instruments, supplies, and assets, by means other than damage.

F = Facilities
E = Equipment
P = Personnel

NA = Not Applicable

Key: Frequency of Occurrence

0 = Less than once in 100 years
1 = Less than once in 10 years
2 = Less than once a year
3 = Less than once a month
4 = Twice a week
5 = Several times daily

FIG. 26-7

Preventive, Limiting, and Recovery Controls for Selected Exposures

Exposure	Preventive Controls	Limiting Controls	Recovery Controls
Fire	■ Fire-resistant facility ■ No-smoking rules ■ Prompt removal of combustibles ■ Frequent fire prevention inspections	■ Sprinklers ■ Fire extinguishers ■ Halon system ■ Nearby fire-fighting capability ■ Offsite back-up capability	■ Recovery plan ■ Duplicate records of vital data ■ System documentation ■ Back-up facility/equipment
Computer outage	■ Overall system design ■ Effective maintenance program ■ Constant power supply ■ Protection against other risks (fire, flood, etc.) ■ Restricted access	■ Solid vendor support ■ Distributed processing ■ Monitoring by operators ■ Detective controls	■ Recovery plan ■ Duplicate records of vital data ■ System documentation ■ Back-up facility/equipment
Malicious programmer	■ Effective employment screening ■ Strict segregation of duties ■ Review and approval of programmer activities ■ Formal programming routines ■ Protective software utilities	■ Segregation of duties ■ Automated logging of changes ■ Review and approval routines ■ Active EDP auditing ■ Application controls (e.g., limit checks, edits, and batch balancing)	■ Effective programming documentation ■ Duplicate program tapes ■ Duplicate vital records ■ Recovery plan
Embezzlement	■ Effective employee screening ■ Strict segregation of duties ■ Restricted access to blank negotiable instrument forms, programs, documentation, etc. ■ Formal procedures for effecting program changes ■ Protective software utilities	■ Segregation of duties ■ Automated logging ■ Active EDP auditing ■ Application controls ■ User controls	■ Pursuit of legal remedies including punitive damages ■ Recovery plan ■ Duplicate records

of participating in the automation revolution are considerable. An added problem is that competing products and services vary a great deal in what they can do, thus making evaluations difficult. Hence, it is a challenge for many companies to spend wisely for the purpose of automating the office. Some of the difficult-to-answer questions include:

- Should automation decisions be left to local units, or should such decisions be centralized?
- What factors are important to consider in deciding automation/telecommunication strategy?
- How can the right vendor system be selected?
- What can be done to minimize installation disruptions and problems?
- What adjustments will be required in daily routines and work habits, if any?

INTERNAL CONTROL IN AN I/S ENVIRONMENT

Applicability of Internal Accounting Control Principles and Objectives

It is clear from the preceding discussion that the uniqueness of the I/S and EDP environment requires specialized control techniques to achieve the broad objectives intended. This is not to say, however, that the principles and objectives outlined in Chapter 18 for internal controls in general do not apply to the EDP environment. A point made in that chapter is worth repeating here: The types of records or I/S within a company do not affect the *objectives* of internal control of each transaction system. But they do influence the *manner* in which the control objectives are achieved.

Thus, the five broad principles of internal control systems apply equally to EDP. These are:

1. Competent and trustworthy personnel
2. Adequate segregation of duties
3. The existence of adequate documents and records
4. Adequate procedures for authorization of transactions
5. Adequate protection for related assets

The objectives noted in Chapter 18, pertaining to authorization, recording, safeguarding, reconciliation, and valuation, also apply in an EDP environment. The reader is reminded that these objectives directly relate to the requirements of the FCPA.

As mentioned earlier in this chapter, accounting or financial I/S are only a portion of the total contribution of I/S toward the company's goals. While external auditors may be concerned only with those aspects related to accounting controls, internal auditors must be concerned with the entire spectrum of information systems and the techniques used to develop, maintain, and operate them.

Other chapters, principally Chapters 4 and 18, note the shifting conceptual underpinnings for assessing the adequacy regarding internal control. Professional auditing standards of the AICPA were amended to make the assessment more directly related to the risk of financial statements being materially misstated. The misstatement would result from errors or irregularities that the system failed to prevent, detect, or correct. This conceptual shift tends to obsolete the distinction between accounting control and administrative control that formed the basis for the professional auditing standards and the FCPA prior to the conceptual shift.

It is believed that this shift, appropriate as it may be for assessing internal control in an audit of financial statements, does not invalidate other means of assessing the adequacy of internal control for other purposes. The objectives of internal control set forth in the FCPA, for example, have not changed. Moreover, management considerations of how much control to establish and maintain go beyond material errors in financial statements. There is a myriad of regulatory, contractual, and internal factors that necessitate a more extensive consideration. Thus, control objectives must be inclusive of all relevant considerations, and techniques must be sufficient to satisfy them. This chapter, developed in recognition of that greater responsibility, also presents internal controls from a minimization of risk standpoint (Figure 26-6), from a responsibility standpoint (Figure 26-7), and by relating control techniques to control objectives. In that way, the control techniques may be studied from three different bases.

Variability of Control Techniques

Like other functions, the control techniques that may be present in an EDP environment will not be constant. The factors that affect the degree of variability are the same as those for other internal control systems. As stated in Chapter 18, these include:

- Overall size of the company
- Geographic dispersion of operating units
- Degree of centralization or decentralization
- Style of management
- Type of industry
- Relative amount of foreign vs. domestic operations
- Management philosophy

Control Techniques Perspective

A perspective on control techniques may help the reader to better understand this challenging subject. Internal control techniques to limit access to, and afford protection of, information include a companywide policy that establishes the principle of information as an asset and that:

- Provides definitions of data classes and establishes responsibilities.
- Makes data owners responsible for specifying control requirements and authorizing individuals permitted access.
- Makes data custodians and data users responsible for complying with requirements established by data owners.
- Establishes a data security administrator to administrate and monitor compliance with information security policy and procedures.
- Classifies data into various categories, such as unrestricted and restricted (e.g., internal use only and company private).
- Specifies control objectives for each class of data.

Among specific control techniques that are used to protect data are:

- Terminal locks
- Passwords
- Secret codes
- Security software systems
- Call-back requirements
- Secure telephone lines
- Distributed and stand-alone computing
- Data back-up and recovery provisions
- Security consciousness
- Firm disciplinary action for security violations

Company managements have been hampered in efforts to provide adequate data security. One reason is that data security weaknesses do not often produce tangible, measurable adverse consequences. The instances of computer tampering, data loss, and data misuse usually go undetected. Some highly publicized hacking incidents have occurred in recent years (see Chapter 25 on computer crime). Except for these, the risks of inadequate data security seem to be more imagined than real.

Related to this reason is the fact that the extent to which vital company information is available usually is not known by managements. The technical knowledge necessary to perceive potential risks caused by expanding communications capabilities simply does not move very far up the organization chart.

Finally, until recently, the extent of available literature on the subject of effective control techniques was not great. This latter factor is changing. As an indication of this change, in 1985, the Bureau of Justice Statistics (BJS) of the U.S. Department of Justice issued a document setting forth over 80 techniques that offer the potential for protecting and securing computer systems of the modern age. The document was prepared for BJS by SRI

International under the project direction of Donn B. Parker. The document is intended to serve as a basic resource in the area of computer security. Figure 26-8 provides a topical listing of the control techniques covered by this work. Note that the controls are categorized by area of responsibility. In this way, it can be easily decided who must perform the control action. Other indices of these controls are provided in the document. They are by:

- Security topic
- Control objective
- Mode or type of implementation
- Area of control environment

The purpose of these several cuts is to make it simpler for computer security practitioners and others to locate all controls under a variety of headings. Each of the more than 80 controls is described in detail following a fixed format. Thus, for any given control, the description provides:

- The control title
- Objective
- Variables (the factors that affect the extent of application of the control)
- Strengths
- Weaknesses
- How to audit
- Purpose
- Control area (refers to the EDP environment element in which the control is implemented, namely, computer center, application system, system development and maintenance, computer system, and management)
- Mode (type of control, e.g., manual procedures, hardware, operating system, applications program, or policy)
- Area of responsibility
- Cost (low, medium, and high)
- Principles of note (e.g., cost-effectiveness, simplicity, and override capability)

This document should assist management and internal auditors alike in their efforts to implement and maintain effective data security.

Internal Control Objectives in an I/S Environment

Over the years, much information has been published that defines I/S objectives and internal control techniques. A brief listing of these is as follows:

☐ *Statement on Auditing Standards No. 48,* "The Effects of Computer Pro-

FIG. 26-8
List of Controls by Area of Responsibility

User

    Suppression of Incomplete and Obsolete Data
    Personal Data Input/Output Inspection
    Human Subjects Review
    Proprietary Notice Printed on Documents
    Completion of External Input Data
    Computer User Trouble Calls Logging
    Minimizing Numbers of Copies of Sensitive Data Files and Reports
    Courier Trustworthiness and Identification
    Responsibilities for Application Program Controls
    Separation of Personal Identification Data
    Sufficient Personal Identifiers for Data Base Searches Access
    Cryptographic Protection
    Exception Reporting
    Data File Access Subcontrol by Job Function
    Remote Terminal User's Agreement

Security

    Low Building Profile
    Physical Security Perimeter
    Security for Sensitive Areas During Unattended Periods
    Minimize Traffic and Access to Work Areas
    Physical Access Barriers
    Universal Use of Badges
    Delivery Loading Dock Access
    Inspection of Incoming/Outgoing Materials
    Passwords for Computer Terminal Access
    Computer Use Access Control Administration
    Computer Terminal Access and Use Restriction

Legal Counsel

    Proprietary Notice Printed on Documents
    Compliance With Laws and Regulations
    Remote Terminal User's Agreement

Audit Management

    Assets Accountability Assignments
    Confirmation of Receipt of Documents
    Data Accountability Assignment to Users
    Suppression of Incomplete and Obsolete Data
    Low Building Profile
    Minimize Traffic and Access to Work Areas
    Independent Control of Audit Tools
    Contingency Recovery Equipment Replacement
    Disaster Recovery
    Independent Computer Use by Auditors
    Separation and Accountability of EDP Functions
    Computer Security Management Committee
    Data Classification EDP Auditor
    Computer Security Officer

(continued)

FIG. 26-8 *(cont'd)*

Requirements and Specification Participation by EDP Auditors
Privileged Information Display Restrictions
Data File Access Subcontrols by Job Function

Insurance

Financial Loss Contingency and Recovery Funding
Monitoring Computer Use

Computer Security

Proprietary Notice Printed on Documents
Placement of Equipment and Supplier
Emergency Preparedness Alternative Power Supply
Separation of Equipment
Computer System Activity Records
Computer Security Officer
Keeping Security Reports Confidential
Cooperation of Computer Security Officer
Remote Terminal User's Agreement

Development and Maintenance

Suppression of Incomplete and Obsolete Data
Completion of External Input Data
Protection of Data Used in System Testing
Separation of Test and Production System
Compliance With Law and Regulations
Computer Programs Quality Assurance
Computer Programs Change Logs
Secrecy of Data File and Program Name
Participation of Computer Users at Critical Development Times
Programming Library Access Control
Data File Access Subcontrols by Job Function

Operations

Proprietary Notice Printed on Documents
Completion of External Input Data
Placement of Equipment and Supplier
Emergency Preparedness
Areas Where Smoking and Eating Are Prohibited
Delivery Loading Dock Access
Separation of Equipment
Isolation of Sensitive Computer Production Job
Correction and Maintenance of Production Systems
Limited Use of System Utility Programs
Tape Management Avoiding External Labels
Separation of Test and Production System
Computer System Activity Records
Minimizing Numbers of Copies of Sensitive Files and Reports
Data Files and Programs Backup
Electrical Equipment Protection
Electrical Power Shutdown and Recovery
Employees Identification on Work
Magnetic Tape Erasures

> Production Programs Authorized Version Validation
> Automation of Computer Operations
> Technical Review of Operating System Changes
> Exception Reporting
> Input Data Validation
> Telephone Access Validation Selection
> Limit Transaction Privileges From Terminal
> Monitoring Computer Use
> Passwords Generated and Printed by Computer in Sealed Envelope
> Remote Terminal User's Agreement
>
> **Input Control**
>
> Suppression of Incomplete and Obsolete Data
> Discarded Document Destruction
> Proprietary Notice Printed on Document
> Minimizing Number of Copies of Sensitive Data Files and Records
> Input Data Validation
>
> **Output Control**
>
> Confirmation of Receipt of Document
> Suppression of Incomplete and Obsolete Data
> Discarded Document Destruction
> Proprietary Notice Printed on Documents
> Minimizing Numbers of Copies of Sensitive Data Files and Reports
> Input Data Validation
>
> Source: *Computer Crime—Computer Security*, prepared for the Bureau of Justice Statistics, U.S. Department of Justice, by SRI International, Donn B. Parker, project leader.

cessing on the Examination of Financial Statements,"[19] American Institute of Certified Public Accountants, 1984.

☐ *Computer Control Guidelines,* the Canadian Institute of Chartered Accountants, 1975.

☐ *Systems Auditability and Control,* The Institute of Internal Auditors, Inc., 1977.

☐ *Control Objectives 1980,* EDP Auditors Foundation.

To these must be added the many texts, authored by knowledgeable I/S experts, that deal with the subject of controls. While the terminology and descriptions vary, the general consensus is to describe the control objectives and techniques in terms of the overall management controls and specific applications. A representative grouping of seemingly similar terminology drawn from these publications is shown in the following:

---

[19] This SAS supersedes SAS No. 3, "The Effect of EDP on the Auditor's Study and Evaluation of Internal Control." SAS No. 48 is integrated in *Professional Standards* Vol. 3, in various AU Sections.

- [ ] Management controls
  - Administrative controls
  - Organizational controls
  - General controls
- [ ] Application controls
  - Input controls
  - Transaction entry controls
  - Data communication controls
  - Conversion controls
  - Processing controls
  - Management controls
  - Computer center controls
  - Hardware and software controls
  - Output controls
  - Output processing controls
  - Physical security controls

Each of the publications mentioned previously provides excellent insight into controls and objectives. Taken together, however, the numerous publications have provided redundant and overlapping concepts and terminology, with the result that there is an absence of any single generally accepted set of control classifications, definitions, and guidelines. In essence, the cited works identify objectives and controls according to functions or processes and activities.

In a typical MIS organization (see Figure 26-4), the following functions are involved:

- EDP management
- Planning
- Systems and programming
- Technical services
- EDP operations

To these may be added such related functions as telecommunications, office automation, and information resource security.

Certain of these functions may be further subdivided. For example, "EDP operations" is made up of data conversion and computer operations and operations support. Under "technical services" are the functions of system software (also known as installation software), equipment analysis and strategy, standards, and quality control. "Systems and programming" includes systems development, applications programming, and procedures and forms. Organized in this way, the MIS department is in a position to achieve both operational and control objectives. While it is admittedly difficult to separate such objectives, both internal and external auditors often make some sort of artificial distinction to facilitate analysis and evaluation. The result may be a hybrid of processing flows, functional organization, organizational activity, and control concerns. The following breakdown is illustrative:

- Organizational objectives
- Operational objectives
- Resource acquisition and utilization objectives
- Record-keeping objectives

INFORMATION SYSTEMS AUDITING

- Accountability objectives
- Security objectives
- System development objectives

DETAILED OBJECTIVES AND CONTROLS

Another way to present internal controls in an I/S environment is to relate them to objectives. The following presents controls in that fashion. The objectives and controls presented are categorized here by activities cited in the preceding discussion.

I/S Organization Controls

☐ *Objectives.* To reasonbly assure that:
- Data processing resources are acquired and managed in such a way so as to result in the delivery of services that meet current and forecasted user requirements efficiently and effectively.
- Data processing operations occur in a manner that results in receiving, processing, storing, and delivering data accurately and completely to authorized users for authorized purposes.
- Data processing operations occur in an environment sufficiently protected from data processing risks. (See Figure 26-6.)

☐ *Techniques:*
- Use of written policy statements covering matters such as:
  — Employment of personnel
  — Acquisition of data processing equipment
  — Use of data processing facilities and services
  — Acquisition of data processing supplies
  — Acquisition of data processing software
  — Development of new systems
  — Changes to existing systems
  — Standards
  — Organization structure
  — Operation manuals, forms, and administrative procedures
- Use of organization charts and functional outlines
- Budgeting controls
- A steering committee
- A statement of control guidelines

With respect to control guidelines, many I/S organizations specify controls along the following lines:

- Use of particular operating systems (such as MVS)
- Use of a particular access control software package (such as RACF or ACF2)
- Use of a specific data base manager (such as IMS)
- Use of specific library and tape management systems
- Separation of functions such as data preparation, scheduling, operations, and application programming
- Use of both preventive and detective controls
- Assigned accountability and proper reporting
- Periodic audit

Other control techniques that might be specified in such guidelines might include:

- Transaction authorization controls
- Written documentation requirements
- Authorization controls
- Instructions for preparing source documents
- Access controls
- Data entry controls
- Data validation controls
- Processing controls
- Storage controls
- Recovery controls
- Correction controls

Specific forms of control techniques may be seen in applicable sections of the EDP Installation Control Questionnaire. (See Figure 27-2.)

Operations Controls

- ☐ *Objective.* To reasonably assure that processing operations occur in a way that results in the efficient storage and production of data accurately and completely and with proper regard for data integrity.
- ☐ *Techniques:*
  - Use of an input/output control group
  - Written procedures for operators
  - Automated software utilities
  - Productivity reporting
  - Access controls
  - Automated inventory (work-in-process) control techniques
  - Temperature and humidity controls
  - Redundancy and backup procedures
  - Cataloging
  - Error detection and correction routines
  - Standards for and review of purging/maintenance of files
  - Retention procedures

INFORMATION SYSTEMS AUDITING

Resource Acquisition and Utilization Controls

- ☐ *Objective.* To reasonably assure the availability and utilization of resources to meet current and future requirements in an optimum fashion.
- ☐ *Techniques:*
  - Maintaining up-to-date reference libraries
  - Maintaining internal information mechanisms
  - Developing current and long-term plans
  - Acquiring resources pursuant to controlled processes and specific authority
  - Monitoring records and reports of equipment and services utilization

Record-Keeping Controls

- ☐ *Objective.* To reasonably assure that the cost of EDP services are allocated to all user groups in a fair and equitable fashion.
- ☐ *Techniques:*
  - A formal set of written procedures
  - A methodology for cost allocation
  - Cost accumulation and reporting techniques
  - Periodic validation of billing rates

Accountability Controls

- ☐ *Objectives.* To reasonably assure that:
  - Physical equipment and facilities are compared with records of same at periodic intervals and any differences disclosed by such comparisons are investigated and resolved in a timely fashion.
  - Management is afforded sufficient insight into data processing activities to enable proper exercise of managerial responsibility.
- ☐ *Techniques:*
  - Procedures and record keeping for all involved computer hardware, including terminals, communications equipment, conversion equipment, storage devices, processors, and printers. Also included are data files and critical forms.
  - Physical inspection of tangible property and subsequent comparisons to records and adjustments made with respect to differences after appropriate investigation.
  - Monitoring via reports, meetings, and reviews of activities such as operations, systems development, and maintenance.

Security Controls

- ☐ *Objective.* To reasonably assure data assets, files and personnel are sufficiently protected from data processing exposures. (See Figure 26-7.)

- ☐ *Techniques:*
  - Proper segregation of duties (e.g., restricting application programmer's access to computers and production programs)
  - Authorization controls for accessing and changing software, documentation, and files
  - Restricting access to the computer area and to computer forms and supplies
  - Restricting access to computer files to authorized personnel
  - Physical protective techniques such as:
    — Fire extinguishers
    — Sprinkler systems
    — Halon systems
    — Temperature and humidity controls
    — Alarm systems
    — Periodic inspection by security guards, fire marshalls, etc.
    — Insurance
    — Fully enclosed facilities
    — Vaults for backup files and tapes
    — Automatic door locks
    — Badge control systems
    — Security checks on employees and others having access to the computer area
    — Backup power source
    — Redundant hardware
    — Passwords and related data entry controls
  - Emergency procedures
  - Disaster recovery procedures

Systems Development Controls

- ☐ *Objectives.* To reasonably assure that new systems are:
  - Developed in an optimum fashion, meaning that the user requirements are fulfilled with a minimum of effort.
  - Developed with sufficient controls for adequacy and completeness of processing and with proper provision for security.
- ☐ *Techniques:*
  - The system development life-cycle concept. This phased aprroach includes:
    — Project definition
    — Systems analysis and design
    — Detail design and programming
    — Testing

- Implementation
- Post review
* Involving users throughout the project development
* Authorization and change controls
* Project management controls
* Compliance with programming standards
* Sufficient system testing
* Sufficient system and program documentation
* Formal user acceptance
* Adequate user training
* User manuals

Other Objectives and Techniques

In addition to the foregoing, control objectives and techniques exist for other EDP functions. These include time-sharing, distributed processing, and computer backup. It should be obvious without specifying objectives and techniques associated with these other functions that the I/S environment requires extensive and specialized controls to reasonably assure attaining EDP objectives.

Personal Computer Control Techniques

Securing PCs against the risk of fire, theft, improper use, and other undesirable events involves the same fundamentals as for large systems. Perhaps the situation is better understood by saying it is simply an extension of the basis problem of information security. According to Dennis D. Steinauer, securing PCs is a matter of applying existing resources, including an organization's data security group, professional organizations, trade publications, consultants, and professional literature. A reprint of a recent article in which Steinauer discusses PC security follows.[20]

> **PROTECTING THE EQUIPMENT**
>
> Protecting the PC (and associated equipment from theft and physical damage) is not a fundamentally new problem—we have had to protect office equipment for years. The only new factors are the higher unit value of PC equipment and the need for somewhat greater concern for environmental controls. Otherwise, the

---

[20] Dennis G. Steinauer, "Security of Personal Computers: A Growing Concern," a draft article prepared by the Institute for Computer Sciences and Technology for publication by the National Bureau of Standards.

physical protection needs of PCs are the same as for other valuable equipment in the workplace. Indeed, if an organization has not addressed such problems prior to introducing personal computers, management should rethink its overall loss protection posture.

If personal computers are being placed in areas which previously had no basic physical access controls (e.g., locks on the doors and people present during working hours), then such controls should be provided. This is only prudent, since the value of a typical PC is well in excess of $2,000. Providing such simple and inexpensive controls will minimize not only the theft risk—it will help reduce exposures to some of the more sophisticated technical problems discussed below.

Personal computers are designed to operate in the "typical" office environment (i.e., without special air conditioning, electrical power quality control, or air contamination controls). In general, it can be argued that "if the people are comfortable, the PCs will be comfortable." Nevertheless, special attention should be given to minimizing the environmental hazards to which such equipment is exposed. Most users understand the need for such controls. Three areas, however, deserve special mention: electrical power, general area cleanliness, and magnetic media protection.

Electrical Power Quality

The typical PC is sensitive to the quality of its electrical power source. Inexpensive devices are available to protect against power surges short of a direct lightning strike. If the local power supply quality is unusually poor (e.g., large fluctuations in voltage or frequency, voltage spikes, or frequent outages), then more expensive power conditioning or uninterruptible power supply (UPS) systems should be considered. In many cases, it will be sufficient just to keep other appliances (e.g., refrigerators or other office equipment) on separate power sources.

Cleanliness

The general cleanliness of the area in which personal computer equipment operates has an obvious effect on reliability—both of equipment and magnetic media. It should be recognized that electronic equipment (including PCs) will naturally attract charged particles in the air. Eliminating such contaminants as smoke and dust will certainly have a beneficial effect on equipment and magnetic media (not to mention people).

Magnetic Media Care

Particular attention should be given to the protection of magnetic media. Not only is this the repository of most of the users' information, it is perhaps the element most vulnerable to damage. Exposure to contaminants (smoke, hair, doughnut crumbs, coffee, etc.) and direct contact with magnetic devices should be minimized. It is worth noting, however, that airport x-ray devices and magnets (kept six or more inches away from magnetic media) pose no danger, despite considerable concerns to the contrary.

Both dangers and proper handling techniques should be well known to all users; most are simply common sense. Nevertheless, it is surprising how carelessly many PC users handle such media.

PROTECTING THE DATA

Although there is considerable value in the physical equipment, the purpose for having computer equipment is to handle information. Information and the ability to produce, store, and analyze it ultimately have considerably more value to the organization than the equipment itself. Protecting that information is a more interesting—and challenging—problem than simply protecting the equipment. This should be our major concern to management.

Although personal computers provide essentially the same function as large systems (i.e., they permit the rapid manipulation and examination of large amounts of text and data), there are some unique characteristics of personal computers and their use that present special security problems.

Physical Accessibility

The large-scale, multi-user computer system represents a sizable investment and is usually provided with considerable physical and environmental protection. This helps ensure the system's reliability and the basic integrity of hardware and software. It is extremely unlikely, therefore, that damage or modifications to the system or its components can occur.

With personal computers, however, physical accessibility is not as easily controlled; indeed, accessibility is inherent in the concept of a "personal" computer. It is seldom necessary or economical to build a protective "shell" around an individual personal computer. This means that protection against damage or modification (either intentional or accidental) is difficult to prevent. Since many technical security mechanisms (e.g., access control software and cryptographic routines) are often dependent on the integrity of the underlying hardware and software, these security mechanisms alone may not provide the intended degree of protection.

Hardware Security Features

A second security problem with most personal computers is the lack of hardware mechanisms needed to isolate users from sensitive, security-related, system functions. For example, the typical personal computer does not support multiple processor states, privileged instructions, and memory protection features that have long been available on larger systems. Without such hardware features, it is virtually impossible to prevent user programs from intentionally or accidentally accessing or modifying parts of the operating system and thereby circumventing any intended security mechanisms.

Because of these two fundamental security weaknesses of personal computers (physical accessibility and lack of hardware security mechanisms), PC users should be wary of claims for products (particularly software) which provide "absolute" security.

It may be argued that a "personal" computer does not need such sophisticated security mechanisms and that the user need only remove and lock away any diskettes containing sensitive data. Indeed, this single-user concept is undoubtedly behind the general lack of security features in personal computers.

In the "real world," however, systems often are too expensive to be sitting idle on someone's desk and, therefore, often must be shared among several users. To compound matters, the introduction of fixed ("hard") disks for data storage makes it difficult or impractical for the user to remove all sensitive data from the system. Thus, personal computers do, indeed, present data sharing and, therefore, real security problems.

SPECIAL CONSIDERATIONS

There are many potential security problems associated with the use of personal computers. Many of them are obvious. However, it will be useful to highlight some of the more important and often overlooked security considerations.

Access Control

If we assume that the threat of theft or physical damage has been addressed, then a primary objective is to limit access to the data handled by the system. Two basic approaches are available to accomplish this: (a) encrypting the data; or (b) controlling physical access to the storage media. It should be noted, however, that the first approach only provides protection against unauthorized disclosure or undetected modification, since even encrypted data is easily destroyed. Critical data, therefore, cannot be protected simply by encrypting it.

The problems of controlling physical access are different for data stored on removable and those stored on fixed media. If the data are resident on removable media, then the simple lock-and-key approach will probably provide the most cost-effective solution. Encryption may be appropriate, however, if diskettes containing sensitive data cannot be protected in this manner (e.g., during shipment).

If data resides on nonremovable media (e.g., a hard disk), then preventing physical access to the media requires controlling access to the machine itself. There are several commercial products available to prevent physical access or use of the equipment. These include lockable enclosures and power switch locks. (For some reason, very few personal computer manufacturers provide a keylock integral to the equipment itself.)

If a given machine must be available for access by several users or cannot be physically locked up when not in use, then more extensive access controls must be considered. Although effective access control to the equipment usually can be provided during working hours (because people are present), this may be impractical at other times.

If equipment must be available for use by many people and cannot be monitored at all times, then hardware- or software-based security mechanisms should be considered. Such mechanisms can limit the type of access available to each user. This can range from limitations on the files which can be accessed to complete denial of system access. It is possible to set up very restricted application environments which will control the activities of all but the most determined of users. Special menu-oriented software and programs which execute automatically at system start-up can be combined to provide such an environment.

There are commercial products which are designed for this purpose, or users may develop such programs themselves, however, when such technical access control mechanisms are employed, it must be remembered that if a user has the opportunity to make modifications to the equipment (e.g., by removing or substituting circuit boards) or to the software (e.g., through programming or debugging facilities), then all bets are off. Nevertheless, such modifications often require "unusual" actions on the part of the user (e.g., opening up the cabinet), and can often be noticed by alert employees.

It should also be recognized that the type of constrained environment suggested above, except for certain well-defined and restricted applications, may negate the benefits for which the personal computer was originally acquired. It may be easier, cheaper, and more effective in the long run to put sensitive applications (i.e., those requiring special protection) on different computers.

Data Residue

Users inadvertently may leave sensitive "residue" on disk or even in memory. Such information often can be read by subsequent users. A common example of disk residue problem is associated with the "erasing" of disk files (e.g., with the ERASE or DELETE commands). This process usually results only in the setting of a "file deleted" indicator in the file directory—not the physical erasure or overwriting of the actual data. It is a simple matter to reset the "file deleted" indicator and thereby "unerase" the file. In fact, there are many available software utilities designed for exactly this purpose. It is dangerous, therefore, to pass files to other users on diskettes which contain "erased" files or sensitive data. The problem also exists for hard disks, since the data remains potentially accessible to subsequent users of the system. Users should also recognize that many programs they use may create and delete "scratch" files, which the user never sees. These files could contain sensitive information and are exposed to the same vulnerability.

This problem can be solved by using a program to "purge" (i.e., overwrite) all file data as part of the deletion process. This might be thought of as the equivalent of an "electronic burn bag." Although such programs are relatively easy to write, they are usually not provided as standard features of PC operating systems. Therefore, they must be acquired or written by the user. If such a utility is not available, then sensitive disk media should not be shared among users. If a fixed disk is used for such data, then the user has three options: use an overwrite utility, encrypt sensitive files, or do not share the system with other users.

Encryption

Much has been said about the value (and need for) encryption in personal computer systems. The majority of commercially-available security products are based entirely or in part on cryptographic protection. However, the PC user must understand the purpose and proper application of cryptography. Otherwise, there is a danger that the user may have security exposures not otherwise expected.

One purpose of the cryptography is to prevent unauthorized disclosure of data while it resides in (or passes through) an environment that cannot be physically protected (e.g., a diskette, a public communications line, or the airwaves). Cryptography also enables detection, but not prevention, of unauthorized modification of data. It does *not* protect against data destruction.

There are many commercially-available cryptographic products designed for PCs. However, these products are not solutions in themselves, and careful planning and evaluation is needed before acquiring them. A weak product or a poor implementation may provide little actual protection. The primary issues that must be addressed when considering the use of cryptography are key generation and management, protecting the integrity of the cryptographic facility itself, and the strength of the underlying algorithm. Most commercial products (whether implemented in hardware or software) do not address these issues to the extent necessary and leave these matters to the user. The following are some comments on these problems.

Key Management. The strength of cryptosystems is dependent on the quality, integrity, and secrecy of the keys used to encrypt and decrypt information. Therefore, such keys must be carefully selected, and they must be protected from unauthorized disclosure or modification. With many commercial cryptographic products for personal computers, it is the user's responsibility to generate and distribute cryptographic keys. This often can result in short or trivial ("weak") keys. In addition to this problem, most commercial products do not provide adequate mechanisms for transmitting and storing keys.

Process Integrity. Some products are implemented in part in software. If this software is modified (e.g., to substitute trivial keys), the basic integrity of the cryptographic process itself can be undermined. Even hardware-based products have some exposures if they use the system bus to pass information. However, these exposures are probably minimal for most applications.

Cryptographic Strength. To date, only one algorithm, the Federal Data Encryption Standard (DES), has undergone detailed examination and been established as a standard for use in U.S. Government (non National Security) and many private sector applications. Although other cryptosystems and algorithms are available, evaluating their cryptographic strength is beyond the ability of most users. Therefore, care should be taken before selecting such systems.

Contingency Planning

With a personal computer "on every desk," there is obviously a need to encourage regular and systematic backup of files, since such backup can no longer be done centrally and systematically as is possible with a large-scale system. Unfortunately, it often takes the loss of an important file before most users become "converts" to the need for regular backup.

Equipment backup must also be considered. Unfortunately, the growing number of identical or "compatible" personal computers in some organizations may lead users to believe that other types of contingency planning are not necessary. However, as application systems on personal computers become more complex, it becomes more difficult simply to move to another PC. Different equipment options, installation variations, and piracy protection mechanisms used in many popular software packages can make "portability" extremely difficult, if not planned in advance.

Auditability

It is questionable whether a single-user PC needs any special audit trail facilities except as an historical record and to aid in recovery from errors. However, designers of important applications will probably require audit trails, and some organizations may wish to monitor use of their personal computers by employees.

INFORMATION SYSTEMS AUDITING

Audit trail information can be recorded as part of an access control process such as those discussed earlier. However, designers should avoid dependence on the PC to provide a safe environment for the storage of such data. It may be too easy for a user to modify or delete such data. If access to a host system is involved, the *host* is the proper location for the placement of audit data capture mechanisms.

Electromagnetic Emanations

All electronic equipment emanates electromagnetic signals. For some equipment (e.g., computers, communication lines, and data terminals), these emanations may carry information that can be detected by appropriately placed monitoring devices. Security measures intended to combat this problem are known as the "Tempest" controls. Applications involving classified (National Security) data generally must be processed on equipment that has been specially shielded or modified to minimize emanations. Although the technical requirements for such shielding are classified, Tempest-certified equipment is available for purchase by non-defense users, at a considerable price premium. Except for classified applications, it is the user's responsibility to determine if the extra cost is justified.

Host System Access

The danger posed to host systems due to increasing availability of personal computers has received considerable attention lately. This is perhaps the greatest security concern expressed by managers regarding personal computers. Although there is certainly some reason for concern, it is important to recognize that almost no new host system security threats result directly from the use of personal computers.

Steinauer also notes that the use of PCs offers some security advantages despite the evident problems. For example, rather than applying strict controls over every user of a large multiuser system, it may be less expensive and more effective to put sensitive applications on their own small stand-alone systems. This offers isolation and security without the usual overhead necessary in larger environments.

IMPLICATIONS FOR AUDITORS

The I/S environment previously described has several implications for auditors, which are noted in the following paragraphs.

Impact of Errors

Because computers do exactly what they are told to do at high speed, errors in programming and processing can have more extensive consequences than is the case in non-I/S environments. As a result, the specially designed processing controls must be tested and evaluated by the auditor.

Access Techniques

In an I/S environment, all information is stored in machine-readable form at the data processing center. This affects the way in which the auditor accesses the information in which he is interested. In non-EDP functions, records and data are easily retrieved and read. EDP records, however, must first be converted from machine language to a language understandable to the auditor. This requires assistance either in the form of audit software or other EDP-supplied aid.

Specialized Knowledge

I/S controls and processing techniques involve specialized technical knowledge. Auditors must possess as much of this knowledge as possible in order to function effectively. It has been said that contemporary auditors should view themselves as the mirror image of the systems analyst (the person responsible for designing computer-based accounting systems) in the same way that traditional auditors may be thought of as the mirror image of the accountant.[21]

Audit Techniques

Evidence-gathering techniques must accommodate the nature of EDP. Often, this works to the advantage of the auditor. The computer can be programmed to do much of the auditor's work, with the advantages of speed and accuracy. Many forms of generalized audit software have been developed for this reason. The reliability of the auditor's work can be enhanced considerably by this process. On the other hand, many computer routines leave no audit trail that evidences their operations. In these situations, the auditor must devise specialized forms of testing. Examples include test decks, integrated test facilities, and embedded audit routines. Chapter 28 discusses these techniques in greater detail.

Independence

In non-EDP situations, the auditor is able to perform his work with a minimum of assistance from the audited entity. Most EDP audit routines are dependent on EDP personnel to execute them. Examples include generalized audit software, test decks, and transaction tagging. Even simple file dumps require the assistance of the EDP department. The auditor must bear this in mind in considering the reliability of the evidence gathered via the com-

---

[21] Joseph Sardinas, John G. Burch, and Richard Asebrook, *EDP Auditing, A Primer* (New York: John Wiley & Sons, 1981), p. 9.

puter. At times, he may wish to devise corroborative tests to provide assurance that the information obtained has not been altered and is a true representation of the original information.

Changing Technology

Auditors are accustomed to changing conditions. However, the rapid rate of EDP technological change requires an extra effort by those involved to keep pace. Thus, the investment in research and training must be more extensive than is required in traditional auditing.

SUMMARY

Despite its relatively recent origin, computer processing has swiftly progressed to the point where it affects virtually all business functions and objectives. The experts predict that the future promises an even greater role of computers affecting not only business, but mankind as well.

Internal accounting control objectives remain the same with or without computers. The computer's presence, however, requires special underlying objectives and control techniques to preserve the broad accounting objectives. EDP objectives and control techniques vary, depending on the same factors that affect internal control environments in general.

Finally, the existence of EDP poses implications for auditors in terms of their requisite knowledge, controls evaluation, access techniques, audit techniques, and independence. Chapters 27 and 28 explain I/S auditing in the context of these implications.

COMPUTER CRIME—A SPECIAL PERSPECTIVE

One of the most commonly cited risks associated with computers is that of computer crime. The term has come to encompass a broad variety of dishonest acts in which the computer is either an unwitting accomplice or a defenseless victim.

In recent years, the news media has sensationalized a handful of embezzlements and frauds in which computers had a role. Ask the average business executive to name the most famous computer crime and the answer will invariably be Equity Funding. Some might also cite the $12 million theft perpetrated by Stanley Rifkin on the Security Pacific National Bank.

It is noteworthy that neither of these is really a computer crime. The Equity Funding incident was much more complex than a simple computer crime. In fact, the computer was not even involved until late in the management-perpetrated fraud. The Rifkin theft involved stealing special codes, which were then used to move sums totaling in excess of $12 million to an account designated by Rifkin. While accessing and using the bank's computer was essential to the theft, so was the availability of internal flight service to facilitate the "get away."

These instances illustrate the difficulty in identifying and measuring computer crime. If every instance in which a computer is a part of a crime is counted as a computer crime, a perception will emerge (if it hasn't already) that the computer is too dangerous an instrument to permit realization of its full potential. Such thinking could have doomed the automobile or the airplane in the early stages of their development.

To be sure, computer crime is a problem that must be recognized and controlled to the extent practicable. However, the truth of the matter is that there are millions of computers in existence in the United States alone, many of which operate in a multishift mode. The number of operations (the effective running of a given application) executed to date must number in the billions. Against that background, computer abuse cases are thought to number in the thousands. Even if this represented only one percent of actual crimes committed but undetected, the total number is a minute fraction of the number of proper operations. This perspective must be borne in mind when contemplating the costs and benefits of preventive- and detective-type controls designed specifically with computer crime in mind. Moreover, certain business segments are more likely to be the target of most criminal efforts. These include banks, insurance companies, government agencies, and others whose operations involve large amounts of cash flow and consumable merchandise.

Continued formal research into this subject is necessary in order to bring the matter into proper perspective. However, from a practical standpoint, there appears to be a widespread and justifiable belief among those within the EDP community that the exposure has been overstated.

On the other hand, company managements in general, and data processing managers in particular, must not take the threat of computer crimes lightly. The risk of such acts must be constantly assessed in the light of each application and computer operation. When risks appear too great, methods must be devised to minimize them with the realization that absolute prevention is unattainable. This process of continuous vigilance and adaptability offers the most practical approach for dealing effectively with computer crime. Chapter 25 provides a complete discussion of computer crime.

GLOSSARY

access time—(1) the time interval between the instant at which data are called for from a storage device and when they are moved to the central processing unit (e.g., the read time). (2) the time interval between the instant at which data is to be stored and the instant at which storage is completed (e.g., the write time).

address—the code used to designate a specific piece of data within computer storage.

analog computer—a device that performs computations by using a nondiscrete representation, such as variations in voltage.

analog transmission—transmission of continuously variable signals, as distinguished from discretely variable signals.

application—the system or problem to which a computer is applied; a computer-based information system for source transaction origination, data processing, record keeping, and report preparation.

assembler—a machine language program that accepts instructions from a source program and produces machine language instructions. Generally, one machine instruction is produced for each symbolic instruction.

asynchronous transmission—transmission in which time intervals between transmitted characters vary. Start and stop bits at the beginning and ending of each character differentiate each transmitted character.

auditability—verifiable features and characteristics of an information system that allow the accuracy and completeness of data processing results to be audited.

backup—files, equipment, and procedures that are available if the originals are destroyed or out of service.

batch processing—a type of application system where homogenous transactions to be processed are collected into groups and concentrated for processing into a brief span of time.

baud—a unit of signaling speed (modulation rate) equal to the number of code elements per second.

binary synchronous communication—an IBM communications protocol originated in 1968, which is now an industry standard. It uses control character sequences for synchronized transmissions of binary data between stations in a data communication system. Also called Bisync.

bit—an on-or-off state in storage, representing the binary digits 0 and 1.

buffer storage—a computer device that stores information temporarily during data transfers from the computer to an input or output device, for the purpose of increasing the throughput of the computer.

bug—a mistake in the logic of a computer program or in the wiring of a circuit.

byte—a set of eight adjacent bits that can be used to represent one alphanumeric character or two decimal digits.

cathode-ray tube (CRT)—a device similar to a television screen on which data can be displayed.

check digit—a digit that is a function of the other digits within a word or number used for testing an accurate transcription.

check point—a specific predetermined point in major programs where a recording of the contents of memory, including all registers, etc., is made for restart purposes.

COBOL—an acronym standing for Common Business Oriented Language, a high-level program language oriented toward business information or data processing problems, as distinguished from engineering, mathematical, or scientific problems.

coding—(1) successive program instructions that direct the computer to execute a particular routine. Also, the act of preparing the code. (2) the recording of values of characters having meanings that are not evident in the code.

common carrier—in data processing, a company that rents or leases transmission lines for communication purposes (e.g., Western Union or AT&T).

compile—to either transform a source program into an assembly language form for subsequent assembly to machine language by the assembler or to directly transform the source program into an equivalent machine language program.

compiler—a computer program that compiles object or machine language instructions from source language statements.

communication protocol—a set of rules that controls information flow on a data link.

console—a component of the computer used for communication and control by operators or maintenance engineers. It usually contains a typewriter keyboard and either a cathode-ray tube or a typewriter printer.

control register (log)—a log or register indicating the disposition and control values of batches or transactions.

data—any representation, such as characters or analog quantities, used to denote alpha, numeric, alphanumeric, and symbolic information.

data base—a structured collection of data items that are related to an enterprise's operations, such as the financial data base, or the customer data base and that is maintained separately from the applications that use it.

data base management system (DBMS)—a set of integrated software routines developed to create, maintain, and control access to a data base. The DBMS handles the mechanics of storing, updating, and accessing the data, thereby allowing the application programmer to view a logical collection of data elements as a file and reducing the programmer's concern with the physical form or structure of these data items.

data dictionary—a structured collection of information elements that define and describe the data elements associated with one or more data bases. Ideally, the dictionary/directory defines each data base and describes its

INFORMATION SYSTEMS AUDITING

attributes related to identification, representation, relationship, security, integrity, and so forth.

data processing—a generic term for all the operations carried out on data or information according to precise rules or procedures. In recent years, it has been generally applied to business-related computer processing.

data storage—a device that stores machine-readable data in a machine-readable media, such as on cards, magnetic tape, or disks.

demodulation—the process of retrieving information from a modulated carrier wave.

digital computer—a computer that processes information represented by combinations of discrete numeric values, in contrast to an analog computer.

direct access—data access method that obtains information from a location in a storage device, such as a disk, without reading the information that precedes it. (Contrast with serial or sequential access.)

direct access storage device—a device in which data are stored so as to permit direct access, such as a magnetic disk device. (Contrast with a serial access device, such as magnetic tape.)

disaster recovery plan—a formal document that describes the manner in which data processing services can be restored following damage or destruction of equipment, data, or facilities.

distributive (distributed) processing—an arrangement of computers within an organization that has several separate computer facility locations. The computers are interconnected to work in a cooperative manner rather than autonomously, as in the instances of conventional single-location facilities.

dump—a printed record of the contents of computer storage usually produced for diagnostic purposes.

edit (noun)—an input control for detecting input data that are inaccurate, incomplete, or unreasonable. This function can be performed either manually or by computer, either before or during regular processing. (verb) To rearrange data for the purpose of clarifying content.

EDP—electronic data processing—a commonly used term for the organized employment of specialized facilities, electronic equipment, programs, systems, procedures, and personnel for the purpose of creating, changing, executing, or storing data in an organized and controlled fashion, by automated methods for specific purposes and uses. Synonymous with information systems (I/S).

field—a set of one or more characters established in a program to provide for the storage or collection of a unit of information for processing (e.g., customer name and inventory quantity).

file (noun)—an organized collection of information or data for some specific purpose, such as an employee's salary file or raw material inventory file. A file may be in the form of a magnetic tape, magnetic disk, or punched cards and may be in alphabetic sequence, numeric sequence, or in a purely random form.

front-end processor—a communications computer, often a minicomputer linked to a mainframe computer, which usually performs communication protocol control.

generalized audit software—computer programs primarily intended to facilitate the access of data or information stored on computer files. Such programs generally provide facilities for random selection, extraction, performance of mathematical functions, and listing.

hardware—the physical equipment or devices that comprise a computer system, including mechanical, magnetic, electrical, and electronic devices, such as central processing unit, card reader, tape drives, disk files, and printers.

hash total—a total developed from accumulated numerical amounts of nonmonetary information used for purposes of control.

header—a control prefix in a message containing source or destination address.

in line—(See *on-line system*.)

input—information or data transferred or to be transferred from an external source into the internal storage of the computer.

interface—a common boundary between automatic data processing systems or parts of a single system.

I/S—information systems—the procedures, techniques, and facilities employed in each function of an enterprise to gather, file, process, store, and analyze data for use in the operation and management of an enterprise. See also EDP.

job control language (JCL)—a series of machine-readable program instructions (card or disk file) that are recognizable to the operating system of the computer and that are used to assign the resources (e.g., tape drives) required for a job, identify the files to be used, and initiate the execution of an application program. The JCL forms the interface between the program to be executed and the operating system, which monitors the allocation and use of resources.

label, external—a specialized record used to identify an assorted collection of data, such as a paper label attached to a reel of magnetic tape to identify its contents, or a label card to identify a box of cards, etc.

label, internal—a record magnetically recorded on tape to identify its contents as an integral part of the program function.

library—a facility for storing punched cards, magnetic tapes, and disks used in computer processing, in order to provide a measure of control over these items so that they can be easily retrieved as required and guarded against loss or destruction.

limit check—tests of specified amount fields against stipulated high or low limits of acceptability. When both high and low values are used, the test may be called a range check.

load module—a computer program that has been converted into a machine executable format.

log—any one of various types of records on paper or machine-readable media, which evidence particular transactions, activities, events, operating instructions, etc., sequenced in the order they occurred. Examples include machine logs and batch control logs.

machine language—instructions written in a form that is intelligible to the internal circuitry of a computer. Usually each computer or family of computers has a unique language of its own.

magnetic tape—refers to a tape made of nylon or plastic, coated or impregnated with magnetic material, on which alphabetic or numeric characters can be represented in code form by means of polarized spots.

master file—a file of semipermanent information that is used frequently for processing data, or for more than one purpose, such as a master customer file that may be used for invoicing purposes, accounts receivable purposes, or sales statistics.

matching—matching of items from the processing stream of an application with others developed independently so as to identify items unprocessed through either of the parallel systems.

memory—an organization of storage units within the computer, characterized by rapid data access rates.

merge—to combine two files into one.

microfiche—computer output microfilm sheets containing rows of microimages of pages of printed matter.

modem—an acronym for modulator/demodulator, meaning a device used to convert serial digital signals to an analog signal suitable for transmission over a telephone or other telecommunications channel, and to reconvert the signal to serial digital signals for acceptance by a receiving terminal.

modulation—the process by which some characteristic of one signal is varied in accordance with another signal.

multiprocessor (multiprocessing)—a computer capable of being able to handle more than one program at the same time. The simultaneous operation of more than one set of processing circuitry within a single computer.

network—an interconnection of computer systems, terminals, and communications facilities.

object code—machine instructions produced from a compiler or assembler program that accepts source language.

object program—a computer program composed of object language instructions.

on-line system—a computer system that maintains files of information in a form that is immediately accessible for either the acceptance of input transactions or the displaying and/or reporting of information through a terminal device that is connected to the main computer system.

operating system—a programmed package provided by the equipment supplier designed to provide the user a facility for scheduling, controlling, and obtaining maximum efficiency of the computer and peripheral equipment. These routines and procedures normally perform some or all of the following functions: (1) scheduling, loading, initiating, and supervising the execution of programs; (2) allocating storage, input/output units, and other facilities of the computer system; (3) initiating and controlling input/output operations; (4) handling errors and restarts; (5) coordinating communications between the human operator and the computer system; (6) maintaining a log of systems operations; and (7) controlling operations in a multiprogramming, multiprocessing, or time-sharing mode. Among the facilities frequently included within an operating system are an executive routine, a scheduler, input/output routines, utility routines, and monitor routines.

operator (operating) instructions—instructions usually prepared by the programmer to inform the computer operator precisely how programs are to be run on the computer, that is, which files are required, what the input is and where it is to come from, the manner in which console switches should be set, the details of halt procedures, which output forms are required, and other program characteristics.

optical scanner—a device that optically scans printed or written data and converts it to machine-sensible form for processing by a computer under appropriate program control.

output—products of a computer system, such as CRT display, printed reports, punched cards, and data sets.

padding—the completion of a block of data with meaningless characters so as to make it the prescribed size.

password—an access restriction technique, using a unique combination of characters known only by a specific user that identifies him to the computer in order to gain access to computer-controlled data from a terminal.

patch—to correct or to modify a computer program by directly altering the object code.

peripheral equipment—the auxiliary storage units of a computer used for input and output of data. All components of a computer other than the central processing unit and core storage.

processing—functions performed electronically by a computer system, such as input, calculating, sorting, storing, and reporting.

program (noun)—The complete sequence of machine instructions and routines necessary to accomplish a given task on a computer. (verb) To plan the method or procedures for accomplishing a task, including the drawing of flow charts and the writing of the instructions referred to as coding.

program language—a source language used to define operations that can be compiled or assembled by software into machine instructions.

programmer—an individual who prepares source language computer programs.

queue—the sequence of tasks in a (computer) job stream awaiting execution.

random access—a manner of storing records in a file so that an individual record may be accessed without reading other records. Also known as direct access.

real time—a computer system that can respond immediately to an inquiry or a command. The performance of a computer process in sufficient time to guide the process (connotes on-line, multiprogramming environments).

record—a group of related fields of information treated as a unit (e.g., an individual employee's information in a payroll master file).

record count—a control that can be included in the program to establish accuracy of processing whereby the number of records is counted before and after processing to protect against loss of a complete record.

recording—the registering of data or information in a reproducible form on magnetic tape or other media.

response time—the elapsed time between the generation of the last character of a message at a terminal and the receipt of the first character of the reply. It includes terminal network and data processing delay.

report file—a machine-readable file containing records that may be directly printed to constitute a report.

rerun—partial or complete reprocessing of a computer run as a result of an error, condition, or defective results.

restart—to go back to a specific checkpoint in a routine, usually because of machine malfunction, for the purpose of rerunning all processing subsequent to the checkpoint or commencement of the program.

routines—a set of coded instructions arranged in proper sequence to direct a computer to carry out a specific desired operation or sequence of operations (e.g., a sort routine).

RPG—abbreviation for report program generator. A high-level computer language designed particularly to facilitate the rapid preparation of reports.

run—one performance of a program on a computer or of several routines linked so that they constitute a complete operation during which manual manipulations are not required of the computer operator. For example, an invoice print run where invoice data are read from a magnetic tape file and printed out on invoice forms.

run manual—a document describing the operating instructions for one or more computer programs within an application system.

run-to-run totals—the utilization of output control totals resulting from one process as input control totals over subsequent processing. The control totals are used as links in a chain to tie one process to another in a sequence of processes, or one cycle to another over a period of time.

self-checking digit—(See *check digit*.)

sequence checking—a verification of the alphanumeric sequence of the "key" field in items to be processed.

serial access—data stored in a manner where all preceding records must be accessed sequentially to locate a specific record (contrasts with random or direct access).

simulator—a computer program that imitates the consequences produced in a real-world environment by variable conditions.

software—all levels of computer programs that control the operation of hardware. Also, the programming aids and programs available for a computer (including library routines, operating systems, assembly routines, utility routines, compilers and application programs), some of which are provided by the suppliers of the equipment while others may be developed by the user or purchased from "software houses."

sort—to arrange items or records in a given sequence.

source code (language)—a computer language used by a programmer and submitted to a translation process to produce object instructions. Examples include COBOL, Basic, and P/L-1.

source document—a document originated for purposes of transmitting source transaction data to the computer; that is, a customer order could serve as a source document for an invoicing, inventory, and accounts receivable computer system.

storage—pertaining to an area of a computer or a peripheral device in which data can be electronically stored and from which it can be obtained at a later time. (Synonymous with the term "memory.")

storage protection—a provision by the software to protect against unauthorized or inadvertent reading or writing between or during intervals of storage.

subroutine—a routine that may be recurringly called on to perform a defined process.

synchronous transmission—transmission in which the data characters and bits are transmitted at a fixed rate with the transmitter and receiver synchronized. This eliminates the need for start/stop elements.

system—a broad term to designate an arrangement of entities that form an organized whole. Generally accompanied by a modifier, such as computer system, application system, and operating system.

system analysis—the analysis of a business activity or computer application system to determine its purpose, function (precisely what must be accomplished), and how, where, and when the function is to be accomplished.

system design (designer)—a person who develops the specifications for new data processing or business information systems.

system programmer—a programmer responsible for implementing upgrades to operating systems and other general systems software and maintaining revisions or modifications to such systems.

tape label check—a programmed check, prior to processing, to ensure that the correct tape file is being used.

telecommunications—the electronic transmission of data over a long distance by means of telephone lines, microwave, satellite, or other medium.

teleprocessing—a form of information handling utilizing telecommunications equipment that may be directly linked with a computer.

terminal—a device used to communicate with a computer.

throughput—a measurement of the amount of useful work performed by a computer system during a given period.

time-sharing—a technique of computer operations that permits a large number of individual users to access general-purpose computer services concurrently.

track—the ring-shaped surface of a disk or drum or the segment of a magnetic tape running parallel to its edge.

trailer label—a record providing a control total of records processed for comparison with accumulated counts or values.

transaction file—a machine-readable file containing transient information that will cause changes to a master file during a file maintenance or updating process.

turnaround time—a measurement of the actual time required to reverse the direction of transmission from sender to receiver or vice versa when using a half-duplex circuit.

validity check—an automatic matching of the characters in a coded field to an acceptable set of values in a table or for a defined pattern of format, legitimate subcodes, or character values, using logic and arithmetic rather than tables.

variable-length record—a machine-readable record that may contain a variable number of fields. (Contrast with fixed-length record.)

voice frequency—any frequency within that part of the audiofrequency range (300–3400 Hz) essential for the transmission of speech of commercial quality.

wideband—communications channel, having a band width greater than a voice-grade channel, characterized by data transmission speeds of 10,000–500,000 bits per second.

SUGGESTED READING

Connor, Joseph E., and Burnell H. DeVos, Jr., eds. *Guide to Accounting Controls.* New York: Price Waterhouse & Co., 1979.

Davis, Keagle W., and William E. Perry. *Auditing Computer Applications,* Chapters 1–3. New York: John Wiley & Sons, 1982.

Doll, Dixon R. *Data Communications Facilities, Networks, and System Design,* Chapter 1. New York: John Wiley & Sons, 1978.

EDP Auditors Foundation. *Control Objectives—1980.* U.S.A.: EDP Auditors Foundation, 1980.

Fitzgerald, Jerry. *Internal Controls for Computerized Systems.* U.S.A.: Jerry Fitzgerald, 1978.

Halper, Stanley D., P. Jarlath O'Neil-Dunne, and Xenia Ley Parker. *Handbook of EDP Auditing.* Copyright by Coopers & Lybrand (United States), 1985, 1986, 1987, published by Warren, Gorham & Lamont.

Mair, William C., et al. *Computer Control & Audit.* U.S.A.: Touche Ross & Co., 1976.

Martin James. *Security, Accuracy and Privacy in Computer Systems.* Englewood Cliffs, New Jersey: Prentice-Hall, Inc., 1973.

Study Group on Computer Control and Audit Guidelines. *Computer Control Guidelines.* Toronto, Canada: The Canadian Institute of Chartered Accountants, 1975.

Systems Auditability and Control, Control Practices. Altamonte Springs, Fla.: The Institute of Internal Auditors, 1977.

Willson, James D., and Jack F. Duston. *Financial Information Systems Manual.* Boston: Warren, Gorham & Lamont, 1986, Chapters 1, 2, and 10 by Steven J. Root.

CHAPTER **27**

How to Establish and Maintain an Information Systems (EDP) Audit Function

Role of Internal Auditing	2	Selling	40
Concern of Management	2		
Response by Auditors	2	**Project Management**	42
Objectives of I/S Auditing	4	Auditing Manuals	42
		Use of Questionnaires and	
I/S Audit Approach	4	Checklists	42
Determining What to Audit	4	Specific Project Authorization and	
Relationship to Basic Internal Auditing		Monitoring	44
Approach	5	Quality Control	45
Types of I/S Auditing	5		
Detailed Functional Auditing	5	**Management of Personnel**	45
Installation Reviews	6	Recruiting	45
Applications Auditing	22	Performance Measurement	46
Developing Systems Auditing	22	Professional Training	47
Concurrent Auditing	23		
Integrated Test Facilities	29	**Management of Personal Computers**	51
Embedded Audit Data Collection ...	29	Automated Workpapers	53
Snapshot/Extended Record	30	Implementation Strategy	57
Other Audit Forms	32		
Prioritizing I/S Audit Projects	32	**Performing I/S Audits**	58
Suggestions for Allocating Audit		Applicability of Basic Audit	
Resources	33	Approach	58
		Preliminary Work	58
Managing the I/S Audit Function	35	Fieldwork	59
Standards	35	Documentation	59
Organizing and Planning I/S Audits	36	Evidential Matter	60
Organizing	36		
Planning	39	**Suggested Reading**	62

Fig. 27-1	Top Management's Data Processing Concerns	3
Fig. 27-2	Questionnaire to Evaluate Controls in an EDP Installation	7
Fig. 27-3	Portion of a Developing System Control Questionnaire	24
Fig. 27-4	Flow Chart of the Snapshot Audit Technique	31
Fig. 27-5	Depiction of the Extended Record Technique	32

Fig. 27-6	Frequencies for I/S Audits	34
Fig. 27-7	Code of Professional Ethics	36
Fig. 27-8	General Standards for Information Systems Auditing	37
Fig. 27-9	Typical I/S Audit Function Organization Chart	39
Fig. 27-10	Excerpt of a Policy Statement Setting Forth I/S Audit Responsibility	40
Fig. 27-11	Audit Manual Contents Page—Excerpt Covering I/S Auditing	43
Fig. 27-12	Audit Software Packages and Vendors	55
Fig. 27-13	Spreadsheet Software	56
Fig. 27-14	Statistical Sampling Computer Report	61

ROLE OF INTERNAL AUDITING

Concern of Management

To understand the role of the internal auditing function in an information systems (I/S) environment, it is first necessary to understand management's EDP concerns. A survey published by the IIA in 1977 indicates that the principal management concern is insufficient internal control.[1] (See Figure 27-1.) Other concerns included the complexity of data processing, insufficient user involvement, lack of standards, and exposure to fraud. A more recent survey published by the Research Foundation of the FEI suggests that, if anything, the concern is growing. That survey disclosed the increasing dependence of companies on computers for operational effectiveness as the aspect of internal control that troubles management executives most.[2] The study cited the increased internal control risks compounded by a shortage of trained data processing and internal auditing personnel as contributing factors. In the years since 1980, little has occurred.

Response by Auditors

It is clear that efforts are being made by both management and internal auditors to deal with this concern. Management has allocated significant resources in recent years to increase internal controls. Also, manufacturers of computer hardware and software have made significant strides in designing controls into new generations of computer hardware and software. System availability and control has become a selling point in marketing strategy for many vendors.

Auditors, too, have responded. The number of auditors skilled in EDP

---

[1] From *Systems Auditability and Control Study—Data Processing Audit Practices Report* (Stanford Research Institute, 1977), p. 16. Copyright © 1977 by the Institute of Internal Auditors, Inc., 249 Maitland Avenue, Altamonte Springs, Fla. 32701, U.S.A. Reprinted with permission.

[2] Robert K. Mautz et al., *Internal Control in U.S. Corporations, The State of the Art* (New York: Financial Executives Research Foundation, 1980), p. 8.

FIG. 27-1
Top Management's Data Processing Concerns

What are your *two* major concerns about data processing in your organization? (Check two)	Percentage of Total*	Percentage of Organizations With Major Concerns Selecting Each Category*†
Organizations indicating no major concerns	5.3%	
Organizations indicating two of the following concerns	94.7	
Insufficient controls		39.4%
Complexity of data processing		29.5
Insufficient user involvement		25.1
Lack of data processing standards		23.9
Exposure to fraud		21.3
Lack of adequate independent review		19.8
Inadequate return on investment		17.1
Other		13.3

Note: Number of respondents = 221

* Percentages are based on actual responses weighted to reflect the probable response distribution of all organizations in the sampling frame. See the appendix for further description of weighting procedures.

† Percentages sum to 189.4% = 2 × 94.7% because respondents with major concerns checked two categories.

auditing has more than tripled during the past 10 years. The professional competence of these auditors has also increased, resulting in part from the body of literature dealing with the subject that has emerged in the last five years. Also, new and powerful audit tools have been developed that greatly leverage the work of the auditor, enabling much more extensive and reliable auditing to occur. Despite these improvements, however, most internal auditing functions are still in a catch-up mode. The incredible pace at which EDP is evolving will make catching up very challenging and probably very costly.

These positive developments must be viewed against the accelerating pace of technological change and the application of those changes to specific functional situations. The result has been not only an expansion in both the number and types of EDP applications but also a decentralization of the responsibility control of those applications. On balance, then, management continues to be concerned about I/S and data processing. In fact, evidence suggests that the dependence on I/S can have strategic consequences if not properly managed.

As an example, in 1987, a major western bank was forced to terminate its Trust Department record-keeping services. This service featured an I/S using the most up-to-date technology. It cost several million dollars to develop and install. A combination of circumstances and events adversely affected the development effort. The result was a system that failed to keep accurate records of the many trust accounts of the bank's clientele. Ultimately, the fiasco cost the bank $80 million and the loss of a major source of bank revenue. Many bank executives and other employees lost their jobs.

Objectives of I/S Auditing

Chapter 2 establishes the objectives of internal auditing. Briefly, internal auditing fulfills its role when it serves the organization's interests. It follows, then, that to meet management's EDP concerns, an audit approach must be designed to provide information regarding the sufficiency of controls to reasonably assure:

- Accurate and complete processing of data.
- Safeguarding of EDP assets, including data.
- Efficient and effective EDP operations.
- Development and maintenance of systems that satisfy user requirements.

How these objectives may be met is discussed in the balance of this chapter.

I/S AUDIT APPROACH

Determining What to Audit

Because of the unique information systems environment described in the preceding chapter, involving a rapidly changing and technically complex set of operating conditions, many internal auditors have found developing an overall information systems audit approach to be difficult initially. However, as experience is gained, most audit managements find it beneficial to devise an approach that can be planned, organized, staffed, directed, and controlled—just as is done with traditional audits—and that fulfills the organization's needs.

Since the size of EDP operations varies from small minicomputer systems to extremely large networks of computers, peripheral equipment, telecommunication devices, and data terminals, the size and skill level of the I/S audit function varies. However, regardless of size and complexity, all EDP systems share a common fundamental objective—to process data accurately and completely in a secure environment. (See Chapter 26.) In recognition of this fact, the vast majority of I/S audit functions may be approached from an auditing standpoint by applying a combination of audit types.

INFORMATION SYSTEMS (EDP) AUDIT FUNCTION

Relationship to Basic Internal Auditing Approach

The approach to internal auditing illustrated in Chapter 2 is not altered by the presence of EDP—a point initially made in that chapter. Thus, the I/S auditing objectives stated in the preceding sections are compatible with the basic internal auditing objectives of providing assurance and information with respect to internal controls, operational efficiency, standards of ethical conduct, and accuracy of information.

Another point made in Chapter 2 having to do with setting priorities also carries over to I/S. There is such a vast array of functions, applications, installations, and developing systems in most medium to large companies and governmental units that a method of prioritizing must be devised. There are several practical methods for deciding what should be audited. A brief discussion of one method later in this chapter sufficiently illustrates the concept.

Types of I/S Auditing

Four basic types of auditing that have gained broad acceptance among I/S auditors are discussed in this section to illustrate the basic point that an overall or strategic approach will best assure effective and efficient auditing. They are (1) detailed functional auditing, (2) installation reviews, (3) applications auditing, and (4) developing systems auditing.

In addition, program verifications and post-implementation audits are also covered. Another form of I/S auditing that has gained importance in recent years—concurrent auditing—is also introduced. It is explained further in Chapter 28.

Detailed Functional Auditing

Detailed functional audits are comparable to the detailed internal control audits discussed in Chapter 18. They may be defined as audits that focus on the internal controls of a single functional aspect of the EDP operation. Examples include audits of such I/S functions as systems programming, data base administration, system hardware and software selection and procurement, applications programming, tape management, documentation control, and security.

Each detailed functional audit is individually planned and performed pursuant to written audit programs. Internal control evaluation is documented either by specially designed questionnaires or by individually designed spreadsheets relating controls and objectives. (See Chapter 18.)

The objective of detailed functional audits is to provide assurance and information to management regarding the internal controls of that particular function. With proper planning and project monitoring, these audits may be performed by a single, experienced auditor within periods ranging from two weeks to three months, depending on complexity.

Some functional areas do not, as a general rule, require extensive technical knowledge. Examples include cost control, budgeting, long-range planning, and the development and maintenance of standards, policies, and procedures. These areas could be assigned to traditional auditors. Among other advantages, this enables traditional auditors to be exposed to the I/S function and saves the more technically oriented staff members for more appropriate work.

Other functional areas require considerable technical knowledge to perform credibly. These include the operating system, telecommunications, and data base management systems.

Installation Reviews

Installation reviews are akin to the internal control surveys that are discussed in Chapter 18. By way of definition, installation reviews may be thought of as audits that survey all important control techniques for each function within a given EDP facility. It resembles the type of general review performed by external auditors under GAAS. There is one important difference, however. External auditors determine the scope of their review by considering the extent to which they plan to use and rely on the EDP controls in their audit of financial statements. Internal auditors need not be concerned about reliability in this context, since they do not certify financial statements for external use. However, reliability would need to be considered if the internal auditor planned to make use of the system for some purpose, such as in performing computer-assisted audit techniques. (See Chapter 28.)

Installation reviews are an effective means of reviewing controls of small- to medium-sized stand-alone EDP installations. The objective is to provide assurance and information regarding internal controls in effect for the installation taken as a whole. The work scope is susceptible to standardization. A single comprehensive internal control questionnaire may be devised that can be used on a recurring basis to evaluate controls. An illustration of such a questionnaire is shown in Figure 27-2. The number of controls tested is usually less than in detailed functional audits due to time constraints. However, key general controls and input, processing, and output controls may be effectively tested within a two- to four-week period by experienced auditors.

It is best to use auditors who possess considerable knowledge of information systems and EDP to perform these reviews. That is because the judgments are not usually based on the type of exhaustive review and testing that would enable less knowledgeable auditors to produce results of suitable quality. Instead, skill and experience are relied on as the principal tools to

(continued on page 27–22)

INFORMATION SYSTEMS (EDP) AUDIT FUNCTION

FIG. 27-2

Questionnaire to Evaluate Controls in an EDP Installation

The attached questionnaire was developed to evaluate the internal controls in electronic data-processing (EDP) installations. It is intended to evidence the determination of the sufficiency to which such internal controls provide reasonable assurance that:

- Information is processed accurately and completely.
- Information-processing activities are properly authorized, recorded, and reported.
- Information-processing activities and operations are efficiently and economically performed.
- Information-processing facilities, including all equipment, software, data files, and documentation, are appropriately safeguarded.

This questionnaire is intended to be completed each year for each location where EDP activities of significance to the location's operations occur. EDP installations of lesser significance should be evaluated by use of this questionnaire at least once every three years.

The facility serving the Southern operating units is too large and complex for this questionnaire alone. Supplemental questionnaires have been developed to serve as a more comprehensive evaluation for the various functions and activities that make up the I/S organization. It is intended that these supplemental questionnaires be completed at least once every three years. The supplements are as follows:

- Planning and budgetary control
- Cost and billing control
- System development control
- Program maintenance control
- Library control
- Data base management system control
- Operating system control
- Data conversion control
- Telecommunications control
- Facilities and equipment acquisition and utilization control
- Software acquisition and utilization control
- Physical security control
- Data security control
- Disaster recovery control

The supplements are designed to be completed in connection with completion of the specific audit projects to which they relate. In other words, each supplemental topic represents a separate audit project. Additional supplements may be developed as circumstances require.

It was not practicable to design this questionnaire so that every question focuses on a specific control, although in many instances that is the case. Because techniques can and do vary, it was necessary in many other instances to focus on a control area as opposed to a specific control. For example, a question may ask if there are "control techniques to reasonably assure that written instructions for preparing source documents are available." A "yes" answer would mean that such control techniques exist. In these instances, the auditor must supplement the questionnaire with spread sheets that identify all of the specific controls in effect. Spread sheets that follow the format used on internal control surveys should be used.

Examples of control techniques are identified for many of the questions which focus only upon a control area. The intent in these instances is to increase the auditor's understanding of the nature of the question. The examples are not intended to be all-inclusive.

Initial completion of this questionnaire may require considerable effort because it

(continued)

FIG. 27-2 *(cont'd)*

involves all facets of an EDP center's activities. To the extent possible, the auditor should seek the assistance of the EDP center personnel and management in completing it. One technique that can be employed is to provide the questionnaire to the EDP center management for their completion in advance of the fieldwork. The accuracy of the responses must be tested by the auditor during the course of performing the fieldwork, regardless of who completes the questionnaire.

If the auditor elects to obtain responses, he may find that responses to certain of the questions may be available from sources other than the EDP installation. This is particularly true where the supplemental questionnaires may provide much useful information. In addition, responses may be available from the external auditors' questionnaires. In these situations, the auditor should incorporate this relevant work to the extent deemed useful in the circumstances.

CORPORATE INTERNAL AUDIT
EDP QUESTIONNAIRE

Completed by: _____   Date: _____

General Information:

1. Division/Subsidiary name:
   Location:
   _____
   _____
   _____ Zip _____

2. I/S organization title (attach I/S organization chart):
   _____

3. Who is in charge of the I/S function?
   Name _____
   Title _____

4. What is the annual budget of this I/S organization?
   Amount _____

5. Indicate number of I/S personnel:
   Supervision   _____
   Systems & programming   _____
   Operations   _____
   Data entry   _____
   Clerical & other   _____
              Total   _____

6. Hardware:
   Annual cost   _____
   Lease expiration date   _____
   CPU   _____
   # Tape drives   _____
   # Disk drives   _____
   # Printers   _____
   Comments: _____
   _____

7. Software:
   Operating system _____
   Multiprocessing _____
   Source libraries _____

   Programming languages _____

   Comments: _____
   _____
   _____

8. Major Applications (5)

	Application	Date Implemented	Processing Hours per Month
(1)	_____	_____	_____
(2)	_____	_____	_____
(3)	_____	_____	_____
(4)	_____	_____	_____
(5)	_____	_____	_____

EDP INSTALLATION CONTROL QUESTIONNAIRE

Response

Yes   No   Reference

I. Installation Organization:

A. Is there a written policy statement or procedure that sets forth the authority for executing the following I/S activities:
1. Employment of personnel ☐ ☐ ....
2. Acquisition of EDP equipment ☐ ☐ ....
3. Use of EDP facilities and services ☐ ☐ ....
4. Acquisition of EDP supplies ☐ ☐ ....
5. Acquisition of EDP software and utility programs ☐ ☐ ....
6. Development of new information systems ☐ ☐ ....
7. Changes to existing information systems ☐ ☐ ....
8. Initiation of or change to system development standards ☐ ☐ ....
9. Initiation of or change to programming standards ☐ ☐ ....
10. Initiation of or change to the I/S organization structure ☐ ☐ ....
11. Initiation of or change to operation manuals, forms, administrative procedures, and cost and billing procedures ☐ ☐ ....

B. Is the management of the I/S function expressed in the form of an organization chart? ☐ ☐ ....

C. Are the activities of the I/S function subject to budgetary controls? ☐ ☐ ....

D. Do procedures require that important decisions such as those set forth in the following tabulation be reviewed and approved by a steering committee or other group comprised of high-level user management members?
1. I/S policies and procedures ☐ ☐ ....
2. I/S management changes ☐ ☐ ....
3. Major acquisitions of equipment and/or systems ☐ ☐ ....
4. Major information systems development efforts ☐ ☐ ....
5. Operating budgets ☐ ☐ ....

(continued)

FIG. 27-2 *(cont'd)*

	Response		
	Yes	No	Reference
E. Do procedures include explicit statements of control guidelines for use in information systems development, programming maintenance, and operations?	☐	☐	....
F. Do control guidelines require the following with respect to information system applications (for both existing systems and those under development):	☐	☐	....
1. Transaction-origination controls to reasonably assure that accurate and complete information is prepared for entry into the system? This would include at a minimum:	☐	☐	....
a. Written documentation of preparation procedures (user's guide or manual)	☐	☐	....
b. Control techniques to reasonably assure that transactions have been properly authorized by user management	☐	☐	....
c. Control techniques to reasonably assure that written instructions for preparing source documents are available	☐	☐	....
d. Control techniques to reasonably assure that errors and/or omissions are detected and corrected on a timely basis	☐	☐	....

For batch-oriented systems these might include:
        ■ Batch control
        ■ Edit checks
        ■ Limit checks
        ■ Balancing (run-to-run) in job-resubmission routines			

For on-line systems these might include:
        ■ Use of feedback dialogues designed to detect and correct errors prior to updating
        ■ Use of input/output control groups located in the user organization to identify and resolve errors			

e. Control techniques to reasonably assure that access to and use of remote terminals is restricted to authorized personnel for authorized purposes.	☐	☐	....

These techniques might include:
        ■ Terminal locks
        ■ User-identification passwords
        ■ Data set access passwords
        ■ Data set update passwords			

2. Data-entry controls to reasonably assure that entry processing results in the accurate and complete conversion of all data submitted in a timely and efficient fashion?	☐	☐	....
This would include at a minimum:			
a. System documentation of procedures required	☐	☐	....
b. Problem-free data conversion hardware	☐	☐	....

	Response	
	Yes No	Reference

c. Software features to facilitate accurate and complete processing such as: ☐ ☐ ....
  - Preformatting
  - Interactive display
  - Computer-aided instruction
  - Master commands
  - Terminal sign-on procedures

d. Techniques to reasonably assure sufficient data-entry validation such as: ☐ ☐ ....

  Batch:
  - Key verification
  - Editing routines
  - Batch balancing

  On-line:
  - Transaction checks
  - Off-line control routines

e. Techniques to reasonably assure that errors and/or omissions in batch-oriented systems are detected and corrected in a timely fashion. ☐ ☐ ....

  These techniques may include:
  - Error listings
  - Proof listings

f. Techniques to reasonably assure that errors and/or omissions in on-line systems are detected and corrected in a timely fashion ☐ ☐ ....

  These techniques may include:
  - Individual transaction checks such as limit tests, range tests, reasonableness tests, sequence checks, etc.
  - Group transaction checks such as periodic item balances and running totals
  - Use of suspense files and/or correction files
  - Use of an input/output control section for on-line file scanning and balancing routines

3. Techniques to reasonably assure that data submitted for batch processing from remote points is received without error or omission in a timely fashion? This would include: ☐ ☐ ....
  a. Documentation of procedures employed ☐ ☐ ....
  b. Techniques to reasonably assure that only authorized messages are sent via terminals ☐ ☐ ....

  These include techniques such as:
  - Identification codes (passwords)
  - Restricted accessibility to transmitting equipment

(continued)

FIG. 27-2 *(cont'd)*

	Response		
	Yes	No	Reference
c. Techniques to reasonably assure that messages are not lost or converted to unauthorized use during transmission	☐	☐	....

These techniques might include:
- Validity checks
- Echo checks
- Encryption techniques
- Automatic storing and switching
- Routine controls
- Line conditioning

d. Control techniques to reasonably assure that messages received are checked for validity and completeness	☐	☐	....

These techniques might include:
- Protocol verification techniques
- Detection with retransmission
- Line usage records
- Message logs
- Modems
- Error recording and correction techniques

4. Techniques to reasonably assure that information processing results in accurate and complete data available for reporting? This would include:	☐	☐	....
a. Written procedures and program-run manuals	☐	☐	....
b. Techniques to reasonably assure that only valid transactions are processed (Note: This involves use of transaction identification codes.)	☐	☐	....
c. Techniques to reasonably assure that the processing and computing procedures are logical	☐	☐	....

These might include use of:
- Label checking
- Control totals
- File completion checks
- File control totals (run-to-run controls)
- JCL standards
- Sysout messages

For real time systems, processing techniques could include the following:
- Provisions to prevent unauthorized access
- Provisions for identification and initiate correction of errors
- System interaction/dialogue to prompt or guide operator in the proper response/sequence of events, or to obtain "HELP" if necessary (i.e., psychological considerations)

INFORMATION SYSTEMS (EDP) AUDIT FUNCTION

	Response		
	Yes	No	Reference

- Sequential logging of transaction
- Dialogue structured to catch errors
- Self-checking operations built into dialogues

d. Techniques to reasonably assure that errors are detected and corrected in a timely fashion   ☐ ☐   ....

For batch-oriented systems these might include:
- Automated suspense files
- Display messages
- Batch balancing
- Error listings and discrepancy reports
- Error re-entry

For on-line systems the control techniques might include:
- Single transaction checks such as descriptive readback displays
- Group transaction checks such as running totals or periodic checkpoints
- Off-line controls techniques effected by a data control function such as file balancing, scanning, or policing
- Comparison of transaction contents with anticipated data (e.g., master file checking/validation and issuance of error messages, cautions, etc.)
- Checks for consistency within a group of transactions
- Checks against previously validated data
- Provisions for a summary of transactions by location
- Procedures for error prevention during system failure

For data-base systems, control techniques might include:
- Controls to restrict access and update capability to authorized persons
- Written procedures for data-base recovery during data-base failures
- Periodic review by specialized software of the physical and logical structure of the data base for gaps or inconsistencies
- Provisions for proper audit trails in the data dictionary
- Provision of sufficient edit tests in the data dictionary to govern operations on data base master records

5. Techniques to reasonably assure that data integrity is maintained during periods when the data is not being used? This would include: ☐ ☐   ....

(continued)

FIG. 27-2 *(cont'd)*

	Response Yes	No	Reference
a. Written procedures pertaining to authorization, access, backup, and recovery, maintenance, and destruction of data libraries.	☐	☐	....
b. Techniques to reasonably assure that all data tapes, disks, files, and documentation are accounted for. This may include use of software utility programs.	☐	☐	....
c. Techniques to reasonably assure that access to data is restricted to authorized personnel for authorized purposes.	☐	☐	....

These may include:
- Passwords
- Data base management system
- Classification/identification of files (private, confidential, etc.)
- Inquiry logging
- Program change control and logging
- Header/trailer label checks
- Tape library custodian

| d. Techniques to reasonably assure recovery in the event that data is lost or destroyed. | ☐ | ☐ | .... |

These might include:
- Automatic transaction taping
- Use of automated techniques for backup of critical files and programs
- Storing backup files in a physically secure location away from the primary record storage area
- Vaulting
- Written recovery procedures
- Written disaster recovery plan

| e. Techniques to reasonably assure that errors in file handling are timely detected and corrected. | ☐ | ☐ | .... |

These include:
- Logging of operating system interruption and processing halts
- Written procedures for restarts

| 6. Techniques to reasonably assure that reports and other output contain complete and accurate data and are delivered to authorized users in a timely fashion? | ☐ | ☐ | .... |

These would include:

| a. Techniques to reasonably assure that data balancing and reconciling and other error-detecting routines are consistently performed by one or more control clerks or groups, and include: | ☐ | ☐ | .... |

Batch-oriented systems:
- Reconciliation of output control totals with corresponding input control totals

	Response		
	Yes	No	Reference

- Review and comparison of transaction logs produced independently by the computer system and output devices (if applicable)
- Recording of all output reports and their disposition
- Review of job control cards for execution of unauthorized programs

On-line systems:
- Off-line file scanning and balancing
- Single transaction checks
- Real-time monitoring of terminal operator activities
- Real-time investigation and resolution of reported errors or other problems by terminal operators

b. Written procedures for report distribution, retention, and destruction. ☐ ☐ ....
c. User organization batch-control reconciliations. ☐ ☐ ....
d. Written procedures for the handling and accounting of documents such as negotiable checks, purchase orders, invoices, etc., to minimize exposure to theft or other loss. ☐ ☐ ....
e. Techniques to reasonably assure that output errors are detected and corrected in a timely fashion. ☐ ☐ ....

These techniques might include:
- Error reporting
- Error logging by control groups or users
- Correction procedures

II. Installation — Operations:

A. Do procedures specify control techniques to be followed for input/output and scheduling to reasonably assure efficient thorough EDP operations? ☐ ☐ ....

These techniques might include:
- An input/output control group
- Written procedures for operators' use
- Automated software utilities for production scheduling/monitoring
- Productivity reports and records

B. Do procedures specify control techniques sufficient to reasonably assure the integrity of data files and program files maintained in media form? ☐ ☐ ....

Such control techniques include:
- Restricted access
- Automated software inventory control techniques
- Temperature and humidity control

(continued)

FIG. 27-2 *(cont'd)*

	Response		
	Yes	No	Reference

- Redundancy and backup procedures for critical files
- Cataloging (O/S — TMS)
- Other

C. Do procedures include sufficient techniques for detecting, reporting, and resolving malfunctions and irregularities? ☐ ☐ ....

D. Do procedures provide sufficient techniques to reasonably assure that facilities and equipment are kept in proper working condition? ☐ ☐ ....

These techniques might include:
- Integration of maintenance time with production scheduling
- Review of equipment usage records and reports for emergency trouble spots
- Evaluation of performance of vendor services

E. Do procedures provide sufficient techniques to reasonably assure appropriate disposition of data files? ☐ ☐ ....

These would include:
- Standards for and review of purging/maintenance of files
- Periodic file backup
- Manual/automated TMS
- Standards for and review of data file retention

III. **Installation — Resource Acquisition:**

A. Do procedures provide for sufficient techniques to reasonably assure the availability of resources to meet future requirements? These techniques include:

1. Maintaining an up-to-date reference library of published technical material. ☐ ☐ ....
2. Maintaining up-to-date internal information from which resource needs can be estimated. ☐ ☐ ....

This might include:
- User-prepared and -approved plans for new systems and major changes to existing systems
- System maintenance requirements based upon historical data kept by the EDP programming department
- Equipment utilization reports
- Information obtained from meetings and other distribution channels indicating the long-term business strategies of the user groups

	Response		
	Yes	No	Reference

- Information obtained through ongoing dialogues with vendors, professional associations, and representatives of I/S departments of other organizational units, both external and internal
- Special research and study projects
- Resource accounting

B. Does the I/S department prepare formal current and long-term plans for the acquisition of:

1. Facilities and equipment ☐ ☐ ....
2. Personnel ☐ ☐ ....
3. Software ☐ ☐ ....

C. Are the plans reviewed and approved by appropriate management levels, such as a steering committee? ☐ ☐ ....

D. Do procedures specify the execution methodology for the acquisition of computer equipment, software, and supplies? ☐ ☐ ....

E. Is the commitment authority vested in persons independent of the I/S group? ☐ ☐ ....

F. Do procedures require advance authorization for use of I/S services? ☐ ☐ ....

IV. Installation — Record-Keeping:

A. Do procedures provide a methodology for allocating the cost of I/S services to user department final cost objectives? ☐ ☐ ....

Such methodology might include:

1. A formal set of written procedures. ☐ ☐ ....
2. A methodology for charging user organizations with the costs reasonably associated with services provided. ☐ ☐ ....
3. A method of actual cost accumulation which permits review and evaluation of billing rates and meets other organizational criteria. ☐ ☐ ....
4. Periodic validation of billing rates. ☐ ☐ ....

V. Installation — Accountability:

A. Do procedures require periodic inspection and comparison of physical assets with the record of such assets? ☐ ☐ ....

At a minimum, the following should be allowed for in this process:

- All computer hardware involved in the automated

(continued)

FIG. 27-2 *(cont'd)*

	Response		
	Yes	No	Reference
processing of data, including terminals, communication equipment, conversion equipment, storage devices, processors, printers, etc. ■ Data sets of all types ■ Blank check stock			
B. Do procedures provide the means for affected management to monitor the following types of activities for efficiency and effectiveness?			
1. EDP operations	☐	☐	....
2. Development of new systems	☐	☐	....
3. Maintenance of existing systems	☐	☐	....
C. Do the techniques specified in Question B above include the following:			
1. Regular reporting or accounting for cost of EDP services to users	☐	☐	....
2. Regular reporting to affected management of actual vs. budgeted expenditures in appropriate detail	☐	☐	....
3. Regular reporting of long-range plans	☐	☐	....
4. Regular performance review meetings	☐	☐	....
VI. Installation — Security:			
A. Do procedures provide sufficient segregation of duties to reasonably assure protection against fraud or other irregularities?	☐	☐	....
Such procedures include:			
1. Preventing applications-programmer's access to computers and production programs (source and object versions)	☐	☐	....
2. Preventing computer operator's access to programs and program documentation	☐	☐	....
3. Requiring program changes to be authorized in writing by management and tested and reviewed prior to implementation by an independent person or group	☐	☐	....
4. Segregating system development activities from computer operations	☐	☐	....
5. Restricting access to the computer area	☐	☐	....
6. Restricting access to stocks of blank checks, purchase orders, invoices and any other vital forms	☐	☐	....
B. Do procedures provide sufficient techniques to reasonably safeguard computer hardware and software from fire, water damage, sabotage, vandalism, or similar acts?	☐	☐	....

	Response		
	Yes	No	Reference

Such techniques might include:
- Fire extinguishers
- Sprinkler systems
- Halon systems under raised floors
- Halon systems — ceiling-mounted
- Temperature and humidity controls
- Alarm systems
- Periodic inspections by security guards, fire marshalls, etc.
- Insurance
- Fully enclosed facilities
- Vaults for backup files and tapes
- Automatic door locks
- Badge control systems
- Security checks on employees and others having access to the computer area
- Backup power source
- Redundant hardware
- Passwords and related remote data entry controls

C. Have emergency procedures been issued and tested for personnel response to emergencies, use of emergency equipment, protection of equipment and data, power and computer shut down, and personnel evacuation in the event of a disaster or other interruptive occurrence? ☐ ☐ ....

1. Do procedures provide for maintaining an up-to-date written disaster recovery plan? ☐ ☐ ....
2. Does the plan identify courses of action to be taken under disaster scenarios of varying proportions to facilities, hardware, software, and personnel? ☐ ☐ ....

For example:
- Facility, personnel, equipment, and software damaged
- Facility, personnel, and equipment intact, but power lost
- Facility intact, but equipment and key personnel lost
- Facility damaged, but equipment and personnel intact
- Facility, equipment, and personnel intact, but access denied

3. Does the plan specify realistic recovery procedures to be performed by specific job positions? ☐ ☐ ....
4. Does the plan provide considerable flexibility? ☐ ☐ ....

D. Do procedures require that the plan be tested periodically? ☐ ☐ ....

E. Do procedures require that the plan be approved by management? ☐ ☐ ....

(continued)

FIG. 27-2 *(cont'd)*

F. Are copies of the plan distributed to all personnel who may be involved?   ☐ ☐ ....

G. Do procedures provide automated record-keeping of changes to computer programs (load modules)?   ☐ ☐ ....

H. Do procedures require implementation of direct-access library maintenance systems or similar techniques for the protection of development and test source programs?   ☐ ☐ ....

I. Do procedures require protection of operating systems, utilities, system support software, etc., from accidental loss or modification?   ☐ ☐ ....

Such protection might include:
- Restricted access
- Documentation and approval of changes
- Approval for all changes
- Software security package
- Backup

VII. Systems Development:

A. Do procedures for developing new systems provide sufficient techniques to reasonably assure that the new system will fulfill system requirements?   ☐ ☐ ....

Such techniques include:
1. Using the system development life-cycle concept, a phased approach to developing new systems which includes:
   a. Project definition   ☐ ☐ ....
   b. System analysis and design   ☐ ☐ ....
   c. Detail design and programming   ☐ ☐ ....
   d. Testing   ☐ ☐ ....
   e. Implementation   ☐ ☐ ....
   f. Post review   ☐ ☐ ....
2. Involving users throughout all phases of system development.   ☐ ☐ ....
3. Requiring explicit user approval for:
   a. Project initiation   ☐ ☐ ....
   b. System requirements definitions   ☐ ☐ ....
   c. System specifications   ☐ ☐ ....
   d. Cost and schedule   ☐ ☐ ....
   e. Controls   ☐ ☐ ....
   f. Test plan   ☐ ☐ ....
   g. Test results   ☐ ☐ ....
   h. Decision to implement   ☐ ☐ ....
   i. Documentation (where appropriate)   ☐ ☐ ....
   j. Changes   ☐ ☐ ....

	Response		
	Yes	No	Reference

4. Using project management controls to reasonably assure efficient development efforts.   ☐ ☐ ....

   These might include:
   - Feasibility studies
   - Development plans
   - Project budgets
   - Cost accumulation and reporting
   - Monitoring of plan vs. actual performance and cost
   - Milestone reviews by affected management
   - Change control

5. Specifying standards to be followed in programming new systems to reasonably assure:
   a. Proper program logic   ☐ ☐ ....
   b. Efficient programmer effort   ☐ ☐ ....
   c. Ease of change in the future   ☐ ☐ ....

   These procedures might include:
   - System "walk through"
   - Naming conventions
   - Permissible programming language
   - A balanced hierarchical approach
   - Fixed column indentations
   - Documentations review of completed programs

6. To the extent that data bases are planned for the new system, do procedures provide sufficient control to reasonably assure optimum anticipated use of the data?   ☐ ☐ ....

   This procedure might include:
   - Use of a data base administrator to coordinate the development of the data so as to comply with data base management system requirements
   - Use of a data base management system
   - Use of controls, including software utilities, to restrict access and update capability to authorized personnel

7. Do procedures require that tests of new systems be sufficient to reasonably assure detection and correction of all problems which could result in processing inaccurate or incomplete data?   ☐ ☐ ....

   These techniques might include:
   - Written testing standards
   - Detailed decks for batch-oriented systems
   - Use of software test facilities for on-line systems

8. Do procedures require users to formally evidence system acceptance prior to implementation?   ☐ ☐ ....

9. Do procedures require that deviations from established system development activities be approved by appropriate management?   ☐ ☐ ....

produce a credible evaluation. However, in small installations, traditional auditors can perform reasonably well with a little preparation.

Installation surveys of extremely large data processing centers should be complemented by detailed functional audits to provide a suitable basis for an overall assessment.

Applications Auditing

As the term implies, applications auditing entails a comprehensive review of specific information systems applications. Since applications are an end product of a controlled process (the system development process), they may be likened to other audits of end products, such as financial statements. The extent of the review of each is affected by the degree of control present in the system development and maintenance functions. Hence, if systems are developed and maintained pursuant to a well-controlled process, the auditor may reasonably restrict the extent of applications auditing. Conversely, weak system development may indicate a need for more extensive work.

The objective of applications auditing is to determine whether the application controls are sufficient to result in the processing of accurate and complete data with adequate provision for security, backup, and recovery. In addition, applications auditing must determine whether the system design results in efficient use of I/S resources and effectively satisfies user requirements.

Theoretically, any application may be audited in this fashion. However, many entities have hundreds of applications covering all aspects of their activities. Some practical method of prioritizing must be employed to be sure that audit resources are allocated sufficiently to those applications for which assurance is of greatest value. Typically, these will be business systems, such as payroll, cash disbursements, customer billing, and inventory ordering.

Applications auditing must usually be performed by a skilled EDP or information systems auditor. This is because the work often entails (1) reviewing system and programming documentation that is technically oriented, (2) performing computer-assisted audit techniques, and (3) reviewing program listings that require a knowledge of applicable program languages. To maximize the utility of applications auditing, it is often advantageous to combine the EDP aspects of a system with the non-EDP aspects. This requires the teaming of traditional and I/S auditors on the given application. The traditional auditor focuses on the user department controls and the I/S auditor focuses on the EDP controls. Application audits can be performed in periods ranging from three weeks to five months, depending on complexity.

Developing Systems Auditing

Developing systems audits are defined as those that review not only the controls being designed for specific new applications, but also the techniques used in the process of developing the application. This type of information systems auditing reflects the internal auditors' attempt to be more useful. The disproportionately high cost of making changes to fully developed systems made the advent of developing systems auditing inevitable. Changes as a result of audit recommendations are less costly to implement when the system is in the development stage. While the auditor's involvement during development may raise some questions regarding independence, the concerns should not be enough to offset the benefits of assuring adequate controls and subsequent system auditability. The objectives of developing systems auditing are threefold:

1. To provide information with respect to the adequacy of controls and appropriateness of the system for user purposes
2. To determine that systems development is occurring efficiently in accordance with prescribed development procedures
3. To implement any devices needed to facilitate system auditability

The nature of systems development auditing gradually changes as the systems take shape. Many practitioners have found that this type of auditing works best if it is performed at specific milestones in the development cycle. Thus, the audit is divided into phases that include requirements definition, system design, programming, and implementation. Questionnaires and checklists can be used in each phase to assist in evaluating controls and progress. An example of a portion of such a questionnaire is shown in Figure 27-3.

It is generally believed that auditing systems in the development stage requires that the auditor possess sound EDP technical skills. Systems development activities can be costly and require from a few months to as much as five years to develop. The resultant orientation required to perform effective auditing in these circumstances suggests that a single auditor be responsible for the work associated with a given system. In major business systems development efforts, it also may be desirable to assign a traditional auditor to evaluate user controls and the adequacy of the system from the user's point of view.

Concurrent Auditing

With the exception of audits of systems in the development stage, the foregoing forms of information systems auditing are after the fact. That is to say, the transactions or activities under review have already occurred. Moreover, the auditor must invariably rely on the data processing department to enable completion of the audit. In questionable situations, where fraud or theft by a programmer may have transpired, the auditor may be unable to prevent the programmer from disguising incriminating evidence. It has also

(continued on page 27–29)

FIG. 27-3

Portion of a Developing System Control Questionnaire

	Yes/No or N/A	Reference
A. SYSTEMS PLANNING:		
1. Is the study team-organized and does the team have adequate skills and time to accomplish the planning phase goals?	....	....
2. Are the project scope and objectives documented and complete?	....	....
3. Is there adequate documented information concerning the existing system to facilitate design of a new system?	....	....
4. Is there a summary of recurring costs in the present system and a determination that those costs are accurate?	....	....
5. Is there a clear description of user information requirements?	....	....
6. Is there an analysis of estimated user and I/S costs and benefits that would permit management to evaluate the system's feasibility?	....	....
7. Is there written approval of the objectives/requirements and general systems concepts from user management?	....	....
B. SYSTEM DEVELOPMENT:		
1. General System Design:		
■ Have specific personnel been given responsibility for the general system analysis and design phase of the project?	....	....
■ Have output requirements been documented?	....	....
■ Have all input requirements been defined?	....	....
■ Have types of file and file organization been defined?	....	....
■ Have the specifications for each of the processing steps been prepared and documented?	....	....
■ Has consideration been given to control and security requirements of the system?	....	....
■ Have required system resources, including hardware, software, user personnel, and scheduling requirements been described?	....	....
■ Has consideration been given to the acquisition of commercial-application software packages?	....	....
■ Has the utility of the system's design been confirmed by the users?	....	....
■ Has appropriate management evaluated requirements, approved system design, and authorized further system development?	....	....
2. Detailed System Design:		
■ Is the organization of personnel appropriate to perform the detailed design phase of the project?	....	....
■ Have output requirements been documented in detail?	....	....
■ Have data formats been documented in detail?	....	....

INFORMATION SYSTEMS (EDP) AUDIT FUNCTION

	Yes/No or N/A	Reference

- Have source documents been designed to permit the gathering and entry of accurate information? ....
- Have specifications been written defining procedures and processes to be followed in converting input data into machine-readable form? ....
- Have program specifications been prepared in sufficient detail to permit programmers to code the application from written specifications? ....
- Are output specifications traceable to either application input or existing file content, and do they include all information needed by user management? ....
- Have control procedures for operation of the new system been prepared in advance? ....
- Have instructions and documentation been prepared for all operating procedures? ....

3. Programming Definition:

- For each program, is there a written statement of program objectives describing purpose, functions to be performed and input and output used? ....
- For each program, is there a detailed narrative description of the processing to be performed and the logic of that processing? ....
- Is there a macro-level block diagram or flowchart of the program to outline pictorially the sequence of the processing steps? ....
- Is there a definition and description of the files, records, and data fields used in both the input and output of all programs? ....
- Are there layouts available that define the data contained in reports and the source of this data? ....
- Does system-level documentation include flowcharts showing the sequence of processing steps, flow of transactions through the system, files maintained by the system, and programs used to maintain the files? Obtain copies of system-level flowcharts and review them to determine their adequacy in describing the flow of data through the system. ....

4. Program Testing:

- Are programming projects completed in accordance with installation programming standards? ....
- Does program testing take place in accordance with installation standards? ....
- Are results of the programming project evaluated by I/S management and user department personnel? ....
- Are the internal controls in the programs tested adequately? ....

(continued)

FIG. 27-3 *(cont'd)*

	Yes/No or N/A	Reference

- Has management reviewed test results of each program and indicated approval of testing in writing?   ....

5. Change Control:
- Has a system of change control been installed to account for all changes to system and programming specifications?   ....
- Has the system design been frozen after an appropriate time interval?   ....
- Are proposed changes evaluated for impact on system development effort and/or system use?   ....
- Are modifications to system design excessive in number?   ....
- Are modifications to system design significant enough to warrant reevaluation of system design?   ....

6. Application Contract Programming:
- If contract programming is used, has it been justified by a written request for service from a project manager?   ....
- Are completed projects tested and reviewed by the I/S development staff prior to authorization for payment?   ....

7. System Testing:
- For system-testing purposes, has the responsibility of personnel engaged in various phases of system testing been defined in advance?   ....
- Has a plan been developed for system testing (an "acceptance" test) as part of the preparation of detailed specifications?   ....
- Are standards for system testing and review of system testing by I/S and user personnel being followed?   ....
- Has a predetermined test plan been prepared outlining sections of the system to be tested, files and data fields to be used, reports to be prepared, and expected results?   ....
- As a part of the final acceptance test (and/or quality assurance testing) have test results been evaluated to determine that the new or revised system is functioning properly?   ....
- Has system testing determined that control features, including input, processing, and output controls, are functioning properly?   ....
- Have security and related procedures been tested?   ....

C. IMPLEMENTATION:

1. Implementation Checklist:
- Is use of a system implementation checklist required?   ....
- Is the checklist used and controlled faithfully?   ....

	Yes/No or N/A	Reference

2. Conversion:
- Has the organization of personnel for conversion been planned and have responsibilities been assigned? ....
- Has a plan been developed for converting files from the existing or manual system(s) to the new system(s)? ....
- Has all system-level and user documentation been completed and made ready for use by computer operations personnel and users? ....
- Prior to implementation of the system, have I/S and user department personnel been given sufficient training to enable them to carry out their responsibilities in the use of the new system? ....
- Has system performance been evaluated by user department personnel to determine if the system meets their needs? ....
- Has user management given final approval of the new systems? ....
- If applicable, has the system been run in parallel for an appropriate period of time and have the results justified switching to the new system? ....

3. System Documentation:
- Does user documentation adequately explain user instructions and expected processing results? ....
- Are there clear instructions for how the user should handle reject-report messages and correct input errors? ....
- Does I/S documentation contain information sufficient to describe the processing, identify data files, identify reports, and permit personnel to determine the programs in which particular functions are being performed? ....
- Do all programs contain documentation providing a detailed description of the contents of the program? ....
- Has documentation been prepared explaining operator instructions and control work procedures necessary for operation of the system? ....
- Are there clear key-processing instructions for the data entry organization? ....
- Have system, programming, operation, and user documentation been prepared in accordance with established documentation standards? ....

4. Security for Data and Programs:
- Have security provisions been provided for in the system? ....
- Have recovery procedures been prepared? ....
- Have responsibility for the identification of sensitive data and authority to provide for appropriate levels of security been established? ....
- Has control over access to program and data files been limited to authorized personnel? ....

(continued)

FIG. 27-3 *(cont'd)*

	Yes/No or N/A	Reference
■ Is access to programs and data files through terminals that are designed to report attempts at unauthorized access and provide information for remedial action?	....	....
■ Have on-line systems been designed to require user identification and authorization?	....	....
■ Is there a backup facility for the security provisions if the primary system goes down?	....	....
■ Is the source and object code operating under an effective management and security system?	....	....

5. **Post-implementation Audit:**
   - Has an analysis been performed comparing originally estimated to actual benefits and costs of system operation?
   - Has a review of the results of processing been performed to determine whether or not original objectives have been met?
   - Does the system meet user requirements?
   - Have backup procedures been tested?

D. **PROJECT MANAGEMENT, ADMINISTRATION, AND AUTHORIZATION:**

1. Has a high-level individual been given overall responsibility for successful development and implementation of the system?
2. Has a project leader been assigned?
3. Has a project management plan been developed?
4. Is project task identification sufficiently definitive to permit effective monitoring?
5. Have cost/schedule budgets/milestones been established and are they reasonable?
6. Has a formal reporting mechanism been created to provide cognizant management with status reports on system development progress?
7. Does the reporting structure address sufficient levels of management to ensure that necessary corrective action will be taken?
8. Does project reporting include:
   - Actual vs. planned costs?
   - Indicated final cost and estimated completion date?
   - Sufficient information to anticipate over-expenditures or project slippage on a timely basis?
9. Is reported data accurate?
10. Are reasons for significant cost or schedule overruns determined and reported to an appropriate level of management?

	Yes/No or N/A	Reference
11. Do solution(s) to overrun problems appear realistic?	....	....
12. Have proper I/S and user management sign-offs been documented at significant project milestones?	....	....
13. Have development funds been authorized in accordance with established policy? (e.g., chart of executive approvals)	....	....
14. Has authority to proceed been properly reviewed and approved by an appropriate agency or steering committee?	....	....
15. Have the users been adequately involved in system development?	....	....
16. Have users evidenced commitment to the system?	....	....
17. Are work authorization and control procedures sufficient to control expenditure of development resources?	....	....

been suggested that it is becoming increasingly difficult to gain an understanding of applications via walk-throughs because systems logic paths are getting more complex.[3] In recent years, new forms of information systems auditing have been developed that minimize the distortions caused by after-the-fact examinations performed in a dependent mode. These techniques involve auditing through the computer in a real-time status using actual or test transactions. The specific techniques involved are discussed in the following paragraphs.

Integrated Test Facilities. The term "integrated test facility" is defined as a technique that enables the auditor to review those functions of an automated application that are internal to the computer.[4] It is integrated because the test transactions are processed at the same time as normal transactions. The facility may be a dummy division, department, customer, or other facilitating object. After completion of processing and evaluation, the test transactions and their effect, if any, are reversed through some appropriate means.

Embedded Audit Data Collection. Embedded audit data collection is defined as one or more specially programmed data collection modules embedded in the computer application system to select and record data for subsequent analysis and evaluation.[5] It involves steps similar to system de-

---

[3] Ron Weber, *EDP Auditing, Conceptual Foundation and Practice* (New York: McGraw-Hill Book Co., 1982), p. 475.

[4] *Systems Auditability and Control Study—Data Processing Audit Practices Report, op. cit.*, p. 119.

[5] *Ibid.*, p. 133.

velopment because embedded audit routines, as their name suggests, are part of the system. One form of embedded routine is actually built into the system during design. This is known as a system control audit review file (SCARF). In a payroll system, for example, audit routines could be designed to accumulate and report, on request or at predetermined intervals, all transactions in excess of authorized levels, such as raises, gross pay, and paid absences. It could also be made to report differences, if any, between gross pay reported on W-2s and gross pay in the individual earnings records.

Snapshot/Extended Record. The snapshot, or extended record, techniques are defined as techniques that, in effect, take "pictures" of a transaction as it flows through the system. In the case of the extended record technique, a large record is built up consisting of images from each snapshot point and is carried through the system.[6] These techniques are illustrated in Figures 27-4[7] and 27-5.[8] The objective is to gain evidence that various controls performed by the computer operate in a real-time environment.

These concurrent audit techniques are discussed in this section as a form of I/S auditing because they require careful planning, staffing, and controlling to assure that the effort is productive. In other words, concurrent auditing requires a considerable investment to identify requirements, create the input data, the routine or the snapshot point, and to review and reconcile test results. In addition, once created, these routines require continuous maintenance (due to underlying system changes).

Concurrent auditing can only be designed, executed, and maintained by a knowledgeable information systems auditor and may require the design and programming assistance of the information systems department. In large companies, one or more individuals may coordinate this work on a full-time basis. Follow-up of reported information may be delegated to others within the audit department, however.

Although concurrent auditing is not yet widely practiced by auditors, the advantages it has over other audit forms increase with the size and complexity of the underlying systems. These advantages include being able to obtain evidence under real operating circumstances as opposed to simulated conditions. Moreover, the embedded or integrated nature of the techniques means that the auditor need not interrupt the normal operation of the computer center, as is necessary when executing general or specialized audit software. The fact that demand is growing for on-line, distributed processing involving centralized data bases promises that concurrent auditing will occupy an increasing proportion of the information systems audit effort.

---

[6] Weber, *op. cit.*, p. 481.

[7] From *EDP Auditing, Conceptual Foundations and Practice* by Ron Weber. Copyright © 1982 by McGraw-Hill Book Co. Reprinted with permission.

[8] From *EDP Auditing, Conceptual Foundations and Practice* by Ron Weber. Copyright © 1982 by McGraw-Hill Book Co. Reprinted with permission.

FIG. 27-4

Flow Chart of the Snapshot Audit Technique

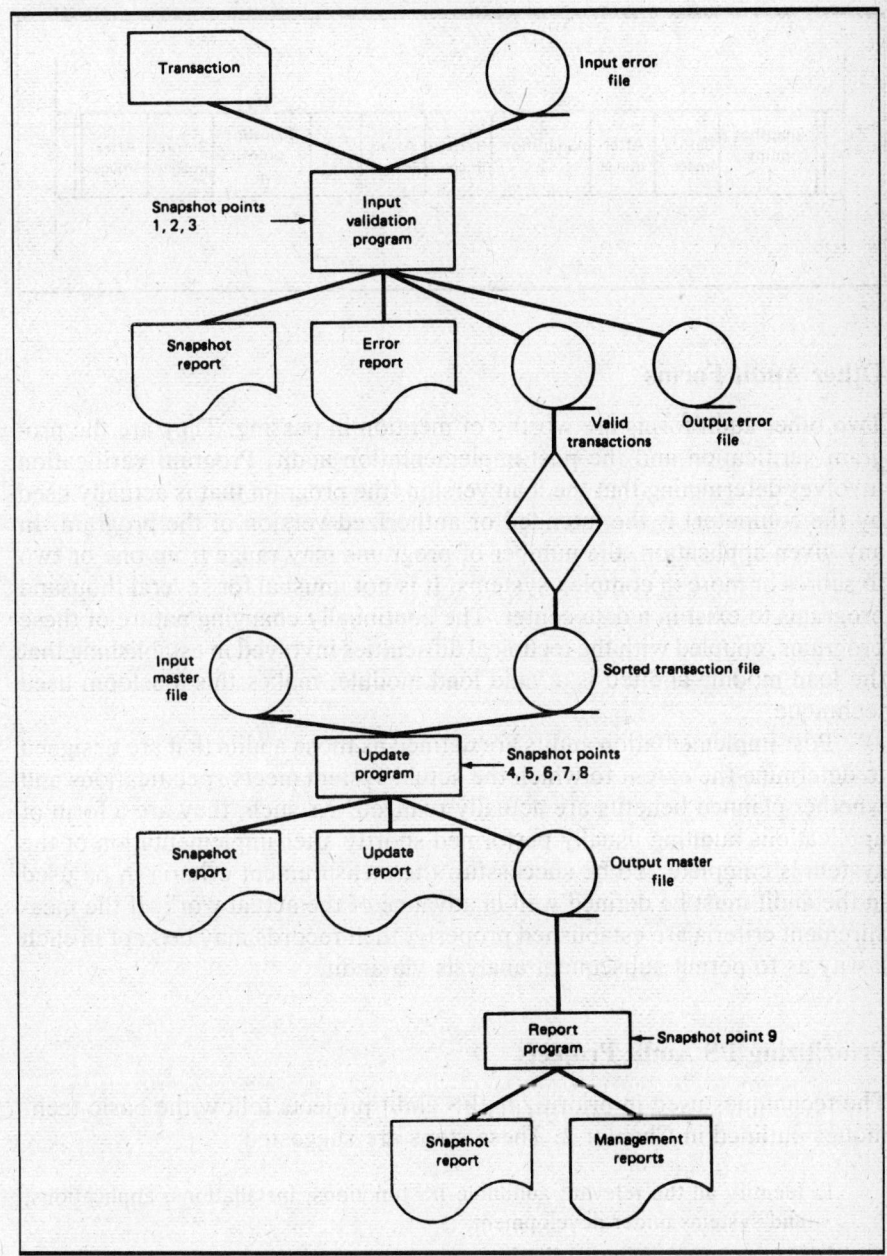

FIG. 27-5
Depiction of the Extended Record Technique

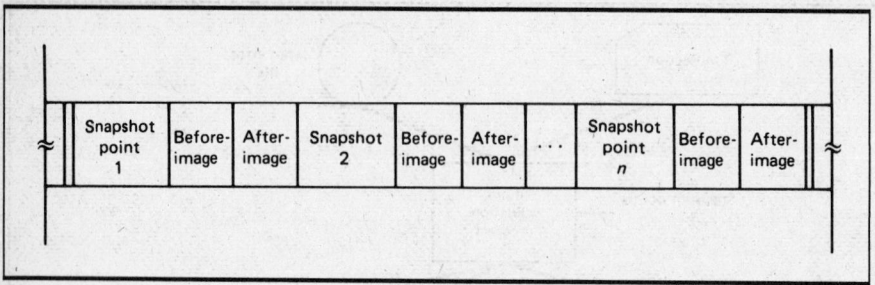

Other Audit Forms

Two other audit forms are worthy of mention in passing. They are the program verification and the post-implementation audit. Program verification involves determining that the load version (the program that is actually used by the computer) is the intended or authorized version of the program. In any given application, the number of programs may range from one or two to scores or more in complex systems. It is not unusual for several thousand programs to exist in a data center. The continually changing nature of these programs, coupled with the technical difficulties involved in establishing that the load module audited is a valid load module, makes this a seldom used technique.

Post-implementation audits are defined as those audits that are designed to determine the extent to which the actual system meets specifications and whether planned benefits are actually realized. As such, they are a form of applications auditing usually performed shortly after implementation of the system is complete. To be successful, the measurement criteria to be used in the audit must be defined well in advance of the actual work. If the measurement criteria are established properly, then records may be kept in such a way as to permit subsequent analysis via audit.

Prioritizing I/S Audit Projects

The techniques used in prioritizing I/S audit projects follow the basic techniques outlined in Chapter 2. These steps are suggested:

1. Identify all the relevant auditable I/S functions, installations, applications, and systems under development.
2. Devise a risk analysis criteria.
3. Perform the analysis (rank the auditable areas).
4. Establish audit frequencies.

INFORMATION SYSTEMS (EDP) AUDIT FUNCTION

Determining the auditable information systems activities requires that the audit manager or director survey all known data processing centers to obtain an inventory of hardware, software, policies and procedures, and existing applications, including those in current development. Other useful information includes budgetary data and long-range plans. The objective in gathering this information is to define the overall information systems audit universe.

The criteria that are used to prioritize that universe are very important and must be developed carefully. Factors used in prioritizing non-I/S audits are applicable for information systems audits as well. These include:

- Impact on decision making
- Complexity of system
- Volume of transactions
- Impact on financial position and operating results
- Source or use of cash
- Regulatory involvement

Other criteria applicable to information systems might include (1) type of system (i.e., batch or on-line), (2) number of uses, and (3) security concern.

The actual performance of the risk analysis that entails ranking the information systems audit subjects is relatively straightforward, once the universe is known and the criteria have been chosen. The analysis should be updated each year when the next year's audit coverage is established.

Since all topics cannot be audited every year, some reasonable frequency for each type of I/S auditing must be devised. These frequencies should be consistent with those established for non-I/S audit projects. For example, if it is determined that the payroll function should be reviewed once every two years, then the I/S application for payroll should also be reviewed at least that frequently. Of course, some I/S audit subjects have no counterpart in the non-I/S world. Examples include data-base management systems, program maintenance, and tape library control. Suggestions for frequency of auditing selected topical areas such as these are given in Figure 27-6.

Suggestions for Allocating Audit Resources

Given the various forms of auditing and number of functions, applications, programs, and installations that might be auditable, the internal auditing director or manager must avoid allocating too much of the audit resource to any single form or undertaking. An approach that utilizes all forms in reasonable proportion offers the best chance for a proper allocation. The apportionment will vary among companies, depending on the number of

FIG. 27-6
Frequencies for I/S Audits

	Suggested Frequency Range in Years
Functional	
Operating system	1 – 2
Telecommunications	1 – 2
Program standards	2 – 3
Program change control	1 – 2
Tape management and control	2 – 3
Hardware planning and acquisition	2 – 3
Software planning and acquisition	2 – 3
Data base management	1 – 2
Applications	
Significant business applications (payroll, customer billing and collection, accounts payable, cash disbursements)	1 – 2
Other business applications	3 – 5
Significant operational applications (production scheduling, material ordering, inventory control)	2 – 3
Other operational applications	3 – 5
Systems Under Development	Varies with importance of system
Installations	
Large	annually
Medium	1 – 2
Small	3 – 5

installations, the number and type of existing applications, the number and type of systems in development, and so on. For a typical large I/S function (operating budget in excess of $25 million), a practicable mix of audit forms might be as follows:

Form	Man Hours per Annum
Functional	2,500– 3,000
Installation	1,000– 1,500
Applications	1,500– 2,000
Developing	2,500– 3,000
Concurrent	1,500– 2,000
Other	1,000– 1,500
	10,000–13,000

This range of resource apportionment places a slight emphasis on developing system audits and functional audits. It is this form of auditing that offers the greatest chance of discovering and preventing major weaknesses in the system. This results because, in the case of functional weaknesses, the ramifications can be and are experienced by many or most applications. In the case of developing systems, the potential for unforeseen system problems is considerably higher than for existing applications whose design has stood the test of time.

MANAGING THE I/S AUDIT FUNCTION

Standards

In Chapter 6, the subject of internal auditing standards is thoroughly discussed. In that chapter, it is noted that the IIA has developed a broad set of auditing standards for the practice of internal auditing. In addition, many internal auditing departments have developed their own standards that are parallel to those of the IIA.

The standards developed by the IIA have considerable applicability to audits in an I/S environment. In particular, the need for independence, technical proficiency, due diligence, and professional care extends to I/S auditors. Perhaps of equal importance are the standards of fieldwork, reporting, and especially the need for gathering sufficient competent evidential matter. (See Chapter 6.) I/S auditors should conform to IIA standards or equivalent standards recently developed by the EDP Auditors Association (EDPAA).

The EDPAA, an international organization of 45,000 EDP auditors, has done much to advance the status of their members toward professionalism. It has been promoting a common body of knowledge and has established a certification program.

In 1976, the EDP Auditors Foundation (EDPAF) was established to engage in educational activities and research in I/S auditing. The EDPAF, in turn, established the Standards Board to promulgate and maintain standards of practice. These standards apply to members of the EDPAF and holders of the Certificate in Information Systems Auditing. The Standards Board issued its *General Standards for Information Systems Auditing* in 1987. They represent the minimum level of acceptable performance required to meet the professional responsibilities set forth in the Code of Professional Ethics (see Figure 27-7). The standards call for independence, technical competence to be maintained through continuing education, proper planning, supervision and due professional care in the performance of the work, and objective reporting of the results, including findings and conclusions. The standards are reprinted in Figure 27-8.

FIG. 27-7
Code of Professional Ethics

The EDP Auditors Foundation, Inc., sets forth this Code of Professional Ethics to guide the professional and personal conduct of members of the EDP Auditors Association and/or holders of the Certificate in Information Systems Auditing.

Information systems auditors shall:

1. **Support** the establishment of and compliance with appropriate standards, procedures, and controls for information systems.
2. **Comply** with Information Systems Auditing Standards as adopted by the EDP Auditors Foundation.
3. **Serve** in the interest of their employers, stockholders, clients and the general public in a diligent, loyal and honest manner, and shall not knowingly be a party to any illegal or improper activities.
4. **Maintain** the confidentiality of information obtained in the course of their duties. This information shall not be used for personal benefit nor released to inappropriate parties.
5. **Perform** their duties in an independent and objective manner, and shall avoid activities which threaten, or may appear to threaten, their independence.
6. **Maintain** competency in the interrelated fields of auditing and information systems through participation in professional development activities.
7. **Use** due care to obtain and document sufficient factual material on which to base conclusions and recommendations.
8. **Inform** the appropriate parties of the results of audit work performed.
9. **Support** the education of management, clients, and the general public to enhance their understanding of auditing and information systems.
10. **Maintain** high standards of conduct and character in both professional and personal activities.

Reprinted by permission of the EDP Auditors Foundation, Inc. Copyright © 1987 U.S.A.

The standards do not supersede auditing standards of other professional organizations or by government bodies. The authors believe these standards parallel those already discussed in Chapters 4–6.

Organizing and Planning I/S Audits

In small companies, all I/S auditing might be performed by a single auditor who has become familiar with general data processing concepts. In other companies, I/S audit specialists may be required. In these situations, organizing and planning the function requires little effort.

For large companies with multiple processing centers, more formalized effort is required to effectively manage the effort. Specific comments applicable to each of these topics are provided in the following paragraphs.

Organizing. Two fundamental points are involved in organizing the function. The first involves the question of to whom should the I/S auditor

FIG. 27-8
General Standards for Information Systems Auditing

Introduction

The EDP Auditors Foundation, Inc., has determined that the specialized nature of information systems auditing, and the skills necessary to perform such audits, require the development and promulgation of Information Systems Auditing Standards which apply specifically to information systems auditing.

Information systems auditing is defined as any audit that encompasses the review and evaluation of all aspects (or any portion) of automated information processing systems, including related non-automated processes, and the interfaces between them.

Standards promulgated by the EDP Auditors Foundation, Inc. are applicable to information systems auditing work performed by members of the EDP Auditors Association, and by holders of the Certificate in Information Systems Auditing.

Further background concerning the EDP Auditors Association, the EDP Auditors Foundation, and their information systems auditing standards program is contained in the "Preface to General Standards for Information Systems Auditing and Statements on Information Systems Auditing Standards."

Objectives

The objectives of these standards are to inform auditors of the minimum level of acceptable performance required to meet the professional responsibilities set forth in the Code of Professional Ethics, and to inform management and other interested parties of the profession's expectations concerning the work of practitioners.

General Standards for Information Systems Auditing

The following ten standards are applicable to information systems auditing as defined above.

Independence

General Standard No. 1: **Attitude and Appearance**—In all matters related to auditing, the information systems auditor is to be independent of the auditee in attitude and appearance.

General Standard No. 2: **Organizational Relationship**—The information systems audit function is to be sufficiently independent of the area being audited to permit objective completion of the audit.

General Standard No. 3: **Code of Professional Ethics**—The information systems auditor is to adhere to the Code of Professional Ethics of the EDP Auditors Foundation.

Technical Competence

General Standard No. 4: **Skills and Knowledge**—The information systems auditor is to be technically competent, possessing the skills and knowledge necessary in the performance of the auditor's work.

General Standard No. 5: **Continuing Professional Education**—The information systems auditor is to maintain technical competence through appropriate continuing education.

(continued)

FIG. 27-8 *(cont'd)*

Performance of Work

General Standard No. 6: **Planning and Supervision**—Information systems audits are to be planned and supervised to provide assurance that audit objectives are achieved and compliance with these standards is met.

General Standard No. 7: **Evidence Requirement**—During the course of the audit, the information systems auditor is to obtain evidence of a nature and sufficiency to support findings and conclusions reported.

General Standard No. 8: **Due Professional Care**—Due professional care is to be exercised in all aspects of the information systems auditor's work, including observance of applicable auditing standards.

Reporting

General Standard No. 9: **Reporting of Audit Coverage**—In preparing reports, the information systems auditor is to state the objectives of the audit, the period of coverage, and the nature and extent of the audit work performed.

General Standard No. 10: **Reporting of Findings and Conclusions**—In preparing reports, the information systems auditor is to state findings and conclusions concerning the audit work performed, and any reservations or qualifications that the auditor has with respect to the audit.

Effective Date

These standards are effective for all information systems audits with periods of coverage beginning January 1, 1988.

Reprinted by permission of the EDP Auditors Foundation, Inc. Copyright © 1987 U.S.A.

---

report? It is believed that most companies prefer to organize the I/S audit function within the overall internal auditing function. In these situations, the I/S auditors usually occupy a level in the organization consistent with other non-I/S auditors possessing comparable skill and experience. They may report to the head of the department or to an I/S audit manager who, in turn, reports to the head of the department. An illustration of this type of organization is shown in Figure 27-9. Under some circumstances, the I/S audit function might report to someone other than the director of internal auditing, such as the financial vice-president or controller. In any event, the reporting should be at a level that reasonably assures independence.

The second point has to do with the charter of the function. It is important that the duties and responsibilities of I/S auditing be clearly established and documented. The form of documentation might be a position description, a functional outline, or a formal policy statement. An example of a formal policy statement is shown in Figure 27-10.

I/S audit charters are important from the standpoint of minimizing the confusion that might otherwise exist as to the role of the I/S auditor. Some managers believe, for example, that I/S auditors should be responsible for internal controls in new systems, and, in many companies, I/S auditors are

INFORMATION SYSTEMS (EDP) AUDIT FUNCTION

FIG. 27-9

Typical I/S Audit Function Organization Chart

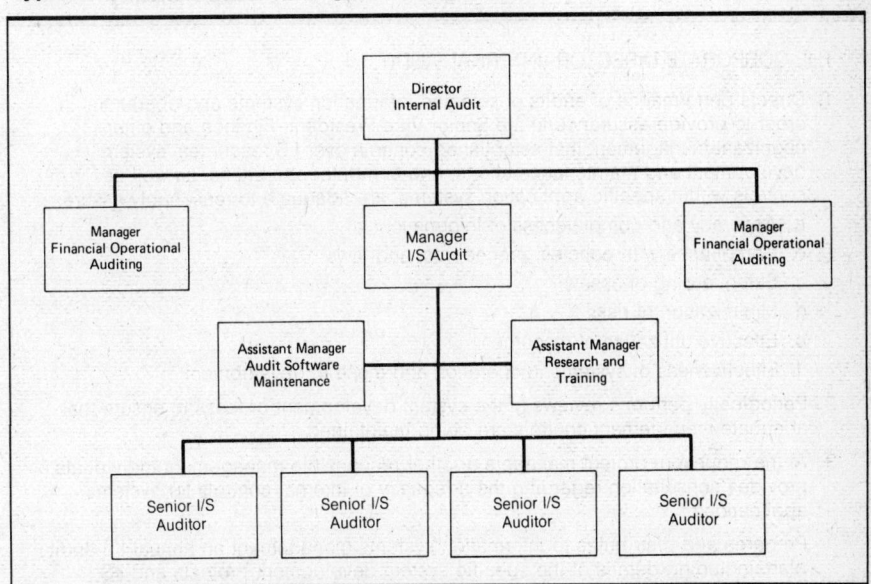

required to sign off on new systems as part of the approval process. Others believe that management is responsible for internal controls in new systems. The authors share this view. In these companies, the I/S audit function may review controls as part of their overall function. Signoffs by auditors are usually not required in these instances.

One final comment: The responsibility of the auditor for reviewing cost-benefit analyses and for conducting post-implementation reviews should be set forth in the charter.

Planning. I/S auditing, like all other functional activities, must be properly planned. This requires long-range or strategic planning, annual planning, specific project planning and, within projects, audit procedural planning. These levels of planning are essentially the same as are required for the entire audit function.

Long-range or strategic planning is necessary to reasonably assure that the I/S audit coverage over a span of years will be sufficient. The rapidly changing and expanding nature of the data processing environment necessitates continuous attention to current and long-term I/S plans. Of particular interest are such matters as equipment and facilities planning, new applications planning, operating systems, and data-base planning.

Annual plans for intended audit projects must be prepared applying the prioritization concept discussed earlier in this chapter. These plans should

FIG. 27-10

Excerpt of a Policy Statement Setting Forth I/S Audit Responsibility

---

THE CORPORATE DIRECTOR—INTERNAL AUDIT:

1. Directs performance of audits of selected information systems and operations in order to provide assurance to the Senior Vice-President—Finance and other cognizant management that established controls over I/S resources, system development and maintenance efforts, and computer operations, as well as controls within specific application systems, are adequate to reasonably assure:
   a. Accuracy and completeness of information
   b. Compliance with policies, procedures, and laws
   c. Safeguarding of assets
   d. Minimization of risks
   e. Effective utilization of resources
   f. Effectiveness of systems in operation and those in development
2. Periodically performs reviews of the system development process to ensure that adequate management controls are being maintained
3. At the request of project managers or other responsible management individuals, provides consultation regarding the adequacy of internal controls for systems applications
4. Prepares and distributes to Information systems management an annual I/S audit plan, including details of the specific system development projects and I/S functions to be reviewed, anticipated starting dates (audits of active, operational systems, as well as special audits which may be performed on an unscheduled basis)
5. Coordinates and assists the efforts of external auditors who are studying and evaluating information systems controls in connection with examinations of corporate financial statements

---

be formally communicated to affected data processing departments and user organizations to facilitate coordination.

Project planning and procedural planning occur in connection with each assigned project to assure that performance will achieve the desired results. Further comments regarding these types of planning are included later in this chapter.

Selling

The "selling" of the I/S audit function must be done following the same techniques recommended in Chapter 7. These include:

- Demonstrating technical competence
- Establishing contact with management (particularly I/S management) in non-audit situations
- Developing good listening habits
- Avoiding impasses to the extent practicable

- Being open and communicative
- Being responsive to requests for special assistance and consultation
- Accepting criticism gracefully

In maintaining relationships with I/S functional management, the audit manager or director must keep in mind that he is dealing with individuals who possess specialized technical knowledge as well as managerial talent. On the basis of unpleasant past experience with auditors, some may lack confidence in the credibility of the auditor in an I/S environment—regardless of whether or not that view is justified. While no amount of salesmanship can compensate for poor audit performance, the combination of good relations and consistent high-quality auditing should secure the necessary level of confidence.

One way to develop satisfactory relationships with the I/S community is to minimize the circumstances that are apt to lead to criticism and ill will. I/S managers most frequently complain that auditors do not give sufficient consideration to the impact that some of their recommendations might have on operational efficiency. Put another way, I/S auditors are often viewed as being too academic or theoretical (not able to put matters in proper perspective) and using hindsight.

To illustrate, consider a situation in which a new on-line purchase order control and status system was proposed and authorized in part because of the estimated savings realizable from the new system over the old. Assume that these savings are based on the cost of six new terminals—the projected user requirement. Assume further that the actual demand for terminals on implementation turns out to be 10. Some auditors might report with hindsight that a portion of the original system justification was invalid. They might recommend that management take steps to assure that accurate estimates be developed so that decisions regarding development are proper. No one can argue that decisions regarding system development should be based upon the most accurate data available. But what evidence is there that more accurate data were available? All that is known for certain is that 10 terminals are now needed. Unless there is evidence to indicate that management either knew, or should have known, that six terminals would be insufficient, there probably is no finding or recommendation to be reported. Auditors who would report the inaccurate terminal demand forecast would probably reinforce the I/S community's belief that auditors are too academic.

Complaints such as that previously described, along with other alleged deficiencies, such as (1) taking too much time away from programmers, operators, and other I/S personnel; (2) not understanding the particular I/S environment in which the audit is occurring; and (3) lacking sufficient technical knowledge, must be addressed by the I/S audit manager.

The point cannot be overemphasized because the essential continuing cooperation of the I/S function depends on its attitude toward the audit department.

PROJECT MANAGEMENT

I/S audit activity is susceptible to the same project controls outlined in Chapter 8 that are applicable to other auditing activity. These controls include:

- Maintenance of an auditing manual
- Development and use of questionnaires and checklists and audit programs
- Use of specific project authorization and monitoring controls
- Quality controls, such as project review

Auditing Manuals

In many companies, the I/S audit function is part of the internal auditing department. The auditing manual of these departments usually contains a section applicable to I/S auditing. Typical topics included in the I/S section are a general discussion of data processing, control, and security; a description of the audit approach and guidelines for the various types of I/S auditing; and terminology. A portion of the table contents of such a section is shown in Figure 27-11.[9]

The audit manager or director responsible for the I/S audit function is advised to obtain assistance in developing the I/S audit section of the manual if he is uncertain as to its form or content. Such certainty is common due to the variety of I/S audit practices and the underlying technical nature of the work. Other practical suggestions regarding an audit manual include these:

- Avoid extensive technical detail. I/S technology is changing so rapidly that details can require constant updating.
- Articulate approaches and audit methods that will apply to the I/S environment of the company and that satisfy management needs. For example, describing how to audit systems in the development phase is superfluous if company management does not look to the audit function for information in this area.
- Specify objectives clearly.
- State any standards that may apply to EDP auditing. Most functions adopt standards for such activities as flow charting, generalized audit software, program languages, and testing techniques.

Use of Questionnaires and Checklists

As is evident from Figures 27-2 and 27-3, questionnaires are particularly useful in conducting audits of internal controls over either selected functional

---

[9] *Contract Audit Manual* (Defense Contract Audit Agency, 1988), Appendix C, page C(1).

FIG. 27-11

Audit Manual Contents Page—Excerpt Covering I/S Auditing

APPENDIX C
Table of Contents

Paragraph		Page
	C-000 ELECTRONIC DATA PROCESSING SYSTEMS	
C-001	Scope of Appendix	C1
	C-100 Section 1—Description of Electronic Data Processing Systems	
C-101	Introduction	C1
C-102	Characteristics of Computer Processing	C1
C-103	Difference Between Manual and Automated Systems	C1
C-104	Computer Components	C3
	C-104.1 Hardware	C3
	C-104.2 Software	C6
	C-104.3 Personnel	C7
C-105	EDPS Processing Modes	C9
	C-105.1 Batch	C9
	C-105.2 Interactive (Online/Data Base)	C9
	C-105.3 EDPS Implementation Modes	C9
	C-200 Internal Controls in EDPS	
C-201	Introduction	C11
C-202	Standards on Study of Internal Controls in EDPS	C11
	C-202.1 Internal Control Objectives	C11
C-203	EDP General Controls	C12
	C-203.1 Organization and Operation Controls	C12
	C-203.2 Systems Development and Documentation Controls	C12
	C-203.3 Hardware and Systems Software Controls	C13
	C-203.4 Access Controls	C13
	C-203.5 Data and Procedural Controls	C14
C-204	EDP Application Controls	C14
	C-204.1 Input Controls	C15
	C-204.2 Processing Controls	C16
	C-204.3 Output Controls	C16
	C-204.4 Audit Effect of a Weakness in Application Controls	C17

Paragraph		Page
	C-300 EDP General and Application System Reviews	
C-301	Introduction	C18
C-302	Audit Scope	C18
C-303	Preliminary Review and System Survey	C18
	C-303.1 Flow of Transactions	C18
	C-303.2 Extent of EDP Utilization	C19
	C-303.3 Basic Accounting Controls Structure	C19
C-304	EDP Internal Control Survey	C19
	C-304.1 Scope of Review	C19
	C-304.2 Audit Objectives	C19
C-305	Audit Risk in EDPS	C19

(continued)

FIG. 27-11 *(cont'd)*

C-306	Transaction Auditing	C20
	C-306.1 Identification	C21
	C-306.2 Retrieval and Testing	C22
C-307	Reporting Audit Results	C22
	C-400 Other EDP Reviews	
C-401	Introduction	C23
C-402	Scope of Section	C23
C-403	Economy and Efficiency Reviews	C23
	C-403.1 Audit Concerns and Procedures	C23
	C-403.2 Capacity Planning, Computer Performance Evaluation (CPE) and System Tuning	C24
C-404	DFARS 70.6 Reviews	C26
	C-404.1 General Requirements	C26
	C-404.2 Audit Procedures	C26

aspects of an EDP installation or over the entire installation. In the latter case, the questionnaire may be designed in such a way as to be applicable to many types of installations. This is possible because all EDP installations involve some common characteristics. These include user submission of data, data conversion, data processing, data storage, and data reporting. Other common areas include hardware and software security, backup, and recovery.

Questionnaires applicable to specific functional areas, such as data-base administration, tape library management, or time-sharing, should be developed following the guidance outlined in Chapter 8. However, these questionnaires will not have the recurring use potential of the installation questionnaire.

In addition to internal control audits, checklists are useful in audits of systems under development and in audits of existing applications.

Specific Project Authorization and Monitoring

On the average, I/S audit projects require greater amounts of time to complete than traditional audits. Hence, project controls, such as authorization, performance monitoring via status reporting, and time budgeting, are perhaps even more important in I/S auditing than normally. The following objectives are applicable regardless of whether the project is an application audit or the design and implementation of an integrated test facility:

- The project must be authorized on the basis of clearly stated auditing objectives.
- The project must be budgeted in terms of time required in sufficient detail to permit review and approval.

- Project completion dates must be specified for important milestones.
- Use of other resources such as audit software and technical assistance must be specified and approved.
- Periodic status reports (weekly for short projects, biweekly for longer ones) indicating progress, problems, if any, and performance against budget should be required and reviewed by audit management.

Quality Control

Some of the foregoing techniques, such as audit manuals, questionnaires, and performance monitoring, double as quality-control mechanisms. Quality-control techniques in addition to these include the project review, which should be performed by an audit manager or the director prior to project completion. The review may be divided into phases to maximize effectiveness and efficiency. Among the matters for review and approval are the audit objectives, proposed audit methodology questionnaire, programs (including generalized and/or specially developed software), workpapers, and report drafts. If the function is too small to permit such reviews to occur within the department, then the person responsible for the I/S audit function outside the department should perform the review—although not necessarily for each department.

MANAGEMENT OF PERSONNEL

The vast majority of I/S audit staffs are comprised of fewer than five individuals per staff; in fact, many have only one or two members. Nevertheless, the vital service provided by I/S auditors makes personnel management every bit as important as it is for other functions. Comments regarding I/S audit personnel management in the following paragraphs cover recruiting, performance measurement, and professional training.

Recruiting

At the outset, it must be declared that the supply of qualified I/S auditors always seems to be exceeded by the demand for them. Two methods have evolved for dealing with this circumstance. Naturally, there are advantages and disadvantages for each.

One method of obtaining I/S auditors is to recruit personnel with skill and experience in auditing and then train them in the technical aspects of I/S. A second method is the opposite of the first—that is, to recruit I/S specialists and then train them to be auditors. Each method has its proponents and detractors. Which method to select will probably be shaped by the underlying conditions in each company. Some auditing functions may be set up and staffed in such a way as to be able to train auditors in the technical aspects of I/S. Others may find it better to offer audit training to EDP specialists. Still others—perhaps the majority—must seek trained personnel in both disciplines.

It is unlikely that qualified candidates can be found on college campuses. As a result, most recruiting for I/S auditors occurs in a sort of cannibalistic fashion. Private industry, governments, and public accounting firms are forced to fulfill their needs by enticing staff members away from each other. Inducements are usually in the form of higher salary offers. Specialized search firms are used to perform the awkward task of finding the candidates in exchange for a percentage of the first-year salary—in the event the candidate is hired.

If the department is seeking I/S auditors with experience in both auditing and I/S, the candidates must be carefully screened by the manager or director. While there are many truly qualified I/S auditors, the field is also populated with a fair share of incompetents. This is due, in part, to the fact that there is no standard evidence indicating minimum acceptable qualifications as there is in other fields. In public accounting, for example, the CPA certificate is evidence of possessing the minimum required by the profession. While a certification program has been developed by the EDP Auditors Association, it is too new to be of much current value.

In screening I/S auditing candidates, the following topical areas will reveal insight into the candidates' real ability:

- Knowledge of trends in I/S technology
- Knowledge of trends in I/S audit technology
- Knowledge of generalized audit software
- Knowledge of authoritative professional and trade publications
- Professional affiliations

Candidates should be asked to describe their most complex I/S audit assignment and their most rewarding assignment. These and similar questions should enable the interviewer to obtain a better idea of the qualifications of the applicant. Employers should be wary of anyone who talks only in generalities. It is fairly easy to learn some of the key buzzwords, such as distributed processing, networking, and structured programming.

Aside from the foregoing, the comments in Chapter 9 pertaining to interviewing candidates, evaluating qualifications, making offers, and following up apply equally to recruiting I/S auditors.

Performance Measurement

Measuring the performance of I/S auditors is not less subjective than is the measuring of the performance of traditional auditors. In both instances, the best approach is to adopt a systematic, rational methodology and apply it

INFORMATION SYSTEMS (EDP) AUDIT FUNCTION

consistently. Like traditional auditors, I/S auditors may be measured on specific abilities, such as planning, testing, documenting, evaluating, and reporting. Other performance indicators peculiar to I/S auditors include:

- Quality of suggestions for control enhancements in developing systems
- Coordination with I/S department
- Ability to design and implement embedded audit routines
- Use of the computer as an audit tool

Of course, I/S auditors may also be evaluated in terms of their technical knowledge, judgment, and diligence.

Professional Training

Obviously, the frequently noted fast pace of change occurring in data processing requires a special effort to keep current. The suggestions in Chapter 9 pertaining to an information distribution network, a program of internal training, on-the-job training, attendance at relevant outside seminars and conferences, and an up-to-date library are all equally applicable to the I/S auditing function.

Among the topics that are appropriate for enhancing auditing practice through training are the following:

- EDP physical and data security
- System development life cycle
- Operating systems
- On-line systems control
- Data base management
- Telecommunications control
- Disaster planning, backup, and recovery
- Generalized audit software
- Integrated test facilities

It is unlikely that sufficient I/S training can be obtained internally. Even the most advanced I/S audit personnel find it necessary to attend seminars and conferences that focus on the above topics as well as several others relevant to I/S auditing. In fact, most I/S audit functions have concluded that these courses offer the most cost-effective training available. The most widely attended are sponsored by professional organizations such as the IIA and the EDPAA. Many seminars, sponsored by private interests, are also available. In addition, vendors such as IBM offer valuable training opportunities—many at little or no direct cost.

The nature and extent of training varies with the skill and experience of each auditor. Each auditor should receive between two and four weeks of training annually. Of course, the training should be integrated with assignments and, accordingly, spread throughout the year.

Training courses are available not only in colleges and universities but also in private companies, CPA firms, and professional and trade associations. Training is available in all aspects of I/S. The material may be general in nature, or it may be focused on a specific topic. The following list, by no means complete and not necessarily current, is representative of the range of courses offered:

Offeror	Training Method	Length	Fee	Course Description
CPA Firms				
Peat, Marwick, Mitchell & Co.	Seminar	3 days	$1850	EDP for Senior Executives
	Seminar	2 days	1150	EDP for Key Users
	Workshop	2 days	650	Realistic Applications of Personal Computers in Business
	Seminar	5 days	750	System 2190 Audit Software
	Seminar	3 days	595	EDP Auditing and Controls
	Seminar	3 days	595	The Auditor's Role in Systems Development
	Seminar	3 days	595	Auditing Advanced Computer Systems
	Seminar	3 days	595	Controlling and Auditing On-Line and Distributed Systems
	Workshop	2 days	425	Advanced Data Communications Workshop
Arthur Andersen & Co.	Seminar	5 days	950	Understanding Computers and Controls
	Workshop	4 days	800	Auditing in an EDP Environment: Controls Evaluation
	Seminar	4 days	900	Systems Project Management

INFORMATION SYSTEMS (EDP) AUDIT FUNCTION

Offeror	Training Method	Length	Fee	Course Description
	Seminar	2 days	500	An Executive Briefing: "Computers—Can you Afford Not To Understand?"
	Seminar	2 days	500	Using Microcomputers in the Business Environment
Professional				
Institute of Internal Auditors	Seminar	4½ days	$875/925*	Auditing Information Processing Facilities
	Seminar	4½ days	875/925	Information Systems Auditing—Concepts and Applications
	Seminar	4½ days	875/925	Information Systems Auditing & Computer Audit Practices
	Seminar	4½ days	875/925	Productive Uses of Microcomputers in Auditing (PUMA)
	Seminar	4½ days	875/925	Microcomputers and Auditing
Other				
American Management Association	Various Seminars	3–4 days	675/735 775/845	Introduction to Data Processing
	Various Seminars	3–4½ days	675/725 775/845	Office Systems and Administrative Support
	Various Seminars	3–4 days	675/775 775/885	Business Applications
	Various Seminars	3–5 days	695/925 800/1065	Technical Skills
	Various Seminars	3–4 days	695/775 800/890	Management Skills

Offeror	Training Method	Length	Fee	Course Description
MIS Training Institute	Seminar	3 days	750	EDP Auditing and Controls
	Seminar	3 days	750	Auditing Advanced Computer Systems
	Seminar	2 days	550	Using Automated Audit Tools
	Seminar	3 days	750	Culprit/EDP Auditor—Concepts and Practice
	Seminar	2 days	595	Auditing MVS Workshop

* The lesser fee is for members.

Some of the offerors present their courses on an in-house basis; some publish fees for this; others negotiate fees on a case-by-case basis. Courses specifically directed at particular industries such as banking, insurance, retail, and oil and gas are also available.

Technology is offering yet another dimension to consider in effecting a program of EDP aid training. Videocassettes are being produced and marketed on a purchase or rental basis, and may be used in self-study programs or in connection with group presentations.

Videocassettes are usually part of an overall course design that includes audio, text, and other materials. The fees for the videocassettes are usually less than $50 if rented, and in the $750 range if purchased. Student handout materials must be purchased, and the fees are on a unit basis, ranging from a few dollars to more than $100 in some instances. A tutorial guide often must be purchased for each course for a slight additional fee. Courses usually are three to four hours in length, but some range much longer—up to 24 hours or more. Course subjects cover the entire range of computers, I/S, telecommunications, and data bases. Courses on non-EDP subjects are also available. The primary source for these courses is Deltak, Inc., 1751 Diehl Road, Naperville, Illinois. The IIA also has produced videos on such relevant topics as Auditing On-Line Systems and Controlling On-Line Systems.

Some internal audit departments may be in a position to develop in-house training that will enable non-I/S auditors to perform some form of limited I/S auditing. Many companies are finding that with proper training, non-I/S auditors perform such projects as I/S applications auditing with acceptable results.

MANAGEMENT OF PERSONAL COMPUTERS

An article in *Internal Auditing Alert* described several ways in which internal auditors are using PCs to ease the administrative work load and improve the efficiency and effectiveness of the audit work itself.[10] A portion of that article is reprinted below:

> **THE PERSONAL COMPUTER IN AUDITING**
>
> ☐ *Audit schedule.* The audit schedule plans the assignment for each auditor over a three-month period. Using the work sheet of Lotus 1-2-3 and listing the auditors' names vertically and the weeks horizontally, the audit plan can be prepared, updated, and revised easily with a clean print-out being available at any time. The work sheet provides space enough for a one-year history and changes are easier than on a wordprocessor.
>
> ☐ *Auditors' profile.* This work sheet lists the auditors and their data, which includes: starting data, grade, education, certification, and their practical experiences. The work sheet helps management to: (1) identify the best suited staff for a particular assignment and (2) select candidates for either additional training or for placement in vacancies that might exist throughout other organizations within the company. The sort and extract features of Lotus 1-2-3 are helpful in identifying the individuals based on predetermined criteria.
>
> ☐ *Department budget.* Preparing annual and monthly department budgets with comparisons to estimated actuals and the prior year's budget is an ideal application for Lotus 1-2-3 that will eliminate the footing and cross footing, and make changes easy once the work sheet is set up.
>
> ☐ *Time sheet control.* Most audit departments with a sizable staff are using weekly time sheets to control the auditors' activities or to generate billing information. Manual control over the receipt of time sheets and follow up on missing ones can be tedious. The Lotus 1-2-3 work sheet can be used for this purpose and for follow-up notices sent using the extract command.
>
> ☐ *Audit plan/ranking.* The audit plan lists all auditable locations within the company and provides for a systematic and formal audit coverage. To facilitate this, the audit plan should have some general information about the facility in addition to data on the last audit and the next scheduled coverage. If this plan is expanded to apply weights to preestablished risk factors, the audit plan can be used to combine both time elapsed and risk to schedule locations for future audit coverage. The risk factors can be the functions within each audit cycle. Once this is set up on the work sheets of Lotus 1-2-3, the updating for risk/weights based on recent audit reports provides for a current data base and helps audit management to focus future audit coverage on high risk areas.
>
> ☐ *Typing.* Many auditors have basic typing skills and would be able to generate a neater audit report draft using the PC. The wordprocessor package

---

[10] "The Personal Computer in Internal Auditing," *Internal Auditing Alert*, Dec., 1983, p. 2.

could be a solution, but the Lotus 1-2-3 basic work sheet can be used as well by setting the column width to 65 or 70 characters. The basic functions, such as insert, delete, etc., are available in the work sheet package and make typing much easier than on a typewriter.

☐ *The work sheet*. There are almost unlimited uses for the work sheet that the auditor can apply during the audit. Once the work sheet is set up, it can be used to generate trial balance with adjustments, balance sheets, income statements, variance calculations, percentage calculations, etc. It will certainly take the auditor some time to understand the capabilities of the basic work sheet and all of its functions, but once these are understood, the auditor will find the PC helpful in his or her basic audit work.

☐ *Graphs*. The Lotus 1-2-3 comes with a graphing capability making it easy to generate bar, line, or pie charts. Since a picture says more than a thousand words, graphs can enhance the readability of an audit report. For example, a graph can dramatically indicate the growth of inventory over a period, or a change in the mix.

☐ *PC talk*. PC talk is a communication software linking the personal computer with timesharing networks or with a main frame. Such a communication link enables the auditor to download data from the main frame and to use this data on his basic work sheet for further analysis. An auditor can also analyze and test an inventory file, accounts payable file, or a receivable file without leaving his or her office. The savings in travel time and expense can be substantial, but more important than that is the fact that the auditor can now look at the total population of the file and perform his audit work thereon, rather than relying on a test population. The technical problems involved with this mode should not be underestimated and it needs the support of the EDP audit staff, and most probably of the MIS group staff. The benefits, however, are well worth the initial setup problems to be encountered.

Training the Audit Staff

As indicated previously, overcoming the reluctance of the audit staff to use the PC is the biggest hurdle that audit management has to face. The basic training in the use of the PC is available as tutorial disks both for the PC and the software. The first step is that auditors should be scheduled to undergo the training and that audit management can demonstrate their familiarity with the equipment during the training phase. Encouraging auditors to bring up the audit schedule so that they know what their next assignments are, or to require the auditors to review the location's audit plan prior to going on assignment, will be a step in the right direction to make the staff more comfortable in the use of the equipment.

Auditing Will Change Over the Next Few Years

The audit staff should understand that the advent of the microcomputers will change the entire audit environment. We are not too far from that day, when every auditor will have a small microcomputer with communication capabilities in his briefcase, when the auditor will be able to review any file on a main frame, and when working papers are generated on floppy disks rather than on paper. The auditor has to prepare today for what will be in store for the profession in the near future. While the young college graduates have no problems adapting to this environment, the "old hands," and that very often includes audit management, seem to be reluctant to face the challenges early on. The PC in the audit department both for administrative tasks and for audit work is a required step that should not be delayed.

Automated Workpapers

Early applications of automating workpapers involve posting adjustments to trial balances, extending trial balances, summarizing and grouping individual accounts into financial statement line items, and performing ratio analyses.

Clearly, these applications have more to do with external auditing, that is, the examination of financial statements, than with internal auditing. However, internal auditors do assist external auditors in financial audits, and many perform limited reviews of interim financial statements.

An article appearing in the August 1985 *Journal of Accountancy* by Jeffrey A. Johnson describes how these applications work. A partial reprint follows:[11]

> There are two types of automated work paper programs: hard coded and template.
>
> The hard-coded programs have been written using a formal programming language such as COBOL and are highly structured. The user enters numbers on an input screen and, subsequently, receives a printed report. This approach can prove to be inflexible because users cannot modify the existing programs or add work papers to the system. In addition, the input screens do not always resemble the printed work papers, although some programs offer limited on-screen viewing of certain reports. Hard-coded systems take considerable time to set up and tend to run slowly. They may, however, be regarded as "idiot proof" because they are good at catching user input errors such as entering an invalid account number.
>
> Template work paper programs are built on existing programs such as Lotus 1-2-3 or dBase II. Although 1-2-3 and dBase are not programming languages in the traditional sense, they do offer significant programming capabilities. Since 1-2-3 and dBase already contain many useful commands, automated work paper programs written as templates within 1-2-3 or dBase can access their commands, making them faster and more efficient than hard-coded programs.
>
> Programs written using dBase II are similar to hard-coded programs because they use input screens and limited on-screen work paper viewing. However, Lotus 1-2-3 based systems provide complete on-screen viewing and editing of account data. The latter is an important feature since it eliminates the constant need for a printer.
>
> Automated work paper programs based on Lotus 1-2-3 possess considerable

---

[11] Jeffrey A. Johnson, "Automated Work Papers: A New Audit Tool," *Journal of Accountancy,* Aug. 1985, pp. 123, 124. Reprinted by permission. Copyright © 1985 by the American Institute of Certified Public Accountants.

flexibility and speed. They also can be adapted to any type of engagement and allow their users to modify or add to the basic program. One detraction of systems based on 1-2-3 is that they require more user knowledge and attention because they have less error-trapping capability. Accountants who are creating other work papers using 1-2-3 will soon realize that compatibility with this popular spreadsheet is an important consideration. More often than not, using a system based on 1-2-3 will help to quickly develop a staff's spreadsheet skills.

A list of software packages and vendors that perform workpaper preparation functions is provided in Figure 27-12.[12]

Software packages that are primarily designed to aid the auditor in preparing workpapers do not constitute all the packages that have potential for aid in this regard. Many software packages exist that permit the user to prepare spreadsheets and offer similar opportunities. Internal auditors are learning to adapt these to their specific work requirements. Some of these spreadsheet packages are generalized, while others are customized for certain functions, such as financial planning. A partial list of some of these packages is shown in Figure 27-13.

Software options for internal auditors go even beyond spreadsheet software. Beginning in 1983, software vendors began to develop and market programs that link together various functions formerly available in separate software packages. Referred to as integrated software, these products permit users to switch from one task to another, as is often required in any given undertaking, without the bothersome procedure of removing the program from the disk drive and inserting another. Perhaps the earliest version of these is Lotus 1-2-3 from Lotus Development Corporation, 161 First Street, Cambridge, Mass. 02142, (617) 494-1270. This package combines spreadsheet, data-base management, and graphics. It is priced somewhat higher than simple spreadsheet packages, at $495. Also, it requires more computer capability to operate than do most spreadsheet packages. Minimum requirements are 192K and two disk drives. Since Lotus 1-2-3, many rival packages have become available. These include *Super Calc 3 Release 2*, *Microsoft Windows*, and *Visi On* from the same vendors of the spreadsheet packages listed in Figure 17-14 for *Multiplan*, *Super Calc*, and *Visi Calc*. More sophisticated packages, such as *Symphony* from Lotus Development Corporation and *Framework* from Ashton-Tate, 10150 West Jefferson Boulevard, Culver City, Cal. 90230, (213) 204-5570, offer even more options and features. Naturally, these are also more expensive, at roughly $700. Also, they require at least 320K and two disk drives to be used effectively. They work best in microcomputers with hard disks. These and similar packages are the most versatile, powerful, and useful multitasking packages yet developed. Features include vastly expanded spreadsheets (more than 8000 rows and

---

[12] *Ibid.*, p. 127. Reprinted by permission of the American Institute of Certified Public Accountants.

FIG. 27-12
Audit Software Packages and Vendors

Software	Vendor
Audit Advantage	Informatics 3400 Lake Park Drive Atlanta, Georgia 38339 (800) 241-3306
Audit Cube	Blackman, Kallick & Company 180 North LaSalle Street Chicago, Illinois 60601 (312) 782-3424
Auditing Performance System	Professional Services Microsystems 1355 South Colorado Boulevard Suite 201 Denver, Colorado 80222 (303) 753-6093
Automated Workpapers	Linton Shafer 2 West Second Street Frederick, Maryland 21701 (800) 638-2220
Fast!	Financial Audit Systems 3801 Wake Forest Road Raleigh, North Carolina 27609 (919) 876-5033
Fast/CPA	McGladrey Hendrickson & Pullen 1300 Midwest Plaza East 800 Marquette Avenue Minneapolis, Minnesota 55402 (612) 332-4300
Fieldwork	Rubin, Brown, Gornstein & Co. 230 South Bemiston Avenue St. Louis, Missouri 63105 (314) 727-8150
Focus: ABC	Hemming Morse, Inc. 1700 South El Camino Real San Mateo, California 94402 (415) 574-1908
Glows Audit	Orion Microsystems, Inc. 910 Lafayette Building 5th and Chestnut Street Philadelphia, Pennsylvania 19106 (215) 928-1119
Pre-Audit	Coopers & Lybrand 1251 Avenue of the Americas New York, New York 10020 (800) 223-0535
Staff Accountant	Specialty Software 1075 North Tenth Street San Jose, California 95112 (408) 286-7936
Working Trial Balance	WTP Software P.O. Box 1164 Yuba City, California 94992 (800) 221-3134

FIG. 27-13
Spreadsheet Software

Product	Vendor	Cost	Requirements	Comments
Multiplan	Microsoft Corp. 10700 Northrup Way Box 97200 Bellevue, Wash. 98009 (800) 426-9400	$195	DOS 1.10-64K 1 disk drive DOS 2.10-128K, 1 disk drive	255 by 63 cell worksheet plus data sorting; spreadsheets can be linked allowing for automated updating
Medallion Spreadsheet	Timberline Software 7180 S.W. Fir Loop Portland, Ore. 97223 (503) 644-8155	$195	192K, 2 disk drives	48 mathematical functions for financial planning, e.g., not present value, rate of return; offers worksheet merging
Super Calc, Super Calc 2	Sorcim/IUS Software 2195 Fortune Drive San Jose, Cal. 95131 (408) 942-1727	1. $195 2. $295	64K, 1 disk drive	254 by 3 cell worksheet, two windows, compatible with *Wordstar*, Version 2 has automated sorting, merging, and other features
Visi Calc, Visi Calc IV	VisiCorp 2895 Zanker Road San Jose, Cal. 95134 (408) 946-9000	$199 IV $250	64K, 1 disk drive 192K, 2 disk drives-IV	254 by 63 cell worksheet, two windows. Visi Calc IV offers sorting and graphics, unlimited number of macros
Easy Calc	Norell Data Systems Corp. 3400 Wilshire Blvd. Los Angeles, Cal. 90010 (213) 257-2026	$100	64K, 1 disk drive	52 column spreadsheet for budgeting, project investment, taxes
Electronic Spreadsheet	American Planning Corp. 4600 Duke St. # 425 Alexandria, Va. 22304 (763) 751-2574	$1,500	64K, hard disk	For large scale spreadsheets; handles up to 2 million numbers; performs math calculations in 3 dimensions

256 columns). They also allow multiple windows for simultaneous viewing of several documents or portions of the same documents.

Other integrated programs have been developed that are more accounting or finance oriented. For a current evaluation of these, the reader is referred to the March 1986 issue of the *Journal of Accountancy*.

Implementation Strategy

Like any other prospective user of microcomputers, internal auditing departments must be prudent and control-conscious when adding the power of microcomputers to their audit resources. Microcomputers, or PCs, must be properly managed, with attention to the following:

- Proper planning and establishing of priorities for events.
- Developing written specifications of what is intended to be done with the PCs. Considerations include volume of data and frequency of use, types of input required, and processing requirements. Reporting requirements must also be identified.
- Acquiring and installing activities.
- System security considerations.
- Documentation disciplines. An up-to-date record must be kept of each application, describing how it works. In addition, a log of diskettes must be maintained, indicating such information as contents and owners.
- Training the users to use the PC in the intended manner.

In deciding which software and hardware to acquire, the following factors are important, according to a recent Price Waterhouse publication:[13]

1. *Software:*
   - ☐ Does the software package have the capabilities you need? Ask for a demonstration; "seeing is believing."
   - ☐ Has the software been widely sold? Does your retail dealer understand the software? Do not help the developer "debug" the software unless you are truly prepared for that approach. Being the "first kid on the block" with microcomputer software packages can bring its share of headaches.
   - ☐ Is the operating system software an established system? Again, being unique and upfront has some real risks.
   - ☐ Does the software provide facilities for an adequate audit trail? Having the ability to know what transactions were processed is important to most users.
   - ☐ Is the software "user friendly"? If you cannot learn to use the software in a matter of hours, chances are a better package can be found.

---

[13] Price Waterhouse, *Microcomputers: Their Use and Misuse in Your Business* (New York: Price Waterhouse, 1983), p. 20. Reprinted with permission.

- ☐ Does the program have editing and balancing controls? Most operators make at least some mistakes; improve the chances of finding them.
- ☐ Do controls exist to prevent programs from being run in the wrong order?
- ☐ Can authorized changes to the program be made by your own personnel? A program written in some programming languages may be difficult for you to modify down the road.
- ☐ Is the documentation adequate? Do not be impressed by a fancy binder or a slick brochure. Read the documentation. Can you understand it?

2. *Hardware:*
   - ☐ Will the software you have selected run efficiently on the hardware under consideration?
   - ☐ Is there sufficient processing and storage capacity to meet current requirements and sufficient expansion capacity to meet anticipated needs?
   - ☐ What are the manufacturer's and retail dealer's reputations and financial stabilities?
   - ☐ How will timely maintenance be provided? Will backup systems be available?
   - ☐ Are there communications capabilities allowing linkage with your other EDP equipment? Plan for the future!
   - ☐ Are delivery arrangements realistic or are they over-optimistic promises? Don't buy a prototype machine; be sure it is really in current volume production.
   - ☐ Is the equipment realistically priced? Discounts are common in the sale of microcomputers. Ask for one!

Copyright © 1983 Price Waterhouse, Microcomputers: Their Use and Misuse in Your Buiness.

Additional criteria to consider in acquiring PCs is presented in Chapter 26.

PERFORMING I/S AUDITS

Applicability of Basic Audit Approach

Effective I/S auditing requires the same organized, disciplined approach that is followed in traditional auditing. The commentary in Chapters 11 and 12 regarding preliminary work and fieldwork are equally applicable to I/S auditing.

Preliminary Work. The nature and extent of preliminary work depends on whether the assignment is recurring or nonrecurring. Installation reviews tend to recur (these are performed at least once every year or two). There

INFORMATION SYSTEMS (EDP) AUDIT FUNCTION

are also recurring aspects of application audits, functional audits, and developing system reviews.

Nonrecurring audit efforts require more extensive planning, research and coordination with users and EDP personnel to enable the I/S auditor to be properly prepared. This is particularly true for the more technical undertakings. Examples of these include audits of telecommunications, operating systems, and data-base management systems. It is important that audit objectives in these reviews be clearly established and the feasibility of accomplishment be carefully assessed. This point is perhaps more important in nonrecurring I/S auditing than it is for other types of auditing. That situation exists because I/S technology is such that the means necessary to accomplish an objective may be beyond the capability of the auditor, or may require excessive use of I/S facilities or staff, or both.

Fieldwork. The concept of fieldwork—that portion of the work done away from the auditor's home office—is not as clear in I/S auditing as it is for traditional auditing. That arises because the I/S auditor's home office is usually at or near the data centers. As a result, much of the fieldwork may be performed at the auditor's office. When aided by a terminal and other computer equipment, a considerable amount of inquiry, inspection, observation, and confirmation may be accomplished without leaving the office and with less coordination than is required in traditional auditing.

In addition, many specific I/S audit tasks take more time to complete than the average non-I/S audit task. For example, common tasks, such as reviewing system documentation, programming documentation, and user manuals, can be quite time-consuming. As a result, day-to-day planning is less critical than for other types of auditing.

Documentation. The purpose of conducting I/S audit fieldwork is to gather evidential matter relevant to the auditor's objectives (i.e., the same as for regular audits). The I/S auditor's workpapers, which document the evidence-gathering activities, are extremely important. Workpapers will usually contain the following items:

- An identification of contents
- A project completion checklist
- Final report copy
- Drafts and related documentation
- Administrative section (work authorization, time budget, actual time record)
- Audit program
- Summary narrative of work performed
- Summary narrative of findings

- Organizational documentation (flow charts, policies, and organization charts, as applicable)
- System/program documentation, as applicable
- Questionnaires
- Tests

In the case of I/S auditing, the documentation of testing can differ considerably from that in traditional auditing—if the computer is used to perform some of the work. In that event, the workpapers would include coding sheets, input data, program cards, and output data. An example of this type of documentation is shown in Figure 27-14. I/S auditors must also document the purpose of the test, the methodology used, and the conclusions drawn, if any.

Evidential Matter

Evidential matter is as critical in I/S auditing as it is in non-I/S auditing. Therefore, the definitions, principles, and concepts discussed in Chapter 14 apply to I/S auditing with equal force.

The nature of evidential matter in an EDP environment differs considerably from that in a non-EDP environment. Typical forms of EDP-oriented evidential matter are shown below. By comparison with the evidential matter shown in Figure 14-1, the difference becomes evident. It is also apparent that most of the evidential matter that can be examined is internally developed, usually from controlled processes. The reference point for the terms "internal" and "external" in the I/S department are given in the following:

1. External evidence
   - User manuals
   - Source documents
   - Batch control logs
   - Policies and procedures
2. Internal evidence
   - Standards, policies, and procedures
   - System documentation
   - Program documentation
   - Source programs—library version
   - Object programs—machine version
   - Data files
   - Machine logs
   - Console messages
   - Run manuals
   - Reports
   - System-generated documents

Because this evidence is generated from or affected by the dynamic data processing surroundings, its reliability is not as high as that for the various types of primary evidence listed in Figure 14-1, unless the auditor has established its reliability through appropriate audit techniques. Needless to say, properly controlled computer-generated data are extremely reliable.

Many of the control techniques that were identified in Chapter 26, such as limit checks and edit routines, operate without leaving any evidential trail.

INFORMATION SYSTEMS (EDP) AUDIT FUNCTION

FIG. 27-14
Statistical Sampling Computer Report

STRATUM	STRATUM SIZE	SAMPLE SIZE	SAMPLE BOOK VAL.	SAMPLE AUDIT VAL.	SAMPLE DIFF.	SAMPLE VARIANCE	SAMPLE STD. DEVN.
1	86,281	14	420.20	420.20	0.00	398.69	19.96
2	64,452	11	1,131.32	1,131.32	0.00	112.31	10.59
3	43,360	13	2,469.57	2,469.57	0.00	1,016.90	81.88
4	20,776	11	3,378.93	3,378.93	0.00	2,253.45	47.62
5	18,818	13	7,610.73	7,610.73	0.00	4,834.86	69.53
6	12,126	13	11,072.03	9,124.61	1,947.42−	110,075.81	331.77
7	4,768	13	23,404.58	23,404.58	0.00	124,746.23	353.19
8	2,813	14	39,260.76	39,260.76	0.00	212,206.34	460.65
9	1,355	12	61,248.90	61,248.90	0.00	530,144.24	728.11
10	835	13	123,358.82	123,358.82	0.00	1,274,895.15	1,129.11
11	492	13	230,571.97	189,385.53	41,186.44−	47,146,832.40	6,866.35
12	304	14	440,768.33	309,078.11	131,690.22−	226,171,135.80	15,038.98
13	186	15	804,847.68	804,847.68	0.00	111,122,829.81	10,541.48
14	110	16	1,538,671.88	1,373,790.77	164,881.11−	1350,456,662.81	36,748.56
15	74	16	2,670,815.93	2,528,280.72	142,535.21−	2133,714,576.14	46,192.14
HIGH-VALUES	137	137	55,527,913.94	55,867,527.85			
TOTALS	258,887	338	71,486,940.57	61,344,314.09	10,142,626.48−		

SAMPLING POPULATION BOOK VALUE 190,865,147.73

SAMPLING RESULTS USING MEAN-PER-UNIT ESTIMATION:

```
ESTIMATE TYPE          1    ESTIMATED POPULATION VALUE   175,541,339.66
RELIABILITY           90    PRECISION OF ESTIMATE          3,215,188.01
                            LOWER CONFIDENCE LIMIT       172,326,150.65
                            UPPER CONFIDENCE LIMIT       178,756,526.67
```

Moreover, unless the evidence obtained by the auditor was produced as part of the actual system operation, there is no absolute assurance that it is valid. For example, the auditor may attempt to simulate the actual operation of a program by running a set of test transactions, using a production program obtained from the library source program. However, there is some risk that this version of the program is not the same version that was used in actual production. In EDP shops, where programmers and others may have access to source programs and production programs (frequently the case), the reliability of the indicated results is less than 100 percent certain.

Another factor affecting evidence-gathering efforts is the auditor's dependence on the organization being audited to complete some of the critical audit steps. For example, if the auditor wishes to select information from an existing data file, he must obtain the assistance of the I/S department to set up and run his selection program, to dump a file, or whatever. This is less of a problem in on-line systems to which the auditor has access via terminal, or in situations in which the auditor is permitted to enter the computer room and operate his own programs.

The foregoing factors influence the methods that are used to gather evidence in a computer-oriented audit. The auditor must often originate evidence to have a proper basis for drawing conclusions. Accordingly, procedures such as the snapshot, transaction test decks, and process simulating have been devised to produce the evidence. These and other I/S auditing techniques are the subject of Chapter 28.

SUGGESTED READING

Auditing Advanced EDP Systems Task Force. *Management, Control and Audit of Advanced EDP Systems.* New York: AICPA, 1977.

Cummings, Barbara K., and Nicholas G. Apostolou. "Expert Systems in Auditing: An Emerging Technology." *Internal Auditing,* Fall 1987, pp. 3–10.

EDP Auditing Committee. *Hatching the EDP Audit Function.* Orlando, Fla.: The Institute of Internal Auditors, Inc., 1975.

Ferris, David. "The Micro-Mainframe Connection." *Datamation,* Nov. 1983, pp. 126–138.

Halper, Stanley D., P. Jarlath O'Neil-Dunne, and Xenia Ley Parker. *Handbook of EDP Auditing.* Copyright © 1987 by Coopers & Lybrand, published by Warren, Gorham & Lamont, Inc.

Macchiaverna, Paul R. *Auditing Corporate Data Processing Activities,* Chapters 2–6. U.S.A.: The Conference Board, Inc., 1980.

Mair, William C., Donald R. Wood, and Keagle W. Davis. *Computer Control and Audit,* 2nd ed., Chapter 24. U.S.A.: Touche Ross & Co., 1976.

Price Waterhouse. "Managing Computer Risks, A Guide for the Policymaker." New York: Price Waterhouse, 1984.

Software Digest, Inc. "How Do Integrated Accounting Programs Compare?" *Journal of Accountancy,* Mar. 1986, pp. 96–104.

Systems Auditability & Control, Audit Practices, Chapters 4–5. U.S.A.: The Institute of Internal Auditors, 1977.

Weber, Ron. *EDP Auditing Conceptual Foundations and Practice,* Chapters 2–3. New York: McGraw-Hill, Inc., 1982.

CHAPTER **28**

Information Systems (EDP) Audit Techniques

Introduction 2	Embedded Audit Routines 23
	Utility Programs 25
Overview 2	Other System Software 26
Definition and Purpose 4	Security Software 27
Sampling Applicability 4	**Improving Performance Efficiency and**
Nonstatistical Sampling 5	**Effectiveness** 28
Statistical Sampling 7	Generalized Audit Software 29
	Utility Programs 35
Traditional Auditing Techniques 7	Other System Software 35
Observation 8	Embedded Routines 36
Inquiry 9	Expert Systems 36
Inspection 10	
Confirmation 11	**Protecting Independence** 38
	The Audit Facility 38
Computer-Assisted Audit Techniques ... 12	Utility Programs 40
Definition and Objectives 12	Program Verifications 40
Applicability 13	Operating System Reviews 41
	Other Operating System Reviews 45
Techniques for Auditing Controls 16	
Tracing 16	**Audit Uses of Personal Computers** 53
Snapshot 17	Criteria in Selecting
Test Data 18	MicroComputers 53
Integrated Test Facility 19	Audit Uses 55
Parallel Simulation 20	
Parallel Simulation Using Generalized	**Final Thoughts** 58
Audit Software 22	**Suggested Reading** 59

Fig. 28-1	Use of I/S Audit Tools and Techniques	3
Fig. 28-2	Selected Activities for Which Nonstatistical Sampling Is Necessary	6
Fig. 28-3	Classification of Computer-Assisted Audit Techniques	13
Fig. 28-4	Narrative Workpaper Illustrating Difficulties in Applying Computer-Assisted Audit Techniques	15
Fig. 28-5	Flow Chart Depicting Parallel Simulation	21
Fig. 28-6	Depiction of Embedded Audit Routines	24
Fig. 28-7	A Tabulation of Generalized Audit Software Packages and Their Vendors	30
Fig. 28-8	Situations in Which Generalized Audit Software May Be of Use	32
Fig. 28-9	Comparison of Audit Techniques Common to I/S and Non-I/S Auditing Indicating the Potential for Independent Performance	39

Fig. 28-10 Suppliers of PC AT Compatibles 56
Fig. 28-11 Software Products for Downloading Data 57

INTRODUCTION

The objective of this chapter is to familiarize practitioners and audit management with the techniques that have evolved to gather evidential matter in an I/S environment. In addition, typical situations in which these audit tools may be used are identified. The discussions are provided in the context of the previous analysis of auditing techniques in Chapters 15 and 16.

The descriptions of I/S auditing techniques will not be so detailed as to constitute "how to" explanations. The circumstances in which I/S auditing procedures are applied vary considerably, making detailed explanations of limited value in a general reference work such as this one. By defining and describing the techniques, relating them to auditing objectives, discussing their applicability, and commenting on advantages, disadvantages, and documentation requirements, it is believed that practitioners, managers, and directors will be sufficiently informed to decide how best to utilize them in their respective auditing organizations.

OVERVIEW

When the subject of I/S auditing is introduced, the imagination invariably conjures up a scene in which the performing auditor, steeped in technical awareness of the EDP environment, is busy scrutinizing some endless listing of program code surrounded by data processing reports in a room with walls covered by bewildering mazes of flow chart diagrams, computer-generated art work, and vendor-supplied calendars.

To be sure, the I/S auditor must spend time reviewing code and doing other things that require specialized knowledge, as we shall see. But much of his time is devoted to performing the same procedures as are completed in the course of non-I/S auditing. Accordingly, the applicability of sampling techniques and the various traditional auditing procedures associated with observation, inspection, inquiry, and confirmation are included in this discussion of I/S auditing.

Before beginning the analysis, it is necessary to put the subject of requisite skill in some perspective. Some very large corporations, particularly banks, have sizeable I/S auditing departments that consist of persons with skill levels ranging from trainees who possess little technical knowledge, to senior auditors who possess a thorough understanding of large-scale systems and communications methods (modems, protocols, teleprocessing software, transmission techniques operating systems, data bases, and utility pro-

FIG. 28-1
Use of I/S Audit Tools and Techniques

I/S Audit Tool/Technique	Percentage Used in Auditing Developments and Modifications*	Percentage Used in Auditing Production Systems*
Generalized audit software	12.5%	32.6%
Manual tracing and mapping routines	22.9	31.2
Test data method (e.g., test-decking)	27.1	26.6
Parallel operation	32.2	23.1
Tagged transactions (flagging transactions in "live" operations for later review)	12.0	20.9
Snapshot (picture-taking of selected transactions through the flow of transactions)	10.0	18.4
Systems performance monitoring and analysis (e.g., System Management Facility (SMF)	8.2	15.8
Program source code comparison	9.6	14.5
Control flowcharting	8.3	9.0
Program object code comparison	4.7	8.9
Integrated test facility (mini- or dummy company)	4.2	5.0
Modeling (simulation)	9.5	7.6
Automatic tracing and mapping routines (analysis of source language and logic to determine if any program segments are not being utilized)	3.6	3.9
Other	6.5	10.5

* Percentages are based on actual responses weighted to reflect the probable response distribution of all organizations in the sampling frame.

Which of the following tools and techniques are used in auditing I/S application systems in your organization?

grams). However, a 1980 survey has shown that most companies' I/S auditing needs are serviced by very small staffs. Indeed, the survey found the size of the average I/S audit staff to be four, including the supervisor or manager, for the 162 companies surveyed.[1] While it is safe to observe that most companies are increasing the size of their I/S audit staffs, it is unlikely that significant increases have yet occurred to materially alter that average. While information pertaining to skill was not presented in the reported results, it is unlikely that the average I/S audit staff possesses the skill level indicated above for a senior I/S auditor.

There are two points that are evident from this state of affairs. First, the absence of high skill within an I/S auditing function does not mean that I/S auditing cannot be performed. Second, the extent of auditing that is performed must be planned and designed in such a way so as to maximize

---

[1] Paul Macchiaverna, *Auditing Corporate Data-Processing Activities* (New York: The Conference Board, Inc., 1980), p. 50.

the use of the skill levels that are available. Most I/S audit projects are time-consuming, and those that involve performing sophisticated evidence-gathering techniques, such as integrated test facilities, are even more costly in this respect. The audit manager and director must carefully assess the benefits of allocating the time required for such techniques against the costs and decide accordingly. Much useful I/S auditing can be accomplished without ever applying the advanced techniques discussed later. However, the auditing of large-scale, advanced information systems must utilize the most sophisticated techniques to achieve maximum effectiveness and efficiency.

As is evident from Figure 28-1, the use of advanced I/S auditing methods is not great, with the possible exception of generalized audit software.[2] This might be explained by the fact that most I/S auditors do not possess the skill level necessary to use them. It might also mean that the instances are rare in which these techniques can be used effectively. It is likely that future technological advances will occur that will enable these, and other techniques yet to be devised, to be applied more easily and universally.

DEFINITION AND PURPOSE

"I/S audit techniques" is the term given to a collection of procedures and tools that are used by the auditor in an I/S environment. The purpose or objective of such techniques is to enable the auditor to gather sufficient competent evidential matter to permit the expression of an opinion regarding system controls and to provide a basis for the reliable reporting of other information of interest to management. Depending on the nature of the project, the opinion may take the form of assurance with respect to the sufficiency of controls in a selected I/S function or an installation, in a specific application, or in a developing system.

The reader will recognize that the objectives of I/S auditing are consistent with the objective of internal auditing in general, as set forth in Chapter 2. That is, that the I/S auditor's objective in providing the aforementioned opinions and other information in the areas noted is consistent with the broad objective of providing information of interest to the organization.

SAMPLING APPLICABILITY

The concept of sampling described in Chapter 15 is applicable to I/S auditing to some extent. However, the speed and efficiency of the computer is such

---

[2] *Systems Auditability & Control; Audit Practices* (Altamonte Springs, Fla.: The Institute of Internal Auditors, 1977), p. 65. Copyright © 1977 by the Institute of Internal Auditors, Inc., 249 Maitland Avenue, Altamonte Springs, Florida 32701, U.S.A. Reprinted with permission.

INFORMATION SYSTEMS (EDP) AUDIT TECHNIQUES

that, in many cases, an entire population can be examined at practically no discernible increase in cost. If the evidence the auditor seeks exists in files resident in the computer system, the computer can be made to divulge the contents accurately, completely, and quickly. Thus, if the auditor is testing compliance with established procedures (e.g., restricting preparation of checks to amounts less than $10,000 in an automated check-writing system), if conditions permit, he may use the computer to report all instances in which compliance did not occur. In such circumstances, the auditor would be 100 percent certain of results—an outcome not attainable in the non-EDP world at a reasonable cost.

It may not always be feasible to examine 100 percent of the population of a given transaction class. When the auditor is interested in evaluating some characteristic of the entire population but examines less than the entire population, then sampling is involved (see Chapter 15).

Nonstatistical Sampling

Most forms of traditional audit techniques—those involving observation, inquiry, inspection, and confirmation—insofar as sample size is concerned, are determined by exercising professional judgment. This is true whether or not the audit project involves EDP. However, in the special instance of I/S auditing, nonstatistical, or judgment, sampling is used even more extensively than in non-I/S auditing. That is because, while I/S organizations process huge volumes of transactions, the number of activities or routines involved to produce those data do not generally occur with sufficient frequency to permit the mathematical laws of statistics to operate.

It is also true that while many EDP operations and activities are recorded, many may occur without leaving a sufficient evidential trail. Examples include mathematical calculations, limit checks, and edit routines. Figure 28-2 contains a tabulation of selected types of I/S auditing for which this often holds true.

While Figure 28-2 is not exhaustive, it serves to illustrate that many important activities in an I/S environment do not occur frequently, or, if they do, there may be no auditable evidence available. Since these characteristics preclude the use of statistical sampling, the auditor must use professional judgment in devising his program of testing. To compensate for the absence of documentary evidence, innovative auditors have devised techniques borrowed from programmers to produce evidence that permits the inference to be made that controls actually operated without, in fact, seeing them operate in a real-time environment. These techniques, which include test decks, transaction tagging, and integrated test facilities, are discussed later in this chapter. Other techniques have been devised, such as embedding audit routines in existing applications, which perform their "audits" as the programs are run. These techniques, also discussed later, are aimed at overcoming the "simulated" nature of the earlier mentioned

FIG. 28-2

Selected Activities for Which Nonstatistical Sampling Is Necessary

Audit Area	Example of Specific Control or Activity	Frequency of Occurrence	Audit Trail Produced?
Functional audits and installation reviews:			
Programming standards	Change in standards	I	Yes
Policies procedures	Change in policies or procedures	I	Yes
Budgets and planning	Preparation	I	Yes
Program maintenance	Change to programs	F	Usually
Operating system	Change to system	I	Usually
Data base management	Access control	VF	Not usually
Data entry	Batch control	VF	Varies
Library control	Access control	VF	Not usually
Computer operation	Restarts	VF	Not usually
Security	Tape backup	F	Not usually
Physical security controls	Computer room entrance controls	VF	Not usually
Developing system audits:			
Project controls	Project feasibility study	I	Usually
Specifications	Preparation	I	Usually
System control	Design of system	F/I	Usually
System test	Test of design	I	Usually
Implementation	Formal approval	I	Usually
Existing applications:			
Input controls	Batch control	VF	Not usually
Access controls	Terminal use	VF	Not usually
Processing controls	Edit routines	VF	Not usually
Update controls	Balancing	VF	Not usually
Output controls	Report distribution	VF	Not usually

KEY

I — Infrequent, fewer than 100 times per year for most installations
F — Frequent, in the range of 100–1,000 times per year
VF — Very frequent, several thousand occurrences per year

INFORMATION SYSTEMS (EDP) AUDIT TECHNIQUES 28-7

methods. In this way, the evidential matter thus generated is believed to be of greater reliability and, thus, more useful to the auditor. The decisions involved in establishing the nature and extent to which any of these techniques is employed are based on exercising professional judgment.

Statistical Sampling

From the preceding discussion, it may appear as though statistical sampling has no place in I/S auditing. That is not the case. Attribute sampling may be used to test the accuracy and validity of the contents of master files, particularly those in which the number of records within the file is quite large. These might include:

- Employee master files in a payroll system
- Vendor master files in a payables system
- Customer files in a billing system
- Bill of material files in a material requirements system
- Mailing lists in an advertising system

The trend toward on-line data-base systems has made it economically feasible to design into new applications the capability to perform statistical sampling selections—and perhaps the actual testing—automatically. It is not difficult to implant a statistical sampling program in a given application during its development, which is executed only by the auditing department whenever desired. Many "stand alone" generalized statistical sampling programs have also been developed that can determine sample size and evaluate sample results. These may be used in lieu of embedded routines. Thus, in a seemingly odd turn of events, auditing "around the computer" may be more feasible because the computer itself can be used to perform the work.

Audits of this type are referred to as auditing around the computer because, rather than understand and confirm the process that generates and maintains the master files, the contents are verified by tracing pertinent details to original source documents. The testing may be done in either a statistical or nonstatistical fashion. If the results are satisfactory to the auditor, he may conclude by inference that the methods used to create the file and keep it current must be adequate.

While the practice has been widely used because of its simplicity, in recent years, it has been giving way gradually to more sophisticated techniques that involve auditing "through the computer."

TRADITIONAL AUDITING TECHNIQUES

Traditional auditing techniques are described in Chapter 16 as comprising various forms of observation, inquiry, inspection, and confirmation. This section describes how these techniques are applicable to I/S auditing. Generally speaking, they are associated with evidence-gathering efforts of installation and functional reviews, developing system audits, program verifications, and certain aspects of application audits.

Persons applying these techniques need not possess an extensive understanding of the technical aspects of data processing. However, they must be familiar with EDP concepts, control objectives, and terminology.

Observation

Observation procedures are described in Chapter 16 as gathering evidence by actually seeing or observing activities in a real-time sense to corroborate management assertions or other data that relate to the auditor's objectives. The nature and extent of the observation effort is usually determined by judgment. Several I/S activities are cited in Chapter 36 as being susceptible to observation. To these, the following may be added:

- ☐ Functional
  - Recovery from system interruptions
  - Monitoring of terminal operator activities
  - Handling of negotiable documents
  - Equipment maintenance activities
  - Controls to restrict access to the computer
  - Tape handling procedures
  - Tests of disaster recovery plans
- ☐ Systems in development
  - Project status review meetings
  - Training sessions
  - System testing
- ☐ Existing applications
  - System operation
  - Debugging activities
  - Report distribution routine

The principal advantage of observation audit procedures is ease of performance. The principal disadvantage is that there is no way to be certain that the observed conduct is reflective of practices occurring when the auditor is not present. Therefore, the results of this work must be considered in the light of results of other procedures to minimize the possibility of drawing invalid conclusions. Documentation of I/S observation techniques are similar to those employed in non-I/S audit efforts.

INFORMATION SYSTEMS (EDP) AUDIT TECHNIQUES

Inquiry

Inquiry is defined in Chapter 16 as the effort to obtain information relevant to the auditor's purpose. While, in a general sense, this is true of all auditing techniques, in the specific instance of inquiry, a sort of querying approach is suggested. Generally, the nature and extent of inquiry is determined by the auditor's judgment. Specific forms of inquiry covered in the chapter include interviewing, researching, analyzing, and reviewing; and they apply to I/S auditing perhaps to an even greater extent than in non-I/S auditing. The objectives of these techniques are as follows:

- ☐ Interviews
  - To gain an understanding of the workings of a particular function or application
  - To corroborate assertions obtained in gaining an understanding
- ☐ Research
  - To enhance the auditor's knowledge of a particular technical aspect, such as data-base management or operating systems
  - To obtain information relative to resolving a particular problem or difficulty encountered during the review
- ☐ Analysis
  - To provide information as to the efficiency and effectiveness of certain activities
  - To detect the existence of breakdowns in controls, which may require remedial action

The interview and research forms are used in virtually every I/S audit. The extent to which the auditor employs them depends on his knowledge of the audit subject and his awareness of the practices in use by the organization under review. Analytical techniques are used less frequently. Typical analytical efforts include:

- ☐ Flow charting of both existing and developing applications to better understand and evaluate system controls. Flow charts often already exist, in which case they may be obtained and reviewed by the auditor for the same purpose.
- ☐ Program analysis in existing and developing system reviews to spot bugs in program logic and to evaluate the efficiency and effectiveness of the program. (Note: Computer-assisted techniques to aid in program analysis are discussed later in this chapter.)
- ☐ Trend analysis to evaluate the effectiveness and efficiency of computer utilization. Analytical data could be accumulated regarding:
  - Programmer and system analyst hours
  - CPU hours
  - Printed lines of data
  - Mean time between equipment failures

- Machine hours
- Percent of available capacity utilized
- Graphic frames produced
- Microfiche masters produced

☐ Regression analysis might be used to obtain insight into the relationships of certain variables, such as:

• Dependent variable	• Independent variable
— Number of requirement changes	— Cost of system development
— Number of emergency changes	— Cost of system maintenance
— Number of terminals	— Response time
— Number of programmers	— Maintenance costs

The advantage of most forms of inquiry is that they are not difficult to perform, provided they are properly planned and executed. This is particularly true with respect to interviews and research. Some types of analytical procedures, on the other hand, require greater skill. The disadvantage of inquiry is the increased chance that inferences that may be drawn are invalid. I/S auditors must devise ways to corroborate information obtained via inquiry. The documentation techniques for inquiry insofar as it pertains to I/S auditing are similar to those previously described in Chapter 16.

Inspection

Inspection, as set forth in Chapter 16, is closely related to observation. If there is a difference between the terms, it may be that inspection implies a more systematic search, in the sense of looking for something. Observation, on the other hand, implies simply seeing what is happening.

The forms of inspection, which include reading, scanning, reviewing, and vouching, all apply to I/S auditing. The extent to which these techniques are used is usually determined by judgment. Much of the I/S auditor's time in connection with audits of systems in the development phase is spent reading, for example. Such documentation as feasibility studies, requirements analysis, and specification statements must be carefully read, although scans may be made of portions of these data, as well as flow charts and program specifications. Records of costs expended and hours consumed may be vouched to source documents.

In existing application audits, system and program documentation may be read or scanned, and flow charts and program listings may be reviewed. Contents of key master files may be selectively vouched to supporting documents. Inspection procedures are also found in a like vein in audits of installations and specific functions.

The advantage of inspection procedures, particularly vouching, is that they usually carry a higher reliability than other forms of gathering evidence. The principal disadvantage is that the techniques are often time-consuming.

INFORMATION SYSTEMS (EDP) AUDIT TECHNIQUES

Documenting inspection routines in I/S audits differs little from documentation techniques for other types of auditing.

Confirmation

Confirmation auditing procedures, as noted in Chapter 16, are used by internal auditors to confirm or corroborate their understanding of controls, which is gained through inquiry, by performing selected compliance tests. I/S auditors also make use of certain forms of confirmation, including reperformance, simulation, and confirmation.

Reperformance is an auditing technique in which the auditor duplicates the performance of a selected control process. Usually, it is done because there is no existing evidence or audit trail indicating original performance. The method is most often used in connection with applications auditing. Thus, the auditor may manually recompute calculations made by the computer (e.g., to derive gross and net pay in a payroll application). Not all computer processes can be confirmed in this manner, however. For example, a limit check on gross pay would only operate if one or more transactions exceeded the limit. This may never occur or may occur very rarely, depending on the relationship of the limit to the range of gross pay calculations.

Under these circumstances, the only way to test the proper functioning of the limited check or a reperformance is to test the entire payroll. However, evidence of proper functioning can be obtained through simulation, a term comprising a variety of computer-assisted audit techniques that simulate, but do not duplicate, the processes that should be occurring. Examples of simulation include running tests desks, parallel simulation, and integrated test facilities. These are described later in this chapter.

Confirmation, as used here, means to corroborate through inquiry the representations and assertions made by management and others to auditors. The confirmations may be obtained orally or in writing, as indicated in Chapter 16. Confirmation may be used in I/S auditing to:

- Corroborate user satisfaction in a developing system audit.
- Confirm sufficiency of computer response time with on-line users.
- Conduct an audit of the time-sharing function.
- Confirm compliance with various policies and procedures through discussions with programmers, operators, and others in connection with functional audits or installation reviews.

Confirmation procedures may be performed on either a nonstatistical or a statistical sampling basis, depending on circumstances.

The advantage of confirmation procedures is that normally they are easy to perform. The disadvantage is that the information gathered may not be as reliable as that from other forms of testing, such as vouching, and thus should be used in connection with other procedures. I/S auditors document confirmation procedures in their workpapers in much the same way as non-I/S auditors.

COMPUTER-ASSISTED AUDIT TECHNIQUES

Definition and Objectives

Computer-assisted audit techniques (CAAT) have been defined as tools used "in carrying out basic verification techniques, additional management verification techniques and compensating audit procedures."[3] The tools make use of the processing power of the computer to help the auditor achieve his audit objectives. In the brief time that computers have been in existence, numerous computer-assisted techniques have been developed, usually by programmers, to aid in testing and debugging new systems in an effort to keep abreast with the rapid pace of new developments. These techniques, along with generalized audit software, utility programs, and embedded audit routines, form the bulk of CAAT.

The objectives of CAAT are inherent in the definition of the term. Three basic objectives are involved, although each is not necessarily present in all instances in which these tools are used. In fact, the techniques are easiest to understand when they are categorized according to objective. The discussion of CAAT is presented in that fashion. The objectives into which CAAT may be classified are:

- ☐ *Auditing controls.* To gather evidence enabling inferences to be drawn by the auditor regarding controls and processes performed by the computer.
- ☐ *Improving performance efficiency and effectiveness.* To expedite the performance of other auditing procedures and to enhance audit quality and reliability.
- ☐ *Protecting independence.* To minimize the degree of dependence by the auditor on EDP facilities and personnel (the auditee) for the performance of his tests and to detect conditions that may suggest wrongdoing.

The techniques employed to accomplish these objectives are shown in Figure 28-3. For ease of reference, the foregoing objectives have been assigned abbreviated headings in the figure. It is clear from this presentation, which is intended to be illustrative and not all-inclusive, that more techniques have been developed to achieve the first objective (having to do with the

---

[3] Study Group on Computer Control and Audit Guidelines, *Computer-Audit Guidelines* (Toronto, Canada: The Canadian Institute of Chartered Accountants, 1975), p. 248.

FIG. 28-3
Classification of Computer-Assisted Audit Techniques

OBJECTIVES

1. **Auditing Controls:**
   - ☐ Walk-through techniques
     - ▪ Tracing
     - ▪ Snapshot routine
     - ▪ Extended record
   - ☐ Testing techniques:
     - ▪ Test data
     - ▪ Integrated test facility
     - ▪ Parallel simulation
     - ▪ Parallel simulation using generalized software
     - ▪ Embedded audit routines
   - ☐ Utility programs

2. **Improving Performance Efficiency and Effectiveness:**
   - ☐ Generalized audit software
   - ☐ Utility programs
   - ☐ Embedded audit routines

3. **Protecting Independence:**
   - ☐ Audit facility
   - ☐ Utility programs
   - ☐ Program verification
   - ☐ Operating system review

---

auditing of controls) than is the case for the others. That is because auditing of controls is generally regarded as probably the most important I/S audit activity. It is also evident from Figure 28-3 that some techniques are more versatile than others (e.g., utility programs and embedded routines).

Many CAATs were not developed by auditors. Rather, they were borrowed from programmers who had devised them primarily to facilitate system testing. Examples include test data, the integrated test facility, and parallel simulation.

Since the early 1970s, auditors as well as others have originated new CAATs on their own. For the most part, these products were developed by CPA firms to help them use the computer primarily for assistance in validation or substantive audit testing.

The classic example usually depicts the external auditor using the generalized package to select easily, from an accounts receivable file, a sampling of accounts. The accuracy of balances for the accounts selected are then corroborated by confirmation, often aided by features designed into the package.

Although not always as easy as represented, using CAATs in this manner did occur. By the 1980s, generalized audit software had become the most frequently applied CAAT. Since most CPA firms have opened usage of their software to others, internal auditors have availed themselves of the new products.

Of course, some internal auditors were using computerized audit software long before then. These packages were either developed by internal auditors, borrowed from programmers, or obtained from other sources. Still, widespread use by internal auditors of computerized audit software followed the development of generalized packages by CPA firms. Needless to say, many found different uses for them, since internal auditors are more often concerned with compliance testing.

Applicability

Deciding when to apply each of the available automated audit techniques is yet another matter of professional audit judgment. As noted earlier, many of the more sophisticated tools are time-consuming to plan and prepare for, and require continuing maintenance and monitoring by properly trained and technically skilled audit personnel.

The audit personnel responsible for deciding on the nature and extent of CAAT should apply a cost vs. benefit approach to each instance where such techniques are being considered. (See Chapter 6.) Cost considerations might include:

- Planning and preparation time for the auditors involved
- Use of I/S department programmers and operators
- Use of the computer and related facilities and software
- Maintenance requirements

Benefit considerations might include:

- Improved quality and reliability of audit results
- Enhanced knowledge of data processing by auditors involved
- Improved relations with the I/S community
- More efficient auditing

Not all of the foregoing factors are susceptible to quantification and, as a result, the decisions will be largely subjective. To assure the propriety of decision in this regard, the responsible auditor should be as certain as possible that all practicable manual procedures have been considered and that the feasibility of applying computer-assisted techniques has been carefully thought through. As is evident from the sample narrative shown in Figure 28-4, attempts to apply CAAT can be frustrating and often end in terminating the effort in favor of something less preferable. It should be noted that the difficulties and obstacles to performing CAAT are disappearing with advances in computer hardware and software technology and as the body of

FIG. 28-4
Narrative Workpaper Illustrating Difficulties In Applying Computer-Assisted Audit Techniques

---

The ABC Division
Accounts Payable

	Initials	Date
Prepared by	BKM	10/31/xx

On-Line Data Entry and Match Process
Audit Observations and Comments

Our original audit objectives as per our work assignment authorization (B-1) included a computer program simulation of the subject program whereby we would create an audit invoice file containing 70 numbers 000 000 to 999 999 and run it against the production file accessing a dummy purchase order receiver data base. Based on our understanding of the program logic (C-1 thru C-14) the result should be that all invoices should be automatically placed on the suspense file for subsequent processing. Any exceptions to this expected result might be indicative of program bugs or possibly unauthorized deviations. The absence of such exceptions should prove that the load module corresponds to the source program contained in the library and that the processing occurs as understood.

The on-line data entry and match process as the name states is an on-line process, and therefore invoices can only be entered on-line from terminals. To accomplish the objective through the original plan would require that we submit one million transactions via terminal — an impractical requirement. As an alternative, we discussed with senior programming personnel the possibility of simulating an on-line process using batch input, but we were informed that this was not feasible from a technical standpoint. We confirmed this discussion with other personnel.

As another alternative, we thought of a manual verification of the subject process if we could interpret the source code and compare the source code to the load module so that we could establish the integrity of the load module. As we do not have software which can make comparisons in this fashion we had no other alternative. A manual effort in bringing the source code into a load module format would be very time consuming, subject to error and would not necessarily indicate which specific program instructions were added or deleted, if any, — it would simply indicate differences. That is because we would only be able to compare the length of the data sets.

The foregoing circumstances necessitated changing our approach to one of comparing program source code per the library program version with a version extracted by a programmer using a time-sharing option. No exceptions were noted and while it is quite likely that these versions are equivalent to the production version, there is a possibility that the actual production version could be different in some unknown respect, since load modules can be changed by a direct modification to machine language instructions without leaving the source (library version) code. As a final test we duplicated the above procedure with another programmer also via TSO with a similar result. See w/p A-4 for further discussion and audit report consideration.

"computer literate" auditors continues to grow. In summary, if conditions in the I/S environment are favorable, and if the auditor possesses or has access to appropriate skills, powerful tools exist to enable the auditor to achieve his objectives effectively and efficiently.

TECHNIQUES FOR AUDITING CONTROLS

As set forth in Figure 28-3, CAAT for auditing internal controls and processes within the computer fall into one of two broad types known generally as "walk-throughs" and "testing." Walk-throughs are familiar to non-I/S auditors as the process whereby the auditor follows a transaction through various manual steps in the process by which it becomes resident in the accounting records of the entity. With respect to I/S, the same process can be made to occur electronically, as shown later. These techniques include tracing, the snapshot, and the extended record.

At best, walk-throughs often serve only to cement an understanding. Usually, they do not provide sufficient evidence that the application under audit complies with that understanding in all material respects during actual operation. To obtain that evidence, methods have been devised that use the computer to produce evidence permitting the auditor to infer compliance. These techniques are identified as test data, parallel simulation, and parallel simulation using generalized audit software.

Other techniques can accomplish both objectives. These include integrated test facilities, the system control audit review file (SCARF), other embedded audit routines, and utility program routines.

Tracing

Tracing has been aptly defined as a technique that:

> provides the internal auditor with the capability of performing an electronic walk-through of a data processing application system. The audit objective of tracing is to verify compliance with policies and procedures by substantiating, through examination of the path through a program that a transaction followed, how that transaction was processed.[4]

Tracing may be used whenever the auditor wishes to obtain evidence that key portions of programs within an application operate in accordance with his understanding. Such sections might include (1) the portion of a payroll program that calculates gross pay, various withholds, and net pay;

---

[4] *Systems Auditability & Control, op. cit.*, p. 155.

(2) the sections of a billing application that calculate and extend prices, sales tax, discounts, and commissions; (3) the portion of a cost system that calculates and applies burden rates; or (4) the portion of a materiel ordering application that determines order quantities. Usually, tracing is performed in connection with acceptance testing of new systems and in connection with audits of existing applications.

To perform tracing, the auditor must have available a software tracing routine. If such a facility is not available from the company's hardware vendors, a special-purpose routine must be developed.

The principal advantage of tracing is that it provides evidence of the operation of important program routines and may disclose the existence of programming bugs. The principal disadvantage is that it is time-consuming to complete the trace, particularly for complex applications. In actual practice, it is a technique that is rarely used due to this limitation.

Auditors who perform tracing should include in their workpapers evidential matter such as flow charts and narratives of the tracing design, applicable programming documentation, memorandums to programmers specifying requirements, trace listings, and any conclusions drawn.

Snapshot

The snapshot is defined in Chapter 27 as a technique that takes pictures of a transaction as it flows through the system. The logic of the snapshot routine must be built into the system. The best time for this to occur is during system design; thus, the auditor must get involved with system development to define his requirements to the design team.

The snapshot technique is similar to that of tracing in that its objective is to provide evidence that certain portions of a system of interest to the auditor operate in compliance with his understanding. The primary difference between tracing and the snapshot technique is that tracing is done after the fact by use of a utility or by a specialized software routine, whereas the snapshot routine is embedded.

The snapshot operates as indicated in the flow chart depicted in Figure 27-4. In essence, the system is programmed to generate a file or a report after each processing step in which the auditor is interested. Examples would include many of the same processes for which tracing is applicable (i.e., payroll calculations, pension plan, entitlement computations, health care claims processing, and calculations of sales discounts and commissions). Accordingly, it is another technique limited primarily to applications auditing. The files or reports contain "before" and "after" information to enable the intervening calculations to be verified.

The advantages of snapshot are that once it is set up, it is easy and economical to operate. Because it focuses on key programming sections, it is an excellent debugging tool. Its disadvantages are that it may require considerable programming and systems effort to establish and its use is limited to those who possess considerable EDP skills.

The workpapers of the auditor who uses the technique simply need to document its use and the resultant follow-up required (if any) and the conclusions drawn. A permanent workpaper record should include the necessary documentation that would be found for any system. This includes flow charts depicting logic, narrative explanations of the purpose of each snapshot point, description of the names in which each snapshot is triggered, and an indication of each report format. Specimen formats may also be included along with instructions for the use of the technique as applicable.

A variation of the snapshot technique is the "extended record" technique.[5] This tool further economizes on the snapshot by accumulating the before and after information in a single file or report. Its logic is depicted in the simple flow chart in Figure 27-5.

Test Data

Test data is defined as "a set of transactions processed by the auditor to test the programmed controls and procedural operations of . . . applications."[6] The test transactions may be selected from actual historical data or may be devised separately by the auditor.

The objective of test data is to provide evidence that selected routines and control processes such as edits and limit checks operate as indicated by the program or system documentation. While evidence indicating proper operation of many controls may be obtained manually by reviewing error listings, not all error detection routines may be exercised in any given run. Therefore, test data offer an opportunity to challenge the full spectrum of controls by introducing invalid, out-of-sequence, incomplete, and inaccurate transactions of all types. It is a technique widely used by programmers to check out new systems and changes to existing ones and is appropriate for use in auditing existing applications. In fact, the auditor should obtain the test data used by programmers, if available, and to the extent possible, use them for his purposes.

In the absence of preexisting test data, the auditor must serve as the test data designer. The following steps are generally required:

1. Obtain an understanding of the application and its controls from interviews and reviewing available system documentation.
2. Perform a system walk-through, noting such information as input submission and processing flow, to help confirm the understanding.

---

[5] Ron Weber, *EDP Auditing: Conceptual Foundations and Practice* (New York: McGraw-Hill Book Co., Inc., 1982), p. 481.

[6] AICPA Computer Services Executive Committee, *Computer Assisted Audit Techniques* (New York: American Institute of Certified Public Accountants, 1979), p. 56.

3. Select the controls to be tested and develop a test plan.
4. Coordinate the plan with appropriate EDP and user personnel.
5. Develop the test data.
6. Perform the test and evaluate the results.

It should be apparent that the foregoing requires considerable time to perform. Thus, the test data technique is often restricted to important applications, such as payroll, billing, cash collections, and cash disbursements.

The advantage of the test data technique is that it provides evidence of the extent to which intrinsic programming controls are functioning. One of the disadvantages of the approach is that it does not operate in a real production environment. The test is normally run with a duplicate version of the program and duplicate data files. It is impracticable in most instances to determine that the duplicates are valid reproductions of the originals. Also, for complete applications involving data bases, it may not be economically possible to use this method due to difficulties in setting aside sufficient computer resources for the purpose.[7]

Workpapers of audit projects in which the test data technique is employed should include a narrative of the objectives, the test plan, the input data, the output data, the program listing used in the test, the predetermined results, a reconciliation of test vs. predetermined results, further follow-up work, and any findings and conclusions.

Integrated Test Facility

An integrated test facility (ITF) enables processing of test data along with actual data in a live production environment. As such, it is a more sophisticated form of the test data technique, and is to be used when running test data off line is impracticable, or when the auditor desires to run the test in as real a situation as possible.

The objective of the ITF technique is the same as that for the simpler test data method, that is, to obtain evidence that selected routines and control processes operate as indicated by the program or system documentation.

The test facility is a dummy file or files that the auditor creates within the existing application. The dummy file may be a department, a division, a customer, an employee, or any other data file item, depending on the application. Once the file is created, the steps involved in executing the technique are similar to those outlined for test data. There is one important additional step, however. Since the dummy file is integrated with actual data, some means must be devised to back the test data out of the file after the test has been completed.

Integrated test facilities offer the advantage of operating in the real EDP

---

[7] *Systems Auditability & Control, op. cit.*, p. 112.

environment. Among other things, this means that special test resources do not have to be allocated away from normal production work. The test results are also thought to be more reliable, since the test occurred during operating conditions.

The disadvantage of the technique is that it may require even more time to prepare for than the test data method—at least initially. Also, some continuing maintenance must occur to keep the ITF operational in the face of system changes, which occur frequently in large, complex applications. Also, programmers may easily foil the test by inserting instructions into the programs, intentionally or otherwise.

The auditor's workpapers, in addition to the items noted in the test data discussion, should also include a description of the ITF, its purpose, any pertinent operating instructions, and an indication of how to remove test data from the dummy files.

Parallel Simulation

Parallel simulation consists of developing a separate set of application programs that emulate the functions performed by the actual subject application programs.[8] The source data are the same as those used in actual production, as are the files. In other words, test data are not used. The results of the simulation are compared with the results of the actual production, and differences are investigated and resolved in terms of their impact on the auditor's understanding of the application.

The objective of parallel simulation is to obtain evidence, by imitating actual processing, that the application produces accurate and complete results. If results are accurate and complete, it may be inferred that a controlled process must have occurred. It is similar, conceptually, to auditing around the computer, the only difference being that the technique is not dependent on manual transaction trails or manual processing capabilities.[9] While the term "parallel simulation" implies a simultaneous running of the test application with the actual production application, in reality, the test is normally run apart from and after the real application is executed. The method is another of the many CAATs that have been "borrowed" from programmers who developed it for acceptance testing purposes in new system development. A flow chart of the functioning of parallel simulation is shown in Figure 28-5.

Parallel simulations may be performed for those applications that involve repetitive financial calculations, such as gross or net pay in payroll applications, interest-earned calculations for banks and savings and loan

---

[8] William C. Mair, Donald R. Wood, and Keagle W. Davis, *Computer Control and Audit*, 2nd ed. (U.S.A.: Touche Ross & Co., Inc., 1976), p. 149.

[9] *Ibid.*, p. 149.

FIG. 28-5
Flow Chart Depicting Parallel Simulation

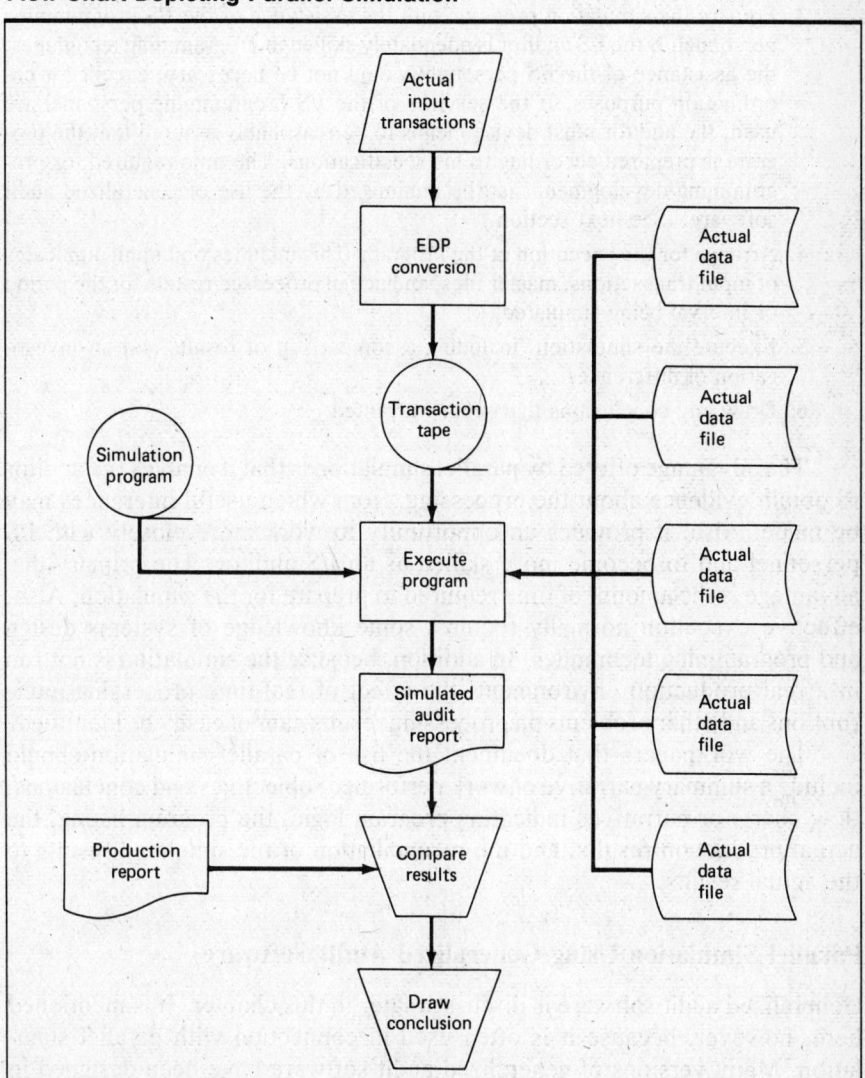

institutions, and finance charges and customer credit billing applications for retail chains.

The typical steps involved in accomplishing parallel simulation are these:

1. Obtain an understanding of the application through reviewing systems and programming documentation and discussing key points with knowledgeable personnel.

2. Devise a statement of requirements and specifications for the simulation program in sufficient detail to permit preparing the program.
3. Prepare the simulation program with the assistance of the I/S programming personnel. If the I/S auditor is adequately skilled in programming techniques, the assistance of the I/S personnel would not be necessary, except for coordination purposes. If the services of the I/S programming personnel are used, the auditor must devise means to be reasonably assured that the program is prepared according to his specifications. The time required for programming development may be minimized by the use of generalized audit software. (See next section.)
4. Arrange for the execution of the program. This includes obtaining duplicates of input transactions, master files, and actual processed results for the period or interval being simulated.
5. Execute the simulation, including a comparison of results and an investigation of differences.
6. Draw any conclusions that seem warranted.

The advantage offered by parallel simulation is that it enables the auditor to obtain evidence about the processing, from which useful inferences may be made. Also, it provides an opportunity to work more closely with I/S personnel and to become more skilled as an I/S auditor. The primary disadvantage is the amount of time required to prepare for the simulation. Also, effective execution normally requires some knowledge of systems design and programming techniques. In addition, because the simulation is not run in a real production environment, the effect of real-time processing interruptions and other problems on processing results cannot easily be identified.

The workpapers that document the use of parallel simulation should include a summary narrative of work performed, objectives and conclusions, flow charts or narratives indicating program logic, the program listing, the actual production results, and the reconciliation of the simulated results to the actual results.

Parallel Simulation Using Generalized Audit Software

Generalized audit software is discussed later in this chapter. It is mentioned here, however, because it is often used in connection with parallel simulation. Many versions of generalized audit software have been designed in such a way that they may be used as a more efficient substitute than the separately developed simulation program. The auditor's objective in this form of parallel simulation is as previously described, namely, to obtain evidence enabling inferences to be drawn about the particular application under audit.

When generalized audit software is used, it is not necessary for the auditor to prepare a full simulation program. Instead, the auditor adapts the generalized software to suit his simulation needs. While this may require some time to accomplish and the results must be tested and checked out, the time required is usually less than that for developing a full simulation program. Moreover, generalized software, because of its flexibility, is often easier to change than is a separate parallel application.

Embedded Audit Routines

Embedded audit data are defined in Chapter 27 as one or more specifically programmed data collection modules embedded in a computer application system to select and record data for subsequent analysis and evaluation. A simple overview depicting the logic of this technique is shown in Figure 28-6.

The objective of embedding data collection modules is to gather evidence during actual system operation that permits inferences to be drawn about the functioning of certain controls of interest to the auditor. Theoretically, any information of interest to the auditor along these lines should also be of interest to management. However, experience suggests that system designers and system users are less inclined to include in the design of the system the ability to generate audit information because to do so tends to increase development cost. In addition, it may make the system more costly to operate. Usually, it is only when the efficiency and effectiveness for audit purposes is considered that management agrees to permit embedded audit routines to be included in system development.

Audit routines may be embedded for virtually any specific objective that may be involved in other I/S auditing techniques. Some specific routines are as follows:

- To provide a running count of transactions processed
- To provide cumulative totals of amounts processed
- To calculate the mean average value and standard deviation of transactions processed
- To select random statistical samples
- To perform various limit checks and edit routines
- To generate reports of desired information

The comparatively high cost of embedding audit routines in existing systems suggest that the auditor wishing to make use of this technique become involved during the initial design of the application. Of course, it is necessary to stay involved after implementation to be certain that subsequent changes do not invalidate the routines.

The procedures to follow in setting up embedded audit routines are similar to those used in parallel simulation or, more precisely, in system development. Thus, it is necessary to:

- Establish feasibility
- Define requirements and specifications

FIG. 28-6
Depiction of Embedded Audit Routines

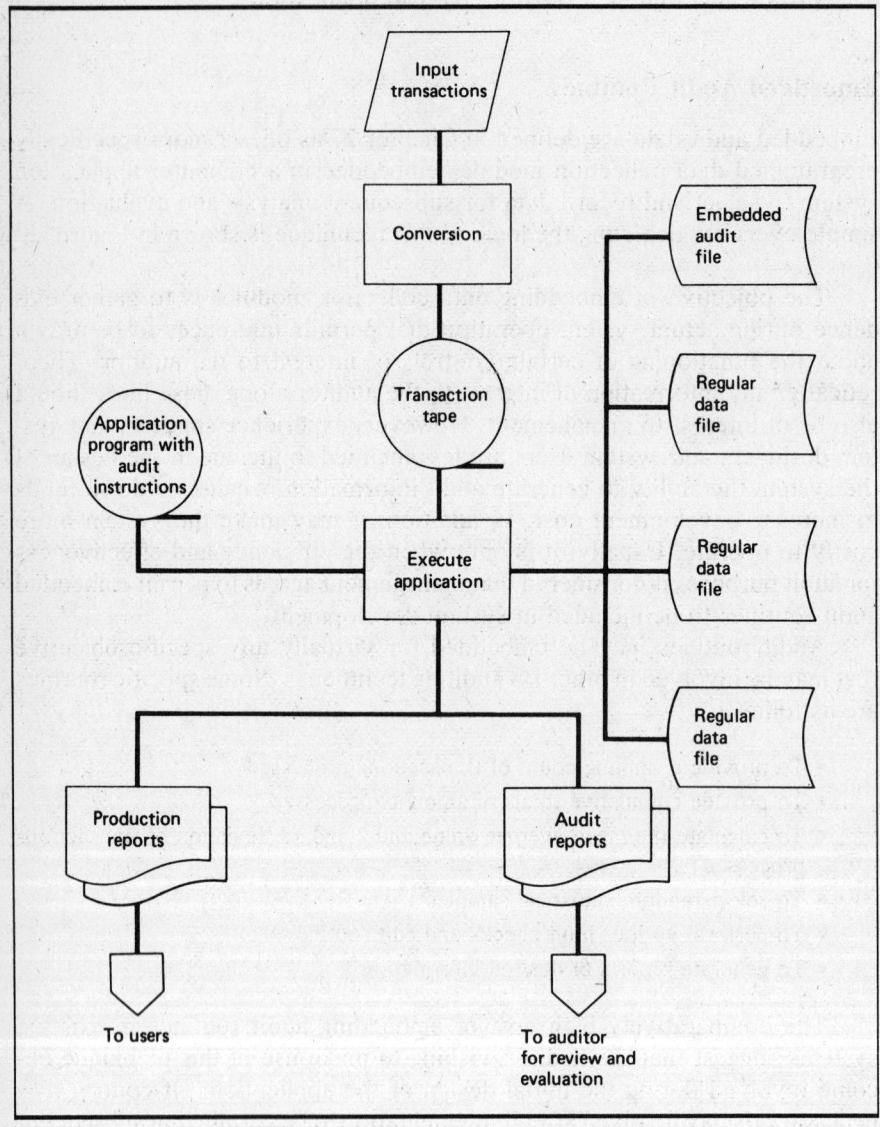

- Design the routines
- Perform design tests
- Implement the system
- Provide continuing maintenance

Auditors should make use of the technical services of the design team to the extent practicable in performing the foregoing steps.

Embedded audit routines are potentially among the most powerful, flexible, and reliable of the audit techniques currently available. Unfortunately, the techniques have not become widely used, possible because many I/S auditors lack sufficient design skills. Another factor may be resistance on the part of the design team to spend the time required to develop the routines. Whatever the reasons, many auditors are missing a chance to increase the efficiency and effectiveness of their I/S auditing.

The advantge of this technique, once it is implemented, is that the costly effort to plan and prepare for executing the routine is almost totally avoided. The routines operate continuously, along with the system itself. This also saves the I/S department considerable time, which would otherwise be required to provide support to the auditor in other types of testing, such as parallel simulation.

The only disadvantage of embedded audit data is the effort required to develop and maintain the routines. In effect, the technique forces the auditor to stay abreast of all developments that might affect the system, just as any user would. Many auditors are not accustomed to the discipline this requires. Moreover, since the audit effort is continuous, the auditor must be prepared to provide timely review and evaluation of reported results. If care is not exercised, the auditor may become overwhelmed by an avalanche of reported audit data.

Typically, embedded audit routines have been developed for systems in which the auditor has exhibited the greatest interest. Hence, payroll systems, procurement systems, and cash collection and disbursement systems have been favorite candidates. The technique also may be used beneficially in financial reporting systems, inventory control systems, and production scheduling.

Workpapers evidencing embedded audit routines look more like systems documentation than workpapers. Permanent file elements include (1) the design specifications, (2) logic flow charts, (3) system tests, (4) record layouts, (5) instructions for use, and (6) a record of changes. Report files must be set up and retention periods determined. Follow-up inquiry and evaluation must be documented in an appropriate fashion.

Utility Programs

"Utility programs" is a term that has gained common usage, referring to programs not specifically associated with any single application but that perform useful routines, such as sorting, merging, duplicating, or dumping. Utility programs have been defined as a subset of system software that performs less global routines than other system software, such as compilers, and that are smaller in size.[10] Most utility programs are supplied by hardware manufacturers and software vendors.

---

[10] Weber, *op. cit.*, p. 432.

I/S auditors may use utility programs to obtain an understanding of computer systems and to collect evidence about the quality of those applications. They are helpful particularly when other I/S audit techniques, such as generalized audit software, are either impractical or limited as to efficiency and effectiveness.

As systems are designed that embrace aspects such as data bases involving complex networks and data interrelationships, developing an understanding of them is made more difficult. In those instances, utility programs may facilitate understanding. For example, utility programs are available that can (1) produce flow charts from source code, (2) display programmed functions in a hierarchical sense to better portray relationships, and (3) make logic paths. Other utility programs enable system documentation existing in machine-readable form to be selectively retrieved, and still other utilities offer the capability to produce charts from the data-base definition that indicate the structure of the data.

Utility programs that help the auditor gather evidence about the operation of an application include various data manipulations, such as sorting, merging, and dumping. Also, query facilities exist, which enable selected retrieval of data and test certain control routines of interest to the auditor.

The advantage of utility programs is that they are a reliable, effective, and efficient family of options. They are more reliable and effective than other available audit techniques because they usually have been tested extensively by several users, not to mention the supplier. They are efficient because they are designed to perform specific tasks as opposed to the general purposes for which their generalized counterparts are designed.

The disadvantage of utility programs is their availability. Normally, utilities are purchased by the I/S department for the use of its programmers. If there is no perceived programming advantage, the utility will not be acquired. Also, utility software may require more technical knowledge to use it than that possessed by most I/S auditors. Other comments on utility programs as an aid improving efficiency and effectiveness and in protecting the auditor's independence are set forth later in this chapter.

Other System Software

Many CPA firms, government audit units, and I/S audit staffs of large internal auditing departments have been developing other audit packages, which are much more specialized than their generalized predecessors. These specialized packages were developed to facilitate extraction, analysis, or other audit testing of particular transaction flows or file types. Others may have been developed for testing data unique to particular industries. Thus, software packages have been developed for:

- ☐ Industry applications
  - Banks
  - Health care
- ☐ Transaction flows and/or files
  - Accounts receivable
  - Fixed assets

- ☐ Industry applications
  - Insurance
  - Brokerage houses
  - Savings and loans
  - Oil and gas
  - Municipal funds
  - Retail chains
  - Utilities
  - Hotels
- ☐ Transaction flows and/or files
  - Accounts payable
  - Payroll
  - General ledger
  - Inventory

Since software packages are specialized, they do not operate in every computer environment. Most are written to be compatible with IBM mainframe environments for obvious reasons. More specialized software is likely to be developed as more industries take advantage of automated processing and as specialization continues among accounting firms and software companies.

Security Software

Recently, IBM devised automated audit tools and embedded them in its Resource Access Control Facility (RACF) security software. Without getting too technical, it is a flexible software package that permits users to set the level of security over access/update privileges that they believe are appropriate for the automated files maintained by the systems they are responsible for. The fact that IBM has embedded audit tools in RACF is evidence of the significance it attaches to the audit function and the value of embedded audit routines.

The embedded routine is, in reality, three routines called RACF Auditor, RACF Report Writer, and The Data Security Monitor (DSMON). With these tools, the auditor is able to determine the extent to which RACF is being used to meet security needs. RACF accomplishes this by:

- ☐ *Logging routines that record information in which the auditor is interested.* RACF Auditor is programmed so that certain events are always logged, certain events are never logged, and certain events may be logged at the option of the auditor. For instance, access attempts using invalid passwords or from an unauthorized terminal are always logged. An example of an event that RACF Auditor would never log is anything that is not essential to security. This includes RACF commands, such as SEARCH or LISTUSER. Optional logging would include such items as:
  - All RACF profile changes
  - All RACF SPECIAL or group SPECIAL user issues
  - All RACF command violations
  - All or some accesses to specific data sets or general resources

- ☐ *Generating reports based on the information the auditor has directed RACF to log.* The information contained in these reports enables the auditor to monitor RACF activities and determine whether they conform to expectations. The reports also provide evidence of the proper functioning of the embedded routines. This reporting can bring to the auditor's attention password violations, access violations, access attempts, and other information. This data can be retained and, over time, trends culled to see if any unusual patterns form. Of course, immediate follow-up would be in order if the auditor believes a serious security incident is involved.

- ☐ *Verifying that the security mechanisms in place are those authorized and intended.* This is done via DSMON, which provides reports of actual RACF characteristics. These reports can be compared with the intended characteristics. Examples of data that may be obtained in this fashion are:
  - Program properties table
  - Authorized caller table
  - RACF exits
  - Selected user attributes

Once these audit tools are embedded in the manner desired by the auditor, they operate in a real-time fashion. Events meeting the criteria present in the program or selected by the auditor are logged as they occur. The individuals able to access these logs are restricted by design. Only those permitted to use the AUDITOR attribute may access this data. Hence, it is believed to be protected from unauthorized viewing or altering. In fact, attempts to do so can be logged and reported.

With these simple-to-use embedded tools, the auditor's objective of measuring the extent to which RACF is providing intended data security can be achieved with greater efficiency and reliability than has been heretofore possible. As with any embedded audit routine, the auditor must make clear what responsibility he is assuming by embedding these routines, and must act accordingly. In some instances, the auditor could be the only person able to receive information indicating violations or other security incidents. Yet, being independent of the functions he is auditing, he is in no position to take preventive or corrective actions. These are the purview of functional management. Therefore, the auditor and functional management must agree on some type of reporting process that brings information to the attention of management in order to permit timely action.

As an alternative, perhaps preferable, the embedded audit routines could be structured in a way that results in simultaneous reports being provided to both the auditor and appropriate management. Indeed, many management teams may demand this arrangement, not wishing to rely on the auditor to convey needed information.

IMPROVING PERFORMANCE EFFICIENCY AND EFFECTIVENESS

From the preceding discussion, it is readily apparent that CAAT may be used constructively by the I/S auditor to gather evidence related to the au-

INFORMATION SYSTEMS (EDP) AUDIT TECHNIQUES

diting of controls existing in computer applications. But, as noted earlier in this chapter, the computer may be used simply to help the auditor perform audit procedures more efficiently and effectively, whether for applications auditing or for other audit undertakings. Here, the objective is not necessarily to gather evidence about the workings of controls internal to the computer but, rather, to expedite completion of the work. Generalized audit software, utility programs, and embedded audit routines are discussed in this context.

Generalized Audit Software

Generalized audit software may be defined as a set of programmed instructions in a high level language, such as COBOL, that perform certain designated routines on data that exist in a machine-readable format. The routines may include retrieval, manipulation (i.e., sorting and merging), and reporting. Because of the flexibility of these devices and the ease with which they may be used, they have become the most frequently used CAAT. Figure 28-7 is a tabulation of several of the leading generalized audit software packages.[11]

The auditor's objective in using generalized audit software, generally, is to enable the computer to be used as a constructive auditing tool. In some instances, it may be the only practicable auditing tool. The following is a partial listing of some of the capabilities common to most generalized software:

- Sorting and merging files
- Extracting from a given file specific data, such as transactions in excess of $100,000
- Performing sample selection and evaluating results for such sampling methods as variables and attributes (See Chapter 15.)
- Executing arithmetic tasks, such as footing files and verifying extensions
- Comparing data on separate files, such as vendor data per the purchase order system and the accounts payable system
- Preparing reports and creating files

While details of how to use generalized audit software vary somewhat with each package, the following steps are often involved:

1. As with other CAATs, when the use of generalized software is contemplated, the auditor must gain an understanding of the EDP environment and the particular circumstances for which use of generalized software is contemplated.
2. The ways in which generalized software may be used to advantage must be decided.

---

[11] Weber, *op. cit.*, pp. 420–421. Used with permission of McGraw-Hill Book Co.

FIG. 28-7
A Tabulation of Generalized Audit Software Packages and Their Vendors

Package	Vendor	Package	Vendor
ASI-ST	Applications Software, Inc. 21515 Hawthorne Boulevard Torrance, Calif. 90503	CARS	Cullinane Corporation Wellesley Office Park 20 William Street Wellesley, Mass. 02181
ASK-360	Whinney Murray 57 Chiswell Street London, ED1 4SY, England	COMPUTER FILE ANALYZER	Price Waterhouse & Co. 1251 Avenue of the Americas New York, N.Y. 10020
AUDASSIST	Alexander Grant & Co. One First National Plaza Chicago, Ill. 60670	DYL-AUDIT	Dylakor Software Systems, Inc. 16255 Ventura Boulevard Encino, Calif. 91436
(AUDEX (AUDEX 100	Arthur Andersen & Co. 69 West Washington Street Chicago, Ill. 60602	EDP-AUDITOR	Cullinane Corporation Wellesley Office Park 20 William Street Wellesley, Mass. 02181
AUDIT	U.S. Department of Commerce Springfield, Va. 22151		
AUDITAID	Seymour Schneidman & Associates 405 Park Avenue New York, N.Y. 10022	EDP-Auditor/3	Cullinane Corporation Wellesley Office Park 20 William St. Wellesley, Mass. 02181
AUDITAPE	Deloitte, Haskins & Sells 1114 Avenue of the Americas New York, N.Y. 10036	HEWCAS	Department of Health, Education & Welfare Audit Office of the Assistant Secretary, Comptroller 330 Independence Avenue Washington, D.C. 20201
AUDITEC	Carleton Corporation 44 Bromfield Street Boston, Mass. 02108		
AUDITFIND	Dataskil Reading Bridge House Reading, England	MARK IV AUDIT	Informatics, Inc. 21050 Vanowen Street Canoga Park, Calif. 91303
AUDITPAK II	Coopers & Lybrand 1251 Avenue of the Americas New York, N.Y. 10020	PANAUDIT	Pansophic Systems, Inc. 709 Enterprise Drive Oak Brook, Ill. 60521
AUDIT REPORTER	Burroughs Corporation World Headquarters 1 Burroughs Place P.O. Box 418 Detroit, Mich. 48232	SCORE-AUDIT	Programming Methods, Inc. 1301 Avenue of the Americas New York, N.Y. 10019
		STRATA	Touche Ross & Co. 1633 Broadway New York, N.Y. 10019
(AUTRONIC-16 (AUTRONIC-32	Ernst & Whinney 1300 Union Commerce Building Cleveland, Ohio, 44115	S/2170	Peat, Marwick, Mitchell & Co. 345 Park Avenue New York, N.Y. 10022
BASE	Computrol, Inc. 187 Baker Avenue St. Louis, Mo. 63119	THE AUDIT ANALYZER	Program Products, Inc. 95 Chestnut Ridge Road Montvale, N.J. 07645

3. The feasibility of using the package must be determined.
4. Since the auditor is creating a sort of one-time application, the "system" must be designed.
5. Instructions must be developed using the coding sheets provided by the supplier.
6. Having worked out the program, the system must be tested and debugged.
7. The system must be executed and the results evaluated.

In practice, these seven basic steps can be performed with surprising ease by individuals with little EDP audit skill. The primary obstacle to overcome is fear of the computer. Many auditors who lack familiarity with EDP fundamentals view the computer as some sort of mysterious, superior force capable of revealing for all to see the auditor's ineptness in EDP. In reality, many non-I/S auditors have overcome this obstacle to attain a remarkable level of proficiency in the use of generalized software.

Another noteworthy limiting factor is the auditor's ability to recognize opportunities for using generalized software. Generally speaking, the package is of potential benefit wherever the auditor wishes to audit data existing in the master files of a given system. Figure 28-8 lists several specific situations in which generalized audit software may be used advantageously.[12]

The advantages offered by generalized audit software include reliability, since it has been thoroughly tested and debugged by repeated uses of countless users. Its ease of use and flexibility is evident from the preceding discussion. However, it would be wrong to assume that its use is without disadvantages. Three principle shortcomings have been associated with generalized audit software. These are as follows:

1. Auditing cannot be done concurrently using generalized audit software.
2. Only limited capabilities exist for validating program logic.
3. It is difficult to measure the propensity of a given application for making mistakes.

To these might be added a fourth drawback in that, occasionally, the use of generalized software may consume more processing resources to execute than would be true for specialized audit software such as utility programs.

If the EDP audit function does not have a generalized audit package, it will have to lease or buy from one or more of the program suppliers. (See Figure 28-7.) The decision as to which program to acquire is not simply a matter of random selection.

Audit software packages are not all the same. Generally speaking, audit software may be classified into two groups: those that are compatible with many types of hardware and those that are not. Generalized software pack-

---

[12] Joseph E. Connor and Burnell H. DeVos, Jr., eds., *Guide to Accounting Controls*, 1982 Supplement (Boston: Warren, Gorham & Lamont, 1982), pp. 142–144. Copyright © by Price Waterhouse & Co. Reprinted with permission.

FIG. 28-8

Situations in Which Generalized Audit Software May Be of Use

	Selecting audit samples	Testing computations and postings	Summarizing, resequencing, and comparing data
	Selecting random samples: • Purchase transactions and payments for vouching with supporting documentation. • Balances for confirmation. **Identifying exceptional transactions and balances:** • Entries from unusual sources (not the usual transaction flow). • Debit balances. • Large purchases, returns, balances, and payments. • Unusual prices. • New suppliers. • Balances with no scheduled payment date. • Overdue accounts. • Major suppliers. • Large purchase variances.	**Testing footing and extension of files:** • Individual entries in purchase journal, suppliers' ledger, and general ledger control account. • Suppliers' account trial balance. • Purchase history file by supplier, etc. **Testing computations:** • Prepaid rent, insurance expenses, etc. **Testing postings:** • Purchase transactions to suppliers' accounts and asset, inventory, or expense accounts. • Payments to suppliers' accounts.	**Resummarizing:** • Purchases by supplier, etc. • Suppliers' accounts in value order. **Comparing data on separate files:** • Discrepancies between quantities received and quantities billed. • Goods received not billed. • Cut-off data. **Comparing audit data with:** • Confirmation replies. • Cut-off data.
Payrolls/employee benefits	**Selecting random samples:** • Individual payroll entries for checking with supporting documentation and testing calculations. • Payroll amendments (pay rate changes, new employees, etc.) for checking with supporting documentation. **Identifying exceptional transactions and balances:** • Unusually large wage payments, pay rates, and overtime hours. • Excessive vacation or sick leave. • Employees who have not taken vacation entitlement. • Entries from unusual sources (not the usual transaction flow). • Unusually small tax deductions.	**Testing footing and extension of files:** • Aggregation of payroll totals. • Individual entries in general ledger labor cost accounts. • Listings of payroll payments. **Testing computations:** • Detailed payroll calculations (gross pay, overtime, bonuses, deductions, etc.). • Vacation pay accruals. • Profit sharing calculations. • Pension accruals. • Labor cost expense distributions. **Testing postings:** • Payroll distribution to asset, inventory, and expense accounts.	**Resummarizing:** • Total year's salary payments to directors, officers, and senior employees. **Comparing data on separate files:** • Discrepancies between payroll and personnel records. **Comparing audit data with client records:** • Returned checks to payroll records.

Inventory/ production costs	Selecting random samples: • Items for physical counting. • Items for pricing tests. • Inventory held by third parties for confirmation. Identifying exceptional transactions and balances: • Entries from unusual sources (not the usual transaction flow). • Large inventory holdings of particular items. • Old or slow-moving inventory. • Large differences between physical and book inventory balances. Omitted physical count sheet numbers: • Negative inventory balances. • Inventory costs greater than net realizable value. • Large cost variances.	Testing footing and extension: • Inventory valuation. • Physical inventory. • Costs of sales summaries. • Production and cost records. Testing computation: • Allocation of labor and overhead costs. • Standard cost computations. • Calculation of variances. • Cost of sales percentages (especially in retail operations). Testing postings: • Accumulation of production costs. • Reduction of inventory for cost of sales. • Physical inventory adjustments.	Resummarizing: • Inventory holdings in value order. • Comparing shipments with inventory holdings by product. • Calculating inventory turnover by product. Comparing data on separate files: • Inventory records with purchase production, and sales records, including cut-off. • Physical inventory with book inventory. Comparing audit data with records: • Physical inventory counts with perpetual records.
Fixed assets/ depreciation	Selecting random samples: • Additions and disposals for vouching to supporting documentation. • Assets for physical inspection. Identifying exceptional transactions and balances: • Fully depreciated assets. • Usually long or short depreciation periods. • Undepreciated assets. • Costs in excess of budget.	Testing footing and extension of files: • Individual entries in fixed assets records. • Fixed assets trial balances, by category of assets. Testing computations: • Depreciation. • Lease capitalization. • Profit or loss on disposal. Testing postings: • Additions and disposals to general accounts. • Profit or loss on disposal to general ledger.	Resummarizing: • Purchases and disposals of assets in value order. • Average rates of depreciation as a percentage of book amount. Comparing data on separate files: • Engineering department records with accounting records.

(continued)

FIG. 28-8 *(cont'd)*

Treasury (cash management, financing, and investments)	**Selecting audit samples** Selecting random samples: • Payments and receipts, (not covered by sales, purchase, or payroll systems) for vouching with supporting documentation. • Deposits, loans, and bank accounts for confirmation. • Securities for physical inspection or confirmation. • Sales and purchases of securities for vouching with supporting documentation. • Interest and dividend payments for vouching with supporting documentation. • Capital and loan stock purchases, sales, transfers, and redemptions for vouching with supporting documentation. Identifying exceptional transactions: • Unusual receipts and payments (not arising from the usual transaction flow). • Unusual interest and dividend rates on deposits, loans, and capital stock. • Missing check numbers. **Testing computations and postings** Testing footing and extension of files: • Receipts and payments listings. • Outstanding checks listings. • Investment and loan stock registers. • Capital and loan stock registers. • Dividend and interest payment listings. Testing computations: • Bank account reconciliations. • Interests and dividend payments, receipts and accruals. • Profits and losses on disposal of investments and redemption of stock. • Amortization of discounts and premiums on investments. Testing postings: • Payments and receipts to relevant general ledger accounts. **Summarizing, resequencing, and comparing data** Resummarizing: • Capital and loan stockholders in holding order. • Investment transactions in value order.

ages of the first group are very portable, meaning they can be executed in many different environments. However, because they are portable, something must be sacrificed in processing efficiency. Software of the second group, being designed for more specific equipment, is more economical to operate but lacks portability. To select the proper package, the chief auditor or his designee must define the needs of the department carefully as a precondition to considering the software alterations.

Some other factors that differentiate generalized audit software are the following:

- ☐ *Auditor involvement.* Some software packages require the auditor to perform some of the coding while others require only that questions be answered.
- ☐ *Applicability.* Some software may be applied in complex on-line data base systems. Others are limited to batch-oriented systems.
- ☐ *Tailoring.* Some software is tailored for specific industries; others are more broad-based. The trend seems to be toward developing industry-tailored packages.
- ☐ *Training and support.* Some variability exists among software suppliers as to this factor. Generally, the variance is greatest in areas of the country that are not included in or near a major concentration of economic activity.

Once the selection is made, the chief auditor or his designee must work closely with the delegated procurement authority to negotiate the acquisition. It may be a good idea to lease or rent the package for an initial period, during which the benefits and costs of actual use may be studied.

Utility Programs

Utility programs are described earlier in this chapter in connection with other CAATs used to audit computer controls. However, like generalized audit software, these packages may be used to assist in applying other audit tools, including generalized software.

Utility programs—also known as system software—that can generate test data, perform tracing and mapping routines, make comparisons of separate versions of source programs, and facilitate program development are available. While these devices were developed primarily to help programmers, I/S auditors who possess comparable skills may make appropriate use of them under the right circumstances.

Other System Software

Some I/S audit functions have prepared unique system software devices to further assist in accomplishing I/S audit objectives. This can only be done by someone able to program in assembler language, a high-skill level. Although this is beyond the ability of most I/S auditors, the technique is listed here to provide an indication of the full range of available tools.

Embedded Routines

Embedded audit routines are among the best methods for facilitating the auditor's work because, once the audit routines have become embedded, they operate automatically. This saves performing the time-consuming planning and preparation procedures associated with other CAATs, such as generalized audit software and simulation. In addition, the embedded routine avoids the wasted effort of searching, either manually or with a CAAT, for unique transactions.

One common form of an embedded routine is the SCARF. This routine is designed to provide continuous monitoring of a given application's transactions in an effort to accumulate in the file specific transactions defined by the auditor. It is usually preferable to design the SCARF as part of the overall application system design effort because it is less costly to do so at that time. The file may accumulate whatever information in that application is of interest to the auditor. Examples include:

- Specific types of erroneous transactions, such as invalid employee numbers in a payroll system, disbursements in excess of stated limits in a check-writing system, or EFT transactions to designated accounts in an EFT system.
- Frequency analysis of data, such as the number of unauthorized access attempts to a vendor master file or an employee master file.
- Duplicating important processing routines, such as calculations of employee earnings, cash discounts, and interest charges, for statistically selected samples of actual transactions processed.

The process of designing and implementing a SCARF is the same as described in the earlier discussion of embedded audit routines.

Expert Systems

The term "expert systems" is a recent addition to information systems jargon, and it is rapidly making its way into the business world.[13] Along with such related terms as artificial intelligence and decision support systems, they presage yet another direction in the application of computer and systems technology. Artificial intelligence is the hot new area for computer hardware and software researchers. It is a generic term intended to apply to computers

---

[13] James M. Conerly, "Ingredients of an Effective Financial Information System," in *Financial Information Systems Manual*, James D. Willson and Jack F. Duston, eds. (Boston: Warren, Gorham & Lamont, 1986), p. 5-5.

that think like humans. While no such computers exist today that even come close to that feat, the day may not be far off. In the meantime, much activity has been directed at developing systems that focus on a more specific setting or task. The result is the advent of the subtechnologies of expert systems, robotics natural language, and vision systems.

An expert system is defined as a program that attempts to capture the knowledge of a particular field or profession.[14] Expert systems are often described as knowledge systems because they contain the knowledge of the facts and heuristics needed to solve particular problems.[15] An early example of an expert system is MYCIN. This system, developed at the Stanford University Medical Experimental Computer Facility, is able to make a diagnosis and form recommendations for treatment of infectious diseases.[16] The success of MYCIN stimulated the development of EMYCIN—a sort of expert systems shell that facilitates developing other expert systems. Other shells also exist now, which have been used by pioneering designers to create expert systems for use in internal auditing.

One early effort is a system known as TICOM, an acronym for The Internal Control Model. It was developed by Messrs. Bailey, Duke, Gerlach, Ko, Meservy, and Whinston.[17] Experts point out TICOM is not a true expert system because humans must still perform the overall evaluation of internal control. Yet, it assists the auditor by providing answers to "what-if" questions posed by him. Accordingly, its principal value is to improve the efficiency and effectiveness of the auditor's evaluation.

Other expert systems are under development. One is EDP-AUDITOR, aimed at assisting in audits of advanced EDP systems.[18] Another is ExperTAP developed by Coopers & Lybrand. This system is intended to aid tax planning for corporations but is reportedly also of use in preparing tax accruals.[19]

These systems provide testimony to the likely future of auditing. It will be a future in which the effectiveness and efficiency of the auditor will be vastly extended. Yet, there will still be room for the auditor—the human ingredient. The observation powers of humans—on the scene—will not likely yield to imitation.

---

[14] Dale L. Flesher and Cindy Martin, "Artificial Intelligence," *The Internal Auditor*, Feb., 1987, p. 32.

[15] Barbara K. Cummings and Nicholas G. Apostolou, "Expert Systems in Auditing: An Emerging Technology," *Internal Auditing*, Fall 1987, p. 4.

[16] P. Harmon and D. King, *Expert Systems: Artificial Intelligence in Business* (Wiley Press, 1985).

[17] Bailey et al., "TICOM and the Analysis of Internal Controls," *The Accounting Review*, Apr. 1985, p. 186.

[18] R. Michaelson and D. Michie, "Expert Systems in Business," *Datamation* (Nov. 1983), p. 243.

[19] D. Shpilberg and L. E. Graham, *"Developing ExperTAP: An Expert System for Corporate Tax Accrual and Planning"* (Coopers & Lybrand, 1986).

PROTECTING INDEPENDENCE

It is stated earlier in this chapter that one of the three primary objectives in applying CAAT is to minimize the degree of dependence on EDP personnel and the EDP facility itself, in order to perform the audit. This objective is best understood by recalling that, in a manual auditing environment, the auditor is free to perform whatever audit steps he may choose. In the EDP environment, however, the data in which the auditor is interested exist only in a machine language and are in the custody of the EDP department. It may be accessed, read, manipulated, and changed by operation of various programs also in the custody of the EDP department. Moreover, unless the auditor is sufficiently familiar with programming and other EDP techniques to obviate assistance, the auditor is almost totally dependent on the EDP department to "see" the data that are contained in EDP files. Under these circumstances, the EDP department can influence the course of the auditor's work intentionally or unintentionally.

Figure 28-9 compares selected audit routines to illustrate how the auditor's independence is compromised by the EDP environment. The dependence of the auditor on the EDP department is changed only marginally, if at all, by CAATs, such as parallel simulation and generalized audit software. That is because their after-the-fact execution is normally performed with varying degrees of assistance from programming and operating personnel of the EDP function, depending on the skill of the auditor and the complexity of the system.

Other forms of CAAT, such as integrated test facilities and embedded audit routines, require much less dependence on EDP personnel once they have been devised. Even these require participation by programmers and others during design and implementation, however.

While dependence cannot be completely overcome, certain CAATs exist that can reduce dependence to more reasonable levels. These include the audit facility, certain utility programs, program verifications, and operating system reviews.

The Audit Facility

The audit facility is a computer that is controlled and operated by the auditor. Its purpose is to perform CAATs, such as test data, generalized audit software, and parallel simulation.

In the early years of EDP auditing, such a facility could not be justified from an economic standpoint due to the high cost of acquiring and operating computer hardware. However, advancing technology has led to the availability of low cost, powerful mini- and microcomputers that do not require high-level EDP skills to operate. Thus, establishing and maintaining one or more of these facilities is within the reach of many internal auditing departments.

FIG. 28-9

Comparison of Audit Techniques Common to I/S and Non-I/S Auditing Indicating the Potential for Independent Performance

Audit Technique	Environment I/S	Non-I/S
■ Read contents of a given file	No	Yes
■ Extract specific data	No	Yes
■ Compare information in one file with information from another file	No	Yes
■ Search for certain transaction types	No	Yes
■ Verify mathematical accuracy	No	Yes
■ Re-perform selected routines	No	Yes
■ Perform analytical procedures	No	Yes

The audit facility eliminates the need for relying on EDP department personnel to execute many of the auditor's CAATs. As a result, the CAAT executed on the audit facility is not exposed to unauthorized tampering. In addition, performing CAATs through a single, controlled computer avoids the difficulties associated with CAAT performance. Also, in instances when several EDP facilities exist in the company, the need to adapt CAATs to differing environments is avoided.

The primary disadvantage of the audit facility is that its cost of acquisition and operation in terms of equipment, personnel, and facilities, despite technological advances, makes it feasible for only the very large EDP audit functions.

Perhaps a more feasible alternative to having a computer in the audit department is to have access to the mainframe. With the advent of on-line, interactive computer systems and sophisticated software, it is possible for the auditor to use the power and speed of the mainframe. In an IBM system, this is accomplished by converting data resident in operating system files, in which the auditor is interested, into the statistical analysis system data bases. The auditor may need technical assistance here to properly code the input and output statements that are required.

Once the data is in a statistical analysis system environment, it can be analyzed and tested using support software consisting of time sharing option C Lists for handling file allocations, space management, and statistical analysis systems in the interactive mode.[20]

---

[20] Stanley D. Halper, P. Jarlath O'Neil-Dunne, and Xenia Ley Parker, *Handbook of EDP Auditing*, 1987 Cumulative Supplement. Copyright © 1987 by Coopers & Lybrand (U.S.A.), published by Warren, Gorham & Lamont, Inc., Boston.

Utility Programs

Several utility programs supplied by vendors may be available to the I/S auditor to help reduce the exposure to unauthorized tampering with audit programs and files by EDP personnel. For example, various utility programs exist that can compare two versions of a given program source code and list differences. This utility enables the auditor to identify unapproved changes and consider their effects. Other utility software may be used to monitor changes to selected program source codes. Still other utilities, designed to provide information relevant to EDP operational efficiency, may be used instead to monitor operating system logs for unusual operating occurrences, such as the execution of unauthorized programs and data set zaps (direct modification without leaving any record thereof) by operating system programmers or others.

In using utility programs, the I/S auditor should devise means to guard against the possibility that the programs may have been altered. One way is to obtain the software directly from the vendor and keep it in a library not accessible to EDP personnel. Another way might be to compare the software with a blueprint or to test critical modules. Whatever technique is employed, only limited assurance can be obtained as to the absence of unauthorized modifications.[21]

Program Verifications

Program verifications entail the review of program listings (source code) to determine the propriety of the coded instructions. While this procedure can be performed manually by those persons familiar with program languages, it is usually preferable to employ some type of automated technique for this purpose. That is because many programs contain several hundred to several thousand lines of complex code, making manual reviews extremely difficult and of questionable reliability.

Utility programs and some generalized audit software are available for this purpose. By applying utility programs, the I/S auditor is able to obtain some evidence as to the validity of the program source code. Of course, the source code may be valid while the compiled machine version may contain unauthorized changes. To reduce this exposure, the I/S auditor might review operating system logs with the help of utility programs or other specialized software for any entries that appear improper.

At best, program verifications are of limited usefulness because the auditor can only conclude as to the condition of the program at the date of his test. The condition of the program previous and subsequent to that date is unknown. For that reason, most I/S auditors perform such tests only for those systems with a high risk factor of irregularities, such as payroll sys-

---

[21] Weber, *op. cit.*, p. 444.

tems, vendor payment systems, and customer accounting systems. Program verifications may be performed in connection with specific applications auditing as part of an installation review or as a separate audit project.

Operating System Reviews

Operating systems are comprised of many hundreds of programs that perform the tasks of managing the various computer resources in the most efficient manner possible. Generally, operating systems perform the following functions:

- Job scheduling
- Initiating and supervising application programs
- Controlling input and output
- Allocating storage and use of peripheral devices
- Managing the use of software and utility programs
- Communicating with other computers and human operators

The operating system for each computer mainframe and each operating system, even those supplied by the same vendor, is unique. Some of the factors affecting uniqueness are as follows:

- Basic design
- Operating system versions
- Maintenance level
- Tuning requirements
- Program content
- Communications requirements
- System description and parameters
- Catalogues and libraries

Operating systems have developed to the point where routine tasks previously performed by equipment operators are now done by the computer. As a result, the auditor cannot determine compliance with procedures simply by observing the action of the operator.

It is necessary to audit such operating systems. The objective in reviewing operating systems is to provide information to management with respect to the integrity of the operating system. It is not possible to provide absolute assurance that a given operating system is reasonably free of exposure to unauthorized access, modification, or detection. However, some effort along these lines may detect weaknesses or irregularities for management attention and action. An important secondary purpose is to study the integrity of the operating system to form a basis for determining any tests or other procedures that might be required to be performed in connection with CAATs to overcome the auditor's dependence on the operating system and its programmers.

The auditing procedures employed involve a combination of manual techniques, such as interviews with key personnel and review of system documentation, and automated techniques, such as use of specialized software, to gather evidence as to the proper operation of the system.

Operating system audits involve highly technical aspects and should be attempted only by auditors possessing the requisite intimate knowledge of the system and its software. Some I/S audit functions employ former operating system programmers for this purpose because of this factor.

A recently published handbook on EDP auditing provides descriptions of additional tools and techniques for use in testing computer-based operating systems. An excerpt of a portion of these descriptions is reprinted below.[22]

> Another example of the need to use comparison programs occurred not long ago when a national company hired a consultant to upgrade its computer system. During his assignment, the consultant did some programming of his own. He modified the system so it would ignore the paid, returned checks written to fictitious people and cashed by him. It was not until the company lost $100,000 in money orders that the unauthorized financial drain was detected.
>
> If appropriate controls had existed in the company's computer system, this unfortunate situation might not have occurred. Software can help detect whether program change controls are operating. One such package is Coopers & Lybrand's Special Linklib Analysis Program Series (SLAPS). This software package provides the auditor with a means of testing load libraries. It can also detect unauthorized changes in modules, as well as unauthorized programs placed in libraries.
>
> Once a compile occurs (after no errors in program syntax have been detected by the compiler), a linkedit is executed. This process joins parts of programs together so that they function properly, in sequence. The linkedit combines the object program with the standard routines necessary to produce a machine-executable program.
>
> The SLAPS audit software consists of programs that extract and print the date of compilation and linkedit, and report any changes that might bypass controls created by the compile and linkedit procedures. The reports include such information as the language that the program was written in, the date the program was compiled and linkedited into the library, and the number of modules (control sections) in the program.
>
> The reports generated are:
>
> - Parameter Card Edit Report, which prints the parameter card exactly as it was read. It also prints any errors or warnings regarding the parameters.
> - Messages and Information Report, which specifies inconsistencies in information regading the user's load modules.

---

[22] Halper, *op. cit.*, pp. 28-18–28-22. Reprinted by permission.

- Serial Partitioned Data Set (PDS) List Report, which lists all load modules, with more recent data listed first.
- The Compile/Linkedit Report, which lists the program name, compiler name, date of compile, and the linkedit date. This information helps the auditor to trace all changes and implementations for the examination period.
- The ZAP Report, which lists ZAPs or Super ZAPs. (ZAPs are a series of programs that can change an object program or an executable program. ZAPs can be used to change programs or data files directly, thereby bypassing the procedures used to control programs or data file changes.) The report provides the control section, but linkedit date, the ZAP date, and the area where the ZAP occurred. It can be used to trace changes to proper documentation.
- The Change Report, which compares two examination periods and lists changed programs, new programs, and programs no longer used. When used in conjunction with source program comparison software (which detects what has been changed within the program), it allows the auditor to continue to rely on programmed procedures. (Programmed procedures include many accounting and control procedures that are executed by computer programs.)

Other categories of audit software packages are available, in addition to comparison programs, which provide the auditor with specialized capabilities for systems activities.

Unexecuted Code Analysis

Software is available that monitors the execution of a program and produces a report showing the number of times each line of source code was executed during processing. This report can be useful when performing code analysis, since it indicates any line of code that is not executed. Unexecuted code should be investigated to find out why it exists in a program. The investigation may make the auditor aware of code that is fraudulent, redundant, or erroneous.

Flowcharting Programs

Flowcharting programs document and analyze programmed procedures. The flowcharts produced by these programs are often too voluminous to be helpful in an audit. However, the verb listings and the cross-referenced data name listings also generated are normally quite worthwhile. Among other uses, they are often helpful in program code analysis. Job control language (JCL) flowchart programs can assist in understanding and confirming system flows.

System Log Analysis

Many installations automatically produce a log of all computer activity (such as IBM's System Management Facility (SMF) log for the OS system). Programs have been developed that analyze the systems log to report specific defined items. Using this software, the auditor can carry out tests to ensure that

- Only approved programs access sensitive data.

- Utilities or service aids that can alter data files and program libraries are used only for authorized purposes.
- Approved programs are being run only when scheduled; conversely, unauthorized runs are not taking place.
- The correct data file generation is being accessed for production purposes.
- Data files reported to be password-protected actually are protected.

System Management Facility

SMF software can be used by auditors, as is shown by the following example. A computer operator, unsupervised during the night shift, decided to make a change to a production program to increase his weekly pay by $1,000. The next day, the payroll was run under the normal supervised procedures; the third shift operator was not even there. The programmer's check was automatically deposited in his account at the bank. To cover his tracks, he then changed the program back to its original version, without the salary increase. Depending on the technique this operator had used to modify the production program, an activity log might have shown that the program was changed twice at irregular times without authorization.

Fortunately, there are operating systems with built-in reporting features that log such activity as system and data file access. SMF has a report feature, used in the IBM OS, SVS (single virtual storage), and MVS (multiple virtual storage) System Control Programs. SMF collects a variety of system- and job-related data. System-related data applies to the computer configuration, paging activity, and workload. Job-related data provides information about job set-up, jobs run, and time-sharing sessions.

The volume and variety of information in the SMF records enable an organization to produce many types of analyses and summaries. This data on accounting and system performance can aid installations in managing their computer resources. The information can be used for billing processing costs to users, and for adjusting hardware and system software configurations for optimal performance. This same information can be quite useful to the auditor.

Much of the information generated by SMF is not of financial audit significance. The auditor, sifting through a veritable mountain of SMF data, must glean only that data necessary to reach the audit objectives. Coopers & Lybrand's SMF Analyzer was developed as an audit tool for extracting SMF data that is pertinent to the audit. This package provides up to 13 different reports containing information on activity within the computer center.

The adaptability of the SMF Analyzer is what makes it a useful tool in the evaluation of general controls. By choosing the appropriate parameters, the auditor can select only those reports necessary for a particular situation. To run the Selected Program Report, for example, the auditor specifies the names of the programs to be reported on, thereby eliminating the necessity of going through extraneous data. The auditor can request this report for all executions of utilities that could have modified production data files. These reported executions can then be traced to records of authorizations for use of the utilities on the files.

The information generated in the reports can assist the auditor in addressing issues such as the following:

INFORMATION SYSTEMS (EDP) AUDIT TECHNIQUES

- Are modifications to production files authorized?
- What data files have been accessed?
- Are accesses to change control records authorized and documented?
- Have all the jobs on the production schedule been executed, and only those?

To assist in the process, the program's reports list information such as executions of specific programs, accesses to program libraries, all jobs and programs executed, all accesses to data files, and scratched and renamed data files.

An analysis program can help determine whether production data files are being accessed by production programs. For example, a large East Coast manufacturing installation uses standard naming conventions for production programs and data files. By scanning the analyzer's reports, the auditors can determine that only production data files are being accessed by production programs.

To augment SMF Analyzer and Coopers & Lybrand's operating system auditing capability, the firm developed APF Analyzer. This software package is designed to help the EDP auditor specialist understand, evaluate, and test integrity controls in the operating system. It is able to analyze MVS operating system tables and produce information about supervisor calls and Program Property Tables.[23]

Other Operating System Reviews

The need to audit operating systems is becoming greater as more and more EDP installations evolve toward using more sophisticated systems. This evolution is happening because the more sophisticated systems, such as IBM's MVS, are more powerful, reliable, and efficient. The fact that MVS and its counterparts have been in existence for over 15 years suggests that new generations soon will become available, which are certain to be even more capable and efficient.

The implication for auditors is that procedures and routines, once performed manually by operators, are now done automatically. The auditor can no longer rely on observation of computer operator routines. Further, sophisticated operating systems are supported by various special utility programs that help operators in monitoring and supervising computer operations and performance. Auditors with appropriate technical skill may use features of operating systems and utility programs to help test the integrity of the system.

An article in the April 1985 *The Internal Auditor* details one approach

---

[23] Coopers & Lybrand, "Analyzing Data Security," *Software Newsletter*, Fall 1985/Winter 1986, p. 10.

to auditing, an IBM/MVS operating system. The following is a reprint of a portion of that article.[24]

> An audit of MVS should include:
> - Verifying that important system-data sets are adequately protected from viewing and modification.
> - Evaluating the adequacy of job segregation for system programmers, application programmers, security administrators, and computer operators.
> - Determining the sufficiency of management controls for promoting operating-system integrity.
> - Determining that certain powerful capabilities are adequately controlled.
> - Evaluating the adequacy of operating-system-backup procedures.
> - Determining if certain audit-trail and diagnostic information is being created and reviewed.
>
> There are several, specific actions to be taken in performing a review of MVS.

Getting Started

First, you should send a letter to the auditee a week or two before the opening conference describing items needed for the review, such as an organizational chart for the data processing function, copies of relevant charters and position descriptions, and READ capability for SYS1 data sets (those starting with the qualifier SYS1 excluding those containing passwords like SYS1.UADS, SYS1.-RACF, PASSWORD).

While you will have to rely considerably upon the accuracy and truthfulness of verbal information from the system programmer during the audit, having READ capability for SYS1 data sets will allow you greater independence in performing certain checks. At the opening conference, you should secure an overview of the operating-system environment and an understanding of the extent and reasons for significant user modifications to MVS.

Maintenance, Monitoring, and Audit Trails

MVS generates several files that serve to document how the operating system has been modified and what it has done or experienced. These files are used for a variety of purposes such as billing data processing expenses back to users, performance measurement and tuning, system troubleshooting, and system monitoring for security and data integrity purposes. Here are a few examples of MVS files.

System Modification Program (SMP). This is, ideally, the tool with which operating-system maintenance is performed.

It's good practice to apply all user modifications (mods) via SMP. This provides a clear audit trail of how the operating system has been modified. It also

---

[24] Chris Bacon, "Auditing MVS." This article was reprinted with permission from the April 1985 issue of *The Internal Auditor*, pp. 49–56, published by the Institute of Internal Auditors, Inc.

assists in identifying user mods that will have to be reinstalled as a result of applying the monthly programming update tapes [program temporary fix (PTF) tapes] from IBM. If user mods are being created by means other than SMP, restoring the system in the event of a problem or disaster could prove more difficult.

In addition to SMP, a formal-approval process should be in place for initiating significant changes to the operating system. A file should be kept that identifies the reason for such modifications along with management's approval.

SYSLOG. This file contains a historical trail of all messages that have been displayed on the master console. As such, it could be useful to the operations department or technical support department in researching operational problems.

If your company employs IBM's RACF (resource access control facility), serious security violations such as unauthorized attempts to enter the system will be routed to the SYSLOG.* You should verify that SYSLOG is being created and retained for an adequate period and that console operators have been adequately briefed on how to react to serious violation messages.

LOGREC. The data set SYS1.LOGREC contains information on hardware errors, serious software errors, and various hardware statistics. It is used by the IBM CE and other vendors' hardware-maintenance engineers, and it's a good idea for operations personnel to also receive reports from this data set. Environmental recording, editing, and printing (EREP) reports can be generated using a standard IBM utility program. These reports could be used by operations people to spot incipient hardware problems before they become serious and to monitor the adequacy of service provided by the hardware vendors.

System-management facility (SMF). This gathers information on resources frequently used for billing, performance-measurement, and audit-trail purposes. Member SMFPR-MOO of SYS1.PARMLIB (see Exhibit 1) is generally the member that defines how SMF data are to be collected. This member should be listed using system-productivity (SPF), full-screen edit (FSE), or a similar facility.

Things to look for would include:

- Whether SMF recording is ACTIVE.
- Whether the SMF parameters do not permit an operator to change the SMF parameters at initial program load (IPL) time.
- Whether all, appropriate SMF record types are set for collection.
- Whether there are adequate reasons for exits (such as IEFU83) that could be used for modifying or deleting SMF records.

Exhibit 1

```
ACTIVE                          /* ACTIVE SMF RECORDING           */
DSNAME(SYS1.MANA,SYS1.MANB)     /* SMF DATASETS USED              */
PROMPT(IPLR)                    /* PROMPT OPERATOR FOR IPL REASONS */
REC(PERM)                       /* TYPE 17 PERM RECORDS ONLY      */
MAXDORM(1500)                   /* WRITE A BUFFER AFTER 15 MIN    */
STATUS(002000)                  /* WRITE SMF STATS AFTER 20 MIN   */
```

---

* In this article, I refer to RACF because it's the package we use at Northrop Corporation. Other security packages may operate differently.

```
          JWT(0020)                     /* 522 AFTER 20 MINUTES            */
          SID(83Y1)                     /* SYSTEM ID IS 83Y1 NODE 8        */
          LISTDSN                       /* LIST DATA SET STATUS AT IPL     */
      SYS(TYPE(0:3,6:19,21:33,36:39,41:255),
          EXITS(IEFU83,IEFU84,IEFACTRT,IEFUSI,IEFUJV,
                IEFUJI,IEFUTL,IEFU29),
          INTERVAL(010000),DETAIL)
      /* WRITE ALL RECORDS EXCEPT 4,5,20,34,35,40 AS THE SYSTEM DEFAULT,
         TAKE ALL KNOWN EXITS, NOTE: JES EXITS CONTROLED BY JES, THERE
         IS DEFAULT INTERVAL RECORDS WRITTEN AND DETAIL TYPE 032 RECORDS
         AS A DEFAULT FOR TSO */

      SUBSYS(TSO,NOEXITS,NOTYPE(20,34,35,40))

      /* TSO WILL TAKE NO EXITS, AND NO RECORDS TYPE 20,34,35, AND 40 */

      SUBSYS(STC,EXITS(IEFU29,IEFU83,IEFU84),NOTYPE(4,5,20,34,35,40))

      /* WRITE RECORDS SAME AS SYSTEM DEFAULT, TAKE ONLY THREE EXITS,
         NOTE: IEFU29 EXECUTES IN THE MASTER ASID WHICH IS A STC ADDRESS
         SPACE SO IEFU29 MUST BE ON FOR STC. */
```

System-Data Protection

Generally speaking, application programmers and analysts should be restricted from WRITE access to all SYS1 data sets. As these data sets define the operating system, they should only be updateable by appropriate technical-support personnel. If employed, the following data sets should be both READ- and WRITE-protected.

PASSWORD	(OS passwords)
SYS1.UADS	(TSO IDs and passwords)
SYS1.RACF	(RACF passwords)

Security package. You may discover a data processing facility places substantial reliance on the effectiveness of a particular security package in protecting its operating-system data sets. If this is the case, an audit of MVS should probably include at least a high-level review of the security administrator's function with a more-detailed look at access rules for important SYS1 data sets and user attributes as defined in the security system.

If your company uses RACF, you'll want to know:

- Who is assigned the SPECIAL attribute? This gives users systemwide control over RACF profiles and provides access to all system data sets.
- Who is assigned the OPERATIONS attribute? Such an individual can modify all data sets that have not had their access lists set to NONE.
- For sensitive operating-system data sets, who is assigned ALTER capability? Such an individual can create new access rules, even add individuals with UPDATE capability.

Claimed RACF protection can be verified by running an IEHLIST (see Exhibits 2 and 3) against the pack containing the protected data sets. This will identify whether the RACF or OS password bits have been set. It will not indicate whether the RACF profiles are adequate.

Exhibit 2

```
**** TSO FOREGROUND HARDCOPY ****    02/26/85    10:58:55
DSNAME=UN35615.UTILITY.PROGRAMS                  (IEHLIST )
VOLUME: 060129     RECFM=FB    LRECL=  80    BLKSIZE=  3120
     //HK35615W JOB '90N3400800,0155','BACON  EXT 6624           C00000010
     //            CLASS=B,MSGCLASS=Q,NOTIFY=UN35615              00000020
     /*JOBPARM SYSAFF=8103
     //         EXEC PGM=IEHLIST                                  00000050
     //DD1     DD   UNIT=3380,VOL=SER=070086,DISP=SHR             00000060
     //SYSPRINT DD  SYSOUT=A,DEST=N8R90                           00001100
     //SYSIN    DD  *                                             00001110
            LISTVTOC ,VOL=3380=070086
     /*
```

Exhibit 3

SYSTEMS SUPPORT UTILITIES---IEHLIST

```
DATE: 85.056   TIME: 14.51.28
               CONTENTS OF VTOC ON VOL 070086
    DATA SET NAME    CREATED  PURGE   FILE TYPE   EXTENTS  FILE SERIAL  VOL. SEQ.  SECURITY
SYS1.JCLIN.XA8103     07984   00000   SEQUENTIAL   00002    MVS1A1       00001      NONE
SYS1.NJEPARMB         13584   00000   SEQUENTIAL   00001    070086       00001      NONE
SYS1.SBLSPNLO         13884   00000   PARTITIONED  00001    070086       00001      NONE
SMPE.JDP1111.F1       14684   00000   PARTITIONED  00002    070086       00001      NONE
SMPE.JDP1111.F2       14684   00000   PARTITIONED  00001    070086       00001      RACF
SYS1.MACLIB           15684   00000   PARTITIONED  00001    070086       00001      NONE
SYS1.TMSLIB           15684   00000   PARTITIONED  00001    070086       00001      RACF
SYS1.IMAGELIB         17484   00000   PARTITIONED  00002    070086       00001      NONE
SYS1.DUMPOO           08184   00000   SEQUENTIAL   00001    MVS1A1       00001      NONE
DATA.DAILY.LOG8401    13184   00000   SEQUENTIAL   00001    MVS1A1       00001      NONE
SYS1.TMSGEN47         13184   00000   PARTITIONED  00001    MVS1A1       00001      RACF
SYS1.PARMLIB          19584   00000   PARTITIONED  00001    070086       00001      NONE
SYS1.LOGREC           24284   00000   SEQUENTIAL   00001    070086       00001      NONE
DATA.DP070086         24284   00000   NOT DEFINED  00000    070086       00001      NONE
HSM.SID8103.HSMLOGY   25584   00000   SEQUENTIAL   00001    070086       00001      NONE
HSM.SI08103.HSMLOGX   25584   00000   SEQUENTIAL   00001    070086       00001      NONE
PASSWORD              26384   00000   SEQUENTIAL   00001    070086       00001      PWD
SYS1.NTXPARM          27284   00000   PARTITIONED  00001    070086       00001      NONE
SYS1.NJEBCKUP         33484   00000   SEQUENTIAL   00001    070086       00001      NONE
SYS1.BLGSRC           35484   00000   PARTITIONED  00001    070086       00001      NONE
SYS1.NJEPARM          01585   00000   SEQUENTIAL   00001    070086       00001      NONE
SYS1.NETEX.PAMFILE    03585   00000   SEQUENTIAL   00001    070086       00001      NONE
SYS1.VTAMLIB          02484   00000   PARTITIONED  00001    TAR00A       00001      NONE
JES2.PARMS            25283   00000   PARTITIONED  00001    TAR00A       00001      NONE
SYS1.BLGPNLS          29783   00000   PARTITIONED  00001    TAR00A       00001      NONE
SYS1.AOS29            21583   00000   PARTITIONED  00001    TAR00A       00001      NONE
SYS1.VTAMLST          02484   00000   PARTITIONED  00001    TAR00A       00001      NONE
SYS1.HSMMAC           21583   00000   PARTITIONED  00001    TAR00A       00001      NONE
SYS1.ISF.R1MO.ISFDLIB 21583   00000   PARTITIONED  00001    TAR00A       00001      NONE
SYS1.ISF.R1MO.ISFSRC  21583   00000   PARTITIONED  00001    TAR00A       00001      NONE
SYS1.DAE              25583   00000   SEQUENTIAL   00001    TAR00A       00001      NONE
SYS1.NPDALIB          02784   00000   PARTITIONED  00001    TAR00A       00001      NONE
SYS1.SBLSMSGO         25583   00000   PARTITIONED  00001    TAR00A       00001      NONE
SYS1.CMDPROC          25583   00000   PARTITIONED  00001    TAR00A       00001      NONE
SYS1.IEVLIB           24483   00000   PARTITIONED  00001    TAR00A       00001      NONE
SYS1.SGIMLMDO         07484   00000   PARTITIONED  00001    TAR00A       00001      NONE
SYS1.BLGMPNL          21583   00000   PARTITIONED  00001    TAR00A       00001      NONE
SYS1.LINKLIB          33483   00000   DIRECT ACC   00001    TAR00A       00001      RACF
SYS1.BRODCAST         21683   00000   PARTITIONED  00001    TAR00A       00001      NONE
SYS1.SGIMMSGO         07484   00000   PARTITIONED  00001    TAR00A       00001      RACF
SYS1.LPALIB           25883   00000   PARTITIONED  00001    TAR00A       00001      RACF
SYS1.PROCLIB          25883   00000   PARTITIONED  00001    TAR00A       00001      NONE
SYS1.SAMPLIB          21683   00000   PARTITIONED  00001    TAR00A       00001      NONE
SYS1.HELP             25883   00000   PARTITIONED  00001    TAR00A       00001      RACF
SYS1.SVCLIB           25083   00000   PARTITIONED  00001    TAR00A       00001      NONE
SYS1.ISRLLIB          26683   00000   PARTITIONED  00001    TAR00A       00001      NONE
SYS1.TMSGEN           07484   00000   PARTITIONED  00031    TAR00A       00001      NONE
SYS1.SGIMPNLO         07484   00000   PARTITIONED  00001    TAR00A       00001      NONE
SYS1.SGIMPRCO         07484   00000   PARTITIONED  00001    TAR00A       00001      NONE
SYS1.SGIMTBLO         21683   00000   SEQUENTIAL   00001    TAR00A       00001      NONE
DVO1.IEF.HASPINDX     21683   00000   PARTITIONED  00001    TAR00A       00001      NONE
SYS1.ISF.R1MO.ISFLOAD 21683   00000   PARTITIONED  00001    TAR00A       00001      NONE
```

Even if the RACF bit is not on, a data set is RACF-protected if the ALWAYS CALL features is employed and a suitable profile exists.

Program-properties table (PPT). This allows an installation to assign special capabilities to program. One property that can be assigned is bypassing password protection (for instance, OS passwords, RACF). The PPT can be dumped using AMASP-ZAP to identify those programs that have this ability.

The PPT normally resides in SYS1.LPALIB (see Exhibit 4 and the resulting report in Exhibit 5). If the 18th hex character in an entry is a 2, 3, 6, 7, A, B, E, or F, the program is set to bypass password protection. The PPT should be protected from unauthorized access.

JES spool space. The job entry subsystem (JES) is a facility for spooling, job queuing, and managing I/O. This spool space holds data that is waiting to be printed. Utilities exist that can be used to view or modify this area. To ensure the security and privacy of sensitive, production data that may temporarily reside on the JES spool, you should study these utilities to certify that adequate controls exist over their use.

Supervisor-call routines (SVCs). These cause hardware interrupts and cause the operating system to pass control to the particular SVC that has been called. Because of this capability, SVCs are sensitive coding and should be released only to a limited number of people in the technical-support department.

Most of an installation's SVCs are supplied by IBM and are formally part of MVS. These SVCs are numbered up to approximately 139. Those with higher numbers have been installed by the data processing facility and are regarded as user SVCs. Documentation should exist that, at least, identifies which package or application each user SVC is associated with.

Authorized-program-facility (APF) libraries. These libraries contain programs that may be able to use restricted MVS functions. The APF libraries are:

- SYS1.LINKLIB and its concatenations as listed in LNKLSTxx of SYS1.-PARMLIB.
- SYS1.SVCLIB.
- Libraries listed in member IEAAPFxx in SYS1.PARMLIB.

A program that resides in an APF library and has the authorized state indicator on can issue sensitive SVC and essentially become an extension of the operating system. It could contain coding to bypass security (such as RACF) checking. As such, WRITE access to APF libraries should be tightly controlled. Documentation should exist to identify which package or application each APF program is affiliated with.

Exhibit 4

```
**** TSO FOREGROUND HARDCOPY ****     02/26/85   10:58:21
DSNAME=UN35615.UTILITY.PROGRAMS                  (AMASPZAP)
VOLUME: 060129      RECFM=FB      LRECL=  80    BLKSIZE=  3120

//HK35615V JOB '90N3400800,0155','BACON   EXT 6624   C00000010
//                CLASS=B,MSGCLASS=Q,NOTIFY=UN35615   00000020
/*JOBPARM SYSAFF=8103
//ZAP          EXEC PGM=AMASPZAP                      00000050
//SYSPRINT DD  SYSOUT=A,DEST=N8R90                    00001100
//SYSLIB    DD  DSN=SYS1.LPALIB,DISP=SHR
//SYSIN     DD  *                                     00001110
 DUMP IEFSD060  IEFSDPPT
 DUMPT IEFSD060  IEFSDPPT
/*
```

Exhibit 5

[Hex dump listing of DUMPT IEFSD060 IEFSDPPT memory contents, showing record length 001780, member name IEFSD060, CSECT name IEFSDPPT, with columns of hexadecimal values and EBCDIC character interpretations on the right side including entries such as IEDQTCAM, ISTINM01, IKTCAS000, AHLGTF, MHLGTF, IHLGTF, IEFIIC, IEFMB660, IEEVMNT2H, IASXWROOM, CSVVFCRE, HASJES20, DFSHVRCO, IATINJK, DXRRLMOO, APSPPIEP, AKPCSIEP, IATINTKF, OSHVASCP, OSNUTILB, IEAVTDSVI, IFASHF, CSVLLCRE, RAXTCAM, ERBMFMFC, HHASMP, DFSNSCOO, COMMON, OMEGAMON, IEWL, SASSICOM, UCC7, AMSTCAM, MINITCAM, MINITCMB, AMSTCAMB, RAXTCAMB, IEDQTCMB, OMINSIN, DBMA]

Other Concerns

The operating system allows certain actions to be initiated or overridden at the master console. For example, a programmer who has submitted a job that is attempting to circumvent date or volume-table-of-contents (VTOC) protection will generate a message at the master console. This message must be responded to before the job will be allowed to proceed. As a result, all terminals that can function as a master console should be located in secure areas (preferably within the computer room) and operators adequately trained in how to react to such messages.

Additionally, if the time-sharing option (TSO) is employed, a study of SYS1.UADS could be performed to verify that only appropriate individuals have been assigned certain, sensitive capabilities. Arrange to have the terminal monitor program run to generate a listing of all TSO users and their attributes; then identify who can add, modify, or delete TSO users. For practical purposes, this individual should have:

- The ACCOUNT attribute (ACCOUNT bit turned on in SYS1.UADS).
- Update capability for SYS1.UADS per any security package that is in place. Identify who can issue the OPERATOR command. Such individuals can answer their own messages that appear on the master console.

Sensitive utilities usually exist in a data processing facility that could represent a security exposure if not adequately controlled. You should determine if any system utilities have been established in such a manner as to bypass password checking. This can be done by locating them in APF libraries and associating them with sensitive SVCs.

Two utilities that can create security exposures are IBM's Fast Dump Restore (FDR) and AMASPZAP (commonly referred to as Superzap). FDR is designed to be used by systems-support personnel for restoring and dumping disk data. It is conceivable that it could be used in assisting an individual to dump a production data set to disk, make an unauthorized modification, and restore the modified data set as the production version. Depending on how FDR has been generated, it may be able to bypass password protection.

AMASPZAP can be used to modify VTOCs to remove RACF protection, or to modify data on production data sets stored in disk. While such actions usually require a positive response from the master-console operator, if individuals have been assigned OPERATOR capability, they could accomplish this activity with no assistance.

Data that is stored on tape may require additional controls to ensure its security. A tape-management system should be in place to assist in administering tapes.

Among other things, this allows all 44 positions of a data set name to be checked during label processing (instead of just the last 17). If sensitive data is kept on tape, use of bypass label processing (BLP) should be controlled. JES exit 6 can limit its use to a specific class requiring provision of a valid password.

Test and production environments should be adequately separated within the data processing facility. There should be controls ensuring that test jobs cannot create files with production names which could be used in a production cycle. JES exit 6 could be used to control this problem. Another method would be to employ RACF. This would involve:

- Specifying automatic data set protection (ADSP) in all user profiles.
- Establishing a common, high-level qualifier for all production data set names.
- Limiting, through GROUP assignments, who has CREATE capability for this qualifier.

Charters and position descriptions should exist to ensure that duties and responsibilities are adequately defined. These documents should explicitly identify responsibilities for operating-system integrity. They should also indicate a sufficient degree of job segregation (subject to staff size) between operations personnel, system programmers and other technical-support staff, and security administration.

Finally, it is imperative that the operating system be re-creatable in the event of a problem or disaster. A copy of the operating system should be kept off-site with tight controls over its recall. System programmers and others involved with operating-system maintenance should not be able to gain physical custody of the backup tapes. A desirable control is to duplicate any tape at the backup site when a recall is requested. This copy should be sent back to the computer operations department and the original retained off-site.

Conclusion

Ensuring that management has properly defined the operating system and that appropriate controls exist to maintain its integrity on a continuing basis are an auditor's goals in a MVS audit. Because of their technical nature, such reviews require a high degree of trust between the auditor and the system programmer.

Only with experience will you be able to operate at your accustomed level of independence.

AUDIT USES OF PERSONAL COMPUTERS

The range of versatility and power of PCs, or microcomputers, is considerable, as is the price. This means that not all uses are feasible on all PC models. Thus, the auditor must develop an awareness of which PCs can do what, and determine what audit use he plans to make of that PC. While there is no single right set of uses, early experience provides a basis for offering selection criteria.

Criteria in Selecting Microcomputers

Most company auditors have only recently begun to use microcomputers. Much of that use has been experimental in nature; thus, the full potential benefit of using microcomputers in internal auditing has yet to be realized. Those that are pioneering the way tend to seek microcomputers that satisfy the following criteria:

☐ *Software availability.* This is one of the most important criteria. At a minimum, the microcomputer should be able to perform word processing, spreadsheet analysis, and graphics. Software is now available that can do each, but some are better than others, and no software operates on all PCs. The most current software products combine such features as spreadsheet analysis and graphics and enable the user to divide the screen into segments or "windows" to permit simultaneous viewing and working on words, graphs, and schedules. The largest selling microcomputers include the Apple IIe, IBM PC, TRS 80 by Tandy, and the Hewlett Packard PC. Software is available for all of these, which supports most auditor uses at present. Care must be taken in considering the other 150–200 microcomputers presently available to avoid being handicapped by insufficient software.

☐ *Ease of operation.* Since most internal auditors know little about computers, the ease of operating one is an important consideration. Virtually all microcomputer manufacturers claim that their computers are simple to use; however, there are deficiencies. Ease of operation is somewhat subjective; what is easy to one person is not necessarily easy to another. Microcomputer vendors are not always helpful in trying to evaluate this factor, so it is a good idea not to place too much reliance on their representations. The best advice is to try as many as is practicable and to talk to present users. One point to keep in mind is that many prospective users do not feel comfortable operating a keyboard. Computers are now available that minimize keyboard use by offering such devices as function keys, touch screen control, and "mouses" to enter commands. These features cost more, but many believe they are worth it.

- *Dependability.* Contrary to manufacturers' claims, microcomputers do break down from time to time. Failures of electronic components are extremely rare; however, there are mechanical components that do wear out and require replacement. The ease with which repair can be made is important. Some manufacturers and independent repair services offer in-plant maintenance, and repair services promptly. This is more preferable to many people than having to take the microcomputer to a service center or back to the vendor.
- *Communication capability.* While some may intend to use their microcomputer in a unique stand-alone fashion, others want to communicate with other computers, even mainframes. Not all microcomputers permit such communication.
- *Speed of operation.* The speed with which a microcomputer performs instructed duties is another important criterion. If the microcomputer is to play an important role in improving auditor efficiency, then its response time must be fast. If the auditor must wait, even for a few seconds, before commencing with the next task, time is wasted. More importantly, the concentration of the auditor may be disrupted or his train of thought lost.
- *Capacity.* Capacity is an obvious limiting factor in what microcomputers can do. The larger the user of internal memory the more powerful and versatile the microcomputer is. At a minimum, the auditor should seek a PC able to offer at least 128K bytes of internal memory. Many microcomputers are currently available that far exceed this minimum. Those auditors who want to make use of the most versatile and powerful software such as Lotus 1-2-3 will have to look to these larger machines.
- *Compatibility.* Some auditors will want to use their PC to interface with the mainframes of the company. This is now possible for IBM shops with IBM's introduction of the IBM PC XT/370. Other manufacturers are sure to build in compatibility in newer models of their products. Eventually, compatibility could become of paramount importance.
- *Portability.* Internal auditors do nearly half their work away from their principal office. Hence, a microcomputer that is powerful, flexible, and portable means that the auditor can take the microcomputer into the field. Many portable models are presently available, and some of these are compatible with others, such as IBM's PC. This is certain to be a factor in the portable computer market, and prospective buyers should keep this in mind.

Other considerations in deciding which microcomputer to buy include:

- Size of the display screen and its resolution
- Keyboard configuration
- Physical size of the computer and how much desktop space it occupies
- Availability of peripheral equipment

No attempt is made in this discussion to set priorities as to the foregoing criteria. Different audit departments have different needs and will attach greater or lesser significance to each criterion as a result.

INFORMATION SYSTEMS (EDP) AUDIT TECHNIQUES 28-55

In 1984, IBM followed up its initial and secondary entries into the PC market with a much more powerful model, the PC AT. This PC differs from its predecessors in many respects. For instance, it offers a larger floppy disk capacity of 1.2M bytes versus 360K for earlier models. Its hard disk offers a whopping 20M or 30M storage capacity. Its microprocessor is Intel's 80286 chip. Prior models were based on the 8088 chip, also from Intel. Processing speeds for the AT are five times faster as a result. Finally, the AT can run on either one or two operating systems, MS-DOS (PC-DOS) and Unix (Xenix). Thus, with Unix, the AT may operate in a multiuser environment.

The development of the AT, like its PC parent, was followed by the development of several competing "look-alikes." Staying compatible with IBM seems essential for most of its rivals in the business marketplace.

The IBM PC AT look-alikes do vary from the AT in some details, although they are similar in the following respects:

- The ability to run Lotus 1-2-3
- The ability to accept IBM PC boards
- The 80286 microprocessor
- Internal memory
- Hard disk capacity

The primary difference is price. Some imitation PC ATs can be purchased for considerably less than the almost $6,000 required for the IBM. In some instances, prices are as low as $2,500. Figure 28-10 lists several of the suppliers of PCs compatible with the PC AT.

Audit Uses

Auditors are only beginning to tap the power of the microcomputer to perform audit tasks. Perhaps the most frequent use at present is to use it as a word processor. Thus, audit programs, working paper narratives, and questionnaires can be prepared expediently.

The best word processing use, however, is in drafting audit reports and memoranda. Many auditors spend more time on this task than on almost any other single undertaking. In part, this is because many find writing, even for internal distribution, to be difficult. With automated word processing, much of the editing and redrafting can be done more quickly and efficiently. Further, some of the word processing packages can check for spelling accuracy and some can perform limited editing. Future enhancements are certain to increase the editing power of the best packages. While these devices are not likely to become a substitute for clear expression of important points, they will eliminate many stumbling blocks.

In addition to word processing, internal auditors can also make use of spreadsheet programs (see Figure 27-13). These can be used to prepare documentation of analytical audit procedures. Trend, ratio, and regression anal-

FIG. 28-10
Suppliers of PC AT Compatibles

Supplier	Model
Compaq Computer Corp. 20555 FM 149 Houston, Tex. 77070 (713) 370-0670	Deskpro
Cordata Systems 275 Hillcrest Drive Thousand Oaks, Cal. 91360 (818) 495-5800	Corona PC 400
Epsom America Inc. Computer Products Division 2780 Lomita Blvd. Torrance, Cal. 90505 (213) 539-9140	The Equity Familily
IBM Entry Systems Division P.O. Box 1328 Boca Raton, Fla. 33432 (305) 998-6048	PC AT
ITT Information Systems Division P.O. Box 52016 Tempe, Ariz. 85281 (602) 894-7000	XTRA
NCR Corp. 1700 S. Patterson Dayton, Ohio 45479	PC 4
Tandy Corporation 1800 One Tandy Center Fort Worth, Tex. 76102 (817) 390-3885	Tandy 3000
Texas Instruments P.O. Box 809063 Dallas, Tex. 75380 (800) 527-3500	TI Professional
Zenith Data Systems 1000 Milwaukee Ave. Glenview, Ill. 60025 (800) 842-8000	ZFA-161-22

Source: Barbara Call, "A Machine For All Seasons," *PC Week Buyers Guide*, pp. 65–78.

FIG. 28-11

Software Products for Downloading Data

Product	Price	Vendor
Answer/DB	$30,000–$45,000 per mainframe $700 per PC	Informatics
Peachlink	$6,000 per PC	Management Science America
Tempus-Link	$6,175–$50,000 per mainframe	Micro Tempus
Interactive PC Link	$25,000 per mainframe $800–$2,500 per PC	McCormack & Dodge

ysis may be documented in this fashion. Graphics software may be used to develop line or bar charts.

If the internal auditor's microcomputer is suitably equipped, the computer may serve as a terminal. Automated research can be performed with this facility to access to research data bases, such as those offered by Mead Data Control, Lockheed, and Systems Development Corporation. Acting as a terminal, the microcomputer is able to access internal data bases.

The ultimate in this direction is to download data from a mainframe for further audit testing in the internal auditor's microcomputer. Many communications software packages are now available that accomplish this. A short list is presented in Figure 28-11.

A recent *Business Week* article detailed the most popular software programs presently being used.[25] These include Wordstar, PFS Write for word processing, and Lotus 1-2-3 for spreadsheet, graphics, and file management, each priced at less than $500. Also mentioned were other popular spreadsheet programs, such as Multiplan and Visicalc, and graphics programs, including Visi Trend/Plot and PFS-graph. The popularity of these programs is a strong indicator that, for the time being, PCs are being used mostly for word processing, analytical work, and developing presentation material.

Other software devices provide more current opportunities to automate manual aspects of auditing. Electronic filing systems are available, which permit storage and retrieval of vast amounts of data. These may be used to store such audit tools as questionnaires, audit programs, and checklists. Audit reports and findings can be stored and cross-filed in such a way that retrieval is permitted in a variety of ways. For example, if the auditor wishes to know all of the instances in which weaknesses in controlling the use of signature plates are identified, the proper query will produce the answer accurately and promptly.

Electronic files can be set up for almost anything of interest to the

---

[25] "Software: The New Driving Force," *Business Week*, Feb. 27, 1984, p. 77.

auditor, provided time and resources are available to load the data and to maintain it. For instance, key controls of important transaction flows by entity can be filed. Thus, when the auditor wants to know how a particular entity controls changes to EDP programs, he can get the answer quickly.

These are but a few examples. Technology has presented internal auditors and others with a golden opportunity in the form of microcomputers to increase substantially the quality of their service and the efficiency with which it is rendered. It is revolutionizing what the auditor can do and how he can do it. This opportunity must be carefully managed in order to ensure that the pitfalls of microcomputer usage are avoided and to realize the potential benefits in full. Techniques for that are discussed in Chapter 27.

FINAL THOUGHTS

As indicated in the beginning of this chapter, it is not possible to cover all aspects of I/S auditing in a general reference work on the broader subject of internal auditing. However, the following thoughts are offered to guide I/S audit managers and practitioners in devising and maintaining an effective program of I/S audit coverage.

- Approach I/S auditing with the same organizational and planning disciplines used in non-I/S auditing.
- A combination of I/S audit approaches, including installation reviews, application audits, and developing system audits, should be adopted.
- While many CAATs have evolved or have been adapted for use in applications auditing, most other I/S auditing involves techniques familiar to non-I/S auditors.
- The computer is a tool that can be used efficiently and effectively only if the performing auditor is properly trained.
- Most CAATs, such as utility software and specialized software, should be used by only the most advanced I/S auditors.
- Use of CAATs requires that the auditor document the objectives, techniques used, and conclusions drawn in such a way as to leave a clear audit trail.
- Some worthwhile CAATs, such as embedded audit routines, require an ongoing commitment to system maintenance, a discipline for which audit organizations must be properly prepared.

As the I/S technology continues to automate manual business functions, the need for I/S auditing will increase. However, it is believed that this trend toward automation will be accompanied by developments that will make auditing simpler and easier. The likely result will be that non-I/S auditors with practically no knowledge of the technical aspects will be able to perform audit routines previously reserved for their technically oriented counterparts. At the same time, however, a need will continue to grow for auditors able to effectively audit the internal technical aspects of an I/S installation, such as its operating system and its network and communications controls.

SUGGESTED READING

AICPA Computer Services Executive Committee. *Computer Assisted Audit Techniques*. New York: AICPA, 1979.

Connor, Joseph E., and Burnell H. DeVos, Jr., eds. *Guide to Accounting Controls*, 1982 Supplement. New York: Price Waterhouse & Co.

Editorial Staff of Auerbach, William E. Perry, and Herbert Zeruld, consultants. *EDP Auditing*, Sections on Audit Methodology and Auditing Case Studies. Pennsacker, N.J.: Auerbach Publishers, Inc., 1978.

Halper, Stanley D., P. Jarlath O'Neil-Dunne, and Xenia Ley Parker. *Handbook of EDP Auditing*, Chapter 28. Copyright © 1987 by Coopers & Lybrand, U.S.A. Published by Warren, Gorham & Lamont, Boston.

Macchiaverna, Paul. *Auditing Corporate Data Processing Activities*. New York: The Conference Board, Inc., 1980.

Mair, William C., Donald R. Wood, and Keagle W. Davis. *Computer Control and Audit*, Chapters 8, 9, and 10. U.S.A.: Touche Ross & Co., 1976.

Study Group on Computer Control and Audit Guidelines. *Computer Audit Guidelines*. Toronto, Canada: The Canadian Institute of Chartered Accountants, 1975.

Systems Auditability & Control, Audit Practices. Altamonte Springs, Florida: The Institute of Internal Auditors, 1977.

Weber, Ron. *EDP Auditing: Conceptual Foundations and Practice*, Chapters 16–21. New York: McGraw-Hill Book Co., Inc., 1982.

CHAPTER **29**

International Operations

Introduction	2
Nature and Purpose of International Business	2
Characteristic Differences in International Operations	4
Advantages and Risks in Multinational Operations	5
Impact of International Operations on Management Functions	6
Impact on Financial Activities	6
Organizational Matters	6
Accounting Activities	9
Financial Planning and Budgets	9
Taxation	10
Investment Decisions	11
Obtaining Funds	11
Controls	11
Impact on Marketing Activities	12
Marketing Organization Structure ..	12
Channels of Distribution	13
Market	13
The Product	13
Marketing Tactics or Methods	13
Impact on Personnel Activities	14
Impact on Manufacturing, and Other Supporting Service, Activities	14
Managing the International Audit Function	15
Special U.S. Laws Relating to International Operations	15
Compliance With Legal Requirements of Host Countries ...	15
Special Need to Interpret Financial Policies and Procedures	16
Differences in Standards of Behavior	16
Performing International Audits	16
Preparation for a Foreign Location Audit	17
Examples of Different Accounting Procedures	19
Improving the Quality of the Overseas Audit	20
International Auditing Standards	21
Diversity in Auditing Standards and Procedures	21
Trends in International Auditing Standards	22
The Changing Multinational	23
Audit Questionnaires and Programs	24
Special Areas for Inquiry	24
Suggested Reading	29

Fig. 29-1	Comparative Horizons or Viewpoints of Domestic (U.S.) vs. International Companies	7
Fig. 29-2	Chart of International Finance Functions—Centralized at Corporate Headquarters	9
Fig. 29-3	International Finance Organization Structure—Decentralized	10
Fig. 29-4	Audit Questionnaire—Foreign Agent Agreements	25

INTRODUCTION

One of the significant developments in American business over the past 20 years has been the growth of international business. Whereas formerly the involvement of a U.S. company in foreign business was nil or represented only a limited amount of exports, now the international business segment may contribute a significant share of sales and earnings. Firms who formerly simply exported goods may now find themselves involved in making major foreign investments and in managing important or extensive foreign operations. Moreover, problems in raising capital abroad to finance these operations, and the need to administer adequate financial controls over the non-U.S. operations, has led to changes in the structure and importance of the international financial function, an activity with which the internal auditors normally would have extensive interface.

The purpose of this chapter is to make the internal auditor aware of the environmental impact on the management of international operations. How the environmental and other cultural or economic factors influence business conduct is commented upon. Matters of organization structure and planning and control are reviewed in the context of possible alternatives. Finally, the direct impact of these factors on conducting an audit and in managing an international auditing function is discussed.

NATURE AND PURPOSE OF INTERNATIONAL BUSINESS

Basically, international business involves transactions across national boundaries. It requires the transfer of some or all of these elements between countries or others: goods, services, technical knowledge, managerial skills and practices, and capital.

The contact or interaction of the parent organization with a host country organization may take any one of several forms, or even different channels for different countries. Among the possibilities are these vehicles or options:

- *Establishment of a simple export department.* When the sales volume is sufficiently high, the firm may establish a separate organization, often called the "export department," to handle all non-U.S. sales. While the initial effort might relate to proper packaging and transportation, it usually expands to handle sales effort, and sales promotion and advertising. In any event, it does not involve extensive overseas investments or operations, except possibly as to sales.

- *Licensing agreements.* When a company does not wish to directly initiate production in other countries and make the related investments in facilities and personnel, it may enter into a licensing agreement to permit another entity, for a fee or royalty, to manufacture the product or provide the services. Sometimes only some of the parts may be manufactured; and under other circumstances, the entire product may be built. Initially, technical know-how or assistance is provided until the foreign enterprise can operate effectively.

Such arrangements provide income and avoid investments. But the degree of control is much weaker than is the case with direct ownership.

- ☐ *Appointment of an agent or distributor.* A third method of handling international sales without the investments or other significant direct involvement is through the appointment of agents or distributors.

    Presumably, reputable businessmen may be found in host countries who know the area, customs, product, customers, and the like. The agent will often be able to market and service the product more effectively than the company. He also may carry inventories, grant credit, service the account, and otherwise perform all the necessary marketing functions. Here, too, there is less involvement and little or no investment in the foreign country.

    The agents and distributors often are under the jurisdiction of a domestically located export or international sales department.

- ☐ *Establishment of an international sales organization.* Where the company is of the opinion that the agents or distributors are not securing an adequate share of the business, or for other reasons, a company may establish its own sales operation in the host country or countries. This usually involves establishing a foreign-based branch or subsidiary, depending on tax law, needs, and so forth. The company may maintain its own sales organization, carry inventories, extend credit, and in most respects handle all marketing activities of the firm. It may lease or own the necessary facilities and equipment.

    In any event, there is much more direct involvement than in the prior alternatives.

- ☐ *Company owned/operated manufacturing and sales facilities, etc.* The company may decide on further involvement by manufacturing and selling the product through its directly controlled subsidiary or other entity. This would be, in effect, a full-fledged operation, substantially similar to its own domestic activities—adjusted to accommodate local customs, laws, and so forth.

    An alternative could be the use of a manufacturing contract with local business executives or companies. Under these circumstances, it may take on the advantages and disadvantages of a local organization.

- ☐ *A joint venture.* Another alternative is the use of a joint venture where the company enters into a joint venture agreement with nationals of the host country. It may assume a minority position for any number of reasons, or may represent the majority interest. Much may depend on the laws of the foreign country. Partial local ownership may mean more acceptance in the host country, and perhaps a more lenient environment on the part of the government.

    Joint venture arrangements raise questions about transfer prices, taxes, and a number of other problems.

Thus, it can be seen that there are a variety of options in the manner of doing international business. Our concern in this chapter will relate principally to those structures involving rather extensive operations.

CHARACTERISTIC DIFFERENCES IN INTERNATIONAL OPERATIONS

It is probably true that business management fundamentals are valid in different cultures, different countries, and in other environmentally different situations. But specific matters do arise that influence the *practice* of business. The success in a given host country in fact may well depend on the attention and care given to some of the local customs.

A partial listing of some of the differences between domestic operations in the United States and international operations are these:

☐ *Cultural differences.* One of the earliest noticeable differences is that of language. Either both parties must know both languages quite well or they must depend on an intermediary. And even when both languages are known, the nuances may not be understood. Further, there may be no exact translation of certain words or meanings.

Different customs exist and a violation can have serious unintended repercussions. Thus, "yes" may not mean assent, but merely a desire not to disagree. Religious and other social traditions may make it difficult to do business in the American style.

☐ *Geographical differences.* Accessibility in terms of distance and terrain may present problems. In some geographic areas, communications between the parent in the United States and the local organization may be very difficult within the host country. Location can also have a major impact on climatic conditions.

☐ *Political factors.* Political factors that must be dealt with may range from problems of stability versus instability to attempts to discriminate against U.S.-owned or operated businesses—some subtle and some not so subtle. There may be varying degrees of government cooperation and interference.

☐ *Legal differences.* The legal environment may be quite different in various host countries as compared to the United States—quite separate from any matters related to government interference. Thus, in some Mideast countries, financial records must be maintained in the local language for legal reasons and, in most instances, in English for operational purposes.

In a multinational company, there will be numerous legal codes, laws, and regulations to be complied with, and disregarding them can be costly.

☐ *Economic environment differences.* These differences may include such matters as great concentrations of wealth and great pockets of poverty; the availability of natural resources; or the economic system—private enterprise versus Socialism versus a mixed economy. Related to this factor is the educational environment.

These economic factors will help determine what products and services are needed. And, of course, the relative rate of return on the investment, with the related risks, may vary from country to country.

☐ *Managerial style.* Finally, managerial style should be mentioned. U.S. businessmen have often come to think that our methods or practices are the best and should be adopted in host countries. Yet, the cultural differences and customs, as other factors, may influence how well managerial functions are carried out. The methods of motivating and communicating may be different. Control systems may not be the same. The attitude towards authority may not be the same. In short, the way managerial functions may be carried out will vary from country to country.

ADVANTAGES AND RISKS IN MULTINATIONAL OPERATIONS

The distinction between domestic enterprise and international operations must be recognized and dealt with effectively. However, that is not to say the differences all constitute negatives. There are many advantages of a multinational operation. For example, the multinational companies (MNCs) can take advantage of many business opportunities. The growth potential of many large companies is closely related to the expanded worldwide market, with domestic operations being quite stable. These firms may benefit by establishing production facilities in certain countries where the product can be manufactured more economically and effectively. Foreign operations may give access to natural resources and materials otherwise limited or not available to domestic firms.

The large MNCs may secure certain advantages through recruiting management and other personnel from a worldwide labor pool.

These same corporations may often utilize capital markets throughout the world. European funds, for example, may be available to finance European operations. Further, more or less "stateless" financial institutions have been created—such as the International Bank for Reconstruction and Development, the Asian Development Bank, or the Inter-American Development Bank—as sources of capital for financing multinational operations.

Yet, while the potential for larger markets, access to raw materials, capital markets, and a large labor pool exists, there are a great many risks and challenges. The potential for earning a higher rate of return than in the United States must be weighed against risks of expropriation, harassment, discrimination, and an unsuccessful effort. The increasing sense of nationalism is a factor that increases these risks. There was a time when the developing country welcomed the introduction of technical skills, management, new facilities, and products. But as the country developed its own capability, it became aware of the value of its own resources and other assets, and some degree of protectionism grew. The political environment may be subject to rapid change; and industries or companies welcomed in one time period may be evicted in other periods. MNCs must cope with political change as well as other factors, and therefore must attempt to maintain good relations with the government of the host country. The rate of return required to offset these added risks must be weighed in considering a foreign business venture.

IMPACT OF INTERNATIONAL OPERATIONS ON MANAGEMENT FUNCTIONS

Managerial practices differ as between international and solely domestic operations. Much will depend, of course, on the type or extent of foreign operation. But those entities having extensive marketing or manufacturing or financial functions in host countries experience substantial influencing factors. Some sense of the horizon or viewpoint characteristics is shown in Figure 29-1.

Some measure of the impact of international operations on specific departmental activities is reviewed in the following sections.

Impact on Financial Activities

With respect to the auditing of international operations, it is probable that the greatest initial interface will take place between internal auditors and the financial function. For this reason, this function is discussed first. It may be helpful to review the impact of international operations on these aspects of financial management, with emphasis on the increased burdens, risks, and opportunities:

- Organizational matters
- Accounting
- Financial planning and budgets
- Taxation
- Investment decisions
- Obtaining funds
- Controls

Organizational Matters. In companies with significant manufacturing and sales activities outside of the United States, the international financial function is becoming, or has become, very important. This arises, among other reasons, from the need to raise capital from non-U.S. sources and the complexity of such financing; the increasingly complicated foreign tax laws and U.S. laws related to foreign taxes; and the growing need for more sophisticated analytical techniques to evaluate risks and opportunities in a multitude of host countries. Moreover, managements are finding that financial practices that are successful in domestic operations do not necessarily produce comparable results when applied to international operations. Many corporate managements find that a specialized knowledge of foreign environmental conditions may be needed for the foreign segment of operations.

There are perhaps two questions to be answered regarding the international financial function: (1) Should financial policy-making and major financial decisions be centralized in the corporate headquarters, or, with adequate controls, in an international headquarters? (2) What should be the

FIG. 29-1
Comparative Horizons or Viewpoints of Domestic (U.S.) vs. International Companies

Functions	Domestic Enterprise	International Enterprise
Planning:		
Monitoring of marketing threats and opportunities	Nationwide markets	Worldwide or regional markets
Selecting facility investments for optimum location	Nationwide only	Worldwide
Locating sources of funds	Usually nationwide	Worldwide or in host countries
Setting goals and objectives	Domestic orientation	Worldwide orientation
Organizing (includes staffing):		
Organization structure	Structure for domestic operations only	Structure for global activities
View of authority	Similar	Various — differing
Sources of managerial talent	Domestic labor pool	Worldwide labor pool
Machinery and equipment	Largely domestic in many cases	Worldwide sources
Material sources	Largely domestic in many cases	Worldwide sources
Directing:		
Leadership and motivational devices	Influenced largely by domestic customs	Influenced by various cultures and customs
Communications	New technology; short geographical distances; rather direct in style	Old technology for local; network with long distances; often indirect
Measuring:		
Reporting system	Substantially similar in nature; newer technology	Diverse in nature; older technology

split of responsibilities and functions as between the corporate financial activities and those of the international unit—if one exists?

The Suggested Readings at the end of the chapter contain useful comments on the desired organization structure. As a general statement, however, it would seem that a domestic financial staff deals with most of the financial problems in the early stages of development—albeit sometimes without the requisite knowledge. But, as the foreign operations grow and management becomes aware of its potential, as well as its complexities, then either a full-time international financial executive is hired, or some of the central domestic staff tend to specialize in foreign financial matters. In summary, the size and makeup of the international financial staff, their duties, and their place in the organization will depend on several factors, including these:

- Size and complexity of the international operations
- Basic management philosophy or organization—centralization vs. decentralization
- Economics and wisdom of centralizing certain financial functions, while decentralizing others
- Capabilities, competence, style of operation, and personality of the chief financial executive
- General importance of the financial function

The basic choice of structure may be between centralization of financial functions as illustrated in Figure 29-2, or decentralization (except as to financial policy) as shown in Figure 29-3. In the latter, the example is a geographical line organization. A product line approach also might be suitable.

The internal auditor, of course, should be interested in the practicality and effectiveness of the organization structure. Closely related to the question of the proper organization structure is the matter of segregation of duties. The company may well have a separate international finance function, but what should be its duties and responsibilities vis-à-vis the central headquarters' finance organization? Many factors may influence how functions are split between the corporate financial headquarters and the many subordinate units, but these fundamentals are basic:

- The international financial function must be held to the basic policies, procedures, and practices as set forth, or agreed to, by the chief financial officer.
- The operating management of the international functions must be properly serviced for all accounting/financial matters.
- Adequate controls of whatever type must be existent and operating: accounting, administrative, and operational.
- The economy of operation must be considered.

It might well be that the full accounting-type services—the basic controllership functions—would be handled on a decentralized, rather self-contained, basis within the international organization, but that financing activities would be centralized. The accounting activities, including related planning, controls, and reporting would be subject to the functional control of the appropriate corporate financial executive but not direct line authority. As to financing, the financial staff in the host country might advise and assist in the providing of funds from non-U.S. sources under policies and practices authorized by the corporate financial headquarters. Some of the complications or considerations, under whatever structure, are commented on under the appropriate functions.

FIG. 29-2
Chart of International Finance Functions—Centralized at Corporate Headquarters

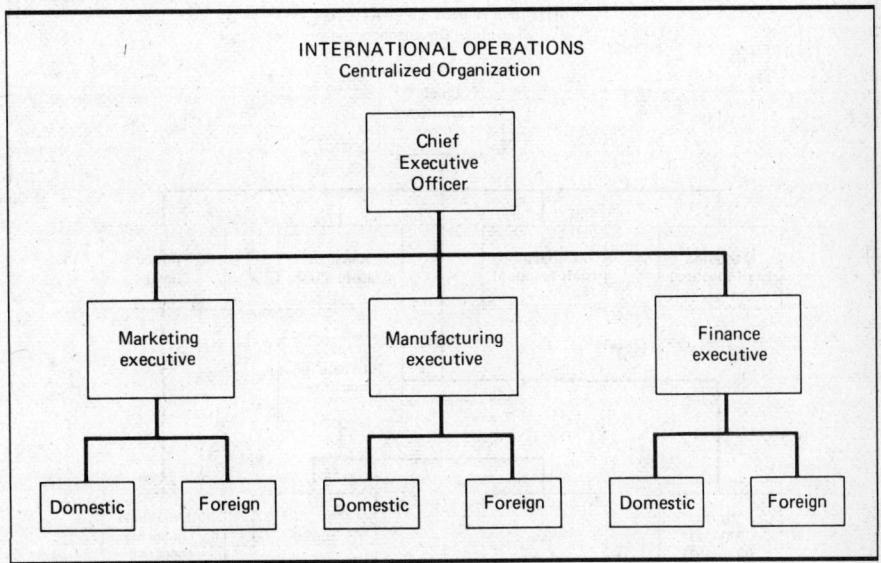

Accounting Activities. The international functions, including each of their units (e.g., plant and sales office), must have the accounting data needed for efficient and effective operation. Ordinarily, this means each such unit will have its own accounting staff, if this makes economic sense. However, since the results must be consolidated, the accounting policies and practices should conform to the company standards as guidelines. Additionally, there may be special accounting requirements in each host country. Thus, the formal accounting records must often be kept in the local language and currency as well as those of the parent. There may also be differences in degree of detail required to support transactions, or there may be special tax records. Often, dual or triple financial records may be practical. The point to be made is that a variety of records must be maintained to serve local management purposes, corporate headquarters management, and governmental needs at several levels. The economic means must be found to provide the needed data under varying conditions. In all operations, there must be adequate internal controls.

Financial Planning and Budgets. Normally, the international operations are subject to the same planning and budgeting requirements as are the domestic units. Each host country activity probably constitutes a profit center or investment center and must submit short-term and long-range plans in a prescribed format that permits ready consolidation. But again, the plans

FIG. 29-3
International Finance Organization Structure—Decentralized

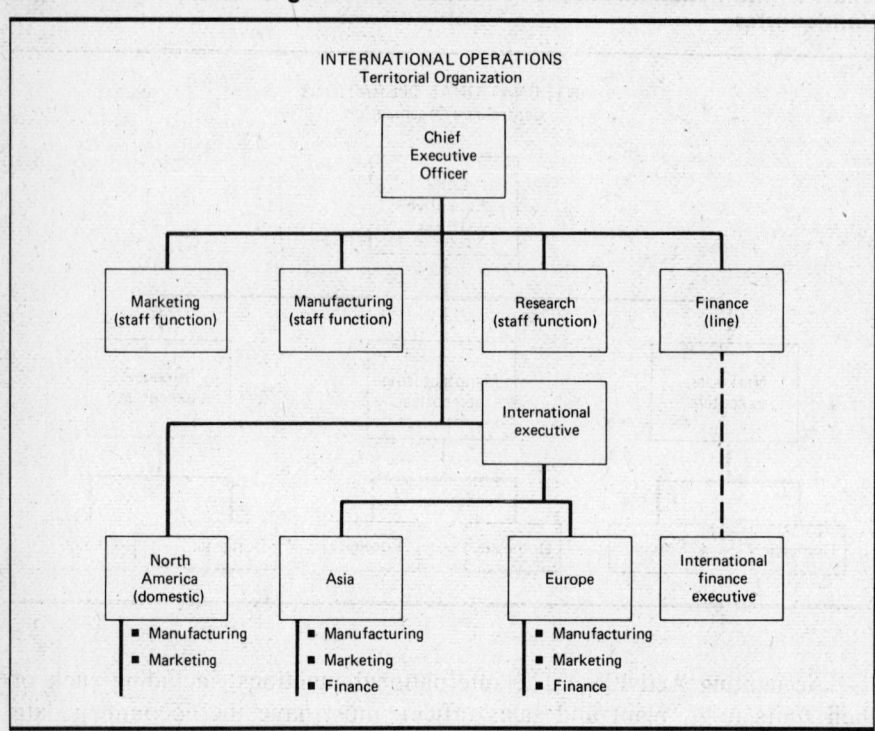

and budgets must often be constructed in local language and currency and then translated into the parent company's currency and terms. Provision must be made for foreign exchange gains or losses, appropriate transfer prices for intercompany transactions, local regulations on fund transfers, and other complications. Additionally, such plans must take into account the impact of local customs and laws—as matters other than currency are affected—as well as the probability of potential harmful governmental actions. Moreover, the absence of some essential market data or the like may make the planning function more difficult.

Taxation. Tax planning assumes special significance in the search for the proper host country, all other factors being considered, to keep the tax burden at a minimum. More than this, the form of doing business must be properly determined because of unequal tax burdens on, say, partnerships versus foreign corporations, or branch offices versus locally incorporated subsidiaries. The financial representatives must know local tax customs as distinguished from what local tax regulations seem to say, or have access to such knowledge. Care must be taken to comply with the appropriate code.

If international operations are conducted in numerous countries, there is a mass of tax returns to be filed—timely and in proper form. Often, local tax counsel must be hired to assist in proper reporting to avoid paying unnecessary taxes.

Investment Decisions. A critical activity in foreign operations is the investment decision itself—be it the initial allocation of funds or subsequent additions. Investments in foreign operations are usually fraught with greater risk than domestic ones. In some countries the risk of expropriation may exist so that the period of investment recovery—the pay-back period—may assume importance, let alone the prospective rate of return. Political winds change, so that a "safe" investment in one time period may not be so classified in another. Cultural differences, competition from a diverse range of products and countries, some perhaps aided by government subsidy, foreign exchange exposures, and lack of adequate market data, to mention a few exposures, require that the company have sound investment criteria. Additionally, because of the greater risks, a higher rate of return should be expected on assets employed. To the extent practical and possible, the investment decisions should be more carefully weighed than with most domestic projects.

Obtaining Funds. Capital must be secured to meet both long-term and short-term needs. Whereas domestic operations may occasionally secure funds from overseas sources (e.g., Eurodollars), the majority of needed monies is usually secured locally. With international operations, the picture is quite different. Given (1) constraints, or possible constraints, in the movement of funds out of certain host countries; (2) foreign exchange risks; (3) problems of convertibility; (4) variations in interest rates; (5) pure availability of funds; (6) government guarantees, government agencies, or special agreements (both host countries and United States); and (7) availability of international financing institutions, there is ample justification to examine the various sources of funds and select the most advantageous.

Quite often a cooperative effort between (1) the corporate headquarters' finance staff or the headquarters' international finance organization group and (2) the local finance group may be the best practical approach. There will be reasons to finance local activities in local currencies to hedge against currency depreciation problems, inconvertibility, or expropriation.

In any event, flexibility is a key consideration, and foreign operations seem to offer more opportunities and require greater ability.

Controls. Finally, a few brief comments should be made about management controls. Foreign operations *should* be subject to the same basic controls as domestic operations. This would apply to operational and financial controls, ranging from controls on capital expenditures, working capital, and the usual daily, weekly, or monthly control of operations through accounting-type reports. However, the scope of activities subject to controls and the type of control that may be practical vary greatly. The technology may not be available locally, the skills needed to operate the system may be absent, or local custom may not make the U.S.-type of reporting and control possible. Again, flexibility and ingenuity are essential. In any event, the local situation may require a special type of control, which is supplemented by strong monitoring and appropriate control reports to international or corporate headquarters.

Given the possible range in the control environment and applications, the use of internal auditors becomes more feasible, as discussed later. The use of internal auditors may be less costly than the maintenance for control reasons of large permanent staffs in the host country.

Impact on Marketing Activities

In a company with extensive foreign marketing activity, in all probability the most suitable type of organizational structure will be determined by marketing—not financial—needs, since this is the function that is the key to a successful international operation. Much of the marketing may be quite autonomous; but great coordination is usually necessary between the corporate marketing headquarters and the various marketing regions. Whether the international activities are organized as a functional, regional, or product group with the proper subdivisions will depend largely on the marketing considerations.

Marketing management will be faced with the same problems—only more so—in international operations as in domestic. But the great variation in local customs, consumer needs, government interference or demands, availability of people, and skill may well require greater flexibility, country by country, in how the products or services are marketed.

To help the internal auditor become aware of some of the difficulties, these differences in domestic versus international marketing are commented upon:

Marketing Organization Structure. Given the variety of circumstances, there is a reasonable chance that different vehicles may be used in different host countries, depending on tax laws, competition, government requirements, and so forth. In country A, an agent may be used; perhaps an independent distributor is more suitable in country B because of contracts, while a company branch office would be most appropriate in another case.

Given the various options, different types of internal audits with differing emphases may be necessary.

Channels of Distribution. The answer as to how best to distribute the product may vary by region or country, or by product. Should the company distribute through a wholesaler, or go directly to the retailer or consumer? Should it perform all of the functions in the distribution chain, or only up to a point? To what extent should the enterprise inventory the goods?

The answers to such questions as these will depend on several factors, including (1) the relative economics or cost of distribution, (2) the availability of qualified distributors, jobbers, and retailers, (3) the existent skills and facilities within the company, (4) the long-term plans of the company for the region or locality, and (5) the time frame within which the company desires to reach certain goals.

Market. Basic to the distribution decision are questions and answers regarding the market itself. Marketing effort should usually be directed according to the market potential. Yet, in some less developed countries, and others, market information might be hard to come by. Data on sales or consumption may simply be nonexistent. Additionally, the product often must be renamed or repackaged to sell effectively. And markets do change, whether due to consumer trends or governmental action such as imposition of import restrictions or tariffs, and the like. Thus, the market and related risks must be carefully studied and monitored before reaching definitive conclusions.

The Product. Initially it might seem that the same products marketed domestically should also be sold in foreign markets. But this does not necessarily follow. Local customs and tastes may preclude distribution of some products without significant changes (such as name or package), as mentioned above. But even more basic product decisions must often be made. Perhaps the product should *not* be exported, but rights to manufacture and sell it should be licensed. Or, support services or technical assistance might only be provided to assist in the manufacture and sale abroad. Perhaps only selected products should be sold in certain countries. Basically, the economics to provide the greatest or optimum return on capital must be studied country by country, or region by region.

Marketing Tactics or Methods. Finally some remarks should be made regarding the methods used in marketing. What may apply in domestic markets may be inapplicable in foreign markets. Advertising and sales promotion campaigns may require a different emphasis if indeed they can be used extensively at all. Language problems, local facilities, and local buying habits must be taken into account. Often it will be helpful to hire local merchandising assistance.

Customer service problems can arise in that (1) users may not properly use or understand the product; (2) technically qualified personnel may not be locally available to provide adequate service; and (3) climate conditions, e.g., humidity and temperature, may create customer service needs. Special training by sales persons and/or customer service personnel may be a necessity.

In summary, there are a host of marketing differences that must be recognized in auditing foreign operations.

Impact on Personnel Activities

Foreign operations will have a great impact on personnel or industrial relations practices in most countries. The degree of difference is often hard to comprehend, but includes such matters as:

- ☐ *Governmental regulations and control.* Host country laws and regulations may establish guaranteed tenure, certain minimum social security, or health-type insurance benefits. Pay levels, working hours and such matters as holiday pay may be legislated. In many countries, the acquisition of local personnel carries with it substantial obligations.

- ☐ *Pay practices.* In many localities, the use of checks for payment purposes is not practical. Banks may not be conveniently located, or may not cash checks for new customers. Accordingly, payment must be made in cash.

- ☐ *Local customers' attitudes and capabilities.* In some countries, well-educated and capable personnel will be available; in others, the nationals simply have neither the education nor experience, and personnel must be imported. Then too, local customs or attitudes may make certain U.S. management patterns unworkable. Government activity and attitudes may not permit the full development of production or other capabilities.

- ☐ *Social stratification.* In some countries, especially in developing ones, there is major social stratification between the privileged (those possessing, education, wealth, social, or governmental position) and the underprivileged (those without education, wealth, or positions of influence).

    From a personnel utilization standpoint, this creates problems in that the manager is restricted as to what he can do with productive ability. These conditions are illustrative of an environment that makes foreign operations much more difficult.

Impact on Manufacturing, and Other Supporting Service, Activities

Comments have been made regarding the impact of international operations on financial, marketing, and personnel activities. These functions were selected as having more relevance for possible internal audit activities. However, *any* activities will be impacted in more or less the same degree. Whatever functions are selected to be pursued in foreign operations, careful analysis should be made of the risks, the availability of the necessary skills, or natural resources, if applicable, and of the economic benefits that might be derived. For various reasons, such activities as these may logically support the domestic operations or foreign marketing efforts:

- Manufacturing, including completely integrated and specialized phases on selected operations only
- Purchasing
- Research and development
- Engineering

MANAGING THE INTERNATIONAL AUDIT FUNCTION

In many respects, management of an international audit function is substantially similar to managing domestic audit activities. However, the task is made immensely more difficult by some of the special circumstances encountered. But, given the increasing importance of international operations, the opportunities are rising. The international auditor is a primary information source for the corporate management on these host country activities. To provide the requisite analyses and evaluations, given the problems of language, greater distances, and cultural differences, the audit manager must be especially sensitive to the factors discussed below.

Special U.S. Laws Relating to International Operations

The manager and his staff must be alert to the provisions and applicability of a series of U.S. laws dealing with international operations, including:

- Export Administration Act of 1969
- Foreign Corrupt Practices Act of 1977
- Export Administration Amendments of 1977
- Anti-Boycott Provisions of the Tax Reform Act of 1976
- Internal Revenue Code, Section 999—International Boycott Determination

Management must be given assurance, where applicable, as to compliance with these laws and any other relevant acts.

Compliance With Legal Requirements of Host Countries

Ordinarily, the audit manager must be sensitive to legal compliance with any law—domestic or foreign. But this topic often assumes more importance as to foreign operations. Failure to comply may result in exceptionally severe penalties. Yet, host countries may pay special attention to aliens operating in their homeland. This is made all the more painful when locally domesticated operations do not comply—with apparent immunity. Use of local counsel may be valuable in securing a proper interpretation of the laws. When the reputation of the company is at stake, the enterprise must be alert to uniform worldwide compliance; and the internal auditors may provide some assistance in getting the facts.

Special Need to Interpret Financial Policies and Procedures

Given the problems of great physical distance from corporate headquarters, possible language difficulties, and personnel untrained in United States or company practices, there is often less understanding of accounting policies and procedures, and other financial practices in the host country than in domestic operations. Currency translation, let alone instructions, can be a source of problems.

In general, the audit manager and his staff should be prepared to carry out special training and education functions. This applies in many areas where internal audits may be undertaken, but the need may be especially critical in the financial accounting functions.

Differences in Standards of Behavior

Under some circumstances, local attitudes and values may increase the risk of wrongful use of company resources, which range from temporary personal use to outright theft. This problem may be compounded by inappropriate activities of U.S. nationals working on foreign assignments. Moreover, in some countries the use of cash instead of checks for local purchases increases the chance of wrongful conversion. The increased possibility of occurrences of this type should be recognized and dealt with through appropriate audit procedures.

These, and other factors, simply increase the need for greater vigilance and creativity in supervising the audit function. It may mean substantial modification of the usual audit techniques.

PERFORMING INTERNATIONAL AUDITS

Something has been said about the increased difficulties of managing international audits and some of the special factors to be considered. But what about actually performing international audits? What about the international auditor? Several observations may be made.

The need for effective internal auditors in international audit situations is likely to increase. This results, among other things, from the pressures from various foreign governments to reduce the large staffs of expatriates and the consequent need for more monitoring of operations. Further, the growth in multinational business, together with the increased recognition of the value of services that the auditor can provide, increases the demand for qualified professionals.

But with these opportunities come some responsibilities. There have been numerous instances where the internal auditor simply lacked the diplomacy or sensitivity that is especially needed on international assignments. This may have arisen from a lack of understanding of the special problems often associated with such efforts, or it may have occurred through an effort to follow a standard audit program that simply was not applicable. To repeat, great flexibility and creativity must be utilized in performing an audit. He should also recognize that in some circumstances, the manager of foreign operations has been allowed great latitude and independence—more so than in decentralized domestic operations. Hence, there have been occasions when the auditor was not exactly welcomed. Accordingly, he should be more than usually sensitive to this attitude. He must conduct himself in such a way that, finally, the local management sees the value of his work. The local manager, in turn, must come to realize that the audits are in his best long-term interests—assuming his interests coincide with the company and top management.

The same skills and professionalism are required of the international auditor as in domestic operations. He must analyze accounts, test for compliance, complete questionnaires, prepare flow charts, use statistical techniques in some instances, interview personnel, and send confirmations—just as in a regular audit. But he often must audit in another language, in some instances through an interpreter, and against records and documents that do not meet normal U.S. requirements. Further, he must adjust for local customs or cultural differences. Phone calls may not be returned, confirmation requests may be ignored, the mail service may be inefficient, the phones may be tapped (by the government), and a host of other problems may arise. Hence, he must be prepared to modify audit procedures and work around special situations. The task can be frustrating, but fun.[1] It can also be challenging to the well-qualified, professional generalist who must know how business operates, and who has enough knowledge of what usually goes awry in foreign assignments to make an effective audit in a relatively short time. The great amount of travel, the frustrations, and inconveniences—for some—are offset by the opportunity to see other cultures and experience living abroad.

Preparation for a Foreign Location Audit

Performing an audit in a foreign location may sound intriguing or fascinating. And it may be in Paris or London or Hong Kong. But many operations are

---

[1] See Marikay Lee, "The International Auditor," *The Internal Auditor*, Dec. 1978, pp. 43–47.

situated in out-of-the way places without many of the conveniences we have come to expect in the United States. In many instances, it can take on the characteristics of a difficult assignment—especially when there is a prolonged stay of one month or so. As stated earlier, foreign internal audits require some of the most capable staff who have the attributes of flexibility, imagination, and self-motivation, and who can perceive what is really being done by the auditee.

A foreign assignment should be carefully planned—even more so than domestic audits. This is because travel is expensive, and the audits usually take longer than comparable ones in the United States, due to different local customs or procedures, need for interpreters, or availability of some audit tools. An in-depth audit by the internal audit staff will often be the only means that corporate headquarters has of getting reasonable assurance that the internal controls are adequate under the circumstances, that the financial reports are reliable, or that the operations are conforming to corporate policies and procedures to the extent necessary and practical. For this reason, they must be planned and executed with care.

These suggestions are made in planning a foreign assignment:

☐ *Arrange for a briefing of the audit team—It might be highly beneficial.* Many companies have sales representatives or other personnel who have visited the country recently discuss the local picture. The audit group could benefit from a briefing by such persons on the economy, living conditions, cultural differences, and "what to expect."

Other sources of help could be some members of the larger public accounting firms who are familiar with audit conditions in the country, various associations, travel brochures, and so forth.

☐ *Plan the size of the audit team carefully.* While a larger audit staff probably could finish an audit more quickly, such an invasion might be very disruptive to the local personnel and activities. It may be wiser to use a smaller audit staff that could still complete a thorough audit within the required time span.

The size of the audit staff should be based on the number of eligible staff, the location and size of the auditee, the availability of adequate hotel space, the relative costs, and so forth.

☐ *Exercise care in selecting team composition.* Given differences in local customs, cultural distinctions, and language, the composition of the audit team is important. The ability to read, write, and speak the native language is highly useful, and experience with local cultural practices can be most helpful in knowing things or actions to avoid. If there is widespread dislike or distrust of a particular religion or race, it may be necessary to avoid raising obstacles in this regard.

☐ *Give recognition to the tariff on transportation costs.* Arrangements made 30 or 60 days in advance can often produce sizeable transportation or hotel cost savings. Certain seasons of the year may be more economical for travel than others.

INTERNATIONAL OPERATIONS

☐ *Do not overlook visa requirements and other related restrictions.* Some locations will require visas, which may take two months or more to secure. Certain countries may demand a temporary working permit for auditors. Others may have restrictions or impediments for particular religions, sex, or color.

☐ *Allow adequate time to do an acceptable audit.* It is far better to spend a few extra days and secure all reasonably necessary data than to leave early with only a partial answer or less than desired audit.

A somewhat longer stay may make some individuals ineligible for personal reasons or conflicting assignments.

Examples of Different Accounting Procedures. A great many differences in accounting/financial practices and procedures are to be expected outside of the United States. A list of some practices widespread in many parts of the world include:[2]

- ☐ Separate cash receipts or disbursement ledgers are not maintained in most European countries and their foreign colonies.
- ☐ Cash and bank transactions are recorded in the general ledger based on bank statements, rather than on the basis of checks issued.
- ☐ Bank reconciliations are not prepared if the recording is based on bank statements.
- ☐ Paid checks are not returned by banks but can be inspected at the bank. (This might require a few days advance warning to the bank.)
- ☐ Bank transfer vouchers may be used rather than checks. These documents are instructions to the bank to transfer the stipulated funds to the specified bank and account number of the payee.
- ☐ Separate payrolls are prepared for staff, middle management, and executives. Local personnel are usually reluctant to show auditors the "confidential" payrolls.
- ☐ Many countries have legally required "bonus" payments. Very often these bonuses appear on separate payrolls.
- ☐ Certain countries require the use of standard charts of accounts, which may differ substantially from U.S. practices.
- ☐ Separate books are often maintained for local legal purposes, and differences will usually occur in inventory valuation, allowances for doubtful accounts, and certain reserves and accruals, including local taxes. Legally required inflation accounting is also a source of major differences. It is important that auditors review the existing differences and that local management maintains a reconciliation of these books on a current basis.

---

[2] From *Internal Auditing Alert*, May 1982, p. 2.

- Imprest funds are not widely accepted; even the principles of the imprest funds are not understood in many countries.
- Added value tax and its accounting requirements should be clearly understood by the auditors. In some countries it can amount to as much as 17 percent of purchase volume and sales.
- Common employee benefits can include mandatory severance pay accruals against which employees can obtain loans, mandatory car loans, housing allowances, and transportation allowances.

Improving the Quality of the Overseas Audit. Given the differences in local customs, language, and procedures, these comments may be helpful:[3]

- Auditors must approach overseas audits with an open mind and accept differences in accounting procedures. These procedures are not necessarily unacceptable just because the auditor is unfamiliar with them. It is easier to have auditors who understand these practices than to train the entire foreign accounting department in U.S. procedures.
- The concept of strict segregation of duties and responsibilities—the cornerstone of U.S. internal control concept—is not accepted universally. Many countries (especially where local management is in control) rely heavily on trust. The internal auditors visiting companies with this attitude have to be missionaries, outlining with patience that "trust is good, controls are better." This educational process is important and has to be carried out in a cooperative relationship.
- Communication is a key factor. Lower-level supervisory and management personnel show great loyalty to top local management and are reluctant to talk to auditors openly and freely on subjects they consider confidential. Auditors should involve higher local management in situations where they notice stalling by supervisory personnel.
- Auditors should arrange for a meeting with local statutory auditors and local attorneys to discuss the validity of issues presented by local management as "customary," "local conditions," "local requirements," etc. Not everything presented as such is really mandatory.
- Prior to completion of the audit and prior to the final meeting, auditors should present a draft report to local management, even if this is not the standard practice of the internal audit department. This enables local management to review the report in its entirety, to get a flavor for the tone of the report, and to recheck the factual contents with their people. This is particularly important if local management's first language is not English. The verbal presentation is different from the formal written report. Misunderstandings can easily occur and are difficult to correct once auditors leave the location.
- A postcompletion audit review with written comments is most important as guidance for future audits at the particular location.

---

[3] *Ibid.*, pp. 2–3.

INTERNATIONAL AUDITING STANDARDS

This chapter has described the nature of international operations, the basic differences between international operations and domestic ones, and some of the special precautions to be taken in managing the international audit function. Given these circumstances, it is understandable that the quality of accounting and related procedures varies country by country, and that the audits differ in quality and procedures. By the same token, uniform auditing standards could be a common objective for internal auditors and business management. Some comments on these subjects are made hereinafter. It is recognized, of course, that audit procedures will always depend on specific findings, condition of records, internal controls, and so forth.

Diversity in Auditing Standards and Procedures

The diversity in *accounting* procedures and practices, with the implications for auditing practices, may be rooted in the cultural, legal, political, and economic differences found in international operations. However, it is probably true that the accounting profession suffers from such international problems as poor quality of accounting education as a result of inadequately trained accounting educators, misinterpretation of the auditor's report due to differences in auditing standards on the meaning of attestation, different standards for independence, and lack of adequately prepared accountants in Third World countries, to name but a few.

Some of the difficulty arises from different audit standards (in part for dissimilar purposes), which may be generated in diverse ways for various countries. Thus, there are four basic ways in which auditing standards may be developed:[4]

1. *By governmental decree.* Thus, France and West Germany issue standards in the body of company law for statutory audits (as distinguished from conventional audits called "contractual audits," which usually are below the standards of quality sought by the accounting profession).

2. *By a legislatively designated professional body.* In Canada, the law refers to the *Canadian Institute of Chartered Accountants Handbook* as the source of auditing standards.

3. *By officially recognized professional bodies, perhaps supported by a government agency.* In the United States, an example would be the ASB, which the SEC oversees.

4. *By importation from other countries with or without modification.* Thus, Indonesia follows U.S. standards.

---

[4] From Paul J. Wendell, ed., *Corporate Controller's Manual, 1984 Update* (New York: Warren, Gorham & Lamont), p. 47-4.

Statutory standards are not acceptable for the usual U.S. type of audit. Standards established through professional bodies (as in 2 and 3 above) may have important differences. Many examples abound in the United States versus the United Kingdom's practices; and importation does not necessarily produce compliance or an understanding of the standard.

In summary, the different sources of standards, the varying cultural, political, and environmental factors, and the quality of the accounting profession cause different auditing standards.

Trends in International Auditing Standards

Given the above reasons for divergency, there are some forces that, nevertheless, are assisting in developing needed international auditing standards. Among these influences are the following:

1. The growth of the transnational auditing firm
   - ☐ The principal firm issues instructions on the extent, scope, and timing of the audit procedures, and expresses on opinion on the consolidated statement and takes responsibility for coordination of the audit. The firm provides guidance on any additional tests needed to express the opinion. Thus, there is a force that helps assure which of the audit procedures, taken as a whole, are adequate.
2. The formation of the International Federation of Accountants (IFAC)
   - ☐ This organization was established in 1977 to aid in the development of a "coordinated, worldwide accountancy profession with harmonized standards."
   - ☐ Various auditing education, ethic, and other guidelines have been issued. *The International Auditing Guidelines* (IAG) are similar to the AICPA's SAS. However, there remain questions as to whether the rules of the IFAC in fact improve practices, and whether they are recognized and enforced.
3. Actions by the internal auditors themselves
   - ☐ The internal auditors have made some progress in respect to internal auditing standards in two ways:
     - In 1978, the IIA issued its own set of auditing standards and, in 1983, SIAS No. 1 (see Chapter 3). SIAS No. 2 (see Chapter 13) was also issued in 1983.
     - Internal auditors have exchanged information as to methods of auditing or audit technology in international operations. Some companies with extensive international commitments have developed a centralized audit group that, among other things, evaluates compliance with professional and corporate standards, and guides the decentralized local audit activities. Thus, U.S. companies directly, and through the IIA, have assisted in elevating the status of internal auditing while encouraging acceptable levels or standards of auditing for international operations.

There will always be differences in conditions of international activities, which will require various standards. But these three groups delineated above are promoting and encouraging the development of elevated levels of practice to the end that the professionals involved, and their companies, can have increased confidence in the adequacy of financial and operational audits conducted by both internal and external auditors.

The Changing Multinational

In this overview of international operations, organization structure and such questions as centralization or decentralization are discussed. It is stressed that the complex political and cultural considerations are factors to be considered along with the economics. The most efficient or appropriate type of operation will depend, for example, on the scope of activity, availability of personnel, and stage of development.

The internal auditor should be sensitive, however, to the changing nature of international operations. In the typical multinational organization, there is a parent company supported by the subsidiaries, or daughters, in specific foreign countries. While major decisions are made in the parent organization as to what products or services are to be sold abroad, as well as key personnel assignments and the conduct of research, a great deal of autonomy is given to each daughter company as to manufacturing, marketing, finance, and human resource management.

However, competitive pressures are such, especially with the impact of automation, that increasing centralization may be required to cover everwidening processes and products. It may be necessary, for example, to centralize the making of engines for South America in one plant, say in Mexico, rather than continue such manufacturing in each country. One authority has stated that financial management may require taking financial operations away from all operating units, including the parent, and running them as systems. Moreover, he states that Japanese multinational management may be ahead of Western-based management precisely because they treat foreign units as branches and not as daughters. Funds, for instance, may be siphoned from American or European outlets and invested in tomorrow's growth markets, such as Brazil or India. Just as a domestic American company would not insist that earnings from New England be reinvested in that geographical area, but could be used in, for example, California, so also should American multinational companies view operations in the broadest context. Just as a subsidiary must become part of a *system* in manufacturing, marketing, and finance, so must management people become transnational. Finally, the authority states:

> Economic realities are thus forcing the multinational to become a transnational system. And yet the political world in which every business has to operate is becoming more nationalistic, more protectionist—indeed more chauvinistic—day by day in every major country. But the multinational really has little choice: if it fails to adjust to transnational economic reality, it will fast become inefficient

AUDIT QUESTIONNAIRES AND PROGRAMS

Enough has probably been said about "flexibility" and "creativity" so that it is evident that standard audit programs may not be utilized to the same extent as in domestic audits. So the authors will not give examples of such documents. To a greater degree than otherwise, the questionnaires must be devised for the special problems that often arise in international audits for different regions or cultures. Thus, if foreign agent agreements are in use, a review of such documents is in order, and a carefully thought-out questionnaire should be prepared to explore this facet of international operations. In addition, similar questionnaires, plus the related audit programs, should be originated for those "special areas." An example of a questionnaire for this specific application is shown in Figure 29-4.

SPECIAL AREAS FOR INQUIRY

To be sure, the individual circumstances will govern the type of audit needed in international operations. However, in addition to the usual domestic-type audits, as modified, the authors have found audits of these activities to be especially beneficial:

- Compliance with U.S. foreign operations laws
- Compliance with local laws as to financial records, taxes, and legal procedures
- Bidding procedures
- Cash purchases of local supplies
- Physical inventory of plant and equipment
- Foreign exchange conversions
- Foreign duty imports
- Host country insurance coverage
- Home leave and vacation practices

(continued on page 29-29)

---

[5] Peter F. Drucker, "The Changing Multinational," *The Wall Street Journal*, Jan. 15, 1986, p. 22.

INTERNATIONAL OPERATIONS

FIG. 29-4

Audit Questionnaire—Foreign Agent Agreements

A. Request for an Agent:

	Yes	No

1. Who is responsible for preparing the preliminary "request for an agent"? . . . .

2. Has the documentation supporting the request for an agent been retained? ☐ ☐

3. In whose possession is the documentation permanently retained? . . . .

4. Does the documentation concerning a request for an agent incorporate the following:
    a. An explanation of the need for an agent? ☐ ☐
    b. Whether alternatives were considered? ☐ ☐
    c. A general statement of the specific services and benefits that the agent will provide in return for the commission payment to be received by the agent? ☐ ☐
    d. A definition of the territory the agent will cover? ☐ ☐
    e. A list of all other agents utilized by the company in the same geographical area? ☐ ☐
    f. An explanation as to how each of these sales organizations relates to one another? ☐ ☐
    g. A statement indicating what relationship the agent will have with the various operating elements of the company (that is, precisely what people, by name and title, within the company will deal with and make use of the concerned agent)? ☐ ☐
    h. Approval by the Vice-President–International? ☐ ☐

B. Qualifications of an Agent:

1. Who is responsible for establishing the qualifications of an agent? . . . .

2. Has the documentation regarding qualifications of an agent been retained? ☐ ☐

3. Where is the documentation located? . . . .

4. Does the documentation concerning qualification of an agent include the following:
    a. An explanation as to why the agent was selected? ☐ ☐
    b. An explanation of the agent's knowledge of the company and its products? ☐ ☐
    c. An opinion whether the agent's knowledge of the company and its products is necessary to sell these products on their merits? ☐ ☐

(continued)

FIG. 29-4 *(cont'd)*

	Yes	No
d. An opinion whether the agent is an established concern, likely to continue business as a commercial or selling agent in the future?	☐	☐
e. Identification of all associated principals, subagents or subcontractors?	☐	☐
f. Where a prior agreement has existed, information concerning:		
▪ The agent's past performance under these agreements?	☐	☐
▪ Whether there are any past or present claims of any kind or character of the company against the representative?	☐	☐
g. A background resumé or brochure which sets forth a statement of qualification, experience, and accomplishments of the organization or individual, to determine if it is professionally capable to perform the services called for by the proposed agreement?	☐	☐
h. Approval by the Vice-President–International of the qualifications of the agent and inclusion of a copy of his approval?	☐	☐

C. Foreign Inquiry:

	Yes	No
1. Has the Division General Manager or Subsidiary President made an inquiry of concerned governments to ascertain their policies concerning the role of commissioned agents in such transactions, including their requirements to disclose such arrangements?	☐	☐
2. Has a written record of these communications been permanently retained?	☐	☐
3. Has a written record of the foreign government's responses been retained?	☐	☐
4. Has a copy of all correspondence with foreign governments been provided to the Vice-President–International?	☐	☐

D. Anticipated Contractual Relationship:

1. Who is responsible for formulating the anticipated contractual relationship? . . . .

2. Where has the documentation in support of the anticipated contractual relationship been retained? . . . .

3. Does the documentation concerning the anticipated contractual relationship include the following:

	Yes	No
a. An explanation as to whether it is anticipated that the agreement will be a continuing relationship or is being entered into on a one-time only basis?	☐	☐
b. An explanation as to whether the agent involved is to obtain business in general for the company or is to be confined to obtaining a specific government contract?	☐	☐

	Yes	No

    c. A justification as to the reasonableness of the proposed initial term of the agreement and whether it is expected the agreement will be renewed after its initial term? ☐ ☐

    d. If it is expected to be renewed, adequate justification to explain why it will be extended and the estimated duration? ☐ ☐

    e. A detailed statement of the specific benefits and services the agent will provide in return for the commission payments to be received by the agent? ☐ ☐

E. Anticipated Financial Relationship:

1. Who is responsible for the determination of the anticipated financial relationship? . . . .

2. Has the documentation in support of the anticipated financial relationship been retained? ☐ ☐

3. In whose possession has the documentation been retained? . . . .

4. Does the documentation in support of the anticipated financial relationship include that:

    a. Fees proposed are generally consistent with the fees paid by it or other entities of the company for similar services in the same general area? ☐ ☐

    b. Compensation is commensurate with the nature and extent of the services to be performed? ☐ ☐

    c. The estimated contract value of the project, including the value of add-ons, has been calculated and included in the documentation? ☐ ☐

    d. The anticipated dollar value of the commission that the organization expects the agent will receive under the agreement has been calculated and included in the documentation? ☐ ☐

    e. A determination has been made that the agent will be paid on a basis consistent with company policy? That is:
- Advance payments will not be made. ☐ ☐
- The agent will not be paid before the company has received payment from the customer. ☐ ☐

    f. Where a prior agreement has existed, a schedule has been prepared setting forth the payment history of the concerned agent, i.e., a chronology of the past commission percentages and payments involved? ☐ ☐

    g. Where a prior agreement has existed, a determination as to whether the company's payments for the agent were allowed for tax purposes? ☐ ☐

F. Instructions — Monitoring, Reporting, and Control:

1. Have instructions been issued that ensure:

    a. Retention and monitoring of periodic reports supplied by the agent? ☐ ☐

(continued)

FIG. 29-4 *(cont'd)*

	Yes	No
b. Proper payment, recording, and financial handling of all agent agreements is being maintained?	☐	☐
c. Procedures and authority have been delegated to assure that full disclosure of the agent agreement is made to the appropriate U.S. government procurement authorities?	☐	☐
d. A written record of all pertinent communications has been maintained?	☐	☐
e. A full flow of pertinent information within the company concerning agency agreement affecting sales to the U.S. government?	☐	☐
f. A system has been established within the finance organization (with the assistance of legal counsel, as required) to audit the compliance of agents with the various covenants contained in their agreements?	☐	☐
g. Sufficient documentation is maintained to ensure the tax deductibility of commissions paid and to ensure their reimbursability to the company under government contracts, if applicable?	☐	☐

G. Compliance With Laws:

1. Who is responsible for determining compliance with laws?
   ....

2. Have explanations regarding compliance with laws been prepared? ☐ ☐

3. In whose possession have those explanations been retained?
   ....

4. Do the explanations for compliance with laws include that:
   a. The agreement is consistent with the laws, rules, and regulations with the United States as well as the laws, rules, regulations, and expressed policies of the foreign purchasing government? ☐ ☐
   b. The commissions are properly includable under such laws and policies in the price of otherwise commissionable sales by the company? ☐ ☐
   c. The commissions are reimbursable to the company under applicable procurement regulations of the U.S. government or of the foreign purchasing government, if applicable? ☐ ☐

H. Standard Agreement Form:

1. Who is responsible for preparing the agent agreement? ....

2. Have executed copies of all agent agreements been furnished to the Vice-President–General Counsel? ☐ ☐

	Yes	No

3. Do the agreements contain as a minimum the following:
   a. Covenants:
      - That the agent will comply with all applicable laws and regulations in the course of his activities on the company's behalf? ☐ ☐
      - A requirement that the agent file periodic reports on his activities on the company's behalf? ☐ ☐
      - An identification of all principals and sub-agents? ☐ ☐
      - A prohibition that the agent will not employ additional sub-agents, nor associate with any additional principals, nor employ public officials, without prior approval of the board of directors? ☐ ☐
      - A provision prohibiting the agent from refunding company funds to any director, officer, or other representative of the company, or from making illegal payments from these funds under applicable law? ☐ ☐
      - A provision providing that the agent's breach of any of these covenants will give rise to a right of termination of the agreement by the company without further liability or obligation on the part of the company? ☐ ☐
   b. Incorporation of all policies and laws of the foreign governments that are necessary to the agent agreement? ☐ ☐
   c. Inclusion of an explanation of any deviations or departures from the Standard Form of Commission Agent Agreement as approved by the Vice-President–General Counsel? ☐ ☐

I. Reporting:

1. Have all cognizant management and staff been informed that any employee dealing with a commission agent engaged by the company, or proposed to be engaged by the company, who has reason to believe that an agent has or may violate any applicable law will report this information to the supervisor and/or to the Vice-President–General Counsel? ☐ ☐

SUGGESTED READING

Bickers, R. L. T. *Marketing in Europe*, Chapters 1–3. London: Gower Press Limited, 1971.

Harris, Philip R., and Robert T. Moran. *Managing Cultural Differences*. Houston: Gulf Publishing Co., 1979.

Koontz, Harold, Cyril O'Donnell, and Heinz Weihrich. *Management*, 7th ed. New York: McGraw-Hill Book Co., 1980, pp. 134–141.

Meister, Irene W. *Managing the International Financial Function*, Studies in Business Policy. No. 133. New York: National Industrial Conference Board, Inc., 1970.

Walter, Ingo, ed., Tracy Murray, assoc. ed., *Handbook of International Business*. New York: John Wiley & Sons, Inc., 1982.

CHAPTER **30**

Financial Analysis for Acquisitions, Mergers, and Divestments

Introduction 2	Capitalized Earnings (P/E Multiples) ... 23
	Discounted Cash Flow 25
Acquisitions as Related to Corporate	Impact of Changes in Accounting
Objectives 3	Policies and Procedures 27
Acquisition Criteria 3	The Accounting Basis for Business
Reasons for Acquisitions or Mergers or	Combinations 29
Divestments 4	**Tax Considerations** 31
Selling a Business 5	Tax Methods of Consummating an
A Trend Toward Concentration 6	Acquisition 31
Public Concern About Takeovers 7	An Asset Acquisition 32
	A 338 Transaction 32
Diversification Can Be a Mistake 9	A Stock Acquisition 32
Alternatives to Acquisitions 10	Type A Reorganizations 32
	Type B Reorganizations 33
Leveraged Buyouts 10	Type C Reorganizations 34
Greenmail 11	Impact of the Tax Reform Act of
	1986 34
Defenses Against Hostile Acquisitions ... 11	**Earnings Per Share** 35
Purpose of Financial Analysis 12	The Combination Package 37
Data Requirements 13	**The Audit Report** 39
Valuing an Acquisition 22	**Financial Analysis Necessary for**
Book Value 22	**Divestments** 45
Appraised Value 22	
Market Value 23	**Suggested Reading** 47

Fig. 30-1	Checklist for Acquisition Review	15
Fig. 30-2	Capitalized Earnings—Weighted and Unweighted	24
Fig. 30-3	Calculation of Purchase Price Based on Historical and Projected Earnings—	
	as Adjusted	25
Fig. 30-4	Present Value of a Business Using the DCF Technique	26
Fig. 30-5	Summary of Comparative Factors for Merger Discussion	28
Fig. 30-6	Comparative Purchase Prices	28

30-1

Fig. 30-7	Rates of Return (DCF)	28
Fig. 30-8	Impact of Accounting Practices	30
Fig. 30-9	Increase in EPS With Acquisition	36
Fig. 30-10	Impact of Different Cash Securities Packages	38
Fig. 30-11	Impact of Various Growth Rates on EPS	39
Fig. 30-12	Illustrative Audit Report	42

INTRODUCTION

In the United States, there have been recurrent waves of corporate acquisitions and mergers. In fact, in the period from 1981 to 1984, given a somewhat different attitude by the Department of Justice about combinations, the prevalence of more business failures or bankruptcies, and competitive pressures, there has been a new surge of takeover bids and friendly corporate marriages. In such an environment, some knowledge of the acquisition process can be helpful to the internal auditor if he becomes involved in these special investigations. But what should his role be?

When a company is considering the purchase or sale of a company or activity, there are many facets to the complicated process. There are many management judgments to be made; there are also many considerations besides financial ones. Moreover, an audit by a firm of independent public accountants may be desirable. But at the center of these multitudinous considerations is the need to secure the financial facts, including an intelligent analysis of them. Very often, the chief financial officer, the controller, and their operating staffs may be involved. In many cases, the chief internal auditor may be called upon, as a part of the financial arm, to gather, analyze, and synthesize data that will assist management in reaching decisions about the proposed acquisition or divestment.

Accordingly, one role of the internal auditor is to be part of the group doing the necessary business analysis and reaching conclusions about values. To avoid accounting myopia, the auditor must know not only the specific financial data needed for a particular project, but also the broader background that may be indirectly helpful in preparing an informative financial report. One purpose of this chapter is to provide such general and useful background as well as concrete examples of data usually found necessary. But in such limited space, only some of the important aspects can be considered.

Aside from the special investigation of a specific acquisition, the internal auditor may be called on to appraise or evaluate the general acquisition policies and procedures. The discussion in this chapter also should be helpful to such an assignment.

ACQUISITIONS AS RELATED TO CORPORATE OBJECTIVES

Most human effort, and this includes business activity, is more productive if properly planned. And what is a plan? It has been defined as a predetermined course of action. Yet, business cannot plan merely one year ahead. Plans must extend to the most remote period as is useful. Thus, a forest products company might plan for three decades, whereas a fashion designer might find a two-year plan adequate. In any event, this longer look ahead, called long-range planning or strategic planning, should include, among other things, these three elements:

1. A statement of the company's basic *purpose* or mission. It is, or should be, a statement of its long-term objectives, giving due recognition to its strengths, weaknesses, and the environment. It may include *one* purpose, such as, "To maintain its existing share of market in the . . . . advanced technology field," or "To be the dominant supplier of fighter aircraft to the U.S. Air Force," or a *series of purposes* relating to such matters as product quality relative to profitability, responsibilities to the community, and so forth.
2. A carefully thought-out *strategy* or means to achieve the basic purpose or purposes. This might include such actions as:
   - Enlarging product line A by acquisition
   - Eliminating Division S
   - Developing research and development competence in product line R
3. Some specific *goals* to be achieved in a defined period. Some illustrative goals might be one of the following:
   - Achieve a sales level of $800 million by 1991.
   - Secure a 15 percent return on shareholders' equity by 1993.
   - Achieve the dominant sales position of 55 percent of market share for product K by 199R.

The point in mentioning corporate objectives and goals is that acquisition analysis really involves three steps: planning; searching and screening; and finally, evaluating. Planning begins with the review and establishment of objectives and strategies. Acquisitions may be one means of achieving the corporate objectives, as distinct from internal developments. Any proposed acquisition should be tested for its consistency with corporate objectives and strategy.

Acquisition Criteria

One other bit of background is useful in reviewing proposed acquisitions. A particular proposed acquisition should be consistent with a set of criteria every company ought to develop. An enterprise should have some rules or guidelines to screen out candidates that are not suitable. For example, a company with $500 million in sales perhaps should not acquire a company, even if in the proper product line, if sales are only $1 million per year. Such an acquisition might not have a significant impact; and undue management time might be taken or required for proper supervision. Some often-used acquisition criteria relate to:

- Line of business
- Market growth rate
- Quality of management
- Share of market
- Sales level
- Ease of entry
- Degree of capital intensity
- Profitability rate (return on investment)
- Profit level—absolute amount
- Capital structure

The point is that good auditing should involve measuring a proposed acquisition against a reasonable set of guidelines. The following discussion contains more specific information about acquisitions.

REASONS FOR ACQUISITIONS OR MERGERS OR DIVESTMENTS

Strategic planning is coming into greater acceptance. Such planning, which should include all the major functions of the enterprise—marketing, manufacturing, finance, research and development, and so forth—should consider the means by which corporate objectives may be achieved. One method is through acquisitions. In fact, it may be argued that an acquisition should not be considered solely on its own, but rather as part of the strategic plan.

There are many reasons why a company may wish to acquire another going business. Some firms may desire to achieve certain objectives by internal means, but this may take many years and cost more than by accomplishing the same purpose through acquiring a suitable existing enterprise. Briefly, the following presents a partial list of some of the reasons for making an acquisition, categorized by the principal objective as viewed by management:

☐ Growth:
- Facilitate growth through diversification, as a means of increasing corporate earnings.
- Promote growth by achieving better operational efficiency.

- Diversification:
  - Reduce the risks related to market, customers, seasonal factors, or cyclical patterns through diversification.
- Product or services:
  - Acquire a completely new product line.
  - Gain specified competitive advantages.
  - Achieve product diversification by completing, broadening, or complementing an existing product line.
  - Improve or implement customer service as related to the product lines (e.g., repairing and maintaining the product and providing repair parts).
- Management-perceived needs:
  - Improve management by replacing aging managers, filling voids, or replacing unsatisfactory segments of management.
  - Acquire badly needed R&D capabilities, such as personnel and know-how.
  - Prevent an unfriendly takeover.
  - Buy time—a stopgap measure until certain capabilities are secured or related plans are completed (e.g., a temporary sales outlet or a channel of distribution).
- Financial reasons:
  - Make a highly profitable investment, producing a higher return than the "usual" business.
  - Invest idle or excess working capital.
  - Improve the financial or capital structure.
  - Secure additional working capital, long-term capital, or additional borrowing capacity.
  - Improve the price-earnings ratio (for acquisition or other purposes).
  - Increase the market value of the stock.
  - Take maximum advantage of tax laws, or minimize adverse government action (foreign or domestic).
  - Exploit a particular short-term opportunity.
- Other reasons:
  - Acquire, on an advantageous and timely basis, needed plant and equipment—e.g., manufacturing, distribution, and laboratories.
  - Improve the corporate image.

Selling a Business

Just as there are prudent reasons why one company should acquire another, there are also valid motives or reasons for selling a going concern. The owners or management of some corporations, especially those of privately held concerns, may wish to sell for a number of reasons, including the following:

- Need to diversify an estate, if it is largely an investment in a single concern

- Lack of succession management
- Lack of necessary funds for needed research and development
- Management dissension
- Inability of management (in its own mind) to cope, for example, with the new technology and the rate of change in business
- Incomplete product line
- Social or environmental difficulties
- Regulatory problems
- Tax advantages
- Lack of funds to build the necessary facilities for expansion
- Declining profitability

When a company is being sold, there may or may not be the need for critical review of the buyer (e.g., where the consideration is shares of a blue chip company) by the seller, as there is for an in-depth study of the seller by the purchaser. But the internal auditor should be alert for clues as to the reasons for sale if he is participating in an audit or investigation on behalf of the buying interests, especially if his principals are uncertain as to the real cause of the decision to sell. Is it a largely obsolete inventory? Major contingent liabilities? Inroads of foreign competition? A dying product line? The decision to sell out may be for stated or unstated reasons, and it is essential to the buyer to know exactly why.

A TREND TOWARD CONCENTRATION

Most mergers or acquisitions, divestments, or purchases or sales of large blocks of stock are done with the intent of someone making money. However, the wave of mergers in the past five or six years is characterized by at least a few differences. The earlier mergers or acquisitions largely stressed diversification. Many free-form conglomerates were formed; management acquired businesses about which they knew very little. This tended to increase the risks. Additionally, given high inflation, some of the "mistakes" were more easily buried, or at least partially offset, by the continually increasing product prices.

Now things are apparently different. To begin with, many of the newer mergers seem to be stressing more economically logical combinations, and managements seem to be concentrating on narrower fields—related fields that they know something about. Moreover, there are increasing investments of unrelated segments. Also, in some industries, joint ventures are being formed between U.S. companies and foreign organizations to improve the competitive posture of the participants and to secure immediate use of new technologies.

Presumably, these moves will benefit the economy as a whole, and well may benefit the companies involved. Of course, at this early stage, the principal beneficiaries have been (1) the shareholders who sold stock at substantially higher prices than just before the merger announcement; (2) the investment bankers who engineered or guided the deal; and (3) the companies that have shed unwanted units.

It should be added, however, that the fear of takeovers is changing corporate tactics and strategy. For example, managers are:[1]

- Sacrificing growth plans that might help the company long term, but could temporarily hurt stock prices.
- Restructuring the company, such as incurring a huge amount of debt, or providing for the contingent issue of stock upon the happening of certain events.
- Acquiring other (less desirable) companies.
- Going private.

Public Concern About Takeovers

With the recent binge of hostile takeovers, there is increasing concern about a direction that threatens many companies and has diverted management attention from running the enterprise to defending its independence. Until quite recently, many business executives decried the trend, but felt there was little to be done. While there was, and is, some opinion that a hostile takeover is a useful instrument to weed out poor managements, it is becoming evident that even well-run companies are frequent targets. Of course, in many such instances, the stock is undervalued.

Be that as it may, Congress has considered a number of measures related to the problem. Some of the proposed actions may treat only symptoms; others attempt to look at the economic causes and consequences. The alert internal auditor may want to be aware of some of the argumentation by members of Congress as well as by others. Some intriguing topics include these:

☐ *Role of pension fund or other large institutional investors.* One of the causes of the hostile takeover trend is the tendency of some large institutional holders to sell out when the opportunity for large profit occurs. According to one source,[2] without the stock of institutional holders, it is doubtful if many hostile takeover attempts would succeed. This same article suggests several possibilities:

- Legislating a set of fiduciary guidelines that would provide a clear rationale

---

[1] "The Raiders, 'They Are Really Breaking the Vice of the Managing Class,'" *Business Week*, Mar. 4, 1985, pp. 80–90.

[2] John F. Lawrence, "Congress Must Act to Control Takeover Binge," *Los Angeles Times*, Nov. 11, 1984, Part VI, p. 1.

for longer-term investments, which would be in the interest of good corporate management and the economy as a whole.
- Requiring a pass-through of voting rights, or a vote that mirrors the vote of the individual investors.
- Providing a tax incentive for longer-term stock ownership, possibly including special provisions for institutions.
- Regulating the central participants—the raiders themselves, or individuals.
- Changing the current federal disclosure laws—which, some say, actually favor hostile takeovers as compared to friendly mergers.

☐ *Slowing the takeover process.* Raiders often use sudden financial maneuvers to acquire undervalued assets. One knowledgeable person, John C. Coffee, Jr., at Columbia Law School,[3] would essentially slow the takeover process, and open up the target to more players with more time to make decisions. Some of his steps would include the following:
- Ban "greenmail."
- Force bidding for the assets.
- Give the bidder's shareholders the right to approve a tender offer and to authorize higher bids in response to any counteroffer.
- Force the owner of more than 30 percent of a company's stock to either sell the excess over 30 percent or buy the remainder at the highest price already paid, within two years. This period would enable the bidder to get more information about a target than usually is available to hostile bidders. Hence a more educated judgment could be made.

Indicative of some congressional effort to make the tender-offer process more considered is legislation approved by the House Commerce Committee that would, among other things:[4]

☐ Require bidders to stop buying a stock as soon as they hold 5 percent of a company's shares outstanding. They would have to announce their holdings within 24 hours and purchase no more stock for two business days after the 5 percent threshold has been reached.

☐ Ban "golden parachutes," the lucrative agreement increasing the compensation of officers or directors of a target company during a takeover, except for normal compensation arrangements that coincide with a tender offer.

☐ Ban the "self-tender," in which a target company repurchases its stock outstanding during a takeover fight, except when a majority of the shareholders approves.

☐ Require shareholder approval for the repurchase at a premium of stock from a hostile bidder holding more than 3 percent of the shares outstanding, unless

---

[3] Stan Crock, "The Right Question to Ask About Corporate Takeovers," *Business Week*, Mar. 11, 1985, p. 88.

[4] Leon E. Wynter, "Some Takeover Defenses Barred in Proposed Bill," *The Wall Street Journal*, Aug. 3, 1984, p. 6.

the shareholder has held the stock for more than two years. This tactic is shown as "greenmail."
☐ Prohibit the issuance of 5 percent or more of a company's voting stock during a takeover. This is done in an effort to dilute the value of the company's shares during a raid.
☐ Require bidders to disclose whether they plan to move the target company's headquarters, or any other significant move on the target's community or employees.

Of course, what secured the attention of Congress in 1984 and 1985 may take a back seat on legislative efforts in 1988 or later. The previous examples are intended to make the internal auditor aware of some of the forces or pressures that influence takeover legislation. It is well to keep in mind, also, that a trend seems to be developing to relegate regulation of mergers to the various *state* legislatures. For example, in 1987, the Dayton-Hudson Company was successful in causing the Minnesota lawmakers to introduce legislation to assist in defeating a proposed hostile takeover.

DIVERSIFICATION CAN BE A MISTAKE

The recent burst of takeovers has been accompanied by an increase in divestments of unwanted operations. And the public press has contained numerous articles about major write-downs of acquired assets. Thus, it is timely to remember that diversification can be costly; that many times the mergers do not accomplish their objectives; and that the internal auditor on financial analyses related to mergers should be aware of some of the causes of failure, and perhaps issue suitable precautions.

Typically, when one company acquires another, it may hope to achieve a synergy through merging the best qualities in both firms. But often, the corporate cultures clash. Corporate culture refers to how things are done in a company; how to do business; and how to manage, organize, and treat people. It arises, in part, from experience in the basic business; some aspects are critical to the success of the business. A new management may alter the culture of the acquired entity at its own peril. Thus, an environment of stringent cost control in a metal stamping operation may not be suitable in an R&D facility. These culture clashes seldom become an issue during takeover talks.

Closely related to this aspect is management expertise. According to Malcolm Salter, professor of business policy at Harvard Business School, "Many managers have come to feel in their gut that the way you create maximum return for minimum risk is by sticking within your area of distinctive competence. Firms are beginning to ask: 'Can we properly manage a wide array of businesses and, even if we can, does it make economic sense?'"

Accordingly, to the extent practical, the internal auditor should raise questions or make observations about this subjective aspect.

To the extent that the internal auditor is involved in financial analysis, in a friendly takeover of a similar or closely related (product) company, he can secure corroborating input from a management more informed about the product or service and the related market than if it were a new field. Of course, being in the same or a related industry, the auditor should be more familiar with the problems and pitfalls.

ALTERNATIVES TO ACQUISITIONS

Given the risks and often unwanted results of acquisitions, some companies enter into joint ventures or partially owned alliances as a means of expanding into a related business or building on existing strengths. These arrangements, however, can present problems in terms of managing the enterprise. A joint venture or a partially owned alliance can involve a 50-50 ownership or a stipulated minority interest. One such partnership was formed by AT&T and N. V. Philips, whereby each owned 50 percent. Most such alliances are successful when a prior relationship, such as that between customer and supplier, exists. In any event, if the internal auditor is called on to explore a means of expanding into a related business, short of an outright acquisition or merger, he should be aware of these alternatives.

LEVERAGED BUYOUTS

During the past two years, a form of takeover known as a leveraged buyout has become more popular. Takeovers are very often set in motion by a company's own management as a means of taking the firm private, that is, out of the public stock market. Typically, the buyers borrow very heavily, using the acquired assets as security, in order to purchase the shares in the hands of the public. Any excess cash of the acquired company, and a dedicated cash flow from operations or from sale of assets, often (for several years) is used to pay off the loans. To keep management in place, the non-majority managers often are allotted 10 to 15 percent of the stock, although in some cases, it has been 20 to 25 percent.

With heavily leveraged buyouts or takeovers come high risks. Since cash flow is used primarily to pay off debt, obsolete equipment may not be replaced when needed, or new oil and gas reserves, for example, will not be discovered. Additionally, rising interest rates or an economic recession may magnify the problems that arise. As John Shad, chairman of the SEC said, "The more leveraged takeovers and buyouts today, the more bankruptcies tomorrow."

The internal auditor may or may not be called on to do some financial analyses, such as projection of the company's ability to service the high level of debt, but he should be familiar with the technique.

GREENMAIL

Takeovers and related activities have several strategies. One is resorting to "greenmail," a play on the term "blackmail." Under these actions, the greenmailer acquires a hold over its corporate victim by buying enough shares in the open market to demonstrate that he has considerable financial muscle. To save itself from the clutches of the tactician, the company buys back its stock at a grossly inflated price over the market. Only the greenmailer wins; the company and shareholders lose, as the shares drop in value after the threat of takeover is removed.

With the flurry of unfavorable publicity in late 1984, greenmail seemed to disappear. However, according to some authorities, it is simply more subtle. As an example, a stock buyback program can hide greenmail. Some of the "privately negotiated transactions" (at a higher price than the public trading) can include these greenmail shares. Holding such stock can force a target company to sell selected assets, part of the consideration being the turning over of such stock.

DEFENSES AGAINST HOSTILE ACQUISITIONS

In a book on internal auditing, emphasis regarding acquisitions, mergers, and divestments should be on the supportive financial analysis, which should be done to assist in the decision making. However, it is important to discuss other related matters so that the internal auditor is not completely unaware of the subject.

With the recent wave of mergers and acquisitions, target companies often have adopted tactics, commonly called shark repellents, to defeat hostile takeover attempts. Although such matters may rest primarily with the lawyers and top management, a few comments may be helpful. Some selected takeover terms that describe devices used against hostile actions follows:

☐ *Fair-price amendment.* This is an antitakeover amendment to the corporate charter that usually includes a supermajority provision, which is triggered by a two-tier bid. Stated otherwise, if a "fair price" is offered for *all* shares, the supermajority requirement is waived. Fair-price amendments generally are effective only against two-tier hostile offers.

☐ *Lock-up option.* To assure the completion of a friendly takeover (or rescue by a friendly second bidder—a white knight), the board of directors of a target company may grant an acquirer options to buy some of its most prized assets or additional equity in the firm. Such options make the target company less attractive to other prospective bidders and thus may prevent shareholders from receiving the optimum value for their interests.

☐ *Poison pill.* This is a complex and usually successful takeover defense, wherein holders of a company's common shares are granted rights to a newly issued class of preferred stock (or other security). The rights are triggered when a tender offer is made or when a large block of the company's shares are acquired. The rights, when activated, permit the holder to purchase shares of the newly merged enterprise at a substantial discount to market value. Hence, a hostile takeover attempt becomes prohibitively expensive.

☐ *Staggered-term board.* The provision classifies a company's board of directors, usually into three groups, so that only a fraction of all directors are elected each year. This makes it difficult for a shareholder with a controlling interest to elect sufficient directors in any one year to gain control of the company.

☐ *Supermajority amendment.* This is any of a broad class of amendments that usually requires from two thirds to as much as 90 percent of a company's shareholders to approve mergers or other important matters. Such amendments usually have a "lock-in" clause requiring the same supermajority of shareholders to change the amendment. They also may have a "board out" clause, which permits the board of directors to determine when a supermajority of shareholders is required to amend the corporate charter.

These few definitions may provide some sense of the more common defenses against hostile takeovers.

PURPOSE OF FINANCIAL ANALYSIS

Having provided some background on mergers and acquisitions, the typical role of the internal auditor should be considered. In a review of a specific acquisition proposal, the major contribution by the internal auditor relates to financial analysis. There are, of course, many reasons for purchasing a company, such as the quality of the product, or the particular know-how that may not be clearly evident in the financial data. But the gathering and proper analysis of the financial information ordinarily is essential to a sound evaluation of the prospect. Before discussing the financial data that might be assembled and specific analyses to be made, an outline of the objectives or purposes of financial analyses may be useful. The data gathered should permit or facilitate conclusions or opinions on such matters as these:

- Financial position of the selling company and the related consolidated financial position of the combined companies
- Historical earnings and cash flow of the proposed acquiree, including:
  —Data based on accounting and tax practices of the acquiree

— Results by employing the accounting and tax practices of the acquiring entity
- Estimated future earning power and cash flow of the prospect
- Identification (in order to judge trends and continuity) of the major income-producing segments of the prospect. Included would be income by:
  — Products or product line
  — Customers
  — Territories or geographical areas
- A determination of the major financial strengths and weaknesses, including:
  — Financial and operating ratios or relationships (e.g., debt to equity, asset turnover, return on assets (segments), return on shareholders' equity, current ratio, quick ratio, and operating margins)
  — Trend of sales by product or product line
  — Trend of operating margin by product or organizational segment
  — Trend of functional expenses (e.g., R&D, marketing, manufacturing, and general and administrative)
  — Unfunded pension liabilities
  — Contingent liabilities, including material purchase commitments, facility commitments, litigation, governmental studies (e.g., environmental impact), liabilities of unconsolidated subsidiaries or investments, and unsettled claims and disputes
- Estimate of the potential range of economies of consolidation, and discontinuances of selected operations (e.g., low margin, items, and unprofitability laws)
- Range of the profit impact of possible synergisms of the acquiring company and acquiree
- Estimate of profit deterioration if selected areas "don't go right"
- Consideration of the best way of financing the acquisition
- Weighting of the preferred method of acquisition, with costs and benefits to both parties, such as:
  — Taxable vs. nontaxable
  — Exchange of common
  — Use of alternate securities (e.g., a package combination)
- Determining an acceptable price range, earning power considered
- Adequacy and capabilities of the acquiree's financial affairs and financial staff (e.g., depth of management)

Proper financial analysis and evaluation of the financial aspects should assist or facilitate management judgment on the desirability and risks of the possible acquisition.

Data Requirements

Having indicated the necessary financial judgments to be reached, it might be helpful to suggest the type of data to be gathered and analyzed. The trends and status disclosed by such information and its analysis provide areas for discussion with the management of the acquiree, as well as the basis for evaluation. Many acquiring companies have standard checklists of desired information, which are modified to fit the particular circumstances or known problem areas. Obviously, the gathering will include much more than the usual financial data and will extend to every major function and aspect of the business. Again, the objective is to gather those facts necessary to evaluate the prospect as a compatible and economically desirable addition to the business.

The usual areas of investigation may be variously grouped, but typically include the following:

- Management
- Personnel and related factors
- Products and services
- Marketing
- Manufacturing
- Research and development
- Engineering
- Facilities
- Finances and financial matters

A checklist for a manufacturing company with a well-developed procedure for acquisition review and appraisal is shown in Figure 30-1. This list is applicable when it is decided a given target should be investigated. It should be modified to fit the specific needs in a particular search.

Another excellent checklist, intended to be used by management, and not actually as an internal audit guide, is a 1982 publication by Coopers & Lybrand, entitled "Checking Into an Acquisition Candidate." It is divided into eight categories to allow management to assign the proper expertise or use outside specialists.

1. General background
2. Product lines and markets
3. Operations
4. Human resources
5. Financial considerations
6. Management styles and practices
7. Research development and engineering
8. Legal matters

The suggested areas of review may be helpful to the internal auditor in preparing his own list of data-gathering requirements.

(continued on page 30-22)

FIG. 30-1
Checklist for Acquisition Review

Preferred Information for Evaluating a Potential Acquisition

Objective. To secure all reasonable and general information to evaluate the suitability of an acquisition, determine its earning power or cash flow, and make judgments as to our ability to successfully integrate it into our method of operation.

	Assigned To	Done

A. General:

1. History of business and significant business factors
2. Corporate structure; chart and description
3. Organization chart
4. List of officers and directors; their affiliation
5. Shareholder information; number, principal holders
6. Policy manual
7. Apparent reasons for selling; indications
8. General reputation of company and its officers; any litigation, regulatory proceedings, etc.?
9. Reasons for selling; any turndowns?

B. Product and Marketing:

1. A listing of product lines, including history and description
2. A five-year record of previous sales performance, unit and dollar volume, if practical
3. A two- to five-year demand estimate for the product type (industry data also)
4. A two- to five- or ten-year sales plan or forecast, including
    a. Share of market
    b. Basic assumptions
    c. Competitive stance
5. Price lists for major products
6. The present strategic sales plan
7. Company estimates as to industry supply and demand for five years

(continued)

FIG. 30-1 *(cont'd)*

	Assigned To	Done
8. Patent status of products	....	....
9. Gross profit and/or contribution margins, by product line, for five years	....	....
10. Description of product/product line strengths and weaknesses. Obsolescence factor?	....	....
11. A review of present and prospective competitors including, for each:		
a. Description of product and its strengths and weaknesses	....	....
b. Estimated share of market or unit sales, etc.	....	....
c. Location	....	....
d. Pricing policies	....	....
e. Distribution methods	....	....
12. Analysis of anticipated increase in volume and/or cost and price reductions on:		
a. Market capacity	....	....
b. Market saturation	....	....
c. Product demand and share of market	....	....
13. A listing (and evaluation) of principal marketing personnel (e.g., age, background)		
14. Channels of distribution:		
a. Description	....	....
b. Any anticipated changes and reasons as to methods of sale	....	....
15. A five-year record of methods of sale	....	....
16. Listing and brief description of marketing facilities:		
a. Purpose (e.g., office, warehouse)	....	....
b. Size	....	....
c. Location	....	....
d. Contemplated changes; reason	....	....
17. Listing of major customers, including:		
a. History	....	....
b. Location	....	....
c. Sales volume	....	....
d. Gross margin or contribution margin	....	....
e. Buying habits	....	....
18. Advertising and sales promotion		
a. Policy	....	....

	Assigned	
	To	Done

    b. Expenditures by product line, geographic location, percentage of sales, for past five years

    c. Participation in trade shows

    d. Catalogs, etc.; general status

19. Market research activity, costs, status

C. Financial:

1. Latest audited financial statements

2. Financial statements for past five years, including:
    a. Statement of consolidated financial position
    b. Statement of consolidated income or expense
    c. Statement of retained earnings
    d. Comparable data, by divisions and subsidiaries
    e. Detail of all costs and expense by account:
        - Administrative
        - Marketing
        - Manufacturing
        - Research and development
        - Financial
        - Engineering

3. Statement or manual of accounting policies

4. Annual plan for the next year, by company segment and consolidated, including:
    a. Statement of income and expense
    b. Statement of sources and uses of cash
    c. Statement of financial position
    d. Capital budget
    e. Major assumptions or premises
    f. Comparative data—prior year
    g. Trends and relationships
    h. Customer orders

5. Long-range plan, next three to five years by organization segment; consolidated, including:
    a. Critical assumptions
    b. Corporate goals or objectives
    c. Income and expense
    d. Financial position
    e. Sources and uses of cash

(continued)

FIG. 30-1 *(cont'd)*

	Assigned To	Done
f. Margin trend by product line and reasons	....	....
g. Analysis of inventories	....	....
h. Sales by customer (which list is reconciled to consolidate financial sales)	....	....
6. Federal income tax status; summary and recent return; analysis of balance sheet accounts	....	....
7. Any state income taxes summary and recent return; analysis of balance sheet accounts	....	....
8. Chart of accounts and accounting manual	....	....
9. Account analysis at recent date for:		
a. Accounts receivable	....	....
b. Inventories	....	....
c. Prepaid insurance	....	....
d. Property accounts	....	....
e. Accounts payable	....	....
f. Notes payable—current and long-term	....	....
g. Long-term leases	....	....
10. Complete listing of insurance policies; coverage, cost, expiration date, claims, etc.	....	....
11. Analysis of pension plans:		
a. Actuarial assumptions	....	....
b. Liabilities, funded and unfunded	....	....
c. Assets	....	....
d. Funding policies	....	....
12. Credit agreements and summary of accounts with:		
a. Commercial banks	....	....
b. Long-term lenders, etc.	....	....
13. Analysis of contingent liabilities, including pending litigation	....	....
14. Capital budget status	....	....
15. Listing of key personnel, age, educational background, experience, etc.	....	....
16. Organizational chart	....	....

	Assigned To	Done

D. Manufacturing:

1. Obtain listing, with brief comments on key personnel

2. Secure organizational chart

3. Obtain plant layout drawings

4. Obtain listings of plants, capacities, bottlenecks, book value, etc.

5. Secure description of plants, age, appraisal of status

6. Get listing of principal profiling and other equipment, age, condition, etc.

7. Comment on need for expansion, availability of land and/or other facilities; load factor

8. Summarize status of dealings with EPA

9. Provide general summary as to status of:
   a. Waste disposal
   b. Water availability
   c. Power supply adequacy

10. Secure analysis of maintenance and repair expense during past three years and generally summarize status of equipment and housekeeping

11. Generally summarize facility status as to:
    a. Building codes
    b. Zoning regulations
    c. Operating restrictions

12. Review and summarize:
    a. Sources, volumes, etc., of principal raw materials, long-term contracts, etc. and availability
    b. Examine trends in costs of major materials, especially those from foreign sources
    c. Purchasing policies and practices
    d. Inbound freight costs and alternatives

E. Personnel:

1. Statement of personnel policies and practices

2. Copies of union contracts

(continued)

FIG. 30-1 (cont'd)

	Assigned To	Done
3. Summary of personnel—number and characteristics, including gross payroll costs and related fringe benefit costs by meaningful segregation, pay rates by classification, etc.	....	....
4. Long-term personnel plans, including:		
a. Needs classified by skill and location	....	....
b. Turnover estimates	....	....
c. Sources	....	....
5. Description and annual costs, etc., of:		
a. Retirement plans	....	....
b. Hospitalization plans	....	....
c. Savings plans	....	....
d. Vacation plans	....	....
e. Incentive plans for executive, salaried, and hourly employees	....	....
6. General appraisal of:		
a. Working conditions	....	....
b. Employee facilities	....	....
c. Relation with union and employer	....	....
7. Accident history, workmen's compensation costs, etc.	....	....
8. Review compliance with various applicable state and federal laws	....	....
9. Check condition and adequacy of employee records (computer applications, etc.)	....	....
10. Appraise community recreation facilities, transportation availability, housing, schools, etc.	....	....
F. Research and Engineering:		
1. Listing of key personnel, with brief statement on background, education, experience, etc.	....	....
2. Organizational chart	....	....
3. Policy manual	....	....
4. Summary of costs or expenses for past five years by appropriate classification; reason for trend	....	....
5. Listing of ongoing projects, including:		
a. Purpose	....	....
b. Number of personnel man-hours	....	....
c. Costs		

	Assigned To	Done

6. Annual plan for function

7. Long-range plan

8. Status of patents, trademarks, etc.

9. Description of facilities
   a. Laboratories
   b. Pilot plants
   c. Special test equipment
   d. Offices

10. Summary of competitive activity and, if possible, related costs (e.g., percentage of sales)

11. Recent developments, both domestic and foreign

12. Product design status, including:
    a. New projects
    b. Recently completed items
    c. Condition of documentation—drawings and specifications
    d. Liaison with marketing

13. An appraisal of the effectiveness of expenditures, if possible

G. Legal Matters:

1. Judgment as to any antitrust problems

2. Pending litigation, including:
   a. Legal opinion as to outcome
   b. Financial exposure (also discuss with independent auditors and financial department)
   c. Legal representations to independent accountants

3. Cost of legal department:
   a. Secure budget for present and next year
   b. Consider whether outside legal charges are most cost effective vs. in-house counsel; nature of outside legal assistance
   c. Secure and analyze legal services bills
   d. Check legal status of corporation, and its stock
   e. Review data regarding state in which company is qualified to do business
   f. Check on compliance with OSHA, ERISA, etc.

4. Consider what legal matters should be dealt with in acquisition agreement.

These lists are to be modified, as necessary, to provide the essential information.

VALUING AN ACQUISITION

The purchase price or stock exchange ratio for two companies considering a business combination will generally be determined by negotiation. Some of the factors that the principals will consider are susceptible to evaluation and some are not. Thus, the competitive status, the existence in the acquired company of a competent management team that will continue with the new organization, a creative and effective research group, an aggressive sales force, facilities in the proper location to suit the acquiring company's plans, know-how in relation to the industry and products, the degree to which the new company can assist in meeting the corporate objectives—all will influence the judgment of the buying principal.

Yet, the analysis of the financial data, the adjustments made, and the financial basis that may be developed by the internal auditor are important starting points in setting the value of the company that may be purchased.

There are several methods used to determine the fair market value of an enterprise that is to be acquired. Some are simplistic and easily applied, and some are more sophisticated. Some need not be given great weight, but neither should they be overlooked. Each may be subject to modification for management reasons. While these techniques may be grouped in several ways, for discussion purposes, they are segregated as follows:

- Book value
- Appraised value
- Market value
- Capitalized earnings (price-earnings multiples)
- Discounted cash flow

Some evaluations are based on a combination of two or more of the above groups.

Book Value

Rightly or wrongly, book value per share (common shareholders' equity ÷ number of shares outstanding) is important to some shareholders as a measure of relative participation in the net worth of the company, and becomes, for them, a factor in measuring the reasonableness of the exchange of stock. These interests are concerned with dilution. Obviously, this factor alone is not a significant measure of an enterprise, since the value relates to original costs and not to present costs or future earning power.

Book value, or net equity value, should be evaluated in the light of needed accounting adjustments.

Appraised Value

Appraised value is determined by an independent appraiser, usually hired by the prospective buyer (perhaps consented to by the seller), to place a value on all the assets of the firm. This method may be used when the acquisition plan calls for the purchase and sale of assets (and not stock). It may be useful when it is desired to have an appraised value, for tax purposes, of each individual asset. A realistic appraisal of tangible and intangible assets can assist in allocating the purchase price to specific assets and produce a related reduction in good will. Such an appraisal assigns a replacement or market value to each asset and may bear little necessary relationship to the productivity of such assets. It can serve as a check against other appraisal methods. Of particular importance is the value of completed research projects, patents, manufacturing know-how, and similar assets whose value might be overlooked.

Obviously, the proper assessment of liabilities to be assumed, which factor usually is not covered by an appraisal, is important in arriving at the net value of the assets.

Market Value

The market value per share, and the related aggregate value, often is an important determinant in setting a price. Where an exchange of stock is involved, and an active market exists, the current price is an indicator of value (before news of a possible merger or other change is made public). In tender offers, the market price plus a substantial premium, such as 50 or 100 percent, may be used to entice the sale of shares to the prospective buyer. The market price plus adjustments may be regarded as a measure of the company's worth.

Capitalized Earnings (P/E Multiples)

From an economic standpoint, a principal reason for acquiring a company is to secure a future stream of earnings. The challenge is to determine what the stream of earnings will probably be and to so value it that both the buyer and seller are satisfied.

The technique is to apply a capitalization rate or its equivalent, a price-earnings (P/E) multiple, to an earnings figure to arrive at a purchase price. This method can be applied to one of the following:

- To *historical* earnings for the current year, or a recent year, or a weighted average (to give more emphasis to recent years) or unweighted average of several years. The recent year might be abnormal for any number of reasons, and an average may be more indicative. Figure 30-2 illustrates the application on both a simple and weighted average for a historical five-year period and a cutoff rate of return, for the limited risk involved, of 8.5 percent after tax, or a P/E multiple of 12. The two companies of equal average earnings are compared to show the impact of weighting the more recent years more heavily. It should be noted that the exact earnings are reversed in years earned. These historical earnings may be adjusted to reflect the accounting policies

FIG. 30-2

Capitalized Earnings—Weighted and Unweighted

Companies X and Y Capitalized Earnings (Historical)
Weighted and Unweighted

($ in thousands)

		Company X		Company Y	
Year	Weighted Factor	Earnings	Weighted Earnings	Earnings	Weighted Earnings
198X	1	$ 8,970	$ 8,970	$12,370	$ 12,370
198X1	2	9,860	19,720	11,680	23,360
198Y2	3	10,400	31,200	10,400	31,200
198Y3	4	11,680	46,720	9,860	39,440
198Y4	5	12,370	61,850	8,970	44,850
TOTAL	15	$53,280	$168,460	$53,280	$151,220
Average Earnings (÷ 5)		$10,656		$10,656	
Average Earnings (÷ 15)			11,231		10,081
Capitalized (P/E of 12)			$134,772		$120,972

of the buying corporation. (See "The Accounting Basis for Business Combinations.")

- To a projection of *future* earnings, based on the judgment of the buyer, taking into account those factors that may influence or modify any plans or estimates prepared by the seller, such as changes in operations contemplated by the buyer, and based on the accounting principles that would be applied to those earnings. The determination of a price based on three years of historical earnings and five years of adjusted future earnings is illustrated in Figure 30-3. It should be noted that the accounting adjustments (depreciation) were more than offset by the cost level reductions (integration) expected. The judgmental adjustment related to a 10 percent per annum (historical) growth rate instead of 20 percent predicted by the seller.

The P/E ratio to be applied may be determined in any one of several ways, including:

- The current P/E ratio at which the stock of the prospective acquiree is being sold if the shares are publicly traded.
- A representative P/E of the industry.
- That P/E ratio representative of the acquiring company's required rate of return—the hurdle rate. Thus, if an enterprise requires a 15 percent after-tax rate of return on its investment, then the equivalent P/E is 6.667. Therefore, if an expected annual net income is $1 million, then the purchase price would be $6,666,700.
- A rate agreed on between buyer and seller.

FIG. 30-3
Calculation of Purchase Price Based on Historical and Projected Earnings—as Adjusted

THE JOHNSON COMPANY
Calculation of Maximum Purchase Price
Based on Adjusted Projections

($ in thousands)

Year	Weighted Factor	Earnings Estimated by Seller	Adjustments Accounting Differences	Adjustments Cost Level Changes	Adjustments Judgmental	Increase (Decrease) Total	Earnings as Adjusted	Unweighted	Weighted
Actual									
1981	1	$ 16,700	$ (420)	$ —	$ —	$ (420)	$ 16,280	$ 16,280	$ 16,280
1982	2	18,370	(460)	—	—	(460)	17,910	17,910	35,820
1983	3	20,207	(490)	—	—	(490)	19,717	19,717	59,151
Subtotal		55,277	(1,370)			(1,370)	53,907		
Projected									
1984	4	24,250	(570)	1,860	(2,022)	(732)	23,518	23,518	94,072
1985	5	29,100	(710)	2,050	(4,650)	(3,310)	25,790	25,790	128,950
1986	6	34,920	(800)	2,250	(8,024)	(6,574)	28,346	28,346	170,076
1987	7	41,904	(840)	2,476	(12,320)	(10,684)	31,220	31,220	218,540
1988	8	50,285	(960)	2,723	(17,741)	(15,978)	34,307	34,307	274,456
Subtotal		$180,459	$(3,880)	$11,359	$(44,757)	$(37,278)	$143,181		
Total	36	$235,736	$(5,250)	$11,359	$(44,757)	$(38,648)	$197,088	$197,088	$997,345
Average Earnings (÷ 8)									24,636
Weighted Average Earnings (÷ 36)									27,704
Capitalized (P/E of 8)								197,088	221,632

Discounted Cash Flow

The more knowledgeable and experienced buyers of companies are using the discounted cash flow (DCF) method of determining value. Thus, *Business Week* reported, even as far back as 1978, that half of the major acquisition-minded companies extensively used the DCF technique to analyze prospective acquisitions. Specifically, an appropriate discount rate is applied to the anticipated stream of cash flow to arrive at a net present value. The discount rate should give consideration to the risk involved. It may be the hurdle rate used by the company for capital budget projects, or a rate based on the estimated cost of capital (perhaps cost of capital plus 5 percentage points) or a subjective rate that measures the minimum rate of return desired by the management.

A simplified application to an estimated net earnings and cash flow, recognizing future capital needs for working capital and fixed assets, is shown in Figure 30-4. The annual earnings and investment requirements may

FIG. 30-4

Present Value of a Business Using the DCF Technique

THE ELECTRONICS CORPORATION
Calculation of Maximum Purchase Price
Based on 15% Return on Investment

($ in thousands)

Year	Estimated Net Income	Depreciation	Operating Cash Flow	Additional Working Capital	Investments Fixed Assets	Net Cash Flow	15% Interest Factor	Present Value
0								
1	$18,970	$2,410	$21,380	$ —	$ —	$21,380	0.870	$ 18,600
2	22,760	2,300	25,060	970	1,400	22,690	0.756	17,154
3	27,310	2,900	30,210	1,210	1,900	27,100	0.658	17,832
4	32,770	3,300	36,070	1,300	—	34,770	0.572	19,888
5	36,050	3,500	39,550	1,900	1,000	36,650	0.497	18,215
6	39,650	3,100	42,750	2,500	2,000	38,250	0.432	16,524
7	43,615	3,500	47,115	3,000	—	44,115	0.376	16,587
8	47,975	3,000	50,975	4,000	—	46,975	0.327	15,361
9 Estimated going value of business (10 ×)						479,750	0.327	156,878
Total								$297,040

be individually estimated, or result from applying historical or other growth rates to sales or net income.[5]

In the illustration, these points may be observed:

- The 15 percent interest factor is secured from present value tables.
- After eight years, the factor is quite low, so cash flow in this year has a much smaller present value than earlier cash flow.
- The value of the business at the close of the period—going concern value, or salvage value, as may be applicable—should be recognized.

Since the DCF method is considered the technically best quantitative method of determining the acquisition price or value to the acquiring company, it may be helpful to the internal auditor to specify the steps in the process:

1. Determine the probable net income of the operation by years for a future period—say five to eight years. This should recognize changes to the acquiror's method of accounting, and special adjustments that may be necessary, e.g., write-off of good will.

---

[5] For a detailed illustration showing the application of the net present value technique, see Paul J. Wendell, ed., *Corporate Controller's Manual* (New York: Warren, Gorham & Lamont, 1981), pp. 30-12–30-14, and Appendix 30-2, on pp. 30-23–30-36.

ACQUISITIONS, MERGERS, & DIVESTMENTS

2. Convert the annual net income to cash flow from operations by recognizing the noncash items, usually, e.g., depreciation.
3. Adjust cash flow to recognize annual cash needs or resources for such things as additional or planned capital assets and working capital, to arrive at net cash generation or usage each year.
4. Determine the going concern value, or salvage value, of the operation at the end of the period used in the valuation process (e.g., the fifth or eighth year). This may be a multiple of the then-year earnings or estimated salvage value.
5. Apply the appropriate discount factor, using tables or preset computer programs to arrive at the yearly value and the sum of the values.

This is the maximum price, or a starting point for negotiation, as the case may be.

Where an exchange of stock is the likely means of consummating the merger, it is often helpful to summarize the ratio of the several valuation factors, as in Figure 30-5.

In presenting any valuation of an acquisition candidate, such appraisal is influenced by the discount rate used, as well as the conservatism of the various assumptions (e.g., growth rate in sales and sales mix). To give the management a sense of the impact of these factors, perhaps a simple tabulation for differing discount rates and assumptions might be a useful part of the audit report. A simple example is shown in Figure 30-6.

Another presentation, Figure 30-7, shows the rate of return of various purchase prices that might be helpful, using the internal rate of return method. This approach can be used where management, or its advisers, has suggested a range of prices.

The principle involved is to summarize in a simple way the significant factors in which the report recipient is or should be interested.

Impact of Changes in Accounting Policies and Procedures

When a company is acquired, presumably it will adopt the accounting policies of the acquiror. This is not an absolute, especially when different industries may be involved, but it does occur most often; and the forecasts of earnings and cash flow, or basis for determining price (e.g., P/E multiple approach), should recognize these differences. Aside from what might be called accounting differences, other new cost levels should be recognized, for example, possible new fringe benefit rates, travel allowances, and so on.

One of the purposes of accounting analysis is to become aware of any policy and practice differences that will have an impact on earnings and to recognize such changes in operating results.

Areas that may cause adjustments include, but are not limited to, the following:

☐ *Inventory basis.* One may use FIFO, while the other may employ LIFO.

FIG. 30-5
Summary of Comparative Factors for Merger Discussion

Summary of Selected Factors for Acquisitions of S by A Through Stock Exchange Per Share

	A	S	Ratio/Share
Market value (before merger talks)	$84.20	$76.10	.90 to 1
Earnings per share—last year	7.60	10.86	1.43 to 1
Earnings per share—average 3 years	5.90	7.08	1.20 to 1
Earnings per share—projected 5 years	14.57	13.80	.95 to 1
Book value	22.10	30.70	1.39 to 1
Dividends	6.50	6.00	1.08 to 1
Net current assets	14.70	12.60	.86 to 1

FIG. 30-6
Comparative Purchase Prices

MAXIMUM ACCEPTABLE CASH PRICE
For Selected Discount Rates and Scenarios

Scenario	Discount Rate		
	11%	13%	15%
A. *Conservative*			
Aggregate Price ($ millions)	$122.00	$ 45.00	$ 75.00
Per Share Price	110.00	90.00	68.18
B. *Most Likely*			
Aggregate Price ($ millions)	143.00	111.00	87.00
Per Share Price	130.00	100.90	79.00
C. *Optimistic*			
Aggregate Price ($ millions)	170.00	132.00	104.00
Per Share Price	150.00	120.00	94.50

FIG. 30-7
Rates of Return (DCF)

Selected Rates of Return Based on Several Offering Prices

	Scenario		
	Conservative	Most Likely	Optimistic
Offering Price ($ millions)			
$50.00	11.46	12.73	14.13
47.50	12.16	13.51	15.00
45.00	12.35	13.72	15.23
40.00	13.50	15.00	16.68

ACQUISITIONS, MERGERS, & DIVESTMENTS

☐ *Depreciation methods.* The acquiror may use some accelerated depreciation or cost recovery procedure, while the acquired might have adopted straight-line depreciation on a very extended life basis.

☐ *Fixed asset capitalization.* Some concerns may expense many items conservatively, such as items with a unit value of $1,000 or less, while another may capitalize items of $100 or over that have a useful life of more than one year. One firm may expense shipping costs, sales tax, installation costs, or plant rearrangement costs, while another may include such items in the total cost of the asset.

☐ *Pension cost funding.* While one firm may amortize unfunded past service costs over, say, 40 years, another may use a 10-year amortization period. The interest rate assumption may be quite different for two pension plans.

☐ *Personnel costs.* An acquired firm may have various different personnel practices, which would be adjusted to conform to the acquiror basis, e.g., vacation plan, savings plan, hospital insurance, travel allowances, overtime policy, moving expense, and deferred compensation. Cost estimates should reflect any changes that are expected to be made.

☐ *Research and development expenses.* While there is less difference now than a few years ago, when many companies capitalized research and development costs, there still may be differences in definition and application as to expense versus capital, a factor that should be addressed.

The point is that earnings and financial condition may be affected in a significant manner by differences in accounting treatment and various other practices. One purpose of an accounting review is to identify such potential adjustments so that management is aware of the fact that net earnings may not be what management has observed in the historical statements prepared by the acquired company.

It might be advantageous for the internal auditor (or independent accountant, if applicable) to prepare a comparative statement of income and expense for a selected year or years, as shown in Figure 30-8, to display the magnitude of the changes.

The Accounting Basis for Business Combinations

The method by which a business combination takes place largely governs the accounting treatment used in preparing the resulting financial statements. Briefly, the Accounting Principles Board (APB), through APB Opinion Nos. 16 and 17 (AC 1091 and 5141), has issued standards. Basically, under stated circumstances, either the purchase method or the pooling-of-interest method may be applicable. The two techniques are defined in AC 1091.11 and 1091.12 as follows:

• *Purchase Method*

11. The purchase method accounts for a business combination as the acquisition of one company by another. The acquiring corporation records at its cost

FIG. 30-8

Impact of Accounting Practices

The Prospective Jeffrey Acquisition Impact of ACQ Accounting Methods for the Years 198X and 198Y
($ in thousands)

	Year	
	198X	198Y
Reported income before income taxes	$22,480	$25,960
Accounting adjustments (deductions):		
(a) Inventory FIFO in lieu of LIFO	1,270	1,750
(b) Depreciation Straight-line vs. accelerated cost recovery	812	714
(c) Fixed asset capitalization Repairs and maintenance	1,040	1,760
Minimum of $100 vs. $500	210	106
(d) Amortization of unfunded pension liability (40 years vs. 10)	178	176
Total Adjustments:	3,510	4,506
Adjusted income before taxes	18,970	21,454
Income taxes (47%)	8,916	10,083
Adjusted net income	$10,054	$11,371
Per Share—Adjusted*	2.33	2.63
Reduction from Reported Income	.43	.56

* Based on 4,316,000 shares

the acquired assets less liabilities assumed. A difference between the cost of an acquired company and the sum of the fair values of tangible and identifiable intangible assets less liabilities is recorded as goodwill. The reported income of an acquiring corporation includes the operations of the acquired company after acquisition, based on the cost to the acquiring corporation.

- *Pooling-of-Interests Method*

12. The pooling of interests method accounts for a business combination as the uniting of the ownership interests of two or more companies by change of equity securities. No acquisition is recognized because the combination is accomplished without disbursing resources of the constituents. Ownership interests continue and the former bases of accounting are retained. The recorded assets and liabilities of the constituents are carried forward to the combined corporation at their recorded amounts. Income of the combined corporation includes income of the constituents for the entire fixed period in which the combination

occurs. The reported income of the constituents for prior periods is combined and restored as income of the combined corporation.

The internal auditor should be aware of the two methods of accounting for business combinations and the consequences regarding operating results and financial condition, and should prepare any projected or historical pro forma financial statements accordingly. When a purchase basis is used, a new basis of cost accountability arises, and the book values of the acquired company will largely be irrelevant.

Reference is made to the several good books containing information on the accounting methods, refinements, various interpretations, and consequences.[6]

TAX CONSIDERATIONS

While the tax specialist of the acquiring company probably will suggest the most appropriate means of effecting the acquisition from a tax viewpoint, the internal auditor should be somewhat knowledgeable about the tax aspects. The report should not contain conclusions or recommendations that do not acknowledge tax effects.

A corporation may acquire another corporation through either a taxable or nontaxable transaction. Moreover, under either basis, a sale of assets or a sale of stock may be accomplished. Obviously, tax considerations are one aspect of selecting the method and, indeed, agreeing on a price.

The impact of taxes most commonly addresses the matter of *federal* income taxes, and this subject is reviewed in the next section. However, the effect of state and local taxes should not be overlooked. For example, the unitary tax laws of some states could subject an entire company's business to state tax, not merely the segment of business done within the state.

Tax Methods of Consummating an Acquisition

There are six basic tax methods of consummating an acquisition, some of which have separate variations:[7]

1. Asset acquisition
2. 338 transaction
3. Stock acquisition
4. Type A reorganizations

---

[6] For example, see John C. Burton, Russell E. Palmer and Robert S. Kay, eds., *Handbook of Accounting and Auditing*, Chapter 30 (New York: Warren, Gorham & Lamont, 1981).

[7] Adopted in large part from James D. Willson, *Budgeting and Profit Planning Manual*, 2nd ed., Chapter 5 (New York: Warren, Gorham & Lamont, 1988).

5. Type B reorganizations
6. Type C reorganizations

An Asset Acquisition. In an asset acquisition, the acquiring company purchases all or a part of the assets of the target entity for cash, stock, other securities, or other consideration. The payment is made by the acquiring company to the target company, and the latter remains in existence subsequent to the transaction. Generally, the transaction is regarded by the IRS as a taxable sale of assets or some of the assets. If the target company adopts a plan of complete liquidation, and distributes all of its assets, it will not be taxed. However, in this circumstance, the owners of the target company must recognize gain or loss on the distribution of the proceeds and the complete liquidation of their interests.

A 338 Transaction. Under this method, the acquiring entity purchases the stock of the target from the latter's shareholders for cash, stock, other securities, or other consideration. Moreover, it elects, pursuant to Section 338 of the IRC, by the fifteenth day of the ninth month, after the month of acquisition, to treat the transaction as if the target sold its assets for a price equal to their fair market value. Such a transaction is viewed by the IRS as a taxable sale by the target's shareholders. (But see the impact of the Tax Reform Act of 1986, discussed later.)

A Stock Acquisition. In this type of transaction, the acquiring company purchases the stock of the target corporation for cash, stock, other securities, or other consideration. This kind of transaction is viewed by the IRS as a taxable sale by the target's shareholders.

A tax-free acquisition is commonly referred to by the tax professionals as a reorganization. Section 368 of the IRC defines six basic reorganizations, of which three (with their modifications) are referred to as acquisition reorganizations (Types A, B, and C), while the others relate to other matters not germane to the substance of this chapter. The three methods of combining corporations, probably without income tax consequences to all parties, are discussed in the following text.

Type A Reorganizations. Transactions that are accomplished as a Type A reorganization may be of four different kinds: (1) Type A statutory merger; (2) Type A statutory consolidation; (3) Type A subsidiary merger; and (4) Type A reverse subsidiary merger.

☐ *Type A statutory merger.* This type occurs when two corporations combine in such a manner that one of the companies disappears and one remains in existence. It must be accomplished pursuant to a state statute. For tax purposes, the merged company is considered to have exchanged its assets for the stock of the surviving (acquiring) company. The merged (acquired) corporation distributes the stock of the acquiring corporation to its own shareholders in exchange for the stock of the target corporation.

These transactions are not taxable.

☐ *Type A statutory consolidation.* A Type A statutory consolidation occurs when two or more corporations are combined into a new corporation. For tax purposes, the combined corporations are considered to have exchanged their assets for the stock of the new company. The combined corporations, on receiving the stock of the new corporation, distribute it to their shareholders in exchange for their shares in the combining corporations.

Again, these transactions are not taxable.

☐ *Type A subsidiary merger.* In this type of merger, which sometimes is called a standard triangular merger, the target corporation merges into a controlled subsidiary of the acquiring entity in exchange for the stock of the acquiring company. The acquiring corporation must acquire substantially all the assets of the target company. Additionally, no stock of the subsidiary may be given to the shareholders of the target company. The merged (target) company is considered to have exchanged its assets for stock. The target company distributes its newly acquired stock to its shareholders in exchange for its stock.

These are not taxable transactions.

☐ *Type A reverse subsidiary merger.* In this transaction, a controlled subsidiary of the acquiring company merges into the target company—because there is a legal need to maintain the target corporation's existence. The shareholders of the target company receive the stock of the acquiring entity, and the acquiring entity receives the stock of the target company. After this transaction, the target company must hold (1) substantially all of the assets it held before the transaction and (2) substantially all of the assets of the subsidiary merged into it.

These are not taxable transactions.

Type B Reorganizations. A Type B reorganization generally may be accomplished in one of two ways: (1) parent stock is exchanged for stock of the target company, or (2) subsidiary stock is exchanged for stock of the target entity.

☐ *Parent stock for target company stock.* In this type of transaction, the acquiring company exchanges its voting stock for stock of the target corporation—sufficient to control the target (i.e., 80 percent of total combined voting power of all voting stock and at least 80 percent of all other classes of target stock). In effect, the target company becomes a subsidiary of the acquirer.

These are not taxable transactions.

☐ *Sudsidiary stock for a stock exchange.* In this transaction, the acquiring company may use its own stock or that of its subsidiary in an exchange—but not a combination of the two.

The acquiring company may pass its stock down to the sudsidiary, who exchanges that stock for the stock of the target, or the subsidiary may issue its own stock in exchange for the stock of the target. The target becomes a subsidiary of the acquiring company's subsidiary.

Again, these are not taxable transactions.

Type C Reorganizations. A Type C reorganization may also be effected in two ways: (1) parent stock is exchanged for assets, or (2) subsidiary stock is exchanged for assets.

- ☐ *Parent stock for assets.* In a parent stock for assets transaction, the acquiring entity exchanges its voting stock for substantially all of the assets of the target company.

- ☐ *Subsidiary stock for assets.* In this transaction, a subsidiary of the acquiring company exchanges its voting stock, or voting stock of the acquiring corporation, for substantially all of the assets of the target company.

Generally speaking, the acquiring company or its subsidiary does not recognize any gain or loss in a Type C reorganization.

The target company and its shareholders recognize no gain or loss if only voting stock is received. When the target is liquidated, its owners will take a basis in the acquiring company stock equal to their target company stock. If "booty" is used in the transaction and distributed to the target's shareholders, it is taxable to them.

It should be understood that the objective in selecting the method of acquisition on behalf of the acquiring corporation is to select the least cost or the most advantageous means of acquiring the target, which is negotiable.

Impact of the Tax Reform Act of 1986

Any law that adjusts the tax rate or tax bases of businesses will be reflected in the net earnings of the entity. Our focus in this section is not on tax rules that would apply to most companies, but specifically those that have an impact on business combination transactions as such. The Tax Reform Act of 1986 may drastically affect the tax consequences of business combinations in these ways:

- Nonuse or restricted use of the target company net operating loss or tax credits
- Repeal of the *General Utilities* doctrine and the consequent recognition of gain or loss on the sale or distribution of property in complete liquidation
- Requirement that purchase price allocation, when asset acquisitions are consummated, must be under the "residual" method, not the "proportional" method

- Nondeductibility of the excess repurchase cost over the fair market value of the stock (i.e., greenmail), or the costs of obtaining a standstill agreement

As would be true in any contemplated acquisition, the specific requirements or limitations of the law then in effect should be reviewed.

EARNINGS PER SHARE

The financial community attaches great weight to earnings per share (EPS), or more specifically, to *growth* in EPS. Business management also keeps an eye on this figure and, particularly in acquisitions, often tries to avoid dilution or at least any significant dilution. Presumably, a sound acquisition will contribute to increased EPS, perhaps immediately, and certainly within a short-term period. Earnings per share growth may not necessarily be an indication of good management. In fact, if the *rate* of return on shareholder's equity remains constant, EPS should increase, if some share of net earnings remains in the company (not paid out as dividends). Moreover, increase in EPS may be achieved, among other ways, by: (1) purchasing and retirement of common shares; (2) increasing leverage through the use of debt, with a subsequent change in capital structure; and (3) acquiring profit-making companies for cash, or with stock if the acquired has a lower P/E ratio than the acquiring company.[8] The chief internal auditor therefore should be sensitive to the impact on per share earnings of any proposed acquisition. He should include such data in his audit report, if within his field of responsibility or competence, possibly including the impact of differing packages of securities and cash.

The type of summary presentation may be simple or complex, depending on the competence, or understanding, of the management (and the internal auditor). A simple EPS comparison, with or without the acquisition, may be made as in Figure 30-9 for instances where an acquisition is made for cash or as stipulated stock exchange ratio. If it is desirable to present the EPS on various packages, or to illustrate the impact on the acquiring company of differing growth rates of the acquiree, graphs may be used, as shown in Figures 30-10 and 30-11, respectively.

The internal auditor should review data on P/E analysis for techniques and ideas.[9] However, the impact on per share earnings of acquirer, company A, by acquisition of (1) a higher P/E ratio company, H, and (2) a lower P/E ratio concern, L, is illustrated by Figure 30-10. Assume these facts:

---

[8] *Ibid.*, Chapter 6.

[9] See, for example, Donald J. Smalter and Roderic C. Lancy, "P/E Analysis in Acquisition Strategy," Merger and Acquisition Series, *Harvard Business Review*, pp. 49–90.

FIG. 30-9
Increase in EPS With Acquisition

The Jones Company Impact on EPS by Acquiring T Corporation

Year	Jones EPS Without Acquisition	T Corporation Impact*	Adjusted EPS
198R	$ 7.82	.34	$ 8.16
198S	9.38	.44	9.82
198T	10.98	.56	11.54
198U	12.63	.82	13.45
198V	15.15	1.07	16.22
198W	17.73	1.23	18.96
198X	20.39	1.49	21.88

* Represents T Corporation earnings less assumed 9.5% interest income before taxes on the $50 million purchase price. For 198R, for example, T Corporation net of $7,500,000 — $2,517,000 after tax interest ÷ Jones' outstanding shares of 14,700,000 = $.34.

Selected Financial Data (before acquisition)
(in millions of dollars, except per share)

	Company		
	A	H	L
Net sales	$700	$300	$300
Net income	63	30	21
Common shares (millions)	10	4	4
EPS	6.30	7.50	5.25
Share price	50.40	82.50	31.50
P/E multiple	8	11	6

Assume the following results of negotiations for the acquisition of companies H or L by company A:

	H	L
Purchase price ($M)	$450	$126
P/E ratio	15	6
A shares to be issued		
$450M ÷ 50.40	10,000,000	
$125M ÷ 50.40		2,500,000

Composite earnings

A		$63,000,000	$63,000,000
H		30,000,000	
L			21,000,000
	Total:	$93,000,000	$84,000,000

Shares outstanding

A		10,000,000	10,000,000
H		10,000,000	
L			2,500,000
	Total:	20,000,000	12,500,000

Per share earnings

With H	4.65	
With L		6.72
Company A without acquisition	6.30	6.30
Increment/(Decrement)	(1.65)	.42
Percentage	(26%)	6.7%

Management may choose *some* dilution, perhaps up to 10 percent, for a limited period on the basis that the rapid growth per year in earnings of an acquired company would soon overcome the dilution. A graphic depiction of the annual growth rate in earnings of a prospective acquiree required to eliminate dilution, at selected P/E ratios paid for the company, might be depicted in a graph as shown in Figure 30-11.

The Combination Package

Several topics have been discussed to provide background for the internal auditor: acquisition criteria, valuation by the DCF method, earnings growth rate of the acquiree, and P/E ratios. But there is a relationship, and sometimes a conflict, among some of these factors. Thus, if the acquisition guidelines provide for no dilution in EPS, and a minimum rate of return, this may not be compatible with a proposed stock exchange. To be sure, cash or a common stock exchange are the usual media of exchange in a merger or acquisition. But under some circumstances, a combination of each, and some senior debt instruments or preferred stock, may meet the needs of a particular situation. A preferred stock, note, or convertible preferred might be helpful, for example, in meeting higher immediate income needs of the seller. Or a convertible preferred might provide the higher income, with the right to convert if the seller subsequently desired to share in capital appreciation.

The internal auditor should be sensitive to the need of suggesting a change in the combination of securities, and/or cash, should that be necessary and within his province. A simple chart, as in Figure 30-10, shows

FIG. 30-10
Impact of Different Cash Securities Packages

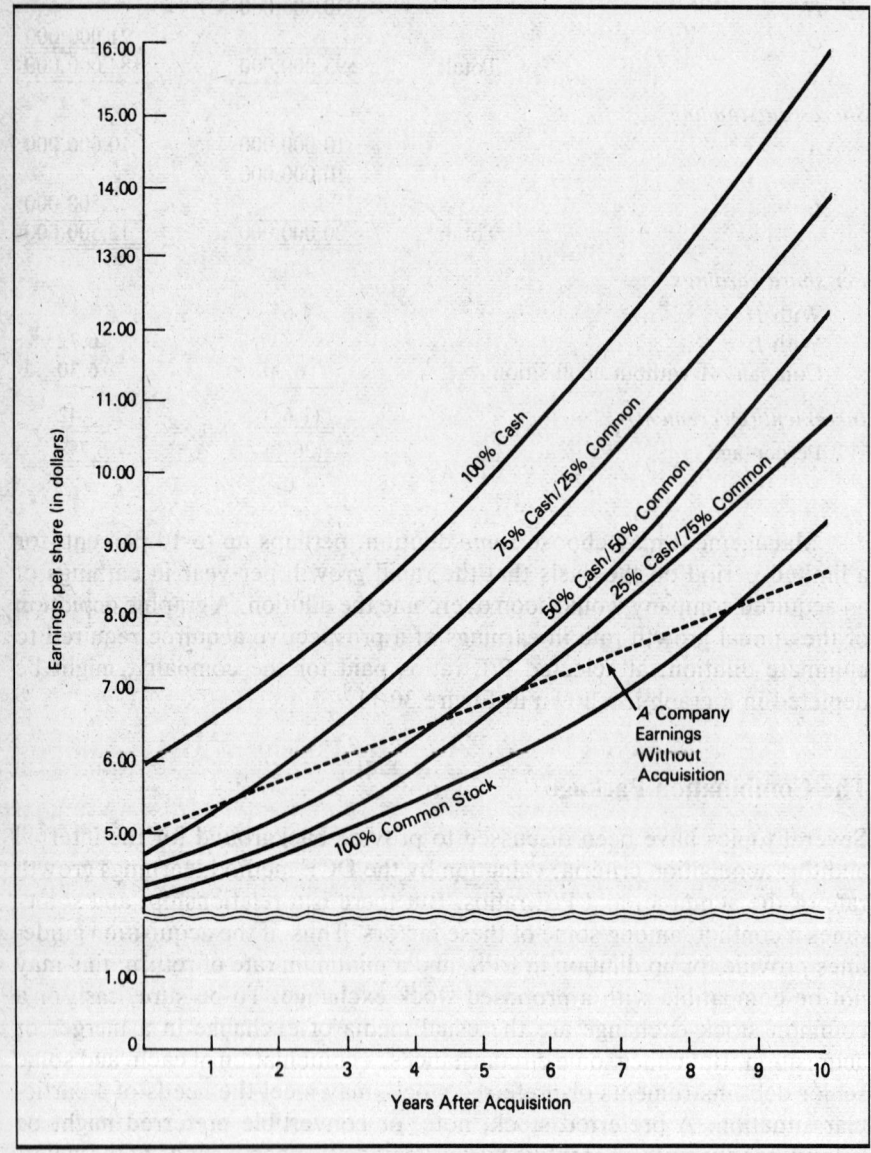

**FIG. 30-11
Impact of Various Growth Rates on EPS**

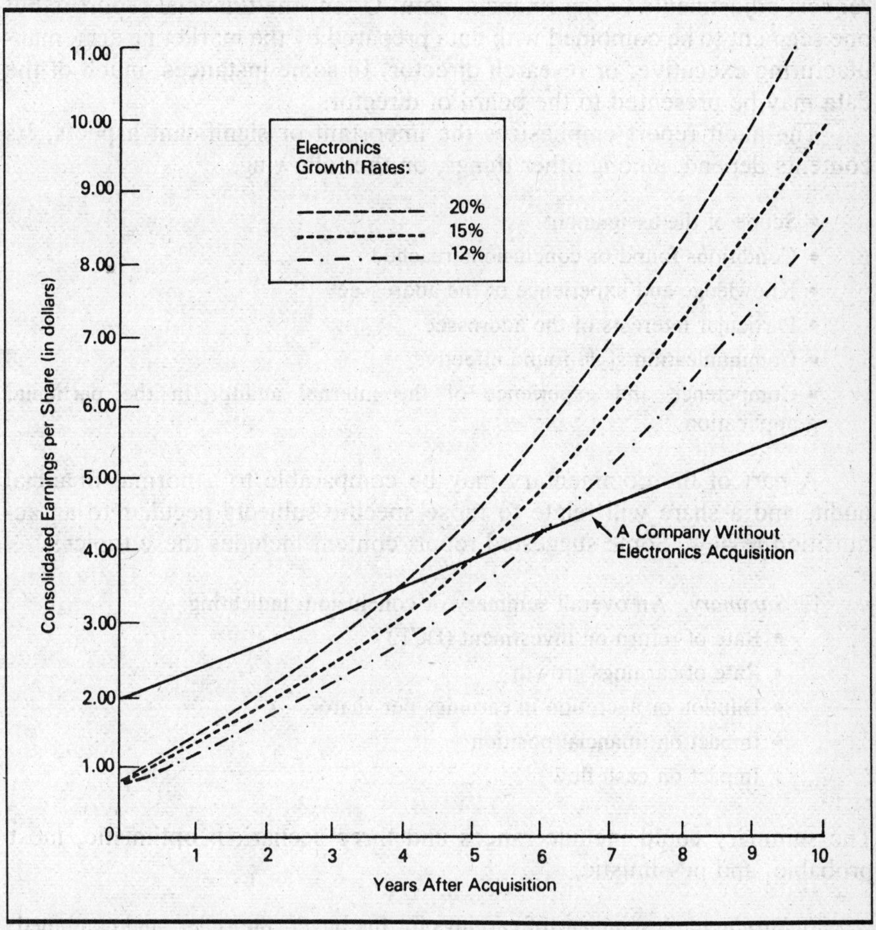

the impact of differing combinations on the buyer, a fact that must not be overlooked.

THE AUDIT REPORT

One end result of a special investigation, such as potential acquisition, is an audit report. If the internal auditor is acting as an arm of the vice-president–finance, controller, or some other management representative, the objective is the same: to communicate the *significant* financial information so that the customer can make a judgment about financial condition, prospective earnings, the desirability of the transactions, and so on. Some of the information may permit the financial arm to reach certain conclusions and perhaps to request adjustments to the financial data. Often, the financial report is but one segment to be combined with data prepared by the marketing arm, manufacturing executive, or research director. In some instances, much of the data may be presented to the board of directors.

The audit report emphasizes the important or significant aspects. Its contents depend, among other things, on the following:

- Scope of the assignment
- Conditions found or conclusions reached
- Knowledge and experience of the addressee
- Particular interests of the addressee
- Communication style found effective
- Competence and experience of the internal auditor in the particular application

A part of the commentary may be comparable to a normal financial audit, and a share will relate to those specific subjects peculiar to an acquisition review. Some suggested report content includes these topics:

☐ *Summary.* An overall summary or conclusion, indicating:
- Rate of return on investment (DCF)
- Rate of earnings growth
- Dilution or accretion in earnings per share
- Impact on financial position
- Impact on cash flow

The summary could include ranges and three scenarios: optimistic, most probable, and pessimistic.

☐ *Earnings.* A summary of earnings for the buyer, the seller, and combined, perhaps for each of the past five years and each of the prospective five years. These related data might be considered:
- Net earnings in nominal terms
- Earnings adjusted for inflation
- Adjustments necessary to seller figures
- Anticipated savings or other benefits of ownership (synergisms)
- Analysis of earnings by significant breakdown (e.g., territory, product, and organizational segment)
- Danger or weak spots in the operation (or assumptions)
- Growth rates
- Contemplated changes in accounting policy of seller that have an impact on income statement (e.g., pension costs, depreciation, and inventory)

ACQUISITIONS, MERGERS, & DIVESTMENTS 30-41

- ☐ *Cash sources and uses of funds.* Pro-forma summary, for the past five years by buyer and seller, and planned for each of the next five years. Among other things, these matters should be summarized, if applicable:
  - Any necessary borrowings
  - Any planned stock issuance
  - Major capital expenditures
  - Dividend payments
- ☐ *Financial position.* Condensed balance sheets of buyer, seller, and consolidated should be included—pro-forma for past five year-ends, and planned for each of the prospective five year-ends. Consideration should be given to this supporting detail:
  - Selected by financial ratios, especially with references to the credit agreements
  - Adjustments contemplated regarding, for example, receivables and inventory turnover rates
  - Summary of income tax status
  - Summary of comments in contingent liabilities
  - Book value
- ☐ *Other general data.* As suitable, data such as the following may be provided:
  - Growth rates—sales and earnings
  - Return on shareholders' equity
  - Impact of alternative securities/cash packages
  - Inventory data—comparative
  - Commentary on expected trouble spots

Some of the formats illustrated in early parts of this chapter may be useful inclusions in the audit report.

To reiterate, the type of audit report, extent of detail, and so on will depend on several factors, including the purpose and the status of negotiations. Figure 30-12, for example, illustrates a highly condensed audit report by the chief internal auditor to the president, for the purpose of establishing a starting point for the negotiation of the purchase of a very small privately owned electronics company that was having some product difficulties as well as aging management. Because the products were substantially similar to those of the purchaser (as to manufacturing process and market) and because the president was particularly interested in the sales volumes that he thought could be substantially increased, emphasis is on that aspect only. It is intended to be an audit report that can be shown to the prospective seller, if requested, and does not consider the impact of the acquiror's contemplated changes in product design, new market approach, and new products. It deals solely with the existing basic product line and facilities.

The majority of audit reports on potential acquisitions are much more detailed than the illustration in Figure 30-12. Because each report should be

FIG. 30-12
Illustrative Audit Report

TO: President
FROM: Chief Internal Auditor
SUBJECT: Electronics West—Acquisition

You have requested an indication of product line sales trends, net income, and a suggested purchase price, based on the preliminary sales and income data you received from the Chairman of Electronics West. We have talked with the sales manager to understand better the basis for the sales projections, and we have reviewed the income projections with the Treasurer to become acquainted with the company accounting policies, etc. Our conclusions are summarized in this brief memo. We believe the historical data to be reliable; however, it is suggested that any purchase price be predicated on an audit by our independent accountants to ascertain the existing financial condition, and the earnings for the nine months ending September 30, 19XX.

Summary

Sales for the year ended December 31, 198Y aggregated $36,220,000, segregated as follows:

Commercial	$16,220,000
Military	20,000,000
Total	$36,220,000

The present management opined that existing product lines should increase to $60,000,000 in the next ten years. Details by product line are provided in Schedule I.

Net income totaled only $1,240,000 for the year ended December 31, 198Y, and adjustment to our corporate basis of accounting would reduce earnings to approximately $1,138,000. It is estimated, based on the Expander Co. accounting principles and practices that in ten years net income would equal $2,180,000, or 3.6% of sales, with the present line of product. The *cash flow* from the company operations in this same time period would aggregate $12,527,000 and would reach a level of $2,160,000 in 19X9. As detailed later, a suggested price, which could provide Expander an acceptable return on equity, could range between $6,900,000 and $10,700,000.

Sales

As reflected in Schedule I, the military products are conservatively estimated to increase by 5% per annum. But some additional research and development should result in product adoptions that could double the growth rate of this product line.

Among commercial products the cellular mobile line, which was introduced in mid-198Y-1, should increase at least 15% annually, despite strong competition. The citizens band radio line is slowly declining and is expected to be phased out in 19X9. The high volume commercial line is the amateur radio, with heavy overseas sales. Growth is erratic and at a rate less than 5%.

Net Income and Cash Flow

Net income of $1,240,000 on the Electronics West accounting basis, increases to $2,380,000 over the ten-year period. However, the income as a percentage of sales, being 3.4% last year and increasing to only 4.0% in 198Y, is below the industry average.

A review of the operating margins on this product line, as projected in ten years, reflects these results:

	Sales	Operating Margin Amount	Percentage
International	$23,115,000	$1,200,000	5.19
Cellular	4,207,000	631,000	15.00
Military	32,578,000	2,932,000	9.00
Total	$59,900,000	$4,763,000	8.00

The cellular and military product lines have acceptable margins, given the relatively modern production facilities. The conglomerate international and amateur line produce only a 5.19% gross margin and reflect on the high cost of manufacture. Clearly, major changes are necessary in this line.

While internal cash generation over the next ten years is expected to be $21,427,000, a sum of $8,900,000 will be applied to (a) limited facility expenditures with (b) the bulk invested in inventory and receivables. The net result is cash generation of $12,527,000 in the ten years. Additionally, it should be recognized that the going value of the business (present product lines) should approximate ten times earnings, or $21,800,000.

Purchase Price

You will recall that the corporate goal is a 15% return on shareholders' equity. However, recognizing the integration possibilities, it may be prudent to accept a somewhat lower return for a limited period. Given the net cash generation shown on Schedule II, aggregating $12,527,000 for the ten years, and using the discontinued cash flow approach, the present value, at selected rates of return, would permit a purchase price as follows:

Desired Return on Investment	Maximum Price
10%	$10,700,000
12%	8,900,000
15%	6,900,000

As previously mentioned, any offer should be conditioned on an independent audit which should disclose a net worth and financial position not significantly less favorable than represented to us.

If you have any questions, please let know.

J. Jones
Chief Internal Auditor

(continued)

FIG. 30-12 *(cont'd)*

Electronics West Summary of Sales Product Price—Schedule I
198Y-4 through 19X9
($ in thousands)

Year	Commercial				Military	Total
	International Amateur	Citizens Band	Cellular Mobile	Total		
Historical						
198Y-4	$ 8,900	$1,000	—	$ 9,900	$ 25,000	$ 34,900
198Y-3	8,825	1,290	—	10,115	25,000	35,115
198Y-2	10,200	1,370	—	11,570	25,000	36,570
198Y-1	11,975	1,310	$ 790	14,075	25,000	39,075
198Y	13,920	1,260	1,040	16,220	20,000	36,220
Total	53,820	6,230	1,830	61,880	120,000	181,880
Projected						
19XX	15,329	1,210	1,196	17,735	21,000	38,735
19X1	16,015	1,100	1,375	18,490	22,050	40,540
19X2	16,791	1,000	1,582	19,373	23,152	42,525
19X3	17,561	1,000	1,819	20,380	24,310	44,690
19X4	18,456	1,000	2,092	21,544	25,526	47,070
19X5	19,127	900	2,406	22,433	26,802	49,235
19X6	19,847	800	2,766	23,413	28,142	51,555
19X7	20,675	700	3,181	24,556	29,544	54,105
19X8	21,630	600	3,659	25,889	31,026	56,915
19X9	23,115	100	4,207	27,422	32,578	60,000
Total	$188,542	$8,410	$24,283	$221,235	$264,135	$485,370

Annual Growth Rates assumed:

Military 5%

Cellular 15%

International, etc. 5%

Schedule II

Year	Per Electronics	Net Income Adjustments	As Adjusted	From Operations	Cash Flow Net Investment	Net
Historical						
198Y-4	$ 521	82	439	834	1,500	$ (666)
198Y-3	983	93	890	1,315	500	815
198Y-2	1,115	96	1,019	1,419	500	919
198Y-1	1,259	104	1,505	1,505	—	1,505
198Y	1,240	102	1,138	1,408	—	1,408
Total	$ 5,118	477	4,641	6,481	2,500	$ 3,981
Projected						
198X	$ 1,370	120	1,250	1,560	700	$ 860
198X1	1,465	140	1,325	1,750	900	850
198X2	1,548	140	1,408	1,923	1,100	823
198X3	1,648	150	1,498	1,983	400	1,583
198X4	1,758	160	1,598	1,978	400	1,578
198X5	1,855	160	1,695	2,085	1,100	985
198X6	1,969	170	1,799	2,284	1,200	1,084
198X7	2,084	170	1,914	2,464	1,200	1,264
198X8	2,230	190	2,040	2,640	1,300	1,340
198X9	2,380	200	2,180	2,760	600	2,160
Total	$18,307	1,600	16,707	21,427	8,900	$12,527

tailored to fit the need, and because many of the figures presented herein may be made part of an acquisition memorandum, no further details are presented. Typically, the summary will cover all important financial and other matters. Substantial supporting details of net sales, income, and financial position by appropriate element would be available and supplementary to the key financial statements. But the key for the executive who doesn't "want to be bothered by details" is concise commentary and a well-presented summary.

FINANCIAL ANALYSIS NECESSARY FOR DIVESTMENTS

Just as care must be taken in selecting proper acquisition candidates, in setting the proper price to be paid, and deciding on the most appropriate security, cash, and type of reorganization, so also the relevant financial analysis must be made of divestment targets. Gathering the necessary historical and relevant plan data for divestments usually is much easier than in the case of acquisitions, since management should already possess much of the information, and is presumed to know the potential earning power (or lack of it) and cash flow or worth of the business segment under study.

The prudent financial planner should be aware of such matters as:

- Probable future earnings of segment.
- Probable future cash flow of segment.
- Present value of segment based on the above data.
- Probable return from alternative use of capital.
- Impact of divestment on corporate earnings and financial position (including impact on pension requirements, contingent liabilities, and tax status).

In summary, the budget director and other financial executives should be aware of the financial impact of divestment of the various targets—just as they should know the comparable values for acquisitions.

If the consideration for a divestment is cash, there is less need for any significant evaluation of an acquirer than if the consideration is stock or some other continuing interest in the acquirer, such as notes payable. When segments of the acquiring entity, such as a product line, division, or subsidiary, are secured in exchange for the divested asset, then much the same review should be made regarding the new potential asset as in other acquisitions.

If the payment for the divestment is in securities of the acquiring company, then a review of the acquirer is appropriate to reach an opinion on the desirability of the new investment and its potential.

Some of the matters to be checked, depending on the type of security received and the likelihood of a continuing relationship and the relative amount involved, include:

- ☐ Some general information about the acquirer and the industry:
    - Reputation of owners and management
    - Standing in the industry, including:
        - Market share and trend thereof
        - Product lines
        - Special advantages and identified handicaps
    - Credit rating
    - Major recent developments in the industry (e.g., foreign inroads)
- ☐ Sufficient financial information to judge the worth of the investment and likely increase or decrease in value (e.g., cash flow, earnings, and contingent liabilities)
- ☐ Factors that account for the success of the company:
    - Perhaps some history of the success of other acquisitions, if any

The amount of data required to reach a sound decision on the divestment, and the exposure involved in the new investment, will relate, in part, to relative risks and terms of sale.

SUGGESTED READING

Burton, John C., Russell E. Palmer, and Robert S. Kay, eds. *Handbook of Accounting and Auditing*, Chapter 30. New York: Warren, Gorham & Lamont, 1981.

Emmett, Robert. "How to Value a Potential Acquisition," *Financial Executive*. Feb. 1982, pp. 16–19.

Godfrey, Robert R. "The Diversification Dilemma: Buy It or Grow It?" *Financial Executive*, Aug. 1983, pp. 38–42.

Hovers, John, Dr. *Expansion Through Acquisition*. London: Business Books Limited, 1973.

Rappaport, Alfred. "Strategic Analysis for More Profitable Acquisitions." *Harvard Business Review*, July/Aug. 1979, pp. 99–110.

Talbott, Frederick, and Robert B. Clayton. "Pluses and Minuses of a Merger." *Financier*, Oct. 1983, pp. 21–24.

Stern, Joel. "A Discussion of Mergers and Acquisitions." *Midland Corporate Finance Journal*, Summer 1983, pp. 21–47.

Wendell, Paul J., ed., *Corporate Controller's Manual*, Chapter 30. New York: Warren, Gorham & Lamont, 1981.

PART IX
Operational Auditing

CHAPTER **31**

A Management Perspective

Internal Auditing—A Continually Changing Emphasis	1	Basic Steps in Operational Auditing	13
		Preliminary Phase	14
A Workable Definition for Operational Auditing	3	Physical Tour of the Facility	14
		Gathering of Written Data	15
		Interviews With Management Personnel	15
Similarity of Activities in Both Financial and Operational Audits	4	Limited Financial Analysis	16
		Preparation of Survey Memorandum	16
Benefits of Operational Audits	6		
		Progressively Difficult Levels of Operational Auditing	17
Areas Suggested for Operational Audits	6	Operational Auditing	17
		Management Auditing	17
Securing an Engagement; Some Limitations	8	Strategic Auditing	18
Knowledge Needed to Perform an Operational Audit	9	Reports on Operational Audits	18
Good Management Practice	10		
Standards for Operational Audits	11	Suggested Reading	19

Fig. 31-1 Nonfinancial Activities and Functions Audited by Internal Auditing, by Industry (282 Companies) 2
Fig. 31-2 Checklist for Expanded-Scope Audits 12

INTERNAL AUDITING—A CONTINUALLY CHANGING EMPHASIS

Originally, a principal function of most internal audit groups was the detection and prevention of fraud and the examination of financial statements to assure their accuracy. As a 1963 report of The Conference Board observed, internal auditing traditionally concentrated its efforts in those areas where

FIG. 31-1

Nonfinancial Activities and Functions Audited by Internal Auditing, by Industry (282 Companies)

Nonfinancial Activity or Function	Number of Mentions					
	Manufacturing		Nonmanufacturing		Total	
	Number	Percentage [1]	Number	Percentage [1]	Number	Percentage [1]
Management information systems	118	70%	72	64%	190	67%
Production	130	77	46	41	176	62
Personnel	100	59	69	61	169	60
Marketing/advertising	102	60	47	42	149	53
Planning systems	59	35	38	34	97	34
Research and development	63	37	24	21	87	31
Energy conservation	42	25	13	12	55	19

[1] Percentage of 169 manufacturing companies, 113 nonmanufacturing, and 282 total companies, respectively.

the exposure to misappropriation or intentional manipulation of the financial statements was the greatest.[1] However, for the next 15 years or so, the auditors began to play down this role, and emphasized a broader scope of so-called management-type audits wherein efficiency and effectiveness were stressed. Then came a series of major frauds involving The Equity Funding Corporation of America, as well as The National Student Marketing Corporation and others. Coupled with this disclosure of major fraudulent activities was the revelation of certain corporate misconduct by a number of companies, involving the use of corporate funds for illegal political contributions and the improper use of corporate monies in securing business abroad. The natural reaction was a swing of the pendulum back to an increased concern about fraud and the importance of adequate internal control, together with a more intensive look at corporate governance.

While there was much written about fraud, internal controls, and corporate governance in the late 1970s and early 1980s, there is evidence that attention, to a degree, is swinging back to nonfinancial audits. Even in a report issued by The Conference Board in 1982, 98 percent of the responding audit staffs surveyed reported *some* activities performed that were of a nonfinancial nature.[2] A tabulation of nonfinancial activities and functions audited by the internal auditing organization for 282 reporting companies is shown in Figure 31-1.[3]

---

[1] Paul Macchiaverna, *Internal Auditing* (New York: The Conference Board, 1978) p. 15.
[2] *Ibid.*, p. 37.
[3] *Ibid.*, p. 39.

A MANAGEMENT PERSPECTIVE

Given the competitive pressures to increase efficiency and the growing recognition that audit techniques may be used to ferret out significant savings, increased interest in most companies probably will again be directed towards operational audits. In other words, internal audit activities will respond to management needs and desires. But it is also quite clear that adequate attention will continue to be paid to internal controls and to financial audits.

A WORKABLE DEFINITION FOR OPERATIONAL AUDITING

A number of different terms have been developed to describe or categorize different types of audit examinations or audit approaches. For our purposes, they have been split into two groups: (1) financial audits and (2) operational audits.

Financial audits, the earlier and traditional field of internal audit, is a term that basically describes examinations relating to the reliability of the accounting records and the financial statements. Included, of course, is the appraisal of the related system of internal control.

An *operational audit* has been defined by one source as follows: "An operational audit is a nonfinancial audit whose purpose is to appraise the managerial organization and efficiency of a company or a part of a company. It can be considered a form of constructive criticism."[4] A report of the Special Committee on Operational and Management Auditing of the AICPA says this:[5]

> An operational audit engagement is a distinct form of management advisory service that may also have some of the characteristics of a financial audit engagement. It involves a systematic review of an organization's activities, or of a stipulated segment of them, in relation to specified objectives. The purposes of the engagement may be (a) to assess performance, (b) to identify opportunities for improvement, and (c) to develop recommendations for improvement or further action.

In fact, operational auditing is a somewhat generic term, described by any one of several names, each of which may have different connotations for different readers: operational auditing, performance auditing, efficiency auditing, expanded scope auditing, management auditing, systems auditing, functional auditing, or organizational auditing. For our purposes, an operational audit is defined as a systematic review and evaluation of an organizational unit (or the entire organization) for the purpose of determining its

---

[4] Dale L. Flescher and Stewart Siewart, *Independent Auditor's Guide to Operational Auditing* (New York: John Wiley & Sons, 1982), p. 3.

[5] Report of the Special Committee on Operational and Management Auditing, *Operational Audit Engagements* (New York: American Institute of Certified Public Accountants, 1982), p. 2.

effectiveness and efficiency. It includes a review of the management control system for any business activity or function, including the financial or accounting organization. This is probably a generally accepted definition.

However, to develop a further idea, some consider *management audits* as synonymous with operational auditing; but others would expand the management audit to include the evaluation of management results in terms of achieving stated objectives and also in terms of selecting those objectives. Thus, some auditors would extend their appraisals, using the same techniques applied to operating or middle management control practices, to upper management areas such as strategic planning, evaluation of organization structure, corporate policies, and profit planning, to name a few.

Some leading internal auditors believe that a traditional financial audit can be broadened to include a review of the administrative controls over the function involved, instead of clinging to the narrower concept of determining the reliability of the accounting records.[6]

What the scope of a particular audit should be may depend a great deal on the capability of the internal audit staff and its co-workers and the attitude of top management regarding the function. Suffice it to say that there is a vast area where audits of operating efficiency can usually be made with good economic results—and where they are only indirectly related to a review of the financial statements. In these operational audits, the internal auditor can become a management consultant and review the operating procedures of the organization from a manager's point of view.

SIMILARITY OF ACTIVITIES IN BOTH FINANCIAL AND OPERATIONAL AUDITS

The Statement of Responsibilities of Internal Auditors, as published by the IIA, even in the 1976 revision, outlined six activities involved in attaining the overall objective of internal auditing. Five of them (excluding the objective of accounting for and safeguarding assets) would normally be included, in whole or part, in operational auditing:

1. Reviewing and appraising the soundness, adequacy, and application of operating controls.
2. Ascertaining the extent of compliance with established policies, plans, and procedures.
3. Ascertaining the reliability of management data developed within the organization.
4. Appraising the quality of performance in carrying out assigned responsibilities.
5. Recommending operating improvements.

---

[6] Richard F. Vancil, ed., *Financial Executive Handbook* (Homewood, Illinois: Dow-Jones Irwin, 1970), p. 229.

Indeed, if there was any question about the desirability of a broadened role for the internal auditor, it was settled in 1971 when the first sentence of the new "Statement of Responsibilities of Internal Auditors" of the IIA was simplified by changing "accounting, financial, and other operations" to merely "operations." It now reads "[i]nternal auditing is an independent appraisal activity within an organization for the review of operations as a service to management. It is a managerial control which functions by measuring and evaluating the effectiveness of other controls."

The expansion of operational auditing procedures was assisted by the efforts of the GAO. Its publication of audit standards contains the following introductory statement:[7]

> This demand for information has widened the scope of government auditing so that such auditing no longer is a function concerned primarily with financial operations. Instead, governmental auditing now is also concerned with whether governmental organizations are achieving the purposes for which programs are authorized and funds are made available, are doing so economically and efficiently, and are complying with applicable laws and regulations.

The publication goes on to state that the audit of or for a governmental unit consists of three elements:[8]

1. *Financial and compliance*—determines (1) whether financial operations are properly conducted, (2) whether the financial reports of an audited entity are presented fairly, and (3) whether the entity has complied with applicable laws and regulations.
2. *Economy and efficiency*—determines whether the entity is managing or utilizing its resources (e.g., personnel, property, and space) in an economical and efficient manner, and determines the causes of any inefficiencies or uncommercial practices, including inadequacies in management information systems, administrative procedures, or organizational structure.
3. *Program results*—determines whether the desired results or benefits are being achieved, the objectives established by the legislature or other authorizing body are being met, and the agency has considered alternatives that might yield desired results at a lower cost.

It can be seen that items 2 and 3 are operational audit techniques. Also, it should be mentioned that the Single Audit Act of 1984 does not include such work as economy and efficiency audits, program results audits, or program evaluation.[9]

Thus, there is ample precedent for internal auditors to use their knowl-

---

[7] *Standards for Audit of Governmental Organizations, Programs, Activities and Functions* (Washington, D.C.: U.S. Government Printing Office, 1974), p. i.

[8] *Ibid.*, p. 2.

[9] W. A. Broadus, Jr., and Joseph D. Comtois, "The Single Audit Act: A Needed Reform," *Journal of Accountancy*, Apr. 1985, pp. 62–70.

edge, background, and audit techniques in expanding into the operational audit area pursuant to their stated purpose of assisting management—and most managements now expect it.

BENEFITS OF OPERATIONAL AUDITS

Having defined and described an operational audit, any mention of the benefits might seem redundant. Yet, it may be helpful to describe some of the benefits that have resulted from operational audits. It could assist in convincing top management of the need for such reviews by providing some details of possible gains—aside from the basic objective of reducing waste and inefficiency. While the benefits will depend on the scope and areas of review, here are a few of the advantages that some firms have gained from operational audits:

- The establishment or identification of previously missing organizational objectives, goals, policies, and procedures.
- Securing an objective evaluation or assessment of a specific segment or operation of the company.
- The development of criteria for assessing management performance and achievement of objectives.
- A determination that a given segment is or is not following policies and procedures, and the development of improved policies and procedures.
- The opening of another avenue to improve communications between the corporate office and widely dispersed operations.
- A determination of the effectiveness and efficiency of management planning and control systems.
- The ferreting out of problem areas and (usually) the underlying causes.
- The development of ideas for cost reduction, or profit improvement for specific segments being reviewed.
- A verification of the validity or attainability of selected corporate or segment objectives and strategies.
- The development of potential alternative strategies or objectives.

AREAS SUGGESTED FOR OPERATIONAL AUDITS

What functions or organizations may be suitable targets for operational auditing will depend on several factors, including the industry, top management's view of the proper internal audit function, the capability of the audit department, and the experience of the internal auditors in particular fields, among other things. The extent or type of a particular audit may be similarly influenced. Thus, because of asset exposure or nature of operations, banks and utilities may have fewer operational audits than manufacturing or retail operations. And again, some managements may feel the auditor can check procedures and controls to see if they are adequate and efficient but would be reluctant to permit them to evaluate operating performance.

There are as many areas for possible review as there are management functions. During the performance of financial audits, most internal auditors will form impressions as to functions that may offer the potential for significant savings or simplifications. The perusal of literature on the subject of operational audits, in addition to discussions with auditors in other companies, will also stimulate thought concerning fruitful areas for audit.

Mindful of the capabilities of the audit staff and realistic limitations in a particular company, the following is a partial list of potential review areas:

- Acquisition and merger policies and procedures
- Budgetary systems and procedures
- Branch office control procedures
- Capital budgeting procedures
- Compliance procedures—laws and regulations (e.g., SEC, IRS, FTC, and ERISA).
- Contracting policies and procedures
- Credit granting and collection procedures
- Dividend policies and procedures
- EDP applications
- Energy conservation procedures
- Facilities management
- Fixed asset control procedures, including government facilities and equipment on loan
- Insurance (risk management) procedures
- Inventory planning and control procedures
- Joint venture agreements
- Long-range (strategic) planning policies and procedures
- Make or buy procedures, including intercompany practices
- Management information systems
- Manufacturing policies and procedures
- Marketing/advertising planning and control systems
- Office equipment—acquisition and utilization
- Payroll policies and procedures
- Personnel policies
- Policy and procedures manuals
- Product pricing policies and procedures
- Purchasing policies and procedures
- Research and development planning and control systems
- Retirement plans
- Special projects (e.g., desirability of a *specific* acquisition, and cost reduction studies)

As a summary, given the many potential areas of audit, these criteria should be considered in identifying areas for audit coverage:

- Materiality of individual decisions (financial impact)
- Complexity of the decision process
- Sources and uses of significant amounts of cash
- Volume of transactions or level of activity
- Level of authority involved
- Regulatory requirements
- Level of documentation

Commonsense consideration of these factors, when weighed in the context of the audit department capabilities and reception by operating management, should assist in selecting audit areas. (See Chapter 2.)

SECURING AN ENGAGEMENT; SOME LIMITATIONS

The initiation of an operational audit assignment or engagement may derive from requests by operating or top management on the one hand, or by the internal audit department itself. Quite often a financial audit will uncover evidence of waste or weak operating controls, and operating management may ask for an audit. Or senior management will request reviews based on information it has received. The chief internal auditor may schedule operational audits in his annual planning activity (see Chapters 2 and 7) based on his judgment as to potential savings. Such audits in many cases will deal with the controls and procedures.

But there will be occasions when an audit will extend to an evaluation of operating performance or efficiency. This is a step beyond an evaluation of systems and procedures, which may let management—and not the auditor—evaluate effectiveness. Indeed, this latter objective—an *effectiveness audit*—is often fraught with danger. Why? Simply because auditors cannot be experts in every phase of operations. Even the presence of engineers or other nonfinancial disciplines on the audit staff does not assure the requisite knowledge. Hence, it is suggested that internal auditors be diligent and prudent in selecting areas for an operational review. Very often the examination will bring to light only obvious deficiencies, unless the audit staff is expert in the field. An organization structure to assist in making more effective audits is discussed in the next section.

Aside from lack of knowledge, there may be other constraints in making an operational-type audit. These may include:

☐ *Time.* Time may be a factor in that the audits often must be performed quickly so that corrective action is taken before major problems develop.

A MANAGEMENT PERSPECTIVE

There is something to be said, therefore, for a continuous program in some areas so that reviews may be made in a relatively short time.

☐ *Cost.* Obviously, cost is a limiting factor. If the cost of an engagement is greater than the potential benefits, it should not be attempted. Perhaps it is well to estimate possible cost savings and other advantages and measure these against the audit cost. (See the section of this chapter on preliminary surveys.)

☐ *Priorities.* There will be occasions when top management requests, for whatever purpose, will take precedence over some operational audits. Then, also, financial audits will quite often be given priority over operating surveys: Existence of potential major fraud or irregularity would be an example inducing a top priority.

☐ *Receptivity.* Finally, there will be times when operating management is hostile to an operational audit. To be sure, this is not a reason to avoid an audit. But such attitudes tend to make audits more difficult and perhaps less effective. Under the circumstances, more congenial areas are often available for review.

In summary, there are some practical limitations as to how many operational reviews may be undertaken in a given company.

KNOWLEDGE NEEDED TO PERFORM AN OPERATIONAL AUDIT

If the question were asked, Who should perform an operational audit? a proper answer might be, Those who are qualified. This raises the point as to what knowledge is required by the auditor to accomplish a quality examination. There is nothing quite so disastrous to the internal audit organization as to have an audit report prepared by untrained people who reach the wrong conclusions, and to have the report discredited by the operating staff. Hopefully, the report review process (see Chapter 13) will catch any major errors or omissions.

Most of those who perform financial audits have acquired a basic knowledge of the principles of accounting, auditing, or internal control from a combination of formal education and on-the-job training. But even in this traditional audit area, much is not known, before audit, of a particular system in a particular company. It must be learned.

Similarly, those who perform "management audits," or operational audits, must learn the specific system. To be sure, the auditor is expected to have at least a general knowledge of the area being reviewed—manufacturing, marketing, information systems, personnel, purchasing, and so forth. This can be gained in part from reading books and periodicals on the subject, as well as studying the procedures or programs of the organization being audited.

But often even such an approach does not equip many auditors with the expertise needed to perform an effective review in many specialty areas. This void can be filled by adding to the audit staff those disciplines that are needed often enough to merit such full-time assistance. Some audit groups include engineers, actuaries, or marketing specialists as staff members.

There is also another method of securing the talent and, at the same time, encouraging more cooperation from the auditee: the use of "task forces" or "teams" made up of some members of the internal audit staff, some members of the organization being audited, and perhaps some non-financial representatives from related functions. These are sometimes called "cooperative audits." For example, the audit team of a manufacturing task force, which includes those knowledgeable in the function and those clearly associated with the function (such as a purchasing member who procures material for the manufacturing group) usually will provide a balanced viewpoint. When the reviews are completed, these temporary team members may return to their regular organization.

Finally, it should be mentioned that independent public accountants are asked to perform operational audits for private-sector clients as well as government clients.

Good Management Practice

Because most operational audits deal with a specific function or subfunction below the general management level, the preceding discussion stresses the need to know the specific functional system, and the use, as part of a team, of "non-auditors" who are specialists. Thus, if a marketing operational audit is being performed, then someone well-versed in the marketing system may provide valuable assistance. But good operational auditing encompasses more than just knowing how a system operates.

Well-conceived operational auditing involves a knowledge of good management practice. To be sure, most internal auditors, with their accounting backgrounds, are somewhat familiar with financial planning and financial controls. But a good operational review must take a broad management view and raise gutty issues, albeit in a diplomatic way—in most instances. All aspects of management must be reviewed. For example, here are some general questions to be investigated—as will be evident from a review of the operational audit questionnaires and programs in the subsequent chapters of Part IX:

- Does management manage? Or do things "just happen"?
- Are authority and responsibility clearly defined?
- Is the organization properly structured?
- Are most levels of management involved to some degree in developing plans?
- Does the financial information allow the performance of each manager, at each echelon, to be measured fairly?

- Does management motivate its employees?
- Is provision made for upgrading skills, and is promoting based on reasonable performance reviews?
- Are there clearly defined relationships between line and staff?

Information pertaining to these and other basic questions relating to good management should be asked by the operational auditor during his interviews at each echelon and as to each related function.

STANDARDS FOR OPERATIONAL AUDITS

In the ordinary examination of financial statements by the independent accountant, the auditor's report, through which he expresses his opinion or disclaims an opinion, states whether or not his examination was made in accordance with GAAS. The GAAS, as approved and adopted by the membership of the AICPA, concern themselves with both the auditor's professional qualities as well as the judgment exercised by him in the performance of his examinations and in his report. Accordingly, there are three categories of such standards.[10]

1. *General standards*—dealing with the qualifications of the auditor and the quality of his work
2. *Standards of field work*—relating to how the examination is to be conducted
3. *Standards of reporting*—dealing with report content

The point to be made is that GAAS exist for financial examinations.

It is highly desirable that those who engage in operational audits should consider applying a somewhat comparable set of standards. One group of standards to be applied in the audit of government activities are those promulgated by the Comptroller General of the United States in cooperation with the AICPA and other federal auditing groups. (See Chapter 5.) Certainly, the standards issued by the IIA should be given due weight.

A checklist for expanded-scope audits has been prepared by the AICPA for the guidance of those interested in such reviews. It is related to the questions of adequate standards, and is outlined in Figure 31-2.[11]

To the extent applicable to operational audits, the reader should review them.

---

[10] Statements on Auditing Standards No. 1, *Codification of Auditing Standards and Procedures* (New York: American Institute of Certified Public Accountants, 1973), p. 5.

[11] Management Advisory Services, Guideline Series No. 6, *Guidelines for C.P.A. Participation in Government Audit Engagements to Evaluate Economy, Efficiency and Program Results* (New York: American Institute of Certified Public Accountants, 1977), pp. 16–18. Copyright © 1977 by the American Institute of Certified Public Accountants.

FIG. 31-2

Checklist for Expanded-Scope Audits

PRE-ENGAGEMENT CHECKLIST

The following checklist for expanded-scope audits involving an evaluation of economy, efficiency, or program results has been prepared to (1) assist CPAs in understanding the nature of each potential engagement; (2) guide those who issue RFPs in providing the desired information; and (3) aid the CPA in structuring a proposal and work program.

The checklist contains a series of questions, which fall into four broad categories:

- *Engagement Environment.* The professional relationship between the CPA and the government entity to be evaluated.
- *Economy and Efficiency.* Elements of the engagement that will affect the CPA's proposal.
- *Program Results.* Elements of the engagement that will affect the CPA's proposal.
- *Professional Proficiency.* The CPA's qualifications to undertake a specific engagement.

Engagement Environment:

1. Who is requesting the evaluation?
2. What motivated the request?
3. Will the requester or recipient be able to implement the report recommendations?
4. Are engagement objectives and scope of work well-defined and attainable?
5. Does the scope entail a constructive piece of work?
6. Is sufficient time allotted for the CPA to complete the engagement?
7. Will the applicable laws and regulations be specified in the engagement agreement?
8. Will the criteria for selecting an independent firm be based on competence as well as price?

Economy and Efficiency:

1. Is there agreement between the CPA and requester on which areas are to be reviewed (e.g., programs, departments, activities, or projects)?
2. Is there a clear understanding of which functional areas are to be reviewed (e.g., personnel utilization, data processing, procurement, financial management, warehousing, inventory management, etc.)?
3. Have there been prior reviews (internal or external) of the same area?
4. Were any actions taken as a result of prior reviews?
5. Will prior reviews be made available to the CPA?
6. Has the requester specified any existing data and reports which may be accepted as reliable without further verification?
7. To what extent does the work to be studied lend itself to measurement?
8. Have criteria for measuring economy and efficiency been established (e.g., does the entity have existing productivity standards)?
9. Have the data related to the established criteria been accumulated?
10. Will the data be available to the CPA?
11. Is routine reporting of productivity a current or feasible practice?
12. To what extent are cost data available?

A MANAGEMENT PERSPECTIVE

Program Results:

1. Are there well-defined program objectives?
2. Are there reasonable, well-defined timetables for achieving program objectives?
3. Have criteria been established for evaluating program results?
4. Are the criteria quantifiable, or at least measureable, and to what extent can the results be measured objectively?
5. Have the data related to the established criteria been accumulated?
6. Will the data be made available to the CPA?
7. Has management prepared a current assessment of the program's results?
8. Have there been any previous external evaluations of the program?
9. Were any actions taken as a result of previous evaluations?
10. Will previous evaluations be made available to the CPA?

Professional Proficiency:

1. Is the CPA familiar with the government environment (e.g., source of funding, related agencies, potential subsequent reviews, etc.)?
2. Does the CPA understand the scope of the engagement?
3. Does the CPA possess or have access to technical skills required to review and evaluate functional areas involved?
4. Does the CPA understand the specific government program and have access to the specific skills needed to evaluate the program results?

BASIC STEPS IN OPERATIONAL AUDITING

Although there is a great similarity in techniques between a financial audit and an operational audit, it is probably fair to state that the latter requires a review that is somewhat more comprehensive than the former, among other reasons because it may be less susceptible to formal structure. Since an operational review must usually satisfy the three purposes of assessing performance, identifying opportunities for improvement, and developing recommendations for such improvements (or further action), an even better understanding of the operations is desirable in an operational audit than in a financial audit.

While the steps of an operational audit may be divided in any number of ways, there are usually at least four basic steps:

1. Familiarization with the physical operations and basic objectives of the segment to be audited. (It is usually a segment, although an entire operation (company) may be involved in a performance audit.
2. Review of the mechanisms used to plan and control the operations and achieve the objective.
3. Appraisal and evaluation of the adequacy and effectiveness of the control mechanisms.
4. Reporting of the findings, usually with recommendations for improvements.

Other authorities segregate the audit into only two phases: the preliminary and the in-depth. The preliminary phase might be said to consist of the familiarization phase and part of the review of the planning and control mechanisms (the latter to be followed by a more in-depth analysis). (See Chapter 11 on how to perform preliminary work.)

This chapter deals with the preliminary phases, and the next nine chapters address specific and in-depth operational audit programs. It should be kept in mind that if the auditor, such as an independent consulting group, is not familiar with the various parts of a company, he may make preliminary surveys of several segments or organizations to determine which ones seem to offer the opportunity of greatest cost savings or improvements. (This assumes he is not directed to make a specific review.) On the other hand, those more familiar with the company, such as its internal auditors, may find that a quick review is helpful in deciding if a particular department in fact does seem to present profit or operational improvement challenges.

Preliminary Phase

Chapter 11 discusses preliminary work. However, with reference to operational audits, especially where the auditor is not unduly knowledgeable of the operations, these comments are applicable. The usual five basic steps in the preliminary phase of a performance audit might include these:

1. Physical tour of the facility
2. Gathering of written data on the potential audit segment
3. Interview with management personnel
4. Limited financial analysis
5. Preparation of survey memorandum

Each of these are commented upon briefly.

Physical Tour of the Facility. The purpose of the preliminary phase is to ascertain whether or not a particular department or segment appears to have sufficient problems to warrant an audit. A survey or "walk-through" of the physical facilities will assist in identifying potential problem areas. Very often there will be a correlation between impressions gained in this physical tour and the problems. Experienced auditors have often observed that sloppy housekeeping is indicative of poor procedures or supervision. Conditions observed by the auditor may be so obvious that they have escaped the attention of the department manager.

This physical inspection, if carefully done with the objective of searching for indications of problem areas, will reveal many things, including the nature of the supervision, subordinates' attitudes about their bosses, the freedom of communication and operation, motivation, and cleanliness. A sense will develop that might not surface in the review of recorded data.

A MANAGEMENT PERSPECTIVE

It is often desirable to have in mind the questions to be asked or conditions to be observed, even though it may be prudent not to take a questionnaire on the tour.[12]

Gathering of Written Data. The auditor, in the context of securing adequate preliminary information on the segment, should secure written data that may be studied for an appraisal of the management practices. In this gathering process, the auditor is not attempting to reach conclusions, but merely to form a data base for planning the audit. The documents may be obtained in the physical tour of the facility or in subsequent interviews with members of management. Examples of the documents that the auditor should attempt to secure include such items as:

- Policy and procedure manuals
- Job descriptions
- Functional outlines (goals and objectives, responsibility and authority of department manager)
- Flow charts
- Organization charts
- Internal audit reports
- Financial statements
- Plan or budget
- Management letter of independent accountants
- Government audit reports
- Catalogs and price lists
- Forms

The absence of some of the basic documents might indicate a problem area. The experienced operational auditor will be familiar with the use of, and need for, documents such as the above.

Interviews With Management Personnel. Ordinarily, the people most knowledgeable about an operation are those who manage it or those closely related to it in terms of related functions, such as the preceding or succeeding sequence of activities. On the other hand, some managers are so immersed in the day-to-day problems—in putting out fires—that problems may not be recognized or the relation between departmental objectives and company objectives may not be perceived. In either event, face-to-face interviews with members of management usually provide essential information as to operational strengths, weaknesses, problem areas, difficulties, and so forth. On this basis, a more complete survey memorandum (and perhaps tentative conclusions) may be developed.

---

[12] See, for example, Flesher and Siewert, *op. cit.*, pp. 29–31.

Among the management types who might be expected to have knowledge of departments other than their own, depending on the area under review, are:

- Chief Executive Officer
- Chief Operating Officer
- Chief Financial Officer
- Other principal functional officers
- Controller
- Chief Internal Auditor
- Department heads:
  —Accounting
  —Payroll
  —Personnel

It may also be desirable to use a questionnaire in the management interview process. Examples of some employed in surveying certain specific departments are illustrated in the book by Flesher and Siewert.[13]

Limited Financial Analysis. The fourth step in the preliminary survey is a limited review of available financial or statistical data. The objective in this phase is to compare both present status and trends of operations with some acceptable standards. These may be industry standards, standards of selected competitors, or even standards within the company. This may be termed "ratio analysis" and compares the surveyed operations with other operations known to be efficient. Suggested ratios include:

- Asset turnover
- Inventory turnover
- Current ratio
- Quick ratio
- Ratio of supervisory to nonsupervisory personnel
- Various expense ratios as related to sales or output (e.g., repairs and compensation)
- Productivity ratios
- Personnel turnover ratios

Related financial analysis would include a review of budget and actual performance, trends in costs, investment per employee, to name a few.

Preparation of Survey Memorandum. The final step in the preliminary survey is the preparation of a relatively short audit report, which is used by

---

[13] *Ibid.*, pp. 38–42.

A MANAGEMENT PERSPECTIVE 31-17

the auditor to determine if an in-depth audit seems appropriate. It is essentially an in-house device that forces the auditor to organize and to briefly summarize his tentative findings from the preliminary work. It is not a definitive document in the sense that final conclusions are not drawn as to any potential weaknesses or problems—if the department is to be audited.

PROGRESSIVELY DIFFICULT LEVELS OF OPERATIONAL AUDITING

Earlier in this chapter, audits were categorized into two types: financial and operational. Operational auditing was further described as covering a broad range—a scope as widely different as are the planning and control activities (i.e., the management activities) of a business.

In developing a program of operational auditing in each company, the chief internal auditor may find it practical to recognize three somewhat distinct management levels that require increasing sophistication and are perhaps fraught with increasing levels of exposure in terms of performing an effective audit. These three levels, which are not necessarily clear-cut in delineation, are as follows:

- Operational auditing—a more restricted definition
- Managerial auditing
- Strategic auditing

Each corresponds with the examination of a different echelon or scope of management function.

Operational Auditing

For differentiation purposes, operational auditing might be defined as relating to operational control. Emphasis is on a review of operational control procedures to assure that specific transactions or tasks are conducted both effectively and efficiently. This type of operational auditing may be regarded as the first echelon. the areas examined in many ways relate to routine activities albeit important ones. The measurements are more objective and involve a lesser knowledge of the activity; they do not relate to the more judgmental activities of the management. Much of the operational auditing at this stage of development takes place at this echelon.

Management Auditing

The second level of operational auditing might be described as management auditing. To be sure, some routine activities are covered, but it extends into areas less susceptible to measurement, including such matters as the compatibility of differing organizational goals; the achievability of the plans, encompassing financial planning, personnel planning, and production planning and scheduling; and the communicating and interacting of the various plan segments and revisions. In this arena, some judgments may be more subjective. And certainly a higher degree of knowledge and experience is required to perform successful auditing in this level of management activity.

Strategic Auditing

The third, and most sophisticated, level of auditing relates to the corporate strategy and involves a critical review of the highest management level in the company: senior management and the board of directors. It seeks to judge the wisdom of the strategic goals and objectives, the allocation of resources (and the means to secure them), and the examination of the ways to arrive at the goals. It obviously would require qualifications and judgments of a high order.

In few companies is this type of operational auditing a reality. And whether it should be is a question to be resolved by each management. To satisfy the political elements of the equations, it might be helpful if a board member were a part of the audit team. Certainly an enlightened management and a courageous board of directors can see the advantage of this type of audit. It provides evidence that most company management decisions are or are not being made on a judicious basis. Given the economic pressures on business, the rapidly changing environment, the quickened growth of new technologies, and so on, at least some thought should be given to the increasingly sophisticated type of operational audit by a competent staff.

REPORTS ON OPERATIONAL AUDITS

While the principles may be the same for an operational audit report, as compared to a financial-type audit, the application may differ in emphasis. It bears mentioning that most addressees of operational audits are (1) not financially trained, (2) not necessarily familiar with financial jargon, (3) not interested in audit procedures, and (4) interested solely in the audit findings.

The purpose of the audit report is to communicate ideas in a simple and easily understood manner, and to get those ideas acted upon. It is, or should be, a sales document, designed to get attention.

The contents of an operational audit report, of course, vary depending on the kinds of problems disclosed, the nature of the operation, and so forth. However, a good report should contain at least these elements:

☐ *The objectives and scope of the engagement.* In many instances not all activities of a department or entity are audited, and the covered items should be made known.

A MANAGEMENT PERSPECTIVE

☐ *The general procedures used, stated briefly.* Perhaps the rationale for their use may be stated, and mention should be made of any limitations imposed on the auditor. Often, the auditor's measurement criteria should be identified.

☐ *Specific findings, which are enumerated.* These should be factual statements supported by the working papers.

☐ *Recommendations, if any, which are clearly stated.* In some instances, the sole recommendation might be further study by the auditee.

Finally, an audit may be judged by the apparent quality of the audit report. Typing errors, misspelled words, inconsistent headings, and handwritten notes all detract from the perceived quality of the audit. A typical reaction: "If the auditor can't even spell correctly, how can I depend on the report?" After spending sizeable sums making an audit, certainly the final report deserves to be proofread for errors and inconsistencies.

This report, in most respects, is substantially similar to one relating to a financial-type audit. For the basic commonsense principles, the reader is referred to Chapter 12.

Just as standards have been developed for auditing procedures, so also reporting standards for economy and efficiency audits and program results audits have been established by the GAO. Inasmuch as they deal specifically with operational audits, the reader may find the GAO Standards helpful. (See Chapter 5.)

SUGGESTED READING

Flesher, Dale I., and Stewart Siewert. *Independent Auditor's Guide to Operational Auditing*. New York: John Wiley & Sons, 1982.

Hubert, Leo. *Auditing the Performance of Management*. Belmont, Calif.: Lifetime Learning Publications, a division of Wadsworth, Inc., 1979.

Lindberg, Roy A., and Theodore Cohn. *Operations Auditing*. New York: American Management Association, 1972.

Sawyer, Lawrence B. *The Practice of Modern Internal Auditing*, 2nd ed. Altamonte Springs, Fla.: The Institute of Internal Auditors, 1981.

CHAPTER **32**

Financial Management

Introduction 1	Basics for an Operating Audit 11
Expanding Role of the Financial Executive 2	The Functional Outline 12
Environmental Changes 2	The Finance Organization Structure ... 12
Technological Changes 3	**Illustrative Audit Questionnaire for Financial Activities** 15
Government Impact 3	
Internal Business Changes 4	**Financial Management Audit Programs** 27
Nature of the Financial Function 5	**Illustrative Audit Findings** 45
Financial Management Objectives 6	**Segment Operational Audits** 55
Organizing and Managing the Financial Function 11	Audit Program for Long-Term Liabilities 56

Fig. 32-1	Functional Outline—Senior Vice-President–Finance	13
Fig. 32-2	Financial Department Organization Chart	15
Fig. 32-3	Cash Management Control Questionnaire	16
Fig. 32-4	Quarterly Cash Forecasting Audit Program	28
Fig. 32-5	Audit Program—Financial Management	30
Fig. 32-6	Audit Report Recommending Improvements in Cash Management Procedures	47

INTRODUCTION

To many it might seem that an operations audit of the financial management function would be a simple task for the professionally trained internal auditor. With his background in accounting, the language of business, and, in many instances, the experience gained as a CPA, many would presume he is fully qualified to review the financial activities and rather quickly reach conclusions as to the efficiency and effectiveness of the operations.

But it is a far cry from a good background in accounting to the ability to perceive what constitutes sound financial policy and practice, what factors of the business must be emphasized in sound financial planning and control, and what relationships must be developed, both internally and externally, to best serve the financial interests of the enterprise.

Even if the internal auditor properly perceives the financial needs of the firm that employs him, it is quite another task to discretely prescribe the remedy in a manner that secures results. This assignment can be made even more difficult if the internal audit organization is not properly situated in the structure, and if the chief financial officers are not sufficiently professional in their outlook.

In this chapter, the authors attempt to take a broad management viewpoint of just what the financial function should encompass to be truly effective, and cover some of the pitfalls and solutions.

EXPANDING ROLE OF THE FINANCIAL EXECUTIVE

What may be said today about the functions of the financial executive could have been stated two decades ago—only now the signals are stronger. The 1960s, in retrospect, seem like a stable, tranquil period. The financially turbulent 1970s have been succeeded by the even more volatile era of the 1980s. Most financial executives would probably agree that these stormy economic conditions have had a great influence in literally catapulting their role from that of recordkeeper, or bookkeeper, or historian, to a forward-thinking highly analytical, highly vital function in modern business.

But there are a great many forces that have combined at the same juncture to cause an explosive change. These influences may be summarized in the following.

Environmental Changes

Environmental changes include both economic and social conditions.

- ☐ *Economic*
  - *High inflation rates.* This condition has fostered greater flexibility and resourcefulness in such matters as cost control, pricing policy, purchasing policy, etc.
  - *Increased competition and greater internationalism.* These influences have demanded quicker responses in the marketplace, as well as in the financial markets.
  - *Changes in the various capital markets.* The continuous need for capital has dramatically changed both the sources and terms for securing the required funds. This condition has increased the analytical demands

placed upon the financial executive, to say nothing of the communication skills, and the need for innovative financial thinking.

- *More volatile economic weather.* Stormy economic conditions require more vigilance in detecting trends or drifts, more critical analyses, and the need for improved instruments to sense threats and opportunities by peering farther into the future.

☐ *Social.* To be sure, the main thrust of business is on economic markets. But there probably also exists a greater social conscience than formerly, which causes business management to weigh some noneconomic factors, undertake more impact studies, and relate to the broader social movements.

Technological Changes

Movement in the technological field is causing a change in the methodology employed by financial executives, and is further accelerating the pace of analysis. More sophisticated analysis is necessary. The technological conversion is twofold:

1. *Computerization.* Much of the tedious record keeping and analysis, account by account, now is done by computer, with the simultaneous treatment of the several accounts involving the same transaction. In some instances, real time reporting is required. And, of course, new systems and procedures and internal controls are a necessity.
2. *Improved communication devices.* Direct link-up between factory and corporate office, among banks and lending institutions, and between foreign and domestic facilities is changing the methods of reporting and the handling of transactions.

Government Impact

While the influence of government on business may or may not be receding in some areas, it remains a significant factor. Again, there are two facets to be reckoned with:

1. *Tax laws and regulations.* Complicated and ever-changing tax laws at the federal, state, and local, as well as foreign, levels affect financing and investing decisions, to say nothing of reporting and monitoring requirements.
2. *Other regulatory agencies.* There is an abundance of regulations that relate to the environment and ways of doing business. Some of the more active areas involve such agencies or acts as the following:
   - SEC
   - FTC
   - IRS
   - Interstate Commerce Commission (ICC)
   - The Economic Recovery Tax Act of 1981 (ERTA)

- Revenue Act of 1978
- FCPA
- ERISA
- Tax Equity and Fiscal Responsibility Act of 1982 (TEFRA)
- Tax Reform Act of 1986

Internal Business Changes

Of course, not all pressures or influences are external. The business world is dynamic, and changes occurring within business itself force behavior modifications. Some of these changes are discussed in the following paragraphs.

- ☐ *Management style and organization structure is changing.* For example, the tendency toward decentralization in management causes changes in internal checks and balances, reporting methods, and accounting systems.
- ☐ *Greater significance of internal cash flow.* Given periodic tightness of credit, greater reliance must be placed on internal cash flow as a source of funds. Ways and means must be found to accelerate internal cash generation and to consider the amount and timing of the cash inflows from new investments, as well as profitability.
- ☐ *Growth in the adaption and use of strategic or long-range planning.* This dimension places new demands on the financial officer, and more closely integrates tactical or short-term planning with the long range plan. It forces a longer time horizon in which to consider financial markets, which is all to the good.
- ☐ *Growth in the sophistication of financial management itself.* Thus, the old methods of handling the finances, making short-term investments, allocating capital resources, reporting performance, and analyzing acquisitions no longer are adequate.

    The Accountants' Method, Payback Method, or Operator's Method of calculating the desirability of a capital investment is passé. The internal rate of return, recognizing the time value of money, is a must. Probability and sensitivity analysis is required. Funds must be invested, even overnight, to improve earnings. Telegraphic transfers of funds are commonplace. Simulation is a necessity. The financial executive must be aware of mathematical techniques, international finance risks and sources, and cost behavior—all of which are useful in supplying better and more rapid answers to complex business problems.

For an effective operational audit of financial management, the internal auditor must be reasonably familiar with the new analytical techniques and their uses. He must see if they are being properly employed, if employed at all, in solving complicated financial issues. There is no longer time for the bookkeeper mentality, the timid agreement with the chief executive officer (CEO), or the rabbit's foot executive. It must be determined whether the

FINANCIAL MANAGEMENT

new techniques are useful, and if they are to be employed; that the financial objectives and goals are proper; that the financial executive is communicating effectively and with the most appropriate tools; and that the right answers are being generated and transmitted in a timely fashion to the other members of management and the outside financial community.

NATURE OF THE FINANCIAL FUNCTION

The financial function may be categorized or broken into any number of segments. The authors believe the following characterization is the most useful in terms of analyzing the function's activities and their effectiveness:

1. Organizational and management activities
   - ☐ Organization structure
   - ☐ Managerial development
   - ☐ Communications—intradepartmental and with other functions
   - ☐ Budgeting and related financial department controls
2. Fund-oriented activities
   - ☐ Cash administration
   - ☐ Fund acquisition
     - Commercial banks
     - Long-term investors
   - ☐ Investor relations
   - ☐ Retirement fund administration
3. Accounting
   - ☐ Policies
   - ☐ Systems and procedures
     - Proper account segregation
     - Proper records
   - ☐ Internal controls
   - ☐ Financial statement preparation
4. Planning
   - ☐ Long-range plan—strategic planning
   - ☐ Annual plan—budgets and tactical plan
   - ☐ Capital budgets as part of the above
5. Accounting controls
   - ☐ Systems and procedures
   - ☐ Setting and revising standards, where applicable
   - ☐ Reporting actual and standard performance
   - ☐ Analysis of trends and relationships
6. Reporting
   - ☐ Internal management reports

- ☐ Shareholder reporting
- ☐ Other external reporting to creditors, financial analysts, etc.
7. Internal auditing
    - ☐ Financial audits
    - ☐ Operational audits
    - ☐ Electronic data processing audits
    - ☐ Internal control audits
    - ☐ Standards of business conduct audits
    - ☐ Special fraud investigations
8. Taxes
    - ☐ Tax planning
    - ☐ Return preparation:
        - Federal
        - State
        - Local
        - Foreign
9. Insurance
    - ☐ Property and casualty
    - ☐ Liability
    - ☐ Health and personal, etc.
10. Other
    - ☐ Relations with independent accountants
    - ☐ Governmental relations, where applicable
    - ☐ Financial analysis—special
    - ☐ Miscellaneous
        - Office management
        - Data processing coordination

These functions and some of the essential characteristics to be examined in the context of an operational audit are reviewed in this chapter.

FINANCIAL MANAGEMENT OBJECTIVES

The principal objective of the financial management of an enterprise should be the successful implementation of the basic financial policy. But financial policy, in the eyes of many, relates chiefly to the acquisition of funds. Yet, financial management extends to activities far beyond the financing of the business, and into the related planning and control aspects. As the starting point in an operational audit of the financial management, the following are suggested as financial management objectives against which the activities should be measured.

1. *Successful implementation of the financial policy objectives, which could include these two objectives:*
    - ☐ To so arrange the financing, and assist in resource allocation, to the end

that the *owners*—the shareholders—over the longer term will secure the maximum benefits. The benefits ordinarily will be two-fold in nature: capital appreciation and dividends. The benefits received by the owners should be consistent with the corporate obligations to the other *stakeholders*, including:
- Suppliers of other capial (e.g., long-term lenders and commercial banks)
- Suppliers of materials and services
- Customers
- Employees
- The general public

☐ To provide for a sound capital and financial structure over the longer term, which will enable the enterprise to:
- Weather any reasonable storm, be it of a general economic nature (e.g., a severe depression), within the industry, or restricted solely to the company.
- Tap the most advantageous pools of capital.
- Secure the necessary funds, on an economical basis, to support corporate growth over the years.

2. *Cash management/long-term investment objectives*. Within the context of the financial policy objectives, these further supplementary objectives should be attained:

☐ *Cash management:*
- Provision of adequate cash to meet operating needs
- Where appropriate, maintenance of adequate cash balances to support commercial bank lines
- Avoidance of excessive cash balances through investment in appropriate short-term vehicles, including overnight
- Adequate internal accounting controls and accountability for cash receipts until such time as they are placed in the proper depository
- Adequate internal controls and procedures to assure that disbursements are made for only approved purposes, including electronic transfers
- Maintenance of adequate, but simple, cash records
- Use of the latest proven technology to improve cash management, including electronic fund transfers, non-check-payment mechanisms, and computer and high-speed data transmission

☐ *Temporary investments:*
- Optimize the return from temporary investments while giving due weight to:
  — Safety of principal
  — Marketability
  — Price stability
  — Yield
  — Maturity

- Give due consideration to the restrictions on temporary investments, as approved by the board of directors, relating to these constraints:
  — Most appropriate instrument as warranted by current market conditions
  — Maximum investment, by type of security
  — Credit rating of issuer
  — Maximum maturity
- Maximize the amount available for temporary investment by control of cash flow, appropriate control of receipts and disbursements, use of most advantageous banks, etc.

☐ *Long-term investments.* This category includes (1) investments in securities of a long-term nature, so classified in the balance sheet, and (2) investments in retirement fund assets. Objectives for these expenditures include the following:
- Long-term investments will be made, consistent with the authorization of the board, (1) in equity or nonequity placement of funds, in the United States, Canada, or overseas, that further the strategic objectives of the enterprise, or (2) as appropriate, in venture capital projects either alone or with suitable partners, or (3) as a minority interest, with the objective of penetrating selected foreign markets.
  — The return on such investments, viewed over a period of time, shall be 5 percentage points above the current cost of capital at the time of expenditure.
- Investment in retirement fund assets will be governed as follows:
  — Corporate policy is to invest in assets for total return over a period of several years, and not to emphasize the return on any particular segment (i.e., real estate, equities, or fixed income investment).
  — Equity investments in the aggregate should yield not less than 15 percent compounded over the period of the business cycle. As a supplemental objective, such funds should outperform the S&P 500 Index by 10 percent.
  — Fixed income securities should earn at least 9 percent over the three- to five-year cycle, and should be 10 percent or more than the Salomon Brothers High Grade Corporate Bond Performance Index (or any comparable index).
  — Real estate investments should be targeted to earn about 20 percent more than the equity securities.
  — All investments shall be governed by the general guidelines issued by the board on 6/17/XX as to risk, restrictions, reporting, and accountability.

3. *Cost-effective implementation of accounting policies such that:*
   ☐ There is developed and maintained an accounting system that accomplishes the proper recording and reporting, on the basis of generally accepted accounting principles, of all operations, transactions, assets, liabilities, and net worth of the company.
   ☐ An appropriate cost accounting system is developed and maintained for

FINANCIAL MANAGEMENT 32-9

the measurement and reporting of operating efficiency, the costing of products, production, shipments, and inventory.

☐ The system of internal controls is developed and maintained sufficient to provide reasonable assurance that (1) transactions are executed in accordance with management's general or specific authorization; (2) transactions are recorded as necessary to permit the preparation of the financial statements in conformity with generally accepted accounting principles or any other criteria applicable to such statements, and to maintain accountability for assets; (3) access to assets is permitted only in accordance with the general or specific authorization of management; and (4) the recorded accountability for assets is compared periodically with the existing assets, and appropriate action is taken.

☐ The accounts are maintained with proper segregation according to accountability and responsibility to meet management needs regarding assets, liabilities, and net worth, and additionally to inform as to behavior pattern for costs, expenses, and revenues.

☐ Proper and effective relations with the independent public accountants are maintained.

4. *With respect to all financial and related planning activities, effective implementation of these actions:*

    ☐ Provide for the installation and maintenance of adequate and practical systems and procedures for the preparation of the annual business plan and related budgets, as well as for the financial aspects of the strategic or long-range plan.

    ☐ Provide assistance to management, at all applicable levels, in the setting of proper financial, or financially expressed, goals and objectives.

    ☐ Coordinate the preparation of the short-term business plans, and the financial aspects of the long-range plan; consolidate the related financial statements and supporting schedules and exhibits.

    ☐ Provide to management a financial appraisal of the short-term plan, including the critical assumptions or premises, as measured by appropriate yardsticks.

    ☐ Provide, as applicable, assistance in the proper allocation of corporate resources to the various functions or profit centers or projects (capital facilities, and working capital).

    ☐ Provide sound criteria and procedures for selecting the proper capital expenditure projects.

5. *In the context of accounting control of operations (i.e., provision of control data to line managers), economic and effective implementation of these functions:*

    ☐ The installation and maintenance of the necessary systems and procedures on a cost-effective basis.

    ☐ Setting of standards, or assisting in setting standards, or evaluating standards as may be applicable, and the revising of the standards for control applications.

    ☐ Reporting actual and standard performance to line management on a timely and economical basis and in an appropriate format.

☐ Analyzing trends and relationships of both costs and revenues for the use of line management in controlling costs.

6. *Cost-effective use of the most modern, but proven, techniques to carry out the reporting function as applied to financial and related data.* The reporting system should communicate effectively the desired information, whether written or oral, and whether computer-produced or otherwise. This objective applies to reports to all addressees, such as shareholders, governmental agencies, stock exchanges, lenders, financial analysts, the general public, creditors, and management.

    It is expected that appropriate management reports will incorporate the established company practices, as long as applicable, as to the principles of responsibility reporting, exception reporting, interpreted reporting, and comparative reporting.

7. *Internal auditing.* The overall objective of the internal audit function is to assist all members of management in the effective discharge of their responsibilities by furnishing them with analysis, appraisals, recommendations, and pertinent comments concerning the activities reviewed.[1]

    Supplementing this basic overall objective, in most companies, the internal audit staff is expected to meet these sub-objectives, among others:

    ☐ Review and appraise the soundness, adequacy and application of accounting, financial and other operating controls, and promote effective control at a reasonable cost.

    ☐ Determine the extent of compliance with the established company policies, plans, and procedures.

    ☐ Ascertain the extent to which the company assets are accounted for and safeguarded against loss.

    ☐ Determine the degree of reliability of management data developed within the enterprise.

    ☐ Appraise the quality and cost-effectiveness of performance in carrying out assigned responsibilities.

    ☐ Where applicable or practical, review efficiency and effectiveness, and the need for the function examined, and make recommendations for operating improvements.

8. *Tax planning and administration.* Given the scope and numerous forms of taxes imposed by federal, state, local, and foreign governments on the private business enterprise, the objectives of tax management should include these:

    ☐ Plan and structure the company tax practices, insofar as possible, to minimize the tax burden. This is but another way of saying take advantage of the tax laws in terms of both strategy and tactics.

    ☐ Ensure that the company tax obligations are satisfied, including the timely filing of the necessary forms and the making of the appropriate payments.

---

[1] See Chapter 2.

9. *Insurance (risk) management:*
   - ☐ Ascertain the insurable hazards of the company as related to people, properties, operations, contract or governmental requirements, or any others.
   - ☐ Determine the extent of exposure and risk, and the most cost-effective manner of reducing the risk to acceptable proportions, and take appropriate action consistent with instructions from management.
10. *Other financial management objectives.* The previous comments have related to the financial management objectives for the major organizational units or functions. However, in given circumstances, there may be other applicable goals to assist line management, or in special circumstances, to:
    - ☐ Maintain an effective relationship as to financial aspects of representatives of the U.S. government or other government agencies in the administration of contracts.
    - ☐ Effectively administer profit improvement programs.
    - ☐ Perform all necessary financial analyses to assist management (e.g., acquisitions and mergers, cost and revenue trends, rate-making in regulated companies, special systems and procedures studies, and electronic data processing installations).
    - ☐ Train an adequate and competent financial staff.

The basic purpose of listing some of the more important financial management objectives is to help make the internal auditor aware of the broad scope of activities covered by the function, matters that should be under the cognizance of an aggressive financial manager, and the objectives the financial officer should be meeting, and that the internal auditor should perhaps be testing or appraising. Hopefully, a comprehensive awareness may cause the auditor to check the validity of the company objectives in some instances.

ORGANIZING AND MANAGING THE FINANCIAL FUNCTION

Basics for an Operating Audit

In most successful businesses, special knowledge is required in each of the major functions to make them effective, and finance is no exception. It is presumptuous to discuss how the many technical aspects of each major activity should be handled. Rather, the approach here is to briefly describe the basic functions included in each activity, and the objectives of each such operation. If the objectives are known, it is easier to review activities and reach a judgment on the efficiency and effectiveness in many instances, without necessarily knowing all of the technical aspects.

The expectations of the functions, as revealed in the job descriptions and other pronouncements, and an understanding of the organization structure, is perhaps an essential preliminary to completing a questionnaire on the function and then developing the audit program.

The Functional Outline

Financial management is a basic function of every business enterprise, regardless of its product, service, or size. To survive and grow, the concern must secure and manage funds and safeguard its assets. In other words it must plan and control the financial activities. Normally, one executive is assigned the responsibility for such activities, and his title is usually vice-president–finance, or treasurer, although numerous others exist.

The duties and responsibilities of the chief financial officer usually emphasize his role in policy-making and in providing a link between the financial organization and other segments of the business, including top management, line management, and the board of directors. A great many factors influence what his duties and responsibilities are and, hence, those of the financial organization. In the final analysis, the needs of the business and the ability and interests of other members of top management play a part in fashioning the exact functions. But a review of the functional outline for the position, and those of other companies, is a good starting point in understanding the activities. The corporate functional outline of the senior vice-president–finance of a major manufacturing company is shown in Figure 32-1.[2] A funcational outline should exist for each financial executive.

The Finance Organization Structure

The organization structure of the financial activities reflects, or should reflect, the assignment of functions to various financial executives. And, of course, the structure affects the effectiveness and efficiency with which the sundry operations are carried out.

There are a number of factors or influences that have substantial bearing on the assignment of functions among the various executives, including:

- Certificate of incorporation of bylaws.
- Size of the company.
- Competence and personality of the individual.
- Historical events pertaining to the company.
- Developing concepts of what each position should be responsible for.

Suffice it to say that some state statutes spell out the duties of certain financial officers, which, with other factors, are reflected in the bylaws of the company. Further, as a company grows in size, the separation of the controllership and treasurer functions assumes new dimensions, as do other

---

[2] Position descriptions for financial executives in several different companies and industries are contained in Edwin P. Harkins, "Organizing and Managing the Corporate Financial Function," *Studies in Business Policy*, No. 129 (New York: National Industrial Conference Board, 1969), and Edward T. Curtis, "Company Organization of the Finance Function," *AMA Research Study 55* (New York: American Management Association, 1969).

FIG. 32-1

Functional Outline—Senior Vice-President–Finance

SUMMARY:

The Senior Vice President–Finance, as the principal financial officer of the corporation, is responsible to the Chairman and Chief Executive Officer for creating and maintaining an effective financial management program. Financial management activities include accounting, budgeting, financial planning, reporting and analysis, internal auditing, insurance, taxes, property administration, financing, cash management, renegotiation, financial aspects of employee group insurance and retirement and savings plans, and such other related financial matters as may be necessary to provide for the continued growth and stability of the company.

SPECIFIC RESPONSIBILITIES:

1. Analyzes the financial and economic aspects of all company business activities as they relate to current, near- and long-term financial requirements
2. Directs regular analyses of the current financial position of the corporation to identify any significant deviations from sound financial planning or the sound allocation of capital funds; develops and recommends corrective action where necessary
3. Analyzes the financial and economic impact of proposals for the acquisition of other companies and/or the sale or lease of major properties, and makes recommendations in relation thereto
4. As specified by the Executive Office, takes the actions necessary to assure that company objectives with respect to acquisitions, joint ventures, licenses, and divestitures are fulfilled
5. Formulates or reviews and approves the principal financial policies of the company
6. Develops and recommends short- and long-term cash, financing, investment, pension plan, and dividend policies and plans for approval by the Board of Directors
7. Represents the company in establishing and maintaining sound relationships with banks, investment bankers, and other financial institutions and groups
8. Maintains relations with existing and potential professional financial community investors on all financial matters
9. Provides for appropriate liaison with regulating bodies at local, state, and national levels
10. Directs the preparation of or authorizes the release of all financial data and reports developed for the Board of Directors, shareholders, or lending institutions
11. Develops and conducts an internal audit program to assist all members of management in the effective discharge of their responsibilities by furnishing them with objective analyses, appraisals, recommendations, and pertinent comments concerning the activities reviewed
12. Determines that all members of top management are provided with operating and financial data as required and on a timely basis to enable them to control their individual areas of responsibility and meet established budgets and goals
13. Furnishes policy direction to division and subsidiary management with regard to overall financial matters and advises and assists them in the fulfillment of their functions

(continued)

FIG. 32-1 (cont'd)

14. Directs the administration of the financial aspects of the company's insurance, employee group insurance, retirement, and savings plans
15. Reviews for concurrence the organizational structure of division and subsidiary financial groups, including proposed changes thereto, and the selection, transfer, or termination of key employees
16. Reviews and evaluates the effectiveness of division and subsidiary financial activities; makes recommendations to the general managers, subsidiary presidents, or the Executive Office, as appropriate
17. Consults with and advises the Executive Office with regard to corporate long-range, worldwide, financial objectives
18. Keeps the Executive Office and the Board of Directors informed regarding operating results and the financial position of the corporation

internal control considerations. Such factors as these change the concept of the board of directors as to what the various positions should entail. As always, the competence, experience, qualifications, and personality of the individual influences the assignment of functions. This factor alone often explains why a given officer will perform certain duties in one company and not in another.

Given different industries, size of companies, and the degree of sophistication in financial management, any number of organization structures are possible. Some, for example, have dual reporting relationships—one for the treasurer and another for the controller.[3] However, for a medium-sized to large company, with one financial executive reporting to the CEO and responsible for all financial matters, the structure reflected in Figure 32-2 is typical.

Several features may be noted:

- Because of influence in policy and substantial interface with top management and the board of directors, the chief financial executive reports to the CEO.
- To give the chief internal auditor adequate status, and permit him to be independent of the treasurer or controller, whose functions he audits, yet provide him with supervision knowledgeable in the financial field, he reports to the senior vice-president–finance. He does, however, have direct access to the chairman of the audit committee (an independent board member).
- Given the desirability of separating the custodial and fund-oriented duties from the control-type duties, the positions of treasurer and controller are held by two different individuals.

A study of the specific needs and circumstances of the company, and the proper finance organization structure, should be an early subject for review in any operational audit of the financial activities.

---

[3] The reader will note many patterns in the reference in note 2 above.

FIG. 32-2
Financial Department Organization Chart

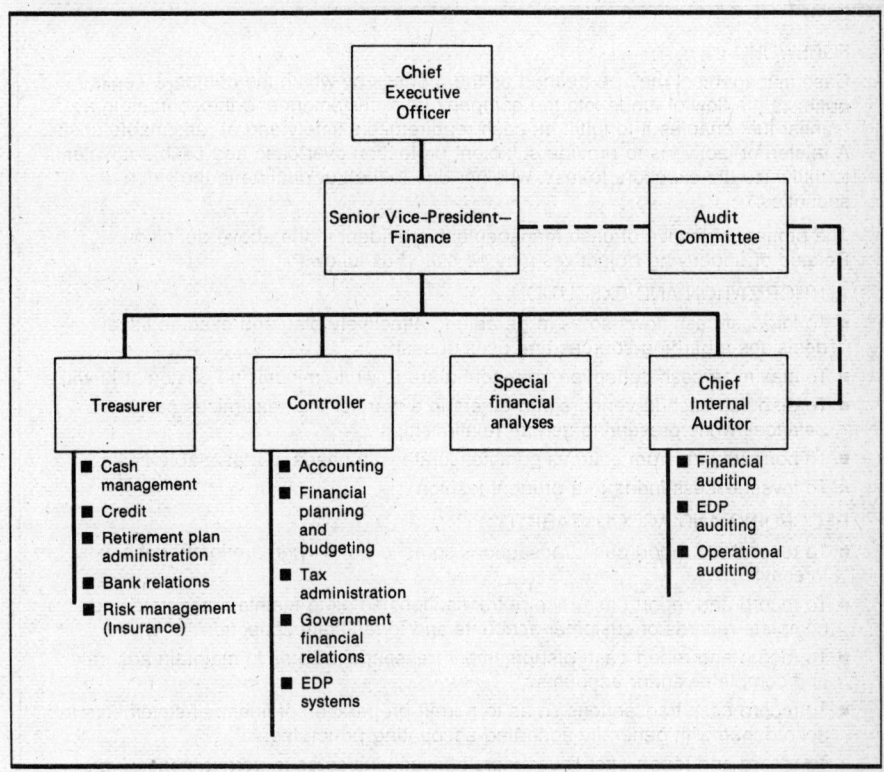

ILLUSTRATIVE AUDIT QUESTIONNAIRE FOR FINANCIAL ACTIVITIES

An audit questionnaire is highly desirable in developing an effective audit program. Among other things, it helps the auditor understand the operation, and usually highlights those areas of special weakness which need an expanded review.

The financial function is so broad in scope and so complex that often it is not practical to do an operation audit on all activities at one time or within a limited time span. Usually, it is accomplished in segments. Because of space and time constraints, an illustrative questionnaire is presented in Figure 32-3 for just one of the many facets: cash management. As always, the questionnaire must be adapted to the specific circumstances.

(continued on page 32-27)

FIG. 32-3
Cash Management Control Questionnaire

FOREWORD:

Cash management may be defined as the process by which the company seeks to optimize the flow of funds into the company from customers and the sources in a manner that enables it to fulfill all cash requirements timely and at reasonable costs. A related objective is to provide sufficient protection over cash and cash equivalents to minimize the exposure to loss, whether due to theft or decline in the value of securities.

The primary objective of cash management is evident in the above definition. Related or underlying objectives may be stated as follows.

AUTHORIZATION AND EXECUTION:
- To forecast cash flows so as to be able to effectively plan and execute fiscal decisions regarding sources and uses of cash
- To maximize cash collection from normal trade while minimizing customer ill will
- To disburse cash to vendors and others in a manner that maximizes cash balances while preserving vendor relationships
- To borrow funds from sources commensurate with needs at reasonable costs
- To invest excess funds in a prudent fashion

RECORDING AND ACCOUNTABILITY:
- To record and report cash transactions so as to permit preparation of cash forecasts
- To record and report cash receipt transactions so as to maintain accurate and complete records of customer accounts and to facilitate collection
- To record and report cash disbursement transactions so as to maintain accurate and complete vendor accounts
- To record cash transactions so as to permit preparation of financial statements in accordance with generally accepted accounting principles
- To record and report cash investment transactions so as to permit monitoring of investment decisions

SAFEGUARDING:
- To restrict access to cash and cash securities to authorized personnel
- To restrict access to cash records and information to authorized personnel
- To reasonably assure that systems of control provide for adequate back-up and recovery in the event of business interruption and that insurable risks are appropriately covered
- To reasonably assure that cash transactions and activities are executed pursuant to management's general or specific authorization

In most companies the foregoing objectives are usually the responsibility of the corporate finance function and involve the offices of the treasurer and controller, respectively. Some responsibilities, such as collections and vendor payments, may be delegated to organizational units.

The extent of involvement of the controller, the treasurer, and the senior financial officer of the company will vary among companies. Accordingly, this questionnaire is designed along functional, as opposed to departmental, lines as follows:

- Cash forecasting
- Cash collection
- Cash disbursements

- Cash borrowing
- Cash investing

In addition, much of the information necessary to effectively manage the finance function is provided by electronic data processing techniques. This questionnaire covers such EDP involvement to the extent applicable.

	Response	
	Yes	No

I. CASH FORECASTING:

A. Authorization and Execution:

1. Do techniques include a formal procedural statement that sets forth techniques used to forecast cash flows? ☐ ☐

2. Has authority for executing the following activities been specified in writing for:
   a. Cash forecasting methodology ☐ ☐
   b. Access to cash forecasting data ☐ ☐
   c. Preparation of cash forecasts ☐ ☐
   d. Approval of cash forecasts ☐ ☐
   e. Distribution of cash forecasts ☐ ☐

3. Are cash forecasts prepared so as to consider all sources and uses of cash within the organizational unit? ☐ ☐
   a. Sources include:
      - Collection of customer accounts
      - Rebates and refunds from suppliers
      - Advances from customers
      - Short-term bank borrowings
      - Long-term debt transactions
      - Sales of company stock
      - Sales of assets
   b. Uses include:
      - Payment of trade accounts
      - Generation of payroll
      - Funding of facilities and equipment needs
      - Payments to discharge indebtedness
      - Payment of taxes
      - Dividend and interest payments
      - Investment

4. Are cash forecasts prepared in sufficient detail (e.g., by company segment or by product line) to permit judgments to be made as to their quality and reliability? ☐ ☐

5. Are cash forecasts prepared consistently and regularly in sufficient frequency to maximize their accuracy and usefulness? ☐ ☐

(continued)

FIG. 32-3 *(cont'd)*

	Response	
	Yes	No
6. Are cash forecasts prepared on both short- and long-term bases?	☐	☐
7. Are cash forecasts prepared from or integrated with other forward-looking reports such as annual budgets and/or business plans?	☐	☐
8. Are cash forecasts prepared from reliable sources? Sources usually considered reliable include: ■ Annual business plans ■ Historical financial statement ■ Cash receipts and disbursement records ■ Knowledgeable personnel	☐	☐
9. Are multiple cash forecasts made under varying assumptions and pursuant to different techniques for maximum flexibility and accuracy? Among the techniques available are: ■ Receipts and disbursements method ■ Adjusted net income method ■ Predetermined balance sheet method	☐	☐
10. Do techniques for cash forecasting utilize electronic data processing services? If the answer to this question is yes, refer to Section V on EDP.	☐	☐
B. Recording and Accountability:		
1. Are cash forecasts recorded in a detailed and organized fashion?	☐	☐
2. Are cash forecasts recorded in a fashion that permits subsequent comparison to actual cash transactions?	☐	☐
3. Are comparisons of cash forecasts with actual results made from time to time?	☐	☐
4. Are such comparisons furnished to the chief general officer and/or the treasurer and controller?	☐	☐
5. Does the cash forecasting report process focus attention on future cash shortages or excesses for management attention and action?	☐	☐
C. Safeguarding:		
1. Is access to cash forecast data restricted to authorized personnel?	☐	☐
2. Are cash forecast records reasonably protected from theft or loss due to fire and similar hazards?	☐	☐
3. Has provision been made for adequate back-up of vital records in the event of loss or destruction?	☐	☐

	Response	
	Yes	No

II. CASH COLLECTION:

A. Authorization and Execution:

1. Do procedures and/or policies specify authority for:
   a. Establishing collection techniques? ☐ ☐
   b. Approving credit and credit policy? ☐ ☐
   c. Approving depository accounts? ☐ ☐
   d. Executing cash transfers, including electronic cash transfers? ☐ ☐
   e. Approving cash transfers, including electronic cash transfers? ☐ ☐

2. Are the company's collection terms communicated to customers in connection with each sale or exchange? ☐ ☐

3. Do procedures provide for prompt billing in accordance with agreed-upon terms? ☐ ☐

4. Is credit policy determined, in part, upon considering the impact of credit policy on competitive posture? ☐ ☐

5. If customer base is broad, does the organizational unit employ decentralized collection techniques so that customer checks may be more promptly deposited? ☐ ☐

6. Has appropriate consideration been given to offering discounts to speed collection? ☐ ☐

7. For organizational units with long-term contracts, are procedures integrated with contractual requirements to minimize administrative delays? ☐ ☐

8. For organizational units with long-term contracts, are cash needs considered in negotiating billing schedules? ☐ ☐

9. Are receipts deposited promptly? ☐ ☐

10. Do techniques provide for the use of cash concentration bank accounts? ☐ ☐

11. Where applicable, do techniques provide for the use of lock-boxes? ☐ ☐

12. Where applicable, do techniques include use of international electronic funds transfer arrangements such as:
    a. New York Clearing House's Interbank Payments Systems (C.H.I.P.S.) ☐ ☐
    b. Society for World Wide Interbank Financial Telecommunications (S.W.I.F.T.) ☐ ☐

(continued)

FIG. 32-3 *(cont'd)*

	Response	
	Yes	No
B. Recording, Accountability, and Safeguarding:		
1. Do procedures require that a record be made of items of cash receipts by the individual who opens the mail?	☐	☐
2. Do procedures require that evidence in support of receipts such as remittance advices be retained?	☐	☐
3. Do procedures require that evidence of amounts deposited be obtained and retained (i.e., authenticated duplicate deposit slips or bank advices)?	☐	☐
4. Do procedures require that the evidence obtained above be promptly given to accounting personnel for recording and filing?	☐	☐
5. Do procedures require that accounting personnel verify the accuracy and validity of deposits by reference to listings of mail receipts, remittance advices, or by other means prior to recording in cash journals or before input to data processing?	☐	☐
6. If receipts are recorded by means of electronic data processing, do procedures require that data input be controlled by item counts, cash totals or by other means prior to submission?	☐	☐
a. If input to data processing is achieved by means of terminals, are all input transactions required to be listed for review and approval prior to input, and is a separate record of input made by the terminal?	☐	☐
b. If the accounting department or profit center is responsible for data conversion, do processing procedures require data verification and a means of concealing source documents subsequent to conversion?	☐	☐
c. Do procedures require that converted data be transferred immediately to a processing center?	☐	☐
d. Do procedures require that accounting personnel receive evidence (i.e., edit listings or proofs) from the processing center that transactions were accepted and reconcile such evidence to control data?	☐	☐
e. Do procedures fix responsibility for error detection and correction and resubmission in a timely fashion?	☐	☐
f. Do procedures require that output reports be reviewed and is control data required to be reconciled to manually prepared data?	☐	☐
7. If posting to cash journal is by means other than data processing, do procedures require that the source for posting be other than the items of cash receipts themselves?	☐	☐
8. Do procedures require the periodic balancing of the totals of the		

	Response	
	Yes	No
postings to the cash receipts journal (or comparable EDP report) with total posting credits to individual accounts receivable records? (Note: This might be performed in connection with reconciling the bank account.)	☐	☐
9. Do procedures cover the handling and recording of checks?	☐	☐
10. Do procedures require that all cash items received, regardless of source, be promptly deposited and recorded?	☐	☐
11. Do procedures require that records of cash receipt transactions periodically be reconciled to bank statements of cash receipts? This procedure normally would be done in connection with reconciling bank and accounting department records. However, reconciliations of bank and accounting department records can occur without performing the procedure outlined above.	☐	☐
12. Do procedures fix responsibility for investigation and correction of differences disclosed by the preceding question?	☐	☐
13. Do procedures require periodic counts of cash items on hand?	☐	☐
14. Are periodic comparisons and evaluations made of cash actually received with projections of cash receipts for specified periods, with investigation of large or unusual differences?	☐	☐
15. Is the authority to receive or transfer cash restricted to designated individuals?	☐	☐
16. Are persons who are authorized to receive cash independent of those in the disbursement functions, those who post accounting records, and those involved in disbursement functions?	☐	☐
17. Do procedures require that cash items be stored in a secure area with restricted access until deposit (i.e., locked box, safe, or locked cabinets)?	☐	☐
18. Are persons empowered to execute transfer of funds between bank accounts independent from related accounting functions?	☐	☐
19. Do procedures provide for appropriate protection for individuals effecting deposits by physically carrying cash items to the bank?	☐	☐
20. Does the method of deposit (e.g., direct receipt by bank, deposits by designated employees, night deposit, armored car service) appropriately safeguard cash items given the nature of the cash items and the accounts involved?	☐	☐
21. Are persons who prepare and effect deposits required to be independent of receiving disbursement and accounting functions?	☐	☐

(continued)

FIG. 32-3 *(cont'd)*

	Response	
	Yes	No
22. Is evidence of bank deposits (e.g., authenticated duplicate deposit slips) required to be received directly from the bank by individuals other than those making the deposit?	☐	☐
23. If recording of cash receipts is effected by means of data processing, are persons involved in receiving, depositing and accounting for cash prohibited from entering the data processing area?	☐	☐
24. If terminals are used to record cash receipts, are there controls over sign on/sign off and transaction entry that restrict access ability (e.g., passwords, employee identifications, lock keys)?	☐	☐
25. If terminals are used, do procedures require periodic review of terminal logs or other control data by designated individuals independent of processing functions?	☐	☐
26. Do procedures require supervisory personnel or management to review and approve journal entries recording cash transactions and the balancing routine described above?	☐	☐
27. Do procedures prohibit cashing personal checks out of current receipts?	☐	☐
28. Have banks been instructed not to cash checks made out to the company?	☐	☐
29. Are all negotiable items (i.e., checks, drafts) restrictively endorsed immediately upon receipt?	☐	☐
30. Are persons involved in depositing and recording cash receipts covered by insurance and fidelity bonds in appropriate amounts?	☐	☐

III. CASH BORROWING:

A. Authorization and Execution:

1. Does company policy specify authority for executing all methods of short- and long-term financing? ☐ ☐
   Note: Available alternatives include, but they are not necessarily restricted to, the following list:
   a. Short-term:
      - Revolving bank credit lines
      - Issuing commercial paper
      - Obtaining advances from customers
      - Factoring
      - Issuing letters of credit

FINANCIAL MANAGEMENT

	Response	
	Yes	No

   b. Long-term:
   - Leasing
   - Mortgaging assets
   - Selling assets
   - Long-term credit agreements with banks and other lending institutions, both domestic and foreign
   - Bonded indebtedness
   - Issuing of stock

2. Are decisions with respect to borrowing made on the basis of:
   a. Reasonably accurate forecasts of cash flows? ☐ ☐
   b. Defining what the refunds will be used for? ☐ ☐
   c. Considering how the debt will be repaid? ☐ ☐
   d. Analyzing the effort of lender restrictions on future activity? ☐ ☐

3. Does the company or organizational unit maintain relations with traditional sources of capital, such as banks, insurance companies, and investment bankers? ☐ ☐

4. Does the company or organizational unit employ any or all of the following techniques to maximize cash balances and obviate the need for borrowing?
   a. Economic ordering and stockpiling of material ☐ ☐
   b. Prompt customer billing ☐ ☐
   c. Discounts for early payment ☐ ☐
   d. Cash concentration accounts ☐ ☐
   e. Electronic fund transfers ☐ ☐
   f. Payment by draft ☐ ☐
   g. Remote disbursement accounts ☐ ☐
   h. Zero balance accounts ☐ ☐
   i. Discounts when offered ☐ ☐

B. Recording and Accountability:

1. Are borrowing transactions such as to permit:
   a. Preparation of financial statements in accordance with generally accepted accounting principles? ☐ ☐
   b. Preparation of reports required by lenders? ☐ ☐
   c. Calculation of compliance with loan restrictions? ☐ ☐
   d. Timely and accurate payment of interest? ☐ ☐
   e. Proper repayment? ☐ ☐

2. Are funding transactions involving the issuance of stock recorded so as to permit:

(continued)

FIG. 32-3 *(cont'd)*

	Response	
	Yes	No
a. Preparation of financial statements in accordance with generally accepted accounting principles?	☐	☐
b. Proper and accurate payment of dividends?	☐	☐
3. Are periodic reports and schedules prepared as required by debt instruments?	☐	☐
4. Does the chief financial officer periodically furnish reports of the financial condition of the company to senior management and/or the board of directors?	☐	☐

C. Safeguarding:

1. Are debt agreements and related documents and records sufficiently safeguarded so to restrict access to only authorized persons?	☐	☐
2. Has provision been made for adequate back-up of vital debt/stock records in the event of loss or destruction?	☐	☐
3. Are records and documents accorded reasonable physical protection from loss or destruction?	☐	☐
4. Are persons assigned duties involving record-keeping for debt and stock activities segregated from receipts and disbursement functions?	☐	☐
5. Is the custodian of unissued stock restricted to person or persons not having access to other company records?	☐	☐

IV. CASH INVESTMENTS:

A. Authorization and Execution:

1. Is the company policy for determining cash investment strategy set forth in writing?	☐	☐
2. Is the authority for approving cash investment decisions set forth in writing?	☐	☐
3. Is the authority for executing cash investments set forth in writing?	☐	☐
4. Does the company strategy give appropriate weight to investment return, liquidity, and investment security?	☐	☐
5. Does the company strategy permit a mix of cash investments? Cash may be invested temporarily in such instruments as: ■ Certificates of Deposit, domestic and foreign ■ Commercial paper	☐	☐

	Response	
	Yes	No

- U.S. Treasury securities
- U.S. government agency issues
- Bankers acceptances
- Repurchase agreements (repos)
- Money market funds

6. Does the company maintain an active program aimed at establishing and preserving relationships with banks and other investing institutions? ☐ ☐

7. Are cash investment transactions initiated based upon reasonably reliable cash forecasts of surplus funds? ☐ ☐

8. Are cash investment transactions effected pursuant to competitive techniques? ☐ ☐

B. Recording and Accountability:

1. Are investment transactions promptly recorded in sufficient detail to permit preparation of financial statements in accordance with generally accepted accounting principals? ☐ ☐
At a minimum the following information should be recorded for each investment transaction:
   - The type of security
   - The issuer
   - Face amount or par value
   - Interest rate
   - Maturity
   - Accrued interest purchased

2. Are records of investment transactions compared with bank advices or other forms of documentation evidencing the transactions? ☐ ☐

3. Are calculations of accrued interest and interest earned to maturity verified? ☐ ☐

4. Are accrued entries calculated and recorded to reflect the recognition of interest income in the proper periods? ☐ ☐

5. Are company detail records of investment balances periodically reconciled to the general ledger investment balance? ☐ ☐

6. Are company records of investment transactions periodically reconciled with bank statements and cash account activity? ☐ ☐

7. Are periodic reports of investment detail balances and activity provided to affected management? ☐ ☐

(continued)

FIG. 32-3 *(cont'd)*

	Response	
	Yes	No
C. Safeguarding:		
1. Are cash investment records and documentation sufficiently safeguarded so as to restrict access to only authorized persons?	☐	☐
2. Has provision been made for adequate back-up of vital records in the event of loss or destruction?	☐	☐
3. Are records and documents accorded reasonable physical protection from loss or destruction?	☐	☐
4. Are persons assigned the responsibility for approving investment transactions independent of those who execute them?	☐	☐
5. Are persons who execute cash investment transactions excluded from record-keeping duties?	☐	☐
6. Is custody of negotiable instruments delegated to a person not having any other duties related to cash or record-keeping?	☐	☐
7. Are persons who review and approve reconciliations independent of those responsible for executing and/or recording cash investments?	☐	☐
8. Are persons involved in cash investment transactions covered by fidelity insurance?	☐	☐

V. ELECTRONIC DATA PROCESSING:

EDP techniques may be involved in any or all of the areas from the previous sections:

- Cash forecasting
- Cash collection
- Cash disbursements
- Cash borrowing
- Cash investing

The following questions should be answered with respect to each application. If the responses to any of the questions are "no," the auditor should consider expanding the inquiry to include a full review of application. If necessary, the assistance of an EDP specialist should be sought.

1. Is authority for developing and/or changing fiscally oriented EDP applications vested in the chief financial officer or his designee?	☐	☐
2. Is authority for accessing and updating EDP records vested in the chief financial officer or his designee?	☐	☐

FINANCIAL MANAGEMENT

	Response	
	Yes	No
3. Is authority for creating or changing input forms and output reports vested in the chief financial officer or his designee?	☐	☐
4. Do user manuals exist that detail instructions for user personnel?	☐	☐
5. Do procedures require current and complete systems and program documentation?	☐	☐
6. Do procedures require that techniques be employed to assure all data input and output is sufficiently controlled?	☐	☐
7. Do procedures require that techniques be employed to reasonably assure errors and omissions are either prevented and/or detected and corrected within a reasonable period?	☐	☐
8. Are back-up and recovery provisions adequate?	☐	☐
9. Is physical security adequate?	☐	☐
If processing involves remote job entry or access, data bases, and/or interactive on-line capabilities, an EDP specialist should be consulted.		

The cash management questionnaire has as one of its objectives the checking of the apparent knowledge of the addressees as to conditions and operations, as well as securing data as to specific phases or conditions.

FINANCIAL MANAGEMENT AUDIT PROGRAMS

From the discussion of the financial function, and the objectives of financial management, it is clear that the financial activities are complicated. Yet, if the product is to be manufactured and sold, the required funds must be available on an economic basis when needed. Further, the use of accounting and statistical data, in their more sophisticated applications as to larger firms, is the means by which the business executive is able to plan, direct, and control operations that reach beyond the range of his own personal observation and supervision. There is little doubt that the executive who is best informed about the operations and economic conditions is in the more suitable position to make the necessary financial decisions and take those actions that enable him to manage the enterprise profitably. Hence, it is essential that the financial organization be operating efficiently and effectively. One

(continued on page 32-45)

FIG. 32-4
Quarterly Cash Forecasting Audit Program

NOTE: Although standard forms are utilized by all company divisions and subsidiaries in the preparation of the cash forecast various methods may exist from division to division for forecasting projected account balances. Thus although this audit program may be utilized it will probably need to be tailored to meet the specific audit testing performed at the various divisions.

	Workpaper Reference	Done by

1. General:

☐ Obtain an organizational chart of the financial planning department or the division or group responsible for preparing the cash forecast.

☐ Obtain applicable policy statements and gain an understanding of the reporting format and the schedule for preparing the cash forecast.

☐ Obtain any written procedures prepared by the division for the preparation of the plan.

☐ Meet with management responsible and obtain understanding of how the cash forecast is prepared, and of the flow of financial information to the financial planning department. If the forecast is prepared by EDP, obtain documentation of user instruction and input forms.

☐ Complete the Internal Control Questionnaire.

2. Authorization:

☐ For a selected period, ascertain that the cash forecast has been reviewed and approved at the appropriate levels prior to submission to the Corporate Office.

☐ Ascertain that any changes in amounts or changes in method of preparing the forecast have been properly approved by management.

☐ If data is obtained from sources outside the department responsible for preparation, ascertain that the data has received departmental approval or has been received from individuals authorized by management to provide the data.

3. Recording/Preparation of the Plan:

☐ For a selected time period, perform the following for cash forecasts prepared during the period:
- Review the plan for completeness and timeliness of submission to the Corporate Office.
- Ascertain that amounts can be traced to supporting detail schedules, and on test basis test the accuracy of supporting schedules and work sheets.
- Compare forecast amounts to actual amounts to determine significant variances, and ascertain reasons for variances.

FINANCIAL MANAGEMENT

	Workpaper Reference	Done by
■ Determine if the reasons for significant differences have been utilized in the preparation of subsequent forecasts in a timely manner.	....	....
☐ Ascertain that assumptions used in preparing the cash forecast are adequately documented.	....	....
☐ Select several forecasts and note differences in assumptions used, and ascertain that explanations are reasonable.	....	....
☐ For a selected cash forecast, to determine if amounts forecasted appear to be reasonable (in terms of the assumptions), perform the following:	....	
■ Ascertain that forecasts of cash receipts relate to forecasted sales activity as reflected in the most current approved forecast of business activity.	....	....
■ Ascertain that direct/indirect costs incurred relate to current projected sales activity level.	....	....
■ For intercompany sales/costs data relate amounts to interdivision work orders or other supporting documentation.	....	....
■ Ascertain that intercompany Corporate allocations are based on estimates of amounts or fringe rates received from the Corporate Office.	....	....
■ Ascertain that balance sheet changes in accounts receivable, inventory, and current liabilities can be related to sales activity and costs incurred amounts in a reasonable manner.	....	....
■ Agree amounts forecast as advance payments to schedules received from contract departments or project controllers, and ascertain reasonableness of amounts (based on past experience or work performed).	....	....
■ Ascertain reasonableness of projected amounts for progress payments and relationship to costs incurred.	....	....
☐ Agree amounts in the cash forecast to line items in the balance sheet and income statement accompanying the cash forecast.	....	....
☐ Ascertain that changes in balance sheet accounts and amounts from the income statement reflect properly in the cash sources and uses statement.	....	....
☐ Ascertain that the required/(excess) cash amount agrees to changes in cash accounts and the net of sources and uses of cash.	....	....

4. **Substantiation/Accountability:**

☐ Ascertain that the forecast amounts are compared with the actual amounts and that significant variances are explained to the Corporate Office. ....

(continued)

FIG. 32-4 *(cont'd)*

	Workpaper Reference	Done by
☐ Ascertain that procedures include contact with appropriate departments to obtain explanations of variances.	....	....
5. Safeguarding:		
☐ Ascertain that documents and workpapers are maintained in adequate safe keeping (i.e., locked in fireproof file cabinets).	....	....

FIG. 32-5

Audit Program—Financial Management

POLICY, ORGANIZATION, AND MANAGEMENT		
	Done by	Date
A. SECURE A COPY OF THE STATEMENT OF THE CORPORATION'S PRINCIPAL FINANCIAL POLICIES AND CHECK FOR COMPLETENESS, ADEQUACY, FLEXIBILITY, AND TIMELINESS AS TO:		
1. Objectives	....	....
2. Capital structure guidelines	....	....
3. Limitations on amount and type of long-term debt, including:		
☐ Term loans	....	....
☐ Straight debt	....	....
☐ Mortgage bonds	....	....
☐ Debentures	....	....
☐ Convertible debentures	....	....
☐ Long-term leases	....	....
☐ Newer types of financing	....	....
4. Dividend policy, including:		
☐ Cash dividends	....	....
☐ Stock dividends	....	....
☐ Payout ratio, or percent of equity	....	....
☐ Extras	....	....

	Done by	Date

☐ Consistency of pattern
☐ Limitations in credit agreements

5. **Available capital, stock adequacy, and practice:**
   ☐ Straight preferred
   ☐ Convertible preferred
   ☐ Common
   ☐ Warrants

B. OBTAIN AN ORGANIZATION CHART OF THE FINANCIAL DEPARTMENT AND APPRAISE:

1. **Departmental segregation, based on the major current functions, short-term expected activity, provision for future international growth, and adequacy of supervision**

2. **The reporting relationship, and independence, of the internal audit function (both corporate and divisional)**

3. **Suitability of tax department structure and placement as related to:**
   ☐ Accounting
   ☐ Tax planning

   Coordination of:
   ☐ Local taxes
   ☐ State income taxes (including division input)
   ☐ Federal income taxes
   ☐ State franchise taxes
   ☐ Foreign taxes

5. **Coordination between treasurer's office and controllers department as to:**
   ☐ Weekly cash planning
   ☐ Quarterly cash forecast
   ☐ Valuation of temporary investments
   ☐ Daily cash transfers and book balances

6. **Management development activities, especially:**
   ☐ Job rotation

(continued)

FIG. 32-5 *(cont'd)*

	Done by	Date
☐ Promotion from division to corporate	....	....
☐ Transfers and promotion from internal audit to divisions and corporate	....	....
☐ Academic pursuits at company expense	....	....
☐ Upgrading of professional level	....	....

C. SECURE THE CORPORATE FUNCTIONAL OUTLINES OF THE VICE-PRESIDENT–FINANCE, ALL OTHER CORPORATE AND DIVISION FINANCIAL OFFICERS, AND ALL FINANCE MANAGERS:

1. **Check all outlines for:**
   - ☐ Currency
   - ☐ Completeness as to reporting status
   - ☐ Recent functional changes in internal auditing relationship
   - ☐ Responsibility of financial analysis
   - ☐ Provision of operating data to line executives

2. **Check the adequacy of the Vice-President–Finance's job description and appraise his responsibilities in regard to:**
   - ☐ Investor relations
   - ☐ Acquisition or divestment financial analyses and reviews (vis-à-vis the divestment officer)
   - ☐ Liaison with regulating bodies at local, state, and federal levels
   - ☐ Review and evaluation of division/subsidiary chief financial officer's salary, incentive pay, and title
   - ☐ Investment of retirement plan assets
   - ☐ Review and evaluation of division/subsidiary financial activities
   - ☐ Establishment of sound relationship with commercial banks, investment bankers, and long-term lenders, including pension funds
   - ☐ Quality of financial advice to CEO, executive management, and the board of directors

D. THROUGH DISCUSSION WITH APPROPRIATE PARTIES AND REVIEW OF CORRESPONDENCE, EVALUATE FOR POSSIBLE IMPROVEMENT THE FOLLOWING FUNCTIONS OF THE CORPORATE VICE-PRESIDENT–FINANCE, THE TREASURER, AND THE CONTROLLER:

1. **Communication with the following persons (noting amount, quality, and extent of understanding):**
   - ☐ Division/subsidiary general managers

FINANCIAL MANAGEMENT

	Done by	Date

☐ Division/subsidiary chief financial officers
☐ Division/subsidiary finance managers
☐ Division/subsidiary public relations officers

2. Meetings with financial analysts:
☐ Individual
☐ Group
☐ Methods and content of presentations

3. Communication with our commercial bankers as to:
☐ Annual business plan review
☐ Current performance
☐ Accounting principles used
☐ Significant news items
☐ Handling of adverse news or other items (e.g., earnings or management)
☐ Trend in line-of-credit requirements and principal credit terms

Note: Discuss with some of the company's commercial bankers and financial officers of other companies the extent of communication with commercial bankers and some of the methods used.

E. MANUALS AND PROCEDURES:

1. Obtain copies of the appropriate section of the Corporate Finance Manual for each organizational segment being reviewed, and check for currency of features specified, evidence of application, and completeness and clarity of instructions, as follows:

☐ Accounting
- Recent AICPA pronouncements
- SEC promulgations
- Policy changes (inventory valuation)
- Computer applications
- Analysis of variations

☐ Taxation
- TEFRA (1982)
- California income allocation

☐ Cash management
- Wire transfers

☐ Investment guidelines
- Diversification

(continued)

FIG. 32-5 *(cont'd)*

	Done by	Date
■ Expected rate of return	....	....
■ Vehicles	....	....
■ Weekly reporting	....	....
■ Compensating balances	....	....
■ Float	....	....
☐ Plans and budgets		
■ Computer programs	....	....
■ Selection of capital budget items	....	....
■ Cutoff rate for capital expenditures	....	....
■ Two-year-plan format	....	....
■ Spare parts pricing	....	....
■ Depreciation changes	....	....
■ Schedule changes — long-range plan	....	....
■ Format changes — programs; actual and planned performance	....	....
☐ Risk management (insurance)		
■ Insurance subsidiary	....	....
■ Re-insurance	....	....
■ Property damage reports	....	....
☐ Retirement and savings — investment		
■ Criteria for managers	....	....
■ Risk	....	....
■ Internal controls	....	....
☐ Internal audit		
■ Operational audits	....	....
■ International operations	....	....
F. CURRENT OPERATIONS — STATUS:		
1. Accounting Policy:		
☐ Review and appraise the ways in which current policies are reviewed and changes are considered, including coordination with independent auditors, industry association groups, and division/subsidiary/financial staff	....	....
☐ Review current policies in line with recent AICPA pronouncements and exposure drafts	....	....
☐ Review impact of any pending changes on the statement of financial position and the statement of income and expense (each separately, by profit center)	....	....
☐ Review and appraise the adequacy of existing policies specifically as they relate to:		
■ Foreign operations	....	....
■ Foreign currency exchange transactions	....	....
■ Depreciation	....	....

FINANTIAL MANAGEMENT

	Done by	Date

- Research and development
- Interest expense — capital projects
- Long-term leases
- Capital expenditures
- Product costing
- Credit terms

2. Reports and Analyses:

☐ Review and appraise all regularly issued financial/accounting reports with specific reference to:
- Timeliness
- Responsibility accounting concept
- Inclusion of user-oriented terms and format (including graphic and other visual aids)
- Extent of interpretation and useful analysis
- Use of exception reporting and elimination of unnecessary detail
- Use of warning signals or extrapolation of trends
- Use of comparative data
- Favorable reaction and usage by addressee
- Application of latest technology, including video presentations

☐ Review and appraise all special analyses for:
- Responsiveness to problem
- Timeliness
- Responsiveness to needs of user
- Conciseness and clarity
- Reference, where applicable, to competitive data, industry data, and probable future economic conditions
- Return on assets employed (or shareholders' equity, if applicable)
- Short- and long-term implications

G. TAX ACTIVITIES:

1. Policy:

☐ By discussions and a review of correspondence, determine if the individuals charged with carrying out tax policies understand the policies and their many nuances, and if they have any suggestions for changing the policies

☐ Review and appraise all policies in light of company expansion to other states and foreign countries

☐ Seek evidence showing the impact of tax policy on strategic planning

(continued)

FIG. 32-5 *(cont'd)*

	Done by	Date

☐ Provide evidence of effective coordination with division/subsidiary personnel as to tax policy in the annual planning cycle   ....

2. Tax Accounting Records:

☐ Where tax policy and accounting policy differ, review and appraise the adequacy of tax accounting records to support company positions and claims: ....
- Secure evidence of a tax balance sheet   ....
- Obtain evidence that the accounting and tax records are reconciled   ....

3. Return Filing:

☐ On a test basis, review the various state and federal tax returns for timeliness and completeness in filing, and:
- Check for any penalties that may have been exacted for late filing   ....
- Ascertain that the company's tax accounting records support the figures in the tax returns   ....
- Ascertain that responsibility for filing has been properly delegated   ....

4. Other Tax Matters:

☐ Tax records
- Review the adequacy of the tax calendar   ....
- Examine the working papers for completeness and orderliness   ....
- Review for adequacy the "tax information record" on all taxes paid or accrued   ....

☐ Tax Personnel
- Review functional outlines for adequacy   ....
- Determine if there is provision for on-the-job training   ....
- Ascertain that the job classifications are appropriate   ....

☐ Other
- Appraise the company's relationship with the various taxing authorities   ....
- Examine evidence indicating the extent of coordination with the independent public accountants   ....

H. CASH MANAGEMENT:

1. Cash Receipts:

☐ Review the internal control questionnaire and follow-up memos since the last financial audit, and:

	Done by	Date

- Ascertain that the suggested procedural changes are operative
- On a test basis, recheck the effectiveness of the internal controls
☐ Review and appraise the program and actual practices for acceleration of cash receipts
☐ In light of the developing technology, check these specific procedures for possible improvement:
  a. Lockbox system
  b. Area concentration banking practices: location and transfer methods of local banks, and timeliness and security of wire transfers to principal banks

2. Cash Disbursements:

☐ Recheck and update the internal control questionnaire
☐ Review and appraise the program for control of disbursements, with special reference to:
  - Controlling the float
  - Location of disbursing banks vs. geographical site for check writing
  - Use of drafts rather than checks
  - Effectiveness of the zero balance accounts
  - Security on wire transfers for temporary investments and inter-company requirements
  - Actual payment schedule on accounts payable vs. minimum requirement

3. Cash Planning:

☐ Review the latest audit of the quarterly cash-forecasting procedures (see Figure 32-4 for audit program) used to test general acceptability of the short-range cash-planning and temporary-investment program, and:
  - Determine how all suggested changes may affect the other cash-planning procedures
  - Through conversations, check on any recent modifications in departmental records and procedures

☐ Review and appraise the updating procedure for expected cash receipts, cash disbursements, and cash balances for the remainder of the year and at year-end, as presented in the monthly financial statements, and:
  - Review the method by which cumulative departures from the cash plan year-to-date are handled as to any projections
  - Review and appraise the procedure for reconciling the actual cash receipts and disbursements, year-to-date, with the cash plan

(continued)

FIG. 32-5 *(cont'd)*

	Done by	Date
■ Review the working papers and compare the actual starting point cash balances, etc., for cash forecasting with the actual figures	....	....
☐ For the annual business plan's statement of estimated sources and uses of cash, review and appraise the procedure, with particular emphasis on these points:		
■ Methodology in determining accounts receivable balances, and accuracy thereof	....	....
■ Methodology in arriving at accounts payable and accrued liabilities balances, and accuracy thereof	....	....
■ Procedure for estimating bank borrowings under revolving credit agreement	....	....
■ Degree of coordination with operations, and procedure for estimating capital expenditures	....	....
■ Procedure for arriving at changes in inventory, and accuracy thereof	....	....
☐ For the long-range cash sources and uses, review the procedures and appraise the methodology. Special attention should be paid to:		
■ Any attempt at excessive detail or accuracy	....	....
■ Method of determining source of long-term capital needs vs. procedures used by Vice-President–Finance	....	....
4. Temporary Investments:		
☐ Review and appraise the internal guidelines for investment of temporary funds, in light of the rapidly changing market. The following features should be examined:		
■ Liquidity constraints	....	....
■ Diversification — limits of investments	....	....
■ Foreign investment limitations	....	....
■ Payment provisions	....	....
■ Maximum maturity limits	....	....
■ Credit rating of issuer	....	....
■ Repurchase agreements, in view of recent market difficulties	....	....
☐ Review and appraise the procedures by which purchases are made, with emphasis on daily securities selection to maximize the return	....	....
☐ Review the adequacy of insurance coverage	....	....
☐ Review the accuracy of the very-short-term cash planning procedure as to daily availability of funds for investment	....	....
5. Cash Reporting:		
☐ Test the accuracy of the daily cash reporting system, especially the data provided the chief financial officer	....	....

	Done by	Date

☐ Review and appraise the month-end closing procedure and account for apparent differences between month-end financial statement and the reports issued by the Treasurer's office   ....

☐ By reference to bank confirmations, or any other source, verify the correctness of the following temporary investment reports as of August 31, 19XX:
- Distribution by issuer   ....
- Maturities and average yield   ....
- Investment portfolio, by type of obligation   ....

6. Other Cash Matters:

☐ Review the procedures and costs and appraise the performance of the in-house investment activities as compared with those of the outside fund manager   ....

☐ Review the bank reconciliation procedures as to timeliness and internal controls   ....

I. PLANNING AND BUDGETING ACTIVITIES:

1. Current Year Financial Updating:

☐ Review and appraise the procedures for monthly updating of the year's operating results and financial condition, as reported in the corporate consolidated financial statement and each of the following division/subsidiary financial statements:
- Income and expense   ....
- Sales, by program   ....
- Financial position   ....
- Status of capital commitments and expenditures   ....
- Cash sources and uses (see cash planning)   ....
- Ascertain the extent of adjustments to subsidiary estimates   ....

2. Annual Business Plan:

☐ Review and appraise the procedure stipulated in the Corporate Finance Manual for preparation of the annual business plan   ....

☐ Note especially the following features:
- Propriety of the corporate goals (ROE) and the nature of establishing it (vs. competition)   ....
- Degree of laxness or tightness in the division subsidiary goals (especially ROA) (indicate your criteria for assessing this)   ....
- Extent to which the business plans of the profit centers are based on financial analysis (vs. hunch, guess, or dictate of Division General Manager)   ....

(continued)

FIG. 32-5 *(cont'd)*

	Done by	Date
■ Extent of internal critical financial analysis: (1) of the profit center plan, at both the profit center and the corporate office; (2) of the consolidated plan by Corporate Finance. Assess adequacy of the tests or criteria used	....	....
■ Degree to which the plan truly motivates the management (suggest possible improvements.)	....	....
■ Extent to which outside factors (such as competitive actions or economic conditions) are considered	....	....
■ Adequacy of the corporate office guidelines	....	....
■ Extent to which Corporate Finance assists or guides the profit centers	....	....

3. Long-Range Plan:

☐ Review and appraise the financial aspects of the long-range planning procedure: ....
- Extent to which finance is involved in nonfinancial aspects (i.e., programs, projects, product lines, and manner of involvement)   ....
- Need for or practicality of continuous updating when major events occur   ....
- Appropriateness of the financially expressed corporate goals (explain your conclusion, assessment criteria used, etc.)   ....
- Degree to which financial criteria are used in project selection   ....
- Reasonableness of the amount of calculations required   ....
- Effectiveness of computer applications   ....
- Utilization of probability and sensitivity analysis (for *each* profit center)   ....
- General usefulness of the manpower data (financial staff only)   ....
- Schedule for plan preparation   ....
- Frequency of revision   ....

☐ Review evidence of consideration of prior years' errors in correcting the plan for the next five years   ....

☐ Review evidence of leakage of sensitive issues, and assess controls designed to prevent such leakage   ....

4. Capital Budget:

☐ Review and appraise the annual capital budgeting procedure, with special reference to the following factors:
- Aggregate limitations on capital budget   ....
- Method of allocating funds to various profit or investment centers   ....
- Project selection techniques within the profit center   ....

	Done by	Date

- Method of evaluating capital expenditures
- Cutoff rate for capital expenditures
- Follow-up procedures for completed projects (e.g., use of Internal Audit)
- Adequacy of control procedures in monitoring expenditures

☐ Review the simple procedure used to determine order of magnitude of capital expenditures in the long-range plan and comment on the usefulness and estimated rate of return

5. Departmental Expense Budgets:

☐ Review and appraise the procedure for annual departmental budget preparation, noting especially the following features:
- Degree of analysis of the need for the activity level
- Adequacy of guidelines provided so the department manager can arrive at the level of effort needed
- Extent of assistance provided by the financial staff, including:
- Historical data
- Format
- Procedures
- Degree to which the department manager is given an opportunity to discuss his budget needs in the budget meeting with the department manager
- Opportunity to simplify the procedures
- Discuss the desirability of flexible budgeting with appropriate management
- Adequacy of the procedure for interim revision of the departmental budget
- Appropriateness and extent of the relationship of budget performance to incentive payments

6. Planning and Budget Reports:

☐ Review and test the suitability of budgetary expense reporting, with attention to the following reporting principles:
- Responsibility reporting
- Exception reporting
- Interpretative (or self-explanatory) reporting
- Timeliness
- Format and terms
- Usefulness
- Frequency

☐ Review and comment on the need for periodic meetings of the cognizant financial group and line executive to provide *oral* commentary on and interpretation of:
- Routine budget matters

(continued)

FIG. 32-5 *(cont'd)*

	Done by	Date

- Reasons for the planning procedure and changes therein
- Special analytical reports relating to planning matters

J. FUND-ORIENTED ACTIVITIES (OTHER THAN CASH MANAGEMENT):

1. Short-Term Capital Requirements:

☐ Review the revolving credit agreement with the company's commercial bankers as to the following points:
  - Availability to meet short-term credit needs as evidenced by the annual business plan
  - Extent of restrictive clauses or limitations vis-à-vis agreements of competitors
  - Competitiveness of terms vis-à-vis other banks supplying the industry, especially as to:
    a. Rate
    b. Working capital requirements
    c. Compensating balance or charges
    d. Debt-to-equity requirements
    e. Events of default
  - Flexibility for expression of borrowings
  - Use of commercial paper

☐ Examine the degree to which short-term credit needs are coordinated with longer-term requirements

☐ Examine what studies were made of alternative sources of short-term funds, noting:
  - Extent to which our investment bankers were consulted
  - Whether or not review was made of possible foreign sources in countries in which the company conducts operations

☐ Provide suggestions to the chief financial officer, as to ways of meeting concerns of the lending banks. Some ideas may be gained from discussions with major suppliers and industry financial analysts

☐ Review and appraise the use of supplier credits on some of the major programs

☐ Determine what competitors are doing

2. Long-Term Capital Requirements:

☐ Review with the chief financial officer the efforts being made to provide for long-term capital needs:
  - Is there any information you can provide for his assistance?

	Done by	Date

- How useful is the long-range plan in revealing the extent of the potential need? Is it sufficiently concrete to use for exploratory talks by the financial executives?
☐ Explore the corporate capital structure and assess:
  - Suitability in our industry (see some investment bankers suggested by the CFO)
  - Desirability of changes to lower the cost of capital
  - Possibility of securing an improved debt rating
☐ Review and appraise dividend policy in light of future capital needs, and note how our pay-out ratio compares with those of our principal competitors
☐ Examine whether or not a dividend reinvestment program would be useful

3. Retirement and Savings Plans:

☐ Review and appraise the following financial aspects of the retirement and employee savings plans:
  - The actuarial assumptions of the retirement plan
  - The following investment policies and practices regarding the fund assets:
    a. Selection of fund managers
    b. Relative performance of the managers
    c. Criteria for fund investments
    d. Treatment of released assets relative to non-vested, terminated employees
    e. Investing practices and procedures
☐ Internal controls regarding:
  - Disbursements to fund managers
  - Disbursements to retired employees or their beneficiaries
  - Reconciliation of bank accounts
  - Determination of estimated funding requirements for annual planning purposes

4. Accounting Control Activities:

☐ Review and appraise the numerous accounting control systems and procedures throughout the corporation and its subsidiaries, noting particularly the following facets:
  - Cost effectiveness
  - Acceptance or use by the line managers
  - Uses of the latest proven techniques including:
    a. Computer printouts
    b. Sampling
    c. Other statistical techniques

(continued)

FIG. 32-5 *(cont'd)*

	Done by	Date
☐ Review and appraise the role of the accountant in setting standards in each of the following areas:		
■ Direct labor		
a. Performance	....	....
b. Rates	....	....
■ Direct material		
a. Usage	....	....
b. Cost	....	....
■ Manufacturing overhead		
a. Rate	....	....
b. Volume	....	....
■ Operating-expense standards		
a. Volume	....	....
b. Rate	....	....
■ Revision of standards	....	....
☐ Review and comment on the reporting system per se, including:	....	....
■ Timeliness	....	....
■ Accuracy	....	....
■ Format	....	....
■ Interpretation	....	....
■ Report system structure	....	....
■ Exception reporting principle	....	....
☐ Review and suggest areas for study, or improvement, as to special (non-routine) analyses of operations. What can be contributed in the following areas:		
■ Revenues — trends and relationships	....	....
■ Costs — trends and relationships	....	....
■ Margins — trends and relationships	....	....
■ Contribution margins by product, territory, etc.	....	....
■ Product price determination and changes	....	....
■ Volume impact	....	....
■ Product mix and margin impact	....	....
■ Asset-to-earnings trends and relationships	....	....
■ Most profitable use of resources	....	....
5. Risk-Management (Insurance) Activities:		
☐ Review and appraise from the standpoint of effectiveness the following operating activities:	....	....
■ Selection of brokers	....	....
■ Selection of specific carriers	....	....
■ Negotiation of specific insurance policy features	....	....

FINANCIAL MANAGEMENT 32-45

	Done by	Date
☐ Review and appraise the policies concerning self-insurance, deductibles, and risks selected for coverage	....	....
☐ Evaluate the adequacy or effectiveness of following insurance records, as to each risk and policy:	....	....
■ Terms of coverage	....	....
■ Cost	....	....
■ Expiration date	....	....
■ Exclusions	....	....
■ Prepaid insurance	....	....
■ Accrued insurance	....	....
■ Claims procedures	....	....
■ Risk-reduction efforts (fire protection procedures, sprinklers, etc.)	....	....
■ Assistance to and education of the operating staff	....	....
■ Coordination of insurance activities with Accounting, Personnel, and Operations	....	....
■ Administration of medical coverage, including adequacy of internal controls	....	....

of the purposes of any operations audit of financial management is to ascertain that this is the case, and to suggest improvements.

It is with this idea in mind that the audit programs in Figures 32-4 and 32-5 have been devised. Not only must the financial operation be reviewed for the usual reasons—adequate internal accounting controls, sound accounting, conformance to designated policies and procedures, and efficiency of operations—but also, it is desirable to review policies, financial objectives, use of the new technology, and a management-oriented information system, as contrasted with the more mundane accounting applications. An attempt has been made to include certain aspects of operations that are often ignored. However, not every facet of financial activity can be covered in one audit; and, as always, the program must be adapted to the specific company and its style of management. Figure 32-4 is an audit program for quarterly cash forecasting. The audit program in Figure 32-5 is intended to follow the complete functional activity of a given finance organization segment for a typical medium-sized to large manufacturing firm.

ILLUSTRATIVE AUDIT FINDINGS

The enormous range and, it should be added, complexity, of financial activities carries with it the potential of sizeable deficiencies; or conversely, opportunities for productive operational audits. With respect to operational deficiencies, under the pressure of limited personnel and increased work load, anything can happen, and it usually does, especially in the cash management area. A brief report on required procedural improvements is illustrated in Figure 32-6.

Rather than attempt to excerpt some of the findings from operational audits of the financial function, a concise listing may indicate the need for observance of some of the simplest, and most basic, principles and procedures. Some weaknesses by type of activity are these:

☐ Organizational/management
- Absence of any statement of financial policy
- Lack of organization charts
- Absence of functional outline (job description) for the financial executives
- Limited knowledge of the importance of capital structure by the financial officers
- No provision for training replacements for financial officers
- No plan for personal development

☐ Absence of required communication skills by financial executives
- Among the management
- With commercial and investment bankers
- With the other financial community members (e.g., financial analysts)
- Lack of key manuals (e.g., accounting, planning, and tax)

☐ Accounting
- Absence of key accounting policy statements
- Failure to follow accounting policies at division/subsidiary level
- Use of outmoded systems and procedures
- Failure to adopt applicable new FASB principles
- Financial statements too late, accounting-oriented, or detailed, or not comparative, interpreted, or organizationally oriented

☐ Tax activities
- No real tax planning
- No use taken of legitimate tax reduction devices
- No separate tex records maintained (where book and tax accounting were dissimilar)

☐ Cash management
- Improper internal controls
- Receipts not deposited intact daily
- Nonuse of newest technology or techniques (e.g., lockbox systems, cash concentration accounts, and wire transfers)
- Excess cash not invested
- Cash planning unrelated to annual plan

(continued on page 32-54)

FIG. 32-6
Audit Report Recommending Improvements in Cash Management Procedures

TO: Senior Vice-President–Finance
FROM: Director of Corporate Audit
SUBJECT: Cash Management — Corporate Office

We have completed a review of cash management and control functions utilized by Corporate Banking Administration for managing cash balances. Our review was performed to determine compliance with established procedures and to evaluate their effectiveness for the purposes intended. Our work was limited by time considerations to a review of cash bank balance control procedures as related to short-term investments, daily cash estimates, average bank balance reporting and monitoring functions, and bank statement reconciliations. Cash receipts and disbursements controls other than wire transfer methods for .... Bank in New York were not reviewed at this time. Corporate Office revolving funds also were not reviewed. These areas will be reviewed at a future date.

In summary, we noted that significant actions have been taken recently to improve the level of control over cash balances and, in particular, over temporary investments. These actions include (1) concentrating the custody of temporary securities in a single institution, (2) segregating incompatible functions, such as executing and recording transactions, and (3) utilizing an outside investment manager to manage $100 million of temporary investments. As a part of the third action, the computer processing techniques utilized by this firm were extended to investment transactions handled by Corporate Banking. These three actions were in response to the need for greater control occasioned by the sharp increase in the amount of surplus cash that must be temporarily invested. As of March 31, 19XX, over $350 million was being managed by Corporate Banking Administration.

Because these actions were taken subsequent to our review and significantly altered the controls, we are not able to express an opinion on their adequacy with respect to temporary investments. We intend to perform another review of these controls in the near future to assess their adequacy. The remaining matters that came to our attention during the review are summarized below. They did not seem to be affected by subsequent actions by the Corporate Banking Administration Group. Accordingly, action in these areas will be required only in order to further improve control over cash and temporary investments and reduce exposure to errors and omissions.

Temporary Investments
- Custodial agreements do not cover all temporary investments.
- Properly approved written confirmations of oral investment instructions are not consistently submitted.

Cash
- Daily cash balance estimating methods have resulted in wide variations from actual balances in February.
- Bank balances are not scheduled and computed on a daily basis to determine and control monthly averages.
- Arrangements regarding cash transfers do not adequately limit opportunities for transfers to non-company accounts.
- Two instances were noted where bank accounts were closed without proper approval and/or instructions.

(continued)

FIG. 32-6 *(cont'd)*

- The bank accounts related to the Corporate Health Care Plans have not yet been reconciled.
- Additional data is required in order to reconcile the Banco de ...., Madrid, Spain, accounts.

Until we have had a chance to verify and evaluate the revised controls over cash and temporary investments and until Banking Administration management has had an opportunity to consider actions in response to this report, we cannot express an opinion on the adequacy of control for managing Corporate cash balances.

A reply to this report is requested within 30 days.

1. Actions subsequent to our review have significantly improved control over temporary investments.

During the time period covered by our review, temporary investments which amounted to over $350 million, were largely controlled by a single individual. This individual was responsible for executing transactions (within prescribed guidelines) recording the transactions, and matching the recorded par value of each transaction at each maturity with substantiating independent records and cash receipts. The adequacy of this method was overly dependent upon the integrity and self-discipline of the individual involved.

In our opinion, adequate control over temporary investments can result only when the functions of executing, recording, and reconciling transactions are segregated and when those individuals who have access to records do not have access to the securities. In addition, the following control elements need to be present:

a. Each transaction must be executed in accordance with predetermined guidelines.
b. Each transaction must be reviewed and approved in writing.
c. Each transaction must be recorded in a manner so as to preserve its identity.
d. Each transaction must be recorded in a manner so as to allow for a proper and accurate accounting for the cost of the securities and the income to be earned from them.
e. Each transaction must be recorded in such a manner so as to permit periodic reconciliation of the carrying value of securities on hand with corresponding amounts maintained by the custodian.
f. Each transaction must be checked individually and verified by reference to customer confirmations.
g. Periodic reconciliation and verification of recorded transactions must occur, including premium/discount and interest, per the general ledger with amounts per the dealer/broker.

Our audit disclosed instances, with respect to items, e, f, and g where available evidence could not substantiate that those control elements had been performed. This was largely due to the informal manner in which procedures had been performed and records maintained. Banking Administration management represents that the vital control elements had been observed to the extent practicable during the time of our review. However, evidence to support this representation is not available. For example, management indicates that it was their policy to verify at the maturity date interest earned and proceeds, but since evidence of this had not been retained, it could not be verified.

The primary exposure during this time period was not the possibility of defalcations or other similar irregularities, in our opinion, because access to securities was effectively restricted and because collusive cooperation by brokers/dealers would have been required. We believe that the primary exposure was to errors and omissions resulting from the informal manner in which procedures were followed and records maintained. However, we believe it is unlikely that any significant error could have occurred, because it would have been discovered at maturity or at the time of reconciling bank accounts. Moreover, the chance of error is further reduced because the transactions were executed with banks, brokers, and other institutions of noted high public trust and confidence. Since these institutions provided the original calculations, the circumstances are not of great concern. As a result, while the possibility of errors existed, it is not likely that any significant distortion of recorded amounts of securities and related interest resulted.

Subsequent to our review, trading functions have been segregated from the accounting functions for securities transactions within the Banking organization, which represents a significant improvement. In addition, $100 million was placed with an outside investment manager to handle a portion of the short-term investment portfolio. This has reduced the volume of transactions to execute, record, and control. An automated investment transaction recording system used by this firm for recording and reporting transactions and holdings has also been installed by Corporate Banking for the same purpose. In our opinion, an automated investment transaction system should be beneficial in providing data at a level of detail necessary to establish and maintain a monthly automated reconciliation of investment balances to the accounting records and outside custodial securities statements. Recent discussions indicate that the automated system adopted by Banking provides such data in a manner that facilitates accomplishing the foregoing control objectives. However, since these events occurred subsequent to our review, we are not in a position to assess or evaluate the changes made. We intend to review this area again at a later date.

RECOMMENDATION NO. 1

Establish a documentary requirement for monthly reconciliation and balancing of securities transactions and holdings, as recorded in the automated investment system, with statements received from custodial banks or other corroborating evidence.

2. Custodial agreements do not cover all temporary investments.

At the time of our review, securities totalling approximately $115 million were being held for the company's account in Corporate bank accounts other than .... Of that amount, approximately $30 million in negotiable securities were being held in three California banks. Custody agreements had not been executed, although letters had been sent to each of them with instructions that effectively limited access to the securities.

In discussions subsequent to our review, we were informed that starting in March 19XX, no new investments were being placed with banks other than .... Bank; and in April all securities held by the various banking institutions were transferred to the .... Bank of Chicago, for which there is a separate custody agreement, and repo (repurchase agreement) investments in other banks). We believe that custodial agreements should be established for investments in negotiable instruments which are not in the custody of .... Bank, so as to extend to all securities the level of control deemed necessary for securities in the hands of .... Bank.

(continued)

FIG. 32-6 *(cont'd)*

RECOMMENDATION NO. 2

Establish custodial agreements and instructions with all banks or institutions selected for security transactions and require monthly reporting of all securities held for the company's account in a manner similar to the custody agreement with .... Bank.

3. **Evidence of properly approved written instructions are not consistently retained.**

   The custody agreement with .... Bank provides that each oral instruction from an authorized employee shall be subsequently confirmed by a written instruction. However, the agreement fails to specify whether the written confirmation should be signed by the individual executing the transaction or approved at a signatory level. In practice, the written confirmation form provides for the signature of an authorized signatory on the commercial bank account; however, we found numerous unsigned confirmations during a review of February 19XX transactions. We were subsequently told that confirmations to .... Bank had been properly signed but that copies were made for the files prior to obtaining the authorized signatures. Since this procedure is intended to prevent unauthorized transactions, it must be clarified for it to be effective. Evidence of signatory compliance should be retained in the files.

RECOMMENDATION NO. 3

Clarify, assure, and retain evidence of compliance with the level of approval required on written instructions in confirmation of oral transactions as specified in the custody agreement with .... Bank, and modify the agreement accordingly.

4. **Daily cash balance estimating methods resulted in wide variations from actual balances in February.**

   Short-term cash forecasts by profit centers are no longer used or requested. An informal daily estimate that recognizes maturing securities and NAR cash receipt and disbursement activities is prepared instead in Banking. For all other profit centers, cash requirements are phoned in daily and a flat estimate of $1.0 million per day is used for all other cash receipts. Profit centers continue to phone in any large or unusual cash receipt items (i.e., in excess of $500,000) as they occur. Our review indicates that daily cash forecasts prepared in the manner described above resulted in wide variations from the actual cash balances in .... Bank as telephoned by .... Bank. During a sample period (February), actual reviewed cash balances at .... Bank often fluctuated over or under estimated amounts by $1 to $2 million, with variances of over $5 and $6 million on two occasions, and $7 million for one day during the 16-day period. If this is representative of activity in other months (Banking management represents that it is not) greater attention to estimating methods may be called for.

   Present cash balance estimating procedures also seem to cause bank overdrafts as we noted in each of four months selected for random testing. For example, bank balances were overdrawn at .... Bank on four separate days, which had an impact of nine days overdrawn during February 1978 (approximately one third of the month). Overdrafts ranged from $200,000 to over $700,000 during this period. In a further test of randomly-selected months, we found two overdrafts in July (four-day impact), two overdrafts in September, and four overdrafts in November 1977, which ranged from $1 million to over $8 million. Since the company is in a surplus cash position, overdrafts probably do no more than strain banking relationships. However, if they occur too frequently, charges or penalties can be assessed, since in effect they represent short-term borrowings from the bank. We recognize that unusual circumstances may have existed during the test periods which gave rise to the unusually large fluctuations and overdrafts. In order to ascertain whether this is a continuing problem, it may be desirable to create and maintain for a reasonable period of time a record of daily cash and bank balance forecasting results.

RECOMMENDATION NO. 4

Establish an appropriate time period to list and monitor daily cash and bank balance forecasting results. Study and determine the cause of variances from actual balances so that a basis for improving forecasting techniques that will minimize day to day fluctuations and eliminate overdrafts can be developed.

5. Bank balances are not scheduled and computed on a daily basis to determine and control monthly averages.

In an extension of our review of daily bank balance forecasting, we reviewed bank balance monitoring and control practices for credit line banks. This review indicated that average balances for the credit line banks, excluding the Bank of ...., exceeded requirements by $.7 million (or 10% of balances required to support account activity, including compensation balances) for 19XX. This indicates a need for improvement in techniques for managing bank balances. The following items represent specific areas where improvements might reduce the average balance. Since Corporate Office balances of $5.5 million were $1.8 million under total balance requirements, the excess occurs when Corporate and profit center balances are combined. In other words, both Corporate and profit center accounts can contribute to excess balances. This suggests a need for establishing profit center bank balance objectives so that Corporate balances which are controllable by Corporate Banking personnel can be adjusted to eliminate the excess.

In addition to the above, we noted that actual Corporate balances are not scheduled and averages are not computed on a daily basis to determine and control the monthly averages. Such monthly determinations are largely informal and occur primarily after the fact. Daily monitoring is essential, in our opinion, in order to minimize average balances.

Average monthly bank balances maintained by the profit centers in the credit line banks are reported by the profit centers and monitored by Banking. There is also an annual study of profit center bank balances to determine trend, etc. However, definite bank balance levels to be attained by the profit centers as a requirement for accounts carried in the main credit line banks have not been established.

Recording and averaging daily bank balances for both .... Bank and Bank of .... (and others as may be applicable), in conjunction with defining and establishing profit center maximum balance requirements, would provide the added visibility required to control the overall Corporate balances at these banks. For example, maximum profit center balance requirements would enable corporate balances to be raised or lowered as necessary to meet predetermined objectives.

(continued)

FIG. 32-6 *(cont'd)*

RECOMMENDATION NO. 5

a. Advise relevant profit centers of Corporate cash balance needs with respect to that profit center's cash position in use by Corporate Banking for managing average balances.

b. Record Corporate bank balances on a daily basis and compute averages on all appropriate main credit line bank accounts to control the averages in accordance with the monitoring activity performed in a., above.

6. **Average bank balances, as reported by Bank of ...., have been erroneous for more than one year.**

Average balances for 19XX, as reported by Bank of .... were approximately $1.0 million in excess of requirements. However, after adjusting for bank overstatement errors the excess actually becomes a balance deficiency of $1.2 million, or an average monthly bank error for the year of $2.2 million. It is our understanding that these errors have continued for a period of at least 14 months and result from failure by the bank to record cash transfers to other banks in a timely manner.

RECOMMENDATION NO. 6

Review the continuing error conditions with appropriate personnel at Bank of .... and explore ways to eliminate the problem.

7. **Arrangements regarding cash transfers do not adequately limit opportunities for transfers to non-corporate accounts.**

Present cash transfer instructions permit an authorized signatory to order cash transfers to non-corporate accounts by telephone without any required additional or confirming authority. Banking Administration management has represented that in those rare instances where funds have been transferred to a non-corporate account, standard expense approval procedures preceded the transfer. While we found no instances of any impropriety and were also informed that none have occurred as a result of these instructions, such arrangements are inconsistent with normal cash control practices, which would preclude any single individual from moving funds out of the company without required involvement, concurrence, or approval by at least one other person. In disbursements involving checks, for instance, the check signer is segregated from the check preparer who prepares checks only for properly approved disbursements. Hence, the check signer cannot move funds via check without the involvement of others.

RECOMMENDATION NO. 7

Revise existing bank instructions to preclude the transfer of funds to non-corporate accounts. If business purposes of certain company operating elements require periodic transfer of funds to non-corporate accounts, these elements and the permissible circumstances should be set forth in the revised instructions as an exception to the general rule, or the bank should confirm

FINANCIAL MANAGEMENT

transfer instructions by any signatory to a non-corporate account with another authorized signatory. Whatever method is followed, revised instructions, as required, should be approved by the Senior Vice-President–Finance. Any subsequent revisions that add or delete exceptions which may be occasioned by changed operating conditions should also be approved by the Senior Vice-President–Finance.

8. Two instances were noted where bank accounts were closed without proper approval and/or instructions.

A Northern Hemisphere commercial account that had been closed in mid-August 19XX was still carried in the bank account manual, and there was no evidence that the account had been closed in writing by a letter to designated signatories signed by a duly authorized person.

Two Northern Pacific accounts that were closed by letter in January 19XX did not revoke prior authorizations as is also required or contain any balance disposition instructions although a minor amount was left after outstanding checks had cleared.

RECOMMENDATION NO. 8

Take steps to assure that all discontinued bank accounts are closed by a letter to the bank revoking all previous signatory authorizations and signed by a person authorized to designate signatories. The closing letter should also contain appropriate disposition instructions for any remaining balance after all outstanding checks have cleared.

9. The bank accounts related to the Corporate Health Care Plans have not yet been reconciled.

Two accounts opened in December 19XX at the Bank of . . . . covering the California Corporation Health Care Plan are not being reconciled at the present time. Discussion with Corporate Accounting indicated that there is a lack of definitive and administrative instructions regarding how the accounts are to function to provide a basis for requesting sufficient banking or other claims data to accomplish reconciliation.

RECOMMENDATION NO. 9

Identify overall responsibilities in connection with administering the Plans and related bank account operations and issue appropriate administrative instructions to provide a basis for adequate bank account control.

10. Additional data is required in order to reconcile the Banco de . . . . accounts.

The Banco de . . . ., Madrid, Spain, is used for collecting a Spanish-based corporation's dividend payments. It is classified as a "savings account," and as such, no bank statements are issued. There is a "savings book" for recording all entries to the account which is retained by Southern, S.A.

(continued)

FIG. 32-6 *(cont'd)*

> in Madrid. However, copies of the "savings book" entries have not been forwarded to Corporate Banking for some time although this organization is evidently notified when the corporation's dividends are deposited. Accordingly, notification was received that a dividend of approximately $49,000 was deposited in January 19XX but has not yet been recorded in the general ledger due to some conflicting documentation regarding the date of the dividend. Also, the funds have not been transferred in dollars. Various efforts have been made by Corporate Banking management to resolve the matter and effect proper recording.
>
> **RECOMMENDATION NO. 10**
>
> Request Southern, S.A. to provide copies of the savings book for all recorded entries. Retain a copy in Banking Administration and forward a copy to Corporate Accounting. This procedure would provide a basis for recording and follow-up of the corporation's dividend deposits.

- ☐ Planning and budgeting
  - No management by objectives
  - Improper goals (percentage return on sales instead of return on assets or return on equity)
  - No tie-in of long range plan and annual plan
  - Plans did not follow organization lines
  - Plans not prepared by those who should carry them out (but by financial staff)
  - No coordination between annual capital budget and long-range plan; between research and marketing
  - Expenses budget was set by dictate, without analysis
  - Analysis or testing of plan for acceptability or reasonableness absent—figures just put together as told
  - No test or cutoff rate for capital expenditures; no ranking of projects
  - No responsibility reporting
- ☐ Fund-oriented activities
  - Credit agreements insufficient for needs—no action
  - Credit agreement not competitive
    — All receivables pledged unnecessarily
    — All inventories assigned—unnecessarily
  - Long-term capital market not cultivated
  - Too much dependence on words of present bankers
  - No established written dividend policy
  - No surveillance of performance of money managers
  - Excessive reliance on actuary

FINANCIAL MANAGEMENT

☐ Accounting control activities
  • Control reports ineffective—late, not accurate, not responsibility-oriented
  • Reports not user-suited—too detailed, no exceptions reporting
  • Inadequate analysis of variances
  • Standards out-of-date
☐ Risk management
  • Too much reliance on insurance broker; no independent checking
  • No competition among brokers for business
  • No analysis of risks to be self-insured

In summary, an audit conducted by alert, knowledgeable, aggressive, analytical operational auditors can suggest many improvements. However, it should be recognized that many financial activities are carried out either personally or by the close and direct supervision of the top management of the company. Accordingly, it is prudent to coordinate any operational audit in these areas with the cognizant management so as to secure its support and an understanding of the viewpoint or reasons for the past actions or procedures.

SEGMENT OPERATIONAL AUDITS

The illustrative audit program shown in Figure 32-5 is of a generalized nature, encompassing, to a limited degree, every usual financial activity in a typical company, including those of the chief financial officer. There will be times, however, depending on the existence of special problems, or the availability of the audit staff, when an operational audit may be made of a single financial function or, indeed, of just a segment activity of a function. Audits, for example, might be made of these activities or segments:

☐ Controller
  • Accounting
  • Financial planning and budgeting
  • Tax planning
  • Tax administration
  • Government financial relations
  • EDP systems
☐ Treasurer
  • Cash management
  • Short-term investments
  • Bank relations
  • Long-term debt

- Retirement plan investing
- Insurance
☐ Chief internal auditor
  - Financial auditing
  - Foreign branch auditing
  - Special investigations
  - EDP auditing
  - Operational auditing

Quite often, when the internal audit is of a segment of a broad activity, the tendency is to probe more deeply or analytically into the operation. Under such circumstances, already prepared audit programs, which can be modified in varying degree to fit the needs, are available from a number of sources, including *Internal Auditing Alert*.

Audit Program for Long-Term Liabilities

In these days of hostile takeovers and leveraged buyouts, the long-term debt structure of an entity may be especially vulnerable. And, of course, such operational/financial audits (the distinction sometimes is not clear in such a review) may provide valuable insight into the activity.[4]

> An audit of long-term obligations such as notes payable, bonds, mortgages, and related accounts may often be performed through substantive procedures rather than reliance on internal accounting control. In many instances, the audit effort required to test compliance, and therefore permit reliance to be placed on the system in applying substantive procedures, will be greater than the effort required to apply substantive procedures without such reliance. For internal auditors who perform financial audits, this article provides audit objectives and audit program steps for audit management to use in cases where minimal reliance will be placed on the internal accounting control system over long-term liabilities.
>
> **Audit Objectives.** The audit procedures to be applied to long-term obligations and related accounts should be designed to determine the following:
>
> ☐ Accounting measurements and classifications are comparable with the prior period or exceptions are clearly described.
>
> ☐ Directly related costs and expenses represent valid transactions, are accurately stated, apply to the period, include all transactions that should be recognized, and are appropriately described and classified.
>
> ☐ The liabilities exist, are bona fide obligations of the enterprise, are fairly stated, include all that should be recognized (e.g., obligations related to capitalized leases), and are properly described and classified.

---

[4] Adopted in part from *Internal Auditing Alert*, (New York: Warren, Gorham & Lamont, Oct./Nov. 1985), pp. 6–8, 8–10.

Unrecorded Obligations. Determine whether or not there are any unrecorded obligations. This can be accomplished by the following procedures:

- ☐ Circularize trade creditors to determine if there are any notes payable or installment purchase arrangements payable to vendors and not recorded.
- ☐ Review repairs and maintenance, rent, expendable equipment, and other expense accounts for indication of repeated monthly payments which could be debt installment payments.
- ☐ Extend review of documents supporting cash receipts and disbursements.
- ☐ Be alert to unusual entries (e.g., officers' advance accounts or interest expense that is not in proportion to recorded debt).
- ☐ Confirm existing security agreements under the Uniform Commercial Code.

If the possibility exists that proceeds or funds are being used for unauthorized purposes, the following additional procedures should be performed:

- ☐ Compare actual expenditure with authorized uses.
- ☐ Extend review of documents supporting cash disbursements.
- ☐ If borrowed funds are advanced to affiliated organization, consider the necessity of extending work to include the disposition of such funds by the affiliate organization.

Additions. With respect to additions to debt during the year, the following procedures should be performed:

- ☐ Ascertain authorization from minutes of Board of Directors meetings or other appropriate authoritative documentation.
- ☐ Read a copy of the indenture, loan, or lease agreement, and compare information on agreements with debt record (e.g., subsidiary records and general ledger accounts). Highlights of the indenture, loan agreement, or lease should be summarized as to the following: description of obligation of and date of issuance, authorized and issued amount and rate of interest, holders, repayment provisions, compliance provisions, description of collateral, and insurance coverage required.
- ☐ Trace proceeds to cash receipts books, bank statements, subsidiary records, and general ledger accounts.
- ☐ Relate use of proceeds to other business activities (e.g., plan expansion, retirement of debt, or preferred stock).
- ☐ Check the reasonableness of interest rate and consider the need to impute interest at an appropriate current rate.

If a public issuance of certificates of indebtedness is involved, the following procedures should be performed:

- ☐ Account for numerical sequence based on certificates received from the printer or confirm issued obligations directly with the trustee.
- ☐ Review authorization for, and computation of, expenses incurred in connection with issuance.

Retirement or Reacquisitions. For retirements or reacquisitions of debt securities during the year, the following procedures should be performed:

- ☐ Check authorization to minutes of Board of Directors' meetings or other appropriate authoritative documentation if reacquisition or retirement is other than according to a scheduled or a previously approved plan.
- ☐ Verify that payments required during the period have been made and are in the proper amount.
- ☐ Trace payments made to cash disbursements, subsidiary records, and general ledger accounts; and inspect vouchers, paid checks, and debit memos or trace to entries in trustee's statements.
- ☐ Count or inspect bonds, notes, and related coupons canceled during the period or verify destruction.
- ☐ If retired obligations were secured by collateral, ascertain if the collateral has been released.
- ☐ Ascertain that deposits to separate redemption accounts, debt service, or sinking fund accounts are made as required.

Interest Expense. Procedures for the verification of interest expense should include the following:

- ☐ Check calculation of interest paid during the period and prepayments accruals at the end of the period.
- ☐ Inspect paid checks for interest payments, or confirm with trustee, and review unclaimed interest, if applicable.
- ☐ Reconcile total interest accrued during the period to recorded interest expense.

Where installment purchase or similar equipment obligations are involved, amortization of unamortized interest and finance charges (i.e., the difference between the cash purchase price and total installments) should also be tested. In general, interest expense for the period and the accrual or prepayment at the balance sheet date should be audited in conjunction with the debt transactions that occurred during the period.

Premium or Discount on Bonds. Audit procedures for the verification of premium or discount on bonds should include the following:

- ☐ Check calculation of amortization and unamortized balance at the end of the period.
- ☐ Reconcile amortization to related expense account.

Premium or discount on bonds should also be audited in conjunction with debt transactions that occurred during the period. Additions and deductions during the period should be related to results of audit procedures performed in connection with additions and retirements of debt.

Compliance With Loan and Security Agreements. A determination should be made as to the company's compliance with requirements of loan and security agreements, bond indentures, etc. Since this information is of continuing interest on an internal audit, copies of the agreement should be maintained in the permanent file.

Agreements usually require that the borrower make principal, interest, sinking fund, or other payments in stated amounts and at particular times, and also may include other provisions. When reviewing loan and security agreements, check whether or not such agreements contain any of the following provisions:

- [ ] Prepayment privileges or restrictions and related penalties.
- [ ] Collateral requirements.
- [ ] Conversion periods, rates, and securities into which conversion is permitted.
- [ ] Report and letters required from the company and their due dates.
- [ ] Insurance coverage required.
- [ ] Ratios and coverage that must be maintained, such as debt-to-equity ratio and working capital ratio.
- [ ] Limitations on dividends.
- [ ] Limitations on types of expenditures, such as property and equipment, lease obligations, and investments.
- [ ] Limitations on types and amounts of additional indebtedness.
- [ ] Limitations on sales of assets, mergers, and dissolution.
- [ ] Limitations on acquisition of other companies for cash and/or debt.
- [ ] Description of events that constitute "events of default."

Confirmation Procedures. Because the amounts are usually material and the number of loan and security holders are usually limited in number, notes and bonds should ordinarily be confirmed directly with the holders designated in the loan agreements. When a corporate trustee is retained, confirmation with the trustee rather than individual creditors is sufficient.

A corporate trustee should also confirm authorized debt and balances in various special accounts (e.g., debt service fund, sinking fund, and redemption fund). The auditor should ascertain that all items on the creditor confirmations are appropriately recorded in the company's accounts or other records.

Control over mailing and receipt of confirmations should be exercised in the same manner as with receivable confirmations. Second requests should be sent to all creditors that do not reply within a reasonable period, usually about one month. If after allowing a reasonable period for replies, the "no" replies are material in relation to the original confirmation, consideration should be given to sending third requests. In some cases, it may also be appropriate to follow up large accounts by telephone or telegram.

CHAPTER **33**

Credit and Collections Management

Introduction	1	Elements of the Credit and Collections Operation	7
Nature and Role of Credit	2		
Basic Objectives of Credit Management	2	Illustrative Audit Questionnaire—Credit and Collections Activity	8
Organizational Status	4	Credit and Collections Operational Audit Program	14
The Three C's of Credit	6	Suggested Reading	20

Fig. 33-1	Functional Credit Organization in a Large Manufacturing Company	5
Fig. 33-2	Audit Questionnaire—Credit and Collections Activity	9
Fig. 33-3	Credit and Collections Operational Audit Program	14
Fig. 33-4	Some Selected Key Business Ratios Developed by Dun & Bradstreet, Inc.	19

INTRODUCTION

Many recent books on business management or on the many facets of financial management stress the importance of liquidity and net working capital. Net working capital, sometimes simply called working capital, is the difference between current assets and current liabilities. Generally, current assets include those assets that are cash or will be converted into cash in one year or in the normal cycle of the business, and those liabilities that must be extinguished in one year or in the normal cycle of the company business, and that involve the use of current assets.

Management of working capital attracts increasing attention for a variety of basically related reasons, including (1) the higher cost of carrying working capital given current interest rates and/or inflation rates; (2) the difficulty of securing outside capital on acceptable terms to finance the business; (3) the increased emphasis on return on assets, or return on equity, as acceptable measures of business management performance; and (4) the losses that may result from inadequate attention to these assets or liabilities.

Accounts receivable constitute a major segment of current assets in most mercantile or manufacturing companies. It is in the context of the need for effective management of these trade accounts receivable that this chapter is written. Some general background material on credit and collections in a typical medium-sized or large manufacturing or wholesaling company may be helpful in developing an acceptable operations audit program of this function.

NATURE AND ROLE OF CREDIT

There are several variant definitions of credit with differing emphasis on certain aspects. Basically, credit may be defined very simply as the power or ability to obtain cash, or goods or services, in exchange for a promise to pay for them in the future. The buyer or purchaser uses his purchasing power as represented by his willingness and ability to pay some time in the future. The seller accepts this promise, and the related risk, in exchange for the cash, goods, or services.

In the United States, a credit economy exists, since the vast amount of sales by far are made for credit as distinguished from cash. From the user standpoint, credit may be public or private, depending on whether the user is a government, an agency thereof, or a private entity. In this chapter, the emphasis is on private credit as distinguished from public finance. Private credit may be divided into consumer credit or business credit, depending on whether the user is a personal consumer or a business entity. This chapter deals largely with business credit used by a typical manufacturer or wholesaler. Emphasis, thus, will be on what is known as mercantile or commercial credit to the exclusion of investment credit (basically long-term obligations given in exchange for money or property), real estate credit (mortgage credit or comparable credit where the security is real estate), or short-term financing provided by commercial banks or other financing institutions.

While there are no known statistics to indicate the total volume of credit business in the United States, it has been variously estimated that 90 to 95 percent of all business involves credit. To the seller, this sales volume is represented by accounts or notes receivable. To the buyer, the obligation to repay is reflected in the statement of financial position as accounts or notes payable.

BASIC OBJECTIVES OF CREDIT MANAGEMENT

Obviously, the manager of the credit and collection function should support the corporate objectives and, within the confines of his authority and responsibility, should contribute to their accomplishment. From the financial viewpoint, the credit manager should assist in meeting the corporate goal for return on assets as one of the factors in achieving the targeted return on shareholders' equity.[1] Further, he should play a role in achieving the annual and long-term net profit objectives and related liquidity objectives.

To be more specific as to the objectives of credit management, the principal credit officer should effectively carry out these functions:

☐ *Assist in maximizing or optimizing the sales or volume objectives of the business.* Credit terms are a major factor in meeting the planned sales volume in the annual business plan or other specific targets related thereto. Through the use of proper credit policies, procedures, and practices, the credit manager should assist the marketing division to maximize the sales volume, which presumably is related to the optimization of the return on shareholders' equity. The number of units sold and the selling price usually are greatly influenced by the credit terms, some of which will be governed by industry practice and others which may reflect the ingenuity of the credit manager (and sales manager).

☐ *Control the investment in trade accounts receivable.* In achieving the return on assets objective, the amount invested in trade receivables is an important factor because of the magnitude of the asset. The credit manager must hold the days of sales outstanding (DSO), or other criterion of receivable level, within acceptable limits. Of course, customary industry credit terms, the stage of the business cycle, or seasonal influences will affect the level of investment. But credit policies and standards in granting credit, and in setting credit limits as well as collection policies and procedures, are important considerations.

☐ *Maintaining the expense of credits and collections within acceptable limits.* This contemplates controlling the usual departmental operating expenses within budgetary or other limits. In addition to the typical costs for most operating departments, there are some unique costs relating to (a) the provision for doubtful accounts and the related write-off of bad-debt losses; (b) costs of outside collection agencies, if any; and (c) fees or other costs for securing credit information.

In this context, controlling costs does not signify minimizing expenses. Thus, bad-debt losses may be kept low by excessively restrictive procedures or standards. It may be far better to accept a higher level of probable doubtful accounts in return for the greater margin to be secured from the higher sales volume.

The principal objectives of the credit and collection department are the three listed above. Of course, other supplementary objectives will contribute to an effective operation. These would include cooperation with outside credit agencies and credit departments and coordination with appropriate

---

[1] For a discussion of corporate profit goals, including return on equity, see James D. Willson, *Budgeting and Profit Planning Manual*, 2nd ed. Chapter 6 (New York: Warren, Gorham & Lamont, 1988).

internal departments, that is, the sales or marketing department and the treasurer's department.

ORGANIZATIONAL STATUS

Before moving on to the more technical aspects of the credit and collection function, one other topic that has a direct bearing on an operational audit and that relates to organizational considerations needs attention. Basically, there are two questions: (1) What is the place of the credit function in the organization (i.e., to whom should it report)? and (2) What should be the organizational structure?

The credit function evolves in any business just as other business functions evolve. In a small organization, the owner may handle the activity, or it may be a part-time function of an accountant, the treasurer, or a salesperson. For operational audit purposes, a medium-sized to large-sized company and extensive credit activity is assumed.

The place of the credit and collection function in a medium-sized to large-sized business will depend on many factors: (1) the capability and personality of the credit manager; (2) the relative importance, management style, and personalities of the financial executive and the marketing executive; and (3) the attitudes of senior management toward the credit function, to name but a few. However, in the typical U.S. manufacturing or wholesaling concern, the credit department is generally found in one of three locations:

1. *As part of the finance function.* In most U.S. companies, the credit department is an integral part of the financial function. The acceptance of credit risks is regarded basically as a financing activity of the concern. Certainly, both the maintenance of trade accounts receivable in an acceptable financial condition and timely collection of funds are essential to the financial health of the company, as are meeting the terms of credit agreements with banks and other lenders. If the function is part of the financial activity, in many instances a financial type might be hesitant to accept credit risks and might thereby injure sales.

2. *As part of the marketing function.* In those cases where the credit department is under the jurisdiction of the marketing executive, some would argue that the selling of merchandise is facilitated and that the sales force cooperates to a greater degree in providing follow-up collection service. The contention often is that since a purpose of both departments is to increase sales, the two departments should be supervised by a common head. However, too much sales orientation can and does lead to unacceptable credit or financial risks.

3. *As a department independent of the financial or marketing executives.* In some instances, such as a wholesale firm, the credit manager might report

FIG. 33-1
Functional Credit Organization in a Large Manufacturing Company

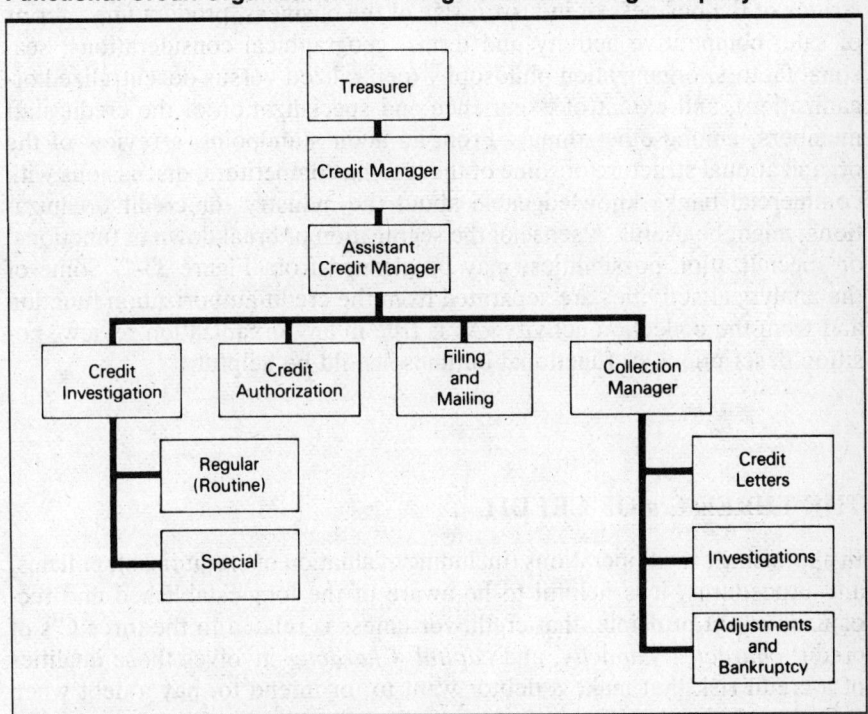

to an operations officer who is on an executive level similar to the sales manager or controller. Under many circumstances, the close relationship to warehousing or purchasing, and the need to avoid undue pressures from either the financial function or the marketing function, makes such an arrangement quite feasible.

The reader should be aware of some alternatives in considering the organizational status of the department and is referred to the available literature on this subject.[2] Obviously, the credit executive must be sensitive to the need to secure profitable sales, yet recognize the financial reality of the proposed transaction. In other words, he must perceive or distinguish the need to take prudent credit risks, or a businessman's risks. He must obviously work closely with the sales and finance departments, must maintain a good relationship with the accounting and accounts receivable departments because of the use of common records, accounting principles, etc., as well as work in concert with the order department, the shipping department, and other departments.

---

[2] See the Suggested Reading at the end of this chapter.

In discussing the organizational structure of the credit department, it is difficult to portray a "standard" department. Much depends on the peculiarities of the business or industry, size of the business, product lines, terms of sale, competitive activity and terms, geographical considerations, seasonal factors, organization philosophy (centralized versus decentralized organization), and extent of experience and specialization of the credit staff members, among other things. From an audit standpoint, a review of the organizational structure of some of the leading competitors, discussions with commercial banks knowledgeable about the industry, or credit organizations, might be useful. A sense of the segregation or breakdown of functions, or specialization possibilities, may be gleaned from Figure 33-1. Some of the analytical activities are separated from the credit authorization function and from the collection activity. As is true in any organization review, position descriptions or functional outlines should be helpful.

THE THREE C's OF CREDIT

In appraising credit operations (including evaluation of credit risks), policies, and procedures, it is helpful to be aware of the long-established and recognized credit principle, that creditworthiness is related to the three C's of credit: *character, capacity*, and *capital. Character* involves those qualities of a credit risk that make a debtor want to, or intend to, pay a debt when it is due. Judgment of this factor must be based on evidence such as a consistent and long history of credit payment. A debtor who has established a good credit reputation and record seldom deviates from his paying pattern. *Capacity* relates to the ability to pay the obligation when due, generally out of the cash flow of the organization. It is basically a question of earning power, or uncommitted cash flow, as distinguished from savings. *Capital* deals with the financial strength of the risk: the existence of equity or net worth. It is evidence that something of value exists to pay the debt if character and capacity fail. However, credit is granted on the basis of continued capacity of cash flow. Resort to capital for repayment usually means the end of a business relationship. Creditworthiness may be dependent on the economic environment or conditions over which the credit risk may have no control. Hence, some credit managers distinguish between the "normal" capacity and capital and look to the short- or long-run conditions in evaluating a risk.

The three C's usually are in fact interrelated. Thus, capital arises from past capacity and in some instances is evidence of future capacity. Character, obviously, is the foundation for capacity.

Given the existence of these three C's, the decision to take a credit risk is largely judgmental and pragmatic as distinguished from mathematical. It depends on the specifics of the case. Nevertheless, there have been some attempts (including the use of computers, as in retail credit) to array the various factors that should be considered in a credit decision and to reach conclusions based on summary scores.[3]

ELEMENTS OF THE CREDIT AND COLLECTIONS OPERATION

An operations audit of the credit and collections function may relate to the entire department or to selected elements. Aside from such matters as departmental objectives, organizational structure, or competence of personnel are such other specific subjects as these, which have a bearing on the effectiveness of the operation:

1. *Credit policy.* General acceptability of the policy and consistency with company overall policies and objectives; and consistency with related departmental policies such as sales, order handling, shipping, and accounting

2. *Credit authorization procedure*
   - ☐ Distinction between large credits and small, and between new accounts and repetitive orders
   - ☐ Standards of financial strength versus competitive practice
   - ☐ Method or factors in setting credit limits
   - ☐ Analysis or identification of risks

3. *Terms of sale.* Competitive posture, financial soundness

4. *Sources of credit information.* Adequacy, currency, practicality
   - ☐ Knowledge of credit manager
   - ☐ Mercantile agencies (general and special)
   - ☐ Interchange bureaus
   - ☐ Attorneys
   - ☐ Salespersons
   - ☐ Personal interviews
   - ☐ Financial statements
   - ☐ Banks
   - ☐ Trade sources

5. *Collection procedures*
   - ☐ Use of aging schedules
   - ☐ DSO

---

[3] For some examples of the factors (such as capacity, business history, ability to pay, future prospects, and return on equity), see Theodore N. Beckman and Ronald S. Foster, *Credits and Collections*, 8th ed. (New York: McGraw-Hill Book Co., 1969), pp. 89–93, or Richard F. Vancil *Financial Executive's Handbook* (Homewood, Ill.: Dow Jones-Irwin, Inc., 1970), pp. 753–756.

- [ ] Collection intervals
- [ ] Collection vehicles or tools
  - Telephone calls
  - Salespersons
  - Mailgrams
  - Standard preprinted forms
  - Statements
  - Form letters
  - Individual letters
- [ ] Collection agencies or attorneys

6. *Measuring credit department performance*
   - [ ] DSO
   - [ ] Percentage of past due receivables
   - [ ] Provision for doubtful accounts and actual write-offs
   - [ ] Collections on accounts written off
   - [ ] Expenses as related to credit sales

7. *Management reports*
   - [ ] Weekly status report; high-risk or high-dollar accounts
   - [ ] Monthly; comparative aging or delinquency reports by appropriate organizational segment
   - [ ] Quarterly; analysis of trade receivables, comparative aging, and comparisons with industry data

8. *Other*
   - [ ] Credit insurance
   - [ ] Computer applications in credit selection
   - [ ] Security measures

These subjects are merely suggestive of the functional areas to be considered in an operations audit.

ILLUSTRATIVE AUDIT QUESTIONNAIRE—CREDIT AND COLLECTIONS ACTIVITY

As in any operational audit, a well-designed questionnaire is helpful in developing an acceptable audit program for the credit and collections function. Such a questionnaire is shown in Figure 33-2. This document must be tailored to fit the needs of the specific circumstances of each audit program. This particular questionnaire has been developed for the activities of an appliance manufacturer and wholesaler.

(continued on page 33-14)

FIG. 33-2

Audit Questionnaire—Credit and Collections Activity

	Response	
	Yes	No
A. Credit and Collections Policy:		
1. Is there a written credit policy statement? Date of latest revision	☐	☐
2. Is it sufficiently specific as to be useful?	☐	☐
3. Are the policy statements consistent with the policy statements for the other related functions?		
a. Marketing	☐	☐
b. Order department	☐	☐
c. Shipping department	☐	☐
d. Finance	☐	☐
e. Accounting	☐	☐
4. Are there any sales customers who do not require credit approval?		
a. U.S. government	☐	☐
b. Major retailers	☐	☐
c. Foreign governments or agencies	☐	☐
d. Foreign subsidiaries	☐	☐
B. Organization:		
1. Is there a written document outlining the functions of the credit and collection department? Date of latest revision	☐	☐
2. Are there position descriptions for each major functional position outlining the authority and responsibility of each?	☐	☐
3. Are there any known inconsistencies between these position descriptions and those of the following?		
a. Marketing	☐	☐
b. Accounting	☐	☐
c. Order	☐	☐
d. Shipping	☐	☐
e. Finance	☐	☐
4. Are there any known inconsistencies within the department itself?	☐	☐
5. Is anyone assigned the responsibility of keeping up-to-date on the latest technical developments for possible departmental uses (e.g., computers)?	☐	☐

(continued)

FIG. 33-2 *(cont'd)*

	Response	
	Yes	No

6. Are the responsibilities clear as between those in the branch credit offices versus the corporate office? ☐ ☐

7. Does any credit executive have direct access to the accounts receivable computer ledgers? ☐ ☐

8. Is provision made for assigning the highest credit risk investigation, etc., to the most experienced persons? ☐ ☐

9. Comment on the ability of the credit manager to give sufficient time to the major credit and/or collection problems with the delegation of routine matters to others. ☐ ☐

C. Credit Authorization:

1. Does final credit approval rest with the general credit manager? ☐ ☐

2. Can any segment be delegated to others? ☐ ☐

3. If an order is rejected on the basis of credit, is provision made for review by higher authority, if requested by the sales department? ☐ ☐
   Who? ....

4. Can provision be made for special terms for a customer? ☐ ☐
   By whom? ....

5. Is special or expedited handling provided for major accounts/orders? ☐ ☐

6. What is the typical credit approval period for the following?
   Regular orders .... days
   Special orders .... days

7. Review with the credit manager what alternatives to irrevocable letters of credit have been used for foreign shipments.
   Do you have any suggestions for the credit manager? ☐ ☐

D. Credit Information Sources and Credit Applications:

1. Which of these sources of information are most frequently used?
   a. Salespersons' reports ☐ ☐
   b. Dun & Bradstreet, Inc. regular reports or reference books ☐ ☐
   c. Dun & Bradstreet, Inc. special reports ☐ ☐
   d. Other mercantile agencies ☐ ☐
   e. Credit interchange reports ☐ ☐
   f. Trade bureau reports ☐ ☐
   g. Credit applications and financial statements secured directly from applicant ☐ ☐

	Response	
	Yes	No

    h. Bankers' reports — ☐ ☐
    i. Direct inquiries from the trade — ☐ ☐
    j. Registers and directories — ☐ ☐
    k. Other — ☐ ☐

2. Is there a standard credit application form? ☐ ☐
   Date of last revision ....

3. Does it provide for an accompanying financial statement? ☐ ☐

4. Are the forms usually completed? ☐ ☐

E. Credit Files:

1. Are the credit files automated? ☐ ☐

2. Is the process of handling new orders differentiated from those of old customers? ☐ ☐

3. Is credit data summarized and transferred to a credit history record? ☐ ☐

4. Are credit files, including orders refused for credit reasons, made available to the salesperson or department? ☐ ☐

5. Does the credit folder on each customer contain all recent data including credit reports, financial statements, and so forth? ☐ ☐

6. Does the credit folder clearly indicate reasons for credit refusal, basis of credit limits, and so forth? ☐ ☐

7. Is there a computer file or card index showing the name, address, and file number for each customer? ☐ ☐

8. Are files segregated into active and inactive accounts? ☐ ☐
   How often are they updated? ....
   As to the last updating:
     Name of account ....
     Date of update ....

F. Terms of Sale:

1. Is the credit period of the company (for the typical sale) competitive? ☐ ☐

2. Are the typical discount terms competitive? ☐ ☐

3. Is abuse of the cash discount extensive? ☐ ☐

(continued)

FIG. 33-2 *(cont'd)*

	Response	
	Yes	No
4. Are seasonal terms in use?	☐	☐
5. Is an anticipation discount rate ever allowed?	☐	☐
6. Is the company in compliance with applicable federal laws, including the Robinson-Patman Act?	☐	☐
7. Must any higher authority approve special terms to the major private brand accounts?	☐	☐
G. Collection Procedures:		
1. Is there a written collection procedure manual?	☐	☐
2. Is an aged accounts receivable report currently available? Frequency of updating? .... Date of last update?	☐	☐
3. Are collection effort results shown thereon?	☐	☐
4. Does the statement or report show all open items by customer?	☐	☐
5. Is the aging minimally as follows?		
a. Current amount	☐	☐
b. Past due:		
30 days	☐	☐
60 days	☐	☐
90 days	☐	☐
120 days	☐	☐
6. Are collection notices sent in accordance with the specified schedule?	☐	☐
7. What form of follow-up is used?		
a. Letter	☐	☐
b. Telegram	☐	☐
c. Phone call	☐	☐
d. Personal call	☐	☐
8. Is the collection procedure computerized for form letter, notices, and so forth?	☐	☐
9. Are copies of collection documents sent to all appropriate parties?	☐	☐
10. Is there periodic notification to the Vice-President–Finance and attorney of all accounts that could result in the following?		
a. Litigation	☐	☐
b. Bankruptcy	☐	☐

	Response	
	Yes	No
c. Notes payable	☐	☐
d. Special payment schedule	☐	☐
e. Collection agency assistance	☐	☐

11. Is approval of the Vice-President–Finance, Controller, or other independent authority required for write-off of doubtful accounts? ☐ ☐

12. Is the counseling on collections adequate or satisfactory? ☐ ☐

13. Is the collection staff sensitive to maintaining good customer relations? ☐ ☐

H. Management Reports:

1. Is an aged comparative summary of accounts receivable made available to the Vice-President–Finance monthly? ☐ ☐

2. Are appropriate analyses of receivables made by customer groups?
   At least quarterly? ☐ ☐
   a. By product line? ☐ ☐
   b. By country of destination? ☐ ☐

3. Is a periodic report made on the following?
   a. Collection efforts—Frequency ☐ ☐
   b. High-risk accounts—Frequency ☐ ☐
   c. High-value accounts—Frequency ☐ ☐

4. Are comparative reports on industry versus company performance made, for example, on the following?
   a. DSO ☐ ☐
   b. Receivable turnover ☐ ☐
   c. Currency ☐ ☐

5. Is any summary or analysis of rejected orders made to the following?
   a. Sales manager ☐ ☐
   b. Vice-President–Finance ☐ ☐

6. Is an annual budget prepared and approved for the department? ☐ ☐

7. Are monthly comparisons of actual and budgeted expenses made and explanations for any variances given? ☐ ☐

CREDIT AND COLLECTIONS OPERATIONAL AUDIT PROGRAM

In the business world, the credit function is critical to sales and profit performance, whether actual or potential. And the success of the credit and collection activity depends greatly on the proper organization of the department and the system, efficiency, or effectiveness with which the work is carried out. For this reason, a periodic operations audit may be helpful and may provide suggestions for improvement.

An audit program for a somewhat limited operations review of the credit and collection department of an appliance manufacturing company is illustrated in Figure 33-3.

(continued on page 33-20)

FIG. 33-3

Credit and Collections Operational Audit Program

Audit Program—Credit and Collections Management

	Done by	Date
A. Policy and Organization:		
1. Secure a copy of the policy statement of the credit and collection department and check it for adequacy, completeness, and timeliness.	....	....
2. Compare the policy statement with that of the marketing department for any conflict or inconsistency.	....	....
3. Obtain a copy of the organization chart of the credit department and all functional outlines and position descriptions. Review for completeness, consistency, and currency with emphasis on:		
a. Stated job description versus actual duties performed	....	....
b. Suitability of functional segregation or job groupings (regarding internal control)	....	....
c. Adequacy of coordination with:		
■ Sales department	....	....
■ Order department	....	....
■ Accounts receivable department	....	....
B. Credit Authorization:		
1. Secure the credit files for:		
a. Current year of the three largest regular customers		
b. About ten smaller commercial accounts selected at random		

	Done by	Date

c. Two U.S. government accounts—Check these for completeness, currency, and orderliness with reference to these points:
- Completeness of credit application form　....　....
- Evidence of review and approval by the credit manager *personally*　....　....
- Written evidence as to basis for credit limits and terms　....　....
- Reasonableness of the credit decision　....　....
- Adequate analysis of current financial statements　....　....
- Existence of current Dun & Bradstreet, Inc. report, or its equivalent　....　....
- Existence of salespersons' report　....　....

2. For two recent disapproved sales orders, secure the files and check for:
   a. Adequacy of support for the decision　....　....
   b. Evidence of review by the salesmanager or salesperson　....　....
   c. Reasonableness of the credit decision　....　....

3. For a limited number of accounts, check the credit history card for:
   a. Currency　....　....
   b. Completeness　....　....
   c. Consistency with credit folder　....　....
   d. Inclusion on computer index　....　....

4. Review some current orders being processed for:
   a. Adequacy of procedures　....　....
   b. Conformance to manual　....　....
   c. Timeliness in processing　....　....

5. For perhaps the ten largest accounts, or those having an exposure of $0.5 million or more, review the extent of the analysis of the financial statements of the customers.
   a. Check for inquiry made as to:
   - Assigned receivables　....　....
   - Pledged inventory　....　....
   - Nature of notes payable　....　....

   b. Review the extent of ratio analysis
   - Current ratio　....　....
   - Net worth to debt　....　....
   - Quick ratio　....　....
   - Operating expense to sales　....　....
   - Return on net worth　....　....
   - Any other ratios considered important　....　....

(continued)

FIG. 33-3 *(cont'd)*

	Done by	Date

    c. Compare such ratios with the business ratios (wholesaling—electrical appliances) prepared by Dun & Bradstreet, Inc.[4] or others

C. Credit Application and Credit Information Sources:

1. Secure credit application forms of some competitors and compare with the company format. Especially review for key data on competitive forms not requested by our corporation. Review questions for clarity and completeness. …. ….

2. On a test basis, review some completed credit applications for degree of completeness. Check for evidence of inadequacies (e.g., clarity of questions, lack of space for answers, key points not discussed). …. ….

3. For some recently completed credit applications, review as to reference checks and limited verification of other answers (e.g., banks, amount of mortgage). …. ….

4. On a test-check basis, review the credit file to verify uses of such selected sources of credit information as:
    a. Salespersons' report …. ….
    b. Dun & Bradstreet, Inc. report …. ….
    c. Dun & Bradstreet, Inc. reference book …. ….
    d. Dun & Bradstreet, Inc. *Special Report* (on larger accounts) …. ….
    e. Current financial statement received directly from applicant …. ….
    f. Bankers' reports (private brand or larger accounts) …. ….

D. Collection Procedures:

1. Secure a recent aged accounts receivable schedule and check for completeness, accuracy, and notations of credit effort. A test-check should be made of the aging by reference to invoices. …. ….

    Determine if the aging summary is supported by the details account analysis for one or two age categories. …. ….

2. Review the collection file for timeliness in follow-up. Is the collection interval observed?

---

[4] For an example of some of the industry ratios made available and periodically undated by Dun & Bradstreet, Inc., see Figure 33-4. Each line of business is represented by three ratios. The middle, or median, ratio is shown in boldface; the upper quartile is the top of the series of three; and the lower quartile is represented by the bottom figure. Those making an operational audit should consult with the appropriate financial officer as to whether the median or a quartile permits the most fair comparison. (And the proper line of business should be selected.)

	Done by	Date

3. On a test-check basis, review for appropriate notice to the salesperson of the collection effort.   . . . .

4. Review, on a selected basis, the adequacy of the following series of collection letters:
   a. Friendly reminder   . . . .
   b. More formal (second) request   . . . .
   c. Final notice   . . . .
   d. Written personal appeal   . . . .

   On a very limited basis, check with some dunned customers as to impression (e.g., courtesy).   . . . .

5. Secure some competitive collection letters and review for new ideas or more appealing content.   . . . .

6. Review the collection effort, perhaps by limited reference to customers, as to the appropriate mix of letters, phone calls, and personal calls. When cost and time are considerations, suggest improvements.   . . . .

7. Review the procedure for provision for doubtful accounts. From an accounting standpoint, is it supportable? Adequate? Have any significant year-end adjustments been necessary?   . . . .

8. As to the write-off of bad accounts, check the adequacy of internal controls, including:
   a. Approval of the write-off   . . . .
   b. Nonaccess to the subsidiary ledger by the collections personnel   . . . .
   c. Treatment of collections on written-off amounts   . . . .

9. Review the limited use of sales personnel on selected collection efforts. Should it be continued? What is the reaction of the customer?   . . . .

10. Review with the credit manager the possible extended use of securing a note payable from the more delinquent accounts. Is this in line with industry practice?   . . . .

11. Review with the credit manager the desirability of credit insurance on all but the private brand accounts.   . . . .

E. Measurement and Control of Departmental Performance:

1. Confirm that monthly aged accounts receivable statements are:

(continued)

FIG. 33-3 *(cont'd)*

	Done by	Date
a. Prepared for and reviewed by the credit manager	....	....
b. Summarized and provided to the Vice-President–Finance and controller	....	....
Comment on timeliness.	....	....
2. Review the trend of days sales outstanding (DSO) and ask for explanations from the credit manager. Compare company results with industry data and/or selected competitors.	....	....
3. Review the available analyses of accounts receivable for completeness and timeliness. Can you suggest other useful reviews or new uses to which existing data can be put?	....	....
4. Is the department using the latest practical devices or methods? Are there opportunities for cost saving?	....	....
5. Is a periodic summary or brief commentary on accounts receivable made to the Board of Directors or the Audit Committee?	....	....
6. Suggest some limited ways to measure the productivity of (a) the credit granting function and (b) the collection function.	....	....
How does company effort and cost compare with the industry?	....	....
7. Review a recent monthly budget report comparing actual and budget performance, and ascertain:		
a. The use made of the report by the credit manager or assistant credit manager	....	....
b. Adequacy of the budget and budget procedure	....	....
c. Suitability of the budget basis (e.g., fixed or variable)	....	....
8. Comment on the availability of other credit and collection procedures, not presently employed, that might be considered by the credit manager.	....	....

CREDIT & COLLECTIONS MANAGEMENT

FIG. 33-4

Some Selected Key Business Ratios Developed by Dun & Bradstreet, Inc.

MANUFACTURING & CONSTRUCTION

Line of Business (and number of concerns reporting)	Current assets to current debt	Net profits on net sales	Net profits on tangible net worth	Net profits on net working capital	Net sales to tangible net worth	Net sales to net working capital	Collection period	Net sales to inventory	Fixed assets to tangible net worth	Current debt to tangible net worth	Total debt to tangible net worth	Inventory to net working capital	Current debt to inventory	Funded debts to net working capital
	Times	Percent	Percent	Percent	Times	Times	Days	Times	Percent	Percent	Percent	Percent	Percent	Percent
2871-72-79 Agricultural Chemicals (43)	3.37 / **1.92** / 1.34	4.21 / **2.51** / 1.66	11.09 / **6.77** / 4.48	26.87 / **15.08** / 8.39	4.75 / **2.96** / 2.14	7.17 / **4.50** / 3.25	33 / **52** / 97	17.0 / **9.5** / 5.7	21.5 / **41.8** / 74.3	25.0 / **56.4** / 124.7	58.3 / **151.1** / 260.8	32.1 / **49.2** / 121.5	109.2 / **139.9** / 223.2	11.1 / **39.2** / 85.9
3722-23-29 Airplane Parts & Accessories (70)	3.54 / **2.32** / 1.73	5.38 / **2.51** / 0.75	12.69 / **8.09** / 1.42	17.00 / **10.65** / 2.87	3.78 / **2.76** / 1.95	5.17 / **3.90** / 2.56	43 / **60** / 73	7.0 / **5.0** / 3.5	36.5 / **53.9** / 81.6	26.2 / **55.1** / 98.1	60.3 / **113.1** / 177.4	51.1 / **82.4** / 116.8	61.3 / **88.0** / 131.9	32.8 / **60.1** / 96.6
2051-52 Bakery Products (62)	3.31 / **1.96** / 1.41	3.22 / **1.56** / 0.46	14.30 / **6.51** / 2.37	38.38 / **21.68** / 5.08	6.85 / **4.34** / 3.50	20.49 / **11.58** / 7.33	16 / **23** / 32	38.8 / **28.9** / 15.5	52.8 / **77.7** / 105.0	19.4 / **36.7** / 60.3	38.6 / **53.6** / 107.4	37.2 / **53.8** / 84.6	118.0 / **200.0** / 284.0	21.7 / **68.4** / 147.9
3312-13-15-16-17 Blast Furnaces, Steel Wks & Rolling Mills (69)	3.21 / **2.24** / 1.68	4.31 / **3.21** / 1.66	11.89 / **6.77** / 3.92	24.57 / **15.28** / 8.59	3.29 / **2.29** / 1.73	6.95 / **4.78** / 3.58	37 / **45** / 51	6.9 / **5.4** / 4.5	60.1 / **78.3** / 107.8	25.4 / **38.5** / 57.5	56.4 / **73.2** / 114.5	74.9 / **87.2** / 112.1	60.1 / **86.3** / 123.0	35.0 / **79.3** / 129.6
2331 Blouses & Waists, Women's & Misses' (53)	1.98 / **1.50** / 1.28	2.19 / **1.23** / 0.49	23.19 / **12.60** / 3.73	30.41 / **14.90** / 4.35	14.68 / **9.98** / 6.49	17.47 / **11.39** / 7.38	30 / **46** / 61	20.0 / **11.2** / 7.2	5.9 / **11.7** / 25.3	90.9 / **141.8** / 314.9	99.5 / **194.7** / 383.7	62.6 / **98.6** / 222.6	136.9 / **211.7**	8.1
2731-32 Books: Publishing, Publishing & Printing (58)	3.55 / **2.36** / 1.92	7.18 / **3.77** / 2.08	14.11 / **9.44** / 5.47	23.63 / **12.61** / 7.16	2.85 / **2.05** / 1.60	5.23 / **3.04** / 2.21	45 / **64** / 82	9.0 / **4.4** / 3.2	14.8 / **36.3** / 50.7	24.1				
2211 Broad Woven Fabrics, Cotton (45)	6.64 / **3.78** / 2.52	3.32 / **2.50** / 1.33	8.27 / **5.24** / 3.48	14.93 / **9.38** / 4.24	2.77 / **2.05** / 1.69	4.63 / **3.26** / 2.83	48	7.9						
2031-32-33-34-35-36-37 Canned & Preserved Frts, Vegs & Sea Fds (80)	2.70 / **1.79**	4.22 / **2.58**	14.06 / **10.32**	26.56	5.60									

SUGGESTED READING

Barzman, Sol. *The Collection Program: A Practical Guide*. New York: National Association of Credit Management, 1979.

Beckman, Theodore N., and Ronald S. Foster, *Credits and Collections*, 8th ed. New York: McGraw-Hill Book Co., 1969.

CHAPTER **34**

Inventory Management

Introduction	2	Scope of Inventory Management	19
		Inventory Planning Applications	20
Pervading Impact of Inventory Management	2	Long-Range Plan	20
		Short-Term Plan	21
		Very Short-Term Plan	21
Key Components of an Effective Inventory Management System	4	Inventory Control Applications	21
		Inventory Levels	22
Organization	5	The ABC Method of Inventory Management	23
Policies	5	Material Requirements Planning	23
Systems and Procedures	5	Reorder Point Systems	24
Functional Objectives and Procedures	6	The Order Quantity	25
Procurement and Inventory Management	6	Importance of Adequate Data	27
Just-in-Time Inventories	7	Inventory Management Control Questionnaire	28
Procurement Objectives	8	Inventory Management Audit Program	37
The Procurement Cycle	8		
Role of the Internal Auditor	9	Inventory Management Audit Findings	41
Procurement Questionnaire and Audit Program	9	Financial Type Inventory Audits	54
Production Management Objectives	18	AICPA Study on Inventory Audits	57
Objectives of Warehousing and Distribution	19	Suggested Reading	59

Fig. 34-1 Illustration of an Integrated Planning and Control System 3
Fig. 34-2 Audit Questionnaire on Purchase of Materials, Supplies, and Services 10
Fig. 34-3 Audit Program for Procurement Review 15
Fig. 34-4 Illustration of EOQ Formula Application 26
Fig. 34-5 Inventory Management Control Questionnaire 28
Fig. 34-6 Audit Program—Inventory Management 38
Fig. 34-7 Audit Report on the Inventory Management System—Small Anodizing and Cutting Plant 41
Fig. 34-8 Audit Report on Inventory Management Showing Unacceptable Conditions —Telecommunications Manufacturer 43

INTRODUCTION

"Inventory management" to some individuals might relate solely to the stores function of maintaining the inventories. However, as will be seen, inventory management in its true sense must encompass a broader view, and relates specifically to several functions, some of which are covered in this chapter.

- Purchasing or procurement
- Transportation
- Receiving and inspection
- Warehousing and stores management
- Production or manufacturing
- Engineering

Inventory, as the term is used here, refers to the stock of goods owned by the enterprise, as evidenced by the "inventory" caption in its statement of financial position. Thus, it will have reference to the on-hand stock of raw materials, work-in-process, finished goods for sale, or merchandise purchased for resale—the tangible current assets which can be seen, weighed, measured, and counted.

The importance of inventories needs little comment. In many companies it is the largest single item among the current assets. From a control standpoint, it has been an asset long used by some managements to manipulate operating results and financial position. While the emphasis of the chapter is on operating management, and not internal control, certainly the control aspects cannot be ignored.

And finally, in summary, the impact of inventory management, including valuation, on the financial status of an enterprise is threefold:

1. The use of a significant amount of financial resources in the investment.
2. The direct impact on income tax liability as a result of costing and valuation practices (e.g., LIFO vs. FIFO).
3. The related influence of costing practices and the cost of carrying inventory on the net income of the corporation.

PERVADING IMPACT OF INVENTORY MANAGEMENT

As just mentioned, inventory management influences the directly related physical activities of the company. But the relationship with the other major functions of the business is extensive, and must be given consideration in an operational audit. In fact, an effective system of inventory management results from the proper interaction and relationship between production,

INVENTORY MANAGEMENT

FIG. 34-1

Illustration of an Integrated Planning and Control System

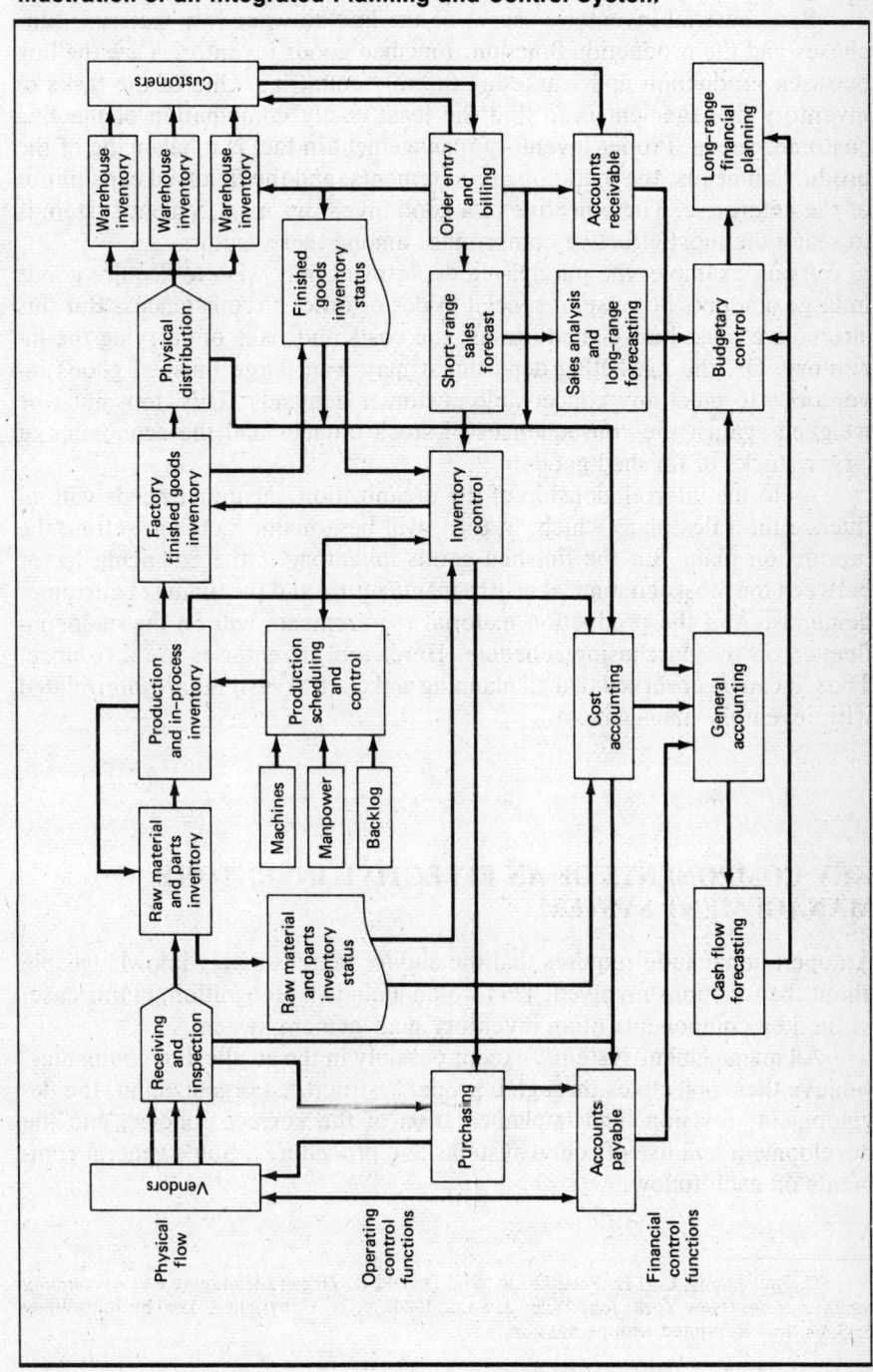

marketing, and finance. The tie-ins of the various functions are illustrated in Figure 34-1.[1] In addition, some explanations may be helpful.

Raw material inventories serve as the link between raw materials purchases and the production function. Finished goods inventories are the link between production and marketing in most countries. One of the tasks of inventory management is to find the least costly combination of meeting customer needs. Proper inventory management in fact is a balancing of the production needs, the marketing requirements, and the financial capabilities of the enterprise. The objective of a good inventory management system is to reach the most effective compromise among these factors.

As an example, the purchasing department may wish to acquire goods in large amounts because of special prices or other circumstances. But this alternative must be weighed against the costs and risks of carrying the inventory. Or, the marketing department may want large finished goods inventories to meet any conceivable customer demands. This, too, must be weighed against the consequences of stock outages and the economics of larger stocks of finished goods.

As to the interrelationship of the organization, customer needs will influence the sales plan, which, in turn, will be a major factor in setting the production plan. But the finished goods inventory is the balancing factor between the most economical way to manufacture and the timing of customer demands. And the production material requirements will be the major influence on the purchasing schedule. Here, too, inventories are a balance. Thus, it can be observed that all planning and control systems are interrelated with inventory management.

KEY COMPONENTS OF AN EFFECTIVE INVENTORY MANAGEMENT SYSTEM

An operational audit requires that the auditor be reasonably knowledgeable about the functions involved. This would include a recognition, in this case, of the key components of an inventory management system.

All management systems, except possibly in the smallest of companies, achieve their objectives through a properly structured organization, the development, revision, and implementation of the correct policies, and the development and use of sound systems and procedures. Some general comments on each follow.

---

[1] C. Paul Jannis, Carl H. Poedtke, Jr., and Donald R. Ziegler, *Managing and Accounting for Inventories* (New York: John Wiley & Sons, 1980), p. 24. Copyright © 1980 by John Wiley & Sons, Inc. Reprinted with permission.

INVENTORY MANAGEMENT

Organization

Effective inventory management may be achieved through a decentralized organization structure or a highly centralized one; from one in which the specific functions of procurement, receiving and storing, and transportation are supervised by executives who report to a divisional production manager, to a highly centralized structure in which the purchasing officer reports to the chief operating officer, as does the manufacturing executive and the stores manager. Regardless, the key to successful operation is (1) a clearly defined statement of authority and responsibility, and functional outline, for each major executive and each department manager; (2) the proper organization structure to fit the needs or peculiarities of the business; and (3) competent personnel who efficiently carry out the function.

Policies

Policies are general statements or understandings that guide thinking and action in the decision-making arena. Policies circumscribe an area within which decisions are to be made, and assume that when they are made, they will fall within certain boundaries.

In the inventory management area, policies should define the scope of the function and set the guidelines for meeting the functional and business objectives. It should set targets or goals which guide the operations. Some subjects for policy statements include method of valuing inventories, inventory investment levels, turnover rates, guides on obsolescence, service to production, and service to marketing.

Systems and Procedures

The third component of an effective inventory management system, and one on which operational audits should be concentrated, is the systems and procedures. The specific key elements of an inventory management system will depend, in part, on the nature of the materials, parts, and finished goods, as well as the system of planning and control. Thus, the system related to vast quantities of chemicals would differ greatly from a producer of machined parts, or minute chips for a computer. Components for an adequate parts type inventory control could include these:

1. *Parts identification*
   - *Part numbering systems.* These should be uniform for ordering, inventory and production control, and engineering use.
   - *Perpetual inventory file.* Record, by part number, of such information as description, unit of measure, stock location, order quantity, receipts, issues, minimum stock quantity, reorder point, physical count data, and on-hand quantity.

- ☐ *Specifications*. The technical data required on each part by the purchasing and inventory management functions.
2. *Quantitative parameters*. Data related to these operating matters, among others, would be included:
   - ☐ *Planned usage*—e.g., sales and production plans and historical usage
   - ☐ *Order point*—the reorder point, minimum/maximum quantities
   - ☐ *Reorder quantities*—economical ordering quantity (EOQ), min-max procedure, and so forth
   - ☐ *Safety stock*—e.g., for emergency needs
   - ☐ *Just-in-time (JIT) Arrangements*—scheduling delivery of inventory items just as needed, with a minimum of stock on hand
3. *Reporting systems:*
   - ☐ *Exception reporting:*
     - Physical inventories
     - Turnover vs. standard
     - Obsolete and slow-moving items
     - Adjustments to the lower of cost or market
     - Critical items
     - Open order status
   - ☐ *Periodic informational/control reports:*
     - Comparison of planned and actual levels—quantities and value
     - Budget revisions

FUNCTIONAL OBJECTIVES AND PROCEDURES

The broad relationship between inventory management and other major functions is somewhat evident from Figure 34-1 and some comments that have been made. However, it is particularly closely related to both procurement and production. The operations audit of inventory management often closely overlaps an audit of these other two functions. A rather complete understanding of the interaction is a necessary prerequisite to an effective operations audit. The degree to which an operations audit on inventory management will delve into substantial detail of the procurement or production function depends on the nature of the processes, organization structure, degree of integration, knowledge of the internal auditors, and audit time available, to mention a few conditions.

PROCUREMENT AND INVENTORY MANAGEMENT

The procurement policies and procedures of a manufacturing company substantially affect the practice of inventory management in several ways.

- The proficiency of the procurement function influences the carrying value of

the inventories through the complete manufacturing process—from raw materials and purchased parts, through work-in-process to finished goods. Securing the minimum cost, substantial volume discounts, or special purchase discounts may increase the total quantity of inventory, but may substantially reduce the unit cost.
- Proper follow-up procedures with vendors and control of deliveries by the purchasing department can substantially reduce the replenishment cycles and minimize the efforts of the inventory management group.
- Good coordination between procurement, inventory management, and production under special circumstances, such as impending major shortages, major price increases, strikes, or business interruptions, can effectively improve the economics of running the business.

So the audit program should take into account the communication between these groups.

JUST-IN-TIME INVENTORIES

No single system of inventory management is necessarily the best for all industries or even all companies within the same industry. This chapter discusses several planning and control techniques, including EOQ. Such models focus on carrying costs, ordering costs, and setup costs.[2] However, there are other costs related to quality, rework, scrap, and worker motivation, which may be significantly affected by manufacturing lot size. Likewise, in material requirements planning (MRP) systems, large lot sizes have been used to reduce average set-up costs and fixed inventory carrying costs.

Under the circumstances, the just-in-time (JIT) inventory technique has been adopted in the automobile industry, and this method is spreading to others. The same philosophy applies to purchasing, delivery, and manufacturing. The central theme is that all inventories are undesirable and should be eliminated or minimized. The JIT goal is to produce and to deliver goods just in time to be sold, subassemblies just in time to be assembled into finished goods, fabricated or purchased parts just in time to go into subassemblies, and purchased materials just in time to be incorporated into fabricated parts. Whereas some systems emphasize large lot sizes, the JIT system focuses on smaller lot sizes that provide benefits through less waste and rework, greater process yield, and higher levels of worker motivation.

The JIT system, of course, has a tremendous effect on suppliers, delivery systems, machine arrangements, and inventory staging areas, to name a few. In the automobile industry, for example, there are fewer suppliers, but the reliability of those selected is substantially improved (e.g., multiple deliveries in small lots to the specific work center specified by production

---

[2] Some of these comments are adapted from James D. Willson, *Budgeting and Profit Planning Manual*, 2nd ed., Chapter 27 (New York: Warren, Gorham & Lamont, 1988).

scheduling, instead of bulk transport systems). This technique often lowers inventory carrying costs and total manufacturing costs.

In some instances, the internal auditor may wish, in conjunction with the manufacturing executive, to consider the benefits of a JIT system or another integrated manufacturing control system, which may help to reduce inventories and costs.

PROCUREMENT OBJECTIVES

The objectives of the procurement function are germane to an operations audit of procurement or inventory management. In a general sense, and in layman's language, the purchasing responsibility is to buy materials of the right quality, in the right quantity, at the right time, at the right price, and from the right source. Much depends on the definition of "right."

In a more specific and sophisticated sense, the procurement objectives are summarized as follows:[3]

- To maintain continuity of supply to support the manufacturing schedule.
- To do so with the minimum investment in materials inventory consistent with safety and economic advantage.
- To avoid duplication, waste, and obsolescence with respect to materials.
- To maintain standards of quality in materials, based on suitability for use.
- To procure materials at the lowest cost consistent with the quality and service required.
- To maintain the company's competitive position in its industry and to conserve its profits, insofar as material costs are concerned.

THE PROCUREMENT CYCLE

It is beyond the scope of a book on internal auditing to delve into all the techniques that make for a well-run procurement function. The reader is referred to good books or manuals on the subject. There are, however, some basic fundamentals that should be mentioned:

☐ *The specific needs must be determined.* Based on the production requirements and the inventory status, the specific needs must be ascertained: the identification of the product and its specifications; the quantities or amount required; the time and place of delivery of specific amounts, and so forth.

☐ *The purchase must be properly authorized.* Procedures should specify who

---
[3] Stuart F. Heinritz and Paul V. Farrell, *Purchasing; Principles and Applications* (Englewood Cliffs, New Jersey: Prentice-Hall, 1971), p. 8.

should buy what items, the limits of authority, the specific approving authority, and the conditions under which it must be bought, e.g., competitive bidding.

☐ *The procurement should be made in the most advantageous manner.* That is to say, the actual purchase order should be placed in the way most advantageous to the enterprise—the proper vendor (e.g., reliable), at the right price, and under the proper terms (e.g., delivery and payment terms).

☐ *As deemed appropriate, the proper follow-up should be made.* This is to assure the timely delivery of the appropriate goods to the proper destination.

☐ *At time of delivery, a check should be made to assure compliance with the terms of the purchase order.* When the goods have been delivered as per contract, proper inspection should be made, claims instituted, or payment authorized per the purchase order terms.

ROLE OF THE INTERNAL AUDITOR

In principle, the role of the internal auditor is the same as to the procurement function as it is to any other operational activity. Specifically, based on a knowledge of the purchasing function and the use of specialists, if required, the auditor should:

- Check compliance with existing policies and procedures.
- Review efficiency in carrying out the existing policies and procedures.
- Consider what improvements can be made in existing policies and practices.
- Review the extent of interaction with other directly related functions in terms of securing economic balance between the procurement function, production, and inventory management, as well as the lesser related functions.
- Check vendor contacts to see if any improvement in operating methods are desirable or feasible.

PROCUREMENT QUESTIONNAIRE AND AUDIT PROGRAM

The audit program for a procurement operational audit as such or, if desired, as part of the inventory management review, will depend on the nature of the industry, nature of the product, organizational structure, environmental constraints, and a host of other considerations. It is difficult to generalize, because the astuteness, experience, and ability of the auditor, as well as the other factors just mentioned, have much to do with just what audit steps or procedures should be accomplished. In the final analysis, judgment will be the governing influence. However, there is presented in Figure 34-2 an audit

(continued on page 34-18)

FIG. 34-2

Audit Questionnaire on Purchase of Materials, Supplies, and Services

	Yes	No
A. General:		
1. Are all purchases of materials and supplies required to be executed by a single purchasing group?	☐	☐
2. Is the purchasing function organizationally separate from receiving, accounting, and disbursing functions?	☐	☐
3. Are written procedures in existence and up-to-date for executing purchasing transactions?	☐	☐
4. Is an organization chart in existence depicting the reporting relationships?	☐	☐
5. Does the purchasing organization have adequate facilities and equipment to accomplish its function?	☐	☐
B. Execution of Transactions:		
1. Are purchases or transactions initiated based upon approved requisitions from user groups or from some other original source such as machine-generated reports or purchasing requirements?	☐	☐
2. Are requisitions or other source data for initiating purchase transactions retained in a manner which permits retrieval?	☐	☐
a. Is procurement action the result of considering:		
■ Quantities required as determined either by user or by some other appropriate means	☐	☐
■ In-house fabrication	☐	☐
■ Economic order quantities	☐	☐
3. If transactions are initiated based upon machine-generated data, is there:		
a. Adequate user department control over data input and output? (Note: In order to answer this question, it is necessary to complete Form .... for each relevant input form and output report.)	☐	☐
b. Segregation of data processing functions from transaction-executing functions?	☐	☐
c. Current and complete system and program documentation?	☐	☐
d. Security over retention of master file data, system and program documentation?	☐	☐
e. Segregation of the functions of computer processing, programming, and systems designing?	☐	☐
f. A method or methods to detect and correct errors and omissions?	☐	☐
g. A user's manual?	☐	☐

INVENTORY MANAGEMENT

	Yes	No
4. Are standard purchase orders that include all relevant terms required to be used in all applicable instances to execute purchase transactions?	☐	☐
5. Do procedures discourage the misuse of blanket purchase orders, use of sole source of supply, or reciprocity in material transactions?	☐	☐
6. Prior to purchase:		
a. Do procedures require a make or buy evaluation?	☐	☐
b. Is a minimum dollar limit established and is it reasonable?	☐	☐
7. Do procedures require obtaining competitive bids?	☐	☐
8. Are procedures in effect for keeping vendor files, price lists, catalogs, and other reference material current?	☐	☐
a. If such files and information are maintained by automated data processing techniques, is there:		
■ Adequate user department control over data input and output?	☐	☐
(Note: In order to answer this question, it is necessary to complete Form .... for each relevant input form and output report.)		
■ Segregation of data processing functions from transaction execution functions?	☐	☐
■ Current and complete system and program documentation?	☐	☐
■ Security and retention of master file data, system and program documentation?	☐	☐
■ Segregation of the functions of computer processing, programming, and system designing?	☐	☐
■ A method or methods to detect and correct errors and omissions?	☐	☐
■ A user's manual?	☐	☐
b. Do procedures require that, where applicable, specifications for materials or parts be set forth in the purchase order?	☐	☐
c. Do procedures require setting forth in writing bidding instructions?	☐	☐
9. Do procedures require obtaining or preparing cost analyses at bids where applicable?	☐	☐
10. Are procedures in existence for analysis and evaluation of bids prior to final selection?	☐	☐
11. Do procedures require assessing the financial strength of vendors and their ability to provide the needed material or supplies?	☐	☐
12. Do procedures require that the basis for selection of vendors be		

(continued)

FIG. 34-2 *(cont'd)*

	Yes	No
clearly documented and approved, particularly in instances where the lowest bid is not selected?	☐	☐
13. Are procedures in effect for negotiating and preparing purchase orders?	☐	☐
14. Do procedures require review by legal counsel in instances involving unusual circumstances, complex arrangements, or omission of standard terms?	☐	☐
15. Are guidelines in existence to aid in selecting the type of purchase order/contract most appropriate in the circumstances?	☐	☐
16. Are there procedures in effect governing review and approval of procurement actions prior to final execution?	☐	☐
17. Is there a formal delegation of authority for approval of purchases?	☐	☐
18. Has provision been made for coordinating certain purchases with the Corporate Office?	☐	☐
19. Are written procedures in effect covering post-award administrative activities such as:		
a. Changes	☐	☐
b. Performance evaluation	☐	☐
c. Disputes	☐	☐
d. Termination	☐	☐
e. Debit memoranda	☐	☐
20. Are there written procedures covering special procurement situations such as government-directed source procurement, purchase of gold, material furnished by the company to suppliers, purchases of equipment, and goods shipped directly to customers?	☐	☐
a. Are advance payments required to be approved?	☐	☐
21. Have standards of procurement practice been established in writing which preclude the existence of conflicts of interest, the acceptance of gifts and gratuities and other similar conflicts?	☐	☐
(Note: For further details regarding evaluation of standards of procurement, see the questionnaire on the subject.)		

C. Processing and Recording of Transactions:

1. Are purchase orders and other related documentation such as change orders and debit memoranda prepared in multiple copies and distributed to all involved functional organizations including receiving and finance (accounts payable and/or accounting)?	☐	☐
2. Are procedures in effect within the purchasing function for		

	Yes	No

reviewing open purchase order files and/or reports and initiating action where required to clear up old items? ☐ ☐

3. Are purchase orders controlled numerically or by some other means in the purchasing group to assure that executed purchase orders are not lost, destroyed, or escape control by other means? ☐ ☐

   Or to prevent the unauthorized use of purchase orders? ☐ ☐

4. Is there a technique in use by accounting personnel to assure that all purchase order copies are received and retained for further processing such as by recording in logs in numerical order or by filing numerically and accounting for numerical sequence? ☐ ☐

5. Are receiving reports or some other evidencing technique in use for all items or services which are received pursuant to purchase orders? ☐ ☐

6. Is there a method to assure that all items and quantities were received pursuant to approved purchase orders? ☐ ☐

   (Note: This is customarily done by matching receiving report data with purchase order data.)

   a. For purchase of services, do procedures require obtaining verification of or information as to performance? ☐ ☐

7. Is the method referred to in the previous question performed by an organization independent from purchasing/receiving functions? ☐ ☐

8. If accounting personnel do not perform the matching function referred to in the sixth question, are they assured by some other means that quantities and items ordered were in fact received? ☐ ☐

9. Do accounting personnel either originate or review for propriety the accounting distribution for purchase transactions? ☐ ☐

   a. Does the individual determining the account distribution have access and refer to up-to-date guidelines such as a chart of accounts, accounting manual, and memoranda? ☐ ☐

10. Are invoice quantities, prices, extensions, approvals, etc., verified and matched to purchase orders where applicable by accounting personnel? ☐ ☐

    a. Is there evidence such as an audit stamp, initial, or check mark present to indicate that the functions in this question have been accomplished? ☐ ☐

    b. Are audited invoices and related receivers and purchase orders stapled, joined together, or otherwise referenced to one another and systematically filed for easy reference? ☐ ☐

    c. Does any independent group (other than Corporate Internal

(continued)

FIG. 34-2 *(cont'd)*

	Yes	No
Audit and external auditors) review purchasing files to check propriety of prices paid, vendors used, and accuracy and completeness of purchase order files?	☐	☐
d. Are errors or differences disclosed by performing the function outlined in this question resolved prior to further processing or payment?	☐	☐
11. If accounting personnel do not perform the function referred to in the tenth question, do they verify that such function occurs?	☐	☐
12. Are purchase transactions recorded subsequent to the completion of the functions outlined in the sixth through eleventh questions above (customarily considered as vouchering)?	☐	☐
13. Are procedures in effect to account for partial shipments?	☐	☐
14. Are procedures in effect requiring periodic review of open receiver, purchase order, and invoice files and follow-up and resolution of unmatched items?	☐	☐
a. Are vendor statements reviewed for old past-due items?	☐	☐
b. Are items disclosed by this review resolved in a reasonably timely manner?	☐	☐
15. Are procedures in effect to assure the receipt, recording, and filing of debit memos?	☐	☐
16. Do procedures require that the total of unpaid vouchered items be balanced periodically (usually monthly) to the related general ledger control account for accounts payable?	☐	☐
17. Do procedures require making appropriate accruals of amounts representing purchases received during the accounting period but not yet recorded by the process in the twelfth question?	☐	☐
18. Where advance payments to vendors are involved, do accounting procedures assure subsequent matching to invoices?	☐	☐
19. If transactions (questions twelve through fifteen) are processed and/or recorded based upon machine generated data, is there:		
a. Adequate user department control over data input and output? (Note: in order to answer this question, it is necessary to complete Form .... for each relevant input form and output report.)	☐	☐
b. Segregation of data-processing functions from transaction-executing functions?	☐	☐
c. Current and complete system and program documentation?	☐	☐
d. Security over retention of master file data and system and program documentation?	☐	☐
e. Segregation of the function of computer processing, programming, and systems designing?	☐	☐

INVENTORY MANAGEMENT

	Yes	No
f. A method to detect and correct errors and omissions in data conversion and processing?	☐	☐
g. A user's manual?	☐	☐
20. Are files evidencing purchase transactions (e.g., paid voucher filed, open P.O. review, invoice files) arranged to facilitate access by authorized personnel?	☐	☐
a. Is access to files restricted to authorized personnel?	☐	☐

D. Authorized Access to Assets:

Note: Purchase transactions do not directly involve access to execute them. However, related functions such as storing and issuing material and disbursing of cash do involve access to assets. For questions related to this aspect of control of these related functions, see the applicable questionnaire.

E. Recorded Accountability for Assets Compared With Existing Assets:

Note: Normally, the purchasing function does not entail comparisons of this type in order to execute, record, and account for purchases of materials and supplies. Such comparisons are customarily found in connection with the function of materials handling. Questions evaluating this aspect of control are set forth in the section of the questionnaire related to that topic.

FIG. 34-3

Audit Program for Procurement Review

	Workpaper Reference	Done by
1. General:		
☐ Obtain a copy of the organization chart and review and discuss it with management to determine the independence and reporting relationship of the procurement function.	....	....
☐ Inquire into the existence of written procedures for procurement function.	....	....
☐ Review procedures, determine that procedures are current, and note last revision date.	....	....
☐ Prepare a schedule cross-referencing procedures to internal control questionnaire.	....	....
☐ By interviews with management and procurement personnel, establish in what way, if any, procedures are not followed or are otherwise not current.	....	....
☐ During the course of the audit, tour facilities and observe personnel at work for any indication of resource problems.	....	....

(continued)

FIG. 34-3 *(cont'd)*

	Workpaper Reference	Done by
2. Execution of Transactions:		
☐ Select at random 50 completed transactions and check for evidence of the following:		
▪ Approval to procure	....	....
▪ Procurement based upon source data (if the transaction is initiated based upon machine-generated data)	....	....
▪ Appropriate item and quantity determination (technique should be stated)	....	....
▪ Use of standard purchase orders or subcontracts	....	....
▪ Appropriate correspondence with bidders (where applicable), which might include bid instructions, specifications, responses to inquiries, etc.	....	....
▪ Evaluation and analysis of bid selection	....	....
▪ Assessing financial strength of bidders	....	....
▪ Basis for vendor selection	....	....
▪ Review by legal counsel (where necessary)	....	....
▪ Review and approval by Corporate Office (if applicable)	....	....
☐ By consultation with knowledgeable personnel, determine an appropriate source from which to select a brief random sample of special procurement transactions, including the following:	....	....
▪ Company-furnished material to suppliers		
▪ Purchase of items shipped directly to customer		
▪ Sole-source procurement		
☐ Verify that proper approval occurred and verify compliance with any special procedure applicable to the source.	....	....
☐ Review written procedures for an adequate statement of standards of procurement practice.	....	....
☐ Discuss standards of procurement practice with management and obtain examples of compliance. Corroborate examples by obtaining examples independently from other procurement personnel.	....	....
☐ Determine that reference files and catalogs are current, and note arrangement, completeness, revision dates, etc.	....	....
☐ Select a brief sample of purchase transactions that have been closed and check for evidence of:		
▪ Approval of changes	....	....
▪ Performance evaluation	....	....
▪ Properly issued debit memoranda (if any)	....	....
▪ Reasonable resolution of disputes (if any)	....	....
3. Processing and Recording of Transactions:		
☐ To test distribution of purchase orders, select a sequence of purchase order numbers and verify distribution to final destination.	....	....

	Workpaper Reference	Done by

☐ Review open purchase order (P.O.) files (or reports of open P.O.s) for old outstanding P.O.s. Obtain explanation for those greater than one year old. ....

☐ Test numerical control over P.O.s. ....

☐ For items selected in the first question in Section 2, determine compliance with procedures for:
- Receipt of item(s) purchased ....
- Matching of receipt to purchase order ....
- Follow-up of unmatched, unacceptable items ....

☐ To the extent members of the accounting group do not perform the function in the fourth question in this section, test the means by which they are assured such functions have occurred for the test items selected. ....

☐ Test items in the fourth question above for evidence of proper matching with related invoices, proper account distribution, and timely recording. ....

☐ Test samples selected in the last question in Section 2 for proper and timely recording. ....

☐ Verify technique used to balance unpaid vouched items with related general ledger control account. ....

☐ To the extent computer processing is involved in recording purchases and accounts payable:
- Test batch control or other techniques used to assure accurate and complete processing ....
- Test error detection and correction routine ....
- Review system and program documentation for currency and completeness ....
- Discuss with data processing personnel the segregation of duties regarding processing of purchase/accounts payable data and the relative security over master file data ....
- Inquire of users as to the adequacy of data-processing services received and the accuracy, completeness, and timeliness of data processing; check problem areas, if any, with data-processing personnel ....

☐ Scan appropriate files of completed transactions for any indication of unusual items such as the following:
- Unauthorized purchases ....
- Purchase of materials at exorbitant prices ....
- Purchase of excess quantities ....
- Procedural violations ....
- Duplicate payments ....
- Unauthorized payments ....
- Improper account distribution ....

(continued)

FIG. 34-3 *(cont'd)*

>   **Workpaper Done**
>   **Reference   by**
>
> Note: To the extent that the public accountants or Eastern Division auditors have performed recent audits of procurements, that work may be used in lieu of performing similar work, provided:
> - Evidence of such work is obtained
> - Evidence is cross-referenced to steps in this audit program
> - The performing auditors (public accountants or Eastern Division) did not raise questions as to the reliability of the procedure being tested
>
> The foregoing does not relieve the Corporate auditor of the burden of performing the balance of the work required by this program not included in the scope of the work of the originating auditor. This includes both the nature of the test and the extent of it.
>
> ☐ Determine that completed certificates regarding interest in suppliers have been completed by appropriate personnel.

questionnaire and in Figure 34-3 an audit program for the operational review of the procurement function of a manufacturing company, in which the auditors are presumed to be reasonably familiar with the operation. Hence, some of the preliminary observation and review procedures have been omitted.

PRODUCTION MANAGEMENT OBJECTIVES

Inventory management is the link between procurement on the one hand and production on the other. Production management has a significant impact on inventories. It is not the intent in this chapter to search into the many techniques that constitute good production management. But some limited comments are germane to inventory management.

    The principal objective of production management is to manufacture the products needed by the marketing management at the least cost. One way to accomplish this is through a substantial buildup of inventory levels of all three types: raw materials, work-in-process, and finished goods. This results from the fact that manufacturing operations can be conducted most efficiently by planning and scheduling long production runs, and consequent higher inventory levels. Setup costs can be minimized with lengthy production runs. Idle time tends to be less. With longer production, employees need less orientation, and higher quality, together with increased productivity, usually result.

    Thus, inventory policies, with the levels established, help determine production costs. The trick is to find the combination that produces

INVENTORY MANAGEMENT

the lowest costs for purchasing, inventory management, and production combined.

OBJECTIVES OF WAREHOUSING AND DISTRIBUTION

Just as there is an interdependence of procurement and production with inventory management, so also there is much interaction, once the goods are produced, between inventory management and the warehousing and distribution of the finished products.

If the product is stocked at more than one location, the inventory management system must be so designed to cope with multilocation inventories, including, perhaps, central computer tie-ins to provide information on the total inventory basis at all locations for proper visibility and safety stock levels. Obviously, the total number of warehouses, the delivery time from warehouse to customer, the geographical tie-in, the storage capacity, and the cost of delivery, all affect inventory requirements. Finally, the aggregate inventory levels influence the risk of obsolescence, theft, and other normal inventory losses as well as the cost of carrying the inventory, and the expense of warehousing space as well as handling.

The comments on procurement, production, and warehousing have been made to be more certain that the internal auditor is sensitive to these ramifications in performing an operations audit on inventory management.

SCOPE OF INVENTORY MANAGEMENT

Inventory management as contemplated herein is a broad activity encompassing the development and implementation of both *planning* and *control* techniques. It seeks to develop and implement those policies, systems, and procedures that minimize the total investment in inventory and the related costs, as well as the allied functional costs of purchasing, material handling, production, transportation (both inbound and outbound), and other related functions (as evidenced by the audit programs included in this chapter). As will be seen by the reference to the multidisciplines more or less involved, it contemplates an effective integrated management information system and coordinated decision making as regards the inventory system.

From the viewpoint of an operational audit, a review of inventory management is wider in scope than the usual audit of the inventory control system, which, in most cases, aims solely to check only adherence to established policies, systems, and procedures. In fact, it calls for knowledge of a higher magnitude than the usual financial auditing and may require use of technical skills in the material and inventory areas.

Inventory Planning Applications

Inventory planning necessarily precedes inventory control. In most companies, it may be segregated into three time phases: (1) long-range or strategic planning, perhaps 5 or 10 years into the future; (2) short-term planning, such as that contemplated in the annual planning cycle, covering a period from six months to two years; and (3) the very short-term planning related to the day-to-day operating needs of the enterprise, for perhaps the next month or two—depending on the procurement and delivery cycle, among other things.

From an operational auditing viewpoint, the importance attached to each type of plan will relate to the ability to reliably plan ahead. For example, is a 10-year plan of any practical value as to the inventory application? Or, is it too broad in nature? In the company or industry, is it useful to attempt to plan inventories, in other than most general terms, for more than, say, two years? Is the answer reasonably accurate and will it remain so for the next year? On the other hand, is the management planning with sufficient focus to anticipate the reasonable needs sufficiently in advance, while there still is time to act in a prudent and cost-effective manner?

Many of the facets to be examined in an operational audit will depend finally on the acumen of the individual auditor, his judgment as to the practicality and need for the direct or inferred procedure, and the findings in the examination.

Some questions that the internal auditor might weigh, depending on the specific circumstances, are these:

Long-Range Plan. In the long-range plan, does the planned investment in inventories recognize the historical (or planned change) relationship to sales? Is it practical to refine it by product line?

Does the plan give consideration, and should it, to these factors:

- Planned change in product mix, such as a substantial addition to inventories by reason of planned new styles, colors and models?
- Changes contemplated in the distribution system?
- Major changes in the manufacturing process that will greatly affect inventory levels?
- Planned changes in geographic distribution of sales, and warehouse requirements?
- Inroads of competition as to directly competitive products and product substitutes?
- Impact of technology in computers and communications that might substantially reduce inventory levels?
- Changes in design and interchange of parts that might reduce required inventory investment?

INVENTORY MANAGEMENT

Short-Term Plan. Points that might be considered in the short-term business plan include these:

- Is the production plan (the quantity of finished product required) "exploded" or multiplied by the specific material requirements for each product to form a reasonable basis for the inventory and purchase requirements?
- Are the inventories tested for turnover rates, or reasonableness as to levels?
- How do the planned inventory levels compare with the prior-year plan, historical experience, industry standards, and competitive levels?
- Have contemplated changes in the income tax law been weighed as to impact on inventory valuation methods?
- Is the proper inventory valuation method recognized in the annual plan? When are write-downs taken?
- Is the short-term planning method as to inventory levels reasonably consistent with the very short-term planning?
- Are any of the points raised with respect to the long-range plan equally (or more) valid as to the short-term plan?

Very Short-Term Plan. As to the very short-term plan, these points are made:

- To the extent necessary and practical, the questions raised in the preceding two planning cycles should be raised here, only with more specificity.
- The accuracy of the input data should be examined.
- The relationship between the planning techniques used and the control techniques employed should be checked for compatability and consistency.
- The application of the specific planning and control techniques should be reviewed, e.g., the basic inventory planning, such as the ABC method of inventory control, EOQ and reorder points.

Inventory Control Applications

Operational audits of the control aspects of inventory management include, of course, a check of adherence to existing policies and procedures; but it should go beyond this application to an examination of whether other improved techniques are practical and useful. This extension of auditing is dependent on the auditor's knowledge of just what might constitute better methods. It may require the use of inventory specialists or industrial engineers. In some companies, this will be practical; in others, it may not.

Inventory control ordinarily will relate to three basic questions:

1. What is an acceptable inventory level, given the expected volume of business?
2. When should specific materials or products be ordered?
3. How much of each specific item should be ordered?

Because each organization has different needs and differing inventory management styles, generalizations may not be too helpful. No single system is necessarily the best for either a company or even an industry. A combination of methods may be found practical. Some of the influences to be considered are these:

- Nature of the business
- Nature of the product
- Nature of the distribution and delivery system, and customer service requirements
- Number of storage locations
- Number of items in the inventory
- Reliability of the information system as to both planning and control

The three phases of inventory control just mentioned will be addressed.

Inventory Levels. One of the first decisions to be made in inventory management, and a matter to be reviewed in an operations audit, is the selection of an acceptable inventory level. Just how was the limit to the total investment in inventories determined?

A *general* guide as to what inventory levels should be is to relate the volume of business done to the cost of the inventory. This is expressed as a turnover ratio, calculated as follows:

$$\text{turnover} = \frac{\text{cost of goods sold (annual)}}{\text{inventory cost (e.g., average or ending)}}$$

Each industry has its own typical turnover ratios (such as those published by Dun & Bradstreet, Inc.). The ratios of a specific company may be checked against industry data or those of specific competitors. They are influenced by type of manufacture and type of distribution system. The key is proper analysis, with greater breakdowns than those evidenced in the statement of financial position. Thus, analysis by type of inventory (raw materials, work-in-process, and finished goods), with subanalyses by specific products and specific territories, may provide useful guides. Of course, the proper usage factor must be used. Thus, cost of goods sold should be related to finished goods. But materials put into production relates to raw materials inventory and is the dividend in the turnover ratio for raw material inventory (which should be current cost, not LIFO carrying value, for example). Then, too, recognition should be given to special conditions and management decisions. Thus, a job shop inventory would be weighted by unusually large special orders; or the imminence of major price increases could influence inventory levels; or seasonal sales would affect inventory levels. What we are saying is that judgment must be applied to the conclusions and varying inventory levels. Differing methods of control may be necessary in specific circumstances.

The ABC Method of Inventory Management. How an item of inventory should be controlled depends, in part, on its value and the cost of control. Thus, if an electric motor costs $20,000, more care should be taken in the number carried in stock because of the unit investment and related carrying costs—e.g., insurance, taxes, and risk of theft—than the stock of a $1.50 steel bolt. One of the most widely recognized types of inventory management is generally known as ABC inventory control. Although originally developed as a manual system to reduce clerical effort and record keeping, the concept is applicable to computer systems.

Under the system, inventory items are categorized into three classes: *A*, *B*, or *C*, depending on the value to be controlled. The primary basis for the classification into the three categories is the yearly usage in monetary terms. This is determined by multiplying the annual usage in units by the unit cost, and then listing all items in descending order of total cost.

Typically, *A* items may represent perhaps 15 percent of the parts and 65 to 80 percent of the dollar amount of inventory. These parts or units generally are controlled on an individual item basis and are ordered more or less on the basis of the exact quantity needed for customer or manufacturing requirements. *B* items, or middle value units, typically represent perhaps 15 to 20 percent of the parts and a corresponding share of the costs. These *B* category items are ordered in quantities that may differ from actual needs for economic reasons, such as EOQ. *C* items represent perhaps 60 to 75 percent of the parts volume, but only 15 percent or so of the value. These low value items may be ordered on an EOQ or min-max basis, as discussed later.

The point to be made is that the internal auditor should be aware of the ABC system of inventory control, as well as other systems, as he examines the inventory management techniques.

Material Requirements Planning. Many manufacturing concerns use a technique called MRP to plan and schedule the materials and parts needed to build either for specific customer orders or for finished goods inventory. Basically, a bill of materials and a master schedule are required. The bill of materials simply is a listing of all the parts and materials needed to manufacture a specified end product. The master schedule is a time-phased listing of when specified quantities of finished articles are needed for finished goods inventory or for shipment to a customer. Given the dates, quantity requirements, and other data, an MRP system breaks out or translates each individual order into the required raw materials and components for the gross requirements; and inventory status determines the net requirements. With the time to manufacture known, and lead time for procurement known, the necessary purchases schedules can be prepared, together with the purchase orders and manufacturing shop orders. Again, the point to be made is that systems to determine manufacturing and procurement requirements range from simple to sophisticated.

Reorder Point Systems. A second basic question in inventory control is, *When* should the item be ordered? This relates basically to what reorder point system is used to initiate action to acquire additional material.

It is not the intent of this chapter to cover in detail reorder point systems. However, it may be mentioned that some such systems are based on known material requirements, such as for plants operating on fixed production schedules, or job shops manufacturing to known orders. The decision to reorder in these circumstances may be based on analyses of lead times for purchases and manufacturing, safety stock, and the use of specialized techniques, including Critical Path Method (CPM), PERT, and Gantt charts.

Another category of reorder point systems assumes a degree of uncertainty about requirements. It may use probability theory in developing the reorder point. The basic formula is:

$$\text{reorder point } (ROP) - L(D) = \text{safety stock}$$

where:
- L = Anticipated lead time in weeks
- D = Forecasted demand in units per week

Be that as it may, the auditor should be aware of some alternative systems. Some of the widely used techniques of determining when to reorder include these:

Reserve Stock System. This method, also called the two bin system, physically separates the amount of material equivalent to the reorder point. It may be in a separate bag in one bin, or a partitioned bin, or a separate bin. When it is necessary to use material from the reserve stock, a material requisition is initiated. No perpetual inventories need be maintained. Although the system is simple, there are three drawbacks: (1) no monthly use data may be readily available; (2) the specific inventory status is not known; and (3) reliance is placed on the stores person to initiate the purchase requisition at the proper time.

Min-Max System. This minimum-maximum method often is used in conjunction with manual inventory records. The minimum quantity level is determined in the same manner as any reorder point. The maximum level is the minimum quantity plus the optimum order lot size. In operation, a purchase requisition is originated when the inventory reaches the minimum level per the perpetual inventory record. The key to the system effectiveness is the reasonableness with which the min-max parameters are established.

Visual Check System. In this highly subjective method, some knowledgeable person, very familiar with the business, simply visually checks the stock on hand periodically and determines what should be ordered. The quality of the decision depends on the frequency of checking and the judgment of the person doing it.

The Reorder Point—EOQ System. This system depends on tables and charts, and related equations to determine, on an objective basis, the reorder point and the EOQ. Computers and models involving many variables can be employed, or tables and charts reflecting selected levels may be used.

Reservation System. In effect, the reservation system recognizes the requirements prior to stock disbursement, and reflects on the tab run, the available stock as well as the physical stock. A reservation is made for known requirements. The available stock usually is the physical stock on hand, less the open requirements, plus the stock on order. The reorder point in this system is based on the available stock balance rather than the physical balance on hand.

As a general statement, there are a number of methods of determining the reorder point. The auditor should look at the practicality of the systems in use, the cost of the inventory, the expense of maintaining the controls and the results being achieved.

The Order Quantity. The final question to be asked is, "How much material should be ordered?" For those instances where the order quantity is based on an analysis of related costs, the quantity to be ordered frequently is referred to as EOQ. The name implies that the designated specific order quantity will result in the lowest total variable expenses.

A formula has been developed which takes into account four variables that determine the order quantity: (1) the forecasted annual usage of the item expressed in units, (2) the variable, or out-of-pocket, expenses associated with handling the order, whether for purchase or manufacture, including issuance and follow-up, (3) the expense of carrying the inventory for one year, expressed as a percentage, and (4) the variable cost of one unit. The formula, in terms which should not scare the nonmathematically inclined, might be stated:

$$Q = \sqrt{\frac{2 \times \text{annual usage} \times \text{set-up or order cost}}{\% \text{ carrying charge} \times \text{unit cost}}}$$

FIG. 34-4
Illustration of EOQ Formula Application

Illustration of Use of Classical Inventory Control Formula

	Valves (High-unit value, low-usage item)	Washers (Low-unit value, high-usage item)
Original practice:		
1. Unit cost	$10.00	$0.10
2. Quantity on hand at inventory date	250	8,000
3. Annual usage	1,200	120,000
4. Average order quantity	300	5,000
5. Expense of carrying inventory, in percent	15%	15%
6. Annual expense of carrying average inventory $\left(\frac{\text{Item 4}}{2} \times \text{Item 1} \times \text{Item 5}\right)$ ignoring safety cushion	$225.00	$37.50
7. Expense of handling an order	$8.00	$8.00
8. Expense of handling year's orders $\left(\frac{\text{Item 3}}{\text{Item 4}} \times \text{Item 7}\right)$	$32.00	$192.00
9. Total expense of carrying and ordering year's requirements	$257.00	$229.50
Indicated practice:		
10. Economic order quantity* (approx.)	115†	11,000
11. Number of orders per year (approx.)	10.5	11.0
12. Annual expense of carrying economic inventory $\left(\frac{\text{Item 10}}{2} \times \text{Item 1} \times \text{Item 5}\right)$	$86.25‡	$82.50‡
13. Expense of handling year's orders (Item 11 × Item 7)	$84.00‡	$88.00‡
14. Total expense of carrying and ordering year's requirements	$170.25	$170.50
Annual Saving:		
Amount	$86.75	$59.00
Percent	34%	26%

* Formula: Economic order quantity is square root of twice annual usage times expense of handling an order, divided by unit cost times carrying expense percentage.

† The application of the formula is:

$$Q = \sqrt{\frac{2 \times 1{,}200 \times 8.00}{15\% \times 10.00}} = 115 \text{ (approx.)}$$

‡ Except for "rounding off" in connection with computation of square roots and number of orders to be placed, amounts on lines 12 and 13 would be equal.

INVENTORY MANAGEMENT

or, in mathematical terms

$$Q = \sqrt{\frac{2\,SE}{KC}}$$

where:
- Q = Economic order quantity
- S = Estimated annual usage of the item
- E = Expense of handling an order
- K = Expense of carrying the inventory, expressed as a percentage of cost of goods on hand
- C = Unit cost of the item

An application of the formula is given in Figure 34-4.[4] The reader is referred to this excellent source for comments on the derivation of the formula, as well as other ideas on inventory accounting and management.

With tools such as the foregoing, an operations audit can well delve into the question of how the order quantity is determined.

IMPORTANCE OF ADEQUATE DATA

Key to the effective operation of an inventory management system is adequate data and the proper use of them. This relates, in the first instance, to the quality, completeness, and reliability of the data base itself, and secondly, to the controls that monitor the data gathering and their proper use.

In terms of adequate information, these points ought to be made:

- The inventory records should reflect the inventory classifications a company should maintain to permit good control, and the extent of detail necessary in each category (e.g., raw materials, work-in-process, and finished goods).
- The system should provide an accurate record of the status of goods in stock, including the specific location, and the exact amount in stock. Depending on the inventory control method for the specific items, the records should include a precise description of the item, and reflect quantities received, quantities disbursed, order quantity, inventory control method, cost of items, amount on order, reserve or minimum stock, and so forth, as well as lead time.
- To assist in keeping records accurate, some periodic verification may be needed, such as a cycle count.

It is this type of information that will assist in determining, for example, proper inventory levels, the EOQ, and the proper reorder point.

---

[4] Jannis et al., *op. cit.*, p. 86.

INVENTORY MANAGEMENT CONTROL QUESTIONNAIRE

The exact depth of an operations audit will depend, as always, on what is appropriate in the circumstances. It will be influenced by the perceived status, importance, or effectiveness of the function. Are there known problems? How knowledgeable is the auditor? How recently has the operation been reviewed? A pattern of examination may be formed through the use of a questionnaire. An illustrative inventory management questionnaire for a multidivision manufacturer of high technology products made to order is given in Figure 34-5. Close coordination between engineering, manufacturing engineering, and manufacturing was especially critical in this situation.

(continued on page 34-37)

FIG. 34-5
Inventory Management Control Questionnaire

FOREWORD:

Inventory management is the term used to describe the combination of techniques and practices or components thereof, employed to produce for profitable exchange a unique line of products or services. Simply stated, the objective of inventory management is to minimize the investment in inventory while attaining all other management goals. This primary objective is not easily met. Effective inventory management requires the utmost management skill, and significant commitment of resources, including facilities, equipment, personnel, systems, and data.

In order to perform a useful, organized evaluation of inventory management, it is necessary to divide the simply stated objective of the preceding paragraph into components. The following detailed objectives are sufficient for this purpose:

AUTHORIZATION AND EXECUTION:

- To provide sufficient resources pursuant to management's authority, such as facilities, equipment, manpower, systems, and data, to enable the investment in inventory to be effectively managed.
- To obtain only those items necessary to fulfill contractual obligations and/or authorized stock levels.
- To incorporate authorized changes to product design and production methods and schedules in a timely and efficient fashion.
- To deviate from primary objectives only upon appropriate management authorization based upon sound, factual information and rationale (e.g., risk inventory, scrap sales, dispositions of slow-moving inventory).

RECORDING AND ACCOUNTABILITY:

- To record and report inventory transactions and activities, including acquisition, conversion, and disposition, so as to permit reasonably effective performance review evaluations and actions by affected management.
- To establish and maintain accountability of inventory activity, including acquisition, conversion, and disposition, so as to reasonably permit preparation of financial statements in accordance with GAAP.

INVENTORY MANAGEMENT 34-29

- To reasonably assure that recorded balances of inventory transactions are periodically compared to valuations of physical counts at reasonable intervals with appropriate action taken with respect to differences.

SAFEGUARDING:

- To store inventory in a manner that offers reasonable protection from loss due to spoilage, damage, waste, and similar physical risks.
- To store inventory in a manner that reasonably restricts access to all personnel other than custodians, while facilitating location and incorporation into the productive process.

Note: The foregoing objectives have been arranged in accordance with the broad objectives of internal control to which they relate. This relationship is displayed in order to reasonably assure that all aspects of internal control are covered by these objectives.

In practice, all organizational units find it necessary to delegate and distribute responsibility and authority for accomplishing these objectives among several functional units. As a result, inventory management is not the responsibility of a single functional unit but rather results from the coordinated efforts of several functions. The following functions are usually involved directly:

- General management
- Engineering
- Manufacturing engineering
- Manufacturing
- Materiel
- Facilities
- Finance
- Security
- Data processing

In order to facilitate the identification and evaluation of internal controls involved in inventory management, the attached questionnaire has been organized by the functions set forth above. In some organizational units certain of the functions may be combined. In others there may be further divisions. The former situation should make even easier the process of obtaining responses since fewer functional departments need to be involved. In the latter situation, however, the auditor may find it necessary to supplement the questionnaire to reasonably assure thorough coverage.

It was not practicable to design the questionnaire so that each question focuses on a specific control, although in many instances that is the case. Because techniques can and do vary it was necessary in many other instances to focus on a *control area* as opposed to a *specific control*. For example, the second question in Section B asks if the procedures employed by the engineering group include "a methodology that reasonably assures that all materials and parts which are necessary are included in the formal system for requirements identification?" The question is followed by a brief listing of several examples of specific techniques that might be in use.

In those instances the auditor must supplement the questionnaire with spread sheets which identify all of the specific controls in effect to reasonably assure that the controls in that area are sufficient. The combination of the predetermined questions and the supplemental spread sheets constitute the documented evaluation of the system.

(continued)

FIG. 34-5 *(cont'd)*

Initial completion of this questionnaire may require considerable effort because of the multiple functions involved. In many instances it is not advisable for one auditor to undertake completing it. The arrangement of the questionnaire is such that it can be easily divided among two or more auditors. Managers should discuss the feasibility of completion with the performing auditor(s) and with the director.

Responses to certain of the questions may already be known by virtue of performing reviews and completing questionnaires of related functional areas, such as procurement, cost control, and data processing. In these situations the auditor should incorporate this relevant work to the extent deemed useful in the circumstances.

INVENTORY MANAGEMENT CONTROL QUESTIONNAIRE

	Yes	No
A. General:		
1. Is there a formal written policy stating management's objective regarding inventory?	☐	☐
2. Is the operational unit organized so as to facilitate managing the investment in inventory? This may include, among other things:	☐	☐

a. Organizing by function to reasonably assure that operational unit objectives are attained.
    These functions might include the following:
    ■ General management
    ■ Engineering
    ■ Manufacturing engineering
    ■ Manufacturing
    ■ Materiel
    ■ Facilities
    ■ Finance
    ■ Security
	☐	☐

b. Organizing by major program to reasonably assure that program-specific objectives are effectively achieved and that customer requirements are efficiently met or exceeded, on time, within cost estimates.
    This may require establishing groups such as the following for each major program:
    ■ Project planning
    ■ Project control
    ■ Design engineering
    ■ Production planning
    ■ Tooling design
    ■ Quality control
    ■ Change control
    ■ Test planning
	☐	☐

	Yes	No

c. Do the organizational units mentioned above involved have established procedures for minimizing the investment in inventory? ☐ ☐

d. Have techniques been developed to reasonably assure intra-organizational review and coordination so as to facilitate achieving inventory management objectives? ☐ ☐
 Such techniques might include:
 - Chartering various committees or boards to administer specific objectives such as: Making or buying decisions; publishing manuals or other documentation; and requiring regular operational meetings of affected management personnel to focus on inventory related matters

e. Do procedures and/or systems provide sufficient periodic information and data to permit effective monitoring of the investment in inventory by the general management group? ☐ ☐
 Such information might include:
 - Reports disclosing estimates of final contract revenue and cost data for contracts
 - Reports disclosing the cost status of contracts in process
 - Reports disclosing comparisons of costs incurred vs. amounts authored or budgeted for projects not covered by contracts
 - Reports disclosing information pertaining to production efficiency
 - Reports which measure actual performance against planned performance and/or contracted requirements

f. Do procedures and/or practices include techniques to identify problem areas evident in the information disclosed in the previous question? ☐ ☐
 These techniques include review and inquiry and may be done informally in meetings and over the telephone or more formally by memo or by special investigation.

g. Do procedures and or practices include techniques to remedy problem areas disclosed by the process in the previous question? ☐ ☐
 These procedures may be informal, such as oral directives, or may be formal, such as special directives, task force efforts, and so forth.

h. Do procedures and/or practices require that all relevant information necessary to determine reasonable courses of action with respect to risk decisions be gathered and reported to appropriate levels of management? ☐ ☐

i. Is there a methodology to reasonably assure that decisions involving material requirements and scheduling that deviate from those derivable from existing system-generated data be based upon other data reasonably susceptible to objective verification? ☐ ☐
 Such decisions might include the following:

(continued)

FIG. 34-5 *(cont'd)*

	Yes	No
■ Advance requests for material ■ Production scheduling in excess of customer requirements ■ Research and development efforts beyond contractual requirements		

B. Engineering:

1. Do the procedures employed by engineering include a requirement for identifying all materials and parts which comprise the designed products? ☐ ☐

2. Do the procedures employed by engineering include a methodology that reasonably assures that all required materials and parts are so identified by the formal system for requirements identification? ☐ ☐
   A methodology might include:
   - Techniques for developing and changing engineering drawings. These may include preparation, verification, approval, and numerical control.
   - Techniques for developing and changing bills of material integrated with engineering drawings and which satisfy customer requirements
   - Techniques to reasonably assure that sufficient up-to-date resources are available to facilitate design efforts

3. Do the procedures include a methodology to reasonably assure that changes in product design take into consideration existing commitments and quantities for the item(s) being changed? ☐ ☐

4. Do the procedures include a methodology to reasonably assure that design changes to component parts are accomplished so that all product designs affected by the change are also changed in a timely fashion? ☐ ☐

5. Do any of the techniques involved in the previous questions in this section involve automated data-processing techniques? ☐ ☐
   Note: If the answer to this question is "yes," refer to Section H of this questionnaire.

C. Manufacturing Engineering:

1. Does the manufacturing engineering function or similar group employ procedures to accomplish the following:
   a. Methodology for assuring that all design-specified materials and parts are organized in a manner that will facilitate fabrication and assembly ☐ ☐
   b. A methodology for determining whether to make or buy all relevant component parts ☐ ☐

INVENTORY MANAGEMENT

	Yes	No

    c. A methodology to reasonably assure that all changes to design specified materials and parts are coordinated so as to minimize the obsolete condition of inventory which might otherwise result ☐ ☐

2. Do any of the techniques involved in the previous questions in this section involve automated data processing techniques? ☐ ☐

 Note: If the answer to this question is "yes," refer to Section H of this questionnaire.

3. Does the design and/or layout of production or manufacturing lines provide for the orderly operation of the various manufacturing/assembly processes? ☐ ☐

D. Manufacturing:

1. Do the procedures employed by the manufacturing function include the following:

 a. A method that reasonably assures that production work occurs pursuant to management's general or specific authorization ☐ ☐

 b. Written procedures or instructions for all relevant production operations ☐ ☐

 c. A provision for sufficient competent inspection throughout all phases of production ☐ ☐

 d. A record of the inspections performed in the previous question and the resolution thereof ☐ ☐

 e. A means by which the written procedures are kept current ☐ ☐

 f. A means of production scheduling designed to meet contractual requirements and to minimize sharp changes in production activity ☐ ☐

 g. A requirement for an ongoing program of sufficient care and maintenance to production equipment to reasonably assure optimum performance and to reasonably minimize production halts ☐ ☐

 h. A production environment with due regard for the personal safety of all involved personnel ☐ ☐

 i. A means to reasonably assure that worker productivity meets acceptable criteria ☐ ☐

 j. Records of production sufficient to:
 - Enable reasonably accurate cost accumulation by contract ☐ ☐
 - Enable actual vs. budget cost comparisons in sufficient detail to identify and correct problems ☐ ☐
 - Meet other customer data requirements ☐ ☐

2. Does affected management receive periodic reports of production activities to permit reasonable monitoring? ☐ ☐

3. Are sufficient resources (manpower, facilities, equipment, and materiel) allocated to the production function to enable efficient inventory management? ☐ ☐

(continued)

FIG. 34-5 *(cont'd)*

	Yes	No
4. Do any of the techniques in the previous two questions employ automated data-processing techniques? Note: If the answer to this question is "yes," see Section H of this questionnaire.	☐	☐

E. Material:

1. Do the procedures employed by the materiel function include the following:

	Yes	No
a. Techniques to reasonably assure that only the materials required to be purchased are in fact purchased? Such techniques include written procedures, bills of materials, requirements integrated with sales orders, and use of contracts, purchase orders, etc.	☐	☐
b. Techniques to reasonably assure that purchase activity occurs pursuant to management's authorization	☐	☐
c. Techniques to reasonably assure that changes in materiel requirements are timely effected to preclude acquiring improper items	☐	☐
d. Techniques to reasonably assure that sufficient sources of supply of needed components are identified insofar as practicable	☐	☐
e. Techniques to reasonably assure that materiels ordering procedures consider lead times which will result in having on hand all material items when needed and in sufficient but not excessive quantities	☐	☐
f. A means by which the effects of price increases are minimized? This might include an economic analysis of procurement quantities which explicitly considers the cost of carrying inventory (35%) vs. the cost of inflation	☐	☐
g. A means by which the supply of critical materials and components is reasonably assured? This might also include consideration of the cost of carrying inventory vs. the cost resulting from stock outages	☐	☐
h. A means by which changes in requirements and specifications are promptly communicated to affected suppliers	☐	☐
i. Procedures to reasonably assure that only materials that were ordered are accepted	☐	☐
j. Procedures to reasonably assure that acceptance of delivered materials occurs only upon sufficient inspection verifying: ■ Description ■ Quantity ■ Specifications and tolerances	☐	☐
k. Procedures to reasonably assure that received materials are sufficiently controlled until issued into or consumed by production including:	☐	☐
■ Storage in designated areas pursuant to procedures which require:	☐	☐

	Yes	No
— Restricting access only to custodians	☐	☐
— Orderly arrangement and storage	☐	☐
— An identification system that facilitates subsequent location	☐	☐
— Periodic physical counts and subsequent comparison to written records by individuals independent of custodians	☐	☐
— Adequate physical protection	☐	☐
■ Techniques to reasonably assure that materials issued into the production process occur pursuant to management's authorization	☐	☐
■ Techniques to reasonably assure that all issue transactions are accurately and timely recorded, including physical counts	☐	☐
■ Techniques to identify and use or otherwise dispose of obsolete or slow-moving materials	☐	☐
■ Techniques to reasonably assure that dispositions of material other than by issues into production are recorded (e.g., scrap, spoiled items, surplus sales, returns to supplies, etc.).	☐	☐

2. Do any of the techniques involved in the previous questions involve automated processing techniques? ☐ ☐

    Note: If the answer to this question is "yes," refer to Section H of this questionnaire.

F. Finance:

1. Do the procedures employed by the finance function include the following:

2. A system of accounting which reasonably assures that the following transactions pertaining to inventory are recorded so as to permit preparation of financial statements in accordance with generally accepted accounting principles: ☐ ☐
    a. Purchase of materiel ☐ ☐
    b. Charging materiel cost to contracts ☐ ☐
    c. Transfer of materiel from one job or contract to another ☐ ☐
    d. Other conversion transactions such as direct labor, other direct costs, and allocable overhead ☐ ☐
    e. Adjustments to record items such as valuation allowances and differences resulting from comparison of physical costs with corresponding recorded amounts ☐ ☐

3. Means by which the funding for the investment in inventory is transferred to the customer, which include, but are not limited to, pricing strategies, contract advances, progress billing, and deferral of income taxes. ☐ ☐

4. A methodology for minimizing the financial risk associated with long-term commitments to subcontractors and suppliers, such as: ☐ ☐

(continued)

FIG. 34-5 *(cont'd)*

	Yes	No
a. Establishing criteria for obtaining performance bonds	☐	☐
b. Evaluating the financial condition of suppliers and subcontractors	☐	☐
c. Establishing appropriate funding through negotiation and approval of contract advances and progress payments	☐	☐
d. Providing for timely payment of invoices	☐	☐
5. Do any of the techniques included in the previous questions involve automated processing techniques?	☐	☐

Note: If the answer to this question is "yes," refer to Section H of this questionnaire.

G. Security:

1. Do procedures employed by the security function include techniques sufficient to reasonably assure that the company investment in inventory items is sufficiently protected from: ☐ ☐
   a. Theft or pilferage
   b. Sabotage
   c. Vandalism
   d. Physical damage from acts of God such as fire, flood, or earthquake.

2. Do procedures employed by the security function include techniques sufficient to reasonably assure that access to classified data is restricted to authorized individuals? ☐ ☐

H. Data Processing:

1. If techniques in effect to minimize the investment in inventory include electronic data processing, this section should be completed for each application.

2. Are the applicable procedures forms, descriptions, and so forth described in a user's manual? ☐ ☐

3. Is the application a batch-oriented application with or without remote job entry features? ☐ ☐

4. Do procedures require current and complete system and program documentation? ☐ ☐

Note: If the answers to the previous questions are all "yes," then the auditor should proceed to obtain responses to the balance of the questions in this section. If the answer is "no," it may

INVENTORY MANAGEMENT

	Yes	No
indicate that the application is too complex for evaluation within the context of this assignment. The auditor should not attempt further EDP evaluation and analysis without either assistance from a Senior EDP Auditor or approval of the manager or director.		
5. Do procedures require that the user departments employ techniques to assure that data input and output are sufficiently controlled? Note: In order to answer this question it is necessary to complete Form . . . . for each relevant input and output report.	☐	☐
6. Do procedures require that techniques be employed to reasonably assure that programs, master files, and other data sets and related documentation are secure and may be reconstructed in the event of data loss or destruction?	☐	☐
7. Do procedures require that techniques be employed to reasonably assure that errors and omissions are detected and corrected within a reasonable time period?	☐	☐

INVENTORY MANAGEMENT AUDIT PROGRAM

It cannot be stressed unduly that an audit program should be tailored to the function to be examined—the known or perceived weaknesses, the critical points for the particular operation, the noncompetitive aspects. Any given audit program in a volume like this can be valuable in suggesting points of review, to be adapted to the specific circumstances.

An illustrative audit program for inventory management for a concern producing a high technology item to specific order is illustrated in Figure 34-6. It is designed to provide rather maximum latitude to the individual audit team, and crosses many functions:

- Engineering
- Manufacturing engineering
- Manufacturing
- Materiel (procurement and stores)
- Finance
- Security
- Data processing

FIG. 34-6

Audit Program—Inventory Management

	Done by	Date
1. General:		
☐ Obtain a copy of the written policy statement regarding inventory. Cross-reference to Internal Control Questionnaire.	....	....
☐ Obtain a copy of relevant organization charts. Cross-reference to Internal Control Questionnaire.	....	....
☐ Obtain copies of relevant procedures issued by various involved functional groups. Cross-reference to Internal Control Questionnaire.	....	....
☐ Study policy statements and charts for propriety of organization for purposes of attaining inventory objectives.	....	....
☐ Note the provision for committees and/or management meetings to coordinate inventory management objectives.	....	....
☐ Obtain or review evidence in the form of minutes of meetings or memos indicating the extent of management review and involvement.	....	....
☐ Obtain or prepare a listing of reports generated by various information systems which bear on inventory management. Test compliance by examining a sample of these reports.	....	....
☐ Inquire into the existence of decisions regarding material requirements or scheduling which deviate from those derived by system generated data. Obtain or prepare documentation of relevant facts and examine evidence of proper approval.	....	....
2. Engineering:		
☐ Obtain copies of all pertinent procedures and control flowcharts relating to inventory management. Cross-reference to Internal Control Questionnaire.	....	....
☐ Devise a statistical or judgmental sample of engineering drawings, checking for attributes of:	....	....
▪ Proper verification	....	....
▪ Proper numbering	....	....
▪ Proper approval	....	....
▪ Listing of parts requirements	....	....
▪ Record of changes	....	....
▪ Considering effects of change on inventory balances.	....	....
☐ Conclude as to evidence indicating compliance with established techniques.	....	....
3. Manufacturing Engineering:		
☐ Obtain copy of relevant procedures, control flow charts, etc.	....	....
☐ Design and perform a test to gather evidence (statistical or judgmental) indicating compliance with requirement to organize manufacturing sequence and actions so as to assure efficient fabrication. Test may include inspection of		

INVENTORY MANAGEMENT 34-39

	Done by	Date

drawings, instruction sheets, and planning documents, as well as observations of actual production operations. Draw conclusions as appropriate. ....

☐ Design and perform a test to gather evidence indicating the extent to which make or buy decisions occur as required. Draw conclusions as appropriate. ....

☐ Design and perform a test to measure compliance with procedures for effecting changes to fabrication designs with emphasis on the extent to which impact on inventory is evidenced. ....

4. Manufacturing:

☐ Obtain copy of relevant procedures. ....

☐ Design and perform a test or tests (statistical or judgmental) to gather evidence of compliance with production control procedures, checking for: ....
- Proper approval of production orders ....
- Coordination with schedule requirements, contractual commitments, and/or market forecasts ....
- Quality control activity ....
- Maintenance of production facilities ....

☐ Discuss with appropriate management and corroborate assertions and representations as necessary in order to obtain evidence indicating the adequacy of resources allocated to production facility. ....

5. Materiel:

☐ Obtain copy of relevant procedures, flow charts, etc. ....

☐ Obtain copy of established statements delegating purchase authority and test by a judgmental sampling of executed procurements. ....

☐ Design and perform a test or tests (statistical or judgmental) designed to measure compliance with:
- Requirement to consider lead times and production schedule requirements ....
- On-hand and on-order quantities ....
- Special monitoring procedures for critical items ....
- Communication of changes to suppliers ....
- Price-minimizing activities ....
- Inspection requirements ....
- Storage procedures ....
- Controls over stores' issues and recordings ....
- Physical counts ....

Draw conclusions as necessary.

☐ Design and perform a test of material dispositions other than

(continued)

FIG. 34-6 (cont'd)

	Done by	Date
by issuance to production (i.e., scrap, spoilage, surplus items) for compliance with established controls.	....	....

6. Finance:
- ☐ Obtain copies of relevant procedures, flowcharts, etc. ....
- ☐ Examine procedures and by analysis and inquiry determine the extent to which the accounting system permits preparation of financial statements and other management information for the following types of transactions: ....
  - Purchasing material ....
  - Charging material costs to contracts ....
  - Transferring materiel costs between contracts ....
  - Ordering conversion transactions such as direct labor, other direct costs, and allocable overhead ....
  - Making adjustments to record items such as valuation allowances and book/physical differences ....
- ☐ Inquire to determine the extent to which the funding of inventory is transferred to the customer. ....
- ☐ Inquire to determine the extent to which financial risks associated with long-term commitments with subcontractors are minimized. ....

7. Security:
- ☐ By inspection and observation, determine the extent of compliance with procedures to minimize exposure to:
  - Theft ....
  - Sabotage ....
  - Pilferage ....
  - Vandalism ....
  - Physical damage ....

8. Data Processing:
- ☐ Obtain copies of relevant documentation (user's manuals, if available) describing application systems involved in processing data related to inventory management. ....
- ☐ By study and analyses, determine the extent to which user's manuals, instructions for preparing inputs, and report formats match actual forms and reports. ....
- ☐ By inspection, determine currency of program documentation. ....
- ☐ By inspection, determine that program changes to application systems occur pursuant to established procedures and approval requirements. ....
  Note: If data processing systems are complex, the program of testing should be marked out in advance with the assistance of EDP audit specialists.

	Done by	Date
☐ Consider simulating certain of the automated data-processing routines with emphasis on error detection and correction or, by use of generalized audit software, extract samples of data from machine-readable files for verification with source documents.	....	....
☐ Inquire to determine the extent to which applicable data sets, programs, related documentation, and applicable equipment are safeguarded.	....	....

INVENTORY MANAGEMENT AUDIT FINDINGS

Audit reports should be tailored to fit the needs and interests of the reader (see Chapter 13). Because findings should be quite specific and presented with the background data as to reasons for the existing conditions, the authors present two very simple reports. The first relates to a very small anodizing and cutting plant inventory management system. A simple straightforward memorandum covers the topic in Figure 34-7.

FIG. 34-7

Audit Report on the Inventory Management System—Small Anodizing and Cutting Plant

> TO: M. Andersen
> FROM: Corporate Audit
> SUBJECT: Review of Inventory Management — Manufactured Systems (MS)
>
> We have reviewed the control techniques in use by MS to manage its investment in inventories. The purpose of the review was to evaluate the effectiveness of related policies and procedures and the degree of compliance therewith.
>
> Our work was based on an audit program specifically designed for that purpose and included the review of the controls over physical quantities including security and arrangement; review and tests of receiving, production, manufacturing, and shipping controls including procedures for controlling scrap; review of the standard cost accounting and reporting system; review of the inventory control system and the related Kardex inventory files; and other tests we considered necessary in the circumstances.
>
> Our audit disclosed the following matters which we believe require your attention:
>
> ▪ The manual Kardex inventory records maintained by the Inventory Control group do not provide management with sufficient visibility to effectively monitor and compare, on an overall basis, actual vs. approved inventory levels.
>
> ▪ Some other monitoring techniques useful in managing inventory and production
>
> *(continued)*

FIG. 34-7 *(cont'd)*

> are not practiced at MS and enhancements are needed in some of the techniques which are used.
> - Sales forecasts are not utilized in inventory planning and production scheduling for catalog products.
> - Standard costs used to account for material annodizing labor and overhead, as well as material usage and labor efficiency, are not current.
> - High unit cost inventory items such as axles, motors, and door closers warrant increased safeguards afforded by perpetual inventory controls and restricted access.
> - Documentation of accounting entries to record the results of the special December and January effort to reduce surplus inventory was not sufficient to reasonably assure all such activity was recorded.
>
> Our findings indicate that the MS system of inventory, production, and accounting controls is not sufficient to reasonably assure the investment in inventory is effectively managed. Moreover, there is an absence of various control techniques usually associated with systems of inventory and production control. For example, a perpetual inventory is not maintained other than for selected metal extrusions for which quantity-only records are maintained for ordering purposes. Also, source documents are not used to evidence and account for material movement between the raw material, work-in-process, and finished goods stages. Further, the modified standard cost system utilized by MS does not provide the capability of measuring material usage and labor efficiency variances. Consequently, inventory controls are highly dependent upon the periodic physical count and comparison to the recorded inventory balance.
>
> We believe, however, that inventory control considerations must recognize the limitations inherent in MS due to its relatively small size. Most production is on a job order basis with production commencing when orders are placed by customers. It appears that the costs of a full-scale cost and perpetual inventory system would exceed the benefits to be derived therefrom. Given this limitation, it is therefore critical that there be consistent and full compliance with the policies and procedures of the present system.
>
> The full implementation of the new inventory and scrap procedures together with the recommendations noted in the body of this report is needed to provide MS with an adequate system of inventory management controls.
>
> A written reply to this report is requested from the action parties within 30 days.

The second illustrative report, in Figure 34-8, covers the completely unacceptable conditions of inventory management in a newly established telecommunications manufacturer on the East Coast, with a sales volume of about $50 million. The audit was performed by the corporate audit staff as a result of a request by the plant manager. Rather than presenting merely excerpts of the findings, it was thought a typical audit report (with its weaknesses) full of the specifics, might be more helpful.

(continued on page 34-54)

INVENTORY MANAGEMENT

FIG. 34-8

Audit Report on Inventory Management Showing Unacceptable Conditions—Telecommunications Manufacturer

---

TO: N. Magraudy
FROM: Corporate Audit
SUBJECT: Review of Inventory Management, Willton Electric, Inc., (WEI)

We have reviewed the internal control techniques in use by Willton Electric, Inc. (WEI) to manage its investment in inventories. The purpose of the review was to evaluate the effectiveness of related policies and procedures and the degree of compliance therewith with particular emphasis on controls over the new Moving Average Cost (MAC) segment of the inventory system. Our findings are summarized as follows:

- The brief operating history of important Accounting controls intended for the MAC system such as cycle counts, shop order closing routines, and reconciliations with general ledger control accounts, coupled with implementation difficulties and system deficiencies, have precluded MAC from attaining the reliability intended by management.
- Control techniques over inventory management did not include the most effective methods for authorizing production, ordering material quantities, tracking inventory movement, and measuring factory efficiency.

Our findings should not be construed to imply that management is unaware of the current status of its efforts to improve inventory accountability, management information, and production efficiency, or is not progressing toward these goals.

Most if not all of the findings were known to management and management has or is in the process of taking corrective action for many of the problems. Also, as noted in the body of this report, during 19XX management instituted significant improvements in production and inventory control. In addition, the MAC system was implemented and several "bugs" have been worked out.

In our opinion, the findings of this report indicate that despite considerable effort during the year, management has not yet implemented sufficient controls to reasonably assure that the investment in inventory is effectively managed.

The balance of this report contains a more detailed description of our findings and recommendations. A written reply to the recommendations of this report directed to Corporate Audit is requested within 30 days.

Implementation difficulties were experienced as follows:

- Formal cycle counts have been done infrequently although physical counts by storeroom personnel have been made in connection with staging shop orders. As a result, the accuracy of perpetual inventory records is uncertain. This could be a significant problem because of the volume of inventory transactions and weaknesses in control over recording material movement.
- Cycle count adjustments are recycled back to inventory through the residual account rather than being written off to cost of sales.
- The weekly shop order closure program has only been run five times since the implementation of the MAC system. This delays the application of the averaging feature of MAC and raises questions about individual MAC values as well as the overall inventory value.
- Reconciliation efforts have not yet resolved significant unreconciled differences between the MAC inventory records and the general ledger.

(continued)

FIG. 34-8 *(cont'd)*

- Since the initial assignment of MAC costs, the MAC inventory has been recosted twice and the last recost was not adequately documented.

The manner in which planned inventory features have been applied caused the following problems:
- The system audit trail and, correspondingly, management's ability to monitor MAC operations have been diminished because the MAC residual account and the unreconciled differences noted earlier are lumped into the discrepancy account.
- Cost of sales adjustments to reflect MAC values have not been booked in a timely manner. As a result valuation errors in inventory may not have been timely corrected.
- Inventory is not being reviewed for slow moving and obsolete items. As a result, slow moving and obsolete items may not be receiving sufficient attention and may be overstating inventory balances.
- "Dummy" shop orders used to accumulate labor and material costs that could not be identified to regular shop orders were being left open in WIP (work in process).

System deficiencies which were identified after MAC was implemented include the following:
- There is no control to assure that changes to MAC parameters are properly authorized.
- There is insufficient documentation of the MAC system and only one person has in-depth knowledge of its details.

Other inventory management findings:

- Procedures do not assure that shop orders are properly authorized.
- Although significant improvements have been made in inventory and production control, some essential control techniques and practices have not been implemented and some established control procedures are not enforced, as follows:
  a. There is no evidence that make or buy decisions have been performed since June, 19XX.
  b. Inventory buy decisions do not include formal consideration of economic order quantities and analysis of lead time requirements.
  c. On-hand inventory quantities in WIP were not considered in the net requirements ordering system. This has probably contributed to overordering and the unnecessary build-up in inventory balances.
  d. There is no system for measuring factory labor efficiency and material usage.
- Because of breakdowns in processing controls, numerous shop orders remain open even though all assembly work is completed and numerous others are shown as open even though production work has not started.
- Inadequate controls have existed to ensure accuracy in the recording of part movement between the production floor and stores, and between stores and shipping.
- Significant system and operational inefficiencies have resulted because the MAC and inventory control systems are based upon two separate EDP systems which are not integrated.

Scope of Work:

Our work was based upon an audit program specifically designed for the WEI inventory and included a review of inventory-related controls in the Engineering Manufacturing, Engineering, Manufacturing, Program Management and Control, and Finance departments. Specifically, we reviewed controls over the processing of engineering changes, production control, physical inventories, material movement (through receiving, stores, production, and shipping), the cost control system, data processing (as it relates to all of the preceding), and other tests as we considered necessary in the circumstances.

DETAILED FINANCIAL AND ACCOUNTING FINDINGS

The following matters relate to difficulties experienced by WEI management in implementing the new MAC system.

1. & 2. Formal cycle counts, have been done infrequently although physical counts by storeroom personnel have been made in connection with staging shop orders. Also, cycle count adjustments are recycled back to inventory through the residual account rather than being written off to cost of sales.

A formal cycle count program was not implemented until October, 19XX, when the top 50 inventory items in terms of dollar value were counted. Previously, the only cycle counting that occurred was as orders were picked in stores and apparent overages or shortages were corrected on-line. Also during October, 19XX, our independent auditors with the assistance of WEI personnel, conducted test counts of an additional 150 inventory items. Although initial results of the sample were not conclusive, it appeared that book quantities were greater than on-hand quantities.

As noted elsewhere in this report, controls over the physical movement of inventory between stores, WIP, and shipping have been inadequate. There is evidence to indicate that material movement is not always recorded in the system. In addition, the physical inventory quantities loaded into the MAC system were taken directly from the old book records which had not been verified by physical count. In light of the lack of controls and evidence to indicate that inventory quantities may be mistated, it is necessary that physical quantities be substantiated. WEI management believes that a wall-to-wall physical inventory would be too disruptive to the operations. In lieu of a complete physical inventory, it is highly desirable that cycle counts be finished for the major portion of inventory before the end of the year. Inventory recaps indicate that 83% of the total dollar value of inventory is attributable to only 5.4%, or 2,400, of the 44,000 parts in the system.

Therefore, it appears possible to substantiate a major portion of the inventory by counting a relatively small percentage of the total items. (Use an ABC approach.)

We also noted that the method employed in booking cycle counts has no immediate effect on inventory. Adjustments are booked as a debit or credit to stores with an offsetting entry to the residual account. Because the residual account is allocated to open shop orders during the closure process, write-ups or write-downs eventually increase or decrease the carrying value of the other inventory items in stores. Adjustments then are not reflected in cost of sales until the remaining quantities in stores inventory items are completed and shipped. Since WEI's inventory has been turning over only about once a year, the effect of current adjustments on inventory values would carryover well into 19XX. Since the legitimacy of inventory quantities is

(continued)

FIG. 34-8 (cont'd)

currently in question, major writedowns can be anticipated. Therefore, to prevent possible distortion of inventory values and profit, cycle count adjustments should be booked to cost of sales.

RECOMMENDATION NO. 1

Conduct physical counts of the high value portion of physical inventory by year end and institute a practice of on-going cycle counts of all inventory items.

RECOMMENDATION NO. 2

Write off cycle count adjustments directly to cost of sales.

3. The weekly shop order closure program has been run only five times since implementation of the MAC system. Reconciliation efforts have not resolved significant unreconciled differences between the MAC inventory records and the general ledger.

The closure program, which is intended to be run weekly, has been run infrequently due to system deficiencies. Closure is fundamental to the MAC system because it is the means by which production orders are closed from WIP to stores to allow eventual relief to cost of sales. Also, it is the means by which the residual account is allocated to open shop orders. Thus, the closure program should be run on a timely basis to ensure accuracy in the inventory pricing.

Near the end of our audit, the manager of Cost Control indicated that systems problems, which prevented the running of closure, have been resolved and that closure would be run on a regular basis.

Management has been unable to identify the causes of the differences but believe that they likely result from uncorrected programming errors and system timing differences. Each month a worksheet is prepared to summarize all MAC activity as support for the inventory journal voucher to the general ledger. The monthly differences between the MAC records and the general ledger are charged to the discrepancy account. The discrepancy account balance is then posted on a graph and monitored on a monthly basis. While this may provide management with some degree of comfort, we feel it is not sufficient because it does not identify the cause of the differences and would not disclose offsetting differences. Furthermore, as discussed later in this report, the discrepancy account includes two components besides the unreconciled differences.

Finance personnel are concerned about the unreconciled differences but feel that the problems will be understood and solved over time as the MAC system matures. In our opinion, monthly reconciliations are essential to the integrity of the MAC system. Therefore, efforts to identify and solve the reconciling differences should be intensified.

RECOMMENDATION NO. 3

Intensify efforts to identify the causes of unreconciled differences between the MAC system and the general ledger and take appropriate corrective action.

INVENTORY MANAGEMENT

4. Since the initial assignment of MAC costs, the MAC inventory has been recosted twice and the last recosting effort was not adequately documented.

When the MAC system was initiated in January 19XX, estimated unit values were used in pricing the MAC inventory in an effort to make it equal to the book value of inventory. The initial values were generally equal to the standard costs in the old system plus an additional factor of 10%. The initial costing, however, resulted in a MAC detail inventory value that was substantially less than the book value. As a result, in May, 19XX, an attempt was made to correct the difference by increasing the individual MAC values by an average of 15%. This recosting caused the MAC detail to be greater than the book inventory, with the difference reflected in a discrepancy account.

During September, 19XX, a second attempt was made to reduce the credit balance in the discrepancy account by recosting the MAC inventory at default value. This effort however, was unsuccessful and resulted in only a minor reduction in the MAC detail inventory value and the discrepancy balance.

The recost was done at the same time a correction was made for a major computer-processing error. Because the recost and the error correction were done at the same time, there was an insufficient audit trail to allow assessment of the effects of the actions on the inventory records. Also, although the recost appeared to have the general approval of the Vice President of Finance, there was no documented evidence of this approval. If recosts are made in the future, they should be approved in writing and done so that there is sufficient visibility to allow after-the-fact evaluation.

RECOMMENDATION NO. 4

Require inventory recosts to be approved in writing by the Vice President of Finance and to be booked in a manner which provides sufficient visibility to allow after-the-fact evaluation.

The manner of application of planned inventory features has caused the following problems:

5. The system audit trail and correspondingly management's ability to monitor MAC operations has been diminished because the MAC residual account and the unreconciled differences are lumped into the discrepancy account.

The discrepancy account represents the difference between the total of the MAC detail inventory and the general ledger book inventory. The MAC residual account represents accumulations for scrap, cycle count adjustments, and cost differences detected during shop order closure. Although the system provides a separate general ledger account for the residual account, the balance has been combined with the discrepancy account for each month except July, 19XX. Also, the unreconciled differences discussed earlier in this report are posted to the discrepancy account. The balances of the residual account and the unreconciled differences should be maintained separately from the discrepancy account to allow proper monitoring and evaluation of the MAC system.

RECOMMENDATION NO. 5

Discontinue the practice of charging miscellaneous adjustments to the discrepancy account and maintain separate monthly

(continued)

FIG. 34-8 *(cont'd)*

> balances for the discrepancy account, the residual account, and unreconciled differences between MAC and the general ledger.
>
> **6. Cost of sales adjustments to reflect MAC values have not been booked in a timely manner.**
>
> Separate adjustments are required for commercial and Foreign government cost of sales. Only two adjustments of each type were made since adoption of MAC. However, although the commercial corrections were not booked monthly, supporting worksheets were prepared monthly which disclosed that the predetermined booking rates were generally overstated. The two commercial adjustments which were recorded were booked to a reserve account, "the Allowance for Booking Rate Adjustment."
>
> The first government contract adjustment was immaterial and the second had been prepared but not yet approved for booking at the time of our review.
>
> With the exception of the first government adjustment, all cost of sales adjustments have been material to WEI's financial position. Consequently, delays in making the adjustments could result in distortion of interim reported earnings. Therefore, future adjustments should be made monthly.
>
> ### RECOMMENDATION NO. 6
>
> > Book cost of sales adjustment for differences between MAC costs and predetermined booking rates on a monthly basis.
>
> **7. Inventory is not being reviewed for slow-moving and obsolete items.**
>
> In August, 19XX, procedures were developed to identify and disposition slow-moving and obsolete items; however the procedures were never approved. We were told that the procedures were not approved because of other priorities. As a result, slow-moving and obsolete inventory may not be receiving sufficient attention and may be overstating inventory.
>
> ### RECOMMENDATION NO. 7
>
> > Initiate ongoing procedures for identification and disposition of slow-moving and obsolete inventory.
>
> **8. "Dummy shop orders," which were used to accumulate labor and material costs that could not be identified to regular shop orders, were being left open in WIP.**
>
> Labor is charged to the dummy orders in cases where additional work is required but the shop order has been closed and where late labor charges funnel in after closure. Material is charged to the dummy orders in cases where an engineering change notice (ECN) has not filtered down to WIP and therefore the system will not accept transfer of the new part to the shop order. To allow completion of the assembly, the new part is issued and charged to a dummy shop order. Also, when materials which can not be identified to a shop order are located on the production floor, they are credited to a dummy shop order and debited back to stores.
>
> We noted that the balances in the dummy accounts were being allowed to accumulate month to month in WIP. This prevented the proper allocation of costs back to stores via open shop orders to allow eventual relief to cost of sales. As of

9/30/XX, the balance of the dummy orders was $55,689 for labor, and $401,118 for material.

Following a discussion of the above noted matters with WEI accounting personnel, a new procedure was established to close dummy balances to the residual account on a monthly basis. We noted that the transfer was made in October, 19XX.

The following are system deficiencies which were identified after MAC was implemented.

There is no control to assure that changes to MAC parameters are properly authorized. The MAC system has a provision for variable parameters which can be loaded into the system to effect changes in the rate of residual allocation, the default values, and other MAC values. Because of the way MAC operates, any change in parameters would be offset by a change in the residual account. Therefore, it does not appear that a long-term misstatement could result from a change in parameters. However, it appears that changes in the parameters could have a short-term effect on reported earnings. Since the adoption of MAC, changes in the parameter percentages have been initiated by the Manager of Cost Control with no requirement for higher approval. To ensure that all future parameter changes are consistent with management's intent, parameter changes should be approved in writing by the Vice President of Finance.

RECOMMENDATION NO. 8

Require that parameter changes in the MAC system be approved in writing by the Vice President of Finance.

9. There is insufficient documentation of the MAC system and only one person has an in-depth knowledge of its details.

We noted an absence of program descriptions and flow charts for the MAC system. Also, there is a lack of documentation of the objectives and function of MAC and how it interacts with the overall accounting system. During the audit we had to direct almost all inquiries concerning the operations of the MAC system to the Manager of Cost Control. This individual is the only person in accounting who has a working understanding of the MAC system. He also is the person most involved with the conceptual development of the system. During our review, a training class was conducted to introduce MAC concepts and operations to the accounting personnel. However, we were aware of no other training efforts being made.

We recognize that the lack of documentation and the narrow knowledge base have resulted, at least in part, from the fact that MAC is a relatively new system. However, because of the uniqueness and complexities of the system and because the system is still in an unrefined state, an improved level of documentation and personnel training is crucial to ensuring continuity of operations. In addition, we feel that the correction of system deficiencies can be accelerated as the knowledge base is broadened.

RECOMMENDATION NO. 9

Initiate action to improve the level of documentation for the MAC system and train other accounting supervisors in the operations of the MAC system.

(continued)

FIG. 34-8 *(cont'd)*

DETAILS OF INVENTORY MANAGEMENT FINDINGS

1. Procedures do not assure that production occurs pursuant to management's authorization.

At the time of our review, most production delays were resulting from the nonavailability of manufactured parts rather than from a shortage of purchase parts. Production orders were being generated primarily on an exception basis to meet immediate sales requirements instead of originating from build schedules. Production orders are generated by the EDP system following batch input of Unplanned Order Release forms (i.e., production order requests input by Manufacturing Engineering). The production order requests are sent to Manufacturing Engineering without any signoff to evidence proper approval and come from three different locations — production control, fabrication, and kit assembly.

We noted that management was in the process of preparing build schedules for most major assemblies and some minor assemblies. The immediate plans called for production order requests to originate from one source in Manufacturing Engineering and to be based primarily upon approved build schedules. However, we are aware of no plans to require written approval of production order requests. Production order requests should not be processed unless they are signed by those designated for approval. Without such control, it is possible for unauthorized production to be initiated.

RECOMMENDATION NO. 1

Institute a requirement that production orders be generated only upon submission of signed request forms evidencing proper approval.

2. Although significant improvements have been made in inventory and production control, some essential control techniques and practices have not yet been implemented and some established control procedures are not being followed.

We noted that during 19XX, WEI management instituted significant improvements in production and inventory control. During this time many procedural and organization changes were made with new management personnel assigned in several key areas, such as manufacturing engineering, production control, and material. To establish greater accountability and control, the overall responsibility for these areas was assigned to the Vice President of Program Management and Control. Also, WEI effected a major improvement in the purchasing system by designing and implementing a net requirements purchasing system known as the 19XX requirements. Under this system, forecasted parts usage is compared with on-hand quantities to determine net-order quantities. At the time of our review a comparable report was being generated for 19XX requirements.

However, although significant improvements have been made, at the time of our review WEI was still experiencing production delays which stemmed primarily from the nonavailability of lower-level manufactured parts, particularly fabricated parts. Most production orders were being generated on an exception basis to meet short-term shipping requirements. Out of necessity, much of management's attention has been focused on the more immediate concerns of reducing backlogs and meeting shipping schedules. Consequently, the implementation of certain longer-term corrective actions has been delayed. In this regard we noted the absence of the following techniques and practices which are normally associated with inventory and production control.

- We saw no evidence that make or buy analyses have been performed since June, 19XX. WEI procedures call for make or buy calculations to be proposed and then reviewed and approved by a make or buy committee, which has been chaired by the Vice President of Manufacturing. However, this individual was recently terminated and at the time of our review, a new chairman had not yet been assigned.
- There is no formal provision in the ordering system for factoring lead time into the ordering process. At the time of our review, management was considering implementation of a system whereby the 19XX forecast of parts requirements would be used to compute an average projected daily usage. Management intends to factor in total order lead time by part and, using the projected daily usage, program the system to alert material analysts when on-hand quantities fall below minimum levels. It appears that the system can be implemented at a reasonable cost since it can be adapted from an existing bulk requirements program.
- There is no formal provision in the ordering system for determining economic order quantities (EOQ). It was represented to us that management performed a manual economic order analysis before proceeding with the large stockpiling of materials for the major product lines. Though such an analysis may have been adequate for two large contract purchases, it appears that the capability should exist for material analysts to determine economic order quantities on an ongoing basis.
- The net parts requirement identification system noted above does not consider on-hand quantities in WIP. As a result, order quantities identified in the system may be overstated. Management is aware of the problem but is unable to take corrective action until the backlog of erroneous open production orders is removed from WIP.
- There is no mechanism for monitoring labor efficiency and material usage in manufacturing. Other than by individual observation, manufacturing personnel have no practical way to measure employee productivity either individually or by department. In addition, there is no means for determining labor hour requirements for outstanding and upcoming production orders in order to schedule work requirements.

Based upon our discussion with personnel in Manufacturing and Manufacturing Engineering, it appears that it would be possible to adapt the current system to accumulate, at point of production order closure, totals of labor hours by individual and by work center. These hours could be compared with routing hours loaded by Manufacturing Engineering to determine labor efficiency. As an alternative (since the routing hours are sometimes inaccurate) the accumulated hours could be compared with statistics and standards accumulated by the Manufacturing supervisors. Also, it appears that by using hour data on the Manufacturing routings, the required labor hours could be estimated for upcoming orders or orders currently in process. Finally, under the MAC system, scrap and rework costs are allocated back to all open production orders. Since rework, spoilage, etc., are reported on nonstandard issue acquisition forms, it appears it would be possible for the system to summarize this data for use in monitoring material usage.

We recognize that there are practical limitations on management and data-processing resources and that corrective actions must therefore be prioritized and dealt with as resources permit. However, we saw no evidence that the relative importance of the matters discussed above had been reviewed and that timetables for corrective action had been established.

(continued)

FIG. 34-8 *(cont'd)*

RECOMMENDATION NO. 2
Review the production and inventory control deficiencies noted above in the context of their relative importance to WEI as a whole and establish individual timetables for corrective action.

3. Because of breakdowns in processing controls, numerous shop orders remain open even though all assembly work is complete, and numerous others are shown as open even though production work has not, and likely never will, take place.

As of 9/30/XX, there were approximately 18,300 open shop orders. According to estimates by personnel in Manufacturing Engineering, the total open orders should only be approximately 12,000. The excess number of orders is caused by:

- Manufacturing personnel not preparing transfer forms for completed assemblies. The system is programmed so that closure occurs only if the quantities issued to and returned from stores zero out. In cases where the quantities do not zero out, the shop order will remain open even if all production work is complete.
- Manufacturing personnel borrowing parts from one shop order to complete another without processing the appropriate paper work. As a result, shop orders may have either an over- or under-allocation of parts.
- As noted earlier, not running the closure program on a timely basis.
- The carry over of approximately 5,000 shop orders from prior years which had been bulk-issued as a means of correcting a system inability to generate shop orders as they were needed. These shops orders are open on paper only, and just sit on shelves in the Material Control area.

The effect, either directly or indirectly, of having an excess number of open orders in the system has been:

- An overstatement of the dollar value of inventory in WIP and correspondingly an understatement of the stores' inventory. Any shop order balance incorrectly held in WIP can not be recycled back to stores for eventual relief to cost of sales. The amount of the overestimate can not be practically estimated.
- An overstatement of the number of open orders on the Open Order Status report, thus significantly diminishing the effectiveness of the report. Production Control personnel can not rely on the report and must often go to the assembly floor to verify that an order is still open. This has the effect of creating inefficiencies in the whole manufacturing process because parts being counted on for higher-level assembly may not be available.
- Overbuying of parts because the WIP quantities are not included in the on-hand inventory when computing order requirements. This occurs because the WIP quantities are overstated and therefore can not be relied upon as a factor in the net requirements ordering system.
- An apparent tendency for labor changes to accrue on the shop orders. Between 1/XX and 9/XX the value of labor in WIP increased by 188% while the material portion of WIP increased by only 25%.

Management is aware of the problems noted above and at the time of our review was in the process of implementing procedures to clear out the erroneous shop orders. We noted that over 2,000 orders were closed during October, 19XX.

In addition to clearing out old shop orders, management was in the process of establishing control to prevent recurrance of the problem. The planned controls include 1) reassigning floor schedules and material movers from Manufacturing to

INVENTORY MANAGEMENT

Program Management (thus, the system of accountability will be independent of manufacturing personnel), 2) establishing floor logs by work center to allow tracking of parts out of WIP, and 3) implementing a revised labor charge system whereby employees will be required to log their time as work is performed. Currently, employees sometimes do not log their time until the end of the day, thus precluding the performance of floor checks to ensure accuracy in labor recording.

We believe that the above actions, if implemented as intended, will substantially improve control over the production process. Inadequate controls have existed to ensure accuracy in the recording of the movement of parts between the production *floor and stores between stores and shipping.*

During our review of inventory movement, we noted that there is no procedure to reasonably assure that all inventory transactions are entered into the MAC system. Transfers from stores to WIP, from WIP back to stores, and from stores to shipping are keyed by terminal operators from material movement forms for direct on-line up-date. The system generates a report, 420, which provides a detailed record of each individual transaction. However it does not recap the total transactions by type nor is there any separate listing or log to which the transactions can be reconciled. Consequently, it cannot be ascertained whether, for example, all completed assemblies have been returned to stores or whether inventory has been properly relieved for shipments. Since several thousand transactions are entered each month, it is not inconceivable that the problem could result in a significant number of errors.

As noted earlier in this report, a major cause of the buildup in the number of open shop orders has been the failure to record the transfer of completed assemblies to stores. During the audit, new procedures were being implemented requiring floor schedules to maintain logs showing material transfers by work center. If the 420 report were recapped by transaction type, daily or weekly transfers could be compared with corresponding production floor logs. Also, transfers from stores to WIP and from stores to shipping could be similarly compared with manual records. These comparisons would provide an ongoing indication of the completeness and accuracy of MAC processing. Our review indicated that only a relatively minor program change would be required to adapt the 420 report as described above.

RECOMMENDATION NO. 3

Adapt the 420 material transaction report to provide a recap of total transactions by type and establish procedures requiring reconciliation of part movement by type between manual records and the MAC system.

4. **Significant system and operation inefficiencies have resulted because the MAC and inventory systems are based upon two separate EDP systems, Vertical Storage Access Method (VSAM) and Disk Bill of Material Processor (DBOMP), which are not integrated.**

The new MAC inventory system was designed as an online system using a VSAM file structure. The old inventory application was designed as a batch system using DBOMP. Because of inherent differences in the systems and because of deficiencies in bridge programs between the two systems, changes in DBOMP often do not get recorded in VSAM as follows:

- The parts number master is fed by DBOMP but is not completely copied to VSAM. As a result, new parts sometimes do not get into the on-line system.

(continued)

FIG. 34-8 *(cont'd)*

- Engineering Change Notices (ECNs) are input to DBOMP and therefore are reflected in all subsequent production orders, since production orders are generated by DBOMP. However, the ECNs often are not reflected in production orders which are already in WIP at the time the ECN is submitted since WIP is driven by VSAM. As a result, issuances of new parts to WIP must often be charged to blanket production orders because the new parts have not been accepted by the VSAM system.
- The open order status report generated by DBOMP does not agree with open orders per the on-line VSAM system. As a result, new orders can be in DBOMP but not VSAM and closures can be reflected in VSAM but not DBOMP. This disparity creates confusion and extra work in production control.
- Production order packets include pick tickets generated by VSAM and production orders, routings, and labor cards generated by DBOMP. In some cases the pick tickets have not corresponded to the other documents in the production packets. This has resulted in production delays.

WEI management is aware of the system differences and believes that all inventory functions should be performed by one common system by the creation and use of an effective data base. It appears that corrective action has been delayed because of the large backlog of system and programming requests already in process. However, we saw no evidence that the DBOMP/VSAM system differences had been compared in terms of priority with other outstanding programming requests. Because of the company-wide significance of the problems noted above, it appears that such an evaluation should be made.

RECOMMENDATION NO. 4

Investigate the feasibility of establishing a common data base for all inventory functions and, as an interim measure, correct bridge programs between the DBOMP and VSAM systems.

FINANCIAL TYPE INVENTORY AUDITS

The preceding discussion has dealt largely with an operational audit of inventory management, and necessarily has related in part to procurement and manufacturing procedures that have an impact on inventories. There will be occasions, however, when the emphasis is on the physical inventory on hand, not on any complicated but related procurement/manufacturing processes. In other words, some inventory review could relate more closely to financial type audits of inventory.

One simple guide may be useful.[5]

> One of the more significant areas for auditing, and for business in general, is inventories and production-related accounts. While the trend today is away from manufacturing to a service-based economy, many organizations still maintain large amounts of goods awaiting production or available for servicing cus-

---

[5] From "Reviewing Inventories and Related Accounts," *Internal Auditing Alert*, Nov. 1985, pp. 6–7.

tomers. In some cases, difficulties arise in accounting for inventory and determining its appropriate valuation. When problems do arise, management is particularly concerned with attaining maximum production and distribution while minimizing costs, investment, and risk.

Many internal and external factors can have an impact on the auditor's review and substantive tests of inventories and production-related accounts. Reporting deadlines, tax considerations, economic conditions, the auditor's assessment of risk and materiality, and the effectiveness of the system of internal accounting controls can all affect the nature, extent and timing of an auditor's review and substantive tests. Following is a guide for auditing inventory and production-related costs.

Observing Physical Inventories. The objectives in observing physical inventories are to ascertain that the merchandise and/or materials exist and to observe that the count and description of the inventories and their condition are accurate and properly recorded.

- ☐ If the inventory is subject to significant volatility of movement or quantities, or if there are weaknesses in the controls over accounting for movement, then inventory should be counted at year-end.
- ☐ If inventory controls are adequate, the count may be taken prior to year-end.
- ☐ If there is a system of cycle counts, inventories might be taken on a staggered basis throughout the year.
- ☐ If inventory is taken at one time, it is not unusual to pick a month in the last quarter of the fiscal year.
- ☐ All written instructions and the memorandum of physical inventory plans should be reviewed and commented on.
- ☐ To facilitate the plan for observing the inventory, one or more instructional meetings should be held with those who are to supervise the inventory-taking.
- ☐ Audit staffing requirements must be determined, based on the timing of inventories at various locations, the number of counting teams available, and the difficulty of the observations to be made.
- ☐ Although an auditor is not an expert appraiser of inventories, he or she should raise questions about an inventory's usefulness and salability. For example, is inventory well arranged? Does it show signs of age and neglect?
- ☐ Considerable time should be spent observing physical inventory procedures and the related controls, including the diligence of the counting teams, the presence of supervisory personnel, and the adherence to instructions.
- ☐ Test counts should be performed by the auditors to confirm the accuracy of the physical inventory and to record the existence of inventory for later tracing into the inventory summarization.
- ☐ An auditor should work with production or operations personnel to deal with problems of work-in-process identification and valuation.
- ☐ During cycle count observation—when the entire inventory is not being

counted at one time—an auditor must take steps to ensure the proper identification of items counted.

Dealing With Difficult Inventories. Certain types of materials may be difficult to count, causing an auditor to use creativity to substantiate quantities on hand. In some situations, an auditor may need the assistance of an expert or specialist in taking or evaluating the inventory. Other cases may require photographic surveys, engineering studies, and similar specialized techniques to take physical inventories.

Sometimes split counts cannot be avoided if operating pressures prevent a plant, warehouse, or other facility from scheduling simultaneous counts. When split counts are required, an auditor should ensure that the cost accounting and perpetual inventory records are accurate and that physical controls and documentation related to transfers from one category of inventory to another are highly reliable.

Another difficult situation that an auditor must deal with is applying alternative procedures if observation of physical inventories is not practicable. Faced with such a situation, an auditor should examine other physical evidence or substantiate inventories through further examination of accounting evidence. These include:

☐ Performing subsequent tests after the physical inventory has been taken.
☐ Examining written instructions for inventory-taking, reviewing the original tags or sheets, and making suitable tests of the inventory summarization.

Purchase Commitments. An auditor should review the record of purchase commitments, giving emphasis to long-outstanding commitments. The examination should include a review of open contracts and purchase orders for materials. Purchase commitments should also be related to inventories and sales orders to determine whether a loss should be recognized and recorded.

Reporting Findings. Inventories and production-related accounts are most important to the operations of a business. When an auditor gathers evidence that questions the existence, ownership, and valuation of inventory or the accuracy of production costs, he should report the finding(s) to management immediately and recommend action to correct the situation in the audit report.

☐ Observing some physical evidence of the existence of inventory and performing appropriate tests of intervening transactions.

Inventory Costing. Inventory costing and summarization is based on the physical inventory results or perpetual inventory records. In either case, the results are compared with recorded book amounts. The extent of testing here depends largely on whether internal controls can be relied on.

☐ In testing the costing of inventories, an auditor can frequently relate costs directly to specific vendor invoices and labor summaries.
☐ In more complex manufacturing operations, the evaluation of material, labor, and overhead may be more difficult, requiring tracking the inventory through its various stages of completion.

- ☐ The accounting method used to price inventory can also affect the substantive tests to be performed (e.g., FIFO, LIFO).
- ☐ In reviewing for obsolete items in inventory, the auditor can compare quantities with those in previous inventories to identify slow-moving items or abnormally large or small balances. Usage records, purchase orders, and production orders may also be examined.
- ☐ An auditor should also test the application of the lower-of-cost-or-market principle and the calculation of net realizable value. Substantive testing is usually based on an auditor's perception of risk.

Cost of Sales. Tests of cost of sales can usually be limited to analytical review procedures that test the proper classification of costs by:

- ☐ Focusing on relationships among various components of costs of sales.
- ☐ Obtaining explanations for fluctuations in expense account balances.

AICPA STUDY ON INVENTORY AUDITS

Another possibly useful guide on inventory audits is that issued by the AICPA.[6]

As part of the Auditing Procedure Study series of the American Institute of CPAs (AICPA) and the Canadian Institute of Chartered Accountants (CICA), the AICPA recently issued "Audit of Inventories." Following is a brief review of the areas covered in this Auditing Procedure Study.

Purpose of Study. The study was designed to provide a discussion of suggested auditing procedures and related problems that auditors may experience regarding inventories such as the following: physical existence, completeness, ownership, valuation, condition, and financial presentation and disclosure. Although the study was designed for independent auditors in obtaining satisfaction concerning client representations on inventories, the guidance provided can also be used by internal auditors during interim audits of a division or plant inventory. The study emphasizes the need for proper planning, including a proper assessment of audit risk as a means of ensuring that sufficient and appropriate audit evidence will be obtained regarding inventories.

Scope of Study. The study covers the following areas:

- ☐ Auditor's objective and initial planning considerations, which include: auditor's objective, initial planning considerations, sampling, the use of computer-assisted audit techniques, use of specialists, and the use of internal auditors.
- ☐ Existence, ownership, and completeness—planning considerations,

---

[6] From "AICPA Issues Study on Inventory Audits," *Internal Auditing Alert*, Aug. 1986, pp. 7–8.

which include: auditor's objective, interrelationship assertions, planning, internal control considerations, multilocation inventories, inventories held by or for others, precount finalization, and using the work of a specialist.
- ☐ Planning considerations for attendance at physical count and postattendance considerations.
- ☐ Valuation, which includes: auditor's objective, planning, cost verification procedures, market verification procedures, and other considerations as they relate to LIFO, retail, and hedged inventories.
- ☐ Other procedures, such as: analytical review, clerical accuracy, reconciliation of physical inventory to book amounts, and year-end cutoff procedures.
- ☐ Financial statement presentation and disclosure.

The study also provides a number of appendices that can be utilized for audits of inventories. Following are the titles of the appendices:

- ☐ Examples of Internal Control Considerations for Inventories
- ☐ Sample Inventory Attendance Planning Questionnaire
- ☐ Sample Confirmation—Inventories Held by Others
- ☐ Sample Confirmation—Inventories Held by Client on Behalf of Others
- ☐ Sample Audit Program
- ☐ Sample Representation Letter for Inventories
- ☐ Examples of Computer-Assisted Audit Techniques

Planning. As indicated in the study, special emphasis is given to planning. In the section under "Auditor's Objective and Initial Planning Considerations," planning is discussed in light of general familiarization, materiality, and audit risk. Under the section entitled "Existence, Ownership, and Completeness—Planning Considerations," there is a discussion of general familiarization, potential errors, and compliance approach versus substantive approach. For example, in the discussion of compliance versus substantive approach, the study discusses the following factors, which may influence the auditor's decision to rely on company count controls:

- ☐ Competence of count personnel.
- ☐ Stock identification procedures.
- ☐ Procedures to reduce the potential for double-counting or missing items.
- ☐ Stock organization.
- ☐ Identification and segregation of consignment or other customer stock.
- ☐ Procedures to check counts.
- ☐ Procedures to control the movement of goods.
- ☐ Procedures to check calculations.
- ☐ Procedures to check work in process.

Finally, under the section "Valuation," planning is discussed with respect to potential errors, assessment of valuation methods, and use of specialists.

Use of Internal Auditors. The study indicates that there may be situations where the work of internal auditors can be used during independent audits, since internal auditors perform routine studies and evaluations of internal control systems and also perform substantive tests. For example, internal auditor assistance might be used in the following tasks:

- ☐ Testing valuations
- ☐ Testing internal control systems
- ☐ Testing cutoffs
- ☐ Inventory counting

Guidance on Inventory Counts. One of the most practical sections for internal auditors to consider is Chapter 3, "Existence, Ownership, and Completeness—Count Attendance and Postattendance Considerations." A discussion is provided on inventory count attendance considerations, which includes the following:

- ☐ Observing the count
- ☐ Performance of test counts
- ☐ Work-in-process considerations
- ☐ Cutoff procedures
- ☐ Documentation
- ☐ Alternative procedures when attendance is not practicable

Postinventory count attendance considerations are also discussed. These include:

- ☐ Testing quantities on final inventory listings
- ☐ Confirmation follow-up
- ☐ Testing cutoff
- ☐ Documentation

SUGGESTED READING

Aggarwal, Sumer C. "MRP, JIT, OPT, FMS? Making Sense of Production Operations Systems." *Harvard Business Review*, Sept./Oct. 1985, pp. 8–16.

Armstrong, David J. "Sharpening Inventory Management; New Graphic and Analytic Techniques Improve Understanding of an Old Management Problem." *Harvard Business Review*, Nov./Dec. 1985, pp. 42–58.

Rogers, Richard L., and Jerrold J. Stern. "When Should LIFO-Liquidated Inventories Be Replaced?" *Management Accounting*, Nov. 1986, pp. 53–57.

Sadhwani, Arjan T., M.H. Sarhan, and Dayal Kiringoda. "Just-in-Time: An Inventory System Whose Time Has Come." *Management Accounting*, Dec. 1985, pp. 36–44.

Sauers, Dale G. "Analyzing Inventory Systems." *Management Accounting*, May 1986, pp. 30–36.

Swalley, Richard W. "Managing Your Inventory: New Use for an Old Tool." *Management Accounting*, May 1984, pp. 52–56.

Swann, Don M. "Where Did the Inventory Go?" *Management Accounting*, May 1986, pp. 26–29.

CHAPTER **35**

Facilities Management

Objectives of Facilities Management 1	Optimum Utilization of Equipment 12
Facilities Organization Structure 2	Records and Reports 12
Facilities Control Cycle 4	Facilities Procurement Review 12
Long-Range Facilities Plan 5	Facilities Management Questionnaire and Program 15
Short-Term Facilities Plan 6	Facilities Management Audit Reports and Typical Findings 31
Project Evaluation Methods 6	
Classifying and Ranking the Projects ... 7	Internal Audit of Capital Investment Projects 34
Steps in the Capital Budgeting Procedure 9	Internal Audit of Ongoing Capital Projects 34
Control and Monitoring of Capital Acquisitions 10	Post-Completion Audits of Capital Projects 37
Custody and Administration of Facilities 11	
Maintenance and Care 11	Suggested Reading 38

Fig. 35-1 Functional Outline—Vice-President–Materiel, Facilities, and Services 3
Fig. 35-2 Priority Schedule for Capital Projects 8
Fig. 35-3 Audit Program for Facilities Procurement Review 13
Fig. 35-4 Facilities Management Audit Questionnaire 16
Fig. 35-5 Audit Program—Facilities Management 25
Fig. 35-6 Facilities Management Audit Report 32

OBJECTIVES OF FACILITIES MANAGEMENT

The extent and methodology of the facilities management function (which relates to the physical assets of land, buildings, machinery and equipment, tools, and furniture and fixtures), and its organizational structure, will obviously depend on the importance of physical facilities to the specific company. To an insurance broker having only one sales and administrative office in a service industry, the function probably would be handled by the office manager, and would be limited in scope. On the other hand, in a capital-intensive industry, such as chemicals or petroleum, the facilities management activity is of major impact.

For the medium- to large-sized manufacturing concerns, where physical facilities are significant, the objectives of facilities management include:

- The procurement of appropriate facilities, under the right terms and conditions, to meet the company needs—both short-term and long-range.
- The most suitable allocation of capital available for fixed asset acquisition among the various processes, or products, or divisions, depending on the method of placing responsibility for results, and the relative profitability.
- The optimum productive use of the capital assets.
- The adequate protection of the physical assets from physical loss, damage, or deterioration.
- Effecting adequate compliance with applicable laws and regulations, such as safety and pollution.

The purpose of an operations audit of facilities management is to assure that these objectives are being met on an efficient and economical basis.

FACILITIES ORGANIZATION STRUCTURE

The organization structure and size of the facilities management group obviously should depend on the job to be done. Influencing factors could be such matters as:

- Importance of the function to the company operations
- Location, extent, and type of physical facilities
- Age and physical condition of the assets
- Planned level of capital expenditures
- Planned major expansion, or modification of the fixed assets
- Extent of operating capacity and degree of utilization
- Whether the company is organized on a centralized or decentralized basis
- Whether or not the board of directors or top management wishes the facilities organization to supervise major construction projects (or contract them out)

The same principles of sound organization apply to facilities management as to any other function. For example:

- The scope of facilities management should be clearly stated, including:
    —Objectives
    —Activities that make it up
    —Corporate policy on facilities

FIG. 35-1

Functional Outline—Vice-President—Materiel, Facilities, and Services

SUMMARY:

The Vice-President–Materiel, Facilities, and Services reports to the President and is responsible for planning, directing, and administering the acquisition, control, and disposition of land, buildings, and equipment to ensure operational support and maximum return and profitability from the use of the company's real and personal property. He is also responsible for coordination of company energy conservation, environmental quality, and telecommunications activities.

SPECIFIC RESPONSIBILITIES:
1. Directs the preparation of a Facilities Master Plan and supporting studies to maintain the company's real estate requirements consistent with the annual and long-range business plans.
2. Prepares, with the assistance of the law department, and administers contracts, leases, and other documents required for the acquisition, utilization, and disposition of real property.
3. Represents the company as required on real estate matters with external individuals and organizations.
4. Maintains current knowledge of local and national developments in the real estate field, including legislation and regulations that affect real property.
5. Administers the capital asset commitment budget.
6. Ensures the approval of capital and operating leases in accordance with corporate policies.
7. Initiates, coordinates, and secures approval of the corporate office capital asset budget.
8. Chairs the Corporate Facilities Committee to ensure that facilities activities and programs are consistent with company strategy and governmental requirements.
9. Acts as the corporate administrative focal point for energy conservation, environmental quality, and telecommunications.
10. Directs the operation of the Corporate Headquarters Building and related corporate facilities.

- The responsibilities of the chief facilities officer should be clearly described, and he should have commensurate authority. A functional outline for the facilities officer of a decentralized high technology company is shown in Figure 35-1.
- There should be adequate staffing, with competent personnel, for the task to be done.
- The staff relationship with the other functions involved with facilities should be clearly spelled out, including those with:
  — Finance   — Materiel
  — Production   — Engineering
  — Plant security

FACILITIES CONTROL CYCLE

We have defined an operational audit as a systematic review and evaluation of an organizational unit for the purpose of appraising its effectiveness and efficiency (see Chapter 31). It necessarily includes a review of the management control system. Accordingly, it is necessary to know what functions are performed (or should be performed), who should perform them, what the basic features and controls should be, and the relationship to various related staff functions.

The functions usually involved in facility management, in all but the most routine and small operations, include these:

- ☐ *Capital asset planning function.* These more specific segments would be a part of this planning phase:
  - Developing the long-range master facilities plan
  - Developing, or coordinating the development of, the short-term or annual facility plan
  - Preparing the technical plans for, and/or evaluating, specific proposed capital projects
  - Initiating and reviewing capital expenditure proposals after approval in principle by the board of directors (the capital commitment and expenditures budget)
- ☐ *Capital asset acquisition control function.* Subdivisions of this function would relate to:
  - Direct acquisition and installation of the equipment, including final acceptance.
  - Where within the scope of the function, the supervision of major construction projects.
  - The monitoring and control of in-progress costs on projects, and approval on completion.
  - Approval of capital disbursements.
  - The post-completion monitoring and review of the equipment or major projects.
- ☐ *Day-to-day asset supervision and control.* These functions would form part of the activity:
  - Maintaining and repairing the equipment
  - Exercising custody of the equipment and protecting it from physical loss or damage
  - Evaluating utilization and productivity of the equipment
  - Coordinating with the insurance department on risk coverage matters
  - Salvaging and disposing of idle and unused and excess fixed assets

All or more of these activities, and any others applicable in the circumstances, should be considered in developing the operational audit program.

Some further elaboration on selected functions is outlined below. In the context of background for auditing, it is not practical, nor should it be necessary, to cover every process, function, or sequence of steps in carrying out an effective facilities management operation.

LONG-RANGE FACILITIES PLAN

One area of weakness in facility management is the frequent absence of a long-range master facilities plan. Yet, capital investment decisions commit an enterprise to specific courses of action for relatively long periods in the future. More than this, once a decision is made, usually it cannot be easily or quickly changed without a significant loss. Not only is the decision not readily undone, but also, in most instances, it may foreclose other profitable decisions because of a limit on the capital resources available and the manpower to manage it.

Given these circumstances, it is easy to realize that the best capital investment decisions must be in concert with the business strategy. Proper capital budgeting procedures should consider a spectrum of long-term investment opportunities with the objective of seeing that the projects selected will contribute to achieving the company's goals and objectives. In so doing, there may be instances where the most profitable near-term expenditure may not be selected! Thus, long-range strategy must consider both market segment growth and relative market share. This is another way of saying that perhaps a company should have a "strategic screening process" *before* it proceeds with other evaluation techniques. In a given instance, the business strategy and the corporation's financial position, meaning adequacy of cash, may result in different capital expenditure decisions than for another company. In the context of corporate strategy, certain key questions must be asked in evaluating capital investment decisions, such as:

- Is the segment of planned expenditure within the area in which the company has certain competitive advantages?
- Is the segment one in which the firm wishes to increase, or maintain, a stream of earnings?
- Is the proposed project still consistent with the corporate decision on:
  — Foreign competition?
  — Foreign parts and raw material sources?

In other words, there must be coordination of strategic plans among facilities management, production management, marketing management, and financial management.

It is recognized that long-range plans are broad-brush in nature and subject to change. But at least a mechanism is needed to be sure that the first year of the strategic plan is consistent, more or less, with the short-term annual plan, and vice versa.

SHORT-TERM FACILITIES PLAN

A segment of the corporate short-term plan is the facilities plan or capital budget. As contrasted to the strategic plan, it is quite specific. Potential projects or items must be analyzed and evaluated; an appropriate selection must be made, approved by higher management, included in the annual facilities plan, and usually submitted to the board of directors for review and approval. While the board may approve a specific project in principle, in that it expects to be advised if circumstances or economics change, and in that management usually will scrutinize the data before specific go-ahead is given to facilities management, generally board approval is a final step before implementation. It is therefore essential that the company have a sound capital budgeting procedure, including these functions:

- Finding attractive investment opportunities
- Possessing a practical way of setting a limit for total capital expenditures
- Having ways of evaluating the economic suitability and worthiness of the projects—at least the major ones
- Possessing the means of ranking the projects, so that the best ones are selected
- Controlling the expenditures so that they are within authorization limits
- Conducting a postaudit, certainly as to the larger expenditures, to compare forecasted and actual economic benefits

A critical element in this whole process is the securing of reliable, accurate and relevant input data on a proposed project.

Project Evaluation Methods

There are certain capital expenditures which must be made if the enterprise is to continue in operation, e.g., replacement of inoperable equipment, acquisition of pollution control facilities, or certain safety devices. On the other hand, some expenditures are made for the hope of future economic benefits—future earnings. Especially in capital-intensive companies, procedures must be developed to provide a reasonably accurate way of measuring the benefits. Factors in this procedure should include:

- An estimate of the expected capital outlay—the cash outflow; and the expected amount and timing of the future benefits—the cash inflow.
- A technique for relating the future benefits to the estimated cost—the rate of return on the capital employed.
- A means of evaluating the risk—of measuring the probability of receiving the future benefits.

It is beyond the scope of this volume to discuss the various methods of evaluating capital expenditures. The readers are referred to the available literature on the subject.[1] A listing of some of the more common techniques to be reviewed include these:

- Payback period
- Operators' method
- Accountants' method
- Discounted cash flow (DCF) methods:
  — Internal rate of return (IRR)
  — Net present value (NPV)

Classifying and Ranking the Projects

Under normal circumstances, the amount of suggested capital expenditures is far greater than the company's financial resources would permit. This is especially true when an environment to encourage proposals does exist. Further, while profitability will be a major factor in project selection, there will be some instances where it will not be the criterion (e.g., where a proposal is inconsistent with corporate strategy). Hence, to simplify the decision-making process, it is suggested the procedures provide that proposals be classified according to basic needs or reasons and, further, that those being made for the measurable economic benefits be ranked in some fashion. A practical method of segregating projects could be:

1. Absolutely essential
   - ☐ Replacement of exhausted or inoperable facilities, without which the company cannot continue in business
   - ☐ Installation of equipment demanded by governmental agencies or laws, such as:
     - Pollution abatement devices
     - Safety controls
     - Items to eliminate health hazards
2. Highly necessary
   - ☐ Sufficient parking space for employees
   - ☐ Competitive quality control equipment
   - ☐ Adequate lighting facilities in profiling area
3. Economically justified projects
   - ☐ Plant expansion
   - ☐ Cost-saving equipment
   - ☐ New product lines, pursuant to corporate goals
   - ☐ New facilities close to foreign markets

---

[1] For example, see James D. Willson, *Budgeting and Profit Planning Manual*, 2nd ed., Chapter 31 (New York: Warren, Gorham & Lamont, 1988).

FIG. 35-2
Priority Schedule for Capital Projects

CAPITAL PROJECT RANKING FOR THE 19XX CAPITAL BUDGET				
Priority	Rate of Return (IRR)	Profitability Index	Description and Location	Estimated Cost
1	34.6%	1.30	New electronics plant — Chicago	$4,870,000
2	30.2	1.21	Modernizing profiler equipment — Los Angeles	3,800,000
3	29.5	1.20	Installing robots — Fabrication — El Segundo	8,920,000
4	26.4	1.14	Mechanizing material handling — New York	2,900,000
5	25.0	1.19	Purchase new trucks — Washington	1,410,000
6	25.0	1.10	Renovate warehouse — Chicago	610,000
7	24.3	1.09	Install new paint facility — Anaheim	2,460,000
8	21.7	1.01	Replace loading dock — El Cerritos	1,110,000

4. Miscellaneous
   ☐ New facade to improve plant appearance
   ☐ Modernizing cafeteria to aid employee morale
   ☐ Refurbishing community center for public relations purposes

It will be observed that these classifications relate more or less to the perceived urgency of making the expenditures. Some projects must be accomplished to permit operation. Others will indirectly contribute to employee efficiency. Some will be justified by the economics. The last category—when funds are available—will contribute to improved employee/community relations.

For projects whose justification lies in the economic gains expected, some means is deemed necessary to separate the clearly more desirable from the remainder. One method is to rank projects in descending order of profitability. Thus, a preliminary screening of profitability rates might produce a schedule such as that illustrated in Figure 35-2. The priority is established by the IRR method, but the profitability index is also shown.

FACILITIES MANAGEMENT 35-9

STEPS IN THE CAPITAL BUDGETING PROCEDURE

This volume addresses some of the key procedures and controls that should exist in an environment of good facilities management. It may be helpful to detail the steps in a sound capital budgeting procedure so that they may be considered in a facilities audit, because proper planning and control of capital expenditures is essential to good management. Planning the capital budget involves committing the funds only after adequate study, with the careful exercise of executive judgment at the highest level. But the screening process must provide the framework for selecting the essential or economically desirable projects from the others, and supporting the recommendations with adequate analysis. Having authorized the project, controls must be instituted to keep expenditures within the planned amount and time limits. Therefore, from the management control viewpoint, these steps at least should be given some consideration in developing the capital budgeting procedure:

1. For the planning period, *establish* the fund limit or a permissible range for the capital budget—as to both commitments and expenditures. This should be provided to those responsible for formulating the specific budget—the division managers, or appropriate line executives and the financial arm, both in total and each for his operation or segment.
2. Through the appropriate channel of organization, and with proper procedures, *encourage* the submission of desirable capital investments. Guidelines should be provided, including cutoff rate of return and method of evaluation, such as DCF for major projects.
3. Provide for a preliminary screening of potential projects. Perhaps there should be a strategic plan screening so that the surviving proposals conform to the corporate long-term objectives and goals, and a rough economic or profitability check might be made.
4. When the preliminary screening has been accomplished, the procedure should provide guidelines to:
    - Classify the projects, e.g., according to need.
    - Specify the detailed method for calculating the economic benefits—including the supporting data that are required.
5. When the proposed capital projects finally are submitted for top management approval, before being presented to the board of directors the items should be tested by the financial analysts (staff of budget director or controller's staff) for:
    - Validity of underlying nontechnical data.
    - Rate of return.
    - Conformity to other criteria and compatibility with financial resources—both individual major projects and overall budget.
6. After top management approval, approval should also be secured from the board of directors. The significant economic and all related data should be presented to the board, and all other information made available upon request.

7. When the board has approved the budget in total, provision should be made for a detailed authorization by the appropriate level of management. At this stage, a rereview of the economics and conformance of the detailed plans with the board authorization should be made.
8. When the project commences, appropriate financial and other status reports should be prepared periodically for the responsible management. Such a report might indicate, among other things, expenditures to date, commitments to data, and estimated cost to complete the project.
9. After the project construction or installation is completed, periodic reports should be made on the larger expenditures, comparing actual and planned economic benefits (cash flow).

CONTROL AND MONITORING OF CAPITAL ACQUISITIONS

Capital assets may be acquired in any one of several ways, or by a combination, including simple purchase, lease, company construction, or external delivery under contract over a period of time. Whatever the method, well-defined policies and procedures with related controls, properly monitored, are essential.

For the most typical mode of acquisition, purchase on a single transaction basis, some basic essentials are:

- Provision for proper competitive bidding
- Appropriate analysis of bids and selection
- Proper testing and acceptance procedures
- Proper authorization for payment

Sometimes the usual procurement practices are adequate, but sometimes special provision, for example, for inspection, is necessary.

Where an acquisition involves delivery or construction over an extended period, a system should be instituted for proper monitoring. A special organization or control system may be required, depending on the magnitude of the project, the skills, experience, and capabilities of company staff; and the role to be played by the purchaser. In any event, the auditor should determine that appropriate procedures are in place for monitoring the purchasing, receiving, inspecting, and monitoring of the work, and for processing invoices. Some of the devices or conditions that must be present include:

- Clear statement of project management responsibility
- Appropriate network planning and scheduling, such as the Critical Path Method (CPM)
- Detailed cost estimates by individual task

FACILITIES MANAGEMENT

- Provision for appropriate inspection and so forth
- Proper system for accumulating commitments, and costs and expenses, by task or appropriate segment (to compare with estimate and percentage of completion)
- Adequate and timely project status reporting—e.g., accumulated costs, commitments, cost to complete, and reasons for over-budget condition
- Periodic internal audit
- Provision for post-completion audit

CUSTODY AND ADMINISTRATION OF FACILITIES

The custody, care, and administration of facilities is important in view of the size of the investment. While there are a multitude of considerations with which it is not practical to deal here, the auditor should be aware of three reference points, regardless of the type and value of the fixed assets:

1. Adequacy of maintenance and care
2. Optimum utilization of the equipment
3. Adequate records

Maintenance and Care

Under this category, two aspects deserve mention: security, and care and maintenance. As to security, it is important that the fixed assets be so handled and controlled as to minimize the danger of theft, unauthorized use, or physical damage. The auditor should see if the costs of protection are weighed against the probabilities of loss or destruction, and if the directed procedures are properly implemented.

The care and maintenance aspects have as an objective the availability of the equipment when it is needed. One facet relates to protection of the asset from unnecessary exposure to deterioration by improper housing and conditioning—whether simply putting it under cover from snow, properly greasing it, or taking other action. The other facet relates to proper repairs and maintenance. Matters to be considered include:

- Proper preventive and corrective maintenance
- Scheduling and budgeting of necessary maintenance activities
- Appropriate analyses of cost of maintenance versus replacement with more productive assets

Again, from an audit viewpoint, the task relates to identifying the programs, if any, and ascertaining that they are being followed with effective results.

Optimum Utilization of Equipment

If funds are spent on capital assets, it is expected that they will be used in an effective manner. It is not unusual, for example, for a company to purchase a new lathe, only to learn later that the other comparable equipment is used only 75 percent of the available time. The auditor should be sensitive to the need for systems and procedures for:

- Measurement of the degree of utilization of specific equipment
- Measure of productivity of specific equipment
- Provision for economic valuation of particular equipment in the light of new processes or new technology

Records and Reports

Policies and procedures should exist that clearly define operating personnel responsibility for equipment. Among other things, there should exist:

- Adequate identification of each (significant) piece of equipment
- Accountability by the department manager in which it is located
- Authorized access to the equipment
- Periodic physical check as to the existence of the equipment
- Adequate property record cards or computer tapes, with, for example, necessary description, location, useful life, depreciation date, cost, and residual value for each piece of equipment

In addition to the procedural aspects just mentioned, there are a vast number of reports that may be of use in facilities management. Some suggested data (many of which can be produced on the computer) include these:

- Current inventory of fixed assets—cost, depreciated value, useful life
- Report on sales or retirements by class of equipment, by department
- Leased facilities
- Fixed assets on loan
- Machine repair histories
- Idle or excess plant and equipment
- Fully depreciated equipment in use
- Maintenance cost history by piece of equipment
- Downtime, by piece of equipment
- Property taxes by equipment item

FACILITIES PROCUREMENT REVIEW

Whether a facility management review should encompass all phases of the function may be a matter of relative urgency, availability of audit staff, and

FIG. 35-3
Audit Program for Facilities Procurement Review

The purpose of this review is to evaluate the efficiency and effectiveness of funds expended for facilities improvements in compliance with established company policies and procedures.

| | **Workpaper Reference** | **Done by** |

1. General:

☐ Obtain copy of organization chart and, by review of chart and discussion with management, determine the independence and reporting relationship of the procurement function.

☐ Inquire into the existence of written procedures for procurement and facilities function.

☐ Review procedures, determine that procedures are current, and note last revision date.

☐ By interviews with management and procurement and facilities personnel, establish in what way, if any, procedures are not followed or are otherwise not current.

☐ During the course of the audit, tour facilities and observe personnel at work for any indication of resource problems.

2. Facilities Operation — Requisitioning:

☐ Ascertain and document from inquiry with knowledgeable personnel this facility's master planning schedule of projects. Identify how future projects are scheduled, administered, designed, reviewed, and coordinated with other departments.

☐ Document design function and ascertain review procedures to ensure drawing integrity.

☐ Determine if target cost budgets are used in drawing design. If so, how are they used in comparison of actual cost?

- Are variance analyses documented and reviewed?
- Are post cost reviews documented at a project's completion?

☐ *Original Drawing Design:*

- Document quality control procedures to ensure integrity.
- Ascertain to what extent original drawings reflect final completed project.
- Are drawings reviewed by person other than assigned designer?
- If "yes" in the previous question, what remedial procedures and documentation procedures are used?

(continued)

FIG. 35-3 *(cont'd)*

	Workpaper Reference	Done by

■ To what extent are job shoppers used within the design function:
  a. Control procedures to ensure integrity
  b. Drawing review procedures
	....	....

☐ *Drawing Change Documentation:*		
■ Ascertain percentage of major drawing change history for period January through August, 198X.	....	....
■ Perform comparison of information obtained above with industry average drawing change history to ascertain division ranking.	....	....
■ Document change authority, source from which change originated, sequence of transaction, and approval procedures.	....	....
☐ *Equipment Facilities Authorization (EFA):*		
■ Document EFA organization source, review, and approval procedures.	....	....
■ Ascertain what projects require EFA documentation.	....	....
☐ *Purchase Requisition:*		
■ Document procedures used and related authority.	....	....
■ Ascertain transaction routing.	....	....
3. Execution of Transactions — Procurement:		
☐ Select at random 15 transactions representing completed transactions to include major construction vendors and check for evidence of the following:		
■ Approval to procure	....	....
■ Appropriate correspondence with bidders (where applicable). This might include bid instructions specifications, responses to inquiries, etc.	....	....
■ Evaluation and analysis of bid selection	....	....
■ Assuring financial strength and performance capability of bidders	....	....
■ Basis for vendor selection	....	....
☐ Select a brief sample of purchase transactions that have been closed and check for evidence of:		
■ Approval of changes	....	....
■ Performance evaluation	....	....
☐ Scan appropriate files of completed transactions for any indication of unusual items such as the following:		
■ Unauthorized purchases	....	....
■ Purchase at exhorbitant prices	....	....
■ Duplicate payments	....	....
■ Unauthorized payments	....	....

	Workpaper Reference	Done by

4. Execution of Transactions — Facilities:

☐ Select a representative sample of completed construction projects (10%) transactions that have been closed for evidence of:
- Statement of work authorization ....
- Approval to procure ....
- Cost estimation and analysis ....
- Approval of changes and cost analysis of cost impact of change ....

5. Estimating Procedures:

☐ Ascertain how facilities project costs are estimated and determine to what extent used in the bidding process and post project cost analyses, if any. ....
- Determine estimating procedures used to control changes to original scope of work and negotiated price. ....
- Do procedures over changes insure bidding process use? ....
- Ascertain to what extent specifications for materials or parts are set forth in the estimating process. ....

6. Payment Authority Procedures:

☐ Ascertain how facilities payments are approved and document procedure used. ....
- Select representative sample of completed transactions to determine approval for payment authority. ....

the period since the last audit. Sometimes it is desirable to check only specific aspects. For a machining company whose interest was focussed primarily on satisfactory procurement procedures, an illustrative audit program is presented in Figure 35-3.

FACILITIES MANAGEMENT QUESTIONNAIRE AND PROGRAM

Because of enormous sums being spent by a decentralized electronics company on capital assets (equal to annual depreciation charges and one-half of the net income), management was insistent on a complete facilities review

(continued on page 35-31)

FIG. 35-4

Facilities Management Audit Questionnaire

"Facilities management" is the term used to describe the techniques and practices employed in order to minimize the expenditures of funds for the acquisition and maintenance of capital asset-type items, while reasonably assuring optimum use of company resources in support of short- and long-term operating plans. The techniques include the coordination, approval, and control of all functions relating to facilities, including architectural decisions and the acquisition, utilization, and disposition of company-owned capital assets, government-owned or leased facilities, and real property.

The objective of the preceding paragraph must be divided into components that will facilitate an organizational approach to the evaluation. The following detailed objectives are outlined for this purpose:

AUTHORIZATION AND EXECUTION OBJECTIVES:

- To acquire and maintain sufficient facilities, including equipment, pursuant to appropriate management authority.
- To obtain only those items necessary to fulfill the commitments and obligations envisioned by the short- and long-term operating plans.
- To deviate from primary objectives only upon appropriate management authorization (i.e., new product design, abandoning old product line, etc.).

RECORDING AND ACCOUNTABILITY OBJECTIVES:

- To record and report facility transactions and activities including acquisition or construction, maintenance and repair, transfers, and dispositions of facilities and equipment so as to permit reasonably effective evaluations and actions by affected management.
- To record facility transactions and activity to reasonably permit preparation of financial statements in accordance with generally accepted accounting principles.
- To verify that recorded balances of facility transactions are periodically compared to valuations of physical counts at reasonable intervals with appropriate action taken with respect to differences.

SAFEGUARDING OBJECTIVE:

- To acquire and maintain facilities and equipment in a manner that offers reasonable protection from loss due to spoilage, damage, waste, fire, vandalism, and other physical and natural risks. Protection would include adequate insurance coverage of the facilities to reduce the risk in the event a loss is incurred.

Note that the foregoing objectives have been arranged in accordance with the broad objectives of internal control to which they relate. This relationship is displayed in order to reasonably assure that all aspects of internal control are covered by these objectives.

In practice, the primary responsibility for attaining the foregoing objectives is delegated to facilities management departments.

Other functions may also be involved in effective facilities management. These include:

- General management
- Facilities engineering
- Constructing or fabricating facilities tooling and equipment

FACILITIES MANAGEMENT

- Materiel (procurement)
- Facilities
- Finance
- Security
- Data processing
- Legal

In order to facilitate the identification and evaluation of internal controls involved in facilities management, the attached questionnaire has been organized by the functions set forth above. In some organizational units, certain of the functions may be combined. In others, there may be further divisions. The former situation should make the process of obtaining responses even easier, since fewer functional departments need to be involved. In the latter situation, however, the auditor may find it necessary to supplement the questionnaire to reasonably assure thorough coverage.

It was not practicable to design the questionnaire in such a manner that each question focused on a specific control, although in many instances that is the case. Because techniques can and do vary, it was necessary in many other instances to focus only on a control area. For example, there is a question in Section B which asks if the procedures employed by the engineering group include "a methodology which reasonably assures that the design for plant equipment and production tooling was fully coordinated with using and other affected departments to ensure maximum design and functional interchangeability and to minimize duplication of design and procurement effort." The question is followed by listing several examples of specific techniques that might be in use.

In those instances, the auditor must supplement the questionnaire with spread sheets that identify all of the specific controls in effect to reasonably assure that the controls in that area are sufficient. The combination of the predetermined questions and the supplemental spread sheets constitute the documented evaluation of the system.

Initial completion of this questionnaire may require considerable effort because of the multiple functions involved. In many instances it is not advisable for one auditor to undertake completing it. The arrangement of the questionnaire is such that it can be easily divided among two or more auditors. Managers should discuss the feasibility of completion with the performing auditor(s) and with the director.

Response to certain of the questions may already be known by virtue of performing reviews and completing questionnaires of related functional areas such as Materiel, Manufacturing, and Data Processing. In these situations, the auditor should utilize this relevant work to the extent deemed useful in the circumstances.

	Yes	No	Reference
A. General:			
1. Is there a formal written policy stating management's objectives regarding facilities management?	☐	☐	....
2. Is the division organized so as to facilitate managing the acquisition, use and disposition of company facilities' resources in support of short- and long-term operating plans?	☐	☐	....

(continued)

FIG. 35-4 *(cont'd)*

	Yes	No	Reference

This may include, among other things, the following:
a. Organizing by function to reasonably assure that organizational objectives are attained, including:
   - General management
   - Facilities engineering
   - Constructing or fabricating facilities, tooling and equipment
   - Materiel
   - Facilities
   - Finance
   - Security
   - Data processing
b. Organizing by major program to reasonably assure that program-specific objectives are effectively achieved and that customer requirements are efficiently met, exceeded, or on time within cost estimates.

3. Do affected functional units have procedures established for minimizing the investment in facilities? If so, do they clearly delineate specific responsibilities and duties? ☐ ☐ ....

4. Do procedures clearly set forth authority for the following transactions and/or activities:
   a. Approval of original facility (capital asset) budgets ☐ ☐ ....
   b. Approval for changes to facility budgets ☐ ☐ ....
   c. Approval of budgets for facility maintenance ☐ ☐ ....
   d. Approval of requests for capital asset expenditures ☐ ☐ ....
   e. Approval and/or acceptance of facility designs and changes thereto ☐ ☐ ....
   f. Approval of movement/relocation of capital assets ☐ ☐ ....
   g. Maintenance programs ☐ ☐ ....
   h. Dispositions of capital assets ☐ ☐ ....
   i. Changes to established procedures, forms, etc. ☐ ☐ ....

5. Do procedures require that decisions involving significant capital asset transactions be based upon sufficient relevant information? ☐ ☐ ....
   Sufficient relevant information might include:
   - Availability of resources (including make or buy analysis)
   - Return of investment (ROI) calculations
   - Cost/benefit analysis
   - Master plans

	Yes	No	Reference

- Financing alternatives
- Financial statement impact
- Environmental impact

6. Do procedures and/or systems provide sufficient information in the form of data processing reports, status reports, presentation material, etc., to permit effective monitoring of facilities management activities? ☐ ☐ ....

7. Do practices involve techniques such as periodic meetings, performance reviews, report analysis, and inquiry to identify emergency problems? ☐ ☐ ....

8. Do practices include techniques such as policy revision, organizational changes, budget revisions, manpower additions, special study teams, etc., to remedy emergency problems mentioned above? ☐ ☐ ....

9. Do procedures require important actions and decisions to be sufficiently documented as to rationale and approval? ☐ ☐ ....

B. Facilities Engineering:

1. Do the procedures employed by Engineering include the following:
   a. A methodology for reasonably assuring that all plant equipment, including production tooling, which is required for designed products, is determined. ☐ ☐ ....
   b. A methodology which reasonably assures that the design for plant equipment and production tooling was fully coordinated with the using and other affected departments to ensure maximum design and functional interchangeability and to minimize duplication of design and procurement effort. A methodology might include: ☐ ☐ ....
      - Techniques for developing and changing engineering drawings that would alter the type and/or size of plant equipment and production tooling. These may include preparation verification, approval, and numerical controls.
      - Techniques for developing materiel requirements.
      - Techniques to reasonably assure that sufficient up-to-date resources are available to facilitate design efforts.

(continued)

FIG. 35-4 *(cont'd)*

	Yes	No	Reference
2. Are automated data processing techniques involved? If so, refer to Section H of this questionnaire.	☐	☐	....
a. Do procedures cover the involvement and coordination activities with representatives of affected disciplines?	☐	☐	....
C. Constructing or Fabricating Facilities, Tooling and Other Equipment:			
1. Do the procedures employed by the above functions include the following:			
a. A method that reasonably assures that fabrication work occurs pursuant to management's general or specific authorization.	☐	☐	....
b. Written procedures, specifications, and/or instructions for all relevant fabrication/assembly operations.	☐	☐	....
c. A means by which the written procedures are kept current.	☐	☐	....
d. A requirement for an ongoing program of sufficient care and maintenance to production equipment to reasonably minimize production halts.	☐	☐	....
e. A production environment with due regard for the personal safety of all involved personnel.	☐	☐	....
f. Sufficient resources (manpower, facilities, equipment, and materiel) allocated to the production function to enable efficient facilities management.	☐	☐	....
g. Employment of automated data processing techniques. If so, refer to Section H of this questionnaire.	☐	☐	....
h. The involvement and coordination activities with representatives of affected disciplines.	☐	☐	....
D. Materiel:			
1. Do the procedures employed by the materiel function include the following:			
a. Techniques to reasonably assure that only facilities (capital asset) items authorized to be purchased are in fact purchased.	☐	☐	....
b. Techniques to reasonably assure that purchase activity occurs pursuant to management's authorization. Purchase activity includes vendor solicitation, bid evaluation, vendor selection, evaluation of vendor performance, etc.	☐	☐	....

FACILITIES MANAGEMENT   35-21

		Yes	No	Reference
	c. Techniques to reasonably assure that changes in capital asset requirements are timely effected to preclude acquiring useless items.	☐	☐	....
	d. Techniques to reasonably assure that sufficient source of supply of needed components are identified insofar as practicable.	☐	☐	....
	e. Techniques to reasonably assure that ordering procedures consider lead times which will result in having on hand all items when needed and in sufficient but not excessive quantities.	☐	☐	....
	f. A means by which the effects of price increases are minimized.	☐	☐	....
	g. A means by which the supply of critical materiels and components is reasonably assured.	☐	☐	....
	h. A means by which changes in requirements and specifications are promptly communicated to affected suppliers.	☐	☐	....
	i. Procedures to reasonably assure that only capital items that were ordered are accepted.	☐	☐	....
	j. Procedures to reasonably assure that acceptance of capital items through receiving departments occurs only upon sufficient inspection verifying:	☐	☐	....
	■ Description			
	■ Quantity			
	■ Specifications and tolerance			
2.	Do any of the techniques involved in the previous question of this section involve automated processing techniques?	☐	☐	....
	Note: If the answer to this question is "yes," refer to Section H of this questionnaire.			
3.	Do procedures cover the involvement and coordination activities with representatives of affected disciplines?	☐	☐	....
E. Facilities:				
1.	Do procedures require establishing and maintaining a master plan for facilities development and utilization?	☐	☐	....
2.	Do techniques involved in preparing such a plan include the following:			
	a. Current business information with respect to marketing (sales) and production forecasts.	☐	☐	....
	b. Current technical information with respect to development in the field of facilities management, such as plant design, construction and installation techniques, communication techniques, manufacturing techniques, etc.	☐	☐	....
				(continued)

FIG. 35-4 *(cont'd)*

	Yes	No	Reference
3. Do techniques involved in maintaining the plan include obtaining sufficient information on an ongoing basis to keep the plan current? Such information may be obtained by attending management meetings, receiving and analyzing forecasts, conducting surveys, etc.	☐	☐	....
4. Does a methodology exist to reasonably assure that routine facility needs of organizational units are met in a timely fashion? Such a methodology might include: ■ Formal requests for facilities ■ Designated approval levels ■ Projectizing the various requests ■ Budgetary controls for projects ■ Progress or status reporting for long-term (six months or more) projects ■ Standards for facility utilization ■ Approvals for deviations from standards ■ Sufficient communication with the requestors ■ Sufficient resources in terms of manpower, systems, and resources	☐	☐	....
5. Does a methodology exist to reasonably assure that significant facility projects such as plant or office building construction or major remodeling occur in a timely fashion at a reasonable cost? A reasonable methodology might include such techniques as: ■ Formal plans ■ Identification of requirements, including security considerations and specifications ■ Configuration/design control ■ Design approved by occupants/management, as appropriate ■ Budgetary controls ■ Competitive bidding ■ Contract execution based upon standard formats or deviations approved by legal counsel ■ Performance monitoring ■ Approval mechanism for changes ■ Performance reporting	☐	☐	....
6. Do any of the techniques involved in the first five items in this section employ automated data processing techniques? Note: If the answer to the previous question is "yes," refer to Section H of this questionnaire.	☐	☐	....

	Yes	No	Reference

F. Finance:

1. Do the procedures employed by the finance function include the following:

   a. A system of accounting which reasonably assures that the following transactions pertaining to facilities are recorded so as to permit preparation of financial statements in accordance with generally accepted accounting principles: ☐ ☐ ....
      - Purchase of capital assets
      - Charging capital asset cost to contracts
      - Transfer of capital asset from one location to another
      - Other conversion transactions such as direct labor, other direct costs, and allocable overhead
      - Adjustments to record items such as valuation allowances, differences resulting from comparison of physical costs with corresponding recorded amounts

   b. A means by which the funding for the investment in facilities minimizes the capital cost to the company. ☐ ☐ ....
   Financing techniques may include consideration of one or more of the following:
      - Revolving credit agreements
      - Commercial paper
      - Long-term bank borrowing, such as via mortgages
      - Debentures
      - Stock offering
      - Leases

   c. A methodology for minimizing the financial risk associated with long-term commitments to subcontractors and suppliers by:
      - Establishing criteria for obtaining performance bonds ☐ ☐ ....
      - Evaluating the financial condition of each supplier or subcontractor ☐ ☐ ....
      - Establishing appropriate funding through negotiation and approval of contract advances and progress payments ☐ ☐ ....
      - Providing for timely payment of invoices ☐ ☐ ....

2. Do any of the techniques included in the previous question in this section involve automated processing techniques? ☐ ☐ ....
   Note: If the answer to the previous question is "yes," refer to Section H of this questionnaire.

(continued)

FIG. 35-4 *(cont'd)*

	Yes	No	Reference
3. Do procedures cover the involvement and coordination with representatives of affected disciplines?	☐	☐	....

G. Security:

1. Do procedures employed by the security function include the following:
   a. Techniques sufficient to reasonably assure that the company investment in facility items is sufficiently protected from:

	Yes	No	Reference
■ Theft or pilferage	☐	☐	....
■ Sabotage	☐	☐	....
■ Vandalism	☐	☐	....
■ Physical damage from acts of God such as fire, flood, earthquake, etc.	☐	☐	....
b. Techniques sufficient to reasonably assure that access to classified data is restricted to authorized individuals.	☐	☐	....

H. Data Processing:

1. If techniques in effect to minimize the investment in facilities include electronic data processing, this section should be completed for each application.

	Yes	No	Reference
2. Are the applicable procedures forms, descriptions, and so forth set in a user's manual?	☐	☐	....
3. Is the application a batch-oriented application with or without remote job entry features?	☐	☐	....
4. Do procedures require current and complete system and program documentation?	☐	☐	....

Note: If the answers to the previous questions in this section are all "yes," then the auditor should proceed to obtain responses to the balance of the questions in this section. If the answer is "no," it may indicate that the application is too complex for evaluation within the context of this assignment. The auditor should not attempt further EDP evaluation and analysis without either assistance from a senior EDP auditor or approval of the manager or director.

FACILITIES MANAGEMENT

FIG. 35-5

Audit Program—Facilities Management

INTRODUCTORY:

Inasmuch as a facilities management audit is performed every other year, the assigned auditors should review the recent audit working papers, audit report, audit responses, and the follow-up notes on compliance with suggested improvements.

On this basis the usual preparatory work should be accomplished, including discussions with the V.P. Facilities at corporate headquarters and his counterparts at the major divisions. Depending on whether or not activities for all sections of the organization are to be examined, the appropriate managers should be contacted regarding the status of operations, recent changes, etc., and any specific questions.

With this information, the facilities management questionnaire should be completed, the tentative audit program designed, and scheduling of the audit arranged with the cognizant executive. The standard facilities audit program is detailed below. Based on answers secured to the questionnaire and a review of prior audits, it should be modified or expanded as required.

The objectives of the audit are to (1) assess performance, (2) examine the necessary management controls, (3) identify opportunities for improvement, and (4) develop recommendations for improvement (or corrective action).

	Workpaper Reference	Done by

1. GENERAL:

☐ Obtain the organization charts and functional outlines for the corporate facilities group and each division audited, including each vice-president, director, or manager. Review the documents for adequacy and completeness as to assigned authority and responsibility, and for relationship with other segments of the organization. Check the reporting relationships for propriety and independence.   ....

☐ Review the systems and procedures manual as to:
- Apparent completeness   ....
- Currency (note the last revision date)   ....
- Nature of recent changes   ....

☐ Discuss with appropriate executives:
- Where procedures are not being followed   ....
- Problems or weaknesses noted in following written procedures   ....

☐ Tour the facility to observe general conditions, tidiness, apparent attitude of staff, etc.   ....

2. OTHER ORGANIZATIONAL MATTERS:

A. Headquarters Organization:

☐ Review the policy statement on facilities management for completeness and consistency with the corporate purpose.   ....

(continued)

FIG. 35-5 *(cont'd)*

	Workpaper Reference	Done by
☐ Review the functional outline with each executive to obtain indications and evidence that each is exercising the required coordination and direction of the division facility activities through appropriate channels. Particularly check what is considered as some of the more difficult assignments in the past two years.	....	....
☐ Review evidence that the staff is adequate and is performing those specified corporate office functions especially relating to:		
■ The master plan	....	....
■ The review of division-proposed projects for suitability, completeness, etc., in the budget	....	....
■ The economic evaluation of major projects, in conjunction with finance	....	....
■ Monitoring costs and construction progress of any major corporate projects	....	....
■ Advising the division facility staff on security and maintenance of sensitive equipment	....	....
☐ Make such a review of the functional outlines as is deemed necessary to determine if the job duties seem fairly and properly distributed or divided; ensure that approval levels for varying acquisition amounts seem appropriate and reasonable.	....	....
3. DIVISION FACILITIES ORGANIZATION:		
☐ To the extent practical, perform the same organizational matters review at the division (except for coordination with all divisions) as is done at the headquarters organization, but in the context of the division, and as expanded below.	....	....
☐ As to the systems and procedures manuals, these specific matters should be checked for adequacy:	....	....
■ Procurement (see separate program)	....	....
■ Receiving and inspection	....	....
■ Payment of invoices	....	....
■ Depreciation policies and procedures	....	....
■ Control of company-managed projects	....	....
■ Authorizations for transfer of capital items	....	....
■ Procedures for retiring assets	....	....
■ Procedures for preventive maintenance, housing and routine care of facilities, and protection from theft	....	....

	Workpaper Reference	Done by

4. PLANNING AND CONTROL OF CAPITAL COMMITMENTS AND EXPENDITURES:

A. Master Facilities Plan:

☐ Review and appraise master facilities plan as to:
- Adequacy of support for projects contained therein
- Consistency with corporate strategic plan, including:
  a. Timing and amount of expenditures
  b. Relation to ROA (return on assets) cut-off point
  c. Balance among divisions and subsidiaries
- Method of eliminating division projects
- Methodology in selecting sites for expansion
- Basis for arriving at the gross cost of projects, including provision for inflation
- Impact of new manufacturing processes
- Consideration given to foreign purchases and/or sites, especially Ireland, Mexico, Canada, and Korea

B. Annual Plan/Annual Capital Budget:

☐ Review and appraise for each division and subsidiary, as well as the corporate headquarters, the following:
- Adequacy of support for projects included in capital budget
- Adherence to corporate guidelines for the divisions and subsidiaries:
  a. Capital budget amount in total
  b. Method of arriving at the contingent budget
  c. Adjustments made by V.P. Facilities to division/subsidiary proposed budgets
- Treatment of projects approved in prior year but not commenced
- Procedures for capital project initiation and approval:
  a. Ways in which capital proposals are encouraged
  b. Methods of screening
  c. Extent of analysis of each project considered
  d. Role played by general manager in review
  e. Method and criteria used in ranking projects

(continued)

FIG. 35-5 *(cont'd)*

	Workpaper Reference	Done by
f. Way in which conservatism, or lack thereof, is introduced into the economic evaluation	....	....
g. Reasonableness of corporate cut-off point (IRR) for capital expenditures as applied to each segment	....	....
h. Steps in the approval chain, and degree of review	....	....
i. Extent to which projects were eliminated from final budget, and procedures used	....	....

C. Project Control Techniques:

☐ For simple purchases (under $100,000 each), the conformance to procedures (see separate facilities procurement review) especially these items: ....
- Adequacy of bidding procedure ....
- Adequacy of receiving, inspection, and acceptance procedures ....
- Basis for vendor selection ....
- Method of handling adjustments ....

☐ For all other major items or projects over $100,000 each, these matters should be reviewed and appraised:
- Procedures for securing data contained in monthly project status report ....
- Consistency of report with underlying records ....
- Methods used to update the cost estimates to complete ....
- Procedure followed for project overruns, delays in schedule, and subcontractor defaults ....
- Procedures for verifying quantity and quality of deliveries, including adequacy of records ....
- Method of accumulating costs on the job site; degree to which these costs agree with subsidiary cost ledger ....
- Basis for approving invoices and/or payroll ....
- Extent to which post-audits are made of the major projects, and time period used for comparison of actual and planned cash flow ....
- Extent to which floor checks are made by division financial staff ....
- Any *major* deficiencies in procedures should be reported when found. Suggestion for improvements should be included, when appropriate. ....

D. Use, Care, and Control of Fixed Assets:

☐ This phase of the facilities should include a physical inspection of selected areas or items of

FACILITIES MANAGEMENT

	Workpaper Reference	Done by

equipment, as well as a review of underlying records and discussions with appropriate personnel.   ....

E. Utilization of Facilities:

☐ Describe the nature of the evidence, and extent of low utilization of:
- Land   ....
- Buildings   ....
- Profilers   ....
- Computers (CAD)   ....
- Machine tools   ....
- Materials handling equipment   ....
- Transportation equipment   ....

☐ Indicate the record mechanism for keeping track of utilization.   ....

☐ Identify the means by which specific machines are selected for utilization. Are they the most efficient?   ....

☐ Identify the programs in place for coordinating machine usage with specific product scheduling.   ....

☐ Explain the procedure for advising other plants of availability of low-use equipment.   ....

F. Care of the Assets:

☐ Explain the program for checking access to the equipment, especially the computer-controlled machines and the other very valuable items.   ....

☐ Explain the check of trucks, cars, and personnel leaving the plants. What is the frequency of such checks?   ....

☐ Identify the security areas patrolled by or protected by electronic devices.   ....

☐ Is the exposure to the elements reasonably limited, considering the costs, especially those close to salt air or those in high temperature areas?   ....

☐ Were any significant pieces of equipment greased or mothballed?   ....

G. Accountability:

☐ Comment on these points.
- Degree to which equipment was properly tagged   ....
- Adequacy of detailed property records, e.g., completeness of data, system or format   ....
- Extent of physical checks against records, especially high-value items   ....

(continued)

FIG. 35-5 *(cont'd)*

	Workpaper Reference	Done by
■ Procedures and records for transfer to other departments	....	....
■ Manner in which unlocated items are handled as to detail (1) records and (2) accounting	....	....
■ Reasonableness of depreciation rates	....	....
■ Manner of determining insurable value	....	....
■ Procedure for handling and accounting for:		
a. U.S. Government property	....	....
b. Property on loan to others	....	....
c. Property temporarily borrowed from others	....	....

H. General Effectiveness of Property Activities:

☐ For purposes of preparing an executive summary, a succinct and candid statement is needed on these points.   ....

I. Policies and Procedures:

☐ Based on your knowledge of industry practice, competitive practice, or policies of "industry leaders" (any industry), comment on our corporate procedures and practices:

- ■ Completeness   ....
- ■ Areas in which the "newest" or most sophisticated (considering the company's size and financial status) techniques are not being applied   ....
- ■ Specific points where the policies may be weakly stated or misdirected, or where the company may be vulnerable to change   ....
- ■ Practices where the company may be too detail-minded or is not delegating sufficient authority   ....
- ■ Success in selecting the truly most economically desirable projects, and related to the cost of capital   ....
- ■ Limitations on the total capital budget, either for a single year, or over a period of, say, five years   ....

J. Quality of Policy/Practice Implementation:

☐ Degree to which major projects meet the cash-flow plan or forecast as to economic results   ....

☐ Degree to which most significant control points are effective   ....

☐ Procedures regarded as practical and workable   ....

☐ General condition and competitiveness of the assets as compared with company A   ....

☐ Extent to which the *reasons* for the policies and procedures are understood   ....

FACILITIES MANAGEMENT 35-31

	Workpaper Reference	Done by
K. Effectiveness of Personnel:		
☐ In responding to these points, please indicate the extent to which you consulted with experienced facilities managers (our own, competitors, or outside consultants).	....	....
■ Did the coordination efforts of the corporate facilities staff meet reasonable acceptance?	....	....
■ Did most of the personnel contacted appear conversant with the points raised, and willing to discuss them?	....	....
■ Were the operations adequately supervised?	....	....

every two years. A questionnaire to guide preparation of the audit program, and to check coordination between the involved departments, is shown in Figure 35-4. A related audit program is shown in Figure 35-5.

FACILITIES MANAGEMENT AUDIT REPORTS AND TYPICAL FINDINGS

A rather short summary report on a facilities management review to provide the newly appointed executive some guidance in points needing review is given in Figure 35-6. Obviously, each report must be adapted to the local circumstances. The possible deficiencies are too numerous to mention. But here are some typical findings—without quoting from the actual reports:

☐ Procurement
  - The head of the facilities department was involving himself in procurement, almost to the total exclusion of the (independent) purchasing department.
  - Competitive bids were secured only in about 75 percent of the cases.
  - Assets were being purchased for one division while another had excess similar items.
  - Assets were being purchased when leasing would have been more advantageous.
  - Excess equipment was being acquired.
  - In an attempt to save money, facilities were purchased from sources unable to adequately service the equipment

☐ Receiving and inspection
  - Slipshod methods were used to check the quantities of small tools being received — with shortages being evident.

FIG. 35-6

Facilities Management Audit Report

TO: J.A. Johnson
FROM: Corporate Audit
SUBJECT: Review of Facilities Management — Nevada Assembly Division (NAD)

We have reviewed the internal control techniques involved in managing the investment in facilities at NAD for the six months ended June 30, 198X. The purpose of our review was to evaluate the techniques and practices employed for minimizing the expenditure of funds for the acquisition and maintenance of capital asset and burden items, while reasonably assuring optimum use of Company resources in support of short- and long-term operating plans. In addition we performed tests to determine that facilities transactions are executed in accordance with management's general or specific authorization, and are properly recorded and reported.

Our review was performed pursuant to department audit standards and included reviewing the related Corporate and NAD policies and procedures, completing a Facilities Management Internal Control Questionnaire, testing of controls identified, following up on prior audit recommendations, discussing facilities and related matters with operating and management personnel, and performing such other procedures as considered necessary in the circumstances.

There has been an increased amount of activity in the past year as indicated in the following statistics:

	198X	198Y	% Increase
Capital asset budget (including revision)	$88,102,000	$106,102,000	20%
Number of facilities requests:			
January to June	1119	1714	53%
July to December	1168		
Number of facilities personnel:	460	598*	30%

* Includes Las Vegas increase of 48 personnel.

NAD has recently developed and implemented a new management program for the planning, acquisition, and control of capital asset and burden items, titled "Capital Asset and Expensed Facilities Program (CAEFP) Management." The objectives of the program are threefold:

1. To assure that the CAEFP Program Plan provides those assets as required by the NAD Business Plan.
2. To manage the CAEFP Program to assure proper budget and schedule performance.
3. To maintain visibility on the status of CAEFP and its subprograms.

Some of the matters of our report may be addressed by the CAEFP, but due to its recent implementation, it was not feasible to perform a complete review and evaluation of its impact on facilities management.

Our review disclosed the following matters which warrant management's attention:
- Post-audit review draft procedures will not result in compliance with Corporate Finance Manual 1020 (CFM).

FACILITIES MANAGEMENT

- Numerous instances were noted in which authorized Facility Request (FR) amounts were exceeded but no supplemental FRs were prepared.
- The FR Scheduling and Tracking System Status Reports (daily & weekly) contain a number of deficiencies, as identified in the balance of this report.
- Plant Services Engineering has an excessive number of machinery and equipment (M&E) items (approximately 8,000) to screen and review for possible preventive maintenance (P.M.) action.
- Some of the supporting documentation was missing from the Facilities Request Master Control Files.
- We noted certain control weaknesses in the processing of Facilities Requests by the project engineers.
- We noted very little control over the processing of Facilities Design Work Orders (FDWOs), which are issued to other NAD departments.
- A budget, approval, and purchase cycle for technical software items has not been established.
- Facilities processed two major Facilities Requests for data acquisition and display systems (totaling $1.1 million) without the approval of NDP as required by NAD-GPD 3-3 "Responsibility for Information Processing Equipment Control."
- Facilities is not in complete compliance with CPD No. 82, "Vital Records Retention."
- Certain NAD policies and procedures require revision.
- CFM 1020 contains dollar value guidelines that have been the same for over ten years, and the volume and dollar value of commitments at NAD has nearly doubled in the past ten years.

The major areas of concern are FRs exceeding authorized amounts and supporting documentation missing from the FR files. These present weaknesses in controls that need to be resolved in order to assure that fixed assets and burden amounts are properly authorized, documented, and accounted for. Approvals and documentation are primary controls to ensure that all facilities transactions are in accordance with management's specific authorization. There are controls after-the-fact, such as budgets for identifying overruns, but this type of control does not reasonably assure allocation of resources to the best use.

The other matters relate primarily to operational inefficiencies and noncompliance with NAD and Corporate policies and procedures, which should also be addressed by management through periodic training sessions and other such enforcement techniques of proper disciplines at all levels of management.

One other item of concern is that cost reduction post-audit reviews have still not been performed, which was also the subject of our prior Audit Report No. XX, dated April 30, 198X, to which a favorable response was issued on June 16, 198X, and revised on February 17, 198Y with new action dates. This is the subject of a special audit currently in progress. Our comments will be presented in a separate report.

In our opinion, the findings of this report raise questions regarding the extent to which internal control techniques are followed to reasonably assure that expenditures for facilities' acquisition and maintenance and the optimum use of resources in support of short- and long-term operating plans. However, we believe other internal control techniques reasonably assure that facilities expenditures are properly recorded and reported. A previous report (No. XX) disclosed weaknesses pertaining to asset accountability for which remedial action is underway. Plant protection is the subject of a separate report.

A detailed description of our findings and recommendations are presented in the balance of this report. A written reply to this report, directed to Corporate Audit (155/CC), is requested from the action parties within thirty days.

- Specifications were not checked against actual performance, with substantial lost time and material.

☐ Accounting
- New equipment was not being tagged.
- Paperwork was not prepared on plant transfers, and equipment accountability was lost.
- Inventory records were not adjusted for differences disclosed by physical count.

☐ Physical custody, etc.
- Valuable electronics equipment was not periodically policed, and valuable parts were removed.
- Preventive maintenance was not accomplished because of an inadequate budget, and costly shutdowns occurred in the critical shipping period (seasonal business).
- Maintenance was performed by the company, at its expense, even though the equipment was still under warranty.

INTERNAL AUDIT OF CAPITAL INVESTMENT PROJECTS

The preceding comments in this chapter have provided a background and a questionnaire and audit program for operational auditing. Aside from an operational audit of facilities management in its total aspects, or segments thereof, an internal auditor may be helpful in the control and monitoring of specific capital projects. These reviews by him may be of two kinds:

1. A periodic internal audit of an ongoing capital project, or
2. A post-completion audit of a capital acquisition.

Comments on each follow.

Internal Audit of Ongoing Capital Projects

The purpose of an internal audit of an ongoing capital project is, in large part, to inform executive management if the proposal is within budget and on schedule. It may also assist operating management by identifying weaknesses in procedures, including internal control. Although such a review normally tends to be largely a financial-type audit, some aspects might be termed operational.

The managing director of Arthur D. Little Valuation, Inc., Chicago, recommends the following audit procedures for an internal audit of a capital

FACILITIES MANAGEMENT 35-35

investment program.[2] Of course, the audit program should be modified, as found necessary, to cover adequately special conditions or practices.

The suggested audit program is as follows:

1. Obtain copies of and review for consistency:
   - All project review and authorization, including economic justification;
   - Project capital expenditure log or ledger;
   - Fixed-asset subsidiary ledger pages related to project;
   - Paid invoice vouchers and other evidential matter supporting entries on fixed-asset subsidiary ledger;
   - Purchase orders, contracts, leases, and other evidential matter documenting purchase commitments related to each expenditure; and
   - Receiving reports and other evidential matter related to assets actually received.
2. Review project and authorization documentation to determine:
   - Proper management approval;
   - Agreement of approved amount with supporting detail; and
   - Adequate support for and proper calculation of projected economic benefit.
3. Review project capital expenditure log to determine:
   - Adequate supporting documentation and reference to properly stated journal entries;
   - Mathematical accuracy;
   - Agreement to fixed asset subsidiary ledger entries; and
   - That expenditures were not made in excess of authorized limits.
4. Review fixed-asset subsidiary ledger pages to determine:
   - Mathematical accuracy;
   - Agreement to supporting paid invoice vouchers, expenditure log, journal entries, etc.;
   - Agreement with appropriate entry in general ledger control accounts; and
   - Proper capitalization and depreciation in accordance with firm policy, GAAP, and federal and state income tax regulations.
5. Review paid income vouchers to determine:
   - Agreement with purchase order or contract regarding quantity and price;
   - Approval by authorized individual before payment;
   - That expenditure appears to relate to project description and supporting details on project authorization documentation;
   - That expenditures appear to be properly capitalized to correct control and subsidiary accounts; and
   - That proper state and local sales and use taxes were paid.

---

[2] From *Internal Auditing Alert*, Jan. 1984, pp. 5–6.

6. Review purchase orders (POs) and other contractual commitments to determine that:
    - PO was properly approved by authorized individual;
    - PO was issued after date of project approval;
    - PO was issued before payment of corresponding invoice;
    - Goods or services ordered on PO correspond to project description on authorization documentation; and
    - No POs for commitments in excess of total project authorized budget were issued.
7. Physically inspect capital investment project in operation to determine that:
    - Assets are in good condition, are being properly maintained, and are being used for the function for which they are authorized;
    - Assets are being used effectively and efficiently;
    - Assets are in location specified in authorization documentation; and
    - There are no assets included with project that were not described on authorization and included on expenditure log and fixed-asset subsidiary ledger.
8. Construct and verify, if possible, the actual economic benefit derived from this project:
    - Review increase in revenue dollars or units;
    - Consider effect of cannibalism of project on revenues from other company products or services;
    - Determine changes in working capital caused by the project;
    - Calculate direct cost reduction associated with the project;
    - Calculate cost reduction in selling, general, and administration expense associated with the project;
    - Verify changes in manpower and personnel costs associated with the project; and
    - Construct measures of actual economic benefit associated with project (e.g., payback, NPV, and IRR).
9. Compare actual and budgeted economic benefits:
    - Compare actual economic benefits calculated in step 8 with projected economic benefits in authorization documentation; and
    - Investigate causes of any significant variances between actual and projected economic results.
10. Prepare report of findings and recommendations related to corrective action and forward to appropriate management. Audit report should be:
    - Reviewed by audit manager;
    - Approved by audit director;
    - Submitted to management; and
    - Followed up with appropriate managers for action on recommendations.

It should be noted that some of these suggested steps can be performed only when the capital project is completed and in operation.

Post-Completion Audits of Capital Projects

Every good capital budgeting procedure should provide for a post-completion audit of selected capital projects. Yet, in reality, this phase is often overlooked. Of course, not every capital acquisition need be reviewed. Each company should select its own criteria. Prudence suggests the following likely prospects:

- Those involving significant sums
- Those relating to areas in which rapid change seems to be taking place
- Those representing expansion into new fields
- Those having experienced difficulty in completion

Perhaps a common characteristic of these groups is the existence of greater than normal risk for the enterprise.

Some companies, for example, may have audits performed only on those projects in excess of $1 million. Often, reviews are made only after the facility has been in operation some time, so most "bugs" have been worked out. As another suggestion, periodic post-completion audits may be made only until the payout period is completed.

The objective of a post-completion review is not a matter simply of determining whether or not the project was kept within authorization limits. Indeed, it goes to the very heart of sound capital budgeting—appraising the economic wisdom of the project and the sufficiency of the policies and procedures that resulted in its approval.

Some of the advantages of a post-completion audit include:

- Generally, an improvement is made in capital budgeting policies and procedures, including the testing and analysis of the input data (markets, potential sales volume, unit prices of output) on which approval was largely based.
- Correction of other projects prior to completion is made possible where the same weaknesses or flaws may exist as in the one audited.
- It permits a reading of the strengths and weaknesses of specific individuals involved in the process (inadequate analysis, undue optimism).
- The practice of making post-completion audits, when publicized among the operating and engineering staff, tends to assure better performance or attention to significant factors, if the individuals know their work will be checked.
- It tends to cause the operating and financial staffs to review practices and procedures and to suggest improvements, before the internal auditors approach.

The nature of the audit and the type of report depend on the circumstances. Some of the steps outlined previously may be used. Key to this post-completion review, of course, is an evaluation of whether or not the key factors that would make for success of the expenditure were properly identified and handled in the analysis (including the application in a financial model). Typical major elements to be considered include these items:

- Competitive environment (including foreign)
- Market conditions
- Technology
- Inflation impact
- Governmental (federal, state, and local) regulations or laws
- Demographic changes
- General economic conditions and stage of business cycle
- Social or political environment

Among other things, the audit report should indicate the probable economic impact on the company as opposed to that planned at the time the project was approved.

An example of a graphic summary illustration of a post-completion capital project report is shown in Figure 13-4.

SUGGESTED READING

Connor, Joseph E., and Burnell H. DeVos, Jr., eds. *Guide to Accounting Controls, No. 6—Productive Assets*. New York: Warren, Gorham & Lamont, 1979.

CHAPTER **36**

Program Management

Introduction	1	**Indicated Final Cost**	11
Programs and Program Management	2	**Program Management Control Questionnaire**	11
The Management Process and PERT	3		
Determine and Define Objectives	4	**Program Management Audit Program**	19
Develop Plans	6		
Determine Schedules	6	**Audit Findings**	19
Progress Evaluation	7		
Management Decisions and Actions	8	**Program Management and Microcomputers**	28
Recycle	8		
PERT Networks	8	**Suggested Reading**	29

Fig. 36-1 The Management Process 5
Fig. 36-2 Work Breakdown Schedule Showing Work Breakdown Packages at Levels 1, 2, 3, 4 5
Fig. 36-3 Relationship of Work Breakdown Package to Functional Activities and Network of Steps 7
Fig. 36-4 PERT Network—Simplified 9
Fig. 36-5 PERT Network With Earliest and Latest Event Time 10
Fig. 36-6 Program Management Control Questionnaire 12
Fig. 36-7 Program Management Audit Program 20
Fig. 36-8 Program Management Audit Report 22

INTRODUCTION

The management process has been variously defined. The tasks of a business manager, or a top government official, might be categorized as four basic functions:

1. Planning
2. Organizing
3. Directing
4. Controlling (measuring)

36-1

Planning may be defined as the continuous process of determining the events and activities essential to the attainment of stated goals. *Organizing* may be described as securing the necessary personnel, materials, and facilities to do the job required. *Directing* relates to carrying out the functions—the doing, getting the job done. *Control*, also called measurement or evaluation, relates to comparing the actual performance with what should have been done, the standard, and taking any necessary action to get back, and stay, on target.

These activites often are viewed and audited on a departmental or functional basis. However, focusing on individual departments or functions sometimes simply is not enough. Individual departments may function efficiently, but the project still may not be completed on time. Some businesses, or aspects of government, have become so complex and intertwined that a new organization structure and concept has evolved, and has been found useful. This has involved a program concept, and has led to the superimposition of a program organization or structure over the usual departmental structures directly involved in the process. A program manager is a sort of coordinator of the entire program, having interface with department managers, in an effort to keep the programs on schedule and within cost estimates.

PROGRAMS AND PROGRAM MANAGEMENT

Program is a very broad term, and might be defined as a plan of procedure, a schedule and/or system, under which action may be taken towards a desired goal. For our purposes, in either business or government, it is defined as a funded effort, usually extending over a period of time, and requiring considerable resources—money, manpower, and material. The term is commonly used in the aerospace business to identify a major operational effort, under contract, requiring the delivery of a product, or documents, or services which may often require research, design, development, and production. A new aircraft or ship would be an example. But it may involve efforts collateral to the total requirements of the organization: a government health program, an employee benefits program, an extensive EDP program, and a diversification program.

The primary objective of program management is to reasonably assure that the product or service is furnished on time, within cost estimates, according to the customer's wishes usually as evidenced in a contract.

The purpose of a program audit would normally be to provide management, or governmental authorities, with information on the costs and status of the program. In other instances, it may be to comment on the results of the program. Stated in other terms, an objective may be to evaluate the program. One technique used is Program Evaluation and Review Technique (PERT), which is discussed later.

Program auditing may entail a study of facets beyond economy and efficiency, depending on the purpose, and who requests it. In any event, terms commonly used in connection with program auditing include these:

- ☐ *Evaluation.* Determining the value of something by comparing with a standard.
- ☐ *Program evaluation.* In its broadest context, it involves evaluating what has been done, or is being done, in relationship to cost. But in some special instances, it may relate to whether the program objectives are proper.
- ☐ *Cost-benefit study.* Basically, this involves measuring the cost input against the benefit or output. In this context, benefit relates to the impact or effect of the output—the increased accuracy of an instrument, for example. Benefits may be more difficult to measure than are the outputs.

    The auditor may be required to suggest or examine alternative approaches to meeting a program objective. He may be required to identify the "biggest bang for the buck"—the most benefits for the amount spent, or conversely, the method which produces the desired level of benefits at the least cost.
- ☐ *Cost-effectiveness study.* In some instances, the benefits cannot be measured in monetary units, and must be judged by such factors as impact on a community.

THE MANAGEMENT PROCESS AND PERT

In the past decade, magazines and newspapers have been replete with stories of cost overruns or behind-schedule conditions of military contracts and wasteful government spending on a number of projects. This arises, in part, because of the difficulty in estimating the time to perform an event—especially for nonrecurring activities involved in research and development. In construction activity, and in many government programs, two facts should be kept in mind. First, when a program is behind schedule costs normally increase, because an organization must remain intact. Literally, "time is money." Second, it is necessary to continuously update the estimated final costs, so that management (or the government) is aware of the trend and magnitude of total costs of the job.

It was because of the difficulty in estimating time and costs on complex programs that the U.S. Government (through the Special Projects Office of the Bureau of Naval Weapons, in cooperation with Booz Allen & Hamilton) developed PERT.[1] As a prelude to program auditing, the internal auditor should be aware of the concept. But it may be helpful to document the basic

---

[1] As quoted in Leonard W. Hein, *The Quantitative Approach to Managerial Decisions* (Englewood Cliffs, N.J.: Prentice-Hall, 1967), p. 289.

steps of the management process in somewhat more detailed steps which closely relate to PERT.

The basic steps of the management process might be outlined as follows:[2]

- Determination and effective communication of the prime and supporting objectives
- Development of a coordinated plan of action for the accomplishment of the objectives
- Conversion of the plan into integrated schedules within allowable resources
- Regular reporting and concurrent evaluation of progress against the scheduled plan and cost estimates
- Recycling of the above process to achieve the incorporation of the desired new action into a new cohesive scheduled plan

The process may be described graphically, as in Figure 36-1. Brief comments on each of these steps, in the context of preparing a PERT network, are described in the next section.

Determine and Define Objectives

The determination of the objectives is the initial step. The current objective or purpose of *each organization segment* must be the yardstick against which requirements and accomplishments should be measured and evaluated. The breakdown of a military system may involve the various work breakdown (packages) elements as shown in Figure 36-2.[3] There are several levels, and objectives must be established for each. The progressive passing down of specific coordinated objectives, from higher to lower echelons of management, sets the targets for, and the authorization of, detailed planning efforts on the part of the receiving organization segment. The sub-objectives of each department support the objectives of each higher level, and the primary objective—delivery of the system.

In the illustrative weapons system in Figure 36-2, each block represents a part, segment, or package of the entire product. Each such block contains these necessary functions:

- Engineering design
- Manufacturing design
- Manufacturing
- Testing

The relationship between the block, or work breakdown package, and

---

[2] Adapted from PERT Coordinating Group, PERT—*Guide for Management Use* (Washington, D.C.: U.S. Government Printing Office, 1963), pp. 1–2.

[3] *Ibid.*, p. 16.

PROGRAM MANAGEMENT

FIG. 36-1
The Management Process

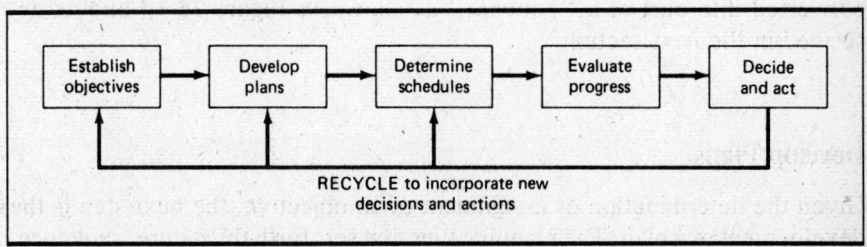

FIG. 36-2
Work Breakdown Schedule Showing Work Breakdown Packages at Levels 1, 2, 3, 4

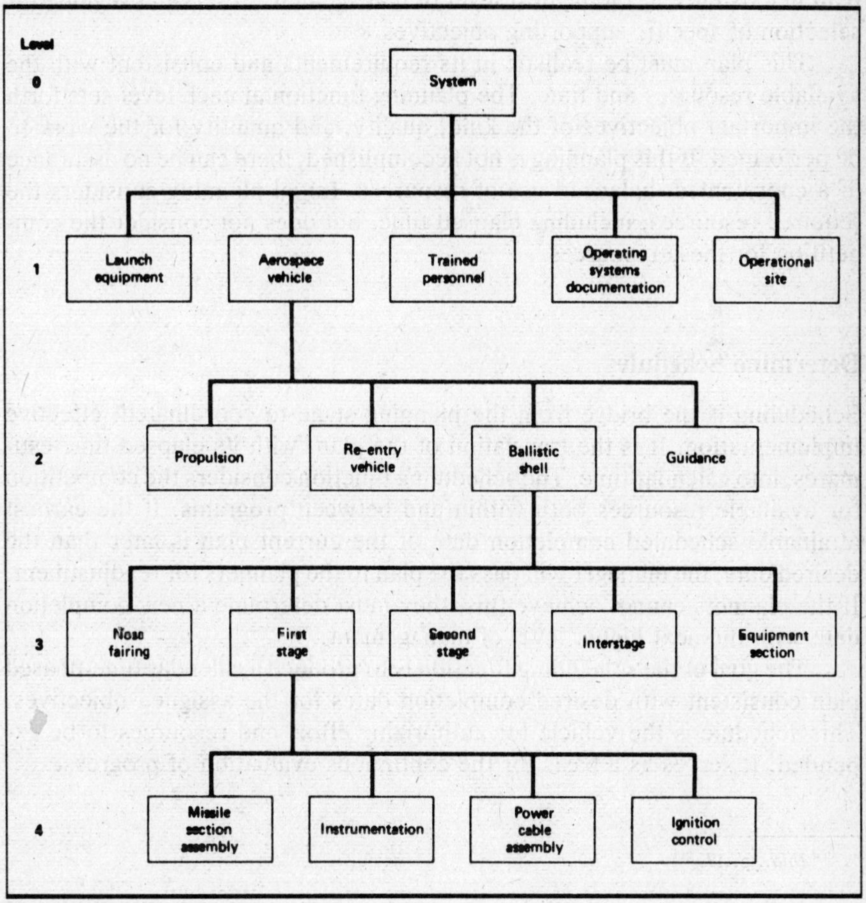

these functions is shown in Figure 36-3. Certain steps must be accomplished before subsequent ones can be started. Hence each step, or milestone, is converted into part of a "network" as shown in Figure 36-3,[4] and as described in the next section.

Develop Plans

Given the determination or assignment of an objective, the next step is the development of a plan. The planning function sets forth the nature, sequence, and interrelationships of the supporting objectives that must be accomplished to achieve the prime objective. Planning is primarily concerned with the structuring and relationships of units of required effort. It considers and answers questions of capability by determining in-house versus subcontracting effort. It establishes the feasibility of meeting the directed due date for the successful attainment of the objective. There must be a broad operating plan in existence at the highest level of management to serve as a guide for selection of specific supporting objectives.

This plan must be realistic in its requirements and consistent with the available resources and time. The planning function at each level sets forth the important objectives of the kind, quality, and quantity for the work to be performed. If this planning is not accomplished, there can be no assurance of a coordinated, balanced use of resources. Initial planning considers the required resources, including elapsed time, but does not consider the competition for these resources.

Determine Schedules

Scheduling is the bridge from the planning stage to coordinated, effective implementation. It is the translation of the plan, with its elapsed time estimates, into calendar time. The scheduling function considers the competition for available resources both within and between programs. If the earliest attainable scheduled completion date of the current plan is later than the desired date, the manager will pass the plan to the planners for readjustment. If the planners cannot achieve this, they must determine a new completion date with the next higher level of management.

The goal of the scheduling function is to produce a calendar time-phased plan consistent with desired completion dates for the assigned objectives. This schedule is the vehicle for authorizing effort and resources to be expended. It serves as a basis for the continuous evaluation of progress.

---

[4] *Ibid.*, p. 17.

PROGRAM MANAGEMENT

FIG. 36-3

Relationship of Work Breakdown Package to Functional Activities and Network of Steps

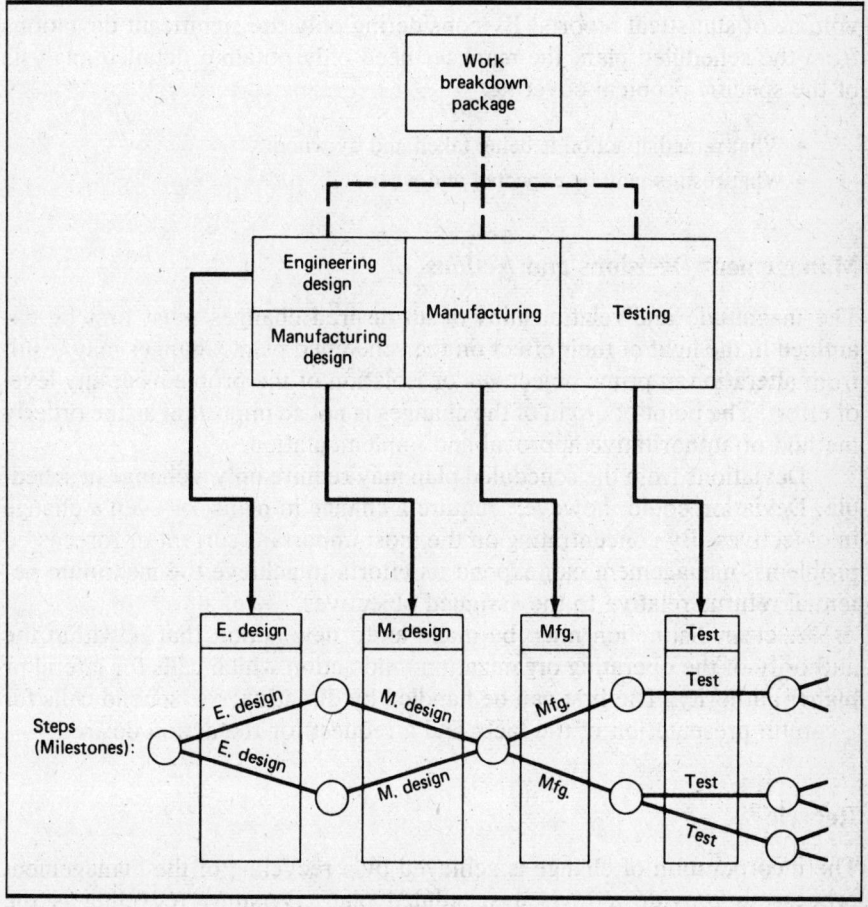

Progress Evaluation

Once the scheduled plan has been activated, a formal procedure for the regular reporting of progress against scheduled plan is necessary. A process for the early detection and specific description of a potentially significant problem area while there is still time for management to seek solutions to that problem is required. The management process described in this discussion therefore emphasizes:

- Regular, continuous, evaluation of actual performance against current scheduled plans; and

- Detection and isolation of significant deviations from the scheduled plan as a forecast of time and cost overrun.

The principle of "significant reporting" effects a great reduction in the volume of statistical reports. By considering only the significant deviations from the scheduled plan, the manager need only obtain a detailed analysis of the specific problem covering:

- What remedial action is being taken and by whom?
- What results may be expected and when?

Management Decisions and Actions

The magnitude and relationships of all desired changes must first be examined in the light of their effect on the scheduled plan. Changes may result from alteration in prime objectives or isolation of the problems at any level of effort. The point of origin of the changes is not so important as the orderly method of authoritative approval and implementation.

Deviations from the scheduled plan may require only a change in schedule. Deviation could, however, require a change in plans, or even a change in objectives. By concentrating on the most important current or forecasted problems, management can expend its efforts to achieve the maximum potential returns relative to the assigned objectives.

A clear distinction must be made as to new action that is within the authority of the operating organization, and action which calls for lateral or higher authority. The first can be handled by direction; the second calls for a careful presentation of the facts and a request for the action desired.

Recycle

The incorporation of change is achieved by a recycling of the management process to provide a revised scheduled plan. Dynamic recycling is the method of achieving and maintaining management control of objective-oriented effort. The formal progress, reviews, and evaluation meetings held by management with their supporting managers provide an opportunity to accomplish the mechanics of the recycling process.

PERT NETWORKS

For many program audits, it is desirable that the auditor review the PERT network and check the related time schedule and costs of the project. The reader is referred to some of the excellent writings on the construction of

FIG. 36-4
PERT Network—Simplified

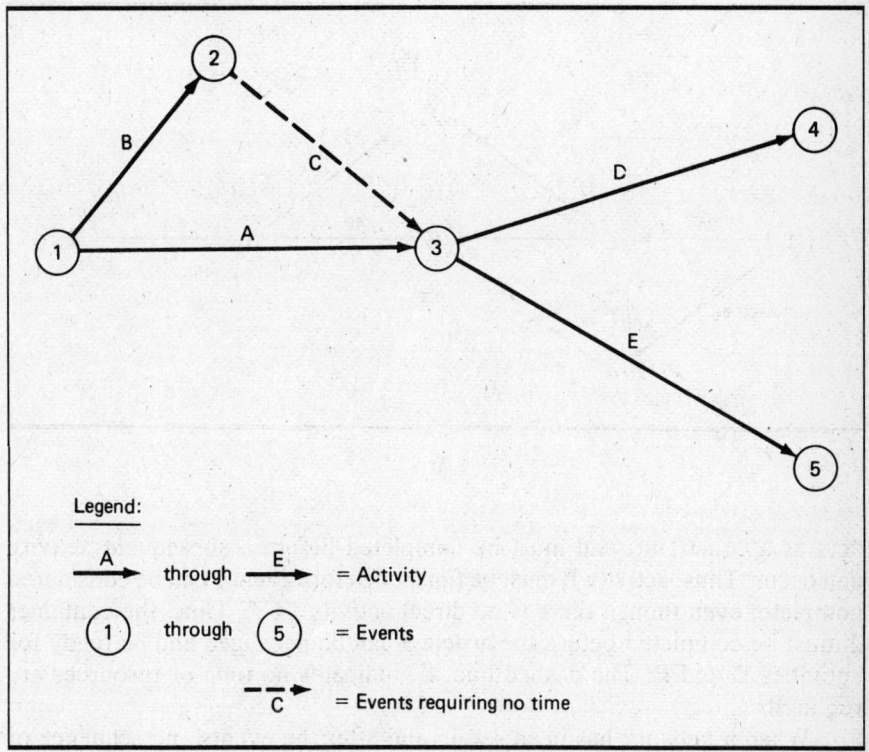

PERT networks.[5] This section covers only some basics. PERT, of course, is used in the planning and control of complex projects or programs. In its evolution, it has drawn upon Gantt charting, milestone reporting systems, and Line of Balance. Basically, a model simulates the program. It consists of a network of estimated activities and events, in which an activity is represented by an arrow, and an event by a circle. By use of the model, a program manager can determine whether schedule requirements will be met, and what function or activities are most critical, and therefore should be watched closely. PERT networks are a combination of related activities and events indicating the sequence in which resources will be applied. Thus, an illustrative network is shown in Figure 36-4. Activity A must be completed before D or E can start. Another convention is use of a dash arrow which signifies a "dummy" activity. No events transpire using resources. But it

---

[5] See, for example, William A. Boccino, *Management Information Systems*, Chapter 10 (Englewood Cliffs, N.J.: Prentice-Hall, 1972).

FIG. 36-5
PERT Network With Earliest and Latest Event Time

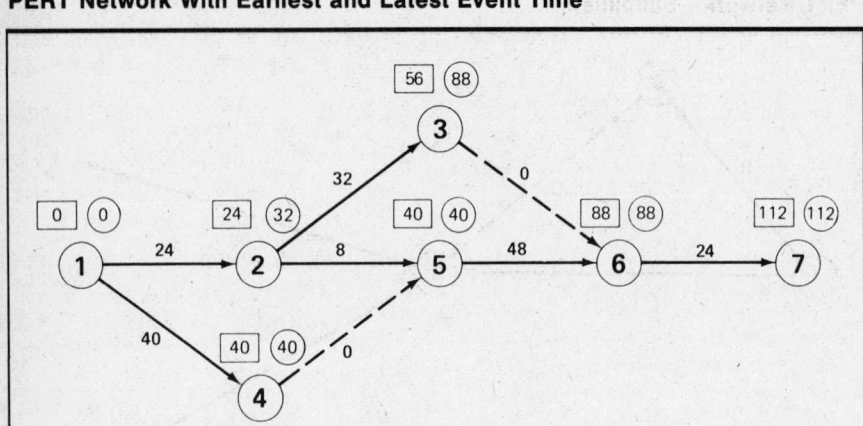

acts as a constraint, and must be completed before a subsequent activity can occur. Thus, activity B must be finished before event 3 can be considered complete, even though there is no direct activity "C." Thus, the container 2 must be completed before the article 3 can be packaged and be ready for activities D and E. The dashed line, C, indicates no time or resources are required.

When a network has been set up and after the events and sequence of activities has been reviewed for accuracy, time estimates are made for each activity, representing lapsed time—and with no constraints, such as a scheduled completion date. The time in weeks, days, or hours is indicated above the arrow. Technically, for the more simple Critical Path Method (CPM), only the single best estimate is used. In PERT, three estimates are needed: (1) optimistic time to complete the activity, (2) pessimistic time to complete it, and (3) the most likely time. The three estimates are combined (unequal weighting) to derive an expected completion time for each activity. It should be mentioned that knowledgeable individuals should preplan the events, the sequence of activities, and the resources needed for each activity. Such preplanning often helps uncover trouble spots before the project begins. Through estimates of the earliest time an activity can be completed, and the latest, a critical path is determined. Usually, the earliest completion time (indicated by a block to the left of the event) is estimated, as well as the latest (indicated by a circle to the right of the event). On the basis of such estimates, the critical path is determined, and it is the schedule particularly monitored. It represents the longest path from commencement to completion of the project. If this schedule is not met, the project is delayed, and costs increase, unless corrective action is taken. A PERT network with the earliest and latest event time is presented in Figure 36-5.

The network illustrated is a PERT/Time network. But a Pert/Cost system usually is also built, based on the PERT network just described. It may be a single estimate for each activity (the most likely), or it may be the three-estimate type. The estimate is made in units called work packages, as mentioned earlier. Technically, it is the unit of work required to complete a specific job, such as a part, a drawing, or a service which is within the responsibility of one operating department or cost center in an organization. To better understand the advantages and pitfalls in a PERT network, the reader should review the designated reference.

INDICATED FINAL COST

As previously mentioned, a primary objective of program management is to assure the customer that the product or service is furnished in accordance with the contract, and assure the contractor, or governmental agency, that it is furnished on schedule and within the cost estimate. One of the features that distinguishes construction or program management from other types of accounting applications is the rather continuous need to update the costs. That is to say, each month, or for other selected periods (week or quarter), the cost to complete the contract must be re-estimated. For each work package, the costs incurred to date, plus the commitments, (if applicable) plus the further estimated cost to complete the program must be totaled to arrive at the new cost estimate for the work package. The sum of all costs for all work packages equals the new estimated cost to complete the program.

Many programs arise because of errors in estimating costs yet to be incurred. Hence, assistance of engineers, or similar disciplines, may be necessary in checking or arriving at new estimates of cost completion.

PROGRAM MANAGEMENT CONTROL QUESTIONNAIRE

As has been previously mentioned, the questionnaire is a highly useful device to assist in developing the audit program for an operations audit—or any type of audit. A portion of a questionnaire for use in developing the audit program for an aerospace contractor, as related to a government contract, is illustrated in Figure 36-6.

(continued on page 36-19)

FIG. 36-6
Program Management Control Questionnaire

FOREWORD:

Program management may be defined as the process by which segments, functions, disciplines, and other resources of a company are brought together in an organized and planned manner to achieve program objectives. A program may be defined as a major undertaking utilizing considerable material, manpower, and resources over long periods of time and involving contractual arrangements. The term is commonly used in the aerospace industry to identify operational effort. It is usually associated with some type of deliverable product or service requiring research, design, development, and long-term production. The product may be either military or commercial (sometimes both) and requires more than the effort and capability of a single contractor.

The primary objective of program management is to reasonably assure that products, systems, and services are furnished in accordance with customer and legal requirements, on time, and within original cost estimates. Related objectives usually include:

- Complying with all applicable contractual terms and conditions
- Preserving competitive posture
- Developing opportunities for additional business
- Enhancing technical and managerial capability

Programs vary in size, affecting the degree of direct and indirect support and the manner in which the program is organized. The most common direct elements of program management are:

- Project planning
- Project control
- Design engineering
- Tooling design
- Materiel production planning
- Quality control
- Change control
- Test planning

Some programs are of such size and duration that they require, in addition to the foregoing, such staff functions as contract administration (including bidding and estimating), materiel, industrial relations, finance, and data processing. This questionnaire is not designed for that type of program. Rather, it assumes that the program is being managed within the context of existing control techniques with respect to such functions. Separate questionnaires would have to be devised for any indirect functions specifically organized and dedicated to a given program.

AUTHORIZATION AND EXECUTION:

- To provide sufficient resources pursuant to management's authority to achieve program objectives.
- To perform only that scope of work necessary to fulfill contractual commitments and approved changes thereto.
- To deviate from primary objectives only upon appropriate management authorization based upon sound, factual information and rationale.

RECORDING AND ACCOUNTABILITY:

- To record and report program activity so as to permit reasonably effective performance review evaluations by affected management.

- To establish and maintain accountability for decisions pertaining to program activities, such as organization, design, production scheduling, customer relations, etc.
- To reasonably assure that actual program or contract status is periodically compared to budgeted or planned progress in order to permit appropriate action to be taken with respect to variances.

SAFEGUARDING:

- To reasonably assure that access to sensitive or confidential program information is restricted to authorized personnel.
- To reasonably assure that access to program facilities is restricted to authorized personnel.
- To reasonably assure that program facilities and equipment are sufficiently protected from insurable hazards.

In practice, the foregoing objectives are usually accomplished by delegating and distributing responsibility among the functional elements previously identified. The attached questionnaire has been organized by these elements. In some organizational units, certain elements may be combined, whereas, in others, there may be further divisions. The former situation should make the process of obtaining responses easier, since fewer functional departments are involved. In the latter situation, however, the auditor may find it necessary to supplement the questionnaire to reasonably assure thorough coverage.

	Yes	No

A. PROJECT PLANNING:

1. **Authorization and Execution:**
   a. Do records reflect that the program objectives have been specified in writing, in sufficient detail and clarity to permit attainment? ☐ ☐
   b. Has authority for executing transactions and activities related to the program been specified in writing? ☐ ☐
   c. Do organization charts exist which depict reporting relationships for the various disciplines necessary to accomplish program objectives? ☐ ☐
   d. Is the total scope of the program documented and approved in writing? ☐ ☐
   e. Do techniques include provisions for continuous planning efforts, so that the impact of current events or intended courses of action can be timely assessed? ☐ ☐
   f. Do written statements exist indicating the levels of approval authority for executing commitments for various transactions essential to achieving program objectives, such as hiring/firing personnel; obtaining facilities, materiel, and services; opening bank accounts; and so forth? ☐ ☐

2. **Recording and Accountability:**
   a. Is the scope of the program documented in writing in a master plan, which includes:

(continued)

FIG. 36-6 *(cont'd)*

	Yes	No
■ Description requirements	☐	☐
■ Interaction of program objectives	☐	☐
■ List of deliverable items	☐	☐
■ Delivery schedule	☐	☐
■ Statement of risks	☐	☐
■ Statement of provisions and plans to minimize risks	☐	☐
■ Master statement of work tasks, such as a work breakdown structure	☐	☐
■ A work breakdown structure organizational matrix, or its equivalent	☐	☐

b. Do detailed planning records identify scheduled start and completion dates for each program task? ☐ ☐

c. Is documentation of program tasks sufficient to:
- ■ Distinguish the task from other tasks ☐ ☐
- ■ Permit measurement of schedule and cost progress ☐ ☐
- ■ Permit cost accumulation (this would usually require some form of cost account numbering system, which allows identification of the program, the task, and the performing organization) ☐ ☐
- ■ Track changes (starting effectively at release dates, for example) ☐ ☐

d. Do techniques include some form of program diagramming, such as networking, PERT, or CPM, which depict suggested steps in a time-phased fashion needed to accomplish program objectives? ☐ ☐

e. Do techniques include some form of periodic reporting to interested program and other management of the following:
- ■ Progress against plan, both schedule and cost, on a task-by-task basis ☐ ☐
- ■ Explanations of significant variances disclosed by such reporting, and an indication of planned remedial actions ☐ ☐
- ■ Graphic presentations of cost/schedule performance ☐ ☐

3. **Safeguarding:**
   a. Are program planning documents and records sufficiently safeguarded to restrict access only to authorized persons? ☐ ☐
   b. Has provision been made for adequate backup of vital records in the event of loss or destruction? ☐ ☐
   c. Are records and documents accorded reasonable protection from loss or destruction? ☐ ☐

B. PROJECT CONTROL:

1. **Authorization and Execution:**
   a. Do procedures and/or policies specify authority for:
   - ■ Signing contracts ☐ ☐
   - ■ Executing contract changes ☐ ☐

	Yes	No

- Performing work not covered by contracts ☐ ☐
- Approving master plans ☐ ☐
- Approving program policies and procedures ☐ ☐
- Approving organization structures and changes thereto ☐ ☐
- Approving job classifications and descriptions ☐ ☐
- Approving salary structures ☐ ☐
- Hiring and firing personnel ☐ ☐
- Approving and executing subcontracts and leases ☐ ☐
- Approving and executing purchase orders ☐ ☐
- Approving budgets of direct and indirect costs ☐ ☐
- Approving burden rates ☐ ☐
- Approving accounting systems ☐ ☐
- Approving estimates of final contract revenue, cost, and margin ☐ ☐

b. Are contract changes that affect both work scope and price required to be executed in a manner similar to that used for original proposal preparation? ☐ ☐

c. Is the budgeting structure integrated with the task or workbreakdown structure so that each discrete task is given a budget cost? ☐ ☐

d. Are requests for additional budget subject to the same approval as the original budget? ☐ ☐

2. **Recording and Accountability:**

a. Are commitments for delivery of program services and/or products expressed in writing, in the form of contracts with the customers? ☐ ☐

b. Do such contracts record all essential terms and conditions, including, but not restricted to:
- Parties to the contract ☐ ☐
- Date of contract and effective period covered ☐ ☐
- Obligations of the parties (deliverables, due dates, etc.) ☐ ☐
- Type of contract ☐ ☐
- Contract price ☐ ☐
- Payment terms ☐ ☐
- Penalties ☐ ☐
- Special conditions ☐ ☐

c. Do procedures prevent performance of work outside the scope of the contracts except for specifically authorized purposes? ☐ ☐

d. Do records include a complete and current set of contractual documents and approved changes? ☐ ☐

e. Do records and procedures permit prompt disclosure of changes to all affected program functions (e.g., engineering, procurement, manufacturing, finance)? ☐ ☐

(continued)

FIG. 36-6 *(cont'd)*

	Yes	No
f. Do record-keeping techniques classify and accumulate program transactions in such manner and detail so as to permit preparation of periodic reports comparing actual and budgeted cost to date?	☐	☐
At a minimum, the records should reflect for each task and/or responsible department, on current period and inception-to-date bases, expenditures categorized according to their nature (labor, material, subcontract, or overhead).		
g. Are record-keeping procedures sufficient to aid in preparing estimates of final contract or program revenue, cost, and margin?	☐	☐
h. Do procedures require preparing or updating estimates of final contract or program revenue, cost, and margin periodically, or when circumstances warrant?	☐	☐
i. Are procedures sufficient for each cost element (labor, materiel, subcontract, overhead) to assure that all costs incurred were charged to the contract as of the cut-off date for preparation of the estimate to complete?	☐	☐
j. Are cost procedures set forth in a disclosure statement?	☐	☐
k. Has the disclosure statement been approved by the customer?	☐	☐
l. Are estimates to complete prepared (1) on the basis of clear instructions and (2) by persons in positions which should afford them a reasonable basis for making such estimates?	☐	☐
m. Are estimates to complete required to be prepared on the basis of all known relevant facts and likely future events, such as:		
■ Budget vs. actual variances	☐	☐
■ Schedule variances	☐	☐
■ Labor rate increases	☐	☐
■ Material price fluctuations	☐	☐
n. Do techniques include review and checking of estimates by persons other than the originators to minimize errors and omissions?	☐	☐
o. Are reports of program status required to be prepared periodically and distributed to interested management?	☐	☐
p. Are reports of indicated final revenue, cost, and margin included in such program status reports, or separately distributed to affected management at regular intervals?	☐	☐
q. Are performance review meetings held periodically to assess program performance in light of all relevant facts and circumstances?	☐	☐
3. Safeguarding:		
a. Are project control records sufficiently safeguarded to restrict access only to authorized persons?	☐	☐
b. Have provisions been made for adequate backup of vital records in the event of loss or destruction?	☐	☐

PROGRAM MANAGEMENT

	Yes	No
c. Are records and documents accorded reasonable protection from loss or destruction?	☐	☐

C. DESIGN ENGINEERING:

1. Authorization and Execution:

a. Is the engineering function organized so as to result in an effective and efficient design of program products? Such organization may include the following segments:
- Policies and procedures ☐ ☐
- Planning ☐ ☐
- Research and analysis ☐ ☐
- Administrative management ☐ ☐
- Data standards ☐ ☐
- Files, records, and supplies ☐ ☐
- Automated systems support ☐ ☐
- Program support ☐ ☐
- Test and evaluation ☐ ☐

b. Are the design engineering objectives divided into reasonably manageable sub-objectives or tasks? ☐ ☐

c. Is there an approved plan of engineering which is integrated with customer specifications? ☐ ☐

d. Is the design effort controlled by use of work authorization forms or similar documents required to be approved by appropriate engineering and/or program management? ☐ ☐

e. Does the design plan include provision for tests and evaluation of components and assemblies? ☐ ☐

f. Does the design plan call for building prototypes to permit testing and evaluation of the final product? ☐ ☐

g. Are designs and changes thereto required to be approved by designated management and the customer? ☐ ☐

h. Are engineers effectively precluded from vendor/supplier negotiations and commitments for the purchase of required materials, parts, or services? ☐ ☐

i. Are engineers effectively precluded from negotiating changes to the scope of the work? ☐ ☐

2. Recording and Accountability:

a. Is the design effort required to be documented in the form of engineering drawings? ☐ ☐

b. Do techniques include requirements for review, check, and approval of engineering drawings? ☐ ☐

c. Do the engineering drawings indicate information as to:
- Materials and parts required ☐ ☐
- Use of item or part ☐ ☐
- Cross-reference to the next assembly ☐ ☐
- Approvals ☐ ☐

(continued)

FIG. 36-6 (cont'd)

	Yes	No
• Effectivity	☐	☐
• A record of changes to original design, including approval and effectivity	☐	☐
d. Does the engineering drawing numbering system enable specific identification, filing, cross-referencing, and retrieval?	☐	☐
e. Is progress toward engineering design objectives monitored by status reports, performance reviews, or other techniques?	☐	☐

3. Safeguarding:

	Yes	No
a. Are engineering drawings, test data, evaluations, and other pertinent documents sufficiently safeguarded to restrict access only to authorized persons?	☐	☐
b. Has provision been made for adequate backup of vital records, such as bills of materials or material parts lists, in the event of loss or destruction?	☐	☐
c. Are records and documents accorded reasonable protection from loss or destruction?	☐	☐

D. TOOLING DESIGN:

1. Authorization and Execution:

	Yes	No
a. Is the tooling design engineering effort organized so as to result in an effective and efficient design of tooling necessary to enable parts to be fabricated and assembled in a proper fashion? (Note: See section on design engineering.)	☐	☐
b. Are the tooling design objectives divided into reasonably manageable sub-objectives or tasks?	☐	☐
c. Is there an approved plan of tooling engineering which is integrated with customer specifications and design requirements?	☐	☐
d. Is the tooling design effort controlled by means of work authorization forms or similar documents required to be approved by specified engineering and/or program management?	☐	☐
e. Are tooling designs and changes thereto required to be approved by designated management and/or the customer?	☐	☐
f. Are tooling engineers effectively precluded from vendor/supplier negotiations and commitments for the purchase of required materials, parts, or services?	☐	☐
g. Are tooling engineers effectively precluded from negotiating changes to the scope of work?	☐	☐

2. Recording and Accountability:

	Yes	No
a. Is the tooling design effort required to be documented in the form of drawings?	☐	☐
b. Do techniques include requirements for review, check, and approval of drawings?	☐	☐

PROGRAM MANAGEMENT 36-19

	Yes	No
c. Do the drawings indicate information as to:		
▪ Materials and parts required	☐	☐
▪ Use of item or part	☐	☐
▪ Approvals	☐	☐
▪ Effectivity	☐	☐
▪ A record of changes to original design, including approval and effectivity	☐	☐
d. Does the drawing numbering system enable specific identification, filing, cross-referencing, and retrieval?	☐	☐
e. Is progress toward tooling design objectives monitored by status reports, performance reviews, or other techniques?	☐	☐
3. Safeguarding:		
a. Are tooling drawings and other pertinent tooling documents sufficiently safeguarded to restrict access only to authorized persons?	☐	☐
b. Has provision been made for adequate backup of vital tooling records in the event of loss or destruction?	☐	☐
c. Are tooling records accorded reasonable protection from loss or destruction?	☐	☐
E. PRODUCTION PLANNING:		
1. Authorization and Execution:		
a. Is there a designated organization responsible for decisions with respect to production planning?	☐	☐

PROGRAM MANAGEMENT AUDIT PROGRAM

A portion of the program management audit program in current use by a defense contractor is shown in Figure 36-7. It presumes a reasonable knowledge by the internal auditor of the accounting system and organization structure, so that much of the preliminary effort is not necessary.

AUDIT FINDINGS

An illustrative audit report covering the control aspects of a program audit is presented in Figure 36-8. It is intended to give the flavor of problems arising in the early stages of a construction program in a foreign country.

(continued on page 36-27)

FIG. 36-7

Program Management Audit Program

	Performed by	Date

A. PROJECT PLANNING:

   1. Authorization and Execution:

     ☐ Obtain a copy of all program policies, procedures, and organization charts and review for completeness in terms of program objectives.   ....

     ☐ Discuss organization structure with program manager and other members of the management team in terms of strengths and weaknesses, problems, challenges, and techniques to accomplish program goals. Note any matters for further inquiry during the course of the audit.   ....

     ☐ Obtain written delegation of authority and review for completeness. Note last date of revision.   ....

   2. Recording and Accountability:

     ☐ Obtain a copy of the master plan and review for completeness such items as:
- Requirements   ....
- Delivery schedule   ....
- Work breakdown structure   ....

     ☐ Compare items to the contract for any inaccuracies or omissions. A sampling will suffice for very large contracts.   ....

     ☐ Obtain a copy of the latest network diagram (PERT, CPM, or Gantt) and test its accuracy and completeness by reference to the contract.   ....

     ☐ Review evidence indicating the extent to which the network diagram is kept current and communicated to other interested management.   ....

     ☐ Review the file of management reports disclosing program status for the following attributes:
- Frequency of preparation   ....
- Approval   ....
- Distribution   ....
- Completeness of content (e.g., actual vs. planned progress, explanations of variances, problems, etc.)   ....

   3. Safeguarding:

     ☐ Observe methods used to safeguard planning documents and note consistency with representation noted in the internal control questionnaire.   ....

     ☐ Obtain evidence in the form of a plan indicating that adequate backup and recovery provisions have been made.   ....

	Performed by	Date

B. PROJECT CONTROL:

1. Authorization and Control:

☐ Obtain a current version of the contract and all change orders and note evidence of proper contract signatures.

☐ Review other documentation indicating evidence of:
- Approved master plan
- Approved policies and procedures
- Approved organization structures
- Approved job classifications and safety structures
- Approved accounting system
- Approved estimates of final contract revenue, cost, and margin
- Approved budget

2. Recording and Accountability:

☐ Review the contract for completeness, noting contract type, price, payment terms, penalties, and special additions.

☐ Test for evidence of controls precluding performance of work outside the scope of the contract or program.

☐ Test the techniques for prompt disclosure of contract charges to all affected parties.

☐ For important cost elements (labor, materiel, overhead), perform a sample test, preferably a statistical sampling, of the propriety of recording (i.e., proper period, proper account charged).

☐ Observe evidence of preparation of estimates of final cost, revenue, and margin on a regular basis. If approved by the assigned audit manager, perform the steps outlined in the audit program for examination of indicated final margin.

3. Safeguarding:

☐ Observe actual techniques used to restrict access to project control records and comment on their consistency with the representation in the questionnaire.

C. DESIGN ENGINEERING:

1. Authorization and Execution:

☐ Review evidence indicating the existence of the following:
- Policies and procedures

(continued)

FIG. 36-7 *(cont'd)*

	Performed by	Date
■ Planning	....	....
■ Administrative management	....	....
■ Standards	....	....
■ Files, records, and supplies	....	....
■ Program support	....	....

FIG. 36-8

Program Management Audit Report

TO: J.D. Williams

FROM: S.O. Proctor

SUBJECT: Audit of Selected Eagle Program Control Functions — Summary Report

We have performed limited reviews of various financial and administrative controls of the Eagle I project at .... as established by the affected divisions and subsidiaries of The Corporation. Our review was performed in order to provide, through our knowledge of corporate policies, a basis for reporting to management such matters which in our opinion require its attention.

Our scope included limited reviews in the following areas with respect to the Construction Division (COND):

■ Change Order Control Procedures
■ Cost and Budget Control Procedures, including Methodology in Developing Indicated Final Cost
■ Subcontract Administration

As to our European-based subsidiary (SATCO) doing work in Southeast Asia, our limited reviews covered the following:

■ Cost and Budget Control
■ Contract Change Order Control Procedures

In addition, we attended separate presentations of control techniques to be used by COND Project Management and SATCO Management, and participated in meetings held for the purpose of establishing the principles of accounting to be followed by SATCO and COND, respectively, in determining the periodic recognition of revenue, costs, and profit for financial reporting purposes. The corporate controller, representatives of the independent accountants, and each division chief financial officer, among others, were in attendance.

The foregoing limited reviews were restricted by time and by the fact that the project is still in the development stage. For many of the new procedures which have been developed, insufficient time has elapsed to permit a determination of compliance or an evaluation of effectiveness. For example, while new procedures have been developed to control contract changes by Eagle project management, there have been no changes which have, as yet, completed the entire change process (several are in progress). Hence, compliance cannot be tested. Our limited reviews, therefore, were not sufficiently extensive to accumulate evidence which would permit an opinion regarding either compliance with established procedures or the effectiveness of such procedures for accomplishing their intended purposes. However, despite the foregoing limitations, we believe that certain observations are appropriate, as set forth in the next paragraph.

Nothing came to our attention that indicated that the following statements are not true:

1. The COND Project Management organization structure is adequate to discharge its functions. The finance structure in particular, including cost and budget control, appeared well organized.
2. The proposed SATCO Project Financial Management organization structure and procedures, as set forth in the November memorandum by L. Roberts, will enable the Project to discharge its function better than it was able to do at the time of the review (October 19XX). The memorandum, among other things, committed SATCO (1) to increase the size of the Eagle Finance Organization by creating the managerial position of Eagle Program Regional Controller, (2) to provide current, accurate monthly cost reports, and (3) to increase the frequency of SATCO internal audit efforts and visits by home office finance management.
3. The principles of accounting established by the respective divisions for the periodic recognition of contract revenue costs and profit are in accordance with generally accepted accounting principles.
4. Procedures used by COND for maintaining accountability of government-furnished property, as approved by the U.S. Air Force, are effective for the purpose intended.

In addition, we searched accounting records, such as cash disbursement records and certain correspondence files maintained by COND and SATCO Project Management personnel, for evidence of any violations of corporate policies with respect to consultant and commission agents, procurement practices, entertainment, and other policies dealing with improper practices. The search, which would not necessarily disclose all matters of concern, disclosed nothing which requires the attention of management.

Notwithstanding the above statements, we are concerned that existing reporting and control mechanisms regarding changes in the scope of the technical construction portion may not be adequate to determine the financial implications of such changes for decisions regarding the change, and for the periodic determination of the overall profitability status of the Eagle Program. Moreover, we are concerned that certain of the changes may be of such magnitude that decisions regarding them warrant the approval of the senior corporate management to assure that such decisions are in the best interests of The Corporation, taken as a whole.

Our concern stems largely from observations in connection with job site tours, the aforementioned attendance at financial review presentations, discussions with representatives of each division, a review of organization structures, and conversations with certain corporate officials. Available evidence is not conclusive, although it is sufficient to form a basis for some concern. In view of the significance of this project to The Corporation's financial position, we believe it is desirable to express that concern and the reasons therefor in order that appropriate consideration of the situation by management may occur. The circumstances contributing to our concern are described in the following paragraphs.

To be successful, COND Project Management must not only complete the project within budget, but also must maintain our competitive advantage so as to be in the best possible position for possible future Eagle work. This means preserving the corporate image of meeting or exceeding contract requirements on time and without cost escalation. Careful judgment must be exercised in balancing these objectives. At times, it may be prudent, for purposes of image maintenance and to augment

(continued)

FIG. 36-8 (cont'd)

relationships between COND and the USAF, to waive the pursuit of increases to the original $1,500 billion NTE despite valid changes in the scope of work. At other times, the converse may be true. A primary determinant, in our opinion, would be the impact of such decisions on the consolidated program operating results. However, we do not believe this impact is required to be considered by any individual or group charged with the responsibility for deciding courses of action. Rather, each division or subsidiary involved tends to assess the impact of events, including the financial impact, as though it stands alone and acts accordingly. We are not aware of any individual or group that, as a matter of policy, is provided sufficient information to assess the impact of events on The Corporation taken as a whole, nor with the decision-making power to coordinate the efforts of the divisions and subsidiaries involved.

In the recent past, consideration of the impact of certain acts on The Corporation taken as a whole has occurred despite the absence of any requirement to do so. The decision to transfer the F&E procurement from SATCO to COND is an example. However, other situations have occurred in which such consideration is not evident, such as the decision to reimburse COND employees for the tax increase resulting from the 19XX change in tax law. While the decision may not have been different had adequate consideration of the impact on The Corporation taken as a whole been made, appropriate concurrent action with respect to other corporate employees might have resulted from such consideration, thereby avoiding the morale difficulties the separate decision has caused. Further decisions on other matters, such as changes in contract scope, could lead to other undesirable consequences in the absence of a requirement to assess the decision from a combined corporate standpoint. Given the size and significance of the Eagle Project and the impact management decisions related to it can have on the entire company, we question whether the delegation of authority to the COND division to act in the best interest of the company taken as a whole, is appropriate. On the other hand, it would be impracticable for senior corporate management to determine the course of events some 15,000 miles away with any degree of frequency. However, it should be practicable for senior corporate management to consider or approve certain decisions which may arise infrequently and which are likely to have long-term significant ramifications.

By way of illustration, the following list of brief captions represents situations, generally known to all involved management, which could become changes to the scope of the technical construction portion of the contract. The dollar estimates shown were provided by SATCO Eagle Project Management and represent a rough estimate of the cost that might be involved in each instance. While the amounts shown may lack precision, they provide a rough indication of the magnitude these potential changes involve.

The list, which is by no means complete, is as follows.

	Rough Cost Estimate of Potential Changes (In Millions)
1. Integrated utilities program	$40–50
2. Firing range fences	14
3. Survival training center	7
4. Tax equalization for 19XX*	4
5. Changes to facilities for which construction has been held up for some reason	Unknown
6. Allowance for special handling and overtime to meet schedule	5

* While the years 19X1 through 19X5 would also be affected, an estimate was provided for 19XX only.

7. Possible increase in scope of work to be performed
by Aranco Electronics 5–15
8. Additional architectural scope changes 1
$76–95

SATCO Management considers all items on the foregoing partial list to be changes outside the scope of the contract. It believes strongly that such situations were clearly known to all interested parties at the time the scope of work was definitized, based on documents, correspondence, and meetings regarding the various subjects which predate such definitization. COND Eagle Project Management does not completely agree. Further, even in situations where it may agree, it may conclude that it is not in the best interest of the division to pursue increases to the original NTE. For example, COND Eagle Project Management apparently will not pursue increases to the NTE for the integrated utilities program according to the pricing proposal, despite the fact that it is a change in scope, unless the ultimate contractual language is made much clearer. The implications of this intent on the company, taken as a whole, have not been developed and conveyed to senior corporate management.

Certain items on the foregoing list, as well as others not on it, will produce differences of opinion as to whether an item is a scope change and, if so, what are the costs involved, among other things. During our recent visit to the project we were furnished a list of approximately 90 items by SATCO Management which it considered to be valid scope changes. We sampled the documentation in support of such items, noting correspondence had been sent to COND Eagle Project subcontract management in all such instances. However, COND subcontract management sees merit in only a few of these items. Some of these items have been pending for a considerable length of time and could involve significant amounts. In the absence of a reporting requirement, the financial implications of these pending items are not known. The longer it takes to resolve these matters, the longer it will be before the financial implications surface under the existing arrangement.

Ultimately, decisions under the present system regarding changes will be made by the COND Eagle Project Change Board (which excludes representation by SATCO). The decisions will be binding and final, and will be made without a requirement to consider the impact, if any, that such decisions will have on the consolidated Eagle Project operating margin. In the foregoing illustration, should the Change Board, for image maintenance purposes, or for other reasons, conclude that none of the items constitute an out-of-scope change, the consolidated operating margin of the company would be adversely affected to an indeterminant degree. Currently, SATCO is using a gross operating margin of 5.4% for financial reporting purposes. Adverse decisions on these changes could nearly eliminate such margin, according to SATCO management. Such ramifications must be considered in making the decisions, but they cannot be unless changes are made. The information is not presently available because the management reporting mechanism of SATCO is not yet sufficiently sensitive to discern the profit impact, if any. Moreover, such information now available regarding SATCO profitability status is not furnished to the Change Board.

To a large extent, the ability of SATCO management to discern financial impact is dependent upon prompt action and timely communication of change order decisions by COND through its subcontract administration function. We are concerned that the mechanism necessary to adequately discharge this function may not be completely in place. Our concern stems from the fact that considerable time elapses between the identification of a change and its ultimate resolution, as mentioned earlier. While valid reasons may exist for some of this time lapse, a contributing factor may also be the degree of responsiveness of the subcontract administration function.

The following are our recommendations.

(continued)

FIG. 36-8 *(cont'd)*

RECOMMENDATION NO. 1

SATCO management must take such steps as are necessary to assure that it is in a position to timely report the financial impact (profitability) of pending changes. These might include the following:

a. Include a Status of Contract Changes Addendum to the cost report which would set forth such information as a brief description of the change, its anticipated cost, the amount of contract contingency, if any, which can be allocated to it, an indication of the current status of the change, and a disclosure of disputes, if any. Disclosure of other information, such as actions or events related to the matter occurring in the period, the age of the item, and an indication of anticipated future actions and events related to the item, might also be appropriate.

b. Provide such information (or suitable abridgements thereof) to the Eagle Project Change Board on a periodic basis and to senior corporate management on a periodic basis which would be of sufficient frequency to permit such timely action as it may deem appropriate.

c. Assess the adequacy of resources allocated to the financial and contract administration functions in light of the disclosures of this report.

RECOMMENDATION NO. 2

COND Eagle Project Management must take such steps as are necessary to assure that the subcontract administration function may be discharged in a prompt, timely fashion. These might include the following:

a. Establish a requirement for periodic meetings between COND Eagle Project Management and SATCO Eagle Project Management for the purpose of resolving differences of opinion with respect to pending scope changes.

b. Prepare a report of the results of such meetings, to be distributed to interested division management and to senior corporate management. We understand COND Management will shortly begin to provide the President and Chief Operating Officer with a monthly status report. This report could include the subject report as an addition.

c. Include consideration of the impact its decisions may have regarding changes in consolidated profitability. Develop means by which all information necessary for such consideration is made available to the Change Board.

RECOMMENDATION NO. 3

Devise and adhere to a procedure for timely arbitration of those situations which cannot be resolved by such meetings. Such procedure should provide for furnishing written position statements by each division for the matter in dispute as an initial basis for arbitration proceedings. The arbitrator should be the

PROGRAM MANAGEMENT 36-27

> Corporate President and Chief Operating Officer, or his appointee.
>
> Decisions should be binding and should be approved by the Senior Corporate Management (President and Chief Operating Officer, Senior Vice President–Finance, Senior Vice President–Operations) for instances involving changes whose financial impact would be material to the consolidated results of operations. Similar procedures should also be employed to appeal decisions of the Change Board which, in the opinion of SATCO Management, will adversely affect its performance to a material extent.
>
> The findings and recommendations of this report have focused on only two of the corporate entities involved in Eagle Project, namely, SATCO and COND, because the scope of our audit work involved only these entities. However, we suspect these recommendations may have applicability to . . . . in its role as subcontractor to each of the other two entities. It would be well to consider establishing similar reporting mechanisms for . . . . Eagle Project management as may be appropriate.
>
> A response to this report by the various action parties is requested within 30 days.

Often, as illustrated in the report, some difficulties arise by reason of:

- Lack of control over, or improper procedures for handling, contract change orders.
- Inadequate or insufficient financial staff to adequately police procedures.
- Improper instructions on the accounting policies and procedures to be followed.
- Lack of control over property items (e.g., construction equipment).

In addition to deficiencies, cited in the audit report, other findings related to major or complex program management projects include such items as:

- Failure to use a program network scheme, such as PERT, to identify the proper sequence of events (with resulting penalties for late work).
- Improper coordination between different organizational segments used on a program (different divisions or subsidiaries, or companies).
- Lack of control over local purchases (e.g., supplies and foodstuffs) for cash.
- Failure to comply with local laws regarding social security or health and safety matters.
- Inadequate insurance coverage.
- Failure to properly update indicated final costs (with consequent error in profit rate pickup).
- Inadequate documentation of costs.
- Failure to secure competitive bids, when it was feasible to maintain competitive practices.

- Delivery of materials to wrong locations (and need to use expensive airfreight to meet schedules).
- Delivery of materials with improper specifications.
- Failure to secure written contracts.
- Selection of subcontractors without requisite capabilities.
- Lack of procedures and controls to prevent work outside the scope of contract.
- Failure to accumulate costs on construction contracts to meet the customer needs.

This list could be expanded considerably, but it does indicate some of the many considerations involved in program management.

PROGRAM MANAGEMENT AND MICROCOMPUTERS

As discussed earlier, both PERT and CPM may typically be used to track individual activities in a large and complicated project or program. For example, they can be employed in managing large construction projects, or weapons-system development, or product development.

But there are a growing number of software vendors who are promoting project management and scheduling programs for any executive charged with completing a job on time and within budget. They assert that such programs can be quite useful, for example, to a small advertising agency beginning a sales campaign to land a new account. In other words, the applications need not be for large and costly projects. Typical programs, which may be run on a personal computer, provide for listing the individual tasks, assigning people to complete them, indicating the time frame, and costs. With proper input, the program can indicate the percent completion of each task, the probability of being completed on time, and identify tasks that are behind schedule. Moreover, the program can be used to reallocate time and resources to get the task back on schedule.

The reader is referred to *PC Week Buyers Guide* and other computer periodicals for some of the presently existing project management software packages. Each year sees improvement in the capability of project management software packages as well as simple explanations of their use. Even those with no claim to expertise in the discipline are finding that their PCs, with the proper software, can assist them in defining, planning, and controlling the execution of either major or minor projects with a minimum of waste and a maximum of efficiency. Selecting the proper software from the plethora of available programs begins with understanding the needs. Thus, if only baseline planning is required, a program that does only planning may be appropriate. If control capabilities are needed, a program that tracks progress and compares to plan is more appropriate.

A recent useful, simple explanation of applying the PC to project management, and explaining two moderately-priced programs, *Advanced Pro-Path 6*, by SoftCorp, and *Time Line*, by Breakthrough Software, is contained in the April 1986 issue of *PC World*.[6]

SUGGESTED READING

Boccino, William A. *Management Information Systems, Tools and Techniques*, Chapter 10 (on PERT scheduling). Englewood Cliffs, N.J.: Prentice-Hall, Inc., 1972.

Brink, Victor Z., and Herbert Witt. *Modern Internal Auditing*, Chapter 27. New York: John Wiley & Sons, 1982.

PERT Coordinating Group (U.S. Department of Defense, NASA, etc.). *PERT Guide for Management Use*. Washington, D.C.: U.S. Government Printing Office, 1963.

Pomeranz, Felix, et al. *Auditing in the Public Sector*. New York: Warren, Gorham & Lamont, 1976.

Sweeny, H. W. Allen, and Robert Rachlin, eds. *Handbook of Budgeting*, Chapter 20. New York: John Wiley & Sons, 1981.

Willson, James D. *Budgeting and Profit Planning Manual*, 2nd ed. New York: Warren, Gorham & Lamont, 1988.

---

[6] See the project management section, *PC World*, Apr. 1986, pp. 144–169.

CHAPTER **37**

Marketing Management

Nature and Scope of the Marketing Function	1	Marketing Management Questionnaire	7
Marketing Objectives	2	Marketing Management Audit Program	14
The Marketing Organization Structure	4	Role of the Internal Auditor	19
Marketing Policies and Procedures	5	Using Computers in Marketing Management	20
Pricing Procedures and Controls	5		
Effectiveness of the Sales Effort	5		
Sales Planning	6	Suggested Reading	20
Performance Reports	6		

Fig. 37-1 Relation of Marketing Objectives, Strategies, and Results 8
Fig. 37-2 Marketing Management Audit Questionnaire 7
Fig. 37-3 Operations Audit Program—Marketing Management 14

NATURE AND SCOPE OF THE MARKETING FUNCTION

As used in this text, marketing is defined as those activities involved in the movement of goods and services from the manufacturer to the consumer. In another sense, it includes those functions which usually are the responsibility of the chief marketing executive.

The concept of the marketing function has changed substantially in the past three or four decades and has evolved beyond that of making a sale to encompass a broad range of activities which support the sales function. Indicative of the general matters that must be addressed by the chief marketing executive in an industrial company are these:

- □ *Marketing objectives.* What should be the marketing objectives? How should they relate to the corporate objectives?

- □ *Marketing strategy.* What should be the basic marketing strategy of the company be? What is the market target or segment? How can it best be reached?

- □ *Organization.* What is the most suitable organization structure? By product?

37-1

by function? By geographical area? By type of customer? And what is the proper relationship of one function to the other?

In more precise terms, the problems to be resolved by the marketing executive relate to such aspects as:

- *Product.* What products should be sold? Where? In what quantities? How many varieties? What quality vis-à-vis competitors?
- *Price.* What price is to be charged? Shall pricing policy be that of meeting any and all competitors? Will it differ in different territories? What should the terms of sale be? Should the company encourage installment selling? Shall a discount be granted for cash?
- *Methods of distribution.* Should the product be sold directly to the ultimate consumer, or through wholesalers? Retailers? Exactly what channels of distribution ought to be used? Should the company market in the entire U.S. or in just certain regions? In Europe? Worldwide?
- *Method of sale.* How should the product be sold—by personal call, catalog, or telephone call? To what extent should advertising be employed? Will sales promotional campaigns be useful—cents off coupons, free gift, etc.?
- *Personnel policies and practices.* How should salespersons be selected and trained? Shall compensation be part salary and part commission? To what extent should sales contests be used? What is the relative job ranking of the various positions?
- *Planning.* How shall the expected sales level for the next year be developed? To what extent should statistical techniques be used? How are individual territorial sales levels to be set? How will sales territories be established? How are allowable expense levels to be established? How is the extent of total advertising expense to be set? How far ahead should the company plan sales—5 years? 10 years? What are acceptable product margins?
- *Control.* What should be used as standards of performance measurements—the sales plan, the expense budget? Standards of individual performance? Costs to results measures? How should traveling expenses be controlled? How should warehousing expense be controlled? What control reports are needed?

The above comments have been made principally to emphasize to the auditor the broad span of the marketing function and the many considerations in carrying out an effective operation. Some are discussed in the context of operational auditing.

MARKETING OBJECTIVES

It will be observed that this section on operational audits usually deals with the functional objectives of any activity early in the chapter. It is quite apparent that the objectives should be known if an audit of the effectiveness

FIG. 37-1
Relation of Marketing Objectives, Strategies, and Results

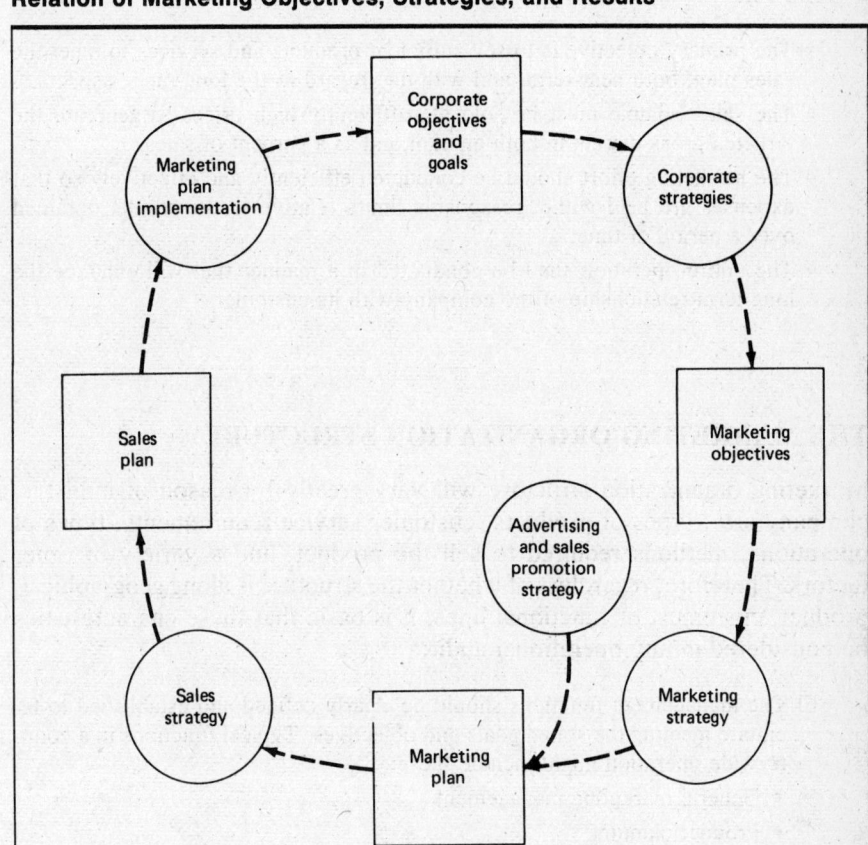

and efficiency with which the function is carried on is to be appraised. What, then, are or should be, the objectives of marketing management?

It will bear mentioning that the marketing objectives should be related to, and supportive of, the corporate objectives. Moreover, the marketing strategy should be the means of reaching the corporate purpose or mission. The relationship may be depicted as in Figure 37-1.

What the marketing objectives are for a particular company, and how they are expressed, will vary with the circumstances. It is not out of line to suggest, however, that marketing objectives should be supportive of the corporate objective (after satisfying customer needs) of earning an acceptable return on shareholders' equity. The overall marketing mission is to sell the desired sales volume at a reasonable price so as to produce adequate margins that provide the desired return on shareholders' equity. In somewhat more precise terms, the marketing objectives of many firms might be outlined as follows:

- The primary objective is to sell sufficient products and services to meet the sales plan, both near-term, and with due regard to the long-range aspects.
- The sales volume must be sold at sufficiently high prices to generate the targeted gross margin in both amount and as a percent of sales.
- The marketing effort should be conducted efficiently and effectively so that expenses are held within reasonable limits relative to the results obtained over a period of time.
- The entire operation shall be conducted in a manner that will enhance the long-term relationship of the company with its customers.

THE MARKETING ORGANIZATION STRUCTURE

Marketing organization structure will vary greatly by reason of industry, company size, types of products, customer service requirements, types of operations, methods required to sell the product, and a variety of other factors. Therefore, regardless of whether the structure is along geographical, product, customer, or functional lines, it is basic that these characteristics be considered in any operational audit:

- ☐ The management functions should be clearly defined and established to facilitate meeting the stated goals and objectives. Typical functions in a countrywide operation might include these:
  - General marketing management
  - Product planning
  - Direct sales operations
  - Advertising and sales promotion
  - Warehousing and storage
  - Transportation (outbound)
  - Market research
  - Customer relations or services
- ☐ The functional outline should be such that the necessary coordination is achieved with other major disciplines that work closely with marketing:
  - Manufacturing
  - Credit
  - Product research
  - Engineering
- ☐ There should exist adequate supervision and staffing to facilitate the carrying out of assigned duties, and enforcement of necessary coordination.
- ☐ The authority delegated to the marketing executives should be sufficient to carry out their responsibilities, but not such as to override the authority

assigned to related functions, e.g., product design, facilities management, accounts payable, and credit.

Review of the organization charts, functional outlines, position descriptions, and policy and procedures manuals should provide a good sense of how the operations should function. A review of the operations and related evidence will show whether or not it does so function.

MARKETING POLICIES AND PROCEDURES

While it is not within the scope of this volume to review all aspects of marketing operations, there are a number of critical procedures that must be closely monitored because of the impact on margins and earnings and the general effectiveness of the functions. Some of the more important areas to be considered in an operational audit are outlined below.

Pricing Procedures and Controls

The methods for setting prices should be formally established, clearly stated, and understood by (1) the general management, (2) those who are concerned with product profitability, and (3) those who deal with the customer on pricing matters.

Care should be taken as to who approves prices, and consideration given to such matters as:

- Contribution margin
- Variable costs
- The cost-volume-profit relationship

Finance concurrence should be considered in determining pricing policies and procedures by reason of the importance of relevant costs and total costs.

Effectiveness of the Sales Effort

Subjects to be covered could include these:

- Extent to which sales effort is directed according to the sales potential
- Degree to which the more profitable products are emphasized
- Whether sales results are measured against some standards, such as sales and gross margin per call and gross margin per dollar of direct selling expense
- Degree to which top marketing executives supervise first line managers and sales persons

- The reporting required; the degree of contact (and encouragement)
- Methods of motivating the sales person
- Methods of selecting sales people
- Extent or degree of training versus the difficulty of the selling task
- Quality of the distribution segments or customers (e.g., wholesalers, retailers, and agents)

Sales Planning

Sales planning would include:

- The method of developing the plan
- Degree of coordination between sales, finished goods inventory levels, and manufacturing both as to the original annual plan and any necessary revisions

Performance Reports

Reports on actual and planned performance and related marketing information include:

- Comparisons of budgeted and actual sales volume
- Most profitable combinations of market effort, product sales, and costs
- Gross margin analysis
- Distribution cost analysis
- Budgeted and actual marketing expenses
- Market share studies
- Competitive activity
- Sales calls and results
- Measurement of sales results by, for example, appropriate organizational segment and product line
- Impact of advertising and sales promotional efforts
- Sales force deployment and effectiveness studies
- Market potentials

Every effort should be made to detect those factors that are crucial to a successful marketing effort for the company (sources include talking with the top sales executives, reading the training manuals), and incorporate them in the questionnaire, which will be used to develop the audit program. An auditor with an extensive marketing background, or an experienced member of the marketing staff might be especially useful in helping to develop the audit program.

MARKETING MANAGEMENT QUESTIONNAIRE

Figure 37-2 is a questionnaire developed for an operational review of the marketing function for an appliance manufacturer with a nationwide distribution system and affiliates in both Canada and Great Britain (the international segment).

(continued on page 37-14)

FIG. 37-2
Marketing Management Audit Questionnaire

The following questionnaire is to be used in evaluating the operational effectiveness of both the corporate marketing organization, the international organization, and the division marketing groups.

The questionnaire contains core questions. However, because of differences in operations between the newer divisions and the original organization, facets may be added which are especially germane to the declining share of market in the Mid-west and East. You are asked to be alert to any practical suggestions for improvement that might be useful to the sales management. The major deterioration in margins requires special care regarding price setting procedures for the private brand business.

	Yes	No	Reference
A. General:			
1. Is there a formal written policy regarding:			
a. The company marketing objectives?	☐	☐	....
b. Date of the latest revision:			
c. Marketing strategy	☐	☐	....
2. Do formal functional outlines and job descriptions exist for:			
a. Marketing vice-presidents	☐	☐	....
b. Directors	☐	☐	....
c. Managers	☐	☐	....
d. Salespersons	☐	☐	....
e. Are they current?	☐	☐	....
3. Is there an organization chart for the marketing function?	☐	☐	....
Date of latest issue:			
a. Is the relationship between the corporate staff and division staff clearly spelled out?	☐	☐	....

(continued)

FIG. 37-2 *(cont'd)*

	Yes	No	Reference
4. Do policy and procedures manuals exist for all major functions, including such matters as:			
a. Pricing policy	☐	☐	....
b. Method of setting prices	☐	☐	....
c. Terms of sale	☐	☐	....
d. Sales planning	☐	☐	....
e. Expense planning	☐	☐	....
f. Advertising policy	☐	☐	....
g. Sales promotion policy	☐	☐	....
h. Product policies	☐	☐	....
i. Direct selling policies	☐	☐	....
j. Marketing information	☐	☐	....
k. Returns	☐	☐	....
B. Organization:			
1. Are all positions of director and above filled?	☐	☐	....
2. Does an up-to-date executive inventory exist?	☐	☐	....
3. Are there back-ups for all executive positions?	☐	☐	....
4. Based on latest job evaluations, are all positions properly classified and related to each other?	☐	☐	....
5. Are comparable positions at the division, corporate offices, and international group evaluated using the same yardstick?	☐	☐	....
C. Strategy:			
1. Has product/marketing strategy been put into writing?	☐	☐	....
2. Does the strategy take into account recent competitive actions re: market share?	☐	☐	....
3. Has the corporate marketing group reviewed the division/international strategy?	☐	☐	....
a. Do they agree?	☐	☐	....
4. Is the strategy compatible with the organization objectives?	☐	☐	....
5. Have industry data and recent intelligence findings been taken into account?	☐	☐	....

	Yes	No	Reference

D. Products:

1. Has each of the following product lines been modified to reflect recent federal energy standards:
   a. Water heaters ☐ ☐ ....
   b. Gas furnaces ☐ ☐ ....
   c. Air-conditioners ☐ ☐ ....

2. In appearance, are the products fully competitive? ☐ ☐ ....

3. Has sales force been briefed in detail on innovations and other changes? ☐ ☐ ....

4. Has there been reasonable coordination between product development and:
   a. Direct selling ☐ ☐ ....
   b. Manufacturing ☐ ☐ ....
   c. Finance ☐ ☐ ....

5. Have the apparently excessive number of sizes and styles been consolidated? ☐ ☐ ....

6. Are sizes of the following products the same as competitors:
   a. Water heaters ☐ ☐ ....
   b. Gas furnaces ☐ ☐ ....
   c. Air-conditioners ☐ ☐ ....

7. Is product performance reported to be as high, or higher than competitors for:
   a. Water heaters ☐ ☐ ....
   b. Gas furnaces ☐ ☐ ....
   c. Air-conditioners ☐ ☐ ....

8. Is warranty fully competitive for:
   a. Water heaters ☐ ☐ ....
   b. Gas furnaces ☐ ☐ ....
   c. Air-conditioners ☐ ☐ ....

9. What is the trend in warranty expense over the past three years? ☐ ☐ ....

E. Direct Selling:

1. Are all territories up to full complement? ☐ ☐ ....

2. Do the field offices seem properly located vis-à-vis the customer? ☐ ☐ ....

(continued)

FIG. 37-2 *(cont'd)*

	Yes	No	Reference
3. Are salespersons fully conversant with the products and recent changes?	☐	☐	....
4. Do the salespersons seem optimistic and motivated?	☐	☐	....
5. Have there been any attempts by salespersons to secure special prices or terms?	☐	☐	....
6. Have orders been filled promptly?	☐	☐	....
7. Have any stock outages been reported?	☐	☐	....
8. Are call reports being analyzed promptly?	☐	☐	....
Are the standards being met?	☐	☐	....
9. Is there evidence of emphasis on the upper ends of the lines?	☐	☐	....
10. Is there customer information interchange for the different product lines?	☐	☐	....
11. Have salesperson routes and/or locations been changed to minimize travel time?	☐	☐	....
12. Are there any reports of distributor noncompliance with pricing and delivery instructions?	☐	☐	....
13. Have any complaints on customer service been received?	☐	☐	....
a. Were they investigated?	☐	☐	....
14. Have the recent packaging changes reduced damage?	☐	☐	....
15. Have returns been reduced?	☐	☐	....
16. Are product deliveries timely?	☐	☐	....
17. Have any significant questions been raised about sales quotas?	☐	☐	....
F. Pricing:			
1. Are f.o.b. prices on the following products fully competitive:			
a. Water heaters	☐	☐	....
b. Gas furnaces	☐	☐	....
c. Air-conditioners	☐	☐	....

	Yes	No	Reference

2. Have regular prices been set to cover all costs and a 30% gross margin minimum? ☐ ☐ ....

3. Do all private brand product prices provide recovery of all direct costs and all manufacturing overhead? ☐ ☐ ....

4. Have discounts and allowances been heavier than last year for:
   a. Water heaters ☐ ☐ ....
   b. Gas furnaces ☐ ☐ ....
   c. Air-conditioners ☐ ☐ ....

5. Have recent quantity discount schedules been put into effect? ☐ ☐ ....
   a. Are they producing results? ☐ ☐ ....

6. Are sales terms essentially competitive for:
   a. Water heaters ☐ ☐ ....
   b. Gas furnaces ☐ ☐ ....
   c. Air-conditioners ☐ ☐ ....

7. Are special campaigns on accessories effective? ☐ ☐ ....

8. Are price changes in the following product lines ahead of the competition's:
   a. Water heaters ☐ ☐ ....
   b. Gas furnaces ☐ ☐ ....
   c. Air-conditioners ☐ ☐ ....

9. Is it practical to introduce seasonal discounts on furnaces and air-conditioners? ☐ ☐ ....

G. Sales and Expense Planning:

1. Has the chief marketing executive reviewed sales plan for 19XX as to each:
   a. Product line ☐ ☐ ....
   b. Territory ☐ ☐ ....
   c. Salesperson ☐ ☐ ....

2. Was any segment of the sales plan reduced by reason of competitive actions? ☐ ☐ ....

3. Were the extrapolations of industry sales:
   a. Increased where we have dominant market share ☐ ☐ ....

(continued)

FIG. 37-2 *(cont'd)*

	Yes	No	Reference
b. Decreased because of local economic conditions Where?	☐	☐	....
4. Was emphasis deliberately placed on higher margin items?	☐	☐	....
5. Were all territorial plans increased in line with the new sales potential figures?	☐	☐	....
6. Were the sales presentations and tactics of all below-plan salespersons reviewed?	☐	☐	....
a. Were any sales plan adjustments made?	☐	☐	....
7. Were product and territory gross margin analyses used in developing the sales plan?	☐	☐	....
8. Was the last total sales plan judged reasonable by the managers?	☐	☐	....
9. Were there any salespersons who judged their plan was:			
a. Too high	☐	☐	....
b. Too low	☐	☐	....
10. Were the planned or budgeted sales expenses related to the planned sales?	☐	☐	....
11. Were budgeted expenses checked against any performance standards?	☐	☐	....
H. Advertising and Sales Promotions:			
1. Do the salespersons feel the advertising and sales promotion support was adequate?	☐	☐	....
2. Was the effort sufficiently coordinated with the sales staff?	☐	☐	....
3. Was the effort related to the expected sales:			
a. For all products	☐	☐	....
b. In each territory	☐	☐	....
4. Was provision made for evaluation of the results of each ad or campaign?	☐	☐	....
5. Was the liaison between the agency and the company sufficient?	☐	☐	....
6. Were company sales promotion efforts as extensive as the competition's?	☐	☐	....

MARKETING MANAGEMENT

	Yes	No	Reference

7. Was the timing of the promotional efforts correct for all markets? ☐ ☐ ....

I. Controls:

1. Were budget reports issued for:
   a. All activities ☐ ☐ ....
   b. Sales territories ☐ ☐ ....
   c. Field offices ☐ ☐ ....
   d. Salespersons ☐ ☐ ....
   e. Advertising and sales promotions ☐ ☐ ....
   f. Product planning ☐ ☐ ....

2. Was any action taken on the basis of the reports? ☐ ☐ ....

3. Were any list prices arbitrarily adjusted by salespersons? ☐ ☐ ....

4. Did any salesperson or manager override the credit office? ☐ ☐ ....

5. Were the private brand contracts reviewed by the chief sales executive? ☐ ☐ ....

6. Were all expense reports approved by the supervisor? ☐ ☐ ....
   Or by the secretary (on his behalf)? ☐ ☐ ....

7. Were all special allowances above $1,000 approved by the senior sales executive? ☐ ☐ ....

8. Were all returned goods returned to point of origin? ☐ ☐ ....

9. Were all sales orders reviewed by a supervisor? ☐ ☐ ....

10. Were all remittances forwarded to the treasurer's office? ☐ ☐ ....

11. Were all project cost reports updated to reflect the latest indicated final cost? ☐ ☐ ....

12. Were all entertainment claims supported by original invoices or receipts? ☐ ☐ ....

13. Were all shipments billed? ☐ ☐ ....

14. Were there any delayed billings? ☐ ☐ ....

15. Did any aggregate sales allowances, by salesperson, seem out of line? ☐ ☐ ....

The marketing management questionnaire was developed to provide a sort of *overall* review of the management of the function. Of course, any questionnaire should be structured to cover the essential facets of the function, which comes about only by knowing (1) how the operation should be directed, (2) a reasonable amount about competitive activity, and (3) what the important success factors are. Under some circumstances, each of the separate functions might be served by an in-depth review of its various aspects. While a questionnaire should be prepared on a specific case basis, some ideas might be gleaned from questionnaires and audit programs in, for example, *Internal Audit Alert*. Functions or aspects that might profit from an operational review include these segments:

- ☐ Advertising
- ☐ Distribution (physical)
- ☐ Market research
- ☐ Sales compensation methods
- ☐ Sales methods
- ☐ Sales person routing
- ☐ Sales training

MARKETING MANAGEMENT AUDIT PROGRAM

Obviously, an operational audit program should reflect the answers given to an audit questionnaire, and should be tailored to fit the needs of the particular case. In part, it should be based on the auditors knowledge of the marketing function and the suspected points of weakness in the system. The objective of an operations audit should be (1) to verify the responses to the operations audit questionnaire and (2) to seek improvements. A *partial audit* program for the appliance manufacturer, which was the object of the marketing management audit questionnaire in Figure 37-2, is presented in Figure 37-3.

(continued on page 37-19)

FIG. 37-3

Operations Audit Program—Marketing Management

> The purpose of this review is to evaluate the efficiency and effectiveness of the marketing operation. Emphasis is changed annually depending in part on the events which have transpired since the last audit.
>
> You should feel free to expand the scope of the review if significant improvement areas seem to exist, or if your review discloses inefficiencies not evident from the questionnaire.

	Workpaper Reference	Done by

1. General:

☐ Obtain a copy of the latest organization chart and do the following:
- Note revision date ....
- Note any vacancies ....
- Check for conformance to the "standard" organization ....
- Verify that it in fact represents the reporting relationship ....

☐ Obtain the functional outlines for all positions of director and above, and:
- Check the completeness of the group ....
- Test-check two or three outlines with the incumbent to ascertain that he performs the functions stipulated, and review evidence ....
- Cross-check against other functions ....
- Check the dates of the revisions ....
- Note the approvals and review signatures ....
- With respect to the coordination with the division and international marketing activities, check on both ends of the organization for the extent, and degree of receptivity, of the "suggestions" ....

☐ Secure the various systems and procedures manuals, and, on a test basis, when checking the activity or function:
- Verify that key procedures are being followed ....
- Note revision dates ....
- Check operation of key control points ....

☐ During the course of the audit, tour the facility and note especially:
- The attitude of the staff ....
- Apparent knowledge possessed by staff of their jobs, the product, and of the marketing and sales promotion effort ....
- The general tidiness of the facility ....

2. Product Pricing:

☐ Obtain the most recent price lists, and select two models from each product line for testing — preferably the high volume items. ....

☐ Secure the product cost sheets and other documents used to establish the prices for the above items, and do the following:
- Compare the list price, and net to the company, with the direct costs and total costs, and extent of mark-up over each ....

(continued)

FIG. 37-3 *(cont'd)*

	Workpaper Reference	Done by
■ Note the approvals	....	....
■ Check for changes in costs from the start of the year, and correspondingly proper price changes	....	....
■ Evaluate the pricing procedure	....	....
■ Check the unit costs per the cost sheets to the costs used to determine the latest monthly income statement and account for any differences	....	....
■ On a test basis, check the support for the costs, with emphasis on direct labor and direct material	....	....
☐ On a limited test basis compare company list prices with those of the competition.	....	....
☐ Test-check some customer invoices throughout the year, but especially for the month of July, against the list prices.	....	....
☐ Review credit memos for returns and allowances to:		
■ Ascertain the approvals	....	....
■ Detect any pattern of excessive allowances (in view of low gross margins) to particular customers, or by a particular salesperson	....	....
☐ Review credit memos for spare parts.	....	....
☐ Select one or two private brand contracts and:		
■ Verify how prices were set	....	....
■ Test-check prices and terms shown on invoices of sale to the contract	....	....
■ Review cost changes vs. price changes allowed in the contract	....	....
■ Note contract approvals	....	....
☐ On a spot-check basis, compare prices being received with those used in the sales plan.	....	....
☐ Evaluate the procedure as to use of unit prices in the planning process.	....	....
3. Planning:		
☐ Secure the supporting documents for the annual sales plan, and, with any related support, do the following:		
■ Check for conformance to the written practices manual	....	....
■ On a test-check basis, by territory:		
a. Compare the sales plan with the market potential	....	....
b. With share of market anticipated	....	....
c. Check reasonableness of change from prior year	....	....
d. On a limited basis, compare the realized gross margin with the planned gross margin and account for the difference	....	....

MARKETING MANAGEMENT

	Workpaper Reference	Done by

- ☐ Evaluate the sales and expense planning procedure:
  - Is the plan "tight enough" to require real effort ....
  - To what extent are the views of the salesperson accepted as to his plan ....
  - How much above the plan is the sales quota for selected sales persons ....
- ☐ Comment on the extent of supervisory review of the underlying sales plans, including:
  - Supporting analyses used ....
  - Marketing intelligence supplied ....
  - Extent of changes made in the plans submitted by the regional offices, and why ....
  - Comparison of company sales trends with industry data for selected territories ....
  - Impact of inflation ....
  - Method of relating advertising and sales promotion efforts to the salesperson ....
- ☐ Review the supporting data for planned marketing expense, and comment:
  - How levels were determined ....
  - What tests of expenses were made as related to results ....
  - Extent of assistance by the marketing accounting group ....
  - Method of determining advertising budget ....
  - How allowable or budgeted expenses compare, as related to sales volume and gross margin:
    - a. For varying sales persons ....
    - b. For field offices ....
    - c. To the extent determinable, with competition ....

4. **Direct Selling Activity:**

- ☐ Secure the following documents for two or three salespersons in each territory:
  - Actual and budgeted sales report ....
  - Call reports ....
  - Expense reports ....

  Ascertain the extent of supervisor review, and corrective action taken or suggestions given on the above items. ....

- ☐ Evaluate the extent of supervision over individual sales staff and field offices. ....

- ☐ Provide your comments on the following sales personnel matters:
  - Qualifications for recruits ....

(continued)

FIG. 37-3 *(cont'd)*

	Workpaper Reference	Done by
■ Source of recruits	....	....
■ Degree or extent of training	....	....
■ Apparent knowledge of products by salesperson	....	....
■ General appearance of sales staff	....	....
■ Motivation levels	....	....
■ Effectiveness of compensation methods	....	....
■ Extent of authority levels in handling customer complaints	....	....
☐ Evaluate the adequacy of field service representatives by reference to service reports and discussion with distributors.	....	....
☐ Comment on the guidance given the field representatives in coordinating the advertising and sales promotion efforts with the individual planned selling effort.	....	....
5. Controls, etc.:		
☐ Evaluate the adherence to policies and procedures as to all control points, specifically:		
■ Prices charged	....	....
■ Quantities shipped	....	....
■ Price or other adjustments	....	....
■ All material and services purchases (e.g., advertising media, space)	....	....
■ Salary approvals	....	....
■ Expense reports	....	....
■ Conformance to applicable state and federal laws and regulations	....	....
■ Remittances to treasury	....	....
☐ Provide your general impressions as to the following:		
■ Adequacy of records to carry out functions	....	....
■ Suitability of control reports	....	....
■ General appearance of facilities	....	....
■ Competence of personnel	....	....
■ Adequacy of staff members	....	....
■ General morale	....	....
■ Comparability location, and suitability of facilities vs. competition	....	....
■ Simplicity of procedures	....	....
■ Attractiveness and use of displays in:		
a. Distributor facilities	....	....
b. Field offices	....	....
■ Effectiveness of the biweekly sales meetings and individual conferences as to:		

	Workpaper Reference	Done by
a. Increasing the number of calls	....	....
b. Selectivity of calls on more likely high volume customers	....	....
c. Coverage of product features	....	....
d. Motivational techniques	....	....
It is suggested each auditor attend at least two meetings.		

ROLE OF THE INTERNAL AUDITOR

Given the complexity of the marketing function and the areas of subjective and creative judgment involving customers and selling methods, there might appear to be little that the internal auditor can do in the way of operational auditing in the marketing area. In this function, in particular, the auditor must be sensitive to the areas where he does not possess the required expertise. On the other hand, marketing is a key activity in most companies, and there are many facets the auditor can check. Moreover, he can be a conduit in providing information on highly effective activities used in one area that might be employed in another. All reasonable assistance should be provided to marketing management to make it an even more effective function.

Chapter 31 discusses several levels of operational or management auditing, and this information can be drawn on as to the marketing activities.

Certainly, the internal auditor can check out the financial controls in the marketing function; and top management should expect this. This might be called the usual financial audit.

Within the marketing operation, there are a vast number of procedures, many routine, wherein the actual method should be monitored or reviewed as compared with the prescribed system set forth in the policy and procedures manual. Emphasis in such a review is to assure that the specific transactions are conducted efficiently and effectively. This is a so-called operational audit—shall we say of the first echelon. Normally, a reasonable auditor should be able to provide assurances to the management as to conformance to procedures or to suggest improved procedures. There should be little problem at this stage.

The next level of review has been described by some as management auditing, and extends into a review of planning and controlling methods and strategy. A certain amount of subjective judgment comes into play. Wisdom and experience enter the picture when judging policy or reviewing objectives and strategy. It is an arena where any auditor must exercise extraordinary care in reaching conclusions. Nevertheless, there are enough procedural aspects that the auditor can provide detached and objective observations that may assist company management.

If the approach to the problem is sound and nonoffensive, and if the internal auditor's personal relations are acceptable, then he should be in a position to render a limited service to management in this key area.

USING COMPUTERS IN MARKETING MANAGEMENT

In the final analysis, the vice-president—marketing is a business manager. To be sure, he must select competent staff and motivate them. In turn, the sales manager, advertising manager, or another manager must do the same. But basically, he is a manager of territories or districts, channels of distribution, products, methods of sale, and accounts. It is his task to assist in increasing the return on assets employed in the business.

To this end, marketing strategies must be developed and tested. Alternatives must be considered and evaluated. The new small microcomputer can be of significant value in an overall marketing strategy. There are numerous software programs marketing executives can use in such evaluations. Most readers are familiar with "electronic spreadsheets." Visi Calc, Super Calc, and Lotus 1-2-3, among others are available and easy to use. The marketing executives should have programs and basic data available (with adequate safeguards to see that they know how to use the figures) to consider the many problems faced in the marketing function. Many "what if" games can be played to determine the impact of alternative actions. Some of the possible applications include:

- Improving the product mix.
- Analyzing the sales potential of customers and territories.
- Checking excessive costs such as freight or delivery expense.
- Analyzing sales performance of individual men (e.g., sales mix, relative costs, and number of calls).

One major advantage of the microcomputer is the ease by which new assumptions or factors, such as rates of growth, can be inputed with a quick, automatic revision of all element figures.

The internal auditor should be familiar with computer applications in the marketing field, ascertain if the techniques are being used properly by marketing management, and be ready to assist.[1]

SUGGESTED READING

Davis, Kenneth R. *Marketing Management*. New York: The Ronald Press Co., 1981.

---

[1] For some illustrative applications, see G. David Hughes, "Computerized Sales Management," *Harvard Business Review*, Mar./Apr. 1983, pp. 102–112.

CHAPTER **38**

Information Systems Management

Overview 2	Negligent or Ineffective I/S
Information Systems and Its	Management 17
Management 2	Computer Dependence 17
Definitions 4	Proliferation of Mini- and
EDP Evolution: Impact on the	Microcomputers 18
Marketplace 4	
	Organizing and Managing the ISM
Expanding Role of ISM 5	**Function** 23
Technology Environment 7	Planning 23
User Environment 8	Auditing ISM Planning Functions 26
EDP Auditing Environment 9	Organizing 28
A Perspective 9	Auditing the Organizing Process 28
	Staffing 29
Nature of the ISM Functions 9	Auditing ISM Staffing 31
Business Within a Business 10	Controlling 31
Service Orientation 10	Controlling Access—The Key 32
Dynamic Environment 11	Auditing the Controlling Function 34
Scarcity of Resources 12	
Interface Challenges 12	**The Auditor's Role and Objectives** 34
ISM Objectives 13	**Audit Techniques** 35
Basic Mission 13	How to Maintain an I/S Audit
Supplemental Objectives 14	Function 35
	Techniques 35
Risks and Concerns 15	I/S Auditing Tools 36
Computer Fraud and Mischievous	
Acts 15	**Suggested Reading** 65
Violations of Laws and Regulations 16	

Fig. 38-1	Phases of I/S Organizational Growth	3
Fig. 38-2	Data Processing Evolution	6
Fig. 38-3	Survey Form for Microcomputer Usage	19
Fig. 38-4	Segment of a Strategic ISM Plan	25
Fig. 38-5	Excerpt From a Tactical ISM Plan	26
Fig. 38-6	Example of a Portion of a System Development Plan	27
Fig. 38-7	Example of a Simple Organization Structure	29
Fig. 38-8	A Typical Roster of Job Positions	30
Fig. 38-9	A List of Functional Areas for Operational Auditing	34
Fig. 38-10	ISM Questionnaire	38

Fig. 38-11 ISM Audit Program 55
Fig. 38-12 ISM Audit Report 64

OVERVIEW

Information Systems and Its Management

In Chapter 26, there is a discussion of information systems (I/S) and internal control. That chapter focuses on orienting the reader to a basic understanding of I/S, control objectives, and techniques by which information may be processed accurately and completely. The modern I/S organization is a complex mixture (1) of sophisticated electronic devices widely dispersed throughout the company; (2) of an extensive concentration of stored programs and data; and (3) involving a sizeable staff of highly technical personnel. However, the discussion is restricted for the most part to internal control and security considerations. The primary concern of Chapter 26 is the control techniques necessary to enable the processing of data accurately and completely with due regard for security and protection.

This chapter discusses I/S in an operational sense, that is, the overall management of information as a resource. This discussion provides the auditor with the proper perspective to perform useful operational audits of the function.

In many companies, I/S responsibility is delegated to a specific department or group. The following illustrate some of the names by which the function is known:

- Data processing (DP)
- Information systems (I/S)
- Data management (DM)
- Information systems management (ISM)
- Business systems management (BSM)
- Information resource management (IRM)

Whatever its name, the span of control exercised by the I/S organization varies considerably among companies, depending on the length of time the organization has been in existence, the degree of recognition by company management, the size of the operation, and certain other factors. It has been stated that the overall approach or structure to managing information contains five phases, as depicted in Figure 38-1.[1]

These phases suggest that, as growth occurs in I/S activities within a

---

[1] International Business Machines, *Organizing the I/S Business* (White Plains, New York: IBM, 1983), p. 20.

FIG. 38-1
Phases of I/S Organizational Growth

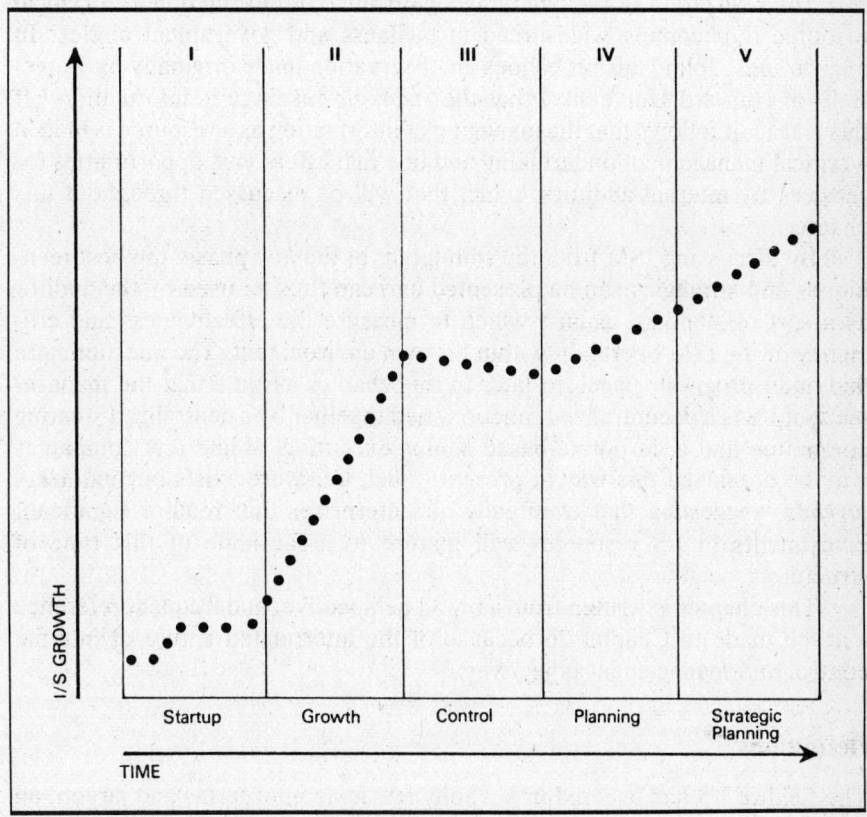

company, the structure changes from the simple processing of data (Phase I) to strategic managing of the related resources (Phase V). It reflects the fact that after an EDP capability is installed, a period of rapid growth follows, during which the challenge to management is to meet the sharply increasing demand for EDP services. This usually involves considerable activity in new systems development, added hardware configurations, operating system conversions, and staff expansion.

This phase is followed by the need to respond to user complaints of poor response time for existing applications, excessive errors and computer malfunctions, and delays in developing new systems. Thus, the importance of control becomes paramount.

In the latter phases, management begins to realize that the investment in resources required to process information is considerable and must be managed in much the same way as are other significant investments, such as those in capital facilities and inventory. This recognition is followed by integrating the DM into the functional organization, most notably at the planning level.

The realization of the emerging significance of information as a critical resource is becoming widespread in business and government circles. In *Megatrends*, John Naisbitt echoes an observation made originally by Daniel Bell, of Harvard University, that the *strategic* resource is information.[2] If this is true, it follows that the managing of information as a resource is indeed a critical management undertaking and one that offers vast opportunities for services by internal auditors, a fact that will be discussed throughout this chapter.

By discussing ISM from the standpoint of the *last* phase, the best techniques and strategies can be presented and can thus be used by the auditor as a sort of standard against which to measure the effectiveness and efficiency of the ISM operation within his own environment. The questionnaire and audit program suggested later in this chapter assume that the management of I/S is a decentralized function, tied together by a centralized steering committee and a corporate-based senior executive. While few companies may be organized this way at present, much literature exists beyond *Megatrends*, suggesting that eventually all enterprises that require significant investments in I/S resources will mature to a facsimile of this type of structure.

This chapter is written from a broad perspective, and frequent reference may be made to Chapter 26 because of the interrelated nature of internal control and management objectives.

Definitions

The field of I/S has ushered in a whole new lexicon of terms and jargon, an extensive list of which is provided at the end of Chapter 26. Similar glossaries can be found in other reference sources. As change occurs, new terms emerge requiring definition, which is the case with ISM. This phrase has been in use for the past few years; however, it has yet to be specifically defined in authoritative literature. ISM is defined here as the process by which the investment in facilities, equipment, systems, and people are organized, planned, controlled, and operated.

EDP Evolution: Impact on the Marketplace

Since the advent of computers in the 1940s, environmental and technological changes, occurring with seemingly increasing rapidity, have spawned a veritable revolution. Some believe it to be as significant as the industrial revolution. Not only have computers become indispensable to business, but they are becoming as commonplace in the home as the television set.

---

[2] John Naisbitt, *Megatrends* (New York: Warner Books, 1982), p. 15.

The management of computer resources has become a significant and substantial management discipline. It is, in effect, a business within a business, covering the resources and methods whereby data is created, filed, processed, distributed, used, and eventually destroyed.

Before computers were available, each function within a business managed the data it needed by itself, as a necessary means to accomplish objectives. The automation of DP required establishing a new function to perform the DM task as a service to the other functions. This was necessary primarily because the technology demanded skills not possessed by other groups. Thus, EDP departments emerged as service organizations to other user organizations within the company, eventually becoming the ISM organizations of today. Some companies are served by one or more massive centralized ISM functions; others are more decentralized, both organizationally and operationally; still others are served by combinations of these approaches.

The EDP evolution has ushered in new and different risks and concerns with which management and auditors must deal. Today, most businesses are heavily dependent on automated I/S and communication networks to conduct operations. This dependence means that errors, omissions, inefficiencies, and interruptions occurring in ISM departments can have serious consequences for the user organizations and the company, even to the point of halting business.

In addition to describing these risks, this chapter defines ISM objectives and examines the means by which ISM objectives are accomplished. Finally, it provides specimen audit tools in the form of a questionnaire, audit program, and report, which offer specific guidance in performing an operational audit of an ISM function.

Most small- or medium-sized ISM departments may be audited from an operational standpoint in a single comprehensive examination by using the tools described in this chapter. Many others, because of their larger size, may be effectively audited only by a continuous program of detailed operational audits of selected segments. This is done by following the techniques outlined in Chapter 27 for establishing I/S audit project priorities.

EXPANDING ROLE OF ISM

Discussing the expanding role of ISM requires discussing the history of DP. However, detailed historical presentation is beyond the purpose of this book. Rather, the commentary is limited only to that needed to make the point that managing EDP resources in the early years of its evolution was comparatively simple. But as growth and technological change expanded the resources under the control and responsibility of the EDP manager, effective management became quite complex. Figure 38-2 displays a composite summary of some of the key events that have paced EDP growth and techno-

FIG. 38-2
Data Processing Evolution

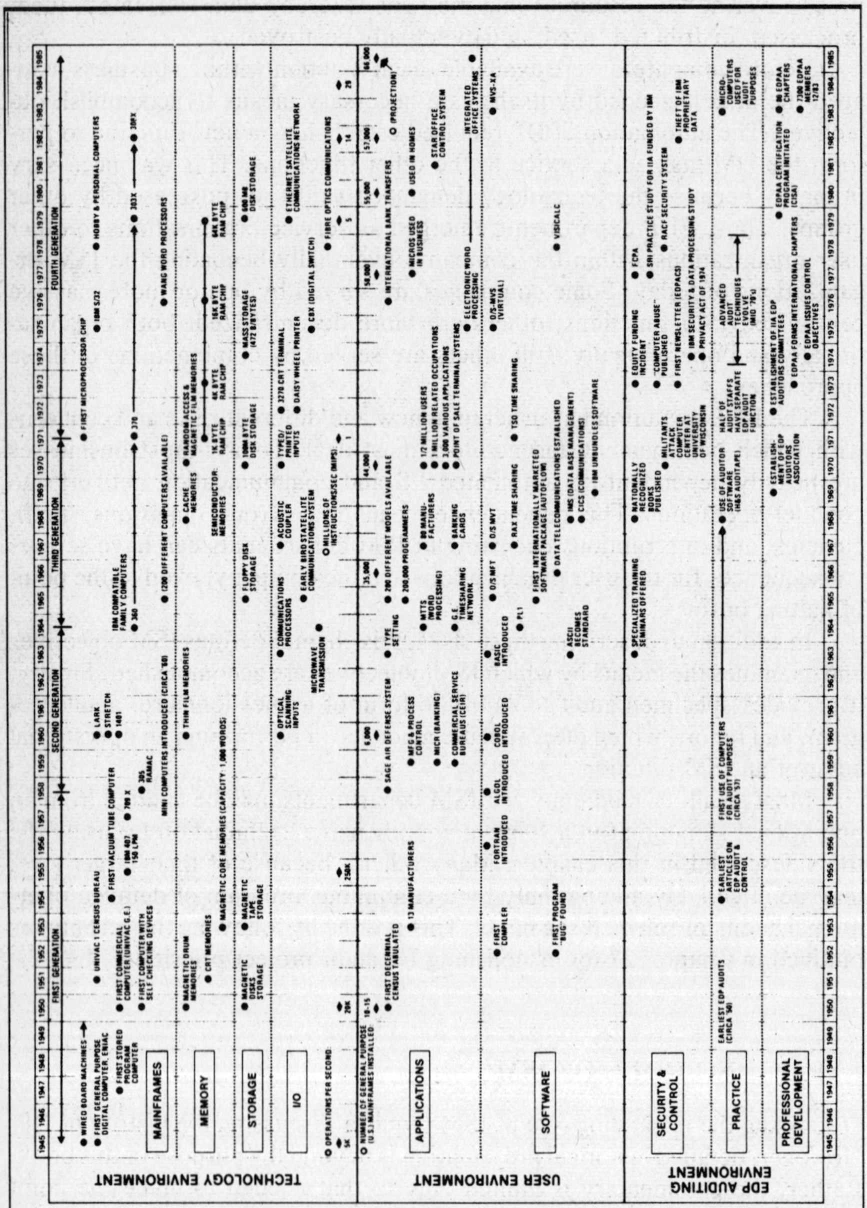

logical change since the first computers were put into use some 40 years ago.

Events are classified in Figure 38-2 by three broad environments: Technology Environment, User Environment and EDP Auditing Environment with subcategories for each of the three. The dates in which events are depicted are approximate. Also included in the figure are estimates of the number of computers in service at selected points in time and the approximate number of instructions per second computers could perform at various historical dates. It is clear that the period following the modest beginning of the computer age is crowded with events of evolutionary consequence. The following paragraphs discuss these according to the environments in which they are presented in Figure 38-2.

Technology Environment

The technology environment includes developments applicable to mainframe computers, memory and storage advances, and input/output or communication-related events.

Mainframe development began with the first general-purpose digital computer, ENIAC, which also probably initiated the EDP community's unbreakable penchant for acronyms. ENIAC stands for Electronic Numerical Integrator and Computer. It could perform 5,000 instructions per second—a marvel at the time.

Developments progressed rapidly in commercial applications, beginning with the introduction of UNIVAC in 1950. Soon a fledgeling company with the novel name of IBM began to gain market attention with its business machine products—notably the Model 407. It was not long before this company grew to a position of dominance within the new industry. It pioneered and capitalized on such developments as transistorized computers and, later, computers based on integrated circuit designs (i.e., chip technology). IBM's dominance did not occur by virtue of exploiting technological advances alone. It gained that position as a result of keen strategic management, innovative manufacturing capability enabling it to mass produce highly technical devices, and superior marketing ability and financial wizardry. Many EDP organizations began to become known as IBM shops, a loyalty forged by the successful formula IBM employed in growing into one of the largest corporations in the world. To be fair, other mainframe manufacturers, such as Sperry Corp., Burroughs (now combined as Unisys), Honeywell, NCR, and Control Data made their share of contributions. However, most observers agree that the history of the computer and its application to business use is the history of IBM.

Technological developments in the memory and storage categories started with magnetic drum memories. The eventual advent of other storage technologies, such as magnetic tape and disks, have greatly expanded the amount of information that can be stored in a centralized DP facility to nearly unbelievable proportions. It is not unusual for these centers to store billions of bytes of information in neat rows of disk drives and tape drives.

Developments in ways information is submitted to and received from computers also occurred in dramatic fashion. In the earliest days, information had to be carefully prepared on input forms, which would be bundled in batches and hand carried or mailed to the central computer for keypunching and processing. Hard copy reports were then sent back after processing. For large computer centers, this required considerable investment in keypunch equipment, operators, and printing devices. Printing and report distribution became a chronic bottleneck in DP. Improvements in printing technology led to increases in printing speeds by powers of 10 in short periods of time. Still, the demand for information and computing speeds were increasing faster. Also, new ways to speed the submission of data and make it more efficient and less error prone were occurring. These included remote job entry via RJE terminals located in or near user areas. Telecommunications developments made it possible to convert digital data into analog data for transmission over telephone lines to central processing areas. Devices there converted the data back to digital data for processing purposes. The speed with which data could be transmitted over telephone lines then became the bottleneck. New ways to minimize the problem involved microwave transmission, satellites, and now, fiber optics.

User Environment

Paralleling, but trailing somewhat the technological hardware developments, were those directly and indirectly involving EDP users. These developments are categorized here as applications and software. It could be argued that software is less of a user-oriented activity. However, it is categorized here as related to the user environment, in part, because software developments are aimed at meeting specific user needs and, in part, arbitrarily.

The early software languages were basically scientific in nature, such as Fortran. Successive improvements in programming language were aimed at making it easier to write programs. Hence, they became more English-oriented. COBOL is an example. However, programming in English-like languages required greater amounts of main computer or core memory than did scientific-oriented languages. Of course, the rapid expansion in memory already described easily accommodated this requirement.

Computer operating systems also underwent constant, significant improvements. These systems, which are designed by the computer manufacturers, contain instructions for scheduling, controlling, and obtaining maximum efficiency of the computer and peripheral equipment. Operating systems such as OS and MVS were developed, which enable the computer to be divided or partitioned into segments that can perform different job routines simultaneously and that permitted on-line interactive contact with users via terminals with video screens and remote printing capability.

Specific applications emerged as technology permitted. The earliest uses were for military purposes. Banks were among the first private users of DP devices, but they were quickly followed by all types of business. Some milestone application systems in the 1960s included the airline reservation system, the various bank accounting systems, and the emergence of time-sharing and service bureaus. In the 1970s, point-of-sales systems, electronic fund transfer systems, national stock quotation system, automated vote tallying, and computer aid design and manufacturing (CAD/CAM) were added. In the 1980s, automatic bank tellers and automated office work stations were developed.

EDP Auditing Environment

As Figure 38-2 illustrates, EDP auditing was quite late in responding to the audit challenges posed by EDP. It was not until 1968, for instance, that the EDP Auditors Association was founded in Los Angeles. It was not until 1972 that the IIA established an EDP audit committee.

From its late beginning, the audit community has been gathering momentum and is now quite well established in performing EDP audit activities. However dramatic the rise in EDP auditing has been in recent years, the pace of EDP developments has been such that much EDP activity is still occurring without being subject to independent audit scrutiny. Catching up will be a challenge facing EDP auditors for some time.

A Perspective

It is evident from this brief discussion that managing an EDP department in 1950 and managing an EDP department in 1985 are vastly different propositions. The EDP manager of 1950 was usually technically oriented. In essence, he was a chief technician who was responsible for only a handful of people and had little budgetary authority.

By contrast, today's I/S manager is responsible for very large numbers of persons, each with a different background. In addition, he is accountable for sizeable investments in facilities and equipment. Effective EDP requires a continuous interface with heads of other company disciplines, such as operations, finance, engineering, and marketing. These and other responsibilities require that the I/S manager possess executive talent. It is much less likely that today's ISM leader is a technician. He has become an indispensable member of the management team.

NATURE OF THE ISM FUNCTIONS

The modern ISM organization is very different from the hardware-oriented technical staffs of a few years ago. The ISM organization has become a large user of overall resources in most companies, consuming as much as 5 percent of total annual expenditures of any given company. ISM can best be described by the following statements, each of which is discussed more fully in the following paragraphs:

- It is a business within a business.
- It is service-oriented.
- It operates in a dynamic, fast-changing environment.
- Despite seemingly large and evergrowing budgets, it often faces resource shortages.
- The users of its services are often unfamiliar with the technology and unaware of their responsibilities.

Business Within a Business

It has been stated that effectiveness in the ISM business can only be achieved by "setting its objectives within the overall objectives of the company it serves, and by constantly seeking the real business opportunities."[3] This means that ISM is a business within a business and must be managed accordingly. Thus, organizing, planning, staffing, controlling, and directing the available resources are as much an integral part of ISM as they are for any other business function.

Being a business within a business also means that ISM must bear in mind that, while there are notable exceptions, the company's primary product lines usually do not include EDP services. Some ISM managers become accustomed to annual escalations in demand for services and the inevitable resulting increases in expenditures. Large organizations can emerge that can take on a life of their own, thereby losing sight of whether their efforts are helping to make the company more efficient and effective in meeting overall business goals. The auditor can serve as a useful check against this possibility through timely operational audits of the ISM function.

Service Orientation

Information Systems Management is similar to other staff functions in that it is a service organization. While the service initially was just a centralized means of delivering computational assistance, technological and environmental changes have occurred that have vastly expanded the services most ISM units now deliver. The following is but a partial list of those services:

- Data processing
  — Batch
  — On-line

---

[3] International Business Machines, *A Management System for the Information Business*, Volume I—Management Overview (White Plains, New York: IBM, 1980), p. 9.

INFORMATION SYSTEMS MANAGEMENT 38-11

- Data storage and retrieval
- Data protection
- Data transmission
- System development
- Programming
- User manual preparation and maintenance
- Training
- Time-sharing
- Office automation support
- Strategic planning
- Technical assistance

Dynamic Environment

The delivery of ISM services occurs in one of the most dynamic environments of any business function. The only thing that seems constant is the increasing pace with which change occurs. It is not unusual for ISM organizations to have experienced the following, at a minimum, during a given five-year interval:

- A major mainframe acquisition
- At least one operating system conversion
- Facilities expansion and/or move
- Organizational and reporting realignment
- Quadrupling of demand for direct access storage
- Developing and installing several major new applications
- Numerous modifications of existing systems
- At least one major systems development bomb
- Vast improvements in software and programming aids
- Significant increase in the number of mini- and microcomputers, many of which are in the custody of and controlled by users
- A doubling of technical staff (e.g., programmers and analysts)
- A tenfold increase in the number of terminals or communication nodes
- High turnover in professional and technical DP positions
- Constant user complaints and criticism
- Many revisions to purchased utilities
- Several interruptions that narrowly averted becoming major catastrophes

While the foregoing poses substantial challenges to ISM managers to maintain proper control and to deliver reliable service efficiently and effectively, the task is far from hopeless. Many ISM managers have successfully developed and used sound techniques to accomplish ISM objectives in spite of the dynamics involved. Unfortunately, others have used the dynamics as a conveniently available excuse to condone inadequate methodologies. Here again, auditors can render a service by ferreting out such inadequacies through operational audits of ISM.

Scarcity of Resources

From the standpoint of many users, ISM organizations seem to be locked into a pattern of constantly escalating costs to deliver needed services. Indeed, EDP costs have escalated at a rate far beyond that of other functional units.

Those within the ISM group feel that the demand for their services is never adequately balanced by company allocations of resources, which they believe are essential to delivering those services. Often, ISM must make difficult choices in deploying its limited resources (e.g., facilities, equipment, and manpower), which sometimes results in forcing ISM to accept greater risks than it ordinarily would to deliver services. These risks run the range from poor response time to losses from outright fraud and theft, all of which are discussed in greater detail later in this chapter.

Whether ISM is an impoverished orphan in the never-ending competition with other functions for the company's scarce resources, or rather an indiscriminate, insatiable glutton is a matter of great interest to management. ISM must obtain sufficient means to carry out its mission within tolerable ranges of risk. Through an operational audit, the internal auditor is able to provide management with valuable assistance in gauging the extent to which this is happening.

Interface Challenges

Competing with other organizations for scarce resources is one illustration of the interface challenges that characterize ISM. If ISM meets with too much success in this competition, it usually faces an adverse backlash reaction from the organizations with which it competes. Overcoming this backlash is a challenge that has stymied many ISM units.

There are other, perhaps more critical, interface challenges. The most critical of these is the challenge posed by the fact that few in the company understand how ISM functions. ISM seems to users and others to be shrouded in a bewildering, unfamiliar technology that makes relations extremely challenging to maintain. Breaking down these technological barriers is essential in order to achieve ISM objectives.

In recent years, ISM groups and users alike have recognized this point and have made great progress in increasing mutual respect, understanding, and cooperation. This task has been facilitated by technology itself with the advent of mini- and microcomputers and more user-friendly software. Thus, users and management are becoming more "computer literate."

Although user and ISM familiarity has been enhanced, another phenomenon is occurring that may limit this effect somewhat. Many executives are thought to be suffering from "technophobia," the fear of being known as a technician.[4] Thus, ISM will continue to face something of a challenge with some members of management to gain the necessary understanding.

From the standpoint of EDP managements, another problem exists. EDP managements have not been able to elevate themselves from the technical service perspective from which they originated in order to adopt the necessary management disciplines to successfully operate and integrate the modern ISM organization into its proper place within the company. ISM is often accused of being unable to perceive the importance of such generally accepted management concepts as formal policy statements, functional outlines, standards, strategic planning, and adequate documentation. Some EDP managements are seen as being uncooperative to the point of adopting a "take it or leave it" attitude when it comes to meeting user requests. Whether deserved or not, ISM units have gained the reputation of having poor management and being difficult to deal with. However, the same forces that are eliminating the technical barriers are also changing the ISM reputation for the better. Technological changes and increased user/ISM contact account for much of this improvement.

Auditors can assist both user management and ISM in achieving the proper level of understanding and cooperation. Internal auditors are increasing their awareness of ISM at a rate much faster than other members of the management team. This awareness places the internal auditor in the unique position of interpreter or consultant, to be used in minimizing interface challenges. Internal auditors must be careful to avoid being "used" by one or the other in ways that might worsen relationships. Effective operational auditing is the key to dealing with these interface challenges.

ISM OBJECTIVES

Basic Mission

The modern I/S organization exists to provide timely and useful DP services to users within the company. This basic mission is usually expressed in terms similar to these:[5]

- Collecting, storing, processing, and distributing data
- Developing new services and applications
- Periodic consultation on the need and use of information

---

[4] John P. Harrison and David C. Goodyear, "Assertiveness Training: Getting What You Want From a Computer," *Corporate Accounting*, Fall 1983, p. 68.

[5] *A Management System for the Information Business, op. cit.*, p. 9.

To be effective, this basic mission must be carried out within the context of the overall business goals and objectives of the organization served by the I/S function. Many I/S units lose sight of the fact that they exist to help achieve broader purposes. Some act as though the basic mission is all that must be considered, which is not the case. In a world of limits, I/S managers must realize that no company can afford each and every technical device and enhancement. The business aim is not to be at the cutting edge of state-of-the-art data processing. Rather, it is to produce and market products and services at a reasonable profit and to achieve satisfactory growth and return for shareholder/owners. Much of the time, the goals of the business are compatible with those of I/S, but occasionally, this is not so. The internal auditor must bear this in mind and realize that, through operational audits, a means exists to help both company and I/S objectives to remain congruent.

Supplemental Objectives

The basic ISM mission defines boundaries for its activities. For clarity, however, it is necessary to state supplemental objectives.

- Authorization and Execution
  - To obtain sufficient resources pursuant to management's authority to achieve objectives
  - To provide services in a timely, economical, and effective manner, in accordance with management's general or specific objective
  - To deviate from established policies and procedures only with appropriate management authority
- Recording and Accountability
  - To record and report DP service activity in order to permit reasonably effective performance evaluations by management
  - To establish and maintain accountability for EDP service and decisions
  - To assure reasonably that actual EDP operations and costs are compared periodically with budget data and standards in order to permit appropriate action to be taken with respect to variances
- Safeguarding
  - To assure reasonably that access to data is restricted to personnel authorized by data owners
  - To assure reasonably that access to EDP facilities, equipment, and records is restricted to authorized personnel
  - To assure reasonably that EDP facilities, equipment, and records are protected from any kind of identifiable hazards.

The foregoing supplemental objectives, although intended to be primarily operationally oriented, have strong internal control overtones. In fact, they are presented in an alignment borrowed from that used in Chapters 17, 18, and elsewhere throughout this volume. This is done intentionally to permit the auditor to understand ISM operations in the familiar context of internal control. It is also useful to present objectives in this manner because of the relationship that can be constructed with internal accounting control requirements of the FCPA. A principal segment of this Act was directed at internal accounting control, for which a smoothly operating I/S function is essential. Techniques for achieving these objectives are presented later in this chapter.

RISKS AND CONCERNS

To understand the importance of achieving ISM objectives, it is worthwhile to consider the ramifications that can result from ISM failures, which is what concerns management, users, and others affected by such failures. The risks vary in terms of importance and consequence from industry to industry and are dependent on whether the point of view is from the perspective of management, users, customers, or other sources.

Chapter 26 details many inherent risks involving computers. This section discusses risk from the oversight perspective of senior management, the group primarily served by internal auditors. Most managements are concerned with the following possible adverse effects on the company:

- Computer fraud and mischievous acts
- Violations of laws and regulations
- Negligent or ineffective I/S management
- Computer dependence
- Proliferation of mini- and microcomputers

Computer Fraud and Mischievous Acts

Computer fraud, despite its relative rare occurrence (see Chapter 25), is perhaps the risk that most concerns management. That is because when it does occur, significant sums of money or other assets are usually involved. Also, these events are often highly publicized in ways that sometimes suggest that the company involved has been lax in minimizing the risk. This adverse publicity undermines the images of prudence and competence most companies try carefully to develop, usually at considerable expense.

In recent years, major frauds involving computers have been reported against government agencies, utilities, banks, insurance companies, and other institutions. With the advent of powerful personal computers with telecommunications capability, fraud through computer time-sharing networks is becoming alarming. While many hackers see "innocent" intellectual sport in foiling expensive and intricate computer security systems, others have more damaging motives in mind. Theft of property and other valuables, such as trade secrets, special formulas, research data, and intelligence records may be the aim. Successful hackers can alter or destroy data in ways that leave no trace or in ways that can wrongfully implicate innocent parties. As more and more people in society gain computer knowledge, this risk is likely to increase. Fraud and hacking are not the only risks in this category. Computers have been and will continue to be the targets of saboteurs, terrorists, disgruntled employees, and others seeking to cause damage and injury.

To help curb the exposures, nearly all of the states have enacted some type of legislation making fraud involving computers and other mischievous acts criminal. (See Chapter 25.) Various efforts at passing federal legislation along these lines has occurred and the IIA, among others, has lent support to these efforts. Whether making computer fraud and mischievous acts felonious crimes will successfully deter would-be perpetrators remains to be seen. The best present defense seems to be a vigilant management and a working system of preventive security measures. Any comprehensive operational audit of ISM must consider the adequacy of these measures. Computer crime is discussed in greater depth in Chapter 25.

Violations of Laws and Regulations

Managements universally intend to achieve their business objectives within the framework of all applicable laws and regulations. Computers are becoming a primary means by which companies are able to comply with the innumerable record-keeping and reporting requirements of federal, state, and local information reporting, as well as other regulatory requirements. At the federal level alone, most business entities are subject to statutory and other regulations by the following:

- Treasury Department
- Internal Revenue Service
- Department of Labor
- Department of Health, Education, and Welfare
- Federal Commerce Commission
- Securities and Exchange Commission
- Department of Commerce
- Department of Defense
- Comptroller General

It is inconceivable that any I/S organization can monitor the innumerable changes in the vast array of rules with which the systems they maintain must comply. They must depend upon users to specify new and changing requirements; however, users are not always able to judge whether the system changes have preserved compliance as intended. Thus, an exposure to filing erroneous, incomplete, or untimely information arises with attendant risks of fines, penalties, and extra legal costs.

Another risk of considerable concern to many companies is that posed by violations of federal laws, such as the Privacy Act of 1974, aimed at securing the individual's right to privacy. Vast amounts of data pertaining to individuals are stored in many company computer files as employees, customers, prospective customers, debtors, or other categories. Unintended misuse of this data can bring about violations of these laws.

While the internal auditor is not a lawyer, he must still be aware of the general applicability of laws and regulations during the conduct of his audits. When circumstances warrant it, the auditor should seek assistance from company lawyers. Together, they can evolve recommendations to help users and I/S organizations with compliance obligations.

Negligent or Ineffective I/S Management

As stated earlier in this chapter, ISM consumes a significant and growing share of company budgets. Many executives are concerned with how efficient and effective I/S organizations are in spending these substantial sums and in managing allocated resources. Often the following questions arise:

- Are user needs for low-cost services being sacrificed to preserve I/S empires?
- Are future I/S requirements adequately anticipated?
- Are system development budgetary goals achieved at the expense of necessary control and security measures?
- Are equipment and software decisions affected more by the desire for keeping pace with technology than by cost/benefit factors?
- Is ISM being overly optimistic in its assessment of risks?
- Are managers too permissive or too restrictive regarding the conduct of technical staff?
- Is computer utilization too high or too low?

Managements are usually able to evaluate the effectiveness of other functional unit performance. However, the I/S business involves unfamiliar technical factors and considerations, thus making it more difficult for them to appraise ISM performance. This is yet another area where the internal auditor's operational auditing can provide valuable assistance. Yet, auditors must be cautious because the same technical barriers limit the extent of the contribution they can make. A properly structured program of I/S operational auditing will do much to improve I/S managerial performance.

Computer Dependence

Many executives express concern that their companies are becoming too dependent on computers to design, market, manufacture, and deliver products and services. Indeed, a significant number of business entities would have to cease operation within a few days if the functioning of their computers were interrupted.

Few computers are interrupted for long periods (i.e., in excess of one day). However, interruptions of short duration (a few minutes to a few hours) are not uncommon. As more and more operations and functions are automated, the effects of interruptions multiply so that excessive computer down time can delay designs, have a negative impact on delivery schedules, and cause unnecessary costs, as well as affect a company's competitive position.

These risks can be minimized by techniques such as distributed processing and adequate backup practices and recovery arrangements. Here too, internal auditors can help management assess whether the risks are being effectively minimized. During operational audits, the auditor can (1) review the extent of distributed processing; (2) observe and test backup techniques and examine the disaster recovery plan; (3) observe disaster simulations and tests of the disaster plan; and (4) compare company techniques with those employed by others in the industry or with those recommended by authoritative sources.

Proliferation of Mini- and Microcomputers

The era of the minicomputer has enabled numerous companies to minimize the risks of loss by distributing the EDP load among several interconnected computers in network configurations. This evolvement also reversed the long-term organizational direction of I/S away from centralization, moving control of I/S operations back to users. In recent years, this trend is being accelerated by the proliferation of small, inexpensive, powerful, and easy-to-use microcomputers. Management is concerned that if this occurs too rapidly, controls may be adversely affected.

Systems and methodologies nurtured by I/S units usually become adequately controlled over time in centralized environments where adequate technical expertise exists. However, users may not yet possess sufficient technical competence to reasonably assure that the same level of control and security is maintained when decentralization occurs. Their ability to evaluate hardware and software alternatives and to obtain suitable programming and other technical support is also less certain. Overall, costs of I/S management could increase due to gaps in coordination, leading to redundancies in data, software, facilities, personnel, and equipment. This could put unwanted pressure on pricing strategies, profitability, and competitive posture.

This is another instance where internal auditors can be useful to both management and I/S organizations. An audit coverage program can be designed to check the adequacy of practices at distributed locations. In order to determine the degree of control necessary over a given system or application, it is important to assess the impact the system or application has on

FIG. 38-3
Survey Form for Microcomputer Usage

Microcomputer Usage Questionnaire

Definition of Microcomputer: For purposes of this questionnaire, a microcomputer will not exceed the neighborhood of $30,000 and/or 16 bits. If a user can use a microcomputer via a terminal or remote station exclusively or on a shared arrangement, this is also considered a microcomputer for this questionnaire as long as there is unconditional availability of the microcomputer to the user. For example, some departments may have several terminals connected to microcomputers contained within one hardware unit, but since they are unconditionally available to each user at any time, the terminal is considered a microcomputer for purposes of this questionnaire. Likewise, a time-sharing terminal would *not* be considered a microcomputer, as the user is queued according to overall usage and demand.

I. Usage

    A. Does your department have exclusive custody and use of one or more microcomputers?
       ☐ Yes   How many? _____
       ☐ No   (Go to Section I.E.)

    B. Does your department use microcomputers on a shared basis with other organizations? _____

    C. How long have you been using microcomputers in this fashion?
_____

    D. Approximately what percentage of available hours are the computers used on the average? _____

    E. If you do not use microcomputers, are you planning to do so?
       ☐ Yes   (Complete remainder of questionnaire under the assumption you will procure the microcomputer system(s) within one year)
       ☐ No   (Go to Section I.G. and then to Section V)

    F. If so, when?
       ☐ Next three to six months
       ☐ Six months to a year

    G. If not, please review Section III of the questionnaire and indicate means of accomplishing audit department tasks.
       ☐ Manual
       ☐ Minicomputer
       ☐ Mainframe
       ☐ Other (please explain) _____

II. Hardware

    A. *Processing unit(s).* Please indicate the type of processing units you have and the number of units (i.e., Apple II, Apple III, IBM PC, IBM XT, etc.)

(continued)

FIG. 38-3 *(cont'd)*

Unit	Number of Units
_____	_____
_____	_____
_____	_____

B. *Printers*. Please indicate the number of printers you have by type.
- Dot matrix—High speed _____
- Dot matrix—Letter quality _____
- Daisy Wheel _____
- Graphics _____
- Laser
- Other _____

C. *Data storage units*. Please indicate the type of data storage used.
- ☐ Floppy diskettes
- ☐ Hard disk
- ☐ Other (please explain) _____

III. Software

A. *Type of software used*. In indicating the type of software used, please write in the names of software programs (i.e., for electronics spread sheets—Lotus 1-2-3, Supercalc), and also indicate the approximate percentage of total software usage represented by use of this type. If you do your own programming, indicate "In-House."

	Package	Percentage of Time
Electronic Spread sheet	_____	_____
Data Management	_____	_____
Word Processing	_____	_____
Project Management	_____	_____
Communications	_____	_____
Statistical Analysis	_____	_____
Integrated	_____	_____
(other; please explain) _____	_____	_____
(other; please explain) _____	_____	_____
(other; please explain) _____	_____	_____
(other; please explain) _____	_____	100%

B. *Programming*. If you do your own programming, what is the most common method used:
- ☐ Application generator
- ☐ Basic

☐ Other languages
☐ Integration of unrelated software packages

C. *Specific applications.* Indicate by approximate percentage of time used, which of the following functions you use the microcomputer for:

Functions	Percentage of Time on Micro
Word Processing	_____
Data and/or Report Transfers (communications)	_____
Project Control	_____
Project Planning and Scheduling	_____
Analytical Procedures	_____
Workpaper Spreadsheets, etc.	_____
Financial Planning	_____
Electronic Mail	_____
Terminal Access to Auditee Database	_____
Timesharing	_____
Department Administration	_____
_____ Other (please explain)	_____
	100%

D. *Word processing.* Approximately what portion, if any, of your word processing applications is used for the following:

Application	Percentage of Time with Word Processing
Correspondence	_____
Reports	_____
Workpaper Narratives	_____
_____ (other; please explain)	_____
_____ (other; please explain)	_____
_____ (other; please explain)	_____
_____ (other; please explain)	_____
	100%

E. *Analytical procedures.* If you use the microcomputer for analytical procedures, approximately what portion, if any, is used for the following:

Application	Percentage of Time with Analysis
Variation analysis	_____
Trend analysis	_____

(continued)

FIG. 38-3 *(cont'd)*

```
            Regression analysis        _____
            Statistical sampling       _____
            Account analysis           _____

            _____        _____
            (other; please explain)

            _____        _____
            (other; please explain)

            _____        _____
            (other; please explain)

            _____        _____
            (other; please explain)             100%
                                        ===================
```

IV. Security

    A. *Data files.* Indicate method or combination of methods you use to provide adequate security of audit data contained in your microcomputer disks:
       ☐ Periodic backup of data files
       ☐ Access codes/passwords
       ☐ Restricted use of data files
       ☐ Offsite storage
       ☐ Other

    B. *Physical security.* Indicate method or combination of methods you use to provide adequate physical security over the microcomputer system.
       ☐ Equipment bolted down
       ☐ Equipment locked up
       ☐ Other (please explain)

the company or department involved.[6] Internal auditors can aid in performing this assessment. Internal auditors cannot audit the use of every personal computer or every application. However, they can measure the adequacy of practices by conducting surveys and by observing and testing practices on a sample basis. An example of such a survey form is shown in Figure 38-3.

Many internal auditors have gained knowledge of personal computers through self-interest, because they own one, or because their auditing department uses them. This knowledge affords an excellent basis for providing consultation to other prospective owners/users. Sharing knowledge helps these units establish sound practices for microcomputer use.

---

[6] Ronald J. Timko, "Controlling Microcomputers—Don't Overreact," *The Internal Auditor*, Dec. 1983, p. 22.

ORGANIZING AND MANAGING THE ISM FUNCTION

The management approach to I/S is basically the same as that for any other business unit or function. To be effective in meeting its objectives, ISMs must organize, plan, staff, and control resources and activities. Much is already written on the general subject of how to manage, not only in this volume but also in other reference works (e.g., Chapter 31). Some brief remarks to put the process into the context of I/S seem in order here.

Planning

Adequate planning is critical to effectively achieving ISM objectives. The planning process is best described in strategic, tactical, and operational terms.

- ☐ *Strategic or long-term planning* must be compatible with the strategic plans of the overall business unit. Thus, assumptions used and objectives developed must be consistent with those used in overall business planning. This seems obvious, but, in many companies, different groups are involved in developing the respective plans, often simultaneously, which makes it difficult to achieve compatibility. In many companies, strategic planning for the ISM unit occurs at the direction of the I/S manager. In some companies with central or corporate-based ISM units, these plans are directed or consolidated and approved by that organization. Strategic plans must provide an indication over the next five- to seven-year period of the following, at a minimum:

    - Projected demand for large processor use
    - Projected demand for small processor use
    - Projected demand for data storage
    - Projected demand for telecommunication equipment
    - Projected demand for terminals, printers, etc.
    - Projected demand for maintenance programming (in hours)
    - Projected demand for new systems programming (in hours) by system
    - Projected demand for technical support (in hours)
    - Projected demand for timesharing
    - Projected demand for systems development efforts (other than programming (in hours)
    - Projected demand for other services
    - Projected costs for each type of service and/or equipment usage
    - Projected manpower requirements

    In order for the projections to be meaningful, the individuals responsible for compiling them must obtain input from all prospective user organizations. Usually, some predetermined methodology is evolved to obtain this data, which involves the use of preprinted forms, written instructions, due dates, and so on.

Some planning organizations keep considerable records of past forecasts, which are used to develop comparisons with actual historical usage. This data enables planners to develop factors in order to adjust inputs received either up or down. In this way, overly optimistic/pessimistic estimates are brought into ranges more in line with what historical models suggest. There are even more sophisticated techniques that may be used involving regression analysis and linear programming, which should be used if circumstances so warrant it.

Whatever the methodology, strategic planning is extremely important in achieving ISM objectives effectively and efficiently. An example of a segment of a strategic plan is shown in Figure 38-4, in this case, for manpower.

☐ *Tactical or short-term planning* usually focuses on the next year or two. Because the period is much shorter, the forecasts are much more accurate and reliable predictors of demand. The kind of data gathered in the tactical plan is very similar to that used in the strategic planning process. Thus, the methodology in gathering the data and developing the projections is similar.

Usually, although not always, tactical planning is done by the same individuals or groups responsible for developing strategic plans. In this way, some of the data gathering for the strategic plan may be used in developing the tactical plan. Other groups believe better tactical plans result from an entirely separate but similar tactical planning effort. An example of a tactical plan for systems development is shown in Figure 38-5.

☐ *Operational planning*. This is the type of planning that occurs at the operational level and is even more focused than tactical planning. Such detailed planning exercises as project planning and production scheduling are involved. This type of planning activity is usually carried out on an as-needed basis by various managers and others responsible for the activities and operations of ISM. These plans may cover periods ranging from a few days to several months. Functions within ISM for which this type of planning occurs include:

- Systems development projects
- Programming
- System programming
- Production job scheduling
- Quality assurance

Operational planning may be as simple as sequencing or time-phasing events and activities or it may be as complex as Performance Evaluation and Review Technique (PERT) or Critical Path Method (CPM) analyses. Some scheduling may be accomplished by means of software utilities. An example of an operational plan for a system development project is shown in Figure 38-6.

FIG. 38-4

Segment of a Strategic ISM Plan

TOTAL MANPOWER PLAN

	Act. 19XY AVG	19XX Forecast												19XZ AVG	19+1 AVG	19+2 AVG	19+3 AVG
		JAN	FEB	MAR	APR	MAY	JUN	JUL	AUG	SEP	OCT	NOV	DEC				
Administrative	66	84	90	93	96	100	100	101	102	104	107	107	107	90	126	130	131
Operations	233	253	261	265	267	270	278	281	283	282	279	279	279	273	296	301	307
Information Systems and Programming:																	
Division Programmer/Analysts																	
Division A	1.5	2	2	2	2	2	3	3	3	3	3	3	3	2.6	2	2	1
Division B	5.9	11	11	11	11	11	11	11	11	11	11	11	11	11	11	11	11
Division C	190.5	181	190	195	201	208	211	213	213	213	213	213	213	205.3	235	263	291
Division D	0.5	0.5	0.5	0.5	0.5	0.5	0.5	0.5	0.5	0.5	0.5	0.5	0.5	0.5	—	—	—
Division E	1.5	1	2	2	2	2	2	2	2	2	2	2	2	2	2	2	2
Division F	12.5	12	13	14	14	15	16	16	16	17	17	17	17	15.4	15	16	16
Division G	7.5	11	11	11	11	12	12	12	12	12	12	12	12	11.7	15	16	16
Multi-Divisional Systems	5.4	5	5	5	5	5	6	6	6	6	6	6	6	5.6	8	4	1
Miscellaneous	0.1	0.1	0.1	0.1	0.1	0.1	0.1	0.1	0.1	0.1	0.1	0.1	0.1	0.1	0.1	0.1	0.1
Corporate Office	21.1	22.4	25.4	28.4	29.4	35.4	35.4	35.4	35.4	42.4	42.4	42.4	42.4	34.7	33.9	28.9	26.9
Total Division Programmer/Analysts	246.5	246	260	269	276	292	297	299	299	307	307	307	307	288.9	322	343	365
XX Internal	65.5	64	65	85	87	77	78	96	96	85	85	85	85	82.7	98	98	109
Total Programmers/Analysts	312	310	326	354	363	369	375	395	397	392	392	392	392	371.6	414	441	474
Total Indirect	96	91	96	99	100	103	104	105	106	106	106	106	106	182.4	115	122	124
Total Information Systems and Programming	488	481	422	453	463	472	479	500	503	498	498	498	498	474	529	563	598
Total	707	738	773	811	826	842	857	882	888	884	884	884	884	846	951	994	1,036

FIG. 38-5
Excerpt From a Tactical ISM Plan

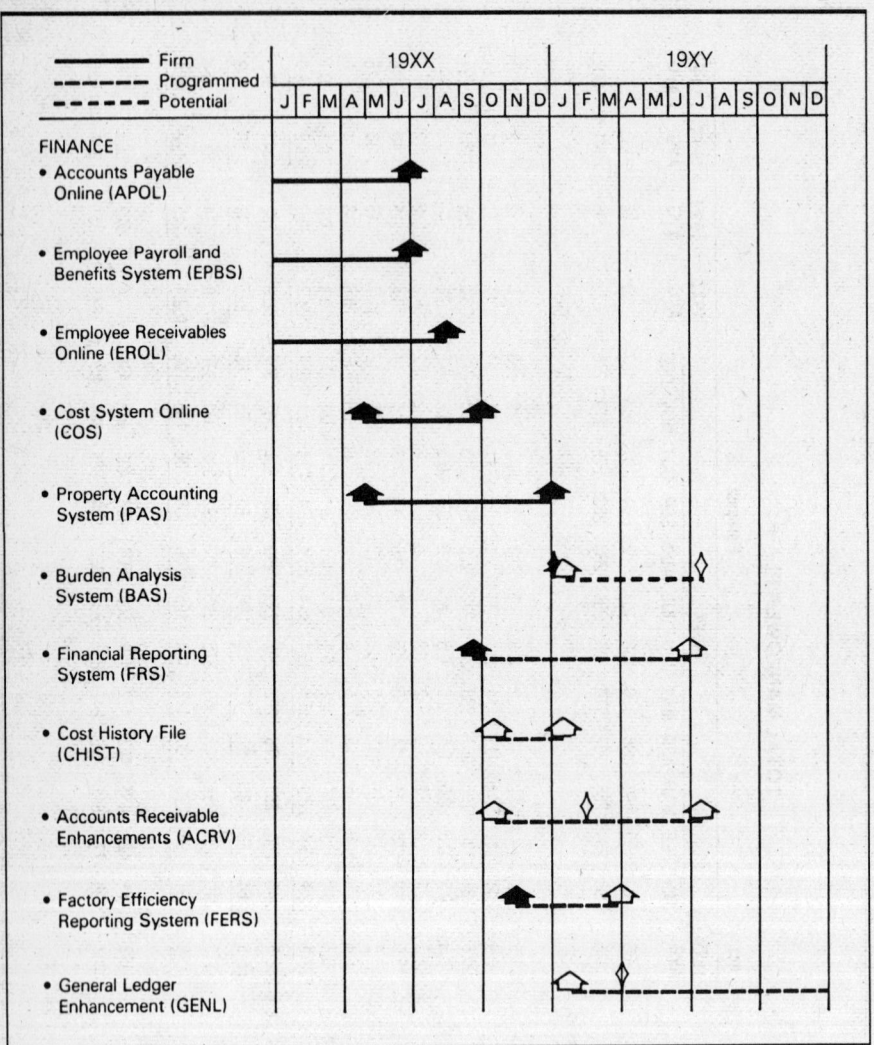

Auditing ISM Planning Functions

Planning at all levels is a subjective process. Accurate plans can be developed by instinct based on the intuitive judgment of experienced and skilled managers; inaccurate plans can be developed even though the most sophisticated planning techniques are employed. Usually though, there is a high correlation between the planning process and the accuracy and reliability of the resultant plans; that is, the better the process, the better the plan.

INFORMATION SYSTEMS MANAGEMENT

FIG. 38-6

Example of a Portion of a System Development Plan

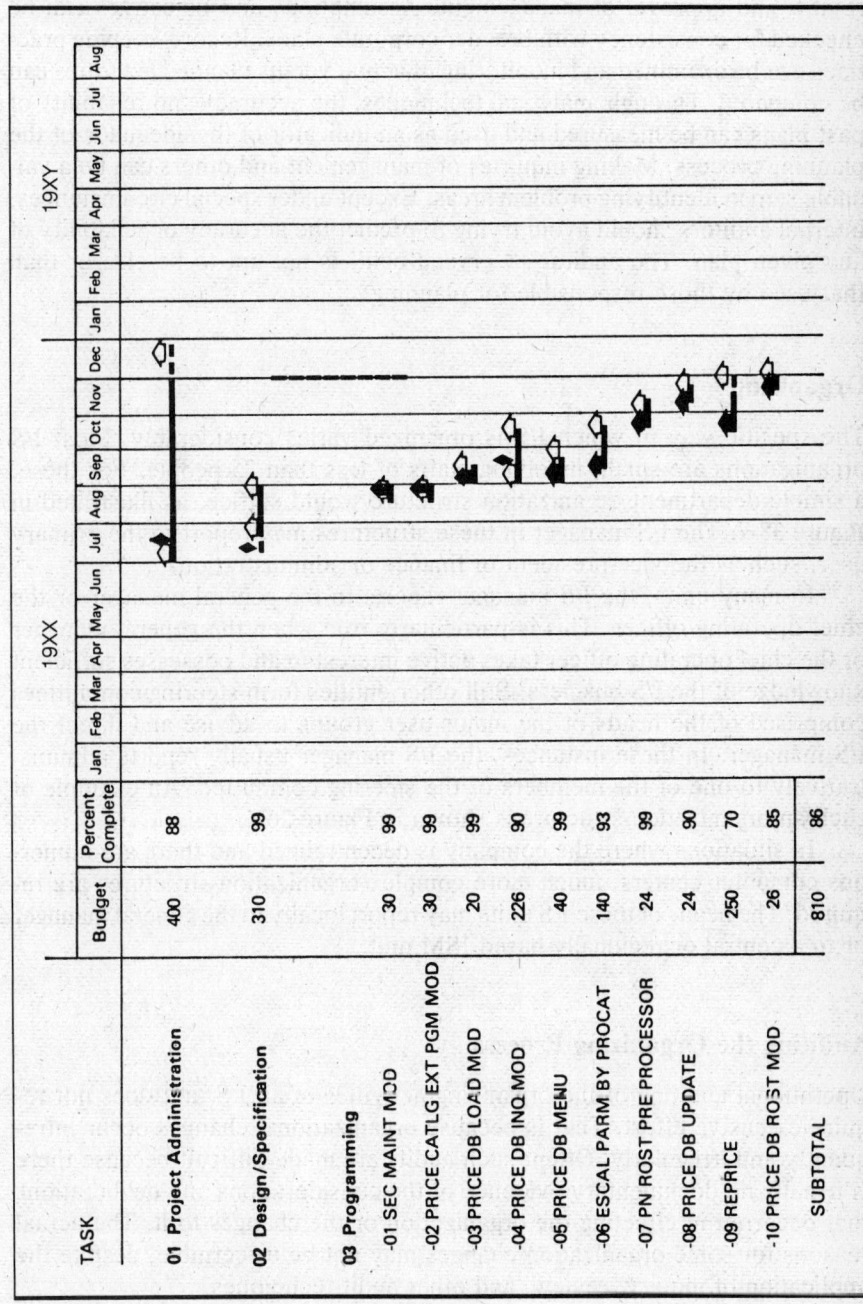

Internal auditors should review the planning process for thoroughness and reasonableness. The involvement of users can be verified as can the review and approval of management. Assumptions and objectives can be checked for consistency with broader corporate plans. Record-keeping practices can be examined and monitoring of actual versus planned activities can be compared. Through analytical techniques, the accuracy and reliability of past plans can be measured and used as an indicator of the adequacy of the planning process. Making inquiries of management and others can be a valuable step in identifying problem areas. Except under special circumstances, internal auditors should avoid trying to predict the accuracy or reliability of any given plan. The auditor's "crystal ball" is not apt to be clearer than that used by those responsible for planning.

Organizing

The specific way in which I/S is organized varies considerably. Most I/S organizations are small, involving staffs of less than 25 people. For these, a simple department organization structure would suffice, as illustrated in Figure 38-7. The I/S manager in these structures may report to the primary user, such as the vice-president of finance or administration.

In many units, the I/S manager reports to the general manager or the chief operating officer. This is particularly true when the general manager or the chief operating officer takes active interest in and possesses sufficient knowledge of the I/S business. Still other entities form steering committees comprised of the heads of the major user groups to advise and direct the I/S manager. In these instances, the I/S manager usually reports administratively to one of the members of the steering committee. An example of such an organization structure is shown in Figure 26-4.

In situations where the company is decentralized and there are numerous computer centers, much more complex organization structures are required. The heads of these I/S units may report locally to the general manager or to a central or regionally based ISM unit.

Auditing the Organizing Process

Operational auditing of the organizing activities of an I/S unit does not require extensive effort. That is because organizational changes occur infrequently and irregularly. Often, such audits are made difficult because there is usually no documentary evidence of the considerations and deliberations that occurred in effecting the organization or the changes to it. The actual reasons for some organization changes may not be discernible, despite the application of inquiry, review, and other audit techniques.

The variety of organizations that actually exist suggests that there is no simple best way to organize, a fact that internal auditors must constantly

INFORMATION SYSTEMS MANAGEMENT

FIG. 38-7
Example of a Simple Organization Structure

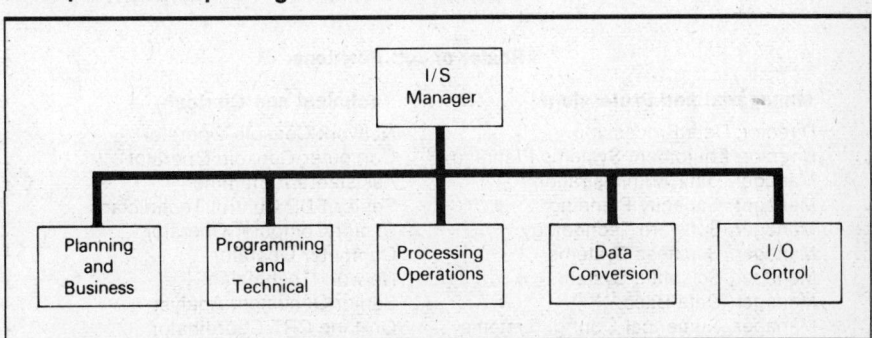

keep in mind. Unless considerable evidence exists to the contrary, the auditor is probably justified in concluding that the existing structure is adequate. Evidence to the contrary may include:

- Frequent organizational realignments—one or more per year for several consecutive years (around three to four)
- High turnover in key positions
- Consistent underachievement of I/S objectives
- Reported clashes with users

The existence of one or more of these conditions does not necessarily mean that an improper organizational alignment exists. Rather, it suggests that the auditor may wish to discuss the matter with appropriate management, although the instances of this are rare.

Staffing

I/S organizations require sufficient, competent staffs in order to function effectively. The types and numbers of personnel to be employed in any given I/S unit will depend on the complexity of the organization, the kinds of services offered, and the extent of the demand for those services. Job positions range from the highly technical, such as operating system programmers, to more clerical types (such as data control clerks operators), while others function "off-line" (such as data base administrators). A typical roster of job positions for an I/S unit is shown in Figure 38-8.

The combination of positions, organizational size, and frequent turnover lead many I/S managers to adopt some or all of the following techniques:

- Written position descriptions
- Minimum qualifications for each position

FIG. 38-8
A Typical Roster of Job Positions

Roster of Job Positions

Managerial and Professional	Technical and Clerical
Director, Data Processing	Network Console Operator
Director, Equipment Systems Planning	Computer Console Operator
Manager, Data Administration	Assistant Programmer
Manager, Capacity Planning	Senior EDP Control Technician
Manager, Software Technology	Senior Computer Operator
Manager, Business Systems	Computer Operator
Manager, Scientific Systems	Network Technician
Manager, Data Base	Senior Document Analyst
Manager, Numerical Control Systems	On-Line CRT Coordinator
Manager, Network Administration and Control	Document Analyst
	Network Maintenance Coordinator
Manager, Communications and Facilities	EDP Control Technician
Manager, Data Entry	Data Entry Operator
Supervisor, Project Billing	Administrative Secretary
DP Senior Technologist	Senior Documentation Clerk
Special Controller, EDP Configurations	Accounting Clerk
Data Base Analyst	Microfilm Data Clerk
Programmer Analyst	On-Line CRT Operator
Project Master Planner	Office Clerk
Project Control Administrator	Documentation Clerk
Management Services Analyst	Data Clerk
Facilities Engineer	Mail Clerk
Network Design Analyst	General Clerk
Data Control Analyst	
Budget Control Analyst	
Accountant	

- Formal recruiting practices including interviews, screening techniques, and reference checks
- Competitive wage ranges
- New employee orientation materials
- Written manuals, standards, and desk procedures
- Performance measurement techniques
- Training programs
- Career development planning, and counseling

The importance of the foregoing techniques cannot be overemphasized. The service nature of the I/S business means that it is labor intensive and people-oriented, despite the considerable investment in facilities and equipment. A properly skilled, trained, and motivated staff is indispensable to delivering quality services.

INFORMATION SYSTEMS MANAGEMENT

Auditing ISM Staffing

Appraising the quality of ISM staffs is no less challenging than appraising the quality of the planning or organizing functions. They are all very subjective undertakings. Unless requested to do so by management, internal auditors should resist any inclination to furnish direct performance appraisals of individual I/S staff members. However, the techniques used by ISM to attract, train, supervise, and evaluate the ISM staff can and should be subjected to periodic audit for consistency and effectiveness.

Also, internal auditors should be alert to signs indicating staffing problems. The fact that high turnover is an unfortunate fact of life in I/S organizations makes an accurate reading of those signs difficult. The demand for highly skilled data processors is such that most find it hard to resist more lucrative offers from other companies. Nevertheless, turnover should be checked and evaluated in light of the foregoing. Other indicators might include:

- Productivity problems
- Frequent overtime
- Excessive errors and omissions
- Inordinate user complaints and dissatisfaction
- Poor work habits
- Low morale

Clues of the existence of these indicators may be discerned by interviewing managers, staff, and users, by reviewing productivity reports, and by observing job performance.

Controlling

The means by which I/S organizations are controlled is the principle subject of Chapter 26, to which the reader is referred for a detailed discussion of organization, operations, resource acquisition and utilization, record keeping, accountability, and security controls. Implications for internal auditors are also presented, as well as a glossary of terms. I/S audit techniques are presented in Chapter 28.

This chapter presents a brief overview of how I/S organizations are controlled. As is true of virtually any other managerial area of responsibility, the internal control principles involved (as discussed in Chapter 17) include:

- Competent personnel
- Adequate segregation of duties
- Existence of adequate documents and records
- Adequate authorization and approval procedures
- Effective planning and accountability

Detailed objectives and control techniques implementing the above principles (described in Chapter 26) are based on the premise that the delivery of reliable and relevant processing service is dependent on a system of preventive, detective, and corrective processes.

Preventive and detective controls may overlap, particularly in critical processes, a fact that helps to assure that errors and omissions are minimized. Thus, input documents may be prepared by one person, reviewed by another, and finally checked for accuracy and propriety by various system-designed checks. Corrective procedures are necessary to assure that errors and their effects caught by the detective process are appropriately overcome.

Controlling Access—The Key

The vast concentration of data in computer files makes critical the controlling of access to data. Before computers, information was generally stored by those who owned it. Limiting access in that environment was comparatively easy primarily because the information was physically visible. Locked desks, files, storage cabinets, vaults, and secure rooms usually offered sufficient protection. Controlling the availability of information in an automated environment is much more challenging because:

- The data are not physically visible to the custodian.
- The data do not have to be removed to gain access.
- The data may be accessed remotely.
- The custodians (the DP group) invariably are not the originators or users of the data; therefore, they must be told who is to have access.
- The originators or owners of the data stored in automated files often do not realize the extent to which their data may be accessed by others, because they do not possess sufficient technical awareness.
- The trend toward large data bases to eliminate redundancy means that a given file or record must be made available to more than one organization. Some types of payroll data, for example, probably must be made available to individuals from employee relations, accounting, law, insurance, and pension administration.
- Personal and small business computers are now able to be used to access information stored in mainframes, thereby greatly multiplying access potential to unprotected data.

The methodology usually employed to control the availability of information requires the development of a companywide policy and involves:

- Defining responsibilities for data owners, users, and custodians.

- Developing definitions for classes of information (e.g., secret and confidential).
- Classifying all information according to definitions.
- Developing controls to apply within each information class.
- Identifying a data security administrator.

This methodology is based on the concept that data owners must accept the responsibility for determining the classifications of data owned by them as well as the level of control desired. Owners are usually also the primary users; they are never I/S personnel. Generally, the custodian of data is the I/S unit, which is responsible for complying with the owner's stipulations as to the level of control.

Also inherent in this methodology is the concept that the owners are involved in risk assessment and cost/benefit analysis. Custodians act in an advisory capacity where technical considerations beyond the capabilities of the owners are involved.

Until recent years, many owners have left the decisions regarding access control to the I/S group. Hence, the foregoing methodology requires these owners to become much more involved in controlling the systems and data for which they bear ultimate responsibility. It also means that I/S groups must be willing to permit the owners to get involved to the extent necessary to effect satisfactory control decisions. For some ISMs and some owner/users, this may prove to be difficult. Internal auditors should watch for any indications of problems in this area and promptly report them as appropriate.

While it is difficult to generalize about specific types of owner controls, the following are usually present in well-controlled systems where remote access is involved:

- ☐ *Secret codes.* A means known only to the accessor to identify him from all others. Passwords are the best and most often used technique, even in the most critical of systems (such as automated bank telling).
- ☐ *Verification.* A means by which the identity of the accessor is verified. This might be a birthdate or some other personalized data. Some systems even have the capability to recognize fingerprints.
- ☐ *Confirmation.* This involves a procedure such as call-back.
- ☐ *Audit trail.* This requires keeping sufficient records of all access attempts.
- ☐ *Restricted directories.* This means restricting access to the records or files of passwords, secret codes, etc.

In the past few years, many software products have been developed by computer manufacturers and others to aid in controlling access to data. In large installations where systems are interactive, software aids are a must. Internal auditors must become familiar with their characteristics to evaluate appropriately the extent to which they are put to use.

FIG. 38-9
A List of Functional Areas for Operational Auditing

Strategy planning	Systems development standards
Documentation control group	Library (tape) management
Disaster planning	Backup and vaulting practices
Data security	Resource acquisition management
Physical security	Records management
Data based administration	Telecommunications management
Operating systems management	Training
Programming change control	Performance measurement

Auditing the Controlling Function

Internal auditors perhaps can make their most significant contribution to management and I/S in this area, because measuring the adequacy of controls is comparatively less subjective than measuring the adequacy of the planning, organizing, and staffing factors.

In small I/S units, an operational audit of the entire unit is possible. In fact, in companies served by multiple I/S units (some large companies have I/S units numbering more than 100), this is a very practical approach. In large installations, however, the I/S organization is more effectively audited in a segmented or subfunctional manner. Figure 38-9 presents a listing of typical functions that might be audited separately.

THE AUDITOR'S ROLE AND OBJECTIVES

The fundamental objective in performing operational audits of ISM is to provide management with independent information regarding ISM and opinions as to its operational effectiveness and efficiency. Management uses the information and opinions as part of the basis on which it assesses ISM performance and decides on courses of action.

A related objective is to assist users and I/S managers in evolving a sound working relationship and a proper division of responsibility for the creation, maintenance, retention, and destruction of data. Also, operational auditing will help develop the ways and means by which ISM delivers relevant and reliable I/S services. If the audit department achieves these objectives, it will fulfill its primary role, that of appraising the adequacy and effectiveness of controls and the quality of performance as a service to others. This service is of particular value in the area of I/S because most managements lack the necessary familiarity to judge ISM performance without assistance.

AUDIT TECHNIQUES

Effective operational auditing of ISM requires the efforts of staff with appropriate technical training and the availability of suitable audit tools. For a great many audit departments, operational auditing of ISM is an ongoing part of the overall I/S auditing activity. This is usually accomplished by a separate group or segment within the internal audit department.

How to Maintain an I/S Audit Function

In Chapter 27, there is a detailed discussion of how these segments are established and maintained. That discussion points out that I/S audit projects are managed in much the same way as are non-I/S audits. Basically, the same standards apply. Control techniques include:

- Properly skilled staff
- Audit manuals
- Programs, questionnaires, and checklists
- Proper authorization and monitoring
- Quality-control practices
- Continuous program of training

Chapter 27 also provides suggestions for establishing priorities for audit projects. Figure 27-6 in that chapter presents frequencies for audit coverage for selected functions. The functional coverage depicted in that figure is an indication of the extent to which operational auditing of ISM should be performed. It is not uncommon to spend as much as 25 percent of available I/S auditing resources in operational (functional) audits. If further information is required on how to establish and maintain an I/S auditing capability, refer to Chapter 27.

Techniques

There is a detailed discussion of I/S auditing techniques in Chapter 28. The discussion indicates that the concept of sampling is applicable to I/S auditing to some extent, and that judgment sampling is probably used more extensively in I/S auditing than in non-I/S auditing. It is also noted that evidence-gathering through the sampling process is obtained by various techniques, such as observation, inquiry, inspection, and confirmation. Examples are:

- Observation
  - Recovery from system interruptions
  - Monitoring of terminal operator activities
  - Handling of negotiable documents
  - Equipment maintenance activities

- Controls to restrict access to the computer
- Tape-handling procedures
- Tests of disaster recovery plans
- Training activities
- Supervisory activities
- Inquiry (via interview and research)
  - Discussions with I/S staff and management
  - Flowcharting of existing and developing system application
  - Program analysis to spot bugs in logic
  - Trend analysis
  - Regression analysis
- Inspection
  - Strategic plans
  - Tactical plans
  - Operating plans
  - Feasibility studies
  - Requirements analyses
  - Specification statements
  - System and program documentation
  - Control logs
  - Machine logs
  - System files
  - Program listings
  - Suspense files
  - Master files
- Confirmation
  - Corroborate user satisfaction
  - Confirm sufficiency of response time
  - Conduct audit of timesharing
  - Confirm various procedural compliance

For a further discussion of I/S auditing working papers with samples, the reader is referred to Chapter 28.

I/S Auditing Tools

The I/S auditing tools are also described in Chapter 28. These include:

- Generalized audit software
- Manual tracing
- Snapshot routines
- Test data method

INFORMATION SYSTEMS MANAGEMENT

- Integrated test facility
- Parallel simulation
- Embedded audit routines
- Audit facility
- Utility programs
- Program verification
- Operating system review

Many of the foregoing techniques have limited applicability in operational auditing. Use of tracing, snapshot, test data, and simulation are used primarily in application auditing. Generalized audit software, embedded audit routines, audit facilities, utility programs, program verifications, and operating system reviews can be used in operational auditing to some extent. The use of these techniques is limited, however, because of the considerable time required to plan and execute them and because they require considerable technical expertise.

Historically, these tools also require considerable involvement of ISM computer facilities. The growing availability of small, but powerful, microcomputers with communication capability is making ISM involvement less of a factor. The time is not far away when internal auditors will easily be able to download data from mainframe computers to their own microcomputers for special examination and analysis using software products.

Not to be overlooked are the analytical techniques described in Chapter 28. In operational audits, trend analysis could be performed, for example, on:

- Programmer and system analyst hours
- CPU hours
- Printed lines of data
- Mean time between failures

Regression analysis could be developed for variables such as:

Dependent variable	Independent variable
• Number of requirement changes	• Cost of system development
• Number of emergency changes	• Cost of system maintenance
• Number of terminals	• Response time
• Number of programmers	• Maintenance costs

By far, the most frequently used audit tools for the future of operational auditing are the questionnaire and the audit program. Figure 38-10 depicts a questionnaire that might be used in a comprehensive operational audit of an I/S organization. Figure 38-11 depicts an audit program integrated with

(continued on page 38-65)

FIG. 38-10
ISM Questionnaire

> The primary objective of the operation of an EDP center is to provide timely and useful DP services to users in accordance with management's general or specific authorization. Such services must be provided efficiently and effectively and in a manner that affords maximum protection for company resources (including data) commensurate with associated economic risk.
>
> The size and scope of the operation of any EDP center is such that effective management requires considerable organization and planning effort, not to mention staffing and control. This effort requires the attention and coordinated involvement, not only of the EDP center management, but also user management and, at times, corporate management. The involvement of these management groups varies with the size of the EDP center and the nature of its services. In view of the foregoing, it is impractical to cover in a single questionnaire all the possible individual situations that the auditor may encounter. However, the following questionnaire is intended to cover most situations that the auditor might examine, including:
>
> - Data processing:
>   a. Batch processing
>   b. On-line processing
> - Data storage and retrieval
> - Data protection
> - Data transmission
> - Documentation and records
> - Facility management
>
> In addition to the foregoing, some EDP centers provide such services not only to internal users but also offer them to users outside the company on a fee basis. There is a separate optional section for these situations in the questionnaire.
>
> All of the services listed above must be provided in order to achieve the primary objective with the following subsets:
>
> *Authorization and Execution*
>
> ☐ To obtain sufficient resources pursuant to management's authority to achieve objectives.
>
> ☐ To provide services timely, economically, and effectively only in accordance with management's general or specific authorization.
>
> ☐ To deviate from established policies and procedures only upon appropriate management authority.
>
> *Recording and Accountability*
>
> ☐ To record and report DP service activity in order to permit reasonably effective performance evaluation by management.
>
> ☐ To establish and maintain accountability for EDP service decisions.
>
> ☐ To reasonably assure that actual EDP operations and costs are compared periodically with budget data and standards to accommodate variances.
>
> *Safeguarding*
>
> ☐ To reasonably assure that access to data is restricted to personnel authorized by data owners.

☐ To reasonably assure that access to EDP facilities, equipment, and records is restricted to authorized personnel.

☐ To reasonably assure that EDP facilities, equipment, and records are protected from all types of identifiable hazards.

In practice, the foregoing objectives are accomplished by distributing authority and responsibility among various functional elements inside and outside the EDP center. The questionnaire that follows has been organized by functional element and by the nature of the service offered. To some extent, it overlaps the EDP Installation Control Questionnaire presented in Chapter 17.

That questionnaire is primarily aimed at evaluating internal control, while this questionnaire is more concerned with operational efficiency and effectiveness. Since the two aims are closely related, some duplication is unavoidable.

	Response		
	Yes	No	Reference

I. Corporate Organization—Organizing Activities:

A. Authorization

1. Is there a written policy covering the following aspects of data?
   a. Basic policy ☐ ☐ .....
   b. Definitions of terms such as applications owner, data owner, data custodian, or data user ☐ ☐ .....
   c. Responsibilities of each ☐ ☐ .....

2. Does the basic policy recognize the concept that data is a resource to be managed like other enterprise resources? ☐ ☐ .....

3. Is the responsibility and authority for managing data resources expressed in the form of an organization chart? ☐ ☐ .....

4. Do written statements exist covering the duties and responsibilities of those assigned to manage data resources? ☐ ☐ .....

5. Is the management of data resources vested in a single corporate executive having a senior position in the overall management structure? ☐ ☐ .....

6. Does the company policy provide for a senior-level steering EDP committee comprised of representatives from all relevant company functions (e.g., finance, law, marketing, administration, and operations), which is chaired by the senior EDP executive? ☐ ☐ .....

7. Is the company policy regarding data management consistent with its fundamental management approach (degree of centralized vs. decentralized operations)? ☐ ☐ .....

(continued)

FIG. 38-10 *(cont'd)*

	Response Yes	No	Reference
8. Does the company policy contain clear statements of authority and responsibility for the following?			
a. Chief executive officer	☐	☐	....
b. Chief operating officer	☐	☐	....
c. Steering Committee	☐	☐	....
d. Senior EDP executive	☐	☐	....
e. Operating unit management	☐	☐	....
f. Auditing units	☐	☐	....
g. Others	☐	☐	....
9. At a minimum, such a statement should cover such activities as			
a. Planning and budgeting	☐	☐	....
b. Acquisition and disposition of hardware, including office automation and telecommunications equipment and services	☐	☐	....
c. Acquisition and/or development of and disposition of EDP software, supplies, and services	☐	☐	....
d. Acquisition and/or development of system applications	☐	☐	....
e. Charges for EDP services	☐	☐	....
10. Is there a written set of guidelines or standards covering such items as the following?			
a. Preferred equipment	☐	☐	....
b. Preferred software	☐	☐	....
c. System development standards	☐	☐	....
d. Documentation standards	☐	☐	....
e. Control standards	☐	☐	....
f. Security standards	☐	☐	....
g. Backup and recovery standards	☐	☐	....
h. Classification of data	☐	☐	....
B. Execution and Recording			
1. Are changes to policy statements, organization charts, and overall standards affecting EDP required to be reviewed and approved in the same manner as other similar policies?	☐	☐	....
2. Are records required to be kept, evidencing such activities as the following?			
a. Revised policies, organization charts, etc.	☐	☐	....
b. Senior EDP executive directives	☐	☐	....
c. Meetings of the Steering Committee	☐	☐	....

INFORMATION SYSTEMS MANAGEMENT

	Response Yes	No	Reference

3. Do procedures require the senior EDP executive or his designee to receive and review periodic reports and other information pertaining to the EDP operations of organizational units? ☐ ☐ ....

4. Is the information sufficient to permit adequate monitoring of all pertinent EDP activities? ☐ ☐ ....

5. Does the senior EDP executive receive copies of audit reports? ☐ ☐ ....

6. Does the senior EDP executive or his designee conduct periodic operational reviews of EDP installations? ☐ ☐ ....

7. Does the senior EDP executive or his designee execute company-wide agreements with EDP equipment and software vendors to take advantage of volume purchasing discounts (where appropriate)? ☐ ☐ ....

8. Does the senior EDP executive or his designee approve in advance deviations from established procedures and standards intended by organizational units? ☐ ☐ ....

C. Accountability and Security

1. Is the senior executive required to provide periodic reports to the chief executive and/or chief operating officer covering such topics as the following?
    a. Strategic and tactical plans ☐ ☐ ....
    b. Cost of resources and services ☐ ☐ ....
    c. Quality of services ☐ ☐ ....
    d. Status of major development projects ☐ ☐ ....
    e. Security and control status ☐ ☐ ....
    f. Specific events or incidents of particular concern ☐ ☐ ....
    g. Other pertinent information ☐ ☐ ....

2. Are records of the activities of the senior EDP executive adequately protected from loss or damage risks? ☐ ☐ ....

3. Is access to records of the senior EDP executive restricted to authorized personnel? ☐ ☐ ....

II. Corporate Organization—Planning:

A. Authorization

1. Do procedures specify authority and responsibility for the preparation and approval of both strategic and tactical (short-term) plans for EDP services? ☐ ☐ ....

(continued)

FIG. 38-10 *(cont'd)*

	Response Yes	No	Reference
2. Do procedures require that changes to strategic and tactical plans be reviewed and approved by the same individuals authorized to review and approve the original plans?	☐	☐	....
3. Do procedures provide the planning group authority to access all relevant data and obtain other information as may be necessary to develop sound plans?	☐	☐	....
4. Do procedures provide the planning group authority to obtain sufficient resources (personnel, office space, equipment) to enable the development of sound plans?	☐	☐	....

B. Execution and Recording

1. Are specific objectives for EDP services stated in short- and long-term plans?	☐	☐	....
2. Are the business objectives of the EDP plans consistent with the business objectives of the overall company?	☐	☐	....
3. Are EDP plans developed on the basis of established procedures and routines at regular intervals?	☐	☐	....
4. Do procedures require gathering relevant, reliable estimates from user groups for future demand of the various types of EDP services?	☐	☐	....

Such procedures might include:
a. Specified forms
b. Instructions for preparation
c. Requirement for user review and approval
d. Due dates
e. Distribution instructions
f. Consolidation routines

5. Do procedures specify the form and content for the formal plans?	☐	☐	....
6. Do procedures require that the plans be prepared in adequate detail to permit independent analysis, understanding, and evaluation?	☐	☐	....

For example, such plans might specify by user both utilization and cost of:
a. Central processing units
b. Storage devices
c. Printers

INFORMATION SYSTEMS MANAGEMENT

	Response	
	Yes No	Reference

    d. Terminals
    e. Other equipment
    f. Programming (maintenance)
    g. Programming (new systems)
    h. Telecommunications services
    i. Office automation equipment

7. Do procedures require that the demand for EDP services be converted into reliable estimates for facilities, equipment, and manpower of all types? ☐ ☐ ....

8. Do procedures include a methodology for estimating EDP costs associated with anticipated demand for EDP services? ☐ ☐ ....

9. Is the method for estimating EDP costs consistent with the method of collecting and recording actual costs? ☐ ☐ ....

10. Do procedures require that the EDP planning group keep accurate and complete records of the following?
    a. Reference material ☐ ☐ ....
    b. User organization input ☐ ☐ ....
    c. Supporting workpapers ☐ ☐ ....
    d. Final plans ☐ ☐ ....

C. Accountability and Security

1. Do procedures require that actual performance be compared periodically to planned performance by responsible management? ☐ ☐ ....

Such comparisons should cover the following topics:
    a. Utilization rates of CPUs
    b. Down time
    c. Response time (for on-line services)
    d. Data storage utilization
    e. Lines printed
    f. Cost/budget comparisons
    g. Progress on new systems development

2. Do procedures require that records of the planning group be adequately protected from loss or damage risks? ☐ ☐ ....

3. Is access to records of the planning group restricted to authorized personnel? ☐ ☐ ....

(continued)

FIG. 38-10 *(cont'd)*

	Response Yes	Response No	Reference
III. EDP Services:			
A. General Management			
1. Is there a written set of policies and procedures by which the EDP department operates?	☐	☐	....
2. Is there a written organization chart?	☐	☐	....
3. Is there a written functional outline for each key managerial function in the organization?	☐	☐	....
For example, functional outlines might be prepared for:			
a. DP manager			
b. Strategy planning manager			
c. Documentation control manager			
d. Security manager			
e. Data base administrator			
f. Operating systems manager			
g. Data conversion manager			
h. Library manager			
i. Quality assurance manager			
j. Technical support manager			
k. Operating systems manager			
4. Are the functional outlines written in order to make clear the authority and responsibility of each?	☐	☐	....
5. Do policies, procedures, and functional outlines appear sufficiently flexible to enable the organization to respond to technological change?	☐	☐	....
6. Does the general management of the department make use of any of the following control techniques?			
a. Budgeting	☐	☐	....
b. Performance review meetings	☐	☐	....
c. Record-keeping and monitoring of relevant operational data such as:			
■ CPU utilization	☐	☐	....
■ Down time	☐	☐	....
■ Response time	☐	☐	....
■ Interruptions	☐	☐	....
■ Security incidents	☐	☐	....
■ Actual cost versus budget comparison	☐	☐	....
■ Other equipment utilization	☐	☐	....
■ Vendor support performance	☐	☐	....
■ Volume of data processed	☐	☐	....

	Response	
	Yes No	Reference

    d. Analyzing, reviewing of records, using microcomputers by other means ☐ ☐ ....
    e. Keeping current with technical developments ☐ ☐ ....

7. Does the general manager of the department meet periodically with other functional organizations (marketing, finance, manufacturing, etc.)? ☐ ☐ ....

8. Does the general manager provide reports to higher management regarding the operational effectiveness of his organization? ☐ ☐ ....

9. Are the emergency duties and responsibilities of the general manager of the department set forth in the disaster recovery plan? ☐ ☐ ....

B. Strategy Planning

1. Is the function of strategy planning expressed formally in a written statement of authority and responsibility? ☐ ☐ ....

2. Is the function of future planning of orderly delivery of DP services integrated with the following?
    a. Other organizational plans ☐ ☐ ....
    b. Corporate-wide EDP strategies ☐ ☐ ....

3. Does the planning function employ such techniques as the following?
    a. Technical research ☐ ☐ ....
    b. User surveys ☐ ☐ ....
    c. Regression analysis ☐ ☐ ....
    d. Cost/benefit analysis of alternative courses of action ☐ ☐ ....
    e. Return on investment analyses of major acquisitions/conversions/expansions ☐ ☐ ....

4. Do individuals involved in strategic planning keep pace with important developments regarding the following?
    a. External
        ■ New products ☐ ☐ ....
        ■ New services ☐ ☐ ....
        ■ New risks ☐ ☐ ....
        ■ Regulatory changes ☐ ☐ ....
    b. Internal
        ■ Organizational changes ☐ ☐ ....
        ■ Policy and procedure changes ☐ ☐ ....

5. Do procedures dictate the frequency of plans and periods to be covered by them? ☐ ☐ ....

(continued)

FIG. 38-10 *(cont'd)*

	Response Yes No	Reference
6. Are the results of planning activities expressed formally in a written plan?	☐ ☐	....
7. Is the written plan distributed to all interested members of management?	☐ ☐	....

C. Documentation Control

1. Is the function of documentation control expressed formally in a written statement of authority and responsibility?	☐ ☐	....
2. Is the operation of the documentation control function covered by written policies and procedures?	☐ ☐	....
3. Do procedures cover such items as the following?		
a. Program documentation	☐ ☐	....
b. Program source codes	☐ ☐	....
c. System documentation	☐ ☐	....
d. Administrative documentation	☐ ☐	....
e. Security	☐ ☐	....
f. Backup and recovery	☐ ☐	....
4. Is a system in effect to reasonably assure that changes to official documentation occur pursuant to management's authorization?	☐ ☐	....
5. Is a system of record-keeping in effect to reasonably assure that the documentation control function can identify custodians of any documentation temporarily loaned out?	☐ ☐	....
6. Is a system in effect to reasonably assure the orderly filing, locating, and retrieving of all documentation?	☐ ☐	....
7. Is there appropriate use of space-saving techniques made?	☐ ☐	....
These might include:		
a. Basic company policy		
b. Legal requirements		
c. User requirements		
8. Is the documentation reasonably protected from destructive hazards and risks?	☐ ☐	....
9. Does the documentation center maintain records of the following:		
a. The documentation it controls	☐ ☐	....

	Response Yes No	Reference

    b. Documentation loaned ☐ ☐ ....
    c. Documentation changes ☐ ☐ ....

10. Does the documentation center periodically conduct physical inventories of documentation under its control for comparison with records thereof? ☐ ☐ ....

11. Is appropriate action taken with respect to any differences disclosed by such comparisons? ☐ ☐ ....

D. Security

1. Is the function of security in the DP department expressed formally in a written statement of authority and responsibility? ☐ ☐ ....

2. Is the operation of the security function covered by written policies and procedures? ☐ ☐ ....

3. Do procedures cover such items as the following?
    a. Maintenance of security standards ☐ ☐ ....
    b. Monitoring and record-keeping of security incidents affecting EDP ☐ ☐ ....
    c. Inspecting security devices and systems ☐ ☐ ....
    d. Consulting on new systems development ☐ ☐ ....
    e. Conducting tests of security, backup, and recovery procedures ☐ ☐ ....
    f. Reporting of security status ☐ ☐ ....

4. Are security standards sufficiently extensive to cover all facilities, personnel, equipment, software, and records of the EDP department? ☐ ☐ ....

5. Are security standards kept up-to-date with changes in systems and technology? ☐ ☐ ....

6. Do records of security incidents indicate the following for each?
    a. The nature of the incident ☐ ☐ ....
    b. The extent of loss or damage ☐ ☐ ....
    c. The reasons contributing to the incident ☐ ☐ ....
    d. Actions taken to limit or halt the incident ☐ ☐ ....
    e. Recovery actions ☐ ☐ ....
    f. Procedures initiated, if any, to avoid recurrence ☐ ☐ ....

7. Are the workings of the following types of security devices and systems inspected at least annually?

(continued)

FIG. 38-10 *(cont'd)*

	Response Yes	Response No	Reference
a. Door locks in computer room, vault, library, and any other critical areas	☐	☐	....
b. Fire extinguishers	☐	☐	....
c. Sprinkler systems	☐	☐	....
d. Halon systems	☐	☐	....
e. Badge recognition systems	☐	☐	....
f. Backup equipment	☐	☐	....
8. Are data security systems reviewed at least annually?	☐	☐	....

These might include:
a. Program security systems
b. Access control security systems
c. Operating system security features

| 9. Are scenarios devised and enacted that test the adequacy of disaster recovery plans? | ☐ | ☐ | .... |

E. Operations

1. Is the function of mainframe computer-room operations expressed formally in a written statement of authority and responsibility?	☐	☐	....
2. Are the several activities of computer-room operations covered by written policies and procedures?	☐	☐	....
3. Do procedures cover the following?			
a. General administration	☐	☐	....
b. Data control	☐	☐	....
c. Data conversion	☐	☐	....
d. Operating system generation and management	☐	☐	....
e. Scheduling and set up	☐	☐	....
f. Run procedures	☐	☐	....
g. Data storage (e.g., tape, disk)	☐	☐	....
h. Testing	☐	☐	....
i. Data base management	☐	☐	....
j. Utilities	☐	☐	....
k. Disaster recovery	☐	☐	....
l. Maintenance	☐	☐	....
4. Does the organization of the EDP operations department facilitate the delivery of EDP services?	☐	☐	....

Such an organization might provide for:
a. General management
b. An input control group or personnel

	Response	
	Yes No	Reference

    c. Data entry operation
    d. Data processing scheduling
    e. Computer operation
    f. Other functions

5. Does general management of the EDP operations function perform the following duties?
    a. Reviewing and approving procedures, standards, forms, budgets, and operating schedules   ☐ ☐   ....
    b. Monitoring job, personnel, equipment, and system performance   ☐ ☐   ....
    c. Reviewing and approving actions to resolve problems presented by abnormal events, deviations from established practices, and processing interruptions   ☐ ☐   ....
    d. Reporting activities and performance to higher management   ☐ ☐   ....

6. Does the data control function
    a. Receive all input batches for all applications?   ☐ ☐   ....
    b. Perform control and balance routines to reasonably assure that all data received will be processed as intended?   ☐ ☐   ....
    c. Maintain files in proper sequence and establish numerical controls?   ☐ ☐   ....
    d. Keep logs, forms, and records to evidence the data received, processed, and distributed?   ☐ ☐   ....
    e. Protect against data loss, destruction, and unauthorized access?   ☐ ☐   ....

7. Does the data entry/conversion function
    a. Perform all data entry/conversion operations?   ☐ ☐   ....
    b. Determine time/resource use?   ☐ ☐   ....
    c. Plan and schedule data entry operations to minimize use of resources and facilitate prompt and accurate data conversion?   ☐ ☐   ....
    d. Employ means to control data during conversion to protect against loss, destruction, duplicate entry, and unauthorized access?   ☐ ☐   ....
    e. Maintain accountability for transactions converted errors, resubmissions, and other information in order to permit monitoring efficiency and effectiveness?   ☐ ☐   ....

8. Is operating system generation and management
    a. Delegated to a specific individual or group?   ☐ ☐   ....
    b. Accomplished by following established policies and procedures approved by higher EDP management covering the following?
        ■ Authority and responsibility   ☐ ☐   ....

(continued)

FIG. 38-10 *(cont'd)*

	Response Yes	No	Reference
■ System generation	☐	☐	....
■ System operation	☐	☐	....
■ Use of supervisory commands and access methods	☐	☐	....
■ Maintenance of system logs and records to permit monitoring and reporting system activity	☐	☐	....
■ Implementation of system changes	☐	☐	....
■ Diagnostic procedures and problem resolution	☐	☐	....
■ System backup	☐	☐	....

9. Do operating system programmers or others responsible for the operating system keep informed with respect to the following?
   a. Vendor-supplied system revisions and enhancements ☐ ☐ ....
   b. Security enhancements ☐ ☐ ....
   c. Difficulties experienced by other operating system users ☐ ☐ ....

10. Do operating system programmers or others responsible for the system make reasonable use of productivity aids supplied by manufacturers, such as the following?
    a. Change tracking ☐ ☐ ....
    b. Mapping ☐ ☐ ....
    c. Display management systems ☐ ☐ ....
    d. Conversion aids ☐ ☐ ....
    e. Source program maintenance aid ☐ ☐ ....
    f. System statistics ☐ ☐ ....
    g. Performance analyzers ☐ ☐ ....
    h. Control and accounting programs ☐ ☐ ....
    i. System test and audit facility ☐ ☐ ....

11. Do operating system programmers or others responsible for the system render periodic reports and other information to higher management to inform them of the performance, effectiveness, and efficiency of the system? ☐ ☐ ....

12. Is the operating environment reasonably protected from security risks? ☐ ☐ ....

Operating systems must be augmented by various utility software, access restrictions on system programmers, detailed logging of system activity, careful review and approval of system changes, and appropriate segregation of duties in order to afford reasonable protection.

INFORMATION SYSTEMS MANAGEMENT

	Response		Reference
	Yes	No	
13. Is the function of production or job scheduling delegated to a specific individual or group?	☐	☐	....
14. Do production schedulers			
a. Receive all requests for data processing jobs?	☐	☐	....
b. Employ means to distinguish the following requests?			
■ Data entry	☐	☐	....
■ Development and test	☐	☐	....
■ Production	☐	☐	....
■ RJE	☐	☐	....
■ Microfiche	☐	☐	....
■ Other	☐	☐	....
c. Utilize job numbering and naming conventions to help organize and schedule production?	☐	☐	....
d. Employ system software or utilities to alternate part or all of the scheduling tasks?	☐	☐	....
e. Determine time/resource availability for processing jobs requested?	☐	☐	....
f. Maintain accurate and complete records and logs of scheduling and operating activity to permit comparisons between scheduled and actual production and to improve future scheduling?	☐	☐	....
g. Provide flexibility sufficient to accommodate reruns, emergencies, unanticipated requests, etc.?	☐	☐	....
15. Are operating instructions and procedures embodied in a run manual(s) or other suitable device covering matters such as the following?			
a. Flow charts	☐	☐	....
b. Data entry instructions	☐	☐	....
c. Operating instructions	☐	☐	....
d. Restart procedures	☐	☐	....
e. Set-up procedures	☐	☐	....
f. Distribution instructions	☐	☐	....
g. Control/balance instructions	☐	☐	....
h. Special instructions	☐	☐	....
16. Is the function of data storage (disk and/or tape) delegated to a specific individual or group?	☐	☐	....
17. Is the function of data storage accomplished by following established policies and procedures approved by higher EDP management covering			
a. Authority and responsibility?	☐	☐	....
b. Method of requesting storage (such as one based on approval requests from systems and programming personnel)?	☐	☐	....

(continued)

FIG. 38-10 *(cont'd)*

	Response Yes	Response No	Reference
c. Procedure for filling requests?	☐	☐	....
d. Maintenance of records and logs?	☐	☐	....
e. Data security requirements?	☐	☐	....
f. Backup?	☐	☐	....
g. Periodic accountability reporting?	☐	☐	....
h. Other?	☐	☐	....
18. Does the method used to fill user requests require consideration of the following?			
a. Alternate storage techniques	☐	☐	....
b. Data compression techniques	☐	☐	....
c. Period of time for which storage is needed	☐	☐	....
19. Is the function of system testing delegated to a specific individual or group?	☐	☐	....
20. Is the function of system testing accomplished by following procedures approved by higher EDP management covering			
a. Authority and responsibility?	☐	☐	....
b. Involvement in internally developed system changes?	☐	☐	....
c. Involvement in externally developed system changes?	☐	☐	....
d. System test methodology?	☐	☐	....
e. Resolution of test findings?	☐	☐	....
21. Do resources permit performing system tests without interruption of normal operations?	☐	☐	....
22. Do procedures preclude performing tests on live production files?	☐	☐	....
23. Do procedures require that system tests be performed on all system changes and the results reviewed and approved by appropriate supervision?	☐	☐	....
24. Is the function of data communications delegated to a specific individual or group?	☐	☐	....
25. Is the function of data communications accomplished by following established policies and procedures covering:			
a. Authority and reponsibility?	☐	☐	....
b. The communication network(s)?	☐	☐	....
c. Methodology for integrating data communication hardware and software current and future requirements with other EDP plans and user requirements?	☐	☐	....
d. Security and control guidelines?	☐	☐	....

INFORMATION SYSTEMS MANAGEMENT

	Response Yes	No	Reference
e. Operating procedures?	☐	☐	....
f. Record-keeping requirements?	☐	☐	....
g. Periodic accountability and reporting?	☐	☐	....

26. Is data communications management accomplished by use of a communications controller and a network control program? ☐ ☐ ....

27. Is there a methodology (usually one or more software modules) for handling such communication tasks as the following?

a. Polling terminals	☐	☐	....
b. Addressing specific terminals	☐	☐	....
c. Dialing services	☐	☐	....
d. Coding	☐	☐	....
e. Redundancy checking	☐	☐	....
f. Error correction	☐	☐	....
g. Queuing	☐	☐	....
h. Message control and editing	☐	☐	....
i. Restarting	☐	☐	....
j. Input/output buffering	☐	☐	....
k. Scheduling of exit routines	☐	☐	....
l. Sequence numbering of outbound messages	☐	☐	....
m. Error data analysis	☐	☐	....
n. Data compression	☐	☐	....

28. Is there a means by which the operation of the telecommunications system is monitored? (Usually this is done by use of a software device such as CICS, ENVIRON/1 or ROSCOE.) ☐ ☐ ....

29. Is network design based on consideration and analysis of the following?

a. User requirements	☐	☐	....
b. Current technology	☐	☐	....
c. Cost/benefit analysis	☐	☐	....
d. System network architecture	☐	☐	....
e. Processor configuration	☐	☐	....
f. Terminal configuration	☐	☐	....
g. Transmission systems	☐	☐	....
h. Security requirements	☐	☐	....

30. Is the function of data base management delegated to a specific individual or group? ☐ ☐ ....

(continued)

FIG. 38-10 *(cont'd)*

	Response Yes	No	Reference
31. Is the function of data base management accomplished by following established policies and procedures covering:			
a. Authority and responsibility?	☐	☐	....
b. Methodology for creating, maintaining, and destroying data elements?	☐	☐	....
c. Minimizing data redundancy?	☐	☐	....
d. Naming conventions?	☐	☐	....
e. User responsibility?	☐	☐	....
f. Approvals?	☐	☐	....
g. Data directories?	☐	☐	....
h. Data dictionaries?	☐	☐	....
i. Maintenance of software?	☐	☐	....
32. Is data base management accomplished by use of a software package such as IMS or TOTO?	☐	☐	....
33. Is access to data bases restricted by means of security software devices such as RACF or ACF2?	☐	☐	....
34. Is use of data base management systems for new applications determined by cost/benefit analysis?	☐	☐	....
35. Is a specified individual or group delegated the responsibility for acquiring and maintaining utility programs?	☐	☐	....
36. Are utility programs acquired on the basis of identified need and cost/benefit analysis?	☐	☐	....
37. Are procedures in effect to restrict use of utilities to authorized purposes by authorized personnel?	☐	☐	....
38. Are all uses of utilities required to be logged or recorded?	☐	☐	....
39. Does the individual or group responsible for utility programs keep current with respect to new programs and revisions to existing ones?	☐	☐	....
40. Is the function of disaster recovery delegated to a specific individual or group?	☐	☐	....
41. Are disaster recovery plans formally expressed in writing and approved by appropriate management?	☐	☐	....
42. Do such plans cover all types of disaster situations? These include:			
a. Facility, personnel, equipment, and software damaged	☐	☐	....

INFORMATION SYSTEMS MANAGEMENT

	Response Yes	No	Reference
b. Facility, personnel, and equipment intact but power lost	☐	☐	....
c. Facility intact but equipment and key personnel lost	☐	☐	....
d. Facility damaged but equipment and key personnel intact	☐	☐	....
e. Facility, equipment, and personnel intact, but access denied	☐	☐	....
43. Do procedures require that disaster recovery plans be periodically tested?	☐	☐	....
44. Do tests cover as many aspects of the plan as possible?	☐	☐	....
45. Is the function of hardware and software maintenance delegated to a specific individual or group?	☐	☐	....
46. Do resources permit carrying on maintenance in a manner in order to minimize disruption to normal processing?	☐	☐	....
47. Do procedures require keeping records of maintenance for each type of equipment?	☐	☐	....
48. Is maintenance activity reported periodically to appropriate supervision?	☐	☐	....
49. Are records required for each machine failure?	☐	☐	....
50. Are statistics of mean time between failure calculated and reported to supervision?	☐	☐	....

FIG. 38-11

ISM Audit Program

	Performed by	Date
I. Organization and Planning:		
A. Corporate Organization		
1. Obtain a copy of the written policy(ies) covering EDP and determine the existence of the following:		
a. Basic policy statement	....	....
b. Definitions of key terms	....	....
c. Clear statements of responsibilities	....	....
2. Obtain a copy of the organization chart for reference and to evidence the organization structure of the DP management.	....	....
	(continued)	

FIG. 38-11 *(cont'd)*

	Performed by	Date
3. Obtain copies of functional outlines for key EDP positions and ascertain that such outlines appear to cover all relevant duties.	....	....
4. Review minutes or other records of steering committee meetings and actions for indications of total management involvement, problem areas, and so forth.	....	....
5. By inquiry of key management, determine whether any problems exist, any higher-than-normal risks, and any current projects or activities that are of particular interest.	....	....
6. Obtain from the executive responsible for overall data management a representation as to the adequacy of overall EDP operations and the extent to which data resources are efficiently and effectively managed.	....	....
7. Obtain copies of any written statements of standards or guidelines covering data management, and review for completeness and currency.	....	....
8. Note evidence of proper approval for any changes during the previous year to policies, procedures, organization charts, and standards.	....	....
9. By inquiry, determine the reasons for and objectives of any changes noted in the preceding audit step.	....	....
10. Consider changing scope of audit as a result of any changes noted above to obtain evidence that the changes are having their desired effect.	....	....

11. Review files of periodic reports and other information received by senior EDP management pertaining to the state of the various EDP operations of organizational units for evidence of the following:
  a. Compliance with reporting requirements
  b. Emerging problems
  c. Remedial actions, if any
	
	....
	....
	....
		
		....
		....
		....

12. Test accuracy and completeness of selected reports on a judgmental basis by tracing to supporting data. This step may be deferred and performed in connection with other audit projects at various field locations.	....	....
13. By inspection of correspondence files and inquiry, ascertain that the senior executive responsible for data management is promptly informed of major problems, security incidents, and projects.	....	....

	Performed by	Date

14. Review files of reports by the senior executive responsible for data management to higher management and/or the board of directors for completeness, accuracy, and as an example of evidence of involvement of all senior management with monitoring data management activities. . . . .

15. If information readily exists, consider performing trend analyses of total expenditures for providing all DP services corporate-wide and for major components thereof (e.g., equipment, software, payroll) . . . .

B. Corporate Organization—Planning

1. Obtain copies of short- and long-term plans and perform the following:
   a. Trace amounts in plans to supporting detail on a test basis (judgmental). . . . .
   b. Review and test supporting data for consistency, completeness, accuracy, and for evidence of user group involvement. . . . .
   c. Evaluate assumptions used in developing plans for consistency with overall assumptions used in corporate goals and strategies. . . . .
   d. Note evidence of senior corporate management review and approval. . . . .

2. By inquiry and confirmation, determine that user groups' needs were satisfied in devising the plans (within economic constraints). . . . .

3. Inspect applicable files and/or records for evidence of periodic comparisons of actual performance with planned performance. In particular evidence of monitoring, the following items should be noted:
   a. Utilization rates of CPUs . . . .
   b. Down time . . . .
   c. Response time . . . .
   d. Data storage utilization . . . .
   e. Lines printed . . . .
   f. Cost/budget comparisons . . . .
   g. Progress on new systems development . . . .

4. By observation and inspection, note compliance with techniques used to afford record and file protection from loss or damage risks and that personnel accessing such data are authorized. . . . .

(continued)

FIG. 38-11 *(cont'd)*

	Performed by	Date
II. EDP Services—Mainframe Data Processing Services:		
A. General Management		
1. Obtain copies of policies, procedures, organization charts, and functional outlines for reference purposes and for evidence of the organizational state of the department.	....	....
2. Review the foregoing documents for consistency and compliance with corporate policy.	....	....
3. By inquiry, determine if any changes have been made since the last review. Obtain explanations concerning the reasons for any changes and ascertain that they have been properly approved.	....	....
4. Consider altering the scope of this audit to include determining compliance with any important changes.	....	....
5. By inquiry and inspection of applicable files and/or records, determine the extent to which the following techniques are used:		
a. Budgeting	....	....
b. Performance reviews	....	....
c. Record-keeping and monitoring of relevant operational data	....	....
6. Observe the extent to which microcomputers and applicable software are used for analysis, record-keeping, and monitoring functions.	....	....
7. By inquiry and confirmation, determine the extent to which the general manager of the department meets with the heads of other functional organizations.	....	....
8. Examine the reports and other information available, which reveal the extent to which the operational effectiveness of the department is reported to higher management.	....	....
B. Strategy Planning		
1. Obtain copies of applicable policies, procedures, organization charts, and functional outlines for reference purposes and for evidence of the organizational state of the function.	....	....
2. By inquiry, inspection, and confirmation, determine the extent of use of techniques such as:		
a. Technical research	....	....
b. User surveys	....	....
c. Regression analysis	....	....

	Performed by	Date

      d. Cost/benefit analysis

      e. ROI analysis

  3. Obtain copies of the most recent department short- and long-term plans and review for

      a. Integration with corporate-based planning

      b. Thoroughness

      c. Relevance and reliability

      d. Evidence of user involvement

C. Documentation Control

  1. Obtain copies of applicable policies, procedures, organization charts, and functional outlines for reference purposes and for evidence of the organizational state of the function.

  2. By inquiry, determine whether any changes to the foregoing occurred during the period under review and ascertain the reasons for them. Determine that key changes, if any, have been properly approved and consider expanding scope to include testing compliance with important changes, if any.

  3. By either statistical or judgmental sampling, measure compliance with the system of record-keeping used to reasonably assure control of:

      a. Documentation on file

      b. Changes to documentation

      c. Documentation loaned out

  4. Observe file and space arrangement and general housekeeping for propriety and effectiveness in finding and retrieving documents.

  5. Observe the techniques in effect to reasonably protect against unauthorized access to files and risks of loss or destruction.

  6. Review records of physical inventories, if any, for compliance and for any indication of significant quantities of missing files.

D. Security

  1. Obtain copies of applicable policies, procedures, standards, organization charts, and functional outlines for reference purposes and for evidence of the organizational state of the function.

  2. By inquiry, determine whether any changes to the forc

(continued)

FIG. 38-11 *(cont'd)*

	Performed by	Date
going occurred during the period under review and ascertain the reasons thereto. Determine that key changes, if any, have been properly approved and consider expanding scope to include testing compliance with and effectiveness of any important changes.	....	....
3. By inquiry and inspection of applicable records, determine that the record of security incidents is in compliance with established procedures.	....	....
4. By inquiry and inspection of applicable files and records, determine the frequency with which security devices and systems are checked for proper functioning. Follow up any reported exceptions to ascertain that remedial actions were taken.	....	....
5. Tour the computer facility and note any observed situations incompatible with sound security procedures. Particular attention should be paid to the proper workings of:		
a. Vaults	....	....
b. Door locks	....	....
c. Badge recognition systems	....	....
d. Backup equipment	....	....
6. During the tour, examine evidence (if any) of inspections of fire-extinguishing equipment and any other physical protective devices to the extent practicable.	....	....
7. Obtain evidence of reviews of data security systems.	....	....
8. If possible, arrange to be present to observe tests of emergency and disaster recovery plans.	....	....
E. Operations		
1. Obtain copies of applicable policies, procedures, standards, organization charts, and functional outlines for reference purposes and for evidence of the organizational state of the function.	....	....
2. By inquiry, determine whether any changes to the foregoing occurred during the period under review and ascertain the reasons for them. Determine that key changes, if any, have been properly approved and consider expanding scope to include testing compliance with and effectiveness of any important changes.	....	....
3. By inquiry of appropriate management and inspection of applicable files and records, obtain evidence of EDP management involvement with and reporting of EDP operations, projects, and other activities.	....	....

	Performed by	Date

4. Review the data control function records and logs for the period under review for evidence of:
   a. Consistency of use ....
   b. Thoroughness and completeness ....
   c. Compliance with procedures for control and balancing ....
   d. Use of numerical control techniques ....

5. By inquiry and confirmation, ascertain the relative frequency of control balancing problems and determine its reasonableness in light of all data processed. Determine whether any unusual balancing errors or difficulties were encountered and investigate as deemed necessary. ....

6. Examine records indicating data conversion activity and review for evidence of:
   - Production efficiency ....
   - Excessive resubmission rate ....
   - Completeness and consistency ....
   - Reporting to higher management ....

7. Obtain copies of applicable operating system policies, procedures, standards, organization charts, and flow charts for reference purposes and for evidence of the organizational state of the function. ....

8. By inquiry, determine if any changes to the foregoing occurred during the period under review and ascertain the reasons for them. Determine that key changes, if any, were properly approved and consider expanding scope to include testing compliance with and effectiveness of any important changes. ....

9. Examine manual records and files, if any, indicating operating system activity for evidence of:
   a. Operating efficiency ....
   b. Operating difficulties ....
   c. Completeness and consistency ....
   d. Reporting to higher management ....

10. If not otherwise available, arrange for and execute through special analyzer software a selected extraction of the following data from the operating system management facility, if present:
    a. Date, time, job name, and program names of all jobs that were abnormally terminated during a one-week period ....
    b. All programs that accessed or attempted to access the following master files:
       - Customer ....

(continued)

FIG. 38-11 *(cont'd)*

	Performed by	Date
■ Payroll	....	....
■ Vendor	....	....
■ Other (at selection of auditor)	....	....
11. By inquiry and observation, determine that SYSGEN occurs in accordance with established procedure.	....	....
12. Confirm the existence and readiness of system backup arrangements.	....	....
13. By inspection of files, logs, and other records and by inquiry of appropriate systems programmers, determine the extent to which use of productivity aids (such as change tracking, mapping, and display management system) occurs.	....	....
14. By inquiry, determine if any security incidents have occurred, their magnitude and impact, and what, if anything, management has done to prevent recurrence.	....	....
15. By inquiry of production schedules and inspection of files, test the following either judgmentally or statistically:		
a. Receipt of all production requests	....	....
b. Consistent use of job numbering	....	....
c. Consistent use of forms, logs, and scheduling software (if applicable)	....	....
d. Scheduling based on user need, resource availability, and the nature of the jobs	....	....
16. Examine the run manual(s) for		
a. Thoroughness (covering all applications)	....	....
b. Completeness (contents include all relevant flow charts, and instructions)	....	....
c. Currency	....	....
d. Evidence of use	....	....
17. Inspect records and logs of data storage as deemed necessary.	....	....
18. Tour library area observing compliance with procedures for orderly arrangement and storage of data tapes.	....	....
19. Examine records and files of system testing activity for:		
a. Evidence of regular testing	....	....
b. Compliance with established procedures	....	....
c. Indications of unresolved problems	....	....
20. By inquiry of data communications personnel and by		

	Performed by	Date

observation and other means as deemed necessary, determine whether

    a. Network design meets user requirements and takes advantage of current technology. ....

    b. Appropriate software is used to aid in monitoring and controlling the network configuration. ....

    c. The network is effective and efficient in transmitting data. ....

    d. Security measures are operative. ....

21. Examine applicable policies for evidence of statement minimizing data redundancy. ....

22. By inquiry of data base administrators and comparative scans of data bases, search for evidence of excessive data redundancy. ....

23. Examine data base administration files or records for compliance with established procedures covering:

    a. Identification of individual(s) responsible for each data item ....

    b. Approvals for changes to authorization for access and update ....

    c. Proper use of data dictionaries ....

    d. Maintenance of data base management system ....

    e. Consistent use of password protection ....

24. By inquiry and confirmation, ascertain the extent to which added use of data base management system is based upon cost/benefit analysis. ....

25. Observe the restoration of a data base. (If this does not occur on a frequent enough basis, it might require that special arrangements be made to demonstrate the restoration process.) ....

26. If records permit, perform analysis to ascertain the extent to which the following occurs:

    a. Unauthorized access/update attempts ....

    b. Incidents of data loss ....

    c. Data base reorganizations to improve efficiency ....

    d. Tests of backup systems ....

27. Review records and files of the disaster recovery function for evidence of disaster.

Plan:

    a. Creation ....

    b. Review and approval by appropriate management ....

    c. Periodic testing ....

    d. Other, as deemed necessary ....

FIG. 38-12
ISM Audit Report

TO: W.M. Soloman

FROM: Corporate Audit

SUBJECT: Operational Review of Information System Management—WCR Division

We have reviewed the Management Information System (MIS) function at the WCR Division. The purpose of the review was to evaluate the adequacy and effectiveness of management controls over operational function within ISM. Generally speaking, actions have occurred over the past two years which have significantly improved the security and control over computer resources and the effectiveness of MIS operations. Division growth, increasing demand, and technological change, which have initiated a requirement for control enhancements, have occurred during this period. Our specific findings are as follows:

- Strategic plans are prepared without regard to business objectives of the division.
- User input is not systematically sought or confirmed in developing strategic and tactical plans.
- Alternatives to acquiring additional direct access storage devices (such as acquiring minicomputers) are not sufficiently explored.
- The incidence of computer down time suggests operating system enhancements are needed.
- The cost of developing new systems often exceeds original estimates, indicating the need for more efficient programming techniques and for better project control and management.
- Data bases contain too much redundancy, suggesting the need for data dictionaries and improved data base administration.
- There are no established policies relating to the acquisition, control, and use of micro/personal computers for business purposes.
- There is inadequate off-site backup of application systems/programming documentation.
- The methodology for distributing ISM costs to the users has not been completely documented.

In our opinion and subject to implementing the corrective action recommended, there are sufficient controls to reasonably assure that data is processed accurately and completely, and that data and other computer resources are effectively safeguarded.

Our detailed findings and recommendations for corrective action are discussed in the balance of the report [omitted]. The scope of our review included an examination of the MIS Installation organization, record-keeping, accountability, security and systems development. Our review was performed in accordance with department audit standards and included a review of a completed questionnaire, applicable procedures and other documentation, discussions with cognizant management and personnel, and the performance of such tests as were appropriate under the circumstances.

A reply to this report, addressed to Corporate Audit, including schedules for contemplated action, is requested from the designated parties within thirty days.

the questionnaire, which might also be used. Finally, Figure 38-12 illustrates a specimen report that might be issued as a result of an ISM operational audit.

SUGGESTED READING

Brink, Victor Z., and Herbert Witt. *Modern Internal Auditing: Appraising Operations and Controls*, 4th ed., Chapters 3, 22. New York: John Wiley & Sons, 1982.

Computer Audit Assistance Group. *Computer Auditing*. Coopers & Lybrand: Use and Distribution Restricted.

Crane, Janet. "The Changing Role of the DP Manager." *Datamation*, Jan. 1982, pp. 97–108.

Harrison, John P., and David C. Goodyear. "Assertiveness Training: Getting What You Want From a Computer." *Corporate Accounting*, Fall 1983, pp. 68–72.

Howe, Charles L. "Coping With Computer Criminals." *Datamation*, Jan. 1982, pp. 118–130.

International Business Machines. *A Management System for the Information Business*, Volume 1—Management Overview. White Plains, New York: IBM, 1981.

———. *Organizing the I/S Business*. White Plains, New York: IBM, 1983.

Naisbitt, John. *Megatrends*. New York: Warner Books, 1982, pp. 11–38.

CHAPTER **39**

R&D Management; Engineering Management

Introduction 2	Organizing for Research and Development 13
Research and Development Activities Defined 2	Outside Resources 14
Corporate Impact of Research and Development 3	Increasing Research and Development Productivity 15
Selected Subjects to Be Reviewed 4	Financial Reports on Research and Development Activity 17
Communication With Top Management 5	Performance Standards 17
Amount Spent on Basic Research 5	
Methods of Determining the Total R&D Budget 5	Research and Development Management Audit Questionnaire and Program 20
Establishment of the Operating Budget: Indirect Costs 8	An Operations Audit of the Engineering Function 34
Project Budgets 8	
Quality of R&D Staff 9	
Limited Use of Economic Measures ... 10	Suggested Reading 41

Fig. 39-1 Interrelationship of Corporate Goals, Objectives, and the Research and Development Activity Plan 6
Fig. 39-2 Twenty-Five Factors Most Likely to Cause Serious Counterproductivity Within Research and Development Organizations 16
Fig. 39-3 Actual and Budgeted Research and Development Expense, by Department 18
Fig. 39-4 Research and Development Project Status Report 19
Fig. 39-5 Audit Questionnaire—Research and Development Management 20
Fig. 39-6 Audit Program—Research and Development Management 31
Fig. 39-7 Audit Questionnaire—Engineering Function 34

INTRODUCTION

In view of a large element of subjective or judgmental decisions, some business functions are less subject to an operational audit than others. Marketing management is one of these; another is R&D management. Nevertheless, an operational audit of some aspects of the R&D function may be helpful to both the general management as well as the manager of R&D operations. This is more apt to be true if the internal auditor takes the view that R&D expenditures, properly managed, should be regarded as an *investment* in the future growth of the company. In some industries, such as aerospace, it is called a business regeneration expense and is vital to the continuity and development of the enterprise.

In many companies, the engineering function and R&D are either closely related or are in the same department. Accordingly, both functions are discussed in this chapter.

RESEARCH AND DEVELOPMENT ACTIVITIES DEFINED

From the internal auditor's point of view, R&D expense might be regarded as those expenses under the jurisdiction of the vice-president or director in charge of R&D. However, the most authoritative definition of R&D expense is that provided by the FASB.[1]

> 8. For purposes of this Statement, research and development is defined as follows:
>   (a) *Research* is planned search or critical investigation aimed at discovery of new knowledge with the hope that such knowledge will be useful in developing a new product or service (hereinafter "product") or a new process or technique (hereinafter "process") or in bringing about a significant improvement to an existing product or process.
>   (b) *Development* is the translation of research findings or other knowledge into a plan or design for a new product or process or for a significant improvement to an existing product or process whether intended for sale or use. It includes the conceptual formulation, design, and testing of product alternatives, construction of prototypes, and operation of pilot plants. It does not include routine or periodic alterations to existing products, production lines, manufacturing processes, and other on-going operations even though those alterations may represent improvements and it does not include market research or market testing activities.
>   9. The following are examples of activities that typically would be included in

---

[1] Statement of Financial Accounting Standards No. 2, *Accounting for Research and Development Costs* (Oct. 1974). Copyright by the FASB, High Ridge Park, Stamford, Conn. 06905. Copies of the complete document are available from the FASB.

research and development in accordance with paragraph 8 (unless conducted for others under a contractual arrangement—see paragraph 2):
(a) Laboratory research aimed at discovery of new knowledge.
(b) Searching for applications of new research findings or other knowledge.
(c) Conceptual formulation and design of possible product or process alternatives.
(d) Testing in search for or evaluation of product or process alternatives.
(e) Modification of the formulation or design of a product or process.
(f) Design, construction, and testing of pre-production prototypes and models.
(g) Design of tools, jigs, molds, and dies involving new technology.
(h) Design, construction, and operation of a pilot plant that is not of a scale economically feasible to the enterprise for commercial production.
(i) Engineering activity required to advance the design of a product to the point that it meets specific functional and economic requirements and is ready for manufacture.

These authoritative definitions are helpful in understanding the broad nature of R&D (as well as some engineering functions). In reviewing activities in a particular company, there is some merit in classifying the R&D functions into the following subdivisions:

☐ *Basic or fundamental research.* This aspect of research is defined as investigation for the purpose of advancing scientific knowledge, with no specific applications in mind. The activity may or may not be in fields of present or potential interest to the company.

☐ *Applied research.* Activity in this area relates to the application of basic research to products or processes in which the firm has or desires a commercial interest.

☐ *Development.* This grouping includes both *product* development and *process* development, and includes effort to bring the product or process into full-scale commercial application.

These distinctions between basic research, applied research, and development become important when considering the allocation of funds to various types of projects. On the other hand, in some industries, the traditional boundaries between basic and applied research are blurring.

CORPORATE IMPACT OF RESEARCH AND DEVELOPMENT

Empirical evidence indicates the existence of some relationship between earnings growth and expenditures made for effective R&D activities. In fact, R&D functions may be both defensive and offensive when related to the strategies of a particular company: defensive in that such efforts may be undertaken to forestall technological or product obsolescence, and offensive in that a competitive advantage is gained by either improving existing products or developing innovative and useful new products (or processes). Innovation or improvement of products and/or processes, coupled with the management of change, is one of the characteristics that distinguishes the progressive company from one on the decline.

Research and development in the United States is undertaken by a number of diverse institutions, encompassing the federal government and other governments, including related agencies; industry; colleges and universities; nonprofit associations and organizations; and professional firms that conduct research for others. In fact, in the late 1970s, there was considerable written commentary about the decline in R&D in the United States, whether the result of unacceptable government regulations or procedures, short-sighted business executives, unstable economic conditions, or lack of incentive. Of course, inadequate R&D could have adverse consequences for the U.S. economy taken as a whole, as well as for a specific company.

Since the late 1970s, as a matter of fact, R&D expenditures by industry—expressed as a percent of GNP—have been increasing.

Each year, *Business Week* publishes its R&D Scoreboard to indicate the magnitude and trend of R&D expenditures of U.S. companies on company-sponsored R&D as reported in Form 10K filed with the SEC. As a matter of interest, in 1986, the 859 *companies* (excluding the U.S. government) included in the survey spent $50.9 billion in R&D expenses, an average of 3.5 percent of sales.[2]

Given the importance of R&D to the continuance and growth of many firms, perhaps the internal auditor should be alert to the need for *reasonable, not minimal,* expenditures, within the company's financial capability.

SELECTED SUBJECTS TO BE REVIEWED

In an operations audit, any number of subjects are usually covered. These become evident as the questionnaire and audit program contained in this chapter are reviewed. However, given the unique nature of R&D activities and the high subjective content, there are some special aspects that should be discussed. Included are these (as well as other) pertinent topics:

- Communication between top management and research staff
- Amount spent on basic research
- Methods of determining the total R&D budget
- Quality of the R&D staff
- Limited use of economic measures

---

[2] *Business Week,* June 22, 1987, p. 158.

As background to an operational audit, each of these subjects is discussed briefly in the following paragraphs.

Communication With Top Management

An area of considerable difficulty in some enterprises is the limited communication between the research staff and top management. The latter often does not understand the workings of the research group. Management does understand output, and often looks for quick output results—new products, new processes, and so on. Yet, much more time than anticipated is required on many occasions. In R&D, a great need is a stable budget for a five-year period rather than an attempt to measure output on a yearly basis.

In interviews with the research directors and staff, as well as top management, the internal auditor may gain some leads about attitudes, expectations, gaps in communications, and methods that can be used to improve the entire communication process.

Amount Spent on Basic Research

In most concerns, there probably should be a balance between funds spent on basic research and monies used for development. A short-sighted management team might be tempted to stress applications to the detriment of basic research and for the increase of near-term profit. Yet, there may be a close relationship between the basic research and other activities, giving promise of immediate rewards. Hence, research management must judge what the requirements are (e.g., whether the technology has reached its limit and whether research on new technologies is vital to the well-being of the concern). The audit report is a useful communication device in this and related matters.

Methods of Determining the Total R&D Budget

In planning the R&D budget, it is highly desirable that a long-term approach be taken. Because project or program costs will be large, and since such activities cannot effectively be turned on and off, it is rather important that the probable outlay over several years be weighed. It is obvious that the planned R&D activities should be consistent with the long-term corporate purpose or mission. The preferred relationship is illustrated in Figure 39-1.[3] If a corporate objective, for example, is growth in the communications or countermeasure fields, then the research projects undertaken should support and enhance this objective. If the concern plans on divesting product lines

---

[3] From James D. Willson, *Budgeting and Profit Planning Manual,* 2nd ed. (New York: Warren, Gorham & Lamont, 1988), Figure 21-4.

FIG. 39-1
Interrelationship of Corporate Goals, Objectives, and the Research and Development Activity Plan

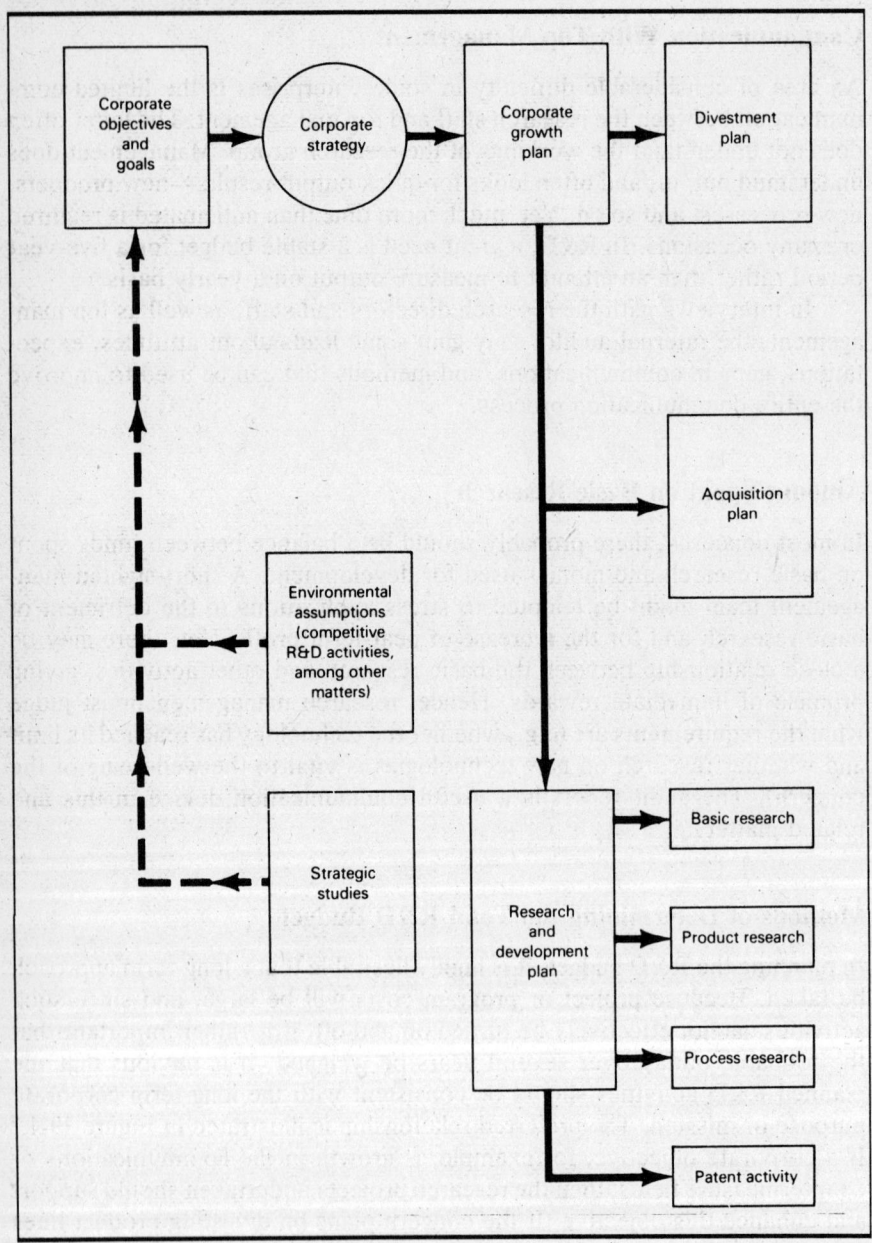

or companies in the aluminum fabrication business, for example, it probably makes little economic sense to spend significant sums that would have only a long-run impact on the business prospects.

The projects to be undertaken should be consistent with the corporate strategy and corporate growth plans (including divestment).[4] With this in mind, management must make an annual decision as to how much should be spent in the aggregate on R&D activities. Of course, this determination must be closely related to the number and extent of R&D programs to be undertaken. Why not simply add up the projected cost of the individual programs? The response is relatively easy. Given the resources—both financial and labor—the potential programs that might be undertaken by a creative director of R&D are almost limitless. There are always new products or processes to be developed, or improvements to be made in existing ones. Hence, more often than not, it is desirable to set an overall limit on the level of expenditures, giving recognition to the multiyear requirements of some programs.

Some of the practical constraints in setting the total amount to be spent include the following factors:

- *The financial position of the company.* No matter how worthy the research objectives, the company must be in a position to make the funds available.
- *The amount necessary to make the program effective.* To spend too little may not permit attainment of the desired results.
- *The expansion program.* The future growth plans of the company will influence both the nature and extent of the research program.
- *Competitive activity.* Action of the principal competitors usually will be considered in reviewing any research plans.
- *General economic outlook.* The future prospects, tax burden, and similar factors must be weighed.
- *Availability of manpower.* Employees with the proper professional background are essential.

With these general considerations in mind, management may select any one of several guideposts to measure the *total* budget:

- Percentage of estimated sales for the next year, or perhaps an average of the next several years
- Percentage of operating profit before R&D expense
- Percentage of net profit
- Expenditures of the preceding year, perhaps adjusted by a flat percentage
- Fixed amount per unit of product sold or estimated to be sold
- Percentage of cash flow for a single year, or perhaps the average of several years

---

[4] *Ibid.* Some of the commentary is adapted from Chapter 21.

- Percentage of investment in capital assets
- Cost of selected projects and related support activities
- Amount per employee

To reiterate, an important point to keep in mind is the need of awareness of the longer-term implications of the R&D budget—and not merely a single year.

Establishment of the Operating Budget: Indirect Costs. The establishment of an overall budget or appropriation merely sets the total limits of expenditure. It becomes necessary to establish (1) the amount for each operating department, which in turn may relate to project costs, and (2) the funds necessary for the supporting services and general administration (the "overhead" or indirect costs). In practice, the project budgets may be planned first, and then the required indirect expenses. For ease of discussion, these indirect expenses are reviewed before touching on the project costs.

While project costs, being the direct outlay applicable to specific projects—the "direct labor" and "direct material"—may be controlled by the project leader, it is probably necessary to consider and control these indirect costs on a total requirement basis. This category of cost results from the many aids and supporting activities that benefit the overall technical program. Costs may include those related to:

- Departmental administration
- Depreciation of technical facilities and equipment
- Authorship of technical papers
- Preparation of technical proposals
- Library services
- Attendance at technical meetings and seminars

In principle, this type of cost must be held to reasonable proportions in relation to the direct costs of the project. Basically, the approach to this expense is similar to that of manufacturing or distribution overhead:

- Definite assignment of responsibility for the budgeted costs
- Establishment of proper amounts, depending on level needed, to support the project activity and direct research effort
- Control by comparison of budget and actual, by responsibility, and by type of expense

Project Budgets. Project budgets ordinarily will be established after an evaluation of the work to be done. In this process, recognition should be given to the various major groupings of R&D activity; and the segregation of total costs budgeted and expended in each category will have considerable significance. As mentioned previously, there should be a proper balance between basic research and other types of research or development, based on the judgment of the research director. The various projects should be classified, based on the type of activity significant in the particular firm. For example, a chemical company segregates its projects into these categories:

- ☐ *Basic research*—having no direct relationship to specific products or processes.
- ☐ *New product research*—related to specific products not now manufactured by the company.
- ☐ *Product improvement*—relating to improvement in the quality or appearance of existing products.
- ☐ *Sales service requests*—projects requested by the sales department to facilitate the servicing of customers.
- ☐ *Factory service requests*—projects requested by the manufacturing arm and representing requests for improved processes.

A great many factors may enter into the selection of specific projects, including:

- Recent breakthroughs in the technical field
- Attitude of top management
- Availability of qualified personnel
- Availability of purchased research (e.g., from a university or professional research group)
- Status of related research
- Needs of the enterprise, and estimated time to find an answer
- Related importance of the project to the company
- Anticipated economic gains (perhaps measured by the discounted cash flow rate of return)
- Potential licensing income

In any event, the judgment of the chief R&D officer, in conjunction with top management, is the primary determinant. The internal auditor must be sensitive to the procedure and the high degree of subjectivity; however, he may have some suggestions after a review of basic data and discussions with appropriate executives.

Quality of R&D Staff

Research and development is largely a people activity, and the achievement of excellence probably depends most on the quality of a properly motivated staff. Therefore, care must be used in applying quantitative measures to the group (i.e., wage rates or salary ranges, relative salaries and fringe benefits, expenses as a percentage of salaries, total costs per man-hour, and so on) either in the absolute, or as measured against other groups, both within and without the company. Tests or reviews of data should relate to the quality of the staff and the assignments given to specific individuals.

Limited Use of Economic Measures

In most well-run companies, approval of capital expenditures on specific programs or projects is given only after a thorough review of the economics. Given the many intangibles, this approach may be used in testing some R&D activities. But the applications might fit only the most conspicuous improprieties or some obvious successes. Thus, it is hardly prudent to spend a significant sum on a development project, only to learn that the market ceased to exist just as the effort was completed. And it would make little business sense to begin a research project if the probable return from the sale of the product simply could never approach the gross outlay. In general, under the private enterprise system, the end product of the research (a product or process) is considered viable only if it does the following:

- Provides for recovery of the cost of research;
- Permits recoupment of the cost of working capital and plant investment; and
- Provides an acceptable rate of return on the cash funds required.

There are occasions when an economic review or test is advisable. But the auditor should be reasonably sure of the facts. Some testing may help avoid the more obvious, ill-planned projects. In some instances, support for the planned amount of R&D can be provided by an economic analysis, where there are not too many "guesses" and the management is analytically inclined.

The cost-volume-profit relationship may provide some insight, albeit with assumptions, that are often gross estimates. Assume these facts:

1. Management expects a return of 8 percent on assets employed, after taxes.
2. The expected sales of the newly developed product should approximate $50 million.
3. The expected product gross margin is 20 percent.
4. The required investment, after research is completed, is:

Working capital	$3,000,000
Plant and equipment	2,000,000
Total	$5,000,000

5. The federal income tax rate is expected to be 40 percent.

The question to be considered, using return on assets as a guide, is, "How much R&D (before taxes) can be spent on this product?"

An indication of the outlay for R&D may be calculated in the following manner:

RESEARCH & DEVELOPMENT MANAGEMENT

$$\text{Return on assets} = \frac{\text{Net income}}{\text{Total assets}}$$

$$\text{Net income} = \text{Gross margin} - \text{R\&D} - \text{Income tax}$$

$$\text{Income tax} = (\text{Gross margin} - \text{R\&D}) \times 40\%$$

$$\text{Gross margin} = \text{Sales} \times 20\%$$

$$\text{Return on assets} = 8\%$$

By substitution:

$$\text{Net income} = \text{Gross margin} - \text{R\&D} - [(\text{Gross margin} - \text{R\&D}) \times 40\%]$$

$$\text{Return on assets} = \frac{\text{Gross margin} - \text{R\&D} - [(\text{Gross margin} - \text{R\&D}) \times 40\%]}{\text{Total assets}}$$

$$8\% = \frac{(50{,}000{,}000 \times 20\%) - \text{R\&D} - [(50{,}000{,}000 \times 20\% - \text{R\&D}) \times 40\%]}{5{,}000{,}000}$$

To simplify:

$$400 = 10{,}000 - \text{R\&D} - [(10{,}000 - \text{R\&D}) \times 40\%]$$
$$-9{,}600 = -\text{R\&D} - 4{,}000 + 0.4\,\text{R\&D}$$
$$0.6\,\text{R\&D} = 5{,}600$$
$$\text{R\&D} = \underline{9{,}333{,}000}$$

Proof:

Sales	$50,000,000
Gross margin @ 20%	$10,000,000
Less: R&D expense	9,333,000
Income before taxes	$ 667,000
Income taxes @ 40%	267,000
Net income	$ 400,000
Total assets	$ 5,000,000
Return on assets ($400,000 ÷ $5,000,000)	8%

Of course, this calculation can be adjusted to an annual basis.

Sometimes management believes it has a sense of the return on a project needed to be acceptable as judged by the percentage return on net sales. Assume these facts:

1. The objective is a net return (after taxes) of 10 percent on sales.
2. The expected sales are $40 million.
3. The federal income tax rate is estimated to be 40 percent.

How much can be spent on R&D? The estimate can be made as follows:

$$\text{Return on sales} = \frac{\text{Net income}}{\text{Sales}}$$

$$\text{Net income} = \text{Gross margin} - \text{R\&D} - \text{Income tax}$$

$$\text{Income tax} = (\text{Gross margin} - \text{R\&D}) \times 40\%$$

$$\text{Gross margin} = \text{Sales} \times 20\%$$

$$\text{Return on sales} = 10\%$$

By substitution:

$$\text{Net income} = (\text{Gross margin}) - \text{R\&D} - [(\text{Gross margin} - \text{R\&D}) \times 40\%]$$

$$\text{Return on sales} = \frac{(\text{Gross margin}) - \text{R\&D} - [(\text{Gross margin} - \text{R\&D}) \times 40\%]}{\text{Sales}}$$

$$10\% = \frac{(40,000,000 \times 20\%) - \text{R\&D} - [(40,000,000 \times 20\% - \text{R\&D}) \times 40\%]}{40,000,000}$$

To simplify:

$$40,000,000 = 8,000,000 - \text{R\&D} - [(8,000,000 - \text{R\&D}) \times 40\%]$$
$$-4,000,000 = -\text{R\&D} - 3,200,000 + 0.4\,\text{R\&D}$$
$$0.6\,\text{R\&D} = 800,000$$
$$\text{R\&D} = \underline{\underline{1,333,000}}$$

Proof:

Sales	$40,000,000
Gross margin (20%)	$ 8,000,000
Less: R&D expense	1,333,000
Income before taxes	$ 6,667,000
Income taxes @ 40%	2,667,000
Net income	$ 4,000,000
Return on sales ($4,000,000 ÷ $40,000,000)	10%

Of course, the derived answers are only rough estimates.

Used properly, analytical techniques may help to convince management of the economic feasibility of a project by showing the steps necessary, converting uncertainty to measured probability and risk, and identifying the cost and time required and the risk/reward relationship.[5] The internal auditor may make tests of the economic benefits or quantify the overall value of

---

[5] As an excellent example, see Philip A. Roussal, "Cutting Down the Guesswork in R&D," *Harvard Business Review,* Sept./Oct. 1983, pp. 154–160.

R&D "successes" over a period of years. However, caution should be used in drawing conclusions.

ORGANIZING FOR RESEARCH AND DEVELOPMENT

In most operational audits, a subject to be reviewed is the organization structure. It is to be emphasized that the organization structure alone does not make for successful R&D. Rather, it is the quality of the people, properly motivated, that largely determines success. Yet, the proper structure facilitates the linkage or communication between the R&D activities and the other key elements of the enterprise: top management, marketing, and especially, manufacturing.

With that proviso, some comments on possible organization structure are in order regarding a decentralized or centralized organization, or some combination of alternatives:

1. Where there are a large number of business units with diverse products and great geographic dispersion, a decentralized structure may be preferred. Of course, it is desirable that the operating unit presidents have a long-term viewpoint, and that they have freedom of action to meet threats and opportunities without the hindrance of a large bureaucracy. It is up to those officers to motivate, stimulate, and direct the R&D activities as well as foster the entrepreneurial spirit. The risk is that too much emphasis is put on short-term results. There might be excessive attention devoted to solving day-to-day needs and less risky projects, with the result that the division's long-term future is neglected. In many circumstances, decentralization permits an easier integration of the R&D activity into the planning and operating functions of the unit.
2. Where economies of scale are possible (as in the use of expensive testing equipment), where the products are related, and research is by technical area (not necessarily product), then a case may be made for a centralized organization. Within such a (large) structure, steps must be taken to avoid stifling initiative.
3. Given the respective advantages and disadvantages of centralized or decentralized R&D, some companies use a mixed mode—with a central or corporate laboratory for the longer-range, higher-risk research, and a decentralized organization for other projects that should have short term applications.

In summary, the types of organization structure of R&D depend on the following, as well as other factors:

- Company history
- Style of management
- Degree of technical diversity

- Geographic dispersion
- Strategic objectives

Further, it should be recognized that some large companies form "venture capital" units within their gigantic organizations in order to motivate and reward certain highly creative R&D types. Individual circumstances govern each situation. These comments are intended to help the internal auditor become aware of the considerations. Reference should be made to recent literature on the matter.[6]

OUTSIDE RESOURCES

The objective of R&D management, after contributing to the continuity and growth of the enterprise, is to secure the maximum benefit from a given investment in R&D, long-term considerations being paramount. But most R&D managers have extensive supplies or reserves above and beyond the internal resources, which include:

- Universities
- Joint research ventures
- Other outside sources, both foreign and domestic, including patents and licensing

An operations audit might explore the use that can be made of these external sources.

Collaboration with a university can benefit both the company and the university. For example, industrial scientists, working with selected academic associates, may gain early insight into the significance of certain basic observations, perhaps covering a wide range of research. Universities can secure financial aid, access to specialized facilities, and a new or different perspective regarding certain phases of research. This can be accomplished without changing the purpose of the university in relation to education and basic research.

Properly planned joint research between companies has some pronounced advantages: (1) the scope of research can be enlarged; (2) duplicative or redundant research can be avoided; and (3) results might be gained more quickly. Such ventures, of course, must comply with the applicable antitrust laws and other legislation.

---

[6] *Research and Development: Key Issues for Management,* James K. Brown and Lita M. Elvers, eds. (New York: National Industrial Conference Board, 1983), Chapters 8 and 9.

Finally, technology may be acquired not only by internal development but also through the purchase of fully developed technology or through license procurement. This practice may save years of research and cost. Indeed, the granting of licenses, or of patents, may be a source of income. Use of outside resources is certainly a proper line of inquiry in some audits.

INCREASING RESEARCH AND DEVELOPMENT PRODUCTIVITY

In business, a continuous aim of most managers is increasing productivity. Improving productivity in the R&D area may be much more elusive and complex, given the nature of the function. This is so because of the interaction of many variables, including (1) personal factors, such as individual competence, motivation, work habits, and attitudes, and (2) job-related causes, such as work environment, work assignments, type and quality of supervision, schedules, and a host of other influences. A purpose of an operational audit in the R&D area is to assist in improving productivity by isolating for the R&D supervisor some of the barriers that exist, which might prevent better results.

It is not within the province of this chapter to describe the myriad things that impede productivity; there is copious literature on that subject, which can be helpful.[7] Figure 39-2, an excerpt from Ranftl, lists 25 factors most likely to cause serious counterproductivity within R&D organizations.[8] An internal auditor should consult this authority before commencing an operational audit of R&D operations.

Technology is becoming more and more important to many companies. In the internal auditor's observation of the R&D operations, and in his check of literature and outside persons, he may learn of items to suggest that the research staff has overlooked. Thus, the 3M Company allows its researchers to spend up to 15 percent of their time "bootlegging," or working on whatever they want.[9] This same company circulates some "product failures" among its scientists to find possible uses. In this manner, the popular Post-it Notes (the yellow stick-on note pads) were thought of for an adhesive that would not stick very well.

---

[7] One of the best references is a study report by Robert M. Ranftl, "R&D Productivity—An Investigation of Ways to Improve Productivity in Technology-Based Organizations," 2nd ed. (1978). Mr. Ranftl is Corporate Director of Engineering/Design Management at Hughes Aircraft Co., El Segundo, Cal.

[8] *Ibid.*, pp. 4–5.

[9] See "3M's Aggressive New Consumer Drive," *Business Week,* July 16, 1984, pp. 114–122.

FIG. 39-2

Twenty-Five Factors Most Likely to Cause Serious Counterproductivity Within Research and Development Organizations

(Factors — identified by study participants)

1. Ineffective planning, direction, and control.
2. Overinflated organization structures.
3. Overstaffing.
4. Insufficient management attention to productivity, and to the identification and elimination of counterproductive factors within the organization.
5. Poor internal communication.
6. Inadequate technology exchange.
7. Insufficient or ineffective investment in independent research and development efforts.
8. Poor psychological work environment.
9. Lack of people-orientation in management — insufficient attention to employee motivation.
10. Misemployment.
11. Ineffective structuring of assignments.
12. Lack of effective performance appraisal and feedback.
13. Insufficient attention to low producers.
14. Technological obsolescence.
15. Ineffective reward systems, which inadequately correlate individual productivity and compensation.
16. Lack of equitable parallel managerial and technical promotion ladders.
17. Lack of equity in operations.
18. Ineffective customer interface.
19. Ineffective engineering/production interface.
20. Ineffective subcontractor/supplier interface and control.
21. Operational overcomplexity — constructive procedures and red tape.
22. Excessive organizational politics and gamesmanship.
23. Excessive provincialism.
24. Ineffective management development.
25. Inadequate investment in and lack of proper maintenance of capital facilities.

Reprinted with permission from *R&D Productivity*, copyright © 1974, 1978 by Robert M. Ranftl, P.O. Box 49892, Los Angeles, Cal. 90049. All rights reserved.

FINANCIAL REPORTS ON RESEARCH AND DEVELOPMENT ACTIVITY

Assuming that a fair and reasonable budget has been approved, with the concurrence of the research director, then R&D activities should be operated within these limitations, just as any other function. Financial reports should be as minimal as possible; however, a few are basic. One simple report is merely a comparison of overall technical (R&D) actual expense by department, with budget for the month and year-to-date. This is illustrated in Figure 39-3. Actual and budgeted expenses are compared for each research department, each development department, and for all other cost centers, including those expenses of a general and administrative nature (nonproject).

Because most R&D activities are planned and controlled on a project basis, a project budget report is highly desirable. Not only should actual expenditures and commitments be shown, but the estimated man-hours and cost to complete the project should be shown as well. This indicated total cost should be compared to budget. Such a project budget report is illustrated in Figure 39-4.[10] To the extent possible, any planning and control reports should be tailored to fit the needs of the executive in charge of R&D activities. The cited examples are only two basic possibilities.

PERFORMANCE STANDARDS

One other subject—performance standards—should be touched upon, before reviewing an audit program or questionnaire. Of course, it is possible to waste funds or use them inefficiently, even while remaining within the budgetary limits. In some circumstances, especially in large operations with many repetitive functions (such as running selected tests), performance standards might be considered in a limited way.

It is true that research and development work is varied and sometimes difficult to predict. Yet, in many instances, performance standards have been used to good advantage.[11] These standards do not serve as a substitute for the watchful eye and necessary guidance of the research supervisors, but they can be of assistance in evaluating the quantitative aspects of some phases of the work. Where the activities are numerous, the benefit of close personal supervision by the higher echelon is lost, but reports on performance can give some indication as to effectiveness.

Standards based on performance of other similar activities can be devised. The ingenuity and guidance of the research staff must be used in gathering the data and selecting bases for measurement and the functions

---

[10] James D. Willson, *op. cit.*, Chapter 21.
[11] *Ibid.*

FIG. 39-3

Actual and Budgeted Research and Development Expense, by Department

THE JONES COMPANY
TECHNICAL EXPENSES BY DEPARTMENT
For the Month Ended October 31, 19XX
(dollars in thousands)

Department/Item	Current Month Budget	Current Month Actual	Current Month (Over)/Under Budget	Year-to-Date Budget	Year-to-Date Actual	Year-to-Date (Over)/Under Budget
Research						
Synthetics	$ 107	$ 87	$20	$ 860	$ 724	$136
Aluminum	82	82	—	810	807	3
Rubber	12	11	1	100	100	—
Total	$ 201	$ 180	$21	$ 1,770	$ 1,631	$139
Development						
Transportation	$ 601	$ 607	$ (6)	$ 5,840	$ 5,862	$ (22)
Testing	47	46	1	450	446	4
Agricultural	802	797	5	7,890	7,870	20
Military	97	99	(2)	930	927	3
Total	$1,547	$1,549	$ (2)	$15,110	$15,105	$ 5
Other						
Pilot plant	$ 106	$ 105	$ 1	$ 99	$ 99	—
Library	20	20	—	200	196	$ 4
Patents	41	35	3	408	370	38
General administrative	62	62	(2)	619	626	(7)
Total	$ 229	$ 227	$ 2	$ 1,326	$ 1,291	$ 35
Grand Total	$1,977	$1,956	$21	$18,206	$18,027	$179
Percentage (Over)/Under Budget			—			0.98%

RESEARCH & DEVELOPMENT MANAGEMENT

FIG. 39-4

Research and Development Project Status Report

THE PLASTIC MANUFACTURING COMPANY
SUMMARY PROJECT STATUS REPORT
For the Month Ended October 31, 19XX

Project	Project No.	Man-Hours	Expenditures Month Salaries and Wages	Expenditures Month Other Expense	Expenditures Month Total	Cumulative to Date Man-Hours	Cumulative to Date Amount	Purchase Order Commitments	Estimated Cost to Complete Man-Hours	Estimated Cost to Complete Amount	Indicated Total Cost	Project Budget	Indicated Cost (Over) or Under Budget
New Product Research													
Urea filler	1152	253	$ 3,790	$ 2,319	$ 6,109	2,140	$32,110	$ 1,519	70	$ 1,200	$ 34,829	$ 34,500	$ (329)
Automobile wax	1154	24	385	475	860	169	1,634	222	—	—	1,856	1,900	44
Phenolic resin	1159	228	3,420	820	4,240	345	6,321	8,301	75	1,200	15,822	16,000	178
Alkyl resin	1160	15	232	120	352	22	352	—	50	1,000	1,352	1,500	148
Total		520	$ 7,827	$ 3,734	$11,561	2,676	$40,417	$10,042	195	$ 3,400	$ 53,859	$ 53,900	$ 41
Product Improvement													
Wet strength resins	1123	45	$ 702	610	$ 1,312	337	$ 5,420		80	$ 1,300	$ 6,720	$ 6,800	$ 30
Brightness—pulp	1124	26	427	410	837	216	3,241	$ 160	25	500	3,901	4,000	99
High quality rayon	1125	186	2,980	2,119	5,099	726	12,342	920	275	5,200	18,462	18,000	(462)
Core binder—adhesion	1126	28	350	722	1,072	63	1,072	—	1,300	22,000	23,072	23,000	(72)
Total		285	$ 4,459	$ 3,861	$ 8,320	1,342	$22,075	$ 1,080	1,680	$29,000	$ 52,155	$ 51,800	$ (355)
Sales Service													
Paint	1129	31	$ 375	$ 10	$ 385	33	$ 307	—	—	—	$ 397	$ 1,000	$ 603
Molding compound	1130	177	2,310	2,460	4,770	959	16,310	$ 2,400	400	$ 7,100	25,810	30,000	4,190
Total		208	$ 2,685	$ 2,470	$ 5,155	992	$16,707	$ 2,400	400	$ 7,100	$ 26,207	$ 31,000	$4,793
Fundamental Research													
Silicone resins	1127	24	$ 415	$ 375	$ 790	54	$ 875	—	30	$ 600	$ 1,475	$ 1,500	$ 25
Electronic appliances	1128	79	1,350	727	2,077	235	3,760	—	5	150	3,910	5,000	1,090
Total		103	$ 1,765	$ 1,102	$ 2,867	289	$ 4,635	—	35	$ 750	$ 5,385	$ 6,500	$1,115
Total Research and Development		1,116	$16,736	$11,167	$27,903	5,299	$83,834	$13,522	2,310	$40,250	$137,606	$143,200	$5,594

to be measured. It is a joint project for both the accountant and the research technician.

Some applications of performance standards are:

- Number of requisitions filled (laboratory supply room)
- Cost per man-hour of supplies
- Cost per man-hour of total research expense
- Number of tests per month
- Number of formulas developed per man-week
- Number of pages of patent applications written per man-day
- Estimated man-hours for function (overall project or part thereof; similar to estimating maintenance or other job orders)
- Cost per patent application
- Pounds of production per man-hour (pilot plant)
- Cost per operating hour

RESEARCH AND DEVELOPMENT MANAGEMENT AUDIT QUESTIONNAIRE AND PROGRAM

Figure 39-5 is a questionnaire concerning R&D activities in an organization consisting of a corporate laboratory (which handles basic research plus a limited number of product development projects) and smaller development

(continued on page 39-30)

FIG. 39-5

Audit Questionnaire—Research and Development Management

The operation of the Corporate Laboratory and the division development function has been characterized by: (1) rapidly rising costs; (2) increasing discontent on the part of the Division General Manager as to the nature of research being conducted by the Laboratory; and (3) a lack of adequate assistance to the Laboratory in the division product development area. With an expenditure of over $30 million in the past year, it is imperative that any further rise in costs be restrained, and that the difference in opinion, and complaints of the Division General Managers (DGMs) with the Vice-President — Technical and the Director of the Corporate Laboratory be brought out and made quite specific. To this end, this questionnaire should be used as a guide to secure leads on problems and possible improvements, as seen by the Laboratory staffs, the division staffs, or you.

	Yes	No	Reference

A. General:

    1. Is there a formal written policy regarding:

        a. The primary objectives of the lab? ☐ ☐ ....
        Date of last revision: ....

	Yes	No	Reference

   b. The manner in which research projects are selected? ☐ ☐ ....
   c. The methods of assisting the divisions in product development? ☐ ☐ ....
   d. The basis of making charges to the divisions? ☐ ☐ ....
   e. The relative cost or effort to be spent on basic research versus product development? ☐ ☐ ....

2. Is there an organization chart for the Corporate Lab? ☐ ☐ ....
   Date of latest issue: ....

3. Are there functional outlines or job descriptions for these positions:

   a. Vice-President — Technology ☐ ☐ ....
   b. Director of the Corporate Laboratory ☐ ☐ ....
   c. Director — Support Services ☐ ☐ ....
   d. Director — Basic Research ☐ ☐ ....
   e. Director — Product Development ☐ ☐ ....
   f. Business Manager ☐ ☐ ....
   g. Manager — Pilot Plant ☐ ☐ ....

4. Do the functional outlines of the Division General Managers spell out their responsibilities regarding research and development? ☐ ☐ ....

   a. Do you have any suggestions for changes? ☐ ☐ ....
      If so, please specify. ....
      ....

5. Do policy and procedure manuals exist covering these matters:

   a. Selection of projects ☐ ☐ ....
   b. Advance review of projects with DGMs ☐ ☐ ....
   c. Cancellation of projects ☐ ☐ ....
   d. Periodic reporting of project status ☐ ☐ ....
   e. Annual planning procedure ☐ ☐ ....
   f. Strategic planning procedure ☐ ☐ ....
   g. Recruitment of professional personnel ☐ ☐ ....

6. Do you have any suggestions for improvements in these areas? ☐ ☐ ....
   If so, please summarize. ....
   ....

7. Are the objectives of the Corporate Lab in concert with the corporate objectives? ☐ ☐ ....
   a. If not, in what ways are there differences? ....
      ....

(continued)

FIG. 39-5 *(cont'd)*

	Yes	No	Reference

B. Personnel:

1. Are all professional positions filled? ☐ ☐ ....
   If not, what positions remain open? ....
   ....

2. What is the mix of professionals and semiprofessionals?
   a. PhDs: ....
   b. Masters: ....
   c. Bachelors: ....

3. Do you have at least two outstanding, experienced professionals in each lab?
   a. Lasers ☐ ☐ ....
   b. Electronics ☐ ☐ ....
   c. Mechanical ☐ ☐ ....
   d. Physics ☐ ☐ ....
   e. Chemical ☐ ☐ ....

4. Briefly, what are the criteria used in selecting the PhDs?
   a. Publications ☐ ☐ ....
   b. Theses ☐ ☐ ....
   c. Reference checks ☐ ☐ ....
   d. Tests ☐ ☐ ....
   e. University ☐ ☐ ....
   f. Other: ....
      ....

5. Are you satisfied with the competence of your professionals? ☐ ☐ ....

6. Would you add increased competence, if available? ☐ ☐ ....

7. Are the salary ranges adequate to attract the type of people you desire? ☐ ☐ ....

8. Are the related fringe benefits sufficiently attractive to serve the quality of staff you need? ☐ ☐ ....
   a. Housing allowances ☐ ☐ ....
   b. Moving allowances ☐ ☐ ....
   c. Hospital and medical ☐ ☐ ....
   d. Retirement pay ☐ ☐ ....
   e. Savings plan ☐ ☐ ....
   f. Incentive plan ☐ ☐ ....
   g. Attendance at professional conferences, etc. ☐ ☐ ....

	Yes	No	Reference

9. Does the supervisor appraise performance of each staff member yearly and advise that staff member of the results? ☐ ☐ ....

10. What turnover have you had in the past year? ....

11. In recruitment, do persons other than the personnel supervisors interview job candidates? ☐ ☐ ....

12. Do you consider the department(s) adequately staffed? ☐ ☐ ....
    If not, what are the deficiencies? ....
    ....

13. Do the various job descriptions spell out the relationship between the Corporate Lab personnel and the division product development personnel? ☐ ☐ ....

14. Are you satisfied with the specified authority and responsibility? ☐ ☐ ....
    Exceptions: ....
    ....

C. Operations:

1. Is the progress or status of basic research projects reviewed periodically with the DGMs? ☐ ☐ ....
   Typical frequency: ....

2. Are the development projects being handled by the Corporate Labs reviewed periodically with the cognizant DGM? ☐ ☐ ....
   Frequency: ....

3. Does each laboratory manager review the status of the department operations—progress, problems—with the supervisor? ☐ ☐ ....
   Frequency: ....

4. Does the V.P.—Technical or the Director of the Corporate Lab review the status of each department at least quarterly? ☐ ☐ ....

5. Are staff meetings held within the Corporate Lab to discuss overall common problems? ☐ ☐ ....
   Frequency: ....

6. Are periodic reviews held with top management on the status or progress of the effort? ☐ ☐ ....

7. In the basic research area, are professionals transferred frequently between departments or projects? ☐ ☐ ....

(continued)

FIG. 39-5 *(cont'd)*

	Yes	No	Reference
Does each department have specific goals for each year? List typical ones.............................	☐	☐	....
9. What is your basic criteria in deciding if a department is efficient?			
10. Is there frequent and informal liaison with the staff members of the appropriate division?			
a. Division development centers	☐	☐	....
b. Division marketing staff	☐	☐	....
c. Division manufacturing staff	☐	☐	....
11. Is there a periodic, planned review by the appropriate central lab staff of the division projects?	☐	☐	....
12. Have there been any complaints by division product development as to corporate staff of:			
a. Excessive supervision	☐	☐	....
b. Inadequate supervision	☐	☐	....
c. Inadequate advice	☐	☐	....

D. Research:

	Yes	No	Reference
1. In your judgment, is there a proper balance between basic research and product development?	☐	☐	....
2. Are the results of basic research conveyed to the product development staffs? Explain when and how.	☐	☐	....
3. Which of these factors influence the selection of basic research projects:			
a. Opinion of V.P.—Technical	☐	☐	....
b. Opinion of Director of the Corporate Lab	☐	☐	....
c. Opinion of department/project manager	☐	☐	....
d. Competitive activity	☐	☐	....
e. University contacts	☐	☐	....
f. Division General Managers	☐	☐	....
g. Top management	☐	☐	....
4. Have any of the results of basic research been useful in new project development? If so, name the three *most* useful.	☐	☐	....
5. Does the attempt to keep within budget ever curtail significant efforts in the basic research area?	☐	☐	....

	Yes	No	Reference

6. Does the selection of basic research projects in any way relate to the corporate objectives? Explain. .... ☐ ☐ ....
7. Are the project leaders given a great deal of latitude in how a problem is to be approached? ☐ ☐ ....
8. Are outside sources used to consult on the seeming correctness of basic procedures or methods? ☐ ☐ ....
9. Are outside sources contracted on possible basic research projects? ☐ ☐ ....
   a. On estimated costs ☐ ☐ ....
   b. On time required ☐ ☐ ....

E. Product Development:

1. Which of these factors influences the selection of product development projects at the corporate level:
   a. Opinion of V.P.—Technical ☐ ☐ ....
   b. Opinion of Director of the Corporate Lab ☐ ☐ ....
   c. Opinion of corporate top management ☐ ☐ ....
   d. Opinion of DGMs or their marketing or development staffs ☐ ☐ ....
   e. Competitive activity ☐ ☐ ....
   f. University contacts ☐ ☐ ....
   g. Articles in professional journals ☐ ☐ ....

2. Has any product development project been cancelled before its "normal" completion? By reason of: ☐ ☐ ....
   a. Negative comments of DGM or marketing staff? ☐ ☐ ....
   b. New technical developments? ☐ ☐ ....
   c. Lack of funds? ☐ ☐ ....
   d. Lack of adequate personnel? ☐ ☐ ....
   e. New insight of product development staff? ☐ ☐ ....

3. Has any attempt been made on any product development to quantify:
   a. The prospective benefits? ☐ ☐ ....
   b. The maximum amount that could be spent economically on the project? ☐ ☐ ....

4. Is it feasible to measure most product development projects on an economic basis? Explain. .... ☐ ☐ ....

5. Has the budget been adequate for most development projects? ☐ ☐ ....

(continued)

FIG. 39-5 *(cont'd)*

	Yes	No	Reference

6. Do you generally rate the senior research staff on product development as equal to or better than the competition? ☐ ☐ ....
   Explain. ....

7. How often is the work on significant projects reviewed by a person higher than the project manager? Frequency: ....

F. Productivity:

1. Are most supervisory employees involved in preparing the annual plan? ☐ ☐ ....

2. Generally speaking, are those responsible for the project cost estimates the same persons who will have responsibility for carrying out the proposal? ☐ ☐ ....

3. In writing proposals, are the risk areas clearly identified? ☐ ☐ ....

4. Is each project supervisor responsible for:
   a. Costs incurred? ☐ ☐ ....
   b. Selection of personnel? ☐ ☐ ....
   c. Status or progress reports? ☐ ☐ ....
   d. Updating of the cost to complete? ☐ ☐ ....

5. Do plans and reports contain excessive, unnecessary detail? ☐ ☐ ....

6. Do contingency plans exist for those potential events that might have a negative impact on the project? ☐ ☐ ....

7. Are computers used in planning? ☐ ☐ ....

8. Are there excess levels of supervision or management? ☐ ☐ ....

9. Does the central lab:
   a. Maintain high performance standards? ☐ ☐ ....
   b. Delegate work effectively, encouraging maximum employee involvement? ☐ ☐ ....
   c. Encourage employee development and growth? ☐ ☐ ....
   d. Recognize achievement? ☐ ☐ ....
   e. Allow "free time" to work on whatever research or development project a professional desires? ☐ ☐ ....

10. Does the R&D organization:
    a. Monitor operational progress and promptly correct deficiencies? ☐ ☐ ....

	Yes	No	Reference
b. Adhere to schedules?	☐	☐	....
c. Attempt to assess its productivity?	☐	☐	....

11. Does the organization:

	Yes	No	Reference
a. Select the most qualified individuals to meet its needs?	☐	☐	....
b. Assign staff so as to best utilize their capability and experience?	☐	☐	....
c. Periodically assess both the performance of the staff and the appropriateness of the organization structure?	☐	☐	....

12. Does the Corporate Lab:

	Yes	No	Reference
a. Keep employees informed about the company and the work?	☐	☐	....
b. Solicit the ideas or opinions of employees?	☐	☐	....
c. Encourage the exchange of technical information?	☐	☐	....
d. Keep top management informed about problems, progress, and needs?	☐	☐	....

13. Does the Corporate Laboratory:

	Yes	No	Reference
a. Keep up-to-date on the various technologies?	☐	☐	....
b. Originate creative concepts that fulfill customer needs?	☐	☐	....
c. Conduct performance/risk/cost trade-offs to seek the best solutions?	☐	☐	....
d. Develop simulation programs and test methods to evaluate accurately the process or product?	☐	☐	....
e. Complete test programs within cost and on schedule?	☐	☐	....

14. Do the Division Development Laboratories:

	Yes	No	Reference
a. Keep up-to-date on the various technologies?	☐	☐	....
b. Originate creative concepts that fulfill customer needs?	☐	☐	....
c. Conduct performance/risk/cost trade-offs to seek the best solutions?	☐	☐	....
d. Develop simulation programs and test methods to evaluate accurately the process or product?	☐	☐	....
e. Complete test programs within cost and on schedule?	☐	☐	....

G. Facilities:

	Yes	No	Reference
1. Are the R&D facilities adequate?	☐	☐	....
2. Is the most modern equipment available in most instances?	☐	☐	....

(continued)

FIG. 39-5 *(cont'd)*

	Yes	No	Reference

3. Does a long-range plan exist for facilities and equipment? ☐ ☐ ....

4. Is the equipment reasonably maintained? ☐ ☐ ....

5. Is the physical location of the labs an impediment to securing adequate staff? ☐ ☐ ....

6. Are library facilities adequate? ☐ ☐ ....

7. Do the computer facilities and related software adequately provide for retrieval of relevant research data? ☐ ☐ ....

8. Is the staff permitted to visit other laboratories? ☐ ☐ ....

9. Has the V.P.—Technical or Director of the Corporate Laboratory toured other laboratory facilities? ☐ ☐ ....
   a. Foreign ☐ ☐ ....
   b. Domestic ☐ ☐ ....

10. Is any attempt made to find uses for "failed" products? ☐ ☐ ....
    Explain. ....

H. Outside Resources:

1. Is there a program for collaborating with selected universities on certain basic research? ☐ ☐ ....

2. Does adequate opportunity exist for contact with the following:
   a. Local universities ☐ ☐ ....
   b. European universities ☐ ☐ ....
   c. U.S. research organizations ☐ ☐ ....
   d. European research organizations ☐ ☐ ....
   e. Japanese research organizations ☐ ☐ ....

3. Are adequate funds provided for use of outside resources? ☐ ☐ ....

4. Have any cross-licensing agreements been concluded with foreign counterparts? ☐ ☐ ....

5. Does a program exist for securing patents on selected work done by all segments of the R&D organization? ☐ ☐ ....

6. In your judgment, is the work done by the patent attorneys competent and reasonable in cost? ☐ ☐ ....

	Yes	No	Reference

I. Budgets and Controls:

1. Are budget reports issued monthly for:
   a. All departments ☐ ☐ ....
   b. Each R&D project, or as a summary of each project ☐ ☐ ....

2. Is any corrective action ever necessary, based on the budget data? ☐ ☐ ....

3. Are the budget reports adequate and self-explanatory? ☐ ☐ ....

4. Do the cost estimates for proposals usually prove accurate? ☐ ☐ ....

5. Are manpower forecasts reasonably accurate? ☐ ☐ ....

6. Are budget reports:
   a. Issued on time? ☐ ☐ ....
   b. Adequate as to explanation? ☐ ☐ ....
   c. Supplemented with additional data, when requested? ☐ ☐ ....
   d. Adequate as to format? ☐ ☐ ....
   e. Excessively detailed? ☐ ☐ ....

7. Have statistical controls been considered in measuring productivity for the more repetitive functions? ☐ ☐ ....

8. For the annual business plan:
   a. Are the instructions, format, and so on clear? ☐ ☐ ....
   b. Is the procedure adequate? ☐ ☐ ....
   c. Does each department/project manager prepare his own plan? ☐ ☐ ....
   d. Are plan revisions ever necessary? ☐ ☐ ....
   e. Are the plans too detailed? ☐ ☐ ....
   f. Are requests for assistance from the budget director treated in a proper and timely fashion? ☐ ☐ ....
   g. Does the V.P.—Technical personally review each department/project budget and discuss it with the cognizant executive? ☐ ☐ ....
   h. Is there any adequate explanation of the total company plan? ☐ ☐ ....
   i. Have you ever been requested to reduce planned expenditures? ☐ ☐ ....
   j. Have any proposed research projects been eliminated from your budget? ☐ ☐ ....

(continued)

FIG. 39-5 *(cont'd)*

		Yes	No	Reference
k.	How is the total R&D budget determined:			
	■ Percentage of sales	☐	☐	....
	■ Percentage of prior year expenses	☐	☐	....
	■ Percentage of pretax profit	☐	☐	....
	■ Needs of specific programs/projects	☐	☐	....
	■ Other			
9.	If absolutely required to permit more new product development, could you reduce your annual expenses by 10 percent and still be about as effective on all present or planned projects?	☐	☐	....
10.	Are there any productivity improvement actions you can take to save 5 percent of the present budget and still be equally effective in your area of responsibility?	☐	☐	....
11.	Do you know of productivity improvements that can be made in other R&D areas? Name three:	☐	☐	....
12.	As to the strategic plan:			
a.	Are instructions, format, and so on adequate?	☐	☐	....
b.	Is there sufficient discussion of the corporate objectives vis-à-vis the Laboratories' long-range plan?	☐	☐	....
c.	Do you have a chance to review the consolidated plan and ask questions?	☐	☐	....
d.	Does your segment make provisions for required facilities and equipment?	☐	☐	....
e.	Is the plan too detailed?	☐	☐	....\
f.	Do you consider the plan practical?	☐	☐	....
g.	Is the level of planned R&D expenses:			
	■ Rising too slowly	☐	☐	....
	■ Rising too quickly	☐	☐	....

facilities in each of the operating divisions, under the line supervision of the Division General Manager. The operating heads are consulted annually about projects they desire be conducted by the corporate laboratory. Charges for the central laboratory activities are made monthly to the operating (using) center, based on (1) a flat amount for basic research and (2) varying charges based on hours spent on the specific division-requested product development. Using this audit questionnaire as a basis, Figure 39-6

RESEARCH & DEVELOPMENT MANAGEMENT

FIG. 39-6

Audit Program—Research and Development Management

A primary purpose of this review is to better understand (1) how projects or programs are selected and (2) the degree of interchange between the Division General Managers (DGMs) and their staffs, on the one hand, and the Vice-President—Technical and his staff, on the other. Also, given the rather sharp cost increases in the past three years, methods of improving the productivity of the R&D organization should be considered.

	Workpaper Reference	Done by

1. General:

☐ Secure a copy of the latest organization chart and do the following:

- Note the revision date: ....
- Check for any vacancies in management position.   ....
- Review for excessive tiers of supervision.   ....
- Consider combinations of organizations.   ....

☐ Obtain the functional outlines for the positions of manager and above in both the central lab and the DGM organizations, and

- Check the revisions dates.   ....
- Check for apparent completeness.   ....
- Check for inconsistencies in the groups.   ....
- Review for responsibility for liaison with appropriate members of:
    a. DGM staff   ....
    b. The division development group   ....
    c. Top management   ....
    d. Marketing executives   ....
    e. Manufacturing executives   ....

2. Projects:

☐ Secure the latest project budget status report and test check for these items:

- Ongoing projects versus those approved in the annual plan   ....
- Accuracy of summarized data   ....
- Adequacy of support for the indicated cost to complete   ....
- Underlying basis for justification of selected projects, including:
    a. Proposal write-up   ....
    b. Discussions with DGM staff and division development groups   ....
    c. Any economic analysis   ....

(continued)

FIG. 39-6 *(cont'd)*

	Workpaper Reference	Done by
d. Availability of qualified professionals	....	....
e. Transfer of "allowable" budget between projects	....	....

☐ Secure a copy of the laboratory long-range plan, and in discussions with the V.P.—Technical:

- Seek to clarify the relationship of present research projects with those outlined in the long-range plan. ....
- Secure a sense of how the V.P.—Technical feels technology is changing, and how the projects are being modified. ....
- Determine how efforts are split between basic research and development projects. ....

☐ Visit with some of the project managers and their staffs to secure ideas on:

- Improving productivity ....
- Level of performance expected ....
- Degree of motivation ....
- Extent of supervision or guildance ....
- Environment created to encourage new ideas ....
- Projects or facets deleted from the program, and reasons therefor ....
- Degree of job satisfaction or needed improvements ....

3. Annual Plan:

☐ Secure a copy of the annual plan, and including discussions with the V.P. — Technical, if appropriate, do the following:

- Compare, by broad category (laser, mechanical, electronics, physics, and chemical projects) and departmental expenses, the planned expenses for the present year versus last year's actual expenses. Secure explanations of reasons for change. ....
- Determine the basis for the total R&D budget. ....
- Seek evidence of discussions with DGMs and their staffs of the amount budgeted for:
  a. Basic research ....
  b. Division-oriented product development ....
- Review projects deleted and the reason why. ....
- Check adequacy of support for the nonproject departmental expenses (library, patent activity, pilot plant, and general and administrative expense). ....
- Check for evidence of review of all departmental budgets by the V.P.—Technical. Were any changes made as a result of such reviews? ....
- Review all data for evidence of provision for reserves, contingencies, and such. ....

	Workpaper Reference	Done by

- Review evidence for degree of review of projects/departmental expenses, and attempt to reduce planned expenditures prudently. …. ….

4. Productivity:

In an R&D organization, the psychological environment or climate plays a major role in determining and improving productivity. The following steps are among those designed to get a sense of the environment. Of course, the auditor is free to choose others.

☐ Undertake discussions with some project supervisors, or department managers, as well as other employees to secure their ideas on these points:

- How does each rate productivity in his area? …. ….
- What factors influence productivity? …. ….
- Does each professional employee have a chance to make a meaningful contribution? …. ….
- Is their judgment valued? …. ….
- Will the company take calculated risks on projects? …. ….
- Is politics a significant factor in decision making? …. ….
- What steps can be taken to increase productivity? …. ….
- Can any measures be used to gauge productivity:
    a. Number of tests per month
    b. Cost per patent application
    c. Number of formulas developed per man-week
    d. Cost per man-hour of R&D
    e. Effectiveness of the activity, such as value of new product (potential sales), savings in a manufacturing process, improved product value (potential sales)

    Are any of these used? …. ….

☐ Review some of the current literature for guides on measuring productivity.
☐ Discuss these with the R&D supervisory staff. …. ….

☐ Discuss R&D productivity with R&D executives, or others, in other industries to solicit ideas for improvement. …. ….

☐ Provide a general appraisal of productivity based on the above steps. Perhaps some sample tests can be made as to measurements. …. ….

Your report should include any suggested changes in interdepartmental communications and productivity improvement measures. The audit program should be modified to follow-up on any avenues you think can lead to improved R&D/DGM relations and cost reduction/productivity improvements.

consists of an operational audit program, undertaken every two years. Obviously, any audit program must be tailored to the conditions in each organization.

AN OPERATIONS AUDIT OF THE ENGINEERING FUNCTION

In many manufacturing plants in capital-intensive industries, it is the engineering department that performs the functions of an R&D department in typical companies. As a matter of fact, some of the examples of R&D activities quoted earlier in this chapter are designated as engineering functions in many manufacturing concerns. Much of the engineering effort is expended on a project-related basis. Many of the same problems in encouraging creativity occur in an engineering department as in an R&D operation. The matter of productivity exists in both activities. However, there may be more controls or discipline exercised in some engineering functions than in many R&D activities.

Given the somewhat close relationship of the two functions, it may be helpful to provide a generalized questionnaire to facilitate an operations audit of the engineering function. It is presented in Figure 39-7.[12]

---

[12] From *Internal Auditing Alert,* Oct. 1983, pp. 4-6; Nov. 1983, pp. 4-5; and Dec. 1983, pp. 5-7.

(continued on page 39-41)

FIG. 39-7
Audit Questionnaire—Engineering Function

Engineering Controls. In order to determine whether engineering controls are adequate, consider the following inquiries:

☐ Are project estimates, covering cost, time, and finishing dates, provided for all identifiable projects over a certain size?
☐ Are project estimates compiled by persons other than those who will work on the project?
☐ Does the department maintain updated and well-organized files of standard costs, past project costs, materials and equipment cost data, and similar information useful in estimating?
☐ Are records kept of current labor costs and standard overhead rates for use in project estimates?
☐ Is a computer used to analyze and project estimating data?
☐ Are estimates developed in sufficient detail for planning and control purposes?
☐ Has the accuracy of recent estimates been satisfactory to department management?

- ☐ Have complaints about estimate quality been heard outside the department?
- ☐ If estimates vary erratically, have steps been taken, or are they being taken, to correct the conditions producing them?
- ☐ Once approved, are plans for major projects prepared in sufficient detail to facilitate the establishment of effective controls?
- ☐ Are there procedures to prevent revising approved plans for major projects without proper authorization?
- ☐ Are schedule and other controls changed when plans are revised?
- ☐ Is there formal authority for approving work in various cost categories?
- ☐ Are in-house and out-of-house labor and material charges that are accumulated by individual projects properly accounted for?
- ☐ Are status reports regularly prepared for major projects to provide comparison against schedules and budgets?

Standards and Records. The following questions apply to standards, records, and schedules:

- ☐ Is there a standards group, committee, or assigned responsibility in the department concerned with design, component, construction, drafting, and other forms of standardization?
- ☐ Does the standards group have specific and known objectives such as component cost reduction, work simplification, and inventory control?
- ☐ Is the standards group or activity also concerned with methods such as drafting simplification, drafting symbols, use of photography, elimination of unnecessary detail, and perspectives?
- ☐ Are records maintained to facilitate modification of work standards as needed?
- ☐ Is the standards activity concerned with materials testing and product evaluation?
- ☐ Is scheduling performed by someone other than the persons responsible for project execution?
- ☐ Are engineering projects assigned priorities and regularly reviewed against due dates?
- ☐ Is there a realistic priority system in effect as an aid to work scheduling?
- ☐ Does planning predict the department's work load to permit early forecasting of manpower or craft bottlenecks and the need to adjust priorities?
- ☐ Are engineering schedules coordinated with construction or production schedules?
- ☐ Are CPM, PERT, and similar scheduling techniques applicable to a project for control purposes used?

Labor and Cost Records. The following questions check whether labor and other costs are properly analyzed:

- ☐ Are determinations routinely made of the total man-hours of work in process, man-hours available for scheduling, and man-hours ahead or backlogged by discipline or specialty?
- ☐ Are comparisons of actual labor hours with estimated hours regularly made and analyzed?
- ☐ Can work imbalances be forecast in time to adjust them?
- ☐ Are work authorization procedures in effect screening out redundant or unnecessary work?

(continued)

FIG 39-7 *(cont'd)*

- ☐ Are adequate procedures in effect to control the design and issue of forms and numbers of copies of documents reproduced, distributed, and filed?
- ☐ Are time expenditures by engineers, technicians, and draftsmen routinely charged, as applicable, to projects?
- ☐ Does engineering have adequate safeguards for confidential materials, drawings, process data, etc.?
- ☐ Are cost records maintained so that management can determine make-or-buy decisions, that is, in-house versus contract for design engineering work?
- ☐ Does engineering participate directly in the preparation of plant capital expenditure estimates?
- ☐ Is there a formal policy regarding engineering charges that should be capitalized versus those that are expensed?
- ☐ Is there a staff group or other specific assignment of responsibility for cost-reduction and methods-improvement studies?
- ☐ Is any form of value analysis used to arrive at the best product cost?
- ☐ Is value analysis applied to major manufacturing processes, equipment groups, or units for the purpose of lowering production costs or achieving improved quality relationships?
- ☐ Are engineering costs charged to the departments or cost centers benefiting directly from the incurred expense?
- ☐ Does accounting use an average rate to distribute engineering labor?
- ☐ Is the engineering staff generally free to accept change in assignment?
- ☐ Do adequate field data such as costs and work progress come in so that an accurate assessment of materials, deliveries, and construction progress is possible?
- ☐ Do estimators occasionally visit construction sites to verify, firsthand, that conditions are as reported?
- ☐ If projects are not on time or over cost budget, and the project manager refuses to take remedial action, may estimating to directly to engineering management?
- ☐ Is a summarized monthly project status report prepared for engineering management to highlight deviations from estimates on an exception basis?
- ☐ Are closed-out-project cost reports analyzed to spot recurring high-cost problems?
- ☐ Once recurring problems are identified, are they turned over to specialists for investigation?
- ☐ Are causes for deviation from schedules and deviation from estimates determined and followed up?
- ☐ Is there a review of proposed projects prior to authorization by a qualified group to determine cash needs, profitability, product life, and similar criteria sufficient for assessment of the priority and value of the project to the company?
- ☐ Is there a satisfactory project cost code that is adequate to break down and assign project costs for purposes of amortization, depreciation, maintenance controls, and other criteria in effect?

Product Engineering. In order to determine that product engineering is adequate, consider the following inquiries:

- ☐ Is there regular feedback from marketing about product performance, client complaints, competitive designs, and suggested improvements?

- ☐ Are the results of quality control, product testing, and evaluation passed on to engineering?
- ☐ Are concepts of configuration management employed?
- ☐ Is there a review procedure for determining manufacturing parts obsolescence?
- ☐ Is it clearly understood who may contact customers and subcontractors and under what circumstances?
- ☐ Is subcontract work inspected and checked against drawings?

Plant Engineering. In order to ascertain whether or not the engineering department is adequate for the needs of the company's plant engineering, consider the following inquiries as they relate to a coordination of activities and related responsibilities:

- ☐ Are equipment purchases, material selections, and project design decisions influenced primarily by first-cost considerations?
- ☐ Is there an understanding between plant engineering and the central engineering department as to responsibilities, authorities, etc.?
- ☐ Are functional responsibilities between plant engineering, quality control, pilot plant engineering, research and development, and other related activities clearly understood?
- ☐ Can plant engineering be incorporated into the central engineering department?

Also, consider the following inquiries as they relate to the intended usage of machinery and equipment:

- ☐ Are capital additions and major changes in plant layout and design over a certain cost subject to engineering review prior to final approval?
- ☐ Are machines and process equipment design modifications over a certain value subject to review prior to final approval?
- ☐ Is a machine and equipment standardization program in effect and under engineering department control?
- ☐ Do the spare parts interchangeability and the materials and equipment standardization programs influence the design of all new construction and purchases of equipment?
- ☐ Are the parts interchangeability and equipment standardization programs taken into account when plant or machine modifications are made?
- ☐ Can production purchasing receive engineering assistance on problems that cannot be solved by the production department?

Drafting. In order to determine whether or not the engineering department maintains appropriate safeguards for the drafting of drawings, make the following inquiries:

- ☐ Is drafting centralized in a group to permit its optimum employment?
- ☐ Is there a satisfactory drawing numbering system that permits easy reference, storage, and retrieval?
- ☐ Is the drawings storage area (vault) adequate for current and near-term future use?
- ☐ Are vault controls in force to limit access to and the removal of drawings?
- ☐ Is protection over original drawings in force, and is their safe custody assured?
- ☐ Is the vault periodically checked for obsolete drawings and are such drawings removed?
- ☐ Is there a system in effect for the microfilming storage of those types of drawings that need to be reproduced?

(continued)

FIG 39-7 *(cont'd)*

In order to check the adequacy of drafting activities and working conditions, consider the following inquiries:

- ☐ Are drafting productivity studies ever made?
- ☐ Are all drawings checked for accuracy, compliance with standards, and customer requirements?
- ☐ Are drawings systematically checked by a responsible person prior to release?
- ☐ Is drafting conveniently located for engineers who rely on it heavily?
- ☐ Are lighting, boards, furniture, and elbow room adequate in drafting?
- ☐ Are drawings released to contractors, plants, and vendors in packaged form in proper sequence?
- ☐ Are drawings accompanied by materials bills per individual drawing, or adequately cross-referenced?
- ☐ Are drawings released to production in accordance with schedule, and to tie in with production schedules and project priority?
- ☐ Are plant drawing files complete and in good order?

Services and Facilities. In order to determine if the engineering function is being run in an efficient manner, an operations audit should cover the services and facilities used by engineering, one of which should be the technical library. In order to audit the adequacy of the technical library, consider the following inquiries:

- ☐ Is there a technical library?
- ☐ Is the technical library maintained on a current basis with the latest engineering professional literature?
- ☐ Is the technical library reasonably supervised and adequately staffed?
- ☐ Is the library actually justified by the volume of information on hand or needed for reference purposes?
- ☐ Is the library accessible to those who need to use the facility?

With regard to the location and supervision of services and facilities other than the technical library, consider the following inquiries:

- ☐ Are vendor catalogs and research material on microfilm?
- ☐ Are files for engineering data and correspondence adequate?
- ☐ Are the files within reach of those who need to use them?
- ☐ Are reproduction facilities adequate and conveniently located?
- ☐ Is there enough suitable reproduction equipment?
- ☐ Is the equipment under proper control?
- ☐ Are the administrative functions in engineering under one supervisor?
- ☐ Is all engineering centralized or decentralized?
- ☐ If decentralized, does the organizational structure appear to be feasible in light of all activities?
- ☐ Are public rooms (conference, training, waiting) adequate for the engineering department needs?
- ☐ Are engineers given privacy for work that requires freedom from distracting noise and movement?
- ☐ Are adequate security systems and procedures in force?

An engineering department may often use models in the course of their work, which should generate inquiries, such as the following:

- ☐ Are models used as extensively as is practical (e.g., for piping)?

- ☐ Are model facilities adequate?
- ☐ Are departments that use engineering facilities charged for the use of those facilities?

In the event that the engineering department employs dictating equipment, make the following inquiries:

- ☐ Are cameras and dictating machines used to aid better and faster communication?
- ☐ Is engineering adequately equipped with dictating machines and other necessary office equipment?

Organization. In order to operate effectively, an engineering department needs to be properly organized. In order to ascertain whether or not responsibilities are clearly delineated, consider the following inquiries:

- ☐ Is the department formally structured; that is, is the segregation of work based on an approved plan?
- ☐ Are personnel so grouped that related functions come under a single supervisor, as far as possible?
- ☐ Is the division of responsibility between production control and engineering clearly defined?
- ☐ Is the division of responsibility between quality control and engineering clearly defined?
- ☐ Are relations between engineering and customer service harmonious, and are responsibilities clearly defined?
- ☐ If the department has organization charts, are they accurate and distributed to those concerned?

Planned Responsibilities. Effective organization is usually the result of effective planning of designated responsibilities. In order to be sure that some form of planned responsibility was implemented, inquire as follows:

- ☐ Are responsibilities the result of some form of analysis?
- ☐ Have studies been made to discover ways to organize engineering work more effectively?
- ☐ Is periodic review made of the distribution of work and authority relationships for the purpose of finding out if efficiency and productivity can be improved?
- ☐ Have steps been taken to improve the utilization of engineers by providing more technical support help?
- ☐ Can work be organized along project lines?

Balanced Work Force. There needs to be a proper balance in the work force in the engineering department among supervisory personnel and subordinates. In order to determine that a balance in the work force does exist, consider the following inquiries:

- ☐ Are current job descriptions covering the supervisor's and subordinates' positions in the hands of each person with supervisory responsibilities?
- ☐ If not, does each man assigned to a project have clearly stated descriptions of project objectives and his responsibilities as a project member?
- ☐ Does the description of staff jobs such as planners, schedulers, and office managers appear adequate?
- ☐ Is management direction diluted by the presence of union leadmen or similar classifications that prevent direct instruction from manager to draftsmen and engineers?

(continued)

FIG 39-7 (cont'd)

- ☐ Does the ratio of supervisors to workers, including engineers, designers, draftsmen, and administrative personnel, appear to be in balance?
- ☐ Does the ratio of graduate engineers to nongraduate technical personnel and draftsmen appear reasonable?
- ☐ Has an effort been made to assign technical work to draftsmen, technical aides, designers, and similar nongraduates to permit graduates to concentrate entirely on design engineering?
- ☐ Are there specialized groups within the engineering department, such as mechanical, electrical, instruments, corrosion, soils, structural, and communications?
- ☐ If engineering is concerned with field work, is there adequate engineering representation in the field?
- ☐ Do project managers have the authority necessary to manage their projects?

Personnel. An engineering department should have some personnel policies so that the right person fits the right job. In order to ascertain that some form of selective process is used, the following questions can help.

- ☐ Are technical and professional staffs generally employed in work that matches their pay grade and skill classification?
- ☐ Have supervisors been given training in cost control and problem solving?
- ☐ Can employees without engineering degrees move into engineering positions?
- ☐ Is there a procedure for identifying the technical abilities or potentials of employees?
- ☐ Have specifications for supervisory positions been defined and made public?
- ☐ Are the specifications followed in selecting supervisors?
- ☐ Does engineering have a procedure for receiving and testing suggestions for solving work and technical problems from other departments in the organization?
- ☐ Are the suggestions received acted upon or are reasons for not acting upon them given to the originators?

Ascertain if there is a formal training program through the following inquiries:

- ☐ Has the supervisory group been given adequate training in management principles and fundamentals?
- ☐ Is there a formal program for the indoctrination and training of new employees?
- ☐ Is there a well-defined plan to upgrade professional skills through company-supported plans and courses, especially those of newly hired engineers?
- ☐ Are nongraduates, technicians, and draftsmen encouraged and given assistance to improve their skills and qualifications?

Personnel Turnover. Sometimes a department, such as engineering, does not operate at peak efficiency because of turnover of personnel. In order to determine the extent of personnel turnover and how to prevent excessive turnover, consider the following questions:

- ☐ Is turnover of department employees equal to or better than industry average?
- ☐ If turnover is in excess of industry average, does it appear that salaries and other rewards are insufficient to retain and motivate competent engineers, technicians, and draftsmen?

- ☐ Is the company seeking to reduce the problem of obsolete engineering techniques by updating the education of senior engineers?
- ☐ Must engineers become managers to obtain recognition beyond middle-management levels?
- ☐ Is compensation equal to or better than the going industry rates for engineers, technicians, and draftsmen?
- ☐ Are annual appraisals made of supervisory performance?

Other inquiries concerning clerical staff, vacations, professional development, and so on, should be made. Therefore, consider the following:

- ☐ Are competent professionals who lack skill or interest in supervision given work that entitles them to equal pay for equivalent contribution?
- ☐ Is the assignment of secretaries and clerical personnel consistent with best employment of those personnel?
- ☐ Are professionals encouraged to publish, seek patents, lecture, and in other ways promote their professional status?
- ☐ Are professionals encouraged to join professional societies?
- ☐ Are vacation schedules coordinated with engineering planning and known peak loads?
- ☐ Are engineers given the opportunity to transfer to other departments to broaden their experience?
- ☐ Can professional managers who lack engineering degrees become managers of the engineering department?

Companies that manufacture products in a capital-intensive industry rely on their engineering function to develop and maintain long-range plans that cover investment, overhead, recruitment, personnel development, and facilities. In order to ascertain whether or not these long-range plans are developed on an integrated basis with corporate plans, internal audit management should periodically schedule an operations audit of their company's engineering function.

The parameters of an operations audit of the engineering function would include: engineering controls, product engineering, plant engineering drafting, services and facilities, organization, and personnel.

SUGGESTED READING

Chambers, John C., Robert L. Emerald, and Albert Rubenstein. "Coupling Corporate Strategy and R&D Planning." *Managerial Planning,* May/June 1985, pp. 35–39, 42–49.

Kimmerly, William C. "R&D Strategic Planning in Turbulent Environments." *Managerial Planning,* Mar./Apr. 1983, pp. 8–13.

Roussel, Philip A. "Cutting Down the Guesswork in R&D." *Harvard Business Review,* Sept./Oct. 1983, pp. 154–160.

Schmitt, Roland W. "Successful Corporate R&D." *Harvard Business Review,* May/June 1985, pp. 124–128.

Willson, James D., *Budgeting and Profit Planning Manual,* Chapter 21. New York: Warren, Gorham & Lamont, 1988.

CHAPTER 40

Retirement Plan Management

Introduction	2	Staffing	22
Background	2	Auditing Retirement Plan	
Definitions	3	Administration Staffing	23
The Employee Retirement Income		Planning	23
Security Act and Other Laws	4	Auditing Retirement Plan Management	
Overview	7	Planning	25
		Controlling	25
Purpose of Plans	9	Design Administration	26
		Participant Record Keeping	27
Nature of Retirement Plan		Plan Management	30
Administration	10	Auditing of Retirement Plan	
Establishing a Plan	11	Controls	31
Maintenance of Plans	12	Internal Accounting Control	
		Surveys	31
Types of Plans	13	Detailed Auditing of Internal	
Defined Benefit Plans	14	Control	31
Defined Contribution Plans	16	Information Systems Applications	
		Auditing	31
Retirement Plan Management			
Objectives	17		
Basic Mission	17		
Supplemental Objectives	18		
		Operational Auditing of Retirement Plan	
Risks and Concerns	19	Management	32
		Auditing Objective	32
Retirement Plan Management		Audit Tools and Techniques	33
Techniques	20		
Organization	20		
Auditing Retirement Plan Management			
Organization	21	**Suggested Reading**	59

Fig. 40-1	Retirement Plan Qualification Requirements Under the Internal Revenue Code	6
Fig. 40-2	Selected Reporting Requirements Under the Employee Retirement Income Security Act	8
Fig. 40-3	A Typical Organization Structure for Retirement Plan Administration	22
Fig. 40-4	Participant Record-Keeping System	28
Fig. 40-5	Flow Chart of Employee Benefits System	29
Fig. 40-6	Illustrative Retirement Plan Management Questionnaire	34
Fig. 40-7	Illustrative Operational Audit Program for Retirement Plan Management	51
Fig. 40-8	Illustrative Audit Report	58

INTRODUCTION

Background

The history of employer/employee relations is a road map of the efforts of a democratic society embued with freedom of choice to fairly reward workers for their labor. The nature of that reward has evolved from the simple concept of a day's wages for a day's work. Now, practically the worker's entire welfare must be considered.

To be sure, the centerpiece of employee compensation is still the basic wage rate. However, employers must also consider offering such other benefits as:

- Vacation pay
- Holiday pay
- Sick leave—with pay
- Group life insurance
- Health care
- Legal aid
- Savings plan
- Stock purchase plan
- Retirement plan

These benefits are supplemented in many companies by such items as subsidized commuting plans, discounting for purchases of company products, childcare centers for working parents, education assistance, credit unions, and company stores. Many companies offer employees low-cost cafeterias, recreational facilities, gymnasiums for fitness programs, and company-sponsored social events of all types.

This evolution has created a very complex world for employers in terms of fiduciary responsibility and regulatory requirements, the most significant of which applies to retirement plans—the subject of this chapter. Auditors must extend their audit scrutiny to all forms of benefit arrangements. That scrutiny must be tailored to each type of benefit. Considerations in an audit of payments for jury duty is much different from those involved in an audit of a health care plan. The number and variety of these arrangements is too extensive for detailed coverage in a reference book such as this. Not only does providing specific guidance on retirement plans guide auditors in this important area, but it also stimulates thinking about other employee benefits auditing.

Retirement plans, although originally conceived in the eighteenth century, are usually thought of as a twentieth-century phenomenon. It is during the period subsequent to the Great Depression that securing a stream of income for employees' retirement years became a paramount objective of society, and therefore of government, business, and labor. While the utilities, banks, railroads, and other institutions had established plans long before this time, much of industrial America omitted retirement benefits from employee

RETIREMENT PLAN MANAGEMENT

entitlements. Even those plans that did exist often were structured in such a way that it was easy for employers to avoid making retirement payments. Suffice it to say that there was much room for improvement. The past 50 years have been marked by significant expansion in the number and types of public and private plans.

In addition, increases have been just as dramatic with respect to:

- Number of persons covered (today, more than half of the workers in the United States are covered by some type of retirement plan)
- Benefit provisions
- Funding requirements
- Laws and regulations
- Record-keeping and reporting requirements
- Benefit payments
- Fund management and administration

As a result of this evolution, today's typical private pension plan requires a significant commitment in terms of management involvement, resources, systems, and personnel in order to achieve essential plan objectives. As management efforts have become significant, so the services of the internal auditor have become a significant requirement as well.

Definitions

Like many other twentieth-century developments, retirement plan administration has a specific body of terms and phrases unto itself. A few key definitions are provided here:

actuarial—of or pertaining to the gathering of statistics and information relating to life expectancy and other retirement factors.

actuary—an individual skilled in the calculation of pension plan costs, insurance premiums, and so forth, and who is usually a member of the American Academy of Actuaries.

actuarial asset value—the value assigned by an actuary to the assets of a plan.

actuarial cost method—a recognized actuarial valuation method, for establishing the amount and incidence of employer contributions and pension costs under a plan. There are several such methods including (1) unit credit method and (2) projected benefit method (varieties of this method include entry age normal, level premium, entry age normal with frozen initial supplemental value, and the aggregate method.[1]

actuarial present value of accumulated plan benefits—a calculated amount using actuarial assumptions and techniques as to development as of a

---

[1] For a thorough explanation of these methods, see Paul Rosenfield, *Accounting and Auditing for Employee Benefit Plans* (Boston: Warren, Gorham & Lamont, 1987), Chapter 8.

certain date, which results in discounting benefit amounts owing under the plan for the time value of money and the probability of actual payments.

break in service—a year in which a covered participant in a plan is credited with less hours than are required by the plan document to continue accruing benefits.

covered employee—an employee who meets the criteria stated in the plan for being included in the plan.

defined benefit plan—a plan that specifies a calculable benefit, usually based on factors such as age, years of service, and salary.

defined contribution plan—a plan that specifies only the contributions that the employer and/or employee will make. It makes no representations or guarantees as to how much, if anything, will be available at retirement age for participants.

multiemployer plan—a plan that covers the workers of two or more companies pursuant to collective bargaining and that is governed by union and employer representatives.

noncontributory plan—a plan in which the participants make no contributions.

net assets available for benefits—the difference between assets and liabilities of a plan.

early retirement age—the age during a time period prior to normal retirement age. In most plans, this age is between 55 and 64.

normal retirement age—the age specified for normal retirement, usually 65.

prior service costs—the amount assigned under the actuarial cost method in use before a given date.

vesting—the elimination, usually by attaining a specific number of years of cumulative service, of any and all contingencies to the eventual payment of benefits earned.

The terms "retirement" plan and "pension" plan can often be used interchangeably. In this chapter, however, every attempt will be made to use the term "retirement" plan. A retirement or pension plan is intended to mean a formal written plan approved by the board of directors, which sets forth the terms and arrangements whereby covered employees receive benefits after fulfilling stipulated conditions. These plans are written to be in accordance with the requirements of applicable income as well as other tax laws.

The Employee Retirement Income Security Act and Other Laws

In the years after 1974, the principal applicable federal law governing retirement plans was ERISA. This was not the first legislation that affected retirement plans. The very nature of these plans makes regulation of them at the federal level a certainty. In 1935, Congress enacted the Social Security Act, which eventually, on subsequent amendments, extended to all private sector workers benefits to replace a portion of earnings lost as a result of old age, disability, or death.[2] It was only natural, then, for Congress eventually to extend its control to cover private retirement plans as well.

In 1947, Congress focused on union-negotiated plans by passing the Taft-Hartley Act. This legislation provided for joint administration of these plans by unions and management. It also required annual audits and placed restrictions on how contributions could be used.

In 1958, Congress adopted the Welfare and Pension Plans Disclosure Act. For the first time, plans were required to file forms describing plans (Form D-1) and an annual report (Form D-2).

Since company sponsors could deduct the costs of pension plan contributions, Congress, through tax law changes starting in 1942, and the IRS began specifying extensive retirement plan rules and regulations. These have been changed and added to many times over the years, most recently in 1986 with the Tax Reform Act. Having a plan qualified under the IRC is extremely advantageous to both employers and employees. Hence, virtually all plans are managed in order to achieve and maintain their qualified status. If the plan is qualified, the following benefits accrue:

- The employer is able to deduct contributions to the retirement plan trust currently.
- The employee is not subject to taxation until retirement benefits are received.
- Favorable tax treatment on lump-sum distributions is afforded terminating employees.
- The retirement plan trust is exempt from income taxes.

The requirements for qualifying plans under the IRC are described briefly in Figure 40-1.

Most, if not all, retirement plans that were in existence before 1974 were exclusively modified to conform with the new requirements resulting from the enactment of ERISA. This was no simple task, for ERISA completely overhauled applicable federal regulations governing retirement plans and the administration of them. Modifications were required again after the Tax Reform Act of 1986.

ERISA was intended to achieve these broad objectives:[3]

- To increase the number of employees covered by retirement plans by establishing minimum age and service eligibility conditions for participation

---

[2] Employee Benefit Research Institute, *Fundamentals of Employee Benefits Programs* (Washington D.C.: Employee Benefits Research Institute, 1983), p. 3.

[3] Geoffrey M. Gilbert, Gregory J. Lachowicz, and James F. Zid, *Accounting and Auditing for Employee Benefit Plans* (New York: Warren, Gorham & Lamont, 1978), p. v.

FIG. 40-1
Retirement Plan Qualification Requirements Under the Internal Revenue Code

---

1. A brief description of the interested parties.
2. The name of the plan, the plan identification number, and the name of the plan administrator.
3. The name and taxpayer identification number of the applicant.
4. A statement that an application for a determination letter is being made to the IRS, identifying the District Director's Office and whether the application relates to initial qualification, a plan amendment, or plan termination.
5. A description of the plan's requirements for participation.
6. A statement as to whether the IRS has issued a previous determination letter on the qualified status of the plan.
7. A statement that any person receiving notification is entitled to submit, alone or with a group of employees, or request the Department of Labor to submit, a comment as to whether the plan satisfies the requirements for qualification. Comments made by employees must be received by the District Director on or before the forty-fifth day after the application for determination is received by the District Director. In Revenue Procedure 80-30, specific deadlines for comment are also provided where the Department of Labor is involved.

- To establish minimum periods during which participating employees must acquire vested interests in the benefits provided under these plans
- To better protect participants' pension interests by increasing the disclosure requirements of plans and establishing minimum standards of conduct by fiduciaries and others who administer plan assets
- To establish minimum requirements for funding promised benefits under such plans
- To make the tax rules more equitable for self-employed persons by reducing the differences in treatment of benefits and allowable deductions that depend on the form of the employer's business organization
- To encourage employees to save for their retirement needs by providing tax incentives for those not covered by plans

Compliance with this comprehensive Act imposed considerable added administrative burdens on retirement plan managers and their staffs in the form of new accounting, reporting, and auditing requirements. ERISA also required that plans be protected by termination insurance and established the Pension Benefit Guaranty Corporation (PBGC) for that purpose. The cost of retirement plan insurance is borne by the plans through premiums paid to the PBGC. Over the years, these premiums have been increasing (more than 250 percent through 1983, since plans terminating during that period exceeded new plan formations, thereby concentrating termination risks among fewer plans).

RETIREMENT PLAN MANAGEMENT

In 1980, additional pension plan regulations arose from the passage of the Multiemployer Pension Plan Amendments Act.

Because of the importance of retirement benefits and the huge sums of money involved, the applicable regulations are subject to constant and continuing change and to interpretation by the federal courts. It is all but impossible to stay abreast of these developments without reference to one or more of the available looseleaf services that track and report these changes (e.g., Commerce Clearing House). The principal regulatory agencies under ERISA are:

- Department of Labor
- Internal Revenue Service
- Pension Benefit Guaranty Corporation

In general, the regulations of these agencies cover:

- Establishing plans
- Plan administration, including forms and procedures for reporting, annual filing requirements, auditing, and financial management of plans
- Participation, vesting, and funding rules, including tax qualification procedures

A brief tabulation of selected reporting requirements under ERISA is presented in Figure 40-2 to further emphasize the administrative burden involved.

ERISA applies only to private retirement plans. However, a study by the House Pension Task Force of the Labor Standards Subcommittee, pursuant to ERISA, revealed that major improvements are needed in public plans. This study cited, among other things, that 29 percent of federal plans and 5 percent of state plans are never audited. In addition, 17 percent of the plans use the pay-as-you-go method, and many of the plans are without fiduciary guidelines.[4] Perhaps future legislation will remedy these and other problems identified in the study.

ERISA has greatly increased the importance of the contribution internal auditors can make to help ensure that retirement plans are properly administered. Since it is required that retirement plan financial statements be audited each year by outside auditors, at least to the level of a limited scope audit, the internal auditors should coordinate coverage to maximize the value of their work for all interested parties.

Overview

Establishing and maintaining one or more retirement plans for a company is but one, albeit significant, aspect of the broader subject of human resource management. Today, private pension plans are created and maintained only

---

[4] *Pension Plan Guide* (Chicago: Commerce Clearing House, 1983), §497.

FIG. 40-2
Selected Reporting Requirements Under the Employee Retirement Income Security Act

Item	Form Number	Due Date
Labor Department		
Summary plan description	—	120 days after plan is in existence
Updated summary plan description	—	Every 5 years
Notice of plan modification	—	60 days after adoption
Terminal reports	—	60 days after termination
Participants		
Summary plan description	—	90 days after employee becomes participant
Summary of material modification	—	210 days after close of plan year in which modification occurs
Summary of annual report	—	9 months after close of plan year
Annual statement of Form 5498	—	May 31 of following year
Internal Revenue Service or Social Security Administration		
Annual registration statement	5500	Filed with IRS, 7 months after end of plan year
Notice of plan changes	—	Filed with IRS, 7 months after end of plan year
Report of merger, consolidation or transfer of assets	5310	Filed with IRS, 30 days prior to action
Periodic plan distributions	W-2P	Filed with Social Security Administration on or before February 28 following year of distribution, with transmittal Form W3
Lump-sum distributions	1099R	Filed with IRS on or before February 28 following year distribution was made, along with Form 1096
Actuarial information	5500 Sched. B	Filed with IRS last day of the 7th month after the end of the plan year
Annual return of fiduciary	5500 Sched. B	Filed with IRS last day of the 7th month after close of plan year
Pension Benefit Guaranty Corporation		
Annual report	5500	Last day of the 7th month after close of plan year
Premium payment declaration	PBGC Form 1	7 months after close of plan year

Item	Form Number	Due Date
Pension Benefit Guaranty Corporation (continued)		
Nature of "reportable event"	—	Within 30 days of event
Plan termination	5310	As soon as possible after issuance of 60-day notice to participants

at considerable expense. Yet, over 55 million persons are covered by private pension and profit-sharing plans.[5] It is estimated that the average retirement plan adds at least 6 to 8 percent to payroll cost. Proper management of retirement plans requires specialized knowledge, a competent staff, extensive records, comprehensive computer applications, and ongoing assistance from outsiders, such as consultants, accountants, lawyers, bankers, and actuaries. Retirement plan administration also requires the frequent attention and action of boards of directors and senior management.

Effective management necessitates proper organization and planning, and adequate internal controls over such areas as:

- Participant records
- Actuarial data
- Contributions
- Benefit payments
- Investment activity
- Reporting

The techniques required above are discussed later in this chapter.

Because of the significance of effective retirement plan management, internal auditors must perform periodic reviews of systems, controls, and records. In addition, an operational audit of the entire retirement management function is desirable from time to time. Techniques for accomplishing this type of audit, including a specimen questionnaire, audit program, and report, are presented. Internal auditors may also render specialized services as requested by management. This may be done, for example, when management is in the process of devising a new plan or making major changes to existing ones.

PURPOSE OF PLANS

Retirement plans are effected by managements as a form of competitive inducement to aid in recruiting and retaining employees. Such plans are

---

[5] Employee Benefit Research Institute, *op. cit.*, p. 21.

attractive to prospective and present employees because, while the entitlements are earned currently, payment of income taxes is deferred until after the participant retires and starts receiving benefits. Usually, the individuals' tax rates are lower in their retirement years.

More importantly, perhaps, is the fact that the retirement years of a covered employee are made more secure, thus offering greater peace of mind during the lifetime of that employee.

If the plan is successful, it should be easier for a company to retain key employees for the duration of their productive careers, thus stabilizing the company's labor force and minimizing recruiting and retraining costs. Retention of a stable work force offers other advantages. Perhaps primary among these is the increased ability to develop more certain long-term plans and enter into longer term commitments.

For companies subject to collective bargaining, retirement plans have become an indispensable bargaining tool for both managements and unions. Difficult union/management wage disputes often have been settled, in part, by altering retirement plans, usually to provide increased benefits. Some believe that this has resulted in disproportionately large pension liabilities, which are becoming increasingly difficult to fund.

Retirement plans are not the only device available to management to attract and retain employees. Other employee benefits that serve that purpose include:

- Health insurance
- Dental insurance
- Long-term disability insurance
- Group life insurance
- Legal services
- Vision care

Each of these benefit plans requires administrative effort, record keeping, and internal controls. However, the techniques involved are different from those used in managing retirement plans and therefore are not covered in this chapter.

NATURE OF RETIREMENT PLAN ADMINISTRATION

Retirement plan administration is a relatively specialized area of management responsibility, a function that is compliance-oriented and executory in nature. That is to say, its primary goal is to execute management's intent with regard to establishing and maintaining the plans in accordance with all applicable laws and regulations. The body of actions necessary to establish or modify a retirement plan differ considerably from those required to maintain it. These differences are discussed subsequently.

Establishing a Plan

When a company establishes a plan for the first time, or makes important changes to an existing plan, several important considerations or decisions are involved:

- Who will be covered?
- What about breaks in service?
- What will the benefits be?
- How will vesting work?
- How will the plan be funded?
- What will be done about past service?
- Should disability benefits be included?
- Who will administer the plan?
- What investment policy should be adopted?
- What new systems and records will be needed?

These primary questions and a host of related ones must be answered satisfactorily, which requires the coordinated efforts of such corporate functional disciplines as finance, tax, law, administration, and labor relations, not to mention general management. If the company is subject to collective bargaining, union representation in these decisions is also a factor for consideration.

In obtaining information on which to base actions to form new plans, management also needs the services of outsiders, such as employee benefit consultants, actuaries, bankers, and accountants. Approval of the plan by regulatory agencies, such as the IRS, Department of Labor, and SEC, may be desirable or required. Also, board of director approval, as well as that of shareholders and even employees, may be needed.

Since the information derived from external and internal services is critical to the decisions that must be made and the approvals that must be obtained, its accuracy and completeness is important. Internal auditors can play a valuable role in helping to ensure accuracy and completeness by reviewing the underlying data and/or the methods employed in its preparation. For example, decisions regarding pension benefits usually are made in the context of what a company can afford and in consideration of other benefits already in existence. Cost compilations of these other benefits can be reviewed by the internal auditor for reasonableness. If preliminary actuarial data has been developed from basic payroll and personnel information, the internal auditor can check to see that the information is consistent with the company's payroll and personnel records.

Internal auditors may also conduct independent surveys of pension practices, perform separate analytical reviews, and undertake specific research tasks. All of these should be done only at the specific request of management.

Generally, management activities involved in devising or changing plans are coordinated by whomever it is that is or will be responsible for plan administration. This usually is the Vice-President—Administration, the Treasurer, or the Vice-President—Human Resources.

Once management has decided on the change, the implementing actions are largely executory in nature, meaning that the necessary actions are authorized either generally or specifically. The steps involved include:

- Coordinating the efforts of outsiders such as actuaries, accountants, and consultants
- Devising plan language
- Creating the trust instrument
- Negotiating agreements with trustees, insurance companies, investment bankers, and others, as necessary
- Preparing and filing the necessary forms and reports
- Communicating with employees
- Obtaining the required approvals
- Establishing and filling resource needs such as staff, systems, records, and facilities

These activities must be carried out effectively and efficiently if management goals are to be realized. This is made more difficult by the fact that creating or changing retirement plans occurs rarely. Hence, few companies can be expected to keep intact the capability to execute all the necessary actions efficiently and effectively, which is why the services of the internal auditor are so important. He can serve as a check to minimize the adverse effects of inefficiencies, errors, and omissions. These services are most useful during the infrequent and irregular intervals when the plans are being formed or changed. However, audit services of plan formation actions and their effects can be provided at other times. Reviews of these actions may bring to light mistakes not detected by other controls. More significant is the greater assurance to management that the process has stood the test of audit scrutiny.

Maintenance of Plans

The body of activities involved in maintaining plans is primarily compliance oriented. It includes:

- ☐ *Record keeping:* Records must be kept that reflect each participant's contributions, accrued benefits, and, for beneficiaries, payments made. In addition, participant records must accurately and completely track participant-related events and data essential to make actuarial valuations, such as seniority dates, job position, years of service, pay rate, and date of birth. Other records must be kept of trust activities, such as payment of administrative expenses and investment changes.

RETIREMENT PLAN MANAGEMENT

- ☐ *Obtaining actuarial data:* This is important in order to determine the periodic contributions that the employer must make to the trust and to enable the preparation of plan financial statements.

- ☐ *Obtaining EDP assistance:* This is essential for most plans to reasonably ensure that accurate and complete records of events and transactions are maintained, and to help in preparing reports.

- ☐ *Preparing and filing reports:* As indicated by Figure 40-2, these activities can be extensive. Reports must be filed with the Department of Labor, IRS, PBGC, and participants and beneficiaries.

- ☐ *Monitoring trustee investment transactions:* Since contributions to retirement plan trusts accumulate to considerable sums (in the billions for large plans), the propriety of investment activity is a significant area of attention. Investment strategies must be developed wisely and carried out effectively and consistently.

- ☐ *Communicating with participants:* Not only does this involve the required reporting, but plan administration must also be responsive to the numerous questions posed by participants. It is best to avoid outright personal financial counseling, however, unless management has authorized such service.

- ☐ *Reporting to management:* Boards of directors and senior managers are deeply interested in their companies' retirement plans inasmuch as they bear ultimate responsibility for the plans' well-being. Of particular interest is the investment activity, the financial condition of the plan, and any particular problems or other matters that demand their specific attention. Thus, reporting to this group is of considerable importance to the effective overall plan administration.

Maintaining retirement plans requires more ongoing time and effort than does the creation or changing of a plan. The activities are susceptible to developing relatively permanent subfunctions, staff positions, systems of record keeping, and data processing in a routine fashion comparable to other administrative and accounting functions. The payment of retirement benefits, for example, is similar in many ways to disbursing payrolls.

Most internal auditors are involved more frequently in operational audits of maintenance activities of retirement plans because of this ongoing nature. There simply is more occasion for that type of auditing than for auditing services related to new plans or major changes to existing ones. The questionnaire and audit program in this chapter are presented with this fact in mind.

TYPES OF PLANS

The two basic types of retirement plans are defined benefit plans and defined contribution plans.

Defined Benefit Plans

These plans may be defined as those in which the company, in effect, guarantees that, on retirement, the participant will receive a benefit determined by a prescribed formula set forth in the plan. The amount is estimated well in advance of retirement for any participant by applying some actuarial assumptions regarding future earnings to the formula, and, by discounting, the present value is calculated for current funding and reporting purposes.

Formulas may specify a flat rate for each year of service, or they may specify a percentage of the participant's average career earnings for each year of service. Another alternative is to apply a percentage of the participant's highest earnings or last earnings for each year of service.

Defined benefit plans may be integrated with Social Security benefits. That is, the retirement benefits formula may be structured in such a way as to provide a targeted benefit using both Social Security and the private plan. Also, it can be designed to provide greater benefits to those with higher salaries. This is intended to offset the built-in tilt of Social Security benefits in favor of lower paid employees. The tilt arises because Social Security benefits are calculated using the FICA taxable wage base, not the full earnings of the individual. Thus, earnings in excess of the base are excluded from the formula.

Defined benefit plans involve more risk for the sponsor than other types of plans and are more regulated, because the sponsor is obligated by the terms of the plan to provide a determinable amount of future benefits. If the assets of the plan trust are insufficient for this purpose, the deficiency must be made up. Thus, companies with defined benefit plans are liable for the excess of the value of vested benefits over the trust assets. If the company has been slow to fund those vested benefits (many have been), this liability can be quite large.

The major private pension plans in the United States, such as that of General Motors, approach $2 billion in unfunded pension liability.[6] The size of these unfunded liabilities stirred controversy among accountants, actuaries, analysts, bankers, and others. At issue were disclosure requirements in financial statements. GAAP under APB Opinion No. 8 and FASB Statement No. 36 required the disclosure in footnotes of the present value of accumulated benefits and the net assets available for plan benefits.

Many financial analysts and others believed that unfunded vested benefits and the related intangible assets should be recorded in the balance sheet. In response, FASB Statement No. 87, Employers' Accounting for Pensions, issued in 1985, altered the accounting principles and disclosure requirements. Effective for fiscal years beginning after December 15, 1986, it requires recording as a liability an estimated amount representing the accrued pension cost payable for plans in which the pension liability exceeds the fair

---

[6] "How Pension Fund Assets Grow So Quickly," *Business Week,* Mar. 21, 1984, p. 226.

value of pension assets. It also requires a schedule reconciling the funded status of a pension plan that is, the projected benefit obligation less the fair value of plan assets as of the date of the employer's financial statements, with amounts reported on the statement of financial position. The reconciliation must reflect the effect, if any, of unrecognized prior service cost, unrecognized net gain or loss, and unrecognized net obligation or (net asset) at the date of initial application of FASB Statement No. 87.

A large body of public accounting firms and publicly held companies voiced opposition to FASB Statement No. 87. For the most part, this group believes that the liability may be real, but measurement difficulties make it almost impossible to calculate with any certainty. For some, recording the liability would destroy debt-to-equity ratios and place many companies in technical default of loan agreements. Others believe that the FASB's views satisfactorily resolve the problems of accounting for pension plans in financial statements.[7]

The prospect of recording unfunded vested benefits in financial statements may have been a factor in the recent surge of terminations of defined benefit plans in favor of other types of plans. According to a recent article in *Dun's Business Week,* companies such as Reynolds Metals, Harper & Row, the Great Atlantic and Pacific Tea Co., GAF, and Occidental Petroleum have initiated or completed retirement plan terminations for one or more of these reasons.[8] For this group, recessionary layoffs and investment fund performance, buoyed by the 1982–1983 surge in bond and stock prices, led to overfunding of pension liability. In these instances, averting takeover and/or obtaining positive cash flow and a boost to earnings were the stated considerations. Nevertheless, the prospect of avoiding potential future debt-to-equity ratio impairment could not have been overlooked. However, 1984 regulations may make it less advantageous for companies to terminate defined benefit plans and substitute defined contribution plans. Under these regulations, issued by the Department of Labor, the Treasury, and the PBGC, companies would first have to fully vest and fund all participants before termination.

The FASB also entered the picture. The frequency of pension plan settlements and/or curtailments and the potential impact on financial reporting of these events was such that accounting principles needed to be specified. The result was FASB Statement No. 88, which became effective for events occurring during and after the fiscal year in which FASB Statement No. 87 was first applied. Briefly, Statement No. 88 specified that the maximum gain or loss recognized in a settlement is the total of the unamortized balance of any unrecognized net gain or loss arising after the date of initial application

---

[7] Gerald I. White, "Pension Accounting: A Challenge for the FASB," *Corporate Accounting,* Spring 1984, p. 12.

[8] John Perham, "Pension Plans: Problems of Plenty," *Dun's Business Week,* Jan. 1984, p. 43.

of FASB Statement No. 87 and/or the unrecognized net asset that arose as a result of the initial application. The amount of the gain or loss is limited to the percentage change in the projected benefit obligation (PBO). If the PBO is reduced by 70 percent, the gain or loss recognized is 70 percent of the total gain or loss. An additional loss may be required to be recognized in a curtailment should unrecognized prior service cost decrease as a result of the curtailment.

Defined Contribution Plans

These plans may be defined as those in which the contribution by the employer (and, in some, the employee) are predetermined and stated in the plan. In effect, the employer agrees to contribute an amount each period for each participant. In addition, the employer administers the plan in accordance with its terms.

The ultimate benefit to be paid to participants under defined contribution plans is not effectively guaranteed, as it is under defined benefit plans. The amounts that are contributed are invested in accordance with the specifications of the plan and applicable ERISA law. However, if the invested assets result in losses, the participant has no recourse to the employer. This is one of the principal differences between the two types of plans. Also, defined contribution plans:

- Do not involve the complex actuarial data requirement of defined benefit plans.
- Are less regulated.
- Usually provide more liberal vesting provisions.
- Are easier to administer and are not subject to the same auditing requirements, accounting rules, and financial statement reporting as are defined benefit plans.

Several types of defined contribution plans are briefly discussed in the following paragraphs:

☐ *Deferred profit-sharing plan:* There are a variety of arrangements that fit into the category of deferred profit-sharing plans. Typically, the amounts contributed vary with the profitability of the company. In loss years, no contributions are made. The regulations affecting profit-sharing plans do not require that the amount to be contributed be predetermined. However, contributions must be substantial and recurring. Thus, considerable discretion is permitted in setting contributions. This is advantageous for many small companies and growth companies that are subject to volatility in periodic earnings but yet desire to provide a form of deferred benefit for either retirement, disability, or death.

- ☐ *Thrift plan:* Also known as savings or savings investment plans, these arrangements usually require employee contributions, with the employer contributing a matching amount, in part or in total. The amounts are then invested by the employer in trust for the participants. Vesting in the employer portion of the contribution is usually quite liberal. From a tax standpoint, the employer receives a current deduction for its contribution and the taxes to the employee are deferred until withdrawal occurs. Since the primary intent is to provide retirement, disability, or death benefits, thrift plans restrict the occasions for withdrawals and/or impose conditions on withdrawal that are not favorable to the participants.

- ☐ *Target benefit plans:* The employer's contribution in this type of plan is based on an actuarially determined target benefit. However, there is no guarantee that the target benefit will be paid.

- ☐ *Stock ownership plans:* Known as ESOPs (for employee stock ownership plans), these arrangements are similar to profit-sharing plans. However, contributions are not necessarily dependent on profits, and the benefits are usually paid in lump-sum distributions of company stock. These plans must be approved by the IRS and, like conventional retirement plans, require the creation of a trust. The primary purpose of ESOPs, aside from providing deferred benefits to employees, is either to obtain financing for company purposes or to transfer ownership. Payroll-based stock ownership plans (PAYSOPs) are a version of this arrangement brought into being by the Economic Recovery Tax Act of 1981. PAYSOP contributions are based on compensation and are intended to replace Tax Reduction Act stock ownership plans (TRASOPs).[9] A description of these, as well as individual retirement accounts (IRAs) and 401K plans, is not pertinent to this chapter.

RETIREMENT PLAN MANAGEMENT OBJECTIVES

Basic Mission

Retirement plan management functions exist to reasonably assure that the employees' retirement benefits intended by management are adequately provided for as authorized by management, efficiently and effectively. Inherent in this mission is responsibility not only for administrative matters but also for investment and actuarial activity.

Successful retirement plan administration results in:

- Preservation of retirement plan capital (company and employee contributions).

---

[9] Employee Benefit Research Institute, *op. cit.*, p. 80.

- Proper balancing of return on investments and investment risk.
- Compliance with the fiduciary requirements of ERISA.
- Satisfactory relationships with actuaries, accountants, bankers, consultants, insurance companies, investment managers, and trustees.

Supplemental Objectives

In addition to the basic mission, there are supplemental objectives that must be satisfied if the administration of retirement plans is to be considered effective and efficient. These objectives are:

- To obtain sufficient resources pursuant to management's authority to achieve objectives.
- To carry out administrative duties in accordance with company policy and applicable federal and state regulations. In this context, administration includes design of the plans and amendments, writing plan language and other material, keeping records of plan data, obtaining actuarial valuations, coordinating audits, preparing and filing various government reports and tax information returns, specifying computer system requirements, developing applicable policies and proceedings, training and monitoring personnel, and assisting in monitoring pension trust assets.
- To deviate from established policies and procedures only on appropriate authority.
- To maintain a current awareness of developments pertaining to retirement plan administration.
- To establish and maintain systems of accounting and reporting to reasonably assure that transactions and data relevant to plan administration are properly classified and recorded. This may include:
  — Separate accounting for each participant
  — Separate accounting for each contributor
  — Adequate records of investments and changes in investments
  — Actuarial records
  — Disbursement records for benefit payments
- To summarize and report information to affected management periodically with respect to:
  — Investment activity
  — Participant data
  — Contributions
  — Benefits paid
  — Actuarial data
- To summarize and report information to participants and regulatory bodies periodically as required by law.
- To reasonably assure that access to retirement plan records and data is restricted to personnel authorized by management.

RETIREMENT PLAN MANAGEMENT

- To reasonably assure that retirement plan data and records are sufficiently protected from identifiable hazards of all types.
- To reasonably assure that retirement plan assets are sufficiently protected from loss, theft, fraud, and similar irregularities.

RISKS AND CONCERNS

To understand the importance of achieving retirement administration objectives, it is worthwhile to consider the ramifications of failing to achieve them. This discussion is confined to defined benefit plan risks and concerns, since most large companies have that type of plan at present. A sample listing follows:

☐ *Overfunding of benefits:* If the overfunding becomes too extreme, the company may become an unwilling takeover target or be tempted to tap the overfunding as a source of financing in ways that could have long-term detrimental effects.

☐ *Underfunding of benefits:* Not only does this cause concern among management, unions, and their members, ERISA imposes a 5 percent excise tax on the deficiency if minimum funding standards are not met. Moreover, underfunding must be made up. If this occurs during periods of higher interest rates, increased costs result.

☐ *Inadequate arrangements with outsiders:* This could adversely affect the quality of services received. If, for example, the actuary is not provided with accurate and complete data, the resultant calculations of pension cost and funding may be misstated. This can, in turn, adversely affect the financial statements of the plan and, in addition, cause overfunding or underfunding.

☐ *Insufficient systems and procedures:* Errors and omissions may occur and, if they become excessive, problems in financial reporting can result and the accuracy and completeness of filings with regulatory agencies can be affected. Also, the calculation and disbursement of benefits may be upset.

☐ *Inadequate investment management:* If the activities of investment managers are not monitored effectively, plan assets could be exposed to risks greater than intended, resulting in possible losses that must be made up in some way. On the other hand, some fund managers may be too conservative in executing investment strategy, possibly underachieving intended return on investment targets. Insufficient attention to accounting for investment income could result in failure to detect errors in accounting for income earned by the investments.

☐ *Inaccurate reporting to participants and others:* This can lead to false impressions of security or needless worry, depending on whether the inaccuracy overstates or understates the participants' vested benefits. Aside from any morale problems this may cause, the company must make costly corrections. This can drain resources and, because the task inevitably falls on the administrative personnel, work routines can become so strained as to affect the quality of other work. This can produce more errors requiring more correction in a seemingly endless cycle.

☐ *Insufficient segregation of duties:* If duties are not sufficiently segregated, increased exposure to fraud, embezzlement, and similar irregularities by administrative personnel will result. Retirement plans are somewhat more exposed than other types of welfare plans because payments by check are ultimately involved.

☐ *Beneficiary fraud:* There is no absolute control technique that assures that, on the retiree's death, payments of retirement benefits will cease, as provided by most plans, or that survivor benefits will kick in. It is easy for heirs and others close to the deceased to continue to receive retirement benefits and to convert them to personal use. Ways of reducing exposure to this possibility are discussed later in this chapter.

These are some of the more important risks and concerns of management, where retirement administration is involved. Internal auditors, in performing operational audits of this function, should keep these risks and concerns in mind when determining audit scope, performing tests, evaluating test results, and drafting reports.

RETIREMENT PLAN MANAGEMENT TECHNIQUES

To be effective, retirement plan management techniques must organize, plan, staff, and control resources and activities. The techniques often employed by plan administrators and management for organization and administration of plan activities are discussed here. A discussion of control techniques for important functional aspects of plan management is also presented. These include:

- Participant records
- Actuarial data
- Contributions
- Benefit payments
- Investment management
- Reporting

Organization

Retirement plan administration is often organized within the finance function, usually as part of the Treasurer's job. That is because many of the important aspects of plan management are finance-related. Examples include maintaining relationships with accountants, insurance companies, bankers, and investment managers. Also finance-related are the functions of income tax administration, payment of benefits, and preparation of financial reports and other data.

For other companies, plan management is organized as a function of

RETIREMENT PLAN MANAGEMENT

the Vice-President—Administration. In these instances, the head of industrial relations and/or employee benefits, in addition to the head of plan management, usually report to this officer, because there is a need for close relationships between these functions for effective plan administration.

However the function is organized, it is important that the head of the function report high in the organization structure. Retirement plan administration is so significant an area of management responsibility that to do otherwise would almost certainly ensure ineffective administration.

Within the plan administration function, the department is usually organized along function lines, such as:

- Accounting
- Benefit payments
- Investments
- Actuarial services
- Information systems

An example of an organization chart depicting these functions is shown in Figure 40-3. In this instance, the retirement plan management is part of the finance organization.

Auditing Retirement Plan Management Organization

Operational auditing of the organizational structure of retirement plan management does not require extensive effort. This is because organizational changes are infrequent and irregular. Often, such audits are made difficult because there is usually no documentary evidence of the considerations and deliberations that occurred in effecting changes. The actual reasons for the changes may not be discernible despite the application of inquiry, review, and other auditing techniques.

The variety of plans and other factors suggests that many organization structures are possible. There is no single best structure to suit all cases, a fact that must be kept in mind when evaluating structure. Unless considerable evidence to the contrary exists, the auditor is probably justified in concluding that the existing structure is adequate. Evidence to the contrary may include:

- Frequent organizational realignments
- High turnover in key positions
- Recurring underachievement of objectives
- Excessive complaints from participants and beneficiaries

The existence of all or some of these conditions does not necessarily mean that an improper structure exists. Rather, it suggests that the auditor may wish to discuss the matter with appropriate management. Instances of this should be rare.

FIG. 40-3
A Typical Organization Structure for Retirement Plan Administration

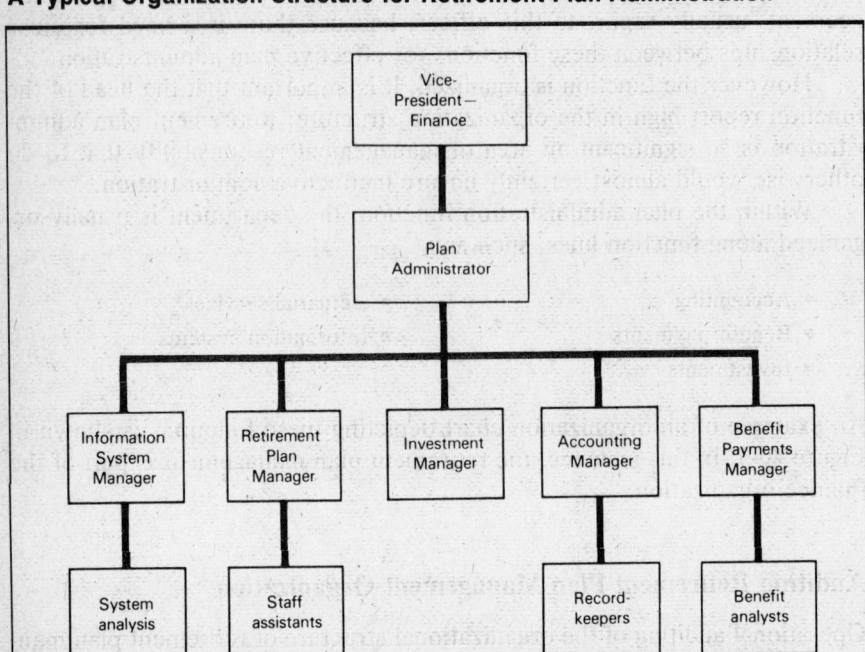

Staffing

Retirement plan administration requires competent staffing in sufficient numbers to carry out all duties and responsibilities effectively and efficiently. The types and numbers of staff depend on the number, size, and complexity of retirement plans in existence. Job positions range from the highly skilled professional plan administrator to the semiskilled clerical worker. Typical positions include:

- *Plan administrator:* This position usually is staffed by someone with formal training and experience in retirement plan administration. The person is usually knowledgeable with respect to actuarial techniques, applicable rules and regulations, and principles of insurance, investment, and finance. The individual is apt to have broad experience in plan design and administration.

- *Benefits analyst:* This position may be staffed by individuals who have formal training in plan administration but lack in-depth experience. Alternatively, this position may be staffed by career analysts whose formal training may be less relevant. Rather, these may be long-term employees familiar with the company, the plan, and department procedures.

- *Investment manager:* This function in many companies is performed by the plan administrator or someone with considerable training, experience, and familiarity with the field of investment management. This would include knowledge of stocks, bonds, real estate, money markets, government securities, and commodities. Also, it is necessary that this individual be familiar with investment strategies, techniques, and risks. Investment managers should also be familiar with analytical techniques and should know analysts, professional investment managers, and brokers.

☐ *Accountant:* This position should be staffed by an individual who is formally trained in accounting with knowledge of accounting procedures and controls applicable to retirement plan record-keeping. The accountant should be familiar with financial statement preparation and GAAP for retirement plans.

Auditing Retirement Plan Administration Staffing

Appraising the quality of retirement administration staffs is no less challenging than appraising the quality of the organization structure. Unless requested to do so by management, internal auditors should resist any inclination to furnish performance appraisals of individual staff members. However, the techniques used to attract, train, supervise, and evaluate staff can and should be subjected to periodic audit for consistency and effectiveness.

Also, internal auditors should be alert to signs indicating staffing problems. Indicators of problems include:

- Productivity decline
- Frequent overtime
- Excessive errors and omissions
- Constant complaints by participants and beneficiaries
- Poor work habits
- Low morale

Clues to the existence of these indicators may be brought to light by interviewing managers, staff, and users; by reviewing evidence of productivity; and by observing job performance.

Planning

Adequate planning is critical to achieving effective retirement plan management. This is particularly true when new retirement plans are being formed or existing plans changed. In these instances, it is necessary to plan and schedule events carefully so as to coordinate the services of actuaries, consultants, lawyers, accountants, and affected government agencies. The role of management and the board of directors must also be considered. Time must be allocated for:

- Deciding issues of coverage, plan type, funding technique
- Drafting, reviewing, and securing approval of plan documents
- Filing applicable reports
- Establishing systems and records, and devising forms and instructions
- Communicating with participants
- Training staff

Aside from the planning activities associated with devising new plans or changing existing plans, retirement plan management must plan on at least two other levels: strategic and tactical.

Strategic planning involves developing a long-term strategy, which ensures that retirement plan benefits remain competitive and continue to aid in recruiting and retaining employees. Matters that might be involved in this long-term strategy are whether and when to incorporate:

- Medical benefits for retirees
- Disability benefits
- Death benefits
- Cost of living allowances
- Vesting changes
- Social Security integration
- Thrift plans
- ESOPs

A related aspect of strategic planning involves investment strategy. Investment strategy must consider the long-term nature of retirement plans. Fluctuations in stock markets and economic factors may necessitate changing strategy in order to consistently ensure a satisfactory return commensurate with risk. Among the matters to consider in developing or changing strategy are whether to (1) manage all or a portion of the investments in-house; (2) manage all or a portion of the assets in stock index funds; (3) manage all or a portion of the investments through professional investment managers; and (4) invest in real estate, foreign securities, or venture capital projects.

Information relevant to strategic planning includes:

- Trends in retirement benefits
- Legislative activity, both federal and state
- Regulatory activity
- Economic forecasts
- Market forecasts
- Performance trends of investment managers, stocks, and bonds
- Actuarial trends

This information must be gathered by the plan administrator from sources inside and outside the system. It is useful to retain this information for future reference and should be filed in a way that permits easy retrieval. In recent years, the availability of electronic filing packages, such as dBASE III, and on-line data retrieval services, such as Dow Jones, have greatly facilitated obtaining, retaining, and retrieving relevant information.

Tactical planning usually focuses on the next year or two and is performed by the same individual or group responsible for strategic planning. Because the periods are shorter, the plans can be much more specific and accurate. The kind of data used in developing tactical plans is similar to that used in strategic planning. Department budgeting is a part of tactical planning.

Auditing Retirement Plan Management Planning

Planning at all levels is a subjective process. Accurate plans can be developed by instinct based on the intuitive judgment of experienced and skilled managers; inaccurate plans can be developed even though the most sophisticated techniques are employed. Usually though, there is a high correlation between the planning process and the accuracy and reliability of the resultant plans; that is, the better the process, the better the plan.

Internal auditors should review the planning process for thoroughness and reasonableness. Assumptions and objectives can be checked with broader corporate plans for consistency. Record-keeping practices can be examined, and monitoring of actual versus planned activities can be performed. Through analytical techniques, the accuracy and reliability of past plans can be checked and used as an indicator of future plans. Except under special circumstances, internal auditors should avoid trying to predict the accuracy or reliability of any given plan. The auditor should balance the accuracy and reliability of the plan against the relative importance of planning in retirement plan management and the nature of the function. Much strategic and tactical planning for retirement plan management must occur on the basis of uncertain data.

Controlling

The means by which retirement plan management achieves its objectives involves a system of preventive, detective, and corrective controls over such critical functions as:

- Effecting proper plan design administration
- Maintaining accurate participant records
- Obtaining reliable actuarial data

- Keeping accurate records of contributions and other plan accounting transactions
- Disbursing benefits timely, accurately, and completely
- Managing investments prudently
- Preparing reports in accordance with established procedures, regulations, and principles

The control principles by which the foregoing is accomplished are the same as for other management undertakings. As discussed in Chapter 17, these include:

- Competent personnel
- Adequate segregation of duties
- Existence of adequate records, forms, and documents
- Adequate authorization and approval procedures
- Effective planning and accountability

The following paragraphs briefly discuss control techniques in accordance with these principles as applied to the functions listed previously.

Design Administration. In this context, design administration refers specifically to the design of the plan, since effective overall administration begins with good plan design. Control techniques include:

- Designs in accordance with management's authorization.
- Clearcut responsibility for plan design.
- Required review by all affected disciplines, such as accountants, lawyers, actuaries, and benefit experts.
- A formal plan design written in clear language in reasonable detail covering all aspects and arrangements, which includes:
  — Definitions
  — General terms
  — Enrollment
  — Employee contributions
  — Company contributions
  — Eligibility for benefits
  — Retirement benefits
  — Other benefits
  — Plan administration
  — Fund management
  — Plan termination
  — Actuarial factors
- Requiring changes to be made only on considering the full impact of such changes.

RETIREMENT PLAN MANAGEMENT

- Obtaining determination letters or other required approvals from regulatory bodies.
- Keeping files and records of official plan documents up-to-date and safe from security risks.

Participant Record Keeping. This function is aimed at maintaining systems and records sufficient to reasonably ensure that all transactions and data relevant to participants and other interested parties are accurately and completely recorded. Records of information must be maintained by participant, such as service record, marital status, salary history, breaks in service, and contributions. For beneficiaries, the records must be complete with respect to the history of payments made. Control techniques include:

- Specifying authority and responsibility for record-keeping practices.
- Utilization of data processing techniques to improve effectiveness and efficiency. Control techniques for this aspect are similar to the control techniques used for any application (discussed in Chapter 26). The data required for participant record keeping in most instances can be taken from payroll/personnel master files. Hence, retirement record-keeping systems are often integrated with payroll and personnel systems. Some companies have established common data bases for those and other employee related applications. A typical system is depicted in Figure 40-4.
- Standard forms and instructions to aid in recording transaction types (adding/deleting employees, changing basic information, such as name and address, and updating service record).
- Specified levels of review and/or approval for charges.
- System checks and edits to detect and correct common entry errors.
- Commencing benefit payments for individual recipients only after evidence exists that a sequence of procedures has been performed to verify and approve the entitlement.
- A means by which the record reflects payments made to recipients. Invariably, an information systems (I/S) application is developed for this purpose. A flow chart depicting such a system is shown in Figure 40-5.
- A methodology for halting payments to beneficiaries upon their death.
- A chart of accounts and an accounting manual, which covers all other types of retirement plan transactions including investment transactions, investment earnings, actuarial transactions, and plan expenses.
- A system of periodic reporting of all types of transactions (proof listings, error reports) to aid error detection and correction.
- Reconciliations to ensure proper balancing and agreement of records, where required.
- Segregation of duties so that no single employee performs two or more functions incompatible with proper internal control and to provide checks and balances in processing and recording retirement transactions. For example:
  —Persons submitting retirement transactions should not have approval authority, and vice versa.

FIG. 40-4
Participant Record-Keeping System

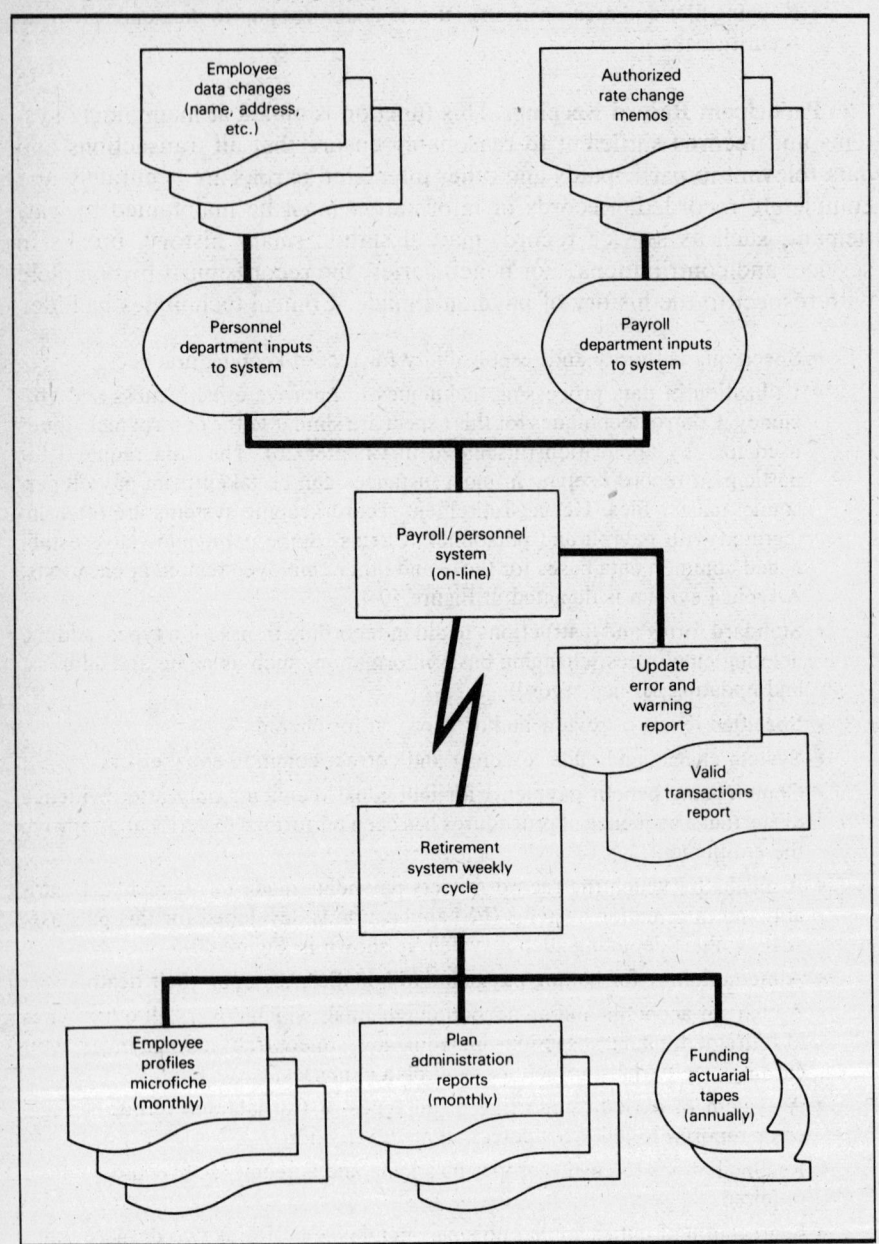

**FIG. 40-5
Flow Chart of Employee Benefits System**

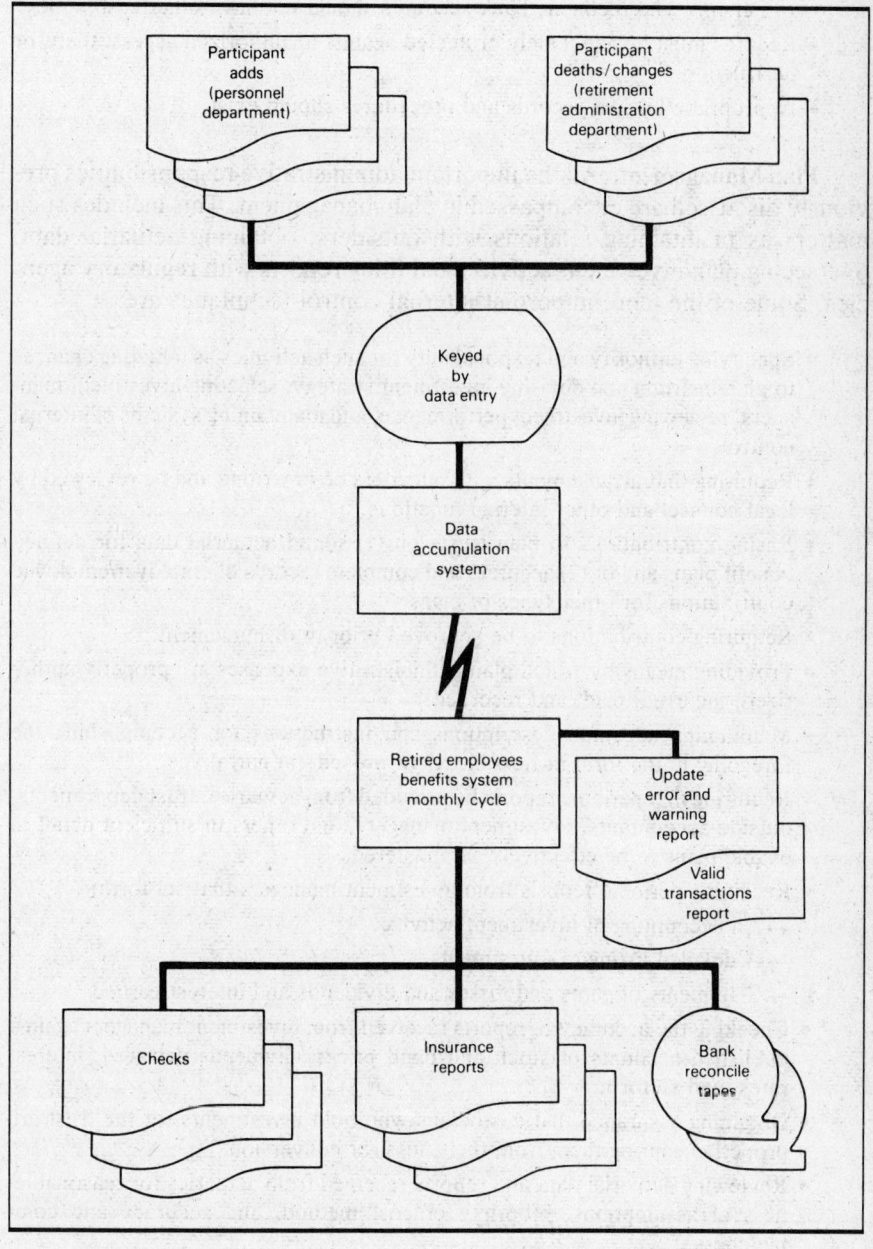

— Persons processing transactions should not be able to submit transactions.
— Persons who calculate benefits should not be able to approve benefits.
— Persons who reconcile bank accounts should not have other cash duties.
- Records must be adequately protected against unauthorized access, theft, or destruction.
- Appropriate backup records and procedures should exist.

Plan Management. All the important administrative responsibilities previously discussed are encompassed in plan management. This includes such matters as maintaining relations with outsiders, obtaining actuarial data, overseeing plan investment activity, and filing reports with regulatory agencies. Some of the more important internal control techniques are:

- Specifying authority and responsibility for such activities as initiating changes to plan instruments, devising investment strategy, selecting investment managers, reviewing investment performance, and maintaining systems of internal control.
- Requiring that arrangements with outsiders be in writing and be reviewed by legal counsel and other internal functions.
- Basing contributions to plan trusts on (1) sound actuarial data for defined benefit plans and/or (2) accurate and complete records of employer/employee contributions for other types of plans.
- Requiring contributions to be approved prior to disbursement.
- Providing means by which plan administrative expenses are properly authorized, incurred, paid, and recorded.
- Maintaining adequate descriptions and instructions for accomplishing the foregoing in the form of flow charts or procedural narratives.
- Requiring that periodic reports be provided from actuaries, trust departments, outside accountants, investment managers, and others in sufficient detail to enable plans to be effectively administered.
- Receiving periodic reports from investment managers that set forth:
  — An accounting of investment activity
  — A detailed listing of investments
  — Statements of gains and losses and dividends and interest earned
- Checking the accuracy of reports received from investment managers against published accounts of stock and bond prices, dividends declared, interest rates, and so forth.
- Obtaining assurance that custodians who hold investments for the trust are properly securing them from theft, loss, or conversion.
- Reviewing actuarial data and reports received from actuaries for reasonableness of assumptions, propriety of cost method, and accuracy and completeness.
- Restricting access to official records, agreements, and other documentation to authorized personnel only.
- Providing adequate backup and recovery procedures.

- Preventing employees who deal with investment managers from engaging in any activities that might give the appearance of a conflict of interest.
- Segregating the duties of custodianship of investments from duties involved in managing investments (buying and selling).
- Requiring periodic physical inspections and/or counts of securities for comparison with records of investments owned.

Auditing of Retirement Plan Controls

The control techniques by which retirement plan management accomplishes objectives may be audited in various ways. These include internal accounting control surveys, detailed auditing of internal controls, I/S applications auditing, and operational audits. The illustrative material at the end of this chapter provides guidelines for conducting a comprehensive operational audit of retirement plan management. Comments in the following paragraphs are restricted to the other forms of auditing.

Internal Accounting Control Surveys. Described in Chapter 18, internal accounting control surveys are aimed at assessing the major components of an overall system of internal accounting control. Applying this approach to retirement plan management, the internal accounting controls over the following transaction cycles could be reviewed:

- Employee/employer contributions cycle
- Actuarial accounting cycle
- Investment cycle
- Benefit payments cycle

The key control techniques to accomplish the internal control objectives within each of these cycles could be identified, documented, evaluated for adequacy, and tested.

Detailed Auditing of Internal Control. As discussed in Chapter 18, these audits focus on a specific cycle or function and review in greater detail the control techniques involved. Aspects of operational auditing may also be included. Any of the previously discussed functions or cycles may be audited by this approach. Questionnaires have to be developed, which serve as a basis for evaluating the internal controls represented to be in effect by management. A program of testing would then be performed in order to gather evidence indicating the extent to which those internal controls actually operated during the period reviewed.

Information Systems Applications Auditing. As discussed in Chapter 27, these audits entail a comprehensive review of specific I/S applications. These audits are undertaken to determine whether internal controls within the application are sufficient to result in processing data accurately and completely with adequate provision for security, backup, and recovery. Applications commonly involved in retirement plan management that may be audited in this way include:

- Participant record-keeping system
- Benefit payment system
- Investment accounting system

I/S applications auditing may be performed in conjunction with detailed internal control audits or internal control surveys or they may be performed in a stand-alone fashion.

OPERATIONAL AUDITING OF RETIREMENT PLAN MANAGEMENT

Perhaps the audit area offering the highest potential for service to management is operational auditing of retirement plan management. The balance of this chapter is devoted to a discussion of how a comprehensive operational audit of retirement plan management may be performed. Objectives and techniques are discussed, and a sample questionnaire, program, and report are presented. The material is presented in a way that permits work to be divided into segments, should a comprehensive review be undesirable for budget or other reasons.

Auditing Objective

The objective of a retirement plan management audit is to determine the extent to which retirement plan management objectives are being achieved effectively and efficiently. The auditor is attempting to determine whether employee benefits as outlined by management are adequately provided for, as well. More specifically, the auditor must try to determine whether:

- Sufficient resources have been allocated to achieve retirement plan objective.
- Administrative duties are carried out in accordance with company policy and applicable federal and state regulations.
- Deviations from policy occur only in accordance with appropriate authority.
- Systems of accounting and reporting reasonably assure that transactions and data relevant to plan administration are properly classified and reported.
- Information reported to management pertaining to retirement plans is accurate, complete, and relevant to evaluating performance.

RETIREMENT PLAN MANAGEMENT

- Information reported to employees is accurate, complete, and in compliance with applicable law.
- Retirement plan records, files, and documents are adequately safeguarded.

Audit Tools and Techniques

Effective operational auditing of retirement plan management requires the use of appropriate audit tools and the application of proper audit procedures. The most important tools are the questionnaire and the audit program, both of which are illustrated at the end of this chapter. In addition to these, the auditor may wish to apply generalized audit software or develop specific extraction programs to obtain samplings of participant data kept on I/S disks or tapes. Also, the auditor may wish to prepare or obtain suitable confirmation forms for use in confirming the existence of recipients and the accuracy of benefit payments.

Auditing procedures used include the following:

- Inquiries and observations to gain an understanding of how management attains retirement plan objectives (e.g., gathering organization charts, policy statements, procedure manuals, and flowcharts).
- Analytical procedures to see if historical data is presenting trends indicative of problems or supportive of effective management. Items that might be analyzed for this purpose include:
  — Investment manager performance (return on investment)
  — Fees paid to consultants, actuaries, and other outsiders
  — Changes made in recent years to the organization, retirement plan, and in methods or systems
  — Retirement plan actuarial costs over the past several years
  — Unfunded liability for vested pension benefits over the past several years
  — Retirement plan administrative expenses over the past several years
  — Overall retirement plan costs as a percentage of payroll over the past several years
- Inquiries of personnel and inspections of records, files, and documents to determine compliance with established control techniques. For these procedures, the auditor should consider, where appropriate, applying statistical sampling techniques. Attribute sampling could be used, for example, to test compliance with procedures for disbursing plan benefits.
- Inquiry and inspection to determine compliance with applicable ERISA and IRC regulations and filing requirements.
- Confirmation procedures for a sampling of beneficiaries to obtain evidence confirming the existence of the beneficiaries (i.e., not deceased or fictitious) and the propriety of benefits paid.
- With programming assistance from the I/S audit staff, a simulation that would reperform the calculation of employee benefits (if automated) for a select group of benefit recipients.

These are but a few of the audit procedures that might be employed in an operational audit of retirement plan management. Retirement plans are susceptible to fraud and other dishonest acts by employees and others. The performing auditor must be alert to the possibility that such acts may have occurred. Special procedures can be devised and performed that could lead to discovering evidence of defalcations or other irregularities.

Since many plans use computers to record and store data pertaining to retirement plans, extraction programs could be developed to disclose the following:

- A list of individuals who receive the highest benefits. By scanning and investigating any unusual amounts, existing fraudulent schemes could come to light.
- A balance range analysis or histogram using computer software. This might reveal to the auditor unusual patterns or bunching of individuals within benefit ranges (e.g., over $100,000) for further investigation.
- A balance range analysis prepared by age group. Any unusual bunchings (e.g., over age 100) could be investigated.
- A sampling of canceled checks, selected either nonstatistically or statistically. The endorsements on these checks could be compared with signatures in retirement plan administration files for consistency. Obvious differences would have to be investigated.

If any of these procedures, or other ones, present strong indications of possible illegal acts, the internal auditor should discuss the matter with company legal counsel before undertaking further action.

As stated previously, the most important audit tools are the questionnaire and the audit program. Figure 40-6 depicts a questionnaire that might be used in a comprehensive operational audit of retirement plan management, and Figure 40-7 shows the operational audit program itself. Figure 40-8 illustrates a specimen report that might result from such an audit.

(continued on page 40-59)

FIG. 40-6

Illustrative Retirement Plan Management Questionnaire

> The primary objective of retirement plan management is to reasonably assure that employees' retirement benefits authorized by management are adequately provided for, efficiently and effectively. Supplementary objectives are:
>
> ■ To obtain sufficient resources pursuant to management's authority to achieve objectives.
>
> ■ To carry out administrative duties in accordance with company policy and applicable federal and state regulations. In this context administration includes design of the plans, amendments, writing plan language and other material, keeping records of plan data, obtaining actuarial valuations, coordinating audits, preparing and filing various government reports and tax information returns,

specifying computer system requirements, developing applicable policies and proceedings, training and monitoring of personnel, and assisting in monitoring of pension trust assets.
- To deviate from established policies and procedures only upon appropriate authority.
- To maintain a current awareness of developments pertaining to retirement plan administration.
- To establish and maintain systems of accounting and reporting to reasonably assure transactions and data relevant to plan administration are properly classified and recorded. This may include:
  — Separate accounting for each participant
  — Separate accounting for each contributor
  — Adequate records of investments and changes in investments
  — Actuarial records
  — Disbursement records for benefit payments
- To summarize and report information periodically to affected management with respect to:
  — Investment activity
  — Participant data
  — Contributions
  — Benefits paid
  — Actuarial data
- To summarize and report information periodically to participants and regulatory bodies as required by law.
- To reasonably assure that access to retirement plan records and data is restricted to personnel authorized by management.
- To reasonably assure that retirement plan data and records are sufficiently protected from identifiable physical hazards of all types.
- To reasonably assure that retirement plan assets are sufficiently protected from loss, theft, fraud, and similar irregularities.

Accomplishing the foregoing objectives requires considerable administrative and managerial effort. This means adequate planning, organizing, staffing, and controlling. It requires the coordinated involvement of these disciplines:

- Plan administration
- Employee relations
- Tax counsel
- Finance

In addition to these internal functions, management is also aided by trust departments of banks, insurance companies, investment advisers, actuarial consultants, and external auditors.

In practice, pension plan administration occurs pursuant to a trust established for the purpose in accordance with applicable provisions of the Internal Revenue Code and the Employee Retirement Income Security Act (ERISA). Usually, the trust instrument specifies administrative and other requirements and names individual fiduciaries who must bear overall responsibility for the trust. Day-to-day plan administration is usually under the direction of one or more plan administrators and staff, along with representation from other affected disciplines.

(continued)

FIG. 40-6 *(cont'd)*

In view of the above, the following questionnaire is organized by functional discipline and covers all applicable objectives. In some instances it may be impractical to cover the entire questionnaire in a single undertaking. The auditor may decide to complete only selected sections at a time based on his professional judgment.

The questionnaire is intended to cover most situations the auditor might encounter. Needless to say, not all questions will necessarily be applicable in a given situation. Conversely, some circumstances could require adding or modifying questions.

RETIREMENT PLAN MANAGEMENT AUDIT QUESTIONNAIRE

	Yes	No	Reference

I. ORGANIZATIONAL

A. Authorization:

1. Is there a written policy stating management's objectives regarding retirement plans? ☐ ☐ ....
2. Does the policy recognize the concept that retirement plans are an integral part of the company's overall employee benefit strategy? ☐ ☐ ....
3. Is the responsibility for managing and/or administering retirement plans expressed in the form of an organization chart or charts? ☐ ☐ ....
4. Do written statements exist covering the duties and responsibilities of those involved in retirement plan administration? ☐ ☐ ....
5. Do written retirement plan instruments exist for each retirement plan subject to administration? ☐ ☐ ....
6. Have retirement plan trusts been established to function as the executory vehicle by which retirement plan interests are handled? ☐ ☐ ....
7. Are specific individuals named to serve in the fiduciary capacity of trustees? ☐ ☐ ....
8. Is a specific individual or group delegated day-to-day trust management and administrative duties? ☐ ☐ ....
9. Does the individual or group occupy a management position in the company high enough to reasonably assure that competent attention to trust matters will occur? ☐ ☐ ....
10. Does the policy statement in retirement plans cover such activities as:
    a. Planning ☐ ☐ ....
    b. Designing and revising basic plans ☐ ☐ ....
    c. Writing plan language ☐ ☐ ....
    d. Record-keeping ☐ ☐ ....
    e. Obtaining actuarial data ☐ ☐ ....
    f. Obtaining I/S assistance ☐ ☐ ....

	Yes	No	Reference

g. Filing various governmental agency reports ☐ ☐ ....
h. Training administrative personnel ☐ ☐ ....
i. Investing strategy and guidelines ☐ ☐ ....
j. Monitoring trustee investment transactions ☐ ☐ ....
k. Communicating with participants ☐ ☐ ....

11. Are the foregoing activities coordinated with applicable functional disciplines such as:
    a. Employee relations ☐ ☐ ....
    b. Law department ☐ ☐ ....
    c. Tax counsel ☐ ☐ ....
    d. Treasurer ☐ ☐ ....
    e. Corporate Secretary ☐ ☐ ....
    f. Controller ☐ ☐ ....

12. Is plan management assisted by outside organizations such as:
    a. Accountants ☐ ☐ ....
    b. Actuaries ☐ ☐ ....
    c. Bank trust departments ☐ ☐ ....
    d. Insurance companies ☐ ☐ ....
    e. Consultants ☐ ☐ ....
    f. Other ☐ ☐ ....

13. Are retirement plan goals and objectives consistent with the overall goals and objectives of the company's employee benefit strategy? ☐ ☐ ....

14. Are changes to policy statements, organization charts, plan instruments, and delegations of authority required to be reviewed and approved? ☐ ☐ ....

B. Execution and Recording:

1. Are records required to be kept evidencing:
    a. Policies, procedures, duties and responsibilities, organization charts, objectives, plans, and so on, and changes thereto ☐ ☐ ....
    b. Meetings of the retirement board ☐ ☐ ....
    c. Directives of senior retirement plan administration executives ☐ ☐ ....
    d. Arrangements and other correspondence with outside organizations, such as accountants, investment managers, bank trust departments, consultants, and actuaries ☐ ☐ ....
    e. Actuarial valuations ☐ ☐ ....
    f. Reports and filings and other correspondence with regulatory agencies such as the IRS and the Department of Labor ☐ ☐ ....
    g. Planning activities ☐ ☐ ....
    h. Meetings of monitoring groups such as investment committees ☐ ☐ ....

(continued)

FIG. 40-6 *(cont'd)*

	Yes	No	Reference
2. Do procedures require that the senior retirement plan executive receive reports of investment activity from investment managers of the trust?	☐	☐	....
3. Do such reports provide sufficient information to permit evaluating investment manager performance?	☐	☐	....

C. Accountability and Security:

	Yes	No	Reference
1. Is the senior retirement plan executive required to report periodically to the board of directors or to senior management such information as:			
a. The financial status of the plans	☐	☐	....
b. Summary actuarial data	☐	☐	....
c. Summary data regarding investment data	☐	☐	....
d. Proposals for changes in plan benefits	☐	☐	....
e. Evaluations of investment manager performance	☐	☐	....
f. Specific events or incidents of particular concern	☐	☐	....
g. Other relevant information	☐	☐	....
2. Are records retained in Question B.1 adequately protected from loss or damage from all identifiable hazards?	☐	☐	....
3. Is access to those records restricted to authorized personnel?	☐	☐	....
4. Is adequate provision for back-up of vital records required?	☐	☐	....

II. PLANNING

A. Authorization:

	Yes	No	Reference
1. Is the authority for retirement plan administration planning delegated to a specific individual, such as the senior retirement plan executive?	☐	☐	....
2. Do procedures require the development of:			
a. Strategic or long-range plans	☐	☐	....
b. Short-term plans	☐	☐	....
c. Tactical plans	☐	☐	....
3. Do procedures require that plans be approved by appropriate management levels?	☐	☐	....
4. Do procedures require that plans be reviewed by and coordinated with all relevant disciplines to reasonably assure the plan is developed in consideration of:			
a. Tax law changes	☐	☐	....
b. Pension law (ERISA) changes	☐	☐	....
c. Other regulatory changes	☐	☐	....

		Yes	No	Reference
d.	Actuarial changes	☐	☐	....
e.	Trends in employee benefits	☐	☐	....
f.	Company objectives and goals	☐	☐	....
g.	Court decisions	☐	☐	....
h.	Changes in plan instruments	☐	☐	....
i.	Financial condition of the plans	☐	☐	....

B. Execution and Recording:

1. Do procedures require gathering relevant, reliable data upon which to develop plans? ☐ ☐ ....
   Note: Sources for this purpose might include reports from actuaries, financial statements, investment reports, and consultant reports.

2. Do procedures require that plans be prepared in sufficient detail to permit independent analysis, understanding, and appraisal? ☐ ☒ ....

3. Do procedures require that anticipated retirement plan administration requirements be converted into reliable forecasts of:
   a. Manpower needs ☐ ☐ ....
   b. Systems needs ☐ ☐ ....
   c. Facilities and equipment needs ☐ ☐ ....
   d. Other ☐ ☐ ....

4. Do procedures require that planning activities be documented in accurate and complete records, such as:
   a. Reference data ☐ ☐ ....
   b. Documentation gathered from other involved organizations ☐ ☐ ....
   c. Supporting workpapers ☐ ☐ ....
   d. Final plans ☐ ☐ ....

C. Accountability and Security:

1. Do procedures require that actual retirement plan administration activities and events be compared with short- and long-term plans by responsible management? ☐ ☐ ....

2. Do procedures require that records be adequately protected from loss or damage from identifiable physical hazards? ☐ ☐ ....

3. Is access to records of the planning group restricted to authorized personnel? ☐ ☐ ....

4. Is adequate provision for backup of vital planning records required? ☐ ☐ ....

(continued)

FIG. 40-6 *(cont'd)*

	Yes	No	Reference
III. DESIGNING OR REVISING BASIC PLANS AND WRITING PLAN LANGUAGE			
A. Authorization and Execution:			
1. Are retirement plans designed or revised pursuant to management's specific authorization (including the board of directors)?	☐	☐	....
2. Is the authority for effecting new plans or changes to existing plans delegated to a specific individual or group?	☐	☐	....
3. Do procedures require that new plans or changes to existing plans be coordinated with:			
a. Employee relations	☐	☐	....
b. Tax counsel	☐	☐	....
c. Legal counsel	☐	☐	....
d. Actuarial consultants	☐	☐	....
e. Other	☐	☐	....
4. Do new plans and/or revisions cover the following aspects:			
a. General terms	☐	☐	....
b. Definitions of terms	☐	☐	....
c. Enrollment	☐	☐	....
d. Employee contributions	☐	☐	....
e. Company contributions	☐	☐	....
f. Disposition of contributions	☐	☐	....
g. Eligibility for benefits	☐	☐	....
h. Retirement benefits	☐	☐	....
i. Commencement and duration of benefits	☐	☐	....
j. Death benefits	☐	☐	....
k. Application and appeal procedures	☐	☐	....
l. Plan administration	☐	☐	....
m. Fund management	☐	☐	....
n. Termination of plan	☐	☐	....
o. Transfer, merger, or consolidation	☐	☐	....
p. Actuarial factors	☐	☐	....
5. Are retirement plans developed or changed only upon consideration of the impact such actions might have on:			
a. Union relations	☐	☐	....
b. Financial condition (funding requirements)	☐	☐	....
c. Compensation posture	☐	☐	....
d. Other employee rights and benefits	☐	☐	....
e. Income tax posture	☐	☐	....
f. Company image	☐	☐	....
6. Are plans written using language that is easy to read and understand?	☐	☐	....

	Yes	No	Reference

7. Does the plan instrument include definitions of such terms as:

	Yes	No	Reference
a. Actuarial equivalent	☐	☐	....
b. Break in service	☐	☐	....
c. Disability	☐	☐	....
d. Effective date	☐	☐	....
e. Employee	☐	☐	....
f. Participating company	☐	☐	....
g. Participant	☐	☐	....
h. Normal retirement age	☐	☐	....
i. Plan year	☐	☐	....
j. Terminated participant	☐	☐	....
k. Vesting	☐	☐	....

8. Are plans or revisions thereof approved by appropriate management and/or the board of directors? ☐ ☐ ....

B. Recording and Accountability:

1. Are terms and conditions of retirement plans set forth in reasonable detail and in an orderly, logical, and understandable fashion? ☐ ☐ ....

2. Are important aspects such as calculation of employee and employer contributions and employee benefits clearly written? ☐ ☐ ....

3. Are any required legal reviews made a matter of record? ☐ ☐ ....

4. Are determination letters and other pertinent correspondence with the Internal Revenue Service retained? ☐ ☐ ....

C. Security:

1. Do procedures require that records of plans and changes thereto be adequately protected from loss or damage from identifiable hazards? ☐ ☐ ....

2. Is access to records of the plan administration restricted to authorized personnel? ☐ ☐ ....

3. Is adequate provision for backup of vital administration records required? ☐ ☐ ....

IV. RECORD-KEEPING

A. Authorization and Execution:

1. Do policies and procedures specify authority and responsibility for establishing and maintaining records of participant data? ☐ ☐ ....

(continued)

FIG. 40-6 *(cont'd)*

	Yes	No	Reference
2. Do such record-keeping systems provide detailed capability for the following:			
a. Active nonvested covered employees?	☐	☐	....
b. Terminated nonvested covered employees?	☐	☐	....
c. Active vested covered employees?	☐	☐	....
d. Terminated vested covered employees?	☐	☐	....
e. Retired nonvested covered employees?	☐	☐	....
f. Retired vested covered employees?	☐	☐	....
3. Are procedures aided by the use of standard forms and instructions for:			
a. Adding new employees to the plan	☐	☐	....
b. Effecting changes to basic participant data such as:			
■ Name	☐	☐	....
■ Address	☐	☐	....
■ Marital status	☐	☐	....
■ Eligibility date	☐	☐	....
■ Service record	☐	☐	....
■ Salary rate	☐	☐	....
■ Contribution rate	☐	☐	....
■ Breaks in service	☐	☐	....
■ Retirement	☐	☐	....
■ Benefit payments	☐	☐	....
c. Deleting participant data	☐	☐	....
4. Does the record-keeping system for keeping participant data include electronic data processing techniques? Note: If the answer to this question is "yes," refer to Section VI of this questionnaire.	☐	☐	....
5. Do procedures require that changes made to correct errors in original data submissions be reviewed and approved for:			
a. Name	☐	☐	....
b. Address	☐	☐	....
c. Marital status	☐	☐	....
d. Eligibility date	☐	☐	....
e. Service record	☐	☐	....
f. Salary rate	☐	☐	....
g. Contribution	☐	☐	....
h. Breaks in service	☐	☐	....
i. Retirement	☐	☐	....
j. Benefit payments	☐	☐	....
6. Do procedures require that benefit payments to retirees commence only after:			

		Yes	No	Reference

    a. Receipt of properly completed application including designations for such items as death benefits, joint survivor election, etc. ☐ ☐ ....
    b. Proof of age report or other evidence verifying age ☐ ☐ ....
    c. Evidence of counselor review and approval ☐ ☐ ....
    d. Withholding information (if applicable) ☐ ☐ ....
    e. Verification of benefit calculation ☐ ☐ ....

7. Do procedures provide a means by which the retirement benefits are stopped upon death of retirees? ☐ ☐ ....
   Note: This method may include receipt of death notice to generate death benefit, receipt of death notice to stop group medical insurance, periodic confirmation procedures with retirees, and other techniques.

8. Is a chart of accounts maintained including descriptions of accounts for classifying and recording plan transactions, such as:
   a. Cash ☐ ☐ ....
   b. Contributions receivable ☐ ☐ ....
   c. Investments ☐ ☐ ....
   d. Claims payable ☐ ☐ ....
   e. Net assets ☐ ☐ ....
   f. Contributions received ☐ ☐ ....
   g. Earnings from investments ☐ ☐ ....
   h. Benefits paid ☐ ☐ ....
   i. Administrative expenses ☐ ☐ ....
   j. Other (describe) ☐ ☐ ....

9. Do procedures provide for keeping records of the following:
   a. Present value of vested benefits for retired participants and for all other participants ☐ ☐ ....
   b. Present value of nonvested accrued benefits ☐ ☐ ....
   c. Number of persons covered (i.e, active, terminated, retired) ☐ ☐ ....
   d. Number of persons not covered ☐ ☐ ....
   e. Total number of employees ☐ ☐ ....

10. Do procedures provide for keeping records of
    a. Normal cost ☐ ☐ ....
    b. Amortization of prior service cost ☐ ☐ ....
    c. Interest ☐ ☐ ....
    d. Actuarial assumptions used ☐ ☐ ....
    e. Actuarial cost method ☐ ☐ ....
    f. Other (specify) ☐ ☐ ....

(continued)

FIG. 40-6 *(cont'd)*

	Yes	No	Reference
B. Recording and Accountability:			
1. Do procedures provide for the prompt and accurate recording of the following types of participant data:			
a. Additions of covered employees	☐	☐	....
b. Deletions of covered employees	☐	☐	....
c. Length of service transactions	☐	☐	....
d. Contributions by employees	☐	☐	....
e. Initiation of benefit payments to retirees	☐	☐	....
f. Changes in benefit payments to retirees	☐	☐	....
g. Cessation of benefit payments to retirees	☐	☐	....
2. Do procedures and systems accommodate situations such as:			
a. Overpayments	☐	☐	....
b. Underpayments	☐	☐	....
c. Insurance refunds	☐	☐	....
d. Death benefits (if applicable)	☐	☐	....
e. Federal withholding (if applicable)	☐	☐	....
f. State withholding (if applicable)	☐	☐	....
g. Retroactive adjustments	☐	☐	....
h. Lump-sum payments	☐	☐	....
i. Miscellaneous	☐	☐	....
3. Do procedures provide for checks and balances in the recording process to reasonably assure the identification of errors?	☐	☐	....
4. Do procedures require that errors identified by Question B.2 above be resubmitted promptly?	☐	☐	....
5. Do procedures require that reports be developed from the records periodically, such as:			
a. Proof listings of transaction inputs	☐	☐	....
b. Edit reports of detected errors	☐	☐	....
c. Valid final transaction reports for transactions such as:			
■ Adds	☐	☐	....
■ Deletes	☐	☐	....
■ Changes	☐	☐	....
■ Contributions withheld	☐	☐	....
■ Benefits paid	☐	☐	....
■ Other (specify)	☐	☐	....
d. Check registers	☐	☐	....
e. Death reports	☐	☐	....
6. Are the various reports required to be reviewed for any unusual items, errors, and reasonableness?	☐	☐	....
7. Do procedures require that the checks issued per			

RETIREMENT PLAN MANAGEMENT

	Yes	No	Reference

the check register be reconciled with the benefits report?   ☐ ☐ ....

C. Security:

1. Does the level of staffing and division of duties allow for proper segregation of the following:
   a. Submission of participant data entries and review of final transaction reports   ☐ ☐ ....
   b. Transaction submission and transaction processing duties   ☐ ☐ ....
   c. Submission of participant data and submission of benefit payment transactions   ☐ ☐ ....
   d. Calculation of benefits and submission of benefit payment transactions   ☐ ☐ ....
   e. Submission of benefit payment transactions and processing of same   ☐ ☐ ....
   f. Submission and processing of checks issued data   ☐ ☐ ....
   g. Reconciling bank accounts and submission/processing of checks issued   ☐ ☐ ....

2. Is access to retirement plan records restricted to authorized personnel?   ☐ ☐ ....

3. Are retirement plan records reasonably safeguarded from loss or destruction as a result of identifiable hazards of all types?   ☐ ☐ ....

4. Is adequate provision for backup of vital retirement plan records required?   ☐ ☐ ....

5. Are retirement plans insured by a fidelity bond against losses through fraud or dishonesty of employees, consultants, bankers, investment managers, or others?   ☐ ☐ ....

6. Are company policies with respect to vacations enforced for all employees involved in retirement plan administration and record-keeping?   ☐ ☐ ....

7. Do procedures require that bank accounts be reconciled periodically?   ☐ ☐ ....

8. Do procedures require the periodic preparation of various summary information and reports to be distributed to:
   a. Participants   ☐ ☐ ....
   b. Retirees   ☐ ☐ ....
   c. Retirement Board   ☐ ☐ ....
   d. Actuary   ☐ ☐ ....
   e. Others   ☐ ☐ ....

9. Do procedures provide for the timely filing of Form 5500, Annual Return/Report of Employee Benefit Plan?   ☐ ☐ ....

(continued)

FIG. 40-6 *(cont'd)*

	Yes	No	Reference
V. PLAN ADMINISTRATION			
A. Authorization and Execution:			
1. Do administrative policies and procedures specify guidelines for maintaining relations with:			
a. Actuaries	☐	☐	....
b. Outside accountants	☐	☐	....
c. Lawyers	☐	☐	....
d. Banks	☐	☐	....
e. Trustees	☐	☐	....
f. Insurance companies	☐	☐	....
g. Consultants	☐	☐	....
h. Investment managers	☐	☐	....
2. Do such policies and procedures specify authority for:			
a. Initiating or executing changes to plan instruments	☐	☐	....
b. Devising overall investment strategy	☐	☐	....
c. Initiating and maintaining trust agreements	☐	☐	....
d. Selecting and approving investment managers	☐	☐	....
e. Reviewing investment manager performance	☐	☐	....
f. Devising and maintaining systems of internal control (including EDP aspects)	☐	☐	....
g. Organizing and staffing involved functions	☐	☐	....
h. Making contributions to trust fund	☐	☐	....
i. Disbursing benefit payments	☐	☐	....
j. Paying administrative expenses	☐	☐	....
k. Communicating with participants and retirees	☐	☐	....
l. Complying with applicable IRS, Department of Labor, and other regulations	☐	☐	....
m. Preparing and submitting various reports to regulators, management, the board of trustees, employees, and others	☐	☐	....
3. Do policies require that arrangements and agreements with involved third parties (actuaries, banks, investment managers, etc.) be in writing?	☐	☐	....
4. Do procedures require that such arrangements and agreements receive appropriate review from interested disciplines including:			
a. Law	☐	☐	....
b. Tax	☐	☐	....
c. Employee relations	☐	☐	....
d. Finance	☐	☐	....
5. Do procedures specify authority for making contributions to pension trusts?	☐	☐	....

	Yes	No	Reference

6. Are such contributions determined on the basis of actuarial reports? ☐ ☐ ....

7. Are such actuarial reports prepared using actuarial assumptions and methods authorized by management? ☐ ☐ ....

8. Are contributions to pension trusts reviewed and approved by appropriate management? ☐ ☐ ....

9. Do procedures specify authority for incurring administrative expenses? ☐ ☐ ....

10. Are payments for administrative expenses made only after receipt, audit, and approval of invoices or statements? ☐ ☐ ....

B. Recording and Accountability:

1. Do procedures require that technique for executing the activities in Question V.A.2 be documented in an appropriate fashion (flow charts, narratives, or desk procedures)? ☐ ☐ ....

2. Do procedures require that reports received from the following be retained in an orderly fashion:
    a. Bank trust departments ☐ ☐ ....
    b. Actuaries ☐ ☐ ....
    c. Outside accountants ☐ ☐ ....
    d. Investment managers ☐ ☐ ....
    e. Consultants ☐ ☐ ....
    f. Others ☐ ☐ ....

3. Do reports of investment managers set forth:
    a. Details of dividends and interest earned ☐ ☐ ....
    b. Details of investments bought and sold showing gains or losses ☐ ☐ ....
    c. Listing of investments held at end of reporting period ☐ ☐ ....

4. Do procedures require periodic validation of details of investment income and performance shown in reports (Question V.B.3) by comparisons with published records of dividends, stock prices, and so on? ☐ ☐ ....

5. Do procedures require periodically comparing the list of investments with the criteria established by management or the board? ☐ ☐ ....

6. Do procedures require periodically obtaining assurance that investment assets held by the custodian(s) agree with listings furnished by the investment manager(s)? ☐ ☐ ....

7. Do procedures require periodically obtaining written assurance that the internal controls of the custodian are sufficient to account for trust transactions and assets? ☐ ☐ ....

(continued)

FIG. 40-6 *(cont'd)*

	Yes	No	Reference
8. Do procedures require periodic reviews of actuarial reports for reasonableness, consistency of assumptions, and methods used, and for indications of funding problems?	☐	☐	....
9. Do procedures require that actuarial reports be reviewed for accuracy and completeness (i.e., that actuarial data is accurately and completely developed from company records of participant data)?	☐	☐	....
10. Are actuarial assumptions and methods periodically reviewed for reasonableness and compared with those used by other private plans?	☐	☐	....
11. Are actuarial assumptions and methods in accordance with applicable ERISA requirements?	☐	☐	....

C. Security:

	Yes	No	Reference
1. Do procedures require that records of agreements, contracts, procedures, flow charts, and reports be adequately protected from loss or damage from identifiable hazards?	☐	☐	....
2. Is access to such records restricted to authorized personnel?	☐	☐	....
3. Is adequate provision for back up of such records required?	☐	☐	....
4. Do policies prevent executive and other employees involved in plan administration from engaging in any activity that might be construed to be a conflict of interest?	☐	☐	....
5. Are executives and other employees who have relations with third parties required to submit statements disclosing any situations that may be construed to pose a conflict of interest?	☐	☐	....
6. Are investment managers who execute investment transactions independent from individuals or organizations (such as bank trust departments) who have custodial responsibility?	☐	☐	....
7. Are periodic inspections and physical counts made of investment securities retained in the custody of the trustee?	☐	☐	....
8. Are the physical counts compared with records of securities on hand?	☐	☐	....
9. Are the physical counts and comparisons performed by someone (usually the outside auditors of the bank) independent of custodial duties?	☐	☐	....
10. Are differences disclosed by the above process followed up and resolved?	☐	☐	....

	Yes	No	Reference

11. Are the results of the process disclosed to all interested parties? ☐ ☐ ....

VI. INFORMATION SYSTEMS

A. Authorization and Execution:

1. Is the responsibility for developing and maintaining retirement plan administration I/S applications expressed in writing? ☐ ☐ ....
2. Do procedures require that changes to the following be authorized by those in Question 1:
   a. Forms ☐ ☐ ....
   b. Programs ☐ ☐ ....
   c. Program documentation ☐ ☐ ....
   d. Passwords ☐ ☐ ....
   e. Number of terminals ☐ ☐ ....
   f. Terminal users ☐ ☐ ....
   g. Extent of accessibility by users ☐ ☐ ....
   h. File update capability ☐ ☐ ....
   i. Back-up requirements ☐ ☐ ....
   j. Special file security protection ☐ ☐ ....
3. Do I/S applications include the following:
   a. Participant master file record-keeping ☐ ☐ ....
   b. Retiree benefit payments ☐ ☐ ....
   c. Participant reporting ☐ ☐ ....
   d. Retirement plan accounting ☐ ☐ ....
   e. Retirement plan investments ☐ ☐ ....
4. Are persons responsible for the above I/S applications involved in the development and/or maintenance of said systems including:
   a. Requirements definition ☐ ☐ ....
   b. System design ☐ ☐ ....
   c. System testing ☐ ☐ ....
   d. Training of use personnel ☐ ☐ ....
   e. Implementation ☐ ☐ ....
5. Are project control techniques used in developing and maintaining the above I/S systems, including:
   a. Project planning ☐ ☐ ....
   b. Project scheduling ☐ ☐ ....
   c. Budgeting and cost control ☐ ☐ ....
   d. Monitoring and reporting ☐ ☐ ....

B. Recording and Accountability*:

1. Do procedures require that systems be developed and maintained in accordance with prescribed standards? ☐ ☐ ....

* This section should be completed for each system.

(continued)

FIG. 40-6 *(cont'd)*

	Yes	No	Reference
2. Are the standards sufficient to reasonably assure the development and maintenance of adequately controlled systems? Note: For this answer, the auditor may wish to consult with I/S auditing evaluations of this process.	☐	☐	....
3. Is the application a batch oriented application with or without remote job entry features?	☐	☐	....

If the answers to the above questions are all "yes," then the auditor should proceed to obtain responses to the balance of questions in this Section. If the answer is "no" to any one of those questions, it may indicate that the application is too complex for evaluation within the context of this assignment. The auditor should not attempt further I/S evaluation and analysis without assistance from a senior I/S auditor or approval of the manager or director.

C. Security:

	Yes	No	Reference
1. Are I/S personnel (including programmers) independent of retirement plan duties and responsibilities?	☐	☐	....
2. Are the following I/S functions segregated:			
a. Conversion	☐	☐	....
b. Computer operations	☐	☐	....
c. File librarian	☐	☐	....
d. System programming	☐	☐	....
e. Application programming	☐	☐	....
3. Are computerized files suitably protected against unauthorized access by use of:			
a. Terminal locks	☐	☐	....
b. Identification codes	☐	☐	....
c. Passwords	☐	☐	....
d. Security software (e.g., Resource Access Control Facility)	☐	☐	....
e. Access attempt logging	☐	☐	....
4. Are vital computer records and files adequately backed up and are duplicate records/files stored off-site?	☐	☐	....
5. Are hardware, software, and facilities adequately protected against loss or destruction from identifiable hazards?	☐	☐	....
6. Are inventories of unused checks adequately protected from theft?	☐	☐	....
7. Is a disaster recovery plan in existence?	☐	☐	....
8. Do procedures call for periodic tests of the plan?	☐	☐	....

FIG. 40-7
Illustrative Operational Audit Program for Retirement Plan Management

The purpose of this audit program is to obtain sufficient evidential matter to afford a basis for expressing an opinion and other observations regarding the efficiency and effectiveness of the controls and techniques used by management to achieve the retirement plan objectives outlined in the related Retirement Plan Management Audit Questionnaire.

	Done by	Date

1. Organizational:

☐ Obtain a copy of the written policy statements regarding retirement plans.

☐ Obtain a copy of relevant organizational charts. Cross reference to questionnaire where applicable.

☐ Obtain copies of relevant procedures, flow charts, trust instruments, agreements, plan documents, and any other pertinent documents for study purposes and to document in the workpapers the organizational activity of management

☐ By inquiry and inspection of policy statements and procedures, determine the extent to which such documentation is kept current.

☐ Review minutes, correspondence files, and other records to determine the extent to which the retirement board is kept aware of retirement plan status, activities, problems, and so forth.

☐ By inquiry and inspection determine the extent to which retirement plan events and actions are coordinated among affected disciplines (e.g., law, tax, treasury, and secretary).

☐ By inquiry and inspection, determine the extent to which services of outside organizations are involved in retirement plan administration.

☐ Obtain or prepare an analysis of fees paid during past five years to consultants, actuaries, fund managers, and others. Determine whether any unusual relationships or fluctuations exist. By inquiry and inspection, determine the reasonableness and propriety of these unusual items and/or fluctuations.

☐ Obtain from the executive responsible for retirement plan management a representation as to the adequacy of techniques for achieving retirement plan objectives and the extent to which such objectives are achieved efficiently and effectively.

☐ By inquiry and confirmation, determine the extent to which any changes in plan instruments, delegations of authority, organization, and/or policies are properly approved.

(continued)

FIG. 40-7 *(cont'd)*

	Done by	Date
☐ By inquiry and observation, determine the existence of the following files:		
■ Policies	....	....
■ Minutes of retirement board meetings	....	....
■ Directives by senior management	....	....
■ Contracts/agreements with outsiders	....	....
■ Actuarial reports	....	....
■ Filings (such as Form 5500) with regulatory agencies	....	....
■ Planning efforts	....	....
■ Minutes of meetings of monitoring groups such as investment committees	....	....
■ Reports to board of directors	....	....
■ Reports from fund managers and other outside experts	....	....
☐ Obtain or prepare a comparative analysis of investment performance by fund manager for the past ten years.	....	....

For purposes of this analysis, return on investment should be calculated from data (if available) reported by the fund managers for each year and cumulatively. Also, the analysis should include common standard measures for comparative purposes, such as the Standard & Poors' 500 Index for equities and the various money rates and/or bond indexes for fixed rate investments.

☐ Obtain explanations from the senior executive responsible for fund managers for any unusual trends or performances indicated by the foregoing comparison. Ascertain whether these matters have been reported to the investment committee.   ....

☐ If information is available, obtain or prepare a comparative analysis of investment performance of the overall retirement plan with that of other plans. Obtain explanations for any unfavorable comparisons and ascertain that such explanations have reported to the investment committee.   ....

☐ By inquiry and observation, determine compliance with procedures aimed at safeguarding records from loss, destruction, and unauthorized access.   ....

2. Planning

☐ By inquiry and inspection, determine compliance with procedures including approval for preparation of short-term and long-term plans.   ....

☐ By inquiry and inspection, determine compliance with record-keeping requirements for short-term and long-term plans.   ....

☐ By inquiry, determine the extent to which actual accomplishments are measured against planned accomplishments.   ....

	Done by	Date
☐ By inquiry and observation, determine compliance with procedures for safeguarding records from loss, destruction, and unauthorized access.	....	....

3. Designing or Revising Basic Plans and Writing Plan Language

☐ By inquiry and inspection, determine that changes to the retirement plan during the year have been reviewed by all relevant disciplines (law, tax, employee relations, etc.) and are properly approved. ....

☐ By reading and studying retirement plan documents and changes thereto, determine that the plan covers all relevant aspects and is written in easy-to-understand language with all technical terms defined. ....

☐ By inquiry and inspection, determine that required determination letters from the Internal Revenue Service and other taxing authorities are present, as applicable. ....

☐ By inquiry and observation, determine compliance with procedures for safeguarding retirement plan documents, IRS correspondence, and related records from loss, destruction, and unauthorized access. ....

4. Record-Keeping

☐ Obtain copies of applicable policy and procedural statements for record-keeping practices applicable to the following:

- Active, nonvested covered employees ....
- Terminated, nonvested covered employees ....
- Active, vested covered employees ....
- Terminated, vested covered employees ....
- Retired, nonvested covered employees ....
- Retired, vested covered employees ....

☐ Obtain copies of all standard forms and instructions used in record-keeping and by review of each, determine that the design of the form and instructions appear effective for the purposes intended. ....

☐ By sampling techniques (nonstatistical or statistical as appropriate), determine compliance with procedures for the following types of transaction flows:

- Employee data changes (name, address, marital status, and so on) ....
- Eligibility changes ....
- Service record changes ....
- Contributions ....
- Benefit payments ....

Attributes to be tested should include where applicable, use of proper form,

(continued)

FIG. 40-7 *(cont'd)*

	Done by	Date

accurate completion of form, evidence of checking, evidence of approval, evidence of processing, evidence of batch control, and evidence of edit.
- By sampling techniques (nonstatistical or statistical as appropriate), obtain by direct correspondence with retirees that retiree is still living, and such other record information as deemed necessary. ....

☐ If records are kept on disk or tape, consider the possibility of performing the following with the assist of generalized audit software:
- An extraction in descending dollar order of the twenty-five individuals who receive the largest benefits and vouch the accuracy of those benefits by tracing to supporting records and by recalculating as necessary. ....
- Trace benefit payments made to canceled checks and compare signature endorsement with records bearing employee signature. Investigate any exceptions. ....
- A balance range analysis (histogram) of the amounts paid to retirees. (A balance range analysis is a stratified listing of the number of retirees and the total amounts paid to those retirees within each defined range, e.g., all those over $100,000, those between $95,000 and $100,000, and so on. Investigate any unusual items. ....
- A balance range analysis showing amounts paid to retirees according to age group. Investigate any extreme items (i.e., payments to individuals over age 100 or over 30 retired years). ....
- An extraction of all instances in which benefit payments were stopped during the year. By sampling (either judgmentally or statistically), determine that all important control techniques for stopping payment were followed. ....

☐ Obtain copy of chart of accounts and review for propriety. ....

☐ Obtain copies of most recent financial statements, independent auditor's report, actuarial valuation, and review for consistency and/or unusual items. Retain such copies as evidence of compliance with administrative procedures requiring periodic preparation of financial statements and examination by independent auditors. ....

☐ By inquiry and inspection, determine compliance with bank account reconciliation procedures. ....

☐ By inquiry and inspection, determine compliance with requirements for reporting financial and other plan data as needed by:
- Participants ....
- Retirees ....
- Retirement board ....

	Done by	Date
■ Actuary	....	....
■ Others	....	....

☐ By inquiry and inspection, determine compliance and filing requirements of regulatory agencies. Obtain copy of most recent Form 5500 and review for accuracy and completeness.   ....

☐ By sampling (either nonstatistical or statistical), determine compliance with procedures for recording the following types of transactions:

- Additions of covered employees   ....
- Deletions of covered employees   ....
- Changes to length of service   ....
- Employee contributions   ....
- Death benefit payments (if applicable)   ....
- Lump-sum payments (if applicable)   ....
- Federal and state withholding (if applicable) on benefit payments to retirees   ....

☐ By inquiry and inspection, determine the existence where applicable of such records as:

- Proof listings   ....
- Edit reports   ....
- Final transaction reports   ....
- Check registers   ....
- Death reports   ....

☐ By inquiry and inspection, determine compliance with procedures for reconciling benefit payment check registers with benefit reports.   ....

☐ By reference to organization charts and by observations and other audit procedures as deemed necessary, test controls aimed at segregating duties and providing for checks and balances in processing and recording transactions, calculating benefits, and so on.   ....

☐ By observation and inquiry, determine compliance with procedures for safeguarding records and limiting access thereto.   ....

☐ Verify existence of fidelity bond.   ....

5. Plan Administration

☐ By inquiry and inspection of correspondence, contracts, and other supporting documentation, as appropriate, determine compliance with procedures or techniques for maintaining relations with:

- Actuaries   ....
- Outside accountants   ....

(continued)

FIG. 40-7 *(cont'd)*

	Done by	Date
■ Lawyers	....	....
■ Banks	....	....
■ Trustees	....	....
■ Insurance companies	....	....
■ Consultants	....	....
■ Investment managers	....	....

☐ Trace all contributions to the retirement plan trust to appropriate sources and examine evidence of proper approval. ....

☐ Review the most recent actuarial report for accuracy, consistency, and reasonableness. ....

☐ By sampling (either nonstatistical or statistical, as appropriate), test payments for retirement plan administrative expenses for compliance with established procedures. ....

☐ By inquiry and inspection, determine compliance with procedures for obtaining and retaining reports and other data from:

- ■ Bank trust department ....
- ■ Actuaries ....
- ■ Outside accountants ....
- ■ Investment managers ....
- ■ Consultants ....
- ■ Others ....

☐ For reports received from investment managers, test statements of dividends and interest received to published data (*Wall Street Journal*) and test gains and losses on dispositions of investments. ....

☐ Review listings of investments owned for compliance with investment guidelines established by investment committee. ....

☐ By inquiry and inspection, determine the existence of a current independent auditor's report on the system of internal controls maintained by the retirement plan's investment custodian (Master Trustee). ....

☐ By inquiry and observation, determine compliance with procedures for safeguarding administration records and for limiting access. ....

☐ By inquiry, determine that individuals responsible for investing plan assets are independent from those with custodial responsibilities. ....

6. Information Systems

☐ Obtain copies of applicable policy statements evidencing the designation of authority and responsibility

	Done by	Date
for developing and maintaining I/S systems applicable to retirement plan activity and record-keeping.	....	....

☐ By inquiry and inspection, determine compliance with procedures for changes to the following during the past year for all key applications:

	Done by	Date
■ Forms	....	....
■ Programs	....	....
■ Program documentation	....	....
■ Passwords	....	....
■ Number of terminals	....	....
■ Terminal users	....	....
■ Extent of accessibility by users	....	....
■ File update capability	....	....
■ Back-up requirements	....	....
■ Special file security	....	....

☐ By inquiry and inspection of minutes, correspondence, or other documentation, determine the extent of involvement of responsible retirement plan administration personnel in systems development and changes thereto. ....

☐ By inquiry and inspection, determine the extent to which project control techniques (project planning, scheduling, budgeting, etc.) are used in developing and maintaining systems. ....

☐ By inquiry, determine whether systems are developed in accordance with established systems and programming standards. ....

☐ By observation and/or inspection, determine for each key application that data processing personnel are independent of retirement plan duties and functions. ....

☐ By observation during actual run conditions, determine that the following functions are segregated:

	Done by	Date
■ Data conversion	....	....
■ Computer questions	....	....
■ File librarian	....	....
■ System programming	....	....
■ Application programming	....	....

☐ By inquiry, observation, and inspection, determine compliance with procedures for protecting retirement plan data sets from unauthorized access. ....

☐ By inquiry and inspection, determine that vital records are identified and backed up as required by procedures. ....

☐ Obtain a copy of the disaster plan and determine the extent to which it has been tested. ....

☐ By inquiry, determine the extent to which retirement plan administration personnel who use the I/S systems are satisfied with such systems and related I/S services. ....

☐ By inquiry, determine when retirement plan I/S applications were last audited. Consider scheduling and performing separate in-depth applications audits. ....

FIG. 40-8
Illustrative Audit Report

TO   Retirement Board
          XYZ Corporation Retirement Board
FROM   Corporate Audit
SUBJECT   Retirement Plan Management

We have performed a review of the functions and techniques involved in the management of the Retirement Plan of the company. Our review was performed to determine the efficiency and effectiveness of such techniques for achieving management objectives. These objectives include reasonably assuring:

- that employee retirement benefits are in accordance with management's authorization and are adequately provided for.
- that administration duties are carried out in accordance with the terms of the plan, company policy and applicable regulations such as the Employee Retirement Income Security Act.
- that internal controls are sufficient to maintain accurate and complete records for such purposes as determining eligibility, calculating benefits, reporting to government agencies, employees and others, and disbursing benefits.

Our work included developing a special computer audit program designed to stratify the retirement file data in a manner that permitted the selection and matching of data from the Retired Employee Payments System (REPS) master files to the data contained in the Personnel Retirement Data Records System (PRS) master files. This program was used to select specific transaction data for detailed testing and analysis. Attachment A to this report contains a detailed listing of the areas included in our review and analysis. Attachment B to this report contains a brief description of the plan, the systems involved in the operation of the plan, and a summary of transactions processed by the plan during 19XX. Our scope did not include any verification of the internal controls over the custodial functions at ABC Trust Company. Also, we didn't verify any controls exercised by each of the investment managers who are authorized to manage, invest, reinvest, acquire and dispose of any plan assets allocated to their respective accounts.
With respect to internal control:

- Changes to participant records in fields such as name, address, and pay rate may be made by several persons without review or approval.
- The weekly error report provided by the Personnel Retirement Data System contains more than 100 entries that are over 1 year old.
- Vital Personnel Retirement Data System records and documentation are not backed up.
- The custodian of the supply of unissued benefit checks is also the custodian of signature plates for the authorized signatures.
- The total of benefit checks issued each month is not reconciled to the total amount transferred to the retirement plan checking account.
- Actuarial assumptions used by the actuary in determining company contributions are not reviewed for reasonableness.

The portions of our scope aimed at aspects of retirement plan management, other than internal control, indicate that in our opinion:

- employee retirement benefits are in accordance with management's authorization and are being adequately provided for.

> ■ that administrative duties are carried out in accordance with company policy and applicable regulations.
>
> In summary, functions and techniques involved in the management of the Retirement Plan of the company, in our opinion, are meeting objectives to the extent practicable with present levels of staffing. The Retirement Administration department appears to lack adequate staff to segregate incompatible duties, and to perform the reconciliations and reviews necessary to reasonably assure that sound internal accounting controls are maintained. Unless remedial actions are taken as suggested in this report, retirement plan management and administration will continue to be unnecessarily exposed to errors and, consequently, inefficiencies. The balance of this report contains a more detailed discussion of our findings, along with our recommendations for improved controls.

SUGGESTED READING

Bankers Trust Company. *Corporate Pension Plan Study: A Guide for the 1980's.* New York: Bankers Trust Company, 1980.

The Conference Board. *Flexible Employee Benefit Plans: Companies' Experience.* New York: The Conference Board, Inc., 1983.

Employee Benefit Plans and ERISA Special Committee. *Audits of Employee Benefit Plans.* New York: AICPA, 1983.

Employee Benefit Plans Under ERISA Federal Regulations. Englewood Cliffs, N.J.: Prentice-Hall, 1983.

Employee Benefit Research Institute. *Fundamentals of Employee Benefit Programs.* Washington, D.C.: Employee Benefit Research Institute, 1983.

Gilbert, Geoffrey M., Gregory J. Lachowicz, and James F. Zid. *Accounting and Auditing for Employee Benefit Plans.* New York: Warren, Gorham & Lamont, 1978.

Hirzel, Patrick S., and Jeffrey D. Mamorsky. "Fiduciary Audits: Defusing the Pension Time Bomb." *Corporate Accounting,* Winter 1983, pp. 60–63.

Price Waterhouse. *Statutory Fringe Benefits.* New York: Price Waterhouse, 1984.

Index

[Chapter numbers are boldface and are followed by a colon; lightface numbers after the colon refer to pages within the chapter.]

A

ABC method of inventory management, **34**:23
Access to workpapers
  and the DCAA, **9**:34–38, 55–59, 64–65
  and the DOD, **9**:34–38, 55–59, 64–65
  Westinghouse and, **9**:34–38, 55–59
Accounting controls, in general, **2**:5–7
Accounting standards, of the FCPA, **17**:8–9
Accounts payable
  audit techniques and, **20**:10–13
  and current financial conditions, **20**:4
  definition, **20**:2–3
  in general, **20**:2
  internal control
    objectives and, **20**:6
    techniques and, **20**:6–9
  legal considerations and, **20**:4–5
  management objectives and, **20**:3–4
  payroll
    audit techniques, **20**:33–36
    the business environment and, **20**:26–27
    definition, **20**:25–26
    in general, **20**:13, 25
    internal control objectives, **20**:29–30
    internal control techniques, **20**:30–33
    risks and, **20**:27–29
    specimen reports, **20**:45
  risks and, **20**:5–6
  type of industry and, **20**:4
  variations in, **20**:3–5

Accounts receivable. *See* Billing and collecting accounts receivable
Acquisitions. *See* Acquisitions and mergers
Acquisitions and mergers
  alternatives to, **30**:10
  the audit report for, **30**:39–45
  corporate objectives and, **30**:3–4
  defenses against hostile acquisitions, **30**:11–12
  diversification versus concentration, **30**:6–10
  earnings per share (EPS) and, **30**:35–39
  in general, **30**:2
  greenmail, **30**:11
  leveraged buyouts, **30**:10–11
  public concern about takeovers, **30**:7–9
  purpose of financial analysis in, **30**:12–21
  reasons for, **30**:3–4
  strategic planning and, **30**:4–6
  tax considerations in, **30**:31–35
  valuing an acquisition, **30**:22–31
Activity and evaluation reports, **13**:32–39
Administrative controls
  See also Accounting controls, in general
  in general, **2**:5–7
AICPA
  audit evidence and the, **14**:3–4
  Code of Professional Ethics, **4**:3–4
  conformity with GAAS, **3**:12–13
  Congress and the, **1**:39–44
  current issues and the, **1**:37–39
  external auditors and the, **8**:26–27, 30–35, 38–39

I-1

[Chapter numbers are boldface and are followed by a colon; lightface numbers after the colon refer to pages within the chapter.]

AICPA (cont'd)
  fraud and the, **22:**3
  GAAS and the, **4:**1–2
  GAO and the, **5:**6
  and GAO standards compared with IIA, **3:**13–14
  in general, **1:**34–36
  guidelines for internal controls, **17:**9–14
  internal controls and the, **17:**3–7
  internal control standards, **18:**20
  membership in, **3:**5–8
  role of the, **1:**36–37
  and standards-setting, **3:**4–5
  standards-setting by the, **3:**9–12
  standards-setting groups, **4:**7–8
  statistical sampling and the, **15:**16–17
  study on inventory audits, **34:**57–59
Allocation of resources, **2:**2–3
Allocation of responsibility for internal control, **17:**47–50
American Institute of Certified Public Accountants. See AICPA
Anderson Committee, recommendations, **4:**4
Anti-Kickback Enforcement Act of 1986, **2:**20–21
Arm's-length activities, defined, **14:**12–13
ASB
  and internal controls, **2:**6
  new standards issued, **4:**6
  role of the, **4:**4–7
  standards of the, **4:**4–5
  and the Treadway Commission, **4:**6–7
Assurances
  different types of, **1:**20–21
  third-party, **1:**18–19
Attestation standards, **4:**18–19
Attest function, CPAs and the, **3:**12–13
Attorney-client privilege
  and the DCAA, **9:**59
  and the NSIA, **9:**59
  and the protection of workpapers, **9:**59
Attributes sampling, method of, **15:**26–30

Audit
  approach to I/S, **27:**4–6, 22–35
  generalized software, **28:**29–37
Audit charters
  defined, **7:**3
  form and content, **7:**3–5
  and management, **7:**5–7
Audit committee
  active versus reactive role, **10:**12–14
  functions of the, **10:**2–14
  guidelines for the, **10:**2–4
  IIA and the, **10:**2–3
  illustrations to present to, **10:**17–20
  independent evaluations and, **10:**11
  and the NCFFR, **10:**2–3
  presentations to the, **10:**14–17
  role of, **10:**1–2, 4, 8–10
Audit evidence
  and the AICPA, GAO, and IIA, **14:**3–4
  defined, **14:**3–4
  relevance, **14:**8
  reliability, **14:**7–8
  selectivity, **14:**4–7
Audit frequency, determining, **2:**50
Audit function
  creating an image, **7:**33–36
  selling the benefits of, **7:**33–34
  techniques for creating an image, **7:**34–35
Audit independence, protecting, **28:**38–53
Auditing
  See also Government accounting; Internal auditing; Public accounting
  allocating resources of, **2:**43–54
  auditors' new functions and roles in, **2:**8–9
  audit sampling and, **15:**2–3
  audit tools and, **11:**27–29
  the changing focus of, **1:**15–16
  common characteristics of, **1:**17–20
  communicating progress and results, **12:**24–34
  competence in, **3:**17–19
  computer-assisted techniques, **28:**12–16

INDEX

I-3

[Chapter numbers are boldface and are followed by a colon; lightface numbers after the colon refer to pages within the chapter.]

confirmation and, **16:**29–35
coordinating efforts, **11:**29–31
and the DCAA, **1:**9–10
definitions of, **1:**4–7
developing the audit plan, **11:**31–32
due diligence in, **3:**19–21
EDP, **1:**12
forces affecting, **2:**23–24
forces in, **1:**14
in general, **1:**4–12
government, **1:**22–34
government standards, **5:**1–2
guidelines for allocating resources, **2:**51–54
historical overview, **1:**13–16
and the IGs, **1:**9–10
and the IIA, **1:**9–10
importance of, **3:**2–3
independence in, **3:**15–17; **7:**23–24
inquiry and, **16:**24
inspection and, **16:**29
internal, **1:**49–55
of internal accounting control, **18:**5–10, 20
internal control, **18:**2–5
I/S, **2:**28
the ISM controlling function, **38:**34
ISM planning functions, **38:**26–28
ISM staffing, **38:**31
keys to effective practice, **1:**56–57
long- and short-range planning, **7:**27–33
1972 standards, **5:**7–8, 12–14
1981 standards, **5:**8–14, 17–18
objectives and organizational needs, **2:**4–23
observation and, **16:**5–7
obtaining resources for, **7:**27
operating systems, **28:**45–52
overall objectives, **2:**23–29
an overview, **1:**4–12
PCs in, **8:**12–13
performing preliminary work, **11:**1–13, 24–32
project reporting and, **8:**17–18
public accounting, **1:**34–49
purpose of, **1:**7–12
and questionnaires and checklists, **8:**4–12
recent changes in standards, **4:**21–22

retirement plan management
  controlling, **40:**31–32
  organization, **40:**21–22
  planning, **40:**25
  staffing, **40:**23
specialized industry, **4:**19–20
standards for international operations, **29:**21–24
surveying prospective areas for, **2:**45–48
techniques in an I/S environment, **28:**2–4, 7–12
three principal branches, **1:**4, 16–21
tools and techniques, **28:**42–45
and the Treadway Commission, **1:**10–11
use of PCs in, **28:**53–58
workpapers, **12:**3–24

Auditing controls, techniques for, **28:**16–28

Auditing internal control
  definitions, **18:**2–3
  evaluations, **18:**6–20
  FCPA and, **18:**4–5
  in general, **18:**2–5
  relevance of, **18:**4

Auditing services, **1:**17–18

Auditing standards
  Cohen Commission and, **3:**2
  defined, **3:**2
  in general, **3:**15–21
  government, **5:**1–2
  internal, **6:**1–2
  for international operations, **29:**21–24
  purpose of, **3:**2
  recent changes, **4:**21–22
  standards-setting practice, **3:**3–8

Auditing Standards Board. *See* ASB

Audit manuals
  contents, **8:**4
  and project management, **8:**2–4

Audit operations, credit and collections, **33:**7–8

Auditor
  independence versus acceptability, **7:**35–36
  role and objectives in ISM, **38:**34

[*Chapter numbers are boldface and are followed by a colon; lightface numbers after the colon refer to pages within the chapter.*]

Auditors
  business combinations and, **2:**9
  data security and, **8:**39–40
  and ethical business practices, **2:**35–43
  independence versus conflict of interest, **7:**23–24
  I/S and, **26:**41–43; **27:**2–4
  new functions and roles in auditing, **2:**8–9
  position descriptions of, **7:**19–22
Audit procedures
  cost-benefit analysis and, **16:**35–40
  and evidential matter, **16:**2–40
Audit program, procurement questionnaire and, **34:**9, 18
Audit programs
  for financial management, **32:**27, 45
  written, **8:**18, 22–23
Audit report
  for acquisitions and mergers, **30:**39–45
  basic principles, **13:**2–3
  classification of, **13:**4–5
  formal written reports, **13:**17–27
  in general, **13:**2
  guidelines for, **13:**3–4
  oral reports, **13:**28
  preparing the report, **13:**39–40
  programs to improve, **13:**40–41
  replies to, **13:**41–43
  requirement for, **13:**2–4
  standards for reporting, **13:**5–17
  visual presentations, **13:**28–32
  writing for senior management, **13:**27–28
Audit reporting structure, factors to consider in, **7:**24–25
Audits
  financial and operational compared, **31:**4–6
  on international operations, **29:**16–20
Audit sampling
  and auditing, **15:**2–3
  concept of limited testing, **15:**4–5
  definitions, **15:**3–4
  in general, **15:**2–3
  minimizing risk, **15:**6–7
  nonstatistical, **15:**7–15
  risk considerations, **15:**4–6
  statistical, **15:**15–26
  statistical methods, **15:**26–36
Audit techniques
  and accounts payable, **20:**10–13
  accounts payable and payroll, **20:**33–36
  and billing and collecting accounts receivable, **19:**8–9
  cost accounting, **21:**14–16
  inquiry, **16:**7–24
Automated workpapers, **27:**53–57

B

Billing and collecting accounts receivable
  audit techniques and, **19:**8–9
  definition, **19:**2–3
  factors to consider, **19:**3–4
  in general, **19:**1–2
  internal control and, **19:**5–7
  risks, **19:**4–5
  sample audit program and, **19:**18
  specimen audit report and, **19:**22
Budgets, project controls and, **8:**14–17
Bulletin board systems, and computer fraud, **25:**10–20
Business climate, and ethics, **2:**18–21
Business combinations
  auditors and, **2:**9
  earnings-per-share and, **2:**8–9
  and internal auditing, **7:**12–13
Business ethics and fraud
  See also Fraud; Ethics
  and the internal auditor, **22:**38–40
  and the Packard Commission, **22:**38–40
  techniques for maintaining, **22:**31–38
Business risks, internal and management control, **17:**2–3

C

Capital investment projects, internal audit of, **35:**34–38

INDEX

I-5

*[Chapter numbers are boldface and are followed by a colon;
lightface numbers after the colon refer to pages within the chapter.]*

Capitalized earnings (P/E multiples),
    valuing an acquisition, **30**:23–24
Career managing, personnel
    management and, **9**:17–19
Certified internal auditor. *See* CIA
Certified public accountant. *See* CPA
CIA
    Code of Ethics, **1**:52–53
    program, **1**:52–53
Code of Ethics
    and data security, **8**:39–40
    of the IIA, **6**:17–19
    in internal auditing, **6**:17–19
Code of Professional Ethics. *See*
    AICPA
Cohen Commission
    and auditing standards, **3**:2
    GAAS and the, **4**:2
    management honesty and the, **14**:11
Collections. *See* billing and collecting
    accounts receivable
Combined attribute variables method
    of statistical sampling, **15**:35–36
Committee on Auditing Procedure
    (CAuP), **4**:1–2
Common characteristics of auditing,
    1:17–20
Communicating, PCs and, **26**:14–15
Communicating progress and results,
    fieldwork, **12**:24–34
Communications software, PCs and,
    26:16–17
Competence, in auditing, **3**:17–19
Computer abuse. *See* Computer fraud
Computer-assisted audit techniques
    (CAAT), I/S and, **28**:12–16,
    28–39
Computer fraud
    See also fraud
    bulletin board systems and, **25**:10–20
    categories of, **25**:3–4
    causes and techniques, **25**:4–10
    computer-related crime, **25**:4–5
    control and responsibility and,
        25:9–10
    definitions, **25**:2

    detection of, **25**:21
    EFTs and, **25**:1–2
    in general, **25**:1–2
    insurance coverage for, **25**:29–30
    ISM and, **38**:15–16
    legislative relief for, **25**:28–29
    new terminology and, **25**:6–9
    operation audits and, **25**:22–24
    prevention of, **25**:20–21
    reasons for growth in, **25**:2–3
    reducing, **25**:20–21
    safeguarding data, **25**:22
    unauthorized access, **25**:10
    vulnerability and, **25**:5–6
Computer security
    operational audit of, **25**:22–24
    safeguarding data, **25**:22
Computer systems, developing internal
    controls for, **25**:24–26
Confirmation
    and auditing, **16**:29–35
    documentation, **16**:32–35
    of evidential matter, **16**:29–35
    procedures, **16**:30–32
    techniques, **16**:32
Conflict of interest, independence
    versus, **7**:23–24
Conflicts of allegiance, in internal
    auditing, **1**:8–10
Congress and the AICPA, **1**:39–44
Control structure
    concept of, **18**:20–22
    and internal control, **18**:20–24
Corporate accountability
    ethics and, **2**:17–21
    fraud and, **2**:17–21
Cost accounting
    audit techniques, **21**:14–16
    definition, **21**:3–5
    in general, **21**:1–3
    internal control objectives, **21**:8
    internal control techniques, **21**:9–14
    risks, **21**:7–8
    sample audit program, **21**:16
    specimen report, **21**:16
    systems, **21**:4–5
    variations in, **21**:5–7

[*Chapter numbers are boldface and are followed by a colon; lightface numbers after the colon refer to pages within the chapter.*]

Cost-benefit analysis
  applicability, **16**:36
  and audit procedures, **16**:35–40
  defined, **16**:35–36
  documentation, **16**:36–39
  techniques, **16**:36–39
Cost-effective controls, for internal accounting, **17**:43–44
Cost systems
  See also Cost accounting
  actual job, **21**:4
  actual process, **21**:4
  standard, **21**:5
CPA
  attest function and the, **3**:12–13
  GAAS and the, **4**:3–4
  and quality assurance, **7**:38–46
  responsibilities of, **3**:5–8
CPAs, internal auditors and techniques of, **18**:26–28
Creating an image
  the audit function and, **7**:33–36
  techniques for, **7**:34–35
Credit and collections
  audit questionnaire, **33**:8
  elements of audit operation, **33**:7–8
  nature and role of, **33**:2
  objectives of, **33**:2–4
  operational audit program, **33**:14
  organizational status, **33**:4–6
  three C's of, **33**:6–7
Credit and collection management, in general, **33**:1–2
Crime, role of computer in, **25**:5

D

Data security
  and auditors, **8**:39–40
  Code of Ethics and, **8**:39–40
  PCs and, **8**:39–40
DCAA
  access to workpapers, **9**:34–38, 55–59, 64–65
  attorney-client privilege and the, **9**:59
  auditing and the, **1**:9–10
  and the DOD, **1**:25–30

efforts to access workpapers, **12**:18–24
  in general, **1**:25–30
  National Security Industrial Association (NSIA) and the, **9**:59
  Westinghouse and the, **9**:55–59
Defective pricing fraud, **24**:38
Defense Contract Audit Agency. *See* DCAA
Defense contractors, ethical practices initiatives and, **2**:19–21
Definitions, auditing, **1**:4–7
Department of Defense. *See* DOD
Detailed auditing of internal control
  advantages and disadvantages of, **18**:36
  defined, **18**:28–29
  objective of, **18**:29–30
  unique characteristics of, **18**:31–36
Developing the audit plan, **11**:31–32
Disclosure
  of financial information, **2**:14–17
  and fraud, **2**:14–17
Discovery sampling, and statistical sampling, **15**:35
Divestment. *See* Acquisitions and mergers
Divestments, financial analysis necessary for, **30**:45–47
Documentation
  confirmation of, **16**:32–35
  cost-benefit analysis, **16**:36–39
Documenting
  performing versus documenting, **12**:10–11
  preparing workpapers, **12**:10–24
  purpose of, **12**:10
DOD
  access to workpapers, **9**:34–38, 55–59, 64–65
  and the DCAA, **1**:25–30
  efforts to access workpapers, **12**:18–24
  Grace Commission and, **2**:13–14
  Packard Commission and the, **2**:14
  and procurement fraud, **24**:1–2

INDEX

I-7

[*Chapter numbers are boldface and are followed by a colon; lightface numbers after the colon refer to pages within the chapter.*]

procurement fraud, indicators of, **24**:5–38
self-policing by contractors, **24**:38
Westinghouse and the, **9**:55–59
Due diligence
   in auditing, **3**:19–21
   defined, **3**:19–21
   internal auditors and, **3**:19–21

E

Earnings-per-share, and acquisitions and mergers, **30**:35–39
Earnings-per-share, and business combinations, **2**:8–9
EDP
   See also I/S
   auditing, **1**:12
   I/S and, **26**:2–4
   and internal accounting controls, **17**:42–43
EDPAA, in general, **1**:55
EDPAF, in general, **1**:55
EDP auditing environment, **38**:9
EFTs, and computer fraud, **25**:1–2
Electronic data processing
   See also EDP; I/S
   in general, **2**:9
Electronic funds transfer. *See* EFTs, and computer fraud
Employee Retirement Income Security Act. *See* ERISA
Environmental Protection Agency. *See* EPA
ERISA
   objectives, **40**:5–6
   principle regulatory agencies under, **40**:7
   retirement plan management and, **40**:4–7
Ethical business practices
   auditors and, **2**:35–43
   defined, **2**:35–43
Ethical practices audit, **2**:36
Ethics

   business climate and, **2**:18–21
   committees on, **2**:19–21
   and corporate accountability, **2**:17–21
   ethical business practices defined, **2**:35–43
   ethical practices initiatives, **2**:19–21
   financial reporting fraud and, **2**:17–21
   training programs and, **2**:20–21
Evidence
   analyzed, **14**:13–22
   characteristics, **14**:13–14
   and the internal auditor, **14**:17–18, 22
   types of, **14**:14–17
Evidential matter
   See also Audit evidence; Evidence
   analyzing evidence, **14**:13–22
   audit procedures and, **16**:2–40
   basic assumptions, **14**:10–13
   confirmation of, **16**:29–35
   definitions, principles, and concepts, **14**:3–8
   for external versus internal auditors, **14**:8–10
   forms of inquiry, **16**:7–24
   GAAS and, **16**:2
   in general, **14**:1–2
   in an I/S environment, **28**:2–4
   importance of, **14**:2–3
   inquiry, **16**:7–24
   inquiry documentation, **16**:19–24
   inquiry techniques, **16**:19
   inspection, **16**:24–29
   observation as, **16**:2–7
   observation documentation, **16**:5
   observation techniques, **16**:3–5
   procedures to gather, **16**:2
External auditors
   and the AICPA, **8**:26–27, 30–35, 38–39
   contrasted with internal auditors, **2**:31–32
   evidential matter and, **14**:8–10
   and the IIA, **8**:27, 32–35, 38–39
   internal accounting controls and the, **17**:45–46
   internal auditors and, **8**:25–39
   management and, **2**:31–32

[*Chapter numbers are boldface and are followed by a colon; lightface numbers after the colon refer to pages within the chapter.*]

External auditors *(cont'd)*
   relationships with, **8:**25–39
   responsibility for internal control, **18:**20–26
   role of, **17:**45–46

F

Facilities
   See also Facilities management
   custody and administration of, **35:**11–12
   maintenance and care, **35:**11
   optimum utilization of equipment, **35:**12
   procurement review, **35:**12–15
   records and reports, **35:**12
Facilities management
   audit reports and typical findings, **35:**31–34
   capital budgeting procedure, **35:**9–10
   classifying and ranking projects, **35:**7–8
   control and monitoring of capital acquisitions, **35:**10–11
   control cycle, **35:**3–5
   long-range plan, **35:**5
   objectives of, **35:**1–2
   organization structure, **35:**2–3
   project evaluation methods, **35:**6–7
   questionnaire and program, **35:**15, 31
   short-term plan, **35:**6–8
FASB
   private sector standards-setting, **3:**4
   R&D activities defined by, **39:**2–3
FCPA
   accounting standards of the, **17:**8–9
   and auditing internal control, **18:**4–5
   effects on internal auditing, **2:**4–5
   in general, **2:**4–5
   internal control and the, **17:**7–9
   and internal control surveys, **18:**39–48
   Public Law 100-418 and the, **2:**5
Federal deficit
   affects of, **2:**10–14
   government spending and, **2:**9–14

Fieldwork
   communicating progress and results, **12:**24–34
   in general, **12:**1–3
   organizing, **12:**4–6
   performing, **12:**7–10
   planning, **12:**3–4
Financial Accounting Standards Board. *See* FASB
Financial analysis, necessary for divestment, **30:**45–47
Financial auditing, achieving objectives in, **2:**24
Financial audits, operational audits and, **31:**4–6
Financial information
   disclosure of, **2:**14–17
   and fraud, **2:**14–17
   importance of, **2:**14–17, 29–31
   management and, **2:**14–21
   reporting defined, **2:**29–35
   SEC and, **2:**14–17
Financial information reporting. *See* Financial information
Financial information systems. *See* FIS
Financial management
   audit findings, **32:**45–46, 54–55
   audit programs, **32:**27, 45
   audit questionnaire for, **32:**15
   in general, **32:**1–2
   nature of the financial function, **32:**5–6
   objectives, **32:**6–11
   operational audits and, **32:**11–15
   role of financial executive, **32:**2–5
   segment operational audits, **32:**55–59
Financial reporting fraud
   and ethics, **2:**17–21
   the Treadway Commission and, **2:**30–31
Financial reports, interim, **2:**32–35
Financial statements
   interim-period, **4:**16
   and the internal auditor, **2:**29–31
   prospective, **4:**17–18
   and the SEC, **2:**29–31
   unaudited, **4:**14–16
Financial type inventory audits, **34:**54–57
FIS, defined, **26:**2–4

INDEX

I-9

[Chapter numbers are boldface and are followed by a colon; lightface numbers after the colon refer to pages within the chapter.]

Foreign Corrupt Practice Act. *See* FCPA
Formal written audit reports, **13**:17–27
Fraud
   See also Computer fraud; Procurement fraud
   and the AICPA, **22**:3
   an antifraud checklist, **22**:40–42
   circumstances that encourage, **22**:5–6
   common forms of, **22**:4–5
   and corporate accountability, **2**:17–21
   defective pricing, **24**:38
   defined, **22**:3–4
   deterrence and prevention of, **22**:11–19
   disclosure and, **2**:14–17
   financial information and, **2**:14–17
   financial statement, **23**:1–9
   a fraud questionnaire, **22**:42–45
   in general, **22**:2
   general preventive measures, **22**:19–25
   indicators in material and labor, **24**:5
   indicia of, **22**:6–11
   investigation and reporting of, **22**:11–19
   and the legal department, **22**:58
   legislative relief for, **25**:28–29
   responsibility for detecting, **22**:45–54
   role of business ethics and, **22**:25–40
   and the SEC, **2**:14–17
   SIAS No. 3 and, **22**:3, 11–19
   special investigations, **22**:54–58
   and a strategic auditing approach, **2**:14–17
   use of "threat teams" to detect and prevent, **25**:26–28
Fraudulent financial reporting
   conditions of, **23**:2–3
   in general, **23**:1–2
   NCFFR and, **23**:3–9
   role of participants, **23**:3
   Treadway Commission and **23**:2–3

G

GAAS
   and the AICPA, **4**:1–2
   AICPA conformity with, **3**:12–13
   the Cohen Commission and, **4**:2
   and the CPA, **4**:3–4
   defined, **4**:1–2
   elements of, **4**:3–4
   and evidential matter, **16**:2
   inspection and, **16**:24–29
   and internal controls, **2**:6
   purpose of, **4**:2
   and the SEC, **4**:1–2
   SEC conformity with, **3**:12–13
   and standards-setting, **3**:4–5
   and statistical sampling, **15**:17–19
   the ten basic standards, **4**:8–9
GAO
   and the AICPA, **5**:6
   and AICPA standards compared with IIA, **3**:13–14
   audit evidence and the, **14**:3–4
   in general, **1**:22–24
   government auditing and the, **5**:2–3, 5–7
   guidelines for internal controls, **17**:21–35
   and the OMB, **5**:6–7
   role of, **5**:5–7
   standards for audit reports, **13**:9–17
   standards-setting and the, **3**:13
   standards-setting in government, **3**:4–5
General Accounting Office. *See* GAO
Generally accepted accounting principles. *See* GAAP
Generally accepted auditing standards. *See* GAAS
Glossary of computer terms, **26**:44–53
Government auditing, **1**:22–34
   the GAO and, **5**:2–3, 5–7
   history of, **5**:3–5
   IGs and, **5**:2–3
   purpose of, **5**:2–3
Government auditing standards, **5**:1–2
Government auditors, **1**:17
   responsibility for detecting fraud, **22**:49–51
Government spending
   affects of, **2**:10–14
   and the federal deficit, **2**:9–14
   in general, **2**:9–14
   Grace Commission and, **2**:12–13
   and operational efficiency, **2**:10–14
   Packard Commission and, **2**:14

[*Chapter numbers are boldface and are followed by a colon; lightface numbers after the colon refer to pages within the chapter.*]

Grace Commission
  DOD and, **2:**13–14
  and government spending, **2:**12–13
  Summary Report, **2:**12–14
Gramm-Rudman-Hollings bill, **2:**11–12
Greenmail, and acquisitions and mergers, **30:**11
Guidelines, for internal controls, **17:**9–35

I

Identifying risk factors, **2:**48–50
IGs
  auditing and the, **1:**9–10
  in general, **1:**30–33
  government auditing and, **5:**2–3
IIA
  and the audit committee, **10:**2–3
  audit evidence and the, **14:**3–4
  Code of Ethics of the, **6:**17–19
  definition of independence, **3:**17
  definition of internal auditing, **1:**4–5
  external auditors and the, **8:**27, 32–35, 38–39
  general and specific internal auditing standards, **6:**7–9
  guidelines for internal controls, **17:**14–21
  internal auditing standards, **6:**1–2
  and personnel recruiting, **9:**5–8
  planning for the internal audit function, **7:**32–33
  and PSBs, **6:**4–6
  and the PSRC, **6:**4–6
  role of the, **1:**53–55
  and SIASs, **6:**4–6
  standards compared with AICPA and GAO, **3:**13–14
  standards for audit reports, **13:**5–9
  standards-setting by the, **3:**12–13
  Statement of Responsibilities, **2:**21–23
  Treadway Commission and standards of the, **3:**13
IIA Research Foundation, **1:**4
Independence
  in auditing, **3:**15–17; **7:**23–24

IIA definition of, **3:**17
SEC definition of, **3:**15–16
versus acceptability, **7:**35–36
versus conflict of interest, **7:**23–24
Independent accountants, responsibility for detecting fraud, **22:**45–47
Indicia of fraud, **22:**6–11
Information distribution, and PCs, **26:**15–16
Information systems. *See* I/S
Information systems management. *See* ISM
Inquiry
  and audits, **16:**24
  as an audit technique, **16:**7–24
  documentation, **16:**19–24
  as an evidential matter, **16:**7–24
  techniques, **16:**19
Insider-trading. *See* Fraud; Ethics
Inspection
  documentation of, **16:**29
  as evidential matter, **16:**24–29
  and GAAS, **16:**24–29
  and specific audit approaches, **16:**29
  specific forms, **16:**25–27
  techniques of, **16:**27–29
Institute of Internal Auditors. *See* IIA
Insurance coverage, for computer fraud, **25:**29–30
Interim financial reports. *See* Financial reports
Interim-period financial statements, **4:**16
Internal accounting control, auditing of, **18:**5–10, 20
Internal accounting controls
  cost-effective controls, **17:**43–44
  EDP and, **17:**42–43
  and the external auditor, **17:**45–46
  objectives, **17:**41–44
Internal accounting systems, elements of, **17:**37–39
Internal audit
  of capital investment projects, **35:**34–38
  IIA planning for, **7:**23–33

INDEX

I-11

[*Chapter numbers are boldface and are followed by a colon;
lightface numbers after the colon refer to pages within the chapter.*]

Internal auditing
See also Auditing
administrative requirements, **7:**16
business combinations and, **7:**12–13
Code of Ethics, **6:**17–19
conflicts of allegiance in, **1:**8–10
definitions of, **1:**4–7
the FCPA and, **2:**4–5
in general, **1:**49–55
geographical considerations, **7:**16
IIA standards, **6:**1–2
and internal controls, **17:**46
intradepartment relationships, **7:**17–19
and I/S, **27:**2–4
keys to effective practice, **1:**56–57
management and, **7:**10–12
a management perspective, **31:**1–3
operational auditing, **2:**7–9
and operational efficiency, **2:**7–9
organization structure, **7:**7–19
organizing and planning, **7:**2–3
personnel resources, **9:**2
POB and self-regulation, **3:**5–8
as a profession, **1:**10–11
quality assurance and, **7:**37–38
regulation of, **3:**5
reporting relationships and standards, **3:**14
reporting relationships in, **7:**22–27
role of, **7:**14
significance of, **1:**55
skill requirements, **7:**14–16
standards for the professional practice of, **6:**1–2
Statement of Responsibilities, **6:**19–22
technology and, **7:**13
Internal auditing standards
applicability, **6:**3–4
defined, **6:**1–2
general and specific IIA standards, **6:**7–9
purpose of, **6:**2–3
Treadway Commission and, **6:**6–7, 9–14
Internal auditors
business ethics and, **22:**38–40
confirmation audit procedures, **16:**29–35
contrasted with external auditors, **2:**31–32
and due diligence, **3:**19–21
effect of internal control standards, on, **18:**26
evidence and, **14:**17–18, 22
evidential matter and, **14:**8–10
and external auditors, **8:**25–39
financial statements and, **2:**29–31
and interim financial reports, **2:**32–35
internal control and, **17:**46
inventory management and, **34:**9
management and, **2:**31–32
and marketing management, **37:**19–20
and the Packard Commission, **2:**14
PCs and, **2:**9
presentations to the audit committee, **10:**14–17
responsibility for detecting fraud, **22:**47–49
role of, **17:**46
services of **1:**50–52
and statements of objectives, **2:**21–23
and techniques of CPAs, **18:**26–28
Internal controls
accounting objectives, **17:**41–44
accounting systems, **17:**37–39
accounts payable objectives and, **20:**6
accounts payable and payroll objectives, **20:**29–30
accounts payable and payroll techniques, **20:**30–33
accounts payable techniques and, **20:**6–9
AICPA and, **17:**3–7, 9–14; **18:**20
allocation of responsibility for, **17:**47–50
ASB and, **2:**6
auditing, **18:**2–5
and billing and collecting accounts receivable, **19:**5–7
business risks and management control, **17:**2–3
control structure and, **18:**20–24
cost accounting objectives, **21:**8
cost accounting techniques, **21:**9–14
defined, **17:**3–7
detailed auditing of, **18:**28–36
EDP and, **17:**42–43

I-12   INDEX

[Chapter numbers are boldface and are followed by a colon; lightface numbers after the colon refer to pages within the chapter.]

Internal controls *(cont'd)*
   effect of standards on internal auditors, **18**:26
   and the external auditor, **17**:45–46
   external auditor's responsibility for, **18**:20–26
   and the FCPA, **17**:7–9
   GAAS and **2**:6
   GAO guidelines for, **17**:21–35
   in general, **2**:5–7; **17**:2
   guidelines for, **17**:9–35
   IIA guidelines for, **17**:14–21
   importance of, **18**:48–49
   and the internal auditor, **17**:46
   management and, **17**:44–45
   for a minicomputer system, **25**:24–26
   the NCFFR and, **17**:30–35
   planning and, **17**:39–41
   reportable conditions and, **18**:24–26
   SIAS No. 1, **17**:15–21
   survey, **18**:37–48
      advantages and disadvantages, **18**:48
      definition, **18**:37
      the FCPA and, **18**:39–48
      objective, **18**:37–39
   unique characteristics, **18**:39–48
   variability of control systems, **17**:35–36

Internal Revenue Service. *See* IRS

International business. *See* International operations

International operations
   advantages and risks in, **29**:5
   auditing standards for, **29**:21–24
   audit questionnaires and programs, **29**:24
   characteristic differences in, **29**:4–5
   in general, **29**:2
   impact on
      financial activities, **29**:6–12
      management functions, **29**:6–15
      manufacturing activities, **29**:14–15
      marketing activities, **29**:12–14
      personnel activities, **29**:14
   legal considerations, **29**:15–16
   management of, **29**:15–16
   managing the audit function, **29**:15–16
   and multinational companies (MNCs), **29**:5
   nature and purpose of, **29**:2–3
   performing audits on, **29**:16–20
   special areas for inquiry, **29**:24–29

Interviewing management, **11**:26–27

Inventory audits
   AICPA study on, **34**:57–59
   financial, **34**:54–57

Inventory control applications, **34**:21–27

Inventory management
   ABC method of, **34**:23
   audit findings, **34**:41–42
   audit program, **34**:37
   control questionnaire, **34**:28
   defined, **34**:2
   functional objectives and procedures, **34**:6
   importance of adequate data for, **34**:27
   just-in-time (JIT) inventories, **34**:7–8
   key components of an effective system, **34**:4–6
   objectives of warehousing and distribution, **34**:18–19
   pervading impact of, **34**:2–4
   procurement and, **34**:6–7
   procurement objectives, **34**:8
   production management objectives, **34**:18–19
   role of the internal auditor, **34**:9
   scope of, **34**:19–27

Inventory planning applications, **34**:20–21

IRS
   auditing and the, **1**:9–10
   in general, **1**:33–34

I/S
   See also ISM
   audit approach, **27**:4–6, 22–35
   auditing, **2**:28
   auditing tools and techniques, **28**:42–45
   auditors and, **26**:41–43; **27**:2–4
   audit techniques, **28**:2–4
   computer-assisted auditing techniques, **28**:12–16

INDEX

I-13

[Chapter numbers are boldface and are followed by a colon; lightface numbers after the colon refer to pages within the chapter.]

definition and purpose of audit
    techniques, **28**:4
definitions, **26**:2–4
and EDP, **26**:2–4
evidential matter and, **28**:2–4
functions that benefit from, **26**:7–10
in general, **2**:9; **26**:4–7
glossary of computer terms, **26**:44–53
improving audit performance
    efficiency and effectiveness,
    28:28–37
internal auditing and, **27**:2–4
internal controls in, **26**:23–31
management and, **27**:2–4
management of personnel, **27**:45–50
managing the audit function,
    27:35–41
objectives and controls, **26**:31–41
organizing and planning audits,
    27:36–40
performing audits, **27**:58–62
prioritizing audit projects, **27**:32–33
project management, **27**:42–45
protecting audit independence,
    28:38–53
sampling applicability, **28**:4–7
selling the audit function, **27**:40–41
standards for the audit function,
    27:35–36
techniques for auditing controls,
    28:16–28
traditional audit techniques, **28**:7–12
ISM
    auditing planning functions, **38**:26–28
    auditing staffing, **38**:31
    auditing the controlling function,
        38:34
    auditor's role and objectives, **38**:34
    audit questionnaire, **38**:37, 65
    audit techniques, **38**:35–37
    computer dependence, **38**:17–18
    computer fraud and, **38**:15–16
    controlling, **38**:31–32
    controlling access, **38**:32–33
    definitions, **38**:4
    dynamic environment, **38**:11–12
    evolution and impact of, **38**:4–5
    expanding role of, **38**:5–9
    in general, **38**:2–4
    interface challenges, **38**:12–13

nature of the ISM functions, **38**:9–13
negligent or inefficient, **38**:17
objectives, **38**:13–15
organizing and managing, **38**:23–24
planning, **38**:23–25
proliferation of mini- and
    microcomputers, **38**:18, 22
risks and concerns, **38**:15–22
scarcity of resources, **38**:12
service orientation, **38**:10–11
staffing, **38**:29–30
supplemental objjectives, **38**:14–15
and the technology environment,
    38:7–8
and the user environment, **38**:8–9
violations of laws and regulations,
    38:16–17

J

Just-in-time (JIT) inventories, *See*
    Inventory management

L

Labor fraud indicators, **24**:5
Legislative relief, for computer fraud,
    25:28–29
Leveraged buyouts
    See also Acquisitions and mergers
    in general, **30**:10–11
Long- and short-range audit planning
    7:27–33

M

Management. *See* Personnel
    management
and accounts payable, **20**:3–4
allocation of responsibility for
    internal control and, **17**:47–50
alternative methodologies of, **7**:10–12
audit charters and, **7**:5–7
business risks and internal control,
    17:2–3

[*Chapter numbers are boldface and are followed by a colon; lightface numbers after the colon refer to pages within the chapter.*]

Management. *See* Personnel management *(cont'd)*
  credit and collections, **33:**1–4
  and external auditors, **2:**31–32
  facilities, **35:**1–2
  financial, **32:**1–2
  of general resources, **9:**19–27
  honesty and the Cohen Commission, **14:**11
  impact of international operations on, **29:**6–15
  and internal auditing, **7:**10–12
  and internal auditors, **2:**31–32
  and internal control, **17:**44–45
  of international operations, **29:**15–16
  interviewing, **11:**26–27
  inventory, **34:**2
  I/S and, **27:**2–4; **38:**2–4
  of I/S personnel, **27:**45–50
  marketing, **37:**1–2
  of PCs, **27:**51–58
  perspective on internal auditing, **31:**1–3
  production objectives, **34:**18–19
  program, **36:**1–2
  R&D, **39:**2
  of records, **9:**27–38, 55–59, 64–65
  retirement plan, **40:**2–9
  writing audit reports for, **13:**27–28
Management accountants, responsibility for detecting fraud, **22:**51–54
Management advisory services, **4:**20–21
Management control, business risks and internal control, **17:**2–3
Management information systems. *See* MIS
Marketing
  nature and scope of the marketing function, **37:**1–2
  objectives, **37:**2–4
  organization structure, **37:**4–5
  policies and procedures, **37:**5–6
Marketing management
  See also marketing
  audit program, **37:**14
  in general, **37:**1–2
  PCs and, **37:**19–20
  questionnaire, **37:**7, 14
  role of the internal auditor, **37:**19–20

Material fraud indicators, **24:**5
Material requirements planning (MRP), **34:**23–24
Mergers. *See* Acquisitions and mergers
Microcomputers, program management and, **36:**28–29
MIS, defined, **26:**2–4
Multinational companies (MNCs), international operations and, **29:**5

N

National Commission on Fraudulent Financial Reporting. *See* NCFFR; Treadway Commission
National Security Industrial Association (NSIA), and the DCAA, **9:**59
NCFFR
  See also Treadway Commission
  and audit committee guidelines, **10:**2–3
  and fraudulent financial reporting, **23:**3–9
  and internal controls, **17:**30–35
1972 auditing standards, **5:**7–8, 12–14
1981 auditing standards, **5:**8–14, 17–18
Nonstatistical sampling
  audit sampling and, **15:**7–15
  definition, **15:**7
  in an I/S environment, **28:**5–7
  techniques, **15:**7–15

O

Objectives, auditing and organizational needs, **2:**4–23
Observation
  and audits, **16:**5–7
  documentation, **16:**5
  as evidential matter, **16:**2–7
  procedures, **16:**3
  techniques, **16:**3–5
Office of Management and Budget. *See* OMB

INDEX

I-15

[Chapter numbers are boldface and are followed by a colon; lightface numbers after the colon refer to pages within the chapter.]

Offices of the Inspector General. *See* IGs
OMB, GAO and the, **5:**6–7
Operational auditing
  achieving objectives in, **2:**25–28
  increase in, **2:**7–9
  ISM, **38:**37, 65
  manufacturing functions of, **2:**27–28
  of retirement plan management, **40:**32–34
  and strategic auditing approach, **2:**14–17
  a workable definition for, **31:**3–4
Operational audits
  areas suggested for, **31:**6–8
  basic steps for, **31:**13–17
  benefits of, **31:**6
  computer fraud and, **25:**22–24
  of computer security, **25:**22–24
  financial audits and, **31:**4–6
  initiation of, **31:**8–9
  knowledge needed to perform, **31:**9–11
  organizing and managing the financial **32:**11–15
  progressively difficult levels of, **31:**17–18
  reports on, **31:**18–19
  for a segment of a function, **32:**55–59
  standards for, **31:**11–13
Operational efficiency
  attempts to improve, **2:**7–9
  government spending and, **2:**10–14
  and internal auditing, **2:**7–9
Operations audit, of the engineering function, **39:**34–41
Organizational culture, importance of, **7:**8–10
Organizational needs and objectives in auditing, **2:**4–23
Organizational planning, **7:**28–29, 32
Organization structure of internal auditing, **7:**7–19
  definition and purpose, **12:**4–6
  techniques in, **12:**4–6
Organizing and planning I/S audits, **27:**36–40
Organizing fieldwork
Overall objectives, of auditing, **2:**23–29

P

Packard Commission
  business ethics and the, **22:**38–40
  DOD and the, **2:**14
  and government spending, **2:**14
  internal auditors and the, **2:**14
  recommendations of, **2:**13–14
Payroll. *See* Accounts payable
PCs
  advent of, **2:**9
  in auditing, **8:**12–13
  audit uses of, **28:**53–58
  availability and use of, **26:**10–12
  communicating with, **26:**14–15
  and communications software, **26:**16–17
  and crime, **26:**43–44
  and data security, **8:**39–40
  glossary of computer terms, **26:**44–53
  implementation strategy, **27:**57–58
  information distribution through, **26:**15–16
  internal auditors and, **2:**9
  and I/S, **26:**10–17
  management of, **27:**51–58
  marketing management and, **37:**19–20
  project management and, **8:**12–13
  risks and concerns with, **26:**12–13, 17. 20–23
  security and control techniques, **26:**35–41
  use in performing fieldwork, **27:**7–10
  word processing with, **26:**13–14
Peer review organization (PRO), SEC rules and, **3:**7–8
Peer review programs
  POB and, **3:**5–8
  SECPS and, **3:**5–8
Peer reviews, and quality assurance, **7:**38–40
Performance measurement
  definition and purpose, **9:**12–13
  of individuals, **9:**12–14
  organizational, **9:**20–22
Performing fieldwork, use of, PCs in, **12:**7–10

[Chapter numbers are boldface and are followed by a colon; lightface numbers after the colon refer to pages within the chapter.]

Performing I/S audits, **27**:58–62
Performing preliminary work
  defining objectives, **11**:6–8
  definition, **11**:2–3
  elements in, **11**:3–13, 24–32
  in general, **11**:1–2
  purpose, **11**:3
  researching authoritative literature, **11**:12–26
  reviewing records, **11**:8–12
  routine versus nonroutine efforts, **11**:4
Performing versus documenting, **12**:10–11
Personal computers. *See* PCs
Personnel management
  and career managing, **9**:17–19
  in general, **9**:2–19
  IIA and, **9**:5–8
  importance of, **9**:2–3
  and professional training, **9**:15–17
  recruiting, **9**:3–8
Personnel resources, and internal auditing, **9**:2
PERT
  management process and, **36**:3–8
  networks, **36**:8–11
  program management and, **36**:2–3
Planning
  and internal controls, **17**:39–41
  and ISM, **38**:23–25
  long- and short-range, **7**:27–33
  organizational, **7**:28–29, 32
  project, **7**:28
  resource, **7**:28
  techniques, **7**:32–33
Planning fieldwork
  purpose of, **12**:3
  techniques in, **12**:3–4
POB
  in general, **1**:40, 44–47
  and internal auditing self-regulation, **3**:5–8
  and peer review programs, **3**:5–8
  and quality assurance, **7**:38–40, 45–46
Position descriptions, defined and discussed, **7**:19–22

Preparing an audit report, **13**:39–40
Preparing and modifying audit tools, **11**:27–29
Presentations
  to the audit committee, **10**:14–17
  illustrations in, **10**:17–20
  by the internal auditor, **10**:14–17
  suggested coverage in, **10**:15–17
  types of, **10**:15
President's Blue Ribbon Commission on Defense Management. *See* Packard Commission
President's Private Sector Survey on Cost Control. *See* Grace Commission
Prioritizing risk factors, **2**:50
PRO, and quality assurance, **7**:38–46
Procurement
  cycle, **34**:8–9
  inventory management and, **34**:6–7
  objectives of, **34**:8
  questionnaire and audit program, **34**:9, 18
Procurement fraud
  DOD and, **24**:1–2
  in general, **24**:1–2
  government publications and, **24**:2–4
  indicators of DOD, **24**:5–38
  minimizing in government contracts, **24**:2
Professional Standards and Responsibility Committee. *See* PSRC
Professional Standards Bulletins. *See* PSB
Professional training, personnel management and, **9**:15–17
Program Evaluation and Review Technique. *See* PERT
Program management
  audit findings, **36**:19, 27–28
  audit program, **36**:19
  control questionnaire, **36**:11
  defined, **36**:2–3
  in general, **36**:1–2
  indicated final cost, **36**:11
  and microcomputers, **36**:28–29

[Chapter numbers are boldface and are followed by a colon; lightface numbers after the colon refer to pages within the chapter.]

PERT, **36:**2–3
  programs and, **36:**2–3
Project controls
  and assignment authorization, **8:**13–14
  and budgets, **8:**14–17
  defined, **8:**13
  in general, **8:**13–25
Project management
  audit manuals and, **8:**2–4
  definition and purpose, **8:**2–4
  in general, **8:**2
  and PCs, **8:**12–13
  project reporting on, **8:**17–18
Project planning, **7:**28
Project reporting
  and auditing, **8:**17–18
  on project management, **8:**17–18
Project review
  in general, **8:**23–24
  proper attitude and, **8:**24–25
Prospective financial statements, **4:**17–18
PSB
  and the IIA, **6:**4–6
  the PSRC and, **6:**4–6
PSRC
  IIA and the, **6:**4–6
  and PSBs, **6:**4–6
  role of the, **6:**4–5
  and SIASs, **6:**4–6
  SIASs issued by the, **6:**14–17
Public accounting
  auditing, **1:**34–49
  in general, **1:**34–49
  self-regulation of, **3:**5–8
  significance of, **1:**48–49
Public Law 100-48 and the FCPA, **2:**5
Public Oversight Board. *See* POB

Q

Quality assurance
  CPAs and, **7:**38–46
  definition and purpose, **7:**36–37
  in general, **7:**36–48
  and internal auditing, **7:**37–38
  issues of, **7:**38–46
  peer reviews and, **7:**38–46
  POB and, **7:**38–40, 45–46
  practical guidelines, **7:**47–48
  SECPS and, **7:**38–40, 45–46
  SIAS No. 4 and, **7:**40–44
Questionnaires and checklists
  auditing and, **8:**4–12
  definition and purpose, **8:**4–12

R

Raids, prevention of, **2:**8–9
R&D
  activities defined, **39:**2–3
  activities defined by FASB, **39:**2–3
  amount spent on basic research, **39:**5
  communication with top management, **39:**5
  corporate impact of, **39:**3–4
  engineering function and, **39:**34–41
  financial reports on activities of, **39:**17
  in general, **39:**2
  increasing productivity of, **39:**15–16
  limited use of economic measures, **39:**10–13
  management audit questionnaire and program, **39:**20–34
  methods of determining the total budget for, **39:**5–9
  organizing for, **39:**13–14
  outside resources, **39:**14–15
  performance standards for, **39:**17–20
  quality of the staff, **39:**9–10
  selected subjects to be reviewed, **39:**4–13
Recommendations to management
  the SEC and, **2:**6
  the Treadway Commission and, **2:**6–7
Records management
  access to workpapers, **9:**29–38, 55–59, 64–65
  in general, **9:**27–38, 55–59, 64–65
Recruiting
  and the IIA, **9:**5–8
  and personnel management, **9:**3–8
  the process of, **9:**8–12

[*Chapter numbers are boldface and are followed by a colon; lightface numbers after the colon refer to pages within the chapter.*]

Reorder point systems, **34:**24–25
Reportable conditions, concept of, **18:**24–26
Reporting relationships, in internal auditing, **7:**22–27
Requirements for audit reports, **13:**2–4
Research and development. *See* **R&D**
Researching authoritative literature, performing preliminary work, **11:**12–26
Resource planning, **7:**28
Resources
  allocating audit, **27:**33–35
  allocation of, **2:**2–3
  management of, **9:**19–27
  techniques of managing, **9:**19–20
Responsibility for detecting fraud
  government auditors, **22:**49–51
  independent accountants, **22:**45–47
  internal auditors, **22:**47–49
  management accountants, **22:**51–54
Retirement plan management
  auditing objective, **40:**32–33
  auditing questionnaire, **40:**34–59
  auditing tools and techniques, **40:**33–34
  controlling, **40:**25–31
  controlling auditing, **40:**31–32
  defined benefit plans, **40:**14–16
  defined contribution plans, **40:**16–17
  definitions, **40:**3–4
  ERISA and, **40:**4–7
  establishing a plan, **40:**11–12
  in general, **40:**2–9
  maintenance of plans, **40:**12–13
  nature of, **40:**10–13
  objectives, **40:**17–19
  operational auditing of, **40:**32–34
  organization, **40:**20–21
  organization auditing, **40:**21–22
  planning, **40:**23–25
  planning auditing, **40:**23–25
  purpose of, **40:**9–10
  risks and concerns, **40:**19–20
  staffing, **40:**22–23
  staffing auditing, **40:**23
  techniques, **40:**20–32
  types of plans, **40:**13–17

Risk, audit sampling and, **15:**4–7
Risk factors
  identifying, **2:**48–50
  prioritizing, **2:**50
Risks
  and accounts payable, **20:**5–6
  accounts payable and the payroll, **20:**27–29
  billing and collecting accounts receivable, **19:**4–5
  cost accounting, **21:**7–8
  inherent in PCs, **26:**17, 20–23
  PCs and concerns with, **26:**12–13

S

Safeguarding data from computer fraud, **25:**22
Sample audit program
  and billing and collecting accounts receivable, **19:**18
  cost accounting, **21:**16
Scientific planning techniques, **7:**32–33
SEC
  conformity with GAAS, **3:**12–13
  definition of independence, **3:**15–16
  and financial information, **2:**14–17
  financial statements and the, **2:**29–31
  fraud and, **2:**14–17
  GAAS and the, **4:**1–2
  peer review organization (PRO) and the, **3:**7–8
  recommendations to management, **2:**6
  role of the, **1:**40–44
  and standards-setting, **3:**4–5
SECPS
  membership in, **3:**5–8
  peer review programs, **3:**5–8
  and quality assurance, **7:**38–40, 45–46
  self-regulation and the **1:**44–47
Securities Exchange Commission. *See* SEC
Selling the benefits of the audit function, **7:**33–34
Selling the I/S audit function, **27:**40–41

INDEX

I-19

[Chapter numbers are boldface and are followed by a colon; lightface numbers after the colon refer to pages within the chapter.]

Services
   management advisory, **4**:20–21
   tax, **4**:20
SIAS
   and the IIA, **6**:4–6
   No. 1, **1**:6
      internal controls, **17**:15–21
   No. 2, standards for audit reports, **13**:5–9
   No. 3
      fraud, **22**:3, 11–19
      and special fraud investigations, **22**:57–58
   No. 4, and quality assurance, **7**:40–44
   the PSRC and, **6**:4–6
   statements issued by the PSRC, **6**:14–17
Single Audit Act of 1984, **5**:14–17
Software
   generalized audit, **28**:29–37
   for statistical sampling, **15**:36–37
Special fraud investigations, **22**:54–58
Specialized industry auditing, **4**:19–20
Specific audit approaches, and observation, **16**:5–7
Specimen audit report, and billing and collecting accounts receivable, **19**:22
Specimen report, cost accounting, **21**:16
Standards for audit reports
   the GAO, **13**:9–17
   the IIA, **13**:5–9
Standards for the I/S audit function, **27**:35–36
Standards of performance, **3**:1–3
Standards for the Professional Practice of Internal Auditing, **1**:7–8; **6**:1–2
Standards-setting
   by the AICPA, **3**:9–12
   and the GAO, **3**:13
   by the IIA, **3**:12–13
Standards-setting practices
   AICPA and, **3**:4–5
   GAAS and, **3**:4–5
   GAO and, **3**:4–5
   by government, **3**:3

   by government and private sector, **3**:4–5
   by private sector, **3**:4
   SEC and, **3**:4–5
Statement of Objectives, IIA *Statement of Responsibilities*, **2**:21–23
Statement of Responsibilities, of internal auditing, **6**:19–22
Statement of Responsibilities, Standards, **1**:6
Statements on Internal Auditing Standards. *See* SIAS
Statistical sampling
   advantages and disadvantages of, **15**:16–17
   and the AICPA, **15**:16–17
   attribute method of, **15**:26–30
   audit sampling and, **15**:15–26
   combined attribute variables method, **15**:35–36
   concepts of, **15**:17–19
   definition, **15**:15
   discovery sampling, **15**:35
   evolution of, **15**:16
   GAAS and, **15**:17–19
   in an I/S environment, **28**:7
   methods, **15**:26–36
   software for, **15**:36–37
   techniques, **15**:19–26
   variable method of, **15**:30–35
Strategic audit, planning, **2**:43–45
Strategic auditing approach
   and department management, **2**:3
   fraud and, **2**:14–17
   operational auditing and, **2**:14–17
   overall strategy, **2**:2
   reasons for a, **2**:2–4
Strategic planning, and acquisitions and mergers, **30**:4–6

T

Takeovers. *See* Acquisitions and mergers
Tax considerations, in acquisitions and mergers, **30**:31–35

[*Chapter numbers are boldface and are followed by a colon; lightface numbers after the colon refer to pages within the chapter.*]

Tax Reform Act of 1986, impact of, **30**:34–35
Tax Services, **4**:20
Techniques of managing resources, **9**:19–20, 22–27
Technology, and internal auditing, **7**:13
Third-party assurances, **1**:18–19
"Threat teams" to detect and prevent fraud, **25**:26–28
Three-step technique for adding specific objectives, **2**:21, 23
Training programs, and ethics, **2**:20–21
Treadway Commission
  ASB and the, **4**:6–7
  and audit committee guidelines, **10**:3–4
  auditing and the, **1**:10–11
  and financial reporting fraud, **2**:30–31
  and fraudulent financial reporting, **23**:2–3
  and IIA standards, **3**:13
  and internal auditing standards, **6**:6–7, 9–14
  recommendations of, **2**:16–17
  recommendations to management, **2**:6–7

U

Ultramares, **3**:9
Unaudited financial statements, **4**:14–16

V

Valuing an acquisition
  appraised value, **30**:22–23
  book value, **30**:22
  capitalized earnings (P/E multiples), **30**:23–24
  discounted cash flow (DCF), **30**:25–27
  in general, **30**:22
  market value, **30**:23
Variability of internal control systems, **17**:35–36
Variables sampling, method of, **15**:30–35
Visual presentations in audit reports, **13**:28–32

W

Warehousing and distribution, objectives of, **34**:18–19
Westinghouse
  and access to workpapers, **9**:34–38, 55–59
  and the DCAA, **9**:55–59
  and the DOD, **9**:55–59
Word processing, and PCs, **26**:13–14
Workpapers
  attorney-client privilege and, **9**:59
  automated, **27**:53–57
  common deficiencies, **12**:11–12
  and confirmations of evidence, **16**:32, 35
  creating, **12**:17–18
  criteria for retention of, **12**:17
  documenting versus performing, **12**:10–11
  and evidential matter, **16**:3–40
  issues of access to, **12**:18–24
  preparing, **12**:10–24
  techniques for organizing, **12**:12–16
  timing of preparation of, **12**:18
Written audit programs, **8**:18–23